Mayflower Births & Deaths

Mayflower Births & Deaths

George Ernest Bowman, ca. 1897

Mayflower Births & Deaths

FROM THE FILES OF GEORGE ERNEST BOWMAN
At the Massachusetts Society of Mayflower Descendants

by
Susan E. Roser

Volume 1

Genealogical Publishing Co., Inc.

Genealogical Publishing Co., Inc.
1001 N. Calvert St., Baltimore, Md. 21202

Second printing 1997
Library of Congress Catalogue Card Number 92-70311
International Standard Book Number, Volume 1: 0-8063-1338-2
Set Number: 0-8063-1340-4
Made in the United States of America

Contents

Preface

George Ernest Bowman (1860-1941) is a well known and respected name in the field of Mayflower research. In 1896 he founded the Massachusetts Society of Mayflower Descendants and served as Secretary, Genealogist and Editor for 45 years, until 1941. He was the Editor of the **Mayflower Descendant,** a quarterly genealogical magazine specializing in primary source material, published between 1899 and 1937. In his book, **Plymouth Colony, Its History & People 1620-1691,** Eugene A. Stratton, FASG, former Historian General of the General Society of Mayflower Descendants, pays tribute to Bowman:

> *The greatest genealogical scholar of Plymouth Colony was George Ernest Bowman . . . He left a living legacy in the Mayflower Descendant, a timeless and unsurpassed collection of original records of the people of colonial Plymouth. Moreover, he left a methodology for precision in acquiring data that has been all too little appreciated in the past, but has been gaining recognition with time.*

Mr. Bowman was a dedicated and disciplined genealogist whose goal was to trace the ancestry of each Mayflower family right up to present-day descendants. Either he did not fully appreciate the enormity of the research involved or he had extremely high expectations of himself (probably the latter), in any case, his goal was never realized although he spent almost half a century trying. Referring to his work as The Mayflower Genealogies, he did manage to accumulate approximately 20,600 pages containing probate, court, church and bible records, cemetery inscriptions, wills, charts, lineages and documentation. The Massachusetts Society admits some of his work "has been superseded by research done since 1941, but the collection remains the largest documented manuscript resource on Mayflower genealogy."

In 1983 the Society filmed the collection on microfiche. The Bowman Files, as it is now referred to, consists of 229 microfiche cards, grouped by family name, with each card containing approximately 96 handwritten and typed pages.

Mayflower Births & Deaths is a compilation of births and deaths extracted and transcribed from these Files. It is hoped that by printing Mr. Bowman's research it will be more accessible to researchers and therefore provide assistance in the advancement of Mayflower research; after all, wasn't that Mr. Bowman's lifelong objective?

Introduction

Mayflower Births & Deaths (MBD) is a two-volume set compiled in the same format as its companion volume, **Mayflower Marriages (MM)** (1990). The intent of these three volumes is to provide a complete account of the births, deaths and marriages of the descendants of the Mayflower passengers as found in the research files of noted genealogist George E. Bowman.

Volume 1 contains data on the descendants of twelve Mayflower families, John Alden through Samuel Fuller, while Volume 2 continues with eleven Mayflower families, Stephen Hopkins through Edward Winslow. Within these covers will be found data on approximately 50,000 ancestors. As well as baptisms, births, deaths and burials the cemetery is often named and in some cases cause of death, occupation and address at death. Deeds and land records, and in particular, wills and probate records are frequently referred to in determining an approximate death date and/or to provide additional data on a person or family. Gravestone epitaphs, excerpts from wills, court and church records and transcripts of personal letters all provide a respite from the seemingly endless listing of names and dates.

Heavy emphasis has been placed on including sources with each piece of data. If the files did not contain a source, I endeavored to find it myself and include it in footnotes. Extensive use has been made of footnotes which, in some of the larger families, number two or three hundred. They serve to expand and add to data within the text as well as to question and correct data. In keeping with the format used in **MM,** lines of descent are again shown which enable the reader to trace back to the first generation any name that is accompanied by a generation number.

At the end of each Mayflower family section will be found a Reference List of genealogical articles pertaining to each particular family. These listings have been compiled to assist the reader in locating research that has been printed on their particular ancestor in the **Mayflower Descendant** and the **Mayflower Quarterly.** The entries under "Miscellaneous" are by no means complete and include only those articles I have come across in my research. Although it was not my intention to include books under Miscellaneous, I have made an exception with the Mayflower research published by the General Society of Mayflower Descendants. The **Mayflower Families in Progress (MFIP)** booklets and the **Mayflower Families For Five Generations (MF5G)** books are of such immense importance to Mayflower research that they could not be ignored. I refer to them often in **MBD** and find them extremely helpful in researching the first four or five generations. Hopefully, in the not too distant future, each Mayflower family will be represented.

It became obvious to me after **Mayflower Marriages** was published in 1990 that although the format used was easy to follow for some, other less experienced researchers required further clarification. In addition, **Mayflower Births & Deaths** employs subtle rules and guidelines of my own which, if not understood, would inhibit the usefulness of these books. Therefore it is suggested that the following be read and referred to as needed.

GUIDELINES

1. Format

MBD & **MM** are compiled in a format which provides the researcher with an easy system of cross-referencing. Each microfiche card in Bowman's Files is numbered. If you have located a marriage of two persons in **MM** under, for example, the Alden family micro #10, you would refer to the Alden family, micro #10, in **MBD** for a listing of this couple's children. If you do not find a listing of children it is because it was not included in the files. The microfiche number is also given so that if the reader wishes to refer to the Bowman Files for additional data on a specific name, he/she will know which card to search (e.g. "Micro #18 of 32" tells you there are 32 microfiche cards in this family (over 3,000 handwritten pages), with the data to follow being found in card #18).

Each Mayflower family section is divided under second generation sub-headings—the children of the Mayflower patriarch (e.g., Jonathan Alden[2] (John[1])). Thus you will know that the entries under this sub-heading are descended through this branch of the family. For those who already know from which branch they are descended, these sub-headings make it easier to locate ancestors, particularly in the larger families. For the same reason I have included headers at the top of each page.

It became apparent after I was underway with the first volume that too much space was being taken listing children with no birth and death dates and with duplicating listings of children whose parents were both Mayflower descendants. Therefore I began listing children with no dates in the footnotes and also began listing children under the father's Mayflower family instead of two duplicate listings under both father's and mother's Mayflower family. Thus, if a listing of children is to be found elsewhere, the text will read: "CHILDREN OF . . ." with accompanying directives, while "**CHILDREN OF . . .**" (bold print) will precede the listing of children. On the same line will be found a number in parenthesis, e.g. "(10)", which refers to the number of children being listed. If it reads "(4 of 10)", only four children will be listed with the remaining six discussed in the accompanying footnote. When birth and death dates of a spouse are included they will be found on the line immediately preceding "**CHILDREN OF...**"

In doing **Mayflower Marriages** I had a problem showing the difference between data which had been written in pen or pencil. I used the words "poss." and "prob." if

Bowman had written data in pencil. Since these words do not properly express the reasoning behind pencilled data I now make use of the asterisk. Names and dates that Bowman wrote in pencil will be accompanied by "*". (Pencilled data that I verified elsewhere will not be labelled as pencilled.) If the "*" is used in numbering a list of children, e.g. "(12*)", this means all names and dates of the children were written in pencil. In cases where a wife's maiden name was in question you will see, e.g., "Elizabeth (Smith*)". If lines of descent were questionable you may find, e.g., "John Smith^7 (*Josiah^6)" or "John Smith^7*". From what I have been able to ascertain, Bowman used a pencil for two reasons: either he was unsure of the data, or he didn't have a pen handy! Since we do not know which was the case with each and every pencilled entry, we must view them cautiously, particularly if they are not accompanied by sources.

2. Lines of Descent

All names bearing a generation number can be traced back to the first generation. Most Mayflower lines are carried to the seventh and eighth generations (with a few to the tenth), so if you are fortunate enough to find, for example, an eighth generation ancestor, you will be able to trace this line back eight generations. Where complete lines of descent are included for a spouse, non-Mayflower descent of said spouse is shown by descent back to the first generation, while Mayflower descent is shown back to the second generation. Please pay particular attention to the line of descent which identifies a person. John Brown^7 (John^6) can be easily confused with John Brown^7 (Jonathan^6), for example. Do not despair if you come across a Mayflower ancestor who is not shown to have Mayflower descent; this does not necessarily mean that your ancestor is not a Mayflower descendant, only that he/she is not shown as such in the files. A line of descent that is deemed questionable is shown thus: "William Alden^8*" or "William Alden^8 (*David^7)". As a reminder that this line is in question, the line of descent for this person's children will not be included.

If you refer to Volume 2, page 2, you will notice that line of descent is shown in two ways and immediately follows the wording "**CHILDREN OF . . .**". First is the example shown at the bottom of page 2: "**CHILDREN OF** Nathaniel SNOW^5 (Edw.^{4}) . . ." In this case, to find the birth of Nathaniel^5 you must backtrack to find Nathaniel's father, Edward^4. The second example is shown on the same page: "**CHILDREN OF** Joseph SNOW^6 . . .". In this case Joseph has a generation number but is not accompanied by a line of descent in parenthesis because he belongs in the family immediately preceding the listing of his own family. You will see Joseph Snow^6 listed under the "**CHILDREN OF** Joseph SNOW^6 & Mary SEARS". Since no backtracking is involved, a line of descent in parenthesis is not needed to assist in his identification.

3. Footnotes and Sources

The text contains only data found in Bowman's Files. In the many instances where I was able to add names, dates and/or sources that were lacking, the additional data was included in footnotes. Footnotes (shown as, e.g., <46>) are employed to expand on data referred to in the text, such as wills. While the files often contain a transcription of a will, I have not included it. I include the date the will was written and the earliest date recorded in the probate records. Therefore, in cases where the death date is not known, you will know the death occurred between, e.g., "16 June 1783 (will) – 20 Apr. 1784 (prob.)". (The word "prob." is the abbreviated "probate" and is never used to mean "probably".) I also state if the wife/husband was mentioned and name any children who are mentioned. This is done to assist in determining an unknown death date for a spouse or child or to support a known date. You will come across the phrases "dec'd, father's will" (person is actually called deceased in father's will) or "not ment. father's will", which are meant to provide a clue in determining an unknown death date.

Sources can be found either in the text in "<>" brackets, or in footnotes. (The <> brackets are used for sources and footnotes only, while the ( ) brackets are used for lines of descent and additional data.) A source may be individual, referring to one entry, or collective, referring to an entire listing of children. Refer again to Volume 2, page 2 for two examples. First, the source for the children of Joseph Snow[5] and Mary Sears reads: "<1-9, Harwich VR, MD 19:116>", which is quite straightforward—the first nine children can be found recorded in the Harwich Vital Records which were printed in the **Mayflower Descendant,** Vol. 19, page 116. The second example is in the listing for Joseph Snow[6] and Priscilla Berry; note the punctuation between the birth and death dates of the children. A comma (",") means that the source cited for the births (in this case, "Harwich VR, MD 34:110") also covers the deaths, while a semicolon (";") signifies that the source covers the birth date only.

Abbreviations used in citing sources include the following: Church Records/ChR; Land Records/LR; Plymouth Colony Records/PCR; Probate Records/PR; Town Records/TR; Vital Records/VR; Mayflower Descendant/MD; Mayflower Quarterly/MQ; New England Historical and Genealogical Register/NEHGR; The Genealogist/TG; The American Genealogist/TAG. Abbreviated words include the following: administration/adm.; Colony/Co.; cemetery/cem.; daughter/dau; gravestone/g.s.; husband/hus; inventory/inv.; probate/prob.; recorded/rec.; witness/wit.

4. Indexing

All names in the text which have the surname in capital letters (e.g. John COOKE) are indexed. Names in parentheses, such as parents' names (e.g. son of John and Mary Smith) are not included.

When searching for a name within the text or in the footnotes, bear in mind that quite often there are multiple entries for the same name on each page. It is also important to remember the variations in surnames. A man may be recorded as John Hayward at birth, John Haward at marriage and John Howard at death. The town clerk often recorded a name the way it sounded, thus speech and dialect contributed to the variations in surnames.

5. Corrections

From time to time in the Files I have come across errors in Bowman's research. These include typographical errors and inconsistencies as well as errors in data and lines of descent. All known errors have been corrected, with the more serious errors discussed in accompanying footnotes.

Errors in lines of descent can be a nightmare as they sometimes involve correcting several generations on several pages. Two such cases proved troublesome. First, the children of Experience Mitchell and Jane Cooke[2]. Although Bowman believed Jane Cooke was the mother of all of Experience's children, researchers today disagree. Unless additional data is discovered which would pinpoint Jane's year of death, we may never know how many children she bore. Unfortunately many of these Mitchell descendants married Mayflower descendants, thus throughout the files can be found inaccurate lines of descent which had to be carefully watched for and corrected. Lines of descent also had to be changed for the William Swift children. Although Bowman states Elizabeth Tomson[3] (Mary Cooke[2]) married William Swift and had ten children, researchers now say she married Thomas Swift and had only one child. As a result, lines of descent for ten Swift children and their descendants had to be corrected.

ADDENDA TO MAYFLOWER MARRIAGES

Extracting the births and deaths from the Bowman Files required a much closer scrutiny of the handwritten data than it did when I extracted the marriages. My second time through the files has resulted in the discovery of errors made by both Bowman and myself. Since **Mayflower Marriages** is a companion volume to **Births & Deaths** I feel it is necessary to use this opportunity to correct errors that have surfaced. (These corrections also appear in footnotes throughout **Births & Deaths**.) The following corrections should be made to your copy of **Mayflower Marriages:**

Pg. 11 – Upon careful examination of the files it can be seen that Lewis L. Keith is mistakenly given 7th generation Mayflower descent, viz: Calvin Keith[6], Jemima Whitman[5], etc. His descent should read: son of Calvin Keith who is the son of David & Charity Keith.

Pg. 35 – The files incorrectly state the father of Francis Billington[4] (who m. Abigail Churchill) was Francis Billington[3]. Line of descent should read: Francis[4] (Jos.[3]). See MQ 52:137-43.

Pg. 54 – Bowman attributes Experience Barnes[6] with marrying Elisha Corban in 1772. However, a careful examination of the probate records cited in the files proves it was her mother, Experience (Rider) Barnes who married

Elisha. In the settlement of the estate of Benjamin Barnes[5], 9 Nov. 1778, the children mention "Elisha Corbin & Experience, his wife (our mother)". <Plymouth Co. PR 25:408> The line "Experience Barnes[6] & Elisha Corban" should be amended to read: Experience (Rider) Barnes & 2nd Elisha Corban.

Pg. 103 – The wife of Nathaniel Thomas is also shown as Jane (Downs) Jackson. She was possibly his second wife, with Priscilla Shaw (same page) possibly his first wife.

Pg. 137 – The last entry under Micro #17 should read: Benjamin Wilcox[4] (Jeremiah[3], Samuel[2], Daniel[1]) and Patience Tucker. Subsequently, the first nine Wilcox entries immediately following under Micro #18 should have the generation numbers changed to reflect the corrected line of descent.

Pg. 146 – Bowman believed Elizabeth Tomson[3] married William Swift, as he also shows in MD 30:110. However, MFIP, Cooke:19 clearly states Elizabeth married Thomas Swift, "not William Swift as stated in MD 20:110". Page 146, line 4 should be corrected to read: Elizabeth Tomson[3] & Thomas Swift, c1687. Accordingly, all the Swift entries on pages 146 and 147 (including Beale, Spear, Rider, Cornish, Savery) should be corrected to show non-Mayflower descent from William Swift[3] (Wm. [2-1]) instead of Elizabeth Tomson[3].

Pg. 160 – "*Joseph* Hatch[3] & Desire Hawes[4]" should be corrected to read *Josiah* Hatch[3].

Pg. 170 – Under Micro #2 the entry should read: Jabez Fuller[4] (John[3]) & *2nd* Priscilla Samson[4].

Pg. 171 – The following changes should be made to the Jabez Fuller[4] listings, to read as follows:

Jabez Fuller[4] (*John*[3]) & 1st Deborah Soule[4]
Jabez Fuller[4] (*Sam.*[3]) & Mercy Gray[5].

Pg. 249 – The entry for Patience Phinny[5] (John[4]) & Ebenezer Holmes should be amended to read: Patience Phinney & Ebenezer Holmes. Therefore the line of descent should be taken out for the five Holmes entries immediately following. MF5G 2:236 states Patience Phinney[5] (John[4]) married 12 Mar. 1727/8, James Coleman. It further states, "No evidence was found to substantiate the claim that this Patience Phinney was the one who married in Plymouth in 1719, Ebenezer Holmes, when she would have been under fifteen years of age. The Mayflower Society has accepted lineages based on this assumed marriage."

Pg. 253 – The two entries for Gideon Samson should be corrected to read: Gideon Samson[4] (Caleb[3]) and Keziah Carver; Gideon Samson & Rebecca Soule.

Pg. 307 – Take out line of descent for David Bradford Bartlett. Although he may indeed have Mayflower descent through Joseph[6], he is most certainly not his son.

Pg. 311 – Line of descent for Jane Swift^{5} should be corrected to read: Jane/Jean Swift^{5} (Jos.^{4}, Wm. $^{3-2-1}$). See correction for p. 146 above.

Pg. 320 – Under Micro #26, line of descent for both Thomas Swift^{4} and Thankful Swift^{4} should be corrected to read: (Wm.$^{3-2-1}$), *not* (Eliz. Tomson^{3}, Mary Cooke^{2}). See p. 146 above.

Inter-Marriages:

Pg. 342 – Joseph Hatch^{3} & Desire Hawes^{4} should read: *Josiah* Hatch^{3} & Desire Hawes^{4}.
Pg. 346 – Delete Thomas Swift & Thankful Morey^{5}.
Pg. 348 – Delete Joseph Bartlett^{5} & Jane Swift.
Pg. 351 – Delete Benjamin Morey^{5} & Thankful Swift.
Pg. 355 – Delete Jeremiah Wilcox & Judith Briggs^{5}.
Pg. 357 – Delete Nathaniel Holmes & Chloe Sears^{6}.
Pg. 361 – Delete Lewis L. Keith & Asaba Churchill^{8}.

Index:

Corrections:
- p. 366, 1st column—"Batlett" should read Ba*r*tlett.
- Joseph Hatch, take out 160, 342.
- Mary Nickerson, p. 178, *not* 175.
- Samuel Rickard, p. 95, *not* 93.
- Gideon Samson, p. 265, *not* 365.
- Lombard/Loring entries: Four entries under Lombard belong under Loring, viz: Experience, 68; John, 66, 68; Jonathan, 68 and Samuel, 68.

Additions:
- Hatch, Josiah, 342.
- Hatch, Ruth, 294.
- Morey, Benjamin, 320.
- Oakman, Faith, 154.
- Sturtevant, Ephriam, 189.
- Winslow, Sarah, 202.

Acknowledgments

My appreciation to the Massachusetts Society of Mayflower Descendants, not only for allowing me to transcribe the Bowman Files, but for their contribution to Mayflower genealogical research, spanning almost a century.

My appreciation to the General Society of Mayflower Descendants who, through their Five Generations Project, has consistently contributed more to Mayflower research since 1975 than any other organization or group in America. We are all beneficiaries of their hard work.

Susan E. Roser

JOHN ALDEN

MICRO #1 of 16

John ALDEN^{1}, b. c1598 <MD 3:120>; d. 12 Sept. 1687, Duxbury <MD 9:129,193>

John ALDEN^{2}, b. c1627 <MD 1:150>; d. 14 Mar. 1701/2, Boston <MD 6:193>

Jonathan ALDEN^{2}, b. c1632; d. 14 Feb. 1696/7

Daniel ALDEN^{4} (Joseph$^{3-2}$), d. 3 May 1767, Stafford CT <VR 2:173>

Abigail ALDEN, wf of Daniel, d. 12 July 1755, Stafford CT <VR 2:169>

Ebenezer ALDEN^{5} (Daniel^{4}), d. 3 July 1755, Stafford CT <VR 2:169>

Hopestill ALDEN, wf of Zephaniah ALDEN, d. 3 Sept. 1749

Hannah (FOSTER) Alden, wf of Capt. Zephaniah ALDEN^{5} (Dan.^{4}), d. 18 Dec. 1777

Anna (DIMMOCK) Alden, wf of Capt. Zephaniah ALDEN^{5} (Dan.^{4}), d. 29 Sept. 1803, Mansfield **<1>**

Ezra ALDEN^{5} (Eleazer^{4}, Jos.$^{3-2}$), b. 22 June 1734, Bridgewater; d. 1818, Greenwich **<2>**

CHILDREN OF Ezra ALDEN^{5} & 1st Miriam RICHARDSON: (4) **<3>**

Sarah ALDEN^{6}, b. 11 July 1761*; d. 2 Dec. 1817, Lebanon N.H. <Alden Mem.:28>

Judith ALDEN^{6}, b. 5 Nov. 1763* <Alden Mem.:28>

Eunice ALDEN^{6}, b. 13 Nov. 1766; d. 17 May 1854 <Alden Mem.:28>

Ezra ALDEN^{6}, b. 25 July 1769; d. 23 Nov. 1846, Greenwich

CHILDREN OF Ezra ALDEN^{5} & 2nd Sarah (RUGGLES) Harwood: (2 of 6)

Miriam ALDEN^{6}, d. 28 Oct. 1784

Abel ALDEN^{6}, d. 11 Nov. 1784

CHILDREN OF Rev. Abishai ALDEN^{6} (Jos.^{5}, Dan.^{4}, Jos.$^{3-2}$) & Mrs. Elizabeth PARKER: (5)**<4>**

Almira ALDEN^{7}, b. 6 July 1793

Dolly Coffin ALDEN^{7}, b. 22 Feb. 1795; d. 29 Jan. 1796

Augustus ALDEN^{7}, b. 26 Nov. 1796

Sophronia ALDEN^{7}, b. 8 Sept. 1799

Betsy Parker ALDEN^{7}, b. 1 Apr. 1802

Joseph ALDEN^{5} (Daniel^{4}), d. aft. 9 Feb. 1769 (inv.) <Stafford CT Probate #24>

John ALDEN^{4} (Andrew^{3}, Jonathan^{2}), d. aft. 17 June 1765 (inv.) <Windham Probate #63-5>

Elizabeth ( ) ALDEN, d. betw. 13 Dec. 1784 (will)- 27 Apr. 1789 (probate) <Windham Prob.#63-3>

James GEER, d. aft. 8 Apr. 1755 (adm.) <New London CT Probate #2191>**<5>**

John SEABURY Jr., d. aft. 15 Jan. 1744/5 (adm.) <New London CT Probate #4720> **<6>**

Rev. Samuel SEABURY, d. aft. 10 Oct. 1796 (adm.) <New London CT Probate #4722>

Jabin ALDEN^{5} (Wm.^{4}, Andrew^{3}, Jonathan^{2}), d. aft. 9 Aug. 1808 (adm.) <Windham Probate #63-4>

Joseph HEWITT, d. betw. 18 Nov. 1784 (will)- 5 Aug. 1786 (prob.) <Stonington CT Probate #1632>**<7>**

Jabez CHESEBOROUGH, d. betw. 30 Dec. 1754 (will)- 10 Mar. 1758 (receipt) <Ston.CT Probate #1166>

Thomas PALMER, d. aft. 12 Dec. 1752 (adm.) <New London CT Probate #3939>

DAVID ALDEN^{2} (John^{1})

David ALDEN^{2}, b. c1646 (MD 7:64); d. betw. 13 Mar. 1717/8 (deed) - 1 Apr. 1719 (adm.), Duxbury <MD 9:145,6:239-43>

Alice ALDEN^{3}, b. c1685 (MD 9:147-150); d. 12 July 1774, 89th yr, bur. Dennis <PN&Q 5:126>

Judah PADDOCK, (son of Zachary) b. 15 Sept. 1681, Yarmouth <MD 3:247>; d. 31 Mar. 1770,bur.Dennis <PN&Q 5:126>

CHILDREN OF Judah PADDOCK & Alice ALDEN^{3}: (7) <MD 13:223>

Reuben PADDOCK^{4}, b. 27 Dec. 1707, Yarmouth

Judah PADDOCK^{4}, b. 27 Mar. 1709/10, Yarmouth

Samuel PADDOCK^{4}, b. 12 Oct. 1711, Yarmouth; d. 27 July 1757*<g.s.>

Mary PADDOCK^{4}, b. 5 Mar. 1714, Yarmouth

Grace PADDOCK^{4}, b. 27 Jan. 1715/6, Yarmouth; d. 17 Sept. 1780* <Brewster g.s.>
Rebecca PADDOCK^{4}, b. 12 May 1718, Yarmouth
Nathaniel PADDOCK^{4}, b. 27 Feb. 1723/4, Yarmouth
John SEARS, b. 18 July 1701, Harwich <MD 3:175>; d. 21 May 1774*<Brewster g.s>
CHILDREN OF John SEARS & Grace PADDOCK^{4}: (11)
Daughter, b. 13 Nov. 1735, Yarmouth*; d. 15 Dec. 1735* <Sears Gen.:71>
John SEARS^{5}, b. 5 June 1737*
Rebecca SEARS^{5}, bpt. 3 May 1741, Harwich <MD 7:147>; d. after 20 July 1779**<8>**
Nathan SEARS^{5}, bpt. 5 July 1741, Harwich <MD 7:147>; d.y.
Phebe SEARS^{5}, bpt. 4 Dec. 1743, Harwich <Sears Gen.:77>
David SEARS^{5}, bpt. 27 Apr. 1746, Harwich <MD 8:120> (wf Phebe Taylor below)
Samuel SEARS^{5}, bpt. 27 Apr. 1746, Harwich <MD 8:120>; d.y.
Rhoda SEARS^{5}, bpt. 16 Oct. 1748, Harwich <MD 9:207>; d. prob. pre 20 July 1779**<8>**
Grace SEARS^{5}, bpt. 12 Aug. 1752, Harwich, d. 1771 <Sears Gen.:77>
Enoch SEARS^{5}, bpt. 11 May 1755, Harwich <MD 10:132>; d. "?1779"**<8>**
Ezra SEARS^{5}, bpt. 12 June 1757, Harwich <MD 10:251>; d. 1778, Plymouth Harbor "frozen" <Sears:7
Phebe TAYLOR^{6} (John^{5}, Abigail Hopkins^{4}, Joshua^{3}, Gyles^{2}), b. 6 May 1746, Eastham
Robert Burnum WHEELER, b. 8 Mar. 1770
Rebecca SEARS, b. 16 Apr. 1775, Harwich
CHILDREN OF Robert Burnam WHEELER & Rebecca SEARS: (7)**<9>**
David Sears WHEELER, b. 17 Aug. 1798
Joseph WHEELER, b. 31 May 1800
Robert Burnum WHEELER Jr., b. 23 Dec. 1801
Phebe Sears WHEELER, b. 17 July 1803; d. 18 July 1803
Williard WHEELER, b. 3 Sept. 1804
Catharine Sears WHEELER, b. 7 Apr. 1806
Dulcia Aurilla WHEELER, b. 12 Dec. 1808
CHILDREN OF Willard WHEELER & Bethiah FREEMAN: (5)**<9>**
Mary Ann WHEELER, b. 26 Feb. 1835; d. 16 July 1867
Emeline Freeman WHEELER, b. 8 May 1837
Delia Tappan WHEELER, b. 21 Feb. 1841; d. 10 Apr. 1893
Charlotte Ellis WHEELER, b. 23 Dec. 1844; d. 12 Aug. 1861
Alice Freeman WHEELER, b. 19 Jan. 1849; d. 26 Nov. 1849
CHILDREN OF Stevens ATWOOD & Rhoda SEARS^{5} (Grace Paddock^{4}): (6)
Stevens ATWOOD^{6}, bpt. 11 July 1773, Harwich/Brewster <MD 13:101>**<10>**
Rhoda ATWOOD^{6}, bpt. 17 Dec. 1775, Harwich/Brewster <MD 13:135>**<10>**
Robert ATWOOD^{6}, bpt. 7 Nov. 1779, Harwich/Brewster <MD 13:137>**<10>**
Rebecca Sears ATWOOD^{6}, bpt. Oct. 1785, Orleans <MD 12:152>
Phebe Sears ATWOOD^{6}, bpt. 3 June 1787, Orleans <MD 13:90>
John ATWOOD^{6}, bpt. 26 July 1789, Orleans <MD 13:91>
Deacon Benjamin ALDEN^{3}, d. 14 Apr. 1741, Duxbury (drowned) <MD 8:233>
Hannah BREWSTER^{4} (Wrestling^{3}, Love^{2}), b. cSept. 1688; d. 8 Jan. 1763, ae.74y4m12d <Dux.ChR 1:2
CHILDREN OF Benjamin ALDEN^{3} & Hannah BREWSTER^{4}:(8) <MD 10:185>
Mary ALDEN^{4}, b. 1 Jan. 1709/10, Duxbury; d. 4 Apr. 1789 <MD 11:79>
Sarah ALDEN^{4}, b. 5 Apr. 1712, Duxbury; d. pre 1741* **<11>**
Elizabeth ALDEN^{4}, b. 12 Sept. 1714, Duxbury; d. 9 July 1771, (apoplexy) <Dux.ChR.1:252>
David ALDEN^{4}, b. 14 Feb. 1717, Duxbury
Ichabod ALDEN^{4}, b. 5 Oct. 1719, Duxbury; d. pre 1741* **<11>**
Bezaleel ALDEN^{4}, b. 15 May 1722, Duxbury; d. 9 Feb. 1799* <Duxbury ChR.1:245>
Wrestling ALDEN^{4}, b. 11 Oct. 1724, Duxbury; d. 7 Sept. 1813*

Abiathar ALDEN^{4}, b. 29 July 1731, Duxbury

CHILDREN OF Wrestling ALDEN^{4} (Ben.^{3}) & Elizabeth ( ): (9 of 12) <MD 12:168>

Michael ALDEN^{5}, (dau.), b. 9 Feb. 1748/9, Duxbury

Bartlett ALDEN^{5}, b. 22 Mar. 1749/50, Duxbury

Wrestling ALDEN^{5}, b. 14 June 17751, Duxbury

Son, b. 24 Jan. 1753, stillborn

Priscilla ALDEN^{5}, b. 19 Oct. 1756, Duxbury

Sarah ALDEN^{5}, b. 21 Mar. 1758, Duxbury

Patmos ALDEN^{5}, b. 12 Aug. 1759, Duxbury

Elizabeth ALDEN^{5}, b. 29 Mar. 1761, Duxbury

Abiathar ALDEN^{5}, b. 16 Apr. 1763, Duxbury

Elizabeth ALDEN^{3}, d. ?4 Jan. 1771, Stonington CT

John SEABURY, d. 17 Dec. 1759, ae. 86, Hampstead L.I.

CHILDREN OF John SEABURY & Elizabeth ALDEN^{3}: (8) <Groton CT VR:8>[<12>]

David SEABURY^{4}, b. 16 Jan. 1698/9

John SEABURY^{4}, b. 25 Nov. 1700, d. same day

Patience SEABURY^{4}, b. 5 May 1702

John SEABURY^{4}, b. 22 May 1704

Samuel SEABURY^{4}, b. 8 July 1706; d. 15 June 1764

Mary SEABURY^{4}, b. 11 Nov. 1708

Sarah SEABURY^{4}, b. 16 Mar. 1710/1

Nathaniel SEABURY^{4}, b. 31 July 1720

CHILDREN OF Samuel SEABURY & Abigail ( ): (2) <Groton CT VR 1:137>[<13>]

Caleb SEABURY, b. 27 Feb. 1728/9

Samuel SEABURY, b. 30 Nov. 1729

CHILDREN OF John SEABURY & Esther ( ): (3) <Groton CT VR 1:147>[<13>]

Easter SEABURY, b. 4 May 1734

John SEABURY, b. 12 Jan. 1735/6

Elizabeth SEABURY, b. 4 July 1738

Abigail SEABURY^{4} (Samuel$^{3-2}$, John^{1}), b. 7 Mar. 1704/5, Duxbury <MD 9:24>; d. 1763, Boston

CHILD OF David SEABURY^{4} (Eliz. Alden^{3}) & Abigail SEABURY^{4} (Samuel^{3}):

Abigail SEABURY^{5}, b. 31 Mar. 1734/5, N. Yarmouth ME, d. 8 May 1781, N.Yarmouth <Cert. Town Clerk>

John MASON, b. 13 Sept. 1734, N. Yarmouth ME, d. 3 Feb. 1769, N. Yarmouth ME <Cert. Town Clerk>

CHILD OF John MASON & Abigail SEABURY^{5} (David^{4}): (1)

Patience MASON^{6}, b. 5 June 1764, N. Yarmouth ME <Cert. Town Clerk>

John OAKES, b. 4 Sept. 1759, N. Yarmouth ME, d. 17 Mar. 1845, Temple ME <Cert. Town Clerk>

CHILD OF John OAKES & Patience MASON^{6} (Abigail Seabury^{5}): (1)

Abigail OAKES^{7}, b. 5 June 1781, N. Yarmouth ME, d. 30 Mar. 1856, Temple ME <Cert. Town Clerk>

Nathaniel STAPLES, b. 1779, Kittery ME, d. 17 June 1829, Temple ME <Cert. Town Clerk>

CHILD OF Nathaniel STAPLES & Abigail OAKES^{7}: (1)

Nathaniel King STAPLES^{8}, b. 7 Apr. 1806, Temple ME, d. 9 Mar. 1886, Temple ME <Cert. Town Clerk>

MICRO #2 of 16

Susan Staples CONANT, b. 7 Feb. 1812, Temple ME, d. 10 Sept. 1890, Temple ME <Cert. Town Clerk>

CHILD OF Nathaniel King STAPLES^{8} & Susan Staples CONANT: (1)

Rachel Hoyt STAPLES^{9}, b. 30 Aug. 1842, Temple ME <Cert.>; d. 16 Dec. 1894, Brookline MA

George Washington MOORE, b. 16 Oct. 1840, Springfield MA; d. 7 Mar. 1925, Brookline MA

CHILD OF George Washington MOORE & Rachel Hoyt STAPLES^{9}: (1)

George Albert MOORE^{10}, b. 29 May 1869

CHILDREN OF Joseph LATHAM^{2} & Patience SEABURY^{4} (Eliz. Alden^{3}): (4 of 6)<Groton CT VR 1:124>[<13>]

David LATHAM^{5}, b. 18 Sept. 1724

Elizabeth LATHAM[5], b. 25 Nov. 1726

Joseph LATHAM[5], b. 27 Jan. 1728

Mary LATHAM[5], b. 11 July 1735

Joseph LATHAM[2] (Joseph[1]), d. aft. 18 Sept. 1746 (will) <New London CT Probate #E/435-6>

Joseph LATHAM[1], d. aft. 14 Mar. 1705/6 (will) <New London CT Probate A/332-3>

Priscilla ALDEN[3], d. aft. 19 Jan. 1735/6 (husband's will) <New London CT Prob.D:248>

Samuel CHEESBOROUGH Jr., d. 2 Mar. 1735/6 <New London CT Probate D:319>

CHILDREN OF Samuel CHEESBOROUGH Jr. & Priscilla ALDEN[3]: (7) <Stonington CT VR 1:101>

Mary CHEESBOROUGH[4], b. 21 Sept. 1702

Priscilla CHEESBOROUGH[4], b. 6 Nov. 1704

Nathaniel CHEESBOROUGH[4], b. 19 Aug. 1706, d. 22 Apr. 1709

Amos CHEESBOROUGH[4], b. 2 Feb. 1708/9

Hannah CHEESBOROUGH[4], b. 16 July 1712

Sarah CHEESBOROUGH[4], b. 14 Aug. 1715

Prudence CHEESBOROUGH[4], b. 28 Feb. 1721/2

CHILDREN OF Amos CHESEBROUGH[4] (Prisc. Alden[3]) & Desire WILLIAMS: (5) <Stonington CT VR 1:129>

Amos CHESEBROUGH[5], b. last of Dec. 1730

Desire CHESEBROUGH[5], b. 14 Mar. 1732/3

Lydia CHESEBROUGH[5], b. 1 Dec. 1735

Priscilla CHESEBROUGH[5], b. 11 June 1738

Mary CHESEBROUGH[5], b. 13 Nov. 1740

Jabez CHESEBROUGH, d. 13 June 1731 <New London CT Probate C/508,509>**<14>**

John STANTON, prob. d. 16 Nov. 1762*, Groton CT

CHILDREN OF John STANTON & Prudence CHEESBOROUGH[4] (Prisc. Alden[3]): (9)<Groton CT VR 1:181>**<13>**

Sarah Chesebrough STANTON[5], b. 31 July 1739

Zerviah STANTON[5], b. 11 Sept. 1742

John STANTON[5], b. 17 May 1745

Samuel STANTON[5], b. 10 Nov. 1747

Amos STANTON[5], b. 29 Nov. 1750

Prudence STANTON[5], b. 7 Nov. 1754

James STANTON[5], b. 28 Dec. 1756

Robert STANTON[5]*, b. 1752; d. aft. 1783 (will), Stonington CT <Chesebrough Gen:310>

Cassandra STANTON[5]*, b. 1762 <Chesebrough Gen:310>

Ruth ALDEN[3], b. c1674 <MD 9:150-1>; d. 2 July 1758, ae 84 <Rochester VR 2:101>

Samuel SPRAGUE, b. c1669; d. 25 July 1740, Rochester, ae 71 <MD 20:192>

CHILDREN OF Samuel SPRAGUE & Ruth ALDEN[3]: (8)

Noah SPRAGUE[4], b. 18 Jan. 1696/7, Duxbury <MD 9:25>; d. 3 Sept. 1773 <Rochester g.s.>

Elizabeth SPRAGUE[4], b. 4 July 1699, Duxbury <MD 9:25>; d. pre 10 Dec. 1763*

Nathaniel SPRAGUE[4], b. 10 Jan. 1701, Duxbury <MD 9:25>; d. 29 July 1739 <Rochester VR 2:100>

Samuel SPRAGUE[4], b. 23 June 1704, Duxbury <MD 9:25>; d. 21 June 1727, Jamaica<Rochester VR 2:100>

Mary SPRAGUE[4], b. 20 Dec. 1706, Duxbury, d. 19 Dec. 1708 <MD 9:25>

Priscilla SPRAGUE[4], b. 18 Mar. 1708/9, Duxbury <MD 9:25>; d. 23 Oct. 1779* <Rochester g.s.>

Micah SPRAGUE[4], d. Sept. 1734, New Providence, W. Indies <Rochester VR 2:100>

Ruth SPRAGUE[4], b. 30 Aug. 1714 <Rochester VR 2:45>; d. 9 Apr. 1733, Rochester <MD 20:190>

Kezia ( ) SPRAGUE, d. 12 May 1790, ae 89 <Rochester VR 2:101>**<15>**

CHILDREN OF Micah SPRAGUE[4] (Ruth Alden[3]) & Elizabeth TURNER: (2)

Ruth SPRAGUE[5], b. 2 Mar. 1734* <Rochester VR>

Mary SPRAGUE[5], b. 1 Nov. 1731* <Rochester VR>

CHILDREN OF Nathaniel SPRAGUE[4] (Ruth Alden[3]) & Kezia ( ): (3)

Lucy SPRAGUE[5], b. 23 Feb. 1731/2*

Micah SPRAGUE^5, b. 31 Jan. 1735*

Nathaniel SPRAGUE^5, b. 21 May 1738*; d. 9 Jan. 1797, ae 59 <Rochester g.s.>

Mary BASSETT*, d. 2 June 1770, ae 23 <Rochester g.s.>

CHILD OF Nathaniel SPRAGUE^5 (Nath.^{4}) & 1st Mary BASSETT*: (1)

Francis SPRAGUE^6, b. 1 Apr. 1770, d. same day

Elizabeth HAMMOND*, d. 10 Mar. 1805, ae 63 <Rochester g.s.>

CHILD OF Nathaniel SPRAGUE^5 & 2nd Elizabeth HAMMOND*:

Ruth SPRAGUE^6, b. Sept. 1775; d. 25 Oct. 1775, ae 5 wks.

Sarah HAMMOND*, (dau. of Lt. John*), b. 23 Dec. 1695* <Rochester VR*>; d. 26 Sept. 1777, ae 82 <Rochester g.s.>

CHILDREN OF Noah SPRAGUE^4 (Ruth Alden^3) & Sarah HAMMOND*: (10) <Rochester VR 2:2>

Joshua SPRAGUE^5, b. 20 Feb. 1722/3, d. 17 Sept. 1725

Alden SPRAGUE^5, b. 27 Sept. 1724

Alathea SPRAGUE^5, b. 24 Mar. 1725/6

Elizabeth SPRAGUE^5, b. 15 Oct. 1727, d. 31 May 1736

Samuel SPRAGUE^5, b. 9 May 1729, d. 17 June 1729

Mary SPRAGUE^5, b. 24 June 1730, d. 4 July 1730

Samuel SPRAGUE^5, b. 19 June 1731

Noah SPRAGUE^5, b. 3 Apr. 1733; d. 30 May 1773 <Rochester g.s.>

Elizabeth SPRAGUE^5, b. 31 Jan. 1736/7

John SPRAGUE^5, b. 21 June 1740

CHILDREN OF Noah SPRAGUE^5 (Noah^4) & Mercy DEXTER: (5) <Rochester VR 2:2>**<16>**

Peleg SPRAGUE^6, b. 10 Dec. 1756

Alden SPRAGUE^6, b. 29 Mar. 1765

Paul SPRAGUE^6, b. 22 Jan. 1767

Hannah SPRAGUE^6, b. 20 Mar. 1769

Nathaniel SPRAGUE^6, b. 29 May 1771, d. 10 July 1776

Benjamin HAMMOND, d. pre 30 Nov. 1763* <2nd marr. of wf>

CHILDREN OF Benjamin HAMMOND & Priscilla SPRAGUE^4 (Ruth Alden^3): (2)

Priscilla HAMMOND^5, bpt. 12 Apr. 1741* <2nd Ch. Rochester>

Hannah HAMMOND^5, bpt. 25 Dec. 1743* <2nd Ch. Rochester>

Anna BARLOW, dau. of Moses, b. 23 Mar. 1699* <Rochester VR>; d. 11 Jan. 1778*<Rochester VR>

CHILD of Samuel SPRAGUE^4 (Ruth Alden^3) & Anna BARLOW: (1)**<17>**

Susanna SPRAGUE^5, b. 28 July 1727*

CHILDREN OF Timothy MENDALL: (7)

Anne Claghorn MENDALL, b. 9 May 1801 <Rochester VR 1:216>

Constant S. MENDALL, b. 6 Oct. 1798 <Rochester VR 1:216>

Joseph Claghorn MENDALL, b. 26 June 1796 <Rochester VR 1:217>

Patty Crandon MENDALL, b. 6 Apr. 1792 <Rochester VR 1:217>

Sally Crandon MENDALL, b. 13 Jan. 1805 <Rochester VR 1:217>

Silvia Record MENDALL, b. 24 Dec. 1815 <Rochester VR 1:217>

Samuel MENDALL, b. 8 Mar. 1794 <Rochester VR 1:217>

CHILDREN OF Seth AMES & Sarah (   ): (5) <Rochester VR 1:15>

Sarah AMES, b. 28 Mar. 1769

Seth AMES, b. 5 Mar. 1772

Deliverance AMES, b. 13 Apr. 1775

Elisabeth AMES, b. 13 Apr. 1775 (twins)

Thomas Crandol AMES, b. 9 Feb. 1779

Samuel ALDEN^3, b. Dec. 1688 <MD 7:64>; d. 24 Feb. 1781, ae 92y2m3d, bur. S.Duxbury <MD 9:159>

Sarah SPRAGUE, b. c1701, d. 28 Mar. 1773, ae 72, bur. S. Duxbury <MD 9:159>

CHILDREN OF Samuel ALDEN^{3} & Sarah SPRAGUE: (8)

Rebecca ALDEN^{4}, b. 4 Jan. 1729/30, Duxbury <MD 11:236>; d. 21 July 1818* <Duxbury g.s.>

Sarah ALDEN^{4}, b. 2 Dec. 1731, Duxbury <MD 11:236>; d. 4 May 1788 <Dux. g.s.>

John ALDEN^{4}, b. 20 Mar. 1733/4, Duxbury <MD 11:236>; d. 1761*

Alice ALDEN^{4}, b. 5 Sept. 1735, Duxbury <MD 11:236>

Samuel ALDEN^{4}, b. 13 Aug. 1737, Duxbury <MD 11:236>

Ichabod ALDEN^{4}, b. 11 Aug. 1739, Duxbury <MD 11:236>; d. 11 Nov. 1778*

Alathea ALDEN^{4}, b. 24 Aug. 1744, Duxbury <MD 12:163>

Abigail ALDEN^{4}, b. 23 Apr. 1750, Duxbury <MD 12:163>

Thomas FRAZIER, b. 1736; d. 18 Nov. 1782, ae 46y9m4d, Duxbury <MD 9:160>

CHILDREN OF Thomas FRAZIER & Rebecca ALDEN^{4} (Sam.^{3}): (2)

Samuel Alden FRAZAR^{5}, b. 12 July 1766; d. 28 Aug. 1838

Rebecca FRAZAR^{5}, b. c1768*; d. 17 Nov. 1840*

ELIZABETH ALDEN^{2} (John^{1})

Elizabeth ALDEN^{2}, b. c1624, Plymouth <MD 3:11>; d. 31 May 1717, ae 93, Little Compton

William PABODIE, b. c1619; d. 13 Dec. 1707, ae 88, Little Compton <MD 6:129,132,134>

CHILDREN OF William PABODIE & Elizabeth ALDEN^{2}: (13)

John PABODIE^{3}, b. 4 Oct. 1645, Duxbury <MD 9:171>; d. 17 Nov. 1669, Duxbury <MD 12:30>

Elizabeth PABODIE^{3}, b. 24 Apr. 1647, Duxbury <MD 9:171>

Mary PABODIE^{3}, b. 7 Aug. 1648, Duxbury <MD 9:171>

Mercy PABODIE^{3}, b. 2 Jan. 1649, Duxbury <MD 9:171>

Martha PABODIE^{3}, b. 24 Feb. 1650, Duxbury <MD 9:171>; d. 25 Jan. 1712* <L.Compton VR 4:6:116>

Priscilla PABODIE^{3}, b. 16 Nov. 1652, Duxbury <MD 9:171>;d. 2 Mar. 1652/3, Duxbury <MD 12:31>

Priscilla PABODIE^{3}, b. 15 Jan. 1653, Duxbury <MD 9:171>

Sarah PABODIE^{3}, b. 7 Aug. 1656, Duxbury <MD 9:171>

Ruth PABODIE^{3}, b. 27 June 1658, Duxbury <MD 9:171>

Rebecca PABODIE^{3}, b. 16 Oct. 1660, Duxbury <MD 9:171>

Hannah PABODIE^{3}, b. 15 Oct. 1662, Duxbury <MD 9:172>; d. 29 Apr. 1723, bur. Plymouth

William PABODIE^{3}, b. 24 Nov. 1664, Duxbury <MD 9:172>; d. 17 Sept. 1744

Lydia PABODIE^{3}, b. 3 Apr. 1667, Duxbury <MD 9:172>; d. 13 July 1748, Saybrook CT<Barbour's VR:54>

John ROGERS^{3} (John^{2}), d. 28 June 1732, Barrington <MD 20:2>

CHILDREN OF John ROGERS^{3} & Elizabeth PABODIE^{3}: (5)

Hannah ROGERS^{4}, b. 16 Nov. 1668, Duxbury <MD 9:172>

John ROGERS^{4}, b. 22 Sept. 1670, Duxbury <MD 9:172>

Elizabeth ROGERS^{4}, b. 16 Apr. 1673, Duxbury <MD 9:173>

Ruth ROGERS^{4}, b. 18 Apr. 1675, Duxbury <MD 9:173>

Sarah ROGERS^{4}, b. 4 May 1677, Duxbury <MD 9:173>

Samuel BARTLETT^{4} (Ben.^{3}, Mary Warren^{2}), d. pre 4 Mar. 1715 <wf's 2nd marr.MD 14:37>

CHILDREN OF Samuel BARTLETT^{4} & Hannah PABODIE^{3}: (2 of 3)

Benjamin BARTLETT^{4}, b. 4 May 1684, Duxbury <MD 9:174>

Joseph BARTLETT^{4}, b. 12 Apr. 1686, Duxbury <MD 9:174>

Daniel GRINNELL, b. c1668; d. 7 Jan. 1740/1, Saybrook CT <Barbour's VR:54>

CHILDREN OF Daniel GRINNELL & Lydia PABODIE^{3}: (9 of 11)[<18>]

Mary GRINNELL^{4}, d. 9 June 1755* <Westbrook g.s.>

Priscilla GRINNELL^{4}, b. c1690*; d. 12 Jan. 1770, ae 81, Killingworth CT

Elizabeth GRINNELL^{4}, b. ( )

Lydia GRINNELL^{4}, b. "?"pre 1696*

Rebecca GRINNELL^{4}, b. ( )

Sarah GRINNELL^4, b. ( )

Jemima GRINNELL^4, b. 26 Jan. 1704/5*

Peabody GRINNELL^4, b. ( )

George GRINNELL^4, d. betw. 29 Apr. 1755 (will) - 23 Nov. 1759 (probate)

John BROOKER, d. 14 Nov. 1731 <Saybrook CT VR 2:410>

CHILDREN OF John BROOKER & Sarah GRINNELL^4 (Lydia Pabodie^3): (7) <Saybrook CT VR 2:410>

John BROOKER^5, b. 21 July 1718

Samuel BROOKER^5, b. 28 May 1720

Mary BROOKER^5, b. 22 Mar. 1723 (twins)

Sarah BROOKER^5, b. 22 Mar. 1723, d. 28 Mar. 1723

Sarah BROOKER^5, b. 14 Aug. 1726

Edward BROOKER^5, b. 22 Mar. 1728/9, d. June 1729

Patience BROOKER^5, b. 10 May 1732

CHILDREN OF George GRINNELL^4 (Lydia Pabodie^3) & Mary BULL: (9)

William GRINNELL^5, b. 26 Feb. 1726/7*

Daniel GRINNELL^5, b. ( )

Mary GRINNELL^5, b. ( )

Anne GRINNELL^5, b. ( )

Phebe GRINNELL^5, b. ( )

Rebecca GRINNELL^5, b. ( )

Lydia GRINNELL^5, b. ( )

Lucy GRINNELL^5, b. ( )

Temperance GRINNELL^5, b. ( )

CHILDREN OF Joseph CLARK & Lydia GRINNELL^4 (Lydia Pabodie^3): (4) <1-3, Saybrook CR VR 2:540>

Joseph CLARK^5, b. 25 Jan. 1713/4

Rebecca CLARK^5, b. 5 June 1716

Lydia CLARK^5, b. 4 May 1718

Daniel CLARK^5, b. ( ) <"deeds">

CHILDREN OF Joseph CLARK Jr. & Lydia ( ): (2)

David CLARK, b. 20 Nov. 1750 <Haddam LR 5:276>

Jonathan CLARK, b. 20 Nov. 1750 (twins) <Haddam LR 5:276>

Robert LAY, d. 1 July 1738, bur. Westbrook* <NEHGR 62:173>

CHILDREN OF Robert LAY & Mary GRINNELL^4 (Lydia Pabodie^3): (8)* <1-6, Saybrook CT VR 2:168>

Robert LAY^5, b. 20 Dec. 1705

Christopher LAY^5, b. 27 Feb. 1707/8

Lydia LAY^5, b. 26 June 1710

Daniel LAY^5, b. 3 Oct. 1712

Jeremiah LAY^5, b. 13 Jan. 1715

Phebe LAY^5, b. 29 May 1717

Jonathan LAY^5, b. 1718; d. Feb. 1779 (smallpox)

John LAY^5, b. ( )

Theophilus REDFIELD, b. 1682; d. 14 Feb. 1759, Killingworth CT

CHILDREN OF Theophilus REDFIELD & Priscilla GRINNELL^4 (Lydia Pabodie^3):(2)

Daniel REDFIELD^5, b. ( )

Peleg REDFIELD^5, b. ( )

CHILD OF Daniel REDFIELD^5 (Priscilla Grinnell^4):

Daniel REDFIELD^6, b. ( )

Samuel SEABURY^2, (son of John & Grace), d. 5 Aug. 1681, Duxbury <MD 8:232>**<19>**

CHILDREN OF Samuel SEABURY^2 & 2nd Martha PABODIE^3: (3)

Joseph SEABURY^4, b. 8 June 1678, Duxbury <MD 9:173>

Martha SEABURY^4, b. 23 Sept. 1679, Duxbury <MD 9:173>

Child, b. ( )<20>

William FOBES, d. 6 Nov. 1712 <Bristol Co. Prob. 3:115>

CHILDREN OF William FOBES & Martha PABODIE^3: (4)

Elizabeth FOBES^4, b. 1683

Constant FOBES^4, b. 1686

Mary FOBES^4, b. 1689; d. 14 Feb. 1712

Mercy FOBES^4, b. 1694; d. 29 July 1712

MICRO #3 of 16<21>

Patience KEMP, d. 29 Oct. 1676, Duxbury <MD 12:31>

CHILDREN OF Samuel SEABURY^2 (John^1) & 1st Patience KEMP: (8) <Duxbury, MD 9:172>

Elizabeth SEABURY, b. 16 Sept. 1661; d. aft. 1718

Sarah SEABURY, b. 18 Aug. 1663

Samuel SEABURY, b. 20 Apr. 1666

Hannah SEABURY, b. 7 July 1668

John SEABURY, b. 7 Nov. 1670; d. 18 Mar. 1671/2 <MD 12:30>

Grace SEABURY, b. 1 Mar. 1672/3; d. 16 Mar. 1672/3 <MD 12:31>

Patience SEABURY, b. 1 Mar. 1672/3, (twins); d. 7 Mar. 1672/3 <MD 12:30>

John SEABURY, b. pre 29 Oct. 1676 <mother's dth.>

Joseph CHILDS, d. 11 Mar. 1717/8, Marshfield <MD 7:133>

CHILDREN OF Joseph CHILDS & Elizabeth SEABURY^3 (Sam.^{2}, John^1): (9) <Marshfield, MD 6:19>

Elizabeth CHILDS, b. 22 Nov. 1691

Priscilla CHILDS, b. 5 Nov. 1693

Mary CHILDS, b. 31 May 1695; d. 10 Apr. 1715 <MD 7:133>

Patience CHILDS, b. 11 Apr. 1696

Joseph CHILDS, b. 14 Jan. 1697/8; d. 14 June 1718

Hannah CHILDS, b. 1 Jan. 1699/1700

Sarah CHILDS, b. 11 Mar. 1702

Richard CHILDS, b. 1 Apr. 1704

Grace CHILDS, b. 18 June 1706; d. 22 Apr. 1716<MD 7:133>

Elizabeth CROCKER, d. 15 Jan. 1716, Barnstable <MD 4:120>

CHILDREN OF Richard CHILDS & Elizabeth CROCKER: (11) <Barnstable, MD 4:120>

Samuel CHILDS, b. 6 Nov. 1679

Elizabeth CHILDS, b. 23 Jan. 1681

Thomas CHILDS, b. 10 Jan. 1682

Hannah CHILDS, b. 22 Jan. 1684

Timothy CHILDS, b. 22 Sept. 1686

Ebenezer CHILDS, b. "latter end" Mar. 1691

Elizabeth CHILDS, b. 6 June 1692

James CHILDS, b. 6 Nov. 1694

Mercy CHILDS, b. 7 May 1697

Joseph CHILDS, b. 5 Mar. 1699/1700

Thankful CHILDS, b. 15 Aug. 1702

CHILDREN OF Samuel SEABURY^3 (Sam.^{2}, John^1) & Abigail ALLEN: (12) <Duxbury, MD 9:24>

Benjamin SEABURY, b. 24 Sept. 1689

Patience SEABURY, b. 11 Apr. 1691, d. 3 Feb. 1698/9

Samuel SEABURY, b. 24 Oct. 1692; d. 25 Sept. 1762, bur. S. Duxbury <MD 10:169>

Son, b. 23 Apr. 1695, d. same day

Son, b. 24 Mar. 1696, d. same day

Dau., b. 14 Feb. 1697, d. same day

Son, b. 3 Sept. 1698, d. 15 Sept. 1698

Barnabas SEABURY, b. 29 Jan. 1700

Dau., b. 13 Apr. 1702, d. same day

Dau., b. 11 Mar. 1703, d. same day

Abigail SEABURY, b. 7 Mar. 1704/5

Patience SEABURY, b. 10 Aug. 1710

Mary JOHNSON*, d. 29 Oct. 1723, Bridgewater <MD 15:91>

CHILD OF Barnabas SEABURY^{4} (Sam.$^{3-2}$, John^{1}) & 1st Mary JOHNSON*: (1)

Rebecca SEABURY, b. 24 Sept. 1723, Bridgewater <MD 15:91>

Deborah WISWALL^{4} (Prisc. Pabodie^{3}, Eliz. Alden^{2}), d. 22 Apr. 1776, ae 83,bur.S.Duxbury<MD 10:169>

CHILDREN OF Samuel SEABURY^{4} (Sam.$^{3-2}$, John^{1}) & Deborah WISWALL^{4}: (9) <Duxbury, MD 9:25>

Sarah SEABURY^{5}, b. 21 July 1718

Hannah SEABURY^{5}, b. 26 June 1720

Hopestill SEABURY^{5}, b. 31 May 1722

Faith SEABURY^{5}, b. 12 Oct. 1724

Paul SEABURY^{5}, b. 26 Nov. 1728

Oliver SEABURY^{5}, b. 26 Dec. 1730

Wiswall SEABURY^{5}, b. 6 Apr. 1733

Deborah SEABURY^{5}, b. 13 Apr. 1727

Mercy SEABURY^{5}, b. 10 Nov. 1735

Joseph SEABURY^{4} (Martha Pabodie^{3}) b. 8 June 1678, Duxbury <MD 9:173>; d. 22 Aug. 1755 <Little Compton RI ":156"*>

Phebe SMITH, b. c1679, d. 21 Apr. 1715 <Little Compton RI ":156"*>

CHILDREN OF Joseph SEABURY^{4} (Martha Pabodie^{3}) & 1st Phebe SMITH: (6)**<22>**

Samuel SEABURY^{5}, b. 5 June 1702; d. Mar. 1768

Martha SEABURY^{5}, b. 7 Feb. 1704

Joseph SEABURY^{5}, b. 2 Dec. 1705

Benjamin SEABURY^{5}, b. 20 Jan. 1708; d. 11 Sept. 1773

Sion SEABURY^{5}, b. 27 Mar. 1713; d. 10 Aug. 1801*

Mary SEABURY^{5}, b. 17 Apr. 1715

CHILDREN OF Joseph SEABURY^{4} & 2nd Mary LADD: (7) <Tiverton RI VR 1:23>

Phebe SEABURY^{5}, b. 2 Mar. 1723/4

Hannah SEABURY^{5}, b. 7 Feb. 1724/5

Gideon SEABURY^{5}, b. 16 May 1726

John SEABURY^{5}, b. 26 Nov. 1727

Elizabeth SEABURY^{5}, b. 2 Feb. 1729/30

Sarah SEABURY^{5}, b. 4 Dec. 1732

Ichabod SEABURY^{5}, b. 18 Jan. 1733/4

Daniel ALLEN, (son of Joseph & Ruth), b. 13 Oct. 1729 <Dartmouth VR 1:255>; d. betw. 16 Mar. 1807 (will) - 30 July 1822 (prob.) <Bristol Co. Probate 59:414>

CHILD OF Daniel ALLEN & Elizabeth SEABURY^{5} (Jos.^{4}): **<23>**

Humphrey ALLEN^{6}, b. 17 Dec. 1754*; d. 17 Jan. 1842*

Phebe BURGES^{6}, b. 14 July 1755*, poss. Dartmouth (wf of Humphrey Allen^{6})

Martha SEABURY^{4} (Martha Pabodie^{3}), b. 23 Sept. 1679, Duxbury <9:173>; d. aft.23 Nov. 1733 (hus. inv.) <Bristol Co. Probate 8:34>**<24>**

Josiah SAWYER, d. betw. 15 Sept. 1733(will) - 15 Nov. 1733(inv.)<Bristol Co.Prob. 8:27,30,34>**<24>**

Constant FOBES^{4} (Martha Pabodie^{3}), b. 29 June 1686, d. 29 June 1771, bur. Marshfield <MD 11:71>

John LITTLE^{4} (Ephraim^{3}, Anna Warren^{2}), b. 18 Mar. 1682/3, Marshfield<MD 2:251> d. 26 Feb. 1767, bur. Marshfield <MD 11:71>

CHILDREN OF John LITTLE^{4} & Constant FOBES^{4}: (12) <1-10,12, Marshfield, MD 7:120>

Anna LITTLE^{5}, b. 29 Dec. 1708; d.y.

Ruth LITTLE^{5}, b. 10 July 1710; d.y.

Mercy LITTLE^{5}, b. 2 Nov. 1711

Fobes LITTLE^{5}, b. 9 Mar. 1712/3

John LITTLE^{5}, b. 30 June 1714

Anna LITTLE^{5}, b. 30 Jan. 1715, Marshfield; d. 11 Mar. 1791<MD 8:199>

Thomas LITTLE^{5}, b. 23 Mar. 1716/7; d.y.

Ephraim LITTLE^{5}, b. 15 Apr. 1718; d. 22 Oct. 1808 <MD 11:71>

Thomas LITTLE^{5}, b. 16 June 1719

William LITTLE^{5}, b. 31 Aug. 1720

Ruth LITTLE^{5}, b. 1723; d. 2 July 1804 <MD 10:247>

Lemuel LITTLE^{5}, b. 8 Dec. 1724; d. 30 Dec. 1798 <MD 11:71>

Elizabeth FOBES^{4} (Martha Pabodie^{3}), b. 1683*; d. aft. 2 Nov. 1750*(hus. will)

William BRIGGS, s. of John, d. 23 Nov. 1751* <Little Compton VR>

CHILDREN OF William BRIGGS & Elizabeth FOBES^{4}: (10)

Judith BRIGGS^{5}, b. 27 May 1710* <Little Compton RI VR 4:6:84*>

Lovet BRIGGS^{5}, b. 1 Feb. 1712*; d. 3 Feb. 1713*

Elizabeth BRIGGS^{5}, b. 17 Dec. 1713*

William BRIGGS^{5}, b. 11 Apr. 1715*

Catherine BRIGGS^{5}, b. 17 Mar. 1717*

Sarah BRIGGS^{5}, b. 1719*

Phebe BRIGGS^{5}, b. 1721*

Mary BRIGGS^{5}, b. 1723*

Fobes BRIGGS^{5}, b. 1725*

Lovel BRIGGS^{5}, b. 1727*

MICRO #4 of 16

Isaac SIMMONS^{4} (Mercy Pabodie^{3}), b. 28 Jan. 1674, Duxbury <MD 9:173>

Martha CHANDLER^{3} (Ben.^{2}, Edmund^{1}), b. 1673, Scituate; d.aft. 19 Aug. 1717<Marshfield 1st ChR>**<25>**

CHILDREN OF Isaac SIMMONS^{4} & Martha CHANDLER^{3}: (4) <1-3, Marshfield, MD 8:178>

Deborah SIMMONS^{5}, b. 30 Apr. 1696

Sarah SIMMONS^{5}, b. 15 Nov. 1699

Isaac SIMMONS^{5}, b. 8 Mar. 1700/01; d. 30 Aug. 1767, Duxbury g.s. <MD 11:58>

Priscilla SIMMONS^{5}, b. 10 Sept. 1709, Marshfield <MD 6:69>

Lydia CUSHMAN, d. aft. 31 Aug. 1764 (hus. will) <Plymouth Co. Prob.19:543 >

CHILDREN OF Isaac SIMMONS^{5} & Lydia CUSHMAN: (8)

Consider SIMMONS^{6}, b. 30 Apr. 1734, Duxbury <MD 11:151>

Martha SIMMONS^{6}, b. 20 Feb. 1735/6, Duxbury <MD 11:151>; d.y.

Jehiel SIMMONS^{6}, b. 14 Apr. 1738, Marshfield

Zeruiah SIMMONS^{6}, b. 20 Sept. 1740, Marshfield

Levi SIMMONS^{6}, b. 6 June 1743, Marshfield; d. 3 July 1798, ae 57, N. Duxbury <MD 11:58>(b. 1741?)

Martha SIMMONS^{6}, b. 13 Mar. 1746, Duxbury <MD 11:151>

Lusanna SIMMONS^{6}, b. 30 Dec. 1749, Duxbury <MD 12:166>

Lydia SIMMONS^{6}, b. 22 Mar. 1752, Duxbury <MD 12:166>

Levi SIMMONS, d. 2 Dec. 1855, ae 82y8m17d, Pembroke Centre g.s.<MD 10:235>**<26>**

Elizabeth M. ( ) SIMMONS, wf of Levi, d. 15 Nov. 1839, ae 60y10m16d, Pembroke Centre g.s. <MD 10:235>

CHILD OF Levi SIMMONS & Elizabeth M.( ):

Elisabeth Magoun SIMMONS, b. 21 July 1818 <"Vol.1, p.292 of copy" - town?>

CHILDREN OF Levi SIMMONS: (3) <"Vol.1, p.292 of copy" - town?>

Nehemiah D. SIMMONS, b. 11 Sept. 1795

Otis SIMMONS, b. 11 Oct. 1808

Betsey SIMMONS, b. 22 July 1818

John SIMMONS^{4} (Mercy Pabodie^{3}), b. 22 Feb. 1670, Duxbury <MD 9:172>; d. pre 6 Aug. 1739 (adm.)

CHILDREN OF John SIMMONS^{4} & Susanna TRACY: (4) <Duxbury, MD 11:25>

John SIMMONS^{5}, b. 22 Aug. 1716

Ruth SIMMONS^{5}, b. 26 Apr. 1719

Joel SIMMONS^{5}, b. 5 Feb. 1722/3

Leah SIMMONS^{5}, b. 7 Sept. 1728

Joseph SIMMONS^{4} (Mercy Pabodie^{3}), b. c1690, d. 20 May 1768, ae 78

Mary WESTON, d. 23 Jan. 1759, ae 70y3m* **<27>**

CHILDREN OF Joseph SIMMONS^{4} & Mary WESTON (4) <Duxbury, MD 12:122>

Nathaniel SIMMONS^{5}, b. 24 Mar. 1710/11

Rebecca SIMMONS^{5}, b. 7 Apr. 1713; d. 25 Jan. 1764, Duxbury g.s. <MD 9:161>

Sarah SIMMONS^{5}, b. 26 Mar. 1718; d. Mar. 1740

Jedediah SIMMONS^{5}, b. 11 June 1725; d. aft. 23 Oct. 1767

Reuben PETERSON^{4} (Jonathan^{3}, Mary Soule^{2}), b. 8 Apr. 1710, Duxbury <MD 8:233>;d. 1 Nov. 1795, Duxbury g.s. <MD 11:57>

CHILDREN OF Reuben PETERSON^{4} & Rebecca SIMMONS^{5}: (8) <Duxbury, MD 12:125> **<28>**

Elijah PETERSON^{6}, b. 12 Mar. 1732/3

Mary PETERSON^{6}, b. 21 Oct. 1734; d. 25 June 1772*

Nehemiah PETERSON^{6}, b. 29 July 1736

Abigail PETERSON^{6}, b. 16 May 1739

Sarah PETERSON^{6}, b. 30 Dec. 1740; d. 5 Dec. 1824 <MD 13:133>

Lydia PETERSON^{6}, b. 14 Nov. 1742

Thaddeus PETERSON^{6}, b. 9 Mar. 1744/5

Luther PETERSON^{6}, b. 8 Apr. 1746

Lydia SOULE^{5} (John^{4}, Joshua^{3}, John^{2}), b. 6 May 1733, Duxbury, d. aft. 23 Oct.1767 (wf of Jedediah Simmons^{5} (Jos.^{4})) **<29>**

Nathaniel SIMMONS^{5} (Jos.^{4}), b. 24 Mar. 1711,Duxbury<MD 12:122>; d. 1 Jan.1789,Waldoborough ME g.s

Mercy SIMMONS^{5} (Moses^{4}, Mercy Pabodie^{3}, Eliz. Alden^{2}), b. 18 May 1720 Duxbury, d. 21 Sept. 1788, Waldoborough, ME g.s.

CHILDREN OF Nathaniel SIMMONS^{5} (Jos.^{4}) & Mercy Simmons^{5} (Moses^{4}): (4 of 7)

Mary SIMMONS^{6}, b. 19 June 1742, Duxbury <MD 12:122>

Joseph SIMMONS^{6}, b. 19 Sept. 1744, Duxbury <MD 12:122>

Stephen SIMMONS^{6}*, b. ( )

Rachel SIMMONS^{6}*, bpt. 6 Nov. 1763*

<u>Waldoboro, ME Cemetary:</u>*

Mary, wf of Zebedee SIMMONS, d. 18 Mar. 1809, ae 60

Miss Rachel SIMMONS, (yo)ungest daughter of Deacon Nathaniel SIMMONS, d. 2 Dec1788, ae 25y2m4d

Mercy SIMMONS, wf of Dea. Nathaniel SIMMONS, d. 21 Sept. 1788, ae 68y3m23d

Deacon Nathaniel SIMMONS, formerly of Duxbury, d. 1 Jan. 1789, ae 77y8m26d

Nathaniel SIMMONS, eldest son of Mr. Joseph SIMMONS, d. 22 Oct. 1788, ae 17y3d

* * * * *

Rizpah RICHARDS^{6} (Hannah Simmons^{5}, Ben.^{4}, Mercy Pabodie^{3}), b. 21 Jan. 1740*;d. 1 Jan. 1832<Bible>

John MITCHELL^{5} (Lydia Hatch^{4}, Sam.^{3}, Mary Doty^{2}), d. 17 Mar. 1830 (hus. of Rizpah) <Bible>

Joshua SIMMONS^{4} (Mercy Pabodie^{3}), b. c1688; d. 15 Jan. 1774, ae 85y8m **<30>**

Martha SIMMONS^{4} (Mercy Pabodie^{3}), b. 17 Nov. 1677, Duxbury <MD 9:173>; d. aft.4 Mar. 1715 <MD 9:26, 29:82>

Ebenezer DELANO^{3} (Phillip$^{2-1}$), d. pre 17 May 1706 < Plymouth Co. Deeds 7:255>

CHILDREN OF Ebenezer DELANO^{3} & Martha SIMMONS^{4}: (3) <Duxbury, MD 8:233>

Joshua DELANO^{5}, b. 30 Oct. 1700; d. 1 Mar. 1750, Boston, bur. Kingston <MD 7:83>

Thankful DELANO^{5}, b. 8 June 1702

Abiah DELANO^{5}, b. 17 Aug. 1704

Samuel WEST, b. 23 Dec. 1672*

CHILDREN OF Samuel WEST & Martha SIMMONS^{4}: (4) <Duxbury, MD 9:26>

Amos WEST^{5}, b. 29 Mar. 1710

Nathan WEST^{5}, b. 18 Aug. 1711

Sarah WEST^{5}, b. 8 Nov. 1712

Moses WEST^{5}, b. 4 Mar. 1715

Hopestill PETERSON^{4} (Jonathan^{3}, Mary Soule^{2}), b. 20 Jan. 1703, Duxbury <MD 8:233>; d. 27 July 1775, Kingston g.s. <MD 7:83>

CHILDREN OF Joshua DELANO^{5} & Hopestill PETERSON^{4}: (11) <Duxbury, MD 11:238>

Lydia DELANO^{6}, b. 12 July 1723

Son, b. 19 May 1726, d. same day

Dau., b. 4 July 1727, d. same day

Rhoda DELANO^{6}, b. 4 July 1728

Thankful DELANO^{6}, b. 28 Feb. 1730/1

Sylvi DELANO^{6}, b. 22 Jan. 1732/3

Hopestil DELANO^{6}, (son), b. 19 June 1735

Beza DELANO^{6}, (dau.), b. 24 Nov. 1737

Martha DELANO^{6}, b. 21 Sept. 1739

Welthea DELANO^{6}, b. 7 Dec. 1741; d. 27 Apr. 1783<MD 7:23>

Joshua DELANO^{6}, b. 30 Sept. 1744; d. 22 July 1816 <MD 7:83>

Moses SIMMONS^{4} (Mercy Pabodie^{3}), b. Feb. 1680, Duxbury**<31>**; 21 June 1761*<Duxbury VR:417*>

Rachel SAMSON^{3} (Caleb^{2}), b. 5 Dec.( ), Duxbury<MD 9:26> (bpt. 20 Apr. 1701,Marshfield)<MD 11:122>

CHILDREN OF Moses SIMMONS^{4} & Rachel SAMSON^{3}: (10) <Duxbury>

Mercy SIMMONS^{5}, b. 18 May 1720 <MD 12:121>

Ichabod SIMMONS^{5}, b. 18 Oct. 1722 <MD 12:121>

Lydia SIMMONS^{5}, b. 18 Apr. 1724 <MD 12:121>

Noah SIMMONS^{5}, b. 31 Aug. 1728 <MD 12:121>

Deborah SIMMONS^{5}, b. 12 Jan. 1732 <MD 12:122>

William SIMMONS^{5}, b. 28 Aug. 1736 <MD 12:122>

Anne SIMMONS^{5}, b. 4 Sept. 1739 <MD 12:122>

Dorothy SIMMONS^{5}, b. 2 Mar. 1741, d.y. <MD 12:122>

Lemuel SIMMONS^{5}, b. 14 Feb. 1743, d.y. <MD 12:122>

Abigail SIMMONS^{5}, b. 10 May 1745, d.y. <MD 12:122>

MICRO #5 of 16

Mary PABODIE^{3}, b. 7 Aug. 1648, Duxbury <MD 1:163>; d. aft. 11 Dec. 1727 <MD 18:244>

Edward SOUTHWORTH^{3} (Constant^{2}, Edw.^{1}), d. betw. 11 June 1719 (will)- 7 Nov.1727 (witnesses sworn) <MD 18:244>

CHILDREN OF Edward SOUTHWORTH^{3} & Mary PABODIE^{3}: (8)<MD 18:245-6>

Elizabeth SOUTHWORTH^{4}, b. Nov. 1672 <MD 9:172>

Thomas SOUTHWORTH^{4}, b. c1675*; d. 2 Sept. 1743, ae 68*

Constant SOUTHWORTH^{4}, b. ( ); d. c1731

Mercy SOUTHWORTH^{4}, b. ( )

Benjamin SOUTHWORTH^{4}, b. c1681*; d. 12 May 1756, ae 75* <Duxbury VR>

John SOUTHWORTH^{4}, b. c1686; d. 10 Aug. 1751, ae 65, Duxbury g.s. <MD 10:170>

Priscilla SOUTHWORTH^{4}, b. c1692*; d. 7 June 1761*, <will - MD 19:115>

Elizabeth SOUTHWORTH^{4}, d. 1(9) Aug. 1750*

Rebecca DELANO^4 (Eliz. Standish^3, Alex.^{2}), Duxbury, d. 6 Sept. 1774, ae 90, <Duxbury VR:425>

CHILDREN OF Benjamin SOUTHWORTH^4 & Rebecca DELANO^4: (10) <Duxbury, MD 12:161>

Hannah SOUTHWORTH^5, b. 29 Oct. 1715

Edward SOUTHWORTH^5, b. 10 Dec. 1717, d. 17 Jan. 1739/40 <MD 12:161>

Elizabeth SOUTHWORTH^5, b. 15 Dec. 1719; d. aft. 5 June 1761**<32>**

Thomas SOUTHWORTH^5, b. 1 Apr 1722

Sarah SOUTHWORTH^5, b. 18 Sept. 1725, d. 6 Jan. 1739/40 <MD 12:161>

Rebecca SOUTHWORTH^5, b. 6 Dec. 1727, d. 8 Jan. 1739/40 <MD 12:161>

Constant SOUTHWORTH^5, b. 9 July 1731

Deborah SOUTHWORTH^5, b. 11 Mar. 1734

Obed SOUTHWORTH^5, b. 11 Nov. 1736

Josher SOUTHWORTH^5, b. 1 Nov. 1738

Anna HATCH, (dau. of Israel & Bethia (Thomas)), b. 22 Nov. 1734, Marshfield*

CHILDREN OF Thomas SOUTHWORTH^5 & Anna HATCH*: (7)*

William SOUTHWORTH^6, b. 18 Feb. 1763 <Duxbury VR:168>

Constant SOUTHWORTH^6, b. 20 Aug. 1764 <Duxbury VR:166>

Lydia SOUTHWORTH^6, b. 8 Nov. 1766 <Duxbury VR:167>

Hannah SOUTHWORTH^6, b. 8 Jan. 1769 <Duxbury VR:166>

Anne SOUTHWORTH^6, b. 23 Dec. 1770 <Duxbury VR:166>

Elizabeth SOUTHWORTH^6, b. 24 Apr. 1773 <Duxbury VR:166>

Thomas SOUTHWORTH^6, b. 24 May 1776 <Duxbury VR:168>

Rebecca SIMMONS^4 (Mercy Pabodie^3), d. aft. 15 Feb. 1750**<33>**

CHILDREN OF Constant SOUTHWORTH^4 (Mary Pabodie^3) & Rebecca SIMMONS^4: (3)

Mercy SOUTHWORTH^5, b. ( )**<34>**

Mary SOUTHWORTH^5, b. c1723, d. 1 May 1765, ae 41y8m <Duxbury VR>

William SOUTHWORTH^5, b. ( )

CHILDREN OF Benjamin SOUTHWORTH^5 (Constant^4) & Mary HUNT* (dau of Tho. & Honor(Stetson)*):(9)**<35>**

Submit SOUTHWORTH^6, b. 1 June 1734, Duxbury <MD 12:124>

Peleg SOUTHWORTH^6, b. 13 Aug. 1736, Duxbury, d. 19 Nov. 1748<MD 12:124,166>

Cynthia SOUTHWORTH^6, b. 13 Feb. 1738/9, Duxbury, d. 4 Dec. 1748<MD 12:124,166>

Abigail SOUTHWORTH^6, b. 11 Nov. 1741, Duxbury <MD 12:124>

Olive SOUTHWORTH^6, b. 25 July 1744, Duxbury, d. 18 Nov. 1748 <MD 12:124,166>

Sylvia SOUTHWORTH^6, b. 22 Nov. 1747, Duxbury <MD 12:124>

Cynthia SOUTHWORTH^6, b. 7 Nov. 1750, Duxbury <MD 12:124>

Honor SOUTHWORTH^6, b. 21 Jan. 1757, Duxbury <MD 12:124>

Olive SOUTHWORTH^{6*}, b. ( )

CHILDREN OF Micah SOULE^4 (Josiah^3, John^2) & Mercy SOUTHWORTH^5 (Constant^4)**<36>**

Thomas WESTON^5 (Mercy Peterson^4, Ben.^{3}, Mary Soule^2), b. 4 Oct. 1726, Duxbury <MD 12:123>; d. 16 May 1776, Duxbury g.s. <MD 10:171>

CHILDREN OF Thomas WESTON^5 & Mary SOUTHWORTH^5 (Constant^4): (4)**<37>**

Joseph WESTON^6, b. aft. 23 May 1756*; d. 3 Feb. 1814*

Thomas WESTON^6, b. aft. 2 Sept. 1755*; d. 29 July 1842*

Mary WESTON^6, bpt. 25 Oct. 1767*; d. 26 Sept. 1776 <Duxbury ChR.>

Jane WESTON^6, bpt. 25 Oct. 1767* <Duxbury ChR.>

CHILDREN OF William SOUTHWORTH^5 (Constant^4) & Mary ( ): (6)

Reumah SOUTHWORTH^6, b. 27 Aug. 1742, Duxbury <MD 12:167>; d. 26 or 27 Dec. 1828*, "in almshouse"

Edward SOUTHWORTH^6, b.27 Mar. 1747, Duxbury <MD 12:167>

John SOUTHWORTH^6, b. 28 Apr. 1752, Duxbury <MD 12:167>

Nathaniel SOUTHWORTH^{6*}, bpt. 12 June 1757*

William SOUTHWORTH^{6*}, bpt. 12 June 1759*

Alice SOUTHWORTH^{6*}, bpt. 13 May 1764*

Elizabeth SOUTHWORTH^{4} (Mary Pabodie^{3}), d. 19 Aug. 1750* <Duxbury VR:436>

Samuel WESTON, d. 7 Dec. 1751* <Duxbury VR:438>

CHILDREN OF Samuel WESTON & Elizabeth SOUTHWORTH^{4}: (6) <Duxbury, MD 11:78>

Samuel WESTON^{5}, b. 5 Mar. 1717/8

Zabdiel WESTON^{5}, b. 22 Jan. 1719/20; d. 12 Oct. 1739 <MD 12:31>

Mary WESTON^{5}, b. 18 July 1722; d. Dec. 1776*

Priscilla WESTON^{5}, b. 24 Jan. 1724/5; d. 7 Jan. 1756*

Elnathan WESTON^{5}, b. 29 Sept. 1727; d. 29 Dec. 1777*<Duxbury VR:436*>

Nathaniel WESTON^{5}, b. 30 Apr. 1730

Jemima BISBEE, (dau of Aaron & Abigail), b. 14 May 1726* <Pembroke VR:36>; d. 6 July 1812*, Duxbury VR:437> (wf of Elnathan Weston^{5})

Thomas SOUTHWORTH^{4} (Mary Pabodie^{3}), b. c1675, d. 2 Sept. 1743, ae 68, Duxbury g.s. <MD 10:170>

Sarah ALDEN^{3} (Jonathan^{2}), b. c1679, d. 26 June 1738, ae 59, Duxbury g.s. <MD 10:170>

CHILDREN OF Thomas SOUTHWORTH^{4} & Sarah ALDEN^{3}: (2)

Jedediah SOUTHWORTH^{5}, b. 13 Apr. 1702, Duxbury <MD 9:231>; d. 8 Sept. 1739, <MD 10:170>

Mary SOUTHWORTH^{5}, b. 18 Sept. 1703, Duxbury <MD 9:231>; d. 12 Nov. 1739 <MD 9:161>

Hannah SCALES*, (dau of Wm.*), b. c1708, d. 18 Oct. 1790, Duxbury g.s. <MD 19:26>

CHILDREN OF Jedediah SOUTHWORTH^{5} & Hannah SCALES*: (5) <Duxbury, MD 12:29>

Sarah SOUTHWORTH^{6}, b. 8 Oct. 1729

Susanna SOUTHWORTH^{6}, b. 27 July 1731

John SOUTHWORTH^{6}, b. 22 Oct. 1733

James SOUTHWORTH^{6}, b. 17 Nov. 1735

Lydia SOUTHWORTH^{6}, b. 11 Oct. 1738

CHILDREN OF James SOUTHWORTH^{6} & Sarah DREW*, (dau of Perez*): (2)

Jedediah SOUTHWORTH^{7}, b. 23 Aug. 1764, Duxbury <MD 9:231>

Abigail SOUTHWORTH^{7}, b. 7 June 1769, Duxbury <MD 9:231>

Thomas LORING, b. c1699, d. 8 Dec. 1739, ae 40, S. Duxbury g.s. <MD 9:161>

CHILDREN OF Thomas LORING & Mary SOUTHWORTH^{5} (Tho.^{4}):(6)

Thomas LORING^{6}, b. 12 Apr. 1725, Duxbury <MD 11:236>

Simeon LORING^{6}, b. pre 13 Aug. 1727 <deeds>

Perez LORING^{6}, b. 26 Aug. 1729, Duxbury <MD 11:236>; d. 22 Oct. 1827 <Duxbury VR:393>

Levi LORING^{6}, b. ( ) <deeds>

Joshua LORING^{6}, b. 5 Feb. 1734/5, Duxbury, d. 3 Feb. 1750 <MD 11:236, 9:161>

Deborah LORING^{6}, b. 31 Mar. 1738, Duxbury <MD 11:236>

Sarah FREEMAN, (dau of Joseph), b. c1731, d. 23 or 26 Aug. 1806, ae 75y5m, <Duxbury VR:393>

CHILDREN OF Perez LORING^{6} & Sarah FREEMAN: (10)**<38>**

Mary LORING^{7}, b. 26 Dec. 1758 <Duxbury VR:105>

Braddock LORING^{7}, b. 21 Aug. 1760 <Duxbury VR:104>; d. Mar. 1822

Zadock LORING^{7}, b. 21 Aug. 1760 (twins) <Duxbury VR:106>

Freeman LORING^{7}, b. 25 July 1762 <Duxbury VR:104>; d. 17 Nov. 1820

Deborah LORING^{7}, b. 22 Oct. 1764 <Duxbury VR:104>; d. 20 Apr. 1836

Baruch LORING^{7}, b. 4 Apr. 1766 <Duxbury VR:104>; d. 1 Jan. 1792

Belinda LORING^{7}, b. 6 Mar. 1768 <Duxbury VR:105>

Sarah LORING^{7}, b. 4 Mar. 1770 <Duxbury VR:106>

Perez LORING^{7}, b. 10 Mar. 1772 <Duxbury VR:105>; d. 29 Mar. 1794

Levi LORING^{7}, b. 13 Feb. 1775 <Duxbury VR:105>

Mary/Polly MATHERS, b. c1760, Scotland; d. 1846, ae 86

CHILDREN OF Braddock LORING^{7} & Mary/Polly MATHERS: (10)

Perez LORING^{8}, b. 21 Aug. 1784, Boston; d. 18 Nov. 1844, Boston

Mary LORING^{8}, b. 4 July 1786

Braddock LORING^{8}, b. 1 Feb. 1788

Sarah Freeman LORING^{8}, b. 19 Sept. 1789

Elizabeth LORING^{8}, b. 26 June 1791

Harriet LORING^{8}, b. 23 Oct. 1792

Charles M. LORING^{8}, b. 23 May 1794

Samuel LORING^{8}, b. 23 Aug. 1795

Deborah LORING^{8}, b. 6 Jan. 1798

Elizabeth LORING^{8}, b. 23 Oct. 1801

Elizabeth SMALLEDGE, b. 1780, Boston, d. 7 Dec. 1858, Boston

CHILDREN OF Perez LORING^{8} & Elizabeth SMALLEDGE: (5)

Elizabeth LORING^{9}, b. 12 May 1808, Boston; d. 2 Oct. 1875 (wf of Stephen Decanter Salmon)

Perez LORING^{9}, b. 1810, Boston; d. 12 May 1856

Braddock LORING^{9}, b. 1813; d. 1 Feb. 1888

George LORING^{9}, b. 27 Nov. 1814; d. 30 Mar. 1882

Sophia LORING^{9}, b. c1817,Cambridgeport d. 18 Aug. 1882, New Bedford, ae 65y6m, <Mass.VR 337:132> (widow of Bartholomew Brown Jr.)

Mercy PABODIE^{3}, b. 2 Jan. 1649, Duxbury <MD 9:171>; 26 Sept. 1728 (will) - 8 Nov. 1728 (inv.), Duxbury <MD 19:53>

John SIMMONS, d. pre 9 Feb. 1715 (adm.) <MD 19:51,52>

CHILDREN OF John SIMMONS & Mercy PABODIE^{3}: (9)**<39>**

John SIMMONS^{4}, b. 22 Feb. 1670, Duxbury <MD 9:172>

William SIMMONS^{4}, b. 24 Feb. 1672, Duxbury <MD 9:173>

Isaac SIMMONS^{4}, b. 28 Jan. 1674, Duxbury <MD 9:173>

Martha SIMMONS^{4}, b. 17 Nov. 1677, Duxbury <MD 9:173>

Benjamin SIMMONS^{4}, b. ( ) <MD 19:52,53>; d. pre 2 May 1748 (adm.) <Plymouth Prob. 11:50,170,172>

Joseph SIMMONS^{4}, b. ( ) < " >

Joshua SIMMONS^{4}, b. ( ) < " >

Joshua SIMMONS^{4}, b. ( ) < " >

Rebecca SIMMONS^{4}, b. ( ) < " >

Moses SIMMONS^{4}, b. Feb. 1680, Duxbury <MD 9:26>

CHILDREN OF Benjamin SIMMONS^{4} & 1st Lorah SAMSON^{4}**<40>**: (5) <Duxbury, MD 12:162>

Mercy SIMMONS^{5}, b. 14 Nov. 1706; d. Feb. 1751

Zachariah SIMMONS^{5}, b. 19 Mar. 1708/9

Benjamin SIMMONS^{5}, b. 13 Mar. 1710/1

Abraham SIMMONS^{5}, b. 9 Nov. 1713

Content SIMMONS^{5}, b. 16 Dec. 1715

Priscilla DELANO^{4} (Eliz. Standish^{3}, Alex.^{2}), d. 7 Feb. 1746/7, Duxbury, <MD 12:33>

CHILDREN OF Benjamin SIMMONS^{4} & 2nd Priscilla DELANO^{4}: (5) <Duxbury, MD 12:162>

Hannah SIMMONS^{5}, b. 16 June 1718

Betty SIMMONS^{5}, b. 25 Feb. 1720/2

Aaron SIMMONS^{5}, b. 25 Mar. 1724; d. 10 May 1790

Priscilla SIMMONS^{5}, b. 30 Dec. 1727

Abiah SIMMONS^{5}, b. 23 Oct. 1730

Aaron SIMMONS, d. 10 May 1790, ae 68, Duxbury g.s.

Sarah HOLMES, b. 17 Sept. 1722*; d. aft. 16 Mar. 1790

CHILDREN OF Aaron SIMMONS & Sarah HOLMES: (3) <"Winsor">

Mary SIMMONS, b. 22 Sept. 1755

Abraham SIMMONS, b. ( )

Jesse SIMMONS, b. 19 Sept. 1760

CHILDREN OF Jesse SIMMONS (Aaron) & Lucy WESTON?*:(6) <"Winsor">

Weston SIMMONS, b. 1783

Ruby SIMMONS, b. 1786

Martin SIMMONS, b. 1788

Sally SIMMONS, b. 1791

Aaron SIMMONS, b. 1797

Lyman SIMMONS, B. 1807

Fear SAMSON^{5} (Nathaniel^{4}, Lorah Standish^{3}, Alex.^{2}), b. 16 Nov. 1708 <Duxbury VR> (wf of Benjamin Simmons^{5} (Ben.^{4}))<41>

CHILDREN OF William RICHARDS & Hannah SIMMONS^{5} (Ben.^{4}): (9) <Pembroke VR:177><42>

Rispah RICHARDS^{6}, b. 21 Jan. 1740

William RICHARDS^{6}, b. 23 Mar. 1742

Erastus RICHARDS^{6}, b. 28 July 1744

Priscilla RICHARDS^{6}, b. 7 Nov. 1746

Benjamin RICHARDS ^{6}, b. 23 Dec. 1749

Nancy RICHARDS^{6}, b. 16 Mar. 1752

Silvina RICHARDS^{6}, b. 22 Mar. 1758

Hannah RICHARDS^{6}, b. 12 Mar. 1755

Bettey RICHARDS^{6}, b. 26 Apr. 1762

Josiah FARROW, (son of John), b. 10 Feb. 1754, Windham; d. 14 Aug. 1819<43>

Ruth RICHARDS, d. 7 May 1834, ae 70 (wf of Josiah Farrow)<43>

Betty Doty SHERMAN^{5}*(Mary Oakman^{4}, Eliz. Doty^{3}, Edward^{2}), b. 11 Apr. 1746<Marshfield VR 2:96,108>

CHILDREN OF Erastus RICHARDS^{6} (Hannah Simmons^{5}) & Betty Doty SHERMAN^{5}: (9)<42>

Jane RICHARDS^{7}, b. Bristol ME

Betsey RICHARDS^{7}, b. Bristol ME

Sally RICHARDS^{7}, b. Bristol ME

Huldah RICHARDS^{7}, b. Bristol ME

Polly RICHARDS^{7}, b. Bristol ME

Deborah RICHARDS^{7}, b. Bristol ME

Doty RICHARDS^{7}, b. Bristol ME

Erastus RICHARDS^{7}, b. Bristol ME

Robert RICHARDS^{7}, b. 1 Oct. 1786, Bristol ME

CHILDREN OF Zachariah SIMMONS^{5} (Ben.^{4}) & Deborah BISHOP: (3)

Nathan SIMMONS^{6}, b. 3 Apr. 1732

Eleazer SIMMONS^{6}, b. 14 Mar. 1738/9

Zachariah SIMMONS^{6}, b. 4 May 1741; d. 1760

MICRO #6 of 16

Ichabod SIMMONS^{5} (Moses^{4}), b. 18 Oct. 1722, Duxbury <MD 12:121>; d. aft.12 Apr. 1794<Plymouth Co. Deeds 78:53><44>

Lydia SOULE^{4} (Josiah^{3}, John^{2}), b. 2 Oct. 1719, Duxbury <MD 11:25>; d. 3 Mar.1779 <Duxbury VR:417>

CHILDREN OF Ichabod SIMMONS^{5} & 1st Lydia SOULE^{4}: (6) <Duxbury Gen'l Rcds.1710-86, p.238>

Consider SIMMONS^{6}, b. 27 Sept. 1744; d. aft. 9 Aug. 1823* < Plymouth Co. Deeds 150:98>

Noah SIMMONS^{6}, b. 2 Sept. 1745; d. 26 June 1832, Duxbury

Lemuel SIMMONS^{6}, b. 22 Feb. 1749

Abigail SIMMONS^{6}, b. 24 May 1753

Nathaniel SIMMONS^{6}, b. 3 Apr. 1757; d. 22 Jan. 1835 <S.Duxbury g.s. - Mayflower Cem.,Tremont St.>

Ichabod SIMMONS^{6}, b. 25 May 1761

Mercy ( ) SPRAGUE, d. 28 Oct. 1815, ae 89, (2nd wf of Ichabod Simmons^{5};former widow of Phineas Sprague who d. 20 Jan. 1776, ae 62)

Nephele/Aphela SOULE^{5} (Micah^{4}, Josiah^{3}, John^{2}), bpt. 19 Apr. 1741; d. ?1 Dec.1827* <Duxbury ChR 1:7, 2:45>

CHILDREN OF Consider SIMMONS^{6} (Ichabod^{5}) & Nephele SOULE^{5}: (4)

Lydia SIMMONS^{7}, bpt. 28 June 1766, d. 1 July 1766 <Duxbury ChR. 1:137,250>

Lucy SIMMONS^{7}, bpt. 26 July 1767 <Duxbury ChR 1:137>

Lydia Soule SIMMONS^{7}, bpt. 24 July 1768 <Duxbury ChR 1:137>

Jonathan Soule SIMMONS^{7}, bpt. 6 June 1773 <Duxbury ChR 1:137>

Lydia SPRAGUE, b. 21 Mar. 1761 <Hist. Dux. :320>; d. 29 Nov. 1829, ae 68, <S.Duxbury g.s.- Mayflower Cemetery, Tremont St.>

CHILDREN OF Nathaniel SIMMONS^{6} & Lydia SPRAGUE: (12)<Hist.Dux.:308>

Parthenia SIMMONS^{7}, b. 1781; d. 15 June 1840, ae 60 <S. Duxbury g.s.>

Sarah SIMMONS^{7}, b. 1784

Anna SIMMONS^{7}, b. 1786

Nathaniel SIMMONS^{7}, b. 1788

Rebecca SIMMONS^{7}, b. 1791

Alathea SIMMONS^{7}, b. 1793

Lydia SIMMONS^{7}, b. 1795

Lucy SIMMONS^{7}, b. 1798

Nancy SIMMONS^{7}, b. 1798 (twins); d. 26 May 1801 <S. Duxbury g.s.>

Ichabod SIMMONS^{7}, b. 1801

Mary SIMMONS^{7}, b. 1804

Joshua SIMMONS^{7}, b. 1807; d. 4 Sept. 1838* <S. Duxbury g.s.>

CHILDREN OF Noah SIMMONS^{6} (Ichabod^{5}) & Sylvia SOUTHWORTH: (9) <Duxbury ChR.>

Welthea SIMMONS^{7}, bpt. 28 Apr. 1771, d. 3 May 1771

Peleg Southworth SIMMONS^{7}, bpt. 1 Mar. 1772

Charles SIMMONS^{7}, bpt. 27 Jan. 1777

Daniel SIMMONS^{7}, bpt. 16 Sept. 1778, d. 23 Sept. 1778

Nathan SIMMONS^{7}, bpt. 25 Apr. 1779, d. 26 Oct. 1779

Daniel SIMMONS^{7}, bpt. Aug. 1781

Welthea SIMMONS^{7}, bpt. 3 May 1783

Infant, d. 27 Sept. 1785

Silvia SIMMONS^{7}, bpt. 29 Sept. 1785, d. 4 Mar. 1796

Lydia SIMMONS^{5} (Moses^{4}), b. 18 Apr. 1724, Duxbury <MD 12:121>

CHILDREN OF Judah DELANO & Lydia SIMMONS^{5}: (10) <2-6, Duxbury, MD 12:164>

Alpheus DELANO^{6}, b. 2 Oct. 1744, Duxbury <MD 12:29>

Salome DELANO^{6}, b. 16 July 1746

Malachi DELANO^{6}, b. 16 Oct. 1748

Judah DELANO^{6}, b. 1 May 1751

Naomi DELANO^{6}, b. 7 Nov. 1753

Priscilla DELANO^{6}, b. 24 Nov. 1755

Jephtha DELANO^{6*}, b. 29 Oct. 1758*

Philip DELANO^{6*}, bpt. 26 July 1761*

Tirzah DELANO^{6*}, bpt. 11 Aug. 1765*

Annis/Eunice DELANO^{6*}, bpt. 27 Mar. 1768*

William SIMMONS^{4} (Mercy Pabodie^{3}), b. 24 Feb. 1672, Duxbury <MD 9:173>; d. c1765, Little Compton RI <will recorded 28 Sept. 1765>

Abigail CHURCH^{4} (Jos.^{3}, Eliz. Warren^{2}), b. c1680; d. 4 July 1720, ae 40, Little Compton RI

CHILDREN OF William SIMMONS^{4} & Abigail CHURCH^{4}: (12)<Little Compton VR>

Mercy SIMMONS^{5}, b. 1 July 1697; d. Nov. 1768*

William SIMMONS^{5}, b. 30 Sept. 1699

Lydia SIMMONS^{5}, b. 15 Dec. 1700

Joseph SIMMONS^{5}, b. 4 Mar. 1702; d. July 1778, Little Compton RI*

John SIMMONS^{5}, b. 14 Aug. 1704

Abigail SIMMONS^{5}, b. 14 July 1706

Rebecca SIMMONS^{5}, b. 8 May 1708

Mary SIMMONS^{5}, b. 15 Oct. 1709

Benjamin SIMMONS^{5}, b. 2 Feb. 1713

Ichabod SIMMONS^{5}, b. 6 Jan. 1715 <June is written in pencil above Jan.>

Peleg SIMMONS^{5}, b. 21 Dec. 1716

Sarah SIMMONS^{5}, b. 26 Aug. 1718; d. 26 Dec. 1718

Rebecca WOOD (dau. of Jonathan*), b. 26 Dec. 1704, Little Compton RI*; d. 17 Nov. 1795, Little Compton RI <VR RI 12:63>

CHILDREN OF Joseph SIMMONS^{5} & Rebecca WOOD: (9*)<Little Compton RI>

John SIMMONS^{6}, b. 29 Jan. 1727

Abigail SIMMONS^{6}, b. 7 Dec. 1728

Edward SIMMONS^{6}, b. 16 Mar. 1730; d. Sept. 1803, Newport <VR RI 14:271>

Betsey SIMMONS^{6}, b. 8 Mar. 1733

Jonathan SIMMONS^{6}, b. 20 Aug. 1736

Ephraim SIMMONS^{6}, b. 29 June 1739

Susanna SIMMONS^{6}, b. 8 July 1742

Rebecca SIMMONS^{6}, b. 7 Feb. 1746

Joseph SIMMONS^{6}, b. 1748

CHILDREN OF Edward SIMMONS^{6} & Mary ROBINSON: (8*)

Martha SIMMONS^{7}, b. 1 Apr. 1754, Newport <"4:2:114">

Jonathan SIMMONS^{7}, b. July 1755, Newport <"4:2:114">; d. Aug. 1803, Newport <VR RI 14:271>

Dau., d. Oct. 1760, ae 1y6m

Son, d. Aug. 1762, ae 2 wks

Son, b. Dec. 1761

Son, b. Jan. 1764, stillborn

Son, b. 3 Apr. 1765

Child, b. Mar. 1768, stillborn

Elizabeth SMITH* (dau. of Henry*), d. Dec. 1819, ae 63*, Bristol

CHILDREN OF Jonathan SIMMONS^{7} & Elizabeth SMITH*:(11*)

Edward SIMMONS^{8}, b. 1779

Mary SIMMONS^{8}, b. 1780

Henry SIMMONS^{8}, b. 1781

Rachel SIMMONS^{8}, b. Apr. 1783

Elizabeth SIMMONS^{8}, b. Feb. 1785

Sarah SIMMONS^{8}, b. 1787

William Smith SIMMONS^{8}, b. 4 Nov. 1788

Robert SIMMONS^{8}, b. 1790

Nathan SIMMONS^{8}, b. 1792

Desire SIMMONS^{8}, b. 28 Mar. 1794

John SIMMONS^{8}, b. 1796

CHILDREN OF Benoni SIMMONS^{7} (? ^{6}) & Nancy BAILEY:(7) <Little Compton RI VR 2:21>[<45>]

Cornelius Baley SIMMONS^{8}, b. 19 Sept. 1785

Lydia SIMMONS^{8}, b. 19 Aug. 1787

Mary SIMMONS^{8}, b. "1th" Feb. 1791

George Washington SIMMONS^{8}, b. 9 Sept. 1793

John SIMMONS^{8}, b. 30 Oct. 1796

Valentine SIMMONS^{8}, (son), b. 19 Apr. 1802

Comfort SIMMONS^{8}, b. 7 July 1803

Priscilla PABODIE^{3}, b. 15 Jan. 1653, Duxbury <MD 9:171>; d. 3 June 1724, Kingston g.s. <MD 7:224>

Rev. Ichabod WISWALL, d. 23 July 1700, ae 63, Duxbury g.s. <MD 10:172>

CHILDREN OF Rev. Ichabod WISWALL & Priscilla PABODIE^{3}: (6)**<46>**

Mercy WISWALL^{4}, b. 4 Oct. 1680, Duxbury <MD 9:229>; d. 12 Nov. 1716<MD 9:231>

Hannah WISWALL^{4}, b. 22 Feb. 1681, Dux.<MD 9:229>; d. 22 Sept. 1722 ("drowned between Duxbury & Boston with dau. Mary") <MD 10:169>

Peleg WISWALL^{4}, b. 5 Feb. 1683, Duxbury <MD 9:229>

Perez WISWALL^{4}, b. 22 Nov. 1686, Duxbury <MD 9:229>; d. pre 25 May 1700

Priscilla WISWALL^{4}, b. c1690 <MD 19:3>; d. 12 Sept. 1780

Deborah WISWALL^{4}, b. c1693 <MD 19:3>; d. 22 Apr. 1776, ae 83, Duxbury g.s. <MD 10:169>**<47>**

Samuel SEABURY^{4} (Sam.$^{3-2}$, John^{1}), b. 24 Oct. 1692, Duxbury <MD 9:24>; d. 25 Sept. 1762, S.Duxbury g.s. <MD 10:169>

CHILDREN OF Samuel SEABURY^{4} & Deborah WISWALL^{4}:(9) <Duxbury, MD 9:25>

Sarah SEABURY^{5}, b. 21 July 1718, Duxbury <MD 9:24>

Hannah SEABURY^{5}, b. 26 June 1720

Hopestill SEABURY^{5}, b. 31 May 1722

Faith SEABURY^{5}, b. 12 Oct. 1724

Deborah SEABURY^{5}, b. 13 Apr. 1727; d. 23 Oct. 1802 <MD 7:24>

Paul SEABURY^{5}, b. 26 Nov. 1728

Oliver SEABURY^{5}, b. 26 Dec. 1730

Wiswall SEABURY^{5}, b. 6 Apr. 1733; d. 20 Sept. 1768 <MD 10:169>

Mercy SEABURY^{5}, b. 10 Nov. 1735

Rev. John ROBINSON, d. 14 Nov. 1745, ae 74, Lebanon CT*

CHILDREN OF Rev. John ROBINSON & Hannah WISWALL^{4} (Prisc. Pabodie^{3}): (7)

Mary ROBINSON^{5}, b. 23 Feb. 1706, Duxbury, d. 22 Sept. 1722 <MD 11:23, 10:169>

Hannah ROBINSON^{5}, b. 2 Nov. 1708, Duxbury <MD 11:23>

Alethea ROBINSON^{5}, b. 26 May 1710, Duxbury <MD 11:23>

Elizabeth ROBINSON^{5}, b. 28 Sept. 1712, Duxbury <MD 11:23>

John ROBINSON^{5}, b. 16 Apr. 1715, Duxbury <MD 11:23>; d. 21 Aug. 1784, Bozrah*

Ichabod ROBINSON^{5}, b. ( )

Faith ROBINSON^{5}, b. ( )

Thankful HINCKLEY, b. 19 Apr. 1723, Lebanon CT* (wf of John Robinson^{5})

John WADSWORTH, (son of John), b. 12 Mar. 1671/2, Duxbury, d. 3 May 1750, Duxbury<MD 9:172,11:79>

CHILDREN OF John WADSWORTH & 1st Mercy WISWALL^{4} (Prisc. Pabodie^{3}): (5) <Duxbury, MD 9:231>

John WADSWORTH^{5}, b. 24 May 1706; d. 26 Mar. 1799 <MD 11:79>

Uriah WADSWORTH^{5}, b. 5 July 1708; d. 29 Apr 1784 <MD 11:79>

Dorothy WADSWORTH^{5}, b. 25 June 1710

Ichabod WADSWORTH^{5}, b. 3 May 1712; d. 21 Apr. 1771, Duxbury g.s. (Old Cem.) <MD 10:170>

Peleg WADSWORTH^{5}, b. 29 Aug. 1715; d. 28 July 1799* <Duxbury VR:432>

Mary ( ) VERDIE, d. 22 July 1742, ae 58, S. Duxbury g.s. <MD 10:171>**<48>**

CHILD OF John WADSWORTH & 2nd Mary ( ) VERDIE: (1)

Mary WADSWORTH, B. 19 JULY 1721, Duxbury <MD 9:231>

Anne HUNT, d. 9 Aug. 1773, ae 59*, Duxbury g.s. (Old Cem.) <MD 10:170>

CHILDREN OF Ichabod WADSWORTH^{5} & Anne HUNT: (5) <1-4, Duxbury, MD 12:29>

Rhodie/Rhoda WADSWORTH^{6}, b. 20 Aug. 1737; d. 24 Dec. 1793, Duxbury g.s. ("large cemetary")

Luna WADSWORTH^{6}, b. 2 Nov. 1739

Luke WADSWORTH^{6}, b. 27 Dec. 1743

Selah WADSWORTH^{6}, b. 25 Jan. 1745/6; d. 24 Dec. 1754

Anna WADSWORTH^{6}, bpt. 16 Oct. 1748; d. 6 Oct. 1818*

Perez CHANDLER^{5} (Philip^{4}, Joseph$^{3-2}$, Edmund^{1}), b. 10 July 1730, Duxbury <MD 11:149>; d. 28 Jan. 1800, Duxbury g.s. ("large cemetery")

CHILDREN OF Perez CHANDLER^{5} & Rhoda WADSWORTH^{6}: (11) <1-3,5-10, Duxbury VR> **<49>**

Betty CHANDLER^{7}, b. 13 June 1758**<50>**; d. 8 June 1835, Duxbury*

Philip CHANDLER^{7}, b. 12 Apr. 1761**<50>**

Perez CHANDLER^{7}, b. 28 Dec. 1763**<50>**

Son, b. 25 Mar. 1766, stillborn <Duxbury ChR 1:250>

Dr. Seth CHANDLER^{7}, b. 22 Feb. 1767**<50>**

Wadsworth CHANDLER^{7}, b. 14 May 1769; d. 10 Oct. 1842, Duxbury g.s

Rhoda CHANDLER^{7}, b. 8 Jan. 1772; d. 3 May 1791, unm.

Wealthea CHANDLER^{7}, b. 20 Apr. 1774

Asenath CHANDLER^{7}, b. 14 July 1777

Daniel CHANDLER^{7}, b. 15 Nov. 1778

Benjamin CHANDLER^{7}, b. 20 Mar. 1782; d. 1827*, Paris ME

Mercy CHANDLER, (dau of Philip & Christian*), d. 10 July 1847, ae 75y2m14d, Duxbury g.s.

CHILDREN OF Wadsworth CHANDLER^{7} & Mercy CHANDLER: (5)*

Son, b. 14 Sept. 1804, stillborn

Almira CHANDLER^{7}, b. 30 Mar. 1806

Wadsworth CHANDLER^{7}, b. 28 Sept. 1807

Elbridge CHANDLER^{7}, b. 15 Oct. 1810

Mercy CHANDLER^{7}, b. 13 Mar. 1814

Nathaniel HOLMES^{7} (Ephraim$^{6-5}$, Mary Brewster^{4}, Wrestling^{3}, Love^{2}), d. 7 Nov.1848, ae 75y3m, Kingston g.s. <MD 7:90>

CHILDREN OF Nathaniel HOLMES^{7} & Asenath CHANDLER^{7} (Rhoda Wadsworth^{6}): (10) <Kingston VR>

Nathaniel HOLMES^{8}, b. 27 Nov. 1799 <VR:96>

Ezekiel HOLMES^{8}, b. 24 Aug. 1801 <VR:92>

Asaph HOLMES^{8}, b. 20 Feb. 1804 <VR:89>

Philip Chandler HOLMES^{8}, b. 21 Dec. 1805 <VR:97>

Asenah HOLMES^{8}, b. 22 Dec. 1807 <VR:89>

Allysa HOLMES^{8}, b. 14 Aug. 1809 <VR:89>

Patrick HOLMES^{8}, b. 28 Aug. 1811 <VR:97>; d. 5 Apr. 1818*

Stephen HOLMES^{8}, b. 10 Sept. 1815 <VR:99>

Harvey HOLMES^{8}, b. 10 Jan. 1818 <VR:92>; d. 10 May 1818*

Henry Smith HOLMES^{8}, b. 21 Oct. 1821 <VR:93>; d. 20 Aug. 1842*

CHILDREN OF Stephen HOLMES^{8} & Mahala BARTLETT: (3) <Kingston VR>

Caroline Brooks HOLMES^{9}, b. 23 Oct. 1847 <VR:90>

Olive Bartlett HOLMES^{9}, b. 17 Sept. 1849 <VR:97>

Susan Brigham HOLMES^{9}, b. 28 Oct. 1845 <VR:99>

Joseph DARLING, (son of Samuel?), b. 1757*; d. 13 May 1793, Duxbury* (1st hus.of Betty Chandler^{7} (Rhoda Wadsworth^{6}, Ichabod^{5}))

Sceva CHANDLER, (son of Ebenezer), bpt. 12 June 1757, Duxbury; d. 14 Mar. 1832, (consumption) <Duxbury ChR> (2nd hus. of Betty Chandler^{7} (Rhoda Wadsworth^{6}))

Edith SAMPSON, d. 1 or 2 June 1796, ae 37y10m18d, Duxbury g.s. (1st wf. of Sceva Chandler)

Mary ALDEN^{4} (Ben.^{3}, David^{2}), b. 1 Jan. 1709/10 <Duxbury VR>; d. 4 Apr. 1789 <Duxbury VR> (wf. of John Wadsworth^{5} (Mercy Wiswall^{4}))

Lusanna SAMSON^{4} (John^{3}, Stephen^{2}), b. 30 Apr. 1720, Duxbury <MD 11:237>; d. 20 July 1788* <Duxbury VR:432>

CHILDREN OF Peleg WADSWORTH^{5} (Mercy Wiswall^{4}) & Lusanna SAMSON^{4}: (10) <Duxbury, 1-6, MD 12:30>

Zilpah WADSWORTH^{6}, b. 21 June 1742; d. 23 Mar. 1743/4 <MD 12:32>

Cephas WADSWORTH^{6}, b. 12 Aug. 1743

Jephtha WADSWORTH^{6}, b. 5 Apr. 1745, d. 2() May 1745 <MD 12:30>

Zilpah WADSWORTH^{6}, b. 8 Apr. 1746

Peleg WADSWORTH^{6}, b. 25 Apr. 1748

Uriah WADSWORTH^{6}, b. 13 Mar. 1750/1

Lucia WADSWORTH^{6}, b. 25 Jan. 1753 <MD 12:164>

Ira WADSWORTH^{6}, b. 18 May 1757 <MD 12:164>

Wealthy WADSWORTH^{6}, b. 21 Sept. 1759 <MD 12:164>

Dura WADSWORTH^{6}, son, bpt. 24 Apr. 1763 <Duxbury ChR>

Peleg WISWALL^{4} (Prisc. Pabodie^{3}), b. 5 Feb. 1683, Duxbury <MD 9:229>; d. 7 Sept. 1767,Boston g.s.

Elizabeth ROGERS, d. 1 Dec. 1743, Boston g.s.

CHILDREN OF Peleg WISWALL^{4} & Elizabeth ROGERS: (5)* <NEHGR 40:61>

Elizabeth WISWALL^{5}, b. 4 Nov. 1720

Daniel WISWALL^{5}, b. 13 Feb. 1722

Priscilla WISWALL^{5}, b. 17 Dec. 1725

Sarah WISWALL^{5}, bpt. 4 May 1729

John WISWALL^{5}, b. 15 Apr. 1731

Priscilla WISWALL^{4} (Priscilla Pabodie^{3}), b. c1690; d. 12 Sept. 1780, Bristol RI g.s. (wf of Gershom Bradford^{4})

Gershom BRADFORD^{4} (Sam^{3}, Wm^{2}), b. 21 Dec. 1691, Plymouth<MD 2:18>; d. 4 Apr. 1757, Bristol RI g.s

Rebecca PABODIE^{3}, b. 16 Oct. 1660, Duxbury <MD 9:171>; d. 3 Dec. 1702*<Little Compton VR 4:6:168>

William SOUTHWORTH^{3} (Constant^{2}, Edw.^{1}), d. 25 June 1719* <L. Compton 4:6:168>

CHILDREN OF William SOUTHWORTH^{3} & Rebecca PABODIE^{3}: (9)

Benjamin SOUTHWORTH^{4}, b. 1681*

Joseph SOUTHWORTH^{4}, b. 1683*

Edward SOUTHWORTH^{4}, b. 1684*

Elizabeth SOUTHWORTH^{4}, b. 1686*

Alice SOUTHWORTH^{4}, b. 14 July 1688

Samuel SOUTHWORTH^{4}, b. 1690*

Nathaniel SOUTHWORTH^{4}, b. 1692*

Thomas SOUTHWORTH^{4}, b. 1694*

Stephen SOUTHWORTH^{4}, b. 1696*

MICRO #7 of 16

John COOK, (son of John & Ruth), b. 5 Nov. 1685, Tiverton RI; d. 1754

CHILDREN OF John COOK & Alice SOUTHWORTH^{4}: (4)*<51><VR RI 4:6:108>

Amey COOK^{5}, b. 11 July 1710, Little Compton

Bathsheba COOK^{5}, b. 30 Mar. 1712, Little Compton

Lillis COOK^{5}, b. 9 Feb. 1714, Little Compton

Samuel COOK^{5}, b. ( ), Little Compton

CHILDREN OF William MANCHESTER & Rebecca COOK: (8)<52><VR RI .4:7:95>

Phebe MANCHESTER, b. 21 July 1743; d. 1 Mar. 1819; Tolland MA<53>

Gilbert MANCHESTER, b. 9 Apr. 1745

Godfrey MANCHESTER, b. 19 Sept. 1746

Rhody MANCHESTER, b. 11 May 1748

John MANCHESTER, b. 7 Nov. 1749

Alice MANCHESTER, b. 21 May 1753

Thaddeus MANCHESTER, b. 1 Jan. 1756

Priscilla MANCHESTER, b. 28 Nov. 1761

David SLOCUM^{5} (Ebenezer^{4}, Eliezer^{3}, Giles^{2}, Anthony^{1}), b. 23 Sept. 1740, Dartmouth; d. 7 Dec. 1818, Tolland MA <53>

CHILD OF David SLOCUM^{5} & Phebe MANCHESTER:
Hull SLOCUM, b. 7 Jan. 1767

Stephen SOUTHWORTH^{4} (Rebecca Pabodie^{3}), b. 31 Mar. 1696* <Southworth Gen.:194,196>
Lydia WARREN^{5} (Rebecca Church^{4}, Caleb^{3}, Eliz. Warren^{2}), b. 3 Nov. 1696* <Southworth Gen.:194,196>

CHILDREN OF Stephen SOUTHWORTH^{4} & Lydia WARREN^{5}: (3) <Freetown VR 1:160>
Rebecca SOUTHWORTH^{5}, b. 7 Oct. 1726
Thomas SOUTHWORTH^{5}, b. 5 Sept. 1728
Steven SOUTHWORTH^{5}, b. 12 Jan. 1731

Ruth PABODIE^{3}, b. 27 June 1658, Duxbury <MD 1:163> (see Warren file)
Sarah PABODIE^{3}, b. 7 Aug. 1656, Duxbury <MD 1:163>
John COE, d. betw. 4 Dec. 1728 (will) - 1 Jan. 1728-9 (probate)

CHILDREN OF John COE & Sarah PABODIE^{3}: (7)
Lydia COE^{4}, b. 26 Feb. 1682/3, Duxbury <MD 9:173>
Sarah COE^{4}, b. 25 Feb. 1684/5, Duxbury <MD 9:173>; d. 2 Jan. 1741*<Little Compton VR 4:6:106,177>
Samuel COE^{4}, b. 12 Dec. 1692* <Little Compton VR>
Elizabeth COE^{4}, b. 28 Mar. 1694* <Little Compton VR>
Hannah COE^{4}, b. ( )
John COE^{4}, b. 1 Feb. 1699*, d. Nov. 1784 <Little Compton VR>
Joseph COE^{4}, b. ( )

CHILDREN OF Edward BURGESS & Elizabeth COE^{4}: (6)*
Benjamin BURGESS^{5}, b. 27 Sept. 1721, d. 5 Feb. 1722 <Little Compton VR>
Thomas BURGESS^{5}, b. 6 Sept. 1723
Esther BURGESS^{5}, b. 27 July 1725
Benjamin BURGESS^{5}, b. 13 July 1728
Sarah BURGESS^{5}, b. 24 Oct. 1730
Lydia BURGESS^{5}, b. 15 Feb. 1734

Rebecca TAYLOR, b. 4 Jan. 1719* <Little Compton VR>

CHILDREN OF John COE^{4} (Sarah Pabodie^{3}) & Rebecca TAYLOR*: (8)*
Lydia COE^{5}, b. 28 Mar. 1742 <Little Compton VR>
Isaac COE^{5}, b. 23 Apr. 1744
Samuel COE^{5}, b. 20 Mar. 1746
William COE^{5}, b. 20 Feb. 1748
John COE^{5}, b. 27 Oct. 1750
Benjamin COE^{5}, b. 3 May 1753
Sarah COE^{5}, b. 11 Feb. 1756
Hannah COE^{5}, b. 9 July 1759; d. 3 Dec. 1850

CHILDREN OF John BAILEY & Lydia COE^{4} (Sarah Pabodie^{3}): (5)*
Joseph BAILEY^{5}, b. 29 Oct. 1710, d. Jan. 1711 <Little Compton VR>
John BAILEY^{5}, b. 13 Apr. 1712
Joseph BAILEY^{5}, b. 22 Sept. 1714
Gideon BAILEY^{5}, b. 1716
Benjamin BAILEY^{5}, b. 1718

CHILDREN OF Samuel COE^{4} (Sarah Pabodie^{3}) & Mary CHADWICK*: (7)*<54>
Isaac COE^{5}, b. 27 May 1717 <Little Compton VR>
Samuel COE^{5}, b. 1 Jan. 1720; d. 25 Dec. 1740
Priscilla COE^{5}, b. 6 May 1723
Sarah COE^{5}, b. 29 June 1725
Matthew COE^{5}, b. 23 May 1727
John COE^{5}, b. 23 Nov. 1728; d. 16 Dec. 1728

CHILDREN OF Samuel TOMPKINS & Sarah COE4 (Sarah Pabodie^{3}): (12)*

Joseph TOMPKINS[5], b. 26 Oct. 1712 <Little Compton VR 4:6:177>
John TOMPKINS[5], b. 14 Sept. 1714
Elizabeth TOMPKINS[5], b. 8 Dec. 1715
Christopher TOMPKINS[5], b. 8 Dec. 1715 (twins)
Abigail TOMPKINS[5], b. 28 Jan. 1717
Nathaniel TOMPKINS[5], b. 19 Nov. 1719; d. 20 Jan. 1724
Gideon TOMPKINS[5], b. 19 Nov. 1720; d. Mar. 1774
Micah TOMPKINS[5], b. 20 Jan. 1722; d. May 1771
Benjamin TOMPKINS[5], b. 26 Jan. 1723
Augustus TOMPKINS[5], b. 19 Mar. 1725; d. 16 Feb. 1747
Priscilla TOMPKINS[5], b. 6 June 1726; d. 18 Aug. 1739
William TOMPKINS[5], b. 17 Oct. 1730; d. Nov. 1768
William PABODIE[3], b. 24 Nov. 1664, Duxbury <MD 1:163>; d. 17 Sept. 1744, Little Compton g.s.
Mrs. Judith PABODIE, wf of William, d. 20 July 1714, ae 45, L. Compton g.s.<54a>
Mrs. Elizabeth PABODIE, 2nd wf of Wm., d. 14 Dec. 1747, ae "about" 45, Little Compton g.s.<54b>
CHILDREN OF William PABODIE[3] & Judith ( ): (9)<54a>
Elizabeth PABODIE[4], b. ( )
John PABODIE[4], b. ( )
William PABODIE[4], b. ( )
Rebecca PABODIE[4], b. ( )
Priscilla PABODIE[4], b. 4 Mar. 1706*
Judith PABODIE[4], b. ( )
Joseph PABODIE[4], b. ( )
Mary PABODIE[4], b. 4 Apr. 1712*
Benjamin PABODIE[4], b. ( )
Nathaniel FISH, (son of Thomas & Margaret (Woodworth)), b. 11 Apr. 1713*
CHILDREN OF Nathaniel FISH & Mary PABODIE[4]: (9) <1-7, Stonington CT VR 3:146>
Miller FISH[5], b. 9 Oct. 1737
William FISH[5], b. 26 Apr. 1739
Elikam FISH[5], b. 2 Feb. 1741
Joseph FISH[5], b. 25 Mar. 1742
Nathaniel FISH[5], b. 6 Feb. 1744
Lydia FISH[5], b. 3 Mar. 1746
Mary FISH[5], b. 5 Mar. 1748
Joseph FISH[5], b. 3 Apr. 1752 <Norwich CT VR 3:39>
Betty FISH[5], b. 19 Apr. 1755 <Norwich CT VR 3:39>
CHILD OF Nathaniel FISH Jr. & Abigail ( ):
Walter FISH, b. 20 May 1770 <Norwich CT VR 3:323>
CHILDREN OF Nathaniel Fish Jr. & Mary ( ): (3) <Norwich CT VR 3:323>
Samuel FISH, b. 30 Mar. 1776
Abigail FISH, b. 11 Oct. 1777
Calvin FISH, b. 15 Dec. 1779
CHILDREN OF Rev. Joseph FISH & Rebecca ( ): (3) <Stonington CT VR 3:49>
Mary FISH, b. 19 May 1736
Rebecca FISH, b. 11 Jan. 1738/9
Joseph FISH, b. 3 Apr. 1742
CHILDREN OF William FISH & Elisabeth HAUGHTON: (2) <Norwich CT VR 2:272>
Molley FISH, b. 23 Oct. 1763
Sarah FISH, b. 11 Feb. 1768
CHILD OF William FISH & Deborah BACKUS:

Lydia FISH, b. 18 Mar. 1773 <Norwich CT VR 3:176>
Deborah WOODWORTH, d. 18 Oct. 1760, Norwich CT
CHILD OF Andrew LOTHROP & Deborah WOODWORTH:
Jesse LOTHROP, b. 22 June 1760, d. 9 Jan. 1761 <Norwich CT VR 2:181>
CHILDREN OF Andrew LOTHROP & Abigail FISH: (7)<55> <Norwich CT VR 2:348>
Abigail LOTHROP, b. 9 Aug. 1764
Deborah LOTHROP, b. 10 June 1766, d. 6 Nov. 1766
Eunice LOTHROP, b. 24 June 1768
Deborah LOTHROP, b. 23 Mar. 1770
Andrew LOTHROP, b. 4 Apr. 1772
Martha LOTHROP, b. 21 June 1774
Wealthy LOTHROP, b. 27 Mar. 1778

JOHN ALDEN[2] (John[1])

John ALDEN[2], b. c1627, Plymouth <MD 6:193>; d. 14 Mar. 1701/2, ae 75, Boston (bur. Old South Church) <MD 6:193>
CHILD OF John ALDEN[2] & 1st Elizabeth ( ):
Mary ALDEN[3], b. 17 Dec. 1659 <Boston Rcd.Com.9:69>
Elizabeth (PHILLIPS) Everill, bur. 7 Feb. 1695/6, Boston <Sewall's Diary>
CHILDREN OF John ALDEN[2] & 2nd Elizabeth (PHILLIPS) Everill: (11)
John ALDEN[3], b. 20 Nov. 1660, d.y. <Boston Rcd.Com.9:73>
Elizabeth ALDEN[3], b. 9 May 1662, d. 14 July 1662 <Boston Rcd.Com.9:83,85>
John ALDEN[3], b. 12 Mar. 1663 <Boston Rcd.Com.9:106>
William ALDEN[3], b. 16 Mar. 1664, d. 7 June 1664 <Boston Rcd.Com.9:91,94>
Elizabeth ALDEN[3], b. 9 Apr. 1665 <Boston Rcd.Com.9:95>
William ALDEN[3], b. 5 Mar. 1666 <Boston Rcd.Com.9:99>
Zachariah ALDEN[3], b. 8 Mar. ( ) <Boston Rcd.Com.9:99><56>
William ALDEN[3], b. 10 Sept. 1669 <Boston Rcd.Com.9:110>
Zachariah ALDEN[3], b. 18 Feb. 1672 <Boston Rcd.Com.9:122>
Nathan ALDEN[3], b. 17 Oct. 1677 <Boston Rcd.Com.9:140>; d. pre 17 Feb. 1701/2
Sarah ALDEN[3], b. 27 Sept. 1681 <Boston Rcd.Com.9:154>
CHILDREN OF Abiel EVERILL & Elizabeth PHILLIPS (dau. of William): (2)
James EVERILL, b. 4 Apr. 1656 <Boston Rcd.Com.9:54>
Abiel EVERILL, bpt. 28 Apr. 1667 <Boston Rcd.Com.9:106>

Alden Deaths - Boston <Miscellaneous Deaths 1700-1800, Vol. 31>
John ALDEN, d. 14 Mar. 1702 <Mass.State Rcds.>
William ALDEN, Esq., d. 9 Feb. 1728/9, ae 60, <Kings Chapel>
Mary ALDEN, wf of above Wm., d. 11 Feb. 1727, ae 56 <Kings Chapel>
Capt. John ALDEN, d. 1 Feb. 1729, ae 67 <Kings Chapel>
Elizabeth ALDEN, wf of above John, d. 26 Nov. 1719, ae 50 <Kings Chapel>
Gilam ALDEN, son of John & Elizabeth, d. 25 Dec. 1726, ae 28 <Kings Chapel>
Nathaniel ALDEN, son of Capt. Nathaniel, d. 25 Feb. 1746, ae 15 <Kings Chapel>
( ) ALDING, child, bur. 14 Aug. 1701 <Old memos & sexton's bills>
Mr. ALDAN, bur. 18 Mar. 1703 <Old memos & sexton's bills>
( ) Alden, child of Wm., bur. 27 Oct. 1702 <Old memos & sexton's bills>
( ) ALLDEN, child, bur. 2 Nov. 1702 <Old memos & sexton's bills>
Capt. William ALDEN, d. 10 Feb. 1729, ae 60 <N.E. Weekly Journal>
Capt. John ALDEN, d. 1 Feb. 1730, ae 65 <N.E. Weekly Journal>

( ) ALDEN, child of Wm. ?, bur. 25 Apr. 1705/6 <Old Sexton's bills>

John ALDEN, d. 14 Mar. 1702 <Farmer's Gen.Reg.>

Will ALDEN, a negro, d. 30 July 1705 <Old sexton's memos>

( ) ALDEN, child of Wm., bur. 23 July 1712 <Old sexton's bills>

( ) ALDEN, child of John, bur. 30 July 1713 <Old sexton's bills>

( ) ALDEN, child of John, bur. 8 Nov. 1706 <Old sexton's bills>

( ) ALDEN, negro woman of John, bur. 7 Mar. 1715 <Old sexton's bills>

John ALDER, bur. 24 Nov. 1712 <Old sexton's bills>

( ) ALDEN, child of John, bur. 29 Dec. 1713 <Old sexton's bills>

( ) ALDEN, child of John, bur. 13 Sept. 1720 <Old sexton's bills>

Mrs. ALDEN, wf of John, bur. 30 Nov. 1719 <Old sexton's bills>

Thomas ALDEN, son of John & Elizabeth, d. 13 Aug. 1701

John ALDEN Sr., d. 14 Mar. 1702

Katherine ALDEN, dau. of John & Elizabeth, d. 31 Oct. 1702

Mary ALDEN, dau. of William & Mary, d. 27 Oct. 1702

William ALDEN, son of John & Elizabeth, d. 27 Dec. 1714

Elizabeth ALDEN, wf of Capt. John, d. 26 Nov. 1719

Mary ALDEN, d. 11 Feb. 1727, ae 56

William ALDEN, d. 10 Feb. 1728, ae 60

John ALDEN, d. 1 Feb. 1729, ae 67

Alden Deaths - King's Chapel <Boston Cemetery Dept.>

Elizabeth ALDEN, wf of John, d. 26 Nov. 1719, ae 50

Gilam ALDEN, son of John & Elizabeth, d. 25 Dec. 1726, ae 28

Katharine ALDEN, dau. of John & Elizabeth, d. 31 Oct. 1702, ae about 5

John ALDEN, son of John & Anna, d. 10 Sept. 1720, ae 9m15d

Mary ALDEN, wf of William, d. 11 Feb. 1727, ae 56

Capt. John ALDEN, d. 1 Feb. 1729/30, ae 67

Nathaniel ALDEN, son of Capt. Nathaniel, d. 25 Feb. 1746, ae 15

William ALDEN, Esq., d. 9 Feb. 1728/9, ae 60

* * * * *

John WALLEY, d. pre 30 Apr. 1702 (adm.)

CHILDREN OF John WALLEY & Elizabeth ALDEN^{3}: (6)

Sarah WALLEY^{4}, b. 25 Aug. 1684; d. 29 June 1690

Abiel WALLEY^{4}, b. 30 Aug. 1686

William WALLEY^{4}, b. 23 Dec. 1687

John WALLEY^{4}, b. 19 July 1688

Elizabeth WALLEY^{4}, b. 4 May 1693; d. aft. 4 Feb. 1719/20

Sarah WALLEY^{4}, b. 27 Apr. 1695

Simon WILLARD, d. betw. 13 Nov. 1709 (will) - 11 Jan. 1713 (probate)

CHILDREN OF Simon WILLARD & Elizabeth ALDEN^{3}: (4) <Boston>

Samuel WILLARD^{4}, b. 19 Jan. 1702/3 <Rcd.Com.24:18>; d. aft. 1717/18

Abigail WILLARD^{4}, b. 19 Jan. 1702/3 (twins) <Rcd.Com.24:18>; d. aft.1 Sept. 1761<mortgage>

Katherine WILLARD^{4}, b. 20 Dec. 1704 <Rcd.Com.24:32>; d. 15 Aug. 1736*,Carver g.s.<Carver VR:148>

George WILLARD^{4}, b. 14 Feb. 1706 <Rcd.Com.24:45>; d.y.

MICRO #8 of 16

Dr. Joseph BRIDGHAM, (son of Joseph & Mercy), b. 16 Apr. 1701*<Boston Rcd.Com.24:5>; d. 25 Sept. 1753*, Carver g.s. <Carver VR:148>

CHILDREN OF Dr. Joseph BRIDGHAM & Abigail WILLARD^{4}: (8)*

Joseph BRIDGHAM^{5}, b. 22 Nov. 1723 <Boston Rcd.Com.24:158>

Abigail BRIDGHAM^{5}, b. 21 Nov. 1724 <Boston Rcd.Com.24:163>

Mercy BRIDGHAM^{5}, b. 27 Dec. 1725 <Boston Rcd.Com.24:168>

Elizabeth BRIDGHAM^{5}, b. ( )

John BRIDGHAM^{5}, b. 27 Aug. 1729 <Boston Rcd.Com.24:190>

Hannah BRIDGHAM^{5}, b. 2 Aug. 1730 <Boston Rcd.Com.24:196>

Sarah BRIDGHAM^{5}, b. ( )

Katherine BRIDGHAM^{5}, b. ( )

Joanna COOMER, (dau. of William & Joanna), bpt. 6 Feb. 1731/2 <Plympton VR:76>

CHILD OF John BRIDGHAM^{5} & Joanna COOMER:

John BRIDGHAM^{6}, b. 16 May 1754*; d. 31 July 1840*, Minot ME

Sibilla SHAW, b. 4 Nov. 1756*; d. 30 Sept. 1835, Minot (wf of John Bridgham^{6})

CHILDREN OF Joseph BRIDGHAM^{5} & Martha BRICKLIN*:(6) <Rehoboth VR:554>

Abigail BRIDGHAM^{6}, b. 1 Dec. 1761

Sarah BRIDGHAM^{6}, b. 6 Aug. 1763

Charlotte BRIDGHAM^{6}, b. 16 May 1765

Joseph BRIDGHAM^{6}, b. 21 Mar. 1770

Martha BRIDGHAM^{6}, b. 21 Mar. 1770 (twins)

Samuel Willard BRIDGHAM^{6}, b. 4 May 1774

Abigail BRIDGHAM, (dau. of Daniel), d. 8 Sept. 1778 <Rehoboth VR:803>

CHILDREN OF Cyrus MARTIN & Charlotte BRIDGHAM: (2)

Willard MARTIN, b. 6 Mar. 1786

Edward MARTIN, b. 12 May 1788

Rev. Othniel CAMPBELL, b. 8 Feb. 1695/6*, Taunton <NEHGR 17:234>, (son of Ebenezer & Hannah (Pratt)); d. Oct. 1778*, Tiverton RI <Plympton VR:455>

CHILD OF Rev. Othniel CAMPBELL & Katherine WILLARD^{4} (Eliz.Alden^{3}, John^{2}):

Katharine CAMPBELL^{5}, b. 3 Feb. 1736 <Plympton VR:53>

CHILDREN OF Samuel ELLIS & Katharine CAMPBELL^{5}: (2)*

Willard ELLIS^{6}, b. 8 Apr. 1767 <Plympton VR:96>

Molly ELLIS^{6}, b. 27 Apr. 1769 <Plympton VR:96> **<57>**

John ALDEN^{3}, b. 12 Mar. 1663, Boston <MD 6:194-5>; d. 1 Feb. 1729/30, Boston <King's Chapel g.s.>

Elizabeth ( ) ALDEN, d. 26 Nov. 1719, ae 50, Boston <King's Chapel g.s.>**<57>**

CHILDREN OF John ALDEN^{3} & Elizabeth ( ): (12) <Boston Rcd.Com.>

Elizabeth ALDEN^{4}, b. 7 Nov. 1687 <9:172>; d. aft. 1747*, unm.

Hannah ALDEN^{4}, b. 20 Nov. 1688 <9:178>; d. betw. 1732-6*

John ALDEN^{4}, b. 20 Sept. 1690 <9:188>; d. pre 31 Mar. 1727, Jamaica <MD 24:165>

Mary ALDEN^{4}, b. 15 Dec. 1691 <9:195>; d. pre 5 May 1727*, unm. (father's will) <MD 10:80-1>

Katharine ALDEN^{4}, b. 19 Aug. 1697 <9:231>; d. 31 Oct. 1762*

Gillam ALDEN^{4}, b. 7 July 1699 <9:246>; d. 25 Dec. 1726*

Ann ALDEN^{4}, b. 7 July 1699 (twin) <9:246>; d. aft. 1741*

Nathaniel ALDEN^{4}, b. 6 July 1700 <24:1>; d. pre 10 July 1740 (adm.) <MD 12:72>

Thomas ALDEN^{4}, b. 13 Aug. 1701 <24:5>; d. 13 Aug. 1701*

Katharine ALDEN^{4}, b. 17 Feb. 1704 <24:26>; d. pre 5 May 1727*,unm. (father's will) <MD 10:80-1>

Thomas ALDEN^{4}, b. 1 Mar. 1707 <24:52>; d. betw. 5 May 1727* (father's will) <MD 10:80-1> - 4 Sept 1739 (wf. 2nd int.) <Boston Rcd.Com.28:231>

William ALDEN^{4}, b. 9 May 1710 <24:66>; d. 27 Dec. 1714*

Anna BRAME, dau of Benjamin & Elizabeth, b. 23 July 1694* <Boston Rcd.Com.9:213>; bur. 24 Apr. 1761*, widow of Dr. Henry Burchsted <Lynn VR 2:444>

Dr. Henry BURCHSTED, d. 31 Mar. 1755*, ae 65, Lynn g.s. <VR 2:444>

CHILDREN OF John ALDEN^4 & Anna BRAME: (3) <Boston Rcd.Com>

John ALDEN^5, b. 29 Nov. 1719 <24:134>

Anna ALDEN^5, b. 29 Jan. 1722 <24:153>; d. 10 Dec. 1795*, Lynn g.s., Western Cem.

Benjamin ALDEN^5, b. 18 Sept. 1724 <24:163>

CHILDREN OF Benjamin BREAME & Anna ( ): (2)

Benjamin BREAME, b. 8 June 1670 <Hingham VR 1:20>

Hannah BREAME, b. 26 July 1668 <Hingham VR 1:15>

Samuel BURRILL, b. 1 Apr. 1717*, Lynn; d. 3 May 1797*, Lynn g.s., Western Cem.

CHILDREN OF Samuel BURRILL & Anna ALDEN^5 (John^4): (6 of 8?)

Samuel BURRILL^6, b. ( )

Alden BURRILL^6, b. 1753*; d. 14 Dec. 1831*, ae 78, Salem <Lynn VR>

Ebenezer BURRILL^6, b. ( )

Elizabeth BURRILL^6, b. ( )

John BURRILL^6, b. ( )

Eunice BURRILL^6, b. ( ); d. 25 Nov. 1816*, Lynn

Joseph HART, d. 15 Dec. 1806*, Lynn

CHILDREN OF Joseph HART & Eunice BURRILL^6: (11)* <Lynn VR>

Anna HART^7, b. 12 Apr. 1766<58>; d. 17 Oct. 1848, ae 81y6m

Child, b. 12 Apr. 1767, d.y.

Joseph HART^7, b. 1 Nov. 1768; d. 15 (or 25) Nov. 1786

Eunice HART^7, b. 8 Nov. 1770

Phebe HART^7, b. 12 June 1773

Burrill HART^7, b. 12 Nov. 1775, d.y.

Burrill HART^7, b. 2 May 1778; d. 8 Dec. 1786

Samuel HART^7, b. 2 May 1778 (twin); d. 18 July 1802

Sarah HART^7, b. 24 Jan. 1781

John HART^7, b. 8 Dec. 1783; d. 26 Aug. 1725 <Bible>

Joseph Burrill HART^7, b. 7 Oct. 1788; d. 19 Nov. 1795 <Bible>

Joseph LYE Jr., d. 16 Oct. 1807*, ae 48

CHILDREN OF Joseph LYE Jr. & Anna HART^7: (9)* <Lynn>

Elizabeth LYE^8, b. 9 Mar. 1788; d. 30 May 1841, unm.

Anna LYE^8, b. 23 Nov. 1789; d. 17 Mar. 1817, ae 30 (?)

Joseph LYE^8, b. 20 Mar. 1792; d. 10 Apr. 1834

Eunice B. LYE^8, b. 17 Mar. 1794; d. 17 Sept. 1817

Child, b. 14 Aug. 1796; d. 14 Oct. 1830

Mary LYE^8, b. 23 Dec. 1798; d. 20 Oct. 1806

John LYE^8, b. 12 Apr. 1801

Robert Gray LYE^8, b. 4 July 1803; d. 14 Feb. 1841

Sally Gray LYE^8, b. 8 Oct. 1805; d. 7 June 1839, unm.

CHILDREN OF Nathaniel ALDEN^4 (John^3) & Mary SMITH*: (3)

Elizabeth ALDEN^5, b. 3 Aug. 1730 <Boston Rcd.Com.24:195>; d. 21 Oct. 1783 <Hopkinton VR:320>

Nathaniel ALDEN^5, b. 1731*, d. 25 Feb. 1746*, ae 15

Hannah ALDEN^5, b. 3 June 1735 <Boston Rcd.Com.24:220>

Anthony JONES, b. 8 June 1723* <NEHGR 51:69>; d. 8 Apr. 1782 <Hopkinton VR:430>

CHILDREN OF Anthony JONES & Elizabeth ALDEN^5: (14) <NEHGR 51:69>

Nathaniel Alden JONES^6, bpt. 21 Aug. 1748

Hannah JONES^6, bpt. 31 Dec. 1749 or 50

Elizabeth JONES^6, bpt. 27 Dec. 1750

Anthony JONES[6], bpt. 1 July 1753; d. 5 Oct. 1786

John JONES[6], bpt. 30 Mar. 1755; d. 25 Nov. 1824, Hopkinton<59>

Isaac JONES[6], bpt. 18 Sept. 1757; d. 26 Oct. 1818

Samuel JONES[6], bpt. 17 Mar. 1759; d. 20 Feb. 1833

Sarah JONES[6], bpt. 5 Oct. 1760

Lydia JONES[6], bpt. 26 Sept. 1762

Anna JONES[6], bpt. 26 Aug. 1764;pre 26 July 1781(father's will)<Middlesex Co.#12792, 62:89;69:123>

Ann JONES[6], bpt. 7 Sept. 1766; d. pre 26 July 1781 (father's will) < " ">

Elisha JONES[6], bpt. 10 July 1768; d. aft. 24 Dec. 1785 (receipt) < " ">

Mehitable JONES[6], bpt. 13 May 1770; d. aft. 24 Dec. 1785 (receipt) < " ">

Simpson JONES[6], bpt. 13 Sept. 1772

CHILDREN OF Alden JONES & Betsey ( ): (7) <Sudbury VR>

George Lewis JONES, b. 3 Jan. 1827, Washington, NH

Henry Francis JONES, b. 3 May 1829

Lyman Alden JONES, b. 17 July 1831

Oliver Pollard JONES, b. 9 Oct. 1833

Mary Elizabeth JONES, b. 4 Oct. 1835

William Hyde JONES, b. 25 Jan. 1838

Sarah Maria JONES, b. 6 July 1840

CHILDREN OF Elijah JONES & Mehitable HAYNES: (10) <1-9, Sudbury VR>

Mehitable JONES, b. 11 Jan. 1801

Maria JONES, b. 19 Nov. 1802

Elijah Fitch JONES, b. 22 July 1804; d. 9 Jan. 1844*

Meshach Haynes JONES, b. 8 June 1807

Avary JONES, b. 17 Aug. 1809

Anthony JONES, b. 3 Mar. 1811

Lydia JONES, b. 28 Sept. 1812

Submit JONES, b. 20 July 1814

Louisa Claflin Jones, b. 28 Jan. 1816

Infant of Elijah Jones, d. 1 Jan. 1818 <ChR>

Elijah JONES, father of above children, d. 12 Apr. 1825, Sudbury

CHILDREN OF John H. JONES[7] (John[6]) & Sally Sears BALLARD: (5)

William B. JONES[8], b. ( )

Mary M. JONES[8], b. ( ) (twin?)

Eliza Curtis JONES[8], b. ( ) (twin?)

John JONES[8], b. ( )

Hannah JONES[8], b. ( )

Rachel HAYNES*, (dau. of Joshua & Susanna), b. 15 June 1758* <Sudbury VR:68>; d. 30 Nov. 1823

CHILDREN OF Samuel JONES[6] (Elizabeth Alden[5]) & Rachel HAYNES: (4 of 8)

Samuel JONES[7], b. ( )

Asa JONES[7], b. ( )

Joshua JONES[7], b. ( )

John JONES[7], b. ( )

(3 daughters & 1 son, not named) <see below>

MICRO #9 of 16

CHILDREN OF Samuel JONES[6] & Rachel HAYNES: (5) (see above)

Lydia JONES[7], b. 12 Mar. 1778 <Sudbury VR:81>

Joshua JONES[7], b. 17 Mar. 1780 <Sudbury VR:81>

Samuel JONES^7, b. 5 June 1784 <Sudbury VR:81>

Joel JONES^7, bpt. 30 Apr. 1786 <West Church>

Asa JONES^7, bpt. 31 Jan. 1790 <West Church>; (see below)

Capt. Samuel JONES, (son of Thomas & Mary) b. 31 May 1741<Concord VR:151>; d. 6 May 1812, Concord g.s. <VR:332>

CHILD OF Capt. Samuel JONES & Hepzebath JONES (dau of Ephraim & Alice):

William JONES, b. 15 Sept. 1772 <Concord VR:234>

Rebecca HOWE, d. 19 Sept. 1886, Sudbury g.s. (widow of Asa Jones^7)

Asa JONES^7 (Sam.^{6}), d. 18 Sept. 1854, ae 64y9m20d, dropsy, farmer, "son of John & Rachel" <Mass. VR 85:125>

CHILDREN OF Thomas ALDEN^4 (John^3) & Jane WHIPPE: (3) <Boston Rcd.Com.>**<60>**

Thomas ALDEN^5, b. 10 June 1725 <24:168>

William ALDEN^5, b. 26 Oct. 1727 <24:179>

John ALDEN^5, b. 30 Oct. 1729 <24:190>

Nathaniel ALDEN^3, d. 1 July 1700 "probably" <MD 10:78, 6:194>

Hephzibah MOUNTJOY, (dau. of George), bpt. 9 (8 mth) 1673 <Boston Rcd.Com.9:131>

CHILDREN OF Nathaniel ALDEN^3 & Hephzibah MOUNTJOY: (5) <MD 10:78>

Mary ALDEN^4, b. 20 Aug. 1692 <Boston Rcd.Com.9:200>

Nathaniel ALDEN^4, b. 6 Aug. 1694 <Boston Rcd.Com.9:213>

Elizabeth ALDEN^4, b. ( ) <Boston Rcd.Com.9:249>

Hephzibah ALDEN^4, b. ( ) <Boston Rcd.Com.9:249>

Phillips ALDEN^4, b. 31 Dec. 1698 <Boston Rcd.Com.9:239>

CHILD OF John MORTEMORE & Hephzibah (MOUNTJOY) Alden:

Anne MORTEMORE, b. 16 Aug. 1704* <Boston Rcd.Com.24:29>

Joseph BRIGHTMAN, (son of Henry & Abiel*), b. 19 July 1693*<Boston Rcd.Com.9:205>

CHILDREN OF Joseph BRIGHTMAN & Mary ALDEN^4 (Nath.^{3}): (2)

Mary BRIGHTMAN^5, b. 7 July 1715 <Boston Rcd.Com.24:103>

Joseph BRIGHTMAN^5, b. 19 Jan. 1716 <Boston Rcd.Com.24:112>

William ALDEN^3, d. 9 or 10 Feb. 1728*, ae 60 (will) <MD 10:80>

Mary DRURY, d. 11 Feb. 1727*, ae 56, Kings Chapel

CHILDREN OF William ALDEN^3 & Mary DRURY: (7) <Boston Rcd.Com.>

Mary ALDEN^4, b. 14 Feb. 1693 <9:205>; d. 27 Oct. 1702*

Elizabeth ALDEN^4, b. 10 Mar. 1695 <9:220>

William ALDEN^4, b. 23 July 1697 <9:231>; d. pre 1729*

Lydia ALDEN^4, b. 22 Dec. 1701 <24:11>

Mary ALDEN^4, b. 12 June 1706 <24:40>

Drury ALDEN^4, b. 12 May 1708 <24:54>; d. pre 1729*

John ALDEN^4, b. 22 Jan. 1711 <24:73>; d. pre 1729*

CHILD OF Thomas BETTERLY & Elizabeth ALDEN^4:

Thomas BETTERLY^5, b. 17 Nov. 1723 <Boston Rcd.Com.24:158>

Zachariah ALDEN^3, d. pre 18 Aug. 1709 (adm.) <MD 10:79>

Mary VIAL, d. aft. 15 Apr. 1736*

CHILDREN OF Zachariah ALDEN^3 & Mary VIAL: (3)

Zachariah ALDEN^4, b. 11 Oct. 1701 <Boston Rcd.Com.24:12>; d. aft. 1736*

Mary ALDEN^4*, b. ( )

Elizabeth ALDEN^4*, b. ( )

CHILD OF Zachariah ALDEN^4 & 1st Jemima HALL*:

Mary ALDEN^5*, b. 8 Mar. 1725* <Boston Rcd.Com.24:168>; d. pre 1733*

CHILDREN OF Zachariah ALDEN^{4} & 2nd Lydia CRANE* (dau. of Ebenezer): (3)*
Lydia ALDEN^{5}, b. 3 June 1730
Zachariah ALDEN^{5}, b. 20 July 1731 <Boston Rcd.Com.24:200>; d. 1733
Mary ALDEN^{5}, b. 6 July 1733 <Boston Rcd.Com.24:210>

JONATHAN ALDEN^{2} (John^{1})

Jonathan ALDEN^{2}, b. c1632 <MD 3:10>; d. 14 Feb. 1697, Duxbury g.s., ae 65 <MD 9:159>
Abigail HALLET, (dau. of Andrew), d. 17 Aug. 1725, Duxbury g.s., ae 81 <MD 9:159>
CHILDREN OF Jonathan ALDEN^{2} & Abigail HALLET: (6)<MD 14:140>
Sarah ALDEN^{3}, b. c1679, d. 26 June 1738, ae 59 <MD 10:170>
John ALDEN^{3}, b. c1681, d. 24 July 1739, ae 58 <MD 9:159>
Jonathan ALDEN^{3}, b. ( )
Andrew ALDEN^{3}, b. ( )
Elizabeth ALDEN^{3}, b. ( )
Anna ALDEN^{3*}, b. pre 1686; d. 8 June 1705, Bridgewater <MD 6:7>
CHILDREN OF Waterman THOMAS & Hannah ( ): (6) <Marshfield TR 2:123>
Abigail THOMAS, b. 5 Dec. 1775, Waldoborough, d. 8 Dec. 1775
Abigail THOMAS, b. 11 Mar. 1777, Waldoborough, d. 21 Sept. 1778
Sarah THOMAS, b. 28 Aug. 1778, Waldoborough
Hannah Briggs THOMAS, b. 1 Dec. 1779, Marshfield
John Anthony THOMAS, b. 30 Nov. 1781, Marshfield
Betsey THOMAS, b. 26 Feb. 1784, Marshfield
CHILDREN OF Andrew ALDEN^{3} & Lydia STANFORD: (4) <Duxbury, MD 10:185>
Jabin ALDEN^{4}, b. 19 Nov. 1714
John ALDEN^{4}, b. 23 July 1716
Prince ALDEN^{4}, b. 28 Oct. 1718
Andrew ALDEN^{4}, b. 20 June 1721
CHILDREN OF Prince ALDEN^{4} & Mary FITCH (dau. of Adonijah): (9)<New London CT VR, 1710-1786,:29>
Mary ALDEN^{5}, b. 1 Dec. 1747
Mason Fitch ALDEN^{5}, b. 25 Oct. 1750
Abigail ALDEN^{5}, b. 11 Aug. 1753
Sarah ALDEN^{5}, b. 6 Feb. 1756
Lydia ALDEN^{5}, b. 31 Oct. 1758
Prince ALDEN^{5}, b. 14 Mar. 1762
Andrew Stanford ALDEN^{5}, b. 5 May 1766
John ALDEN^{5*}, b. ( )
Daniel ALDEN^{5*}, b. ( )
Josiah SNELL, (son of Thomas), b. 5 May 1674, Bridgewater <MD 2:242>; d. 4 Apr.1753, Bridgewater <MD 6:7>
CHILDREN OF Josiah SNELL & Anna ALDEN^{3}: (3) <MD 6:7>
Josiah SNELL^{4}, b. 23 Feb. 1701, Bridgewater
Abigail SNELL^{4}, b. 9 Sept. 1702, Bridgewater
Zachary SNELL^{4}, b. 17 Mar. 1704, Bridgewater
Abigail FOBES, b. 4 May 1709, Bridgewater; d. 3 Feb. 1793, Bridgewater
CHILD OF Josiah SNELL^{4} & Abigail FOBES:
Anna SNELL^{5}, b. 19 Mar. 1732, Bridgewater; d. 14 May 1776, Bridgewater
Edmund HAYWARD, b. 12 May 1720, Bridgewater; d. 12 Feb. 1781, Bridgewater

CHILD OF Edmund HAYWARD & Anna SNELL^{5}:
Waldo HAYWARD^{6}, b. 27 Mar. 1758, Bridgewater; d. 18 Mar. 1834, Bridgewater
Lucy BARTLETT, b. 28 Mar. 1762, Bridgewater; d. 20 Aug. 1831, N. Bridgewater
CHILD OF Waldo HAYWARD^{6} & Lucy BARTLETT:
Ira HAYWARD^{7}, b. 18 Sept. 1782, Bridgewater; d. 14 Feb. 1850, Kingston
Sarah EDSON, b. 17 Nov. 1783, Bridgewater; d. 29 June 1819, N. Bridgewater
CHILD OF Ira HAYWARD^{7} & Sarah EDSON:
Ambrose HAYWARD^{8}, b. 6 or 10 Jan. 1810, Bridgewater; d. 9 Nov. 1870, N.Bridge.
Hannah HOWLAND^{7} (Jabez^{6}, Ansel^{5}, Jabez^{4}, Shubael^{3}, John^{2}), b. 18 Nov. 1806, Barnstable; d. 14 Mar 1885, Brockton
CHILD OF Ambrose HAYWARD^{8} & Hannah HOWLAND^{7}:
Albert Francis HAYWARD^{9}, b. 26 Sept. 1842, Brockton; d. 9 Nov. 1920, Quincy
Louisa Miranda BELDEN, b. 29 May 1846, Amherst; d. 3 Nov. 1911, Quincy
CHILD OF Albert Francis HAYWARD^{9} & Louisa Miranda BELDEN:
Carle Reed HAYWARD^{10}, b. 27 Oct. 1880, Yankton, South Dakota
Mary Gordon MURRAY, b. 15 July 1889, Quincy (wf of Carle Reed Hayward)
Elizabeth ALDEN^{3}, d. betw. 21 Feb. 1738 - 2 May 1757
Edmund CHANDLER^{3} (Joseph^{2}, Edmund^{1}), d. betw. 4 Apr. 1715 - 8 Oct. 1717
CHILDREN OF Edmund CHANDLER^{3} & Elizabeth ALDEN^{3}: (4)
John CHANDLER^{4}, b. c1696
Nathaniel CHANDLER^{4}, b. c1700
Mercy CHANDLER^{4}, b. c1704
Zebedee CHANDLER^{4}, b. b. Jan. 1712/3
Pelatiah WEST, b. 8 Mar. 1674; d. 7 Dec. 1756 <Duxbury ChR. 1:248>
John ALDEN^{3}, d. 24 July 1739, ae 58, Duxbury g.s. <MD 9:159>
Hannah BRIGGS, d. 8 Feb. 1739/40, ae 56, Duxbury g.s. <MD 9:159>
CHILDREN OF John ALDEN^{3} & Hannah BRIGGS: (7) <Duxbury, MD 11:22>
John ALDEN^{4}, b. 7 Oct. 1710; d. 15 Oct. 1712 <MD 9:159>
Samuel ALDEN^{4}, b. 7 Nov. 1712; d. 10 Oct. 1757*, Bitton, Gloucestershire, Eng. <NEHGR 14:190>
Judah ALDEN^{4}, b. 10 Aug. 1714
Anna ALDEN^{4}, b. 2 June 1716; d. 1 July 1804, Old Cemetery, S. Duxbury g.s. <MD 9:160>
Deborah ALDEN^{4}, b. 16 May 1721; d. 2 Oct. 1730 <MD 9:159>
Briggs ALDEN^{4}, b. 8 June 1723; d. betw. 23 Dec. 1793* (will) - 8 Oct.1796* (probate)
Abigail ALDEN^{4}, b. 27 Feb. 1726/7, Duxbury; d. 24 July 1802, Marshfield g.s.<MD 13:246>
Edith ( ) WILLIAMS, d. 29 Nov. 1775*, Bitton, Gloucestershire, Eng. (wf of Samuel Alden^{4}) <NEHGR 14:190>
Anthony THOMAS^{5} (Lydia Waterman^{4}, Sarah Snow^{3}, Abigail Warren^{2}), b. 25 Mar.1719, Marshfield, d. 14 July 1781, Marshfield g.s. <MD 7:122, 10:49>
CHILDREN OF Anthony THOMAS^{5} & Abigail ALDEN^{4} : <see Warren file>
Benjamin LORING, d. 1 Mar. 1781, Old Cemetery, S. Duxbury g.s. <MD 9:160>
CHILDREN OF Benjamin LORING & Anna ALDEN^{4}: (10)
Mary LORING^{5}, b. 1739, d. 12 Jan. 1739/40, ae 8 weeks, Duxbury <MD 9:161>
Benjamin LORING^{5}, b. 1741, d. 8 Aug. 1745, ae 4, Duxbury <MD 9:160>
Sarah LORING^{5}, b. 1743, d. 11 Aug. 1745, ae 2, Duxbury <MD 9:161>
Benjamin LORING^{5}, b. 1745, d. 11 Nov. 1752, ae 7, Duxbury <MD 9:160>
Samuel LORING^{5}, b. ( )
Judah LORING^{5}, b. ( )
Daniel LORING^{5}, b. ( )

John LORING^{5}, b. Sept. 1752, d. 27 Oct. 1753, ae 1y1m, <MD 9:161>

Seth LORING^{5}, b. ( )

Lucy LORING^{5}, bpt. 19 Nov. 1758*; d. 25 Oct. 1847, ae 89 <MD 7:87>

Mercy WADSWORTH, (dau of Ichabod), b. 7 Sept. 1724

CHILDREN OF Briggs ALDEN^{4} (John^{3}) & Mercy WADSWORTH: (10)<Bible>

Hannah ALDEN^{5}, b. 24 Oct. 1743; d. 22 Apr. 1789

John ALDEN^{5}, b. 24 Jan. 1745; d. 17 Nov. 1766, drowned on passage Casco Bay to Duxbury <MD 9:159>

Son, b. 5 Sept. 1746, d. same day

Deborah ALDEN^{5}, b. 7 Aug. 1748; d. 7 Mar. 1793

Judah ALDEN^{5}, b. 31 Oct. 1750

Nathaniel ALDEN^{5}, b. 30 Mar. 1752

Edith ALDEN^{5}, b. 3 Jan. 1754; d. 7 Jan. 1814

Abigail ALDEN^{5}, b. 7 July 1755; d. Dec. 1800

Samuel ALDEN^{5}, b. 1 July 1757; d. 2 Nov. 1779

Amherst ALDEN^{5}, b. 22 July 1759; d. 20 Dec. 1804

MICRO # 10 of 16

Jonathan ALDEN^{3}, b. c1686, d. 10 July 1770*, ae 84y4m, Forham ME <History of Gorham:387>

Elizabeth (ARNOLD^{5}) Waterman (Elizabeth Gray^{4}, Mary Winslow^{3}, Mary Chilton^{2}), d. aft. 3 Apr. 1727 <Plymouth Deeds 22:61>

CHILDREN OF Jonathan ALDEN^{3} & Elizabeth (ARNOLD^{5}) Waterman: (5) <Marshfield>

Jonathan ALDEN^{4}, bpt. 8 Mar. 1718/9 <MD 31:124>

Anthony ALDEN^{4}, bpt. 11 Sept. 1720 <MD 31:162>

Seth ALDEN^{4}, bpt. 27 May 1722 <MD 31:163>

Josiah ALDEN^{4}, bpt. 16 Aug. 1724 <MD 31:164>

Austin ALDEN^{4}, bpt. 26 Oct. 1729 <MD 31:168>

Son, (date worn off records) <MD 9:180>

Salome LOMBARD, (dau of Solomon), b. 10 June 1736 <Truro VR:37>

CHILDREN OF Austin ALDEN^{4} & Salome LOMBARD: (5)

Elizabeth ALDEN^{5}, b. 3 or 31 Oct. 1757*; d. 4 May 1824*, Hampden ME

Josiah ALDEN^{5}, b. 31 Mar. 1760*

Humphrey ALDEN^{5}, b. 21 Jan. 1763*

Anner ALDEN^{5}, b. 14 Apr. 1765*

Hezekiah ALDEN^{5}, b. 15 July 1767*; d. 27 Nov. 1768*

CHILD OF Humphrey ALDEN^{5} & Mary ( ):

Humphrey Austin ALDEN^{6}, b. 26 Sept. 1794 <Boston Rcd.Com.24:342>

CHILDREN OF Jesse HARDING & Elizabeth ALDEN^{5}: (7)*

Elizabeth HARDING^{6}, b. 17 Jan. 1778, Gorham ME

Jesse HARDING^{6}, b. 21 Sept. 1779, Gorham ME; d. 1781

Samuel HARDING^{6}, b. 14 July 1781, Gorham ME

Austin HARDING^{6}, b. 1 May 1784, Hampden ME; d. ?24 May 1861, ae 67 ("1851?")

Eunice HARDING^{6}, b. 3 Oct. 1788, Hampden ME

Salome HARDING^{6}, b. 26 June 1790, Hampden ME

Josiah HARDING^{6}, b. 21 Jan. 1794, Hampden ME

Polly MURCH, dau of William & Hannah, b. 1788, Hampden ME; d. 14 Dec. 1880, ae 92y8m, apoplexy, Boston (bur. Hampden ME) <Mass. VR:321:315>**<61>**

CHILDREN OF Austin HARDING^{6} & Polly MURCH: (11)

Huldah HARDING^{7}, b. ( )

Sarah HARDING^{7}, b. ( )

Hannah HARDING^{7}, b. 17 July 1809; d. 6 Aug. 1849

Susan Alden HARDING^{7}, b. ( ); d. Bellevue Hospital N.Y. (bur. Hampden ME)

Melissa HARDING^{7}, b. ( ); d. Fall River

Eliza HARDING^{7}, b. 19 Aug. 1823, Hampden ME; d. 26 Mar. 1915, Boston, bur. Hampden ME <Mass VR 1:466>**<62>**

Mary Jane HARDING^{7}, d. 25 Apr. 1913, ae 94, unm., Boston <Mass.VR 11:397>**<63>**

Nellie HARDING^{7}, b. ( )

Elizabeth HARDING^{7}, b. ( )

Austin HARDING^{7}, b. ( ); d. E. Boston (policeman)

Martha HARDING^{7}, b. ( )

CHILDREN OF Enoch HOLBROOK & Hannah HARDING^{7}: (2)

Isaac HOLBROOK^{8}, b. 20 Dec. 1837; d. 30 Sept. 1928

Abby HOLBROOK^{8}, b. ( )

Sarah ALDEN^{3}, b. c1679 <MD 14:140>; d. 26 June 1738, ae 59, S. Duxbury g.s. <MD 10:170, 19:25>

Thomas SOUTHWORTH^{4} (Mary Pabodie^{3}, Eliz. Alden^{2}), b. c1675, d. 2 Sept. 1743, ae 68, S. Duxbury g.s. <MD 10:170,19:25>

CHILDREN OF Thomas SOUTHWORTH^{4} & Sarah ALDEN^{3}: (2)

Jedediah SOUTHWORTH^{4}, b. 13 Apr. 1702, Duxbury <MD 9:231>; d. 8 Sept. 1739 <MD 10:170>

Mary SOUTHWORTH^{4}, b. 18 Sept. 1703, Duxbury <MD 9:231>; d. 12 Nov. 1739 <MD 9:161>

JOSEPH ALDEN^{2} (John^{1})

Joseph ALDEN^{2}, d. 8 Feb. 1696/7, Bridgewater <MD 6:73>

CHILDREN OF Joseph ALDEN^{2} & Mary SIMMONS (dau of Moses): (6)

Isaac ALDEN^{3}, b. pre 1670* <MD 6:71>

Joseph ALDEN^{3}, b. c1667, d. 22 Dec. 1747, ae 80, Bridgewater <MD 6:71, 3:143>

John ALDEN^{3}, b. 1674, d. 29 Sept. 1730, ae 56, Middleborough <MD 6:111,72>

Elizabeth ALDEN^{3}, b. pre 1678* <MD 6:110-1>

Mercy ALDEN^{3}, b. ( ) <MD 6:110-1>

Hopestill ALDEN^{3}, b. ( ) <MD 6:110-1>

Joseph SNOW^{3} (Rebecca Brown^{2}), d. 18 Dec. 1753, Bridgewater <MD 14:209>

CHILDREN OF Joseph SNOW^{3} & Hopestill ALDEN^{3}: (7) <Bridgewater, MD 14:208>

Joseph SNOW^{4}, b. 7 Sept. 1690

Mary SNOW^{4}, b. 1 Nov. 1691

James SNOW^{4}, b. 16 Aug. 1693

Rebecca SNOW^{4}, b. 25 June 1696

Isaac SNOW^{4}, b. 22 July 1700

Jonathan SNOW^{4}, b. 27 Sept. 1703

David SNOW^{4}, b. 27 Sept. 1703 (twin)

Isaac ALDEN^{3}, b. pre 1670*; d. 24 June 1727, Bridgewater <MD 20:49,51>

Mehitable ALLEN, (dau of Samuel), b. 20 Jan. 1664, Bridgewater <MD 2:91>; d. aft. 30 Oct. 1727 (hus. probate) <MD 20:51>

CHILDREN OF Isaac ALDEN^{3} & Mehitable ALLEN: (9) <1-8, Bridgewater, MD 3:9>

Mehitable ALDEN^{4}, b. 7 Mar. 1687; d. pre Nov. 1722

Sarah ALDEN^{4}, b. 24 Sept. 1688

Mary ALDEN^{4}, b. 10 July 1691

Isaac ALDEN^{4}, b. 10 Mar. 1692; d. 20 Oct. 1781 <MD 32:157>

Ebenezer ALDEN^{4}, b. 5 Jan. 1693; d. 31 Dec. 1776* <E. Bridgewater:331>

Mercy ALDEN^{4}, b. 30 Oct. 1696

Abigail ALDEN^{4}, b. 28 July 1699

Jemima ALDEN^{4}, b. 9 Jan. 1702; d. 5 Mar. 1766, Bridgewater <MD 15:172>

John ALDEN^{4}, b. ( )

Anna KEITH, (dau of Joseph), b. 19 Apr. 1695, Bridgewater <MD 14:207>; d. 11 Jan. 1775*<E.Bridgewater:332>

CHILDREN OF Ebenezer ALDEN^{4} & Anna KEITH: (5) <Bridgewater, MD 15:85>

Anna ALDEN^{5}, b. 19 Feb. 1717/8

Susanna ALDEN^{5}, b. 9 Apr. 1719

Abigail ALDEN^{5}, b. 27 Dec. 1721; d. 22 Nov. 1738*

Nathan ALDEN^{5}, b. 7 Aug. 1727

Ezra ALDEN^{5}, b. 12 Mar. 1732; d. 3 Nov. 1767*, E. Bridgewater g.s.

Jephtha BYRAM, d. c1805*

Susanna WASHBURN, (dau of Eleazer), b. 27 Apr. 1740, Bridgewater; d. 1 Nov. 1813, Morristown NJ

CHILDREN OF Jephtha BYRAM & Susanna WASHBURN: (5) <Bridgewater VR>

Eleazer BYRAM, b. ( )

Eliab BYRAM, b. ( )

Jephtha BYRAM, b. ( )

Susanna BYRAM, b. ( )

Abigail BYRAM, b. 1 Sept. 1772

Mary HUDSON, d. 1755

CHILD OF Nathan ALDEN^{5} (John^{4}) & Mary HUDSON:

Nathan ALDEN^{6}, b. 1751

Sarah BARRELL^{7} (Wm.$^{6-5}$, Lydia Turner^{4}, Mary Brewster^{3}, Jonathan^{2}), b. c1755, d. 1816, ae 61

CHILDREN OF Nathan ALDEN^{6} & Sarah BARRELL^{7}: (6)

Mary ALDEN^{7}, b. 2 Jan. 1777

Lydia ALDEN^{7}, b. 27 Aug. 1779

Marcus ALDEN^{7}, b. 9 Aug. 1782

Isaac ALDEN^{7}, b. 3 Sept. 1786

Sarah ALDEN^{7}, b. 13 Sept. 1792

Lucius ALDEN^{7}, b. ( )

Ebenezer BYRAM, (son of Ebenezer), b. 17 Sept. 1716, Bridgewater <MD 7:56>

CHILDREN OF Ebenezer BYRAM & Abigail ALDEN^{5} (Ebenezer^{4}): (10)*

Huldah BYRAM^{6}, b. 1739 <Mitchell>; d.y.

Huldah BYRAM^{6}, b. 8 Nov. 1740 <VR>

Edward BYRAM^{6}, b. 11 June 1742 <VR>

Ebenezer BYRAM^{6}, b. 1744 <Mitchell>

Naphtali BYRAM^{6}, b. c1749; d. 1812, ae 63

Joseph BYRAM^{6}, b. ( )

Abigail BYRAM^{6}, b. ( )

Anna BYRAM^{6}, b. ( )

Mary BYRAM^{6}, b. ( )

Phebe BYRAM^{6}, b. ( )

Rebecca KEITH, (dau of Josiah), d. 30 Aug. 1777 <Bridgewater 2:438>

CHILDREN OF Ezra ALDEN^{5} (Ebenezer^{4}) & Rebecca KEITH: (5)

Son, d.y.

Abby ALDEN^{6}, b. ( ), d.y.

Abigail ALDEN^{6}, b. 19 Mar. 1761*, Bridgewater

Isaac ALDEN^{6}, b. ( )

Susanna ALDEN^{6}, b. ( )

George VINING, (son of George & Ruth) b. 24 Dec. 1754*<Norton VR:145>;d. 8 Apr. 1822*, Plainfield

CHILDREN OF George VINING & Abigail ALDEN^{6}: (11)**<64>**

Thomas WHITMAN, b. 1702*, d. 15 Dec. 1788*, E. Bridgewater g.s.

CHILDREN OF Thomas WHITMAN & Jemima ALDEN^{4} (Isaac^{3}): (8) <Bridgewater, MD 15:172>

Simeon WHITMAN[5], b. 9 Sept. 1728
Peter WHITMAN[5], b. 4 May 1730
Benjamin WHITMAN[5], b. 2 Feb. 1732
Jemima WHITMAN[5], b. 27 June 1734; d. 1771*
Nathan WHITMAN[5], b. Feb. 1736
Amos WHITMAN[5], b. 17 Feb. 1738; d. 12 Nov. 1791*
William WHITMAN[5], b. 21 May 1740
Isaac WHITMAN[5], b. 28 Mar. 1742; d. 1 June 1747 <MD 15:172>
David KEITH, (son of Joseph), b. 1728*, d. 1812*, ae 84
CHILDREN OF David KEITH & 1st Jemima WHITMAN[5]: (5)*
David KEITH[6], b. 1755, d. 1778
Abigail KEITH[6], b. 1758, d. 1778
Levi KEITH[6], b. 1760
Molly KEITH[6], b. 1763
Zenas KEITH[6], b. 1766
CHILDREN OF David KEITH & 2nd Charity (KINGMAN) Brett*: (2)*
Calvin KEITH, b. 1775
David KEITH, b. 1778
CHILD OF Calvin KEITH & Bethiah STETSON*:
Lewis L. KEITH, b. ( )**<65>**
Asaba CHURCHILL[7] (Cynthia Packard[6], Solomon[5], Susanna Kingman[4], Mary Mitchell[3],Jacob[2], Experience[1]), d. 2 Apr. 1875, E. Bridgewater**<66>**
CHILDREN OF Lewis L. KEITH & Asaba CHURCHILL[7]: (11) <E. Bridgewater>
Harriet L. KEITH, b. 24 Feb. 1820 <VR:77>
Eliza Ann KEITH, b. 2 June 1821 <VR:76>, d.y.
Eliza Ann KEITH, b. 18 July 1823 <VR:76>
Lurania Churchill KEITH, b. 11 Mar. 1825, d. 4 Apr. 1844 <VR:78>
Marcus Morton KEITH, b. 20 Mar. 1827 <VR:78>
Adeline Cushman KEITH, b. 22 Mar. 1829 <VR:78>; d. 2 Aug. 1845
Lewis KEITH, b. 4 July 1831 <VR:78>; d. 3 Apr. 1860, E. Bridgewater <Mass.VR 139:293>
Nahum Packard KEITH, b. 29 May 1833 <VR:78>
Maria B. KEITH, b. 26 June 1835, d. Apr. 1846 <VR:78>
Joshua Sears KEITH, b. 26 Apr. 1837 <VR:78>
Elizabeth C. KEITH, b. 8 Apr. 1839, d. 30 Sept. 1839 <VR:77>
CHILDREN OF Samuel G. ALDEN & Harriet L. KEITH: (2)
Ella Green ALDEN, b. 2 Nov. 1841 <E. Bridgewater VR:11>
Samuel ALDEN, b. 6 Aug. 1848 <E. Bridgewater VR:12>

Misc. Aldens <from the town records of Minot ME>

CHILD OF Jonathan & Abigail ALDEN:
John ALDEN, b. 15 Dec. 1775, Bridgewater
CHILDREN OF John & Dabey ALDEN: (4) <Minot ME>
Benjamin ALDEN, b. 15 July 1799
Mary ALDEN, b. 24 Sept. 1802
Susannah ALDEN, b. 27 Oct. 1804
Charles ALDEN, b. 4 May 1808
CHILD OF Daniel & Deborah ALDEN:
Cyrus ALDEN, b. 5 Aug. 1804, Minot ME
CHILDREN OF Benjamin & Sarah ALDEN: (3) <Minot ME>

Asa A. ALDEN, b. 12 July 1826
Angerona ALDEN, dau., b. 4 Dec. 1831
Nelson H. ALDEN, b. 31 Mar. 1836
CHILDREN OF Daniel & Deborah ALDEN: (2)
Elvira ALDEN, b. 14 Aug. 1799, Poland ME
Hannah ALDEN, b. 10 Aug. 1801, Poland ME
Daniel ALDEN, d. 12 July 1831, Minot ME
"In a little cemetery in Mechanic Falls, ME: John R. ALDEN, son of Charles & Nancy, d. 26 Mar. 1832, age 3 yrs 6 mos., also 2 small pieces of granite beside this stone mark 2 other graves."

"**Notes** from a book that contains inscriptions from surrounding cemeteries:"
Brookvale Cemetery, West Auburn ME:
Daniel ALDEN, d. 12 July 1831, ae 56
Clarissa L. ALDEN, d. 15 Sept. 1810, ae 20
Rosina ALDEN, dau. of Daniel & Deborah, d. 16 Nov. 1812, ae 25
Eliza P. ALDEN, wf of Charles, d. 23 Dec. 1887
Charles ALDEN, d. 17 Dec. 1869, ae 61y7m
Caleb N. ALDEN, son of Charles & Eliza P., d. 27 July 1855, ae 17y1m23d
William H. ALDEN, d. 5 Mar. 1918, ae 78y1m20d
Capt. Cyrus ALDEN, 30 May 1783 - 5 Mar. 1877
Nabby Keith Kinsley, his wife, 8 Aug. 1788 - 6 Mar. 1848

* * * * *

Benjamin RICHARDS, d. 4 Apr. 1741, Bridgewater <MD 14:181>
CHILDREN OF Benjamin RICHARDS & 1st Mehitable ALDEN^4 (Isaac^3): (5) <Bridgewater, MD 14:180>
Mehitable RICHARDS^5, b. 6 Dec. 1712
Joseph RICHARDS^5, b. 15 Aug. 1714
Daniel RICHARDS^5, b. 20 Mar. 1716
James RICHARDS^5, b. 3 Mar. 1717/8 <Bridgewater VR 1:277>
Sarah RICHARDS^5, b. 30 July 1720
Lydia FAXON, (dau of Josiah & Mehitable (Adams)), b. 30 Nov. 1695; d. 23 Apr. 1788
CHILDREN OF Benjamin RICHARDS & 2nd Lydia FAXON: (6) <Bridgewater, MD 14:180-1>
John RICHARDS, b. 29 Sept. 1723; d. 27 Dec. 1812
Josiah RICHARDS, b. 6 Dec. 1724; d. 6 Apr. 1815
Seth RICHARDS, b. 31 Mar. 1726
Ezra RICHARDS, b. 10 Aug. 1728
Lydia RICHARDS, b. 19 June 1732
Hannah RICHARDS, b. 2 Dec. 1736; d. 19 Dec. 1816
CHILDREN OF James RICHARDS & Susanna PRATT (dau of Joseph & Lydia (Leonard)): (3)
Nathan RICHARDS, b. ( )
Child, d. 5 Oct. 1745
Child, d. 25 Oct. 1747
CHILD OF John RICHARDS & Keziah ( ):
James RICHARDS, b. 14 Dec. 1766 <Bridgewater VR 1:277>
James RICHARDS, d. 12 Dec. 1749 <Bridgewater VR 2:549>
Zaccheus PACKARD, (son of Zaccheus & Sarah*), b. 4 Sept. 1693, Bridgewater <MD 14:206>
CHILDREN OF Zaccheus PACKARD & Mercy ALDEN^4 (Isaac^3): (5 of 6) <Bridgewater, MD 15:170-1>
Eliezer PACKARD^5, b. 24 Sept. 1727
Benjamin PACKARD^5, b. 5 Aug. 1730, d. 19 Sept. 1730, Bridgewater
Jesse PACKARD^5, b. 26 Oct. 1731, d. 29 Mar. 1732, Bridgewater
Seth PACKARD^5, b. 23 May 1733

Simeon PACKARD^{5}, b. 30 Mar. 1736

Seth BRETT^{4} (Sarah Hayward^{3}, Sarah Mitchell^{2}, Experience^{1}), b. 24 Feb. 1687/8, Bridgewater <MD 14:84>; d. 11 Feb. 1721/2, smallpox, Bridgewater <MD 14:84>(see <66>)

CHILDREN OF Seth BRETT^{4} & Sarah ALDEN^{4} (Isaac^{3}):(5) <Bridgewater, MD 5:247>

Samuel BRETT^{5}, b. 22 Aug. 1714

Silas BRETT^{5}, b. 28 Feb. 1715/6

Sarah BRETT^{5}, b. 3 Mar. 1717/8

Seth BRETT^{5}, b. 13 Apr. 1722

CHILD OF Recompense CARY & Sarah ALDEN^{4} (Isaac^{3}):

Abigail CARY^{5}, b. 11 Aug. 1729, Bridgewater <MD 15:87>

Hannah WHITE, (dau. of Ebenezer), b. 5 May 1680*<Weymouth VR 1:339>; d. 5 Oct. 1732,Middleborough <MD 6:111>

CHILDREN OF John ALDEN^{3} & Hannah WHITE: (13) <Middleboro>

David ALDEN^{4}, b. 18 May 1702 <MD 2:104>; d. 14 May 1763*

Priscilla ALDEN^{4}, b. 2 Mar. 1703/4 <MD 2:104>**<67>**

Thankful ALDEN^{4}, b. 30 May 1706 <MD 2:201>; d. 29 Oct. 1732, Middleboro <MD 13:5>

Hannah ALDEN^{4}, b. 24 Mar. 1708/9 <MD 2:201>

Lydia ALDEN^{4}, b. 18 Dec. 1710 <MD 2:201>; d. 1 Mar. 1803* <MD 6:111>

Mary ALDEN^{4}, b. 18 Nov. 1712 <MD 2:201>; d. 1 Aug. 1787, Middleboro g.s. <MD 14:216>

Abigail ALDEN^{4}, b. 28 Sept. 1714 <MD 3:85>>

Joseph ALDEN^{4}, b. 11 Sept. 1716 <MD 3:85>; d. 26 Jan. 1787* <Alden Mem.:144>

John ALDEN^{4}, b. 8 Oct. 1718 <MD 3:234>

Ebenezer ALDEN^{4}, b. 8 Oct. 1720 <MD 3:234>

Lemuel ALDEN^{4}, b. ( ), d.y. <MD 6:111-2>

Nathan ALDEN^{4}, b. 12 June 1723; d.y. <MD 6:112,179>

Noah ALDEN^{4}, b. 31 May 1725 <MD 6:228>; d. Bellingham <MD 6:112>

CHILDREN OF Francis EATON^{4} (Ben.$^{3-2}$) & Thankful ALDEN^{4}: (2)

Joseph EATON^{5}, b. 26 Nov. 1728* <Kingston VR:68>

Jabez EATON^{5}, b. 29 Jan. 1730/1, Middleboro <MD 12:131>

CHILDREN OF David ALDEN^{4} & Judith ( ): (9) <Middleboro>

Solomon ALDEN^{5}, b. 21 Nov. 1728 <MD 7:243>

David ALDEN^{5}, b. 14 Jan. 1729/30 <MD 8:28>

Rufus ALDEN^{5}, b. 19 Nov. 1731 <MD 9:47>

Huldah ALDEN^{5}, b. 8 Oct. 1733 <MD 12:232>

Hannah ALDEN^{5}, b. 18 Jan. 1735/6 <MD 8:248>

Job ALDEN^{5}, b. 24 Sept. 1737 <MD 16:17>

Silas ALDEN^{5}, b. 10 Oct. 1739 <MD 16:17>; d. pre 5 Nov. 1764*(adm) <Plymouth Co. Probate #180, 17:135>

Abigail ALDEN^{5}, b. 19 May 1744 <MD 16:18>

Peter ALDEN^{5}, b. 17 Feb. 1747 <MD 16:132>

CHILDREN OF David ALDEN^{5} & Rhoda LEACH^{7*} (Joseph^{6}, Hephzibah Washburn^{5}, Jos.^{4},Eliz. Mitchell^{3}, Jane Cooke^{2}): (3) <Middleboro>

Rufus ALDEN^{6}, b. 18 May 1757 <MD 16:132>

Caleb ALDEN^{6}, b. 26 Oct. 1759 <MD 23:47>

Huldah ALDEN^{6}, b. 18 Dec. 1762 <MD 23:47>

Darius ALDEN, (poss. son of Rufus^{6}), b. 2 Oct. 1783*; d. 29 Dec. 1808*

Lydia HOLMES, (dau. of Francis & Lydia), wf of Darius Alden, d. 29 Aug. 1808,ae 25 <MD 8:150>

CHILDREN OF Silas ALDEN^{5} & Silence ( ): (1 of 2)

Rosinda ALDEN^{6}, b. betw. 1756-64*

John FOBES, (son of Josiah & Freelove (Edson)), b. 12 Mar. 1758*

CHILDREN OF John FOBES & Rosinda ALDEN^{6}: (10)*
Silas Alden FOBES^{7}, b. 1 Dec. 1783
Selinda FOBES^{7}, b. 22 May 1785
Enoch FOBES^{7}, b. 22 Feb. 1787
Elijah FOBES^{7}, b. 11 Mar. 1754
John FOBES^{7}, b. 5 Nov. 1791
Horatio FOBES^{7}, b. 10 May 1794 <bpt. 1814 - Windsor VR:30>
Clarissa Leonard FOBES^{7}, b. 28 Aug. 1797 <bpt. 1814 - Windsor VR:30>
Mary FOBES^{7}, b. c1805
Freelove FOBES^{7}, bpt. 4 Mar. 1814 <Windsor VR:30>; d. 11 Jan. 1821, Bridgewater, ae "about" 20
Susan A. FOBES^{7}, bpt. 4 Mar. 1814 <Windsor VR:30>
Thomas WOOD, d. pre 12 Feb. 1744 (adm.) <Plymouth Co. Probate 9:414>
CHILDREN OF Thomas WOOD & Hannah ALDEN^{4} (John^{3}): (8) <Middleboro>
Priscilla WOOD^{5}, b. 26 Feb. 1729/30 <MD 8:29>
Thomas WOOD^{5}, b. 24 Feb. 1731/2 <MD 12:130>
Abner WOOD^{5}, b. 24 Feb. 1731/2, (twin) <MD 12:130>
Amasa WOOD^{5}, b. 8 Feb. 1733/4 <MD 12:231>
Zephaniah WOOD^{5}, b. 12 Apr. 1737 <MD 4:70>
Lemuel WOOD^{5}, b. 15 or 16 Oct. 1739 <MD 17:21>
Hannah WOOD^{5}, b. 7 Feb. 1741/2, d. 4 Dec. 1749 <MD 17:22>
Abigail WOOD^{5}, b. 8 Mar. 1743/4, <MD 17:22>

MICRO #11 of 16

Lydia LAZELL^{5} (Margaret Cooke^{4}, Jacob$^{3-2}$), b. 5 Jan. 1722/3, Plym. <MD 12:225>;d. 17 Apr. 1749 <MD 6:111>
CHILDREN OF John ALDEN^{4} (John^{3}) & 1st Lydia LAZELL^{5}: (5) <MD 6:111-3>
John ALDEN^{5}, b. 7 Feb. 1740
Mary ALDEN^{5}, b. 22 Nov. 1741; d. pre 1801*
Nathan ALDEN^{5}, b. 22 Aug. 1743; d. 9 Dec. 1820, Middleboro <MD 12:66>
Susanna ALDEN^{5}, b. 29 Aug. 1745
Lydia ALDEN^{5}, b. 11 Dec. 1747; d. 19 June 1775
Rebecca WESTON^{5} (Zachariah^{4}, Rebecca Soule^{3}, John^{2}), b. 25 Nov. 1730 <MD 6:112>
CHILDREN OF John ALDEN^{4} (John^{3}) & 2nd Rebecca WESTON^{5}: (14) <MD 6:112-3>
Priscilla ALDEN^{5}, b. 15 May 1751; d. 22 Oct. 1751
Ruth ALDEN^{5}, b. 15 Oct. 1752; d. 25 Aug. 1753
Elijah ALDEN^{5}, b. 13 June 1754
Rebecca ALDEN^{5}, b. 18 Apr. 1756
Hannah ALDEN^{5}, b. 15 Apr. 1758
Sarah ALDEN^{5}, b. 9 Feb. 1760
Lucy ALDEN^{5}, b. 12 Aug. 1762; d. 29 Apr. 1795 (wf of Eleazer Carey)
Jael ALDEN^{5}, b. 27 June 1764
Son, b. 26 Mar. 1766, d.y.
Dau, b. 16 Apr. 1767, d.y.
Ruth ALDEN^{5}, b. 13 Mar. 1768
Seth ALDEN^{5}, b. 7 Feb. 1770
Betsey ALDEN^{5}, b. 13 Apr. 1773
Elihu ALDEN^{5}, b. 20 May 1775
CHILDREN OF Daniel THOMAS & Betsey ALDEN^{5}: (5) <MD 6:113>
Daniel THOMAS^{6}, b. ( )
Hercules THOMAS^{6}, b. ( )
Lewis THOMAS^{6}, b. ( )

Eliza THOMAS^{6}, b. ( )

Rebecca THOMAS^{6}, b. ( )

CHILDREN OF Elihu ALDEN^{5} (John^{4}) & Lydia MITCHELL: (2) <MD 6:113>

Lucy ALDEN^{6}, b. ( )

Millbury Weston ALDEN^{6}, b. ( )

CHILDREN OF Elijah ALDEN^{5} (John^{4}) & Mary ALDEN^{6} (Solomon^{5}, David^{4}, John^{3},Jos.^{2}): (10)<MD 6:113>

Israel ALDEN^{6}, b. ( )

Lucinda ALDEN^{6}, b. ( )

Vienna ALDEN^{6}, b. ( )

Serena ALDEN^{6}, b. ( )

Jared ALDEN^{6}, b. ( )

Elijah ALDEN^{6}, b. ( )

Mary ALDEN^{6}, b. ( ), d.y.

Polly ALDEN^{6}, b. ( )

Daniel ALDEN^{6}, b. ( )

Olive ALDEN^{6}, b. ( )

CHILDREN OF Isaiah JONES & Jael ALDEN^{5} (John^{4}): (4) <MD 6:113>

Child, b. pre 1801

Child, b. pre 1801

Alden JONES^{6}, b. ( )

Philander JONES^{6}, b. ( )

CHILDREN OF John ALDEN^{5} (John^{4}) & Lois SOUTHWORTH (dau of Gideon): (9) <MD 6:113>

Mary ALDEN^{6}, b. ( )

Sarah ALDEN^{6}, b. ( ), d.y.

John ALDEN^{6}, b. 9 Sept. 1771* <Alden Mem.>; d. 8 Aug. 1843*

Lydia ALDEN^{6}, b. ( )

Sally ALDEN^{6}, b. ( )

Lois ALDEN^{6}, b. ( )

Gideon ALDEN^{6}, b. ( )

Seth ALDEN^{6}, b. ( )

Nathan ALDEN^{6}, b. ( )

Ruth POPE, (dau of Samuel), b. 14 Mar. 1773*; d. 18 Sept. 1845*

CHILDREN OF John ALDEN^{6} & Ruth POPE: (3) <MD 6:113>

Ebenezer ALDEN^{7}, b. 30 July 1794*

Betsey ALDEN^{7}, b. 10 Feb. 1796*

Samuel ALDEN^{7}, b. 17 Apr. 1799*; d. 14 July 1825*

CHILDREN OF Gamaliel CHURCH & Lydia ALDEN^{6} (John^{5}): (3) <MD 6:113>

Isaac CHURCH^{7}, b. ( )

James CHURCH^{7}, b. ( )

Lydia CHURCH^{7}, b. ( )

CHILDREN OF Rev. Isaac TOMPKINS & Mary ALDEN^{6} (John^{5}): (2) <MD 6:113>

Lois TOMPKINS^{7}, b. ( )

Sally TOMPKINS^{7}, b. ( )

John SPOONER, d. Feb. 1773 <MD 6:112>

CHILDREN OF John SPOONER & Lydia ALDEN^{5} (John^{4}): (2) <MD 6:112-3>

John SPOONER^{6}, b. ( )

Thomas SPOONER^{6}, b. ( ); d. 31 May 1799

CHILDREN OF Calvin DELANO & Mary ALDEN^{5} (John^{4}): (3) <MD 6:112>

Lydia DELANO^{6}, b. ( )

Alden DELANO^{6}, b. ( ); d. pre 1801*

Deborah DELANO^{6}, b. ( )

Priscilla MILLER, (dau of John & Priscilla), b. 19 May 1745*, Middleboro <MD 16:107>; d. 19 Sept. 1807, Middleboro g.s.**<68>**

CHILDREN OF Nathan ALDEN^{5} (John^{4}) & Priscilla MILLER: (7) <MD 6:112-3>

John ALDEN^{6}, b. 1767*

Priscilla ALDEN^{6}, b. 1769*; d. 16 Oct. 1773, ae 4y12d <MD 12:66>

Otis ALDEN^{6}, b. 1773*

Lydia ALDEN^{6}, b. 1771*

Polly ALDEN^{6}, b. 1776*

Earl ALDEN^{6}, b. 2 Nov. 1778, d. 18 June 1864 <Middleboro g.s.>

Nathan ALDEN^{6}, b. 1788*

Mercy NELSON, (dau of Samuel), b. 22 Apr. 1775 (Middleboro) <g.s.>; d. 14 Aug. 1856, Middleboro g.s. <Mass.VR 103:210> (wf of Earl Alden^{6})

Susanna DUNHAM, b. 20 May 1763*; d. 2 Jan. 1814, Middleboro <MD 12:67>

CHILD OF John ALDEN^{6} (Nathan^{5}) & Susanna DUNHAM:

Andrew ALDEN^{7}, b. 30 Dec. 1790*; d. 8 Aug. 1792 <MD 12:66>

CHILDREN OF Walter HOWARD & Ruth ALDEN^{5} (John^{4}): (2) <MD 6:113>

Alden HOWARD^{6}, b. ( )

Ruth HOWARD^{6}, b. ( )

CHILDREN OF Joseph TRIPP & Susanna ALDEN^{5} (John^{4}): (2) <MD 6:112>

Child, b. pre 1801

Joseph TRIPP^{6}, b. ( )

CHILDREN OF Samuel PROCTER & Susanna ALDEN^{5} (John^{4}): (3) <MD 6:112>

Susanna PROCTER^{6}, b. ( ); d. 15 Sept. 1865, ae 83y9m, Fairhaven MA (widow of Levi Jenney^{7})

William PROCTER^{6}, b. ( )

Charles PROCTER^{6}, b. ( )

Levi JENNEY^{7} (Levi^{6}, Cornelius^{5}, Desire Blackwell^{4}, Sarah Warren^{3}, Nathaniel^{2}), b. 26 Feb. 1778*

CHILDREN OF Joseph ALDEN^{4} (John^{3}) & Hannah HALL: (5) <Middleboro, MD 16:132>**<69>**

Ebenezer ALDEN^{5}, b. 4 Feb. 1742/3; d. 6 Jan. 1773*

Joseph ALDEN^{5}, b. 11 Feb. 1745/6

Mercy ALDEN^{5}, b. 23 July 1747

Phebe ALDEN^{5}, b. 25 Apr. 1749

Hannah ALDEN^{5}, b. 24 Aug. 1750

Ruth FOBES, (dau of Joshua*), d. 1816

CHILDREN OF Ebenezer ALDEN^{5} (Joseph^{4}) & Ruth FOBES: (6)

Hannah ALDEN^{6}, b. 2 Feb. 1765; d. 19 Jan. 1816

Orpah ALDEN^{6}, b. Jan. 1766

Polly ALDEN^{6}, b. 1767; d. 7 Jan. 1831

Ruth ALDEN^{6}, b. 18 Dec. 1768; d. 20 Feb. 1858

Ebenezer ALDEN^{6}, b. 8 Aug. 1770; d. 31 Oct. 1853

Joseph ALDEN^{6}, b. 1772

Daniel FAUNCE, d. 2 May 1803

CHILDREN OF Daniel FAUNCE & Ruth (FOBES) Alden: (5)

Sarah FAUNCE, b. ( )

Phebe FAUNCE, b. ( )

Eunice FAUNCE, b. ( )

Alden FAUNCE, b. ( )

Ezra FAUNCE, b. ( )

CHILDREN OF Simon BACKUS & Hannah ALDEN^{6} (Eben.^{5}): (7)

Andrew BACKUS^{7}, b. ( )

Ebenezer BACKUS^{7}, b. ( )

Adam BACKUS^{7}, b. ( )

Eunice BACKUS^{7}, b. ( )

Isaac BACKUS^{7}, b. ( )

Joseph Alden BACKUS^{7}, b. ( )

Hannah BACKUS^{7}, b. ( )

CHILDREN OF Zadock PERSHO & Orpah ALDEN^{6} (Eben.^{5}): (11)

Asa PERSHO^{7}, b. ( )

Laura PERSHO^{7}, b. ( )

James PERSHO^{7}, b. ( )

Sullivan PERSHO^{7}, b. ( )

Isaac PERSHO^{7}, b. ( )

Zadock PERSHO^{7}, b. ( )

Ruth PERSHO^{7}, b. ( )

Elmira PERSHO^{7}, b. ( )

Daniel PERSHO^{7}, b. ( )

Thomas PERSHO^{7}, b. ( )

William F. PERSHO^{7}, b. ( )

CHILDREN OF Nehemiah JONES & Polly ALDEN^{6} (Eben.^{5}): (7)

Maria JONES^{7}, b. ( )

Nehemiah JONES^{7}, b. ( )

Clarissa L. JONES^{7}, b. ( )

Mary W.F. JONES^{7}, b. ( )

Emeline JONES^{7}, b. ( )

Louisa JONES^{7}, b. ( )

William H. JONES^{7}, b. ( )

Samuel EDDY, d. 3 Nov. 1746* <Eddy Fam. (1881):208>

CHILDREN OF Samuel EDDY & Lydia ALDEN^{4} (John^{3}): (5) <Middleboro>

Nathan EDDY^{5}, b. 8 Sept. 1733 <MD 13:6>

Joshua EDDY^{5}, b. 6 Mar. 1734/5 <MD 13:7>

Susanna EDDY^{5}, b. 22 Nov. 1736 <MD 13:7>; d. ?29 July 1817*,ae 81,unm. <MD 12:202>

Samuel EDDY^{5}, b. 12 Jan. 1742/3 <MD 13:7>

Seth EDDY^{5}, b. 11 Feb. 1744/5 <MD 16:19>

John FULLER^{4} (John^{3}, Samuel$^{2-1}$*), b. c1692*; d. 24 Apr. 1766*, ae 74 <Halifax g.s.*> (2nd hus. of Lydia Alden^{4} (John^{3}))

Eunice SAMSON^{5}* (Ephraim^{4}, Lydia Standish^{3}, Alex.^{2}), b. 15 May 1737* <Plympton VR>

CHILDREN OF Nathan EDDY^{5} & Eunice SAMSON^{5}: (7)* <Giles Mem.:389; Eddy Gen. (1881):208>

Ephraim EDDY^{6}, b. 1759

Lydia EDDY^{6}, b. 176()

Hannah EDDY^{6}, b. 1766

Nathaniel EDDY^{6}, b. 1768

Nathan EDDY^{6}, b. 1771; d. c1843

Isaac EDDY^{6}, b. 1774; d. 1833

Zachariah EDDY^{6}, b. 1775; d. 1872

Noah THOMAS, (son of Edward), b. 22 Oct. 1709, Middleboro <MD 3:83>; d. 20 Dec. 1758, Middleboro g.s. <MD 14:216>

CHILDREN OF Noah THOMAS & Mary ALDEN^{4} (John^{3}): (11) <Middleboro>

Lucia THOMAS^{5}, b. 17 Dec. 1733 <MD 12:231>

Fear THOMAS^{5}, b. 17 Aug. 1735 <MD 8:249>

Mary THOMAS^{5}, b. 29 Apr. 1737 <MD 8:249>

Noah THOMAS^5, b. 19 Mar. 1738/9, d. 26 Nov. 1758 <MD 14:245, 216>

Abiel THOMAS^5, b. 16 May 1741, d. 1 Feb. 1759 <MD 13:6, 14:214>

Daniel THOMAS^5, b. 8 June 1743 d. 14 May 1789 <MD 13:6, 14:214>

Job THOMAS^5, b. 16 Mar. 1744 <MD 17:20>; d. pre 1758*

Elias THOMAS^5, b. 19 Jan. 1746/7 <MD 18:151>; d. pre 1758*

Hannah THOMAS^5, b. 9 Jan. 1748/9, d. 7 Apr. 1821 <MD 18:151,2:154>

Priscilla THOMAS^5, b. 2 Nov. 1751 <MD 18:152>

Enoch THOMAS^5, b. 7 Dec. 1753, d. 16 Dec. 1758 <MD 19:36, 14:215>

Thankful ( ) THOMAS, (wf of Daniel^5), d. 13 Oct. 1778, ae 37, Middleboro g.s.<MD 14:217>

CHILD OF Daniel THOMAS^5 & Thankful ( ):*

Elias THOMAS^6, b. 1774, d. 26 Nov. 1786, ae 12 <MD 14:215>

Joanna VAUGHAN, (dau of John & Jerusha), b. 12 Sept. 1725, Middle. <MD 7:240>(wf of Noah Alden^4 (John^3))

Lydia ALDEN, (dau of Noah & Joanna (Vaughan)), b. 1 Apr. 1751, Stafford CT <VR Barbour Coll.:4>

CHILDREN OF Caleb THOMSON & Lydia ALDEN: (8) <Bellingham VR>

Joel THOMSON, b. 13 Feb. 1770 <VR:68>; d. 13 Sept. 1835, "ae 67","at the poor house"

Silence THOMSON, b. 21 June 1771, d. 22 June 1771 <VR:68>

Hannah THOMSON, b. 3 June 1773, d. 9 Aug. 1788 <VR:67>

Freelove THOMSON, b. 10 June 1776 <VR:67>

Zenas THOMSON, b. 9 Mar. 1779, Milford <VR:68>

Rufus THOMSON, b. 9 July 1782, Mendon <VR:68>

Susanna THOMSON, b. 21 Oct. 1785 <VR:68>

Hannah THOMSON, b. 7 Oct. 1789 <VR:67>

Hannah DUNHAM, (dau of Daniel), b. c1670, d. 14 Jan. 1747, ae 78, Bridgewater <MD 3:143>

CHILDREN OF Joseph ALDEN^3 & Hannah DUNHAM: (10) <Bridgewater>

Daniel ALDEN^4, b. 29 Jan. 1690, <MD 3:142>; d. 3 May 1767*, Stafford CT g.s. <NEHGR 66:39>

Joseph ALDEN^4, b. 24 Aug. 1693, d. 19 Dec. 1695 <MD 3:142>

Eleazer ALDEN^4, b. 27 Sept. 1694, d. 29 Jan. 1773 <MD 3:142,14:207>

Hannah ALDEN^4, b. 1 Feb. 1696 <MD 3:142>; d. 1777*, Easton

Mary ALDEN^4, b. 10 Apr. 1699 <MD 3:142>; d. 14 Feb. 1782* <Stafford CT 1st ChR>

Joseph ALDEN^4, b. 5 Sept. 1700, d. 25 Oct. 1704 <MD 3:143>

Jonathan ALDEN^4, b. 3 Dec. 1703, d. 10 Nov. 1704 <MD 3:143>

Samuel ALDEN^4, b. 20 Aug. 1705 <MD 3:143>

Mehitable ALDEN^4, b. 18 Oct. 1707 <MD 3:143>

Seth ALDEN^4, b. 6 July 1710 <MD 3:143>; d. 6 Sept. 1784*, Bridgewater g.s.

Abigail SHAW, (dau of Joseph), d. 12 July 1755*, Stafford CT g.s.<NEHGR 66:39>

CHILDREN OF Daniel ALDEN^4 & Abigail SHAW: (11) < 1-10, Bridgewater, MD 15:85>

Joseph ALDEN^5, b. 20 Nov. 1718; d. 2 Jan. 1765*

Daniel ALDEN^5, b. 5 Sept. 1720; d. 18 May 1790*

Abigail ALDEN^5, b. 3 Dec. 1722

Zephaniah ALDEN^5, b. 13 June 1724

Hannah ALDEN^5, b. 23 May 1726, d. 2 July 1726

Hannah ALDEN^5, b. 17 Dec. 1727

Mehitable ALDEN^5, b. 23 May 1729, d. 13 July 1729

Barnabas ALDEN^5, b. 10 Sept. 1732; d. betw. 4 Oct. 1793(will)- 19 Feb. 1794 (probate),Ashfield MA

Ebenezer ALDEN^5, b. 11 Aug. 1734 <MD 15:86>

Mary ALDEN^5, b. 12 May 1737, d. 6 Mar. 1737/8 <MD 15:86>

Mary ALDEN^5*, b. ( ) <Alden Mem.:15>

Elizabeth PATTERSON, d. aft. 19 Feb. 1794 <hus. probate>

CHILDREN OF Barnabas ALDEN^5 & Elizabeth PATTERSON: (8)

Barnabas ALDEN^{6}, b. ( )

Mary ALDEN^{6}, b. ( )

Lydia ALDEN^{6}, b. ( )

Susanna ALDEN^{6}, b. 1 July 1768 <Stafford CT VR>; d. 6 Oct. 1852, Ashfield MA

Deborah ALDEN^{6}, b. ( )

Esther ALDEN^{6}, b. ( )

Abigail ALDEN^{6}, b. ( )

Zephaniah ALDEN^{6}, b. ( )

Mark HOWES, (son of Thomas), b. 1765, Dennis; d. 8 July 1853, ae 88y1d, Ashfield MA

CHILD OF Mark HOWES & Susanna ALDEN^{6}:

Barnabas Alden HOWES^{7}, b. 1797, Ashfield MA; d. 24 June 1861, ae 63y11m16d, Ashfield MA

Polly Clark LAWTON, (dau of Benjamin & Susanna), b. 1803; d. 23 Jan. 1875, ae 71y9m23d, (widow of Barnabas Alden HOWES^{7})

Martha SHAW, b. c1691*; d. 6 Jan. 1760, Bridgewater <MD 14:207>

CHILDREN OF Eleazer ALDEN^{4} (Jos.^{3}) & Martha SHAW: (8) <Bridgewater, MD 14:207>

Jonathan ALDEN^{5}, b. 22 June 1721; d. 1801 or 1805*

Eleazer ALDEN^{5}, b. 30 Aug. 1723

Abraham ALDEN^{5}, b. 31 Aug. 1725; d. 2 Sept. 1726

David ALDEN^{5}, b. 18 June 1727

Joshua ALDEN^{5}, b. 19 Apr. 1729

Caleb ALDEN^{5}, b. 20 Apr. 1731; d. 21 Apr. 1733

Ezra ALDEN^{5}, b. 22 June 1734

Timothy ALDEN^{5}, b. 24 Nov. 1736; d. 13 Nov. 1828, Yarmouth g.s.

Experience HAYWARD*, (dau of Nathaniel), d. 1809* ae 90 (widow of Jonathan Alden^{5} (Eleazer^{4}))

Sarah WELD, (dau of Rev. Habijah), d. 28 Oct. 1796, ae 59, Yarmouth g.s.

CHILDREN OF Timothy ALDEN^{5} & Sarah WELD: (6)*

Rev. Timothy ALDEN^{6}, b. 28 Aug. 1771, Yarmouth; d. 5 July 1839, Pittsburg PA

Isaiah ALDEN^{6}, b. 22 Sept. 1772; d. 1843

Martin ALDEN^{6}, b. 17 Oct. 1773; d. 1839

Oliver ALDEN^{6}, b. 1775

Sarah Weld ALDEN^{6}, b. 1776; d. July 1847

Martha Shaw ALDEN^{6}, b. 1778; d. 1857

CHILD OF Rev. Timothy ALDEN^{6} (Tim.^{5}) & Elizabeth Shepherd WORMSTED:

Martha Wright ALDEN^{7}, b. 19 May 1798* <Marblehead VR 1:10>

Polly KINGMAN, b. 14 Aug. 1783

CHILDREN OF Martin ALDEN^{6} (Tim.^{5}) & Polly KINGMAN: (7) <Bible>**<70>**

Albert ALDEN^{7}, b. 26 Aug. ( )

Caleb ALDEN^{7}, b. 10 Dec. ( )

Mary K. ALDEN^{7}, b. 10 Dec.? ( )

Timithy ALDEN^{7}, b. 14 June ( )

Isiah ALDEN^{7}, b. 17 Dec. ( )

Martin ALDEN^{7}, b. 3 Apr. ( )

Osman ALDEN^{7}, b. 8 May, Tuesday, ( )

Mark LATHROP, (son of Samuel), b. 9 Sept. 1689, Bridgewater <MD 15:45>; d. 1777*, Easton

CHILDREN OF Mark LATHROP & Hannah ALDEN^{4} (Joseph^{3}): (3)*

Jonathan LATHROP^{5}, b. 11 Mar. 1722/3

Joseph LATHROP^{5}, b. 23 Mar. 1725

Seth LATHROP^{5}, b. 7 July 1729

Timothy EDSON, b. 1695*, d. 20 Jan. 1782*, ae 87y10m <Stafford CT ChR>

CHILDREN OF Timothy EDSON & Mary ALDEN^{4} (Joseph^{3}): (6)*

Hannah EDSON^{5}, b. 10 Oct. 1720, Bridgewater <MD 15:86>; d. 23 Apr. 1792, Stafford CT

Timothy EDSON^{5}, b. 19 June 1722, Bridgewater <MD 15:86>

Anna EDSON^{5}, bpt. 31 Oct. 1725 <E. Bridgewater:48>

Abijah EDSON^{5}, bpt. 31 Oct. 1725 <E. Bridgewater:48>

Jonathan EDSON^{5}, bpt. 10 Mar. 1727/8 <E. Bridgewater:49>

Mary EDSON^{5}, bpt. 13 Sept. 1730 <E. Bridgewater:49>

Israel HOWE, b. c1716*; d. 8 Feb. 1796*, ae c80, Stafford CT* (hus of Hannah Edson^{5})

Abiah EDSON, (dau of Josiah & Sarah), b. 6 Apr. 1706, Bridgewater <MD 14:45>

CHILDREN OF Samuel ALDEN^{4} (Jos.^{3}) & Abiah EDSON*: (9)

Abiah ALDEN^{5}, b. 24 Feb. 1729 <Bridgewater VR 1:17>

Mehitable ALDEN^{5}, b. 27 Apr. 1732 <Bridgewater VR 1:20>

Sarah ALDEN^{5}, b. 25 Mar. 1734 <E. Bridgewater VR 1:21>

Samuel ALDEN^{5}, b. 7 Apr. 1736 <E. Bridgewater VR 1:21>

Josiah ALDEN^{5}, b. 26 May 1738 <E. Bridgewater VR 1:20>

Simeon ALDEN^{5}, b. 10 May 1740 <E. Bridgewater VR 1:21>

Silas ALDEN^{5}, d. ae 21*

Mary ALDEN^{5}, b. ( )*

Hosea ALDEN^{5}, b. ( )*

CHILDREN OF Seth HARRIS & Abiah ALDEN^{5}: (7) <Abington VR>

Seth HARRIS^{6}, b. 20 Sept. 1752 <VR 1:101>

Abiel HARRIS^{6}, (son), b. 20 Dec. 1754 <VR 1:101>

Rebecca HARRIS^{6}, b. 19 Sept. 1759 <VR 1:102>

Oliver HARRIS^{6}, b. 19 Mar. 1763 <VR 1:102>

John HARRIS^{6}, b. 27 Sept. 1765 <VR 1:101>

Abiah HARRIS^{6}, (dau), b. 16 Mar. 1768 <VR 1:101>

Samuel HARRIS^{6}, b. 5 Aug. 1770 <VR 1:102>

Solomon ALDEN, b. c1767*; d. 4 May 1815*, ae 48 <Lynn VR 2:410>

Hannah STONE, d. aft. Apr. 1813*

CHILDREN OF Solomon ALDEN & Hannah STONE: (9)* <Lynn VR 1:15>

Hannah ALDEN, b. 10 Oct. 1795

Betsey ALDEN, b. 25 May 1797

John ALDEN, b. 23 Feb. 1799

Joseph ALDEN, b. 23 Aug. 1801

Solomon ALDEN, b. 16 Apr. 1803

Mary ALDEN, b. 29 Sept. 1805

David ALDEN, b. 17 Dec. 1807

William ALDEN, b. 30 Mar. 1810

Child, d. 24 Nov. 1813, ae 6mths <Lynn VR 2:410>

Mary ALDEN, widow, d. 11 Apr. 1802, ae 62 (strangury) <Brookline VR:178>

John ALDEN, d. 14 Oct. 1798, ae 11 (putrid fever) <Brookline VR:178>

Silas ALDEN^{6} (Simeon^{5}), b. 30 June 1766; d. 1 June 1845

Polly FRENCH, (dau of Thomas*), b. 27 Oct. 1765; d. 11 Oct. 1810

CHILDREN OF Silas ALDEN^{6} & Polly FRENCH: (13) <MD 16:46>

Silas ALDEN^{7}, b. 24 Oct. 1786; d. 19 Jan. 1855

Calvin ALDEN^{7}, b. 23 Aug. 1788; d. 27 July 1825

Samuel ALDEN^{7}, b. 19 Nov. 1790

Polly ALDEN^{7}, b. 21 Feb. 1792; d. 21 May 1883

Adoniram ALDEN^{7}, b. 9 Feb. 1794; d. 24 Apr. 1816

Leonard ALDEN^{7}, b. 13 July 1796; d. 23 July 1822

Thomas ALDEN^{7}, b. 11 Aug. 1798; d. 7 Feb. 1820

Cintha F. ALDEN^{7}, b. 20 Jan. 1801; d. 5 Feb. 1805

Melinda ALDEN^{7}, b. 9 Mar. 1803; d. 31 Dec. 1887

Sally F. ALDEN^{7}, b. 23 Feb. 1805; d. 14 July 1876

Sukey F. ALDEN^{7}, b. 23 Feb. 1805 (twin); d. 30 Nov. 1880

Cintha ALDEN^{7}, b. 9 June 1808; d. 3 June 1886

Silence F. ALDEN^{7}, b. 16 Apr. 1810; d. 16 Apr. 1858

Mehitable CARVER^{4} (*Eleazer^{3}, John^{2}, Robert^{1}*), d. 14 Oct. 1757*, ae 52, Bridgewater g.s.

CHILDREN OF Seth ALDEN^{4} (Jos.^{3}) & Mehitable CARVER^{4}: (4) <Bridgewater VR>

Oliver ALDEN^{5}, b. 6 Aug. 1740*, d. 29 Sept. 1825* <VR 1:21,2:425>

Seth ALDEN^{5}, b. 22 Mar. 1741* <VR 1:21>; d. 29 Aug. 1775*

Caleb ALDEN^{5}, b. 6 Apr. 1744*, d. 20 Aug. 1747 <VR 1:17,2:423>

Joseph ALDEN^{5}, b. 16 Aug. 1747* <VR 1:20>; d. 8 Apr. 1803

Bethiah CARVER^{6} (*Eleazer^{5-4-3}, John^{2}, Robert^{1}*), b. 6 July 1754*; d. 19 May 1821, Bridgewater <NEHGR 88:316>

CHILDREN OF Joseph ALDEN^{5} & Bethiah CARVER^{6}: (9) <NEHGR 88:316>

Mehitable ALDEN^{6}, b. 28 Aug. 1775

Joseph ALDEN^{6}, b. 24 May 1777

Daniel ALDEN^{6}, b. 29 Feb. 1780

Thomas ALDEN^{6}, b. 6 Dec. 1782

Cyrus ALDEN^{6}, b. 20 May 1785

Eunice ALDEN^{6}, b. 20 Mar. 1788

Bethiah ALDEN^{6}, b. 14 June 1790

Seth ALDEN^{6}, b. 21 May 1793

Betsey ALDEN^{6}, b. 16 Oct. 1796

Experience LEONARD, (dau of Solomon), b. 22 Oct. 1743*, Bridgewater; d. 24 Oct. 1818*,Bridgewater

CHILDREN OF Oliver ALDEN^{5} (Seth^{4}) & Experience LEONARD: (4) <Bridgewater>

Caleb ALDEN^{6}, b. 14 Nov. 1766; d. 22 Aug. 1845

Oliver ALDEN^{6}, b. 30 May 1770; d. 12 Nov. 1775

Cromwell ALDEN^{6}, b. 13 Feb. 1773; d. 31 Oct. 1775

Experience ALDEN^{6}, b. 25 Feb. 1779

Mary CARVER^{6} (*Eleazer^{5-4-3}, John^{2}, Robert^{1}) b. 28 Aug. 1748*; d. 1 or 2 Dec. 1811*<NEHGR 88:316>

CHILDREN OF Seth ALDEN^{5} (Seth^{4}) & Mary CARVER^{6}: (3)

Seth ALDEN^{6}, b. 15 Feb. 1769*; d. 10 Aug. 1775

Mehitable ALDEN^{6}, b. 29 Apr. 1771*; d. 11 Aug. 1775

Betsey ALDEN^{6}, b. 1773, d. 8 Aug. 1775*

Amander ALDEN, (son of Joseph & Mary), d. 27 Mar. 1860, ae 49y9m24d, Bridgewater, shoemaker, (kidney disease) <Mass.VR 139:283>

John BURRILL, d. 16 Nov. 1731 <Weymouth VR 2:252>

CHILDREN OF John BURRILL & Mercy ALDEN^{3}: (5) <Weymouth VR>

Elizabeth BURRILL^{4}, b. 25 Sept. 1689, d. 24 Mar. 1714 (measles) <VR 1:67,2:252>

Thomas BURRILL^{4}, b. 26 Mar. 1692 <VR 1:68>

John BURRILL^{4}, b. 19 Feb. 1694 <VR 1:68>; d. 26 Jan. 1754* <Abington VR 2:260>

Marcy BURRILL^{4}, b. 22 Jan. 1700 <VR 1:65>

Mary BURRILL^{4}, d. ?14 Dec. 1802*, ae 104, (old age) <Weymouth ChR>**<71>**

Mary HUMPHREY, (dau of Joseph), b. 20 Mar. 1697/8, d. aft. Aug. 1766 <father's will>

CHILDREN OF John BURRILL^{4} & Mary HUMPHREY: (6) <Weymouth VR>

John BURRILL^{5}, b. 30 Nov. 1717 <VR 1:64>

Joseph BURRILL^{5}, b. 24 Sept. 1719 <VR 1:64>

Abraham BURRILL^{5}, b. 26 Sept. 1721 <VR 1:62>

Humphrey BURRILL^{5}, b. 20 Dec. 1723 <VR 1:64>; d. 25 Oct. 1767*, Lake George <Abington VR 2:260>

Thomas BURRILL^{5}, b. 4 Mar. 1730 <VR 1:64>

Mary BURRILL^{5*}, b. ( )

MICRO #12 of 16

Joseph HUMPHREY^{3} (Thomas^{2}, John^{1}), d. Aug. 1766 <will - 14 Aug. 1766, probate - 5 Sept. 1766>

Mary ( ) HUMPHREY, d. 23 June 1742, ae 70, Hingham <Hist. Hingham 2:361>

CHILDREN OF Joseph HUMPHREY & Mary ( ): (3)

Mary HUMPHREY, b. 20 Mar. 1697/8; d. aft. 1766

Joseph HUMPHREY, b. 14 Apr. 1705; d. 24 Jan. 1723/4

Abigail HUMPHREY, d. 1711

CHILDREN OF Humphrey BURRILL^{5} (John^{4}) & Hannah THAYER: (3)* <Abington VR>

Mercy BURRILL^{6}, b. 14 Feb 1746 <VR:44>

Hannah BURRILL^{6}, b. 13 Sept. 1750 <VR:45>

Humphnes BURRILL^{6}, b. 7 Mar. 1755 <VR:45>

Anna VINTON, (dau of Thomas*), b. 7 Sept. 1718* <Vinton Mem.:50>

CHILD OF John BURRELL^{5} & Anna VINTON*:

Mary BURRELL^{6*}, b. 22 Feb. 1741***<72>**

Jane DYER, b. 2 May 1729* <Weymouth VR>

CHILDREN OF Abraham BURRELL^{5} (John^{4}) & Jane DYER, (dau of Jos. & Jane): (5)

Isaac BURRELL^{6}, b. 24 Mar. 1747/8 <Weymouth VR 1:64>

Abraham BURRELL^{6}, b. 20 Aug. 1750 <Abington VR 1:44>

Jane BURRELL^{6}, b. 29 Sept. 1753 <Abington VR 1:44>

Cloe BURRELL^{6}, b. 18 May 1757 <Abington VR 1:45>

Benjamin BURRELL^{6}, b. 17 Jan. 1760 <Abington VR 1:43>

CHILDREN OF Joseph DYER & Jane STEPHENS: (11) <Weymouth VR 1:99>

Sarah DYER, b. 20 Mar. 1727

Jane DYER, b. 2 May 1729

Joseph DYER, b. 7 Sept. 1731

Hannah DYER, b. 8 Jan. 1734, d. 9 Jan. 1734

Mary DYER, b. 8 Jan. 1734, (twins), d. 9 Jan. 1734

Benjamin DYER, b. 9 Feb. 1735

Joanna DYER, b. 2 July 1737

Asa DYER, b. 26 July 1739

Stevens DYER, b. 20 Oct. 1741

Mary DYER, b. 13 Mar. 1744

James DYER, b. 14 June 1746

CHILDREN OF Josiah RIPLEY & Mary BURRILL^{4} (Mercy Alden^{3}): (7) <Weymouth VR>

Eliphalet RIPLEY^{5}, b. 21 Apr. 1720

Lemuel RIPLEY^{5}, b. 6 Sept. 1722

Josiah RIPLEY^{5}, b. 6 Feb. 1725

Elizabeth RIPLEY^{5}, b. 6 July 1727

William RIPLEY^{5}, b. 25 Nov. 1729

Mary RIPLEY^{5}, b. 25 May 1732

Lydia RIPLEY^{5}, b. 31 Mar. 17(39)

REBECCA ALDEN^{2} (John^{1})

Dr. Thomas DELANO, b. pre 1 Apr. 1646*; d. betw. 5 Oct. 1722(will)- 22 Apr.1723(probate)<MD 6:22>

CHILDREN OF Dr. Thomas DELANO & Rebecca ALDEN^{2}: (8) <MD 6:23>

Benoni DELANO^{3}, b. c1667; d. 5 Apr. 1738, ae 71, Duxbury g.s. <MD 9:160>

Thomas DELANO^{3}, b. ( )

Jonathan DELANO^{3}, b. 1675; d. 6 Jan. 1765, ae 89y2wks <Duxbury ChR 1:250>
David DELANO^{3}, b. ( )
Mary DELANO^{3}, b. ( )
Sarah DELANO^{3}, b. ( ); d. aft. 15 May 1746 <MD 7:117>
Ruth DELANO^{3}, b. ( )
Joseph DELANO^{3}, b. ( )
Elizabeth DREW, (dau of John), b. 5 Feb. 1673, Plymouth <MD 20:31>; d. pre 21 Aug. 1733<MD 20:31>
CHILDREN OF Benoni DELANO^{3} & Elizabeth DREW: (4) <MD 20:31,33,34>
Beriah DELANO^{4}, d. 1748*, Duxbury <div.- 10 Mar. 1759, Plymouth Co. Probate #6233, 15:106>
Lemuel DELANO^{4}, b. 1712*; d. 6 Sept. 1778, ae 65y10m <Duxbury VR:370>
Hannah DELANO^{4}, b. ( )
Rebecca DELANO^{4}, d. 6 Jan. 1750 <Lancaster VR:323>
CHILDREN OF Beriah DELANO^{4} & Naomi MERITT*: (6) <1-5, Duxbury, MD 12:33>
Ichabod DELANO^{5}, b. 7 June 1735; d. pre 1756*
William DELANO^{5}, b. 31 May 1737
Silvanus DELANO^{5}, b. 15 June 1739
Lemuel DELANO^{5}, b. 24 Sept. 1741
Elizabeth DELANO^{5}, b. 28 May 1743
Benjamin DELANO^{5}, bpt. 27 Aug. 1746*
Lydia BARTLETT^{6} (Ebenezer$^{5-4}$, Ben.^{3}, Mary Warren^{2}), b. 17 Aug. 1721, Plymouth <MD 13:115>
CHILDREN OF Lemuel DELANO^{4} (Benoni^{3}) & Lydia BARTLETT^{6}: (8) <1-6, Duxbury, MD 12:119>
Beriah DELANO^{5}, b. 16 Oct. 1742
Lydia DELANO^{5}, b. 15 Jan. 1744; d. 13 Aug. 1832*, ae 88
Esther DELANO^{5}, b. 15 Nov. 1745
Mary DELANO^{5}, b. 1 Jan. 1747/8; d. 20 Dec. 1828*, ae 81
Hannah DELANO^{5}, b. 26 Sept. 1749
Rebecca DELANO^{5}, b. 6 Dec. 1753
Elizabeth DELANO^{5}, b. 2 Mar. 1756, Duxbury <MD 12:120>
Amy DELANO^{5}, b. 29 Jan. 1759, Duxbury <MD 12:120>
Amasa TURNER, (son of Amasa & Ann*), b. ? 20 Aug. 1705* <Scituate VR>; d. aft.5 Dec. 1763* <deed>
CHILDREN OF Amasa TURNER & 1st Rebecca DELANO^{4} (Benoni^{3}): (12) <1-7, Hanover VR:12>
Elizabeth TURNER^{5}, b. 4 June 1729
Hannah TURNER^{5}, b. 28 Apr. 1731
Ichabod TURNER^{5}, b. 3 Mar. 1732/3
Zilpah TURNER^{5}, b. 30 Dec. 1734
Nathaniel TURNER^{5}, b. 31 Jan. 1736/7; d. 16 Jan. 1823*, shaker, Shirley MA
Samuel/Lemuel TURNER^{5}, b. 10 July 1738
Ezra TURNER^{5}, b. 22 July 1740
Joseph TURNER^{5}, bpt. 3 July 1743 <Hanover ChR 1:125>
Abner TURNER^{5}*, b. 7 Oct. 1745, Lancaster
Susanna TURNER^{5}*, bpt. 6 Sept. 1747 <Hanover ChR 1.128>
Amasa TURNER^{5}*, bpt. 6 Sept. 1747 <Hanover ChR 1:128>
Rebecca TURNER^{5}*, bpt. 1 Apr. 1750 <Lancaster VR:295>
Eunice SANDERSON, d. 8 Dec. 1753 <Lancaster VR:323>
CHILD OF Amasa TURNER & 2nd Eunice SANDERSON:
Sarah TURNER, bpt. 15 Oct. 1752 <Lancaster VR:297>
Margaret GROSS, d. 28 Oct. 1763 (3rd wf of Amasa Turner) <Lancaster VR:325>
Anna GROSS, b. 7 June 1741, Hingham
CHILDREN OF Nathaniel TURNER^{5} (Rebecca Delano^{4}) & Anna GROSS: (3)
Anna TURNER^{6}, bpt. 18 May 1760 <Lancaster VR:301>

Susanna TURNER^{6}, bpt. 23 Nov. 1760 <Lancaster VR:301>

Asenath TURNER^{6}, bpt. 16 Jan. 1763 <Lancaster VR:303>

Anna TURNER, d. 7 Sept. 1806 <Lancaster VR:197>

Mrs. ( ) TURNER, wf of Ichabod TURNER^{5} (Rebecca Delano^{4}), d. 6 Feb. 1761<Lancaster ChR 1:324>

Eleazer HARLOW^{5} (Sam.^{4}, Rebecca Bartlett^{3}, Mary Warren^{2}), b. 18 Apr. 1694, Plymouth <MD 2:18>

CHILDREN OF Eleazer HARLOW^{5} & 1st Hannah DELANO^{4} (Benoni^{3}): (3) <Plymouth, MD 13:35>

Eliphaz HARLOW^{5}, b. 5 Mar. 1716

Lemuel HARLOW^{5}, b. 29 Nov. 1717

Eleazer HARLOW^{5}, b. 17 Oct. 1719; d. 15 Aug. 1812 <MD 13:35>

CHILDREN OF Eleazer HARLOW^{5} & 2nd Hannah PRATT: (2) <Plymouth, MD 13:35>

Elizabeth HARLOW, b. 21 Apr. 1721

Patience HARLOW, b. 1 Oct. 1722

Hannah DOTEN^{3} (Thomas^{2}), b. Dec. 1675, Plymouth <MD 1:143>; d. ?12 Apr. 1764*,ae "87 4/12 " <Duxbury ChR 1:250>

CHILDREN OF Jonathan DELANO^{3} & Hannah DOTEN^{3}: (11) <Duxbury, MD 12:33>

John DELANO^{4}, b. 11 Oct. 1699; d. aft. Dec. 1763*

Jonathan DELANO^{4}, b. 3 Nov. 1701; d. betw. 7 Mar. 1744(will)- 20 May 1744 (probate), Rochester

Nathan DELANO^{4}, b. 26 Oct. 1703

Amasa DELANO^{4}, b. 15 Nov. 1705; d. 14 May 1706

Ruth DELANO^{4}, b. 25 May 1707

Amasa DELANO^{4}, b. 7 Aug. 1709; d. "5-7" Aug. 1790* <Duxbury VR>

Hannah DELANO^{4}, b. 28 Dec. 1711

Dorothy DELANO^{4}, b. 3 Apr. 1714

Dorothy DELANO^{4}, b. 14 Oct. 1715

Ebenezer DELANO^{4}, b. 29 Nov. 1717

David DELANO^{4}, b. 3 June 1720

Ruth SAMSON^{5} (Abraham^{4}, Lorah Standish^{3}, Alex.^{2}), b. 2 July 1713, Duxbury <MD 10:185>; d. pre 22 May 1764* (father's will)

CHILDREN OF Amaziah/Amasa DELANO^{4} & Ruth SAMSON^{5}: (9) <Duxbury, MD 12:162>

Ezekiel DELANO^{5}, b. 19 Dec. 1731

Thomas DELANO^{5}, b. 30 Aug. 1734, d. 9 Oct. 1747

Hannah DELANO^{5}, b. 18 Feb. 1736/7

Zenas DELANO^{5}, b. 8 Dec. 1739

Cornelius DELANO^{5}, b. 10 Oct. 1742; d. 24 Apr. 1801, Duxbury g.s.

Jemima DELANO^{5}, b. 8 Feb. 1744/5

Thomas DELANO^{5}, bpt. 1 May 1748 <Duxbury VR>

Silva DELANO^{5}, bpt. 12 Aug. 1750 <Duxbury VR>

Ruth DELANO^{5}, bpt. 5 Aug. 1753 <Duxbury VR>

CHILDREN OF Jonathan DELANO^{4} (Jonathan^{3}) & 1st Elizabeth WINSLOW, (dau of Samuel):(4) <Rochester VR 2:2>

Elizabeth DELANO^{5}, b. 11 Nov. 1725

Jonathan DELANO^{5}, b. 25 Feb. 1727/8

Hannah DELANO^{5}, b. 11 June 1730

Samuel DELANO^{5}, b. 6 Oct. 1734

CHILDREN OF Jonathan DELANO^{4} (Jonathan^{3}) & 2nd Elizabeth SPRAGUE: (3) <Rochester VR 2:2>

Amasa DELANO^{5}, b. 26 Jan. 1737

Samuel DELANO^{5}, b. 11 May 1739

Iranea DELANO^{5}, b. 25 Oct. 1740

CHILDREN OF Jonathan DELANO^{4} (Jonathan^{3}) & 3rd Rachel BUMP: (2) <Rochester VR 2:2>

Joanna DELANO^{5}, b. 22 July 1742

Martha DELANO^5, b. 5 Feb. 1743

John DREW, (son of John), b. 29 Aug. 1676, Plymouth <MD 1:146>; d. betw. 17 Apr. 1742 (will) - 10 July 1745 (probate) <MD 7:114>

CHILDREN OF John DREW & Sarah DELANO^3: (6) <MD 7:114 - names>

John DREW^4, b. ( )

Thomas DREW^4, b. c1706, d. 14 June 1770, ae 64, Halifax g.s. <MD 12:243>

Elizabeth DREW^4, b. ( )

Jemima DREW^4, b. ( )

Mary DREW^4, b. ( )

Abigail DREW^4, b. c1715, d. 26 May 1726, ae 11 <MD 12:200>

Isaac BENNET^4 (Priscilla Howland^3, Isaac^2), b. 7 Jan. 17( )* <MD 1:220>

CHILDREN OF Isaac BENNET^4 & Mary DREW^4: (6) <Middleboro>

Isaac BENNET^5, b. 16 May 1733

Susanna BENNET^5, b. 22 Mar. 1734/5 <MD 12:233>; d. pre 9 July 1760*

Joseph BENNET^5, b. 31 Jan. 1739/40 <MD 14:245>

Nathan BENNET^5, b. 14 June 1742 <MD 15:217>

Jedediah BENNET^5, b. 5 May 1745 <MD 16:107>

Mary BENNET^5, b. 6 Jan. 1748 <MD 16:133>

Susanna BENNET^4 (Priscilla Howland^3, Isaac^2), b. 10 July 1707, Middleboro <MD 2:105>

CHILDREN OF John DREW^4 (Sarah Delano^3) & Susanna BENNET^4: (10)

Peter DREW^5, b. 25 Oct. 1728, Middleboro <MD 8:28>

Mary DREW^5, b. 7 May 1731, Middleboro <MD 12:230>

Silvanus DREW^5, b. 14 Dec. 1732, Middleboro <MD 12:230>

Lydia DREW^5, b. 4 Dec. 1735 <Halifax VR:45>

Deborah DREW^5, b. 9 Apr. 1737 <Halifax VR:45>

Hannah DREW^5, b. 5 Aug. 1739 <Halifax VR:45>

Priscilla DREW^5, b. 20 Feb. 1741/2 <Halifax VR:45>

John DREW^5, b. 7 Aug. 1744 <Halifax VR:45>

Cornelius DREW^5, b. 23 Nov. 1747 <Halifax VR:45>

Jedediah DREW^5, b. 12 Oct. 1749 <Halifax VR:45>

CHILDREN OF Dr. Stephen POWERS & Lydia DREW^5: (2) <Middleboro, MD 25:106>

Susanna POWERS^6, b. 14 Dec. 1760

Mary POWERS^6, b. 2 Mar. 1766

Abigail HARRIS^6 (Samuel^5, Mercy Latham^4, Susanna Winslow^3, Mary Chilton^2), d. 9 Sept. 1789, ae 69 Halifax g.s. <MD 12:243>

CHILDREN OF Thomas DREW^4 (Sarah Delano^3) & Abigail HARRIS^6: (7)

Thomas DREW^5, b. c1740, d. 30 Apr. 1824, ae 84, Halifax g.s. <MD 12:243>

Isaac DREW^5, b. pre 1742*

John DREW^5, b. ( )

Abigail DREW^5, b. ( )

Mary DREW^5, b. ( )

Jemima DREW^5, b. c1746*, d. 7 May 1825*, ae 79

Child, b. ( )

"Sarah (BARROWS) Pratt, widow, d. 31 May 1877, ae 76y4m, Watertown MA. She was born at Wareham, dau. of Thomas & Mary Barrows who were born at Carver." <Mass.VR 293:224>

Lucy TOMSON^5 (Reuben^4, Thomas^3, Mary Cooke^2), b. 4 Dec. 1755 <Halifax VR:47>; d. 5 Jan. 1818, Halifax g.s. <MD 12:243> (wf of Thomas Drew^5)

Peleg BARROWS^3 (Peleg^2, George^1), b. Feb. 1747/8*; d. 2 Mar. 1835, ae 87y22d,S. Carver g.s.,Union Cemetery (hus. of Jemima Drew^5)

CHILDREN OF Peleg BARROWS & Jemima ( ): (8): <Carver VR>**<73>**

Thomas BARROWS, b. 4 Aug. 1776

William BARROWS, b. 1 Nov. 1778

Mary BARROWS, b. 14 Aug. 1780

George BARROWS, b. 16 Feb. 1783

Stephen BARROWS, b. 6 Feb. 1785

Nelson BARROWS, b. 4 June 1787

Abigail BARROWS, b. 8 Sept. 1789

Joseph BARROWS, b. 8 Nov. 1792

CHILDREN OF Thomas DELANO^{3} & Hannah ( ) BARTLETT: (3)<74>

Thomas DELANO^{4}, b. ( )

Deborah DELANO^{4}, b. ( )

Elkanah DELANO^{4}, b. ( )

CHILDREN OF Elkanah DELANO^{4} & Mary SANDERS: (8) <Plymouth, MD 15:210>

Son, b. 1729, d. ae 3 wks, smallpox <MD 15:209>

Elkanah DELANO^{5}, b. 2 Nov. 1730

Hannah DELANO^{5}, b. 19 Dec. 1732

Mary DELANO^{5}, b. 7 May 1735

Barzillai DELANO^{5}, b. 10 Sept. 1737

Eunice DELANO^{5}, b. 1 Aug. 1741

Deborah DELANO^{5}, b. 22 May 1743

Sarah DELANO^{5}, b. 6 Dec. 1746

Humphrey RICHARDS, (son of Humphrey), b. 4 Apr. 1721

CHILDREN OF Humphrey RICHARDS & Sarah DELANO: (6)<75>

Polly RICHARDS, b. ( )

Sarah RICHARDS, b. ( )

Betsey RICHARDS, b. ( )

Susanna RICHARDS, b. ( )

Barzillai RICHARDS, b. ( )

John RICHARDS, b. 14 Aug. 1767 "the youngest"

Abigail DYER, d. 22 Feb. 1836, Cape Elizabeth (wf of John Richards)

CHILDREN OF Thomas DELANO^{4} (Tho.^{3}) & Sarah ( ): (7)

Thankful DELANO^{5}, b. 9 Aug. 1727, Provincetown <MD 9:103>

Sarah DELANO^{5}, b. 17 June 1729, Provincetown, d. 18 July 1730 <MD 9:103,12:80>

Sarah DELANO^{5}, b. 24 May 1731, Provincetown <MD 9:103>

Hannah DELANO^{5}, b. 4 Aug. 1733, Provincetown <MD 9:103>

Mary DELANO^{5}, b. 19 Apr. 1735, Provincetown <MD 11:47>

Abigail DELANO^{5}, b. ( )

Barzillai DELANO^{5}, b. ( )

RUTH ALDEN^{2} (John^{1})

Ruth ALDEN^{2}, b. pre 1644*; d. 12 Oct. 1674* <Braintree VR:640>

John BASS, b. c1632*; d. 12 Sept. 1716*, ae 84 <Braintree VR:724>

CHILDREN OF John BASS & Ruth ALDEN^{2}: (7)

John BASS^{3}, b. 26 Nov. 1658 <MD 4:203; Braintree VR>; d. betw. 10 July 1723 (will) - 30 Nov. 1724 (probate) <MD 18:105>

Samuel BASS^{3}, b. 25 Mar. 1660 <MD 4:203; Braintree VR:642>; d. 20 Feb. 1751*, Bridgewater

Ruth BASS^{3}, b. 28 Jan. 1662* <MD 4:204,206; Braintree VR>; d. 5 June 1699* Braintree VR:694; Giles Mem.:501>

Joseph BASS^{3}, b. 5 Dec. 1665 <MD 4:204>; d. 22 Nov. 1733, Boston <MD 18:107>

Hannah BASS[3], b. 22 June 1667, d. 24 Oct. 1705 <Braintree VR:646,695>

Mary BASS[3], b. 11 Feb. 1669 <MD 4:204; Braintree VR:647>; d.aft. 31 Dec. 1716*

Sarah BASS[3], b. 29 Mar. 1672 <MD 4:204; Braintree VR:649>; d. 19 Aug. 1751<Thayer Gen.(1874):590>

MICRO #13 of 16

Joseph ADAMS[3] (Jos.[2], Henry[1]), b. 24 Dec. 1654*, d. 12 Feb. 1736/7 <Braintree VR:630,732> <will - MD 18:112>

Mary CHAPIN, b. 27 Aug. 1662, d. 14 June 1687 <Braintree VR:819,660>

CHILDREN OF Joseph ADAMS[3] & 1st Mary CHAPIN: (2)

Mary ADAMS, b. 6 Feb. 1682/3

Abigail ADAMS, b. 17 Feb. 1683/4

CHILDREN OF Joseph ADAMS[3] & 2nd Hannah BASS[3]: (8) <Braintree VR>

Joseph ADAMS[4], b. 4 Jan. 1688/9 <VR:665>; d. 26 May 1783*, NH

John ADAMS[4], b. 8 Feb. 1690/1 <VR:669>; d. 25 May 1761*

Samuel ADAMS[4], b. 28 Jan. 1693/4 <VR:669>; d. 17 July 1751*

Josiah ADAMS[4], b. 18 Feb. 1695/6 <VR:673>

Hannah ADAMS[4], b. 21 Feb. 1697/8 <VR:675>

Ruth ADAMS[4], b. 21 Mar. 1700 <VR:678>

Bethiah ADAMS[4], b. 13 June 1702 <VR:681>

Ebenezer ADAMS[4], b. 30 Dec. 1704 <VR:685>; d. betw. 9 Jan. 1769 (will) - 29 Aug. 1769 (probate) <Suffolk Co. Wills 68:227-29>

CHILD OF Joseph ADAMS[3] & 3rd Elizabeth ( ):

Caleb ADAMS, b. 26 May 1710, d. 4 June 1710 <Braintree VR:690>

Elizabeth, wf of Joseph ADAMS[3], d. 14 Feb. 1739/40, ae 71

"Benjamin H. ADAMS, d. 3:31:76, comsumption, ae 63y11m16d, b. Portsmouth NH, son of Benjamin & Elizabeth T." <Dedham Rcds.: Abstracts of Deaths, 1844-90>

CHILDREN OF Capt. Ebenezer ADAMS[4] (Hannah Bass[3]) & Anne BOYLSTON*, (dau. of Peter*): (6)

Peter ADAMS[5], b. & d. 1730*

Anne ADAMS[5], b. 24 July 1731*, Braintree; d. 11 July 1794*, Braintree (widow of 2nd hus. Thomas Thayer) <Hist. Old Braintree & Quincy:127>

Boylsten ADAMS[5], b. 28 Feb. 1734*, Braintree; d. 1761*

Ebenezer ADAMS[5], b. 15 Mar. 1737*

Zabdiel ADAMS[5], b. 1739*

Micajah ADAMS[5], b. 1741*, d. 1769*

Dr. Elisha SAVIL, (*son of Sam. & Patience), b. 19 Aug. 1724* <Braintree:755>;d. 30 Apr. 1768*, Hancock Cem. g.s. <Hist. Old Braintree & Quincy:127>

CHILDREN OF Dr. Elisha SAVIL & Anne ADAMS[5]: (5) <Braintree VR>

Ann SAVIL[6], b. 17 May 1754* <VR:804>; d. 2 Apr. 1826* (wf of William Saunders, d. 27 Oct.1830, ae 83) <Hist. Old Braintree & Quincy:124>

Susanna SAVIL[6], b. 12 May 1756* <VR:812>

Edward SAVIL[6], b. 30 May 1759* <VR:813>

Lucretia SAVIL[6], b. 21 Aug. 1761* <VR:815>; d. 17 Apr. 1804 <Town Clerk, Wilton >

Samuel SAVIL[6], b. 15 Dec. 1763* <VR:822>

Jeriah BASS, (son of Samuel & Alice (Spear)), b. 25 Feb. 1759 <Braintree VR>; d. ?1813, Wilton ME

CHILDREN OF Jeriah BASS* & Lucretia SAVIL[6]: (7) <Town Clerk, Wilton >**<76>**

Charles BASS[7], b. 21 Apr. 1785; d. 23 May 1862, Weld ME

Lucretia BASS[7], b. 28 Mar. 178()

Samuel BASS[7], b. 3 May 1790

Elisha BASS[7], b. 2 June 1793

Jeriah BASS[7], b. 5 Feb. 1796

John BASS[7], b. 1 Mar. 1799

Seth BASS^{7}, b. 25 July 1803

Susanna LANE, b. 6 Sept. 1791; d. 16 Aug. 1869, ae 78

CHILDREN OF Charles BASS^{7} & Susanna LANE: (8)**<76>**

Charles BASS^{8}, b. 18 Mar. 1811

Susan BASS^{8}, b. 25 Mar. 1812

Anna BASS^{8}, b. 2 June 1816, Weld ME

Sarah BASS^{8}, b. 7 Mar. 1818

Phebe BASS^{8}, b. 10 May 1820

Mary Raulstone BASS^{8}, b. 12 Mar. 1822

George BASS^{8}, b. 10 Mar. 1826

Seth L. Bass^{8}, b. 4 Apr. 1832

Mary ALLEN^{5} (Tho.^{4}, Ben.^{3}, Jos.^{2}, Sam.^{1}), b. 12 Sept. 1737*

CHILDREN OF Boylston ADAMS^{5} (Ebenezer^{4}) & Mary ALLEN^{5}: (3)*

Mary ADAMS^{6}, b. 1755

Anne ADAMS^{6}, b. 1757

Elizabeth ADAMS^{6}, b. 1759

Benjamin OWEN, b. 1 Nov. 1691, Braintree

CHILDREN OF Benjamin OWEN & Hannah ADAMS^{4} (Hannah Bass^{3}): (6) <Braintree VR>

Hannah OWEN^{5}, b. 23 Nov. 1725 <VR:757>

Ruth OWEN^{5}, b. 9 Oct. 1727 <VR:759>

Bethiah OWEN^{5}, b. 23 Nov. 1729 <VR:766>

Lydia OWEN^{5}, b. 19 Jan. 1731/2 <VR:766>

Benjamin OWEN^{5}, b. 4 Feb. 1733/4 <VR:770>

Timothy OWEN^{5}, b. 12 Jan. 1735/6 <VR:774>

Abigail ADAMS^{3} (Jos.^{2}, Henry^{1}), b. 27 Feb. 1658*, d. 26 Oct. 1696* <Braintree VR:818, 693>

CHILDREN OF John BASS^{3} & 1st Abigail ADAMS^{3}: (2)

John BASS^{4}, b. 8 June 1688* <Braintree VR:665>; d. betw. 7 Aug. 1761 (will) - 2 Apr. 1762 (prob.)

Samuel BASS^{4}, b. 17 June 1691 <Braintree VR:667>

CHILD OF John BASS^{3} & 2nd Rebecca SAVIL:

Ebenezer BASS^{4}, bpt. 11 Oct. 1702*

CHILD OF Ebenezer BASS^{4} & Sarah MOSELEY*:

Ebenezer BASS^{5}, b. 11 Dec. 1741?*

Lydia SAVIL, d. 4 Feb. 1715*

CHILD OF John BASS^{4} (John^{3}) & 1st Lydia SAVIL:

Child, d. 4 Feb. 1715*

Hannah NEALE, b. 15 Mar. 1692*; d. 15 May 1761*

CHILDREN OF John BASS^{4} & 2nd Hannah NEALE: (6)*

John BASS^{5}, b. 26 Mar. 1717, Braintree

Benjamin BASS^{5}, b. 17 Sept. 1719; d. 24 Sept. 1808

Jedediah BASS^{5}, b. 29 Apr. 1721; d. 12 Mar. 1806

Joseph BASS^{5}, b. 29 Feb. 1723; d. 23 Sept. 1800

Jonathan BASS^{5}, b. 23 Apr. 1729 <Braintree VR:762>; d. 20 July 1778

Hannah BASS^{5}, b. 12 Mar. 1731/2 <Braintree VR:767>

Josiah RAWSON^{4} (David^{3}, Wm.^{2}, Edw.^{1}), b. 31 Jan. 1727/8 <Braintree VR:760>;d. 24 Feb. 1812, *Warwick MA*

CHILDREN OF Josiah RAWSON & Hannah BASS^{5}: (12)*

Josiah RAWSON^{6}, b. 1751

Simeon RAWSON^{6}, b. 1753; d. Apr. 1835

Abigail RAWSON^{6}, b. 14 Nov. 1755 <Grafton VR>; d. 15 Apr. 1831

Mary RAWSON^{6}, b. 23 Nov. 1757 <Grafton VR>

Anna Batcheller RAWSON^{6}, b. 11 Oct. 1759 <Grafton VR>

Jonathan Bass RAWSON^{6}, b. 10 Sept. 1761 <Grafton VR>

Lydia RAWSON^{6}, b. 1763; d. c1781

Elizabeth RAWSON^{6}, b. 1765

Lemuel RAWSON^{6}, b. 18 Jan. 1767

Amelia RAWSON^{6}, b. 1769

Hannah RAWSON^{6}, b. 1771; d. Warwick MA

Secretary RAWSON^{6}, b. 19 Sept. 1773; d. 24 Oct. 1842, Jericho VT

Seth ELLIS, d. 22 Jan. 1855, Orange, ae 70, farmer, b. Orange, son of Seth <Mass.VR 93:206>

CHILDREN OF Rev. John BASS & Mary DENESON: (3)<Ashford CT>**<77>**

John BASS, b. 5 June 1746

Mary BASS, b. 24 Dec. 1747

John BASS, b. 24 Oct. 1751

CHILDREN OF Jonathan BASS^{5} (John^{4}) & Hannah HAYWARD*: (3)<Thayer Mem.1:57>

Jonathan BASS^{6}, bpt. 7 Aug. 1763*; d. 9 June 1859, ae 95y10m7d, Quincy, old age, bootmaker, b. Quincy <Mass.VR 130:166>

Hannah BASS^{6}*, bpt. 4 Aug. 1765*; d. pre 4 July 1778 (father's will) <Suffolk Co.Probate #16676, 77:527>

Susanna BASS^{6}, bpt. 22 May 1768*

Elizabeth Marston CHANNEL, b. 13 Jan. 1767

CHILDREN OF Jonathan BASS^{6} & Elizabeth Marston CHANNEL: (9)

Susanna BASS^{7}, b. 17 Dec. 1793

Lewis BASS^{7}, b. 20 June 1795; d. 18 June 1873, Quincy, pneumonia, married <Mass.VR 257:322>

Isaac BASS^{7}, b. 15 Mar. 1797; d. 9 Jan. 1849, Quincy, widower, suicide <Mass.VR 41:37>

Jonathan Howard BASS^{7}, b. 31 Dec. 1798; d. 6 Oct. 1803

Elizabeth BASS^{7}, b. 12 Aug. 1800

Benjamin BASS^{7}, b. 6 Sept. 1802; d. 23 Oct. 1877, ae 75y1m17d, Quincy <Mass.VR 293:279>

Mary BASS^{7}, b. 20 Sept. 1804

Jonathan Howard BASS^{7}, b. 19 Apr. 1806

Hannah Maria BASS^{7}, b. 30 Aug. 1808

MICRO #14 of 16

Grace Hall STEVENS, (dau. of Solomon & Martha) b. Amherst, d. 28 June 1873, ae 71y6m10d <Mass.VR 257:322>

CHILDREN OF Benjamin BASS^{7} & Grace Hall STEVENS: (4)**<78>**

Mary Jane BASS^{8}, b. c1833, d. 18 Apr. 1880, ae 46y9m26d, Quincy (widow of Wm.Adams) <Mass.VR 320:246>

John B. BASS^{8}, b. ( )

Joseph A. BASS^{8}, b. ( )

Edward W.H. BASS^{8}, b. ( )

Georgianna (HAYDEN) Bass, b. 1 Aug. 1838 <Braintree VR 3:78>; d. 20 Sept. 1865, Braintree

Sarah SAVIL, d. 25 Jan. 1727*

CHILD OF Samuel BASS^{4} (John^{3}) & 1st Sarah SAVIL*:

Samuel BASS^{5}*, b. 29 Dec. 1724*; d. cApr. 1807*

CHILD OF Samuel BASS^{4} & 2nd Hannah GOULD*:

Abigail BASS^{5}*, b. 31 Jan. 1728*

Mary BELCHER, (dau. of Moses & Mary), b. 8 Sept. 1668, d. 2 Nov. 1707 <Braintree VR:647, 694>

CHILDREN OF Joseph BASS^{3} & 1st Mary BELCHER: (8) <Braintree VR>

Mary BASS^{4}, b. 22 June 1690 <VR:666>; d. Oct. 1760

Joseph BASS^{4}, b. 5 July 1692 <VR:669>; d. 9 Jan. 1752, Dorchester

Benjamin BASS^{4}, b. 19 Dec. 1694 <VR:670>; d. 23 May 1756, Hanover

Moses BASS^{4}, b. 23 Oct. 1696 <VR:674>; d. 15 Jan. 1780

Ruth BASS^{4}, b. 21 Mar. 1699 <VR:678>; d. 16 Jan. 1752

John BASS^{4}, b. 19 Jan. 1702, d. 31 Jan. 1702 <VR:681,721>

Elizabeth BASS^{4}, b. 2 Feb. 1703 <VR:682>; d. 17 Oct. 1776

Alden BASS^{4}, b. 21 Oct. 1705 <VR:685>; d. Apr. 1737

CHILD OF Alden BASS^{4} & Mercy DOWDING:

Alden BASS^{5}, b. 1 Oct. 1735*; d. 4 May 1803, Boston

Hannah TYLER, d. Aug. 1801 (wf of Alden Bass^{5})

Mary GARDNER, (dau. of James), d. 25 Feb. 1772*

CHILDREN OF Rev. Benjamin BASS^{4} (Jos.^{3}) & Mary GARDNER: (3)*

Mary BASS^{5}, b. 30 Oct. 1730; d. 21 Mar. 1802

Elizabeth BASS^{5}, b. 18 Mar. 1733

Benjamin BASS^{5}, b. 6 June 1741

Robert BASS^{7} (Ben.$^{6-5}$), b. Hanover, d. 22 June 1886, Rockland, ae 73y10m13d, blacksmith, "softening brain", bur. Hanover <Mass.VR 374:352>

Lydia LOUD, (dau. of Horatio & Sally), b. Weymouth, d. 14 Apr. 1889, Rockland, spinal chlorosis, bur. Hanover <Mass.VR 401:392>

CHILD OF Robert BASS^{7} & Lydia LOUD:

Alden BASS^{8}, b. Hanover, d. 18 Jan. 1893, ae 56y18d, Bridgewater, bur. Abington, chronic diarrhea shoecutter <Mass.VR 437:583>

CHILD OF Alden BASS^{8} & Phelinda R. GREY:

Edwin Alden BASS^{9}, b. 15 Oct. 1856, Abington <Mass. VR 98:1>

CHILDREN OF Daniel HENSHAW & Elizabeth BASS^{4} (Jos.^{3}): (10)* <Boston Rcd.Com.>

Daniel HENSHAW^{5}, b. 13 Feb. 1724 <24:165>

Joshua HENSHAW^{5}, b. 21 July 1726 <24:176>

Joseph HENSHAW^{5}, b. 20 Dec. 1727 <24:181>

Mary HENSHAW^{5}, b. 3 Feb. 1728 <24:187>

Benjamin HENSHAW^{5}, b. 12 Jan. 1729 <24:193>

John HENSHAW^{5}, b. 5 Dec. 1732 <24:208>

Elizabeth HENSHAW^{5}, b. 22 Dec. 1733 <24:212>

William HENSHAW^{5}, b. 20 Oct. 1735 <24:222>

Elizabeth HENSHAW^{5}, b. 27 Sept. 1737 <24:229>

Mary Belcher HENSHAW^{5}, b. 20 June 1739 <24:237>

Elizabeth BRECK, (dau. of Edward), b. 30 Apr. 1700 <Dorchester Rcd.com.21:44>;d. 21 June 1751 <Dorchester Rcd.Com.21:249>

CHILDREN OF Joseph BASS^{4} (Jos.^{3}) & 1st Elizabeth BRECK: (11) <Boston Rcd.Com.>

Elizabeth BASS^{5}, b. 15 Nov. 1719 <21:67>

Elizabeth BASS^{5}, b. 5 May 1721 <21:69>

Joseph BASS^{5}, b. 28 Sept. 1723, Dorchester <21:72>

Edward BASS^{5}, b. 23 Nov. 1726 <21:77>

Mary BASS^{5}, b. 10 Sept. 1728 <21:79>, d. 19 Aug. 1751 (wf of Joseph Williams) <21:249>

William BASS^{5}, b. 12 Nov. 1729 <21:80>, d. 24 Jan. 1729/30 <21:134>

William BASS^{5}, b. 8 Jan. 1730/1 <21:82>, d. 29 Sept. 1752 <21:250>

Susanna BASS^{5}, b. 11 Feb. 1732/3 <21:85>, d. 15 Dec. 1752 <21:250>

Benjamin BASS^{5}, b. 22 Nov. 1734 <21:87>

John BASS^{5}, b. 29 Sept. 1738 <21:92>

Hannah BASS^{5}, b. 9 May 1741 <21:97>

Hannah GLOVER, d. 3 Nov. 1766, (2nd wf of Joseph Bass^{4})<Boston Rcd.Com.21:258>

CHILD OF Benjamin BASS^{5} & Mercy TOLMAN:

Mercy BASS^{6}, b. c1766, d. 9 June 1794, ae 28, (wf of Heman Holmes) <MD 7:90>

Lydia SEARL, (dau. of Jabez?), b. 12 Feb. 1723*?, Dorchester; d. Dec. 1788*?

CHILDREN OF Joseph BASS^{5} (Jos.^{4}) & Lydia SEARL: (7) <Dorchester Rcd.Com.>

Sarah BASS^{6}, b. 14 Aug. 1748, d. 27 Sept. 1750 <21:144,248>

Alden BASS^{6}, b. 12 July 1750 <21:145>

Sarah BASS^{6}, b. 12 Nov. 1751 <21:147>

Elizabeth BASS^{6}, b. 8 May 1753 <21:150>; d. 14 May 1843, Minot ME <MD 8:84>

William BASS^{6}, b. 22 Nov. 1755 <21:153>

Lydia BASS^{6}, b. 11 Oct. 1757 <21:156>

Edward BASS^{6}, b. 26 Feb. 1760 <21:159>

Jonathan SCOTT,(son of John) b. 12 Oct. 1744, Lunenburg MA, d. 15 Oct. 1819, Minot ME<MD 8:81,80>

CHILDREN OF Jonathan SCOTT & Elizabeth BASS^{6}: (7) <Yarmouth N.S.- MD 8:82>

Joseph SCOTT^{7}, b. 5 June 1785; d. 8 Apr. 1800, Minot ME <MD 8:83>

Elizabeth SCOTT^{7}, b. 29 Dec. 1786; d. 18 Aug. 1869 <MD 8:84>

Lucy SCOTT^{7}, b. 10 Mar. 1788; d. 23 Oct. 1793 <MD 8:83>

Benjamin SCOTT^{7}, b. 10 Sept. 1789; d. 1870, Mechanic Falls ME <MD 8:84>

George SCOTT^{7}, b. 21 Aug. 1791; d. 1825 "lost at sea" <MD 8:84>

Mary SCOTT^{7}, b. 6 Mar. 1793; d. 11 June 1827, Temple ME (wf of John Scales)

Sylvanus SCOTT^{7}, b. 24 Oct. 1795, Minot; d. 8 Feb. 1807 "in ye flames of his father's house" <MD 8:83>

Hannah BUTLER, (dau. of Peter & Mary), b. 5 July 1707 <Boston Rcd.com.24:46>;d. 2 Nov. 1796, bur. "Phillips Tomb, Granary Bur. Ground"

CHILDREN OF Moses BASS^{4} (Jos.^{3}) & Hannah BUTLER: (7)

Moses Belcher BASS^{5}, b.27 Aug. 1731 <Boston Rcd.com.24:201>; d.y.

Henry BASS^{5}, bpt. 19 Aug. 1733; d.y.

Moses Belcher BASS^{5}, bpt. 20 July 1735; d. 31 Jan. 1817

Hannah BASS^{5}, bpt. 2 July 1738

Henry BASS^{5}, bpt. 9 Mar. 1740; d. 5 June 1813

Joseph BASS^{5}, b. 1 Feb. 1743

Gillam BASS^{5}, bpt. 13 Apr. 1746, Boston

Rebecca WIMBLE, (dau. of Capt. Wm. & Elizabeth), b. 24 Feb. 1750, Boston; d. 2 May 1801, bur. "Grandfather Phillip's Tomb, Granary Bur. Ground"

CHILDREN OF Gillam BASS^{5} & Rebecca WIMBLE: (8) <Family Rcds. of Gillam Bass>

Faith BASS^{6}, b. 23 Oct. 1769, Boston <Northboro VR:18>

Rebecca BASS^{6}, b. 27 Sept. 1771, Boston <Northboro VR:18>

Hannah BASS^{6}, b. 26 Aug. 1772 <Westboro VR:14>

Gillam BASS^{6}, b. 1 May 1775 <Northboro VR:18>

Elizabeth BASS^{6}, b. 9 June 1777, d. 11 Aug. 1778 <Northboro VR:18,128>

Mary BASS^{6}, b. 21 May 1779 <Northboro VR:18>

Nancy BASS^{6}, b. 14 Aug. 1781 <Northboro VR:18>

William Wimble BASS^{6}, b. 10 May 1787 <Northboro VR:18>

Elizabeth WIMBLE, d. July 1770

CHILD OF Moses Belcher BASS^{5} (Moses^{4}) & Elizabeth WIMBLE:

Elizabeth Wimble BASS^{6}, b. 25 Dec. 1769 <Boston Rcd.com.24:318>

CHILDREN OF Moses Belcher BASS^{5} & 2nd Margaret SPRAGUE, (dau of John & Margaret of Hingham): (7)

Margaret BASS^{6}, b. 11 Feb. 1774, d. 24 Sept. 1774

Moses BASS^{6}, b. 18 Feb. 1775, d. 22 Sept. 1776

Elijah BASS^{6}, b. 3 Aug. 1776, d. 2 Oct. 1778

Joseph BASS^{6}, b. 26 Aug. 1778, d. 22 Dec. 1803

Margaret BASS^{6}, b. 19 Feb. 1780, d. 15 Aug. 1781

Margaret BASS^{6}, b. 15 Feb. 1782

Mary Butler BASS^{6}, b. 4 Jan. 1784

Christopher WEBB, (son of Christopher), b. 25 Mar. 1663* <Billerica VR>; d. Mar. 1689/90,smallpox <Braintree VR:658>

CHILDREN OF Christopher WEBB & Mary BASS^{3}: (3) <Braintree VR>

Hannah WEBB^{4}, 16 Dec. 1686* <VR:664>; d. 1725*

Sarah WEBB^{4}, b. 10 "10th mth" 1688* <VR:665>

Christopher WEBB^{4}, b. 19 Aug. 1690 <VR:666>

William COPELAND, (son of Laurence & Lydia), b. 15 Nov. 1656*, d. 30 Oct. 1716 <Braintree VR:636,724>

CHILDREN OF William COPELAND & Mary BASS^{3}: (9) <Braintree VR>

William COPELAND^{4}, b. 7 Mar. 1694/5*, d. 29 June 1727* <VR:672,728>

Ephraim COPELAND^{4}, b. 1 Feb. 1697* <VR:676>

Ebenezer COPELAND^{4}, b. 16 Feb. 1698* <VR:676>

Jonathan COPELAND^{4}, b. 31 Aug. 1701 <VR:680>; d. 1790

David COPELAND^{4}, b. 15 Apr. 1704* <VR:684>

Joseph COPELAND^{4}, b. 18 May 1706*<VR:685>; d. 26 Jan. 1793 <PN&Q 5:40>

Benjamin COPELAND^{4}, b. 5 Oct. 1708* <VR:688>; d. 2 or 20 Oct. 1790*, Norton

Moses COPELAND^{4}, b. 28 May 1710* <VR:689>

Mary COPELAND^{4}, b. 28 May 1713* <VR:696>

Anne WHITE, b. 6 Mar. 1696*?, Boston?

CHILDREN OF Christopher WEBB^{4} (Mary Bass^{3}) & Anne WHITE: (14)

Samuel WEBB^{5}, b. 5 Oct. 1716 <Boston Rcd.Com.24:118>; d. 27 Aug. 1773

Mary WEBB^{5}, b. 17 Aug. 1718, Braintree, d. 1719 <Giles Mem.:511>

Christopher WEBB^{5}, b. 5 Oct. 1720, d.y. <Braintree VR:708>

Christopher WEBB^{5}, b. 4 Dec. 1721 <Braintree VR:709>; d. late in 1761

Joseph WEBB^{5}, b. 29 Mar. 1724 <Braintree VR:753>

Ann WEBB^{5}, b. 2 Aug. 1726 <Braintree VR:758>

Mary WEBB^{5}, b. 22 Dec. 1727 <Braintree VR:760>

Nathaniel WEBB^{5}, bpt. 6 Apr. 1729 <Braintree 1st ChR:72>; d. 20 July 1772

Sarah WEBB^{5}, b. 14 July 1730, d. 1731 <Braintree VR:764>

Ebenezer WEBB^{5}, b. 17 Jan. 1731, d. 1731 <Braintree VR:766>

Thomas WEBB^{5}, bpt. 15 Oct. 1732 <Braintree 1st ChR:75>

Ebenezer WEBB^{5}, bpt. 23 Dec. 1733 <Braintree 1st ChR:76>

John WEBB^{5}, bpt. 30 Mar. 1734/5 <Braintree 1st ChR>

Lydia WEBB^{5}, b. 13 Feb. 1736/7 <Braintree VR:774>

Samuel ARNOLD, (son of Ephraim & Mary), b. 7 Jan. ( ) <Braintree VR:665>**<79>**; d. "about" 9 Feb. 1743* <Thayer Mem.1:49> (bur. 23 Mar. 1743*)

CHILDREN OF Samuel ARNOLD & Sarah WEBB^{4} (Mary Bass^{3}):(11)* <Braintree VR>

Samuel ARNOLD^{5}, b. 16 May 1713 <VR:696,710>

Joseph ARNOLD^{5}, b. 16 May 1713 (twin) <VR:696,710>

Mary ARNOLD^{5}, b. 21 or 22 Dec. 1714 <VR:698,710>

Sarah ARNOLD^{5}, b. 14 Sept. 1716 <VR:710>

Joseph ARNOLD^{5}, b. 11 Oct. 1718 <VR:710>

John ARNOLD^{5}, b. 4 Oct. 1720 <VR:710>

Moses ARNOLD^{5}, b. 11 June 1722 <VR:712>

Abigail ARNOLD^{5}, b. 12 Feb. 1724/5 <VR:755>

Nathaniel ARNOLD^{5}, b. 18 Oct. 1726 <VR:758>

Deborah ARNOLD^{5}, b. 14 Nov. 1729 <VR:763>

David ARNOLD^{5}, b. 23 July 1732<VR:767>; d. Dec. 1810*<Norton VR:355>

Phebe PRATT, b. c1735*; d. 27 Aug. 1818* <Norton VR:356>

CHILDREN OF David ARNOLD^{5} & Phebe PRATT: (9) <Norton VR>
David ARNOLD^{6}, b. 23 Dec. 1757
Phebe ARNOLD^{6}, b. 1 Apr. 1760
John ARNOLD^{6}, b. 23 May 1763
Samuel ARNOLD^{6}, b. 13 Jan. 1766
Asa ARNOLD^{6}, b. 3 Feb. 1768
Salmon ARNOLD^{6}, bpt. 28 July 1771
William ARNOLD^{6}, bpt. 4 Sept. 1774
Lemuel ARNOLD^{6}, bpt. 10 Oct. 1779
Sarah ARNOLD^{6}, <mentioned last in father's will, dated 28 Mar. 1803 - Bristol Co.Probate 46:140>
CHILDREN OF Joseph ARNOLD^{5} (Sarah Webb^{4}) & Mary ( ): (5)*
Sherebiah ARNOLD^{6}, b. ( )
Benjamin ARNOLD^{6}, b. ( )
Moses ARNOLD^{6}, b. c1751
Joseph ARNOLD^{6}, b. 23 Apr. 1754 <Braintree VR:827>
Mary ARNOLD^{6}, b. ( )

MICRO #15 of 16

CHILDREN OF Moses ARNOLD^{6} & Sarah VINTON: (4)* <Braintree VR:845>
John Vinton ARNOLD^{7}, b. 25 Oct. 1774
Moses ARNOLD^{7}, b. 16 Nov. 1777
Samuel ARNOLD^{7}, b. 2 Oct. 1780
Ralph ARNOLD^{7}, b. 29 Apr. 1783
"Charles D. HAYDEN, married, d. 21 Nov. 1876, Braintree, ae 71; b. Braintree, son of Robert & Huldah (Cleverly)" <Mass.VR 284:212>
"Rebecca S. HAYDEN, widow, d. 30 Jan. 1893, Walpole, ae 85y8m; b. Braintree, dau. of Samuel V. & Rebecca M. (Soper) Arnold" <Mass.VR 437:563>
"Elizabeth Jane THORNDIKE, widow of Samuel, d. 8 Sept. 1902, Braintree,ae 61y5m1d,bur. Cambridge; b. Stoughton, dau. of Charles L. & Rebecca(Thayer)Hayden" <Mass.VR 530:11>
"Samuel W. THORNDIKE, married, d. 20 May 1896, Braintree, ae 60y2m27d; b. Boston, son of James P. & Martha E. (Hodgdon)" <Mass.VR 464:482>
"Samuel V. ARNOLD, married, d. 2 Oct. 1858, Braintree, ae 78, paralysis, farmer; b. Braintree, son of Moses & Sarah" <Mass.VR 121:182>
"Rebecca ARNOLD, widow, d. 18 Aug. 1869, Braintree,ae 90; b. Braintree, dau. of Edmond & Rebecca" <Mass.VR 221:234>
Sarah ALLEN, d. 20 Mar. 1801*, ae 96
CHILDREN OF Benjamin COPELAND^{4} (Mary Bass^{3}) & Sarah ALLEN: (10)*<3-10, Norton VR>**<80>**
Benjamin COPELAND^{5}, b. 7 June 1736 <Braintree VR:773>; d. 13 May 1749
Sarah COPELAND^{5}, b. 10 Apr. 1738 <Braintree VR:777>
Susanna COPELAND^{5}, b. 1 Apr. 1740
Elizabeth COPELAND^{5}, b. 3 Apr. 1742
Eunice COPELAND^{5}, b. 17 Nov. 1743
Moses COPELAND^{5}, b. 16 Nov. 1745
William COPELAND^{5}, b. 20 Mar. 1747/8
Samuel COPELAND^{5}, b. 30 May 1750
Asa COPELAND^{5}, b. 8 May 1752
Lydia COPELAND^{5}, b. 16 Oct. 1755
"Joseph COPELAND, widower, d. 15 Feb. 1883, Lyons, Iowa, ae 52y8m23d, consumption; b. Norton, son of Thomas & Eliza" <Mass.VR 346:139>
Bettie SNELL, b. 1705* <Mitchell:245>; d. 5 Sept. 1775, Sharon
CHILDREN OF Jonathan COPELAND^{4} (Mary Bass^{3}) & Bettie SNELL: (11) <Bridgewater VR 2:127>

Abigail COPELAND^{5}, b. 9 Dec. 1724, d. 27 Mar. 1809 <Bridgewater VR 1:84,2:496>

Bettie COPELAND^{5}, b. 17 Apr. 1726; d. 14 June 1750

Jonathan COPELAND^{5}, b. 9 Aug. 1728

Mary COPELAND^{5}, b. 26 Mar. 1731

Joseph COPELAND^{5}, b. 28 Apr. 1734

Hannah COPELAND^{5}, b. 13 May 1737

Elijah COPELAND^{5}, b. 3 June 1739; d. 8 Sept. 1817*, Easton*

Daniel COPELAND^{5}, b. 13 Sept. 1741

Sarah COPELAND^{5}, b. 13 Feb. 1744/5

Ebenezer COPELAND^{5}, b. 27 July 1746

Bettie COPELAND^{5}, b. 23 Sept. 1750

George HOWARD, b. 30 Jan. 1722, d. 3 Apr. 1815 <Bridgewater VR 1:138,2:496>

CHILDREN OF George HOWARD/HAWARD & Abigail COPELAND^{5}: (12) <Bridgewater VR>

Hannah HOWARD^{6}, b. 26 July 1746 <VR 1:133>; d. betw. 1771-1775

Abigail HOWARD^{6}, b. 26 Sept. 1748 <VR 1:135>

Betty HOWARD^{6}, b. 9 May 1751 <VR 1:136>

George HOWARD^{6}, b. 8 Sept. 1753 <VR 1:138>

Oliver HOWARD^{6}, b. 21 Dec. 1755 <VR 1:140>

Job HOWARD^{6}, b. 17 May 1758 <VR 1:138>

Caleb HOWARD^{6}, b. 15 Dec. 1760 <VR 1:136>

Rachel HOWARD^{6}, b. 20 Apr. 1763 <VR 1:140>

Patty HOWARD^{6}, b. 2 Aug. 1765 <VR 1:140>

Asaph HOWARD^{6}, b. 19 Mar. 1768 <VR 1:136>

Nehemiah HOWARD^{6}, b. 20 Aug. 1770 <VR 1:140>

Polly Brett HOWARD^{6}, b. ( )

Misc. - Howard

Daniel W. GREENE, d. 27 Nov. 1879, Newburyport, ae 43y6m27d; b. Lancaster, son of Williams & Sarah M. <Mass.VR 310:256>

Sarah A. GREENE, widow, d. 21 Apr. 1858, Lancaster, ae 48; b. Bridgewater, dau. of George & Sarah Howard <Mass.VR 122:110>

George HOWARD, married, farmer, d. 7 Mar. 1860, Lancaster, ae 74; b. Bridgewater, son of George & Parnel (Ames) <Mass.VR 140:200>

Sarah Worthen GREEN, b. 25 May 1861, Newburyport, dau. of D.W. & Mary Green (father b. Clinton, mother b. P.E.I.) <Mass.VR 141:306>

Persis Lucinda HOWARD, b. 18 Feb. 1848, dau. of Henry A. & Sally F. (Wood) <Lancaster VR:262>

Elizabeth HOUGHTON, d. 2 June 1837, ae 27 <Lancaster VR:183>

CHILD OF George W. HOWARD & 1st Elizabeth HOUGHTON:

Mary Frances HOWARD, b. 1 Apr. 1837 <Lancaster VR:209>

CHILD OF George W. HOWARD & 2nd Martha F. RUGG:

John Henry HOWARD, b. 18 Dec. 1847, d. 5 Aug. 1849 <Lancaster VR:262,397>

CHILDREN OF Sydney HOWARD & Sally ( ): (7) <Lancaster VR:209>

Caleb Alden HOWARD, b. 26 Dec. 1817

Parney HOWARD, b. 8 Nov. 1819; d. 18 Mar. 1847 <VR:267>

Sarah Ann HOWARD, b. 3 Jan. 1824

George Frederic HOWARD, b. 9 Oct. 1821

Sidney Thomas HOWARD, b. 22 Apr. 1827

Susan Sawyer HOWARD, b. 9 Feb. 1830

Francina HOWARD, b. 19 May 1832 <VR:210>

Moses HOWARD/HAYWARD, d. 26 Mar. 1829, ae 85, "a shaker" <Lancaster VR:197>

CHILDREN OF Levi HOWARD & Mary ( ): (3) <Lancaster VR>

Amasa HOWARD, b. 28 Sept. 1828, d. 9 July 1830 <VR:209,183>

Sarah Elizabeth HOWARD, b. 24 Mar. 1831 <VR:209>

Sarah MANLEY, d. 7 Sept. 1830, ae 39 <VR:183>

CHILD OF George HOWARD & Sarah MANLEY:

Daniel Manley HOWARD, b. 25 Mar. 1829 <Lancaster VR:209>

Sarah MANLEY, widow, d. 11 Sept. 1833, "at the house of George Howard" <Lancaster VR:186>

CHILD OF George HOWARD & Elizabeth BUSS:

Louisa M. HOWARD, b. 7 Aug. 1834 <Lancaster VR:209>

* * * * *

Daniel LOTHROP, b. 10 Dec. 1745, W. Bridgewater; d. 1837, Wilton ME

CHILDREN OF Daniel LOTHROP & 1st Hannah HOWARD^{6} (Abigail Copeland^{5}): (4)

George LOTHROP^{7}, b. 13 ( ) 1765 <Bridgewater VR 1:202>; d. 1839

Daniel LOTHROP^{7}, b. 28 Mar. 1767 <Bridgewater VR 1:202>

Thomas LOTHROP^{7}, b. 1768

Hannah LOTHROP^{7}, b. 1771

CHILDREN OF Daniel LOTHROP & 2nd Lydia WILLIS (dau. of Samuel): (2)

Samuel LOTHROP, b. 1777

Sullivan LOTHROP, bpt. 18 Oct. 1778

CHILD OF Daniel LOTHROP & 3rd Mary TURNER (dau. of George):

Alson LOTHROP, b. ( )

CHILDREN OF Elijah COPELAND^{5} (Jonathan^{4}) & Rhoda SNELL: (3)<Bridgewater VR 3:344>

Elijah COPELAND^{6}, b. 7 Aug. 1766

Josiah COPELAND^{6}, b. 13 Oct. 1768

Luther COPELAND^{6}, b. 17 Sept. 1770

Elizabeth TOLMAN, (dau. of Paul & Eliz.), b. 5 Nov. 1713 <Scituate VR 1:363>; d. 13 Nov. 1798 <PN&Q 5:40>

CHILDREN OF Joseph COPELAND^{4} (Mary Bass^{3}) & Elizabeth TOLMAN: (14) <PN&Q 5:40>

Elizabeth COPELAND^{5}, b. 6 May 1736, d. 26 Aug. 1828

Joseph COPELAND^{5}, b. (or bpt.?) 6 Aug. 1737*, d. "an infant"

Ruth COPELAND^{5}, b. 16 Sept. 1738, d. 27 May 1831**<81>**

Mary COPELAND^{5}, b. 3 Nov. 1740, d. 27 Jan. 1829

Hannah COPELAND^{5}, b. 24 Feb. 1743, d. 16 Dec. 1836

Rhoda COPELAND^{5}, b. 22 Apr. 1745, d. 3 Dec. 1839

Lydia COPELAND^{5}, b. 20 July 1747, d. 4 Oct. 1841

Joseph COPELAND^{5}, b. 22 Aug. 1749, d. Aug. 1841

William COPELAND^{5}, b. 21 Sept. 1751, d. 2 July 1839

Ebenezer COPELAND^{5}, b. 20 Oct. 1753, d. 3 Dec. 1810

Rebecca COPELAND^{5}, b. 30 Aug. 1755, d. 27 Dec. 1840

Sarah COPELAND^{5}, b. 2 Jan. 1758, d. 16 Oct. 1842

Elisha COPELAND^{5}, b. 20 Dec. 1759, d. 20 Oct. 1831

Huldah COPELAND^{5}, b. Nov. 1761, d. 12 Feb. 1763

Micah FORD^{6} (*Michael^{5}, James^{4}, Abigail Snow^{3}, Abigail Warren^{2}), b. 20 Feb. 1747* <Marshfield VR>

CHILDREN OF Micah FORD^{6} & Rhoda COPELAND^{5}: (6)* <Scituate VR>

Rhoda FORD^{6}, b. 7 Feb. 1776

Sarah FORD^{6}, b. 16 Nov. 1777

James FORD^{6}, b. 3 May 1780

Lucy FORD^{6}, b. 26 Oct. 1782

Michael FORD^{6}, b. 22 Jan. 1784

Lydia FORD^{6}, b. 14 Apr. 1786

William BRIGGS, (*son of James & Hannah), b. 23 July 1731*<Scituate VR 1:49>; d. 5 Dec. 1815* <Scituate VR 2:359>

CHILDREN OF William BRIGGS & Elizabeth COPELAND^{5} (Jos.^{4}): (10)*<Scituate VR>

Rachel BRIGGS^{6}, b. 19 Aug. 1755 <VR 1:48>

Ruth BRIGGS^{6}, b. 13 Aug. 1757 <VR 1:48>

William BRIGGS^{6}, b. 15 Mar. 1780 <VR 1:49>

Elijah BRIGGS^{6}, b. 17 July 1762 <VR 1:45>

Lemuel BRIGGS^{6}, b. 25 Mar. 1765 <VR 1:47>

Elizabeth BRIGGS^{6}, b. 15 July 1767 <VR 1:45>

John BRIGGS^{6}, b. 24 Feb. 1770 <VR 1:47>

Charles BRIGGS^{6}, b. 8 Feb. 1773 <VR 1:44>

Cornelius BRIGGS^{6}, b. 2 Aug. 1776 <VR 1:44>

Huldah BRIGGS^{6}, b. 3 Sept. 1780 <VR 1:46>

Mary THAYER, (*dau. of Richard & Rebecca (Micall)), b. Feb. 1689/90* <Braintree VR>

CHILDREN OF William COPELAND^{4} (Mary Bass^{3}) & Mary THAYER*: (7)*<Braintree VR>

Rebecca COPELAND^{5}, b. 16 Mar. 1718/9 <VR:705>

Lydia COPELAND^{5}, b. 25 Oct. 1720 <VR:709>

William COPELAND^{5}, b. 19 Aug. 1722, d. 29 June 1727 <VR:711,728>

James COPELAND^{5}, b. 19 Mar. 1724 <VR:754>

Mary COPELAND^{5}, b. 31 May 1726 <VR:757>

Anna COPELAND^{5}, b. 4 Aug. 1728 <VR:761>

William COPELAND^{5}?, b. Dec. 1730 <Thayer Mem.>

Peter WEBB^{3} (Christopher$^{2-1}$),b. 1 Dec. 1657, Braintree, d. 12 Feb. 1717,Salem g.s.<Giles Mem:501>

CHILDREN OF Peter WEBB^{3} & 1st Ruth BASS^{3}: (10) <Braintree VR>

Ruth WEBB^{4}, b. 7 May 1684 <VR:663>

Peter WEBB^{4}, b. 25 Dec. 1685 <VR:662>

David WEBB^{4}, b. 27 Nov. 1687 <VR:664>

Christopher WEBB^{4}, b. 30 Dec. 1689 <VR:663>

Hannah WEBB^{4}, b. 14 May 1692, d. 17 May 1693 <VR:663,660>

John WEBB^{4}, b. 10 Mar. 1693 <VR:663>

Hannah WEBB^{4}, b. 8 Sept. 1694 <VR:663>

Joseph WEBB^{4}, b. 17 June 1696 <VR:693>

Priscilla WEBB^{4}, b. 1 Sept. 1697 <VR:694>**<82>**

Mary WEBB^{4}, b. 5 Oct. 1698 <VR:694>

Amy HAYDEN^{3} (Jonathan^{2}, John^{1}), b. 16 Sept. 1672, Braintree; d. 8 Nov. 1732, Boston <Vinton Mem.: 324; Giles Mem.:501-2>

CHILDREN OF Peter WEBB^{3} & 2nd Amy HAYDEN: (5) <Braintree VR>

Amy WEBB, b. 25 Dec. 1704 <VR:684>; d. 24 Feb. 1717

Richard WEBB, b. 3 May 1707 <VR:686>

Samuel WEBB, b. 24 Mar. 1709 <VR:688>

Jonathan WEBB, b. 13 Oct. 1710, d. 12 Oct. 1710/1 <VR:690,694>

Sarah WEBB, b. 14 Aug. 1712 <VR:692>; d. 2 Jan. 1714

Mary ADAMS^{3} (Jos.^{2}, Henry^{1}), b. 25 Feb. 1667*, d. 9 Mar. 1706* <Braintree VR:646,695>

CHILDREN OF Samuel BASS^{3} & 1st Mary ADAMS: (5)*<Thayer Mem.1:59>**<83>**

Jonathan BASS^{4}, bpt. 3 Oct. 1697, d. aft. 22 Feb. 1749* (will)

Abigail BASS^{4}, bpt. 3 Oct. 1697

Mary BASS^{4}, bpt. 14 Aug. 1698, Braintree

Samuel BASS^{4}, b. 26 July 1700 <Braintree VR:679>; d. 3 Apr. 1768

Bethiah BASS^{4}, b. 2 Feb. 1704 <Braintree VR:683>

CHILD OF Samuel BASS^{3} & 2nd Bethia NIGHTINGALE?*:

Bathsheba BASS^{4}, bpt. 29 Mar. 1711 <Thayer Mem.1:59,60>

Susanna BYRAM, (dau. of Nicholas & Mary), b. 15 Jan. 1694/5, Bridgewater <MD 2:145> (wf of Jonathan Bass^{4})

"Rhoda V. KEEN, married, d. 29 July 1877, E. Bridgewater, ae 69y13d,; b. W. Bridgewater, dau. of Eleazer & Lucy Churchill" <Mass.VR 293:308>

"Samuel KEEN, widower, d. 21 Nov. 1884, E. Bridgewater, ae 79y3m22d; b. E.Bridgewater, son of Samuel & Margaret O. (Clift)" <Mass.VR 356:302>

"Samuel KEEN, married, d. 14 Mar. 1850, E. Bridgewater, ae 71; b. Pembroke" <Mass.VR 49:152>

"Margaret O. KEEN, widow, d. 27 Nov. 1874, E. Bridgewater, ae 90y2m; b. E.Bridgewater, dau. of Anthony W. & Bethia (Orr) Clift" <Mass.VR 266:299>

William BOWDITCH, (*son of Jonathan & Temperance), b. 20 Jan. 1683* <Braintree VR:662>; d. pre 10 May 1748* (adm.) <Suffolk Co.Prob.#8986, 41:124>

CHILDREN OF William BOWDITCH & Mary BASS^{4} (Sam.^{3}): (9) <Braintree VR>

Mary BOWDITCH^{5}, b. 2 Apr. 1720 <VR:707>

Bethiah BOWDITCH^{5}, b. 25 Mar. 1722 <VR:710>

Ruth BOWDITCH^{5}, b. 7 Mar. 1724 <VR:753>

William BOWDITCH^{5}, b. 19 Sept. 1726 <VR:758>; d. pre 27 Nov. 1793 <Norfolk Co.Probate #2245>**<85>**

Samuel BOWDITCH^{5}, b. 25 Feb. 1728/9 <VR:763>

Abigail BOWDITCH^{5}, b. 8 June 1731 <VR:765>

Susanna BOWDITCH^{5}, b. 19 May 1733 <VR:768>

Bathsheba BOWDITCH^{5}, b. 7 Mar. 1736/7 <VR:775>

Jonathan BOWDITCH^{5} b. 13 Mar. 1738 <VR:779>

CHILD OF Ephraim GROVES & Bathsheba BOWDITCH^{5}:

Deborah GROVES^{6}, d. 1 Dec. 1843, Wrentham, ae 80 (wf of Elias Ware)**<84>**

Elias WARE, d. 29 June 1841, Wrentham, ae 87 **<84>**

CHILD OF Galen BOWDITCH^{6} (Jonathan^{5}) & Sadie ( ):

Grenville BOWDITCH^{7}, b. Newton Upper Falls, d. 28 Jan. 1884, Ashland, ae 73y3m22d, bur. South Framingham, married, mechanic <Mass.VR 356:41>

Susanna ALLEN, (*dau. of Benjamin & Deborah), b.? 12 Apr.1738* <Braintree VR:777>**<85>**

Susanna BOWDITCH^{6} (Wm.^{5}), b. c1760, d. 23 Mar. 1806, ae 46 <Weymouth VR 2:289>

Ebenezer HUNT, d. 3 Nov. 1832 <Weymouth VR 2:287>

CHILDREN OF Ebenezer HUNT & 1st Susanna BOWDITCH^{6}: (4)

Ebenezer HUNT^{7}, b. 17 July 1783; d. 27 Jan. 1823

William HUNT^{7}, b. 7 July 1786; d. 24 Sept. 1722

Susanna HUNT^{7}, b. ( ); d. 1862

Elias HUNT^{7}, bpt. 5 Oct. 1800; "conductor of King's Chapel Choir"

CHILD OF Ebenezer HUNT & 2nd Tirzah BATES:

Albert HUNT, b. 6 May 1809; d. 1 July 1810

CHILD OF Elias HUNT^{7} & Eliza SOPER:

Edmund Soper HUNT^{8}, b. 1826, d. Sept. 1909, ae 83

Hannah WHITE^{4} (Sam.^{3}, Tho.$^{2-1}$), b. 11 Dec. 1704*, Braintree; d. 6 June 1743*

CHILDREN OF Samuel BASS^{4} (Sam.^{3}) & Hannah WHITE^{4}*: (3)

Abigail BASS^{5}, b. 31 Jan. 1727/8*

Col. Jonathan BASS^{5}, b. 14 Nov. 1733*; d. 12 May 1790, Randolph <Thayer Mem.1:60>

Hannah BASS^{5}, b. ( )

CHILD OF Jonathan WILD & Hannah BASS^{5}:

John WILD^{6}, b. 3 June 1751* <Braintree VR:801>; d. 31 Aug. 1831, bur.Randolph Central Cemetery

Jemima SPEAR, d. 8 Jan. 1839*, ae 89, bur. Randolph Central Cem., Randolph

CHILDREN OF John WILD^{6} & Jemima SPEAR: (2 of 7)**<86>**

Polly/Mary WILD^{7}, b. 14 Jan. 1783*; d. 9 Apr. 1859, Boston, ae 77y2m <Mass.VR 131:21>

Betsy WILD^{7}, b. 1778*, d. 11 Aug. 1806*, ae 28

Daniel CURTIS, d. 12 Mar. 1861, ae 67y2m4d <N. Stoughton g.s.>

Zilpha CURTIS, d. 1 Sept. 1889, ae 86y11m19d <N. Stoughton g.s.>

Thomas CODMAN, b. 15 Sept. 1764, Boston <Family Records>; d. 23 June 1822, apoplexy <Boston City Rcds, Deaths & Interrments>

CHILD OF Thomas CODMAN & Polly/Mary WILD^{7} (John^{6}):

Harriet M. CODMAN^{8}, d. 1 Mar. 1901, Boston, ae 82y1m3d, widow of Tho. E. Lillie <Mass.VR 519:134>

CHILDREN OF Col. Jonathan BASS^{5} (Sam.^{4}) & Susanna BELCHER: (2)

Samuel BASS^{6}, b. 15 May 1757 <Braintree VR:810>

Sarah BASS^{6}*, b. 24 Jan. 1759*; d. 2 June 1833*

<u>MICRO #16 Of 16</u>

Ephraim THAYER, b. 17 Jan. 1669* <Braintree VR:647>; d. betw. 10 Apr. 1755 (will) - 15 July 1757 (probate) <MD 18:113> ("88th yr"*)

CHILDREN OF Ephraim THAYER & Sarah BASS^{3}: (4 of 14)**<87>**

Sarah THAYER^{4}, d. 12 June 1753* <Braintree VR:736* ("widow Sarah Dorman, eldest child of Mr. Ephraim Thayer")

Ruth THAYER^{4}, b. 1 Apr. 1704* <Braintree VR:684*>

Esther THAYER^{4}, b. 24 July 1705, Braintree; d. 13 Dec.1800, Braintree <Thayer Gen.(1874):590,625>

Naphtali THAYER^{4}, d. 1760* (inv.- 10 Nov. 1760) <Suffolk Co.Probate 57:341>

Moses FRENCH, b. 16 Feb. 1700 <Braintree VR:678>; d. 19 Sept. 1768, Braintree <Thayer Gen.:625>

CHILDREN OF Moses FRENCH & Esther THAYER^{4}: (4 of 5)* <Braintree VR>**<88>**

Moses FRENCH^{5}, b. 16 Sept. 1731 <VR:766>

Elisha FRENCH^{5}, b. 12 Jan. 1733/4 <VR:769>

Esther FRENCH^{5}, b. 21 Dec. 1735 <VR:772>

Jonathan FRENCH^{5}, b. 19 Jan. 1739 <VR:780>

CHILD OF Moses FRENCH^{5} & Elizabeth HOBART* (dau of Caleb & Eliz. (Hollis)):

Asa FRENCH^{6}, b. ( )

Mehitable HOLLIS, (*dau of Thomas & Lydia), b. 12 Aug. 1779*<Braintree VR:857>

CHILD OF Asa FRENCH^{6} & Mehitable HOLLIS:

Jonathan FRENCH^{7}, b. Braintree; d. 4 Feb. 1882, Braintree

Sarah Brackett HAYWARD, d. 15 Mar. 1890, Braintree (widow of Jonathan French^{7})

Bathsheba BASS^{4} (Sam.^{3}, Ruth Alden^{2}), d. betw. 29 Oct. 1761*-5 May 1768*

CHILDREN OF Naphtali THAYER^{4} (Sarah Bass^{3}) & Bathsheba BASS^{4}: (5)

Bathsheba THAYER^{5}, b. 14 Apr. 1733*; d. aft. 5 May 1774 <Suffolk Co.Deeds 125:268>

Bethiah THAYER^{5}, b. 4 Nov. 1734*

Naphtali THAYER^{5}*, b. 30 July 1739*

Hannah THAYER^{5}*, b. ( )

Susanna THAYER^{5}*, b. 20 May 1743*

Nathan BEALS, (son of Sam.); b. 9 Oct. 1727*, Bridgewater (see p.63); d. aft. 5 May 1774<Suffolk Co.Deeds 125:268>

CHILDREN OF Nathan BEALS & Bathsheba THAYER^{5}: (8)*

Mary BEALS^{6}, b. 15 Jan. 1750 <Bridgewater VR:47>

Nathan BEALS^{6}, b. 30 Nov. 1752 <Bridgewater VR:47>

Nehemiah BEALS^{6}, b. 22 Jan. 1755 <Bridgewater VR:47>

John BEALS^{6}, b. 15 June 1759 <Bridgewater VR:47>

Enos BEALS^{6}, b. 19 June 1761 <Mendon VR>

David BEALS^{6}, b. 25 Mar. 1763 <Mendon VR>

Asa BEALS^{6}, b. 22 Nov. 1765 <Mendon VR>; d. 30 July 1849 <Medway VR:291>

Bethiah BEALS^{6}, b. 30 July 1770 <Mendon VR>

Samuel BEALS, d. 5 May 1750

CHILDREN OF Samuel BEALS & Mary BASSETT (dau of Elnathan): (9) <Bridgewater VR>

Samuel BEALS, b. 16 Aug. 1726

Nathan BEALS, b. 9 Oct. 1727 (see p.62)

Daniel BEALS, b. 25 Mar. 1729

Jonathan BEALS, b. 10 Dec. 1730

Joseph BEALS, b. 2 July 1733, d. 19 Apr. 1736

Benjamin BEALS, b. 2 July 1733 (twin)

Seth BEALS, b. 23 Aug. 1736, d. 22 Oct. 1736

Mary BEALS, b. 23 Feb. 1742, d. 9 Aug. 1747

Joseph BEALS, b. 11 Apr. 1744, d. 1 Aug. 1747

Olive CHENEY, (dau of Caleb), b.? 14 Apr. 1772*; d. Nov. 1826*, Medway

CHILDREN OF Asa BEALS^{6} (Bathsheba Thayer^{5}) & Olive CHENEY: (17!)*<Cheney Gen.:86-7>

Sabra BEALS^{7}, b. 4 Nov. 1790, Milford; d. 19 Aug. 1798

Betsy BEALS^{7}, b. 29 Nov. 1791

Samuel BEALS^{7}, b. 18 June 1793

Bersheba BEALS^{7}, b. 6 Oct. 1794

Sophia BEALS^{7}, b. 5 Jan. 1796

Nathan BEALS^{7}, b. 29 Apr. 1797; d. 9 Aug. 1798

Hannah BEALS^{7}, b. 6 June 1798

Joshua BEALS^{7}, bpt. 18 Dec. 1800

Olive BEALS^{7}, b. 25 Feb. 1800

Lorana BEALS^{7}, b. 24 May 1801

Lucinda BEALS^{7}, b. 24 May 1801 (twin) <Milford VR>; d. 31 Mar. 1859, Milford, tumor, <Mass.VR 131:127> (widow of Nathan White, below)

Adolphus BEALS^{7}, b. 31 Mar. 1803

Asa BEALS^{7}, b. 19 Sept. 1804

Mary Wheelock BEALS^{7}, b. 3 Jan. 1806

Nathan Thayer BEALS^{7}, b. 12 July 1807

Sabraan BEALS^{7}, b. 3 May 1810

Sally Cheney BEALS^{7}, b. 21 Jan. 1812

Nathan WHITE, b. Franklin MA; d. 16 Apr. 1854, Milford, ae 57, lung fever,painter, son of Nathan <Mass.VR 86:144>

CHILDREN OF Joseph FORD & Priscilla THAYER^{4} (Sarah Bass^{3}): (3) <Braintree VR>

Joseph FORD^{5}, b. 18 Sept. 1740 <VR:782>

James FORD^{5}, b. 13 June 1743 <VR:786>

Nathaniel FORD^{5}, b. 23 June 1746 <VR:791>

* * * * * * * * * * *

FOOTNOTES

<1> p.1, In giving the marriage date she is called Mrs. Ann Dimmock. The death date of Zephaniah Alden is not given. His will was dated 2 Feb. 1796 and proved 6 Feb. 1801 <Stafford Probate #28>.

<2> p.1, Although no sources are given for data on Ezra Alden and his children, at the top of the page is written "Stafford Conn. Rec.".

<3> p.1, Preceeding these entries is written in pencil "3 rec. Stafford" which probably refers to the births of the first three children.

<4> p.1, Birth places are not given, at the top of the page is written "Willington Conn.".

<5> p.1, Sarah Greer, admx. Across the bottom of the page is pencilled, "Sarah Cheesborough^{4}, Priscilla Alden^{3}, David^{2})".

<6> p.1, Across the bottom of the page is written, "John Seabury^{4}, Eliz. Alden^{3}, David^{2} ".

<7> p.1, The accompanying note reads, "he m. Mary Cheseborough".

<8> p.2, The date of the will of her mother, Grace (Paddock) Sears.

<9> p.2, Source: Certified copy of original records, Bangor ME.

<10> p.2, Records of 1st church in Brewster, formerly 1st church in Harwich.

<11> p.2, Not listed in settlement of father's estate.

<12> p.3, Births of children found in "oldest book - small, square, no cover".

<13> p.3,4, "Groton CT Rcds. BMD I, copy made 20 Nov. 1861 by C.M. Morgan, Town Clerk".

<14> p.4, Husband of Priscilla Cheesborough[4] (Prisc. Alden[3], David[2]); no children listed.

<15> p.4, Widow of Nathaniel Sprague[4] (Ruth Alden[3], David[2])

<16> p.5, Although Bowman adds two !!, no explanation is given for the nine year span between the 1st two children. The date of marriage intentions is 20 Nov. 1756, three weeks before the birth of the 1st child. The marriage date is not given, could it possibly have been postponed a few years?

<17> p.5, This couple did not marry, nor are marriage intentions given. Samuel died one month before the birth of their child.

<18> p.6, Two other children are listed in pencil but are so faint they are difficult to make out. They could read Ruth Grinnell (no dates) and Daniel Grinnell, b. 11 Jan. 1717/8.

<19> p.7, Date of birth is extremely faint in pencil but could read 10 Dec. 1640 <Boston Rcd.Com. 9:10>

<20> p.8, A codocil to Samuel Seabury's will, dated 8 Oct. 1680, states "hee did judge his present wife Martha Saberrey to be with child" <Plymouth Col. Wills 4:1:93-94>

<21> p.8, The order of the data extracted on the family and descendants of Samuel Seabury has been changed slightly for easier reference. If you were to refer to the files you would find charts on his daughter's family before his own.

<22> p.9, Source for the children is given only as Little Compton p.156.

<23> p.9, Although only one child is listed, Daniel's will mentions eight Allen children, viz: Wesson, Humphrey, Pardon, Joseph, Gideon, John, Mary "Cornell" and Rhoda "Macomber".

<24> p.9, Eight children are listed for Josiah & Martha but the penciled entries are too faint to read. Josiah's will of 1733 mentions six Allen children, viz: John & Josiah (both under age), Hannah "Williston", Marcy, Mary, Abigail and Priscilla.

<25> p.10, The date of the baptism of her four children, although "one so frowered would not be baptised" (Priscilla) <MD 12:109>. Martha's death occured after this date but before 22 Apr. 1728 as she is not mentioned in her mother's will <MD 13:111>

<26> p.10, From source 94:202 (no town) is added: "Dec. 1 1855, Levi Simmons, age 85 yrs, died at Bridgewater of old age, shoemaker, born at Duxbury." Note the discrepancy in the age.

<27> p.11, The descent of Mary Weston is shown twice, as Mary Weston[3] (Elnathan[2], Edmund[1]) and Mary Weston (Elnathan & Desire (Standish) Weston), however this seems to be an error. Mary married Joseph Simmons in 1710 <MD 11:23>,five years before the marriage of her alledged parents.

<28> p.11, Although only eight are listed here, MF5G 3:106 gives fifteen children. The remainder Peterson children are: Reuben, bpt. 14 May 1749; Joshua, b. 20 Aug. 1751; Samuel, b. c1753; Rebecca; Thomas Whittemore, b. 24 Mar. 1766; William, b. c1768.

<29> p.11, MF5G 3:195

<30> p.11, His marriage to Sarah Delano[4] (Eliz. Standish[3], Alex.[2]) is given but no children are known. According to MFIP, Standish:23, Sarah Delano[4] m. Joshua Simmons, son of Aaron & Mary (Woodworth) Simmons, not the son of Mercy Pabodie[3] as stated here.

<31> p.12, With this entry is written "an error? youngest son".

<32> p.13, Mentioned in will of cousin Priscilla Southworth <Plymouth Co. Probate 16:204>

<33> p.13, Mentioned in will of brother-in-law, John Southworth[4].

<34> p.13, Probably b. aft. 1714, Duxbury; d. 1797, Duxbury <MF5G 3:59>

<35> p.13, Benjamin Southworth[5] is called the illegitimate son of Constant Southworth[4] and Abigail Cole.

<36> p.13, The children of Micah Soule & Mercy Southworth are listed here with no dates. See the Soule family for complete data.

<37> p.13, MF5G 3:310 provides the births of the children of Thomas Weston and second wife Martha Chandler: Peleg, bpt. 1767; Mercy, b. 29 June 1767; Edmond, bpt. 1770, d.y.; Rebecca, b. 16 June 1774.

<38> p.14, See "Loring Genealogy by Pope, 1917, pp.62,63".

<39> p.15, The charts for Mercy Pabodie[3] and her children are out of order. Data on her children and descendants can be found under Micro #4.

<40> p.15, Lorah Sampson's parentage is shown thus - "?Abraham not Caleb". However, MFIP, Standish:7 shows a Lora in the family of Caleb & Mercy (Standish[3]) Samson[2] <TAG 28:1-11>.

<41> p.16, No children are listed for Benjamin & Fear Simmons. An accompanying extract of guardianship records dated 22 Mar. 1748 give the names of five children of "Benjamin Simmons Jr., late of Duxbury", viz: Lucy (minor dau.), Micah, Benjamin, Elizabeth and Keturah.

<42> p.16, Additional data on this family is given from "A Genealogical Register of the Descendants of Several Ancient Puritans", Vol. III, by Rev. Abner Morse, A.M., Boston 1861.

<43> p.16, Farrow, John Pendleton. History of Islesborough ME. Bangor. 1893.(p.205)

<44> p.16, MF5G 3:60 gives his date of death as Feb. 1798, Duxbury. See the same, p.193-4 for further data on this family.

<45> p.18, Although his generation number is shown, line of descent is not. His chart follows that of John Simmons[6] (Jos.[5]) and wife Lydia Grinnell with no children shown.

<46> p.19, "His daughter Elizabeth, by former wife, marr. Elisha Wadsworth"

<47> p.19, The VR, copied from Duxbury Church Records (ChR):253, repeat the error that she was 73 at the time of death. Bowman notes this would place her birth "3 yrs. after father's death!!"

<48> p.19, Bowman notes that she may be the Mary Jarvis who married Luke Verdey, 13 July 1716 <Boston Rcd.Com.28:67>.

<49> p.20, The baptisms can be found in Duxbury ChR 1:134,145. Also, from the same 1:177 is the entry "Peres Chandler & his wife, their child being dangerously sick had it baptized at their own house". Although this entry was not dated it immediately followed an entry for 15 June 1779. Bowman added in pencil "probably Daniel".

<50> p.20, Source: "General Records 1710-1786, Town of Duxbury".

<51> p.21, On a following page nine children are listed for John Cook and Alice Southworth,

with the source being "Putnam 6:77", viz: Amy, b. 1712; Bathsheba, b. 1714; Samuel, b. 1716; William, b. 1718; Abiel, b. 1720; Lillias, b. 1722; Rebecca, b. 1724; Ruth, b. 1725; Elizabeth, b. 1727. (Note the discrepéncies.) Two children are also listed for John Cook Jr., viz: Samuel, b. 4 Nov. 1716 and William, b. 2 Feb. 1718 <VR RI 4:7:69>

<52> p.21, On the same page is given the marriage of Rebecca Cook and "William Manton, Manchester", 7 Oct. 1742 <VR RI 4:7:16>. The entry from <VR RI 4:7:37> shows his name as "William Manton, of John" with the notation, "under Manchester".

<53> p.21, Source: Slocum Family. 1882. pp.95-6. Phebe Manchester is called the daughter of "Godfrey" Manchester, not William as stated here.

<53a> p.23, Her name was Judith Tilden, b. 1 June 1670, Scituate; d. 20 July 1714, Little Compton <NEHGR 115:263>. They were married 27 June 1693 <TAG 53:246-8>.

<53b> p.23, Her name was Elizabeth (Throope) Peck, b. 1672, Barnstable; d. 14 Dec. 1717, Little Compton. They were married 20 Mar. 1715/6 <TAG 53:246-8>.

<54> p.22, An eighth child is listed but with a (?) instead of the customary check mark, viz: "Elizabeth (Peckham)", b. 30 Apr. 1732. No explanation is given for the name in brackets. What is interesting is that Samuel's 2nd wife was Elizabeth Peckham whom he married in 1746. (She was born 28 Aug. 1726 <Little Compton VR>.)

<55> p.24, It is later shown that Abigail Fish was the only daughter of Capt. Moses & Martha Fish. The will of widow Martha Fish of Norwich (1773) mentions her daughter and sons, Moses, Thomas, Elisha & Jonathan <Norwich PR 5:14>.

<56> p.24, He was baptized "19th day 3rd mth. 1667" <Boston Rcd.Com.9:106>.

<57> p.26, Source is listed as "Historical Sketches of King's Chapel:42,(Cemetery Dept.,Boston)

<58> p.27, Bowman makes note of this interesting year of birth with the "66" underlined. The reason? - her parents were married seven months <u>later</u> .

<59> p.28, The children of John Jones^{6} & his wife Hannah Holmes are not given. However his accompanying will, dated 10 Apr. 1823 names nine children, viz: sons, Lawson, Washington, John H. and daughters, Sally, Mary, Ann, Betsey "Ballard", Melicent "Loring" and Emily "Bliss".

<60> p.29, Intentions were published in December, six months <u>after</u> the birth of the first child. (His father forbid the banns.) A marriage date is not given.

<61> p.32, Her address is given as 114 Thornton St., Boston.

<62> p.33, Her address is given as 284 Warren St., Boston.

<63> p.33, Her address is given as 22 Juniper St., Boston.

<64> p.34, The 11 Vining children are listed without dates, viz: Polly, Freeman, Melvin, Nabby, Scott, George, Marcus, Ruth, Leah, Rebecca (d.y.) and Rebecca.

<65> p.35, Upon careful examination of the files it can be seen that Lewis L. Keith is mistakenly given a 7th generation number and is shown as having Mayflower descent, viz: (Calvin Keith^{6}, Jemima Whitman^{5}, etc). However as is also shown, his descent should read: son of Calvin Keith, the son of David & Charity Keith.

(Note: In **Mayflower Marriages**, companion volume to this **Mayflower Births & Deaths**, the descent of Lewis L. Keith (p.11) is shown incorrectly.)

<66> p.35, This line of descent was incorrectly numbered in the files and has been amended here. See Jane Cooke in the Cooke family for an explanation.

<67> p.37, The accompanying note reads: "Her brother John Alden says she married Abraham Borden and died soon after. <MD 6:111>"

<68> p.40, Possibly a descendant of Howland & Priest.

<69> p.40, A pencilled date of death is given for Hannah - "1 July 1766, ae 48 <Alden Mem:144>" However, a 2nd marriage is attributed to Joseph in 1757 <MD 26:27> - 9 years <u>before</u> this date.

<70> p.43, The accompanying note reads: "The following record was written in the almost illegible hand of a very aged person on the fly leaf of a Bible dated 1696 and once the property of the Rev. Timothy Alden." (The years of birth are omitted.) The last entry is "Martin Alden, d. 9 Sept. Sunday 1838." Across the bottom of this page is written "Yale Library".

<71> p.45, The will of John Burrill, 28 July 1727, mentions daughter Mary Ripley. <Suffolk Co. Probate #6180, 29:321>

<72> p.46, Vinton Mem.:88 attributes a marriage by her to Er Cushing, 1774. However, Bowman's note reads: "This is not correct! It was the daughter of Joseph Burrill & Hannah Birknell who married Er Cushing."

<73> p.49, The children of "Peleg & Jemima Barrows" are written on a piece of scrap paper. They appear to be the children of Peleg Barrows^{3} & Jemima Drew^{5}. After the names of the children is the following entry: "Peleg, bpt. 7 Sept. 1802, ae 93 less a few days" which could be the father of Peleg above.

<74> p.50, MFIP, Warren:34 confirms Bowman's pencilled notations that she was the widow of Ebenezer Bartlett^{4} (Ben.^{3}, Mary Warren^{2}) and possibly the daughter of John & Abigail Bryant.

<75> p.50, The source is in pencil and difficult to read; it appears to be "Mosse's Anc. Puritans 3:181". (See <42>) The parentage of Sarah Delano is not given.

<76> p.51,52, See also "Maine Genealogical Recorder 2:95" for data on this family.

<77> p.53, Source: Ashford VR:11, Barbour Collection in the Connecticut State Library Vol.2:36. This page follows the chart for John Bass^{5} (John^{4}) who m. Mary Danielson (no additional data).

<78> p.53, The names of the children are found in their father's will, dated 9 Sept. 1875 <Suffolk Co.Probate #154, 138:109-110>

<79> p.56, His year of death is smudged, it could read 1679.

<80> p.57, This chart is entirely in faint pencil and, although accompanied by a check mark in pen, difficult to read. The names Sarah & Asa are an "educated" guess from the visible letters.

<81> p.59, Thirteen children are listed for Robert Lenthal Eells & Ruth Copeland without additional data, viz: Ruth, Betsey, Huldah C., Anne Lenthal, Robert, Nabby, John, Nathaniel, Joseph, Lucy, Edward, Sarah and Samuel.

<82> p.60, Eight children are listed for Samuel Hayden & Priscilla Webb without additional data. They are as follows: Samuel, Amy, Christopher, Richard, Jeremiah, Nehemiah, Nathaniel and William Hayden <Vinton:326>
<83> p.60, For additional data see "American Genealogist, Jan. 1949,p.11".
<84> p.61, Source - Pension applications (1817,1843), Bureau of Pensions, Washington D.C. Their children are listed as Elias, Preston, James (b. c1785), Ephraim G., Deborah Ann Fisher (b. c1805), Clarissa Spooner, Maria (b. c1797) and Addison Ware.
<85> p.61, The probate records list seven children of William Bowditch & Susanna Allen: William, Susanna Hunt (wf of Ebenezer), Jonathan, Mary Hunt (wf of Elihu), James, Benjamin and Abigail. In the files, data is given only for Susanna.
<86> p.61, The remaining five Wild children are listed with no dates, the names are taken from their father's will (1807): Joshua, Simon Willard, Jemima, Sally Curtis (wf of Daniel), Eunice, and Betsey (dec., wf of Oliver Vinton) <Norfolk Co.Probate #20331, 56:318>
<87> p.62, The remaining ten Thayer children are listed with no additional data: Ephraim, Philip, Hannah, Joseph, Shadrack, Christopher, Peter, Priscilla, James and Abigail.
<88> p.62, The fifth name (a daughter) is so faint it is impossible to read (it possibly begins with "D" - Deliverance?); the dates for this name are, b. 18 Nov. 1742 <Braintree VR:785>; d. 22 June 1778.

* * * * *

REFERENCE LIST:

GENEALOGICAL ARTICLES PERTAINING TO ALDEN FAMILY RESEARCH

Mayflower Descendant (MD) (1899-1937)

2:152-54 - The Family Records of Nathaniel Thompson And His Son Rev. Otis Thompson
3:10-12 - Inventory & Settlement of Estate of John Alden[1]
3:120-21 - Deposition of John Alden, 1682 (age)
4:202-206 - Will & Inventory of John Bass
6:22-25 - Will & Inventory of Dr. Thomas Delano
6:71-74 - Will & Inventory of Joseph Alden[2]
6:110-14 - Genealogical Letter from John Alden[4]
6:129-35 - Will & Inventory of William Pabodie
6:174-78 - Estate of Capt. Jonathan Alden[2]
6:193-200 - Will & Inventory of Capt. John Alden[2]
6:239-43 - Estate of David Alden[2]
7:114-17 - Will & Inventory of John Drew, Sr. (1745)
8:80-84 - Family Bible of Rev. Jonathan Scott (1744-1850)
9:129-31 - A Rare Broadside on the Death of John Alden (printed shortly after his death, 1687)
9:145- - Alden Notes (Deeds - Jonathan[2], David[2], Paddock, Seabury, Cheeseborough, Sprague)
9:193-96 - The Original Broadside by J.C. On The Death of John Alden
10:76-83 - Alden Notes (records pertaining to children of Capt. John Alden[2])
11:249-51 - Delano Notes (Phillip[1], Samuel[2])
12:72-75 - Alden Notes (John[5], Capt. Nathaniel[4])
12:108-12 - Benjamin Chandler's Children (Edmund & Eliz. (Alden) Chandler)
14:65-70 - Chandler Notes
14:140-42 - Alden Notes (children of Capt. Jonathan Alden[2])
16:46-46 - A Record of Silas Alden[6]'s Family by His Son Leonard Alden
17:129-31 - An Autograph of William Pabodie
18:105- - Wills - Alden/Bass/Adams/Thayer
18:242-44 - The Children of Benjamin & Ruth (Pabodie[3]) Bartlett
18:244-47 - Will of Edward Southworth of Duxbury
19:1-5 - Will of Rev. Ichabod Wiswall
19:25-30 - Will of Thomas Southworth[4] of Duxbury And The Estate of His Son Jedediah[5]
19:51-54 - Estate of John Simmons of Duxbury And The Will of His Widow Mercy (Pabodie[3])
19:112-15 - Wills of John Southworth[4] of Duxbury And His Sister Priscilla Southworth[4]
19:165-72 - Wills of John Little[4] of Marshfield And His Widow Constant (Fobes[4])
20:1-11 - Estates of John Rogers[3] And His Second And Third Wives (Eliz. Pabodie[3])
20:12-15 - Estate of Col. John Alden[3] of Duxbury And The Will of His Widow Hannah
20:31-34 - The Wife of Dr. Benoni Delano of Duxbury And The Settlement of His Estate
20:49-51 - Will of Isaac Alden[3] of Bridgewater
20:76-78 - Will of Capt. Samuel Alden[3]
20:190-92 - Ruth Sprague[4] Did Not Marry John Haskell
20:89-93 - Estate of Deacon John Wadsworth
21:126-28 - Will of Anna (Alden[4]) Loring
22:142-44 - False And Faked Mayflower Claims (Mercy Simmons, wf of Benjamin Chase was not a daughter of John & Mercy (Pabodie) Simmons
22:189-92 - Will of Isaac Alden[4]
23:105-107 - Will of Deacon William Pabodie[3]
23:111-117 - Wills of John Alden[3] And His Widow Hannah
23:129-133 - Estate of Ebenezer Alden[4]
23:192 - Delano Notes: Mercy Delano (dau of Jonathan, m. a Hatch, not Wm. Spooner)
24:74-81 - Estate of Deacon Benjamin Alden[3], Widow Hannah Alden's Death, Estate of Eliz. Alden[4]
24:104-109 - Micah Soule of Duxbury MA, His Wife And Children And His Will
24:165 - Misc. Death Records: The Weekly Newsletter (Capt. John Alden[4])

29:80-82 - Simmons/Delano/West Notes (Martha Simmons[4] & husbands)

31:49-52 - The Rare Broadside On The Death of John Alden Esq.

31:144 - Error in above broadside

31:156-162 - James Cary His Book, 1720

34:49-53 - Broadsides On The Death of John Alden

34:97-101 - Gravestones of William Pabodie And His Wife Elizabeth (Alden[2]) With The Boston Newsletter Notice of Elizabeth's Death

PN&Q 2:49-52 - Alden/Bass/Adams/Webb (children of John & Ruth (ALden[2]) Bass)

PN&Q 3:77 - An Alden Record: Joseph & Joanna (Macomber) Alden

PN&Q 5:40 - Family Records: Joseph Copeland[4]

Mayflower Descendant (MD) (1985-1990)

35:176-177 - Notes on Samuel Proctor

36:169-172 - Mary Butler (Bass[7-6]) Smith Bible

37:73-74 - Bible Records: Nathan Delano (b. 1814)

38:47-48 - A Delano Item (Thomas Delano[6])

39:88 - Proof that Joseph Delano[6] was son of Barzillai Delano[5]

39:111-122 - John Alden: Theories On English Ancestry (Part 1)

39:179-180 - The Parentage of Keziah, Wife of Nathaniel Sprague of Duxbury & Rochester

39:187-194 - Thomas Caswell of Taunton & His Descendants

40:133-136 - John Alden: Theories On English Ancestry (Part 2)

40:197 - Josiah Allen's Wife Was William Read's Daughter

Mayflower Quarterly (MQ) (1975-1990)

42:87-90 - President John Adams & His Alden Ancestry

45:88-90 - The Alden Family: Where Did These Descendants Go?

45:196-199 - The Enigma of Reuben Doane of Cape Cod: A New Alden Line

46:18-19 - Two Matthew Allens of Bridgewater Mass.

46:120-127 - Joseph Southworth[5] of Durham CT, A New Alden Line

46:186-189 - Jonathan Crane - "Gone West"

47:68-69 - The Problem of Confused Identities, 1. Joseph Barrows

48:136 - Benjamin Southworth's Maternal Ancestry
- (error - line 2 should read Benjamin[5] not Constant[5])

48:172-176 - The Secret Life of Jonathan Sampson[5]

49:18-20 - Loyalists in N.S.: Peleg Wiswall[6]

49:135-137 - Ebenezer[4] & Lydia (Delano)(Wormall) Delano, A New Sampson Line

50:77-78 - The Alden Family: Where Did These Alden Descendants Go?

52:144-147 - "Gypsy Frank" McFarland, Yankee Peddler, Descendant of John Alden & Myles Standish

54:208-209 - Famous Americans of Mayflower Descent: John Quincy Adams

55:25 - Woods Family: Record of Births
- (Jane Churchill[6], MF5G 3:169)

55:196-198 - The Marriage of Deborah (Loring[5]) Finney, An Alden/Mullins LIne

55:296-297 - Sylvia Sturtevant and Her Seven Mayflower Lines

56:312-315 - Bible Records: The Francis Woods Puzzle

Miscellaneous

TAG 53:235 - John Alden - Beer Brewer of Windsor?

NEHGR 54:181 - Alden Genealogy

* * * * * * *

ISAAC ALLERTON

MICRO #1 of 9

Isaac ALLERTON^{1}, b. c1586 <MD 4:109><1>; d. Feb. 1658/9, New Haven CT <MD 2:155>
Mary NORRIS, d. 25 Feb. 1620/1, Plymouth <MD 1:88>
CHILDREN OF Isaac ALLERTON & 1st Mary NORRIS: (5)
Bartholomew ALLERTON^{2}, b. ( )<2>
Remember ALLERTON^{2}, b. ( )
Mary ALLERTON^{2}, b. ( ); d. 28 Nov. 1699, Plymouth <MD 16:63>
Child, bur. 5 Feb. 1620, Leyden, Holland
Son, 22 Dec. 1620, stillborn <Mourt's Relation (Dexter Ed.):66>
CHILDREN OF Isaac ALLERTON & 2nd Fear BREWSTER^{2}: (2)
Sarah ALLERTON^{2}, b. ( )<3>
Isaac ALLERTON^{2}, b. ( ); d. aft. 25 Oct. 1702 <MD 7:173>
Joanna ( ) ALLERTON, d. aft. 14 May 1680 <MD 2:254><4>

ISAAC ALLERTON^{2} (Isaac^{1})

CHILDREN OF Isaac ALLERTON^{2} & Elizabeth ( ): (2)<5>
Elizabeth ALLERTON^{3}, b. 27 Sept. 1653 <MD 7:174>
Isaac ALLERTON^{3}, b. 11 June 1655<6>
CHILDREN OF Isaac ALLERTON^{2} & Elizabeth (WILLOUGHBY)(Overzee) Colclough: (3) <MD 7:174-6><5>
Willoughby ALLERTON^{3}, b. ( )
Sarah ALLERTON^{3}, b. ( )
Frances ALLERTON^{3}, b. ( )
CHILDREN OF John ALLERTON & Elizabeth ( ): (9) <Norwich CT VR 1:26>
Esther ALLERTON, b. 11 July 1713
Sarah ALLERTON, b. 14 Oct. 1715
Mary ALLERTON, b. 24 Mar. 1717/8
John ALLERTON, b. 23 Aug. 1720
Richard ALLERTON, b. 2 Mar. 1722/3
Isaac ALLERTON, b. 15 Aug. 1725
Elizabeth ALLERTON, b. 25 Nov. 1728
Ann ALLERTON, b. 10 Oct. 1731
Jonathan ALLERTON, b. 18 Sept. 1735
CHILDREN OF John ALLERTON & Rosanna (BURLINGAME) Cooper: (8)<7>
Jerusha ALLERTON, b. 21 July 1755
Sarah ALLERTON, b. 8 June 1757
Freelove ALLERTON, b. 11 Aug. 1759
Roger ALLERTON, b. 1 Oct. 1761
John ALLERTON, b. 13 Feb. 1764
Elizabeth ALLERTON, b. 3 July 1766
Russell ALLERTON, b. 27 Nov. 1768
Rosanna ALLERTON, b. 11 Mar. 1771

MARY ALLERTON^{2} (Isaac^{1})

James CUSHMAN^{5} (Allerton^{4}, Elkanah^{3}, b. 27 May 1715
James CUSHMAN^{5} (Elkanah$^{4-3}$), b. 29 Aug. 1709; d. c1742

CHILDREN OF Edward THOMAS Jr. & Abigail PARLOUR: (6) <Middleboro VR>

Son, b. 26 Feb. 1720/1 <VR 1:77>

Jennet THOMAS, b. 6 Dec. 1722 <VR 1:77> (name later changed to Rhoda, 1:251>

Mary THOMAS, b. 1 Dec. 1725 <VR 1:79>

Jesse THOMAS, b. 26 Oct. 1728 <VR 1:80>

Rosamond THOMAS, b. 28 Nov. 1730 <VR 1:131>

Hushaie THOMAS, b. 27 May 1732 <VR 1:131>

CHILDREN OF Hushai THOMAS & Lucy VAUGHAN: (4) <Middleboro VR 2:2:111>

Lucy THOMAS, b. 17 Apr. 1764

Hushai THOMAS, b. 27 Mar. 1766

Daniel THOMAS, b. 3 Apr. 1769

Lewis THOMAS, b. 18 Jan. 1771

Thomas CUSHMAN, bpt. 8 Feb. 1607/8, Canterbury, Eng. <NEHGR 68:183>; d. 10/11 Dec. 1691, Plymouth <MD 4:37> **<8>**

CHILDREN OF Mary ALLERTON[2] & Thomas CUSHMAN: (8)<MD 4:39>

Thomas CUSHMAN[3], b. 1637 <MD 4:38>**<8a>**

Rev. Isaac CUSHMAN[3], b. 8 Feb. 1648, Plymouth <MD 15:27>;d. 21 Oct. 1732,Plympton g.s.<MD 10:111>

Elkanah CUSHMAN[3], b. 1 June 1651, Plymouth <MD 16:237>; d. 4 Sept. 1727, Plympton <MD 5:20>

Eleazer CUSHMAN[3], b. 20 Feb. 1656 <MD 17:71>; d. aft. 14 Oct. 1723 (deed)<Plymouth Co.LR 18:140>

Sarah CUSHMAN[3], b. ( )

Lydia CUSHMAN[3], b. pre 1668* **<8b>**

Mary CUSHMAN[3], b. ( ); d. pre 22 Oct. 1690 (father's will) <MD 4:40>

Fear CUSHMAN[3], b. 20 June 1653 <MD 17:70>; d. pre 22 Oct. 1690* (father's will) <MD 4:40>

Elizabeth COOMBS, (dau. of John & Elizabeth ( )(Barlow)), d. aft. 14 Oct. 1723 (deed) <Plymouth Co. LR 18:140>**<9>**

CHILDREN OF Eleazer CUSHMAN[3] & Elizabeth COOMBS: (6)**<10>**

Lydia CUSHMAN[4], b. 13 Dec. 1687, Plymouth <MD 1:212>; d. 7 July 1771, Halifax g.s.<MD 10:105>

John CUSHMAN[4], b. 13 Aug. 1690, Plymouth <MD 1:212>

Moses CUSHMAN[4], b. c1693/4; d. 12 Aug. 1766, ae 74, Halifax g.s. <MD 12:243>

James CUSHMAN[4], d. betw. 14 Mar. 1775 (will) - 6 Oct. 1778 (probate) <Bristol Co.PR 25:265, 267>

Eleazer CUSHMAN[4], b. ( ); d. Plympton, betw. 22 Feb. 1758 (will) - 2 May 1758 (probate)<Plymouth Co. Probate #5806, 14:509-10>

William CUSHMAN[4], b. 27 Oct. 1710

CHILDREN OF James CUSHMAN[4] & Sarah HATCH: (11)

Lydia CUSHMAN[5], b. 4 Sept. 1723, Plymouth <MD 13:173>; d. pre 14 Mar. 1775 (father's will above)

James CUSHMAN[5], b. 4 May 1725, Plym. <MD 13:173>; d. aft. 14 Sept. 1796 <Bristol Co.Deeds 81:436>

Ebenezer CUSHMAN[5], b. 4 June 1727 <Dartmouth VR 1:289>; d. 9 Jan. 1813 <Cushman Gen.:141>

Thomas CUSHMAN[5], b. 28 Jan. 1728 <Dartmouth VR 1:289>

Mary CUSHMAN[5], b. 1 Nov. 1730 <Dartmouth VR 1:289>

Sarah CUSHMAN[5], b. 1 Dec. 1732 <Dartmouth VR 1:289>

Seth CUSHMAN[5], b. 16 Oct. 1734 <Dartmouth VR 1:289>

Elisha CUSHMAN[5], b. 20 May 1737, Dartmouth, d. 8 May 1814 <Cushman Gen.:141>

Elizabeth CUSHMAN[5], b. 29 July 1739 <Dartmouth VR 1:289>

Temperance CUSHMAN[5], b. ( )**<11>**

Patience CUSHMAN[5], b. ( )**<12>**

Phillip CANNON, d. pre 23 June 1768 (inv.) (hus. of Mary Cushman[5])

CHILDREN OF Ephraim JENNEY & Lydia CUSHMAN[5]: (2) <mentioned in will of James Cushman[4] above>

Dau., b. ( )

Dau., b. ( )

Hannah NEGUS, d. aft. 14 Sept. 1796 (wf of James Cushman[5])<Bristol Co. Deeds 81:436>

Reliance EASTLIN, b. 11 Apr. 1736, d. 3 Feb. 1795 (wf of Elisha Cushman^5) <Cushman Gen.:141>
Joanna PRATT, (dau. of John & Margaret), b. 26 Oct. 1690, Plymouth <MD 1:212>
CHILDREN OF John CUSHMAN^4 (Eleazer^3) & Joanna PRATT: (3) <Cushman Gen.:139>
John CUSHMAN^5, b. ( )
Eleazer CUSHMAN^5, b. c1720*, d. 1797*
Charles CUSHMAN^5, b. Plymouth, d. Rutland VT <:140>
John WATERMAN, (son of John), b. 23 Sept. 1685, Marshfield<MD 3:189>; d. 8 June 1761, Halifax g.s <MD 10:105>
CHILDREN OF John WATERMAN & Lydia CUSHMAN^4 (Eleazer^3): (7) <Plympton, MD 5:184>
Sarah WATERMAN^5, b. 8 Nov. 1709,
Joseph WATERMAN^5, b. 2 Feb. 1710/11
Perez WATERMAN^5, b. 8 Oct. 1713; d. 9 Aug. 1793* <Bridgewater VR 2:576>
Anthony WATERMAN^5, b. 23 June 1716; d. 1 Dec. 1769, Halifax g.s. <MD 10:104>
John WATERMAN^5, b. 3 July 1718; d. 26 Apr. 1790, Halifax g.s. <MD 10:105>
Eleazer WATERMAN^5, b. 3 Aug. 1721
Lydia WATERMAN^5, b. 7 Apr. 1724
Hannah VAUGHAN, d. betw. 26 Sept. 1782 (will) - 1 Oct. 1798 (probate)<Plymouth Co.Probate 36:425>
CHILDREN OF Anthony WATERMAN^5 & Hannah VAUGHAN: (10) <Halifax VR:43>
Joanna WATERMAN^6, b. 21 Oct. 1736
Sarah WATERMAN^6, b. 24 Aug. 1738
James WATERMAN^6, b. 20 Apr. 1740
Hannah WATERMAN^6, b. 12 Mar. 1741/2
Anthony WATERMAN^6, b. 21 Mar. 1743/4; d. betw. 28 Oct. 1769 (father's will) <Plymouth Co.Probate #22126, 20:348> - 6 Aug. 1770 (adm.)<Plymouth Co.Probate #22125, 20:395>
Elisha WATERMAN^6, b. 12 June 1746; d.? 19 June 1747 <MD 10:104>
David WATERMAN^6, b. 12 June 1746 (twins); d.? 19 June 1747 <MD 10:104>
Elisha WATERMAN^6, b. 29 Aug. 1748
David WATERMAN^6, b. 4 May 1751; d. 11 Mar. 1761 <MD 10:104>
Phebe WATERMAN^6, b. 19 Sept. 1757
Sarah CURTIS, (*dau. of Elisha & Sarah), bpt. 19 Dec. 1742*, Scituate <Norwell Ch.>
CHILDREN OF Anthony WATERMAN^6 & Sarah CURTIS: (2)
James WATERMAN^7, b. 20 Sept. 1766, Halifax; d. 9 Dec. 1824
Calvin WATERMAN^7, b. ( ); d. 19 Oct. 1823, ae 55
Hannah BATES, b. 20 Oct. 1766, Abington; d. 6 May 1794
CHILD OF James WATERMAN^7 & 1st Hannah BATES:
Anthony WATERMAN^8, b. 19 July 1791
Polly PAYSON, b. 26 July 1772, Braintree
CHILDREN OF James WATERMAN^7 & 2nd Polly PAYSON: (11)
Polly WATERMAN^8, b. 3 Dec. 1796; d. 8 Feb. 1797
Achsah WATERMAN^8, b. 17 Mar. 1798
James C. WATERMAN^8, b. 14 June 1800
Oren WATERMAN^8, b. 3 Mar. 1803; d. 12 Mar. 1803
Hannah WATERMAN^8, b. 18 Oct. 1804; d. 25 Aug. 1805
Polly WATERMAN^8, b. 18 Oct. 1804 (twins); d. 22 Oct. 1804
John WATERMAN^8, b. 2 Sept. 1806; d. 27 Dec. 1867
Sally WATERMAN^8, b. 28 Apr. 1809; d. 21 Mar. 1819
Joseph W. WATERMAN^8, b. 21 Dec. 1811
Philena WATERMAN^8, b. 22 Dec. 1813
Harriet N. WATERMAN^8, b. 23 Apr. 1816
Fear STURTEVANT^5 (Fear Cushman^4, Isaac^3, Mary Allerton^2), b. 7 Apr. 1719, Plympton <MD 5:180>;

d. 17 Jan. 1790, Halifax g.s. <MD 10:104>

CHILDREN OF John WATERMAN^{5} (Lydia Cushman^{4}) & Fear STURTEVANT:(7) <Halifax VR:50>

Child, b. 25 or 26 Feb. 1741, d. 27 Feb. 1741, Halifax g.s.

Betty WATERMAN^{6}, b. 17 Sept. 1744; d. 8 Mar. 1836 <MD 10:104>

John WATERMAN^{6}, b. 29 Jan. 1746

William WATERMAN^{6}, b. 13 Aug. 1749

Isaac WATERMAN^{6}, b. 14 June 1752; d. 17 Mar. 1754 <MD 10:104>

Isaac WATERMAN^{6}, b. 23 Feb. 1755; d. 23 June 1813, Halifax g.s. <MD 10:105>

Fear WATERMAN^{6}, b. 25 Dec. 1758

Lucy SAMPSON^{6} (Bethiah^{5}, Jonathan Samson^{4}, Lydia Standish^{3}, Alex.^{2}), b. 6 Mar. 1761* <Giles Mem. :418>; d. 4 Sept. 1844, Plympton g.s. <MD 11:162> (see Mrs. Lucy Soule below)

CHILDREN OF Isaac WATERMAN^{6} & Lucy SAMPSON: (8)<1-4, Halifax VR:25; 5-8, Giles Mem.:418>

Phebe WATERMAN^{7}, b. 4 Mar. 1782; d. 18 Dec. 1802 <MD 10:105>

Isaac WATERMAN^{7}, b. 13 Feb. 1784

Joseph Samson WATERMAN^{7}, b. 7 July 1785

Lucy WATERMAN^{7}, b. 6 Nov. 1788

Bethiah Sampson WATERMAN^{7}*, b. ( )

Elizabeth WATERMAN^{7}*, b. ( )

Melzar WATERMAN^{7}*, b. ( )

Fanny WATERMAN^{7}*, b. ( )

"Lucy W. STONE, d. 1 Mar. 1905, ae 92y1m7d, at 9 Crescent Ave., Chelsea, asthma & old age, wf of Benjamin F.; b. Malden, dau. of Ephraim Barker (b. England) & Lucy S. Waterman (b. Halifax)" <Mass.VR 31:435>

Mrs. Lucy SOULE, d. 4 Sept. 1844, E. Bridgewater,ae 84, widow of Daniel <Obituary>[<13>](see above)

Abigail ( ) WATERMAN, b. c1716*, d. 19 Jan. 1782*, ae 66, Bridgewater g.s.

CHILDREN OF Perez WATERMAN^{5} (Lydia Cushman^{4}) & Abigail ( ): (5) <Halifax VR:45>

Perez WATERMAN^{6}, b. 19 June 1739; d. 13 Dec. 1820*, Oakham

Abigail WATERMAN^{6}, b. 9 Apr. 1740

Thaddeus WATERMAN^{6}, b. 25 Mar. 1743

Lucy WATERMAN^{6}, b. 12 Apr. 1745

Jonathan WATERMAN^{6}, b. 20 Feb. 1747/8

Abigail WASHBURN, (dau of Josiah), d. 15 June 1790*, ae 41 <Brookfield VR:543>

CHILDREN OF Jonathan WATERMAN^{6} & 1st Abigail WASHBURN*: (9) <Brookfield VR:228>

Son, b. 10 Feb. 1769, d. 15 Feb. 1769, g.s.

Lavinia WATERMAN^{7}, b. 14 Jan. 1770; d. 7 Feb. 1770 <VR:543>

Sarah WATERMAN^{7}, b. 7 June 1771; d. 6 May 1801 <VR:543>

Josiah WATERMAN^{7}, b. 10 Aug. 1773; d. 7 Jan. 1777

Levina WATERMAN^{7}, b. 21 May 1776; d. 1 May 1800 <VR:543>

Betsey WATERMAN^{7}, b. 17 Nov. 1780

Ambrose WATERMAN^{7}, b. 15 Feb. 1783

Cynthia WATERMAN^{7}, b. 8 June 1786

Abigail WATERMAN^{7}, b. 4 Oct. 1788

Hannah BARTLETT, d. 24 June 1812, ae 50, g.s. <Brookfield VR:543>

CHILDREN OF Jonathan WATERMAN^{6} & 2nd Hannah BARTLETT: (2) <Brookfield VR>

Rebecca WATERMAN^{7}, b. 28 Dec. 1797

Hannah WATERMAN^{7}, b. 26 Sept. 1808

CHILDREN OF Perez WATERMAN^{6} (Perez^{5}) & Abigail ( ): (9)* <Bridgewater VR>

Stephen WATERMAN^{7}, b. 22 July 1766

Calvin WATERMAN^{7}, b. 2 June 1768

Ruth WATERMAN^{7}, b. 7 Apr. 1770

Bethiah WATERMAN^{7}, b. 15 May 1772

Lydia WATERMAN^{7}, b. 13 June 1774

Barnabas WATERMAN^{7}, b. 23 Sept. 1776

Abigail WATERMAN^{7}, b. ( )

Lucy WATERMAN^{7}, b. ( )

Benjamin WATERMAN^{7}, d. 30 Oct. 1817*, St. Mary's, GA

CHILDREN OF Benjamin WATERMAN^{7} & Lucy STONE: (4)*

Harrison Gray Otis WATERMAN^{8}, b. 15 May 1806

Benjamin H. WATERMAN^{8}, b. 27 Dec. 1809

Harriet Stone WATERMAN^{8}, b. 27 Oct. 1812

Henry Starbuck WATERMAN^{8}, b. 14 Oct. 1814

Mary JACKSON, (dau. of Eleazer), b. 15 Apr. 1701, Plymouth <MD 3:123>

CHILDREN OF Moses CUSHMAN^{4} (Eleazer^{3}) & Mary JACKSON: (11)<1-6 at Plympton; 7-11, Halifax VR:42>>

Abner CUSHMAN^{5}, b. 10 Mar. 1722 <MD 5:208>; d. pre July 1777 (wf 2nd marr.- Halifax VR:20>

Elijah CUSHMAN^{5}, b. 14 Feb. 1724/5, d. 6 Jan. 1725/6 <MD 5:208>

Mary CUSHMAN^{5}, b. 21 Sept. 1725 <MD 5:209>

Sarah CUSHMAN^{5}, b. 20 Oct. 1727 <MD 5:209>

Isaac CUSHMAN^{5}, b. 19 Feb. 1730 <MD 5:209>

Hannah CUSHMAN^{5}, bpt. 13 Feb. 1731/2 <Plympton VR:84>

Bettee CUSHMAN^{5}, b. 3 Sept. 1735

Deborah CUSHMAN^{5}, b. 8 July 1737; d. 9 Sept. 1815, Halifax g.s. <MD 12:243>

Huldah CUSHMAN^{5}, b. 16 May 1739

Moses CUSHMAN^{5}, b. 22 Mar. 1740

Eleazer CUSHMAN^{5}, b. 30 Aug. 1744

Mary TILSON, (*dau. of John Jr. & Joanna), b. 1 Jan. 1729, d. 10 Oct. 1816 (wf of 2nd hus. James Faunce <Halifax VR:94>

CHILDREN OF Abner CUSHMAN^{5} & Mary TILSON: (5)**<14>**

Unice CUSHMAN^{6}, b. 5 Mar. 1746/7 <Halifax VR:53>; d. 25 Jan. 1788*

Fear CUSHMAN^{6}, b. 6 Aug. 1749 <Halifax VR:53>

Lydia CUSHMAN^{6}, b. 20 Oct. 1751 <Halifax VR:53>; d. 27 Oct. 1820*

Joanna CUSHMAN^{6}*, b. c1757*, d. Mar. 1805*, ae 50

Rebecca CUSHMAN^{6}*, b. ( )

MICRO #2 of 9

Thomas HOOPER^{4} (Tho.^{3}, John^{2}, Wm.^{1}), b. bpt. 31 July 1737, Bridgewater, d. 1777, Saratoga NY <Family Rcds.>**<15>**

CHILDREN OF Thomas HOOPER & Deborah CUSHMAN^{5} (Moses^{4}): (3)***<15>**

Cushman HOOPER^{6}, b. 1763, "enlisted in the Revolutionary Army but died before performing service"

Thomas HOOPER^{6}, b. 1765, "..a hatter. He went to Ohio to buy fur, capsized from boat and died"

Chloe HOOPER^{6}, b. 15 May 1768, d. May 1845, E. Bridgewater

Ebenezer HATHAWAY, (son of Josiah & Hannah (Latham)), b. 13 July 1768, d. 30 June 1830**<15>**

CHILDREN OF Ebenezer HATHAWAY & Chloe HOOPER^{6}: (13)**<15>**

Isaac HATHAWAY^{7}, b. 1789

Cushman HATHAWAY^{7}, b. 1 Mar. 1790

Deborah HATHAWAY^{7}, b. Oct. 1791

Seabury HATHAWAY^{7}, b. 24 Jan. 1793

Chloe HATHAWAY^{7}, b. 4 May 1794

Ruth HATHAWAY^{7}, b. 11 Mar. 1798

Sarah HATHAWAY^{7}, b. 7 July 1800

Wadsworth Phillips HATHAWAY^{7}, b. ( )

John HATHAWAY^{7}, b. 21 May 1802

Ebenezer HATHAWAY^{7}, b. 7 Aug. 1804
Thomas HATHAWAY^{7}, b. 27 Mar. 1807
Josiah HATHAWAY^{7}, b. 16 Mar. 1810
Isaac HATHAWAY^{7}, b. 13 Apr. 1814
Silvanus LEACH, (son of Micah), b. 22 July 1749 <Halifax VR:53>
CHILDREN OF Silvanus LEACH & Rebecca CUSHMAN^{6} (Abner^{5}): (3)
Tomson LEACH^{7}, b. 19 Nov. 1772 <Halifax VR:49>
Rebecca LEACH^{7*}, b. 20 June 1786*
Sarah LEACH^{7*}, b. 21 Sept. 1792*
Asa PRATT, (son of Samuel & Betty), b. 8 July 1742 <Weymouth VR 1:223>
Asa PRATT, (son of Ephraim Jr. & Lucy), b. 5 or 12 Dec. 1766 <Weymouth VR 1:223>
Asa PRATT, (son of Ezra & Abigail), b. 15 or 18 Mar. 1780 <Weymouth VR 1:223>
Asa PRATT, (son of Peter & Anna), bpt. 21 Mar. 1785 <Weymouth VR 1:223>
Asa PRATT, (son of Samuel 3d & Molly), b. 10 Apr. 1787 <Weymouth VR 1:223>
Asa PRATT, (son of Asa & Sarah), b. 20 June 1794 <Weymouth VR 1:223>
Asa PRATT 2d, b. c1785, d. 1 July 1821 ae 36 <Weymouth VR 2:317>
Asa PRATT, d. 28 Nov. 1824 <Weymouth VR 2:317>
Asa PRATT, b. c1787, d. 18 Aug. 1837, ae 50 <Weymouth VR:2:317>
Elizabeth COLE, d. 4 Jan. 1681/2, Plymouth <MD 13:203>**<16>**
CHILDREN OF Elkanah CUSHMAN^{3} & 1st Elizabeth COLE: (3) <MD 1:142>
Elkanah CUSHMAN^{4}, b. 15 Sept. 1678, Plymouth; d. pre 22 June 1715***<17>**
James CUSHMAN^{4}, b. 20 Oct. 1679, Plymouth
Jabez CUSHMAN^{4}, b. 28 Dec. 1681, Plymouth; d. May 1682
Martha COOKE^{3} (Jacob^{2}), b. 16 Mar. 1659, Plymouth, d. 17 Sept. 1722, Plympton <MD 17:182, 2:141>
CHILDREN OF Elkanah CUSHMAN^{3} & 2nd Martha COOKE: (5) <MD 1:142>
Allerton CUSHMAN^{4}, b. 21 Nov. 1683, Plymouth; d. 9 Jan. 1730/1, Plympton g.s. <MD 10:111>
Elizabeth CUSHMAN^{4}, b. 17 Jan. 1685, Plymouth; d. 13 Mar. 1724/5, Plympton g.s. (wf of Robert Waterman) <MD 2:139>
Lieut. Josiah CUSHMAN^{4}, b. 21 Mar. 1687/8, Plymouth; d. 13 Apr. 1750, Plympton g.s. <MD 10:112>
Martha CUSHMAN^{4}, bpt. 1691*
Mehitable CUSHMAN^{4}, b. 8 Oct. 1693, Plymouth
Mary BUCK, b. c1688, d. 15 Dec. 1725, Plympton g.s., ae 37 <MD 10:112>**<18>**
CHILDREN OF Allerton CUSHMAN^{4} & 1st Mary BUCK: (4) <MD 3:164>
Allerton CUSHMAN^{5}, b. 16 Dec. 1712, Plympton**<19>**
James CUSHMAN^{5}, b. 27 May 1715, Plympton
Mary CUSHMAN^{5}, b. 5 June 1718, Plympton
Ephraim CUSHMAN^{5}, b. 25 Oct. 1720, Plympton; d. 15 or 17 Nov. 1725 <MD 10:111>
CHILDREN OF Allerton CUSHMAN^{4} & 2nd Elizabeth SAMPSON^{3} (George^{2}, Abraham^{1}): (2)**<20>**
Alice CUSHMAN^{5}, b. June 1727, d. 18 July 1727, ae 3wks6d <MD 10:111>
Joseph CUSHMAN^{5}, b. 4 Feb. 1729/30, Plympton, d. 26 July 1731 <MD 3:164, 10:112>
Alethea SOULE^{4} (Jos.^{3}, John^{2}), b. 9 Jan. 1713/4, Duxbury <MD 11:235>; d. 3 Mar. 1747/8
CHILDREN OF Allerton CUSHMAN^{5} & 1st Alethea SOULE: (8)**<21>**
Asenath CUSHMAN^{6}, b. 22 Nov. 1735
Zilpah CUSHMAN^{6}, b. 3 Feb. 1736/7
Allerton CUSHMAN^{6}, b. 4 May 1738; d. 19 Aug. 1739 <MD 10:111>
Allerton CUSHMAN^{6}, b. 3 May 1740
Lydia CUSHMAN^{6}, b. 2 Oct. 1741
Ephraim CUSHMAN^{6}, b. 20 Feb. 1742/3
Mary CUSHMAN^{6}, b. 23 Dec. 1744
Luther CUSHMAN^{6}, b. 14 Oct. 1747

CHILDREN OF Allerton CUSHMAN[5] & 2nd Deborah ( ): (2)*<22>

Caleb CUSHMAN[6], b. 21 Oct. 1749, Woodstock CT

Deborah CUSHMAN[6], b. 26 Sept. 1751, Woodstock CT

Hester BARNES, (dau. of Jonathan), b. 18 Feb. 1682; d. 1 Nov. 1770<23>

CHILDREN OF Elkanah CUSHMAN[4] (Elkanah[3]) & Hester BARNES: (4)

Elizabeth CUSHMAN[5], b. 5 Dec. 1703, Plymouth <MD 2:226>; d. aft. 1747 <Plymouth Co.Deeds 39:28>

Elkanah CUSHMAN[5], b. 10 July 1706, Plymouth <MD 2:226>; d. c1742* <wf 2nd marr.- MD 14:160>

James CUSHMAN[5], b. 29 Aug. 1709, Plymouth <MD 2:226>; d. pre 6 Mar. 1741/2 <Plymouth Co.Probate #5847, 8:471>

Hannah CUSHMAN[5], b. ( ); d. aft. 1747*<Plymouth Co.Deeds 39:28>

CHILD OF Ichabod DELANO & Elizabeth CUSHMAN[5]:

Lemuel DELANO[6]*, b. ( )

Lydia BRADFORD[4] (David[3], Wm.[2]), b. 23 Dec. 1719, Plymouth <MD 12:85>; d. 28 Oct. 1756<24>

CHILD OF Elkanah CUSHMAN[5] (Elkanah[4]) & Lydia BRADFORD:

Elkanah CUSHMAN[6], b. 13 Nov. 1741, Plymouth <MD 15:159>

CHILDREN OF John WATERMAN & Hannah CUSHMAN[5] (Elkanah[4]): (7) <Plymouth, MD 15:41><25>

Elkanah WATERMAN[6], b. 20 Mar. 1732/3

John WATERMAN[6], b. 27 July 1735, d. 9 Mar. 1735/6

Elizabeth WATERMAN[6], b. 15 Aug. 1737

John WATERMAN[6], b. 17 Oct. 1739, d. 17 Aug. 1741

Hannah WATERMAN[6], b. 10 Mar. 1741/2

John WATERMAN[6], b. 27 Mar. 1744, d. 27 July 1744

James WATERMAN[6], b. 11 May 1745

Hannah COBB[4] (Elisha[3], John[2], Henry[1]), b. 11 Nov. 1716*

Susanna SHURTLEF[3] (Wm.[2-1]), b. c1690, d. 27 July 1763, ae 73, Plympton g.s. <MD 10:112>

CHILDREN OF Lieut. Josiah CUSHMAN[4] & Susanna SHURTLEF: (9) <1-7, Plympton, MD 5:181>

Susanna CUSHMAN[5], b. 16 Sept. 1710; d.y.

Martha CUSHMAN[5], b. 12 Jan. 1712/3

Susanna CUSHMAN[5], b. 24 May 1715; d. 6 Feb. 1756*, Lakenham Cem., N. Carver <VR:173>

Anna CUSHMAN[5], b. 20 May 1717

Josiah CUSHMAN[5], b. 12 Aug. 1719; d. 17 Sept. 1784, Plympton g.s., Old Cem.<MD 10:112>

Elkanah CUSHMAN[5], b. Sept. 1721; d. 6 Aug. 1803, Plympton g.s. <MD 10:111>

William CUSHMAN[5], b. 26 Feb. 1723/4

Elizabeth CUSHMAN[5]*, b. 22 Sept. 1728*; d. 10 Oct. 1808*

Isaiah CUSHMAN[5], b. 2 Feb. 1730/1, d. 2 Nov. 1818*

Hannah STANDISH[5] (Zachariah[4], Ebenezer[3], Alex.[2]), b. 15 Dec. 1723, Plympton <MD 2:53>; d. 16 Oct. 1756, Plympton g.s. (1st wf of Elkanah Cushman[5] above) <MD 10:111>

Patience (PADDOCK*) Perkins*, d. 10 Dec. 1772, ae 45y27d, Plympton g.s. (2nd wf of Elkanah Cushman[5]) <MD 10:112>

Sarah RING[5]* (*Andrew[4], Eleazer[3], Deborah Hopkins[2]), b. 2 Sept. 1737*, N. Yarmouth

CHILD OF Isaiah CUSHMAN[5] & Sarah RING:

Sarah CUSHMAN[6], b. 19 Apr. 1763*, Plympton (wf of Jos. Perkins below)

Joseph PERKINS[6] (Deborah Soule[5], Ebenezer[4], Ben.[3], John[2]), b. 23 Dec. 1754*, Plympton

Sarah STANDISH[5] (Zachariah[4], Eben.[3], Alex.[2]), d. 11 Feb. 1752, ae 23, Plympton g.s., Old Cem. <MD 10:112> (1st wf of Josiah Cushman[5-4])<26>

Deborah RING, d. 6 Sept. 1823, ae 81y1m5d, Plympton g.s., Old Cem. <MD 10:111> (2nd wf of Josiah Cushman[5-4])<27>

Benjamin SHURTLEFF[3]*(*Abiel[2], Wm.[1]), b. 17 Apr. 1710*, Plymouth <MD 2:79>; d. 23 Nov. 1788*, Lakenham Cem., N. Carver <VR:171>

CHILDREN OF Benjamin SHURTLEFF & Susanna CUSHMAN[5] (Josiah[4]): (4)*

Hannah SHURTLEFF^{6}, b. 23 Mar. 1746

Benjamin SHURTLEFF^{6}, b. 14 Oct. 1748

Susanna SHURTLEFF^{6}, b. 1 Feb. 1751; d. 26 Dec. 1842

Ruth SHURTLEFF^{6}, b. 25 July 1753; d. Aug. 1785

CHILDREN OF Nathaniel HOLMES & Martha CUSHMAN^{4}: (5) <Middleboro, MD 9:48>

Nathaniel HOLMES^{5}, b. 21 June 1718

Jedediah HOLMES^{5}, b. 19 May 1720

Jabez HOLMES^{5}, b. 13 Sept. 1723

Elkanah HOLMES^{5}, b. 7 Aug. 1725

John HOLMES^{5}, b. 30 Apr. 1727

Rebecca HARLOW?^{4*} (Rebecca Bartlett^{3}, Mary Warren^{2}), d. 3 Sept. 1727, ae 73, Plympton g.s. <MD 10:112>**<28>**

CHILDREN OF Rev. Isaac CUSHMAN^{3} & Rebecca HARLOW*: (6) <Plymouth, MD 1:210>

Lieut. Isaac CUSHMAN^{4}, b. 15 Nov. 1676; d. 18 Sept. 1727, Plympton g.s. <MD 10:111>

Rebecca CUSHMAN^{4}, b. 30 Nov. 1678; d. 8 July 1756*, N. Yarmouth ME <Desc. Edw. Small 1:406> (wf of Jacob Mitchell^{3}, below)

Mary CUSHMAN^{4}, b. 12 Oct. 1682; d. 13 Mar. 1722/3, Plympton g.s. <MD 11:194>

Sarah CUSHMAN^{4}, b. 17 Apr. 1684

Ichabod CUSHMAN^{4}, b. 30 Oct. 1686; d. 26 Oct. 1732, Middleboro Green g.s. <MD 12:199>

Fear CUSHMAN^{4}, b. 10 Mar. 1689; d. 13 July 1746, Halifax g.s. <MD 10:10>

Jacob MITCHELL^{3} (Jacob^{2}, Experience^{1}), d. 21 Dec. 1744, ae 73, N. Yarmouth ME g.s.<Small 1:404>

William STURTEVANT, d. 28 Aug. 1753, ae 70, Halifax g.s. <MD 10:11>

CHILDREN OF William STURTEVANT & Fear CUSHMAN^{4}: (5) <Plympton, MD 5:180>

Isaac STURTEVANT^{5}, b. 10 Aug. 1708; d. 7 Feb. 1750 <MD 10:10>

Hannah STURTEVANT^{5}, b. 20 Aug. 1711

Rebecca STURTEVANT^{5}, b. July 1715

Fear STURTEVANT^{5}, b. 7 Apr. 1719; d. 17 Jan. 1790, Halifax g.s. <Halifax VR:6>

Elizabeth STURTEVANT^{5}, b. 7 Apr. 1719 (twins)

John WATERMAN^{5} (Lydia Cushman^{4}, Eleazer^{3}, Mary Allerton^{2}), b. 3 July 1718, Plympton <MD 5:184>; d. 26 Apr. 1790, Halifax g.s. <Halifax VR:6>

CHILDREN OF John WATERMAN & Fear STURTEVANT^{5}: (7) <2-7, Halifax VR:50, MD 10:105>

Son, b. 25 or 26 Feb. 1741, d. 27 Feb. 1741, Halifax g.s. <MD 10:105>

Betty WATERMAN^{6}, b. 27 Sept. 1744

John WATERMAN^{6}, b. 29 Jan. 1746

William WATERMAN^{6}, b. 13 Aug. 1749

Isaac WATERMAN^{6}, b. 14 June 1752; d. 17 Mar. 1754 <MD 10:104>

Isaac WATERMAN^{6}, b. 23 Feb. 1755; d. 23 June 1813 <MD 10:105>

Fear WATERMAN^{6}, b. 25 Dec. 1758

Jonathan RIPLEY, (*son of Wm. & Mary), b. 5 Mar. 1707*; d. 10 Aug. 1772 <Halifax VR:5>

CHILDREN OF Jonathan RIPLEY & Hannah STURTEVANT^{5} (Fear Cushman^{4}): (7) <Halifax VR:47>

Abigail RIPLEY^{6}, b. 28 May 1732

Rebecca RIPLEY^{6}, b. 20 July 1734

Perez RIPLEY^{6}, b. 20 Feb. 1737/8; d. 3 Jan. 1816*

Jonathan RIPLEY^{6}, b. 14 Aug. 1740

Abner RIPLEY^{6}, b. 7 (?) 1742/3

Hannah RIPLEY^{6}, b. 16 Apr. 1746

Silvanus RIPLEY^{6}, b. 29 Sept. 1749; d. 5 Feb. 1787*

Sarah FULLER^{5} (Nathaniel^{4}, Sam.$^{3-2-1}$), b. 28 Sept. 1712, Plympton <MD 3:163>; d. 21 July 1763, Halifax g.s. (wf of 2nd hus. Austin Bearse) <MD 9:152>

CHILDREN OF Isaac STURTEVANT^{5} (Fear Cushman^{4}) & Sarah FULLER: (9) <3-9, Halifax VR:52>

Deborah STURTEVANT^{6}, b. 12 Feb. 1731/2 <Plympton VR:203>
William STURTEVANT^{6}, b. 9 Oct. 1733 <Halifax VR:43>
Martha STURTEVANT^{6}, b. 18 Nov. 1735
Sarah STURTEVANT^{6}, b. 14 Mar. 1737/8; d. 25 Sept. 1747 <Halifax VR:3>
Isaac STURTEVANT^{6}, b. 11 Mar. 1739/40
Simeon STURTEVANT^{6}, b. 11 May 1742; d. 2 Mar. 1822, Halifax g.s., Monpouset Cem. <MD 10:11>
Samuel STURTEVANT^{6}, b. 19 Jan. 1744/5; d. 8 Jan. 1839 <MD 10:10>
Jesse Fuller STURTEVANT^{6}, b. 27 Mar. 1748
Nathaniel STURTEVANT^{6}, b. 2 Aug. 1750
Capt. Isaac STURTEVANT, d. 10 July 1806, ae 66, bur. Jamaica Plain Cem., W. Roxbury <NEHGR 10:20>
Mrs. Rebecca STURTEVANT, d. 7 June 1827, ae 69, bur. Jamaica Plain Cem., W. Roxbury <NEHGR 10:20>
Ruth TOMSON^{5}, (Amasa^{4}, Tho.^{3}, Mary Cooke^{2}), b. 14 Jan. 1744/5 <Halifax VR:50>; d. 8 May 1831, Halifax g.s., Monpouset Cem. <MD 10:10>

CHILDREN OF Simeon STURTEVANT^{6} & Ruth TOMSON: (10) <Halifax VR:50>
Amasa STURTEVANT^{7}, b. 28 Aug. 1765
Simeon STURTEVANT^{7}, b. 20 Aug. 1768
Levi STURTEVANT^{7}, b. 15 Aug. 1770; d. 21 June 1853, Pembroke g.s. <MD 10:238>
Son, b. 7 May 1772, d. 8 May 1772 <MD 10:11>
Nathaniel STURTEVANT^{7}, b. 18 Mar. 1773; d. 5 Mar. 1850 <MD 10:10>
Daniel STURTEVANT^{7}, b. 24 Nov. 1775; d. 15 Mar. 1840 <MD 10:9>
Solomon STURTEVANT^{7}, b. 2 Nov. 1777; d. 17 Aug. 1844 <MD 10:11>
William STURTEVANT^{7}, b. 14 Oct. 1779; d. 27 May 1811 <MD 10:11>
Ward STURTEVANT^{7}, b. 12 Mar. 1782
Ruth STURTEVANT^{7}, b. 20 June 1784
Mary CHAMBERLAIN^{6} (Freedom^{5}, Mary Soule^{4}, Aaron^{3}, John^{2}), d. 3 Oct. 1848, ae 81 (hus. g.s.)

CHILDREN OF Levi STURTEVANT^{7} & Mary CHAMBERLAIN: (11) <Pembroke VR:198>
Maria STURTEVANT^{8}, b. 10 Aug. 1794*; d. 6 Oct. 1796, ae "2y2m wanting 4 days" <MD 10:238>
Emily STURTEVANT^{8}, b. 21 Apr. 1796*
Levi STURTEVANT^{8}, b. 28 Dec. 1797*
Washington STURTEVANT^{8}, b. 3 Feb. 1800*
Matilda STURTEVANT^{8}, b. 2 May 1802*
Alphonso STURTEVANT^{8}, b. 28 Mar. 1804*
David STURTEVANT^{8}, b. 22 May 1806, d. 22 May 1806, ae 4 hours <MD 10:237>
Jonathan STURTEVANT^{8}, b. 22 May 1806, d. 22 May 1806, ae 4 hours <MD 10:237>
Maria STURTEVANT^{8}, b. 22 May 1806, d. 22 May 1806, ae 4 hours <MD 10:237> (triplets!)
Amos Tomson STURTEVANT^{8}, b. 16 Aug. 1807*
Solomon STURTEVANT^{8}, b. 30 Jan. 1810
Margaret JOHNSON, (*?dau. of John & Mary), b.? 30 Mar. 1766 <Kingston VR>

CHILDREN OF Simeon STURTEVANT^{7} (Simeon^{6})& Margaret JOHNSON: (5) <Halifax VR:25>
Ward STURTEVANT^{8}, b. 12 May 1791
Zadock STURTEVANT^{8}, b. 23 May 1795
Thomas STURTEVANT^{8}, B. 11 JULY 1799
Simeon STURTEVANT^{8}, b. 26 July 1803
Henry STURTEVANT^{8}, b. 19 Mar. 1807
Patience HOLMES, (*dau. of John),d. 8 Sept. 1755, ae 65, widow of 2nd hus. Elnathan Wood, Middleboro Green g.s. <MD 14:224>

CHILDREN OF Ichabod CUSHMAN^{4} (Isaac^{3}) & 2nd Patience HOLMES: (9) <Plympton, MD 3:165>
Johanah CUSHMAN^{5}, b. 17 Dec. 1713
William CUSHMAN^{5}, b. 13 Oct. 1715; d. 27 Aug. 1768, Middleboro Green g.s. <MD 12:200>
Sarah CUSHMAN^{5}, b. 8 Nov. 1717, Middleboro; d. 1 Feb. 1791*<Middleboro ChR:92>

Experience CUSHMAN^{5}, b. 12 July 1719

Patience CUSHMAN^{5}, b. 8 Apr. 1721; d. 1 Jan. 1769

Mary CUSHMAN^{5}, b. 22 Dec. 1723

Ichabod CUSHMAN^{5}, b. 12 May 1725

Rebecca CUSHMAN^{5}, b. 11 July 1727

Isaac CUSHMAN^{5}, b. 12 Aug. 1730

CHILDREN OF Jonathan SMITH Jr. & Experience CUSHMAN^{5}: (3) <Middleboro, MD 15:218>

Susanna SMITH^{6}, b. 2 June 1738

Thomas SMITH^{6}, b. 17 Apr. 1740

Ichabod SMITH^{6}, b. 21 Aug. 1742

Susanna THOMAS, d. 11 May 1724, ae 30, Middleboro Green g.s. <MD 4:73,14:133>

CHILDREN OF Jonathan SMITH & 1st Susanna THOMAS: (2) <Middleboro, MD 3:233>

Samuel SMITH, b. 30 Aug. 1714

Jonathan SMITH, b. 14 Feb. 1715/6

Sarah CHURCHILL, d. 5 June 1744, ae 49, Middleboro Green g.s. <MD 14:133>

CHILDREN OF Jonathan SMITH & 2nd Sarah CHURCHILL: (6) <1-5, Middleboro, MD 12:233>

Susanna SMITH, b. 30 Apr. 1726; d. 8 Oct. 1736, ae 11, Middleboro Green g.s. <MD 14:133>

Sarah SMITH, b. 16 Jan. 1727/8

John SMITH, b. 13 Feb. 1729/30

Mary SMITH, b. 23 Mar. 1731/2

Ebenezer SMITH, b. 29 Mar. 1734

Joseph SMITH, b. 17 July 1738 <MD 14:244>

Capt. Jonathan SMITH, d. 6 Sept. 1767, ae 79, Middleboro Green g.s. <MD 14:132>**<29>**

CHILDREN OF Capt. Jonathan SMITH & Rhoda (   ): (4) <Middleboro, MD 22:153>

Rhoda SMITH, b. 12 May 1754

Abigail SMITH, b. 17 Feb. 1756; d. 12 May 1776, ae 21, Middleboro Green g.s. <MD 14:132>

Lois SMITH, b. 7 Jan. 1759

Benjamin SMITH, b. 9 Nov. 1761

CHILDREN OF Holmes CUSHMAN^{6} (Ichabod^{5}) & Molly PADDOCK: (2)

Isaac CUSHMAN^{7}, b. 22 Jan. 1788 <Middleboro VR 4:1:48>

Andrew CUSHMAN^{7}, d. 28 Sept. 1789, ae 6m24d

Daniel VAUGHAN^{4} (*Jabez^{3}, Jos.^{2}, George^{1}), b. 29 Oct. 1712* <Middleboro VR>; d. 8 Jan. 1812* <Middleboro ChR:92>

CHILDREN OF Daniel VAUGHAN & Sarah CUSHMAN^{5} (Ichabod^{4}): (5)

Betty VAUGHAN^{6}, b. 20 Sept. 1736 <MD 8:249>

Lucia VAUGHAN^{6}, b. 9 June 1738 <MD 14:244>

Jabez VAUGHAN^{6}, b. 25 May 1740 <MD 14:246>

Sarah VAUGHAN^{6}, b. 11 July 1742 <MD 16:107>

Deborah VAUGHAN^{6}, b. 24 June 1749 <MD 24:39>

Lois SOULE^{5} (Zachariah^{4}, Ben.^{3}, John^{2}), b. 17 Dec. 1742 <Plympton VR>**<30>**

CHILDREN OF Jabez VAUGHAN^{6} & Lois SOULE: (8) <1-4, Middleboro VR>**<31>**

Asenath VAUGHAN^{7}, b. 9 Dec. 1765 <MD 24:39>

Daniel VAUGHAN^{7}, b. 18 Sept. 1768 <MD 24:39>

Deborah VAUGHAN^{7}, b. 27 Mar. 1771 <MD 24:39>

Lucy VAUGHAN^{7}, b. 7 Mar. 1773 <MD 32:6>

Jabez VAUGHAN^{7}, b. 30 July 1775*

Ebenezer VAUGHAN^{7}, b. 1 Dec. 1778*

Jonah VAUGHAN^{7}, b. 15 Aug. 1781*; d. 24 May 1855*, New Vineyard ME

Lois VAUGHAN^{7}, b. 13 Apr. 1783*

Rebecca MORTON, b. 25 Sept. 1785*, Middleboro; d. 10 July 184()

CHILD OF Jonah VAUGHAN^{7} & Rebecca MORTON:

Ira VAUGHAN^{8}, b. 12 July 1807*, New Vineyard ME; d. 8 Feb. 1849*

CHILDREN OF Thomas JOHNSON: (3)<32>

Abigail Luce JOHNSON, b. 26 Feb. 1810*; d. 21 May 1830* (1st wf. of Ira Vaughan*)

Katherine JOHNSON, b. 1 July 1814; d. 2 May 1839, New Vineyard ME (wf of Z. Morton Vaughan)

Emily JOHNSON, b. 31 Dec. 1816*; d. 17 Sept. 1837*

CHILD OF Ira VAUGHAN^{8} (Jonah^{7}) & 2nd Emily JOHNSON:

Joseph Warren VAUGHAN^{9}, b. 8 Nov. 1833*; d. 5 Apr. 1892*

Nehemiah COBB, b. 12 Jan. 1783* <Cobb Gen.:169>

CHILDREN OF Nehemiah COBB & Lois VAUGHAN^{7} (Jabez ^{6}): (4)* <Cobb Gen.:169>

Nathan COBB^{8}, b. 27 Feb. 1807

Nehemiah COBB^{8}, b. 6 Oct. 1808

Jabez Vaughan COBB^{8}, b. 13 Apr. 1811

Lucius COBB^{8}, b. 5 Dec. 1812

Susanna SAMPSON^{4} (*Jos.^{3}, George^{2}, Abraham^{1} <Giles Mem.:384>), d. 13 Sept. 1749,ae 34, Middleboro Green g.s. <MD 12:200>

CHILDREN OF William CUSHMAN^{5} (Ichabod^{4}) & 1st Susanna SAMPSON: (7) <Middleboro>

Joseph CUSHMAN^{6}, b. 19 Jan. 1736/7 <MD 8:248>; d. 5 Nov. 1800, Middleboro Green g.s. <MD 12:199>

Joanna CUSHMAN^{6}, b. 3 Apr. 1739 <MD 14:244>

William CUSHMAN^{6}, b. 12 Apr. 1741 <MD 15:121>; d. 30 Nov. 1815, Middleboro Green g.s. <MD 12:200>

Zenas CUSHMAN^{6}, b. 1 May 1743 <MD 15:121>

Noah CUSHMAN^{6}, b. 14 May 1745 <MD 16:107>; d. 29 Mar. 1818, Middleboro Green g.s. <MD 12:199>

Son, b. 3 Mar. 1747, d. 3 Mar. 1747, Middleboro Green g.s. <MD 12:200>

Ichabod CUSHMAN^{6}, d. 27 Sept. 1749, ae 23d, Middleboro Green g.s. <MD 12:199>

Priscilla (TINKHAM^{5}) Cobb (Shubael^{4}, Eben.^{3}, Mary Brown^{2}), b. 10 June 1726, Middleboro <MD 6:229> d. 15 Apr. 1769, Middleboro Green g.s. <MD 12:199>

CHILDREN OF William CUSHMAN^{5} & 2nd Priscilla (TINKHAM) Cobb: (7) <Middleboro>

Priscilla CUSHMAN^{6}, b. 23 Oct. 1751 <MD 18:154>

Isaac CUSHMAN^{6}, b. 27 Feb. 1754 <MD 18:155>

Susanna CUSHMAN^{6}, b. 13 Jan. 1756 <MD 18:155>

Andrew CUSHMAN^{6}, b. 26 Mar. 1757 <MD 20:35>

Perez CUSHMAN^{6}, b. 26 Jan. 1759 <MD 23:44>

Patience CUSHMAN^{6}, b. 16 Sept. 1764 <MD 23:44>

Welthea CUSHMAN^{6}, b. 13 Sept. 1767, d. 3 June 1768, Middleboro Green g.s. <MD 12:200>

Mercy SOULE^{6} (Jabez^{5}, Zachariah^{4}, Ben.^{3}, John^{2}), b. 28 Apr. 1748 <Halifax VR:53>; d. 24 Mar. 1788 Middleboro Green g.s. <MD 12:199>

CHILDREN OF Noah CUSHMAN^{6} (Wm.^{5}) & 1st Mercy SOULE: (10) <Middleboro>

William CUSHMAN^{7}, b. 17 Dec. 1769 <MD 29:185>

Jacob CUSHMAN^{7}, b. 27 Apr. 1771 <MD 30:11>

Noah CUSHMAN^{7}, b. 4 Apr. 1773 <MD 31:134>

Soule CUSHMAN^{7}, b. 29 Jan. 1775 <MD 31:134>

Mercy CUSHMAN^{7}, b. 12 Dec. 1776 <MD 31:134>

Andrew CUSHMAN^{7}, b. 26 Oct. 1778 <MD 31:134>

Zenas CUSHMAN^{7}, b. 11 Dec. 1780 <MD 31:134>

Abigail CUSHMAN^{7}, b. 25 June 1782 <MD 32:11>

Hercules CUSHMAN^{7}, b. 29 Nov. 1785 <MD 32:11>; d. 15 July 1832, Nemasket g.s.,Middleboro<MD 15:3>

Susanna CUSHMAN^{7}, b. 7 Mar. 1787 <MD 32:11>

Zilpha THOMPSON^{6} (Francis^{5}, Tho.^{4}, John^{3}, Mary Cooke^{2}), d. 23 June 1806, ae 43y3m10d, Middleboro Green g.s. <MD 12:200>

CHILDREN OF Noah CUSHMAN^{6} & 2nd Zilpha THOMPSON: (8) <5-8, Cushman Gen.:292>

Rebecca CUSHMAN^{7}, b. 12 June 1790 <MD 32:163>

Joanna CUSHMAN^{7}, b. 6 Aug. 1791 <MD 32:163>

Elias CUSHMAN^{7}, b. 4 July 1793 <MD 33:77>

Daniel CUSHMAN^{7}, b. 11 Sept. 1795 <MD 33:77>

Zilpah CUSHMAN^{7}, b. 5 Oct. 1798*

Joseph CUSHMAN^{7}, b. 31 Oct. 1800*

Priscilla CUSHMAN^{7}, b. 20 Apr. 1803*

Salome CUSHMAN^{7}, b. 12 Sept. 1804*

CHILD OF Noah CUSHMAN^{6} & 3rd Zerviah THOMAS (*dau. of Ben.)

Zerviah CUSHMAN^{7}, b. 18 Sept. 1811* <Cushman Gen.:292>

Mary WASHBURN^{8} (Abiel^{7}, Edw.$^{6-5}$, James^{4}, Eliz. Mitchell^{3}, Jane Cooke^{2}), b. 13 Oct. 1792, Middleboro<MD 33:78>;d. 26 Aug. 1813, Nemasket g.s., Middle.(1st wf of Hercules Cushman^{7})<MD 15:3>

CHILDREN OF Jacob CUSHMAN^{8} (Jacob^{7}) & Roxa SHAW: (7)

Harriet Peirce CUSHMAN^{9}, b. 26 Sept. 1824 <Middelboro VR 7:206>

James C. CUSHMAN^{9}, b. 1826, d. 11 Sept. 1827, ae 1y3m

Sarah H. CUSHMAN^{9}, b. 1828, d. 14 June 1830, ae 2y2m

George Harris CUSHMAN^{9}, b. 11 Mar. 1830 <Middleboro VR 7:206>

Sarah Eliza CUSHMAN^{9}, b. 29 Feb. 1832 <Middleboro VR 7:206>; d. 30 Sept. 1837*

William Jacob CUSHMAN^{9}, b. 1838, d. 20 June 1838, ae 3m3d

Florella Gertrude CUSHMAN^{9}*, b. Jan. 1848* <Cushman Gen.:596>

Sarah GIBBS^{4} (Alice Warren^{3}, Nathaniel^{2}), d. 28 Oct. 1716, ae 34, Plympton g.s. <MD 10:112>

CHILDREN OF Lieut. Isaac CUSHMAN^{4} (Isaac^{3}) & 1st Sarah GIBBS: (5) <Plympton, MD 3:166>**<33>**

Phebe CUSHMAN^{5}, b. 14 Mar. 1702/3

Alice CUSHMAN^{5}, b. 26 June 1705; d. 13 Aug. 1724 <MD 8:152>

Rebecca CUSHMAN^{5}, b. 14 Oct. 1707

Sarah CUSHMAN^{5}, b. 2 Dec. 1709

Nathaniel CUSHMAN^{5}, b. 28 May 1712

Mercy (BRADFORD^{4}) Freeman (John^{3}, Wm.^{2}), b. 20 Dec. 1681, Plymouth <MD 1:147>; d. 27 June 1738, Plympton g.s. <MD 10:112>

CHILDREN OF Lieut. Isaac CUSHMAN^{4} & 2nd Mercy (BRADFORD) Freeman: (4)**<34>**

Fear CUSHMAN^{5}, b. 10 July 1718

Priscilla CUSHMAN^{5}, b. 12 Dec. 1719

Isaac CUSHMAN^{5}, b. 29 Sept. 1721, d. 18 Oct. 1721, Plympton g.s. <MD 10:111>

Abigail CUSHMAN^{5}, b. 31 Dec. 1722; d. 8 Feb. 1784*

Nathaniel SPOONER, b. 21 Apr. 1709*, d. Nov. 1732* <Spooner Gen.:39,73>

CHILDREN OF Nathaniel SPOONER & Phebe CUSHMAN^{5}: (2)* <Spooner Gen.:73>

Alice SPOONER^{6}, b. 23 Aug. 1730

Rebecca SPOONER^{6}, b. 9 Jan. 1732

CHILD OF Barnabas HATCH & Phebe CUSHMAN^{5} (Isaac^{4}):

Abigail HATCH^{6}, bpt. Dec. 1742, Kent CT

MICRO #3 of 9

CHILDREN OF Nehemiah STURTEVANT Jr. & Fear CUSHMAN^{5} (Isaac^{4}): (4) <Plympton VR>

Peleg STURTEVANT^{6}, b. 25 Jan. 1735/6 <VR:201>

Perez STURTEVANT^{6}, b. 15 Nov. 1737 <VR:201>

Phear STURTEVANT^{6}, b. 6 Dec. 1745 <VR:206>

Ruth STURTEVANT^{6}, b. 12 Sept. 1747 <VR:206>

Robert WATERMAN^{3} (John^{2}, Robert^{1}), b. 9 Feb. 1681, Marshfield <MD 2:250>; d. 16 Jan. 1749/50, Monponsett g.s., Halifax <MD 10:105>

CHILDREN OF Robert WATERMAN & 1st Mary CUSHMAN^{4} (Isaac^{3}): (8) <Halifax VR:40>**<35>**

Isaac WATERMAN^{5}, b. 10 May 1703

Josiah WATERMAN[5], b. 5 Mar. 1704/5

Thomas WATERMAN[5], b. Oct. 1707; d. 22 Aug. 1789, Old Cem. g.s., Plympton <MD 11:194>

Rebecca WATERMAN[5], b. 9 Oct. 1710

Robert WATERMAN[5], b. 2 Mar. 1712/3; 8 Sept. 1761, Halifax g.s. <MD 10:105>

Mary WATERMAN[5], b. 25 Feb. 1715/6

Samuel WATERMAN[5], b. 11 Aug. 1718; d. 16 Nov. 1787* <Watermans of ME:40>

Anna WATERMAN[5], b. 6 Mar. 1720/1

Abigail (   ) WATERMAN, d. 28 Nov. 1771, ae 84y4m12d, Monponsett g.s., Halifax <MD 10:104>

CHILD OF Robert WATERMAN & 2nd Abigail (   ):

Abigail WATERMAN, b. 5 Mar. 1728/9, d. 9 Apr. 1729 <Halifax VR:40>

Joanna BRIANT, (dau. of Sam.), b. 1 Mar. 1701/2, Plymouth <MD 3:121>; d. 12 Feb. 1765, Plympton g.s. <MD 11:194>

CHILDREN OF Josiah WATERMAN[5] & Joanna BRIANT: (3) <Plympton, MD 2:52>

Ichabod WATERMAN[6], b. 3 Nov. 1723

Ephraim WATERMAN[6], b. 20 Oct. 1725

Josiah WATERMAN[6], b. 2 Aug. 1728

Hannah ROGERS[6] (Ben.[5], John[4-3], Joseph[2]), b. 5 Apr. 1735, Plymouth <MD 15:42>

CHILDREN OF Ichabod WATERMAN[6] & Hannah ROGERS: (8)* <Kingston>

Lydia WATERMAN[7], b. 5 Nov. 1758

Benjamin WATERMAN[7], b. 8 Aug. 1760

Zenas WATERMAN[7], b. 29 Dec. 1762

James WATERMAN[7], b. 21 Mar. 1765

Ichabod WATERMAN[7], b. 12 Aug. 1767

Hannah WATERMAN[7], b. 9 June 1770

Phebe WATERMAN[7], b. 30 Dec. 1771

Thomas WATERMAN[7], b. 10 Mar. 1776

Martha CUSHMAN[5]* (*Josiah[4], Elkanah[3], Mary Allerton[2]), d. 25 Sept. 1770, ae 59, Halifax g.s. <MD 10:105>

CHILDREN OF Robert WATERMAN[5] (Mary Cushman[4]) & Martha CUSHMAN: (7) <Halifax VR:42>

Abigail WATERMAN[6], b. 3 Aug. 1735; d. 9 Oct. 1735 <VR:1>

James WATERMAN[6], b. 17 Mar. 1737; d. 9 July 1737 <VR:1>

Abigail WATERMAN[6], b. 3 Jan. 1739; d. 3 Feb. 1739 <VR:1>

Susanna WATERMAN[6], b. 6 Feb. 1742

Martha WATERMAN[6], b. 6 Mar. 1744/5; d. 13 Sept. 1761 <VR:4>

Robert WATERMAN[6], b. 15 Sept. 1748; d. 18 Dec. 1748 <VR:3>

Rebecca WATERMAN[6], b. 5 Mar. 1750/1

CHILDREN OF Rev. Ephraim BRIGGS & Rebecca WATERMAN[6]: (12) <Halifax VR:16>

Ephraim BRIGGS[7], b. 3 Mar. 1769

William BRIGGS[7], b. 19 Feb. 1771

Rebecca BRIGGS[7], b. 19 Feb. 1773

Isaac BRIGGS[7], b. 26 May 1775

Thomas BRIGGS[7], b. 12 Jan. 1778

Robert Waterman BRIGGS[7], b. 25 Sept. 1779; d.y.

Richard BRIGGS[7], b. 2 Mar. 1782

Martha BRIGGS[7], b. 12 Apr. 1784

Polly BRIGGS[7], b. 17 Feb. 1786

Sally BRIGGS[7], b. 25 Jan. 1788

Charles BRIGGS[7], b. 17 Jan. 1791

John Kingsbury BRIGGS[7], b. 9 Dec. 1794

Mary TOMSON[4] (Tho.[3], Mary Cooke[2]), b. 8 May 1718, Middleboro <MD 3:86>; d. 9 Apr. 1756,Monsonsett g.s., Halifax <MD 10:105>

CHILDREN OF Samuel WATERMAN^{5} (Mary Cushman^{4}) & 1st Mary TOMSON: (10) <Halifax VR:46>

Ebenezer WATERMAN^{6}, b. 12 May 1738, d. 17 Aug. 1738

Zebadiah WATERMAN^{6}, b. 17 June 1739; d. 4 or 5 May 1756 <MD 10:106>

Seth WATERMAN^{6}, b. 1 Feb. 1740/1

Samuel WATERMAN^{6}, b. 25 June 1743; d. 10 Aug. 1825, Duck Creek g.s., Wellfleet <MD 12:137>

Thomas WATERMAN^{6}, b. 9 May 1745; d. 29 May 1745 <MD 10:106>

Nathaniel WATERMAN^{6}, b. 9 June 1746; d. 14 Jan. 1749/50 <MD 10:105>

Benjamin WATERMAN^{6}, b. 15 July 1748; d. 8 Jan. 1754 <MD 10:104>

Mary WATERMAN^{6}, b. 14 Nov. 1750; d. 20 Dec. 1753 <MD 10:105>

Nathaniel WATERMAN^{6}, b. 23 Sept. 1752; d. 11 Jan. 1754 <MD 10:105>

Robert WATERMAN^{6}, b. 15 Jan. 1755; d. 27 Sept. 1756 <MD 10:105>

CHILDREN OF Samuel WATERMAN^{5} & 2nd Mary FULLER: (5)

Asaph WATERMAN^{6}, b. 30 Sept. 1757, d. 17 Oct. 1757 <Halifax VR:46, MD 10:104>

Olive WATERMAN^{6}, b. 26 Oct. 1758, d. 14 Jan. 1759 <Halifax VR:38, MD 10:105>

Oliver WATERMAN^{6}, b. 5 May 1760 <Halifax VR:46>

Robert WATERMAN^{6}, b. 26 June 1762, d. 1 Feb. 1763 <Halifax VR:46, MD 10:105>

Abigail WATERMAN^{6}, b. 10 Nov. 1763 <Halifax VR:46>

Sarah ( ) WATERMAN, d. 4 Mar. 1795, ae 48, 1st wf of Sam., Duck Creek g.s., Wellfleet<MD 12:137>

CHILDREN OF Samuel WATERMAN^{6} & Sarah ( ): (2*)

Molly WATERMAN^{7}, b. c1769, d. 20 Dec. 1771, ae 1y8m <MD 12:137>

Samuel WATERMAN^{7}, b. c1786, d. 24 Mar. 1805, ae 19 <MD 12:137>

Lydia ( ) WATERMAN, d. 9 Apr. 1827, ae 76, 2nd wf of Sam., Duck Creek g.s., Wellfleet

Mercy FREEMAN^{6} (Jonathan^{5}, Tho.^{4}, Mercy Prence^{3}, Patience Brewster^{2}), b. 24 Apr. 1711, Harwich <MD 5:86>; d. pre 1763*

CHILDREN OF Thomas WATERMAN^{5} (Mary Cushman^{4}) & Mercy FREEMAN: (7*) <Freeman Gen.:99>**<36>**

Jonathan WATERMAN^{6}, b. 17 Dec. 1730

Abigail WATERMAN^{6}, b. 16 May 1733

Dau., b. 19 Apr. 1736

Mercy WATERMAN^{6}, b. 16 June 1739

Thomas WATERMAN^{6}, b. 23 July 1742

Priscilla WATERMAN^{6}, b. 22 Apr. 1745

Freeman WATERMAN^{6}, b. 16 July 1748 <Plympton VR:220>; d. 5 Apr. 1830, Thompson St. g.s., Halifax <MD 14:11>

CHILDREN OF Benjamin Franklin FARNSWORTH & Harriet N. JOSCELYN: (3) <Farnsworth Gen.:274>

Ella Frances FARNSWORTH, b. 19 Apr. 1846, New York, N.Y.

Edward Everett FARNSWORTH, b. 16 May 1847, New York, N.Y.

Mary deRose FARNSWORTH, b. 21 Jan. 1849, New York, N.Y.

Joanna TOMSON^{5} (John^{4}, Jacob^{3}, Mary Cooke^{2}), b. 9 Aug. 1751 <Halifax VR:49>; d. 10 Sept. 1833, Thompson St. g.s., Halifax <MD 14:11>

CHILDREN OF Freeman WATERMAN^{6} (Tho.^{5}) & Joanna TOMSON: (8) <Halifax VR:39>

Tomson WATERMAN^{7}, b. 26 June 1769

Rebecca WATERMAN^{7}, b. 30 Nov. 1771

Mercy WATERMAN^{7}, b. 3 Feb. 1774

Jonathan WATERMAN^{7}, b. 25 Dec. 1776; d. 25 Apr. 1784 <MD 14:11>

Joanna WATERMAN^{7}, b. 14 Apr. 1780

Priscilla WATERMAN^{7}, b. 16 May 1782

Abigail WATERMAN^{7}, b. 14 July 1784; d. 27 Dec. 1784 <Halifax VR:6>

Abigail WATERMAN^{7}, b. 24 Nov. 1786; d. 9 Dec. 1786 <Halifax VR:6>

William HARLOW^{4} (Rebecca Bartlett^{3}, Mary Warren^{2}), b. 2 June 1657, Plymouth <MD 12:195>; d. 28

Jan. 1711/12, Plymouth <MD 16:64> (hus. of Lydia Cushman^{3})

John HAWKS, b. 1633* <Essex Co. CT 11:85>; d. 5 Aug. 1694, Lynn CT <MD 17:224>

CHILDREN OF John HAWKS & 2nd Sarah CUSHMAN^{3}: (8) <MD 17:224>

Susan/Susana HAWKS^{4}, b. 29 Nov. 1662, Lynn; d. last of Nov. 1675

Adam HAWKS^{4}, b. 12 May 1664; d. pre 18 Nov. 1691 (adm.) <MD 17:227>

Anna HAWKS^{4}, b. 3 May 1666; d. last of Nov. 1675, Lynn

John HAWKS^{4}, b. 25 Apr. 1668

Rebecca HAWKS^{4}, b. 18 Oct. 1670; d. last of Nov. 1675

Dr. Thomas HAWKS^{4}, b. 18 May 1673, Lynn; d. pre 4 June 1722 (adm.)<Essex Co.Prob.#12943,313:450>

Mercy HAWKS^{4}, b. 14 Nov. 1675, Lynn; d. aft. Dec. 1710*

Ebenezer HAWKS^{4}, b. betw. 1673-77*; d. 9 Dec. 1766 <Lynn VR 2:498>**<37>**

Rebecca MAVERICK^{3} (Remember Allerton^{2}), bpt. 7 Aug. 1639*; d. 4 Nov. 1659

CHILD OF John HAWKS & 1st Rebecca MAVERICK^{3}:

Moses HAWKS^{4}, b. Nov. 1659

CHILDREN OF James HINDS & Anna HAWKS: (2) <Marblehead 2nd Ch.>

Anna HINDS, bpt. 6 Mar. 1790

Mary HINDS, bpt. 5 Aug. 1792

CHILD OF Adam HAWKS^{4} (Sarah Cushman^{3}) & Elizabeth ( ):

John HAWKS^{5}, b. 10 Apr. 1690 <MD 17:225>; d. pre 11 Sept. 1738 (adm.)

Mary WHITFORD, (dau of John), b. c1691; d. 21 Apr. 1758*, ae 67 <Lynn CT ChR>

CHILDREN OF John HAWKS^{5} & Mary WHITFORD: (6)

Adam HAWKES^{6}, b. pre Sept. 1717*; d. pre 11 Jan. 1774* (adm.)

Mary HAWKES^{6}, b. pre 1717*; d. 18 Nov. 1747*

Eve HAWKES^{6}, b. pre 1724*

Lydia HAWKES^{6}, b. ( )

Eunice HAWKES^{6}, b. ( )

Elizabeth HAWKES^{6}, b. ( )

Huldah BROWN, (dau of Josiah), d. pre 11 June 1747 <hus.2nd marr.- Lynn VR 2:177>

CHILD OF Adam HAWKES^{6} & 1st Huldah BROWN:

Huldah HAWKES^{7}, b. c1743, d. 1 Jan. 1818*, ae 75 <Westminster MA VR:215>

Lydia WILEY, (*? dau of Timothy & Mary, b. 17 Apr. 1724 <Reading VR:253>)

CHILDREN OF Adam HAWKES^{6} & 2nd Lydia WILEY: (5) <Lynn VR 1:181-3, 3:213>**<38>**

Lydia HAWKES^{7}, b. 28 Jan. 1748

John HAWKES^{7}, b. 14 July 1754

Mary HAWKES^{7}, b. 25 Dec. 1756

Benjamin HAWKES^{7}, b. 20 Sept. 1761

Adam HAWKES^{7}, b. 8 June 1764

Jonathan BROWN, d. 14 Mar. 1821*, ae 79 <Westminster MA VR:215>

CHILDREN OF Jonathan BROWN & Huldah HAWKES^{7}: (7) <Westminster VR>

Jonathan BROWN^{8}, b. 30 Aug. 1765*, d. 14 Mar. 1842*

Benjamin BROWN^{8}, b. 9 Mar. 1769*, d. 24 June 1804*

Joseph BROWN^{8}, b. 6 Apr. 1772*, d. 11 Sept. 1777

Huldah BROWN^{8}, b. 18 Oct. 1773*

Sally BROWN^{8}, b. 14 Dec. 1778*, d. 23 Oct. 1802*

Joseph BROWN^{8}, b. 13 Oct. 1780*, d. 31 Mar. 1826*

John BROWN^{8}, b. 13 Mar. 1785*, d. 29 Mar. 1809*

CHILDREN OF Jacob WALTON & Eunice HAWKES^{6} (John^{5}): (4*) <Reading VR>

Jacob WALTON^{7}, b. 19 Jan. 1745

Israel WALTON^{7}, b. 13 Feb. 1747/8

Mary WALTON^{7}, b. 7 Mar. 1749

Lois WALTON^{7}, b. 15 Mar. 1752

Ebenezer GILES, (*son of Eleazer & Lydia), bpt. 23 May 1714*

CHILD OF Ebenezer GILES & Eve HAWKES^{6} (John^{5}):<39>

Mary GILES^{7}, bpt. 25 May 1740* <Beverly 1st Unit. Ch.>

CHILDREN OF Nathaniel FELCH & Mary HAWKES^{6} (John^{5}): (7*)

Nathaniel FELCH^{7}, b. 23 July 1733, d. Aug. 1753

Nathaniel FELCH^{7}, b. 23 Apr. 1735

Mary FELCH^{7}, b. 9 Feb. 1736/7

Elizabeth FELCH^{7}, b. 21 Dec. 1739

Eunice FELCH^{7}, b. 19 Sept. 1741, d. 25 Sept. 1741

Abijah FELCH^{7}, b. 30 Sept. 1741 (sic)

Eunice FELCH^{7}, b. 21 Aug. 1746, d. 26 Aug. 1746

Elizabeth COGSWELL, (?dau. of John*), b.? 1 Aug. 1677* <Ipswich Court Rec.1:96>; d. 16 June 1718 <Lynn VR 2::499>

CHILDREN OF Ebenezer HAWKS^{4} (Sarah Cushman^{3}) & 1st Elizabeth COGSWELL: (3) <Lynn VR>

Ebenezer HAWKS^{5}, b. 14 July 1702 <VR 1:184>; d. 9d 11m 1741/2* <Lynn CT VR 2:498>

Elizabeth HAWKS^{5}, b. 24 Apr. 1704 <VR 1:184>

Samuel HAWKS^{5}, b. 12 May 1716 <VR 1:184>

Sarah (BASSETT)(Griffin) Newhall, (dau of Wm.), d. 27 3mth 1732*, Lynn, "cancer of breast", (2nd wf. of Ebenezer Hawks^{4})

Ruth ( ) GRAVES, d. 15 Jan. or July 1760*, Lynn (*3rd wf. of Ebenezer Hawks^{4}) <Z. Collins diary>

Anna BREED^{4} (*Sam.^{3}, Allen$^{2-1}$), b. 28 July 1706* <Lynn CT VR 1:61>

CHILDREN OF Ebenezer HAWKES^{5} & Anna BREED: (5)

Ebenezer HAWKES^{6}, b. ( )

Benjamin HAWKES^{6}, b. 31 Jan. 1730; d. 16 Apr. 1772, ae 42y3m <Marblehead g.s.> (family rcd.-28th)

Amos HAWKES^{6}, b. ( )

Nathaniel HAWKES^{*6}, b. ( )

James HAWKES^{*6}, b. ( )

Deborah KIMBALL, (dau of Joshua), b. 24 Oct. 1741; d. Oct. 1794

CHILDREN OF Benjamin HAWKES^{6} & Deborah KIMBALL: (7)<40>

Anna HAWKES^{7}, b. 30 Apr. 1761

Deborah HAWKES^{7}, b. 13 Sept. 1762; d. Oct. 1763

Benjamin HAWKES^{7}, b. 24 Jan. 1764; d. 30 Jan. 1806

Joshua HAWKES^{7}, b. 12 May 1766

Deborah HAWKES^{7}, b. 7 Mar. 1768; d. 18 Aug. 1769

Deborah HAWKES^{7}, b. 25 Jan. 1770

Elizabeth HAWKES^{7}, b. 5 Nov. 1771

CHILDREN OF Edward BOWEN & Deborah (KIMBALL) Hawkes: <40>

Sarah BOWEN, b. 23 Oct. 1775; d. 7 Nov. 1775

James BOWEN, b. 16 Oct. 1776; d. 1795/6, "ae 21", St. Bartholomew, W. Indies

Edward BOWEN, b. 23 Jan. 1779; d. Nov. 1805

Sarah BOWEN, b. 21 Feb. 1781

Elizabeth BOWEN, b. 3 Oct. 1783; d. 3 Oct. 1784

CHILDREN OF Samuel HAWKES^{5} (Eben.^{4}) & Philadelphia ( ): (5 of 9)<41>

Ebenezer HAWKES^{6}, d. 21 Aug. 1791 <Lynn VR 4:357>

Matthew HAWKES^{6}, b. ( )

Deliverance HAWKES^{6}, b. 23 Oct. 1753 <Lynn VR 4:234>

Patience HAWKES^{6}, b. 25 Jan. 1755 <Lynn VR 4:234>

Hannah HAWKES^{6}, d. 13 Oct. 1756

CHILDREN OF Ebenezer HAWKES^{6} & Rebecca ALLEY (dau of Sam.): (9) <Lynn VR 4:357>

Ebenezer HAWKES[7], b. 8 Jan. 1766
Abijah HAWKES[7], b. 10 Dec. 1767
William HAWKES[7], b. 14 Oct. 1769, d. 20 Oct. 1822
Rebecca HAWKES[7], b. 10 Dec. 1771, d. 12 Jan. 1776
Abigail HAWKES[7], b. 4 Sept. 1773
Rebecca HAWKES[7], b. 22 Mar. 1776
Elizabeth HAWKES[7], b. 12 June 1778
Lydia HAWKES[7], b. 9 Oct. 1780
Anna HAWKES[7], b. 28 Sept. 1785
Ruth BREED, (*dau of Ben. & Ruth), d. 19 Aug. 1776 <Lynn CT ChR.1> (wf of Matthew Hawkes[6](Sam.[5]))
CHILDREN OF Matthew HAWKES: (7) <Lynn>**<42>**
Miriam HAWKES, b. 11 Jan. 1777
Ruth HAWKES, b. 5 Oct. 1780
Matthew HAWKES, b. 4 Sept. 1782
Samuel HAWKES, b. 16 July 1785, d.y.
Micajah HAWKES, b. 16 July 1785 (twins)
Samuel HAWKES, b. 17 Aug. 1787
Nabby HAWKES, b. 4 May 1792

MICRO #4 of 9

Abigail FLOID, (dau of John & Sarah), d. c19 Oct. 1732, Lynn <Z. Collins Diary>
CHILDREN OF John HAWKS[4] (Sarah Cushman[3]) & Abigail FLOID: (3) <Lynn VR 2:49>
Sarah HAWKS[5], b. 14 Dec. 1699; d. 4 Mar. 1764* <Lynn ChR:2>
Abigail HAWKS[5], b. 7 June 1701
John HAWKS[5], b. 18 Nov. 1706
CHILDREN OF Cornelius JONES & Abigail HAWKS[5]: (5*)**<43>**
Thomas GOWING, (*son of John & Johannah), b. 30 Oct. 1690*<Lynn VR>; d. 19 Dec. 1769*<Lynn ChR:2>
CHILDREN OF Thomas GOWING & Sarah HAWKS[5]: (4) <Lynn VR 3:88>
John GOWING[6], b. 16 Nov. 1721; d. 28 Nov. 1737*
Timothy GOWING[6], b. 6 May 1727
Joseph GOWING[6], b. 7 May 1730
Thomas GOWING[6], b. 20 Feb. 1737
Capt. Nathaniel GOODHUE, b. c1670, d. 18 Aug. 1721*, ae 51 <Ipswich g.s.>
CHILDREN OF Capt. Nathaniel GOODHUE & Mercy HAWKS[4] (Sarah Cushman[3]): (7) <1-6, Ipswich VR 1:165>
William GOODHUE[5], b. 15 Oct. 1699; d. 23 Oct. 1772 <Ipswich VR 2:570>
Sarah GOODHUE[5], b. 8 Feb. 1701*
Nathaniel GOODHUE[5]*, b. 22 Nov. 1702*; d. 16 Sept. 1721*
John GOODHUE[5], b. 5 Jan. 1707*
Mercy GOODHUE[5]*, b. 19 Feb. 1709*; d. 12 Oct. 1721*
Elizabeth GOODHUE[5], b. 1 Dec. 1710*
Ebenezer GOODHUE[5], b. ( )
Ruth PRESTON, b. c1710, d. 3 Mar. 1787, ae about 77 <Ipswich VR 2:570>**<44>**
CHILDREN OF William GOODHUE[5] & Ruth PRESTON: (1 of 11)**<45>**
Ruth GOODHUE[6], bpt. 8 Nov. 1747; d. 20 June 1834
Sarah HAVEN, (dau of Richard), d. aft. 7 Mar. 1748/9* (will of brother Joseph) <Essex Co.Probate 328:430> (see next pg.)
CHILDREN OF Dr. Thomas HAWKS[4] (Sarah Cushman[3]) & Sarah HAVEN: (5) <Essex Co.Prob.328:430>
Hannah HAWKS[5], b. pre 1722
Sarah HAWKS[5], b. pre 1722
Elkanah HAWKS[5], b. pre 1722; d. aft. 16 Jan. 1778 (will) <Essex Co.Prob. 353:144>
Jonathan HAWKS[5], b. c1715; bur. 6 Feb. 1762*, ae 47 <Chelsea VR:492>

Thomas HAWKS[5], b. pre Sept. 1715; d. 4 Sept. 1736, drowned <Lynn VR 2:49>

CHILDREN OF Richard HAVEN & Susanna ( ): (3) <46>

Hannah HAVEN, b. 10 Aug. 1677

Joseph HAVEN, b. 17 Aug. 1680

Susanna HAVEN, b. 1 Oct. 1686

CHILDREN OF Elkanah HAWKES[5] (Thomas[4]) & Eunice NEWHALL: (4) <Lynn VR 4:32><47>

Thomas HAWKES[6], b. 5 Feb. 1742/3

Eunice HAWKES[6], b. 25 May 1745

Sarah HAWKES[6], b. 19 Mar. 1746/7

Elizabeth HAWKES[6], b. 11 Feb. 17( ) <last 2 figures not entered>

CHILDREN OF Thomas HOAKS/HAWKS & Esther NEWHALL: (7) <Lynn VR 4:518>

Joseph Haven HAWKS, b. 11 June 1769

Levi HAWKS, b. 1 June 1771

Simeon HAWKS, b. 3 May 1773

Love HAWKS, b. 14 Feb. 1775

Esther HAWKS, b. 8 June 1777

Samuel HAWKS, b. 1 Apr. 1779

Ruth HAWKS, b. 27 June 1781

CHILDREN OF Joseph Haven HAWKS & Mary HITCHINS: (5) <Lynn VR 5:140>

Thomas HAWKS, b. 21 Aug. 1792

Joseph Haven HAWKS, b. 26 July 1794

Lucinda HAWKS, b. 16 Feb. 1797

Mary HAWKS, b. 26 May 1800

Ruth HAWKS, b. 11 June 1802

CHILD OF Jonathan HAWKS[5] (Thomas[4]): (see below)

Hannah HAWKS[6], b. 7 Feb. 1751/2 <Lynn VR> (marr. Samuel Cheney)

Elizabeth BLAKE, widow, d. 16 Dec. 1855, ae 77y8m, Boston, old age; b. Boston, dau of Samuel & ( ) Cheney <Mass.VR 95:88>

James BLAKE, d. 3 July 1851, ae 71y3m, Boston; b. Milton <Mass. VR 59:43>

James BLAKE, (son of James & Thankful), b. 13 Mar. 1780, Milton<48>

CHILD OF Jonathan HAWKES[5] (Thomas[4]) & 1st Sarah NEWHALL:

Sarah HAWKES[6], b. 26 Apr. 1736 <Lynn VR 3:42>

Abigail FARRINGTON, (*?dau of John & Abigail), ?b. 28 Feb. 1725/6* <Lynn VR>

CHILDREN OF Jonathan HAWKES[5] & 2nd Abigail FARRINGTON: (7) (1-4, Lynn VR 3:218>

Elizabeth HAWKES[6], b. 21 May 1744

Joseph Haven HAWKES[6], b. 1 Mar. 1749/50

Hannah HAWKES[6], b. 7 Feb. 1751/2

Jonathan HAWKES[6], b. 19 July 1753; d. pre 31 Oct. 1786* (guardianship)<Suffolk Co.Prob.#18774>

William HAWKES[6], b. 4 3mth 1756*, Chelsea

Abigail HAWKES[6], b. 5 4mth 1761*, Chelsea

Edward HAWKES[6], bpt. 27 Nov. 1768*, Chelsea

CHILDREN OF Thomas CUSHMAN[3] & 1st Ruth HOWLAND[2]: (3) <Plymouth>

Robert CUSHMAN[4], b. Oct. 1664, d. 7 Sept. 1757, ae 92y11m3d, Kingston g.s. <MD 7:28><49>

Thomas CUSHMAN[4], b. c1670*; d. 9 Jan. 1726/7, ae 57<50>

Desire CUSHMAN[4], b. c1668; d. 8 Feb. 1762*, ae about 94, g.s. Tylers Point<51>

Abigail FULLER, b. c1652, d. 31 May 1734, ae 82, g.s. <Attleboro VR:656><52>

CHILDREN OF Thomas CUSHMAN[3] & 2nd Abigail FULLER: (4) <Plymouth>

Job CUSHMAN[4], b. ( ); d. pre 5 Mar. 1739 (adm.) <Plymouth Colony Probate 8:165>

Bartholomew CUSHMAN[4], b. 1683; d. 21 Dec. 1721, ae 38, Plympton g.s., Old Cem. <MD 10:111>

Benjamin CUSHMAN[4], bpt. 1 Mar. 1691 <Plymouth ChR 1:271>; d. 17 Oct. 1770, " <MD 10:111>

Samuel CUSHMAN^{4}, b. 16 July 1687* <Cushman Gen.:125>; d. 19 Feb. 1766, ae 79, Attleboro g.s.<53>

Sarah EATON^{4} (Ben.$^{3-2}$), b. 20 Oct. 1695, Plymouth <MD 2:78>; d. 13 Sept. 1737, Plympton g.s., Old Cemetary <MD 10:112>

CHILDREN OF Benjamin CUSHMAN^{4} & 1st Sarah EATON: (10) <Plympton, MD 3:165>

Jabez CUSHMAN^{5}, b. 11 Aug. 1713

Caleb CUSHMAN^{5}, b. 15 May 1715

Solomon CUSHMAN^{5}, b. 9 Sept. 1717

Jerusha CUSHMAN^{5}, b. 7 Dec. 1719; d. 22 May 1727 <MD 10:112>

Benjamin CUSHMAN^{5}, b. 25 May 1722

Sarah CUSHMAN^{5}, b. 29 Sept. 1725; d. 24 Jan. 1745/6 <MD 10:112>

Abigail CUSHMAN^{5}, b. 22 Nov. 1727; d. 4 May 1751, Plympton g.s. <MD 11:117>

Thomas CUSHMAN^{5}, b. 11 Oct. 1730; d. 30 Oct. 1777 <MD 10:112>

Jerusha CUSHMAN^{5}, b. 18 Oct. 1732*

Huldah CUSHMAN^{5}, b. 6 Apr. 1735*

Sarah ( ) BELL, b. c1694, d. 16 Jan. 1783, Plympton g.s., Old Cem. <MD 10:112><54>

Zabdiel SAMSON^{5} (Hannah Soule^{4}, Ben.^{3}, John^{2}), b. 26 Apr. 1727, Plympton <MD 3:93>; d. 16 Sept. 1776, Harlem N.Y., "killed in battle", Plympton g.s. <MD 11:119>

CHILD OF Zabdiel SAMSON & Abigail CUSHMAN^{5}:

Sarah SAMSON^{6}, b. 2 June 1749*

CHILDREN OF Jabez CUSHMAN^{5} (Ben.^{4}) & Sarah PADELFORD: (4 of 8*)<55>

Zebedee CUSHMAN^{6}, b. 17 Feb. 1740, Middleboro, d. 17 Mar. 1831, Taunton g.s.

Samuel CUSHMAN^{6}, b. 6 Apr. 1742; d. pre 13 July 1794 <wf 2nd marr.>

Phebe CUSHMAN^{6}, b. c1737, d. 25 Feb. 1796, ae 59, Bridgewater g.s. <Scotland Cem.>

Capt. Jabez CUSHMAN^{6}, b. 9 July 1756, Middleboro; d. 3 June 1827, New Gloucester ME

Ursula BEARCE, d. 18 Apr. 1840

CHILDREN OF Capt. Jabez CUSHMAN^{6} & Ursula BEARCE: (12) <Cushman Gen.:161,257>

Sally CUSHMAN^{7}, b. 25 May 1783, d. 26 Dec. 1846

Betsy CUSHMAN^{7}, b. 31 Jan. 1786

Samuel CUSHMAN^{7}, b. 13 Apr. 1787

Polly CUSHMAN^{7}, b. 17 July 1789

Isaac CUSHMAN^{7}, b. 10 Oct. 1791, d. 1852

Celia CUSHMAN^{7}, b. 25 Nov. 1793

Jabez CUSHMAN^{7}, b. 12 Feb. 1796

Sophronia CUSHMAN^{7}, b. 7 Feb. 1798, d. June 1798

Rosamond CUSHMAN^{7}, b. 13 Apr. 1799, d. 10 May 1808

Solomon Paddleford CUSHMAN^{7}, b. 10 May 1801

Ammi R.M. CUSHMAN^{7}, b. 8 Feb. 1803, d. 26 Feb. 1837

Joseph E. Foxcroft CUSHMAN^{7}, b. 21 May 1806

Sally CUSHMAN, widow of Alvah, d. 5 July 1893, ae 93y3m6d, Taunton, senile debility,housekeeper; b. Taunton, dau of William Leonard & Sally Seavy/Leavy <Mass VR 436:338>

Benjamin HUTCHIN, d. 2 Sept. 1811, Minot ME <U.S. Pension Rcd.>

Nancy RIDER^{7} (*Hannah Cushman^{6}, Jabez^{5}), b. c1772 <age 66 in Sept. 1838*>; d. aft.1848*<56>

CHILDREN OF Benjamin HUTCHIN & Nancy RIDER^{7}: (5) <NEHGR 88:58>

Nancy HUTCHIN^{8}, b. 20 Apr. 1789, Paris ME

Merum HUTCHIN^{8}, b. 3 June 1792, Poland ME

Jonathan HUTCHIN^{8}, b. 28 Dec. 1793

Lydia HUTCHIN^{8}, b. 29 July 1796

Jabez HUTCHIN^{8}, b. 30 Dec. 1798

Sarah PADELFORD, b. c1757, d. 16 Feb. 1833, ae 76, Taunton g.s.

CHILDREN OF Zebedee CUSHMAN^{6} (Jabez^{5}) & Sarah PADELFORD: (7) <Cushman Gen.:161,255>

Apollos CUSHMAN^{7}, b. 9 Aug. 1782

Betsy CUSHMAN^{7}, b. 9 June 1785

Sarah CUSHMAN^{7}, b. 28 Feb. 1788

Selina CUSHMAN^{7}, b. 25 May 1790; d. 21 Apr. 1835, Taunton g.s.

Ann CUSHMAN^{7}, b. 5 Nov. 1793

Christianna CUSHMAN^{7}, b. 18 Oct. 1795; d. 27 June 1805 <Taunton VR>

Alvah CUSHMAN^{7}, b. 10 Oct. 1797

Lydia GANO, b. 11 Aug. 1752

CHILDREN OF Samuel CUSHMAN^{6} (Jabez^{5}) & Lydia GANO: (6) <Cushman Gen.:161,254>

Sarah CUSHMAN^{7}, b. 15 Feb. 1772, d. aft. 1852

Lewis CUSHMAN^{7}, b. 20 May 1774

Jane CUSHMAN^{7}, b. 19 Aug. 1776

Samuel CUSHMAN^{7}, b. 18 Sept. 1778, d. at sea

Adoniran CUSHMAN^{7}, b. 28 June 1780

George Washington CUSHMAN^{7}, b. 1 Aug. 1782, d. 3 Oct. 1849

Lt. Joseph BASSETT, b. 1731; d. 6 May 1803

CHILDREN OF Lt. Joseph BASSETT & 1st Phebe CUSHMAN^{6} (Jabez^{5}): (8) <Hist. Bridgewater:112>

Caleb BASSETT^{7}, b. 11 Nov. 1757

Phebe BASSETT^{7}, b. 19 Aug. 1759

Nathan BASSETT^{7}, b. 12 Aug. 1763

Abigail BASSETT^{7}, b. 12 Sept. 1765

Joseph BASSETT^{7}, b. 5 Jan. 1769

Hannah BASSETT^{7}, b. 1771

David BASSETT^{7}, b. ( )

Rev. Cushman BASSETT^{7}, b. ( )

Sarah (PRIOR)(Fobes) Eaton, d. 1839, ae 100 (2nd wf of Lt. Joseph Bassett)

Anna CHIPMAN^{5} (Jacob^{4}, Sam.^{3}, Hope Howland^{2}), b. 31 Mar. 1730 <Halifax VR:41>; d. 4 Jan. 1778, Plympton g.s. <MD 11:64> (wf of Tho. Cushman^{5}, Ben.^{4})

Lydia BREWSTER^{4} (*Wm.^{3}, Love^{2}), b. 11 Feb. 1680, Duxbury <MD 9:229>; d. betw. 27 Sept. 1744(will) - 16 Mar. 1749 (bond) <Plymouth Colony Probate 11:216, 12:366>**<57>**

CHILDREN OF Job CUSHMAN^{4} (Tho.^{3}) & Lydia BREWSTER: (3) <Plymouth, MD 7:176>

Maria CUSHMAN^{5}, b. 16 Feb. 1706/7

Job CUSHMAN^{5}, b. 10 Feb. 1710/11; d. 12 Nov. 1729 <g.s.>

Lydia CUSHMAN^{5}, b. 31 Oct. 1718

Persis ( ) CUSHMAN, b. c1671, d. 14 Jan. 1743/4, Kingston g.s. <MD 7:28>

CHILDREN OF Robert CUSHMAN^{4} (Tho.^{3}) & Persis ( ): (7) <Plymouth, MD 4:111>

Robert CUSHMAN^{5}, b. 2 July 1698; d. 13 Sept. 1751, Kingston g.s. <MD 7:28>

Ruth CUSHMAN^{5}, b. 25 Mar. 1700

Abigail CUSHMAN^{5}, b. 3 July 1701

Hannah CUSHMAN^{5}, b. 25 Dec. 1705

Thomas CUSHMAN^{5}, b. 14 Feb. 1706; d. 13 June 1768, Kingston g.s. <MD 7:28>

Joshua CUSHMAN^{5}, b. 14 Oct. 1707; d. 25 Mar. 1764, Marshfield g.s. <MD 12:56>

Jonathan CUSHMAN^{5}, b. 28 July 1712; d. 7 Dec. 1775, Kingston g.s. <MD 7:28>

Mary SOULE^{4} (Jos.^{3}, John^{2}), b. 18 Dec. 1711, Duxbury, d. 25 June 1750, Duxbury<MD 11:235, 12:167>

CHILDREN OF Joshua CUSHMAN^{5} & 1st Mary SOULE: (8) <Duxbury, MD 12:122>

Joseph CUSHMAN^{6}, b. 6 Oct. 1733

Joshua CUSHMAN^{6}, b. 25 Nov. 1734

Mary CUSHMAN^{6}, b. 17 May 1736

Ezra CUSHMAN^{6}, b. 29 Jan. 1738

Paul CUSHMAN^{6}, b. 7 June 1741

Apollos CUSHMAN^{6}, b. 8 Apr. 1744

Cephas CUSHMAN^{6}, b. 15 Nov. 1745; d. 12 Feb. 1808*, Rochester g.s. <VR 2:371>

Soule CUSHMAN^{6}, b. 9 Jan. 1748; d. 15 Nov. 1795*, Littleton NH

Deborah FORD, d. 1 July 1789, ae 71, Marshfield g.s. <MD 12:56>

CHILDREN OF Joshua CUSHMAN^{5} & 2nd Deborah FORD: (4) <1-2, Duxbury, MD 12:165>

Mial CUSHMAN^{6}, b. 23 May 1753

Consider CUSHMAN^{6}, b. 12 Apr. 1755

Robert CUSHMAN^{6}, b. 11 Feb. 1758* <Cushman Gen.:153>

Deborah CUSHMAN^{6}, b. 11 Apr. 1762* <Cushman Gen.:153>

Judith CLARK, b. 26 Sept. 1749* <Rochester VR 1:81>; d. 1 Oct. 1832 <Rochester VR 2:371>

CHILDREN OF Cephas CUSHMAN^{6} & Judith CLARK: (15)**<58>**

CHILD OF Joshua CUSHMAN^{6} & Mercy WADSWORTH* (*dau of John):

Joshua CUSHMAN^{7}, b. ( ); d. 12 Nov. 1776, ae 12y2m28d <MD 9:160>

MICRO #5 of 9

Lydia KEMPTON, (dau of Ephraim), b. 16 Feb. 1753 <Dartmouth VR>; d. pre 1776*

CHILD OF Soule CUSHMAN^{6} (Joshua^{5}) & 1st Lydia KEMPTON:

Thomas CUSHMAN^{7}, b. ( ); d. 1815*

Thankful DELANO, b. 8 Feb. 1757*

CHILD OF Soule CUSHMAN^{6} & 2nd Thankful DELANO*:

Delano CUSHMAN^{7}, b. 30 Jan. 1776*

Mercy WASHBURN^{5} (Lydia Billington^{4}, Isaac^{3}, Francis^{2}), b. 21 Apr. 1702, Plymouth <MD 2:165>; d. 3 May 1796, Kingston g.s. <MD 7:87>

CHILDREN OF Robert CUSHMAN^{5} (Robert^{4}) & Mercy WASHBURN: (1 of 13)**<59>**

Lydia CUSHMAN^{6}, b. c1726, d. 3 Apr. 1784, ae 58 (wf of Josiah Fuller^{5})

John FULLER^{4} (Sam.$^{3-2-1-}$), d. 25 Sept. 1778, ae 80, Kingston g.s. <MD 7:87> (2nd hus. of Mercy Washburn)

CHILDREN OF John MAGRAY & Abigail ( ): (4) <Yarmouth N.S. VR 2:88>

Eliza MAGRAY, b. 16 Dec. 1804

Nabby Jane MAGRAY, b. 30 Jan. 1806

John MAGRAY, b. 9 Dec. "1806"

Sophia MAGRAY, b. 3 Dec. 1807

Jebogne Pt. "Old Town" Cemetery, Yarmouth N.S.:

Capt. John MAGRAY, d. 9 Nov. 1845, ae 71, on same stone with:

Robbins MAGRAY, d. 5 Sept. 1841, ae 17y5m

Abigail, wf of Capt. John MAGRAY, d. 2 Apr. 1870, ae 82y9m, on same stone with:

Mrs. Catharine CROWELL, d. 1 May 1861, ae 41

Joseph ROBINS Sr., d. 8 July 1839, ae 82y6m27d, side by side with:

Mrs. Elizabeth ROBBINS, wf of Joseph Robbins Sr., d. 27 Oct. 1845, ae 85y7m12d

* * * * *

CHILDREN OF Luke PERKINS & Ruth CUSHMAN^{5} (Rob.^{4}): (3*) <Plympton VR>

Ignatius PERKINS^{6}, b. 15 July 1720

Hannah PERKINS^{6}, b. 27 May 1723

Mary PERKINS^{6}, b. 28 June 1726

Alice HAYWARD^{4} (Tho.^{3}, Sarah Mitchell^{2}, Experience^{1}), b. 7 Apr. 1707, Bridgewater <MD 7:55>

CHILD OF Thomas CUSHMAN^{5} (Rob.^{4}) & Alice HAYWARD:**<60>**

Thomas CUSHMAN^{6}, b. 25 Sept. 1736*, d. 15 Oct. 1820*

Mehitable FAUNCE^{5} (Lydia Cooke^{4}, Jacob$^{3-2}$), b. 11 Apr. 1722, Plymouth <MD 5:100>; d. 19 June 1761 Kingston g.s. <MD 7:28>

CHILDREN OF Thomas CUSHMAN^{5} (Rob.^{4}) & Mehitable FAUNCE: (12) <*Cushman Gen.:131,146 (dates*)>

Lydia CUSHMAN^{6}, b. 23 Nov. 1739, d. 4 Jan. 1747/8

Job CUSHMAN^{6}, b. 18 Jan. 1741/2, d. 30 Dec. 1747
Elkanah CUSHMAN^{6}, b. 18 Jan. 1741/2 (twins), d. 30 Dec. 1747
Bartholomew CUSHMAN^{6}, b. 18 Feb. 1743/4, d. 30 Dec. 1747
Mary CUSHMAN^{6}, b. 24 Feb. 1745/6, d. 30 Dec. 1747
Desire CUSHMAN^{6}, b. 24 July 1748, d. 25 Oct. 1822
Sarah CUSHMAN^{6}, b. 19 Sept. 1750
Amaziah CUSHMAN^{6}, b. 17 Oct. 1752, d. 1 June 1800
Elisha CUSHMAN^{6}, b. 15 Jan. 1755, d. 17 May 1790
James CUSHMAN^{6}, b. 22 Dec. 1756, d. 15 Nov. 1832
John CUSHMAN^{6}, b. 15 Jan. 1759, d. Apr. 1799
Samuel CUSHMAN^{6}, b. 20 Feb. 1761, d. 21 July 1761
Bethiah THOMPSON, (dau of Tho. & Jane (Washburn)), b. 15 Nov. 1755*, Bridgewater
CHILD OF Thomas CUSHMAN^{6} (Tho.^{5}) & Bethiah THOMPSON:
Thomas CUSHMAN^{7}, b. c1796; d. 20 Aug. 1889, ae 93y9m18d, Bridgewater, heart disease, farmer, b. Bridgewater <Mass.VR 401:348>
Lucy CUSHMAN, d. 21 July 1883, ae 84y3m1d, Bridgewater, consumption, marr., housewife, b. Bridgewater, dau. of Cornelius & Martha Pratt <Mass.VR 347:303>
Fear CORSSER, b. c1685, d. 2 Dec. 1767, ae 82, Attleboro g.s.
CHILDREN OF Samuel CUSHMAN^{4} (Tho.^{3}) & Fear CORSSER: (8) <1-6, Plympton, MD 5:181>
Desire CUSHMAN^{5}, b. 18 Sept. 1710
Mercy CUSHMAN^{5}, b. 8 Feb. 1712/3; d. 11 Jan. 1797 <Attleboro Epitahs by Ira B.Peck,:113>
Samuel CUSHMAN^{5}, b. 10 July 1715; d. 27 Apr. 1727 <MD 10:112>
Joseph CUSHMAN^{5}, b. 7 Jan. 1717; d. ()9 May 1727 <MD 10:112>
Jacob CUSHMAN^{5}, b. 20 Mar. 1719/20; d. betw. 19 Nov. 1792 (will)- 1 Aug. 1796 (prob.)<Bristol Co. Prob. 34:170,173>**<61>**
Jemima CUSHMAN^{5}, b. 23 Oct. 1724, d. 2 May 1727 <MD 5:182, 10:111>
Bartholomew CUSHMAN^{5}, b. c1726, d. 26 Aug. 1736*, ae 10, Attleboro g.s.
Jemima CUSHMAN^{5}, b. c1729, d. 2 Apr. 1736*, ae 7, Attleboro g.s.
Mrs. Abigail CUSHMAN, d. 31 May 1734, ae 82, g.s. (wf of Tho.) <Attleboro Epitaphs, by Ira Peck>
Ebenezer FOSTER^{4} (*John^{3-2-1}), b. 20 Aug. 1709*, Dorchester, d. 18 June 1749* <Foster Gen.(1899)>
CHILDREN OF Ebenezer FOSTER & Desire CUSHMAN^{5} (Sam.^{4}): (12*) <Foster Gen.(1899): 713,14,17>
Huldah FOSTER^{6}, b. 21 Sept. 1731
Mercy FOSTER^{6}, b. 19 June 1733, d. 20 June 1733
Mercy FOSTER^{6}, b. 22 May 1734
Fear FOSTER^{6}, b. 24 Feb. 1736, d. 26 Feb. 1736
Fear FOSTER^{6}, b. 9 Mar. 1737
Ebenezer FOSTER^{6}, b. 9 Apr. 1739
Jemima FOSTER^{6}, b. 6 July 1741
Samuel FOSTER^{6}, b. 14 June 1743
Desire FOSTER^{6}, b. 10 June 1745, d. Aug. 1745
Desire FOSTER^{6}, b. 12 Aug. 1746
Bartholomew FOSTER^{6}, b. Sept. 1748, d. Nov. 1748
Bartholomew FOSTER^{6}, b. Sept. 1749, d. 1776
Oliver PECK, d. June 1796*, Norway NY <Foster Gen.(1899):714>
CHILDREN OF Oliver PECK & Fear FOSTER^{6}: (9*) <Foster Gen.:714>
Nancy PECK^{7}, b. 25 Nov. 1759
Oliver PECK^{7}, b. 22 Nov. 1761
Joseph PECK^{7}, b. 13 Nov. 1763, d. 1840
Foster PECK^{7}, b. 20 Dec. 1765
Amos PECK^{7}, b. 16 May 1768

Ira PECK^{7}, b. 15 Oct. 1771, d. 4 May 1864

Lewis PECK^{7}, b. 17 Dec. 1773

Eli PECK^{7}, b. 23 Jan. 1776

Polly PECK^{7}, b. 23 Jan. 1778

CHILDREN OF Ira PECK^{7} & Lydia PALMER* (dau of Caleb): (9*) <Foster Gen.(1899):714>

Olive PECK^{8}, b. 9 Dec. 1799

Eliza PECK^{8}, b. 30 June 1802

Mary PECK^{8}, b. 6 Nov. 1804

Ann M. PECK^{8}, b. 9 July 1807

Sarah PECK^{8}, b. 22 Dec. 1809

Ira L. PECK^{8}, b. 18 Aug. 1812

Jane PECK^{8}, b. 24 Dec. 1814

Anna C.T. PECK^{8}, b. 12 June 1817

Louisa A. PECK^{8}, b. 28 Dec. 1819

Noah FULLER, d. 10 Aug. 1786, ae 74 <Attleboro Epitaphs by Ira B. Peck, p.113>

CHILDREN OF Noah FULLER & Mercy CUSHMAN^{5} (Sam.^{4}): (5) <Attleboro TR, Jillson Mss.,p.67>

Mercy FULLER^{6}, b. 2 May 1742

Noah FULLER^{6}, b. 10 Jan. 1743/4; d. 21 June 1788 <Attleboro TR, Jillson Mss.,p.555>

Sibulah FULLER^{6}, b. 6 Jan. 1745/6

Chloe FULLER^{6}, b. 6 Aug. 1747

Comfort FULLER^{6}, b. ( )

Noah FULLER, d. 12 Jan. 1715/6 <Attleboro TR, Jillson Mss., p.193>

John BATES, d. pre 15 Dec. 1834 (prob.) <Thompson CT Probate Court>

CHILDREN OF John BATES & Chloe FULLER^{6}: (1 of 3)**<62>**

Alanson BATES^{7}, b. 30 Jan. 1772 <Attleboro VR>, d. 21 Aug. 1842, dysentry <Webster VR 3:287>

CHILD OF Alanson BATES^{7}:

Nelson BATES^{8}, b. Webster, d. 2 Feb. 1889, ae 87y6m21d, apoplexy, farmer <Webster VR 402:567>

Lucia BATES, d. 31 Dec. 1895, ae 91y4d, widow, debility; b. Thompson, dau of Ira Jacobs & A. Joslin <Webster VR 456:723>

Sarah STRONG, (dau of Jedediah), d. 25 Dec. 1726*, ae 52, Lebanon g.s.

CHILDREN OF Thomas CUSHMAN^{4} (Tho.^{3}) & Sarah STRONG: (6)**<63>**

CHILDREN OF Thomas CUSHMAN^{5} (Tho.$^{4-3}$) & Mary ( ): (7) <Lebanon CT>

Oliver CUSHMAN^{6}, b. 24 Nov. 1729*; d. 1759*

Sybil CUSHMAN^{6}, b. 7 Apr. 1732*

Rhoda CUSHMAN^{6}, b. 4 Feb. 1733/4*

Mercy CUSHMAN^{6}, b. 23 Oct. 1735*

Mary CUSHMAN^{6}, b. 16 May 1737*

Thomas CUSHMAN^{6}, b. 19 Dec. 1739*

Sarah CUSHMAN^{6}, b. 6 Nov. 1743*

REMEMBER ALLERTON^{2} (Isaac^{1})

Moses MAVERICK, d. 28 Jan. 1685/6, Marblehead <MD 5:130>**<64>**

CHILDREN OF Moses MAVERICK & 1st Remember ALLERTON^{2}: (7) <Salem, Essex Inst.Hist.Coll.6:228-43>

Rebecca MAVERICK^{3}, bpt. 7 Aug. 1639 <6:228>; d. 4 Nov. 1659, Lynn <MD 17:223>

Mary MAVERICK^{3}, bpt. 14 Feb. 1640/1 <6:237>**<65>**

Abigail MAVERICK^{3}, bpt. 12 Jan. 1644/5 <6:240>; d. pre Jan. 1685* <MD 5:129, 132>

Elizabeth MAVERICK^{3}, bpt. 13 Dec. 1646 <6:240>, d.y.

Samuel MAVERICK^{3}, bpt. 19 Dec. 1647 <6:241>; d. pre 1686

Elizabeth MAVERICK^{3}, bpt. 30 Sept. 1649 <6:242>; d. pre 29 Nov. 1698*

Remember MAVERICK[3], bpt. 12 Sept. 1652 <6:243>

CHILDREN OF Moses MAVERICK & 2nd Eunice ( ) ROBERTS: (4)<66>

Mary MAVERICK, bpt. 6 Sept. 1657 <Salem, Essex Coll.6:244>

Moses MAVERICK, bpt. 1m 3d 1660 <Boston Rcd.com.9:77>

Sarah MAVERICK, b. ( ); d. aft. 31 Aug. 1706

Aaron MAVERICK, bpt. 20 Mar. 1663 <Salem, Essex Coll.7:13>

John NORMAN, b. c1660 (ae about 26 on 16 July 1686)<MD 5:136>

CHILDREN OF John NORMAN & Sarah MAVERICK[2] (Moses[1]): (10) <Marblehead VR>

Richard NORMAN, b. 4 Sept. 1684

Eunice NORMAN, b. 14 Mar. 1686

Moses NORMAN, b. 23 Feb. 1687

John NORMAN, b. 2 Mar. 1690

Sarah NORMAN, b. 26 Jan. 1693

Benjamin NORMAN, b. 18 Aug. 1694

John NORMAN, bpt. 26 Apr. 1696

Benjamin NORMAN, bpt. 8 Oct. 1699

Jonathan NORMAN, bpt. 9 Mar. 1700/01

Elizabeth NORMAN, b. 31 Aug. 1706

Sarah HAWKES, d. 18 June 1792 <Lynn VR>

CHILDREN OF Richard SHUTE Jr. & Sarah HAWKES: (3) <Lynn VR>

Sarah SHUTE, b. 3 Apr. 1788

Thomas Hawks SHUTE, b. 12 Mar. 1790, d. 18 Aug. 1791

Polley SHUTE, b. 15 June 1792, d. 15 Aug. 1792

MICRO #6 of 9

Samuel WARD[2] (Sam.[1]), bpt. 18 Nov. 1638, Hingham; d. betw. 30 July 1690 - 12 Mar. 1690/1 (prob.) <Essex Co.Probate #28928><67>

Samuel WARD[1], b. c1593, d. 30 Aug. 1682, ae 89, Charlestown MA

Mrs. Samuel WARD, d. 28 Nov. 1638, Hingham

Frances ( ) WARD, d. 11 June 1690, ae 83, Copps Hill g.s. <2nd wf of Samuel[1]>

CHILDREN OF Samuel WARD[2] & Abigail MAVERICK[3] (Remember Allerton[2]): (4)<68>

CHILD OF Samuel WARD[2] & 2nd Sarah (BRADSTREET) Hubbard:<69>

Mercy WARD, b. ( )

Capt. William HINDS, d. betw. 9 Feb. 1735 (will) - 30 June 1736 (prob.) <Essex Co.Prob.#13381, 320:335-7>

CHILDREN OF Capt. William HINDS & Abigail WARD[4] (Abigail Maverick[3]): (4) <Marblehead VR>

John HINDS[5], b. 14 Feb. 1682

Abigail HINDS[5], bpt. 1 Feb. 1684/5

Rebecca HINDS[5], bpt. 10 Apr. 1686; d. aft. 9 Feb. 1735*

William HINDS[5], bpt. 22 July 1688; d.y.

CHILDREN OF Joseph HORMAN & Abigail HINDS[5]: (2) <Marblehead ChR><70>

Joseph HORMAN[6], bpt. 21 Oct. 1711*

Mary HORMAN[6]*, bpt. 9 May 1714*

CHILDREN OF John HINES/HINDS[5] (Wm.[4]) & Constance BENNETT: (4) <Marblehead VR 1:259>

Abigail HINDS[6], bpt. 26 May 1706; d.y.

John HINDS[6], bpt. 22 June 1707

Abigail HINDS[6], bpt. 11 June 1710

Susanna HINDS[6], bpt. 8 Nov. 1713

CHILDREN OF Thomas ROLLS & Abigail HINDS[6]: (7*) <Marblehead VR 1:439>

Thomas ROLLS[7], bpt. 5 Jan. 1730

Mary ROLLS[7], bpt. 10 Oct. 1731

Abigail ROLLS^{7}, b. 16 June 1734

Elizabeth ROLLS^{7}, bpt. 20 Nov. 1737

Susanna ROLLS^{7}, bpt. 30 Dec. 1739

Sarah ROLLS^{7}, bpt. 11 July 1742

John ROLLS^{7}, bpt. 25 Aug. 1745

John NORTHEY, d. betw. 20 Dec. 1744 (will) - 28 Jan. "1744" (prob.)<Essex Co.Probate #19601,

CHILDREN OF John NORTHEY & Susanna HINDS^{6}: (4*) <Marblehead VR 2:211,307> 326:139-41>

John NORTHEY^{7}, bpt. 17 Dec. 1732

Sarah NORTHEY^{7}, bpt. 26 Jan. 1734/5; d.y.

Joseph NORTHEY^{7}, bpt. 14 Aug. 1737

Sarah NORTHEY^{7}, bpt. 14 Jan. 1738/9; d. pre 7 May 1769 <hus.2nd marr.>

CHILDREN OF Roger VICKERY & Susanna HINDS^{6}: (3) <Marblehead VR>

Hannah VICKERY^{7}, bpt. 1 Oct. 1749

Elizabeth VICKERY^{7}, bpt. 24 Nov. 1751

Mary VICKERY^{7}, bpt. 1 Aug. 1756

Mercy LeCRAW, (dau. of John & Hannah), bpt. 8 Apr. 1744*

CHILDREN OF Joseph NORTHEY^{7} (Susanna Hinds^{6}) & Mercy LeCRAW: (7) <Marblehead VR 1:367>

John NORTHEY^{8}, bpt. 26 Sept. 1762

Mercy NORTHEY^{8}, bpt. 9 June 1765; d. betw. 5 Sept. 1793 <Essex Co.Deeds 189:51> - 1 May 1795 <hus 2nd marr.int.>

Joseph NORTHEY^{8}, bpt. 25 Feb. 1770

Sarah Craw NORTHEY^{8}, bpt. 2 Feb. 1772

Joseph NORTHEY^{8}, bpt. 23 Jan. 1774

Roger NORTHEY^{8}, bpt. 23 Jan. 1774 (twins)

Hannah NORTHEY^{8}, bpt. 8 Feb. 1778

CHILD OF Capt. Joseph NORTHEY & Elizabeth ( ):

Ebenezer NORTHEY, b. 30 Jan. 1786*, Scituate

CHILDREN OF John NORTHEY^{8}. & Mary CROSS: (8) <Marblehead VR 1:367>

John NORTHEY^{9}, bpt. 19 Feb. 1786

Samuel Bartol NORTHEY^{9}, bpt. 19 Feb. 1786 (twins)

John NORTHEY^{9}, bpt. 21 Sept. 1788

Mercy Craw NORTHEY^{9}, bpt. 20 Feb. 1791

John NORTHEY^{9}, bpt. 27 Oct. 1793

Joseph NORTHEY^{9}, bpt. 4 Mar. 1798

Samuel NORTHEY^{9}, bpt. 30 Aug. 1801[<71>]

Samuel NORTHEY^{9}, bpt. 18 Aug. 1805[<71>]

CHILDREN OF Levi MORSE, (son of Joseph & Mary (Randall)) & Mercy Craw NORTHEY^{9}: (11) <Marblehead VR 3: >[<72>]

Child, d. 19 or 20 May 1817, ae 9m

Mercy MORSE^{10}, bpt. 7 Sept. 1817, ae 5y

Mary Jane MORSE^{10}, bpt. 7 Sept. 1817, ae 3y

Louisa MORSE^{10}, bpt. 6 Sept. 1818, ae 6m

Levi MORSE^{10}, b. 6 Aug. 1820

Child, d. 11 Feb. 1823, ae 6wks

Deborah Northey MORSE^{10}, b. 28 Dec. 1823

Abigail S. Graves MORSE^{10}, bpt. 16 June 1827, ae 9m

Lucy Maria MORSE^{10}, b. 18 Jan. 1829

Hannah MORSE^{10}, b. 1 Feb. 1832

James Laskey MORSE^{10}, b. 5 Nov. 1834

Samuel BARTOL, d. 23 Feb. 1835, Salem[<73>]

CHILDREN OF Samuel BARTOL & Mercy NORTHEY[8] (Jos.[7]): (2)
Samuel BARTOL[9], bpt. 24 Dec. 1786, d. 28 Dec. 1837, ae 51 <Marblehead VR 1:34, 2:484>
Mercy BARTOL[9]*, b. 2 Feb. 1790*?
Mercy Craw BARTOL, d. 11 Sept. 1844 (wf of Levi Wallis)
Levi WALLIS, d. 23 Jan. 1827
Sally RUSSELL, d. 2 Feb. 1827 <Marblehead VR 2:484>
CHILDREN OF Samuel BARTOL[9] & 1st Sally RUSSELL: (9) <Marblehead>
Samuel BARTOLL[10], bpt. 11 June 1809; d. 19 June 1809
Thomas Russell BARTOLL[10], bpt. 11 June 1809 (twins); d. 19 June 1809
Sally Elizabeth BARTOLL[10], b. 18 Nov. 1811
Samuel F. BARTOLL[10], b. 27 Dec. 1813
Thomas R. BARTOLL[10], b. 18 Apr. 1816
John A. BARTOLL[10], b. 11 Feb. 1818
Child, b. 1820, d. 10 Dec. 1821, ae 15 or 17 mths.
Marcia Ann BARTOLL[10], b. 27 Jan. 1823
Child, d. 22 Jan. 1827
CHILD OF Samuel BARTOL[9] & 2nd Hannah RUSSELL:
Franklin BARTOLL[10], b. 2 July 1834
Richard WOOD, d. 8 Feb. 1805*, ae 73
CHILDREN OF Richard WOOD & Sarah NORTHEY[7] (Susanna Hinds[6]): (6*) <poss. Marblehead>
Sarah WOOD[8], bpt. 28 Aug. 1757
Richard WOOD[8], bpt. 12 Aug. 1759
Roger WOOD[8], bpt. 7 Nov. 1762
Sarah WOOD[8], bpt. 16 Sept. 1764
Charles WOOD[8], bpt. 23 Nov. 1766
Hannah WOOD[8], bpt. 27 Dec. 1768
CHILDREN OF William GROSS & Rebecca HINDS[5] (Abigail Ward[4]):(9) <Marblehead 1st Ch.>
William GROSS[6], b. 10 Feb. 1711
Rebecca GROSS[6], b. 7 Oct. 1712
Harrison GROSS[6], b. 28 Apr. 1714
Deborah GROSS[6], bpt. 22 Apr. 1716
Susanna GROSS[6], bpt. 21 Dec. 1718
Jerusha GROSS[6], bpt. 26 Nov. 1721
John GROSS[6], bpt. 15 Mar. 1723/4
Abigail GROSS[6], bpt. 9 July 1727
Elizabeth GROSS[6], bpt. 29 Mar. 1730
John TUTTLE, d. 26 Feb. 1715/16, ae 48y10m5d, Ipswich g.s. <Ipswich VR 2:698>
CHILDREN OF John TUTTLE & Martha WARD[4] (Abigail Maverick[3]): (7) <Ipswich VR>
Martha TUTTLE[5], b. 1690* <VR 1:372>; d. 15 May 1763*, ae 73, Ipswich g.s. <VR 2:580>
Mary TUTTLE[5], b. 7 July 1696* <VR 1:373>
Abigail TUTTLE[5], b. 25 Apr. 1701* <VR 1:373>
Remember TUTTLE[5], b. ( ); d. pre 30 Sept. 1735 <hus.2nd marr.>
William TUTTLE[5], bpt. 30 Sept. 1705* <VR 1:374>; d. 10 Dec. 1726*, ae 22, Ipswich
Sarah TUTTLE[5], b. c1707 <*age about 17 in 1724>
Susanna TUTTLE[5], b. c1709 <*age about 16 in 1725>; d. 8 May 1790*, ae "87", Andover g.s. (wf of Dr. Nicholas NOYES, who d. 17 May 1765*, ae 63, Andover <Noyes Gen.1:310>)
Mark HASKELL, (son of Mark & Elizabeth), b. 16 Sept. 1687 <Gloucester VR 1:331>; d. 25 Aug. 1775* <Ipswich VR 2:580>
CHILDREN OF Mark HASKELL & Martha TUTTLE[5]: (12) <1-9, Gloucester; 10-12, Ipswich>**<74>**
Elizabeth HASKELL[6], b. 23 Dec. 1710 <VR 1:336>

Martha HASKELL[6], b. 18 Feb. 1711/2 <VR 1:342>

Mark HASKELL[6], b. 19 Aug. 1713 <VR 1:342>

Lucy HASKELL[6], b. 21 May 1715 <VR 1:341>

Priscilla HASKELL[6], b. 18 Oct. 1718 <VR 1:343>

Jane HASKELL[6], b. 22 or 24 June 1722 <VR 1:339>

Jane HASKELL[6], b. 31 May 1723 <VR 1:339>

Jeanna/Johanna HASKELL[6], b. 27 Sept. 1724 <VR 1:339>

George HASKELL[6], b. 3 Aug. 1726 <VR 1:337>

Tuttle HASKELL[6], bpt. 29 Dec. 1728 <VR 1:179>; d. 8 Jan. 1728* <VR 2:580>

Eunice HASKELL[6], bpt. 4 July 1731 <VR 1:178>

Rebecca HASKELL[6], bpt. 27 Aug. 1732 <VR 1:178>

Sarah LORD, d. 6 Oct. 1771, ae 24 <Ipswich VR 2:594>

CHILD OF Jonathan INGERSOLL & Sarah LORD:

Sarah INGERSOLL, bpt. 10 Mar. 1771, d. 11 Feb. 1791 <Ipswich VR 1:205, 2:595>

CHILDREN OF Nathaniel LORD:

Sarah LORD, bpt. 21 May 1749 <Ipswich VR 1:248>

Mary LORD, bpt. 21 May 1749 (twins) <Ipswich VR 1:246>

CHILDREN OF Mark HASKELL & Elizabeth ( ): (3) <Gloucester VR>

George HASKELL, b. 18 Oct. 1686 <VR 1:330>

Mark HASKELL, b. 16 Sept. 1687 <VR 1:331> (see pg. 92)

William HASKELL, b. 1 Jan. 1689/90 <VR 1:331>

CHILDREN OF Mark HASCALL & Jemima ( ): (9) <Gloucester VR>

Francis HASCALL, b. 18 June 1722 <VR 1:337>

Mark HASCALL, b. 20 Oct. 1723 <VR 1:342>

Mary HASCALL, b. 13 Aug. 1725 <VR 1:342>

Sollomon HASCALL, b. 16 July 1729 <VR 1:330>

Mary HASCALL, b. 16 July 1729 (twins) <VR 1:332>

Jane HASCALL, b. 26 Sept. 1730 <VR 1:339>

Solomon HASCALL, b. 16 July 1731 <VR 1:345>

Abigail HASCALL, b. 14 Apr. 1732 <VR 1:329>

Solomon HASCALL, b. 4 Dec. 1734 <VR 1:330>

CHILDREN OF Mark HASKELL: (3) <Gloucester VR>

Lucy HASKELL, bpt. 5 June 1727 <VR 1:341>

Abigail HASKELL, bpt. 23 Apr. 1732 <VR 1:333>

Mark HASKELL, bpt. 12 Oct. 1746 <VR 1:342>

Nathaniel WARNER, (*son of John & Mary), b. 6 July 1693* <Ipswich VR 1:384>; d. 2 Aug. 1763*<Newbury VR>

CHILDREN OF Nathaniel WARNER & Mary TUTTLE[5] (Martha Ward[4]): (12) <Ipswich VR>

Mary WARNER[6], bpt. 2 June 1717, ae 4m <VR 1:384>

Abigail WARNER[6], bpt. 3 Aug. 1718 <VR 1:382>

John WARNER[6], bpt. 20 Dec. 1719, ae 10m <VR 1:384>

Nathaniel WARNER[6], bpt. 5 Feb. 1720 <VR 1:384>

Martha WARNER[6], bpt. 13 Jan. 1722/3 <VR 1:384>

John WARNER[6], bpt. 25 Sept. 1726 <VR 1:384>

William WARNER[6], bpt. 17 Mar. 1727 <VR 1:385>

Joseph WARNER[6], bpt. 22 Nov. 1730 <VR 1:384>

Benjamin WARNER[6], bpt. 1 Feb. 1735 <VR 1:383>

Susanna WARNER[6], bpt. 29 Jan. 1737 <VR 1:385>

Lucy WARNER[6], bpt. 27 July 1740*

Sarah WARNER[6], b. ( )

CHILD OF Nathaniel WARNER Jr.:
Susanna WARNER, bpt. 20 Sept. 1746 <Ipswich VR 1:385>
CHILDREN OF John WARNER^{6} (Nath.^{5}) & Susanna HODGKINS: (9) <Ipswich VR 1:384>
Susanna WARNER^{7}, bpt. 24 Sept. 1749
Joanna WARNER^{7}, bpt. 23 Aug. 1752
John WARNER^{7}, bpt. 23 Aug. 1752 (twins)
Mary WARNER^{7}, bpt. 26 Jan. 1755
Lois WARNER^{7}, bpt. 6 Feb. 1757
Lucy WARNER^{7}, bpt. 18 Feb. 1759
Benjamin WARNER^{7}, bpt. 5 July 1761 <VR 1:383>
Joseph WARNER^{7}, bpt. 5 July 1761 (twins)
Stephen WARNER^{7}, b. 9 June 1769
Job HARRIS, d. 17 Sept. 1771*, shopkeeper <will - Essex Co.Prob.#12490, 347:226>
CHILDREN OF Job HARRIS & 1st Remember TUTTLE^{5} (Martha Ward^{4}): (9*) <Ipswich VR>
Elizabeth HARRIS^{6}, bpt. 21 Sept. 1723, d. 3 Oct. 1723
Job HARRIS^{6}, bpt. 30 Aug. 1724, d. 4 Nov. 1728
Nathaniel HARRIS^{6}, bpt. 30 July 1727
Sarah HARRIS^{6}, bpt. 1 Dec. 1728, d. 24 Sept. 1729, ae 21m
Job HARRIS^{6}, bpt. 15 Jan. 1729, d. 17 Nov. 1731
Sarah HARRIS^{6}, bpt. 12 Sept. 1731, d. 18 Nov. 1732
Job HARRIS^{6}, bpt. 14 Jan. 1732
Edward HARRIS^{6}, bpt. 30 June 1734
Sarah HARRIS^{6}, b. ( ) <mentioned in deed>
CHILDREN OF Job HARRIS & 2nd Ruth ( ) GOODALE: (2*)
Elizabeth HARRIS, bpt. 6 Feb. 1736, d. 20 June 1737
Elizabeth HARRIS, bpt. 28 Jan. 1737
"Widow of Job Harris, d. 5 Jan. 1786*"
CHILDREN OF Nathaniel HARRIS^{6} (Remember Tuttle^{5}): (2)
Nathaniel HARRIS^{7}, b. ( )
Sally HARRIS^{7}, b. ( )
CHILD OF Robert CALDER & Sally HARRIS^{7}:
Frances Wentworth CALDER^{8}, bpt. 13 Sept. 1772*, St. Paul's Ch., Newburyport
Joseph DOLIVER, d. 1688*?, <Marblehead ChR.>
CHILD OF Joseph DOLIVER & Mary WARD^{4} (Abigail Maverick^{3}):
Margaret DOLIVER^{5}, b. ( )
CHILD OF William WATERS & Mary WARD^{4} (Abigail Maverick^{3}):
Hannah WATERS^{5}, bpt. 11 Aug. 1700 <Marblehead ChR.>
CHILDREN OF Philip TEWKSBERRY & Hannah WATERS^{5}: (4) <Marblehead ChR.>
Nathaniel TEWKSBERRY^{6}, b. 7 Sept. 1722
Samuel TEWKSBERRY^{6}, bpt. 16 Aug. 1724
William TEWKSBERRY^{6}, bpt. 16 July 1727
Mary TEWKSBERRY^{6}, bpt. 22 Mar. 1729/30
CHILDREN OF Mary DOLIVER/DOLLABER: (8) <Marblehead ChR.>
Joseph DOLIVER, bpt. 6 Sept. 1684
Abigail DOLIVER, bpt. 13 Dec. 1685
Peter DOLIVER, bpt. 12 May 1689
Samuel DOLIVER, bpt. 8 Mar. 1690/1
John DOLIVER, bpt. 19 May 1695
Hannah DOLIVER, bpt. 19 May 1695
Thomas DOLIVER, bpt. 27 Sept. 1696

Peter DOLIVER, bpt. 19 Mar. 1698/9

<u>MICRO #7 of 9</u>

CHILD OF Peter DOLIBER & Mary ( ):

Mary DOLIBER, bpt. 25 Feb. 1732/3 <Marblehead ChR>

CHILDREN OF John CURTIS & Margaret DOLIVER^{5} (Mary Ward^{4}): (4) <Marblehead ChR.>

Deliverance CURTIS^{6}, bpt. 22 June 1712

John CURTIS^{6}, bpt. 9 Nov. 1712

John CURTIS^{6}, bpt. 25 May 1714

Agnes CURTIS^{6}, bpt. 28 Aug. 1720

William WILSON, d. pre 8 Nov. 1732* (adm.)

CHILDREN OF William WILSON & 1st Remember WARD^{4} (Abigail Maverick^{3}): (2*)**<75>**

John WILSON^{5}, b. 29 Sept. 1681

Samuel WILSON^{5}, b. 17 Aug. 1683, d. 26 June 1686

CHILD OF William WILSON & 2nd Mary PEARSE*, (*dau. of John & Isabel):

Mary WILSON*, b. 4 Nov. 1690*

CHILDREN OF Samuel WARD^{4} (Abigail Maverick^{3}) & Sarah TUTTLE*,(*dau. of Simon):(4)<Ipswich VR:704>

Samuel WARD^{5}, b. 16 June 1702*, d. 8 July 1702*

Sarah WARD^{5}, d. 7 May 1703*

Sarah WARD^{5}, b. pre 14 July 1705***<76>**

Abigail WARD^{5}, b. pre 14 July 1705*, d.? 23 Oct. 1730***<76>**

Nathaniel GRAFTON, d. 11 Feb. 1670/71*, Barbadoes <Salem VR, Essex Inst.Hist.Coll.2:97>

CHILDREN OF Nathaniel GRAFTON & Elizabeth MAVERICK^{3}: (3) <Salem VR>

Elizabeth GRAFTON^{4}, b. 18 Dec. 1667*; d. 26 Mar. 1754/5

Remember GRAFTON^{4}, b. 29 Sept. 1669*; d. pre 25 June 1695*

Priscilla GRAFTON^{4}, b. 12 Mar. 1670/1*

Thomas SKINNER, d. 28 Dec. 1690*, baker <Boston Rcd.Com.9:194> (2nd hus. of Eliz.Maverick)

John HAWKS, d. 5 Aug. 1694, Lynn <VR 17:224>

CHILD OF John HAWKS & Rebecca MAVERICK^{3}:

Moses HAWKS^{4}, b. Nov. 1659 <MD 17:223, 5:132>; d. 1 Jan. 1708/9, Lynn <MD 17:225>**<77>**

Margaret COGSWELL,(*dau. of John), b. 6 Sept. 1675*<Ipswich VR 1:97>;d.aft. 7 Dec. 1719<MD 17:234

CHILDREN OF Moses HAWKS^{4} & Margaret COGSWELL: (5) <Lynn, MD 17:225>

Moses HAWKS^{5}, b. 4 Mar. 1698/9; d. 1 Dec. 1760* <Lynn VR, Z.Collins Diary>

Margaret HAWKS^{5}, b. 5 Nov. 1700

Adam HAWKS^{5}, b. 15 Dec. 1702, d. 22 July 1729, Lynn g.s.

John HAWKS^{5}, b. 27 Jan. 1704/5; d. 20 8mth 1748* <"PR5", Zach Collins Diary>

Rebecca HAWKS^{5}, b. 12 Aug. 1708

Daniel HITCHENS, d. "c15:2:1731, ae about 100" <Lynn VR, Z. Collins Diary>**<78>**

Mrs. Daniel HITCHENS, widow, bur. "12:5:1737" <Lynn VR, Z. Collins Diary>**<78>**

Hannah PREAST, d. aft. 23 Apr. 1765 (wf of 2nd hus Thomas Fuller, below)<Essex Co. Deeds 113:137>

CHILDREN OF John HAWKES^{5} & Hannah PREAST: (8) <Lynn VR 3:208>

Mary HAWKES^{6}, b. 28 June 1733

Hannah HAWKES^{6}, b. 13 May 1735

Rebecca HAWKES^{6}, b. 21 Apr. 1737, d.y.

Lydia HAWKES^{6}, b. 24 July 1739

Sarah HAWKES^{6}, b. 26 Aug. 1741

Adam HAWKES^{6}, b. 3 or 5 Dec. 1743

Rebecca HAWKES^{6}, b. 13 Apr. 1746

Dr. John HAWKES^{6}, b. 3 June 1749; d. 26 Jan. 1827 <Lancaster VR:183>

Thomas FULLER, (*?son of Elisha & Eliz.), b. ?4 July 1691* <Lynn VR 1:155>; d. c14 Aug. 1766**<79>**
<Lynn VR 2:483> (will - Essex Co. Prob.#10424, 343:194,270,272, 343:194, 344:235>

Hannah JAMES, (*dau of Ben. & Mary), b. 2 Feb. 1748/9*, Marblehead*; d. aft. 1834*

CHILDREN OF John HAWKES^{6} & Hannah JAMES: (6)

Hannah HAWKES^{7}, b. 3 Feb. 1772 <Willard Gen.(1915):202>; d. 7 Apr. 1843, Schuyler, N.Y.

John HAWKES^{7}, b. c1773, d. 8 Oct. 1847, ae 74, Middle Cemetary <Lancaster ChR:431>

Mary HAWKES^{7}, b. ( )

Sally HAWKES^{7}, b. 1779, d. 12 Mar. 1813, ae 34 <Lancaster VR:185>

Catherine HAWKES^{7}, b. 24 Mar. 1784, Lancaster, d. 18 Aug. 1838 <Bible>

Benjamin HAWKES^{7}, b. 1787, d. 27 Jan. 1860, Templeton MA, ae 72y2m, paralysis, cabinet maker <Mass.Vital Stat.140:245>

Alice ALLEN, d. aft. 4 Jan. 1848

CHILDREN OF John HAWKES^{7} & Alice ALLEN: (14) <1-9, 11 & 12 - Lancaster VR:208>

Alice HAWKES^{8}, b. 10 Mar. 1796

John HAWKES^{8}, b. 7 May 1797

Sally HAWKES^{8}, b. 10 Oct. 1798

Daniel A. HAWKES^{8}, b. 20 Apr. 1800

James HAWKES^{8}, b. 19 Mar. 1802

Hariot HAWKES^{8}, b. 18 Nov. 1803

Benjamin HAWKES^{8}, b. 15 May 1805

Sewall HAWKES^{8}, b. 22 Jan. 1807; d. 22 Mar. 1809

Cynthia HAWKES^{8}, b. 10 June 1809; d. 6 Sept. 1811

Rebecca HAWKES^{8}, b. 29 Apr. 1811

Austiss HAWKES^{8}, d. 1 Apr. 1817, ae 6mths <Lancaster VR:182, ChR;359>

Mary Plimpton HAWKES^{8}, b. 20 Jan. 1817; d. pre 25 Mar. 1844* <father's will>**<80>**

Cynthia Austiss HAWKES^{8}, b. 25 Jan. 1818 <Lancaster VR:209>

Child, b. Sept. 1822, d. ae 2wks <Lancaster ChR:361>

Silas WILLARD^{6} (Nathaniel^{5}, Wm.^{4}, Henry$^{3-2}$, Simon^{1}), b. 29 Aug. 1771, Lancaster, d. 18 Nov. 1819 <Willard Gen.(1915):202>

CHILDREN OF Silas WILLARD & Hannah HAWKES^{7} (John^{6}): (5)

Jonas WILLARD^{8}, b. 7 May 1795; d. 1877

Silas WILLARD^{8}, b. 25 Sept. 1799; d. 5 Oct. 1850, Schuyler, N.Y.

Benjamin Hart WILLARD^{8}, b. 27 Sept. 1807, "Hoosick Falls"; d. 5 Dec. 1891, Rome, N.Y.

Joel WILLARD^{8}, b. 1809

Harriet WILLARD^{8}, b. 1811

MICRO #8 of 9

Jonas WHITNEY, (son of Jonathan & Mary), b. 27 Aug. 1772 <Lancaster VR:108>; d. 14 Jan. 1846, dropsy <Lancaster VR:372>

CHILD OF Jonas WHITNEY & Mary HAWKES^{7} (John^{6}):

Mary WHITNEY^{8}, b. 7 Mar. 1804 <Lancaster VR:224>

Jonas LANE, b. c1762, d. ?6 June 1848, ae 87 <Lancaster VR:268, ChR:396>

CHILDREN OF Jonas LANE & Sally HAWKES^{7} (John^{6}): (3)

Sarah Ann LANE^{8}, bpt. 4 Aug. 1811* <Lancaster ChR:344>**<81>**

Mary Hawkes Kendall Ballard LANE^{8}, bpt. 4 Apr. 1813*; d. 30 July 1814* <Lancaster ChR:450>

Daughter, d. 31 July 1813*, ae 5mths (mother d. 12 Mar. 1813)

Samuel PHELPS, b. 22 Jan. 1757, Lancaster <Phelps Family 2:1616>**<82>**

CHILDREN OF Samuel PHELPS & Lovenia MORSE, (dau of Jonas & Mary): (2) <Phelps Family 2:1616>**<82>**

Anthony PHELPS, b. 20 Jan. 1786 <Marlboro VR:145>

Jonas PHELPS, b. 20 Aug. 1788, Lancaster

CHILDREN OF Anthony PHELPS, (son of Sam.) & Catherine HAWKS^{7} (John^{6}): (9)

Anthony PHELPS^{8}, b. 11 May 1812

Benjamin Hawkes PHELPS^{8}, b. 7 Dec. 1813

Jonas PHELPS^{8}, b. 5 Aug. 1815

Catherine May PHELPS^{8}, b. 9 May 1817, Lunenburg VT, d. 19 Sept. 1847 <Bible>**<83>**

Samuel PHELPS^{8}, b. 5 May 1819

Joseph PHELPS^{8}, b. 18 Feb. 1821

Merrick PHELPS^{8}, b. 23 July 1823

Henry Cleveland PHELPS^{8}, b. 29 May 1826

Maryann PHELPS^{8}, b. 29 May 1826 (twin)

Andrew Jackson FARNSWORTH, (son of Ben. & Dorcas), b. 23 Mar. 1815; d. 18 Aug. 1873 <Bible>

CHILD OF Andrew Jackson FARNSWORTH & 1st Catherine May PHELPS^{8}:

Mark Anthony FARNSWORTH^{9}, b. 7 Sept. 1843, Lancaster; d. 2 June 1925

Mary C. POTTER, d. 16 Apr. 1880, ae 68y10m24d

CHILD OF Andrew Jackson FARNSWORTH & 2nd Mary C. POTTER:

Merrick P. FARNSWORTH, b. 16 Jan. 1849

CHILDREN OF Benjamin HAWKES^{7} (John^{6}) & Polly BALLARD: (7) <2-7, Templeton VR:33>**<84>**

Thomas Ballard HAWKES^{8}, b. 20 July 1809* <Lancaster VR:208>

Benjamin James HAWKES^{8}, bpt. 6 Oct. 1811*

Abigail Sophia HAWKES^{8}, bpt. 4 Sept. 1814*

Edwin HAWKES^{8}, bpt. 8 June 1817*

Josiah HAWKES^{8}, bpt. 25 June 1820*; d. 8 Sept. 1843*

George HAWKES^{8}, bpt. 9 ( ) 1824*

Martha Ballard HAWKES^{8}, bpt. 2 Sept. 1827*; d. 3 Apr. 1831*, ae 4 <ChR>

Hannah NEWHALL, (*?dau of Moses & Susanna), b. 6 June 1748; d. 1826*, Boston

CHILDREN OF Adam HAWKES^{6} (John^{5}) & Hannah NEWHALL: (8)

Hannah HAWKES^{7}, b. 31 Oct. 1765

Rebecca HAWKES^{7}, b. 29 Nov. 1767

John HAWKES^{7}, b. 7 Sept. 1769

Lydia HAWKES^{7}, b. 30 Nov. 1770

Mary HAWKES^{7}, b. 7 Apr. 1772

Susanna HAWKES^{7}, b. 13 Nov. 1774

Sally HAWKES^{7}, b. 3 Oct. 1776

Adam HAWKES^{7}, b. 22 Jan. 1778

Simon FRANCIS, (son of Ben.), d. 18 Oct. 1803, ae 32

CHILDREN OF Simon FRANCIS & Lydia HAWKES^{7}: (4)

Lucy FRANCIS^{8}, b. 18 Feb. 1796

Mary FRANCIS^{8}, b. 12 Dec. 1797; d. 14 July 1798

Simon FRANCIS^{8}, b. 31 Jan. 1799

Nathaniel FRANCIS^{8}, b. 9 Nov. 1801

Jonathan PEIRCE, d. 2 Sept. 1825, Charlestown, ae 80y4m

CHILDREN OF Jonathan PEIRCE & Lydia (HAWKS^{7}) Francis: (2)

Jonathan PEIRCE^{8}, b. 18 Oct. 1809

Joshua Hawkes PEIRCE^{8}, b. 29 July 1812

CHILDREN OF Daniel HICHINS & Susanna TOWNSEND: (4)

Daniel HICHINS, b. 19 Oct. 1709

Susanna HICHINS, b. 22 Mar. 1711; d. aft. 9 Dec. 1784* <deed>

Elkanah HICHINS, b. 23 July 1712

Timothy HICHINS, b. 23 May 1715

CHILDREN OF Moses HAWKS^{5} (Moses^{4}) & Susanna HICHINS: (9) <Lynn VR 3:193>

Moses HAWKS^{6}, b. 24 Nov. 1730 <VR 1:183>; d. 1771*

Mary HAWKS^{6}, b. 25 Sept. 1732

Susanna HAWKS^{6}, b. 13 Feb. 1736; d. ?8 Jan. 1763*, (wf of Michael Newhall*) <Lynn VR; PR5, Zach

Collins Diary>

Abijah HAWKS^{6}, b. 11 Aug. 1739 <VR 1:181>; d. aft. 30 July 1808 <letter to brother Nathan>

Anna HAWKS^{6}, b. 15 June 1742; d. ?aft. 12 Aug. 1794*, Brookfield, unm.

Nathan HAWKS^{6}, b. 1 July 1745; d. 17 Oct. 1824*, Saugus <will - Essex Co.Prob.#12937, 404:228>

Lois HAWKS^{6}, b. 30 June 1747

Daniel HAWKS^{6}, b. 20 Oct. 1749; d. 1831*, Richfield N.Y.

James HAWKS^{6}, b. 27 June 1752

Hannah HICHINGS, (*dau of Daniel & Hannah (Ingalls)), b. 19 Feb. 1745* <Lynn VR 1:191>; d. prob. aft. 30 July 1808*

CHILDREN OF Abijah HAWKS^{6} & Hannah HICHINGS: (4)[<85>]

Abijah HAWKS^{7}, b. 9 Oct. 1766; d. 13 Mar. 1843, Richfield, Otsego Co., N.Y.

Nancy HAWKS^{7}, b. ( )

Hannah HAWKS^{7}, b. ?1789*

Amos HAWKS^{7}, b. 1788, Richfield N.Y., d. 4 Oct. 1865, ae 77

Sanford BABBIT^{5} (*Sam.^{4}, Elkanah$^{3-2}$, Edw.^{1}*), b. 17 Dec. 1765* <Babbitt Gen.:165>

CHILD OF Sanford BABBIT & Nancy HAWKS^{7}:

John BABBITT^{8}*, b. 17 Aug. 1801*, Pelham <Babbitt Gen.:165>

Lois FRIZZELL, (*dau of Samuel), b. 23 Sept. 1773*; d. 1 Feb. 1862 <g.s.>

CHILDREN OF Abijah HAWKS^{7} (Abijah^{6}) & Lois FRIZZELL: (10)*

Harriet Thency HAWKS^{8}, b. 7 Mar. 1792

Dolly HAWKS^{8}, b. 11 Dec. 1794

Joel HAWKS^{8}, b. 15 Apr. 1796

Polly HAWKS^{8}, b. 24 June 1800

Lois HAWKS^{8}, b. 13 June 1803

George HAWKS^{8}, b. 19 July 1806

Charles HAWKS^{8}, b. 2 May 1809

Nathan HAWKS^{8}, b. 15 Jan. 1812

Abijah HAWKS^{8}, b. 7 Dec. 1815; d. 28 May 1902*, bur. Jordanville N.Y.

James HAWKS^{8}, b. 28 Oct. 1819

Susanna BOARDMAN, b. c1816*, d. 17 Apr. 1900*, ae 84

CHILDREN OF Abijah HAWKS^{8} & Susanna BOARDMAN: (2)

Ellen S. HAWKS^{9}, b. c1840[<86>]

George HAWKS^{9}, b. ( )

CHILDREN OF David TAFT & Lois HAWKS^{8} (Abijah^{7}): (2)

Delevan TAFT^{9}, b. ( )

Ovid V. TAFT^{9}, b. c1831* <ae 78, 14 May 1909>

Harriet Arethusa HAWKS^{8} (*Abijah$^{7-6}$, Moses$^{5-4}$, Rebecca Maverick^{3}, Remember Allerton^{2}), b. 1794, Richfield N.Y., d. 13 June 1872, ae 78

CHILDREN OF Amos HAWKS^{7} (Abijah^{6}) & Harriet Arethusa HAWKS: (7)

Giles HAWKS^{8}, b. 6 Mar. 1820

Amos HAWKS^{8}, b. 1 July 1823; unm.

Joel HAWKS^{8}, b. 9 Mar. 1825; unm.

Thomas HAWKS^{8}, b. 18 July 1828; d. 20 Mar. 1880; unm.

Arethusa/Thucy Ann HAWKS^{8}, b. 28 Oct. 1831 or 32; d. 6 Apr. 1896; unm.

Samuel HAWKS^{8}, b. 14 Feb. 1834 or 35

Alfred HAWKS^{8}, b. 1836; d. Apr. 1895; unm.

CHILDREN OF Giles HAWKS^{8} & Harriet A. HOLLISTER: (6)[<87>]

CHILDREN OF John William THAYER & Hannah HAWKS^{7} (Abijah^{6}): (6)[<88>]

CHILDREN OF Daniel HAWKS^{6} (Moses^{5}) & Rhoda PERHAM: (3 of 10)*[<89>]

Lois HAWKS^{7}, b. 1771*

James HAWKS^{7}, b. 1775*; d. 2 Oct. 1865*

Thomas HAWKS^{7}, b. 2 Apr. 1784*, Petersham; d. 24 Mar. 1870*

CHILDREN OF James HAWKS^{6} (Moses^{5}) & Olive WILLIS: (2) <Petersham VR:29>

Sally HAWKS^{7}, b. 24 Nov. 1776*

William HAWKS^{7}, b. 3 Oct. 1778*

CHILDREN OF Thomas MANSFIELD & Mary HAWKS^{6} (Moses^{5}): (7)*<Lynn VR>

Daniel MANSFIELD^{7}, b. 2 May 1759

Thomas MANSFIELD^{7}, b. 25 Aug. 1761

Mary MANSFIELD^{7}, b. 4 June 1763

Margaret MANSFIELD^{7}, b. 9 Aug. 1765

Susanna MANSFIELD^{7}, b. 29 Jan. 1768

Anna MANSFIELD^{7}, b. 18 Nov. 1771

Moses MANSFIELD^{7}, b. 27 Feb. 1774; d. 29 July 1806

CHILDREN OF Moses HAWKES^{6} (Moses^{5}) & Mary RIDDAN: (7) <Lynn, 1-5, 4:246>

Jerusha HAWKES^{7}, b. 23 Nov. 1755*

Thomas HAWKES^{7}, b. 22 Dec. 1757*

Sarah HAWKES^{7}, b. 30 June 1760*

Mary HAWKES^{7}, b. 27 Apr. 1762*

Moses HAWKES^{7}, b. 7 May 1764*

Benjamin HAWKES^{7}, b. 1766*; d. 30 Sept. 1854, ae 88y4m, Marblehead

William HAWKES^{7}, b. 1768*

MICRO #9 OF 9

Sarah HITCHINGS, b. c1750, d. 19 Dec. 1837*, ae 87, Saugus <will - Essex Co.Prob.#12942, 410:204>

CHILDREN OF Nathan HAWKES^{6} (Moses^{5}) & Sarah HITCHINGS: (8) <Lynn VR 4:527>

Hannah HAWKES^{7}, b. 3 Mar. 1773; d. betw. 15 Dec. 1857 (will) - Feb. 1861 (prob.) <Essex Co.Prob. #41963, 421:132, 227:108>

Nathan HAWKES^{7}, b. 22 Jan. 1775; d. betw. 22 Feb. 1861 (will) - 2 June 1863 (prob.) <Essex Co. Prob.#41973, 422:339, 234:253>

Daniel HAWKES^{7}, b. 15 Nov. 1777; d. 13 May 1847, Saugus, consumption <Mass.VR 32:125>

James HAWKES^{7}, b. 29 Jan. 1779

Susanna HAWKES^{7}, b. 24 July 1782; d. unm. betw. 30 Sept. 1842 (will) - Sept. 1854 (prob.) <Essex Co.Prob.#41983, 417:480, 206:3>

Mary HAWKES^{7}, b. 17 Oct. 1784; d. betw. 1 Mar. 1861 (will) - 2 Feb. 1864 (prob.) <Essex Co.Prob. #41969, 423:34, 234:407>

Moses HAWKES^{7}, b. 21 July 1788

Aaron HAWKES^{7}, b. 26 July 1791; d. 14 Oct. 1793

Rachel ALLEN, (dau of Samuel & Mary (Robey)), b. c1785, Saugus, d. 29 Jan. 1863, ae 77y9m7d, Melrose <Mass.VR 166:140>

CHILD OF Daniel HAWKES^{7} & Rachel ALLEN:

Sarah R. (HAWKES^{8}) Evans, b. c1820, Saugus, d. 29 Jan. 1871, ae 50y6m, diabetes <Mass VR.239:143>

Elizabeth TARBELL, b. c1785, d. 22 July 1822, ae 37, Saugus g.s.

CHILDREN OF Nathan HAWKES^{7} (Nathan^{6}) & Elizabeth TARBELL: (5) <1-3, Lynn VR, 4-5, Saugus VR>

Elizabeth Cook HAWKES^{8}, b. 24 Aug. 1806*

Sarah Ann HAWKES^{8}, b. 18 Nov. 1808*

Nathan Douglas HAWKES^{8}, b. 4 May 1811

Hannah HAWKES^{8}, b. 13 Mar. 1815*

Susanna HAWKES^{8}, b. 12 Jan. 1818*

Edward WOODMAN, d. betw. 22 Oct. 1691 - 22 Sept. 1693 <MD 5:138-9>

CHILDREN OF Edward WOODMAN & Remember MAVERICK^{3}: (2) <MD 5:138, 140>**<90>**

Remember WOODMAN^{4}, b. c1673; d. betw. 18 Dec. 1701 (hus inv.) - 31 Dec. 1702 (letter) <Suffolk Co

Prob.#2648, 14:428, 15:109>

John WOODMAN[4], b. c1676

Thomas PERKINS, d. pre 27 Mar. 1701 (adm.) <Suffolk Co.Prob.#2648, 13:319>

CHILDREN OF Thomas PERKINS & Remember WOODMAN[4]: (6) <Boston Rcd.Com.>

Edward PERKINS[5], b. 1 May 1695 <9:223>; d. 2 May 1695 <9:225>

Thomas PERKINS[5], b. 24 Apr. 1696 <9:227>; d. 10 June 1697 <9:237>

Thomas PERKINS[5], b. 19 Oct. 1697 <9:234>

Mary PERKINS[5], b. 13 Dec. 1698 <9:242>; d. 1 Jan. 1699 <9:253>

Mary PERKINS[5], b. 27 Mar. 1700 <9:243>

Elizabeth PERKINS[5], b. 13 Oct. 1701 <9:249>

CHILDREN OF James LOVEL & Elizabeth PERKINS[5]: (3) <Weymouth VR>

James LOVEL[6], b. 10 May 1719*

Thomas LOVEL[6], b. 11 Nov. 1720*

Job LOVEL[6]*, bpt. 22 Feb. 1735/6*, Abington

CHILDREN OF Joseph GURNEY & Mary PERKINS[5] (Remember Woodman[4]): (8) <Abington VR>

Sarah GURNEY[6], b. 15 Jan. 1720/1* <VR 1:98>

Perkins GURNEY[6], b. 13 Apr. 1723* <VR 1:97>; d. 27 Feb. 1792*, Abington

Mary GURNEY[6], b. 15 Jan. 1725/6* <VR 1:95>

Betty GURNEY[6], b. 19 June 1728* <VR 1:91>

Lydia GURNEY[6], b. 15 June 1730* <VR 1:95>; d. 23 Mar. 1791* <Abington VR 2:244>

Joseph GURNEY[6], b. 4 Feb. 1735* <VR 1:95>

Benoni GURNEY[6], b. 3 Apr. 1737* <VR 1:91>

Remember GURNEY[6], b. 11 Oct. 1742* <VR 1:97>

CHILDREN OF Benoni GURNEY[6] & Caroline WILKS: (4) <Abington VR>

Benoni GURNEY[7], b. 13 Oct. 1764 <VR 1:91>

Thomas GURNEY[7], b. 5 Jan. 1767 <VR 1:98>

Samuel GURNEY[7], b. 29 Apr. 1769 <VR 1:98>

Caroline GURNEY[7], b. 16 July 1772 <VR 1:91>

Benoni GURNEY, d. 22 June 1806, ae 67 (ae 69 in P.R.47) <Abington VR 2:286>

Mrs. Benoni GURNEY, d. 23 Jan. 1790, ae 48 <Abington VR 2:290>

William HERASEY, (*son of Wm. & Abigail (Tirrell)), b. 24 May 1719*; d. 7 or 8 May 1817, ae 97, (hus of Lydia Gurney[6]) <Abington VR 2:295>

Jane DERBY, (*dau of Jonathan & Ruth), b. 21 July 1725* <Weymouth VR 1:92>

CHILDREN OF Perkins GURNEY[6] (Mary Perkins[5]) & Jane DERBY: (11) <Abington VR>

Jane GURNEY[7], b. 5 Oct. 1747 <VR 1:94>

Thomas GURNEY[7], b. 21 Feb. 1748/9 <VR 1:98>

Jonathan GURNEY[7], b. 9 Oct. 1750 <VR 1:94>

Thomas GURNEY[7], b. 9 Oct. 1752 <VR 1:98>

Ruth GURNEY[7], b. 19 May 1755 <VR 1:97>

Jonathan GURNEY[7], b. 24 Apr. 1757 <VR 1:94>

David GURNEY[7], b. 1 Mar. 1759 <VR 1:92>

Hannah GURNEY[7], b. 12 Mar. 1761 <VR 1:93>

Adam GURNEY[7], b. 28 Mar. 1763 <VR 1:91>

Seth GURNEY[7], b. 17 Apr. 1766 <VR 1:98>

Molley GURNEY[7], b. 19 June 1768 <VR 1:96>

CHILDREN OF Isaac HERSEY & Mary GURNEY[6] (Mary Perkins[5]): (5) <Abington VR>**<91>**

Lydia HERSEY[7], b. 5 Nov. 1744*; d. 13 Nov. 1816*

David HERSEY[7], b. 3 Nov. 1746*; d. 17 Nov. 1827*

Isaac HERSEY[7], b. 24 Nov. 1750*; d. 2 Mar. 1822*

Daniel HERSEY[7], b. 24 Aug. 1752*; 8 Dec. 1752*

Gideon HERSEY[7], b. 3 Dec. 1761*

Elizabeth JENKINS, b. c1744, d. 8 June 1803*, ae 59

CHILDREN OF David HERSEY[7] & Elizabeth JENKINS: (5) <Abington VR>

Molley HERSEY[8], b. 26 July 1766*

Elizabeth HERSEY[8], b. 6 Sept. 1767*

Desire HERSEY[8], b. 11 May 1769*; d. 9 Nov. 1849, Abington, consumption (wf of Nathan Stoddard) <Mass VR 41:74>

Lydia HERSEY[8], b. 12 July 1774*

Martha HERSEY[8], b. 11 Feb. 1782*

Nathan STODDARD, b. Hanover, d. 28 May 1855, ae 83y3m, Abington, consumption <Mass.VR 94:175>**<92>**

Dianthia WHITING, d. 6 Sept. 1884, ae 79y11m, married, "softening of brain", b. Rockland, dau of Nathan (b. S. Abington) & Carintha (b. Rockland) (no surname) <Mass.VR 356:304>

Mary BICKNELL, d. 15 Oct. 1822*, ae 70 <Abington VR>

CHILDREN OF Isaac HERSEY[7] (Mary Gurney[6]): (4)* <Abington VR>

James HERSEY[8], b. 11 Mar. 1775

Isaac HERSEY[8], b. 30 May 1777; d. 5 Dec. 1793

Daniel HERSEY[8], b. 18 Aug. 1781; d. 1 Sept. 1836

Avery HERSEY[8], b. 27 Mar. 1793

Zenas HARDEN[8] (Lydia Hersey[7]), b. 1794, d. 22 Jan. 1875, ae 80y2m2d, E. Bridgewater (son of John & Lydia) <Mass.VR 275:303>

Sally GANNETT[7] (Seth[6-5], Hannah Brett[4], Sarah Hayward[3], Sarah Mitchell[2], Experience[1]), b. 1798, Abington, d. 3 June 1881, ae 83, E. Bridgewater, neuralgia of heart, dau of Seth & Caroline Gannett <Mass.VR 329:307>

CHILD OF Zenas HARDEN[8] & Sally GANNETT:

Lucins HARDING[9], b. 1820, E. Bridgewater, d. 20 Apr. 1895, Lynn, ae 74y11m28d, old age, bur. E. Bridgewater <Mass.VR 454:489>

Rebecca L. PRATT, (dau of Asa & Rebecca (Leach), b. 1821, Halifax, d. 29 Oct. 1877, ae 55y10m20d, S. Abington, cancer, (wf of Lucins Harding[9]) <Mass.VR 293:339>

* * * * * * * * * * *

FOOTNOTES

<1> p. 67, b. Suffolk, England <MQ 47:14-18; MD 40:7>.

<2> p. 67, No further data on Bartholomew Allerton is given in the files. Recent investigations have shown he was b. c1612 and d. betw. 15 Oct. 1658 - 19 Feb. 1658/9, probably at Bramfield, Co. Suffolk, England. His second wife was Sarah Fairfax, dau. of Benjamin & Sarah (Galliard) Fairfax, who d. betw. 13 Sept. 1678 - 6 Nov. 1679. Mentioned in her will are four children: Isaac, Mary Auger, Dorothy Rousham and John. See MD 40:7-10, Bartholomew Allerton and the Fairfax Family of Bramfield, Suffolk by Newman A. Hall.

<3> p. 67, Although Bowman attributes daughter Sarah Allerton to first wife Mary, she is now believed to be the daughter of second wife Fear, b. c1627 and d. pre 1651. <MQ 47:17>

<4> p. 67, Her name was Joanna Swinnerton. <see MQ 47:15, NEHGR 124:133> A later pencilled note states she d. 1682 <NEHGR 44:291>.

<5> p. 67, All five children are attributed to this wife. However, further research has shown that two (b. New Haven CT) were by this first wife with the remaining three (b. Westmoreland, VA) by a second wife (whose name has been added here but does not appear in the files).<MFIP, Allerton:4>

<6> p.67, Vital Records of New Haven CT, 1649-1850 (1917) 1:12. He apparently died before 25 Oct. 1702, the date of his father's will. <MFIP, Allerton:5>

<7> p. 67, The possibility that he was the son of the John Allerton & Elizabeth ( ) immediately preceeding is questioned.

<8> p. 68, The son of Robert Cushman & Sarah Reder.

<8a> p. 68, d. 23 Aug. 1726, ae 89 "wanting a month", Plympton <MD 10:112>.

<8b> p. 68, d. 11 Feb. 1718/9, Plymouth <NEHGR 14:229>.

<9> p. 68, Elizabeth Coombs, b. 30 Nov. 1662 <Boston VR 9:83>.

<10> p. 68, MFIP, Allerton:12 adds two children, Sarah and poss. Mary Cushman.

<11> p. 68, bpt. 6 June 1742, Dartmouth <MFIP, Allerton:40>.

<12> p. 68, bpt. 13 May 1744, Dartmouth <MFIP, Allerton:40>.

<13> p. 70, The newspaper clipping appears in the files without a source. She is described as the "mother of Israel", having "a superior mind", meek, cheerful and devoted to her family. Seven

Seven of her eight children chose "her God for their God".

<14> p. 71, Source for births of first three children is later given as Halifax VR:55.

<15> p. 71, Family records of Mrs. C.H. Smith, Auburn St., Bridgewater (1911).

<16> p. 72, Daughter of James Cole & Abigail Davenport <MFIP, Allerton:11>.

<17> p. 72, d. 9 Jan. 1714/5, Plymouth <Epitahs From Burial Hill, by Kingman:10>.

<18> p. 72, Her Mayflower descent is as follows: Mary Buck^5 (Abigail Church^4, Nath.^{3}, Eliz. Warren^2) <MFIP, Allerton, 36>.

<19> p. 72, d. Jan. 1777, Coventry CT <MF5G 3:58>.

<20> p. 72, Elizabeth Sampson, b. 22 Dec. 1692, Plymouth <MD 1:247>; d. 17 Apr. 1744 <Plympton VR>.

<21> p. 72, Almost entirely in faint pencil and without sources, the children are confirmed in Plympton VR <MF5G 3:58>.

<22> p. 73, Deborah Lyon, (dau of Caleb & Margaret), b. 23 Jan. 1728/9, Rehoboth, d. 1 Dec. 1751, Plympton <MF5G 3:58>.

<23> p. 73, Daughter of Jonathan Barnes & Elizabeth Hedge <MFIP, Allerton:36>. Sources: birth, (Plymouth) <Savage 1:121>; death, (Plymouth) <Kingman:10>.

<24> p. 73, Wife of Dr. Lazarus LeBaron, Plymouth <MD 16:87>.

<25> p. 73, John Waterman, son of Samuel & Bethiah, b. 12 Jan. 1704, Plymouth <MD 2:19>; d. 15 Oct. 1781, Plymouth.

<26> p. 73, b. 5 Aug. 1729 <MD 2:53>

<27> p. 73, Was she the daughter of Andrew Ring^4 (Eleazer^3, Deborah Hopkins^2) who was b. 21 July 1742, N. Yarmouth ME? <MFIP, Hopkins:112-3>.

<28> p. 74, It has not been firmly established that Rebecca Harlow was the wife of Isaac Cushman. See TAG 26:144-7 which supports this marriage.

<29> p. 76, Middleboro VR <MD 26:30> states he was in his 77th year.

<30> p. 76, d. 26 Oct. 1831, Pomfret VT <MF5G 3:165>.

<31> p. 76, Jabez & Ebenezer were born at Lyme NH, Jonah & Lois at Pomfret VT <MF5G 3:165>. Across this page is written "MD 22:150, Jabez Vaughan, reputed son of Jabez Vaughan Jr. & Sarah L(ea)ch Jr., b. 12 Nov. 1763, Middleboro VR 2:63."

<32> p. 77, A History of Farmington, Franklin Co., Maine...1776-1885, by Francis Gould Butler. Farmington. 1885. (p.511).

<33> p. 78, First two children born at Plymouth <MD 2:226>; a sixth child, a daughter, d. 25 Feb. 1714/5, age 7 days <Plympton g.s. MD 10:111>.

<34> p. 78, Plympton, MD 3:93.

<35> p. 78, First two children born at Plymouth <MD 2:226>, rest born at Plympton <VR>.

<36> p. 80, The names and dates are written very faintly in pencil, with the names particularly difficult to read. The third name, a daughter, is too faint to make a guess.

<37> p. 81, Ebenezer Hawkes, b. 7 Sept. 1677, Lynn CT <MFIP, Allerton:31>.

<38> p. 81, An accompanying note states the Lynn VR erroneously credits these children to his first wife.

<39> p. 82, Several question marks on this chart cast doubt as to whether she did indeed marry Ebenezer Giles.

<40> p. 82, This data appears to have come from an unidentified family record.

<41> p. 82, No data is given on the remaining four Hawkes children, viz: Joseph, John, Philadelphia and Sarah.

<42> p. 83, The name of his wife is not given, nor is his line of descent. He appears to be Matthew Hawkes^6 (Samuel^5). (If so, these children would bear the generation number 7 in Mayflower descent.) Preceeding this list of names are three pages, each containing a marriage only as follows: Matthew^6 & Ruth Breed (1774), Matthew & Ruth Collins (1778) and Matthew & Betsey Sweetser (1792). By the marriage dates given, it would appear that Ruth Collins was the mother of the children.

<43> p. 83, No data is given on the remaining Jones children, viz: Joseph, John, Jonathan, Abigail and Benjamin.

<44> p. 83, A note reads, "probably dau. of Wm. & Priscilla, b. 25 Mar. 1710, Beverly<VR 1:266>

<45> p. 83, No data is given on the remaining Goodhue children, viz: Marcy, Nathaniel, William, Ebenezer (d.y.), Elizabeth, Sarah, Lucy, Hannah, Mary & Ebenezer. (Ruth is number nine.)

<46> p. 84, Genealogy of the Descendants of Richard Haven of Lynn. Josiah Adams. Boston. 1849. 2nd Ed. (p.8-9). Only three children are listed here; however, in his will, Joseph Haven mentions "my sister Sarah Hawkes of said Lynn, widow". <Essex Co.Prob.328:430>

<47> p. 84, The will of Elkanah Hawkes^5 mentions eight children; the remaining four are Ezra, Elkanah, Love & Grace.

<48> p. 84, Milton Records, Births, Marriages & Deaths, 1662-1843. Boston. 1900. (p.11).

<49> p. 84, His birth date has been derived from his age at death. Some feel this date should be 1665, probably because his parents were married in Nov. 1664. An interesting entry in PCR 4:83 shows his parents were fined on 7 Mar. 1664/5 for committing "carnal coppulation" before marriage but after contract. Although this does not necessarily mean Robert Cushman was born before their marriage, it would seem presumptuous of researchers to question his age at death and alter his birth date to 1665 to accomodate his parents' marriage.

<50> p. 84, He died at Lebanon CT. <MFIP, Allerton:25>

<51> p. 84, Included is the following note with no source: "Mrs. Desire Kent, wife of Mr. Samuel Kent of Barrington, was English woman, Daughter on New England, died Feb. 1762, aged about 94 years."

<52> p. 84, She was Abigail (Titus) Fuller, daughter of John Titus & Abigail Carpenter, b. 18 Feb. 1652/3, Rehoboth <VR:755>.

<53> p. 85, Plymouth ChR 1:259 gives his year of baptism only - 1687.

<54> p. 85, The 2nd wife of Benjamin Cushman, she is most probably the Sarah Phipeny who marr. 1st John Bell, 8 Aug. 1715 <Boston VR 28:62>. John Bell d. 14 May 1736 ae 45.<Plympton VR>
<55> p. 85, The remaining four Cushman children are without dates, viz: Hannah, Sarah, Huldah and Molly
<56> p. 85, Nancy Rider's line of descent is questioned as is the year of birth of her first child, Nancy in 1789. (Nancy & Benjamin were married in Apr. 1790.)
<57> p. 86, Her name is first written as Lydia "Arnold" with the surname crossed out and the Brewster name and descent added in pencil. Her will mntions her "brother" Edward Arnold.
<58> p. 87, The childrens' names are given without data as follows: Ezekiel, Cephas, Ezra, Joshua, Mary, Rebecca, Allerton, Hannah, Judith, Aaron, Benjamin, Gardner, Asenath, Deborah and Thomas Cushman.
<59> p. 87, No dates accompany the remaining 12 Cushman children, viz: Jerusha, Rebecca, Mercy, Hannah, Thankful, Ruth, Abigail, Robert, Elkanah, Martha, Isaac and Job.(See Billington <15>)
<60> p. 87, Thomas Cushman and Alice Hayward were not married.
<61> p. 88, Jacob Cushman and Elizabeth Read had 12 children, viz: Cynthia, Samuel, Elizabeth, Lois, triplets - Joseph, Mary & stillborn child, Sarah, Rebecca, Eunice, Lucy & Rowland. Jacob's will mentions the 11 surviving children.
<62> p. 89, Two additional children are given without dates - Jacob & Molly Bates. The will of John Bates mentions the following children: Alanson, John Jr., and daughter "Ballard".
<63> p. 89, The six Cushman children, without dates, are William, Thomas, Eleazer, Zibiah, Ruth & Lydia.
<64> p. 89, Moses Maverick, bpt. 3 Nov. 1611, Hiush, Devon co., England, son of John Maverick & Mary Guy. <NEHGR 96:232>
<65> p. 89, d. 24 Feb. 1655, Boston <VR 9:52>
<66> p. 90, Eunice Cole widow of Thomas Roberts.
<67> p. 90, Maj. Samuel Ward of Ipswich wrote his will 29 July 1689; it begins, "Whereas the Governor & Counsill have orderid me upon an expedition to Canade..." In a deposition, the witnesses stated his will was sealed & delivered to one of the witnesses - "and This was don on his goeing to Canada on ye 30th July 1690." It would seem more probable that he would have made his will the day before he left, not a year before. The deposition further states that Samuel was "seriously melancholy In haste to Looke after his Souldiers." He did not return from this expedition.
<68> p. 90, No dates or sources accompany the four Ward children, viz: Samuel, Abigail, Mary & Martha. However, MFIP, Allerton:12 provides a complete list of seven children including baptisms <Salem 1st Ch.:29, 30, 33>:

Abigail, bpt. 6 Aug. 1669 <29>	Martha, bpt. 16 Sept. 1672 <30>
Remember, bpt. 6 Aug. 1669 <29>	Samuel, bpt. Feb. 1673/4 <30>
Mary, bpt. 6 Aug. 1669 <29>	Rebecca, bpt. 1 Oct. 1678, d.y. <33>
Elizabeth, bpt. 8 May 1670, d.y. <29>	

<69> p. 90, They had another child, Ann Ward, bpt. 19 July 1685,d. 23 Aug. 1685.<Marblehead Ch>
<70> p. 90, One other child is listed in pencil, Abigail Horman, bpt. 3 Jan. 1717, with the note, "? of Joseph & Abigail (Merret) Horman, m. 21 Dec. 1715?".
<71> p. 91, The following death date is given below the list of these childrens' names -"Samuel B., s. of John & Mary, d. Porto Cavallo, rec. 3 Sept. 1825, ae 25y". If he is the Samuel Northey bpt. in 1801 one wonders why the name Samuel was given to the next child bpt. in 1805.
<72> p. 91, Mercy Craw Northey is also shown as Mercy Cross Northey.
<73> p. 91, Determining Samuel Bartol's death date proved interesting. On various pages and in various forms, 5 dates are given for what seem to be 3 different Samuels. The dates which appear to refer to Samuel, husband of Mercy Northey & 2nd wf. Hannah (Calley) Hanover are:
Probate records quote his death as 23 Feb. 1835. Recorded within one week of his death we must assume this record to be correct. Pension application data from the Bureau of Pensions gives the date as 23 Jan. 1835. North Church, Salem, Centennial Exercises, List of Proprietors, 1772-1836 states he died 24 Jan. 1835, ae 70. This same source gives his widow Hannah's death as 9 Mar. 1836, ae 78, while Essex Inst.Hist.Col.9:111 gives the date of death of a Mrs. Bartol, widow of Samuel, Feb. 1836, ae 73.

Of the remaining two dates, that of 28 Dec. 1837, ae 51, is attributed to his son Samuel, which leaves the date of a Samuel Bartol, who d. 22 Jan. 1835, ae 50, unaccounted for.

An interesting account of Samuel Sr. is given on his revolutionary pension application. Age 54 in 1818 when he applied, he was born c1764, therefore was 11 yrs old when he enlisted as a drummer in 1775 and served 9 months, 5 days. In 1820 he states he was formerly a marine, but after his right leg was amputated he became a painter. (Other records confirm he was an ornamental painter.)
<74> p. 92, These names are not listed on Martha Tuttle's sheet but appear on the proceeding page under "Mark & Martha Haskell".
<75> p. 95, See <68>.
<76> p. 95, The approximate birth dates are derived from a bond dated 14 July 1719 which states "Sarah Ward upwards of 14 years & Abigail Ward, minor children of..." <Essex Co.Probate 313:12>.
<77> p. 95, Since his mother died 4 Nov. 1659, he must have been born within the first four days of November.
<78> p. 95, Although these two are listed as husband & wife, there appears to be a question as to which Daniel Hitchens was her husband. An accompanying pencilled note reads "?Wid. of old Daniel, buried 15:1:1734/5 <Z. Collins>". On the proceeding page is the marriage intention of Daniel Huchings Sr. and Sarah (Cushman[3]) Hawks.
<79> p. 95, Thomas Fuller was the 2nd husband of Hannah (Preast) Hawkes. His first wife, the mother of his children, is not named. No data is listed for the children whose names are taken

from his will, viz: Thomas (eldest son), Edward, Elizabeth, Elisha, David (4th son), Abigail, Ebenezer and Jonathan (youngest son).

<80> p. 96, Her brother Austiss was born cOct. 1816, so her date of birth should probably be Jan. 1818, not 1817.

<81> p. 96, Her mother, Sally (Hawkes) Lane was baptized 3 Sept. 1810 due to sickness<Lancaster ChR:344>. It is possible Sarah Ann was born around this time and her mother, on the verge of dying, was baptized. Sally Lane finally did succumb to childbirth in 1813.

<82> p. 96, The Phelps Family of America, compiled by Judge Oliver S. Phelps and Andrew T. Servin. 2 Vols. Pittsfield MA. 1899.

<83> p. 97, Mrs. Catherine P. Farnsworth, married, d. 18 Sept. 1847, typhus fever, wf of A.J. Farnsworth <Mass. Vital Stat.33:186>.

<84> p. 97, The files give a Polly Ballard, b. 9 May 1788, dau of Thomas & Abigail Ballard <Lancaster VR:119>, but fail to identify her as Benjamin Hawke's wife.

<85> p. 98, The data on Abijah Hawks and his children is out of order in the files. For easy clarification, he has been included here before the files of his children. Also, mention is made of a child of a Abijah Hawkes who d. 9 or 10 Nov. 1775 <Lancaster 1st ChR:327>

<86> p. 98, Reference is made to a letter dated 11 Jan. 1903, Jordanville, in which Ellen S. (Hawkes) Eastwood stated she was 3 years old when her grandfather, Abijah Hawkes, died in 1843.

<87> p. 98, No dates accompany the names of the six Hawks children, viz: Laura, Webster, Mary (dy), Hattie, Amos (dy) and Luretta.

<88> p. 98, No dates accompany the names of the six Thayer children, viz: William H., Amos John, Mary Eliza, Susan, Louisa and Lydia. On a later page the date of birth is given for Mary Eliza Thayer[8], 25 Mar. 1812.

<89> p. 98, The remaining seven Hawks children are listed without dates, viz: Lydia, Daniel, Moses, Anna, Rhoda and 2 unnamed children who died young.

<90> p. 99, Salem 1st Church gives the baptism of all seven children of Edward Woodman and Remember Maverick. The 1st six were all baptized on the same day, 15 June 1684, viz: Remember, Edward (prob. d.y.), John, b. c1676, Moses, Maverick, Samuel (d. pre 15 Feb. 1708/9) and Cornelius, b. c1684, bpt. 13 Aug. 1684, Marblehead <VR>. See MFIP, Allerton:8.

<91> p.100, The remainder of the files are out of sequence so their order has been corrected here for easier reference.

<92> p.101, No children are listed on the sheet of Nathan Stoddard and Desire Hersey. In an extract from his probate records, the following heirs are listed: Edward & Betsey J. Estes, Gilman C. & Diantha Whiting, George & Lydia Hamman and a guardian appointed for Adaline Stoddard. (Are these four women his daughters?) Across this page is written, "Richmond Stoddard is eldest son <PLymouth Co.Probate #19585>.

* * * * *

REFERENCE LIST:

GENEALOGICAL ARTICLES PERTAINING TO ALLERTON FAMILY RESEARCH

Mayflower Descendant (MD) (1899-1937)

2:155-57 - Will & Inventory of Isaac Allerton
4:37-42 - Will & Inventory of Elder Thomas Cushman (incl. records of death).
4:109-110 - Deposition of Isaac Allerton, 1639 (age)
5:20-22 - Will of Deacon Elkanah Cushman[3] and Bond of his sons, Josiah[4] & Allerton[4]
5:129-141 - Will & Inventory of Moses Maverick
7:129-130 - Mayflower Marriage Records at Leyden & Amsterdam (Degory Priest & Isaac Allerton[1])
7:173-176 - Will of Isaac Allerton[2]
9:81-82 - Will & Inventory of James Cushman, 1648
10:193 - Marriage of Robert Cushman & Mary Shingelton
11:100-104 - Estate of Robert Waterman, 1652
17:139-140 - Will of Rev. Isaac Cushman[3]
17:222-234 - Hawkes Notes: John Hawkes (m. Rebecca Maverick[3])
21:102-104 - Will of Lt. Josiah Cushman[4]
22:15-16 - Marriage Record of Isaac Allerton, Leyden
22:126-128 - Will of Robert Waterman, 1744
25:97-98 - An Autograph of Isaac Allerton The Mayflower Passenger, 1653

Mayflower Descendant (MD) (1985-1990)

35:59-62 - Smith Family Bible Links Mayflower Descendant (error on chart, p.62 see MD 35:175)
40:7-10 - Bartholomew Allerton[2] and the Fairfax Family of Branfield, Suffolk, Eng.
40:145-152 - Thomas Caswell of Taunton And His Descendants

Mayflower Quarterly (MQ) (1975-1990)

44:39-44 - Pilgrim Ancestry of Revolutionary Soldiers: The Taylor Family of Virginia
45:23-24 - The Unproved Allerton Family Lineage (Isaac[3])
45:70-80 - Joseph Howland of North Yarmouth, ME & Burton, N.B. (1717-1796)
47:14-18 - The Children of Isaac Allerton
48:119-122 - Nathaniel Holmes of Canterbury CT & Dutchess Co. NY (m. Martha Cushman[4])
48:170-171 - Isaac Allerton, The First Yankee Trader (error, p.171, line 8 should read Mary not Remember)

52:28-32 - Mary Cushman[3], Wife of Francis Hutchinson, An Isaac Allerton Line
54:186-88 - A Sixth Generation Mayflower Descendant, Thomas Cushman
- (error, p.187, Sarah m. Morris Morris not Thomas Morris. See MQ 55:222)
55:18-19 - Going Another Route - Tracing the Parry/Perry Family

Miscellaneous

Mayflower Families In Progress: Isaac Allerton Of The Mayflower and His Descendants for Four Generations (MFIP), pub. by General Society of Mayflower Descendants. 1990.

NEHGR 124:133 - Joanna Swinnerton: The Third Wife of Isaac Allerton Sr.
TAG 26:144 - Rebecca, Wife of Rev. Isaac Cushman

* * * * * * * * *

JOHN BILLINGTON

MICRO #1 of 2

John BILLINGTON[1], d. 1630, Plymouth<1>

CHILDREN OF John BILLINGTON[1] & Elinor ( ): (2)

John BILLINGTON[2], d. pre 1630<1>

Francis BILLINGTON[2], b. c1604-06 <MD 1:222>; d. 3 Dec. 1684 <MD 2:46><1>

Thomas BILLINGTON, d. pre 1 May 1662, Taunton (inv.) <MD 17:216>

Mrs. Abraham BILLINGTON, d. 1825 <Bangor Hist.Mag.4:216>

CHILDREN OF Samuel BILLINGTON & Eliza Nickerson (dau of David): (4) <Bangor Hist.Mag.4:216>

Levi BILLINGTON, b. ( )

Eliza BILLINGTON, b. ( )

Samuel BILLINGTON, b. ( )

Mary BILLINGTON, b. ( )

FRANCIS BILLINGTON[2] (John[1])

CHILDREN OF Francis BILLINGTON[2] & Christian (PENN) Eaton: (9) <Plymouth><2>

Elizabeth BILLINGTON[3], b. 10 July 1635; d. aft. 22 Mar. 1709/10, Providence RI

Joseph BILLINGTON[3], b. pre Feb. 1736/37; d. betw. 7 Jan. 1684/5 - 1692, prob. Block Island RI

Martha BILLINGTON[3], b. c1638; d. aft. 9 June 1704, Plainfield CT

Mary BILLINGTON[3], b. c1640; d. aft. 28 June 1717

Isaac BILLINGTON[3], b. c1644, d. 11 Dec. 1709, ae 66, Middleboro <MD 1:223>

Child, b. pre 1651, d.y.

Rebecca BILLINGTON[3], b. 8 June 1647; poss. d.y.

Dorcas BILLINGTON[3], b. c1650; d. aft. 1711

Mercy BILLINGTON[3], b. 25 Feb. 1651/2; d. 28 Sept. 1718, Rehoboth

Edward MAY, d. 10 Aug. 1691, Plymouth <MD 16:62><3>

CHILDREN OF Edward MAY & Dorcas BILLINGTON[3]: <4>

CHILDREN OF Richard BULLOCK & Elizabeth BILLINGTON[3]: (4) <Rehoboth VR:563><5>

Israel BULLOCK[4], b. 15 July 1661

Mercy BULLOCK[4], b. 13 Mar. 1662

John BULLOCK[4], b. 19 May 1664; d. 20 June 1739, E. Providence, Little Neck Cem.

Richard BULLOCK[4], b. 15 Mar. 1666/7

Elizabeth BARNES, (dau of Thomas), b. 14 Feb. 1674/5 <Swansea VR>; d. 20 July 1761, E. Providence

CHILDREN OF John BULLOCK[4] & Elizabeth BARNES:<6>

CHILDREN OF Francis BILLINGTON[4] (Joseph[3]) & Abigail CHURCHILL: (7) <Plymouth, MD 13:33><7>

Sarah BILLINGTON[5], b. 11 Dec. 1702

Mercy BILLINGTON[5], b. 1 Jan. 1704/5<8>

Francis BILLINGTON[5], b. 16 Feb. 1708

Jemima BILLINGTON[5], b. 12 June 1710

Content BILLINGTON[5], b. 2 Feb. 1712/3

Abigail BILLINGTON[5], b. 21 Oct. 1716; d. 14 Aug. 171()

Joseph BILLINGTON[5], b. 11 Jan. 1718/9

Matthew LEMOTE, d. pre 20 Feb. 1767 (adm.)<9>

CHILDREN OF Matthew LEMOTE & Mercy BILLINGTON[5]: (9) <Plymouth, MD 14:241>

Mathew LEMOTE[6], b. 18 Aug. 1730, d. 15 July 1733

Joseph LEMOTE[6], b. 30 Nov. 1732, d. 22 July 1733

Abigail LEMOTE[6], b. 6 June 1733, d. 25 Oct. 1734

Mercy LEMOTE[6], b. 29 Oct. 1734

Susanna LEMOTE[6], b. 30 June 1736

Mathew LEMOTE^{6}, b. 25 June 1738, d. Sept. 1739

Mary LEMOTE^{6}, b. 17 Feb. 1739

George LEMOTE^{6}, b. 24 Dec. 1741

Abigail LEMOTE^{6}, b. 2 Feb. 1743/4

William BARNES^{6} (Seth^{5}, Mary Bartlett^{4}, Jos.^{3}, Mary Warren^{2}), b. 1 Oct. 1732, Plymouth<MD 13:166> d. pre 31 Mar. 1764 (wf 2nd int.) <MD 26:43>

CHILDREN OF William BARNES & Mercy LEMOTE^{6}: (3) <Plymouth, MD 18:214>

Abigail BARNES^{7}, b. 7 Aug. 1755

Mercy BARNES^{7}, b. 15 Dec. 1757

William BARNES^{7}, b. 2 Jan. 1760

Richard HOLMES, (son of Gershom & Lydia), b. 20 Oct. 1743, Plymouth <MD 15:112>

CHILDREN OF Richard HOLMES & Mercy (LEMOTE^{6}) Barnes: (4) <Plymouth, MD 18:214>

Elizabeth HOLMES^{7}, b. 15 Oct. 1764

Richard HOLMES^{7}, b. 5 July 1766

William HOLMES^{7}, b. 26 Mar. 1768

Lydia HOLMES^{7}, b. 8 Jan. 1770

CHILDREN OF James HOWARD & Sarah BILLINGTON^{5}: (6)**<10>**

Hannah GLASS, b. 24 Dec. 1651, Plymouth <MD 16:237>

CHILDREN OF Isaac BILLINGTON^{3} & Hannah GLASS: (6)**<11>**

Mary DUNHAM, b. c1705, d. 24 July 1777, ae 72 <Middleboro 1st ChR:86>

CHILDREN OF Isaac BILLINGTON^{4} (Isaac^{3}) & Mary DUNHAM: (4) <Middleboro>

Isaac BILLINGTON^{5}, b. 14 Feb. 1730/1 <MD 9:48>

Nathaniel BILLINGTON^{5}, b. 7 Feb. 1732/3 <MD 12:131>

Seth BILLINGTON^{5}, b. 11 May 1735 <MD 13:3>

Ichabod BILLINGTON^{5}, b. 23 May 1737 <MD 8:249>

John WASHBURN, b. c1671, d. 17 June 1750, Kingston g.s. <MD 7:223>

CHILDREN OF John WASHBURN & Lydia BILLINGTON^{4} (Isaac^{3}): (10) <Plymouth, MD 2:165>**<12>**

John WASHBURN^{5}, b. 19 Apr. 1699; d. 22 May 1768 <Plymouth ChR:397>

Ichabod WASHBURN^{5}, b. 7 Feb. 1700/1

Mercy WASHBURN^{5}, b. 21 Apr. 1702; d. 3 May 1796, Kingston g.s. <MD 7:87>

Elisha WASHBURN^{5}, b. 5 Nov. 1703; d. 20 July 1734**<13>**

Ephraim WASHBURN^{5}, b. 6 June 1705

Barnabas WASHBURN^{5}, b. 12 Feb. 1706/7**<14>**

Jabez WASHBURN^{5}, b. 10 Apr. 1708; d. 1 Apr. 1794, Kingston g.s. <MD 7:222>

Ebenezer WASHBURN^{5}, b. 18 Aug. 1709

Thankful WASHBURN^{5}, b. 24 Feb. 1714/5; d. 15 Jan. 1805, Kingston g.s. <MD 7:21>

Child, b. 22 or 23 Sept. 1716, d. same day <MD 16:85>

CHILDREN OF Robert CUSHMAN^{5} (Robert^{4}, Tho.^{3}, Mary Allerton^{2}) & Mercy WASHBURN^{5}: (13)**<15>**

CHILDREN OF Barnabas WASHBURN^{5} (Lydia Billington^{4}) & Hannah SEARS:**<16>**

CHILDREN OF Ebenezer WASHBURN^{5} (Lydia Billington^{4}) & Lydia FAUNCE: (3)**<17>**

Lydia WASHBURN^{6}, d. pre 1 July 1765 (mother's will) <Plymouth Co.Prob.#22049, 29:147>

Ebenezer WASHBURN^{6}, d. aft. 24 June 1784 (div. mother's estate) <" ", 29:173>

Simeon WASHBURN^{6}, d. betw. 23 Feb. 1764 (will) - 4 Apr. 1764 (prob.) <Plymouth Co.Prob.#22099>

CHILDREN OF Elisha WASHBURN^{5} (Lydia Billington^{4}) & Martha PERKINS:**<18>**

CHILDREN OF Ephraim WASHBURN^{5} (Lydia Billington^{4}) & Eglah STETSON:**<19>**

CHILDREN OF Ichabod WASHBURN^{5} (Lydia Billington^{4}) & Bethiah PHILLIPS:**<20>**

MICRO #2 OF 2

Judith FAUNCE, (dau of John), b. 1 Jn. 1710/1, Plymouth <MD 5:100>; d. 3 Mar. 1752, Kingston g.s. <MD 7:223>

CHILDREN OF Jabez WASHBURN^{5} (Lydia Billington^{4}) & 1st Judith FAUNCE: (7) <Kingston, Gen.Adv.2:43>

Jabez WASHBURN^{6}, b. 22 Apr. 1733; d. 17 Feb. 1775, Kingston g.s. <MD 7:222>

Elisha WASHBURN^{6}, b. 17 Mar. 1734/5; d. 29 June 1754, Kingston g.s. <MD 7:222>

Susanna WASHBURN^{6}, b. 7 May 1737; d. 26 Apr. 1756, Kingston g.s. <MD 7:223>

John WASHBURN^{6}, b. 18 July 1739; d. June 1763, Kingston g.s. <MD 7:223>

Molly WASHBURN^{6}, b. 15 May 1742; d. 14 June 1754, Kingston g.s. <MD 7:223>

Rebecca WASHBURN^{6}, b. 14 Apr. 1744; d. 24 July 1827, Kingston g.s. <MD 7:223>

Judah WASHBURN^{6}, b. 10 July 1746; d. 8 May 1824*

Deborah THOMAS, b. c1717, d. 8 Oct. 1802, ae 85, Kingston g.s. <MD 7:222>

CHILDREN OF Jabez WASHBURN^{5} & 2nd Deborah THOMAS: (2)

Thomas WASHBURN^{6}, b. 30 Sept. 1755; d. 11 Mar. 1759, Kingston g.s. <MD 7:223>

Susanna WASHBURN^{6}, b. 3 July 1762; d. ?28 Feb. 1824

Mary SHERMAN, b. Feb. 1735*, d. 17 Feb. 1779*, ae 44y10d (wf of Jabez Washburn$^{6-5}$)

CHILDREN OF John WASHBURN^{5} (Lydia Billington^{4}) & Abigail JOHNSON: (7) <Plymouth, MD 14:242>**<21>**

John WASHBURN^{6}, b. 8 May 1730

Abigail WASHBURN^{6}, b. 17 Feb. 1731/2

Mary WASHBURN^{6}, b. 21 Nov. 1734

Mercy WASHBURN^{6}, b. 31 July 1736, d. 4 Mar. 1737/8

Seth WASHBURN^{6}, b. 17 Apr. 1738, d. 27 Apr. 1826, Plymouth <MD 14:242>

Philip WASHBURN^{6}, b. 5 Sept. 1739

Thankful WASHBURN^{6}, b. 14 Aug. 1742 **<22>**

Lydia PRINCE^{6} (Ben.^{5}, Ruth Turner^{4}, Mary Brewster^{3}, Jonathan^{2}), b. c1735, d. 12 May 1782, ae 47

CHILDREN OF John WASHBURN^{6} & Lydia PRINCE: (6) <Plymouth, MD 18:213>

John WASHBURN^{7}, b. 28 Dec. 1755

Abiah WASHBURN^{7}, b. 21 Nov. 1757

Benjamin WASHBURN^{7}, b. 14 Aug. 1761

Prince WASHBURN^{7}, b. 9 Sept. 1763

Lydia WASHBURN^{7}, b. 1 Oct. 1765

Thomas WASHBURN^{7}, b. 16 Dec. 1767

Bathsheba CHURCHILL^{5} (Ben.^{4}, Stephen^{3}, Eleazer^{2}, John^{1}), b. c1762, d. 13 July 1788, Plymouth g.s. (1st wf of Benjamin Washburn^{7})**<23>**

Fear HOWARD, b. c1739, d. 9 Apr. 1682, Kingston g.s. (wf of Seth Washburn^{6}, John^{5}) <MD 7:222>

John ADAMS, (son of Francis), b. 14 June 1714; d. 15 Apr. 1806, Kingston g.s. <MD 7:20>**<24>**

CHILDREN OF John ADAMS & Thankful WASHBURN^{5} (Lydia Billington^{4}): (10)**<25>**

Mary BILLINGTON^{4} (Isaac^{3}), b. c1685, d. 30 May 1733, ae 48, Middleboro g.s., Nemasket <MD 15:109>

Elnathan WOOD, (son of Abiel), b. 14 Apr. 1686, Middleboro<MD 2:106>; d. 20 Apr. 1752, Middleboro g.s., Nemasket <MD 15:107>

CHILDREN OF Elnathan WOOD & Mary BILLINGTON^{4}: (6) <Middleboro, 1-5, MD 4:68>

Jemima WOOD^{5}, b. 21 July 1712

Jedidah WOOD^{5}, b. 27 Mar. 1715

Ephraim WOOD^{5}, b. 8 May 1716; d. 4 Dec. 1781 <MD 14:224>

Mary WOOD^{5}, b. 5 Oct. 1719

Lydia WOOD^{5}, b. 1 July 1722

Judah WOOD^{5}, b. 11 Apr. 1728 <MD 7:242>

Samuel SABIN, d. 23 Sept. 1699 <Rehoboth VR:875>

CHILDREN OF *Samuel* SABIN & Mary BILLINGTON^{3}: (6) <Rehoboth VR>

Samuel SABIN^{4}, b. 27 Nov. 1664 <VR:736>

Mercy SABIN^{4}, b. 8 Mar. 1666 <VR:736>

Sarah SABIN^{4}, b. 10 Aug. 1667 <VR:737>

Israel SABIN^{4}, b. 8 June 1673 <VR:737>

Experience SABIN^{4}, b. 5 Oct. 1676 <VR:737>; bur. 28 Nov. 1676 <VR:875>

Mary SABIN[4], b. 4 Mar. 1678/9 <VR:737>

CHILDREN OF Israel SABIN[4] & Mary ORMSBEE: (10) <Rehoboth VR:737>

Sarah SABIN[5], b. 26 Mar. 1697

Elizabeth SABIN[5], b. 31 Mar. 1698

Samuel SABIN[5], b. 21 Jan. 1699/1700

Israel SABIN[5], b. 8 Oct. 1701

Jeremiah SABIN[5], b. 26 Aug. 1703

Josiah SABIN[5], b. 3 June 1705

Margaret SABIN[5], b. 5 Feb. 1706

William SABIN[5], b. 14 Oct. 1708

Eleazer SABIN[5], b. 21 Feb. 1710

Mary SABIN[5], b. 1 June 1711

CHILDREN OF Josiah SABIN[5] & Mary GAY: (6) <Rehoboth VR:738>

Uriah SABIN[6], b. 25 July 1725

William SABIN[6], b. 31 July 1728

Mary SABIN[6], b. 6 Aug. 1733

John SABIN[6], b. 30 Apr. 1736

Nathaniel SABIN[6], b. 11 Aug. 1738

Daniel SABIN[6], b. 31 July 1741

CHILDREN OF James WELCH & Mercy SABIN[4] (Mary Billington[3]): (9)**<26>**

John WELCH[5], b. 25 June 1685, Swansea; d. 14 Aug. 1685

Elizabeth WELCH[5], b. 27 Sept. 1688, Rehoboth

Mercy WELCH[5], b. 1 Mar. 1689/90, Rehoboth

James WELCH[5], b. 27 July 1692, Rehoboth

Samuel WELCH[5], b. 15 Oct. 1693, Rehoboth

Thomas WELCH[5], b. 1 Mar. 1694/5, Rehoboth

Ebenezer WELCLH[5], b. 13 Feb. 1697, Bristol

John WELCH[5], b. 17 Apr. 1699, Bristol

Martha WELCH[5], b. 25 Oct. 1704, Plainfield

CHILDREN OF John MARTIN & Mercy BILLINGTON[3]: (4) <Rehoboth VR>

John MARTIN[4], 10 June 1682

Robert MARTIN[4], b. 9 Sept. 1683

Desire MARTIN[4], b. 20 Mar. 1684/5

Francis MARTIN[4], b. 7 May 1686

Desire CARPENTER[5] (Desire Martin4), b. 3 June 1716; d. 28 May 1800, Stevens Corner Cem., Rehoboth

Hezekiah HIX, b. c1715, d. 5 Feb. 1788*, ae 73, Stevens Corner Cem., Rehoboth

CHILDREN OF Hezekiah HIX & Desire CARPENTER[5]: (8) <Rehoboth VR:635>**<27>**

Hannah HIX[6], b. 17 May 1740

James HIX[6], b. 21 Apr. 1742

Hezekiah HIX[6], b. 10 Aug. 1744

Mary HIX[6], b. 17 Mar. 1746/7

Desire HIX[6], b. 27 Dec. 1750

Gideon HIX[6], b. 26 May 1752

Jotham HIX[6], b. 26 May 1752 (twin)

Nathan HIX[6], b. c1761*

Renew CARPENTER[5] (Desire Martin[4]), b. 6 June 1714; d. 9 Feb. 1787, Stevens Corner Cem., Rehoboth

Jabez ROUND, b. c1708, d. 14 Mar. 1790, Stevens Corner Cem., Rehoboth**<28>**

CHILDREN OF Jabez ROUND & Renew CARPENTER[5]: (11) <Rehoboth VR:733>

Isaac ROUND[6], b. 23 Jan. 1733/4

Jabez ROUND[6], b. 8 Jan. 1735/6; d. 20 May 1806*

Abigail ROUND^6, b. Jan. 1740

Isaiah ROUND^6, b. 30 Jan. 1741

Rebecca ROUND^6, b. 21 Mar. 1742

Sibbel ROUND^6, b. 10 Sept. 1744

Oliver ROUND^6, b. 1 Apr. 1747

Rhoda ROUND^6, b. 26 Jan. 1750

Esther ROUND^6, b. 8 Oct. 1752 <VR:734>

Simeon ROUND^6, b. 4 Feb. 1755 <VR:734>

* * * * * * * * * * *

FOOTNOTES

<1> p. 106, John Billington, b. c1580, poss. Lincolnshire, Eng. <NEHGR 124:116-18>, d. in Sept. 1630 when he was executed for murder. His wife was Elinor (not Helen or Ellen), maiden name unknown, and was living 2 Mar. 1642/3, the wife of Gregory Armstrong <PCR 12:28-9, 33-4>.

John Billington^2 was living at the time of the May 1627 Cattle Division but deceased at the time of his father's death in Sept. 1630. <Bradford's Hist. (1952):234,446>

Francis Billington^2's year of birth is uncertain due to conflicting records. He was thought to be "aged forty years or thereabouts" in 1649 (b. c1609) <NEHGR 124:116-18>; age 68 in 1674 (b. c1606) <MD 2:46>; and age 80 when he died in 1684 (b. c1604) <Middleboro Dths.:20>.

<2> p. 106, There is no file sheet listing all the children of Francis & Christian so they have been added for easier reference. <Mayflower Increasings:20, 21>

Christian (Penn) Eaton is said to have died c1684 (Stoddard:115 says July 1684). The petition of her son, Isaac Billington, (1 Mar. 1703/4), implies she died the same year as her husband Francis..."They were near 80 years old when they dyed; & it is now 18 years since." Unfortunately, the time span he mentions does not prove Christian died in 1684 but rather 1686. His referral to "18 years since" could refer not to the death of his parents but to the death of his last surviving parent, Christian, in 1686. <Petition - Plymouth Co.Probate #2001>

<3> p. 106, Bowman gives his date of death as 20 Aug. although in checking the reference given (MD 16:62) it clearly says <u>10</u> Aug.

<4> p. 106, Four unnamed children (2 sons & 2 daus.) are attributed to Edward May & Dorcas Billington <distribution of his estate - MD 31:104>. However, MFIP, Billington:13 identifies Edward, Israel and a daughter as possibly the children of Edward by his 2nd wife Dorcas.
Dorcas also had an illegitimate son c1672, father unknown as is the child's name.

<5> p. 106, Richard Bullock was b. c1622, England and d. pre 22 Oct. 1667 (Inv.) <MD 17:28>. By her 2nd marriage to Robert Beers, Elizabeth Billington had a son, Benjamin Beers, b. 6 June 1674 <Rehoboth VR> and d. 3 July 1714, Providence RI <MFIP:8>.

<6> p. 106, No children are listed for John Bullock and his wife. MFIP, Billington:15, provides the following nine children, viz: Ann, Elizabeth, Zerviah, Esther, Israel, Prudence, Mary, John and Richard.

<7> p. 106, If you refer to the files you will find reference made to Francis Billington^3, the father of Francis^4 who married Abigail Churchill. Researchers have proven this to be in error, it should read Joseph Billington^3, father of Francis^4. This error is repeated throughout.
<Note: This error of descent is repeated in **Mayflower Marriages**, companion volume to this book. On p.35, descent should read: Francis Billington^4 (Joseph^3) <u>not</u> (Francis^3)>.

<8> p. 106, Her date of death is given as aft. 20 Feb. 1767, the administration of her husband's estate. However, in the brief transcript included, her name is not mentioned.
<Plymouth Co.Prob. #12568, 17:178; 19:436, 558, 560> Burial Hill by Benjamin Drew (p.214, #1492) lists her death as 8 Aug. 1758 "in ye 34 year of her age" - the age obviously an error.

<9> p. 106, Matthew Lemote, d. 27 Oct. 1762, ae 50y20d <Burial Hill by Drew, p.214, #1491>

<10> p. 107, James Howard d. 12 Apr. 1763, Plymouth <ChR:430>. No children are listed, the following are found in MD 13:170, viz: John, b. 12 Jan. 1723/4; Mary b. 28 Feb. 1725/6; James, b. 18 Jan. 1727/8 (d. 9 May 1749, Jamaica <MD 16:86>); Francis, b. 12 Sept. 1731; Sarah, b. 1 Jan. 1733/4; William, b. 10 June 1742.

<11> p. 107, No data accompanies the names of the six Billington children, viz: Desire, Lydia, Eleanor, Mary, Seth and Isaac.

<12> p. 107, Lydia (Billington) Washburn d. 22 Sept. 1716 <Plymouth ChR 1:215> or 23 Sept. <MD 16:85>, probably the same day she gave birth to a stillborn child. She is mistakenly called Desire in the vital records <MD 16:85>.

<13> p. 107, Kingston <MD 7:222>

<14> p. 107, d. 21 Mar. 1770 <Kingston VR:288>

<15> p. 107, The Cushman children are not listed here but found in the Allerton family <59>. MFIP, Billington:58 provides birth (Kingston) and death dates, viz: Lydia, b. 29 Sept. 1726; Jerusha, b. 15 Jan. 1727/8; Rebecca, b. 9 Apr. 1730; Mercy, b. 5 June 1731; Hannah, b. 2 July 1732; Thankful, b. 10 Mar. 1733/4, d. 23 Aug. 1748; Ruth, b. 22 Dec. 1735; Abigail, b. 3 Apr. 1737; Robert, b. 27 Oct. 1738; Job, b. 27 Jan. 1739/40, d. 28 Jan. 1739/40; Elkanah, b. 29 Dec. 1740, d. 18 Aug. 1748; Martha, b. 14 Sept. 1742, d. 23 Aug. 1748; and Isaac, b. 10 Mar. 1745.

<16> p. 107, Bowman calls her Hannah Sears but she is identified in vital & church records as both Hannah Shear & Hannah Thears. She d. 19 May 1787, ae 67 <Kingston VR:389>. MFIP, Billington:60 lists their three Washburn children, b. Kingston, viz: Barnabas, b. 1 Apr. 1749; Elkanah, b. 3 Jan. 1750/1; and Elisabeth, b. 1 Aug. 1754, d. 1 Jan. 1770.

<17> p. 107, Lydia Faunce was b. 10 June 1714, Plymouth and d. 3 Apr. 1784, Halifax <MD 5:100, 14:11>. The births of the Washburn children are found in the Kingston VR, viz: Lydia, b. 1 Oct.

1733 <VR:150>; Ebenezer, b. 14 Sept. 1735 <VR:153>; and Simeon, b. 20 Jan. 1737/8 <VR:155>. MD 7:222 gives the death dates (Kingston) of Simeon Washburn, 16 Mar. 1764, ae 26y1m (5 or 15 d) and Ebenezer Washburn, 26 Jan. 1810, ae 74.
<18> p. 107, Martha Perkins, dau. of Luke & Martha (Content), was b. 14 Aug. 1707 <Beverly VR 1:254>. The three children of Elisha & Martha Washburn are found in Kingston VR:150, 153, 389 (& MFIP, Billington:59), viz: Lydia, b. 12 Dec. 1729; Martha, b. 5 May 1732 & Elishaba, b. 13 Apr. 1735, d. 6 Jan. 1747/8
<19> p. 107, Eglah/Egloth Stetson, dau. of Elisha & Abigail (Brewster) Studson, was b. 7 Oct. 1710, Plymouth <MD 7:178> and d. 18 Nov. 1792, Plymouth <ChR 1:420>. MFIP, Billington:60 gives the 8 Washburn children, b. Kingston, viz: Ezekiel, b. 22 Nov. 1733; Deborah, b. 15 Nov. 1735; Marcy, b. 23 Sept. 1738; Ephraim, b. 16 Mar. 1741; Alithea, b. 18 Aug. 1743; Eunice, b. 20 July 1746; Nehemiah, b. 11 June 1749, d. 13 Apr. 1751 <MD 7:223> and Sarah, b. 22 Mar. 1752.
<20> p. 107, Bethiah Phillips, dau. of Benjamin & Sarah (Thomas), was b. 27 Feb. 1704/5 <Marshfield VR:30> and d. 25 Jan. 1789 <Norton VR:399>. MFIP, Billington:57 provides the four Washburn children, viz: Bethiah, b. 24 May 1729; Ichabod, b. 13 Apr. 1731, d. 14 Nov. 1746, Norton; Malatiah, b. 29 Mar. 1733; Sarah, b. 12 Feb. 1736/7, d. 31 May 1750, Norton.
<21> p. 108, MFIP, Billington:57 shows her to be Abigail (Phillips) Johnson, dau. of Benjamin & Sarah (Thomas) Phillips, b. 29 Oct. 1699, Marshfield <MD 18:149> and d. 24 Sept. 1782, Plymouth <Marshfield VR:30>.
<22> p. 108, Burial Hill (by Benjamin Drew), p.31, #214.
<23> p. 108, Ibid., p.31, #213.
<24> p. 108, b. Plymouth <MD 2:227>
<25> p. 108, The ten Adams children are listed with no data, with the exception of death dates for John and Joseph. MFIP, Billington:62 provides birth dates for all ten, b. Kingston, viz: Joseph, b. 2 Oct. 1740, d. 7 Aug. 1815 <MD 7:21>; Francis, b. 14 Dec. 1741; John, b. 12 Mar. 1742/3, d. 10 Jan. 1833 <MD 7:20>; Ebenezer, b. 17 Nov. 1744; Jemima, b. 6 Oct. 1746; Melzar, b. 3 July 1750; Sarah, b. 7 Jan. 1752; Mercy, b. 7 July 1753; Lydia, b. 25 Feb. 1755; and Susanna, b. 7 July 1759
<26> p. 109, The childrens' names & dates are written very faintly in pencil and are difficult to read. This list is taken from MFIP:20.
<27> p. 109, MFIP:80 gives a ninth child, Abel Hix^6, b. 1755 and provides the birth date for Nathan Hix^6, 20 Apr. 1762.
<28> p. 109, Jabez Round (son of John & Abigail) was b. 28 Sept. 1708, Swansea. It would appear that his first two children, Isaac & Jabez were also born at Swansea <MQ 51:197>.

* * * * *

REFERENCE LIST:

GENEALOGICAL ARTICLES PERTAINING TO BILLINGTON FAMILY RESEARCH

Mayflower Descendant (MD) (1899-1937)

15:247-253 - Washburn Notes: Will of John Washburn

Mayflower Quarterly (MQ) (1975-1990)

46:14-15 - Presidential Mayflower Connections (correction - MQ 46:197)
48:67-71 - Esther (Carpenter)(Bardeen) Bowen, An Elusive Billington Descendant
49:170-179 - The Martins of Swansea & The Martins of Rehoboth
50:21-30 - Judah Fuller^6, The Bloomer's Daughter
50:71-76 - The Additional Children of Joseph & Mercy (Canedy) Williams & Their Migrations to Western MA & Groton NY
50:180-187 - There Were Three Hezekiahs, Not One, In The Round Family
51:196-198 - The Family of Jabez & Renew (Carpenter) Round, A John Billington Line
52:137-143 - Desire Billington And Her Grandfather Francis Billington's Estate
55:296-297 - Sylvia Sturtevant and Her Seven Mayflower Lines

Miscellaneous

Mayflower Families In Progress: John Billington of the Mayflower and His Descendants for Five** Generations (MFIP), pub. by General Society of Mayflower Descendants, 1988.

NEHGR 124:116 - Francis Billington of Lincolnshire
TG 3:228-248 - Some Descendants of Francis Billington of the Mayflower

* * * * * * * * * *

**Now available: Mayflower Families Through Five Generations: John Billington of the Mayflower (MF5G), pub. by General Society of Mayflower Descendants. 1991.

WILLIAM BRADFORD

MICRO #1 of 15

William BRADFORD[1], bpt. 19 Mar. 1589/90, Austerfield, Eng., d. 9 May 1657, Plymouth <MD 7:65, 2:228>

Dorothy MAY, b. c1597 (age 16 at marr.), d. 7 Dec. 1620, Cape Cod Harbour <MD 9:115, 31:105>**<1>**

CHILD OF William BRADFORD[1] & 1st Dorothy MAY:

John BRADFORD[2], b. ( ) **<2>**

Alice (CARPENTER) Southworth, b. c1590, d. 26 Mar. 1670, ae about fourscore, Plymouth <MD 31:144>

CHILDREN OF William BRADFORD[1] & 2nd Alice (CARPENTER) Southworth: (3) <Plymouth>**<3>**

William BRADFORD[2], b. 17 June 1624, d. 20 Feb. 1703/4, Plymouth <MD 1:151, 15:212>

Mercy BRADFORD[2], b. pre 22 May 1627 (Cattle Division)

Joseph BRADFORD[2], b. c1630, d. 10 July 1715, "neare 84 yrs.", Plymouth <MD 15:212> **<4>**

Susan B. DAVIS, d. 18 May 1865, ae 62, Acton, b. Medford, dau of Seth & Abigail Bradford <184:35>

Ebenezer DAVIS, d. 20 July 1890, ae 78y11m5d, Acton, son of Ebenezer & Abigail (Faulkner)<410:50>

Mary BRADFORD, d. 28 June 1853, ae 68, dropsy, bur. Eel River, Plymouth, widow of Josiah, b. Plymouth <Plymouth BDM 4:400>

CHILDREN OF Zabdiel BRADFORD & Mary ( ): (2) <Marshfield VR 3:2>

Mary BRADFORD, b. 22 May 1807

Zabdiel BRADFORD, b. 13 July 1809

John BRADFORD, d. 27 Mar. 1724 <Kingston VR 1:5>

Major John BRADFORD, d. 8 Dec. 1736 <Kingston VR 1:5>

Mercy BRADFORD, widow of Major John, d. Mar. 1747 <Kingston VR 1:5>

Jael BRADFORD, d. 14 Apr. 1730 <Kingston VR 1:5>

Deborah BRADFORD, (dau of Ephraim & Eliz.), d. 10 June 1732 <Kingston VR 1:5>

Lewis BRADFORD, d. 5 July 1854, ae 62, Worcester, married, carpenter, b. Duxbury, son of Lewis & Priscilla <86:192> (Mass.VR?)

Lucy BRADFORD, d. 14 Feb. 1854, ae 90, Duxbury, wf of William, b. Duxbury, dau of John & Abigail Sampson <85:199> (Mass.VR?)

Lewis BRADFORD, d. 10 (or 16) Aug. 1851, ae 83y4m20d, Plympton, accident, b. Plympton, son of Levi, unm., town clerk <58:188> (Mass.VR?)

Olive BRADFORD, d. 22 Apr. 1859, ae 66, Duxbury, consumption, widow, b. Duxbury, dau of Charles & Hannah Delano <130:203> (Mass.VR?)

Mrs. Edward G. BRADFORD, d. 18 Jan. 1828 <Conway VR:21>

Daughter of Edward G. Bradford, d. 17 Sept. 1828, ae 17, dysentery <Conway VR:21>

Son of Edward G. Bradford, d. 25 Sept. 1828, ae 11, dysentery <Conway VR:21>

Infant of John Bradford, d. 24 Oct. 1828 (Conway?)

CHILDREN OF John BRADFORD & Susanna ( ): (6) <Conway VR:66>

Anna C. BRADFORD, b. 17 Jan. 1815

George Washington BRADFORD, b. 22 Feb. 1817

Lydia F. BRADFORD, b. 8 Mar. 1818

Mary F. BRADFORD, b. 11 May 1825

John Lalabarron BRADFORD, b. 28 Nov. 1827, d.y.

John Lalabarron BRADFORD, b. 5 Jan. 1831

Mary BRADFORD, d. 17 July 1826, consumption <Conway VR:37>

CHILDREN OF Shubal BRADFORD Jr. & Mary ( ): (6) <Conway VR:97>

Melvin Munroe BRADFORD, b. 4 Mar. 1834

Josephine Maria BRADFORD, b. 15 Dec. 1835

Elias F. BRADFORD, b. 21 Nov. 1837

John Wrisley BRADFORD, b. 14 Oct. 1842

Susan Farley BRADFORD, b. 14 Oct. 1842 (twin)

Caroline Elizabeth BRADFORD, b. 9 Oct. 1849

Shubal BRADFORD, d. 26 Mar. 1837, ae 73 <Conway VR:30>

CHILDREN OF Shubal BRADFORD & Anna ( ): (8) <Conway VR:73>

John BRADFORD, b. 13 Aug. 1791

Pamela BRADFORD, b. 21 Aug. 1793

Abigail BRADFORD, b. 8 Mar. 1796

Phebe BRADFORD, b. 18 Feb. 1798

Parthena BRADFORD, b. 29 Dec. 1800

Anna BRADFORD, b. 22 Dec. 1803

Minerva BRADFORD, b. 28 Aug. 1807

Shubal BRADFORD, b. 13 July 1809

Infant of Mr. Bradford, d. 7 Mar. 1795, ae 7d <Conway VR:239>

CHILDREN OF Edward BRADFORD & Charlotte ( ): (8) <Conway VR:57>

William BRADFORD, b. 16 June 1798

Samuel BRADFORD, b. 14 Apr. 1800

Nancy BRADFORD, b. 18 May 1802

Lyman BRADFORD, b. 17 Oct. 1803

Alvin BRADFORD, b. 8 Sept. 1805

Parlinthia BRADFORD, b. 13 June 1807

Charlotte BRADFORD, b. 1 June 1811

Edward Gray BRADFORD, b. 26 Mar. 1813

Lyman BRADFORD, d. 1837 <Conway VR:30>

MICRO #2 of 15

Bradford Deaths, Bristol RI, "from gravestones, from small book in Town Clerk's office":

Mrs. Hannah BAYLIES, wf of Dr. Gustavus & dau of Hon. William Bradford, d. 6 July 1811, ae 41

Gershorm BRADFORD, d. 4 Apr. 1757, ae 67

Mary BRADFORD, wf of William, d. 3 Oct. 1775, ae 47

Priscilla BRADFORD, wf of Gershorm, d. 12 Sept. 1780, ae 90

LeBaron BRADFORD, d. 25 Sept. 1793, ae 39

Abby BRADFORD, wf of Capt. Hersey Bradford, d. 6 May 1803, ae 26

Jemine BRADFORD, b. 25 May 1808, d. 17 Sept. 1808, dau of John & Jemine

Hon. William BRADFORD, d. 6 July 1808, ae 80 <RI VR 3:19>

Capt. Henry BRADFORD, d. Dec. 1808, at sea

Hon. Daniel BRADFORD, d. 22 July 1810, ae 89 <RI VR 3:20>

Major William BRADFORD, 1st son of Hon. William, d. 29 Oct. 1810, ae 59 <RI VR 3:21>

Capt. Leonard J. BRADFORD, d. 27 July 1812, ae 33 <RI VR 3:21>

Susannah BRADFORD, wf of Hon. Daniel, d. 31 Dec. 1815, ae 76 <RI VR 3:23>

Abby BRADFORD, wf of Capt. Hersey Bradford, d. 16 Apr. 1822, ae 24

Hon. John BRADFORD, d. 7 July 1833, ae 67

Hersey BRADFORD Jr., d. 6 July 1842, ae 22 (see Henry, next pg.)

Jemima BRADFORD, wf of Hon. John, d. 5 Sept. 1842, ae 68 <RI VR 4:72>

Seraphine BRADFORD, dau of Hersey Bradford, d. 12 July 1847, ae 29 <RI VR 4:98>

Capt. Hersey BRADFORD, d. 1 Sept. 1849, ae 77 <ae 79, at Middletown, RI VR 4:114>

Bradford Deaths, Bristol RI VR:

Levi BRADFORD, "old Mr. Potters grandson", d. 7 Nov. 1756, ae 19 <VR 2:2, 2:16>

Capt. Gershom BRADFORD, d. 4 Apr. 1757, ae 66 <VR 2:3, 2:16>

Dr. BRADFORD's negro child, d. 30 Dec. 1760 <VR 2:7>

Child of Dr. BRADFORD, d. 5 Sept. 1763, ae 10 mths (Hannah is added in pencil) <VR 2:9, 2:16>

Stillborn child of Elijah BRADFORD, d. Dec. 1763 <VR 2:10>

Infant child of Dr. BRADFORD, 1764 (betw. entries 29 Aug. - 12 Dec.) <VR 2:10>
John BRADFORD, son of Dr. Wm. & Mary, d. 30 Oct. 1765, ae 8 <VR 2:11, 2:10>
Dr. BRADFORD's negro child, d. 16 Aug. 1766 <VR 2:12>
Mrs. Mary BRADFORD, d. 16 Apr. 1772 <VR 2:17>
Dr. BRADFORD's negro child, d. 15 Feb. 1773 <VR 2:18>
Mrs. Mary BRADFORD, d. 3 Oct. 1775, ae 44 <VR 2:21, 2:18> (wf of Wm. is added in pencil)
Son of Capt. Job BRADFORD, d. 12 Mar. 1776, ae 11 <VR 2:22>
Mrs. Priscilla BRADFORD, d. 12 Sept. 1778, ae 85 <VR 2:24, 2:18>
LeBaron BRADFORD, d. 25 Sept. 1793, ae 40y <VR 3:8>
Major William BRADFORD, d. 29 Oct. 1811 <VR 2:28, 3:21>
Leonard J. BRADFORD, d. 27 July 1812, ae 32 <VR 2:29>
Francis BRADFORD, d. Dec. 1814 (at sea with schooner O.H. Perry) <VR 3:22>
John BRADFORD, d. 7 July 1833 <VR 3:32>
Henry BRADFORD Jr., d. 6 July 1842, ae 22 <VR 4:70> (see Hersey, previous pg.)
Robert Nimme BRADFORD, son of Durfee T., d. 24 Dec. 1847 <VR 4:100>
Ann P. BRADFORD, wf of Capt. Samuel, d. 6 July 1850, ae 35 <VR 4:124>
Capt. William BRADFORD, d. 23 Apr. 1851, ae 70 <VR 4:130>

Bradford Births, Bristol RI VR:[5]

CHILDREN OF Daniel BRADFORD & Mary CHURCH: (2) <RI VR>[6]
Elizabeth BRADFORD, b. 5 June 1750 <VR 1:149>[7]
Priscilla BRADFORD, b. 1 Mar. 1752 <VR 1:151>

CHILDREN OF Dr. William BRADFORD & Mary ( ): (5) <RI VR>
William BRADFORD, b. 15 Sept. 1752, Warren <VR 1:150>
Lebarron BRADFORD, b. 31 Mar. 1754 <VR 1:150>
John BRADFORD, b. 9 Oct. 1758 <VR 1:151>
Mary BRADFORD, b. 3 Sept. 1760 <VR 1:151>
John BRADFORD, b. 1768 <VR 1:152>

CHILDREN OF Daniel BRADFORD & Susannah JARVIS (dau of Leonard): (3) <RI VR>
Daniel BRADFORD, b. 27 June 1778, Attleboro <VR 1:153>
Leonard J. BRADFORD, b. 22 May 1780 <VR 1:153>
Samuel BRADFORD, b. 6 May 1783 <VR 1:153>

CHILDREN OF Maj. William BRADFORD Jr. (son of Hon. Wm.) & Elizabeth/Betsey Bloom JAMES: (6) <RI>
Mary BRADFORD, b. 30 Dec. 1778, Taunton <VR 1:153>
Elizabeth Bloom BRADFORD, b. 18 Feb. 1785, Rehoboth <VR 1:153>
Henry BRADFORD, b. 18 Feb. 1787, Rehoboth <VR 1:153>
Peter James BRADFORD, b. 6 Feb. 1790, Rehoboth <VR 1:153>
John Willis BRADFORD, b. 26 Dec. 1793, Rehoboth <VR 1:154>
Sarah BRADFORD, b. 29 Jan. 1799, Bristol <VR 1:154>

CHILDREN OF John BRADFORD & Jemima ( ): (7) <RI VR>
Mary LeBarron BRADFORD, b. 18 June 1801 <VR 1:154>
Eleanor BRADFORD, b. 18 Dec. 1804 <VR 1:154>
Lydia BRADFORD, b. 9 Feb. 1806 <VR 1:154>
Walter BRADFORD, b. 13 Aug. 1809 <VR 1:156>
Nancy BRADFORD, b. 16 Aug. 1795 <VR 1:156>
Benjamin Wardwell BRADFORD, b. 24 June 1797 <VR 1:155>
LeBarron BRADFORD, b. 18 Apr. 1799 <VR 1:155>

CHILDREN OF Daniel BRADFORD Jr. & Sarah REYNOLDS (dau of Joseph): (8) <RI VR 1:157>
Charles Jarvis BRADFORD, b. 17 Aug. 1800
Joseph Reynolds BRADFORD, b. 15 Nov. 1802
Sally Russell BRADFORD, b. 10 Mar. 1805

Mary Sparhawk BRADFORD, b. 23 Nov. 1806
Jane Augusta BRADFORD, b. 22 Aug. 1809
Daniel BRADFORD, b. 9 Mar. 1811
CHILDREN OF Leonard Jarvis BRADFORD & Sally TURNER (dau of Capt. Moses): (5) <RI VR 1:158>
Susannah Jarvis BRADFORD, b. 18 Mar. 1802
Sally Leonard BRADFORD, b. 18 Nov. 1803
Harriet Turner BRADFORD, b. 11 Feb. 1806
Leonard Jarvis BRADFORD, b. 29 Mar. 1808
Durfee Turner BRADFORD, b. 14 Mar. 1810
CHILDREN OF William BRADFORD, 3d (son of Maj. Wm. & Eliz.) & Mary SMITH (dau of Nathaniel & Parnel): (4) <RI VR 1:156>
William Parnell BRADFORD, b. 29 May 1805
Edward James BRADFORD, b. 29 Sept. 1806
Allen Taylor Smith BRADFORD, b. 2 Sept. 1808
Nancy Smith BRADFORD, b. 7 Apr. 1811
CHILDREN OF Samuel BRADFORD & Elizabeth REYNOLDS (dau of Joseph): (4) <RI VR 1:158>
Samuel BRADFORD, b. 10 May 1807
William Greenwood BRADFORD, b. 4 Mar. 1809
Elizabeth BRADFORD, b. 2 Feb. 1811
Ann Peck BRADFORD, b. 1 Dec. 1814
Deaths, from the Newport Mercury Newspaper: (3) <Arnold VR 12:40>[8]
Mrs. William BRADFORD, d. 9 Oct. 1775 (?paper of), Bristol
William BRADFORD, of Providence, d. 16 Apr. 1785 (?paper of), Virginia
William BRADFORD, Att.Gen. N.S., d. Philadelphia, "a few days since", paper of 1 Sept. 1795
CHILDREN OF Theophilus BRADFORD & Ruth GOODSPEED: (2) <Arnold VR 4:83>[9]
John BRADFORD, b. 27 Nov. 1732
Mary BRADFORD, b. 5 Sept. 1736
Polly TUPPER, b. c1771, d. 19 Dec. 1807, ae 35 or 36, consumption <Kingston VR>
CHILDREN OF Stephen BRADFORD & Polly TUPPER: (2) <Kingston VR>
Mary Ann BRADFORD, b. 14 June 1805, d. 2 Sept. 1807
Stephen BRADFORD Jr., b. 4 June 1807
CHILDREN OF Stephen BRADFORD Jr. & Rebecca M. Hayward: (3) <Kingston VR>
Mary Elizabeth BRADFORD, b. 20 Sept. 1835
Orrin Winslow BRADFORD, b. 31 July 1839
Charles Stephen BRADFORD, b. 5 Feb. 1849
Deborah SAMPSON, (dau of Jeremiah & Sarah (Washburn)), b. c1780, d. 22 Dec. 1817, childbed fever <Kingston VR>
CHILDREN OF Peleg BRADFORD & Deborah SAMPSON: (2) <Kingston VR>
Charles BRADFORD, b. 23 July 1814
Peleg Sampson BRADFORD, b. 10 Dec. 1817
Joanna BRADFORD, b. 9 Aug. 1796 <Kingston VR> (marr. Francis Drew)
Joanna BRADFORD, b. 11 Feb. 1772 <Kingston VR>
Jason BRADFORD, b. Nov. 1809
Phebe ( ) BRADFORD, b. July 1813
CHILDREN OF Jason BRADFORD & Phebe ( ): (4) <Kingston VR>
Zuma BRADFORD, b. 20 Sept. 1833, poss. d. 3 May 1835
Henry Austin BRADFORD, b. 1 Sept. 1836
Zuma Ann BRADFORD, b. 6 June 1838
Albion BRADFORD, b. 23 Dec. 1840
Mrs. Betty THOMAS, b. 16 Sept. 1755; d. 7 June 1825 <Kingston VR>

CHILD OF David BRADFORD & Mrs. Betty THOMAS:

Lucy BRADFORD, b. 26 Oct. 1778 <Kingston VR>

Melatiah HOLMES, b. 30 Mar. 1745, d. 19 June 1827 <Kingston VR>

Benjamin DELANO, b. 31 Mar. 1778, d. 19 Jan. 1868 <Kingston VR>

Susannah HOLMES, d. 12 Aug. 1866 <Kingston VR>

CHILD OF Benjamin DELANO & Susannah HOLMES:

Catherine DELANO, b. 4 Dec. 1820 <Kingston VR>

JOSEPH BRADFORD[2] (William[1])

Jael HOBART, (dau of Rev. Peter), b. c1643, d. 14 Apr. 1730, ae 87, Kingston g.s. <MD 7:23>**<10>**

CHILDREN OF Joseph BRADFORD[2] & Jael HOBART: (3)

Joseph BRADFORD[3], b. 18 Apr. 1665, Plymouth; d. pre 8 Oct. 1712 (father's will) <MD 5:218>

Elisha BRADFORD[3], b. c1669*, d. 16 June 1747, ae 78, Kingston <Bible>

Peter BRADFORD[3], b. 1 Mar. 1676/7 <Hingham VR 1:39>

Mrs. Hannah BRADFORD, d. Sept. 1754 <Hingham VR 2:15, 59>

Hannah Cole, (dau of James), d. Aug. 1718 (1st wf of Elisha Bradford[3])**<11>**

Bathshua BROCK, b. 21 May 1703 <Scituate VR 1:50>**<12>**

CHILDREN OF Elisha BRADFORD[3] & 2nd Bathshua BROCK: (15!) <1-5, MD 13:112; 6-15, NEHGR 1:276>**<13>**

Hannah BRADFORD[4], b. 10 Apr. 1720, Plymouth; d. 22 May 1758 (marr. Joshua Bradford[4])**<14>**

Joseph BRADFORD[4], b. 7 Dec. 1721, Plymouth; d. 4 Sept. 1743

Silvanus BRADFORD[4], b. 6 July 1723, Plymouth; d. 12 July 1723

Nehemiah BRADFORD[4], b. 27 July 1724, Plymouth; d. pre 15 Feb. 1747

Laurania BRADFORD[4], b. 27 Mar. 1726, Plymouth (marr. Elijah MacFarland)

Mary BRADFORD[4], b. 1 Aug. 1727; d. 21 Aug. 1727

Elisha BRADFORD[4], b. 6 Oct. 1729; d. Mar. 1753

Lois BRADFORD[4], b. 30 Jan. 1730/1; d. 10 Oct. 1752, unm.

Deborah BRADFORD[4], b. 18 Nov. 1732 (marr. Jonathan Sampson)

Alice BRADFORD[4], b. 3 Nov. 1734; d. 6 July 1795, Stoughton

Asenath BRADFORD[4], b. 15 Sept. 1736 (m. Daniel Waters, son of Sam. & Bethiah (Thayer))

Carpenter BRADFORD[4], b. 7 Feb. 1738/9

Abigail BRADFORD[4], b. 20 June 1741; d. 17 Dec. 1760

Chloe BRADFORD[4], b. 6 Apr. 1743; d. 21 Feb. 1747/8

Content BRADFORD[4], b. 21 May 1745; d. 22 May 1745

Zebulon WATERS, (son of Sam. & Bethiah), b. 3 Jan. 1734/5 <Stoughton VR:22>; d. 29 May 1790

CHILDREN OF Zebulon WATERS & Alice BRADFORD[4]: (10) <Stoughton VR>

Nehemiah WATERS[5], b. 9 July 1758 <VR:52>

Asa WATERS[5], b. 11 Feb. 1760 <VR:10>; d. 1845 <Waters Fam.of Marrietta, (1882):10>

Matilda WATERS[5], b. 31 May 1761 <VR:94>

Rebecca WATERS[5], b. 8 Oct. 1762 <VR:97>

Daniel WATERS[5], b. 5 July 1765 <VR:89>

Hannah WATERS[5], b. 12 Jan. 1767 <VR:100>

Zebulon WATERS[5], b. 23 Aug. 1768 <VR:100>; d. 5 Jan. 1831

Samuel WATERS[5], b. 6 Oct. 1770 <VR:115>

Molly WATERS[5], b. 6 Apr. 1773 <VR:115>

Chloe WATERS[5], b. 19 Sept. 1775 <VR:115>

Lemuel MONK, b. 7 May 1769* <Canton VR:117>

CHILD OF Lemuel MONK & Chloe WATERS[5]:

Polly MONK[6], d. 27 June 1800* <Canton VR:168>

CHILDREN OF Zebulon WATERS[5] & Zilpha LOVEL: (2)

Nancy WATERS[6], b. 25 Nov. 1794* <Canton VR:124>

William Bradford WATERS[6], b. 3 Aug. 1797* <Canton VR:122>

Lydia SMITH, (?dau of Joseph & Experience), b. 10 Jan. 1763 <Stoughton VR:114>; d. 22 June 1809

CHILD OF Asa WATERS[5] (Alice Bradford[4]) & Lydia SMITH*:

Asa WATERS[6], b. 14 Dec. 1786* <Stoughton VR:121>

WILLIAM BRADFORD[2] (William[1])

Alice RICHARDS, b. c1627, d. 12 Dec. 1671, ae about 44, Plymouth <MD 18:68>**<15>**

CHILDREN OF William BRADFORD[2] & 1st Alice RICHARDS: (10) <Plymouth, MD 9:91>**<16>**

John BRADFORD[3], b. 20 Feb. 1652/3 <MD 16:238>

William BRADFORD[3], b. 11 Mar. 1654/5, d. 5 July 1687 <MD 17:71, 15:213>

Thomas BRADFORD[3], b. c1657; d. 1 Oct. 1731, Windham CT g.s.

Alice BRADFORD[3], b. c1659; d. 15 Mar. 1745, ae 84 <Canterbury CT g.s.>

Mercy BRADFORD[3], bpt. 2 Sept. 1660, Boston

Hannah BRADFORD[3], b. 9 May 1662; d. 28 May 1738 <Windham CT VR; MD 28:101>

Melatiah BRADFORD[3], b. 1 Nov. 1664

Samuel BRADFORD[3], b. c1667/8; d. 11 Apr. 1714, Duxbury g.s. <MD 9:160>

Mary BRADFORD[3], b. 1668

Sarah BRADFORD[3], b. 1671; d. betw 18 Oct. 1705 (last child) - 29 Sept. 1712 (hus will) <MD 24:27>

CHILD OF William BRADFORD[2] & 2nd (   ):**<16,17>**

Joseph BRADFORD[3], b. 18 Apr. 1675, Plymouth; d. 16 Jan. 1747, New London CT

Mary (WOOD) Holmes, d. 6 Jan. 1714/5, Plymouth <MD 15:212>

CHILDREN OF William BRADFORD[2] & 3rd Mary (WOOD) Holmes: (4) <Plymouth>**<16,18>**

Israel BRADFORD[3], b. c1677/78

Ephraim BRADFORD[3], b. 1685; d. betw 16 Dec. 1741 (will)- 6 Oct. 1746 (prob.) <MD 21:189>

David BRADFORD[3], b. pre 1687; d. pre 1 Apr. 1730 (adm.) <MD 23:181>**<18a>**

Hezekiah BRADFORD[3], b. pre 1687

MICRO #3 of 15

Rev. William ADAMS, b. 27 May 1650, Ipswich; d. 17 Aug. 1685, Dedham <VR:20>

CHILDREN OF Rev. William ADAMS & Alice BRADFORD[3]: (4) <Dedham VR>

Elizabeth ADAMS[4], b. 23 Feb. 1680 <VR:17>; d. 21 Dec. 1766, New Haven CT

Alice ADAMS[4], b. 3 Apr. 1682 <VR:18>**<19>**

William ADAMS[4], b. 17 Dec. 1683 <VR:18>

Abiell ADAMS[4], (dau), b. 15 Dec. 1685

James FITCH, b. 2 Aug. 1649, d. 10 Nov. 1727, Canterbury CT <NEHGR 70:344>

CHILDREN OF James FITCH & Alice (BRADFORD[3]) Adams: (4 of 8)**<20>**

Abigail FITCH[4], b. 22 Feb. 1687/8

Ebenezer FITCH[4], b. 10 Jan. 1689/90

Daniel FITCH[4], b. Feb. 1692/3

Jabez FITCH[4], d. 31 Jan. 1784*, ae 81, Canterbury CT g.s. <NEHGR 70:344>**<20a>**

Sibel BISSELL, (dau of Daniel), b. 1 June 1761 ("marr. a Pember") <Stiles' Ancient Windsor 2:83>

CHILDREN OF Elijah PEMBER: (4) <Stiles' Ancient Windsor 2:561>

Thomas PEMBER, b. 2 Mar. 1757

Elizabeth PEMBER, b. 20 July 1758

Stephen PEMBER, b. 14 Oct. 1760

Elizabeth PEMBER, b. 16 Nov. 1762

Rev. Joseph METCALF, d. 24 May 1723, Falmouth**<21>**

CHILDREN OF Rev. Joseph METCALF & Abiell ADAMS[4] (Alice Bradford[3]): (9) <Gen.Adv.4:113-4>**<22>**

Abigail METCALF[5], b. 13 June 1708

Abel METCALF[5], b. 15 Nov. 1709 (twin)

Hannah METCALF[5], b. 2 May 1712

Alice METCALF[5], b. 2 May 1712 (twin)

Mary METCALF[5], b. 17 Dec. 1715

Elizabeth METCALF[5], b. 6 Mar. 1716/7

Delight METCALF[5], b. 1 May 1719

Sarah METCALF[5], b. 10 Feb. 1720/1

Sybil METCALF[5], b. 10 Nov. 1722

CHILD OF Nathaniel COLLINS & Alice ADAMS[4] (Alice Bradford[3]):**<23>**

John COLLINS[5], d. pre 20 Nov. 1746 (adm.) <Hist. Enfield CT:2221>

Mary MEACHAM, d. 21 May 1766, wf of 2nd hus. Joseph Sexton <Barbour, Somers CT VR:119>

CHILDREN OF John COLLINS[5] & Mary MEACHAM: (6)

John COLLINS[6], b. pre 6 Oct. 1732

Giles COLLINS[6], b. 3 Dec. 1734

Ariel COLLINS[6], b. 9 June 1737; d. 28 Aug. 1820 <Springfield VR 2:126>

Isaac COLLINS[6], b. 21 Aug. 1741

Ambrose COLLINS[6], b. 23 Dec. 1743

Elijah COLLINS[6], b. 12 June 1746

Mary STEBBINS, (dau of Joseph & Mary), b. 14 Feb. 1740, d. 25 May 1810 <Springfield VR 2:45, 108>

CHILD OF Ariel COLLINS[6] & Mary STEBBINS:

Hannah COLLINS[7], b. 10 June 1777 <Springfield VR 3:22>

Jonathan PEASE 2nd, d. 5 Apr. 1839 <Springfield VR 2:164>

CHILD OF Jonathan PEASE & Hannah COLLINS[7]:

Betsey Collins PEASE[8], b. 29 July 1813 <Springfield VR 3:169>

Charles BLAKE, (son of Harvey & Lucinda), b. 22 Mar. 1811 <Springfield VR 3:155>

CHILD OF Charles BLAKE & Betsey Collins PEASE[8]:

Sarah BLAKE[9], b. 22 Aug. 1845 <Springfield VR 4:47>

Betsey BLAKE, d. 20 Nov. 1846 <Springfield VR 3:329> (not identified)

Rev. Samuel WHITING, b. 22 Apr. 1670, Hartford CT; d. 27 Sept. 1725*, Enfield CT g.s.**<24>**

CHILDREN OF Rev. Samuel WHITING & Elizabeth ADAMS[4] (Alice Bradford[3]): (2)**<25>**

Samuel WHITING[5], b. 15 May 1720, Windham CT; d. 15 Feb. 1803, Stratford CT g.s. <Hist.:258>

Sybil WHITING[5], b. ( ); d. 7 Aug. 1755 <Hist.Windham CT:61>**<26>**

Elizabeth JUDSON, (?dau of Joshua), b. c1723, d. 5 Dec. 1793, ae 70, Stratford g.s.<Hist.:258>

CHILDREN OF Samuel WHITING[5] & Elizabeth JUDSON: (10) <Hist. of Stratford CT:1345>

Samuel WHITING[6], bpt. Mar. 1744

Judson WHITING[6], bpt. Mar. 1746

John WHITING[6], bpt. Nov. 1748; d. Jan. 1822, ae 73, Bridgeport CT

Elizabeth WHITING[6], bpt. Nov. 1751

Joseph WHITING[6], bpt. Apr. 1754

Sarah WHITING[6], bpt. Sept. 1756

Martha WHITING[6], bpt. Dec. 1759

David WHITING[6], bpt. May 1762

William Nathan WHITING[6], bpt. Sept. 1764

Seymour Conway WHITING[6], bpt. July 1766; d. 26 July 1841

John BACKUS, d. June 1769 <Hist.Windham CT:61>**<26>**

CHILDREN OF John BACKUS & Sybil WHITING[5] (Eliz. Adams[4]): (7 of 12) <Hist.Windham CT:61>**<27>**

Nathaniel BACKUS[6], b. 5 Feb. 1726, d. 29 Nov. 1727

John BACKUS[6], b. 23 Mar. 1728

Sybil BACKUS[6], b. 1 Mar. "1728-30"

Elizabeth BACKUS[6], b. 17 Feb. 1731/2, d. 21 Oct. 1747

Lucretia BACKUS^{6}, b. Feb. 1733/4
Lydia BACKUS^{6}, b. 15 July 1736
Sylvanus BACKUS^{6}, b. 6 July 1738
CHILDREN OF Sylvanus BACKUS^{6} & Elizabeth GAMBLE: (6) <Hist.Windham CT by Weaver:61>
John BACKUS^{7}, b. 25 Feb. 1759
Simon BACKUS^{7}, b. 20 Oct. 1761
Sybil BACKUS^{7}, b. 14 June 1764, d. 13 June 1766
Elizabeth BACKUS^{7}, b. 25 Nov. 1765
Sybil BACKUS^{7}, b. 13 June 1766
Eunice BACKUS^{7}, b. 16 Jan. 1769
John DYER, b. 9 Apr. 1692, Weymouth; d. 25 Feb. 1779, Windham CT
CHILDREN OF John DYER & Abigail FITCH^{4} (Alice Bradford^{3}): (8) <Canterbury CT VR>
Sybil DYER^{5}, b. 26 Oct. 1714
Elijah DYER^{5}, b. 10 Sept. 1716
Abigail DYER^{5}, b. 10 Apr. 1718
James DYER^{5}, b. 16 Feb. 1720
John DYER^{5}, b. 9 May 1722
Joseph DYER^{5}, b. 15 Feb. 1724
Sarah DYER^{5}, b. 14 Nov. 1727
Ebenezer DYER^{5}, b. 19 Sept. 1729; d. 1757
CHILDREN OF James DYER^{5} & Ann WHITING: (7) <Canterbury CT VR>**<28>**
William DYER^{6}, b. 29 Jan. 1755; d. 22 July 1756
John DYER^{6}, b. 24 Mar. 1757; d. 1 Jan. 1777
James DYER^{6}, b. 2 Nov. 1759
Abigail DYER^{6}, b. 10 May 1761
Anna DYER^{6}, b. 19 May 1766
Samuel DYER^{6}, b. 2 Feb. 1773
Parmelia DYER^{6}, b. 21 June 1775
CHILDREN OF David BUTTS & Anna DYER^{6}: (6) <Canterbury CT VR>
Hiram BUTTS^{7}, b. 26 Oct. 1796
Lyman BUTTS^{7}, b. 22 Apr. 1798
Sarah BUTTS^{7}, b. 31 Mar. 1801
Mary Ann BUTTS^{7}, b. 15 Mar. 1803
David BUTTS^{7}, b. 8 June 1805
John Dyer BUTTS^{7}, b. 9 July 1807
Mary DeFOREST, b. c1749, d. 16 June 1823, ae 74, Bridgeport CT**<29>**
CHILDREN OF John WHITING^{6} (Sam.^{5}) & Mary DeFOREST: (4) <Hist.Stafford CT:1345>
Elizabeth WHITING^{7}, b. Sept. 1770; d. 18 Oct. 1842, Westmoreland, NY g.s.
Ephraim WHITING^{7}, b. 19 Oct. 1772 <Bible>; d. 12 Oct. 1855*
John William WHITING^{7}, b. Apr. 1788
William John WHITING^{7}, b. Apr. 1788 (twin)
Sally YOUNGS, b. 8 Dec. 1772 <Bible>
CHILDREN OF Ephraim WHITING^{7} & Sally YOUNGS: (8) <Bible>
William Youngs WHITING^{8}, b. 10 Sept. 1796
Elvira WHITING^{8}, b. 15 June 1798
Judson WHITING^{8}, b. 24 Aug. 1800, d. 11 Sept. 1800
Minerva WHITING^{8}, b. 29 Oct. 1801
Harry Willis WHITING^{8}, b. 17 Nov. 1804
Betsey WHITING^{8}, b. 6 Mar. 1807, d. 20 Sept. 1828
Elizabeth Mary WHITING^{8}, b. 10 Sept. 1809, d. 2 Aug. 1838

Sally Cornelia WHITING^{8}, b. 10 Apr. 1814; d. betw. 7 Apr. 1883 (will) - 19 Nov. 1885 (prob.)

CHILD OF Otis BOOTH & Sally Cornelia WHITING^{8}: (1) <will>**<30>**

Hattie C. BOOTH^{9}, b. July 1840 (m. Nelson King)

Charles BANKS, b. 1804, Eng., d. 19 June 1870, Bridgeport CT

CHILDREN OF Charles BANKS & Sally Cornelia (WHITING^{8}) Booth: (3) <will>

Georgia L. BANKS^{9}, b. 11 Aug. 1847

Charles BANKS^{9}, b. ( )

Warren H. BANKS^{9}, b. ( )

James LeWORTHY, b. 1754, London, Eng.; d. 27 Mar. 1829, Westmoreland, NY g.s.

CHILD OF James LeWORTHY & Elizabeth WHITING^{7} (John^{6}):

Eliza LeWORTHY^{8}, b. 17 Feb. 1807, New York, NY; d. 11 Nov. 1876, Pahnyra, NY

CHILD OF Artemas TROWBRIDGE & Eliza LeWORTHY^{8}:

Susan A. TROWBRIDGE^{9}, b. 14 Aug. 1828

Betty WELLS, (*dau of Robert & Eunice (Curtis)), b. c1728, d. 1783, ae 55

CHILDREN OF Ephraim BURTON & Betty WELLS: (5) <Hist.Stafford CT:1170>

Mary BURTON, bpt. Sept. 1749**<29>**

Samuel BURTON, b. 12 Dec. 1750

Lewis BURTON, b. ( )

Nathaniel Judson BURTON, b. ( )

Ann BURTON, bpt. Feb. 1756

Lydia GALE, b. c1700, d. 20 Aug. 1753, ae 53, Canterbury CT g.s. <NEHGR 70:344>**<31>**

CHILDREN OF Jabez FITCH^{4} (Alice Bradford^{3}) & Lydia GALE: (8) <Canterbury CT ChR>**<32>**

Jerusha FITCH^{5}, bpt. 23 June 1723*

Alice FITCH^{5}, bpt. 11 Apr. 1725*

Perez FITCH^{5}, bpt. 11 Dec. 1726*

Lydia FITCH^{5}, b. ( )

Lucy FITCH^{5}, bpt. 27 June 1736*

Asel FITCH^{5}, bpt. 27 Aug. 1738*

Abigail FITCH^{5}, bpt. 19 Apr. 1741***<33>**

Jabez FITCH^{5}, b. ( )

Phineas ADAMS, d. 7 Jan. 1779 <Norwich CT VR 1:232>

CHILDREN OF Phineas ADAMS & Lydia FITCH^{5}: (11) <Norwich CT VR (1-6) 1:315, (7-11) 1:232>

William ADAMS^{6}, b. 17 Oct. 1752

Asael ADAMS^{6}, b. 13 Sept. 1754

Abigail ADAMS^{6}, b. 7 Dec. 1756

Lydia ADAMS^{6}, b. 22 Dec. 1758, d. 16 Feb. 1759

Welthean ADAMS^{6}, b. 22 Feb. 1760

Phineas ADAMS^{6}, b. 17 Aug. 1762

Roger ADAMS^{6}, b. 6 Nov. 1764

Dr. Jabez ADAMS^{6}, b. 23 Aug. 1768; d. 24 May 1848, Mansfield g.s.<ChR:435>

Fitch ADAMS^{6}, b. 20 Jan. 1772

Lydia ADAMS^{6}, b. 4 May 1774

Alice ADAMS^{6}, b. 8 Oct. 1776

Lucy SWIFT^{7} (Barzilla^{6}, Rowland^{5}, Abigail Gibbs^{4}, Alice Warren^{3}, Nathaniel^{2}), b. 27 Aug. 1772 <Mansfield CT VR:177>; d. 11 Jan. 1814 <Mansfield CT ChR:428; Hist.Windham 1:29>

CHILDREN OF Dr. Jabez ADAMS^{6} & 1st Lucy SWIFT: (11) <Hist.Windham 1:29, (4-11) 1:30>**<34>**

Harriet ADAMS^{7}, b. 25 Aug. 1794; d. 18 Dec. 1844, Springfield, consumption <Mass.VR 14:147> **<35>**

Henry ADAMS^{7}, b. 30 Mar. 1796, d. 29 Apr. 1858

Abigail L. ADAMS^{7}, b. 28 Feb. 1798; d. 1 Oct. 1813 <Mansfield ChR:428>

Lucy Swift ADAMS^{7}, b. 13 Dec. 1799 (m. Reuben Bishop)

Washington Swift ADAMS[7], b. 6 Jan. 1803; d. 1 Oct. 1813 <Mansfield ChR:428>

Eliza ADAMS[7], b. 23 Apr. 1805 (m. Ezra Bingham)

David A. ADAMS[7], b. 6 Feb. 1807

Sarah Fearing ADAMS[7], b. 20 Mar. 1809

Alice R. ADAMS[7], b. 10 Feb. 1811 (m. Col. E.S. Fitch)

Fitch ADAMS[7], b. 25 Feb. 1813, d. 18 Mar. 1814

Lydia ADAMS[7], b. 25 Feb. 1813 (twin)

CHILDREN OF Dr. Jabez ADAMS[6] & 2nd Lucy ENSWORTH (dau of Dr. Jedediah): (2) <Hist.Windham 1:30>

Abigail Ann ADAMS[7], b. 15 Apr. 1816, d. 2 July 1848

Jabez F. ADAMS[7], b. 10 Sept. 1820, d. 4 July 1851

James BREWER, (son of Daniel & Anna), b. c1789, Springfield, d. 20 July 1856, ae 67, Springfield, consumption <Mass.VR 102:230>

CHILD OF James BREWER & Harriet ADAMS[7] (Jabez[6]):**<36>**

James Dwight BREWER[8], b. 24 Apr. 1819, Thompsonville CT <Hist. CT Valley (1879) 2:888>; d. 7 Feb. 1886, ae 66y9m14d, Springfield, paralysis <Mass.VR 373:395>

Sarah PORTER, (dau of Col. Solomon & Nancy), b. 1821, Hartford CT, d. 18 Apr. 1886, ae 65y1m7d, Springfield <Mass.VR 373:298>

CHILDREN OF James Dwight BREWER[8] & Sarah PORTER: (2) <Springfield>**<36>**

Edward L. BREWER[9], b. 13 June 1846 <Mass.VR 22:227>

Harriet Porter BREWER[9], b. 30 May 1850 <Mass.VR 42:272>

Elizabeth PHINNEY[3] (Jonathan[2], John[1]), bpt 1695, Bristol RI <NEHGR 60:68>; d. aft 9 Oct. 1746**<37>**

CHILDREN OF David BRADFORD[3] & Elizabeth PHINNEY: (5) <Plymouth, MD 12:85>

Nathaniel BRADFORD[4], b. 10 Dec. 1715; d. 27 Mar. 1751, Plymouth <MD 16:87>

Jonathan BRADFORD[4], b. 13 Nov. 1717; d. pre 1742*

Lydia BRADFORD[4], b. 23 Dec. 1719; d. 28 Oct. 1756, Plymouth g.s.

Nathan BRADFORD[4], b. 3 Apr. 1722; d. 14 Oct. 1787, consumption, Kingston g.s. <VR, MD 7:23>

Lemuel BRADFORD[4], b. 1 Mar. 1726/7; d. pre 1746*

Elkanah CUSHMAN[5] (Elkanah[4-3], Mary Allerton[2]), b. 10 July 1706, Plymouth <MD 2:226>

CHILD OF Elkanah CUSHMAN & Lydia BRADFORD[4]:

Elkanah CUSHMAN[5], b. 13 Nov. 1741, Plymouth <MD 15:159>

Dr. Lazarus LeBARRON, (son of Francis), b. 26 Dec. 1698, Plymouth, d. 3 Sept. 1773 Plym.<MD 2:78>

CHILDREN OF Dr. Lazarus LeBARRON & Lydia (BRADFORD[4]) Cushman: (7) <Plymouth, MD 15:161>

Isaac LeBARRON[5], b. 25 Jan. 1743/4; d. 23 Dec. 1819 <Plymouth VR>

Elizabeth LeBARRON[5], b. 21 Dec. 1745

Lemuel LeBARRON[5], b. 1 Sept. 1747

Francis LeBARRON[5], b. 3 Sept. 1749

William LeBARRON[5], b. 8 Aug. 1751; d. 23 Oct. 1816

Priscilla LeBARRON[5], b. 3 Aug. 1753

Margaret LeBARRON[5], b. 5 July 1755; d. 20 Nov. 1756

Martha HOWLAND[5] (Consider[4], Tho.[3], Jos.[2]), b. 22 Dec. 1739, Plymouth <MD 13:175>; d. 26 June 1826 <Plymouth VR>

CHILDREN OF Isaac LeBARRON[5] & Martha HOWLAND: (4)

Isaac LeBARRON[6], b. 11 Mar. 1777; d. 29 Jan. 1849

Martha Howland LeBARRON[6], b. 14 June 1778; d. 24 Aug. 1850

Francis LeBARRON[6], b. 29 Apr. 1781; d. 20 June 1829

Mary Howland LeBARRON[6], b. 14 May 1786; d. 11 Apr. 1867

CHILDREN OF Nathan BRADFORD[4] (David[3]) & Elizabeth (   ): (5) <Kingston VR>**<38>**

Lydia BRADFORD[5], b. 17 Jan. 1750, d. 31 July 1751

Jonathan BRADFORD[5], b. 15 May 1752

Elizabeth BRADFORD[5], b. 11 Apr. 1754

Thomas BRADFORD^5, b. 18 June 1755

David BRADFORD^5, b. 27 Mar. 1757, d. 29 Feb. 1840, old age

MICRO #4 of 15

Sarah SPOONER, (*dau of Tho.), b. 31 Jan. 1726/7*, Plymouth <MD 13:33>; d. 1 July 1782*, Bridgew.

CHILDREN OF Nathaniel BRADFORD^4 (David^3) & Sarah SPOONER: (2) <Plymouth, MD 12:13>

Nathaniel BRADFORD^5, b. 26 July 1748; d. 24 Nov. 1837*, Plymouth**<39>**

Lemuel BRADFORD^5, b. 20 Feb. 1750/1; d. 22 May 1828, Plymouth <Burial Hill:159>

Mary SAMPSON, (dau of Ebenezer & Hannah (Harlow)), b. 4 June 1755; d. 21 Dec. 1790, Plymouth g.s. <Burial Hill:65>

CHILDREN OF Lemuel BRADFORD^5 & 1st Mary SAMPSON: (5) <Plymouth VR>

Lemuel BRADFORD^6, b. 1 Dec. 1775; d. 17 Sept. 1814 "killed in battle"

Thomas BRADFORD^6, b. 25 Feb. 1778; d. 1837

Mary BRADFORD^6, b. 19 Dec. 1780; d. 1856*

George BRADFORD^6, b. 19 Sept. 1783; d. 1849, Bangor ME

Eleanor BRADFORD^6, b. 25 Aug. 1785

Lydia HOLMES, (dau of Cornelius & Lydia (Drew)), b. Aug. 1750; d. 6 June 1838 <Burial Hill:159>

CHILDREN OF Lemuel BRADFORD^5 & 2nd Lydia HOLMES: (6) <Plymouth VR>

Cornelius BRADFORD^6, b. 20 or 28 Mar. 1793; d. 16 Aug. 1824*, New Orleans

Lydia BRADFORD^6, b. 25 Jan. 1795, d. 14 Apr. 1868***<40>**

David BRADFORD^6, b. 28 Apr. 1796; d. 22 July 1860***<41>**

William Holmes BRADFORD^6, b. 12 Feb. 1798

Lewis BRADFORD^6, b. 1 Apr. 1801; d. 13 Apr. 1802*

Lewis BRADFORD^6, b. 6 Dec. 1802

Capt. Ephraim HOLMES, b. 30 Oct. 1776; d. (4) Aug. 1811 "at sea 3 days out from Havana"

CHILDREN OF Capt. Ephraim HOLMES & Mary BRADFORD^6: (4)

Maj. Ephraim HOLMES^7, b. 29 Oct. 1801

Joan HOLMES^7, b. 23 Jan. 1803

Ephraim HOLMES^7, b. 29 Aug. 1805

Mary Ann HOLMES^7, b. 6 Aug. 1808

CHILDREN OF John TRIBBLE & Mary (BRADFORD^6) Holmes: (3)

Maria TRIBBLE^7, b. 9 Sept. 1817

Albert TRIBBLE^7, b. 21 Apr. 1819; d. 14 Oct. 1841

Leventha TRIBBLE^7, b. 31 May 1821; d. 9 May 1824

Mary Ann ATWOOD, (dau of John & Nancy (Churchill)), b. 18 Sept. 1807, Plymouth

CHILDREN OF Maj. Ephraim HOLMES^7 (Mary Bradford^6) & Mary Ann ATWOOD: (5)

William Walace HOLMES^8, b. 17 Mar. 1832; d. 2 Feb. 1834

Ann Maria HOLMES^8, b. 30 Nov. 1834

William Walace HOLMES^8, b. 13 Apr. 1837; d. 4 Sept. 1838

Mary Bradford HOLMES^8, b. 22 July 1841

Ephraim HOLMES^8, b. 7 Aug. 1845

Frank LEWIS, (son of Sam. & Mercy (Sears)), b. 14 Oct. 1835

CHILD OF Frank LEWIS & Ann Maria HOLMES^8:

Frank Clifton LEWIS^9, b. 28 Nov. 1857

Jacob JACKSON, (son of Daniel & Rebekah (Morton)), b. 9 Jan. 1794; d. 22 Oct. 1857

CHILDREN OF Jacob JACKSON & Joan HOLMES^7 (Mary Bradford^6): (9)

Gustavus JACKSON^8, b. 24 Mar. 1826

Joan JACKSON^8, b. 4 Mar. 1829

Leventha JACKSON^8, b. 14 June 1831; d. 22 Sept. 1851

Sophia JACKSON^8, b. 25 Mar. 1833; d. 20 Sept. 1849

Mary Ann JACKSON^8, b. 11 Mar. 1835

Lydia E. JACKSON^{8}, b. 26 Feb. 1837

Andrew JACKSON^{8}, b. 7 Mar. 1839; d. 9 July 1845

Marcia JACKSON^{8}, b. 15 Dec. 1840

Maria E. JACKSON^{8}, b. 16 Aug. 1843

Lewis Gould LOW, (son of Dr. Abram & Emma (Burr)), b. 17 Aug. 1828 ("of Bridgewater, formerly of Boston")

CHILDREN OF Lewis Gould LOW & Joan JACKSON^{8}: (7)

Charles Abram LOW^{9}, b. 17 July 1852

George Hale LOW^{9}, b. 28 Feb. 1855

Gustavus Jackson LOW^{9}, b. 10 Mar. 1857

Emma Burr LOW^{9}, b. 3 May 1859

Ann Jackson LOW^{9}, b. 29 Aug. 1861

Lewis Gould LOW^{9}, b. Aug. 1864; d. Oct. 1864

Elizabeth Cummings LOW^{9}, b. 1 Mar. 1866

Corban BARNES, (son of Corban & Phebe (Holmes)), b. 3 Mar. 1805

CHILDREN OF Corban BARNES & Mary Ann HOLMES^{7} (Mary Bradford^{6}): (9)

Albert Corban BARNES^{8}, b. 3 Mar. 1838; d. 23 June 1843

Corban BARNES^{8}, b. 11 Dec. 1839; d. 2 Sept. 1841

Lemuel BARNES^{8}, b. 20 July 1841; d. 16 June 1842

Mary Ann BARNES^{8}, b. 4 Feb. 1843; d. 8 Oct. 1844

Mary Clifton BARNES^{8}, b. 9 Oct. 1844

Frances Sophia BARNES^{8}, b. 11 Oct. 1846

Albert Corban BARNES^{8}, b. 31 Aug. 1848

George Bradford BARNES^{8}, b. 11 July 1851

Corban BARNES^{8}, b. 14 July 1853

CHILD OF Cornelius BRADFORD^{6} (Lemuel^{5}) & Elizabeth HINCKLEY: <42>

Cornelius BRADFORD^{7}, b. ( )

CHILD OF Cornelius BRADFORD^{7} & Mary BAKIN:

Joseph Morey BRADFORD^{8}, b. 2 Sept. 1812*

CHILDREN OF Joseph Morey BRADFORD^{8} & Anna Roberson RAYMOND: (1 of 6)<43>

Cornelius Francis BRADFORD^{9}, b. 4 Mar. 1845*; d. 3 Mar. 1908*

CHILDREN OF Capt. David BRADFORD^{6} (Lemuel^{5}) & Betsey BRIGGS: (13)<44>

David Lewis BRADFORD^{7}, b. 11 Apr. 1821; d. 31 Aug. 1838<45>

Betsey BRADFORD^{7}, b. 10 Aug. 1822

Desire Harlow BRADFORD^{7}, b. 22 Dec. 1823; d. 28 July 1825<45>

Cornelius BRADFORD^{7}, b. 22 Mar. 1825

Desire Harlow BRADFORD^{7}, b. 9 Aug. 1826

Lemuel BRADFORD^{7}, b. 4 Aug. 1828

Nathaniel BRADFORD^{7}, b. 27 Apr. 1830

Andrew Jackson BRADFORD^{7}, b. 27 Jan. 1832; d. 10 June 1833<45>

Lydia Holmes BRADFORD^{7}, b. 5 Dec. 1833; d. 9 Aug. 1834<45>

Lydia Holmes BRADFORD^{7}, b. 26 July 1835; d. 27 Sept. 1837<45>

Allen BRADFORD^{7}, b. 27 Aug. 1837

Harriet BRADFORD^{7}, b. 21 Jan. 1841

Mary Briggs BRADFORD^{7}, b. 14 Apr. 1842

William BRIGGS, (son of John & Rachel), b. 15 Jan. 1822; d. 21 Mar. 1854

CHILD OF William BRIGGS & Betsey BRADFORD^{7}:

Betsey Williams BRIGGS^{8}, b. 18 June 1849

William B. COREY, (son of Barnum & Ann), b. 26 Aug. 1824

CHILDREN OF William B. COREY & Betsey (BRADFORD^{7}) Briggs: (3)

Martha Ann COREY^{8}, b. 15 Nov. 1858

David Bradford COREY^{8}, b. 11 Feb. 1860; d. 11 Aug. 1860

David Bradford COREY^{8}, b. 4 Mar. 1861

Hannah Jane RIPLEY, (dau of Alexander & Hannah (Flemming)), d. May 1857

CHILDREN OF Cornelius BRADFORD^{7} (David^{6}) & Hannah Jane RIPLEY: (2)

David Lewis BRADFORD^{8}, b. 19 Dec. 1849

Abby Lincoln BRADFORD^{8}, b. 22 Feb. 1857

Mary P. DELANO, (dau of Charles), b. 17 Feb. 1825 (2nd wf of Cornelius Bradford^{7})

Elizabeth Bartlett WHITING, (dau of Ephraim & Patience (Everson)), b. 6 Dec. 1827

CHILDREN OF Lemuel BRADFORD^{7} (David^{6}) & Elizabeth Bartlett WHITING: (6)

Eugene Russell BRADFORD^{8}, b. 1849, d. 1850

Eugene Russell BRADFORD^{8}, b. 13 Dec. 1850; d. 7 Feb. 1857

Lemuel Allen BRADFORD^{8}, b. 20 Apr. 185()

Lizzie Everson BRADFORD^{8}, b. 7 Feb. 1857; d. 2 Jan. 1860

Charles Eugene BRADFORD^{8}, b. 27 May 1861

Herbert Everson BRADFORD^{8}, b. 3 June 1862

Solomon FAUNCE, (son of Thadeus & Elizabeth (Sylvester)), b. 1784; d. May 1815

CHILDREN OF Solomon FAUNCE & Eleanor BRADFORD^{6} (Lemuel^{5}): (3)

Solomon FAUNCE^{7}, b. ( )

Lemuel Bradford FAUNCE^{7}, b. ( )

Rev. William FAUNCE^{7}, b. ( )

Mary Olive HARLOW, (dau of Nathaniel & Sallie (Holmes)), b. 16 Sept. 1811

CHILDREN OF Solomon FAUNCE^{7} & Mary Olive HARLOW: (2)

Solomon FAUNCE^{8}, b. 14 Apr. 1838; d. Apr. 1838

Solomon Elmer FAUNCE^{8}, b. 1() Sept. 1841

Lydia Vaughn WOOD, (dau of Eliab & Pursis (Record)), b. 9 Sept. 1814; d. 15 Feb. 1845

CHILDREN OF Lemuel Bradford FAUNCE^{7} (Eleanor Bradford^{6}) & 1st Lydia Vaughn WOOD: (4)

Lemuel Bradford FAUNCE^{8}, b. 20 Sept. 1831(?)

George Frederick FAUNCE^{8}, b. 15 Mar. 1837

Caleb Winslow FAUNCE^{8}, b. 27 Oct. 1841

Lydia Emely FAUNCE^{8}, b. 10 Nov. 1844

CHILDREN OF Lemuel Bradford FAUNCE^{7} & 2nd Elizabeth A. MORTON, (dau of Ephraim & Sally A.): (4)

Cassandria Raymond FAUNCE^{8}, b. 30 Dec. 1849

Joshua Bradford FAUNCE^{8}, b. 17 Oct. 1852

Elizabeth Ann Evelin Faunce^{8}, b. 29 Mar. 1857

George Winslow FAUNCE^{8}, b. 12 Sept. 1859

CHILDREN OF Rev. William FAUNCE^{7} (Eleanor Bradford^{6}) & Matilda Bradford BRADFORD, (dau of Josiah & Polly (Robbins)): (6)**<46>**

CHILDREN OF Weston VAUGHAN & Matilda Bradford FAUNCE^{8} (Wm.^{7}): (4)

Weston VAUGHAN^{9}, b. 1853

Frank VAUGHAN^{9}, b. 1855

Ann VAUGHAN^{9}, b. 1857

Child, b. 1861

CHILD OF William Thomas FAUNCE^{8} (Wm.^{7}) & Hannah PIERCE:

William Peirce FAUNCE^{9}, b. 1858

CHILDREN OF Capt. George BRADFORD^{6} (Lemuel^{5}) & Harriet CHURCHILL: (5)

George BRADFORD^{7}, b. 24 Aug. 1808

Edmund BRADFORD^{7}, b. 7 June 1810

Lemuel BRADFORD^{7}, b. 10 Mar. 1813

Henry Churchill BRADFORD^{7}, b. 21 May 1816; "lost on board the Lexington when she was burned on

Long Island, 12 Jan. 1840".
Harriet BRADFORD^{7}, b. 19 Aug. 1819; d. 14 Apr. 1847
Sarah Prince BROWN, b. 3 Aug. 1808, poss. Newburyport
CHILDREN OF George BRADFORD^{7} & Sarah Prince BROWN:(6)**<47>**
George Henry BRADFORD^{8}, b. 20 Nov. 1835
Joseph Moss BRADFORD^{8}, b. 25 Feb. 1838; d. 31 July 1857
Amy Ann Earl BRADFORD^{8}, b. 12 May 1841
Sarah Prince BRADFORD^{8}, b. 10 May 1845
Edmund Davis BRADFORD^{8}, b. 9 Feb. 1848
William BRADFORD^{8}, b. 7 Nov. 1849
Mary E. HALL, b. 1 Dec. 1815, poss. Newburyport
CHILDREN OF Edmund BRADFORD^{7} (George^{6}) & Mary E. HALL: (6)
Mary Harriet BRADFORD^{8}, b. 7 Nov. 1834
Edmund Churchill BRADFORD^{8}, b. 8 Jan. 1837
Henry Clay BRADFORD^{8}, b. 5 Sept. 1839
Selina Hall BRADFORD^{8}, b. 20 Feb. 1842; d. 6 Feb. 1844
Silas Stone BRADFORD^{8}, b. 3 Aug. 1844
Oscar Hall BRADFORD^{8}, b. 14 May 1851
CHILDREN OF Lemuel BRADFORD^{7} (George^{6}) & Lucy Ann DAMON: (6)**<48>**
Frederick BRADFORD^{8}, b. 5 Apr. 1837; d. 13 Jan. 1861
Matilda Ann BRADFORD^{8}, b. 26 Mar. 1839
Lucy Ellen BRADFORD^{8}, b. 16 Dec. 1840; d. 6 Mar. 1848
William Henry BRADFORD^{8}, b. 14 Dec. 1843
Harriet BRADFORD^{8}, b. 31 Aug. 1845; d. 6 Aug. 1846
George BRADFORD^{8}, b. 26 Aug. 1850; d. 3 Sept. 1851
Hetty HINCKLEY, (dau of Ebenezer & Esther (Mayo)), b. 1780, d. 9 Feb. 1809, 29th yr<Old Cemetery, Barnstable>
CHILDREN OF Capt. Lemuel BRADFORD^{6} (Lemuel^{5}) & Hetty HINCKLEY: (4)
Abagail Hinnkley BRADFORD^{7}, b. 10 Feb. 1801
Hetty Amelia BRADFORD^{7}, b. 11 Apr. 1803
George Frederick BRADFORD^{7}, b. 5 Apr. 1805; d. 1822
Charles Augustus BRADFORD^{7}, b. 24 May 1808
Isaac Jackson BICKNELL, b. 10 Sept. 1801; d. 6 Feb. 1855 (m.Brooklyn NY)
CHILDREN OF Isaac Jackson BICKNELL & Abagail Hinnkley BRADFORD^{7}: (3)
William Jackson BICKNELL^{8}, b. 23 Aug. 1827
Julia Ellen BICKNELL^{8}, b. 18 Oct. 1830
Lucy Amelia BICKNELL^{8}, b. 3 Jan. 1835
Abagail Clapp BEAL, (dau of Ebenezer & Joan (Withington)), b. 8 Feb. 1810, Randolph
CHILDREN OF Charles Augusta BRADFORD^{7} (Lemuel^{6}) & Abagail Clapp BEAL: (3)
Charles Frederick BRADFORD^{8}, b. 6 June 1844
William Hinkley BRADFORD^{8}, b. 23 Mar. 1847
Henry Withington BRADFORD^{8}, b. 24 Jan. 1853
Dr. Andrew MACKIE, (son of Dr. Andrew & Charity (Fearing)), b. 24 Jan. 1794, d. 9 May 1871
CHILDREN OF Dr. Andrew MACKIE & Hetty Amelia BRADFORD^{7} (Lemuel^{6}): (5)
Rev. Andrew MACKIE^{8}, b. 21 Feb. 1823, Plymouth
John Howell MACKIE^{8}, b. 24 Aug. 1826
George Frederick MACKIE^{8}, b. 25 Dec. 1830, New Bedford; d. 28 Sept. 1853, Staten Island
Elizabeth Crocker MACKIE^{8}, b. 18 Dec. 1833
Amelia Bradford MACKIE^{8}, b. 18 Mar. 1840, d. 9 Apr. 1855
Sarah COWELL, (dau of Ben & Elizabeth), b. 30 Apr. 1824, poss. Providence RI; d. 2 Mar. 1857

CHILDREN OF Rev. Andrew MACKIE^{8} & Sarah COWELL: (2)

Olivia Hitchcock MACKIE^{9}, b. 13 Oct. 1850, Providence RI

Andrew MACKIE^{9}, b. 29 Dec. 1852; d. 18 Jan. 1853, Newark NJ

Mary HOLMES, (dau of Richard & Abagail (Damon)), b. 29 Nov. 1780, poss. Plymouth

CHILDREN OF Thomas BRADFORD^{6} (Lemuel^{5}) & 1st Mary HOLMES: (8)

Mary Sampson BRADFORD^{7}, b. 25 Aug. 1800

Thomas BRADFORD^{7}, b. 21 Feb. 1803, d. 1 Jan. 1804

Abagail BRADFORD^{7}, b. 21 Sept. 1804, d. 11 Sept. 1823

Thomas Lewis BRADFORD^{7}, b. 21 Oct. 1806, d. Mar. 1832

Amos Sturtevant BRADFORD^{7}, b. 22 June 1808

David A. BRADFORD^{7}, b. 19 Aug. 1812

Sarah Spooner BRADFORD^{7}, b. 5 Dec. 1814

Lewis BRADFORD^{7}, b. 20 June 1816

Sophia (PARMENTER) Russell, (dau of Artemas & Lucy), b. 9 Oct. 1793, d. 9 Dec. 1845 (m.1st James Russell of Chilcotha OH)

CHILDREN OF Thomas BRADFORD^{6} & 2nd Sophia (PARMENTER) Russell: (6)

James Russell BRADFORD^{7}, b. 12 Mar. 1824

Lydia BRADFORD^{7}, b. 8 Nov. 1826

Maria BRADFORD^{7}, b. 19 Nov. 1829

Thomas BRADFORD^{7}, b. 7 June 1833

Artemas BRADFORD^{7}, d.y.

Elizabeth BRADFORD^{7}, b. 29 Dec. 1837

Cervilla Frances OLDAKEN, (dau of John & Mary), b. 3 Nov. 1818

CHILDREN OF James Russell BRADFORD^{7} & Cervilla Frances OLDAKEN: (6) (poss.Richmondale Ross Co.OH)

Sophia Frances BRADFORD^{8}, b. 17 Oct. 1845

Mary BRADFORD^{8}, b. 23 Feb. 1847

Sarah Elizabeth BRADFORD^{8}, b. 22 Oct. 1848

Julia Ann BRADFORD^{8}, b. 11 Dec. 1850

John Edson BRADFORD^{8}, b. 26 Aug. 1853

James Bartlett BRADFORD^{8}, b. 26 May 1857

Elizabeth CLARK, (dau of Jos. & Sarah (Tucker)), b. 14 Feb. 1811

CHILDREN OF Amos Sturtevant BRADFORD^{7} (Tho.^{6}) & Elizabeth CLARK: (9) (poss. Clarks co., OH)

Mary Holmes BRADFORD^{8}, b. 21 May 1830

Joseph BRADFORD^{8}, b. 26 May 1831, d. July 1832

David BRADFORD^{8}, b. 20 Aug. 1832, d. "Sept. 1833(??)" (his marriage is below)

Sarah Spooner BRADFORD^{8}, b. 16 Aug. 1834

Williams Holmes BRADFORD^{8}, b. 1 Mar. 1836, d. Nov. 1840

Amos BRADFORD^{8}, b. 15 Oct. 1837

Phebe BRADFORD^{8}, b. 4 Sept. 1841

Minerva BRADFORD^{8}, b. Sept. 1843

Martha BRADFORD^{8}, b. 20 Sept. 1845

Mary BURK, (dau of Tho. & Mary (Coffee)), b. 1 Oct. 1826

CHILDREN OF David BRADFORD^{8} & Mary BURK: (4) (poss. Golconda co., IL)

Thomas A. BRADFORD^{9}, b. 30 July 1850, d. 1 Nov. 1851

Thomas A. BRADFORD^{9}, b. 9 June 1853

David BRADFORD^{9}, b. 27 Sept. 1857

Mary Bell BRADFORD^{9}, b. 21 Nov. 1860, d. 7 Oct. 1861

CHILDREN OF Thomas M. PIERCE & Sarah Spooner BRADFORD^{8} (Amos S.^{7}): (6) (poss.Paris, Edgar co.,IL)

"Marth" PIERCE^{9}, b. 16 Dec. 1853

Harriet R. PIERCE^{9}, b. 20 Dec. 1854

Frances Jane PIERCE[9], b. 7 Dec. 1857

Charlot K. PIERCE[9], b. 8 Feb. "1858"

Child, b. ( )

Amos PIERCE[9], b. 16 May 1862

CHILDREN OF Thomas Lewis BRADFORD[7] (Tho.[6]) & Mary ( ): (2) (poss. Chillecotha, OH)

Albert BRADFORD[8], b. ( )

Elizabeth BRADFORD[8], b. ( )

John CAMPBELL, b. 4 June 1798 (of Shaw's Crossing, Mercer co., OH)

CHILDREN OF John CAMPBELL & Mary Sampson BRADFORD[7] (Tho.[6]): (8)

Mary Jane CAMPBELL[8], b. 4 Mar. 1828

Thomas S.B. CAMPBELL[8], b. 4 Aug. 1830

Elizabeth A. CAMPBELL[8], b. 5 June 1832 (m. Dr. A. Tolan, OH)

Sarah Spooner CAMPBELL[8], b. 7 Mar. 1834

George W. CAMPBELL[8], b. 5 Oct. 1835

Harriet F. CAMPBELL[8], b. 2 Aug. 1837

Rebekah E. CAMPBELL[8], b. 22 Jan. 1840

John W. CAMPBELL[8], b. 31 July 1842

CHILD OF John EXLINE & Sarah Spooner CAMPBELL[8]:

Harriet EXLINE[9], b. 17 Oct. 1859

Delia HILL, (dau of Stephen & Anna (Anderson)), b. 4 June 1833

CHILDREN OF Thomas S.B. CAMPBELL[8] & Delia HILL: (5) (poss. Kensia, Neb.)

John CAMPBELL[9], b. 10 Jan. 1852

Stephen CAMPBELL[9], b. 1 July 1853, d. 10 Sept. 1856

Mary Ann CAMPBELL[9], b. 11 May 1855, d. 1 Sept. 1856

Elizabeth CAMPBELL[9], b. 2 Dec. 1857

George W. CAMPBELL[9], b. 1 Dec. 1860

CHILDREN OF David EXLINE & Mary Jane CAMPBELL[8] (Mary S. Bradford[7]): (2)

Alice EXLINE[9], b. 4 Aug. 1859, d. 19 July 1861

David EXLINE[9], b. 9 Feb. 1862

Mary HOLMES, b. 6 Aug. 1803, d. 25 May 1852

CHILDREN OF William Holmes BRADFORD[6] (Lemuel[5]) & Mary HOLMES: (7)

Mary Holmes BRADFORD[7], b. 28 Aug. 1828

William Holmes BRADFORD[7], b. 8 July 1830, d. 4 Mar. 1843

George Frederick BRADFORD[7], b. 6 Apr. 1831, d. 27 Sept. 1841

Lydia Amelia BRADFORD[7], b. 5 Oct. 1834, d. 5 July 1837

Lydia BRADFORD[7], b. 28 Jan. 1838

George Frederick BRADFORD[7], b. 4 Jan. 1842

William Holmes BRADFORD[7], b. 26 Jan. 1845

Samuel HARLOW[9], (son of George[8] & Lydia (Ellis)), b. 14 July 1824<49>

CHILDREN OF Samuel HARLOW & Mary Holmes BRADFORD[7]: (2)

Frank HARLOW[8], b. 23 Sept. 1852

Mary Elizabeth HARLOW[8], b. 25 May 1854

Rebecca HOLMES, (*dau of Ichabod & Hannah (Sylvester)), b. c1753, d. 15 June 1838, ae 85 <Plymouth ChR:682><50>

CHILDREN OF Nathaniel BRADFORD[5] (Nathaniel[4]) & Rebecca HOLMES*: (8) (prob. Plymouth)

Nathaniel BRADFORD[6], b. 26 Nov. 1775; d. 11 June 1830<51>

Joseph BRADFORD[6], b. 18 May 1778; d. 17 Apr. 1853

John Howland BRADFORD[6], b. 14 July 1780; d. 7 Dec. 1863<52>

Sarah BRADFORD[6], b. 8 Jan. 1783

Ephraim BRADFORD[6], b. 28 June 1785, ship carpenter

Rebecca BRADFORD^{6}, b. 4 Feb. 1788; d. 13 Feb. 1870

Benjamin Willis BRADFORD^{6}, b. 15 Jan. 1791, cabinet maker

Elizabeth BRADFORD^{6}, b. 25 Dec. 1794, d. 1800<53>

Nancy BARNES, (dau of Jos. & Hannah (Rider)), d. 22 June 1844, Plymouth

CHILDREN OF Joseph BRADFORD^{6} & Nancy BARNES: (5) (prob. Plymouth)

Joseph BRADFORD^{7}, b. 24 Mar. 1801, d. 20 Oct. 1802

Nathaniel Barnes BRADFORD^{7}, b. 6 May 1803, d. Sept. 1818, lost at sea

Joseph BRADFORD^{7}, b. 10 Aug. 1806, d. 11 June 1839, died at sea

Edward Winslow BRADFORD^{7}, b. 4 Aug. 1807

James Madison BRADFORD^{7}, b. 10 Feb. 1810<54>

Mary DILLARD, (dau of Ben & Mary (Holmes)), b. 25 Dec. 1808, Plymouth; d. 18 Mar. 1870, Plymouth

CHILDREN OF Edward Winslow BRADFORD^{7} & Mary DILLARD: (10)

Nathaniel Barnes BRADFORD^{8}, b. 28 Feb. 1830, d. 31 July 1831

Mary Winslow BRADFORD^{8}, b. 3 Jan. 1832 (m. Wm. Alfred Dimon)

Catharine Edward BRADFORD^{8}, b. 13 May 1834

Nathaniel Barnes BRADFORD^{8}, b. 7 Feb. 1837

Josephine BRADFORD^{8}, b. 5 Mar. 1839

Ann Elizabeth BRADFORD^{8}, b. 1 Mar. 1841

Hannah Barnes BRADFORD^{8}, b. 28 Sept. 1843

Emma Francis BRADFORD^{8}, b. 23 Aug. 1846

Alice May BRADFORD^{8}, b. 30 Oct. 1848

Edward Winslow BRADFORD^{8}, b. 13 Nov. 1850

Charles Henry THOMAS, (son of Stephen & Sally (Everson)), b. 27 Nov. 1833 (of Boston)

CHILD OF Charles Henry THOMAS & Catharine Edward BRADFORD^{8}:

Charles Edward THOMAS^{9}, b. 30 May 1859

Joan BARNES, (dau of Corban & Phebe (Holmes)), b. 2 Sept. 1808, ?Plymouth

CHILDREN OF Joseph BRADFORD^{7} (Jos.^{6}) & Joan BARNES: (3)

Nancy Barnes BRADFORD^{8}, b. 26 May 1830

Sarah Ellis BRADFORD^{8}, b. 30 Mar. 1834

Joseph BRADFORD^{8}, b. 27 Apr. 1836, d. 10 Nov. 1841

Josiah Carver FULLER, (son of Calvin & Eliza (Carver)), b. 23 June 1828

CHILDREN OF Josiah Carver FULLER & Nancy Barnes BRADFORD^{8}: (3)

Annie Bradford FULLER^{9}, b. 30 May 1858, d. 5 Aug. 1859

Russell Bradford FULLER^{9}, b. 5 Oct. 1859, d. 10 Aug. 1860

Joseph Calvin FULLER^{9}, b. 10 Dec. 1860

Hannah CLOW, b. 18 Jan. 1786, d. 26 Aug. 1846, of Salem

CHILDREN OF Benjamin Willis BRADFORD^{6} (Nathaniel^{5}) & Hannah CLOW: (2) (Boston or Salem?)

Benjamin Willis BRADFORD^{7}, b. 8 Aug. 1826, d. 26 Aug. 1829

Anna Elizabeth BRADFORD^{7}, b. 29 Nov. 1831

Hannah MORTON, b. 29 June 1782, d. 27 Apr. 1817, of Duxborough

CHILDREN OF Ephraim BRADFORD^{6} (Nath.^{5}) & 1st Hannah MORTON: (3) (Duxbury?)

Ephraim BRADFORD^{7}, b. 27 Nov. 1807

Sally BRADFORD^{7}, b. 7 Oct. 1810

Morton BRADFORD^{7}, b. 2 Apr. 1817, ship carpenter

Lucy Peterson, b. 1 May 1799, ?Duxbury

CHILDREN OF Ephraim BRADFORD^{6} & 2nd Lucy PETERSON: (3)

John BRADFORD^{7}, b. 27 Nov. 1823

Rev. George BRADFORD^{7}, b. 3 June 1828, d. 17 Feb. 1859 (no issue)

Lucy BRADFORD^{7}, b. 7 Feb. 1831

Lucy KEENE, b. 28 July 1814, of Duxborough

CHILDREN OF Ephraim BRADFORD^{7} & Lucy KEENE: (3) (?Duxbury)

Hannah Morton BRADFORD^{8}, b. 11 June 1837, d. Apr. 1839

Lucy Ann BRADFORD^{8}, b. 10 Aug. 1841

Edna S. BRADFORD^{8}, b. 19 July 1844

Briggs Bradford DELANO, b. 30 Oct. 1808, ship carpenter

CHILDREN OF Briggs Bradford DELANO & Sally BRADFORD^{7} (Ephraim^{6}): (3)

Briggs Bradford DELANO^{8}, b. 11 Nov. 1835

Herbert DELANO^{8}, b. 27 Apr. 1838

Sally Bradford DELANO^{8}, b. 7 Apr. 1853

Catherine Elizabeth BURT, b. 1825, of Plymouth

CHILDREN OF Morton BRADFORD^{7} (Ephraim^{6}) & Catherine Elizabeth BURT: (2)

Catherine Morton BRADFORD^{8}, b. 16 Aug. 1844

Edward Everet BRADFORD^{8}, b. July 1848

Jane West MAGLUTHLIN, b. June 1825, of Duxbury

CHILD OF John BRADFORD^{7} (Ephraim^{6}) & Jane West MAGLUTHLIN:

Ellen BRADFORD^{8}, b. ( )

Francis NICKERSON, b. 8 Feb. 1824, of Duxbury

CHILDREN OF Francis NICKERSON & Lucy BRADFORD^{7} (Ephraim^{6}): (4)

Lizzie NICKERSON^{8}, b. 21 Mar. 1853

George NICKERSON^{8}, b. 15 Nov. 1855

Henry NICKERSON^{8}, b. 2 Aug. 1857

Lucy Bradford NICKERSON^{8}, b. 4 Apr. 1860

Deborah (SAMPSON) Wright, (dau of George & Mary (Kempton)), b. 29 Mar. 1776, d. 28 Feb. 1861

CHILDREN OF Nathaniel BRADFORD^{6} (Nath.^{5}) & Deborah (SAMPSON) Wright: (6) (?N.Y. City)

Nathaniel BRADFORD^{7}, b. 7 May 1801, d. 20 Mar. 1802

Deborah BRADFORD^{7}, b. 25 Aug. 1802

Nathaniel Governeur BRADFORD^{7}, b. 13 Aug. 1804

Benjamin Wright BRADFORD^{7}, b. 13 Feb. 1806

Elizabeth Holmes BRADFORD^{7}, b. 6 Mar. 1811

Rebekah BRADFORD^{7}, b. 16 Nov. 1812

Catherine ALLEN, b. 22 May 1810, of N.Y. City (wf of Ben.Wright Bradford^{7}, "No.2 Varice Place, New York City")

Rachel MILLER, b. 4 Sept. 1805

CHILDREN OF Nathaniel Governeur BRADFORD^{7} & Rachel MILLER: (3) (?N.Y. City)

Nathaniel Barnes BRADFORD^{8}, b. 31 Aug. 1831

Rachel Louisa BRADFORD^{8}, b. 1 Oct. 1836

Benjamin Wright BRADFORD^{8}, b. 28 July 1839

Abagail SACKET, b. 7 July 1831, d. 1 May 1857 (?N.Y. City)

CHILDREN OF Nathaniel Barnes BRADFORD^{8} & Abagail SACKET: (3) (?N.Y. City)

Mary Estelle BRADFORD^{9}, b. 23 Sept. 1854

Emely BRADFORD^{9}, b. 4 Mar. 1856

Alice BRADFORD^{9}, b. 18 Apr. 1857

Martin WILLARD, b. 9 July 1811, Shirley Village, Mass.

CHILDREN OF Martin WILLARD & Elizabeth Holmes BRADFORD^{7} (Nath.^{6}): (5) (N.Y. City?)

Joseph WILLARD^{8}, b. 26 Apr. 1839, d. 25 Apr. 1849

Mary WILLARD^{8}, b. 25 Nov. 1841

Bradford WILLARD^{8}, b. 19 May 1844

Eliza Leach WILLARD^{8}, b. 21 Dec. 1847

Gates WILLARD^{8}, b. 22 Sept. 1851

Capt. Samuel DOTEN, (son of Sam. & Eunice (Robbins)), b. 11 June 1783, Plymouth; d. 8 Sept. 1861

CHILDREN OF Capt. Samuel DOTEN & Rebekah BRADFORD[6] (Nath.[5]): (9)
Samuel Holmes DOTEN[7], b. 5 June 1812
Rebekah Holmes DOTEN[7], b. 26 Feb. 1814
Laura Ann DOTEN[7], b. 14 Mar. 1816
Euphelia Frances DOTEN[7], b. 21 May 1820, d. 4 Aug. 1850
Cornelia DOTEN[7], b. 20 July 1822
Eunice DOTEN[7], b. 2 Sept. 1824
Elizabeth DOTEN[7], b. 1 Apr. 1827
Alfred DOTEN[7], b. 27 July 1829
Charles Carrol DOTEN[7], b. 9 Apr. 1833 **<55>**
Elizabeth BREWSTER[4] (Wrestling[3], Love[2]), b. c1690, d. 5 Dec. 1741, 51st yr,Kingston g.s.<MD 7:23>
CHILDREN OF Ephraim BRADFORD[3] & Elizabeth BREWSTER: (14!) <Plymouth, 1-10, MD 13:32>
Deborah BRADFORD[4], b. 21 June 1712; d. 10 June 1732, Kingston g.s. <MD 7:22>, unm.
Son, b. June 1714; d.y. <MD 13:32>
Anna BRADFORD[4], b. 25 July 1715
Dau., b. Oct. 1716; d.y. <MD 13:32>
Elizabeth BRADFORD[4], b. 3 Nov. 1717
Ephraim BRADFORD[4], b. 1 Jan. 1718/9; d. pre 1741*
Abigail BRADFORD[4], b. 28 Feb. 1719/20
Lusanna BRADFORD[4], b. 3 May 1721
Elijah BRADFORD[4], b. 23 Jan. 1722/3 <MD 13:32>; d. pre 1741*
Son, b. c28 Mar. 1723/4; d.y. <MD 13:32>
Ruth BRADFORD[4], b. c1725, d. 26 Aug. 1767, ae 42
Ezekiel BRADFORD[4], d. 1816, Turner ME**<56>**
Simeon BRADFORD[4], b. 28 Aug. 1729 <Kingston VR:30>; d. 7 Oct. 1793 <Springfield VT VR>
Wait BRADFORD[4], b. ( ) <MD 21:189>
CHILDREN OF Peleg HOLMES & Abigail BRADFORD[4] (Ephraim[3]): (9) <Kingston, Gen.Adv.4:69,70>**<57>**
Abigail HOLMES[5], b. 4 June 1741; d. 20 June 1742
Deborah HOLMES[5], b. 3 Apr. 1743; d. 26 Jan. 1748
Abigail HOLMES[5], b. 6 July 1746
Peleg HOLMES[5], b. 6 Jan. 1749
Elizabeth HOLMES[5], b. 18 Feb. 1751
Lydia HOLMES[5], b. 29 June 1753
Nathaniel HOLMES[5], b. 21 Oct. 1753
Mary HOLMES[5], b. 20 Feb. 1758
Sarah HOLMES[5], b. 23 Apr. 1760
Ebenezer CHANDLER[4] (Jos.[3-2], Edmund[1]), b. 8 Sept. 1712, Duxbury <MD 11:150>
CHILDREN OF Ebenezer CHANDLER & Anna BRADFORD[4] (Ephraim[3]): (4) <Duxbury, MD 12:121>**<58>**
Lydia CHANDLER[5], b. 14 Mar. 1740/1
Zilpah CHANDLER[5], b. 15 Feb. 1741/2
Simeon CHANDLER[5], b. 23 June 1744
Anna CHANDLER[5], b. 14 June 1746
CHILDREN OF Azariah WHITON, (son of John & Bethiah) & Elizabeth BRADFORD[4] (Ephraim[3]): (5) <Plympton VR>**<59>**
John WHITON[5], b. 6 Aug. 1754
Ephraim WHITON[5], b. 21 Jan. 1757
Patience WHITON[5], b. 21 Jan. 1757, d.y.
Elizabeth WHITON[5], b. 6 Oct. 1759
Patience WHITON[5], b. ( )
Betty CHANDLER[5] (Philip[4], Jos.[3-2], Edmund[1]), b. 21 Oct. 1728, Duxbury <MD 11:149>; d. 24 Oct.

1811, Turner ME

CHILDREN OF Ezekiel BRADFORD^{4} (Ephraim^{3}) & Betty CHANDLER: (10) <Kingston VR>

Ephraim BRADFORD^{5}, b. 13 Dec. 1750 <VR:27>

Deborah BRADFORD^{5}, b. 18 Aug. 1752 <VR:26>

William BRADFORD^{5}, b. 9 Mar. 1754 <VR:30>

Rebecca BRADFORD^{5}, b. 22 Sept. 1756 <VR:29>

Jesse BRADFORD^{5}, b. 7 Mar. 1758 <VR:27>; d. 20 May 1829, Turner ME

Ezekiel BRADFORD^{5}, b. 15 Dec. 1759 <VR:27>

Chandler BRADFORD^{5}, b. 15 Aug. 1761 <VR:25>

Martin BRADFORD^{5}, b. 17 Oct. 1763 <VR:28>

Philip BRADFORD^{5}, b. 8 June 1765 <VR:29>

Betty BRADFORD^{5}, b. 22 Aug. 1767 <VR:25>

Judith WESTON, b. 17 Aug. 1762 <Kingston VR:58>; d. 15 Nov. 1842, Turner ME

CHILDREN OF Jesse BRADFORD^{5} & Judith WESTON: (1 of 9)* **<60>**

Philip BRADFORD^{6}, b. 15 July 1789; d. 24 June 1863, Turner ME

Lucy GREENWOOD, b. c1788, d. 27 Feb. 1822, ae 34, Turner ME

CHILD OF Philip BRADFORD^{6} & Lucy GREENWOOD:

Marcia BRADFORD^{7}, b. 19 Aug. 1819, Turner ME, d. 30 Oct. 1884, Turner ME

William Riley FRENCH, b. 8 June 1814, Turner Center ME, d. 7 Aug. 1893, Turner ME

CHILD OF William Riley FRENCH & Marcia BRADFORD^{7}:

Lucy Greenwood FRENCH^{8}, b. 9 Mar. 1844, Lewiston ME, d. 13 Jan. 1940, Portland ME

Merritt Bradford COOLIDGE, b. 8 Apr. 1839, Hallowell ME, d. 1 Feb. 1926, Portland ME

CHILD OF Merritt Bradford COOLIDGE & Lucy Greenwood FRENCH^{8}:

Arthur William COOLIDGE^{9}, b. 13 Oct. 1881, living 1944

MICRO #5 of 15

Nathan CHANDLER^{5} (Philip^{4}, Jos.$^{3-2}$, Edmund^{1}), b. 28 Oct. 1726, Duxbury <MD 11:149>; d. 21 Sept. 1795, S. Duxbury Cem. near Town Hall

CHILD OF Nathan CHANDLER & Ruth BRADFORD^{4} (Ephraim^{3}): **<61>**

Ephraim CHANDLER^{5}, b. c1750, d. 28 Jan. 1794, 44th yr, Kingston **<62>**

CHILDREN OF Ephraim CHANDLER^{5} & Molly DOTEN: (8) **<63>**

Selah CHANDLER^{6}, b. 16 Aug. 1776

Rizpah CHANDLER^{6}, b. 23 June 1778, d. 1779 **<64>**

Nathan CHANDLER^{6}, b. 5 Sept. 1780

Isaac CHANDLER^{6}, b. 3 Sept. 1782

Rizpah CHANDLER^{6}, b. 22 June 1785

Molly CHANDLER^{6}, b. 5 Apr. 1788; d. 23 Dec. 1793 **<65>**

Ephraim CHANDLER^{6}, b. 22 Apr. 1790

John CHANDLER^{6}, b. Nov. 1792

Phebe WHITON, (dau of Azariah & Eliz. (Barrows)), b. 16 Mar. 1736/7 <Plympton VR:229>; d. aft 16 Nov. 1793 (adm. husband's estate)

CHILDREN OF Simeon BRADFORD^{4} (Ephraim^{3}) & Phebe WHITON: (4 of 10) <1-3,Kingston,Gen.Adv.4:72> **<66>**

Asa BRADFORD^{5}, b. 5 July 1758

Simeon BRADFORD^{5}, b. 3 Sept. 1760

Lucy BRADFORD^{5}, b. 2 Oct. 1762

Ruth BRADFORD^{5}, b. 17 Jan. 1768 <Springfield VT VR>

Isaac SMITH, b. 22 Dec. 1766*, d. Mar. 1803* (hus of Ruth Bradford^{5})

CHILDREN OF Simeon BRADFORD^{5} & Mary SMITH: (4)

Orin BRADFORD^{6}, b. 1800

Otis BRADFORD^{6}, b. 1801

Alden BRADFORD^{6}, b. 1804

Enos BRADFORD^{6}, b. ( )

CHILDREN OF Wait BRADFORD^{4} (Ephraim^{3}) & Welthea BASSETT^{6} (Lydia Cooke^{5}, Wm.^{4}, Jacob$^{3-2}$): (4)

Sarah BRADFORD^{5}, b. c1768, bpt. 9 Oct. 1774 <Kingston VR:30>

Simeon BRADFORD^{5}, b. c1770, bpt. 9 Oct. 1774 <Kingston VR:30>

Deborah BRADFORD^{5}, b. c1777

Ephraim BRADFORD^{5}, b. c1783, bpt. 14 Aug. 1785 <Kingston VR:27>

Joshua RIPLEY, (son of John & Eliz. (Hobart)), b. 9 Nov. 1658, Hingham <MD 28:97>; d. 18 May 1739 <Windham CT VR; MD 28:97>

CHILDREN OF Joshua RIPLEY & Hannah BRADFORD^{3}: (12) <1-4, Hingham, 6-12, Windham CT, MD 28:100>

Alice RIPLEY^{4}, b. 17 or 18 Sept. 1683; d. 18 Dec. 1768* <Norwich CT VR>

Hannah RIPLEY^{4}, b. 2 Mar. 1685; d. Mar. 1751

Faith RIPLEY^{4}, b. 20 Sept. 1686; d. 11 Feb. 1720/1 <Windham VR>

Joshua RIPLEY^{4}, b. 13 May 1688; d. 18 Nov. 1773 <Windham CT VR, Barbour 1:55>

Margaret RIPLEY^{4}, b. 4 Nov. 1690, Norwich CT; d. 3 May 1774, Lebanon CT g.s.

Rachel RIPLEY^{4}, b. 17 Apr. 1693; d. aft 6 Jan. 1738/9*

Leah RIPLEY^{4}, b. 17 Apr. 1693 (twins); d. betw 9 Sept. 1772 (will) - 8 May 1775 (witnessed)

Hezekiah RIPLEY^{4}, b. 10 June 1695; d. 7 Feb. 1779 <Windham CT VR, Barbour 1:262>

David RIPLEY^{4}, b. 20 May 1697; d. 16 Feb. 1781 <Windham CT VR A:242>

Irena RIPLEY^{4}, b. 28 Aug. 1700; d. 20 Jan. 1726/7 <Windham CT VR A:77>

Jerusha RIPLEY^{4}, b. 1 Nov. 1704; d. 8 Oct. 1792 <Windham CT VR A:253>

Ann RIPLEY^{4}, b. 1 Nov. 1704 (twins); d. betw 6 Jan. 1738/9 (fath. will)- 17 Feb. 1747(hus.remarr)

Samuel EDGERTON, d. 7 June 1748 <Norwich CT VR>**<67>**

CHILDREN OF Samuel EDGERTON & Alice RIPLEY^{4}: (10) <Norwich CT VR:60>

Samuel EDGERTON^{5}, b. 15 Mar. 1704

Peter EDGERTON^{5}, b. 14 Jan. 1705/6

Joshua EDGERTON^{5}, b. 26 Feb. 1707/8

John EDGERTON^{5}, b. 25 Apr. 1710; d. 13 July 1730

William EDGERTON^{5}, b. 25 Apr. 1710 (twins)

Mary EDGERTON^{5}, b. 17 May 1713

Elijah EDGERTON^{5}, b. 1 Dec. 1715

David EDGERTON^{5}, b. 28 Aug. 1718

Alice EDGERTON^{5}, b. 25 Dec. 1721

Daniel EDGERTON^{5}, b. 10 July 1725, d. 31 Aug. 1726

CHILDREN OF Solomon WHEAT & Ann RIPLEY^{4} (Hannah Bradford^{3}): (3) <Windham>**<68>**

Sarah WHEAT^{5}, bpt. 3 Oct. 1731

Anna WHEAT^{5}, b. 8 July 1736 <VR A:21>

Hannah WHEAT^{5}, b. 16 July 1738 <VR A:21>

CHILDREN OF David RIPLEY^{4} (Hannah Bradford^{3}) & Lydia CARY: (12) <Windham CT VR A:61>

Faith RIPLEY^{5}, b. 6 May 1722

Lydia RIPLEY^{5}, b. 24 Feb. 1723/4

Ann RIPLEY^{5}, b. 27 Aug. 1726

Irena RIPLEY^{5}, b. 11 Feb. 1728/9

David RIPLEY^{5}, b. 7 Feb. 1730/1

William RIPLEY^{5}, b. 12 July 1734

Gamaliel RIPLEY^{5}, b. 19 Apr. 1736; d. 29 May 1737 <VR A:149>

Alathea RIPLEY^{5}, b. 24 Apr. 1738 <VR A:149>

Gamaliel RIPLEY^{5}, b. 20 Oct. 1740 <VR A:149>

Hezekiah RIPLEY^{5}, b. 3 Feb. 1742/3 <VR A:149>

Bradford RIPLEY^{5}, b. 26 Dec. 1744 <VR A:149>

Hannah RIPLEY^{5}, b. 23 Feb. 1750 <VR A:149>

Samuel BINGHAM, b. 28 Mar. 1685, d. 1 Mar. 1760, Windham CT

CHILDREN OF Samuel BINGHAM & 1st Faith RIPLEY[4] (Hannah Bradford[3]): (5) <Windham CT VR A:3>

Jerusha BINGHAM[5], b. 2 Feb. 1708/9

Abishai BINGHAM[5], b. 29 Jan. 1709/10

Lemuel BINGHAM[5], b. 20 Sept. 1713

Anne BINGHAM[5], b. Nov. 1716

Marah BINGHAM[5], b. 10 Feb. 1720/1, d. 22 Feb. 1720/1

Elizabeth MANNING, d. 27 Mar. 1780 <Windham CT VR:69>

CHILDREN OF Samuel BINGHAM & Elizabeth MANNING: (6) <Windham CT VR:69>**<69>**

Elizabeth BINGHAM, b. 14 Dec. 1722, d. 26 Dec. 1722

Samuel BINGHAM, b. 11 Nov. 1723

Thomas BINGHAM, b. 12 Sept. 1725, d. 9 July 1726

Thomas BINGHAM, b. 20 June 1727

Deborah BINGHAM, b. 4 May 1729

Mary BINGHAM, b. 18 Oct. 1731

CHILDREN OF Abishai BINGHAM[5] (Faith Ripley[4]) & Mary TUBBS: (2)

Abishai BINGHAM[6], b. ?28 Feb. 1735*

Abner BINGHAM[6], b. ( )

Ann SAWYER, (*dau of Elijah & Hannah (Terrill)), b. 28 Feb. 1734/5, Windham CT; d. 29 Oct. 1813*

CHILDREN OF Abishai BINGHAM[6] & Ann SAWYER: (8)* <Windham CT, Bingham Family:377,378>

Elias BINGHAM[7], b. 10 Dec. 1756; d. 1820

Sarah BINGHAM[7], b. 24 July 1758

Lucretia BINGHAM[7], b. 3 July 1760

Levi BINGHAM[7], b. 14 July 1762, unm.

Asahel BINGHAM[7], b. 15 May 1765

Irena BINGHAM[7], b. 29 July 1767, d. 31 Dec. 1842, unm.

Lucy BINGHAM[7], b. 23 Aug. 1770, d.y.

Anne BINGHAM[7], b. 7 Oct. 1772

CHILDREN OF Abner BINGHAM[6] (Abishai[5]): (2)

John Clark BINGHAM[7], b. 22 Feb. 1765, d. 11 Mar. 1826, Middletown Cem., Londonderry VT, "a Revolutionary soldier"

Ripley BINGHAM[7], b. ( )

CHILDREN OF Ripley BINGHAM[7] & Elizabeth MACK: (4 of 7)**<70>**

Ripley BINGHAM[8], b. c1786, d. 2 Oct. 1859*, ae 73, Sutton VT g.s.

Clarissa BINGHAM[8], b. ( ) (m. Charles Baldwin)

Betsey Elizabeth BINGHAM[8], b. ( )

Sally BINGHAM[8], b. ( ) (m. Samuel Horton)

Betsey CARY, (dau of Elezur), b. c1790, d. 5 May 1857, ae 67, Sutton VT g.s.

CHILDREN OF Ripley BINGHAM[8] & Betsey CARY: (2)

Horace BINGHAM[9], b. ( )

Eliza Ann BINGHAM[9], b. ( )

CHILDREN OF Stephen Eldridge HARTSHORN & Betsey Elizabeth BINGHAM[8] (Ripley[7]): (1 of 9)**<71>**

Theresa Lucina Sobeiska HARTSHORN[9], b. 12 Aug. 1829, Freedom NY, d. 22 Mar. 1904, Bainbridge OH

CHILDREN OF Faber Enos KINGSLEY & Theresa L.S. HARTSHORN[9]: (3)

Lyman Faber KINGSLEY[10], b. ( )

Mary L. KINGSLEY[10], b. ( )

Laura Alice KINGSLEY[10], b. 8 Apr. 1864

Frank Clayton BALL[10] (Maria Bingham[9], Ben.[8], Ripley[7]), b. 24 Nov. 1857, Greensburg OH

Elizabeth Wolfe BRADY, b. 24 Mar. 1867, Muncie Ind.

CHILD OF Frank Clayton BALL[10] & Elizabeth Wolfe BRADY:

Edward Arthur BALL[11], b. 10 Dec. 1894

CHILDREN OF Joseph TAYLOR & Hannah ( ): (6) <Concord VR>**<72>**

Anne TAYLOR, b. 14 Oct. 1759 <VR:202>

Nathan TAYLOR, b. 11 Feb. 1761 <VR:210>

Samuel TAYLOR, b. 7 Jan. 1763 <VR:225>

Hannah TAYLOR, b. 31 Dec. 1764 <VR:225>

Joseph TAYLOR, b. 5 Apr. 1767 <VR:225>

Sarah TAYLOR, b. 10 Sept. 1769 <VR:230>

CHILDREN OF Samuel WEBB & Hannah RIPLEY[4] (Hannah Bradford[3]): (4) <Windham CT VR A:7>**<73>**

Ebenezer WEBB[5], b. 26 Apr. 1712; d. 8 June 1713

Hannah WEBB[5], b. 29 June 1715

Ebenezer WEBB[5], b. 12 Jan. 1718/9

Joshua WEBB[5], b. 9 Feb. 1721/2

CHILDREN OF Joshua WEBB[5] & Hannah ABBE: (4) <Windham CT VR A:244>

Jehiel WEBB[6], b. 23 Jan. 1744/5

Joseph WEBB[6], b. 3 May 1746

Azariah WEBB[6], b. 11 Oct. 1748

Hannah WEBB[6], b. 19 June 1752

Deborah PALMER, (dau of David of Norwich CT), b. c1745, d. 20 July 1823, 78th yr

CHILDREN OF Darius WEBB, (son of Eben.) & Deborah PALMER: (11) <Family Rcd.>

Nathan WEBB, b. 13 June 1768, d. 26 Sept. 1807

Loren WEBB, b. 13 Aug. 1770

Thomas WEBB, b. 29 June 1772

Ruby WEBB, b. 25 May 1774

Lucius WEBB, b. 13 Apr. 1776

Lucy WEBB, b. 13 Apr. 1776 (twins), d. 21 Apr. 1776

David WEBB, b. 24 July 1778

Lucy WEBB, b. 27 Oct. 1780

Polly WEBB, b. 11 Nov. 1782

Susannah WEBB, b. 8 Feb. 1784

Judith K. WEBB, b. 25 Nov. 1790

Miriam FITCH, d. 19 Dec. 1744 <Windham CT VR A:205> (1st wf Hezekiah Ripley[4])

Mary SKINNER, b. c1703, d. 17 Nov. 1787, 84th yr <Windham CT VR A:256>

CHILD OF Hezekiah RIPLEY[4] (Hannah Bradford[3]) & 2nd Mary SKINNER:

Hezekiah RIPLEY[5], b. 25 Sept. 1748 <Windham CT VR A:256>

Samuel MANNING, (son of Sam.), b. 14 Jan. 1690*, Billerica MA; d. 3 June 1727 <Windham CT VR>

CHILDREN OF Samuel MANNING & Irena RIPLEY[4] (Hannah Bradford[3]): (6) <Windham CT VR>

Josiah MANNING[5], b. 18 Mar. 1720

Hezekiah MANNING[5], b. 8 Aug. 1721

Abigail MANNING[5], b. 25 Nov. 1722

Sarah MANNING[5], b. 22 Feb. 1723/4

Samuel MANNING[5], b. 22 Oct. 1725

David MANNING[5], b. 14 Jan. 1726/7

Deborah MANNING, (wf of Samuel), d. 8 Aug. 1727 <Windham CT VR A:77>

Samuel MANNING Sr., d. 20 Feb. 1755 <Windham CT VR A:77>

Sarah MANNING, (wf of Samuel), b. 11 Oct. 1746 <Windham CT VR A:77>

CHILDREN OF David MANNING[5] & 2nd Miriam SIMONSON*: (3)

Eunice MANNING[6], b. c1764, d. 23 May 1776, 12th yr <Sharon CT BMD:39>

Ripley MANNING[6], bpt. 11 Sept. 1768 <Sharon CT BMD:84>

Eunice MANNING[6], bpt. Sept. 1777 <Sharon CT BMD:84>

Maj. David MANNING, d. 1816, Manningville, Lisle, NY <Manning Gen.:251>

Anne JACKSON, (dau of Col. Giles & Anne (Thomas)), b. 15 May 1761, d. 5 Aug. 1847 <Manning Gen.: 251> (2nd wf of Maj. David Manning)

Edward BROWN, d. 28 July 1791 <Windham CT VR A:253>

CHILD OF Edward BROWN & Jerusha RIPLEY^{4} (Hannah Bradford^{3}):

Hubbard BROWN^{5}, b. 11 Dec. 1745, d. 1779, lost at sea <Windham CT VR A:253>

Mary BACKUS, b. c1792, d. 19 Oct. 1770, 78th yr, Windham CT g.s.<Windham CT VR, Barbour 1:55>

CHILDREN OF Joshua RIPLEY^{4} (Hannah Bradford^{3}) & Mary BACKUS: (9) <Windham CT VR, Barbour 1:39>

Mary RIPLEY^{5}, b. 18 Nov. 1714

Phineas RIPLEY^{5}, b. 25 Nov. 1716; d. 4 Aug. 1746

Hannah RIPLEY^{5}, b. 12 Jan. 1718/9; d. 8 Nov. 1750, unm.

Nathaniel RIPLEY^{5}, b. 30 June 1721

Elizabeth RIPLEY^{5}, b. 4 Nov. 1724

Joshua RIPLEY^{5}, b. 30 Oct. 1726; d. 19 Dec. 1787 <Windham Ct g.s.>

Ebenezer RIPLEY^{5}, b. 27 June 1729

William RIPLEY^{5}, b. 12 Feb. 1733/4

John RIPLEY^{5}, b. 31 Mar. 1738

CHILDREN OF Ebenezer RIPLEY^{5} & Mehitable BURBANK: (12) <Windham CT VR B:11>

Hannah RIPLEY^{6}, b. 28 Apr. 1753

Elioner RIPLEY^{6}, b. 16 Aug. 1754

Jerusha RIPLEY^{6}, b. 28 May 1756

Juliania RIPLEY^{6}, b. 31 July 1757, d. 18 July 1759

Justin RIPLEY^{6}, b. 1 Jan. 1759, d. 25 Oct. 1761

Abraham RIPLEY^{6}, b. 25 Feb. 1761

Abiah RIPLEY^{6}, b. 12 Dec. 1762 (dau)

Dwight RIPLEY^{6}, b. 7 Aug. 1764

Ebenezer RIPLEY^{6}, b. 26 Mar. 1766[<74>]

Thaddeus RIPLEY^{6}, b. 22 Oct. 1767

Anna RIPLEY^{6}, b. 20 June 1770

Horace RIPLEY^{6}, b. 20 Aug. 1772

Elizabeth LOTHROP, b. c1730, d. 30 June 1778, 48th yr, Windham CT g.s.

CHILDREN OF Joshua RIPLEY^{5} (Joshua^{4}) & 1st Elizabeth LOTHROP: (10) <Windham CT VR A:290>

Eliphalet RIPLEY^{6}, b. 28 Oct. 1749

Ralph RIPLEY^{6}, b. 25 Oct. 1751

Elizabeth RIPLEY^{6}, b. 22 May 1754

Olive RIPLEY^{6}, b. 13 Sept. 1756

Roger RIPLEY^{6}, b. 10 Apr. 1759

Joshua RIPLEY^{6}, b. 16 May 1761

Lydia RIPLEY^{6}, b. 30 July 1763

Nathaniel RIPLEY^{6}, b. 14 Feb. 1768

Erastus RIPLEY^{6}, b. 17 June 1770

Mary RIPLEY^{6}, b. 4 Oct. 1774

Thomas EATON, b. c1773, d. 18 May 1819, ae 46 <Fayetteville NY Cem.Rcds.>

Annie HIBBARD, b. c1779, d. 13 May 1834, ae 55 <Fayetteville NY Cem.Rcds.>

CHILD OF Thomas EATON & Annie HIBBARD:

Hiram EATON, b. 20 June 1808, d. 15 June 1882 <Fayetteville NY Cem.Rcds.>

Zaide AVERY, (dau of Melbourn & Lucretia), b. 26 MAY 1812, Duanesburg, d. 29 Oct. 1883, Fayetteville NY (wf of Hiram Eaton) <Fayetteville NY Cem.Rcds.>

Joshua ABBE, (son of Eben.), b. 20 Jan. 1710/1 <Windham CT VR>; d. 13 Jan. 1807, Windham CT g.s.

CHILDREN OF Joshua ABBE & Mary RIPLEY^{5} (Joshua^{4}): (10) <Windham CT VR A:164>

Zibeiah ABBE^{6}, b. 11 June 1737
Rachel ABBE^{6}, b. 6 Feb. 1738/9
Mary ABBE^{6}, b. 21 Dec. 1740
Zeruiah ABBE^{6}, b. 7 Jan. 1743
Shubael ABBE^{6}, b. 9 Nov. 1744
Phineas ABBE^{6}, b. 22 Nov. 1746
Lucretia ABBE^{6}, b. 10 Mar. 1749
Joshua ABBE^{6}, b. 9 Jan. 1751
Elisha ABBE^{6}, b. 15 May 1753
Elizabeth ABBE^{6}, b. 6 Dec. 1758, d. 20 Jan. 1759
Ebenezer ABBE, d. 5 Dec. 1758 <Windham CT VR A:35>
CHILDREN OF Ebenezer ABBE & Mary ( ): (14) <Windham CT VR A:35>
Ebenezer ABBE, b. 27 July 1708
Elizabeth ABBE, b. 11 Sept. 1709
Joshua ABBE, b. 20 Jan. 1710/1 (see p.135)
Mary ABBE, b. 21 Sept. 1712
Nathan ABBE, b. 6 May 1714
Gideon ABBE, b. 13 Feb. 1715/6
Samuel ABBE, b. 30 Oct. 1717, d. beginning of Mar. 1718
Samuel ABBE, b. 24 Apr. 1719
Zeruiah ABBE, b. 17 Mar. 1720/1
Lilly ABBE, b. ( ) (not in rcds.)
Jerusha ABBE, b. 22 Oct. 1722 <VR A:64>
Abigail ABBE, b. 1 Aug. 1724
Miriam ABBE, b. 1 Aug. 1726
Solomon ABBE, b. 29 May 1730 <VR A:113>
Ann RIPLEY^{5} (David^{4}, Hannah Bradford^{3}), b. 27 Apr. 1726; d. 6 Sept. 1792* <Windham VR B:148>[<75>]
CHILDREN OF Nathaniel RIPLEY^{5} (Joshua^{4}) & Ann RIPLEY: (3) <Windham CT VR A:273>
Phineas RIPLEY^{6}, b. 20 Mar. 1746/7
Anne RIPLEY^{6}, b. 20 Aug. 1749
Ama RIPLEY^{6}, b. 20 Nov. 1751
Capt. Samuel BINGHAM, b. c1723, d. 25 July 1805, ae 82 <Windham CT VR B:148>
Samuel COOK, d. 27 Aug. 1745, Windham <Windham Dist.Prob. 3:368>
CHILDREN OF Samuel COOK & Leah RIPLEY^{4} (Hannah Bradford^{3}): (7) <Windham CT VR A:38>
Phineas COOK^{5}, b. 6 Dec. 1716; d. 22 Jan. 1729/9
Rebecca COOK^{5}, b. 26 Nov. 1718; d. 15 July 1764* (m. Caleb Jewett)
Jerusha COOK^{5}, b. 20 Feb. 1721/2
Welthean COOK^{5}, b. 20 Aug. 1724 (m. Thomas Pardee)
Mary COOK^{5}, b. 25 July 1729
Samuel COOK^{5}, b. 25 Aug. 1732; d. pre 18 May 1758 (inv.), Plainfield CT
Phineas COOK^{5}, b. 7 June 1736; d. 12 Jan. 1784, Newton

MICRO #6 of 15

Benjamin SEABURY, b. c1689, d. 9 Apr. 1787, Lebanon CT g.s.[<76>]
Old Cemetery, Lebanon CT: (8) <NEHGR 74:67>
Miss Abigail SEABURY, d. 12 June 1802, 88th yr
Mrs. Ann SEABURY, d. 13 Feb. 1692, 76th yr
Benjamin SEABURY, d. 9 Apr. 1787, 56th yr
Elisha SEABURY, d. 3 Nov. 1776, 56th yr
Elizabeth SEABURY, d. 5 May 1787, 68th yr, wf of Elisha

Margaret SEABURY, d. 3 May 1774, 84th yr, wf of Benjamin

Samuel SEABURY, d. 16 Mar. 1800, 83rd yr

Sudhai SEABURY, d. 10 Dec.1751, ae 3, dau of Elisha & Hephzibah

CHILDREN OF Winslow TRACY & Rachel RIPLEY^{4} (Hannah Bradford^{3}): (7) <Norwich CT VR 1:24>**<77>**

Joshua TRACY^{5}, b. 19 June 1715; d. 13 Dec. 1715

Perez TRACY^{5}, b. 13 Nov. 1716

Josiah TRACY^{5}, b. 10 May 1718

Eliphilate TRACY^{5}, b. 14 Nov. 1720

Nehemiah TRACY^{5}, b. 18 Mar. 1722/3

Samuel TRACY^{5}, b. 5 Dec. 1724

Solomon TRACY^{5}, b. 23 May 1728

Sarah BARTLETT^{5} (Ben.$^{4-3}$, Mary Warren^{2}), b. c1681, d. 3 Apr. 1761, 80th yr,Kingston g.s.<MD 7:23>

CHILDREN OF Israel BRADFORD^{3} & Sarah BARTLETT: (7) <Plymouth, MD 13:167>

Ruth BRADFORD^{4}, b. 11 Dec. 1702, d. beginning Feb. 1702/3

Bathsheba BRADFORD^{4}, b. 8 Nov. 1703

Benjamin BRADFORD^{4}, b. 17 Oct. 1705; d. 16 Nov. 1783, Kingston g.s. <MD 7:22>

Abner BRADFORD^{4}, b. 25 Dec. 1707; d. 18 June 1784, Kingston g.s. <MD 7:22>

Joshua BRADFORD^{4}, b. 23 June 1710; d. 22 May 1758, Maduncook ME

Ichabod BRADFORD^{4}, b. 22 Sept. 1713; d. 6 Apr. 1791*, Kingston g.s.

Elisha BRADFORD^{4}, b. 26 Mar. 1718

CHILDREN OF Abner BRADFORD^{4} & Susanna ( ): (12) <Kingston VR>**<78>**

Elijah BRADFORD^{5}, b. 11 Apr. 1735

Levi BRADFORD^{5}, b. 1 Oct. 1737, d. June 1758

Zenas BRADFORD^{5}, b. 6 July 1739, d. July 1749

Mary BRADFORD^{5}, b. 13 June 1742

Abigail BRADFORD^{5}, b. 21 Aug. 1744

Israel BRADFORD^{5}, b. 17 July 1748, d. July 1749

Lydia BRADFORD^{5}, b. 20 Dec. 1749

Hannah BRADFORD^{5}, b. 28 Feb.1751

Elisha BRADFORD^{5}, b. 10 May 1753; d. 31 May 1809, Cheshire MA g.s.

Lucy BRADFORD^{5}, b. 10 May 1755

Peggy BRADFORD^{5}, b. 8 May 1757

Levi BRADFORD^{5}, b. 1 July 1759; d. 21 Sept. 1820, Kingstown RI <VR 13:201>

Eunice BENNETT, b. c1764, d. 17 Dec. 1822, 58th yr, Cheshire MA g.s.

CHILDREN OF Elisha BRADFORD^{5} & Eunice BENNETT: (11) <Family Rcds.>

Susanna BRADFORD^{6}, b. 15 Feb. 1782, Chesire; d. 22 Jan. 1876*, Adams <Mass.VR 283:28>

Lucy BRADFORD^{6}, b. 18 Mar. 1784

William BRADFORD^{6}, b. 3 Mar. 1786

Joseph BRADFORD^{6}, b. 30 Mar. 1788

Hopestill BRADFORD^{6}, b. 1 Mar. 1790

Levi BRADFORD^{6}, b. 25 Dec. 1791; d. 3 July 1856*, Lanesboro MA g.s.

Simeon BRADFORD^{6}, b. 9 Mar. 1794

Sarah BRADFORD^{6}, b. 18 Mar. 1796

George BRADFORD^{6}, b. 9 Mar. 1798

Twins, b. 23 Feb. 1800, d.y.

Amanda ( ) BRADFORD, d. 11 Aug. 1842*, ae 43, Lanesboro MA g.s. (wf of Levi Bradford^{6})

Isaac BROWNE, (son of Eleaser & Sarah), b.c Aug. 1776, Adams, d. 31 Aug. 1865, ae 89y7d, S. Adams <Mass.VR 183:25>

CHILDREN OF Isaac BROWNE & Susanna BRADFORD^{6}: (8) <Adams MA, Family Rcds.>

Lucy BROWNE^{7}, b. 11 Dec. 1800

Maria BROWNE^{7}, b. 25 July 1802; d. 23 Jan. 1890, Adams, cerebral hemorrhage <Mass.VR 409:27>

Daniel BROWNE^{7}, b. 13 Apr. 1804

Daniel BROWNE^{7}, b. 13 Apr. 1804

Eunice BROWNE^{7}, b. 28 Feb. 1806

Sarah BROWNE^{7}, b. 10 Mar. 1808

Albert Gallatin BROWNE^{7}, b. 3 Oct. 1810

Jerome BROWNE^{7}, b. 25 Apr. 1813

Eliza BROWNE^{7}, b. 8 Aug. 1823

CHILDREN OF Albert Gallatin BROWNE^{7} & Adaline Lavinia BABBITT: (5) <Family Rcds.>

Francis BROWNE^{8}, b. 7 Mar. 1838

Ann Eliza BROWNE^{8}, b. 30 Mar. 1840

Charles BROWNE^{8}, b. 17 July 1842

Isaac BROWNE^{8}, b. 23 Sept. 1850

William BROWNE^{8}, b. 9 Jan. 1854

CHILDREN OF Charles BROWNE^{8} & Susan McCALLUM: (5) <Family Rcds.>

Charles BROWNE^{9}, b. 12 Aug. 1870

Frances BROWNE^{9}, b. 31 Aug. 1872

William Bradford BROWNE^{9}, b. 7 May 1875

Sarah BROWNE^{9}, b. 2 May 1879

Agnes BROWNE^{9}, b. 13 Nov. 1881

George A. LAPHAM, (son of George & Darcus), b. c1798, S.Adams, d. 19 Oct. 1865, ae67y6m, S.Adams, typhus fever <Mass.VR 183:25>

CHILD OF George A. LAPHAM & Maria BROWNE^{7} (Susanna Bradford^{6}):

Susan M. LAPHAM, b. c1825, d. 1 July 1901, ae76y2m24d, Adams <Mass.VR 517:124> (wf of Lawrence D. Smith)

Sylvanus BRADFORD, d. 21 Feb. 1823, Glocester RI, ae 30, formerly of Kingston MA, masonic honours <VR RI 18:287>**<79>**

Calvin RIPLEY, b. 18 Mar. 1748*, Pembroke; d. aft 27 May 1810 <Bristol Co.Deeds 91:268>**<80>**

CHILDREN OF Calvin RIPLEY & Peggy BRADFORD^{5} (Abner^{4}): (13) <Kingston VR>

Charles RIPLEY^{6}, b. 14 May 1775 <VR:122>

Levi RIPLEY^{6}, b. 16 May 1777 <VR:123>

Lucy RIPLEY^{6}, b. 16 July 1779 <VR:123>

Luther RIPLEY^{6}, b. 16 June 1781 <VR:123>

Bradford RIPLEY^{6}, b. 1 Oct. 1785 <VR:122>

Nancy RIPLEY^{6}, b. 16 Nov. 1787 <VR:123>

Betsey RIPLEY^{6}, b. 23 Jan. 1790 <VR:122>

Sally RIPLEY^{6}, b. 15 May 1792 <VR:124>

Polly RIPLEY^{6}, b. 27 Apr. 1794 <VR:124>

Sophia RIPLEY^{6}, b. 12 Feb. 1797 <VR:124>

Calvin RIPLEY^{6}, b. 23 Nov. 1800, d. 25 Feb. 1802 <VR:122>

Peggy RIPLEY^{6}, b. 23 Nov. 1800 (twins) <VR:124>

Thomas ADAMS, (son of Francis), b. 5 May 1709, Plymouth <MD 2:227>**<81>**

Zerash STETSON^{5} (Abigail Brewster^{4}, Wrestling^{3}, Love^{2}), b. 29 Nov. 1712, Plymouth <MD 7:178>; d. 6 Apr. 1765, Kingston g.s. <MD 7:23>

CHILDREN OF Benjamin BRADFORD^{4} (Israel^{3}) & Zerash STETSON: (8) <Kingston VR>

Thomas BRADFORD^{5}, b. 9 Feb. 1732/3, d. 7 July 1748

Mikell BRADFORD^{5}, b. 16 May 1735, d. 2 Oct. 1735

Peres BRADFORD^{5}, b. 3 Sept. 1736, d. 12 July 1748

Lydia BRADFORD^{5}, b. 22 June 1739, d. 16 July 1748

Benjamin BRADFORD^{5}, b. 8 Feb. 1742, d. 19 July 1748

Marcy BRADFORD^{5}, b. 13 Mar. 1745, d. 9 Aug. 1745

Lemuel BRADFORD^{5}, b. 16 June 1747, d. 12 July 1748

Lydia BRADFORD^{5}, b. 7 June 1749

Esaias PETERSON, (son of Nehemiah & Prince (Dillingham)), d. 5 Jan. 1865, ae 81y24d, Duxbury, farmer <Mass.VR 175:306>

John CUSHING, (son of John & Lydia (Holmes)), d. 30 Mar. 1882, ae 81y1m27d, Duxbury, heart disease, widower <Mass.VR 338:303>

Betsey D. CUSHING, (dau of Asa & Betsey Krug), d. 6 Nov. 1872, ae 71y4m19d, Duxbury <Mass. VR 248:383>

Lydia PETERSON, (dau of Levi & Lydia Holmes), b. c1779, Duxbury, d. 9 Aug. 1856, ae 77y3m14d, Duxbury, dropsy, married <Mass.VR 103:197>

Benjamin B. CUSHING, (son of John & Betsey (Darling)), b. c1822, Duxbury, d. 22 Mar. 1893, ae 71y5m6d, Duxbury, typhoid fever, farmer, married <Mass.VR 437:613>

Mary JOHNSON, d. 13 July 1761, Kingston g.s.

CHILDREN OF Ichabod BRADFORD^{4} (Israel^{3}) & 1st Mary JOHNSON: (5) <Kingston VR>

Ichabod BRADFORD^{5}, b. 28 Aug. 1744

Elizabeth BRADFORD^{5}, b. 10 July 1747

Rhoda BRADFORD^{5}, b. 20 July 1751

Lemuel BRADFORD^{5}, b. 22 Aug. 1755

Anne BRADFORD^{5}, b. 15 Apr. 1758

CHILD OF Ichabod BRADFORD^{4} & 2nd Mary COOK:**<82>**

Israel BRADFORD^{5}, b. c1765**<83>**

CHILDREN OF Lemuel BRADFORD^{6} (Israel^{5}) & Bathsheba NELSON: (6) <Plymouth, MD 19:149>**<84>**

Lemuel BRADFORD^{7}, b. 22 May 1813

Charles BRADFORD^{7}, b. 28 Jan. 1821**<85>**

Winslow BRADFORD^{7}, b. 4 Nov. 1826

Lydia Nelson BRADFORD^{7}, b. 29 Mar. 1830

Hannah Everson BRADFORD^{7}, b. 26 Mar. 1833**<86>**

Ebenezer Nelson BRADFORD^{7}, b. 31 Oct. 1836

Hannah BRADFORD^{4} (Elisha^{3}, Jos.^{2}), b. 10 Apr. 1720, Plymouth <MD 13:112>; d. 22 May 1758, Maduncook ME**<87>**

CHILDREN OF Joshua BRADFORD^{4} (Israel^{3}) & Hannah BRADFORD: (9) <Kingston VR>**<87>**

Cornelius BRADFORD^{5}, b. 10 Dec. 1737; d. pre 15 Sept. 1790 (adm.)

Sarah BRADFORD^{5}, b. 16 Oct. 1739

Rachel BRADFORD^{5}, b. 28 Jan. 1741

Mary BRADFORD^{5}, b. 16 Mar. 1744

Melatiah BRADFORD^{5}, b. 16 Mar. 1744 (twins)

Joshua BRADFORD^{5}, b. 2 Apr. 1746

Hannah BRADFORD^{5}, b. 9 Mar. 1748

Joseph BRADFORD^{5}, b. 19 Mar. 1751; d. Nov. 1811* <Sterling Gen.2:1037>

Benjamin BRADFORD^{5}, b. 28 May 1753

Abigail STERLING, b. 13 Nov. 1752*, New Marblehead ME, d. 16 Jan. 1832 <Sterling Gen.2:1037>**<88>**

MICRO #7 of 15

Mercy WARREN^{3} (Jos.^{2}), b. 23 Sept. 1653, Plymouth<MD 18:69>; d. Mar. 1747, Kingston g.s.<MD 7:23>

CHILDREN OF John BRADFORD^{3} & Mercy WARREN: (7) <Plymouth, MD 1:47>

John BRADFORD^{4}, b. 29 Dec. 1675; d. 27 Mar. 1724, Kingston g.s. <MD 7:23>

Alice BRADFORD^{4}, b. 28 Jan. 1677; d. 14 July 1746 <Hist.Hingham 2:300>

Abigail BRADFORD^{4}, b. 10 Dec. 1679; d. 4 May 1697, unm., Plymouth <MD 16:63>

Mercy BRADFORD^{4}, b. 20 Dec. 1681; d. 27 June 1738, Plympton g.s.<MD 10:112>

Samuel BRADFORD^{4}, b. 23 Dec. 1683; d. 26 Mar. 1740, Plympton g.s. <MD 8:154,23:20>

Priscilla BRADFORD^{4}, b. 10 Mar. 1686; d. aft 2 Oct. 1732 (father's will)

William BRADFORD^{4}, b. 15 Apr. 1688; d. 7 or 8 May 1728, Kingston g.s. <MD 7:23; VR>

Edward MITCHELL, (son of Experience), d. 15 Mar. 1716/7 <MD 20:141>

CHILDREN OF Edward MITCHELL & Alice BRADFORD^{4}: (3) <Bridgewater, MD 14:184>

Mary MITCHELL^{5}, b. 19 July 1709

Alice MITCHELL^{5}, b. 23 Dec. 1714

Edward MITCHELL^{5}, b. 7 Feb. 1715/6

CHILD OF Joshua HERSEY & Alice (Bradford^{4}) Mitchell:**<89>**

Sarah HERSEY^{5}, bpt. 27 Dec. 1719, Hingham

Rebecca BARTLETT^{5} (Ben.$^{4-3}$, Mary Warren^{2}), d. aft. 20 June 1724 <MD 16:120>

CHILDREN OF John BRADFORD^{4} (John^{3}) & Rebecca BARTLETT: (2) <Plymouth, MD 12:13>

Robert BRADFORD^{5}, b. 18 Oct. 1706; d. 12 Aug. 1782, Kingston g.s. <MD 7:23>

Rebecca BRADFORD^{5}, b. 14 Dec. 1710 (m. John Brewster^{4}, Wrestling, Love^{2})

Sarah STETSON^{5} (Abigail Brewster^{4}, Wrestling^{3}, Love^{2}), b. 26 Aug. 1708, Plymouth <MD 7:178>; d. 23 Feb. 1792* <Kingston ChR:322>

CHILDREN OF Robert BRADFORD^{5} & Sarah STETSON: (12) <Kingston VR>

Peleg BRADFORD^{6}, b. 9 Mar. 1727* <VR:29>; d. 13 May 1804* <Kingston VR:321>

Zilpha BRADFORD^{6}, b. 6 Apr. 1728*

Rebecca BRADFORD^{6}, b. 31 Dec. 1730*; d. 25 ( ) 1778*

John BRADFORD^{6}, b. 18 Oct. 1732*; d. 15 Jan. 1811*, dropsy & asthma <Kingston ChR>

Alethea BRADFORD^{6}, b. 13 Dec. 1734*; d. 11 June 1737*

Orpha BRADFORD^{6}, b. 28 Dec. 1736*; d. 3 May 1830*

Stetson BRADFORD^{6}, b. 17 Feb. 1738/9* <VR:30>; d. 5 Oct. 1826, Kingston g.s. <MD 7:23>

Robert BRADFORD^{6}, b. 1(4) Jan. 1740/1*; d. Sept. 1747*

Sarah BRADFORD^{6}, b. 1 Jan. 1741/2*; d. Sept. 1747*

Consider BRADFORD^{6}, b. 13 Feb. 1744/5*; d. Sept. 1747*

Sarah BRADFORD^{6}, b. 4 Feb. 1747/8*

Robert BRADFORD^{6}, b. 11 July 1750*

CHILDREN OF James BRADFORD & Sarah ( ): (8) <Kingston VR> (see p.142 <112>)

CHILDREN OF Spencer BRADFORD & Lydia ( ): (4) <Kingston VR>

Alden Spencer BRADFORD, b. 4 Aug. 1815

Lydia Smith BRADFORD, b. 8 Oct. 1817

Lucy Holmes BRADFORD, b. 3 Sept. 1820

Frances Adelia BRADFORD, b. 1 Sept. 1824 (m. Simeon W. McLaughlin)

Sally JOHNSON, (dau of John & Deborah), b. c1790, d. 4 July 1847, ae 57y8m19d <Kingston VR>**<90>**

CHILD OF Peleg BRADFORD & Sally JOHNSON:

William Stetson BRADFORD, b. 31 Jan. 1825, d. 3 Apr. 1842, scarlet fever <Kingston VR>**<90>**

CHILD OF Robert BRADFORD:

Sophy BRADFORD, bpt. 24 May 1789 <Kingston VR>

CHILDREN OF Nathaniel BRADFORD & Sarah COOK: (8) <Kingston VR>**<91>**

Deborah A. BRADFORD, b. 27 Dec. 1800

Levi BRADFORD, b. 11 Sept. 1802

Charles BRADFORD, b. 10 Dec. 1804**<92>**

Nathaniel BRADFORD, b. 11 Mar. 1807

Bartlett BRADFORD, b. 21 June 1809

Caleb C. BRADFORD, b. 15 Aug. 1811

Julia BRADFORD, b. 17 Jan. 1816

George Anson BRADFORD, b. 6 Mar. 1818

CHILDREN OF Ellis BRADFORD & Dorothy ( ): (8) <Kingston VR>**<93>**

Rufus Bartlett BRADFORD, b. 9 Aug. 1797**<94>**

Ellis BRADFORD, b. 2 Sept. 1799**<95>**

Dorothy Bartlett BRADFORD, b. 19 Aug. 1802 (m. Peleg Bryant)

George BRADFORD, b. 24 Aug. 1805
Rufus BRADFORD, b. 5 Oct 1807
William BRADFORD, b. 21 Aug. 1810
Sarah Ellis BRADFORD, b. 10 Oct. 1813
Ann Gurley BRADFORD, b. 14 Aug. 1815
CHILDREN OF Rufus B. BRADFORD & Elizabeth Ann ( ): (2) <Kingston VR>**<96>**
Henry Jackson BRADFORD, b. 13 Apr. 1832
Ellis BRADFORD, b. 31 May 1833**<97>**
CHILDREN OF Consider BRADFORD & Betsey WILDER: (3) <Kingston VR>
Alexander BRADFORD, b. 16 Oct. 1808
Elizabeth Wilder BRADFORD, b. 12 Sept. 1812
Louisa BRADFORD, b. 17 Apr. 1815
Martha Drew PERLEY, (dau of Amos & Joanna), b. c1811, d. 13 Nov. 1845, ae 34y11m4d, child bed <Kingston VR>
CHILDREN OF George BRADFORD & Martha Drew PERLEY: (2) <Kingston VR>
Amos Perley BRADFORD, b. 20 Feb. 1832, d. 2 Nov. 1840, dysentery **<98>**
Amos Perley BRADFORD, b. 6 Nov. 1845
CHILDREN OF Thomas BRADFORD & Lydia ( ): (8) <Kingston VR>
Maria BRADFORD, b. 2 Oct. 1817
Mary BRADFORD, b. 11 Jan. 1819
Lydia Thomas BRADFORD, b. 25 Mar. 1821
Thomas Bartlett BRADFORD, b. 12 Sept. 1823
William Harrison BRADFORD, b. 4 Mar. 1827
Horace Smith BRADFORD, b. 2 Jan. 1828
Priscilla Cooke BRADFORD, b. 13 Apr. 1829
George Lewis BRADFORD, b. 25 Jan. 1832
CHILDREN OF John BRADFORD[6] (Robert[5]) & 1st Ruth COBB: (4) <Kingston>**<99>**
Silvanus BRADFORD[7], b. 10 June 1755; d. 7 Dec. 1810, "bleeding" <Kingston ChR>
Exzuma BRADFORD[7], b. 30 Mar. 1757; d. 26 June 1844, Kingston g.s.(wf of Ben.Waterman)<MD 7:223>
Priscilla BRADFORD[7], b. 12 May 1760; d. 29 May 1760
Noah BRADFORD[7], b. 29 May 1761; d. 20 or 21 Dec. 1841
Hannah EDDY, b. 25 Oct. 1737, d. Mar. 1820 <Kingston ChR>
CHILDREN OF John BRADFORD[6] & 2nd Hannah EDDY*: (4) <Kingston VR>**<99>**
Stephen BRADFORD[7], b. 23 Dec. 1771; d. 22 Apr. 1837
Hannah BRADFORD[7], b. 12 Jan. 1775
Pelham BRADFORD[7], b. 12 Jan. 1778; d. 23 Nov. 1829* <Kingston ChR>
Daniel BRADFORD[7], b. 29 Oct. 1780
Sarah BRADFORD, d. 23 Feb. 1792, ae 84, widow, apoplexy <Kingston VR:322>
CHILDREN OF Benjamin WATERMAN & Lucy BRADFORD[7] (John[6]): (2)**<100>**
Otis WATERMAN[8], b. 20 Aug. 1792
Sally WATERMAN[8], b. 10 Aug. 1794, d. 24 Dec. 1824, unm.**<101>**
Polly TUPPER, d. 19 Dec. 1807**<102>**
CHILDREN OF Stephen BRADFORD[7] (John[6]) & 1st Polly TUPPER: (2)
Mary Ann BRADFORD[8], b. 14 June 1805, d. 2 Sept. 1807**<103>**
Stephen BRADFORD[8], b. 4 June 1807
Ruth CUSHING, d. 19 May 1820, ae 43**<104>**
CHILD OF Stephen BRADFORD[7] & 2nd Ruth CUSHING:
Mary BRADFORD[8], b. 23 Feb. 1810; d. 30 Apr. 1833, childbed (wf of Charles Bradford)**<105>**
Lucy BROOKS, b. 1769, d. 1818
CHILDREN OF John BRADFORD[7] (John[6]) & Lucy BROOKS: (6)**<106>**

Austin BRADFORD^{8}, b. 1799, d. 1856<107>

Lucy BRADFORD^{8}, b. 1800, d. 1818, unm.

Sophronia BRADFORD^{8}, b. 5 Apr. 1803, Randolph VT; d. 8 Sept. 1878

Elmira BRADFORD^{8}, b. 6 Apr. 1806, East Bethel VT

Paschal BRADFORD^{8}, b. 1808; d. 1860

Hon. Philander D. BRADFORD^{8}, b. 1811

Hon. Jonah BROOKS, b. 15 Sept. 1801, Alstead NH; d. 2 Oct. 1882 (m. Sophronia Bradford^{8})<108>

Ehud DARLING, b. 16 Mar. 1804, Hancock VT (m. Elmira Bradford^{8})<109>

CHILDREN OF Pelham BRADFORD & Selah ( ): (2) <Kingston VR>

Selah BRADFORD, b. 12 May 1799

John BRADFORD, b. 20 Aug. 1803

Jane BRIGGS, b. c1751, d. 24 Feb. 1813*, ae 62, consumption <Kingston ChR><110>

CHILDREN OF Silvanus BRADFORD^{7} (John^{6}) & Jane BRIGGS: (7) <Kingston VR>

Ruth BRADFORD^{8}, b. 5 Mar. 1781

Remember BRADFORD^{8}, b. 15 Feb. 1784

Deborah BRADFORD^{8}, b. 12 Apr. 1786; d. 1809*

Jane BRADFORD^{8}, b. 29 Sept. 1789; d. 1816*

Silvanus BRADFORD^{8}, b. 1 Aug. 1792

Robert BRADFORD^{8}, b. 9 July 1795; d. 1818*

Noah BRADFORD^{8}, b. 27 Oct. 1798

CHILDREN OF Robert BRADFORD^{6} (Robert^{5}) & Keziah LITTLE*: (2)

Polly Otis BRADFORD^{7}, b. 1782, d. 5 Oct. 1783, ae 11m4d, Kingston g.s. <MD 7:23>

Sophy BRADFORD^{7}*, bpt. 24 May 1789*

Lydia STURTEVANT, b. 1724, d. 26 Mar. 1812 <Kingston VR:320>

CHILDREN OF Peleg BRADFORD^{6} (Robert^{5}) & Lydia STURTEVANT: (7) <Kingston VR>

Elizabeth BRADFORD^{7}, b. 23 Sept. 1747 <VR:26>

James BRADFORD^{7}, b. 2 May 1749 <VR:27>; d. Feb. 1836 <Kingston VR:320><111>

Bartlett BRADFORD^{7}, bpt. 14 Apr. 1751 <VR:25>

Consider BRADFORD^{7}, bpt. 31 Mar. 1755 <VR:26>

Rebecca BRADFORD^{7}, bpt. 8 May 1757 <VR:29>

Lydia BRADFORD^{7}, bpt. 8 Aug. 1762 <VR:28>

Sarah BRADFORD^{7}, bpt. 5 May 1765 <VR:30>

Sarah ELLIS, b. 10 Mar. 1755, Plymouth <MD 18:212>; d. 25 Nov. 1834, Plymouth <Kingston VR:322>

CHILDREN OF James BRADFORD^{7} & Sarah ELLIS: (7) <Kingston VR><112>

Ellis BRADFORD^{8}, b. 7 Sept. 1773<113>

Nathaniel BRADFORD^{8}, b. 10 Apr. 1776 <VR:29><114>

Lydia BRADFORD^{8}, b. 20 July 1778 <VR:28>

Consider BRADFORD^{8}, b. 9 May 1781 <VR:26>

Bartlett BRADFORD^{8}, b. 7 May 1784 <VR:25>

James BRADFORD^{8}, b. 25 Sept. 1786 <VR:27>

Thomas BRADFORD^{8}, b. 12 Oct. 1790 <VR:30>

Lurana HOLMES^{6}, (Jos.^{5}--), b. 18 Apr. (1750)* <Kingston VR:23>; d. 13 Mar. 1825, ae <u>84y1m6d</u>, influenza, Kingston g.s. <ChR; MD 7:23>

CHILDREN OF Stetson BRADFORD^{6} (Robert^{5}) & Lurana HOLMES: (6) <Kingston VR>

Elisabeth BRADFORD^{7}, b. 29 Aug. 1772; d. 24 May 1831*, unm.

Zilpha BRADFORD^{7}, b. 30 Dec. 1773; d. 31 Oct. 1849*, unm.

William BRADFORD^{7}, b. 4 Apr. 1776

Charles BRADFORD^{7}, b. 14 Sept. 1777 <VR:25>

Peleg BRADFORD^{7}, b. 16 May 1787

Spencer BRADFORD^{7}, b. 1 June 1781

Elizabeth P. (BROWN) Clark, b. 3 Apr. 1776; d. 6 Jan. 1835

CHILDREN OF Charles BRADFORD^{7} & Elizabeth P. (BROWN) Clark: (7)

Charles Otis BRADFORD^{8}, b. 16 June 1804

Lucy Holmes BRADFORD^{8}, b. 23 June 1806

Harvey Stetson BRADFORD^{8}, b. 27 Sept. 1809

Nancy Lutia BRADFORD^{8}, b. 3 July 1811; d. 2 July 1825

Sophia Maria BRADFORD^{8}, b. 17 Mar. 1813

William Spencer BRADFORD^{8}, b. 5 July 1816

Sally Jane BRADFORD^{8}, b. 2 June 1818

Jonathan FREEMAN^{5} (Tho.^{4}, Mercy Prence^{3}, Patience Brewster^{2}), b. 11 Nov. 1678, Eastham <MD 8:93>; d. 27 Apr. 1714, Harwich <MD 6:55>

CHILDREN OF Jonathan FREEMAN & Mercy BRADFORD^{4} (John^{3}): (4) <Harwich, MD 5:86>

Jonathan FREEMAN^{5}, b. 26 Mar. 1709/10

Mercy FREEMAN^{5}, b. 24 Apr. 1711

Bradford FREEMAN^{5}, b. 15 Aug. 1713

Ichabod FREEMAN^{5}, b. 2 Aug. 1714

Isaac CUSHMAN^{4} (Isaac^{3}, Mary Allerton^{2}), b. 15 Nov. 1676, Plymouth <MD 1:210>; d. 18 Sept. 1727, Plympton g.s. <MD 10:111> (4 Sept. in Plympton VR)

CHILDREN OF Isaac CUSHMAN & Mercy (BRADFORD^{4}) Freeman: (4) <Plympton>

Fear CUSHMAN^{5}, b. 10 July 1718

Priscilla CUSHMAN^{5}, b. 12 Dec. 1719

Isaac CUSHMAN^{5}, b. 29 Sept. 1721; d. 18 Oct. 1721 <MD 10:111>

Abigail CUSHMAN^{5}, b. 31 Dec. 1722

Sarah GRAY^{3} (Edw.$^{2-1}$), b. 8 Apr. 1697, Tiverton, d. 16 Oct. 1770, Chilmark g.s. <MD 28:105,106>

CHILDREN OF Samuel BRADFORD^{4} (John^{3}) & Sarah GRAY: (10)<1-6, Plympton, MD 3:94; 7-10, PN&Q 3:106>

John BRADFORD^{5}, b. 8 Apr. 1717; d. 28 Sept. 1770, Plympton g.s. <MD 8:153>

Gideon BRADFORD^{5}, b. 27 Oct. 1718; d. 18 Oct. 1793, Plympton g.s. <MD 8:153>

Dr. William BRADFORD^{5}, b. 16 Dec. 1720; d. 15 Feb. 1724/5 <MD 8:154>

Mary BRADFORD^{5}, b. 16 Oct. 1722

Sarah BRADFORD^{5}, b. 4 Apr. 1725

William BRADFORD^{5}, b. 4 Nov. 1728; d. 6 July 1808, Bristol RI <PN&Q 3:106>

Mercy BRADFORD^{5}, b. 12 Apr. 1731; d. 1 June 1731 <PN&Q 3:106>

Abigail BRADFORD^{5}, b. 12 June 173( ); d. 31 Jan. 1776, 44th yr, Plympton g.s. <MD 11:163>

Phebe BRADFORD^{5}, b. 30 Mar. 1735

Samuel BRADFORD^{5}, b. 13 Apr. 174(0)

William HUNT, d. betw 19 Mar. 1760 (will) - 19 July 1769 (prob.) <MD 28:107>(2nd hus./Sarah Gray)

CHILDREN OF Abial COOK & Mary BRADFORD^{5}: (7) <VR RI, Little Compton>

Mary COOK^{6}, b. 8 Aug. 1744

Joseph COOK^{6}, b. 21 Aug. 1746

Alice COOK^{6}, b. 6 June 1752

Samuel COOK^{6}, b. 4 Oct. 1754

Nathaniel COOK^{6}, b. 28 Dec. 1756

Sarah COOK^{6}, b. 2 July 1759

Priscilla COOK^{6}, b. 10 Dec. 1761

CHILDREN OF Caleb STETSON & Abigail BRADFORD^{5} (Sam.^{4}): (2) <Plymouth, MD 18:216>

Caleb STETSON^{6}, b. 12 Aug. 1755

Bradford STETSON^{6}, b. 20 May 1757

Jane PADDOCK, (dau of Ichabod), b. 30 Aug. 1717, Yarmouth <MD 23:108>; d. 18 Apr. 1795, Plympton g.s. <MD 8:153>

CHILD OF Gideon BRADFORD^{5} (Sam.^{4}) & Jane PADDOCK: (2 of 7)[<115>]

Calvin BRADFORD^6, b. ( )

Gideon BRADFORD^6, b. c1753, d. 5 Apr. 1805, ae 52, Plympton g.s. <MD 8:153>

CHILDREN OF Calvin BRADFORD^6 & Lucy PRATT*: (4 of 9)**<116>**

Mary BRADFORD^7, b. c1781, d. 29 Nov. 1863, ae 82y5m21d, unm., Plympton <Mass.VR 166:314>

Luther BRADFORD^7, b. c1787*, d. 26 June 1861, ae 74y29d, Plympton, surgeon <Mass.VR 148:345>

Phebe BRADFORD^7, b. c1792, d. 6 Dec. 1795, ae 3y10m17d, Plympton g.s. <MD 8:154>

Joseph Warren BRADFORD^7, b. c1795, d. 9 Apr. 1796, ae 13m2d, Plympton g.s. <MD 8:153>

Ruth HOLMES, b. c1792, d. 6 Mar. 1815, 23rd yr, Plympton g.s. <MD 8:154>

CHILD OF Luther BRADFORD^7 & Ruth HOLMES:**<117>**

Lydia H. BRADFORD^8, d. 9 June 1891, ae 78y3m21d, Whitman, bur. Middleboro, shock following fractured hip <Mass.VR 419:568> (wf of George H.Barrows)**<118>**

Elizabeth HOLMES^6 (Hannah Sylvester^5, Hannah Bartlett^4, Jos.^{3}, Mary Warren^2), b. 13 Oct. 1723, Plymouth <MD 12:12>; d. 30 Dec. 1806, Plympton g.s. <MD 8:153>

CHILDREN OF John BRADFORD^5 (Sam.^{4}) & Elizabeth HOLMES: (11)

Elizabeth BRADFORD^6, b. 9 Aug. 1744*

Mary BRADFORD^6, b. 15 May 1746*; d. 13 Nov. 1814, Pittsfield MA g.s.

John BRADFORD^6, b. 18 July 1748*; d. 11 June 1807, ae 58y24d, Plympton g.s. <MD 8:153>

Priscilla BRADFORD^6, b. 4 Sept. 1750*

Perez BRADFORD^6, b. 10 Nov. 1752*

Hannah BRADFORD^6, b. 16 Jan. 1755*

Lydia BRADFORD^6, b. 16 Feb. 1757* (m. Levi Bryant)

Oliver BRADFORD^6, b. 10 Jan. 1759*; d. 14 Nov. 1835*, Fairhaven MA

Mercy BRADFORD^6, b. 20 Dec. 1761*

William BRADFORD^6, b. 8 June 1766*

Sarah BRADFORD^6, b. 8 Oct. 1769*

Eunice ( ) BRADFORD, b. c1751, d. 15 Nov. 1813, 62nd yr, Plympton g.s. <MD 8:153>

CHILDREN OF John BRADFORD^6 & Eunice ( ): (7)**<118a>**

John CHURCHILL, (son of Barnabas), b. 9 May 1739, Plymouth <MD 12:86>; d. 19 Mar. 1819, Pittsfield MA

CHILD OF John CHURCHILL & Mary BRADFORD^6 (John^5):

Sarah CHURCHILL^7*, b. 19 Oct. 1771* <Churchill Gen.>

Sarah CHIPMAN^6 (Seth$^{5-4}$, Sam.^{3}, Hope Howland^2), b. 5 May 1764* <Kingston VR>; d. 1 June 1839, Fairhaven MA

CHILDREN OF Oliver BRADFORD^6 (John^5) & Sarah CHIPMAN: (10)*

Julah/Abigail BRADFORD^7, b. 31 Aug. 1782 (named was changed to Abigail)

Seth Chipman BRADFORD^7, b. 22 Dec. 1783

Vollentine BRADFORD^7, b. 4 Sept. 1785

Matilda BRADFORD^7, b. 11 Oct. 1787

Molborough BRADFORD^7, b. 10 Sept. 1789

Melvin BRADFORD^7, b. 30 Nov. 1791

George BRADFORD^7, b. 30 Sept. 1793

Priscilla BRADFORD^7, b. aft 30 Sept. 1793

Aaron Wing BRADFORD^7, b. ( )

Sophia BRADFORD^7, b. ( )

Mary LeBARON^6 (Lydia Bartlett^5), Jos.$^{4-3}$, Mary Warren^2), b. 20 Mar. 1731/2, Plymouth <MD 13:112>; d. 2 Oct. 1775, Bristol RI <PN&Q 3:105>

CHILDREN OF Dr. William BRADFORD^5 (Sam.^{4}) & Mary LeBARON: (11) <Bristol RI 2:19; PN&Q 3:105>

William BRADFORD^6, b. 14 Sept. 1752, Warren; d. 29 Oct. 1810*

LeBaron BRADFORD^6, b. 31 May 1754, d. 25 Sept. 1793

John BRADFORD^6, b. 9 Oct. 1758, d. 31 Oct. 1765

Mary BRADFORD^{6}, b. 2 Sept. 1760 <Bristol RI 2:19>; d. 14 Jan. 1834, Newport RI <VR RI 6:136>
Hannah BRADFORD^{6}, b. 22 Nov. 1762, d. 5 Sept. 1763
Son, b. 15 July 1764, d. 5 Aug. 1764
Hannah BRADFORD^{6}, b. 14 June 1767 <Bristol RI 2:19>
John BRADFORD^{6}, b. 14 July 1768 <Bristol RI 2:19>
Nancy BRADFORD^{6}, b. 1770
Ezekiel Hersey BRADFORD^{6}, b. c1770, d. 1 Sept. 1849, ae 79
Lydia BRADFORD^{6}, b. Apr. 1773

MICRO #8 of 15

CHILDREN OF William BRADFORD 3rd & Mary ( ): (4) <Bristol RI 2:96>
William Parnell BRADFORD, b. 29 May 1805
Edward James BRADFORD, b. 29 Sept. 1806
Allen Taylor Smith BRADFORD, b. 2 Sept. 1808
Nancy Smith BRADFORD, b. 7 Apr. 1811

CHILDREN OF John BRADFORD^{6} (Wm.^{5}) & Jemima WARDWELL: (8) <Bristol RI VR>
Nancy BRADFORD^{7}, b. 16 Aug. 1795 <VR 2:86>
Benjamin Wardwell BRADFORD^{7}, b. 24 June 1797 <VR 2:86>
LeBaron BRADFORD^{7}, b. 18 Apr. 1799 <VR 2:86>; d. May 1821*
Mary LeBaron BRADFORD^{7}, b. 18 June 1801 <VR 2:74>
Ellinor BRADFORD^{7}, b. 18 Dec. 1804 <VR 2:74>
Lydia BRADFORD^{7}, b. 9 Feb. 1806 <VR 2:74>
Jemima BRADFORD^{7}*, b. 1808, d. 14 Sept. 1808*, ae 5m
Walter BRADFORD^{7}, b. 13 Aug. 1809 <VR 2:86>

Henry GOODWIN, b. c1761, d. 31 May 1789, Bristol RI <VR RI 6:136> (hus of Mary Bradford^{6}, Wm.^{5})

CHILDREN OF William BRADFORD^{6} (Wm.^{5}) & Elizabeth Bloom JAMES, (dau of Peter): (7) <Bristol RI 2: 74; 2-6, Rehoboth>
Mary BRADFORD^{7}, b. 30 Dec. 1778, Taunton
William BRADFORD^{7}, b. 2 Feb. 1781
Elizabeth Bloom BRADFORD^{7}, b. 15 Feb. 1785
Henry BRADFORD^{7}, b. 18 Feb. 1787
Peter James BRADFORD^{7}, b. 6 Feb. 1790
John Willys BRADFORD^{7}, b. 26 Dec. 1793
Sarah BRADFORD^{7}, b. 29 Jan. 1799, Bristol RI

Hannah FOSTER, (dau of John), b. 25 July 1694, Plymouth <MD 2:20>; d. 17 Dec. 1778, S. Duxbury g.s. <Duxbury VR, MD 9:161>

CHILDREN OF William BRADFORD^{4} (John^{3}) & Hannah FOSTER: (6) <1-4, Plymouth, MD 12:224>
James BRADFORD^{5}, b. 2 July 1717; d. 10 Dec. 1801 <Bible Rcds>
Zadock BRADFORD^{5}, b. 30 July 1719; d. pre 12 Mar. 1745 (adm.) <Plymouth Co.Prob.#2635, 10:85>
Samuel BRADFORD^{5}, b. 4 Apr. 1721; d. 4 Feb. 1735 <MD 12:56>
Eliphalet BRADFORD^{5}, b. 20 Jan. 1722/3 <Kingston VR 1:9>; d. 7 June 1795, Duxbury g.s.**<119>**
Hannah BRADFORD^{5}, b. 29 May 1724 <Kingston VR 1:9>
William BRADFORD^{5}, b. 25 Jan. 1726/7 <Kingston VR 1:9>; d. 7 Dec. 1753*, unm.

Hannah PRINCE^{6} (Tho.^{5}, Ruth Turner^{4}, Mary Brewster^{3}, Jonathan^{2}), b. 22 Oct. 1730, Duxbury <MD 11:237>; d. 11 July 1756, Duxbury g.s. <MD 12:167>

CHILDREN OF Eliphalet BRADFORD^{5} & 1st Hannah PRINCE: (3) <Duxbury, MD 12:170>
Hannah BRADFORD^{6}, b. 30 May 1752
Lydia BRADFORD^{6}, b. 15 Jan. 1754
Eunice BRADFORD^{6}, b. 8 May 1756

Hannah OLDHAM, b. c1733, d. 4 Nov. 1804, Duxbury g.s., ae 71y3d, Mayflower Cem. <Duxbury VR:352>

CHILDREN OF Eliphalet BRADFORD^{5} & 2nd Hannah OLDHAM: (6)* <Duxbury VR>

Lucy BRADFORD^{6}, b. 9 Nov. 1758

Abigail BRADFORD^{6}, b. 26 Dec. 1759

William BRADFORD^{6}, b. 17 Nov. 1761

Zadock BRADFORD^{6}, b. 11 Aug. 1765; d. 1 July 1833*, S. Duxbury g.s.

Deborah BRADFORD^{6}, b. 26 Dec. 1767

Mary BRADFORD^{6}, b. 1773, d. 16 May 1774, ae 9m

Lucy GRAY, b. 24 Oct. 1772*, d. aft. 1 Aug. 1833*

CHILDREN OF Zadock BRADFORD^{6} & Lucy GRAY: (8) <Duxbury VR>

Zadock BRADFORD^{7}, b. 11 June 1798

Nancy BRADFORD^{7}, b. 22 Mar. 1800

George BRADFORD^{7}, b. 30 Sept. 1801

Lucy G. BRADFORD^{7}, b. 7 Oct. 1803

Caroline BRADFORD^{7}, b. 24 June 1805

Charles BRADFORD^{7}, b. 13 Dec. 1806; d. 13 May 1831*

Lewis Eldridge BRADFORD^{7}, b. 15 Nov. 1809; d. 22 Sept. 1867, Quincy <Mass.VR 203:250>

James BRADFORD^{7}, b. 22 Sept. 1812

Lewis E. BRADFORD^{8} (Lewis^{7}), b. c1843, Duxbury, d. 18 May 1874, ae 30y7m22d, Quincey, scarlet fever <Mass.VR 266:260>

Priscilla ( ) BRADFORD, d. 11 Feb. 1743, ae 24 (1st wf of James Bradford^{5}, Wm.^{4})

Zeruiah THOMAS^{5} (Lydia Waterman^{4}, Sarah Snow^{3}, Abigail Warren^{2}), b. 3 Oct. 1715, Marshfield <MD 8:176>; d. 23 Nov. 1808 <Bible Rcds>

CHILDREN OF James BRADFORD^{5} (Wm.^{4}) & 2nd Zeruiah THOMAS: (7) <Bible Rcds.>

Samuel BRADFORD^{6}, b. 6 Sept. 1747, d. 26 Sept. 1790

Anthony BRADFORD^{6}, b. 6 Sept. 1749, d. 16 July 1819

James BRADFORD^{6}, b. 20 Jan. 1751, d. 3 Dec. 1777, ae 20 (sic)

Priscilla BRADFORD^{6}, b. 14 Dec. 1752

Keziah BRADFORD^{6}, b. 15 Oct. 1754, d. 23 Oct. 1809, Windham CT <VR RI 18:344> (wf of Waterman Clift)**<120>**

Hannah BRADFORD^{6}, b. 8 Oct. 1756, d. 25 June 1778

Joseph BRADFORD^{6}, b. 30 Dec. 1758, d. 26 May 1759

Susannah SMITH, b. 11 Oct. 1737, d. 22 Mar. 1776 <Bible Rcds>

CHILDREN OF John DOUGLAS & Susannah SMITH: (9) <Bible Rcds, James Bradford Family>

Olive DOUGLAS, b. 28 Feb. 1758

Mary DOUGLAS, b. 3 Oct. 1759, d. 3 Dec. 1759

Sarah DOUGLAS, b. 17 Nov. 1760

Rebecca DOUGLAS, b. 29 May 1763

Susannah DOUGLAS, b. 22 July 1765

Micah DOUGLAS, b. 11 July 1767

John DOUGLAS, b. 5 Dec. 1769

Mary DOUGLAS, b. 14 Oct. 1771, d. 14 Nov. 1771

William DOUGLAS, b. 15 May 1774

CHILDREN OF Anthony BRADFORD^{6} (James^{5}) & Olive DOUGLAS: (3)**<121>**

Anne FITCH, d. 7 Oct. 1715 <Lebanon CT VR>**<122>**

CHILDREN OF Joseph BRADFORD^{3} & 1st Anne FITCH: (10) <Lebanon CT VR:20>

Anne BRADFORD^{4}, b. 26 July 1699; d. 9 Oct. 1788, Mansfield CT g.s., Gurley Cem.

Joseph BRADFORD^{4}, b. 9 Apr. 1702; d. pre 5 Jan. 1778 (adm.)

Priscilla BRADFORD^{4}, b. 9 Apr. 1702 (twins); d. 14 May 1778*, Lebanon CT

Alithea BRADFORD^{4}, b. 6 Apr. 1704, d. Apr. 1704

Ireny BRADFORD^{4}, b. 6 Apr. 1704 (twins), d. 16 Apr. 1704

Sarah BRADFORD^{4}, b. 21 Sept. 1706

Hannah BRADFORD^{4}, b. 24 May 1709

Elizabeth BRADFORD^{4}, b. 21 Oct. 1712

Alithea BRADFORD^{4}, b. 19 Sept. 1715

Irene BRADFORD^{4}, b. 19 Sept. 1715 (twins)

Mary ( ) BRADFORD, d. 16 Sept. 1752 <Hist.Montville:344>**<123>**

CHILD OF Joseph BRADFORD^{3} & 2nd Mary ( ):

John BRADFORD^{4}, b. 20 May 1717 <New London CT TR:261>; d. 10 Mar. 1787 <g.s.>

Esther BRADFORD, wf of John^{4}, d. 10 Dec. 1799, ae 82 <g.s.>

William BRADFORD, b. c1774, d. 5 Sept. 1800, 26th yr <g.s.>

Mary BRADFORD, wf of John Jr., d. 15 Nov. 1780, ae 35 <g.s.>

Sherwood BRADFORD, b. c1776, d. 16 Nov. 1805, 29th yr <g.s.>

David HYDE, (son of Sam.*), bpt. 22 Mar. 1719*, Lebanon CT; d. pre 12 May 1741* (adm.)

CHILD OF David HYDE & Alathea BRADFORD^{4} (Jos.^{3}):

David HYDE^{5}, bpt. 4 Jan. 1741*, Lebanon CT <Hyde Gen.:16>

Timothy DIMMICK^{4} (John^{3}, Shubael^{2}, Tho.^{1}), b. July 1698, Barnstable <MD 4:222>; d. 27 Dec. 1783, Mansfield CT g.s., Gurley Cem.

CHILDREN OF Timothy DIMMICK & Anne BRADFORD^{4} (Jos.^{3}): (9) <Mansfield CT VR:63>

Ann DIMMICK^{5}, b. 23 May 1724 <VR:62>

Timothy DIMMICK^{5}, b. 8 Apr. 1726 <VR:62>; d. ?Feb. 1795* <Coventry CT VR:229>

John DIMMICK^{5}, b. 24 Mar. 1727/8

Joannah DIMMICK^{5}, b. 28 Aug. 1730

Josiah DIMMICK^{5}, b. 2 Mar. 1732/3

Simeon DIMMICK^{5}, b. 19 Sept. 1735, d. 9 Mar. 1737/8 <VR:315>

Sylvanus DIMMICK^{5}, b. 18 June 1738

Oliver DIMMICK^{5}, b. 31 Dec. 1740

Daniel DIMMICK^{5}, b. 13 May 1743

CHILDREN OF Ebenezer CLARK & Ann DIMMICK^{5}: (13) <Mansfield CT VR:42>

Temperance CLARK^{6}, b. 21 Apr. 1741

Simon CLARK^{6}, b. 11 Mar. 1744

Timothy CLARK^{6}, b. 26 Dec. 1745

Joanna CLARK^{6}, b. 23 Jan. 1747/8

Wilcome CLARK^{6}, b. 8 Apr. 1750 (son)

Abigail CLARK^{6}, b. 28 Feb. 1752

Ebenezer CLARK^{6}, b. 10 Mar. 1754

Daniel CLARK^{6}, b. 6 May 1756

Anna CLARK^{6}, b. 9 May 1759

Eunice CLARK^{6}, b. 11 May 1761

Jonathan CLARK^{6}, b. 20 May 1763 <VR:43>

Mary CLARK^{6}, b. 7 May 1765 <VR:43>

Solomon CLARK^{6}, b. 7 Oct. 1767 <VR:43>

Mehitable SLATE, (dau of Ezekiel & Mehitable (Hall)), b. 19 Feb. 1749 <Mansfield CT VR:159> (m. a Daniel Clark)

MICRO #9 of 15

Desire DIMMICK^{6} (Tho.^{5}, Desire Sturgis^{4}--), b. c1732, d. 10 May 1802, ae 70 <Coventry CT VR:232>

CHILDREN OF Timothy DIMMICK^{5} (Anne Bradford^{4}) & Desire DIMMICK: (11) <Coventry CT VR:36>

Desire DIMMICK^{6}, b. 22 Jan. 1751

Eunice DIMMICK^{6}, b. 9 Feb. 1753

Anne DIMMICK^{6}, b. 15 Sept. 1754

Lois DIMMICK^{6}, b. 12 May 1756

Sibel DIMMICK^{6}, b. 18 Mar. 1758

Lucy DIMMICK^{6}, b. 22 May 1760

Timothy DIMMICK^{6}, b. 22 Aug. 1762

Daniel DIMMICK^{6}, b. 20 Feb. 1765, d. 1 Aug. 1833, Coventry CT <VR:243>

Mason DIMMICK^{6}, b. 22 June 1767; d. May 1843* <Mansfield CT 2nd ChR:458>

Rhoda DIMMICK^{6}, b. 10 Aug. 1770

Roger DIMMICK^{6}, b. 5 Aug. 1772

Anne WRIGHT, b. c1767, d. 26 Jan. 1832, ae 65 <Coventry CT VR:242>

CHILDREN OF Daniel DIMMICK^{6} & Anne WRIGHT: (9) <Coventry CT VR:37>

Anna C. DIMMICK^{7}, b. 18 Aug. 1787

Parthena DIMMICK^{7}, b. 9 Apr. 1789

Lucinda DIMMICK^{7}, b. 18 Mar. 1791

Salle DIMMICK^{7}, b. 23 June 1793

Harty DIMMICK^{7}, b. 24 Dec. 1794

Clara Maria DIMMICK^{7}, b. 14 Sept. 1796, d. 21 Aug. 1849, unm. <VR:180>

Eliza DIMMICK^{7}, b. 24 May 1798

Timothy DIMMICK^{7}, b. 17 Apr. 1799

Desire DIMMICK^{7}, b. 31 Mar. 1802

Anna ROBERTSON, b. c1757, d. 14 Nov. 1839* <Mansfield CT 2nd ChR:457>

CHILDREN OF Mason DIMMICK^{6} (Tim.^{5}) & Anna ROBERTSON: (8) <Coventry CT VR:37>

Mason DIMMICK^{7}, b. 26 July 1787

Rufus DIMMICK^{7}, b. 21 Mar. 1789

Clarissa DIMMICK^{7}, b. 7 May 1791

Samuel DIMMICK^{7}, b. 18 Sept. 1793

Desiah DIMMICK^{7}, b. 26 Sept. 1795

Wealthy DIMMICK^{7}, b. 22 Mar. 1798

Chauncey DIMMICK^{7}, b. 16 Nov. 1801

John A. DIMMICK^{7}, b. 16 Sept. 1806

CHILDREN OF Ralzamon BELKNAP & Desiah DIMMICK^{7}: (3) <Coventry CT VR:10>

Maria Ann BELKNAP^{8}, b. 13 Mar. 1826

Emma Virginia BELKNAP^{8}, b. 13 Feb. 1837

Roxana Bingham BELKNAP^{8}, b. 25 Dec. 1840

CHILDREN OF Andrew LISK & Elizabeth BRADFORD^{4} (Jos.^{3}): (8) <Lebanon CT VR:182>

William LISK^{5}, b. 17 Dec. 1738

Ann LISK^{5}, b. 24 Mar. 1740

Martha LISK^{5}, b. 30 May 1742

Andrew LISK^{5}, b. 4 Nov. 1744

Betty LISK^{5}, b. 22 Nov. 1746

Sarah LISK^{5}, b. 7 Mar. 1748/9

Amey LISK^{5}, b. 15 Jan. 1752

Huldah LISK^{5}, b. 18 Aug. 1754

CHILDREN OF Jonathan JANES & Irene BRADFORD^{4} (Jos.^{3}): (11) <1-7, Lebanon CT VR>

David JANES^{5}, b. 23 Dec. 1736

Jonathan JANES^{5}, b. 28 Jan. 1738/9

Irene JANES^{5}, b. 3 Apr. 1741, d. 28 June 1743

Eliphalet JANES^{5}, b. 23 Feb. 1742/3

Irene JANES^{5}, b. 30 July 1745

Solomon JANES^{5}, b. 20 June 1748

Daniel JANES^{5}, b. 17 Mar. 1751

Mary JANES^{5}, b. 28 Apr. 1753 <Janes Gen.(1868):116>

Jonathan JANES^{5}, b. 8 Jan. 1756 <Janes Gen.:116>

Abigail JANES^{5}, b. 24 Jan. 1759 <Janes Gen.(1868):116>

Ann JANES^{5}, b. 12 Dec. 1761 <Janes Gen.:116>

Henrietta SWIFT, b. c1701, d. Oct. 1758, 57th yr, Haddam, Higgauum Cem.

CHILDREN OF Joseph BRADFORD^{4} (Jos.^{3}) & Henrietta SWIFT: (7) <New London CT VR>

Elizabeth BRADFORD^{5}, b. 17 Jan. 1730/1 <VR:4>

Ann BRADFORD^{5}, b. 23 July 1732 <VR:4>

William BRADFORD^{5}, b. 16 Apr. 1734 <VR:5>

Henry Swift BRADFORD^{5}, b. 21 Aug. 1736 <VR:5>

Robert BRADFORD^{5}, b. 21 July 1739 <VR:5>; d. betw 26 Sept. 1803 (will) - 7 Feb. 1808 (prob) <Middletown CT Prob.9:61,65>

Hannah BRADFORD^{5}, b. 10 Mar. 1740/1 <VR:40>

Joseph BRADFORD^{5}, b. 10 Jan. 1744/5 <VR:40>

CHILD OF Richard MAYO & Elisabeth BRADFORD:

Ruth Elisabeth MAYO, b. 9 Feb. 1775 <Chatham CT VR 1:123>

CHILDREN OF Richard LYMAN & Ann BRADFORD^{5} (Jos.^{4}): (4)

Ann LYMAN^{6}, b. 13 Apr. 1759*

Richard LYMAN^{6}, b. 22 Sept. 1761*

Joseph Bradford LYMAN^{6}, b. 1 Sept. 1767 <Lebanon CT VR:183>

Rachel LYMAN^{6}, b. 19 Sept. 1769 <Lebanon CT VR:183>

Penelope ( ) BRADFORD, d. pre 1822 (adm) <Middletown CT Prob.12:268>

CHILDREN OF Robert BRADFORD^{5} (Jos.^{4}) & Penelope ( ): (2)

Joseph BRADFORD^{6}, b. ( )

Perez BRADFORD^{6}, b. ( )

CHILDREN OF William BRADFORD^{5} (Jos.^{4}) & Sarah RICH: (4) <Chatham CT VR 1:60>

Amos BRADFORD^{6}, b. 24 Aug. 1763

Henrietta BRADFORD^{6}, b. 4 Oct. 1765

Mercy BRADFORD^{6}, b. 19 May 1769, d. 16 Mar. 1770

William BRADFORD^{6}, b. 17 June 1776

CHILDREN OF Israel HIGGINS & Henrietta BRADFORD^{6}: (3) <Chatham CT VR 1:189>

Livia HIGGINS^{7}, b. 12 May 1789

Jared HIGGINS^{7}, b. 24 Dec. 1790

Duel HIGGINS^{7}, b. 6 Apr. 1792

Samuel HIDE, b. 10 Sept. 1691*, Windham CT; d. 14 Feb. 1776*, Lebanon CT

CHILDREN OF Samuel HIDE & Priscilla BRADFORD^{4} (Jos.^{3}): (9) <Lebanon CT VR:146>

Samuel HIDE^{5}, b. 24 Oct. 1725

Anne HIDE^{5}, b. 22 Oct. 1727

Priscilla HIDE^{5}, b. 16 Apr. 1731, d. 5 Oct. 1732

Sybil HIDE^{5}, b. 16 Apr. 1731 (twins)

Daniel HIDE^{5}, b. 7 May 1733

Priscilla HIDE^{5}, b. 4 June 1735, d. 4 July 1759, Litchfield CT

Hannah HIDE^{5}, b. 19 July 1738

Zerviah HIDE^{5}, b. 15 Dec. 1740

Abigail HIDE^{5}, b. 4 Nov. 1744; d. 20 Dec. 1830*

Lieut. Samuel HIDE, d. 6 Nov. 1742 <Lebanon CT VR:149>

Israel LOTHROP, d. pre 22 Mar. 1758* (will)

CHILD OF Israel LOTHROP & Sarah (BRADFORD^{4}) Tuthill:

Prudence LOTHROP^{5}, b. 16 Mar. 1747/8* <Norwich CT VR:255>

CHILDREN OF William HUNT & Mary BRADFORD^{3}: (2) <Weymouth>**<124>**

Mary HUNT^{4}, b. 18 Feb. 1687/8 <NEHGR 4:59>

William HUNT^{4}, b. 17 May 1693 <NEHGR 4:71>

John STEELE, (son of James),b. c1660, d. 6 Mar. 1698 <Early CT Prob.Rcds.1:587

CHILDREN OF John STEELE & Melatiah BRADFORD^{3}: (3)

Bethiah STEELE^{4}, b. ( )

John STEELE^{4}, b. ( ), d.y.

Ebenezer STEELE^{4}, b. 1695; d. betw. 26 June 1745 (will) - 3 Mar. 1746/7 <Early CT Prob.3:655>

CHILD OF Samuel STEVENS & Melatiah (BRADFORD^{3}) Steele:<125>

Elizabeth STEVENS^{4}, b. c1703 (m. John Hubbard)

Samuel STEELE, b. 15 Mar. 1652<126>

CHILDREN OF Samuel STEELE & Mercy BRADFORD^{3}: (7)<Hartford CT, Savage 4:181><127>

Thomas STEELE^{4}, b. 9 Sept. 1681

Samuel STEELE^{4}, b. 15 Feb. 1684/5; d. 1710*

Jerusha STEELE^{4}, b. 15 Feb. 1684/5 (twins)

William STEELE^{4}, b. 20 Feb. 1687/8; d. 1713*

Abiel STEELE^{4}, b. 8 Oct. 1693 (dau) (m. John Webster)

Daniel STEELE^{4}, b. 3 Apr. 1697; d. 11 Mar. 1788*, Hartford CT<128>

Eliphalet STEELE^{4}, b. 23 June 1700

Mary HOPKINS, bpt. 13 Jan. 1703/4, Hartford; bur. 19 Aug. 1796*, Hartford CT (wf of Daniel Steele^{4})<129>

CHILD OF Josiah STEELE & Elizabeth COLTON:

Rachel STEELE, b. 12 Aug. 1764, d. 24 July 1847 (m. Jonas Barnes of Tolland CT)<130>

West Hartford CT, Births & Deaths: (misc.*)

John Kellogg BELDING, (son of John Jr.), bpt. 20 or 25 May 1740 <VR (1):39

Noah WEBSTER, (son of Daniel), bpt. 28 Mar. 1722 <VR (1):28>

Mercy STEELE, (dau of Eliphalet), bpt. 8 Oct. 1727 <VR (1):31>

Mercy WEBSTER, (dau of Noah), bpt. 12 Nov. 1749 <VR (1):46>

Betsey BELDING, (dau of John), bpt. 15 May 1786 <VR 2:78>

Benjamin BELDEN, (son of John), bpt. 10 Aug. 1799 <VR 2:83>

Mary Ann BELDEN, (dau of John), bpt. 19 Apr. (1780 or 1800) <VR 2:84>

Mercy Webster BELDEN, (dau of John), bpt. 25 Apr. 1802 <VR 2:86>

Lucy Benjamin BELDEN, (dau of John Jr.), bpt. 29 Apr. 1804 <VR 3:87>

Edwin Webster BELDEN, (son of John Jr.), bpt. 3 Nov. 1805 <VR 3:88>

Henry John BELDEN, (son of John Jr.), bpt. 23 May 1813 <VR 3:91>

Patience BELDING, (dau of John), d. 31 Jan. 1759, ae 17 <VR 6:141>

Capt. Daniel WEBSTER, d. 22 Dec. 17()5, ae 72y3m, pneumonia <VR 6:144>

Eliphalet STEELE, d. July 1773 <VR 6:146>

Rachel BELDING, (dau of John Jr.), d. 9 Sept. 1777, dysentery <VR 6:150>

Widow STEELE, d. 21 Mar. 1779, old age <VR 7:151>

John BELDEN, d. 20 Dec. 1785 <VR 7:154>

Catherine STEELE, widow, d. 3 June 1788, ae (87?) <VR 7:154>

Child of John BELDEN, d. 8 July 1813, ae 4m <VR 9:217>

Noah WEBSTER, d. 9 Nov. 1813, ae 92 <VR 9:218>

John Kellogg BELDEN, d. 23 Nov. 1813, ae 75, typhus fever <VR 9:220>

Mercy BELDEN, widow, d. 11 Aug. 1820, ae 71 <VR 9:222>

CHILDREN OF John Kellogg BELDING: (5)* <W.Hartford CT 4th ChR>

Mercy BELDING, bpt. 2 June 1771 <ChR:65>

Lucinda BELDING, bpt. 17 May 1772 <ChR:66>

John BELDING, bpt. 23 Jan. 1774 <ChR:68>

Rachel BELDING, bpt. 15 Sept. 1776 <ChR:71>

Ebenezer BELDING, bpt. 25 Oct. 1778 <ChR:73>

Hannah ROGERS^{4} (John$^{3-2}$), b. 16 Nov. 1668, Duxbury <MD 9:172>

CHILDREN OF Samuel BRADFORD^{3} & Hannah ROGERS: (7) <Plymouth, MD 2:18>

Hannah BRADFORD^{4}, b. 14 Feb. 1689

Gershom BRADFORD^{4}, b. 21 Dec. 1691; d. 4 Apr. 1757, Bristol RI g.s. <MD 19:1>

Perez BRADFORD^{4}, b. 28 Dec. 1694

Elizabeth BRADFORD^{4}, b. 15 Dec. 1696; d. 10 May 1777, Stonington CT

Jerusha BRADFORD^{4}, b. 10 Mar. 1699

Welthea BRADFORD^{4}, b. 15 May 1702

Gamaliel BRADFORD^{4}, b. 18 May 1704; d. 24 Apr. 1778, Duxbury g.s. <MD 9:160>

Charles WHITING, b. 1 July 1692, Hartford CT; d. 7 Mar. 1738, Montville CT(hus of Eliz.Bradford^{4})

Abigail BARTLETT^{5} (Ben.$^{4-3}$, Mary Warren^{2}), d. 30 Aug. 1776, ae 73y3m26d, Duxbury g.s. <MD 9:160>

CHILDREN OF Gamaliel BRADFORD^{4} & Abigail BARTLETT: (10) <Duxbury, MD 11:149>

Abigail BRADFORD^{5}, b. 24 Sept. 1728

Samuel BRADFORD^{5}, b. 2 Jan. 1729/30; d. 17 Feb. 1777, Duxbury g.s. <MD 9:160>

Gamaliel BRADFORD^{5}, b. 2 Sept. 1731; d. 4 Jan. 1807, S. Duxbury g.s.

Seth BRADFORD^{5}, b. 14 Sept. 1733

Paybodie BRADFORD^{5}, b. 8 Mar. 1734/5; d. 5 Sept. 1782, Kingston g.s. <MD 7:23>

Deborah BRADFORD^{5}, b. 17 Aug. 1738; d. 1 Aug. 1739

Hannah BRADFORD^{5}, b. 30 July 1740

Ruth BRADFORD^{5}, b. 5 July 1743

Peter BRADFORD^{5}, b. 2 June 1745

Andrew BRADFORD^{5}, b. 2 June 1745 (twins)

Wait WADSWORTH, (son of Elisha & Eliz.), b. 23 Oct. 1714, Duxbury <MD 11:148>; d. 5 June 1799*, Duxbury g.s.

CHILDREN OF Wait WADSWORTH & Abigail BRADFORD^{5}: (14)

Abigail WADSWORTH^{6}, b. 3 June 1749, d.y.

Joseph WADSWORTH^{6}, b. 7 July 1750

Alvira WADSWORTH^{6}, b. 1 Nov. 1751

Seneca WADSWORTH^{6}, b. 9 Apr. 1753

Wait WADSWORTH^{6}, b. 7 Oct. 1754; d. 11 Mar. 1840*

Clynthia WADSWORTH^{6}, b. 25 Mar. 1756

Robert WADSWORTH^{6}, b. 26 Sept. 1757; d. 1760**<131>**

Eden WADSWORTH^{6}, b. 12 May 1759; drowned 30 Apr. 1818* (g.s. says 26 Apr.)

Beulah WADSWORTH^{6}, b. 8 June 1762

Celanah WADSWORTH^{6}, b. 9 Dec. 1763

Elisha WADSWORTH^{6}, b. 15 June 1765

Zenith WADSWORTH^{6}, b. 5 Oct. 1766

Abigail WADSWORTH^{6}, b. 25 Oct. 1768

Wiswall WADSWORTH^{6}, b. ( )

Sarah ALDEN^{4} (Sam.^{3}, David^{2}), b. 2 Dec. 1731, Duxbury <MD 11:236>; d. 4 May 1788

CHILDREN OF Gamaliel BRADFORD^{5} (Gamaliel^{4}) & Sarah ALDEN: (8)*

Perez BRADFORD^{6}, b. 14 Nov. 1758

Sophia BRADFORD^{6}, b. 16 Nov. 1761

Gamaliel BRADFORD^{6}, b. 4 Nov. 1763, d. 17 Nov. 1824

Alden BRADFORD^{6}, b. 19 Nov. 1765

Sarah BRADFORD^{6}, b. 24 Feb. 1768

Jerusha BRADFORD^{6}, b. 30 Jan. 1770

Daniel BRADFORD^{6}, b. 27 Dec. 1771

Gershom BRADFORD^{6}, b. 3 Feb. 1774

Joshua STANFORD, (*son of Robert & Fear), b. 30 Nov. 1729, Duxbury <MD 12:126>

CHILDREN OF Joshua STANFORD & Hannah BRADFORD^{5} (Gamaliel^{4}): (5) <Duxbury VR>

Robert STANFORD^{6}, bpt. 11 July 1760*

Rebecca STANFORD^{6}, bpt. 11 Apr. 1762*

Hannah STANFORD^{6}, bpt. 17 July 1763*

Joshua STANFORD^{6}, bpt. 30 Nov. 1766*

Samuel Bradford STANFORD^{6}, bpt. 3 Aug. 1777*

Welthea DELANO^{6} (Joshua^{5}--), b. 7 Dec. 1741, Duxbury, d. 27 Apr. 1783, Kingston <MD 11:238,7:23>

CHILDREN OF Paybodie BRADFORD^{5} (Gamaliel^{4}) & Welthea DELANO: (10) <Kingston VR>**<132>**

Lewis BRADFORD^{6}, b. 24 Aug. 1761* <VR>

Ira BRADFORD^{6}, b. 27 June 1763*, d.y. <VR>

Pamela BRADFORD^{6}, b. 30 Nov. 1764* <VR>; d. 30 Oct. 1823

Charles BRADFORD^{6}, b. 2 Aug. 1767* <VR>

Cynthia BRADFORD^{6}, b. ( ) (mentioned in father's will)

Joanna BRADFORD^{6}, b. pre 1777* (mentioned in father's will)

Sylvia BRADFORD^{6}, b. pre 1777* (mentioned in father's will)

Deborah BRADFORD^{6}, bpt. Sept. 1777* <VR>

Lucy Foster BRADFORD^{6}, b. 28 Oct. 1778* <VR>; d. 6 Sept. 1850, Kingston, congestion of brain <Mass.VR 49:159>

Ira BRADFORD^{6}, b. 17 or 27 Apr. 1783* <VR>

Joseph BARTLETT^{7} (son of Joseph^{6} & Lurana), b. 10 Jan. 1770*; d. 9 Nov. 1851, jaundice, Kingston, master mariner <Mass.VR 58:179>

CHILDREN OF Joseph BARTLETT & Lucy Foster BRADFORD^{6}: (8)*

Betsey Bradford BARTLETT^{7}, b. 10 Sept. 1799

Lucy Foster BARTLETT^{7}, b. 10 May 1801; d. 22 Aug. 1804

Nancy BARTLETT^{7}, b. 6 Jan. 1804

David Bradford BARTLETT^{7}, b. 11 Aug. 1806

Ichabod BARTLETT^{7}, b. 1 July 1809, d. 17 Aug. 1828

Cornelius Adams BARTLETT^{7}, b. 23 Dec. 1811

Lucy Foster BARTLETT^{7}, b. 5 Jan. 1814

Walter Scott BARTLETT^{7}, b. 22 June 1818

Laurana BARTLETT, (dau of Jos. & Lurana), d. 20 Apr. 1851, ae 83y2m, Kingston, apoplexy, unm. <Mass.VR 58:179>

Peabody BRADFORD^{6} (son of Paybodie^{5} & Lydia (Freeman)), b. 15 Mar. 1758, d. 17 Jan. 1852, Auburn ME g.s. <NEHGR 4:234,242>**<132>**

Hannah BRADBURY, b. 19 July 1766; d. 26 Nov. 1852, Auburn ME g.s.

CHILD OF Samuel FREEMAN & Hannah BRADBURY:

Olive FREEMAN, b. 23 Nov. 1785, d. 4 Apr. 1836 <Bible Rcd.>

CHILDREN OF Peabody BRADFORD^{6} (Paybodie^{5}) & Hannah (BRADBURY) Freeman: (9) <Bible Rcd.>

Benjamin BRADFORD^{7}, b. 4 July 1789

Lydia BRADFORD^{7}, b. 28 July 1791, d. Sept. 1850

Samuel BRADFORD^{7}, b. 16 July 1793

Abigail BRADFORD^{7}, b. 22 June 1795

Mary BRADFORD^{7}, b. 28 Aug. 1797

Eleanor BRADFORD^{7}, b. 22 Dec. 1799

Freeman BRADFORD^{7}, b. 24 May 1802

Lewis BRADFORD^{7}, b. 22 Aug. 1804

Charles BRADFORD^{7}, b. 21 July 1809, d. 17 Oct. 1863

CHILD OF Lewis BRADFORD^{6} (Paybodie^{5}) & Priscilla TUPPER:

Charles BRADFORD^{7} b. ( )

CHILDREN OF Charles BRADFORD^{7} & Emeline INGRAHAM: (3)

Alden BRADFORD^{8}, b. 7 Oct. 1843, Boston (of Washington D.C. in 1866)

Henry BRADFORD^{8}, b. 1835

Emeline P. BRADFORD^{8}, b. 1827, d. 25 Jan. 1896

Nathaniel LITTLE Jr., b. c1759, d. 20 Nov. 1808, ae 49

CHILDREN OF Nathaniel LITTLE Jr. & Pamela BRADFORD^{6} (Paybodie^{5}): (6)

Welthea LITTLE^{7}, b. 6 May 1793

Charles LITTLE^{7}, b. 31 Jan. 1795

Henry Otis LITTLE^{7}, b. 5 Mar. 1797

Lewis Bradford LITTLE^{7}, b. 25 July 1800

Nathaniel LITTLE^{7}, b. 21 Oct. 1802

George LITTLE^{7}, b. 11 Sept. 1804

Grace RING^{5} (Sam.^{4}, Eleazer^{3}, Deborah Hopkins^{2}), b. 6 Apr. 1730 <Kingston VR:121>

CHILDREN OF Samuel BRADFORD^{5} (Gamaliel^{4}) & Grace RING: (10) <Duxbury VR>

Deborah BRADFORD^{6}, b. 11 Dec. 1750; d. 15 July 1827*, Kingston g.s. <MD 7:20>(m. Melzar Adams)

Samuel BRADFORD^{6}, b. 27 Mar. 1752; d. 1816*

Lydia BRADFORD^{6}, b. 6 Apr. 1754; d. 1769*

William BRADFORD^{6}, b. 25 Nov. 1755

Welthea BRADFORD^{6}, b. 15 Nov. 1757 (m. Isaac Drew)

Lyman BRADFORD^{6}, b. 1 Oct. 1760; d. 1776*

Elihu BRADFORD^{6}, bpt. 16 June 1765; d. 1781*

Grace BRADFORD^{6}, b. 6 Apr. 1765; d. 1848*

George BRADFORD^{6}, b. 20 Nov. 1767; d. 1791*, Havana

Isaiah BRADFORD^{6}, b. 25 Nov. 1769; d. 7 or 27 Jan. 1849*

William DREW, (son of Isaac & Welthen), b. c1798, Duxbury, d. 12 Jan. 1853, ae 55, Boston, master mariner <Mass.VR 77:3>

Caroline DREW, widow of William, b. S. Carolina, d. 1 July 1854, ae 51y5m, Boston <Mass.VR 86:50>

Priscilla WISWALL^{4} (Priscilla Pabodie^{3}, Eliz. Alden^{2}), b. c1690, d. 12 Sept. 1780, 90th yr, Bristol RI g.s. <MD 19:1>

CHILDREN OF Gershom BRADFORD^{4} (Sam.^{3}) & Priscilla WISWALL: (5 of 10)**<133>**

Priscilla BRADFORD^{5}, b. c1716, d. 18 Nov. 1811 <Newport Mercury>

Daniel BRADFORD^{5}, b. c1721, d. 22 July 1810, 89th yr, Bristol RI g.s. <Prov.Gazette>

Job BRADFORD^{5}, b. c1723, Kingston, d. Apr. 1789*, ae 63

Dr. Solomon BRADFORD^{5}, b. 1727, d. 8 Apr. 1795*, Providence <Arnold VR 13:200>

Dr. Jeremiah BRADFORD^{5}, b. c1734

Mary CHURCH, d. 16 Apr. 1772, Bristol RI <Prov.Gazette>

CHILDREN OF Daniel BRADFORD^{5} & 1st Mary CHURCH: (2) <Bristol RI VR 2:8,23>

Elizabeth BRADFORD^{6}, b. 5 June 1750; d. 29 Apr. 1837 (widow of Nathaniel Fales)

Priscilla BRADFORD^{6}, b. 1 or 12 Mar. 1752, d. 9 Jan. 1832**<134>**

Susanna JARVIS, (dau of Col. Leonard), d. 31 Dec. 1811 or 1815, Bristol RI g.s., ae 76 <RI American>

CHILDREN OF Daniel BRADFORD^{5} & 2nd Susanna JARVIS: (3) <Bristol RI VR 2:49>

Daniel BRADFORD^{6}, b. 27 June 1778, Attleborough

Leonard Jarvis BRADFORD^{6}, b. 22 May 1780; d. 27 July 1812

Samuel BRADFORD^{6}, b. 6 May 1783

MICRO #10 of 15

Bristol RI Deaths <"Original #2">

Levi BRADFORD, d. 7 Nov. 1756, ae 19, "old Mr Potters grand son" <2:2>

Capt. Gershom BRADFORD, d. 4 Apr. 1757, ae 66 <2:3>

Dau., of Isaac GORHAM, d. 10 May 1759, ae 3y <2:5>

Isaac GORHAM, d. 1 Dec. 1760, ae 50 <2:7>

Stillborn child, of Elijah BRADFORD, d. Dec. 1763 <2:10>

Infant, of Dr. BRADFORD, d. 1764 <2:10>
John BRADFORD, son of Dr., d. 30 Oct. 1765, ae 8 <2:11>
Stillborn child, of John HOWLAND, d. 1771 <2:16>
Mrs. Mary BRADFORD, d. 16 Apr. 1772 <2:17>
Mris. Mary BRADFORD, d. 3 Oct. 1775, ae 44 <2:21>
Child, of John HOWLAND, d. 31 Dec. 1775 <2:22>
Son, of Capt. Job BRADFORD, d. 12 Mar. 1775, ae 11 <2:22>
Mrs. Priscilla BRADFORD, d. 12 Sept. 1778, ae 85 <2:24>
CHILDREN OF Leonard Jarvis BRADFORD^6 (Dan.^{5}) & Sally TURNER, (dau of Moses):(5)<Bristol RI 2:121>
Susannah Jarvis BRADFORD^7, b. 18 Mar. 1802
Sally Leonard BRADFORD^7, b. 18 Nov. 1803
Harriett Turner BRADFORD^7, b. 11 Feb. 1806
Leonard Jarvis BRADFORD^7, b. 29 Mar. 1808
Durfee Turner BRADFORD^7, b. 14 Mar. 1810
CHILDREN OF Daniel BRADFORD^6 (Dan.^{5}) & Sarah REYNOLDS, (dau of Jos.): (8) <Bristol RI 2:120>
Charles Jarvis BRADFORD^7, b. 17 Aug. 1800
Joseph Reynolds BRADFORD^7, b. 15 Nov. 1802
Sally Russell BRADFORD^7, b. 10 Mar. 1805
Mary Sparhawk BRADFORD^7, b. 23 Nov. 1806
Jane Augusta BRADFORD^7, b. 22 Aug. 1809
Daniel BRADFORD^7, b. 9 Mar. 1811
Leonard Jarvis BRADFORD^7, b. 4 Feb. 1813
Susanna Jarvis BRADFORD^7, b. 4 June 1815
Rebecca DART, (dau of Eben. & Ruth (Loomis)), b. 25 Nov. 1728; d. aft. 4 Apr. 1811 (deed)<Chatham CT Rcds.13:483>
CHILDREN OF Dr. Jeremiah BRADFORD^5 (Gershom^4) & Rebecca DART: (4) <Chatham CT Fam.:251>
Vienna BRADFORD^6, b. 5 Nov. 1757* (m. George Talcott)**<135>**
Jeremiah BRADFORD^6, b. 15 Oct. 1758***<136>**
William BRADFORD^6, b. 10 Nov. 1760*, d. 21 Sept. 1824, Rocky Hill CT g.s.
Joel BRADFORD^6, b. 7 June 1764*; d. 5 Mar. 1837*, silversmith
Sally/Sarah STOCKING, (dau of Lamberton & Sarah), b. 18 June 1770, d. 3 Mar. 1842**<137>**
CHILDREN OF Joel BRADFORD^6 & Sally STOCKING: (9) <Chatham Fam.:251, by Martin Roberts>
Harry BRADFORD^7, bpt. 14 Oct. 1792, d.y.
Harry BRADFORD^7, bpt. 4 May 1794; d. 1827 or 1832, Cuba <Family Rcds>
Halsey Dart BRADFORD^7, bpt. 12 June 1796; d. c1830, NY <Family Rcds>
Rebecca BRADFORD^7, b. July 1802; (m. Diodate Brainerd, removed to NY) <Family Rcds>**<138>**
Susan BRADFORD^7, b. 10 Nov. 1805; (m. Hezekiah Young, removed to Summit Co., OH) <Family Rcds>
Hezekiah BRADFORD^7, b. 28 Mar. 1808; (resided NY) <Family Rcds>
Louisa BRADFORD^7, b. 20 Nov. 1810, d. unm.
George Talcott BRADFORD^7, b. 31 Dec. 1814; (resided San Iago, Cuba) <Family Rcds>
Dr. Charles Mansfield BRADFORD^7, b. 27 Feb. 1817
Mary SMITH, (dau of Enoch & Ruth), b. 10 May 1763, d. 17 Apr. 1810 <Chatham CT Fam.:251>
CHILDREN OF Jeremiah BRADFORD^6 (Jeremiah^5) & Mary SMITH: (9) <Chatham CT Fam.:251>
Child, b. 5 May 1783, d. ae 1 hour
Harriet BRADFORD^7, b. 25 Dec. 1784
Vienna BRADFORD^7, b. 5 Nov. 1786
Jeremiah BRADFORD^7, bpt. 4 Sept. 1791
Ruth BRADFORD^7, b. 26 June 1795
William Henry BRADFORD^7, b. 8 Mar. 1798
Gershom Wiswall BRADFORD^7, bpt. 20 July 1800

Gershom Wiswall BRADFORD^{7}, bpt. 31 Dec. 1803 (called Jeremiah), d. 9 Apr. 1810

Chauncy D. BRADFORD^{7}, b. 7 Sept. 1808

Lavinia Martha PEARSON, b. 23 Aug. 1825 <Family Rcds>

CHILDREN OF Dr. Charles Mansfield BRADFORD^{7} (Joel^{6}) & Lavinia Martha PEARSON: (7)<MO)>**<139>**

Helen Eliza BRADFORD^{8}, b. 17 June 1843

Charles Hardeman BRADFORD^{8}, b. 11 June 1845

Sarah Mildred BRADFORD^{8}, b. 1 Nov. 1847

Ida Isadore BRADFORD^{8}, b. 11 Apr. 1850

Isabella BRADFORD^{8}, b. 8 May 1852

Louisa Ellen BRADFORD^{8}, b. 16 Mar. 1854

George Herbert BRADFORD^{8}, b. 8 May 1858, d. 27 July 1860

CHILDREN OF Charles Hardeman BRADFORD^{8} & Suzan Lacy SMITH: (3) <Missouri>

Charles Ernest BRADFORD^{9}, b. 25 Mar. 1870

Dr. Thomas Glyndon BRADFORD^{9}, b. 15 Dec. 1872

Helen Louise BRADFORD^{9}, b. 9 Feb. 1875**<140>**

Elizabeth SEARS, b. c1757, d. 13 Oct. 1828, ae 71, Rocky Hill CT g.s.

CHILDREN OF William BRADFORD^{6} (Jeremiah^{5}) & Elizabeth SEARS: (7) <Stiles Ancient Wethersfield CT 2:127>

William BRADFORD^{7}, bpt. 26 Sept. 1784

Nancy BRADFORD^{7}, b. c1786, d. 21 Oct. 1872, ae 86 (wf of Sylvester Bulkley)

George BRADFORD^{7}, bpt. 28 Mar. 1790, d. 30 Sept. 1846, ae 58, Fayetteville NC

Horace BRADFORD^{7}, bpt. 27 Oct. 1793, 3rd Ch. Wethersfield; d. 27 June 1827, Fayetteville NC

Fanny BRADFORD^{7}, bpt. 8 Nov. 1795

Charlotte BRADFORD^{7}, bpt. 30 July 1797 (m. Richard Grimes)

Sophia BRADFORD^{7}, bpt. 18 Oct. 1801, d. 24 Feb. 1841, ae 40, NY (m. Charles H. Hill)

William BRADFORD^{7}, b. ( )

Betsey BRADFORD, widow of Ralph Bulkley, b. 28 Aug. 1782, d. 26 Nov. 1876, Rocky Hill <Wethersfield Inscriptions:212>**<141>**

Grace BRADFORD^{9} (Wm.$^{8-7-6}$), b. 2 Sept. 1868, New York, NY

Lindsay FAIRFAX, b. 5 May 1857

CHILDREN OF Lindsay FAIRFAX & Grace BRADFORD^{9}: (2)

Bradford Lindsay FAIRFAX^{10}, b. 11 Feb. 1893, New York, NY

Grace Lindsay FAIRFAX^{10}, b. 21 Apr. 1898, Eastbourne, Eng.

MICRO #11 of 15

Elizabeth PARKMAN, (dau of Samuel & Dorcas (Bowes)), b. 30 Apr. 1732

CHILDREN OF Job BRADFORD^{5} (Gershom^{4}) & Elizabeth PARKMAN: (7) <Boston>

Elizabeth BRADFORD^{6}, b. 1760 (m. Ben. Reynolds)

Dorcas BRADFORD^{6}, b. 1762 (m. Silas Noyes)

William Barnes BRADFORD^{6}, b. June 1764

Abigail BRADFORD^{6}, b. 1765 (m. Rev. John Allyne, Barnstable)

Rufus BRADFORD^{6}, b. 1767

Joseph Nash BRADFORD^{6}, b. 1769, d. 1818

Huldah BRADFORD^{6}, b. ( )

Ann TUFFTS, b. 1765, Boston, d. 24 Feb. 1826 (m. 1st John Merchant)

CHILDREN OF Joseph Nash BRADFORD^{6} & Ann (TUFFTS) Merchant: (6)

Claudius BRADFORD^{7}, b. 20 Jan. 1801, d. 2 Feb. 1863, Anti(uck) OH

Eleanor BRADFORD^{7}, b. 6 Mar. 1802 (m. Ben. Kent)

Lawrence BRADFORD^{7}, b. 10 Feb. 1803, lost at sea 1824

Lewis H. BRADFORD^{7}, b. 11 Jan. 1804, d. 17 Feb. 1884

Louise E. BRADFORD^{7}, b. 5 Mar. 1806 (m. Charles Thomas)

Charles F. BRADFORD^{7}, b. 5 Mar. 1806 (twins)

CHILDREN OF William Barnes BRADFORD^{6} (Job^{5}) & Mary TUFTS: (7) <Boston Rcd.Com.>

Mary BRADFORD^{7}, b. 7 Oct. 1786 <24:335>

William Barnes BRADFORD^{7}, b. 31 Oct. 1787 <24:336>

Elizabeth BRADFORD^{7}, b. 26 May 1789 <24:337>

John BRADFORD^{7}, b. 19 Sept. 1790 <24:338>

Rufus BRADFORD^{7}, b. 7 Oct. 1792 <24:340>

Samuel BRADFORD^{7}, b. 18 Jan. 1795 <24:343>

Joseph BRADFORD^{7}, b. 20 Jan. 1796 <24:344>

Moses NORMAN, b. c1718, d. 8 July 1776 <Newport Mercury>

CHILDREN OF Moses NORMAN & Priscilla BRADFORD^{5} (Gershom^{4}): (5)

Moses NORMAN^{6}, b. 1751, d. 25 Mar. 1806

Ann NORMAN^{6}, b. 1753, d. 21 July 1848 <Bristol RI VR 4:104> (m. Edw. Talbee)

Priscilla NORMAN^{6}, d. 1785 (m. Wm. Thurston)

Hope NORMAN^{6}, b. 1762, d. 18 July 1845 (m. Caleb Hargill)

John Bradford NORMAN^{6}, b. 1765, d. 13 Aug. 1805

CHILDREN OF Moses NORMAN^{6}: (8) <Newport Mercury>

Thomas NORMAN^{7}, b. 1782, d. 1847

Elizabeth NORMAN^{7}, b. 1785, d. 1841

Moses NORMAN^{7}, b. 1788, d. 1861

Ann NORMAN^{7}, b. 1790, d. 1852

Hope NORMAN^{7}, b. 1793, d. 1851 (m. Jason Butler)

Richard Cornell NORMAN^{7}, b. 1795, d. 1847

George Washington NORMAN^{7}, b. 1797

Priscilla Bradford NORMAN^{7}, b. 9 Apr. 1800 (m. Philip Stevens)

Bettey GREENWOOD, d. 22 Apr. 1759 <Rehoboth VR>

CHILDREN OF Solomon BRADFORD^{5} (Gershom^{4}) & 1st Bettey GREENWOOD: (5) <Rehoboth VR>

Noah BRADFORD^{6}, b. 26 Oct. 1750

Solomon BRADFORD^{6}, b. 11 Nov. 1751, d. 23 Nov. 1751

Bette BRADFORD^{6}, b. 6 Oct. 1752, d. 5 June 1753

Huldah BRADFORD^{6}, b. 7 May 1754; d. 18 Aug. 1804, Keene NH <Arnold VR 14:121> (m. James Morse)

Bette Greenwood BRADFORD^{6}, b. 26 June 1756, d. 21 June 1759

Mary RUTTENBURG, b. c1732, d. 21 May 1816, 84th yr <Arnold VR 20:601> (m.1st Mr. Owen, 2nd Solomon Bradford^{5})

CHILDREN OF Samuel BRADFORD & Elizabeth REYNOLDS, (dau of Jos.): (4) <Bristol RI 2:121>

Samuel BRADFORD, b. 10 May 1807

William Greenwood BRADFORD, b. 4 Mar. 1809

Elizabeth BRADFORD, b. 2 Feb. 1811

Ann Peck BRADFORD, b. 1 Dec. 1814

Nathaniel GILBERT, (son of Tho.), b. 19 July 1683, d. 17 Aug. 1765 <Taunton VR 1:176, 3:88>

CHILDREN OF Nathaniel GILBERT & Hannah BRADFORD^{4} (Samuel^{3}): (7 of 9)**<142>**

Hannah GILBERT^{5}, b. c1711, d. 10 Aug. 1747*, 36th yr, Taunton, Gilbert Cem.

Welthea GILBERT^{5}, b. ( ); d. aft. 15 Mar. 1792*

Thomas GILBERT^{5}, b. c1715 (eldest son), Berkley; d. 1 July 1797* (of Gagetown N.B.)

Mary GILBERT^{5}, b. c1715/6, Berkley; d. 7 Nov. 1811 <Norton VR:372>

Nathaniel GILBERT^{5}, b. ( ), d. pre 2 June 1757 (father's will)

Samuel GILBERT^{5}, b. ( )**<143>**

Abigail GILBERT^{5}, b. c1727, d. 17 Sept. 1747, 20th yr <Taunton VR 3:87>

Ebenezer SMITH, d. pre Aug. 1747*

CHILDREN OF Ebenezer SMITH & Hannah GILBERT^{5}: (7)**<144>**

James GODFREY, b. c1715, d. 3 Apr. 1795 <Norton VR:371>

CHILDREN OF James GODFREY & Mary GILBERT^{5} (Hannah Bradford^{4}): (8) <Norton VR:63>

Bathsheba GODFREY^{6}, b. 9 May 1738

Mary GODFREY^{6}, b. 4 May 1740

James GODFREY^{6}, b. 19 Mar. 1742, d. 18 May 1754 <VR:371>

Gershom GODFREY^{6}, b. 29 Feb. 1744

Samuel GODFREY^{6}, b. 7 July 1746; d. 12 Mar. 1801

Rachel GODFREY^{6}, b. 2 Sept. 1748

Abbe GODFREY^{6}, b. 10 Mar. 1752

Hannah GODFREY^{6}, b. 5 July 1754, d. 19 Dec. 1758 <VR:371>

CHILDREN OF Thomas GILBERT^{5} (Hannah Bradford^{4}) & Mary GODFREY*: (7)**<145>**

Ebenezer HATHAWAY, (son of Eben.), b. 13 July 1718 <Freetown VR 1:168>; d. 16 June 1791*,Freetown g.s. <NEHGR 8:2(52)>

CHILDREN OF Ebenezer HATHAWAY & Welthea GILBERT^{5} (Hannah Bradford^{4}): (8) <1-6, Freetown VR 1:155>

Gilbert HATHAWAY^{6}, b. 6 Feb. 1745/6

Triphena HATHAWAY^{6}, b. 6 Feb. 1745/6 (twins)

Ebenezer HATHAWAY^{6}, b. 25 July 1748; d. 3 Feb. 1811, Burton N.B.<Family Bible>**<146>**

Welthea HATHAWAY^{6}, b. 1 Sept. 1750

Shadrack HATHAWAY^{6}, b. 9 June 1752

Calvin HATHAWAY^{6}, b. ( ); d. betw. 15 Mar. 1792 - 1823*

Luther HATHAWAY^{6}, b. ( )

Hannah HATHAWAY^{6}, b. pre 1770*; d. betw. 21 Nov. 1823 (will) - 2 Dec. 1823 (notice), unm.<Bristol Co.Prob.61:224,180>

CHILDREN OF Ebenezer HATHAWAY & Hannah ( ): (5) <Family Bible>

Abigail HATHAWAY, b. 25 Mar. 1714

Ebenezer HATHAWAY, b. 13 July 1718

Silas HATHAWAY, b. 2 Sept. 1721

Hannah HATHAWAY, b. 12 May 1724

Benjamin HATHAWAY, b. 12 Jan. 1725

Mary HATHAWAY, (dau of Joshua), b. 12 Mar. 1751 <Freetown VR 1:208>;d. 30 May 1835, St. John**<146>**

CHILDREN OF Ebenezer HATHAWAY^{6} (Welthea Gilbert^{5}) & Mary HATHAWAY: (7) <1-3, Freetown VR 2:327>

Ebenezer HATHAWAY^{7}, b. 19 Mar. 1772; d. 2 July 1835 <Family Bible>

Warren HATHAWAY^{7}, b. 9 Jan. 1774 <Family Bible>

Cushi HATHAWAY^{7}, b. 1 June 1776

Calvin Luther HATHAWAY^{7}, b. 17 Sept. 1786; d. 27 Aug. 1865 <Family Bible>**<147>**

Charles Ruggles HATHAWAY^{7}, b. 30 Jan. 1789 <Family Bible>

James Gilbert HATHAWAY^{7}, b. 30 Jan. 1789 (twins) <Family Bible>, d. 1 June 1818 <Family Bible>

Thomas Gilbert HATHAWAY^{7}, b. 25 Feb. 1791, d. 24 Apr. 1855 <Family Bible>

Sarah HARRISON, b. 12 Aug. 1789, d. 7 Dec. 185(4) <Family Bible>

CHILDREN OF Calvin Luther HATHAWAY^{7} & 1st Sarah HARRISON: (11) <Family Bible>

Charles James HATHAWAY^{8}, b. 10 Aug. 1810, d. 29 Sept. 1819

Frederick William HATHAWAY^{8}, b. 12 Dec. 1811, d. 5 May 1866

George Luther HATHAWAY^{8}, b. 4 Aug. 1813, d. 5 July 1872

Wealthy Jane HATHAWAY^{8}, b. (1) Nov. 1815

James Gilbert HATHAWAY^{8}, b. 30 May 1818, d. 23 July 1851

Mary HATHAWAYS^{8}, b. 16 Apr. 1820

Charles Harrison HATHAWAY^{8}, b. 19 Aug. 1822

Ebenezer HATHAWAY^{8}, b. 11 Sept. 1824

Sarah Elizabeth HATHAWAY^{8}, b. 20 Dec. 1826, d. 14 Jan. 1848

Julia Caroline HATHAWAY^{8}, b. 27 July 1828

Ann Amelia HATHAWAY[8], b. 27 July 1828 (twins)

Mary BARKER, b. 29 May 1804 (2nd wf of Calvin Hathaway[7])

Elizabeth LITTLEHALE, (dau of John), b. 26 June 1834 <Family Bible>

CHILDREN OF Charles Harrison HATHAWAY[8] & Elizabeth LITTLEHALE: (4) <Portland, Family Bible>

Frederick William HATHAWAY[9], b. 5 Oct. 1854

John C.L. HATHAWAY[9], b. 27 Sept. 1856

Charles Harrison HATHAWAY[9], b. 28 Sept. 1858

Gertrude Annie HATHAWAY[9], b. 19 (Nov.) 1861

Ann CANBY, (dau of Jos.), b. 9 Sept. 1794, d. 5 Apr. 1827, Old Burial Ground, St. John N.B. <ME Hist.Gen.Recorder 7:226>

CHILDREN OF Thomas Gilbert HATHAWAY[7] & 1st Ann CANBY: (4) <Family Bible>

Thomas Ebenezer HATHAWAY[8], b. 17 June 1816

Joseph Canby HATHAWAY[8], b. 31 July 1820

William Henry HATHAWAY[8], b. 5 May 1825

Canby HATHAWAY[8], b. 8 Mar. 1827

<u>MICRO #12 of 15</u>

Harriet Eliza BATES, b. 16 Apr. 1812 (2nd wf of Tho. Gilbert Hathaway[7]) <Family Bible>

Elizabeth WILLIAMS[6] (Nathaniel[5-4], Eliz. Rogers[3], John[2]), bpt. 1 July 1750*; d. 2 Feb. 1779*, 29th yr, Freetown g.s., Old Forge Cem. <NEHGR 8:286>

CHILDREN OF Gilbert HATHAWAY[6] (Welthea Gilbert[5]) & 1st Elizabeth WILLIAMS: (5)<Freetown VR 3:151>

Tryphena HATHAWAY[7], b. 3 Dec. 1768; d. 10 May 1850*

Welthea HATHAWAY[7], b. 4 Aug. 1771; d. Feb. 1851*

Polly HATHAWAY[7], b. 28 June 1773; d. Oct. 1856*

Gilbert HATHAWAY[7], b. 29 Sept. 1775

Elizabeth HATHAWAY[7], b. 22 May 1777

Mary EVANS, (dau of David & Anna (Weaver)), b. 12 Feb. 1751 <Freetown VR 16:28>; d. aft. 2 Jan. 1797* (m. 1st Jonathan Weaver of Swansea)

CHILDREN OF Gilbert HATHAWAY[6] & 2nd Mary (EVANS) Weaver: (9) <Freetown VR 3:151>

Anne HATHAWAY[7], b. 17 Dec. 1780

Phebe HATHAWAY[7], b. 18 Mar. 1783

Sarah HATHAWAY[7], b. 11 Nov. 1784

Luther HATHAWAY[7], b. 14 Aug. 1786

David HATHAWAY[7], b. 24 Sept. 1788

Bailey HATHAWAY[7], b. 26 Aug. 1790

Amy HATHAWAY[7], b. 27 June 1792

Patience HATHAWAY[7], b. 8 Oct. 1794

Ebenezer HATHAWAY[7], b. 6 Nov. 1796

Richard RUGGLES, b. 4 Mar. 1744, d. 1832, of Clements N.S. <Ruggles Fam.:86>**<148>**

CHILDREN OF Richard RUGGLES & Wealthea HATHAWAY[6] (Welthea Gilbert[5]): (8) <Ruggles Fam.:86>

Bathsheba RUGGLES[7], b. 22 Sept. 1772 (m. John Hutchinson)

Cynthia RUGGLES[7], b. 1774 (m. John Durland)

Thomas RUGGLES[7], b. 1775

Sophia RUGGLES[7], b. 1777 (m. John Ryarson)

Richard RUGGLES[7], b. 1780

Wealthy RUGGLES[7], b. 1783 (m. Charles Tucker) <:87>

Tryphena RUGGLES[7], b. 1786 <:87>

Gilbert RUGGLES[7], b. 1788, d. 1841 <:87>

Ebenezer GAY, (son of Nathaniel), b. 15 Aug. 1696, Dedham; d. 18 Mar. 1787 <Hist.Hingham 2:264>

CHILDREN OF Ebenezer GAY & Jerusha BRADFORD[4] (Sam.[3]): (11) <Hist.Hingham 2:264-65>**<149>**

Samuel GAY[5], b. 15 Jan.1720/1; d. 1746

Abigail GAY^{5}, b. 8 Sept. 1722; d. 1729

Calvin GAY^{5}, b. 14 Sept. 1724; d. 1765*

Martin GAY^{5}, b. 29 Dec. 1726

Abigail GAY^{5}, b. 20 Aug. 1729; d. 1804, unm.

Celia GAY^{5}, b. 13 Aug. 1731, unm.

Jotham GAY^{5}, b. 11 Apr. 1733; d. 1802, Hingham

Jerusha GAY^{5}, b. 17 Mar. 1734/5

Ebenezer GAY^{5}, b. 3 Mar. 1736/7; d. 1738

Persis GAY^{5}, b. 2 Nov. 1739; d. 1752

Joanna GAY^{5}, b. 23 Nov. 1741; d. 1772, unm.

Abigail BELCHER, b. 23 Aug. 1695, Dedham; d. 15 Nov. 1746, S. Attleboro g.s.<VR:553>

CHILDREN OF Perez BRADFORD^{4} (Sam.^{3}) & Abigail BELCHER: (4 of 9)**<150>**

Perez BRADFORD^{5}, b. ( )

George BRADFORD^{5}, bpt. 22 Oct. 1732, Milton <NEHGR 23:446>; d. 11 May 1795*, Attleboro

John BRADFORD^{5}, d. 25 Apr. 1781* <Rehoboth VR:803>

Hannah BRADFORD^{5}, b. ( )

Sarah CARPENTER, b. 25 Feb. 1737*, Attleboro; d. 1836*, Cooperstown NY

CHILDREN OF George BRADFORD^{5} & Sarah CARPENTER: (4) <Attleboro VR:120>

George BRADFORD^{6}, b. 19 May 1757

Carpenter BRADFORD^{6}, b. 7 Mar. 1762

Sarah BRADFORD^{6}, b. 2 Dec. 1759

Perez BRADFORD^{6}, b. 25 July 1764

Martha JENCKES, (dau of Nath. & Catharine), b. 22 Feb. 1724/5 <Providence VR 5:446>

CHILDREN OF David HARRIS & Martha JENCKES: (3) <Providence VR 5:446>

Sarah HARRIS, b. ( )

Amey HARRIS, b. 9 (1st mth) 1756

George HARRIS, b. 22 (2nd mth) 1766

Jabez GAY, d. pre 26 Oct. 1801, Attleboro (prob.) <Bristol Co.Prob.38:392>

CHILDREN OF Jabez GAY & Hannah BRADFORD^{5} (Perez^{4}): (9) <Attleboro VR 1:143>

Hannah GAY^{6}, b. 4 Feb. 1747/8

Selah GAY^{6}, b. 13 July 1750

Philena GAY^{6}, b. 8 Apr. 1752

Monica GAY^{6}, b. 19 Feb. 1754

Molly GAY^{6}, b. 29 Nov. 1755

Jabez GAY^{6}, b. 12 Feb. 1758

Lucy GAY^{6}, b. 31 Oct. 1759 (m. Joel Metcalf)

Eleanor GAY^{6}, b. 14 Dec. 1763 <VR 1:128>

Lydia GAY^{6}, b. 10 July 1766 <VR 1:128>

Phebe STEARNS, d. 23 May 1770* <Rehoboth VR:803>

CHILDREN OF John BRADFORD^{5} (Perez^{4}) & 1st Phebe STEARNS:(5)* <Rehoboth VR:553>

John BRADFORD^{6}, b. 24 Jan. 1762

William BRADFORD^{6}, b. 23 Apr. 1763

Mary BRADFORD^{6}, b. 20 Nov. 1764

Phebe BRADFORD^{6}, b. 9 June 1767

Walter BRADFORD^{6}, b. 11 Dec. 1769

CHILDREN OF John BRADFORD^{5} & 2nd Sarah DOGGETT: (3)* <Rehoboth VR:553>

Hannah BRADFORD^{6}, b. 11 July 1772

Israel BRADFORD^{6}, b. 3 May 1775

Joel BRADFORD^{6}, b. 17 May 1777

CHILDREN OF Walter BRADFORD^{6} & Sarah MANN*: (5) <Medfield VR:23>

Hannah BRADFORD^{7}, b. 23 Jan. 1796
Stephen Sabin BRADFORD^{7}, b. 17 Aug. 1797
Olive BRADFORD^{7}, b. 4 Aug. 1799
Mary Ann BRADFORD^{7}, b. 28 Apr. 1804
Phebe BRADFORD^{7}, b. 29 Sept. 1810

CHILD OF Joseph BRADFORD^{5} (Perez^{4}) & Beulah MORSE*:
Joel BRADFORD^{6}, b. ( )

CHILDREN OF Joel BRADFORD^{6} & (Alsey) MOSIER: (12)**<151>**

CHILDREN OF Joseph JACKSON & Zipporah ( ): (8) <Cumberland, VR RI 3:5:105>
Mary JACKSON, b. 15 May 1732, Wrentham
Benjamin JACKSON, b. 5 Mar. 1735
Joseph JACKSON, b. 24 Feb. 1737
Jeremiah JACKSON, b. 2 Aug. 1739
Zipporah JACKSON, b. 14 May 1742
Nehemiah JACKSON, b. 11 Sept. 1744
Eleazer JACKSON, b. 10 Aug. 1747
Michael JACKSON, b. 7 June 1750

CHILDREN OF Perez BRADFORD^{5} (Perez^{4}) & Mary JACKSON, (dau of Jos.): (2) <Attleboro VR:9>
Perez BRADFORD^{6}, b. 13 Aug. 1750; d. 13 Mar. 1814*, fever, ae 61 <Sturbridge VR:310>
Betty BRADFORD^{6}, b. 17 Sept. 1753; d. 5 Aug. 1791 <Dudley VR:285>
Wife of Perez BRADFORD^{6}, d. 23 Feb. 1814, fever, ae 50 <Sturbridge VR:310>

CHILD OF Dr. James WOLCOTT & Betty BRADFORD^{6}:
Amy WOLCOTT^{7}, b. c1779, d. 7 Aug. 1813, ae 34 <Dudley VR:288>

Peter LANE, b. 25 May 1697, Hingham; d. 17 Mar. 1764, Hingham

CHILDREN OF Peter LANE & Welthea BRADFORD^{4} (Sam.^{3}): (7) <Hist.Hingham 2:414>
Hannah LANE^{5}, b. 27 May 1724 <2:415>
Irene LANE^{5}, b. 6 Jan. 1725/6
Lucy LANE^{5}, b. 6 June 1728, d. 9 Feb. 1733/4
George LANE^{5}, bpt. 6 June 1731, d. 12 May 1790
Lucy LANE^{5}, b. 16 Mar. 1734/5
Sybil LANE^{5}, b. 26 July 1741
Sarah LANE^{5}, bpt. 6 Oct. 1745

CHILDREN OF Samuel JOHNSON & Hannah LANE^{5} (Welthea Bradford^{4}): (7) <Hist.Hingham>
Hannah JOHNSON^{6}, b. 16 Jan. 1745/6 <2:386>; d. Deering NH, bur. Francestown NH
Celia JOHNSON^{6}, b. 8 Apr. 1748, d. 15 Feb. 1751/2
Esther JOHNSON^{6}, b. 22 Jan. 1749/50
Celia JOHNSON^{6}, b. 5 Aug. 1752, d. 9 Apr. 1754
Perez JOHNSON^{6}, b. 10 Dec. 1754, d. 8 Dec. 1757
Celia JOHNSON^{6}, b. 28 Oct. 1756
Benoni JOHNSON^{6}, ("alias Adrianensens"), bpt. 13 June 1762

Peleg EWELL, b. 19 Oct. 1739, Scituate(?); d. 30 Nov. 1823, Deering NH

CHILDREN OF Peleg EWELL & Hannah JOHNSON^{6} (Hannah Lane^{5}): (4) <Hist.Francestown NH:673-4>
Perez EWELL^{7}, b. 25 Sept. 1769, Scituate(?); d. 14 Mar. 1842 <Andover VR 2:428>
Hannah EWELL^{7}, b. ( )
Sally EWELL^{7}, b. ( )
Charlotte EWELL^{7}, b. 1 Sept. 1781, Lyndeborough, d. 4 Mar. 1869, Francestown

Betsey LORD, b. 27 Sept. 1770, Exeter NH; d. 28 July 1850, Walden VT

CHILDREN OF Perez EWELL^{7} & Betsey LORD: (8) <Hist.Francestown NH:673>
Isaac Watts EWELL^{8}, b. 10 June 1795
Betsey EWELL^{8}, b. 3 Apr. 1797

John EWELL[8], b. 2 July 1799
Hannah EWELL[8], b. 14 Nov. 1801
Sally EWELL[8], b. 24 Mar. 1804
Mary EWELL[8], b. ( )
Samuel EWELL[8], b. 7 June 1809
Julia EWELL[8], b. ( )
Kenelm BAKER, (son of Sam.), b. 23 Mar. 1657, Marshfield <MD 2:7>; d. betw. 29 Sept. 1712 (will)-6 Apr. 1713 (prob.) <MD 24:27>
CHILDREN OF Kenelm BAKER & Sarah BRADFORD[3]: (10) <Marshfield, 1-4, MD 5:234
Sarah BAKER[4], b. 28 Oct. 1688
Alice BAKER[4], b. 3 Nov. 1690; d. 14 June 1715, Marshfield g.s. <MD 10:49>
Elinor BAKER[4], b. 31 Mar. 1692
Abigail BAKER[4], b. 23 Dec. 1693; d. 25 Sept. 1753, Marshfield g.s.
Kenelm BAKER[4], b. 3 Nov. 1695 <MD 5:234>; d. 22 May 1771, Marshfield g.s. <MD 12:55>
Bethiah BAKER[4], b. 12 May 1699 <MD 6:20>
Keziah BAKER[4], b. 15 Aug. 1701 <MD 6:20>
Samuel BAKER[4], b. 5 Feb. 1702/3 <MD 6:20>; d. 4 Nov. 1793, Marshfield g.s. <MD 12:55>
William BAKER[4], b. 18 Oct. 1705 <MD 6:21>; d. aft. 22 May 1721 (guardian app'td) <MD 24:30>
Edward BAKER[4], b. 18 Oct. 1705 (twins) <MD 6:21>
Nathan THOMAS, (son of Sam. & Mercy), b. 21 Nov. 1688, Marshfield <MD 3:187>; d. 3 Nov. 1741, Marshfield g.s. <MD 13:131> (hus. of Alice Baker[4])
CHILD OF Gideon THOMAS & Abigail BAKER[4]:**<152>**
Anna THOMAS[5], bpt. 16 Apr. 1727, Marshfield; d. 1 Oct. 1812* <Pembroke VR:408>
Nathaniel OLDS, d. pre 15 May 1753 (wf. 2nd marr.)
CHILD OF Nathaniel OLDS & Anna THOMAS[5]:
Nathaniel OLDS[6], b. c1749
Elijah DAMON, b. c1729, d. 11 July 1810 <Pembroke VR:425>
CHILDREN OF Elijah DAMON & Anna (THOMAS) Olds: (4 of 7) <Marshfield VR 2:118>
Abigail DAMON[6], b. 15 July 1754
Mary DAMON[6], b. 13 Feb. 1756
Elizabeth DAMON[6], b. 5 Mar. 1758
Reuben DAMON[6], b. 30 Nov. 1759
Nancy DAMON[6], b. ( )
Mercy DAMON[6], b. ( )
Elijah DAMON[6], b. c1770, d. 15 Nov. 1811, ae 41 <Pembroke VR:407>
Deborah SOPER, (dau of Alex. & Molley), b. 7 June 1769 <Pembroke VR:358>; d. 25 Jan. 1830, Pemb.
CHILDREN OF Elijah DAMON[6] & Deborah SOPER: (8) <Pembroke VR:461>
Gideon Thomas DAMON[7], b. 26 Mar. 1791
William P. DAMON[7], b. 16 Jan. 1793
Betsey DAMON[7], b. 16 Dec. 1794
Elijah DAMON[7], b. 15 Apr. 1797
Nathaniel DAMON[7], b. 27 July 1799
Deborah DAMON[7], b. 9 Dec. 1801
Mary DAMON[7], b. 21 Mar. 1803
Anna Thomas DAMMON[7], b. 10 Apr. 1805
Emily JOSELYN, b. 28 Aug. 1805 <Family Bible>
CHILDREN OF Elijah DAMON[7] & Emily JOSELYN: (3) <Family Bible>
Emily DAMON[8], b. 10 June 1828
Elijah DAMON[8], b. 3 Nov. 1829
William DAMON[8], b. 3 Nov. 1829 (twins)

Patience DOTY^{3} (John^{2}), b. 3 June 1697, Plymouth<MD 1:206>; d. 18 Feb. 1784, Marshfield<MD 12:55>

CHILDREN OF Kenelm BAKER^{4} (Sarah Bradford^{3}) & Patience DOTY: (7) <Marshfield>

John BAKER^{5}, b. 18 Oct. 1719 <MD 30:154>; d. ?1 July 1804*, Marshfield g.s. <MD 12:55>

Alice BAKER^{5}, b. 26 Jan. 1722 <MD 30:154>

Sarah BAKER^{5}, b. 21 Apr. 1726 <MD 9:186>; d. 29 Nov. 1792 <MD 11:72>

Kenelm BAKER^{5}, b. 1 July 1728 <MD 9:186>

Elizabeth BAKER^{5}, b. 29 July 1730 <MD 9:186>

William BAKER^{5}, b. 16 Oct. 1734 <MD 30:147>

Lucy BAKER^{5}, b. 15 May 1737 <MD 30:147>

Hannah FORD^{5} (James^{4}, Abigail Snow^{3}, Abigail Warren^{2}), b. 18 Oct. 1705*, Marshfield <MD 6:70>; d. 28 Apr. 1800, Marshfield g.s. <MD 12:55>

CHILDREN OF Samuel BAKER^{4} (Sarah Bradford^{3}) & Hannah FORD: (9) <Duxbury, 4-9, MD 11:239>

Eleanor BAKER^{5}, b. 21 Sept. 1727 <MD 11:238>

Hannah BAKER^{5}, b. 25 Feb. 1729 <MD 11:238>

Bethiah BAKER^{5}, b. 11 May 1733 <MD 11:238>; d. 19 Jan. 1822* <Hanover VR>

Samuel BAKER^{5}, b. 26 Feb. 1735

James BAKER^{5}, b. 4 Jan. 1737

Thomas BAKER^{5}, b. 24 Jan. 1739

Charles BAKER^{5}, b. 26 Apr. 1741

Elijah BAKER^{5}, b. 1 July 1744

Abigail BAKER^{5}, b. 24 Sept. 1746

CHILDREN OF Joseph THOMAS & Eleanor BAKER^{5}: (2)*

Joseph THOMAS^{6}, b. 13 May 1756

Ichabod THOMAS^{6}, b. 17 Mar. 1758; d. 24 Feb. 1845

Henry PERRY, d. 23 Mar. 1815*, ae 80, Pembroke (hus. of Bethiah Baker^{5})

CHILDREN OF Charles BAKER^{5} (Sam.^{4}) & Deborah WILLIAMSON*: (6) <Marshfield VR>

Eleanor BAKER^{6}, b. 21 Jan. 1769

Abigail BAKER^{6}, b. 18 May 1770

Charles BAKER^{6}, b. 28 Dec. 1771

Samuel BAKER^{6}, b. 24 Mar. 1774

Deborah BAKER^{6}, b. 10 Jan. 1781

John BAKER^{6}, b. 28 Mar. 1788

John SHERMAN, (son of John), b. 17 Oct. 1682, Marshfield <MD 2:251>

CHILDREN OF John SHERMAN & Sarah BAKER^{4} (Sarah Bradford^{3}): (9) <Rochester VR 1:41>

Sarah SHERMAN^{5}, b. 15 Aug. 1714

Jane SHERMAN^{5}, b. 2 Oct. 1716

Alice SHERMAN^{5}, b. 29 July 1719

John SHERMAN^{5}, b. 27 July 1721

Abigail SHERMAN^{5}, b. ( )

Bethiah SHERMAN^{5}, b. 26 Jan. 1724

William SHERMAN^{5}, b. 11 Jan. 1726

Keziah SHERMAN^{5}, b. 28 Oct. 1728

Samuel SHERMAN^{5}, b. 2 Jan. 1730/1

MICRO #13 of 15

CHILDREN OF Thomas BRADFORD^{3} & Ann RAYMOND, (dau of Joshua): (4) <Norwich CT>**<153>**

Joshua BRADFORD^{4}, b. 23 Nov. 1682

Susanna BRADFORD^{4}, b. ( )

James BRADFORD^{4}, b. c1688, d. 26 Mar. 1762, Canterbury CT g.s.

Jerusha BRADFORD^{4}, bpt. 28 May 1693, Norwich CT; d. 4 Nov. 1739 <Lebanon CT VR:223>

CHILDREN OF James BRADFORD^{4} & 1st Edith ( ): (5) <Canterbury CT VR>**<154>**

Thomas BRADFORD[5], bpt. 12 July 1713
John BRADFORD[5], bpt. 27 Feb. 1714, d.y.
Jerusha BRADFORD[5], bpt. 1 July 1716
William BRADFORD[5], b. 1 July 1718
Sarah BRADFORD[5], bpt. 2 Oct. 1720
Susanna ADAMS, (dau of Sam.), d. 17 Mar. 1752 <Canterbury CT VR>
CHILDREN OF James BRADFORD[4] & 2nd Susanna ADAMS: (3)
Ann BRADFORD[5], bpt. 10 July 1726
Mary BRADFORD[5], bpt. June 1728
James BRADFORD[5], bpt. 1733; d. pre 1762 (father's estate)
Zerviah LOTHROP, d. 22 Oct. 1740 <Canterbury CT VR>
CHILD OF William BRADFORD[5] & 1st Zerviah LOTHROP: <Canterbury CT VR>
Zerviah BRADFORD[6], b. 6 Sept. 1740
Mary CLEAVELAND[6] (Abigail Paine[5], Elisha[4], Mary Snow[3], Constance Hopkins[2]), d. 6 Aug. 1765
CHILDREN OF William BRADFORD[5] & 2nd Mary CLEVELAND: (13) <MD 15:66>
Mary BRADFORD[6], b. 1 Mar. 1744
William BRADFORD[6], b. 4 Mar. 1745
Ebenezer BRADFORD[6], b. 29 May 1746
David BRADFORD[6], b. 8 May 1748
John BRADFORD[6], b. 27 July 1750
Joshua BRADFORD[6], b. 17 Oct. 1751
Abigail BRADFORD[6], b. 2 Sept. 1753
James BRADFORD[6], b. 12 Feb. 1755
Olive BRADFORD[6], b. 13 July 1756
Josiah BRADFORD[6], b. 25 Nov. 1757
Lydia BRADFORD[6], b. 2 July 1760
Beulah BRADFORD[6], b. 3 Sept. 1763
Moses BRADFORD[6], b. 6 Aug. 1765
CHILD OF William BRADFORD[5] & 3rd Martha WARREN:
Joseph BRADFORD[6], b. 22 Jan. 1767 <MD 15:66>
CHILDREN OF Hezekiah NEWCOMB & Jerusha BRADFORD[4] (Tho.[3]): (9) <Lebanon CT VR:223>**<155>**
Silas NEWCOMB[5], b. 2 Sept. 1717
Peter NEWCOMB[5], b. 28 Nov. 1718
Anne NEWCOMB[5], b. 4 Mar. 1720
Hezekiah NEWCOMB[5], b. 27 Dec. 1722
Thomas NEWCOMB[5], b. 3 Sept. 1724
Jerusha NEWCOMB[5], b. 24 Mar. 1726
Elizabeth NEWCOMB[5], b. 19 Dec. 1727
Samuel NEWCOMB[5], b. 2 Sept. 1729
Jemima NEWCOMB[5], b. 14 Dec. 1730
James NEWCOMB[5], b. 7 Feb. 1732/3
Rebecca BARTLETT[4] (Ben.[3], Mary Warren[2]), d. pre 3 June 1742 <MD 6:45, 17:254>**<156>**
CHILDREN OF William BRADFORD[3] & Rebecca BARTLETT: (3)**<157>**
Alice BRADFORD[4], b. ( ) <MD 6:45>; d. aft. 23 Jan. 1749**<158>**
Sarah BRADFORD[4], b. c1686; d. 11 Apr. 1718, ae about 32, Plymouth g.s. <Kingman:11>
William BRADFORD[4], b. pre 18 Dec. 1686 <MD 4:144, 16:116>; d. 9 Mar. 1729/30, Kingston<MD 24:155>
William BARNES, b. c1670, d. 31 Mar. 1751, 81st yr, Plymouth g.s. <Burial Hill by Drew:256>
CHILDREN OF William BARNES & Alice BRADFORD[4]: (5) <Plymouth, MD 5:53>
William BARNES[5], b. 5 Jan. 1706; d. 16 Apr. 1730 or 31, drowned
Lemuel BARNES[5], b. 16 Feb. 1707; d. 1751 <MD 5:53>

Mercy BARNES^{5}, b. 19 Dec. 1708; d. 25 Dec. 1791, Plymouth g.s. <Burial Hill by Drew:197>

Benjamin BARNES^{5}, b. 11 Dec. 1711, d.y.

Benjamin BARNES^{5}, b. 20 Dec. 1717; d. 12 Apr. 1760, Plymouth <MD 5:53>**<159>**

Experience RIDER, (dau of Josiah), b. 13 Jan. 1724/5, Plymouth <MD 13:167>

CHILDREN OF Benjamin BARNES^{5} & Experience RIDER: (8) <Plymouth, MD 15:161>

Alice BARNES^{6}, b. 2 Apr. 1743

Mercy BARNES^{6}, b. 8 July 1745; d. pre 7 Mar. 1786* (adm.), unm. <Plymouth Co.Prob.#1036>**<160>**

Bradford BARNES^{6}, b. 1 Aug. 1747; d. 1816*, Danby VT <Hist.Danby (1869)>

Benjamin BARNES^{6}, b. 14 Jan. 1749/50; d. 26 Sept. 1838 <Plymouth TR 3:30>

Josiah BARNES^{6}, b. 15 Jan. 1752

Isaac BARNES^{6}, b. 16 June 1754; d. aft. 5 May 1800*

Experience BARNES^{6}, b. 11 May 1756**<161>**

Sarah BARNES^{6}, b. 13 June 1760

MICRO #14 of 15

Samuel BATTLES, b. c1734, d. 31 July 1812, ae 78, Plymouth**<162>**

CHILDREN OF Samuel BATTLES & Alice BARNES^{6}: (6) <1-2, Plymouth, MD 21:166>

Elizabeth BATTLES^{7}, b. 17 Sept. 1763

Polley BATTLES^{7}, b. 2 Dec. 1765 (m. Joseph Holmes)**<163>**

Samuel BATTLES^{7}, b. ( )**<164>**

Sarah BATTLES^{7}, b. ( ) (m. John Gray)

Experience BATTLES^{7}, b. ( ) (m. George Perkins)**<165>**

John BATTLES^{7}, b. ( )**<166>**

George PERKINS, d. 6 Feb. 1834*, 54th yr, Plymouth g.s. <Burial Hill by Drew:177>**<165>**

Deborah HOLMES^{7} (Ichabod^{6}, Hannah Sylvester^{5}, Hannah Bartlett^{4}, Jos.^{3}, Mary Warren^{2}), b. 19 June 1755; d. 7 Feb. 1833 <Plymouth TR 3:30>

CHILDREN OF Benjamin BARNES^{6} (Ben.^{5}) & Deborah HOLMES: (5)

Benjamin BARNES^{7}, b. 1775

Bradford BARNES^{7}, b. 1777

Samuel BARNES^{7}, b. ( )

Deborah BARNES^{7}, b. 1786, d. 1871 (m. John Gooding)

Ellis BARNES^{7}, b. ( )

CHILDREN OF Bradford BARNES^{6} (Ben.^{5}) & Sarah HOWARD: (4)**<166a>**

Lucy HARLOW^{7} (Jonathan^{6}, Tho.^{5}, Wm.^{4}, Rebecca Bartlett^{3}, Mary Warren^{2}), b. 9 Mar. 1758, Plymouth <MD 15:161> (wf of Isaac Barnes^{6} (Ben.^{5}))

Lydia BARNES^{5} (Mary Bartlett^{4}, Jos.^{3}, Mary Warren^{2}), b. 4 Dec. 1713, Plymouth <MD 2:20>

CHILDREN OF Lemuel BARNES^{5} (Alice Bradford^{4}) & Lydia BARNES: (8) <Plymouth, MD 15:162>

Hannah BARNES^{6}, b. 6 Aug. 1735

Lydia BARNES^{6}, b. 9 Sept. 1737

William BARNES^{6}, b. 4 Mar. 1740/1

Lemuel BARNES^{6}, b. 30 Mar. 1743, d. 29 July 1743

Alice BARNES^{6}, b. 30 June 1744

Lemuel BARNES^{6}, b. 11 Aug. 1746

John BARNES^{6}, b. 11 Sept. 1748

Isaac BARNES^{6}, b. 2 May 1750, d. Oct. 1750

Samuel COLE, (*son of Ephraim), d. 18 Aug. 1731, ae 23, Plymouth g.s.<Burial Hill by Drew:198>

CHILDREN OF Samuel COLE & Mercy BARNES^{5} (Alice Bradford^{4}): (3) <Plymouth, MD 14:240>

James COLE^{6}, b. 12 Sept. 1729, d. 10 Dec. 1729

Ephraim COLE^{6}, b. 14 Nov. 1730, d. 25 Jan. 1730/1

Samuel COLE^{6}, b. 14 Nov. 1731, d. 18 Mar. 1811**<167>**

Barnabas HEDGE, (*son of John & Thankful), b. 27 Dec. 1704*, Yarmouth <MD 11:112>; d. 18 Jan.

1762, Plymouth g.s. <Burial Hill by Drew:197>

CHILDREN OF Barnabas HEDGE & Mercy (BARNES^{5}) Cole: (9) <Plymouth, MD 15:41>

Mercy HEDGE^{6}, b. 27 Nov. 1734, d. 20 Sept. 1779, Plymouth g.s. <MD 15:41>

Lemuel HEDGE^{6}, b. 20 Sept. 1736, d. 3 Oct. 1736

Abigail HEDGE^{6}, b. 2 Dec. 1737, d. 9 Dec. 1763, unm.**<168>**

Barnabas HEDGE^{6}, b. 3 May 1740, d. Feb. 1814, Plymouth

Lemuel HEDGE^{6}, b. 25 June 1742, d. 7 July 1742

Lothrop HEDGE^{6}, b. 5 Nov. 1744, d. 20 Jan. 1744/5

Sarah HEDGE^{6}, b. 5 June 1746

John HEDGE^{6}, b. ( )

William HEDGE^{6}, b. ( )

CHILDREN OF Barnabas HEDGE^{6} & Hannah HEDGE: (2) <Plymouth, MD 21:21>

Dau., b. 14 Oct. 1763, d. 14 Oct. 1763, about 1 hour

Barnabas HEDGE^{7}, b. 15 Sept. 1764; d. pre 10 Aug. 1840 (adm.) <"10:386A">**<169>**

Eunice Dennie BURR, b. c1772, d. 13 Nov. 1849, ae 77, lung fever, Boston, bur. Plymouth <Plymouth TR 4:370,371> (see below)

CHILDREN OF Barnabas HEDGE^{7} & Eunice Dennie BURR: (15) <Plymouth, MD 21:21>

Barnabas HEDGE^{8}, b. 13 Nov. 1791; d. ?12 July 1841*

Hannah HEDGE^{8}, b. 19 Jan. 1793, d. 2 Feb. 1796

Eunice Dennie HEDGE^{8}, b. 17 Aug. 1794, d. 29 Sept. 1794

Eunice Dennie HEDGE^{8}, b. 1 Sept. 1795, d. 18 Oct. 1795

Isaac Lothrop HEDGE^{8}, b. 8 Mar. 1797, d. 22 Sept. 1797

Isaac Lothrop HEDGE^{8}, b. 7 Dec. 1798

Thomas HEDGE^{8}, b. 22 Oct. 1800

Abigail HEDGE^{8}, b. 22 Nov. 1802

Hannah HEDGE^{8}, b. 1 Aug. 1804

Eunice Dennie HEDGE^{8}, b. 28 June 1806

Ellen Hobart HEDGE^{8}, b. 5 July 1808

John Sloss Hobart HEDGE^{8}, b. 8 Mar. 1810, d. 17 Oct. 1810

Priscilla Lothrop HEDGE^{8}, b. 5 May 1811, d. 31 Oct. 1814

Elizabeth HEDGE^{8}, b. 28 Nov. 1813

Priscilla Lothrop HEDGE^{8}, b. 11 July 1816; d. 18 Oct. 1816 <Col.Soc.Coll.23:664>

CHILDREN OF Gershom BURR & Priscilla LOTHROP: (4) <Burr Gen.(1891):156>

Gershom BURR, bpt. 5 Aug. 1768

Abigail BURR, bpt. 9 Sept. 1771

Eunice Dennie BURR, bpt. 11 Oct. 1772

Priscilla BURR, bpt. 10 July 1774

CHILDREN OF Thomas HEDGE^{8} (Barnabas^{7}) & Lydia Coffin GOODWIN: (7) <Plymouth, MD 21:22>

Mary Ellen HEDGE^{9}, b. 12 May 1825

Abby Burr HEDGE^{9}, b. 17 Sept. 1826

Edward Goodwin HEDGE^{9}, b. 11 Oct. 1828

Albert Goodwin HEDGE^{9}, b. 19 May 1832

Lydia Goodwin HEDGE^{9}, b. 24 Jan. 1834

Thomas B. HEDGE^{9}, b. 6 July 1838

William HEDGE^{9}, b. ( )

CHILDREN OF Barnabas HEDGE^{8} (Barnabas^{7}) & Tryphena COVINGTON: (3) <Plymouth, MD 21:21>

James Gorham HEDGE^{9}, b. 13 Oct. 1812

Sarah Thomas HEDGE^{9}, b. 11 Aug. 1814

William HEDGE^{9}, b. 9 Nov. 1815

Thomas DAVIS, b. c1722, d. 7 Mar. 1785, 63rd yr, Plymouth g.s. <Kingman:57>

CHILDREN OF Thomas DAVIS & Mercy HEDGE[6] (Mercy Barnes[5]): (9) <Plymouth, MD 18:211>
Sarah DAVIS[7], b. 29 June 1754, d. 10 Nov. 1821, Plymouth (m. LeBaron Bradford)**<170>**
Thomas DAVIS[7], b. 26 June 1756, d. 21 Jan. 1805, Boston
William DAVIS[7], b. 13 July 1758, d. 6 Jan. 1826, Plymouth**<171>**
John DAVIS[7], b. 25 Jan. 1761
Samuel DAVIS[7], b. 5 Mar. 1765; d. 10 July 1829**<172>**
Dau., b. 7 Aug. 1766; d. 14 Aug. 1766 <MD 18:211>
Isaac DAVIS[7], b. 7 Oct. 1771
Wendell DAVIS[7], b. 13 Feb. 1776**<173>**
Son, b. 18 Sept. 1779, stillborn
Jonathan BARNES[3] (Jonathan[2], John[1]), d. pre 27 Dec. 1736 (adm.) <Plymouth Co.Prob.#1012, 9:171>
CHILDREN OF Jonathan BARNES & Sarah BRADFORD[4] (Wm.[3]): (4) <Plymouth, 1-3, MD 7:176>
Sarah BARNES[5], b. 9 Oct. 1709
Rebecca BARNES[5], b. 14 Mar. 1711 (m. Ebenezer Phinney)
Lydia BARNES[5], b. 30 Jan. 1714/5
Hannah BARNES[5], b. 1718; d. 15 June 1793, 75th yr, Plymouth g.s.**<174>**
Stephen CHURCHILL, (son of Stephen), b. 24 Aug. 1717, Plymouth <MD 12:13>; d. 5 Sept. 1751, Plymouth g.s.**<175>**
CHILDREN OF Stephen CHURCHILL & Hannah BARNES[5] (Sarah Bradford[4]): (7) <Plymouth, MD 15:210>
Sarah CHURCHILL[6], b. 18 July 1739; d. 13 Aug. 1740
Mercy CHURCHILL[6], b. 18 July 1739 (twins); d. 13 July 1740 <MD 15:210>
Stephen CHURCHILL[6], b. 17 July 1741; d. 14 Sept. 1742 <MD 15:210>
Stephen CHURCHILL[6], b. 7 June 1743
Hannah CHURCHILL[6], b. 14 Feb. 1744/5
Zadock CHURCHILL[6], b. 16 July 1747; d. pre 10 Oct. 1793 <Plymouth Co.Prob.#3995, 26:181>
Peleg CHURCHILL[6], b. 9 July 1749; d. 5 Oct. 1750 <MD 15:210>
CHILDREN OF John OTIS* & Hannah CHURCHILL[6]: (2) <Plymouth, MD 22:106>
Temperance OTIS[7], b. 18 June 1766
Hannah OTIS[7], b. June 1768
CHILD OF Rufus ROBBINS & Temperance OTIS[7]: <Plymouth>
Hannah ROBBINS[8], b. c1792, d. 31 Oct. 1890, ae 98y4m20d, old age & cancer, Paxton, bur. Worcester (widow, Hannah Laforest) <Mass.VR 411:534>
Lucy BURBANK, (*dau of Tim. & Mary), b. 4 May 1745, Plymouth <MD 14:240>(m. Stephen Churchill[6])
Eleanor (CHURCHILL) Leach, (dau of David & Sally (Collins)), b. c1811, Plymouth, d. 4 July 1886, ae 75y5m, endocarditis, Plymouth, widow <Mass.VR 374:347>
Bathsheba RIDER[7] (Jos.[6], Mary Southworth[5], Desire Gray[4], Mary Winslow[3], Mary Chilton[2]), b. 7 Nov. 1750 <Plymouth VR 2:69>
CHILD OF Zadock CHURCHILL[6] (Hannah Barnes[5]) & Bathsheba RIDER:
Bathsheba RIDER, b. c1776 (ae 17 in 1793) <Plymouth Co.Prob.#3995, 26:281>
CHILDREN OF Joseph SMITH & Lydia BARNES[5] (Sarah Bradford[4]): (2) <Plymouth TR 1:178>
Sarah SMITH[6], b. 9 Feb. 1738/9
Lydia SMITH[6], b. 23 May 1744
Thomas DOANE, b. 10 Jan. 1701/2*, Eastham <MD 9:8>; d. pre 13 May 1747 (adm.)
CHILDREN OF Thomas DOANE & Sarah BARNES[5] (Sarah Bradford[4]): (5)**<176>**
Betsey DOANE, (*dau of Sarah Barnes[5]), b. c1743, d. 10 June 1832, S. Dennis g.s. <MD 11:14>
Israel NICKERSON, b. c1740, d. 30 Sept. 1791, S. Dennis g.s. <MD 11:14>
CHILDREN OF Israel NICKERSON & Betsey DOANE: (11) <Dennis, MD 7:67; dths, MD 11:14>
Israel NICKERSON, b. 19 Sept. 1768
Betsey NICKERSON, b. 23 Aug. 1770; d. 12 Oct. 1791
Nehemiah NICKERSON, b. 5 Mar. 1772; d. 11 Oct. 1791

Jonathan NICKERSON, b. 4 Jan. 1774

Hannah NICKERSON, b. 16 Apr. 1776; d. 12 Oct. 1791

Sarah NICKERSON, b. 22 Mar. 1778; d. 4 Oct. 1791

Bathsheba NICKERSON, b. 30 Apr. 1780

Mulford NICKERSON, b. 28 July 1782 <MD 7:68>

Polly NICKERSON, b. 1 Dec. 1784 <MD 7:68>; d. 29 May 1867

Horace NICKERSON, b. 7 May 1787 <MD 7:68>; d. 1 Oct. 1791

Thomas NICKERSON, b. 14 Dec. 1789 <MD 7:68>; d. 11 July 1827

Elizabeth FINNEY^{4} (Elizabeth Warren^{3}, Jos.^{2}), b. 8 Feb. 1690, Plymouth <MD 1:208>; d. betw. 31 Dec. 1772 <Plymouth Co.Deeds 57:44>- 15 July 1778 (adm.) <Plymouth Co.Prob.#2521> <MD 25:25>

CHILDREN OF William BRADFORD^{4} (Wm.^{3}) & Elizabeth FINNEY: (9) <1-4, Plymouth, MD 12:87>

Elizabeth BRADFORD^{5}, b. 10 Jan. 1714, d. 21 Jan. 1714

Charles BRADFORD^{5}, b. 4 Jan. 1715/6

Sarah BRADFORD^{5}, b. 15 Dec. 1718

Jerusha BRADFORD^{5}, b. 20 Dec. 1722; d. 23 Apr. 1820, Middleboro g.s. <MD 12:142>

Josiah BRADFORD^{5}, b. betw. 29 Nov. 1722 - 1730; d. 26 Apr. 1777* <Plymouth ChR:407>

William BRADFORD^{5}, b. 9 May 1726, Kingston <MD 24:155>; d. 16 or 23 July 1726 <MD 7:23>

Mercy BRADFORD^{5}, b. 15 Jan. 1728/9, Kingston <MD 24:155>; d. 4 July 1762*, Plymouth g.s.

Elizabeth BRADFORD^{5}, b. 15 Sept. 1730, Kingston, d. 10 Oct. 1730 <MD 24:155>

Samuel HARLOW^{6} (Wm.^{5}, Sam.^{4}, Rebecca Bartlett^{3}, Mary Warren^{2}), b. 7 Sept. 1726,Plymouth<MD 12:87> d. 17 June 1767, Plymouth g.s. <Kingman:40> (hus of Mercy Bradford^{5}) (see Warren Family)

Edward SPARROW, d. betw. 24 Aug. 1744 - 5 June 1745 (adm.) <MD 25:27>

CHILD OF Edward SPARROW & Jerusha BRADFORD^{5}:

Edward SPARROW^{6}, b. 2 Apr. 1745, Plymouth, d. 29 Jan. 1817 <MD 13:169, 14:135>

Josiah CARVER, (son of Josiah & Dorothy), b. 25 Sept. 1724, Plymouth <MD 13:173>; d. 5 Apr. 1799, Middleboro g.s., The Green <MD 12:142> (2nd hus of Jerusha Bradford^{5})

Rhoda BUMP/BUMPAS, (*dau of Philip & Mary (Burge)), b. 22 Feb. 1748*, Wareham; d. 10 Jan. 1816, Middleboro g.s., The Green <MD 14:135>

CHILDREN OF Edward SPARROW^{6} & Rhoda BUMP/BUMPAS: (2 of 11)**<177>**

Edward SPARROW^{7}, b. 10 Jan. 1768*, Wareham

Elizabeth SPARROW^{7}, b. 15 Mar. 1778*; d. 5 Sept. 1856, Middleboro, ae 78 <Mass.VR 103:210>

CHILD OF Gorham WOOD & Elizabeth SPARROW^{7}:

Melinda WOOD, b. c1806, Middleboro, d. 14 Sept. 1887, ae 81y5m7d, Foxboro, bur. Middleboro <Mass. VR 383:286> (widow Melinda Curtis)

Hannah RIDER^{6} (Sam.^{5}, John^{4}, Sarah Bartlett^{3}, Mary Warren^{2}), b. 26 Nov. 1726, Plymouth <MD 15:38>

CHILDREN OF Josiah BRADFORD^{5} (Wm.^{4}) & Hannah RIDER: (3 of 9) <Plymouth, MD 3:121>**<178>**

William BRADFORD^{6}, b. 30 Oct. 1749; d. 14 Jan. 1794*, Roxbury, Plymouth g.s.**<179>**

Hannah BRADFORD^{6}, b. 9 July 1751

Josiah BRADFORD^{6}, b. 7 Feb. 1754

Ruth DUNHAM, (dau of Amos), b. 1753*, Plymouth; d. 22 May 1813, ae 60, Plymouth g.s.**<179>**

CHILD OF William BRADFORD^{6} & Ruth DUNHAM:**<180>**

Josiah BRADFORD^{7}*, b. ( )

MICRO #15 of 15

Zephaniah HOLMES, (*son of Nathaniel & Joanna), b. ?16 Jan. 1712/13, Plymouth <MD 2:80>

CHILDREN OF Zephaniah HOLMES & Sarah BRADFORD^{5}: (5) <Plymouth, MD 15:162>

Bradford HOLMES^{6}, b. 9 Oct. 1739, d. 14 May 1740

Zephaniah HOLMES^{6}, b. 30 July 1741

Sarah HOLMES^{6}, b. 23 Dec. 1743

Luce HOLMES^{6}, b. 13 June 1747

Deborah HOLMES^{6}, b. 8 Apr. 1750

FOOTNOTES

<1> p.112, Dorothy is believed to be the daughter of John May or Henry May but further research is needed. See Eugene Stratton's Plymouth Colony:324-36 for discussion.
<2> p.112, Alice Southworth was bpt. 3 Aug. 1590, Wrington, co. Somerset, England. <MD 38:90>
<3> p.112, A fourth child is listed, an unnamed daughter with a question mark.
<4> p.112, The source of the volume & page number is not given. (poss. Mass.VR)
<5> p.114, The deaths of many of those listed here can be found in the preceeding two lists of "Bradford Deaths".
<6> p.114, She is called Mrs. Mary Church in the marriage record.
<7> p.114, Possibly the "child of Daniel" who d. 14 June 1750 <Bristol RI VR 2:15>.
<8> p.115, Bowman is not certain whether these are death dates or the date the obit appeared in the newspaper.
<9> p.115, Theophilus Bradford is called "of Dorsetshire, England".
<10> p.116, Jael Hobart, dau of Rev. Peter Hobart & Elizabeth Ilbrook, bpt. 30 Dec. 1643, Hingham <Hingham Hist.2:90>.
<11> p.116, Hannah Cole, dau of James Cole & Abigail Davenport. Although she was married to Elisha Bradford for over 15 years they had no children. MFIP, Bradford:14 gives her date of death as the 15th of Aug. with the source being Plymouth ChR 1:219. However, a check of the church records shows they do not give the day, only Aug. 1718.
<12> p.116, She has also been called Bathsheba LeBrock/LaBrock, dau of Francis Brock & Sarah Hobart.
<13> p.116, Every time I come across Elisha Bradford I have to chuckle to myself. Although his first marriage of 15 years ended with no children he certainly made up for it with his second wife, Bathshua. She was just 16 years old when she married 50 year old Elisha in 1719. Over the next 25 years she bore him 15 children, the equivalency of one child every 18 months. Elisha was 76 years old when his last child was born. Sturdy stock those Bradford men!
<14> p.116, Descent of Joshua Bradford^{4} - (Israel^{3}, Wm.^{2}). Joshua, wife Hannah and baby Winslow were killed by Indians 22 May 1758 at Friendship ME.
<15> p.117, Alice Richards, dau of Thomas Richards & Welthean Loring, b. England.
<16> p.117, Bowman makes note of the fact that only 10 children are by his 1st wife, however all 15 children are listed out of order. For easier reference the order of birth has been corrected with birthdates, or aproximate dates, added for children #2-15. <Mayflower Increasings:23-25>
<17> p.117, Although her identity has not been found, there is speculation that her maiden name was Fitch and she was the widow of a Wiswall. <Mayflower Increasings:23>
<18> p.117, Mary Wood, dau of John Wood/Atwood & Mary Masterson.
<18a>p.117, d. 16 Mar. 1729/30 <Kingston VR>
<19> p.117, d. 19 Feb. 1734/5, Enfield CT <VR 1:119>
<20> p.117, Bowman lists four additional Fitch children, viz: John, Bridget, Jerusha and William, the source appears to be NEHGR 17:42. MFIP, Bradford:7 lists the following 3 additional children, (b. Canterbury CT), viz: Jerusha b. c1696, Lucy b. c1698 and Theophilus b. c1701.
<20a>p.117, Jabez Fitch, b. 30 Jan. 1702, Canterbury CT. MFIP, Bradford:27 gives his date of death as 3 Jan. 1784, not 31 Jan. as stated here.
<21> p.117, His date of birth is given as 11 Apr. 1682 (no source), while MFIP, Bradford:24 states he was b. 2 Apr. 1683 (no source). He was the son of Jonathan Metcalf and Hannah Kenric.
<22> p.117, Two children are missing from this list, viz: Abijah, b. 15 Nov. 1709, d.y. (twin of Abiel) and the last child Azuba born a few months after her father's death in 1723. Sybil Metcalf d. 26 Dec. 1722, Falmouth.
<23> p.118, There is no listing of the children of Nathaniel Collins & Alice Adams. Their eight children can be found in MFIP, Bradford:24, viz: Mary, Ann, John, Alice, Nathaniel, William, Edward and Alice, all recorded at Enfield CT.
<24> p.118, MFIP, Bradford uses this date of 27 Sept. 1725 as the date his estate was divided, and says he died pre this date.
<25> p.118, The children of Rev. Samuel Whiting & Elizabeth Adams are not given, only Sybil and Samuel are carried further. They had 14 children, viz: Anne, Samuel d.y., Elizabeth, William, Joseph d.y., John, Sybil, Martha, Mary, Eliphalet, Elisha, Samuel, Joseph and Nathan. <See MFIP, Bradford:23>
<26> p.118, History Of Ancient Windham CT, William L. Weaver. Willimantic, 1864.
<27> p.118, Ibed., The remaining five Backus children are without data, viz: Ebenezer, Mary DeLucena, Whiting and Charles.
<28> p.119, An undocumented notation states Ann Whiting was the dau. of William Whiting^{5} & Ann Raymond, with William being the son of Rev. Samual Whiting and Elizabeth Adams^{4}.
<29> p.119, There appears to be some question as to which Mary married John Whiting. On John Whiting's chart, she is called Mary DeForest with the name "Burton?" in pencil. On her daughter Elizabeth's chart, the maiden name of DeForest is underlined twice. On Ephraim Burton's chart, his daughter Mary Burton is credited with marrying John Whiting.
<30> p.120, She is also called Sarah Cornelia Whiting.
<31> p.120, Lydia Gale, dau of Abraham Gale & Sarah Fiske, b. 6 July 1699, Watertown CT. MFIP, Bradford:27 gives her date of death as 22 Aug. 1753, not 20 Aug. as stated here, with the source being Canterbury CT VR 1:147.
<32> p.120, MFIP, Bradford:28 provides the birth dates of six of the Fitch children in Canterbury CT, viz: Jerusha, b. 30 Jan. 1723; Alice, b. 8 Jan. 1724/5; Perez, b. 5 Dec. 1726; Jabez, b. 23 May 1729, Norwich CT; Lydia & Lucy, b. 24 June 1736 (twins). Bowman gives Lydia a baptism date of 27 Jan. 1734 but this is obviously an error.
<33> p.120, d. 1 May 1749 <Canterbury CT VR 1:147>.

<34> p.120, The deaths of two unnamed children are cited from Mansfield ChR:427,428. The first child d. 25 Jan. 1813, ae 6 hours. If the twins, Fitch & Lydia were indeed b. 25 Feb. 1813, then this date of a child b. 25 Jan. 1813 cannot be correct. It could possibly be an error for 25 Feb. and refer to Lydia's death. The second date refers to a child who d. 21 Apr. 1814, ae 1 yr. This date could refer to Fitch who, Weaver says, d. 18 Mar. 1814. There are numerous inconsistencies between the Mansfield Church records and Weaver's, History of Ancient Windham CT. As well as the above noted discrepencies, the church records are interpreted to include Daniel and Ellis, while Weaver names them David & Alice. Jabez is given a baptism date of 28 Nov. 1819, while Weaver says he was not born until 10 Sept. 1820.
<35> p.120, Weaver's Hist. of Ancient Windham mistakenly states she m. James Brown.
<36> p.121, History of the Connecticut Valley in Mass., with Illustrations and Biographical Sketches of Some of its Prominent Men & Pioneers. 2 Vols. 1879. Philadelphia.
<37> p.121, Elizabeth Phinney, dau of Jonathan Phinney & Joanna Kinnicut, bpt. 27 Oct. 1695.
<38> p.121, His wife was Elizabeth Groce, dau of Isaac Groce & Dorothy Cobb, bpt. 12 July 1730, Hingham, d. 30 Apr. 1773, Kingston. <Hist.Hingham 2:281>
<39> p.122, Burial Hill, by Benjamin Drew, p.205, #1428.
<40> p.122, Ibed., p.206, #1435.
<41> p.122, Ibed., p.144, #983.
<42> p.123, Eight Bradford children are listed very faintly in pencil with no additional data. Only 3 names can be positively read, viz: William, Thankful and Betsey. The source listed is Davis' Ancient Landmarks:309.
<43> p.123, The remaining five Bradford children are written in pencil without dates, viz: Adreanna, Edgar, Joseph, Seth Russell, Anna Robinson and George Russell.
<44> p.123, Betsey (Briggs) Bradford, b. 1797, d. 26 Nov. 1843, ae 46y4m, Plymouth g.s. <Burial Hill by Drew:144, #982>
<45> p.123, Ibed., All five children are on the same stone as their mother.
<46> p.124, No data accompanies the names of the six Faunce chldren, viz: Matilda Bradford, William Thomas, Ellen, Mary Sampson, David Brainerd and David Brainerd.
<47> p.125, George Bradford was a printer, 52 Green St., Charlestown MA.
<48> p.125, "1st Street, Bangor ME" is included.
<49> p.127, Samuel Harlow was a dealer in stoves, hardware, etc. on Main St., Plymouth. The generation numbers given to Samuel suggest Mayflower descent although it is not shown.
<50> p.127, A later page states her mother was Rebecca Ellis.
<51> p.127, d. New York City <Burial Hill by Drew, p.206, #1428>
<52> p.127, Ibed.
<53> p.128, d. Oct. 1800 <Ibed.>
<54> p.128, Six children are listed (without dates) for James Madison Bradford and Betsey Mason Holmes, (dau. of Samuel Holmes & Betsey Johnson), viz: Elizabeth Mason, James Madison, Branch Johnson, William Briggs, Joseph and Frances Maria. This family removed to California.
<55> p.130, Although MFIP, Bradford:12 says "5 Dec. or Feb. 1741", Bowman makes note of the month, saying "Dec. is plainly shown in photo" which probably refers to g.s.
<56> p.130, b. 14 Mar. 1738 <Kingston VR>; d. Sept. 1816, Turner ME <MFIP, Bradford:57>.
<57> p.130, b. 28 Sept. 1715, son of John Holmes & Mercy Ford <MD 7:209>. MFIP, Bradford:57 states Peleg and wife Abigail died in N.S.
<58> p.130, MFIP, Bradford:55 gives three additional Chandler children, viz: Nathaniel, bpt. 14 Nov. 1756, d. 14 June 1773, ae 20y9m, Duxbury; Judah, bpt. 14 Nov. 1756, d. 24 Apr. 1772, ae 21y2m, Duxbury and Sceva, bpt. 12 June 1757.
<59> p.130, b. 9 Aug. 1711 <Plympton VR>.
<60> p.131, The remaining eight Bradford children are in pencil with no dates, viz: Hira, D( ), Ethel, Judith, Jeanette, Solome and 2 unnamed sons <The Bradford Family in Maine>.
<61> p.131, Four additional children are named in Nathan Chandler's will, dated 26 Feb. 1795. He mentions wife, Esther (2nd wife Esther Glass?) and children, Ira, Ruth, Lucy and Hannah. He also names four sons of his "eldest son dec'd" (Ephraim). <Plymouth Co.Prob.#3795, 35:324,325>
<62> p.131, MD 7:24
<63> p.131, Molly (Doten) Chandler, d. 27 Apr. 1808, ae 53, Kingston g.s. <MD 7:25>
<64> p.131, d. Nov. 1779, ae 17m, Kingston g.s. <MD 7:25>
<65> p.131, Kingston g.s. <MD 7:25>
<66> p.131, The six additional Bradford children are listed without dates. MFIP, Bradford:57, 58 provides birth dates, (prob. b. Springfield VT) as well as an 11th child, Rebecca, viz: Hosea; Abigail, b. 23 Jan. 1765; Deborah; Joel, b. 25 Jan. 1773; Ephraim, b. 1780; Rebecca, prob. d.y. and Cynthia.
<67> p.132, b. May 1670, son of Richard & Mary <Norwich CT VR 1:35>.
<68> p.132, MFIP, Bradford:35,36 gives three additional Wheat children, viz: Solomon, bpt. 19 Dec. 1731, Cantebury CT, d.y.; Mary, bpt. 1 July 1733, Old Lyme CT and Jemima, bpt. 28 July 1740, Ashford CT.
<69> p.133, An accompanying note reads, "Bingham Gen.(1927) 1:10 gives 2 more children - Jonathan Bingham, b. 19 Mar. 1734, d. 4 May 1824, unm. and Abigail Bingham, b. 18 July 1736, d. 12 Feb. 1814, unm.".
<70> p.133, Throughout the files, three additional Bingham children are mentioned, viz: Abner, Jacob and Benjamin.
<71> p.133, The additional nine Hartshorn children are listed without dates, viz: Elias Humphrey, Elisha Eldridge, Laura Adaline, Harriete Ann, Lorenzo Dow, James Ripley, and two unnamed children who died young.
<72> p.134, She is possibly Hannah Wheat^5 (Anna Ripley^4).
<73> p.134, Samuel Webb, son of Samuel & Mary (Adams), b. 14 May 1690, Braintree, d. 6 Mar.

1779, Rockingham VT. <MFIP, Bradford:31>
<74> p.135, "Statement of Settlement with Administrator on Estate of Mr. Ebenezer Ripley late of Windham dec^d Feb. 19th 1823." His identity is not shown. An interesting note - the cost of his gravestone was $14.00. <Windham CT 16:65>
<75> p.136, This date of death is based on the possibility of her being the wife of Capt. Samuel Bingham who died on this date.
<76> p.136, Benjamin Seabury, son of Samuel Seabury & Abigail Allen, b. 24 Sept. 1689, Duxbury. No children are listed for Benjamin and wife, Margaret Ripley^4 (Hannah Bradford^3), however, MFIP, Bradford:32 lists three born Lebanon CT, viz: Abigail, Elisha and Sarah.
<77> p.137, Winslow Tracy, (son of John Tracy & Mary Winslow), b. 9 Feb. 1688/9 <Norwich CT VR> 1:8> He died c1767 and his wife Rachel Ripley, d. 4 Apr. 1782, Norwich CT.<MFIP, Bradford:32>
<78> p.137, "Susanna Porter, dau of Nicholas who d. 1773, Bridgewater" is written in pencil. Although Bradford Descendants (1951):34 repeats this claim, MFIP, Bradford:53 states the evidence points to her being Susanna Potter, dau of Hopestill & Lydia, b. 15 Oct. 1715.
<79> p.138, VR RI 13:201 states he d. <u>21 Mar.</u> 1823.
<80> p.138, Possibly the Calvin Ripley whose estate was administered 6 Sept. 1842. <Bristol Co. Prob. 84:402>
<81> p.138, d. 12 Dec. 1768 <Kingston VR>. Thomas Adams and Bathsheba Bradford^4 (Israel^3) had six children recorded at Kingston, viz: Sarah, b. 3 Dec. 1732; Joshua, b. 21 Nov. 1735; Bartlett, b. 19 Mar. 1738/9; Nathaniel, b. 18 Nov. 1740; Mary, b. 3 Sept. 1744 and Deborah, b.17 Oct. 1747.
<82> p.139, MFIP, Bradford:54 shows her to be Mary Samson, (dau of Peleg Samson & Mary Ring), b. 6 Jan. 1724, Pembroke, widow of Nathaniel Cooke.
<83> p.139, b. 28 Oct. 1766 <Plympton VR>.
<84> p.139, Lemuel Bradford d. 1 Mar. 1855, ae 66, Plymouth; his wife Bathsheba Bradford d. 22 Jan. 1861, ae 68y10m12d. <Burial Hill by Drew:103>

Bowman includes three additional Bradford children in pencil which are confirmed in Burial Hill by Drew:104, as follows: Ebenezer Nelson, b. c1817, d. 20 June 1833, ae 15y7m; Lydia Nelson, b. c1824, d. 13 Sept. 1826, ae 2; Bathsheba, b. c1815, d. 15 Jan. 1837, ae 22.
<85> p.139, Lost at sea Sept. 1846, ae 25y8m. <Burial Hill by Drew:103>
<86> p.139, d. 23 Mar. 1854, ae 21. <Burial Hill by Drew:104>
<87> p.139, Joshua Bradford, his wife Hannah and youngest child, Winslow, were killed by Indians 22 May 1758 at Friendship ME.

MFIP, Bradford:54 lists two additional Bradford children, viz: Elisha (Bowman has "Philip*") b. 15 Oct. 1755 and Winslow, bpt. 30 July 1757, Marshfield.
<88> p.139, An accompanying note states Joseph Bradford and Abigail Sterling had nine children, not named here but listed in Sterling Gen.2:1037.
<89> p.140, Joshua Hersey, (son of William Hersey & Rebecca Chubbuck, b. 29 Mar. 1678/9, Hingham, d. 30 Sept. 1740, Hingham. <MFIP, Bradford:16>
<90> p.140, MD 7:23.
<91> p.140, Is he the Nathaniel Bradford shown in <114> below? MD 7:23 lists a Sarah Bradford, widow of Nathaniel, who d. 24 July 1834, 54th yr.
<92> p.140, MD 7:22 shows a Charles Bradford who d. 5 Mar. 1837, 34th yr.
<93> p.140, See <113> below.
<94> p.140, d. 2 Sept. 1802, Kingston g.s. <MD 7:23>.
<95> p.140, MD 7:23 shows an Ellis Bradford who d. 28 Aug. 1829, 30th yr, Charleston SC, bur. Kingston.
<96> p.141, Elizabeth Ann Bradford, dau of Rufus & Elizabeth, d. 8 Jan. 1838, ae 3y3m14d, Kingston g.s. <MD 7:23>.
<97> p.141, d. 12 May 1834, Kingston g.s. <MD 7:23>.
<98> p.141, Kingston g.s. <MD 7:23>.
<99> p.141, Two additional children are listed for John Bradford but it is not clear by which wife, viz: John, b. 26 Dec. 1763 and Lucy, b. 14 Dec. 1767, d. 27 Dec. 1800.
<100> p.141, Benjamin Waterman d. 17 Oct. 1845, 86th yr and 1st wife Lucy d. 27 Dec. 1800, Kingston g.s. <MD 7:223>. Benjamin remarried Lucy's sister Exzuma, no issue. See <99> for Lucy.
<101> p.141, Kingston g.s. <MD 7:223>.
<102> p.141, 36th yr, Kingston g.s. <MD 7:23>.
<103> p.141, Kingston g.s. <MD 7:23>.
<104> p.141, (Ibed.,)
<105> p.141, (Ibed.,)
<106> p.141, See <99> above for John's birth.
<107> p.142, Three children are listed for Austin Bradford & Aurelia C.E. Bissell without dates, viz: Austin E., Aurelia R.F. and Lucy A.
<108> p.142, Seven Brooks children are listed without dates, viz: Lucy A., Charles L., Lucy A., Mills S., Laura P., Herbert J. and Eugene H.
<109> p.142, Two Darling children are listed without dates, viz: John B. and Mary J.
<110> p.142, A later note states she was b. 8 Mar. 1760.
<111> p.142, Kingston ChR say he d. <u>17 Jan.</u> 1836.
<112> p.142, Two separate pages provide lists of James Bradford's children. The first appeared after the Robert Bradford & Sarah Stetson list on p.140 but did not identify James or his wife Sarah. (The fact that this data apeared there implies the unidentified listings following it on pp. 140 & 141 could be his descendants, e.g. Ellis Bradford). Two children are included in the first list who are not included in the second listing, viz: Nathaniel, b. 9 Apr. 1768 and Ellis, b. 1773 <Kingston VR>. It seems unlikely however that James & Sarah would have a child born in 1768. Sarah would have been only 13 yrs old at the time, plus, the Kingston VR:245,320 give their marriage intention as occurring on 30 Jan. 1773.

<113> p.142, MD 7:23 shows a Capt. Ellis Bradford who d. 5 Nov. 1848, ae 75, Kingston g.s. as well as Dorothy, wife of Capt. Ellis, who d. 13 Mar. 1830, ae 55 and Priscilla, widow of Capt. Ellis, who d. 4 Apr. 1850, ae 59y11m11d.
<114> p.142, MD 7:23 shows a Nathaniel Bradford who d. 23 Mar. 1820, 45th yr Kingston g.s.
<115> p.143, Although only one child is listed for Gideon Bradford & Jane Paddock, Gideon's will, dated 11 May 1784, mentions the following seven children: Levi, Samuel, Joseph, Gideon, Calvin, Sarah (wf of Freeman Ellis) and Jane/Jenny (wf of Noah Bisbee). <Plymouth Co.Prob.#2533>.
<116> p.144, The remaining five Bradford children are listed in pencil with an approximate date of birth, viz: Jane, c1779; Lucy, c1783; Calvin, c1785; Sarah, c1789 and Lydia, c1797.
<117> p.144, A second wife for Luther Bradford is written in pencil, Mary Standish[7] (Jonathan[6], Moses[5-4], Eben.[3], Alex.[2]). Luther's will dated 23 Mar. 1858 mentions wife Mary and 10 children, viz: Lydia (wf of Jacob Barrows), Ruth Cook (wf of Thomas A. Pratt), Irene Shaw (wf of Simeon Pratt), Sarah Ann (wf of Jonathan B. Waterman), Aroline Bartlett (wf of Prince E. Penniman), Clara L. (minor), Joseph Warren, Dewitt Clinton and William Harrison (minor). <Plymouth Co.Prob.>
<118> p.144, Her age at death would put her year of birth c1817 which is impossible since her mother Ruth (Holmes) Bradford died in 1815.
<118a> p.144, There is no listing of their children, John Bradford's will mentions his seven children, viz: John, eldest dau. Polly (wf of Ellis Standish), 2nd dau. Eunice (wf of Asa Washburn), Nancy, Sukey, Sopha and Jane. <Plymouth Co.Prob.42:130>. A later note gives the birth of Mary Bradford, 10 Oct. 1777 and that of her husband Ellis Standish, 26 Feb. 1773.
<119> p.145, A copy of a letter appears in the files from George Partridge to James Bradford of Plainfield CT, dated at Duxbury, 12 June 1795. In the letter, George informs James of the death of his brother, Eliphalet Bradford. The following excerpt may be of interest to his descendants: "...Last sunday your Brother Eliphlet expired, after a lingering sickness of 4 or 5 months. He had a bad cold & cough in ye winter, tho' he continued to walk out to his neighbours till 8 or 10 days before he dyed. He expired in the full possession of his reason & was calm & resigned to the will of heaven..."
<120> p.146, The Bible records give this child's name as "Josiah" (1754-1809).
<121> p.146, Three Bradford children are listed in pencil without dates, viz: Henry, Edward Anthony and Sidney.
<122> p.146, b. 6 Apr. 1676, dau of James & Priscilla Fitch. <Norwich CT VR 1:39>
<123> p.147, Mary (Sherwood) Fitch, dau of Mathew Sherwood & Mary Fitch, and widow of Daniel Fitch. <MFIP, Bradford:11>
<124> p.149, William d. 2 Jan. 1727, Chilmark. His wife, Mary Bradford d. 7 May 1720, Chilmark <Mayflower Source Rcds.:108,111>.
<125> p.150, Samuel Stevens, son of William Stevens & Mary Meiggs, b. 1 Mar. 1656, Guilford CT <VR:A60>. MFIP, Bradford:9 gives a 2nd child of Samuel & Melatiah, William, b. 2 Feb. 1705/6, Killingworth CT <VR 2:160>.
<126> p.150, Samuel Steele, son of John & Mary (Warner), b. Farmington CT <MFIP, Bradford:7>.
<127> p.150, MFIP, Bradford:8 lists an 8th child, Elizabeth, bpt. 25 Feb. 1682/3, d. pre 5 Feb. 1711/12.
<128> p.150, MFIP, Bradford:29 says he d. 13 Mar.
<129> p.150, MFIP, Bradford:30 says she was the dau of Ebenezer Hopkins & Mary Butler and was bpt. 30 Jan..
<130> p.150, An accompanying note reads, "She was brought up by her uncle Rev. George Colton of Bolton CT who had adopted her".
<131> p.151, d. 25 Apr. 1760, Duxbury g.s. <MD 10:171>.
<132> p.152, Paybodie Bradford & Lydia Freeman[5] (Jos.[4], Edmund[3-2-1]) had an illegitimate chld, Paybodie, b. 1 Mar. 1758. <Bible Rcd.>
<133> p.153, The remaining five Bradford children are without dates, viz: Alexander, Noah, Hopestill, Eliphalet and Rachel.

MFIP, Bradford:38,39 states that Solomon, b. c1711 and Alexander, b. c1713 were Gershom Bradford's children by his unnamed first wife who died before his second marriage in 1716, however, no reason (or source) is given for this claim.
<134> p.153, Priscilla Bradford married Col. Sylvester Child and had three children (no dates), viz: Mary R., Priscilla Bradford and Abigail Miller.
<135> p.154, A later note, citing Haddam Neck Cong. Church (F.F. Starr copy), says Vienna was bpt. 16 Oct. 1757.
<136> p.154, On separate pages are given two dates of death for Jeremiah Bradford. Chatham CT Fam.:251 (mss.) by Martin Roberts gives the date of 21 June 1836, Berlin VT. Yale Biogaphies & Annals 4:103 gives the date as 25 Dec. 1835, Berlin VT "at the house of his youngest dau." This reference also states he married Mary Smith, dau. of Capt. Enoch Smith & Ruth Goodrich and had 3 sons and 3 daughters. History of Middlesex Co. CT:202 also supports the death date of 25 Dec.
<137> p.154, Haddam Neck, Old Cem., CT has her death as 3 Mar. 1841, ae 66.
<138> p.154, (Ibed.,) says she d. 11 July 1858, ae 55.
<139> p.155, According to the family records, Charles Mansfield Bradford graduated in medicine from the Univ. of Penn. Mar. 1839, immediately moved to Missouri and began his medical practice at Arrow Rock, July 1840.
<140> p.155, Unmarried in 1946 and residing at 4807 Gaston Ave, Dallas, Texas.
<141> p.155, Betsey and her husband witnessed the deed of release of the children of William & Elizabeth Bradford. <Hartford CT Prob.37:220,279>
<142> p.156, Nathaniel's will dated 2 June 1757, mentions two daughters, dec'd and bur.Taunton.
<143> p.156, A pencilled note suggests he married Sarah Dean. Is he the Samuel Gilbert & wf Sarah mentioned in Bristol Co.Prob.147:163, 149:147 thus: "Samuel Gilbert...Inhabitant of Berkley Mass. has absented himself for near two year...said Samuel Gilbert volenterily went to our

Enimies and is still absent from his Habitation", dated 10 May 1777. He is called deceased by 6 Sept. 1796.
<144> p.156, No dates accompany the names of the following seven Smith children, viz: Lemuel, John, Ebenezer, Mary, Sible, Hannah and Abigail.
<145> p.157, Seven Gilbert children are listed without data, viz: Thomas, Peres, Bradford, Molly, Bathsheba, Hannah and Deborah.
<146> p.157, The Family Bible of Calvin Hathaway states Ebenezer was b. 6 Aug. 1742, and his wife Mary was born 23 Mar. 1750.
<147> p.157, Calvin L. Hathaway was the author of The History of N.B., Fredericton, 1846. N.B. Bibliography:41 says he was born at Burton, Sunbury co., N.B. and died 20 Aug. 1866, Burton N.B.
<148> p.158, The Ruggles Family of England & America, by Henry Stoddard Ruggles. Boston. 1893.
<149> p.158, The year of birth only is listed, the dates have been added.
<150> p.159, The nine Bradford children are listed without dates. MFIP, Bradford:40 provides the birth dates, b. Swansea, viz: Abigail, b. 15 May 1721, Dedham; Hannah, b. c1724; Elizabeth; Perez, bpt. 5 Jan. 1728/9, Milton; Joel, bpt. 30 Sept. 1730, Milton; George, John, b. 1734; Joseph, b. 1737 and Mary.
<151> p.160, Twelve Bradford children are listed in pencil without dates, viz: Abigail, Beulah, Lydia, Eunice, Isaac, James, Seth, Anne, Joel, Gardner, Gamaliel and Joseph.
<152> p.161, This particular file sheet is missing from the files. They were married 9 Feb. 1720/1, Marshfield and the following six Thomas children are recorded there, viz: Abigail, b. 4 Dec. 1722; Mercy, b. 27 June 1725; Anna, b. 7 Aug. 1726; Elizabeth, b. 10 May 1729; Sarah and Eleanor, b. 10 Feb. 1732/3 (twins).
<153> p.162, Ann Raymond, (dau of Joshua Raymond & Elizabeth Smith), b. 12 May 1664 <New London CT VR1:14>. MFIP, Bradford:6 gives two additional children, William, bpt. 1695, prob. d.y. and a dau. who m. Edward Dewolfe c1712. The birthdate is also given for James, 24 Mar. 1689.
<154> p.162, She is identified by MFIP, Bradford:21 as Edith Adams, dau. of Pelatiah & Ruth, b. 25 June 1688, Chelmsford.
<155> p.163, Hezekiah Newcomb, son of Simeon & Deborah, b. Edgartown, d. 15 Aug. 1772, ae 79, Lebanon CT. <MFIP, Bradford:22>
<156> p.163, MFIP, Warren:33 states she d. 14 Dec. 1741 <Duxbury VR>, the wife of 3rd husband, Caleb Samson.
<157> p.163, Mentioned here is the inquest held into the death of William Bradford[3], "a cart overurned on him". <Quarter Sessions, 1687-1721, p.26>
<158> p.163, MFIP, Bradford:19 states she was b. 28 Jan. 1680, prob. Plymouth and d. 1775.
<159> p.164, Burial Hill by Drew:258.
<160> p.164, Is she the Mercy Barnes who d. 16 Dec. 1783?. <Plymouth ChR 1:413>
<161> p.164, Bowman attributes Experience Barnes[6] with marrying Elisha Corban in 1772. However, a careful examination of the probate records proves it was her mother, Experience (Rider) Barnes who married Elisha. In the settlement of the estate of Benjamin Barnes[5], 9 Nov. 1778, the children mention "Elisha Corbin & Experience his wife (our mother)". <Plymouth Co.Prob.25:408>

(NOTE: In **Mayflower Marriages**, companion volume to this book, p.54, the line should read: Experience (RIDER) Barnes and 2nd Elisha Corban not Experience Barnes[6] and Elisha Corban.)

<162> p.164, Burial Hill by Drew:176.
<163> p.164, Is she the Polly Holmes, wf of Joseph who d. 3 July 1794, ae 26yr? <Drew:257>.
<164> p.164, William Battles, (son of Samuel Battles & Deborah Atwood), d. 12 Dec. 1802, ae 2m18d. <Burial Hill by Drew:176>.
<165> p.164, Written in pencil next to her name is "?Pella?" Burial Hill by Drew:177 lists a Pella, wife of George Perkins, who was b. 5 Feb. 1782, d. 2 Feb. 1826. Also listed are two children, viz: William, b. 19 June 1810, d. 4 Sept. 1811 & Hannah, b. 2 Mar. 1816, d. 16 Sept. 1825.
<166> p.164, Is he the John Battles listed in Burial Hill by Drew:241? b. 26 Feb. 1778, d. 20 Sept. 1855; first wife Elizabeth d. 29 Sept. 1800, ae 23y5m and second wife Lydia, d. 20 Apr. 1865, ae 86y3m.
<166a> p.164, History of Danby VT (1869) gives the following four Barnes children, viz: Hosea, Benjamin, Bradford Jr. & Sally. Sarah Howard is said to have d. 1830. Bradford Barnes[7] moved to Buffalo NY, living in 1869. Benjamin Barnes[7] d. 1861, ae 72. He and his wife Zilphia Gifford had four children, viz: Clarissa, Sophronia, Harriet and Heman. Heman Barnes[8] d. 1859 "from the effects of cancer".
<167> p.164, Burial Hill by Drew:196.
<168> p.165, Plymouth g.s. <Burial Hill by Drew:81>
<169> p.165, A Barnabas Hedge, d. 12 July 1841 <Plymouth TR 3:57>. Could the administration date be wrong and these are the same men?
<170> p.166, Sarah (Davis) Bradford is buried next to her son, LeBaron Bradford, b. 1780, d. Nov. 1846, Plymouth g.s. <Burial Hill by Drew:81>
<171> p.166, William's wife, Rebecca Morton, b. 30 Dec. 1762, d. 1 Apr. 1847, Plymouth g.s. Their son, Thomas Davis[8], b. 3 Apr. 1791, d. 14 Sept. 1848. <Burial Hill by Drew:82>
<172> p.166, Plymouth g.s. <Burial Hill by Drew:81>
<173> p.166, The Hon. Wendell Davis, d. 30 Dec. 1830, Sandwich, Plymouth g.s. <Drew:81>
<174> p.166, Wife of 2nd husband Jeremiah Howes, buried next to 1st husband <Drew:225>
<175> p.166, Burial Hill by Drew:225.
<176> p.166, The five Doane children are listed without dates, viz: Nehemiah, Thomas, Reuben, Mary and Elizabeth.
<177> p.167, The remaining nine Sparrow children are listed without dates, viz: Jerusha, Susanna, Rhoda, Philip, Josiah, William, James, Bradford and Polly.
<178> p.167, The remaining six Bradford children are in pencil without dates, viz: Samuel,

Charles, Zephaniah, Betsey, Lois and Mercy. All nine children are mentioned in a deed dated 30 Jan. 1797. At this time Wiliam was deceased, Hannah, Lois and Betsey were "spinsters" and Mercy was married to Thomas Perkins. <Plymouth Co.Deeds 82:40>
<179> p.167, Burial Hill by Drew:80.
<180> p.167, (Ibed.,) Four additional Bradford children are given, all buried in Plymouth,viz: Amos, b. c1777, d. 3 Aug. 1794, ae 17y, in "Marinico"; Isaac, b. c1785, d. 16 Mar. 1806, ae 21; Elizabeth, d. 15 Nov. 1787, ae 7 wks and James, d. 28 Dec. 1788, ae 7 wks 6 days.

* * * * *

REFERENCE LIST

GENEALOGICAL ARTICLES PERTAINING TO BRADFORD FAMILY RESEARCH

Mayflower Descendant (MD) (1899-1937)

2:228-34 - Will & Inventory of Gov. William Bradford
3:144-49 - Will & Inventory of Alice Bradford
4:143-47 - Will & Inventory of Maj. William Bradford
5:5-16 - Gov. Bradford's Letter Book
5:75-81 - Gov. Bradford's Letter Book
5:164-71 - Gov. Bradford's Letter Book
5:198-210 - Gov. Bradford's Letter Book
5:217-24 - Will of Joseph Bradford[2]
6:141-47 - Gov. Bradford's Letter Book
6:207-15 - Gov. Bradford's Letter Book
7:5-12 - Gov. Bradford's Letter Book
7:65-66 - Record of Baptism of Gov. William Bradford
7:79-82 - Gov. Bradford's Letter Book
7:151-59 - Gov. Bradford's Account of N.E. (verse form)
9:1-3 - Gov. Bradford's Letter to Gov. Winthrop, 1631/2
9:65-66 - Gov. Bradford's Marriage Settlement On His Son William
9:89-91 - Wills of Thomas & Welthian Richards
9:115-17 - Mayflower Marriages in Leyden & Amsterdam
10:1-2 - The Marriage of Edward Southworth & Alice Carpenter
13:233 - Deed, Mrs. Alice Bradford Sr., 1659
14:65-70 - Chandler Notes: Mary Chandler m. Hezekiah Bradford
15:65-67 - The Bible Record of William Bradford[5] of Canterbury CT
16:114-20 - Bradford Notes: Wills of Jael Bradford, William[3], Samuel[3], John[4]
17:65-66 - An Autograph of Maj. William Bradford Son of Gov. William Bradford
17:99-100 - Will of John Sunderland
17:254-56 - Bradford Notes: Rebecca Bartlett, wf of William Bradford[3] & daughters Alice & Sarah
18:127-28 - Notes: Data on Brock/Hobart
18:177-83 - Will of Benjamin Bartlett of Duxbury And The Division of His Real Estate (Israel & Gamaliel Bradford[3])
19:1-5 - Will of Rev. Ichabod Wiswall (Gershom Bradford[4])
19:187 - Notes: Hobart/Bradford/Rogers/Turner
20:133-37 - Will of Maj. John Bradford[3] of Kingston MA
21:117-20 - Will of Capt. Nathaniel Gilbert (Hannah Bradford[3])
21:189-91 - Will of Lieut. Ephraim Bradford[3]
22:63-64 - Marriage Record of William Bradford, Amsterdam
22:123-25 - A Norman Family Record (1800's)
23:14-23 - Will of Lieut. Samuel Bradford[4]
23:155-61 - Estate of William Bradford[4] Jr. Son of Major John Bradford of Kingston MA
23:165-68 - Will of Jonathan Phinney of Swansea And The Estate of His Widow Joanna
23:181-85 - David Bradford[3] And His Wife Elizabeth Phinney
24:24-26 - Will of Deacon John Foster (William Bradford[4])
24:27-30 - Will of Kenelm Baker (m. Sarah Bradford[3])
24:154-64 - Estate of William Bradford[4] Son of William Bradford of Kingston MA
25:25-30 - Estate of Widow Elizabeth (Finney) Bradford (William Bradford[4])
27:41-44 - Deeds: Cole/Bradford/Howland (Elisha Bradford[3])
27:129-31 - Autograph of Maj. John Bradford[3] on Hezekiah Bradford[3]'s Deed to Wrestling Brewster
28:97-104 - The Gravestones of Joshua Ripley, Esq. And Hannah Bradford His Wife With Joshua Ripley's Will (Hannah Bradford[3])
28:105-08 - Gravestone of Widow Sarah Hunt (Samuel Bradford[4])
- Notes: Hunt/Bradford
28:119 - Gov. Bradford's Letter Book
29:97-102 - Gov. William Bradford's First Wife Dorothy (May) Bradford Did Not Commit Suicide
29:114-21 - Rev. Cotton Mather's Account of Four Plymouth Colony Governors From His "Magnalia Christi Americana"
31:105 - Death of Dorothy (May) Bradford
34:14-15 - False & Faked Mayflower Claims (Mercy Barnes[6] did not m. Richard Holmes)

PN&Q 3:104-06 - Family Records: Two Bradford Bibles (William[5], William[7])

Mayflower Descendant (MD) (1985-1990)

38:190 - Notes: Identification of Alice Carpenter
39:88 - Correction to MFIP, Bradford:28 (Lydia Fitch)
39:179-80 - The Parentage of Keziah, Wife of Nathaniel Sprague of Duxbury & Rochester

Mayflower Quarterly (MQ) (1975-1990)

46:186-89 - Jonathan Crane - "Gone West"
47:200-04 - Some Weston & Maglathlin Descendants of Gov. William Bradford & Pilgrim George Soule
48:161-65 - The Mystery of the Bradford Manuscript
48:172-77 - The Secret Life of Jonathan Sampson (Deborah Bradford^4)
54:96-98 - The Spear Family Register From The Burned File
55:320-22 - The Reverand Jonathan Hascell/Haskell, A Soule & Bradford Descendant

Miscellaneous

Mayflower Families In Progress: William Bradford of the Mayflower and His Descendants for Four Generations (MFIP), pub. by General Society of Mayflower Descendants, 2nd Ed., 1988.

NEHGR 83:439, 84:5 - Ancestry of the Bradfords of Austerfield, County York - Records Extending The Ancestral Line of Gov. William Bradford
NEHGR 144:26-28 - More About Mary (Wood)(Holmes) Bradford of Duxbury & Plymouth MA
TAG 46:117, 47:87 - A Royal Line From Edward I to Dorothy May Bradford of Plymouth MA (note: this line is based on her parentage which has not been definitely proven.)

* * * * * * * *

WILLIAM BREWSTER

MICRO #1 of 18

William BREWSTER[1], d. 10 Apr. 1644, Plymouth <MD 1:7><1>

Mary ( ) BREWSTER, d. 17 Apr. 1627, Plymouth <MD 1:7><2>

CHILDREN OF William BREWSTER[1] & Mary ( ): (6)

Child, d.y.

Jonathan BREWSTER[2], b. 12 Aug. 1593, Scrooby, Nottinghamshire, Eng., d. 7 Aug. 1659 <MD 1:7, 72>

Love BREWSTER[2], b. ( )

Patience BREWSTER[2], b. ( )

Fear BREWSTER[2], b. ( )

Wrestling BREWSTER[2], b. ( )

Mrs. Miriam BREWSTER, d. 9 Dec. 1818, 91st yr, wf of Peter, Strong Cem. g.s., N. Coventry CT

Silver St. Cemetery, Coventry CT:

Jacob BREWSTER, d. 31 Mar. 1823, 81st yr

Mrs. Delia BREWSTER, d. 20 Oct. 1835, 86th yr, wf of Jacob

Mrs. Asenath BREWSTER, d. 21 May 1814, 48th yr, wf of Shubael

Mrs. Rube BREWSTER, d. 28 Oct. 1796, 42nd yr, wf of Jesse

Mrs. Mary BREWSTER, d. 17 Sept. 1784, 74th yr, wf of Peter

Peter BREWSTER, d. 27 Jan. 1802, 95th yr

Brewster Inscriptions, "Central" Cemetery, Kingston:

Deacon Wrastling BREWSTER, d. 1 Jan. 1767, ae 72y14m28d

Hannah BREWSTER, d. 20 Aug. 1788, ae 90 wanting 21 days, widow of Deacon Wrastling

Miss Mary BREWSTER, d. 25 Aug. 1795, ae 54y3m16d

Deborah BREWSTER, d. 3 Oct. 1802, 76th yr, wf of Wrestling

Wrestling BREWSTER, d. 8 Feb. 1810, ae 86

Judith BREWSTER, d. 19 July 1849, ae 43

Thomas BREWSTER, d. 10 Aug. 1815, ae 85

Hosea BREWSTER, d. 18 Jan. 1832, ae 38

Capt. Hosea BREWSTER, d. 28 Aug. 1794, ae 32

Rebecca BREWSTER, d. 30 Oct. 1801, 36th yr, widow of Capt. Hosea

Capt. Martin BREWSTER, d. 22 Aug. 1833, ae 75

Sally BREWSTER, d. 26 Sept. 1846, ae 80y2m10d, widow of Capt. Martin

John BREWSTER, son of John & Rebecca, d. 23 July 1748, ae 17y9m16d

Sarah BREWSTER, d. 1 June 1826, ae 71y6m, widow

Spencer BREWSTER, d. 28 Dec. 1843, ae 67

Clynthia D. BREWSTER, his wife, d. 18 Mar. 1809, ae 33

Experience BREWSTER, d. 24 Nov. 1824, ae 48

Persis BREWSTER, his widow, d. 21 Sept. 1848, ae 65

Aaron BREWSTER, d. 14 July 1841, ae 31, New Orleans

Brewster Inscriptions, "Fern Hill" Cemetery, Hanson:

William BREWSTER, d. 6 Feb. 1825, 62nd yr

Adah BREWSTER, d. 31 June 1829, ae 64, widow of William

Christiana BREWSTER, dau of Wm. & Adah, d. 4 Sept. 1823, 24th yr

Anna BREWSTER, dau of Wm. & Adah and wf of Earl Joslen, d. 10 May 1821, 27th yr

Brewster Inscriptions, "Oak Grove" Cemetery, Plymouth: (2)

Ellis BREWSTER, d. 27 Aug. 1817, 49th yr, at sea, 1st hus. of Nancy (widow of Dan. Churchill),

William E. BREWSTER, their son, d. 13 Dec. 1809, ae 4

CHILD OF Seabury BREWSTER & 1st Sally BRADFORD: <Norwich CT VR 4:139>

William BREWSTER, b. 24 Aug. 1787

CHILDREN OF Seabury BREWSTER & 2nd Lucy LEFFINGWELL: (3) <Norwich CT VR 4:139>

Elisha BREWSTER, b. 21 Dec. 1790

Levi BREWSTER, b. 24 Apr. 1793

Henry BREWSTER, b. 27 Feb. 1797

CHILDREN OF Seabury BREWSTER & 3rd Fanny BAKER*: (2) <Norwich CT VR 4:139>

Christopher S. BREWSTER, b. 27 June 1799

Seabury BREWSTER, b. 7 June 1805

Brewster Inscriptions, Old Cemetery, Unitarian Church, Duxbury:

Joseph BREWSTER, d. 3 Sept. 1791, 74th yr

Jedidah BREWSTER, d. 26 Mar. 1794, 73rd yr, widow of Joseph

Joseph BREWSTER, d. 19 June 1807, drowned, 60th yr

Deborah BREWSTER, d. 19 Sept. 1814, 61st yr, wf of Joseph

Miss Welthea BREWSTER, dau of Joseph & Deborah, d. 22 May 1802

Araunah BREWSTER, son of Joseph & Deborah, d. 28 Oct. 1793, 20th yr

Asa BREWSTER, son of Joseph & Deborah, d. 31 Dec. 1792, ae 5y2m27d

Arunah BREWSTER, d. 10 Nov. 1814, ae 17y5m24d

Eunice BREWSTER, dau of Joseph & Sarah, d. 15 Dec. 1805, ae 1y9m

Stephen BREWSTER, d. 4 Mar. 1840, ae 57y2m4d

Stephen BREWSTER, son of Stephen & Phillippi, d. 29 Sept. 1824, ae 3m21d

Joshua BREWSTER, d. 20 Sept. 1832, 72nd yr (Rev. Soldier)

Ruth BREWSTER, d. 8 Feb. 1811, ae 48, wf of Joshua

Deborah BREWSTER, d. 3 Jan. 1820, ae 32

Rachel BREWSTER, d. 21 Oct. 1812, 24th yr

Ruth BREWSTER, d. 10 May 1806, ae 40y17d, wf of Cyrus

Zadock BREWSTER, d. 28 Aug. 1827, ae 28y17d, St. Ubes, son of Capt. Cyrus & Ruth

Lydia W. BREWSTER, dau of Capt. Daniel & Polly, d. 17 Dec. 1824, ae 11y2m

Old Cemetery, South Duxbury:

Joseph BREWSTER, d. 20 Apr. 1767, 74th yr

Elizabeth BREWSTER, d. Apr. 1786, 83rd yr, wf of Joseph

Deacon William BREWSTER, d. 3 Nov. 1723, ae near 78th yr

* * * * *

Jonah BREWSTER, d. 3 June 1750 <CT Hist.Soc., Weaver papers>

CHILDREN OF Jonah BREWSTER & Joanna WALDO: (5) <CT, Weaver papers> (1-4, bpt. Scotland CT Ch.)

Jonathan BREWSTER, b. 25 Aug. 1744

Nathan BREWSTER, b. 31 Jan. 1745/6; d. ae nearly 90, "Penna." (no date)

Ezekiel BREWSTER, b. 19 July 1747

Ann BREWSTER, b. 12 Feb. 1748/9

Jonah BREWSTER, b. 1 Sept. 1750

CHILDREN OF Jonathan BREWSTER[5] (Jonathan[4], Wrestling[3], Love[2]) & Eunice KINGSLEY: (8) <CT, Weaver>

Orson BREWSTER[6], b. 30 Aug. 1767

Dau., b. 25 Jan. 1769, d. 9 Feb. 1769

Eunice BREWSTER[6], b. 8 Jan. 1770

Ohel BREWSTER[6], b. 28 Aug. 1771

Oramel BREWSTER[6], b. 31 Oct. 1773

Joanna BREWSTER[6], b. 29 July 1775

Lydia BREWSTER[6], b. 2 Jan. 1779

Jonathan BREWSTER[6], b. 17 Oct. 1781

William DURKEE[1], d. 2 Mar. 1732, ae about 60, of Gloucester <CT Hist.Soc., Weaver papers>

CHILDREN OF William DURKEE[1] & Rebecca GOULD (dau of Henry of Ipswich): (3 of 8) <" " >

Martha DURKEE, b. 11 Dec. 1705

Jerusha DURKEE, b. 12 Apr. 1707

William DURKEE[2], b. 28 Feb. 1710; d. betw. 10 Jan. 1795 (will) - 1 Mar. 1795 (prob.)

CHILDREN OF William DURKEE[2] (son of Wm.[1]) & Abigail HOVEY (dau of Nathaniel): (4) <Weaver papers>

Abigail DURKEE, b. 14 Apr. 1734

Sarah DURKEE, b. 31 Aug. 1736, d. 15 June 1742

Hannah DURKEE, b. 26 Jan. 1738/9

Mary DURKEE, b. 29 Nov. 1741, d. 4 June 1783 (wf of John Brewster, below)

Asa BREWSTER, d. 10 Mar. 1811, ae 73 <CT Hist.Soc., Weaver's Windham Deaths>

CHILDREN OF Asa BREWSTER & Ruth BADGER: (4) <CT Hist.Soc., Weaver papers>

Edmund BREWSTER, b. 12 Jan. 1767

Oliver BREWSTER, b. 17 Mar. 1769

Erastus BREWSTER, b. 15 Mar. 1773, d. 15 Oct. 1775 <Weaver's Windham Deaths>

Abigail BREWSTER, b. 28 Oct. 1775

CHILD OF William BREWSTER & Mehitable ( ): <Mansfield VR>

Son, b. 13 Mar. 1729/30

John BREWSTER, b. 14 June 1739, Scotland CT <CT, Weaver papers> (m. Mary Durkee)

CHILDREN OF John BREWSTER & Mary DURKEE (dau of Capt. Wm. & Abigail): (7) <CT, Weaver papers>

Mary BREWSTER, b. 9 Sept. 1762

William BREWSTER, b. 17 June 1764, d. 4 Jan. 1789

John BREWSTER, b. 31 May ( ), deaf & dumb

Augustus BREWSTER, b. 30 May 1768, d. 3 Jan.1789

Royal BREWSTER, b. 13 July 1770, d. Mar. 1835

Abel BREWSTER, (twin), d.y.

Sophia BREWSTER, (twin), d.y.

CHILDREN OF John BREWSTER & Ruth AVERY: (2) <CT, Weaver papers>

Dr. John BREWSTER, b. c1739, d. 18 Aug. 1823, ae 84

Ruth BREWSTER, b. c1754, d. 18 May 1823, ae 69

Capt. James BREWSTER, d. 2 Oct. 1755, ae 40

CHILDREN OF James BREWSTER (son of Jonathan) & Faith RIPLEY: (6)

Lydia BREWSTER, b. 18 Mar. 1739/40

Faith BREWSTER, b. 30 May 1742, d. 28 Sept. 1745

Olive BREWSTER, b. 18 June 1744

James BREWSTER, b. 8 Jan.1748/9

Marcy BREWSTER, b. 30 June 1751

David BREWSTER, b. 21 Dec. 1753

Elizabeth BREWSTER, d. 20 Oct. 1758 <Weaver's Windham Deaths>

Wife of David BREWSTER, d. 29 Nov. 1803 <" " >

Wife of Benjamin BREWSTER, d. 18 or 24 Mar. 1808, ae 47 <" ">

Joseph BREWSTER, d. 29 Oct. 1813, ae 20, in prison <" ">

Benjamin BREWSTER, d. 23 Mar. 1725, ae 72 <" ">

CHILDREN OF William BREWSTER & Ruth ( ): (7) <CT Hist.Soc., Weaver papers>

Benjamin BREWSTER, b. 6 Feb. 1753

Hannah BREWSTER, b. 26 Oct. 1754

Elizabeth BREWSTER, b. 19 Jan. 1759

Cynthia BREWSTER, b. 25 July 1762

William BREWSTER, b. 21 Jan. 1765

Cyrus BREWSTER, b. 5 Aug. 1769; d. 28 Sept. 1818, suddenly <Weaver's Windham Deaths>

Bowen BREWSTER, b. 19 Apr. 1773

Peleg BREWSTER (son of Jonathan), b. Feb. 1717, d. 2 Apr. 1801, ae 84, Canterbury CT <Weaver>

Jonathan BREWSTER[4] (Wrestling[3], Love[2]), d. 24 Nov. 1753 <CT, Weaver papers>**<3>**

CHILD OF Benjamin BREWSTER: <1st Ch. Windham, Weaver papers>
Elijah BREWSTER, bpt. 12 Sept. 1731
CHILDREN OF Peleg BREWSTER: (4) <3rd Ch. Scotland CT>
John BREWSTER, bpt. 18 Nov. 1739
Mary BREWSTER, bpt. 12 Oct. 1740
Jedediah BREWSTER, bpt. 6 June 1742
Mary BREWSTER, bpt. 18 Mar. 1744

JONATHAN BREWSTER[2] (William[1])

Lucretia OLDHAM, d. 4 Mar. 1678/9 <MD 1:168>
CHILDREN OF Jonathan BREWSTER[2] & Lucretia OLDHAM: (8) <MD 1:7,8; 32:2>
William BREWSTER[3], b. 9 Mar. 1625, Plymouth
Mary BREWSTER[3], b. 16 Apr. 1627, Plymouth; d. aft. 23 Mar. 1697/8 <PN&Q 2:158>
Jonathan BREWSTER[3], b. 17 July 1629, Plymouth
Ruth BREWSTER[3], b. 3 Oct. 1631, Jones River, Plymouth; d. 1 May 1677, New London CT <MD 1:73>
Benjamin BREWSTER[3], b. 17 Nov. 1633, Duxbury; d. 14 Sept. 1710, Norwich CT <MD 1:8>
Elizabeth BREWSTER[3], b. 1 May 1637, Duxbury; d. Feb. 1708*, g.s. <Hist.New London CT:317>
Grace BREWSTER[3], b. 1 Nov. 1639, Duxbury; d. 22 Apr. 1684 <MD 1:75>
Hannah BREWSTER[3], b. 3 Nov. 1641, Duxbury
Ann DARTE, d. 9 May 1708, Norwich CT <MD 1:73<4>
CHILDREN OF Benjamin BREWSTER[3] & Ann DARTE: (8) <1-4, MD 1:72; 5-8, MD 1:74>
Mary BREWSTER[4], b. 10 Dec. 1660
Ann BREWSTER[4], b. 29 Sept. 1662, Mohegin
Jonathan BREWSTER[4], b. last of Nov. 1664, Mohegin; d. 20 Nov. 1704 <MD 1:73>
Daniel BREWSTER[4], b. 1 Mar. 1667, Mohegin; d. 7 May 1735 <MD 1:173>
William BREWSTER[4], b. 22 Mar. 1669, Mohegin
Ruth BREWSTER[4], b. 16 Sept. 1671, Mohegin
Benjamin BREWSTER[4], b. 25 Nov. 1673, Mohegin; d. betw. 14 Jan. 1755 (will) - 6 Feb. 1755 (prob.)
Elizabeth BREWSTER[4], b. 23 June 167(); d. 9 Mar. 1744 <MD 1:74>
Mary SMITH, b. c1673, d. 27 Mar. 1747*, 74th yr
CHILDREN OF Benjamin BREWSTER[4] & Mary SMITH: (7) <1-3, MD 1:193>
Benjamin BREWSTER[5], b. 24 Sept. 1697
John BREWSTER[5], b. 25 May 1701
Mary BREWSTER[5], b. 24 Apr. 1704; d. 27 Feb. 1777, Lebanon CT g.s.
Jonathan BREWSTER[5]*, b. 1706*, d. 1717*
Nehemiah BREWSTER[5]*, b. 1709*, d. 1719*
Comfort BREWSTER[5]*, b. 1711*
Daniel BREWSTER[5]*, b. 1714*
Benjamin PAYNE, (son of John), d. 14 Jan. 1755, ae 55, Lebanon CT g.s. (hus of Mary Brewster[5])<5>
CHILDREN OF Stephen PAYNE[6] (Mary Brewster[5]) & Rebecca BUSHNELL,(dau of Nathan):(5)<Coventry CT VR
Sarah PAYNE[7], b. 20 May 1758
Rebecca PAYNE[7], b. 20 May 1760
Ebenezer PAYNE[7], b. 27 Sept. 1762; d. 19 Dec. 1834
Allin PAYNE[7], b. 31 Mar. 1765
Tilla PAYNE[7], b. 1 Nov. 1767
Capt. Stephen PAYNE, d. 28 Aug. 1815, 70th yr, Lebanon CT g.s.
Martha PAYNE, wf of Capt. Stephen, d. 24 Sept. 1804, 56th yr, Lebanon CT g.s.
CHILDREN OF Ebenezer PAYNE[7] & Keziah ( ): (13) <Hinsdale VR>
Ebenezer PAYNE[8], b. 10 Dec. 1784
Alpha PAYNE[8], b. 13 Feb. 1787

Daniel PAYNE[8], b. 13 Feb. 1789; d. 21 Jan. 1827

Stephen PAYNE[8], b. 27 May 1791

Bushnal PAYNE[8], b. 3 Mar. 1793

Noah PAYNE[8], b. 21 Sept. 1795

Chancy PAYNE[8], b. 12 Aug. 1798; d. 15 Dec. 1803

Sally PAYNE[8], b. 8 Dec. 1800

James PAYNE[8], b. 27 Jan. 1804

Elijah PAYNE[8], b. 15 Nov. 1806

Keziah PAYNE[8], b. 18 Apr. 1809

Lyman K. PAYNE[8], b. 8 July 1811

Alvira PAYNE[8], b. 27 Dec. 1813

Hannah GAGER, b. Feb. 1666*; d. 25 Sept. 1727 <MD 1:173>

CHILDREN OF Daniel BREWSTER[4] (Ben.[3]) & 1st Hannah GAGER: (10) <2-10, Preston>

Daniel BREWSTER[5], b. 11 Oct. 1687, Norwich, d. 14 June 1756, Preston <MD 1:168, 73-4>

Hannah BREWSTER[5], b. 2 Dec. 1690 <MD 1:168>

Mary BREWSTER[5], b. 2 Jan. 1692 <MD 1:169>

John BREWSTER[5], b. 18 July 1695 <MD 1:169>

Jerusha BREWSTER[5], b. 18 Nov. 1697, d. 17 Apr. 1704 <MD 1:169>

Ruth BREWSTER[5], b. 20 June 17(00) <MD 1:169>

Bethiah BREWSTER[5], b. 5 Apr. 1702 <MD 1:169>

Jonathan BREWSTER[5], b. 6 June 1705 <MD 1:171>

Jerusha BREWSTER[5], b. 15 Oct. 1710, d. 7 Mar. 1711 <MD 1:170>

Ebenezer BREWSTER[5], b. 19 Sept. 1713, d. 7 Oct. 1739 <MD 1:170, 173>

Joseph FREEMAN, (son of John*), d. 12 May 1733 <MD 1:173>

CHILDREN OF Joseph FREEMAN & Hannah BREWSTER[5]: (10) <1-9, Preston CT>

Joseph FREEMAN[6], b. 4 Mar. 1709 <MD 1:171>

Daniel FREEMAN[6], b. 1 Apr. 1712, d. 28 Apr. 1733 <MD 1:171, 173>

Hannah FREEMAN[6], b. 23 Feb. ( ) <MD 1:171>

Caleb FREEMAN[6], b. 27 Feb. 1716/17 <MD 1:172>

Phineas FREEMAN[6], b. 23 Oct. 1718 <MD 1:172>

Nathan FREEMAN[6], b. 23 Sept. 17( ) <MD 1:172>

Benjamin FREEMAN[6], b. 27 Nov. 1723 <MD 1:172>

Samuel FREEMAN[6], b. 26 June 1726 <MD 1:172>

Mary FREEMAN[6], b. 12 July 1728 <MD 1:172>

Jemima FREEMAN[6]*, b. ( ) <Brewster Gen.:72>

Lucy BLODGETT, b. c1628, d. 2 Nov. 1753, 25th yr, Preston CT <MD 1:196>

CHILD OF Nathan FREEMAN[6] & 1st Lucy BLODGETT:

Ruth FREEMAN[7], b. 24 Oct. 1749, d. 24 Apr. 1750, Preston CT <MD 1:196>

CHILDREN OF Nathan FREEMAN[6] & 2nd Lucy BARNES: (2) <Preston CT VR 2:27>

Daniel FREEMAN[7], b. 29 June 1754

Lucy FREEMAN[7], b. 2 or 10 Nov. 1755; d. 4 Nov. 1835

Nathan FREEMAN[7], b. 22 Oct. 1757

Mary FREEMAN[7], b. 10 Jan. 1760, d. 23 Dec. 1773

Sarah FREEMAN[7], b. 22 Oct. 1761

Ruth FREEMAN[7], b. 1 Mar. 1764

Matilda FREEMAN[7], b. 6 Apr. 1766

Margaret FREEMAN[7], b. 1 Aug. 1768

Caleb FREEMAN[7], b. 9 Dec. 1772

Gideon SAFFORD Jr., b. 4 Nov. 1754; d. 7 Mar. 1838

CHILDREN OF Gideon SAFFORD Jr. & Lucy FREEMAN[7]: (13) <1-5, Preston CT VR 2:193; Family Bible>

Mary SAFFORD^{8}, b. 27 Sept. 1775
Elizabeth SAFFORD^{8}, b. 13 Jan. 1777
Gideon SAFFORD^{8}, b. 29 Nov. 1778
Chester SAFFORD^{8}, b. 10 June 1780
Nathan SAFFORD^{8}, b. 14 Aug. 1783
Ira SAFFORD^{8}, b. 4 June 1782, d.y.
Adin SAFFORD^{8}, b. 20 Dec. 1785
Hannah SAFFORD^{8}, b. 6 June 1788
Matilda SAFFORD^{8}, b. 25 Nov. 1790
Lucy SAFFORD^{8}, b. 27 Aug. 1792
Thomas SAFFORD^{8}, b. 13 Apr. 1795
Sarah SAFFORD^{8}, b. 18 Oct. 1796
Phoebe SAFFORD^{8}, b. 24 Oct. 1798
James TURNER, b. 16 Nov. 1791 <Family Bible>
CHILDREN OF James TURNER & Matilda SAFFORD^{8}: (8) <Family Bible>
William TURNER^{9}, b. 18 Apr. 1815
Gideon S. TURNER^{9}, b. 15 Oct. 1817
James G. TURNER^{9}, b. 20 May 1820
Eleanor E. TURNER^{9}, b. 18 June 1823
Chester TURNER^{9}, b. 20 Mar. 1825
Lucy M. TURNER^{9}, b. 12 Mar. 1827
Elizabeth L. TURNER^{9}, b. 20 Aug. 1830
CHILDREN OF John BREWSTER^{5} (Dan.^{4}) & Dorothy TREAT: (10) <1-4, Preston CT, MD 1:194>
Oliver BREWSTER^{6}, b. 20 July 1726
Dorothy BREWSTER^{6}, b. 22 Jan. 1727/8
Hannah BREWSTER^{6}, b. 26 Sept. 1729; d. 15 Dec. 1736* <Brewster Gen.>
Sarah BREWSTER^{6*}, b. 25 May 1733*
Sybil BREWSTER^{6*}, b. 20 Aug. 1735*
John BREWSTER^{6*}, b. 9 Jan. 1737/8*, d. 7 Aug. 1752* <Brewster Gen.>
Eunice BREWSTER^{6*}, b. 17 Oct. 1740*
Levi BREWSTER^{6*}, b. 17 Mar. 1743*, d. 11 Dec. 1750
Asaph BREWSTER^{6*}, b. 7 Mar. 1745/6*, d. 13 Dec. 1750
CHILDREN OF Jonathan BREWSTER & Mary PARRISH: (7) <Preston CT VR 1:58>
Lucresha BREWSTER, b. 14 Aug. 1727
Ruth BREWSTER, b. 6 Apr. 1730
Ephraim BREWSTER, b. 20 Aug. 1731
Jonathan BREWSTER, b. 8 June 1734
Mary BREWSTER, b. 2 Dec. 1735
Lydia BREWSTER, b. 1(3) Mar. 1738
Hannah BREWSTER, b. 5 Mar. 1739/40
CHILD OF Jonathan BREWSTER Jr. & Zipporah SMITH:
Moses BREWSTER, b. 8 Sept. 1769 <Preston CT VR 2:73>
John FOBES, d. 18 Feb. 17( ) <MD 1:197>
CHILDREN OF John FOBES & Ruth BREWSTER^{5} (Dan.^{4}): (5) <MD 1:197, 2-5, Preston CT>
Simeon FOBES^{6}, b. 14 Jan. 171()
Mary FOBES^{6}, b. 19 Jan. ( )
Jerusha FOBES^{6}, b. 19 Dec. 1724, d. 25 Feb. 1727
Hannah FOBES^{6}, b. 29 May 1727
Ebenezer FOBES^{6}, b. 22 Oct. 1728
Judith STEVENS, b. cDec. 1670 (ae 20 wanting 7 days when marr. 18 Dec. 1690) <MD 1:172>

CHILDREN OF Jonathan BREWSTER[4] (Dan.[3]) & Judith STEVENS: (2) <MD 1:172>

Lucretia BREWSTER[5], b. 3 Nov. 1691

Jonathan BREWSTER[5], b. 2 Apr. 1694

Samuel FITCH, (son of James), b. 16 Apr. 1655, Saybrook CT

CHILDREN OF Samuel FITCH & Mary BREWSTER[4] (Dan.[3]): (10) <1-5, MD 1:75; 6-10, MD 1:76>

Mary FITCH[5], b. 10 Mar. 1679/80

Samuel FITCH[5], b. 5 Oct. 1681

Hezekiah FITCH[5], b. 7 Jan. 1682, d. 1738

Elizabeth FITCH[5], b. 15 Feb. 1684

Abigail FITCH[5], b. 1 Feb. 1686

Samuel FITCH[5], b. 28 Nov. 1688

Benjamin FITCH[5], b. 29 Mar. 1691

John FITCH[5], b. 17 May 1693

Jabez FITCH[5], b. 3 Ju() 1695, d. 28 Mar. 1779

Peltiel FITCH[5], b. 18 Feb. 1698

CHILDREN OF Jabez FITCH[5] & Anna KNOWLTON: (7) <MD 2:21>

Elisha FITCH[6], b. 6 Mar. 1720, d. 4 Aug. 1789

Pelatiah FITCH[6], b. 26 May 1722, d. 16 Apr. 1803

Asa FITCH[6], b. 1 June 1730, d. 16 Apr. 1755

Lurene FITCH[6], b. May 1732, d. 20 Jan. 1781

Jabez FITCH[6], b. 15 Feb. 1737; d. 29 Feb. 1812, Hydepark VT <MD 2:23>

Cordilla FITCH[6], b. 15 Oct. 1738, d. June 1762

Cynthia FITCH[6], b. 8 June 1743

Hannah PERKINS, d. 13 Aug. 1808, Hydepark VT <MD 2:22>

CHILDREN OF Jabez FITCH[6] & Hannah PERKINS: (8) <MD 2:21>

Cordilla FITCH[7], b. 6 Apr. 1762

Darius FITCH[7], b. 2 Jan. 1764

Theophilus Wilson FITCH[7], b. 15 July 1765; d. 28 Feb. 1845 <MD 2:23>

Samuel Perkins FITCH[7], b. 15 July 1765 (twins); d. 13 June 1841 <MD 2:23>

Jabez FITCH[7], b. 26 Mar. 1770; d. 17 July 1847 <MD 2:23>

Betsy FITCH[7], b. 7 June 1771

Hannah FITCH[7], b. 10 May 1773

Lurene FITCH[7], b. 10 June 1775; d. 19 Nov. 1798 <MD 2:22,23>

Peter BRADLEY, d. 3 Apr. 1662 <MD 1:72, 5:194>

CHILDREN OF Peter BRADLEY & Elizabeth BREWSTER[3]: (4) <New London CT>

Elizabeth BRADLEY[4], b. 16 Mar. 1654/5 <VR 4:328; MD 1:71>

Hannah BRADLEY[4], b. 17 Sept. 1656 <MD 1:71>

Peter BRADLEY[4], b. 7 Sept. 1658 <VR 4:328>; d. 25 Aug. 1687 <MD 1:72,77>

Lucretia BRADLEY[4], b. 16 Aug. 1661 <MD 1:72>; d. 7 Jan. 1690/1, New London CT

Christopher CHRISTOPHERS, d. 23 July 1687 <MD 1:77>

CHILDREN OF Christopher CHRISTOPHERS & Elizabeth (BREWSTER[3]) Bradley: (2)[<6>]

John CHRISTOPHERS[4], b. 3 Sept. 1668 <MD 1:77>; d. Feb. 1702, Barbadoes (will & prob.)

Child, b. ( )[<6>]

CHILDREN OF Thomas DYMOND & Elizabeth BRADLEY[4] (Eliz. Brewster[3]): (5) <New London CT VR>

Elizabeth DYMOND[5], b. 14 Aug. 1672 <VR 4:320>

Thomas DYMOND[5], b. 22 July 1675 <VR 4:317>

Moses DYMOND[5], b. 14 May 1677 <VR 4:315>

Ruth DYMOND[5], b. 12 Sept. 1680 <VR 4:311>

John DYMOND[5], b. 25 July 1686 <VR 4:303>

MICRO #2 of 18

CHILDREN OF Christopher CHRISTOPHERS[1] & 1st Mary ( ): (2)<6>

Richard CHRISTOPHERS[2], b. 13 July 1662, Devon, Eng.; d. 9 June 1726, New London CT

Mary CHRISTOPHERS, b. ( )

CHILDREN OF Richard CHRISTOPHERS[2] & Lucretia BRADLEY[4] (Eliz. Brewster[3]): (4) <New London CT VR>

Christopher CHRISTOPHERS[5], b. 2 Dec. 1683 <VR 4:306>

Richard CHRISTOPHERS[5], b. 18 Aug. 1685 <VR: 4:303>

Peter CHRISTOPHERS[5], b. 18 July 1687 <VR 4:301>

John CHRISTOPHERS[5], b. 15 Mar. 1689/90 <VR 4:299>

CHILDREN OF Richard CHRISTOPHERS & 2nd Grace TURNER[4] (Mary Brewster[3], Jonathan[2]):<7>

CHILD OF Peter BRADLEY[4] (ELiz. Brewster[3]) & Mary CHRISTOPHERS, (dau of Christopher):

Christopher BRADLEY[5], b. 11 July 1679 <New London CT VR>

CHILDREN OF Christopher CHRISTOPHERS[5] (Lucretia Bradley[4]) & Sarah PROUT: (8)* <New London CT VR>

Peter CHRISTOPHERS[6], b. 28 Aug. 1713, d. 30 Aug. 1713

Mary CHRISTOPHERS[6], b. 25 Aug. 1714

Christopher CHRISTOPHERS[6], b. 10 Oct. 1717, d. 25 Oct. 1775

John CHRISTOPHERS[6], b. 27 Feb. 1718/9

Sarah CHRISTOPHERS[6], b. 10 Mar. 1719/20

Lucretia CHRISTOPHERS[6], b. 24 June 1721

Lydia CHRISTOPHERS[6], b. 21 June 1723, d. 2 July 1723

Margaret CHRISTOPHERS[6], b. 7 Mar. 1724/5, d. 23 Aug. 1725

CHILDREN OF Richard CHRISTOPHERS[5] (Lucretia Bradley[4]) & Mrs. Elizabeth SALTONSTALL: (6)* <New London CT VR>

Richard CHRISTOPHERS[6], b. 29 July 1712

Elizabeth CHRISTOPHERS[6], b. 13 Sept. 1714

Mary CHRISTOPHERS[6], b. 17 Dec. 1716

Sarah CHRISTOPHERS[6], b. 6 Dec. 1719

Joseph CHRISTOPHERS[6], b. 31 Nov. 1722

Katharine CHRISTOPHERS[6], b. 5 Jan. 1724/5

CHILDREN OF John CHRISTOPHERS[4] (Eliz. Brewster[3]) & Elizabeth MULFORD: (4) <New London CT>

Samuel CHRISTOPHERS[5], b. 24 July 1697

Elizabeth CHRISTOPHERS[5], b. 15 Feb. 1698/9

John CHRISTOPHERS[5], b. May 1701

Hester CHRISTOPHERS[5], b. 20 June 1703

List of New London CT VR:<8>

CHILDREN OF Ezekiel TURNER, (son of John) & Susannah KEYNEY, (dau of John): (4)

Sarah TURNER, b. 28 Oct. 1683 <VR 4:305>

Susannah TURNER, b. 2 Jan. 1685 <VR 4:303>

Mary TURNER, b. 30 May 1686 <VR 4:303>

Ruth TURNER, b. 2 Mar. 1688 <VR 4:301>

CHILDREN OF Adam PICKETT & Hannah WETHERELL, (dau of Daniel): (3)

Adam PICKETT, b. 7 Sept. 1681 <VR 4:309>

John PICKETT, b. 28 July 1685 <VR 4:303>

Hannah PICKETT, b. 6 June 1689 <VR 4:299>

CHILDREN OF Benjamin SHAPLEY, (son of Nicholas) & Mary PICKETT, (dau of John): (6)

Ruth SHAPLEY, b. 21 Dec. 1672 <VR 4:320>

Benjamin SHAPLEY, b. 20 Mar. 1675 <VR 4:317>

Mary SHAPLEY, b. 26 Mar. 1677 <VR 4:315>

Joseph SHAPLEY, b. 15 Aug. 1681 <VR 4:309>

Anne SHAPLEY, b. 31 Aug. 1685 <VR 4:303>

Daniel SHAPLEY, b. 14 Feb. 1689 <VR 4:299>

CHILDREN OF Samuel FOSDICK & Marcy PICKETT, (dau of John & Ruth): (4)
Samuel FOSDICK, b. 16 Aug. 1683, d. 18 Nov. 1683 <VR 4:305>
Samuel FOSDICK, b. 18 Sept. 1684 <VR 4:303>
Marcy FOSDICK, b. 30 Nov. 1686 <VR 4:303>
Ruth FOSDICK, b. 27 June 1689 <VR 4:299>
CHILDREN OF John PICKETT & Ruth BREWSTER: (3)
John PICKETT, b. 25 July 1656 <VR 4:328>
Adam PICKETT, b. 15 Nov. 1658 <VR 4:328>
Marcy PICKETT, b. 16 Jan. 1660 <VR 4:327>
CHILD OF John KEYNEY & Sarah ( ):
Susanna KEYNEY, b. 6 Sept. 1662 <VR 4:326>
CHILDREN OF Charles HILL & 1st Ruth (BREWSTER) Pickett: (5)
Jane HILL, b. 9 Dec. 1669 <VR 4:323>
Charles HILL, b. 16 Oct. 1671 <VR 4:321>
Ruth HILL, b. & bur. Oct. 1673 <VR 4:319>
Jonathan HILL, b. Dec. 1674 <VR 4:318>
Son, b. 27 Apr. 1677, lived half hour <VR 4:315>
Ruth, wife, d. 30 Apr. 1677 <VR 4:315>
"Rachell, ye beloved wife of Charles Hill was snached away by death in child bearing on daughter being borne dead another child at ye birth, 4 Apr. 1679" <VR 4:314>[<9>]

* * * * * * * *

Richard CHRISTOPHERS, (son of Richard), d. 28 Set. 1736 <New London CT Rcds.>
Mary PICKETT, (dau of John), d. 11 May 1754
CHILDREN OF Richard CHRISTOPHERS, (son of Richard) & Mary PICKETT, (dau of John): (2)<New London>
Mary CHRISTOPHERS, b. 23 May 1734
Elizabeth CHRISTOPHERS, b. 24 Dec. 1735, d. 11 Mar. 1748
CHILDREN OF Nathaniel GREEN & Mary (PICKETT) Christophers: (2) <New London CT Rcds>
Katharine GREEN, b. 5 June 1740
Lydia GREEN, b. 22 Apr. 1742
CHILDREN OF Amos CHESEBROUGH & Mary CHRISTOPHERS: (4) <New London CT Rcds>
Mary CHESEBROUGH, b. 30 Mar. 1757
Desire CHESEBROUGH, b. 11 Feb. 1759
Abigail CHESEBROUGH, b. 26 Jan. 1761
Richard Christopher CHESEBROUGH, b. 20 Feb. 1763
Daniel WETHERELL, (son of Wm.), b. 29 Nov. 1630, Maidstone, Kent, Eng. <MD 1:74>; d. 14 Apr. 1719 <New London CT Rcds>
CHILDREN OF Daniel WETHERELL & Grace BREWSTER[3]: (9) <1-8, MD 1:74-75>
Hannah WETHERELL[4], b. 21 Mar. 1659/60, d. 16 Sept. 1689 <New London CT VR 4:327, 299>
Mary WETHERELL[4], b. 1662, "lived but 2 month"
"4 sons successiv() borne and dyed nameless immediately after their births <MD 1:75>
Mary WETHERELL[4], b. 7 Oct. 1668 <New London CT VR 4:323>
Daniel WETHERELL[4], b. 26 Jan. 1670 <New London CT VR 4:322>
Samuel WETHERELL[4]*, bpt. 19 Oct. 1679* <Hist.New London CT>
Thomas HARRIS[3] (Gabriel[2], Walter[1]), d. 9 June 1691*, Barbadoes <Hist.New London CT:271>
CHILD OF Thomas HARRIS & Mary WETHERELL[4]:
Mary HARRIS[5], b. 4 Nov. 1690*
CHILDREN OF George DENISON & Mary (WETHERELL[4]) Harris:(8)
Grace DENISON[5], b. 4 Mar. 1695*
Phebe DENISON[5], b. 16 Mar. 1697*
Hannah DENISON[5], b. 28 Mar. 1698*

Borradell DENISON^{5}, b. 17 May 1701*

Daniel DENISON^{5}, b. 27 June 1703*

Wetherell DENISON^{5}, b. 24 Aug. 1705*

Ann DENISON^{5}, b. 15 Aug. 1707*

Sarah DENISON^{5}, b. 20 June 1710*

CHILDREN OF Samuel STARR & Hannah BREWSTER^{3}: (3) <1-2, New London CT VR>

Samuel STARR^{4}, b. 11 Dec. 1665 <VR 4:325>

Thomas STARR^{4}, b. 27 Sept. 1668 <VR 4:324>

Jonathan STARR^{4}*, b. ( )

CHILD OF Jonathan STARR^{4} & Elizabeth MORGAN:

Samuel STARR^{5}, b. 1699*, d. 1786*

CHILD OF Samuel STARR^{5} & Ann BUSHNELL*:

Anna STARR^{6}, b. 25 Apr. 1731* <Norwich CT VR:36>

CHILD OF Stephen PRENTICE & Anna STARR^{6}:

Anna PRENTICE^{7}, b. c1759, d. 20 Nov. 1837, ae 78y10m, Waterford Township OH, g.s.

CHILDREN OF Joseph* CHAMPLIN & Anna PRENTICE^{7}: (2)

Joseph CHAMPLIN^{8}, b. ( )

Nancy CHAMPLIN^{8}, b. ( ); d. 5 Sept. 1830

CHILDREN OF Elnathan HATCH & Anna (PRENTICE^{7}) Champlin: (2)

Hannah Prentice HATCH^{8}, b. aft. 1794*

Silence HATCH^{8}, b. aft. 1794*

Alpha DEVOL^{3} (Wanton^{2}, Gilbert^{1}), b. 12 Sept. 1789*, Marietta, O.; d. 30 June 1871 (hus of Nancy Champlin^{8})

CHILDREN OF Philip DEVOL^{3} (Wanton^{2}, Gilbert^{1}) & Hannah Prentice HATCH^{8}: (2)

Maria DEVOL^{9}, b. c1839*; d. 8 Apr. 1918*

Julia DEVOL^{9}, b. ( )

CHILD OF Andrew Jackson BEACH & Julia DEVOL^{9}:

Will T. BEACH^{10}, b. ( )

MICRO #3 of 18

CHILD OF Stephen DEVOL & Silence HATCH^{8} (Anna Prentice^{7}):

Louise P. DEVOL^{9}

John TURNER, d. betw. 4 Mar. 1695 (will) - 20 May 1697 (inv.), prob. shortly before inv., Scituate <MD 5:41>

CHILDREN OF John TURNER & Mary BREWSTER^{3}: (13) <MD 32:30; 1-9, Scituate Rcds>

Jonathan TURNER^{4}, b. 20 Sept. 1646 <4:3:8; MD 17:75>; d. 18 Apr. 1724* <Cohasset VR:232>

Joseph TURNER^{4}, b. 12 Jan. 1647, d. 15 Jan. 1647 <4:3:9; MD 17:75>

Joseph TURNER^{4}, b. 12 Jan. 1648/9 <4:3:10; MD 17:75>; d. 13 Feb. 1724*, Norwell g.s. <MD 32:29>

Ezekiel TURNER^{4}, b. 7 Jan. 1650 <4:3:12; MD 17:75>; d. 16 Jan.1703/4*,New London CT<Caulkins:346>

Lydia TURNER^{4}, b. 24 Jan. 1652 <4:3:14>; d. 20 June 1714 <Scituate Rcds. 4:4:7>

John TURNER^{4}, b. 30 Oct. 1754 <4:3:16; MD 17:75>

Elisha TURNER^{4}, b. 8 Mar. 1656 <4:3:18; MD 32:30>; d. 24 Apr. 1700, Scituate <MD 32:71>

Mary TURNER^{4}, b. 10 Dec. 1658 <4:3:20>

Benjamin TURNER^{4}, b. 5 Mar. 1660 <4:3:22>; d. betw. 10 May 1731 (will) - 21 Feb. 1734 (prob.)

Ruth TURNER^{4}, bpt. 17 May 1662 or 63* <MD 5:43>

Isaac TURNER^{4}, bpt. 30 Apr. 1665*; d. pre 4 Mar. 1695/6 (father's will)

Grace TURNER^{4}, bpt. 2 Aug. 1668* <MD 5:43>

Amos TURNER^{4}, bpt. 4 June 1671*, d. 13 Apr. 1739, Scituate g.s. <MD 5:43, 8:118>

Mary HILAND, (dau of Thomas), b. 15 May 1667 <Scituate Rcds 4:3:27>; d. 5 Nov. 1729, Scituate g.s. <Scituate VR 2:457>

CHILDREN OF Amos TURNER^{4} & Mary HILAND: (8) <Scituate Rcds 4:2:84>

Amos TURNER^{5}, b. 16 Nov. 1695; d. pre 13 Apr. 1739

Jane TURNER^{5}, b. 4 May 1697

Anne TURNER^{5}, b. 7 Apr. 1699

Ezekiel TURNER^{5}, b. 23 Mar. 1700/01; d. 10 Aug. 1773* <Hanover ChR:192>

Mary TURNER^{5}, b. June 1702, d.y.

Mary TURNER^{5}, b. 23 Apr. 1704; d. 19 Aug. 1775, Scituate g.s. <MD 8:118>

Seth TURNER^{5}, b. 28 Nov. 1705; d. betw. 3 Oct. 1743 (will) - 14 Oct. 1743 (prob.)

Lydia TURNER^{5}, b. 26 May 1707

Joseph WITHEREL, d. pre 16 June 1748 (adm.) (hus of Lydia Turner^{5})

James TURNER, (son of Samuel), b. 18 Dec. 1706* <Scituate VR 1:375>; d. 30 May 1776, Scituate g.s <MD 8:118>

CHILDREN OF James TURNER & Mary TURNER^{5} (Amos^{4}): (7) <Scituate>

James TURNER^{6}, b. 13 July 1733, d. 24 Oct. 1803* <Scituate VR 1:375, 2:456>

Desire TURNER^{6}, b. 4 Apr. 1735 <VR 1:372>; d. 17 Aug. 1775 <Scituate VR 2:374>

Lydia TURNER^{6}, b. 16 Feb. 1736; d. 26 Mar. 1740, Scituate g.s. <MD 8:118>

Mary TURNER^{6}, b. 12 Feb. 1739

Nathaniel TURNER^{6}, b. 12 Apr. 1741

Mehitable TURNER^{6}, b. 1 Jan. 1743 <VR 1:379>

Samuel TURNER^{6}, b. 12 Mar. 1746, d. 1775-77*

CHILDREN OF Amos TURNER^{5} (Amos^{4}) & Elizabeth STOCKBRIDGE: (4) <Scituate ChR>

Priscilla TURNER^{6}, bpt. 29 Dec. 1727

Jane TURNER^{6}, bpt. 29 Dec. 1727

Ann TURNER^{6}, bpt. 13 Apr. 1729

Amos TURNER^{6}, bpt. 4 July 1731; d. 1 Aug. 1780* <Medway VR:340>

Hannah BASS, b. c1741, d. 12 Aug. 1878*, ae 87 <Medway VR:324>

CHILDREN OF Amos TURNER^{6} & Hannah BASS: (6) <Medway VR>

Amos TURNER^{7}, b. 7 Sept. 1760

Charles TURNER^{7}, b. 19 Dec. 1764; d. 1 May 1766

Polly TURNER^{7}, b. 22 Oct. 1767

Vesta TURNER^{7}, b. 26 Sept. 1772

Hannah TURNER^{7}, b. 27 Aug. 1775

Charles TURNER^{7}, b. 14 Sept. 1778

CHILDREN OF Amos TURNER^{7} & Rachel HAMMOND: (8) <Medway VR>

Amos TURNER^{8}, b. 17 Nov. 1785; d. 22 Jan. 1815

James TURNER^{8}, b. 22 July 1787

Cyrus TURNER^{8}, b. 10 Apr. 1789; d. Sept. 1830, New Orleans

Irene TURNER^{8}, b. 6 Feb. 1791; d. 28 Jan. 1819

Charles TURNER^{8}, b. 12 Apr. 1793; d. 18 Sept. 1816

Cynthia TURNER^{8}, b. 13 May 1795; d. 4 Aug. 1817

Asa TURNER^{8}, b. 25 Feb. 1797; d. 30 July 1817

Louisa TURNER^{8}, b. 26 Aug. 1801

William PEAKES, (son of Eleazer & Rachel), b. 8 Dec. 1719 <Scituate Rcds 4:3:162> (hus of Priscilla Turner^{6})

Bathsheba STOCKBRIDGE, (dau of Joseph & Margaret (Turner)), d. 14 July 1731* <Hanover ChR 1:180>

CHILDREN OF Ezekiel TURNER^{5} (Amos^{4}) & 1st Bathsheba STOCKBRIDGE: (2)*<Hanover:12>**<10>**

( ), (dau) b. 4 June 1729

( ), b. 24 June 1731

Ruth RANDALL, b. c1720, d. 25 May 1806*, ae 86

CHILDREN OF Ezekiel TURNER^{5} & 2nd Ruth RANDALL: (6)*<Hanover:12,13>

Ruth TURNER^{6}, b. 12 June 1737

Bathsheba TURNER^{6}, b. Apr. 1739

Ezekiel TURNER^{6}, b. 18 July 1740; d. 18 Oct. 1746

Amos TURNER^{6}, b. 16 July 1741

Elizabeth TURNER^{6}, b. 30 Mar. 1743

Abigail TURNER^{6}, b. 9 Apr. 1744

Eli CURTIS, (s. of Tho. Jr. & Ruth), b. 23 Feb. 1733*, d. 26 Jan. 1818*<Scituate VR 1:107, 2:374>

CHILDREN OF Eli CURTIS & Desire TURNER^{6} (Mary Turner^{5}): (6)

Eli CURTIS^{7}, b. 9 Mar. 1760*; d. 21 Mar. 1830

Abner CURTIS^{7}, b. 31 May 1762*

Luther CURTIS^{7}, b. 16 Jan. 1766*

Desire CURTIS^{7}, b. 28 July 1767*; d. 28 Dec. 183()*

Seth CURTIS^{7}, b. 4 June 1769*

Asa CURTIS^{7}, b. 13 May 1773*

Deborah LINCOLN, (*?dau of Joshua & Mercy (Dwelly)), b. 12 Apr. 1740*, d. 1817 <Scituate VR 1:220 & 2:455>

CHILDREN OF James TURNER^{6} (Mary Turner^{5}) & Deborah LINCOLN: (9) <Scituate VR>

Debe TURNER^{7}, b. 28 July 1763*

Nathaniel TURNER^{7}, b. 28 Sept. 1765*; d. 24 Mar. 1846, Scituate <Mass.VR 21:116>

Lydia TURNER^{7}, b. 28 Oct. 1767*

Mercy Dwelly TURNER^{7}, b. 3 Jan. 1770*; d. 5 Apr. 1810* <Scituate VR 2:396>

Desire TURNER^{7}, b. 26 Aug. 1773*

Mary TURNER^{7}, b. 20 Nov. 1775*

James TURNER^{7}, b. 23 Jan. 1778*; d. 24 Jan. 1835*

Bettey TURNER^{7}, b. 21 Apr. 1782*; d. 1 Oct. 1814*

Samuel Humphrey TURNER^{7}, b. 15 Sept. 1754*; d. 25 Oct. 1806*

Jonathan HATCH, (son of Jonathan & Lucy), b. 27 July 1764*, d. 10 Nov. 1846* <Scituate VR 1:174, 2:395> (hus of Mercy Dwelly Turner^{7})

Sarah JAMES^{8} (Ben.$^{7-6}$, John^{5}, Lydia Turner^{4}, Mary Brewster^{3}, Jonathan^{2}), b. 1 Feb. 1772, d. 13 Nov. 1834* <Scituate VR> (wf of Nathaniel Turner^{7})

Mary MANSON, d. 15 Oct. 1862, ae 66y4m13d, Scituate, widow, dau of Nathaniel & Sally Turner Turner <Mass.VR 157:376>

Gideon CHITTENDEN, (*son of Israel Jr. & Deborah), b. 20 Mar. 1749*, d. Oct. 1799 <Scituate VR 1:67, 2:362>

CHILDREN OF Gideon CHITTENDEN & Mehitable TURNER^{6} (Mary Turner^{5}): (2*) <Scituate VR 1:66>

Deborah CHITTENDEN^{7}, b. 10 Sept. 1777

Israel CHITTENDEN^{7}, b. 14 Aug. 1781

Elizabeth HAWKINS, d. betw. 14 Jan. 1740 (will) - 8 Mar. 1744 (prob.) <Plymouth Co.Prob.#21337>

CHILDREN OF Benjamin TURNER^{4} (Mary Brewster^{3}) & Elizabeth HAWKINS: (7) <Scituate VR>

John TURNER^{5}, b. 1 Jan. 1692/3*; d. 20 Mar. 1778*, Scituate g.s., Norwell

Joseph TURNER^{5}, b. 18 Apr. 1694*

Grace TURNER^{5}, b. 17 Dec. 1695*; d. 16 Feb. 1715

Benjamin TURNER^{5}, b. 5 Aug. 1698* <VR 1:370>; d. 12 Aug. 1748* <Scituate VR 2:455>

William TURNER^{5}, b. 5 Aug. 1698* (twins)

Hawkins TURNER^{5}, b. 27 Aug. 1704***<11>**

Elizabeth TURNER^{5}, b. c1703; d. Apr. 1786, Duxbury g.s. <MD 9:160>

Joseph BREWSTER^{4} (Wm.^{3}, Love^{2}), b. 17 Mar. 1692/3, Duxbury <MD 9:232>; d. 20 Apr. 1767, Duxbury g.s. <MD 9:160> (hus of Elizabeth Turner^{5})

Mercy TURNER^{3} (Charles^{2}, Tho.^{1}), b. 24 Sept. 1703*; d. 19 Feb. 1787* <Norwell ChR>

CHILDREN OF Benjamin TURNER^{5} (Ben.^{4}) & Mercy TURNER: (9) <Scituate Rcds, old vol.:19>

Benjamin TURNER^{6}, b. 25 June 1724; d. 7 July 1724*

Lucy TURNER^{6}, b. 17 Jan. 1726; d. 5 Apr. 1738*

Capt. Elisha TURNER^{6}, b. 24 Feb. 1729; d. c1793 <Plymouth Co.Prob.#21333>

Benjamin TURNER^{6}, b. 1 June 1733

Joseph TURNER^{6}, b. 27 Feb. 1735

Mercy TURNER^{6}, b. 28 May 1738 <Scituate VR 1:379>

Peleg TURNER^{6}, b. 13 Apr. 1741

Susanna TURNER^{6}, b. 12 Sept. 1744; d. 21 June 1746*

Elizabeth TURNER^{6}, b. 5 Apr. 1747

Abigail FOSTER, (dau of Jos. & Abigail), b. 2 Feb. 1738* <Scituate VR 1:154>; d. 13 Apr. 1764* <Scituate VR 3:455> (1st wf of Capt. Elisha Turner^{6})

Prudence JAMES^{7} (John$^{6-5}$, Lydia Turner^{4}, Mary Brewster^{3}, Jonathan^{2}), b. 23 Dec. 1740 <Scituate VR 1:197>; d. aft. 1793*

CHILDREN OF Capt. Elisha TURNER^{6} & Prudence JAMES: (10) <Scituate VR>

Prudence TURNER^{7}, b. 25 Mar. 1768*

Benjamin TURNER^{7}, b. 31 Oct. 1769*; d. 26 Sept. 1775*

Elisha TURNER^{7}, b. 25 Aug. 1771*; d. 13 Sept. 1771*

Abigail TURNER^{7}, b. 20 Jan. 1773*; d. 4 Sept. 1775*

Rhoda TURNER^{7}, b. 5 Mar. 1775*

Benjamin TURNER^{7}, b. 19 Mar. 1777*

Abigail TURNER^{7}, b. 12 Jan. 1779*

Lucy TURNER^{7}, b. 23 Feb. 1781*

Elisha TURNER^{7}, b. 5 Mar. 1784*; d. 16 Aug. 1848, Hull g.s.

Sophia TURNER^{7}, b. 29 July 1786*

Elizabeth DILL, b. c1787, d. 15 Apr. 1831, ae 44, Hull g.s.

CHILDREN OF Elisha TURNER^{7} & Elizabeth DILL: (4)**<12>**

Benjamin STETSON, (son of Anthony & Anna), b. 7 July 1736* <Scituate VR 1:348>

CHILDREN OF Benjamin STETSON & Mercy TURNER^{6} (Ben.^{5}): (4) <Scituate Rcds, old vol.:51>

Lucy STETSON^{7}, b. 26 Apr. 1766

Mercy STETSON^{7}, b. 30 Mar. 1768

Benjamin STETSON^{7}, b. 8 Jan. 1771

Joseph STETSON^{7}, b. 8 Jan. 1771 (twins)

CHILDREN OF Richard DWELLY, (son of Richard) & Grace TURNER^{5} (Ben.^{4}): (2) <Scituate VR>

Richard DWELLY^{6}, b. 9 Feb. 1713/14

Grace DWELLY^{6}, b. 16 Feb. 1715**<13>**

Mercy BARTLETT^{5} (Ben.$^{4-3}$, Mary Warren^{2}), b. c1694, d. 6 Oct. 1757, Scituate, Norwell g.s.

CHILDREN OF John TURNER^{5} (Ben.^{4}) & 1st Mercy BARTLETT: (3) <1-2, Scituate VR>

Grace TURNER^{6}, bpt. 9 Oct. 1715*

Bartlet TURNER^{6}, bpt. 12 Oct. 1718*

Deborah TURNER^{6}, b. ( )

CHILDREN OF John TURNER^{5} & 2nd Mary VINAL: (4)**<14>**

Mary TURNER^{6}, b. 23 June 1769*

Lucy TURNER^{6}, b. 2 Jan. 1772*

Ruth TURNER^{6}, b. 19 Jan. 1774*

Rachel TURNER^{6}, b. 18 Apr. 1776*

MICRO #4 of 18

Susanna KEYNEY, (dau of John & Sarah), b. 6 Sept. 1662 <New London CT VR>

CHILDREN OF Ezekiel TURNER^{4} (Mary Brewster^{3}) & Susanna KEYNEY: (11) <1-4, New London CT VR>

Sarah TURNER^{5}, b. 28 Oct. 1683 <VR 4:305>

Susanna TURNER^{5}, b. 2 Jan. 1685 <VR 4:303>

Mary TURNER^{5}, b. 30 May 1686 <VR 4:303>

Ruth TURNER^5, b. 2 Mar. 1688 <VR 4:301>

Lydia TURNER^5, b. 5 Sept. 1690*

Grace TURNER^5, b. 29 Aug. 1692*

Hannah TURNER^5, b. 8 Sept. 1694*

Elizabeth TURNER^5, b. 5 Dec. 1696*

Ezekiel TURNER^5, b. 14 Mar. 1699*; d. betw. 3 June 1769 (will) - 13 Mar. 1770 (prob.) <Stonington Prob.#3319>

Lucretia TURNER^5, b. 20 Jan. 1701*

Abigail TURNER^5, bpt. 14 Mar. 1703, New London CT; d. 23 Sept. 1756

Elizabeth JACOB, (dau of John), b. 11 Apr. 1666 <Hingham VR 1:8; MD 32:71>; d. betw. 28 Oct. 1710 (will) - 17 Jan. 1710/11 (prob.) <MD 32:30>

CHILDREN OF Elisha TURNER^4 (Mary Brewster^3) & Elizabeth JACOB: (6) <Scituate, MD 32:71>

Elisha TURNER^5, b. 11 Mar. 1688, d. 7 May 1688 <MD 32:72>

Mary TURNER^5, b. 10 June 1690; d. aft 16 Apr. 1774 (bond) <Plymouth Co.Prob.#20005>

Elizabeth TURNER^5, b. 3 Apr. 1692

Jael TURNER^5, b. 5 Apr. 1694, d. 1 Jan. 1694/5 <MD 32:72>

Jael TURNER^5, b. 17 Aug. 1696; d. ?10 Oct. 1778* <Duxbury VR:374>

Elisha TURNER^5, b. 24 July 1700; d. aft. 24 Oct. 1726 <Plymouth Co.Deeds 21:115>

CHILD OF Josiah TURNER & Hannah HOLBROOK:

Elisha TURNER, b. Mar. 1702 <Scituate VR 1:372>

Waitstill TURNER, (son of Isaac), b. c1722, d. 25 Oct. 1815, ae 93, "a pauper", poss. Hanover

Mary STAPLES, d. 15 July 1768

CHILDREN OF Waitstill TURNER & Mary STAPLES: (3 or 4) <Hanover>

Elisha TURNER, b. 15 Mar. 1762, "prob. d.y.?"

Mary TURNER, bpt. 6 Oct. 1764, in private "not one year old!"

Hannah TURNER, b. 23 July 1765, "d.y.?"

Hannah TURNER, bpt. 14 Dec. 1766, ("same Hannah as above?")

Joshua TURNER, (*?son of Thomas Sr.), b. 7 July 1689* <Scituate VR 1:376>

CHILDREN OF Joshua TURNER & Elizabeth TURNER^5 (Elisha^4): (7)* <3-7, Norwell Ch>

Elizabeth TURNER^6, b. 27 Mar. 1712 <Scituate VR 1:373>

Joshua TURNER^6, b. 5 Feb. 1713/4

Elizabeth TURNER^6, bpt. 26 Feb. 1726/7

Jael TURNER^6, bpt. 26 Feb. 1726/7

Lurana TURNER^6, bpt. 26 Feb. 1726/7

Princess TURNER^6, bpt. 26 Feb. 1726/7

Mary TURNER^6, bpt. 12 Nov. 1732

John DILLINGHAM, d. betw. 10 Feb. 1769 (will) - 1 May 1769 (prob.), Hanover <Plymouth Co.Prob.#6474, 20:241> (hus of Jael Turner^5 (Elisha^4))

CHILDREN OF John DILLINGHAM & Jael TURNER^6: (5 of 10) <Hanover Ch & Cem.Rcds>**<15>**

Child, b. ( ), d. 15 June 1730/1 <:180>

Child, b. May 1732 <:108>

Child, b. Mar. 1733/4 <:109>

Child, b. May 1736 <:111>

Child, b. Nov. 1738 <:112>

CHILDREN OF Henry DILLINGHAM & Elizabeth ( ): (2) <Hanover BMD:31>

Elizabeth Jacobs DILLINGHAM, b. 15 Oct. 1755

Deborah DILLINGHAM, b. 23 Mar. 1764

Zebulon SILVESTER, (son of Israel), b. 25 Jan. 1689 <Scituate VR >; d. betw 26 Apr. 1766 (will) - 4 Aug. 1766 (prob.) <Plymouth Co.Prob.#20030, 19:380>

CHILDREN OF Zebulon SILVESTER & Mary TURNER^5 (Elisha^4): (9)

Olive SILVESTER^{6}, b. 7 Jan. 1713/14

Martha SILVESTER^{6}, b. 30 Mar. 1716 <Scituate VR>; d. aft. 1766* (father's will)(m. Elisha Prouty)

Israel SILVESTER^{6}, bpt. 24 Apr. 1720, Norwell <NEHGR 58:261>; d. 25 Jan. 1812, ae 95 <Scituate VR 2:440>

Elisha SILVESTER^{6}, bpt. 24 Apr. 1720, Norwell <NEHGR 58:261>; d. betw. 17 July (will) - 7 Dec. 1807

Jacob SILVESTER^{6}, b. 17 Aug. 1722; d. 25 or 26 July 1806 <Hanover Ch, VR:198>

Luke SILVESTER^{6}, bpt. 10 Oct. 1731, Norwell Ch, Scituate <NEHGR 59:79>

Zebulon SILVESTER^{6}, bpt. 10 Oct. 1731, Norwell Ch, Scituate <NEHGR 59:79>

Nathaniel SILVESTER^{6}, bpt. 10 Oct. 1731, Norwell Ch, Scituate <NEHGR 59:79>

Mary SILVESTER^{6}, bpt. 13 Aug. 1732, Norwell Ch, Scituate <NEHGR 59:135>

Norwell Church Records:<15a>

Lillis SYLVESTER, (widow of Elisha^{6}), d. 9 Aug. 1812, ae 75 <ChR:2>

Deborah SYLVESTER, (widow of "Zac."), d. 17 Dec. 1815, ae 96 <ChR:3>

Samuel SYLVESTER, d. 5 Feb. 1823, ae 77 <ChR:5>

Marcy TURNER, widow, d. 15 Feb. 1823, ae 67 <ChR:5>

Elisha TURNER, d. 10 Mar. 1823, ae 64 <ChR:5>

Lydia SYLVESTER, d. 27 Mar. 1823, ae 90 <ChR:5>

Elijah TURNER, d. 10 Apr. 1823, ae 74 <ChR:5>

Thomas SYLVESTER, d. 25 Mar. 1827, ae 72 <ChR:7>

Widow of Thomas SYLVESTER, d. 8 Nov. 1831, ae 81 <ChR:9>

CHILDREN OF Elisha SYLVESTER: (2)

Elisha SYLVESTER, bpt. 18 Feb. 1753 <Norwell ChR:15>

Thomas SYLVESTER, bpt. 3 Feb. 1755 <Norwell ChR:18>

Elisha SYLVESTER, (son of Lemuel), bpt. 8 or 15 May 1757 <Norwell ChR:19; Scituate VR 1:351>

* * * * * * * *

Edward PROUTY, d. pre 5 Apr. 1755

Elizabeth HOW, d. betw 13 Nov. 1751 <NEHGR 60:175> - 5 Apr. 1755

CHILDREN OF Edward PROUTY & Elizabeth HOW: (10)

Edward PROUTY, b. 6 Oct. 1702

Elizabeth PROUTY, b. 30 May 1704; d. pre 20 June 1731<16>

James PROUTY, b. 16 Oct. 1706

Richard PROUTY, b. 8 Jan. 1708/9

John PROUTY, b. 17 Oct. 1710; d. 16 Feb. 1710/11

Eunice PROUTY, b. 1 Mar. 1711/12; d. 12 pre Apr. 1788 <Plymouth Co.Prob. 30:353>

Hannah PROUTY, b. 15 May 1714

Elisha PROUTY, b. 19 Mar. 1715 <Scituate VR 1:301> (m. Martha Silvester^{6} (Zebulon^{5}))

Mary PROUTY, bpt. 2 Mar. 1718

Mary PROUTY, b. 22 Oct. 1719

Elisha SILVESTER, b. pre 1718*; d. betw. 29 June 1747 (will) - 6 Dec. 1767 (prob.) <Plymouth Co. Prob.#19960, 19:525>

CHILDREN OF Elisha SILVESTER & Eunice PROUTY (dau of Edw.): (4) <Scituate VR>

Elisha SILVESTER, bpt. 30 Nov. 1735 <VR 1:318>

Elisha SILVESTER, bpt. 4 June 1738 <VR 1:318>

James SILVESTER, bpt. 23 Nov. 1740 <VR 1:319>; d. pre 9 Feb.1781 <Plymouth Co.Probate 27:61>

Simeon SILVESTER, bpt. 5 June 1743 <VR 1:321>; d. pre 29 June 1747 (father's will)

Joanna BROOKS, b. 21 Nov. 1748*; d. 4 Nov. 1820*

CHILDREN OF James SILVESTER (son of Elisha) & Joanna BROOKS: (3)

Eunice SILVESTER, b. c1766*, d. 1833, ae 67 <Scituate VR 2:365>

Bethiah SILVESTER, b. ( )

Miriam SILVESTER, d. pre 15 June 1821

Michael CLAPP^{5} (Sam.^{4}, Jos.^{3}, Sam.^{2}, Tho.^{1}), b. 15 Oct. 1760; d. 19 Oct. 1800*, Hanover<17>

CHILDREN OF Israel SILVESTER: <NEHGR 57:323>

Zebulon SILVESTER, bpt. 1695

Barshua SILVESTER, bpt. 1695

CHILD OF Israel SILVESTER: <Scituate VR 1:317>

Elisha SILVESTER, b. 3 Jan. 1685; living 1727

MICRO #5 of 18

Hannah HUNT, (*dau of Capt. Eben.), b. 4 Oct. 1726*, Weymouth; d. 10 Aug. 1749*<Scituate VR 2:439

CHILD OF Elisha SILVESTER^{6} (Mary Turner^{5}) & 1st Hannah HUNT:<18>

Lurana SILVESTER^{7}, b. 30 May 1748 <Scituate VR 1:320>; d. aft 17 July 1805*

Grace RUGGLES, (dau of John & Joanna), b. 11 Sept. 1725, d. Apr. 1776 <Scituate VR 1:314, 2:439>

CHILDREN OF Elisha SILVESTER^{6} & 2nd Grace RUGGLES: (5) <Scituate VR>

Elisha SILVESTER^{7}, b. 28 Nov. 1752*, d. 31 Dec. 1834 <1:318, 2:449>

Thomas SILVESTER^{7}, b. 26 Nov. 1754* <VR 1:319>; d. 25 Mar. 1827 <Norwell ChR:7><19>

Hannah SILVESTER^{7}, b. 29 Nov. 1758* <VR 1:319>; d. pre 17 July 1805

Chloe SILVESTER^{7}, b. 23 July 1765* <VR 1:318>

CHILD OF Elisha SILVESTER^{6} & 3rd Lillis YOUNG:

Lillis SILVESTER^{7}, b. 7 Aug. 1778 <Scituate VR 1:319>; d. pre 1865*

John RUGGLES, b. c1695, d. 5 Dec. 1772, 77th yr, Norwell g.s., Scituate

Joanna BROOKS, b. c1696, d. 26 Mar. 1779, 83rd yr, Norwell g.s., Scituate

CHILDREN OF John RUGGLES & Joanna BROOKS: (6) <Scituate VR>

Thomas RUGGLES, b. 31 July 1721; d. 10 May 1740

Hannah RUGGLES, b. 22 June 1723; d. 9 Apr. 1742, unm.

Grace RUGGLES, b. 11 Sept. 1725 (see above)

John RUGGLES, bpt. 10 Sept. 1727; d. 26 Mar. 1728

John RUGGLES, b. 13 June 1729; d. 12 May 1812

Sarah RUGGLES, b. 22 May 1731

CHILDREN OF Elisha SILVESTER^{7} (Elisha^{6}) & Abigail PALMER: (3) <Scituate VR 6:births:25>

Ruggles SILVESTER^{8}, b. 26 Dec. 1776

Hervey SILVESTER^{8}, b. 1 June 1779

Mercy SILVESTER^{8}, b. ( )

CHILDREN OF Thomas SILVESTER^{7} (Elisha^{6}) & Relief JORDAN: (8) <Scituate VR 2:169, 258><20>

Relief SILVESTER^{8}, b. 25 July 1773

Warren SILVESTER^{8}, b. 24 Sept. 1775

Mercy SILVESTER^{8}, b. 14 Mar. 1778

Rachel SILVESTER^{8}, b. 16 Mar. 1782

Thomas SILVESTER^{8}, b. 1 Oct. 1784

Charles SILVESTER^{8}, b. 20 Dec. 1787

Tryphena SILVESTER^{8}, b. 25 Sept. 1790

Tryphosa SILVESTER^{8}, b. 19 May 1793

CHILDREN OF Caleb TORREY & Hannah SILVESTER^{7} (Elisha^{6}): (2)

Daniel TORREY^{8}, b. 11 May 1782*

Caleb TORREY^{8}, b. 23 June 1784*

CHILD OF Elnathan CUSHING & Lillis SILVESTER^{7} (Elisha^{6}):

Mary Stockbridge CUSHING^{8}, b. 26 Jan. 1803*

Abiel TURNER, (*?son of Abiel & Eliz. (Robinson)), b. ?3 May 1741*, Scituate

CHILDREN OF Abiel TURNER & Lurana SILVESTER^{7} (Elisha^{6}): (5) <Scituate VR>

Robinson TURNER^{8}, b. 12 Sept. 1767 <VR 1:381>

John TURNER^{8}, b. 19 Apr. 1769 <VR 1:376>

Abial TURNER^{8}, b. 11 Jan. 1779 <VR 1:369>

Pegge TURNER^{8}, b. 3 June 1790 <VR 1:380>

Clarissa TURNER^{8}, b. 14 Dec. ( ) (bpt. 25 June 1791) <VR 1:371>

Deborah LEWIS*, (*dau of John & Deborah (Hawks)), b. 28 June 1720 <Hingham VR 2:443>

CHILD OF Jacob SILVESTER^{6} (Mary Turner^{5}) & 1st Deborah LEWIS:

Deborah SILVESTER^{7}, b. 17 July 1753 <Scituate VR 1:318>; d. 26 Feb. or 16 Mar. 1830

Paul WEBB, b. c1759, d. 12 July 1824, ae 65 (m. Deborah Silvester^{7})

Mary/Molly SILVESTER, (widow of Jacob Silvester^{6}), d. 24 Dec. 1811, ae 81 or 84 <Hanover VR:201, ChR:206> (she was blind in 1806)

CHILD OF Luke SILVESTER^{6} (Mary Turner^{5}) & Mary DAMON:

Luke SILVESTER^{7}, bpt. 3 June 1753 <Norwell ChR:82 (printed)>

Edmund GROSS, b. 10 May 1705* <Hist.Hingham 2:280>; d. c1799 <Plymouth Co.Prob.#8743>

CHILDREN OF Edmund GROSS & Olive SILVESTER^{6} (Mary Turner^{5}): (11) <Scituate Rcds I>

John GROSS^{7}, b. 13 Nov. 1738

Edmund GROSS^{7}, b. 3 Dec. 1739

Olive GROSS^{7}, b. 23 Oct. 1740

Martha GROSS^{7}, b. 13 Jan. 1743

Thomas GROSS^{7}, b. 3 Jan. 1745; d. 8 Oct. 1811

Mary GROSS^{7}, b. 6 June 1748

Elisha GROSS^{7}, b. 16 Mar. 1749; d.? Sept. 1829*

Lucy GROSS^{7}, b. 22 Nov. 1751

Deborah GROSS^{7}, b. 31 Dec. 1756

Joshua GROSS^{7}, b. 8 Apr. 1758

Elijah GROSS^{7}, b. 16 Aug. 1760

Clement MINER Jr., b. 14 Dec. 1700, New London CT; d. 9 Aug. 1775

CHILDREN OF Clement MINER Jr. & Abigail TURNER^{5} (Ezekiel^{4}): (9)<1-6, New London; 7-8, Norwich>

Lucy MINER^{6}, b. 8 Mar. 1722/23

Lydia MINER^{6}, b. 23 Oct. 1724

Abigail MINER^{6}, b. 29 Nov. 1726; d. 10 Aug. 1755, Lyme CT

Jonathan MINER^{6}, b. 10 Feb. 1728/29

Ebenezer MINER^{6}, b. 5 Jan. 1730/31

Martha MINER^{6}, b. 7 Mar. 1732/33

Clement MINER^{6}, b. 14 Apr. 1735

Daniel MINER^{6}, b. 20 May 1737

William MINER^{6}, bpt. 1 Apr. 1747

Richard SMITH, d. betw 27 May 1792 (will) - 6 Mar. 1793 (prob.)

CHILDREN OF Richard SMITH & 1st Abigail MINER^{6}: (5) <Lyme CT>

Anna SMITH^{7}, b. 1 Feb. 1746/47; d. 17 Nov. 1781, West Springfield ("Feeding Hills")

Betsey SMITH^{7}, b. ( )

Richard SMITH^{7}, b. 25 Nov. 1750

Abigail SMITH^{7}, b. 23 Dec. 1752

Lydia SMITH^{7}, b. ( )

CHILDREN OF Richard SMITH & 2nd Grace (LEACH) Moore, (dau of Clement & Eliz. (Keeny)): (8)<21>

Timothy FLOWER, b. 12 Oct. 1743, Wethersfield CT; d. 18 Oct. 1834, West Springfield MA

CHILDREN OF Timothy FLOWER & 1st Anna SMITH^{7}: (7) <"Feeding Hills" (West Springfield)>

Roswell FLOWER^{8}, b. 23 May 1767

Anna FLOWER^{8}, b. 29 Apr. 1769

Timothy FLOWER^{8}, b. 26 Oct. 1771; d. 17 Jan. 1861, Rupert VT

Betsey FLOWER^{8}, b. 25 Nov. 1773

Lydia FLOWER^{8}, b. 16 Jan. 1776

Joseph Warren FLOWER^{8}, b. 9 May 1778

Bernice FLOWER^{8}, b. 10 Aug. 1780

Hannah SPENCER, d. 10 Apr. 1809

CHILDREN OF Timothy FLOWER & 2nd Hannah SPENCER: (3) <Feeding Hills>

Spencer FLOWER, b. 3 Jan. 1785

Ebenezer FLOWER, b. 13 Sept. 1787

Daniel FLOWER, b. 10 Aug. 1790

Clarissa PHILLIPS, b. 16 Feb. 1785, Rupert VT; d. 11 Apr. 1863, Rupert VT

CHILDREN OF Timothy FLOWER^{8} & Clarissa PHILLIPS: (11) <Rupert VT>

Elizabeth FLOWER^{9}, b. 2 July 1802

Clarissa FLOWER^{9}, b. 23 June 1804

Bernice FLOWER^{9}, b. 29 Aug. 1806

Thankful FLOWER^{9}, b. 29 Apr. 1809

Timothy Smith FLOWER^{9}, b. 11 Nov. 1811

Elihu Spear FLOWER^{9}, b. 27 Aug. 1813; d. 18 Feb. 1897

Horace Spencer FLOWER^{9}, b. 13 Feb. 1816

Legrand Sherwood FLOWER^{9}, b. 9 June 1819

Cynthia Maria FLOWER^{9}, b. 11 Mar. 1821

Lydia Ann FLOWER^{9}, b. 14 July 1823

Lucinda FLOWER^{9}, b. 19 Apr. 1827

CHILDREN OF Ezekiel TURNER^{5} (Ezekiel^{4}) & 2nd Borodel DENISON^{5} (Jos.^{4}, Mercy Gorham^{3}, Desire Howland^{2}): (5) <Groton CT VR 1:144, Barbour Coll.>**<22>**

Theody TURNER^{6}, b. 14 Aug. 1730*; d. 5 June 1752* <Stonington CT VR 3:196>

Prudence TURNER^{6}, b. 8 Mar. 1731/2*; d. 24 Jan. 1823, Salem CT

Ezekiel TURNER^{6}, b. 27 Jan. 1733/4*; d. 7 Apr. 1826*

Eunice TURNER^{6}, b. 24 July 1740*

Amos TURNER^{6}, b. 1 Sept. 1744*; d. 15 Feb. 1826*

Samuel FOX, (*son of Sam. & Mary), b. 15 June 1724* <Preston CT VR>; d. 13 Dec. 1809, New London

CHILDREN OF Samuel FOX & Prudence TURNER^{6}: (10)

Amos FOX^{7}, b. 4 July 1752*; d. 21 Dec. 1755*

Jesse FOX^{7}, b. 8 Feb. 1754*; d. 13 Feb. 1834*

Ezekiel FOX^{7}, b. 19 Apr. 1756*; d. 6 Apr. 1844*

Asa FOX^{7}, b. 29 Dec. 1758*; d. 7 Mar. 175(9)*

Elijah FOX^{7}, b. 29 Dec. 1758* (twins); d. 12 Mar. 175(9)*

Thankful FOX^{7}, b. 27 Feb. 1759*; d. 5 Mar. 1838*

Elijah FOX^{7}, b. 1 Mar. 1761*; d. 2 Jan. 1847*

Jabez FOX^{7}, b. 26 May 1763*; d. 15 Apr. 1783*

John FOX^{7}, b. 29 May 1765*; d. 28 Mar. 1856*, Boston

Borradell FOX^{7}, b. 21 May 1768*; d. 11 Mar. 1839*

MICRO #6 of 18

CHILDREN OF Daniel BROWN & Theody TURNER^{6}: (2) <Stonington CT VR 1:196>

Daniel BROWN^{7}, b. 3 Feb. 1751*

Theodaty BROWN^{7}, b. 5 June 1752*

Samuel FOSDICK^{5} (Mercy Pickett^{4}, Ruth Brewster^{3}, Jonathan^{2}), b. 18 Sept. 1684 <New London VR 4:303> (hus of Susanna Turner^{5} (Ezekiel^{4}))

Richard CHRISTOPHERS, b. 13 July 1662*, d. 9 June 1726* <Hist.New London CT:317>

Lucretia BRADLEY^{4} (Eliz. Brewster^{3}, Jonathan^{2}), b. 16 Aug. 1661 <MD 1:72>; d. pre Sept. 1691 (1st wf of Richard Christophers.

CHILDREN OF Richard CHRISTOPHERS & 2nd Grace TURNER^{4} (Mary Brewster^{3}): (7) <New London CT VR>

Joseph CHRISTOPHERS^{5}, b. 14 July 1692 <VR 4:297>

Mary CHRISTOPHERS^{5}, b. 18 Sept. 1694 <VR 4:295>

Jonathan CHRISTOPHERS^{5}, b. 19 Sept. 1696, d. 12 Oct. 1696 <VR 4:295>

Grace CHRISTOPHERS^{5}, b. 14 Oct. 1698 <VR 4:293>; d. 9 Nov. 1745 <New London CT VR>

Lydia CHRISTOPHERS^{5}, b. 10 Aug. 1701 <VR 4:290>

Ruth CHRISTOPHERS^{5}, b. 26 Sept. 1705 <VR 4:285>

Joanna CHRISTOPHERS^{5}, b. 19 Mar. 1706 <VR 4:284>

CHILDREN OF Richard CHRISTOPHERS & Mrs. Elizabeth SALTONSTALL: (3) <New London CT VR>

Richard CHRISTOPHERS, b. 29 July 1712

Elizabeth CHRISTOPHERS, b. 13 Sept. 1714

Mary CHRISTOPHERS, b. 17 Dec. 1716

John COIT, (son of John & Mehitable (Chandler)), b. 25 May 1696 <New London CT VR:76>

CHILDREN OF John COIT & 1st Grace CHRISTOPHERS^{5} (Grace Turner^{4}): (5) <New London CT VR>

John COIT^{6}, b. 7 Apr. 1720, d. 26 Mar. 1745, drowned, Middletown CT

Richard COIT^{6}, b. 8 July 1722 <VR 4:249>

Elizabeth COIT^{6}, b. 31 Dec. 1724, d. 25 Apr. 1725

Samuel COIT^{6}, b. 14 Oct. 1726

Joseph COIT^{6}, b. 3 Oct. 1728

CHILDREN OF John COIT & 2nd Hannah (GARDNER) Potter (dau of Henry): (3) <Coit Gen.:29,30>

Desire COIT, b. 15 Oct. 1749

John COIT, b. 30 Oct. 1752

Mehitable COIT, b. 16 June 1755

CHILD OF John COIT^{6} & Mary PEIRCE, (dau of Robert & Ann):

Grace COIT^{7}, b. 27 Aug. 1744

Elizabeth RICHARDS, (dau of David), b. 9 Feb. 1733; d. 14 Aug. 1826**<23>**

CHILDREN OF Samuel COIT^{6} (Grace Christophers^{5}) & Elizabeth RICHARDS: (10) <Coit Gen:49; 1-3, New London CT VR 2:109>**<23>**

Elizabeth COIT^{7}, b. 25 Nov. 1753

Samuel COIT^{7}, b. 22 Dec. 1755; d. 10 Sept. 1756

Rhoda COIT^{7}, b. 1 Sept. 1757

Lydia COIT^{7}, b. Apr. 1759

Samuel COIT^{7}, b. 17 June 1761

David COIT^{7}, b. 29 Dec. 1764; d. 13 May 1831, Cedar Grove Cem., New London CT

John COIT^{7}, b. 12 Mar. 1767

Grace COIT^{7}, b. 26 June 1770

Lucretia COIT^{7}, b. 26 Jan. 1773

Richard COIT^{7}, b. 31 Jan. 1776

Sarah OGDEN, (dau of David & Mary (Wilkinson)), b. 23 Apr. 1768 <1st Presb.Ch, Morristown NJ:174> d. 30 Apr. 1841, Cedar Grove Cem., New London CT

CHILDREN OF David COIT^{7} & Sarah OGDEN: (9)**<24>**

Mary COIT^{8}, b. 5 Jan. 1792

Richard COIT^{8}, b. 28 Sept. 1794

Elizabeth COIT^{8}, b. 31 Mar. 1797

Nancy COIT^{8}, b. 14 Oct. 1799; d. 13 Nov. 1800

Nancy COIT^{8}, b. 11 Dec. 1802

David COIT^{8}, b. 1 July 1805

Sarah COIT^{8}, b. 10 Apr. 18( ); d. 11 Feb. 1892, Newton

William COIT^{8}, b. 30 Dec. 1811

Harriot COIT^{8}, b. 20 Nov. 1814; d. Jan. 1878, unm.

CHILDREN OF John TURNER^{4} (Mary Brewster^{3}) & Abigail PADISHAL* (*dau of Richard): (8)

Abigail TURNER^{5}, b. 29 June 1690*

Child, d. 21 Jan. 1693/4*

John TURNER^5, b. 23 Apr. 1695*

Lydia TURNER^5, b. 5 July 1699*

Richard TURNER^5, b. 5 June 1702*<Scituate VR>; d. betw. 26 Jan. 1752 (will) - 29 Apr. 1752 (prob) <Plymouth Co.Prob.13:41>

Deborah TURNER^5, b. 14 Sept. 1704*

Abiel TURNER^5, b. 4 Oct. 1706* (son); d. 20 Sept. 1798*, Norwell g.s. ("98th yr"), Scituate

Joseph SYLVESTER, d. betw 2 May 1771 (will) - 14 Aug. 1771 (prob.) <Plymouth Co.Prob.21:62>

Lydia TURNER, d. pre 2 May 1771 (hus. will)<25>

CHILDREN OF Joseph SILVESTER & Lydia TURNER: (5)<25>

Lemuel SILVESTER, b. 9 Dec. 1728

Ruth SILVESTER, bpt. 9 May 1731, Norwell Ch

Lydia SILVESTER, bpt. 9 Nov. 1735, Norwell Ch

Deborah SILVESTER, bpt. 5 Aug. 1739, Norwell Ch

Joseph SILVESTER, bpt. 16 May 1742, Norwell Ch

Mehitable COLE, (*dau of James & Sarah), b. 6 Nov. 1753* <Scituate VR 1:86> (wf of Jos.Silvester>

Lydia ROSE, (*dau of Gideon & Lydia), bpt. 30 Apr. 1732*, Norwell Ch, Scituate; d.? 26 Mar. 1823* ae 91 <Scituate VR>

CHILD OF Lemuel SILVESTER (son of Jos.) & Lydia ROSE:

Elisha SILVESTER, bpt. 8 May 1757, Norwell Ch, Scituate

Elizabeth ROBINSON, b. 1713*, d. 28 May 1784*, ae 71y3m20d, Norwell g.s., Scituate

CHILDREN OF Abiel TURNER^5 (John^4) & Elizabeth ROBINSON*: (10) <Scituate VR>

Robinson TURNER^6, b. 17 Feb. 1737 <VR 1:381>

Elizabeth TURNER^6, b. 15 Nov. 1739 <VR 1:373>

Abiel TURNER^6, b. 3 May 1741 <VR 1:369>

Abigail TURNER^6, b. 24 Sept. 1743 <VR 1:369>

Margaret TURNER^6, b. 27 June 1745, d. 15 Dec. 1755 <VR 1:378, 2:457>

Anna TURNER^6, b. 29 June 1747 <VR 1:370>

Rowland TURNER^6, b. 29 June 1747 (twin) <VR 1:381>; d. 18 Dec. 1838*

Bethiah TURNER^6, b. 4 May 1751, d. 6 Nov. 1752 <VR 1:371, 2:455>

Bethiah TURNER^6, b. 4 Jan. 1753 <VR 1:371>

Martha TURNER^6, b. 8 Feb. 1755 <VR 1:378>

CHILDREN OF Abiel TURNER^6 & ?Lurana SILVESTER: (5) <Scituate VR>

Robinson TURNER^6, b. 12 Sept. 1767 <VR 1:381>

John TURNER^6, b. 19 Apr. 1769 <VR 1:376>

Abial TURNER^6, b. 11 Jan.1779 <VR 1:369>

Clarissa TURNER^6, b. 14 Dec. 1790 (sic) <VR 1:371>, bpt. 5 June 1791, Norwell Ch

Pegge TURNER^6, b. 3 June 1790 <VR 1:380>

CHILDREN OF Samuel BRYANT & Abigail TURNER^5 (John^4): (4)*<26>

CHILDREN OF Benjamin WOODWORTH & Abigail BRYANT: (2) <Scituate, Woodworth Desc.:9><27>

Benjamin WOODWORTH, b. 29 Dec. 1782

Samuel WOODWORTH, b. 13 Jan. 1784, d. 9 Dec. 1842, NY

CHILDREN OF Samuel WOODWORTH (son of Ben.) & Lydia REEDER:<28>

Ruth FOSTER, d. betw 12 July 1753 (will) - 18 Aug. 1753 (prob.)

CHILDREN OF Richard TURNER^5 (John^4) & Ruth FOSTER: (7)<29>

Martha BISBEE, (dau of Elisha), bpt. 27 Apr. 1651*, Norwell Ch <Scituate VR 1:34>; d. 24 Mar. 1687 <Scituate Rcds 4:4:4>

CHILDREN OF Jonathan TURNER^4 (Mary Brewster^3) & 1st Martha BISBEE: (5) <Scituate Rcds 4:3:87>

Deborah TURNER^5, b. 2 Dec. 1678

Jemima TURNER^5, b. 9 Oct. 1680

Isaac TURNER[5], b. 27 Feb. 1682; d. aft. 25 Apr. 1725* (father's estate)

Keziah TURNER[5], b. 3 May 1687

Jonathan TURNER[5], b. 13 Mar. 1687; d. 7 June 1687 <Scituate Rcds 4:4:4>

Mercy HATCH, (dau of Jeremiah), b. 15 Apr. 1665 <Scituate Rcds 4:3:26>

CHILDREN OF Jonathan TURNER[4] & 2nd Mercy HATCH: (6) <Scituate Rcds 4:3:87>

Mercy TURNER[5], b. 27 Oct. 1690

Ruth TURNER[5], b. 6 Mar. 1693/4

Ignatius TURNER[5], b. 15 Mar. 1697/8

Martha TURNER[5], b. 24 Apr. 1700

Jesse TURNER[5], b. 24 Dec. 1704

Mary TURNER[5], b. 28 July 1706

CHILDREN OF Isaac TURNER[5] & Ruth TURNER (dau of Ezekiel): (6) <Norwell Ch, Scituate VR>

Susanna TURNER[6], b. 12 Aug. 1712 <VR 1:382>

Jonathan TURNER[6], b. 27 May 1714 <VR 1:376>

Isaac TURNER[6], bpt. 5 Apr. 1719 <VR 1:375>

Lemuel TURNER[6], bpt. 14 Aug. 1720 <VR 1:377>

Ezekiel TURNER[6], bpt. 23 Sept. 1722 <VR 1:373>

Waitstill TURNER[6], bpt. 29 Nov. 1724 <VR 1:383>

Polly/Mary ANDREWS, d. 31 May 1869, ae 94y2m26d, New Salem, widow, b. Baynham, dau of Michael & Batheba Turner <Mass.VR 220:285> (wf of Daniel Andrews)

Joshua CLAPP, b. 7 Jan. 1729, d. 1812, ae "about 80" <Clapp Mem.:115>

Lydia SHORT, b. c1728, d. 17 July 1786, 58th yr <Clapp Mem.>

CHILDREN OF Joshua CLAPP & Lydia SHORT: (6) <Clapp Mem.>

Lydia CLAPP, b. 14 Sept. 1758, d.y.

Bela CLAPP, b. 2 July 1760, d. 12 July 1812, Claremont NH

Lydia CLAPP, b. 3 July 1762

Caleb CLAPP, b. 9 May 1764, d. 19 May 1829, Westminister VT

Matthew S. CLAPP, b. 4 Oct. 1766

Ann CLAPP, b. 30 Aug. 1771

Polycarpus JACOBS, d. 1852, Milton

CHILDREN OF Polycarpus JACOBS & Lydia CLAPP (dau of Joshua): (8)

Lusanna JACOBS, b. 3 May 1798

Malinthe JACOBS, b. 15 June 1799

Elizabeth JACOBS, b. 15 June 1802

Leah JACOBS, b. 15 Mar. 1804

Edward Foster JACOBS, b. 2 Feb. 1805

Almena JACOBS, b. 23 July 1808

Rachel JACOBS, b. 28 Oct. 1810

Thales JACOBS, b. 3 Sept. 1812

CHILDREN OF Samuel COFFIN & Elizabeth GARDNER: (11) <Nantucket VR 3:310>

Elihu COFFIN, b. 9 7mth 1745

Thomas COFFIN, b. 7 11mth 1747

Simeon COFFIN, b. 5 4mth 1750

Samuel COFFIN, b. 7 Sept. 1752

Tristram COFFIN, b. 5 Apr. 1755

Obed COFFIN, b. 14 Sept. 1757

Phebe COFFIN, b. 10 Nov. 1760

Barnabas COFFIN, b. 7 Mar. 1763

Miriam COFFIN, b. 14 Sept. 1765

Rebecca COFFIN, b. 29 May 1770<30>

CHILDREN OF Jesse TURNER^{5} (Jonathan^{4}) & 2nd Lydia NEAL: (7) <Scituate VR>**<31>**
Mercy TURNER^{6}, b. 9 Dec. 1741; d. 11 Dec. 1741
Jonathan TURNER^{6}, b. 27 Dec. 1742; d. Nov. 1821
Abigail TURNER^{6}, b. 19 Oct. 1744
Seth TURNER^{6}, b. 19 Dec. 1746, d.y.
Seth TURNER^{6}, b. 29 Nov. 1748
Lydia TURNER^{6}, b. 3 Feb. 1753
David TURNER^{6}, b. 4 Dec. 1754
Jonah STETSON, (*son of Samuel), b. Apr. 1691* <Scituate VR>; d. Apr. 1766*, Norwell g.s.Scituate
CHILDREN OF Jonah STETSON & Mercy TURNER^{5} (Jonathan^{4}): (3)
Jonah STETSON^{6}, bpt. 25 Feb. 1721/2; d. Dec. 1782
Eunice STETSON^{6}, bpt. 29 Nov. 1724
Micah(?) STETSON^{6}, bpt. 4 July 1729; d. July 1729, ae 2m
Amos PERRY, (*son of Wm.), b. 10 Mar. 1690/91* <Scituate VR 1:292>; d. pre 5 July 1756 (adm.)<Plymouth Co.Prob.#15670, 14:406, 15:13>
CHILDREN OF Amos PERRY & Ruth TURNER^{5} (Jonathan^{4}): (9) <Scituate>**<32>**
Ruth PERRY^{6}, bpt. 10 Sept. 1721
Priscilla PERRY^{6}, bpt. 13 Oct. 1723
Mary PERRY^{6}, bpt. 18 July 1725
Amos PERRY^{6}, bpt. 11 Oct 1726 (sick)
William PERRY^{6}, bpt. 30 Aug. 1729 (sick, not likely to live)
Hannah PERRY^{6}, bpt. 31 May 1731 (sick, in great danger)
Amos PERRY^{6}, bpt. 17 Mar. 1733/4
Isaac PERRY^{6}, bpt. 5 Sept. 1736
Jonathan PERRY^{6}, bpt. 17 July 1740
CHILD OF Isaac PERRY^{6} & 1st Betty CHUBBUCK:
Ruth Turner PERRY^{7}, b. Oct. 1777; d. 8 Mar. 1855
Jemima FARROW, bpt. 4 May 1746; d. Nov. 1824, ae 78 (2nd wf of Isaac Perry^{6})**<33>**
Bathsheba (HOBART) Leavitt, b. c1641, d. 14 Ar. 1724, ae 83, Norwell g.s. <MD 32:111>**<34>**
CHILDREN OF Joseph TURNER^{4} (Mary Brewster^{3}) & Bathsheba (HOBART) Leavitt: (3)* <Scituate VR>
Margaret TURNER^{5}, b. 20 Sept. 1677 <VR 1:378>; d. 17 Oct. 1732* <Hanover TR:192>
Bathshua TURNER^{5}, b. 30 Dec. 1679 <VR 1:370>; d. 16 Mar. 1744, Norwell g.s. <MD 32:108>
Joseph TURNER^{5}, bpt. 11 June 1682 <VR 1:376>

MICRO #7 of 18

Hatherly FOSTER^{4} (*Timothy^{3}, Edw.^{2}, Timothy^{1}), b. 22 Sept. 1671*, Dorchester; d. 11 July 1751, ae 79y11m, Norwell g.s. <MD 32:108>
CHILDREN OF Hatherly FOSTER & Bathshua TURNER^{5}: (8)* <Scituate VR>
Margaret FOSTER^{6}, b. 20 Aug. 1699 <VR 1:156>
Joseph FOSTER^{6}, b. 8 Aug. 1702 <VR 1:156>
Ruth FOSTER^{6}, b. 14 May 1704, d. 3 Oct. 1704 <VR 1:156>
Timothy FOSTER^{6}, b. 4 Mar. 1706 <VR 1:157>; d. 13 Sept. 1730
Elisha FOSTER^{6}, b. 28 May 1708 <VR 1:155>; d. 23 Apr. 1771
John FOSTER^{6}, b. 12 Jan. 1711/12 <VR 1:156>
Ruth FOSTER^{6}, bpt. 4 Aug. 1717 <VR 1:156>
Elizabeth FOSTER^{6}, b. 14 Feb. 1721 <VR 1:155>
CHILDREN OF Joseph FOSTER^{6} & Abigail STEEL: (7)* <Scituate VR>
Margaret FOSTER^{7}, b. 20 May 1734 <VR 1:156>
Hatherly FOSTER^{7}, b. 21 Apr. 1737 <VR 1:155>
Abigail FOSTER^{7}, b. 2 Feb. 1738 <VR 1:154>
Betty FOSTER^{7}, b. 19 May 1741 <VR 1:154>

Joseph FOSTER^{7}, b. 27 Feb. 1742 <VR 1:156>

Timothy FOSTER^{7}, b. 23 Mar. 1744 <VR 1:157>

Steel FOSTER^{7}, b. 17 Dec. 1750 <VR 1:157>

Joseph STOCKBRIDGE, (*son of Charles), b. 28 June 1672* <Scituate VR 1:336>; d. 11 Mar. 1773* <Hanover TR:192>

CHILDREN OF Joseph STOCKBRIDGE & Margaret TURNER^{5} (Jos.^{4}): (7)* <Pembroke VR:197>

Joseph STOCKBRIDGE^{6}, b. 1 Oct. 1698

Grace STOCKBRIDGE^{6}, b. 12 Aug. 1700

John STOCKBRIDGE^{6}, b. 11 Apr. 1704; d. 28 Oct. 1704 <VR 1:451>

Barsheba STOCKBRIDGE^{6}, b. 12 Oct. 1706

Margaret STOCKBRIDGE^{6}, b. 19 Oct. 1708

Lu(ci)anna STOCKBRIDGE^{6}, b. 12 Aug. 1711; d. 28 Dec. 1711 <VR 1:451>

David STOCKBRIDGE^{6}, b. 14 Sept. 1713; d. 23 Dec. 1788* <Hanover ChR 1:196>

Deborah CUSHING, d. 27 Mar. 1747* <Hanover ChR 1:184>

CHILDREN OF David STOCKBRIDGE^{6} & 1st Deborah CUSHING: (3)* <Hanover VR:13>

Joseph STOCKBRIDGE^{7}, b. 20 Aug. 1737; d. 5 Apr. 1761*, ME <Hanover VR:192>

Betty STOCKBRIDGE^{7}, b. 22 Apr. 1739

John STOCKBRIDGE^{7}, b. 7 Dec. 1741 <VR:14>; d. 10 Feb. 1768*

CHILDREN OF David STOCKBRIDGE^{6} & 2nd Jane (REED): (4)* <Hanover VR:14>

Child, d. 18 July 1751 <Hanover ChR 1:185>

William STOCKBRIDGE^{7}, b. 20 Dec. 1752

David STOCKBRIDGE^{7}, b. 19 May 1755; d. 26 Feb. 1843* <Hanover Cem.1:285>

Deborah STOCKBRIDGE^{7}, b. 18 Aug. 1761; d. 2() May 1829

Ruth CUSHING, (*dau of Joseph), b. c1761, d. 11 Apr. 1833*, 72nd yr <Hanover Cem.1:285>

CHILDREN OF David STOCKBRIDGE^{7} & Ruth CUSHING: (8)* <Hanover VR:40>

Joseph Reed STOCKBRIDGE^{8}, b. 6 Oct. 1780

Benjamin STOCKBRIDGE^{8}, b. 7 Nov. 1781

David STOCKBRIDGE^{8}, b. 25 Nov. 1783

Martin STOCKBRIDGE^{8}, b. 20 Dec. 1785

Horatio STOCKBRIDGE^{8}, b. 27 Apr. 1788

Deborah STOCKBRIDGE^{8}, b. 4 Nov. 1790

Ruth STOCKBRIDGE^{8}, b. 23 Mar. 1793

Joseph Cushing STOCKBRIDGE^{8}, b. 4 July 1798

John JAMES, d. pre 5 Mar. 1678 <MD 19:97,98>

CHILD OF John JAMES & Lydia TURNER^{4} (Mary Brewster^{3}):

John JAMES^{5}, b. 10 Jan. 1676/7, Scituate <MD 5:42>; d. 28 Sept. 1761, Scituate g.s., Norwell Old Cem., Main St. <MD 20:153>

William BARRELL, b. c1654, d. 7 Nov. 1689*, ae 35, Norwell g.s.

CHILDREN OF William BARRELL & Lydia (TURNER^{4}) James: (5) <Scituate Rcds.4:-:47>

Mary BARRELL^{5}, bpt. 22 May 1681, d.y.

William BARRELL^{5}, b. 28 Mar. 1683; d. betw. 19 Oct. 1745* - 4 Nov. 1752 (adm.)

Lydia BARRELL^{5}, b. 25 May 1684; d. pre 4 May 1768 (adm.)

Mary BARRELL^{5}, b. 10 Sept. 1686

James BARRELL^{5}, b. 20 Sept. 1687; d. 1 June 1710 <4:-:5>

Norwell Church Rcds., Scituate <NEHGR>

CHILDREN OF William BARRELL & Abigail ( ): (7) <NEHGR>

Abigail BARRELL, bpt. 5 May 1728 <59:74>

James BARRELL, bpt. 5 May 1728 <59:74>

Mary BARRELL, bpt. 1 Aug. 1731 <59:78>

John BARRELL, bpt. 31 Mar. 1734 <59:136>

Elisha BARRELL, bpt. 28 Sept. 1735 <59:138>

Coleburn BARRELL, bpt. 7 May 1738 <59:314>

CHILDREN OF William BARRELL & Lydia ( ): (2) <NEHGR>

Joshua BARRELL, bpt. 30 Nov. 1746 <59:392>

Lydia BARRELL, bpt. 16 Dec. 1748 (mother dec'd) <60:64>

CHILDREN OF James BARRELL & Deborah ( ): (2) <NEHGR>

James BARRELL, bpt. 30 June 1751 <60:66>

William BARRELL, bpt. 14 Oct. 1753 <60:179>

CHILD OF James BARRELL Jr. & ( ): <NEHGR>

Elias BARRELL, bpt. 3 July 1791 <60:271>

CHILDREN OF William BARRELL & ( ): (2) <NEHGR>

Lucy BARRELL, bpt. 9 Sept. 1792 <60:271>

Ruth BARRELL, bpt. 9 Sept. 1792 <60:271>

CHILDREN OF Luther BARRELL & ( ): (3) <NEHGR>

Luther BARRELL, bpt. 13 Jan. 1793 <60:272>

Nabby Leavet BARRELL, bpt. 9 Aug. 1795 <60:273>

Fanny D. BARRELL, bpt. 30 Sept. 1798 <60:274>

* * * * * * * *

CHILDREN OF John BARREL & Judith ( ): (2) <Bridgewater VR 3:228>

Molley BARREL, b. 1 Oct. 1757

John BARREL, b. 11 Mar. 1760, d. 7 Mar. 1762

CHILDREN OF William BARREL & Sarah ( ): (7) <Bridgewater VR 3:299>

James BARREL, b. 20 May 1753, d. 4 Sept. 1753

Sarah BARREL, b. 24 Nov. 1754

Lydia BARREL, b. 26 June 1757

Hannah BARREL, b. 4 Dec. 1759

Ruth BARREL, b. 3 Feb. 1762

Content BARREL, b. 6 Sept. 1764

James BARREL, b. 11 Dec. 1766

CHILDREN OF Joshua BARREL & Olive ( ): (4) <Bridgewater VR 3:407>

Susanna BARREL, b. 12 Oct. 1771

Jannet BARREL, b. 29 June 1774

William BARREL, b. 11 Nov. 1776

Jonathan BARREL, b. 13 Apr. 1779, d. 16 Nov. 1779

Content BARRELL, d. 20 Jan. 1823, ae 58 <Bridgewater VR 4:66>

Major James BARRELL, d. 11 Oct. 1810, ae 45 <Bridgewater VR 4:73>

James C. BARRELL, d. 5 Jan. 1812, ae 25 <Bridgewater VR 4:73>

William BARRELL, d. betw 18 Aug. 1806 (will) - 1 Sept. 1806 (prob.), Scituate <Plymouth Co.Prob. 40:493>

Rebecca WILDER^{4} (Isaac^{3}, John^{2}, Edw.^{1}), b. 29 Dec. 1749, Hingham; d. pre Aug. 1806*

CHILDREN OF William BARRELL & Rebecca WILDER: (7) <Scituate VR>

William BARRELL, b. 7 Feb. 1776

Rebecca BARRELL, b. 25 Nov. 1777

Bathsheba BARRELL, b. 8 June 1779

Betsey BARRELL, b. 11 Aug. 1782

Lucinda BARRELL, b. 11 Jan. 1784

Lucy BARRELL, b. 18 Apr. 1787

Ruth BARRELL, b. 25 Dec. 1789

CHILDREN OF William BARRELL & Elizabeth ( ): (3) <Scituate>

Hannah BARRELL, bpt. 26 Sept. 1714

William BARRELL, b. 23 June 1714

James BARRELL, b. 29 Dec. 1727, "lived 99 yrs."

Eunice STETSON, (*dau of Benjamin), bpt. 27 May 1683*, Norwell Ch, Scituate<35>; d. 29 Aug. 1717, ae 35, Scituate g.s., Norwell Old Cem., Main St.

CHILDREN OF John JAMES^{5} (Lydia Turner^{4}) & Eunice STETSON: (8) <Scituate TR 4:112>

Eunice JAMES^{6}, b. 25 Mar. 1703, d.y.

Mary JAMES^{6}, b. 5 Oct. 1704

Eunice JAMES^{6}, b. 5 Feb. 1706/7 <VR 1:198>; d. 16 Aug. 1798*, Scituate g.s., Norwell <VR 2:456>

John JAMES^{6}, b. 5 June 1709; d. 3 Sept. 1764, Scituate, S. Parrish g.s., Main St., Norwell

Benjamin JAMES^{6}, b. 12 May 1711; d. 28 Nov. 1788, Union St. g.s., Scituate

Lydia JAMES^{6}, b. 13 May 1713, d. 7 Aug. 1714

Elisha JAMES^{6}, b. 5 Apr. 1715

Zipporah JAMES^{6}, b. 22 Aug. 1717

Rhoda KING, d. 24 July 1731 <Scituate TR 4:10>

CHILD OF John JAMES^{6} & 1st Rhoda KING: <Scituate TR 4:112>

John JAMES^{7}, b. 12 July 1731; d. 19 Oct. 1775, Scituate, S. Parish g.s., Main St., Norwell

Prudence STANTON, b. c1710, d. 6 Aug. 1783, ae 73, Scituate, S. Parrish g.s., Main St.

CHILDREN OF John JAMES^{6} & 2nd Prudence STANTON: (9) <Scituate TR 4:112>

Staunton JAMES^{7}, b. 13 Oct. 1738

Prudence JAMES^{7}, b. 23 Dec. 1740

Rhoda JAMES^{7}, b. 29 Sept. 1742

Elisha JAMES^{7}, b. 13 Aug. 1744; d. 28 Dec. 1833*

William JAMES^{7}, b. 1 June 1746; d. 6 Jan. 1832*

Eunice JAMES^{7}, b. 9 Mar. 1747

Lydia JAMES^{7}, b. 27 Nov. 1749

Lucy JAMES^{7}, b. 8 Oct. 1751

Thomas JAMES^{7}, b. 9 June 1753

Mercy STOCKBRIDGE^{5} (*Mercy Tilden^{4}, Hannah Little^{3}, Anna Warren^{2}), b. 6 May 1707* <Scituate VR>; d. 6 Jan. 1788, Union St. g.s., Scituate

CHILDREN OF Benjamin JAMES^{6} (John^{5}) & Mercy STOCKBRIDGE: (2) <Scituate TR 4:134>

Mercy JAMES^{7}, b. 11 Sept. 1737

Benjamin JAMES^{7}, b. 23 Feb. 1744/5; d. 23 Mar. 1797, James Cem., Greenbush, Scituate <MD 10:28>

Sarah HOLMES, b. c1750, d. 30 Mar. 1796, 46th yr, James Cem., Greenbush, Scituate <MD 10:28>

CHILDREN OF Benjamin JAMES^{7} & Sarah HOLMES*: (6) <Scituate TR>

Sarah/Sally JAMES^{8}, b. 1 Feb. 1772

Benjamin JAMES^{8}, b. 10 May 1774; d. 31 Aug. 1827, Scituate g.s. <MD 10:28>

John JAMES^{8}, b. 12 Sept. 1776; d. 14 Oct. 1862, Scituate g.s., James Cem. <MD 10:28>

Mercy JAMES^{8}, b. 27 July 1778

Polly JAMES^{8}, b. 25 Apr. 1781

Elisha JAMES^{8}, b. 29 Apr. 1785; d. 25 Feb. 1854, Scituate g.s. <MD 10:28>

CHILD OF Peleg FORD & Mercy JAMES^{8}: <(Mass.VR) 419:361>

Harriet FORD^{9}, b. 24 Nov. 1801, Scituate, d. 10 Apr. 1891, Scituate (widow of Elijah Clapp)

Nathaniel TURNER^{7} (James^{6}, Mary Turner^{5}, Amos^{4}, Mary Brewster^{3}, Jonathan^{2}), b. 28 Sept. 1765*, <Scituate VR>; d. 24 Mar. 1846

CHILDREN OF Nathaniel TURNER & Sally/Sarah JAMES^{8} (Ben.^{7}): (6) <Scituate VR>

Sally James TURNER^{9}, b. 26 July 1792; d. 1834<36>

Mary TURNER^{9}, b. 2 June 1796

Lydia TURNER^{9}, b. 10 Sept. 1798

Nathaniel TURNER^{9}, b. 25 June 1802

Marcy TURNER^{9}, b. 13 Apr. 1808; d. 2 Sept. 1822<37>

Samuel Humphrey TURNER^{9}, b. 13 Aug. 1811

Augustus COLE, (son of Charles & Esther), b. 24 Nov. 1789

CHILDREN OF Augustus COLE & Sally James TURNER^{9}: (5) <Scituate VR>

Sarah James COLE^{10}, b. 28 May 1820

Mercy James COLE^{10}, b. 23 Oct. 1825

Augustus COLE^{10}, b. 1 Jan. 1828

Charles COLE^{10}, b. 2 Apr. 1831

Esther COLE^{10}, b. 2 Apr. 1831 (twins)

Anna JAMES, wf of Ben. James^{8} (Ben.^{7}), d. 11 Feb. 1827, 55th yr, Scituate g.s.

Abigail TURNER, (*dau of Elisha & Prudence (James)), b. c1779, d. 15 Feb. 1862, ae 83, Scituate g.s., James Cem., Greenbush <MD 10:28> (wf of John James^{8} (Ben.^{7}))

Charles TURNER^{3}, (*Charles^{2}, Tho.^{1}), b. 30 Sept. 1705* <Scituate VR 1:371>; d. 3 Oct. 1782*, Scituate g.s., Norwell Cem. <VR 2:455>

CHILDREN OF Charles TURNER & Eunice JAMES^{6} (John^{5}): (6)* <Scituate>**<38>**

Eunice TURNER^{7}, bpt. 3 May 1730

Rev. Charles TURNER^{7}, bpt. 5 Aug. 1733

George TURNER^{7}, bpt. 26 May 1738 (sick)

Edward TURNER^{7}, bpt. 3 Sept. 1739 (sick)

Child, bpt. 6 May 1741 ("sick & not like to live")

William TURNER^{7}, bpt. 25 Jan. 1746/7; d. Turner ME*

Sarah TILDEN^{5} (Desire Oldham^{4}, Mercy Sprout^{3}, Eliz. Samson^{2}), b. c1732, d. 25 Sept. 1761, ae 29, Scituate g.s., S. Parish Cem., Main St., Norwell

CHILD OF John JAMES^{7} (John^{6})& 1st Sarah TILDEN:

John JAMES^{8}, b. 15 Jan. 1759* <Scituate VR>; d. 15 Oct. 1761

Hannah JACOB, (*dau of Jos. & Marcy*), b. 9 May 1739* <Scituate VR>; d. 17 Nov. 1816, Scituate g.s., S. Parish Cem., Main St., Norwell

CHILDREN OF John JAMES^{7} & 2nd Hannah JACOB: (6) <Scituate VR>

Sarah JAMES^{8}, b. 27 Mar. 1764*

John JAMES^{8}, b. 27 July 1766*

Hannah JAMES^{8}, b. 5 Sept. 1768*; d. 30 Dec. 1782

George JAMES^{8}, b. 15 Feb. 1771*

Joseph JAMES^{8}, b. 11 July 1773*

Charles JAMES^{8}, b. 30 ( ) 1775*

CHILDREN OF John JAMES^{8} & Patience CLAPP: (12) <Scituate VR>

John JAMES^{9}, b. 19 Jan. 1789

Galen JAMES^{9}, b. 29 Sept. 1790

Hannah JAMES^{9}, b. 30 Mar. 1792

Horace JAMES^{9}, b. 3 Jan. 1794

Harriet JAMES^{9}, b. 1 Jan. 1796

Lucy JAMES^{9}, b. 30 Dec. 1797

Charles JAMES^{9}, b. 18 Aug. 1800

Joseph JAMES^{9}, b. 27 Nov. 1802

Almira JAMES^{9}, b. 11 Mar. 1805

Eliza JAMES^{9}, b. 14 Aug. 1807

Mary JAMES^{9}, b. 9 Mar. 1810

Thomas JAMES^{9}, b. 30 June 1812

Sally Cole WADE, (*dau of Snell & Charlotte (Otis)), b. 17 Mar. 1789* <Scituate VR>

CHILDREN OF John JAMES$^{9?}$ & Sally Cole WADE: (3)*

Charlotte JAMES, b. 27 Sept. 1815, Scituate

Harriet Maria JAMES, b. 25 July 1817, Scituate

Elizabeth Ha(v)ard JAMES, b. 10 June 1819, Medford

Samuel STOCKBRIDGE, b. c1679, d. 20 July 1758*, ae 79, Norwell g.s., Scituate

CHILDREN OF Samuel STOCKBRIDGE & Lydia BARRELL^{5} (Lydia Turner^{4}): (6) <Scituate Rcds 4:3:113>

Lydia STOCKBRIDGE^{6}, b. 7 Jan. 1704/5

Persis STOCKBRIDGE^{6}, b. 22 Jan. 1707/8

Samuel STOCKBRIDGE^{6}, b. 13 May 1711

James STOCKBRIDGE^{6}, b. 4 Apr. 1714

Abigail STOCKBRIDGE^{6}, b. 3 June 1719

Abiel STOCKBRIDGE^{6}, b. 14 Feb. 1720 (dau); d. aft. 13 Aug. 1768* <Plymouth Co.Prob.20:219>

CHILD OF Joseph BENSON & Abiel STOCKBRIDGE^{6}:

Joseph BENSON^{7}, bpt. 16 Dec. 1744*, Scituate <NEHGR 59:340>

CHILDREN OF John BRYANT & Abiel (STOCKBRIDGE^{6}) Benson: (3)*

John BRYANT^{7}, bpt. 1 (Dec.) 17(51), Norwell Ch, Scituate

Abiah BRYANT^{7}, b. 9 July 1755

Elizabeth BRYANT^{7}, b. 1763; d. July 1808 <Scituate VR 2:420>

Noah MERRITT, (*son of Obadiah & Deborah), b. 26 Feb. 1759*, d. 31 May 1831* <Scituate VR 1:250, 2:422> (hus of Eliz. Bryant^{7})

CHILDREN OF James CUSHING & Mary BARRELL^{5} (Lydia Turner^{4}): (5)*

Lydia CUSHING^{6}, b. 15 Dec. 1714

James CUSHING^{6}, b. 16 Sept. 1716

Sarah CUSHING^{6}, b. 30 Nov. 1718; d. 15 Sept. 1722

Content CUSHING^{6}, b. 19 July 1722

Sarah CUSHING^{6}, bpt. 12 June 1726

CHILDREN OF William BARRELL^{5} (Lydia Turner^{4}) & 1st Elizabeth BAILEY, (dau of John): (3)<Scituate>

Hannah BARRELL^{6}, b. 12 Jan. 1706/7 <VR 1:25>

Lydia BARRELL^{6}, b. 15 Dec. 1709 <VR 1:25>**<39>**

William BARRELL^{6}, b. 23 June 1714 <VR 1:26>; d. 7 Mar. 1806*, g.s. <E. Bridgewater:220>

CHILDREN OF William BARRELL^{5} & 2nd Abigail BOWKER: (7)**<40>**

James BARRELL^{6}, b. 29 Dec. 1729*; d. 17 Apr. 1827, ae 99 <Scituate VR>

Abigail BARRELL^{6}, bpt. 5 May 1728

Mary BARRELL^{6}, bpt. 1 Aug. 1731

John BARRELL^{6}, bpt. 31 Mar. 1734

Elisha BARRELL^{6}, bpt. 28 Sept. 1735; d. 21 May 1829*, Hanover

Colburn BARRELL^{6}, bpt. 7 May 1738

Abigail BARRELL^{6}, bpt. 18 July 1742

Mary COLLAMORE, (*dau of John), b. c1736, d. 8 Jan. 1831*, ae 95

CHILDREN OF Elisha BARRELL^{6} & Mary COLLAMORE: (3)*

Mary BARRELL^{7}, b. 21 Sept. 1774; d. aft. 1850

Elisha BARRELL^{7}, b. 7 Mar. 1777; d. aft. 1850

Sarah BARRELL^{7}, b. 4 Feb. 1779; d. 1845

Deborah BOWKER, d. 10 Mar. 1813 <Scituate VR>

CHILDREN OF James BARRELL^{6} (Wm.^{5}) & Deborah BOWKER: (4)* <1-2, Norwell Ch, Scituate >

James BARRELL^{7}, bpt. 30 June 1751

William BARRELL^{7}, bpt. 14 Oct. 1753

Noah BARRELL^{7}, b. ( )

Bartlett BARRELL^{7}, b. ( )

CHILDREN OF James BARRELL Jr.$^{7?}$ Martha FARROW: (11) <Scituate VR>

James BARRELL, b. 5 Aug. 1773

Benjamin BARRELL, b. 27 Mar. 177(5)

Martha BARRELL, b. 3 Oct. 1777

Jemima BARRELL, b. 5 Dec. 1779

Abel BARRELL, b. 28 Jan. 1784

Anna BARRELL, b. 2 June 1785

Colburn BARRELL, b. 25 Apr. 1787

Lydia BARRELL, b. 18 May 1789

Elias BARRELL, b. 8 June 1791

Desire BARRELL, b. 4 Dec. 1793

Thomas BARRELL, b. 21 Jan. 1796

Joseph YOUNG^{4} (Sarah White^{3}, Peregrine^{2}), b. 10 Oct. 1701 <Scituate VR>

CHILDREN OF Joseph YOUNG & Lydia BARRELL^{6} (Wm.^{5}): (3) <Scituate>

Ruth YOUNG^{7}, b. 24 Nov. 1729

Ezekiel YOUNG^{7}, b. 22 June 1731

Sarah YOUNG^{7}, b. 10 June 1733

Lydia SIMMONS^{4} (Ebenezer^{3}, Aaron^{2}, Moses^{1}), b. 10 Sept. 1719 <Scituate VR>; d. pre June 1751

CHILDREN OF William BARRELL^{6} (Wm.^{5}) & 1st Lydia SIMMONS: (2)

Joshua BARRELL^{7}, bpt. 30 Nov. 1746*; d. 25 May 1828*, Turner ME

Lydia BARRELL^{7}, bpt. 16 Dec. 1748*, d.y.

Sarah CARY, (dau of James), b. 10 June 1723; d. 5 Nov. 1806*, g.s. <E. Bridgewater:220>

CHILDREN OF William BARRELL^{6} & 2nd Sarah CARY: (7)

James BARRELL^{7}, b. 1753*, d.y.

Sarah BARRELL^{7}, b. 1754*

Lydia BARRELL^{7}, b. 1757*

Hannah BARRELL^{7}, b. 1759*; d. 1784*, unm.

Ruth BARRELL^{7}, b. 1762*

Content BARRELL^{7}, b. 1764*; d. 1823*, unm.

James BARRELL^{7}, b. 1766*

Eliphalet PACKARD, (son of Ebenezer), b. c1758, d. 1819*, ae 61

CHILDREN OF Eliphalet PACKARD & Lydia BARRELL^{7}: (5)

Son, b. 7 Dec. 1782; d. 12 Oct. 1784

Robert PACKARD^{8}, b. 15 Oct. 1784

Ruth PACKARD^{8}, b. 19 Sept. 1786

Bela PACKARD^{8}, b. 10 Feb. 1793*

Lydia PACKARD^{8}, b. 14 Mar. 1795*

Olive BASS^{6} (Jonathan$^{5-4}$, Sam.^{3}, Ruth Alden^{2}), d. 20 July 1834*, Turner ME

CHILDREN OF Joshua BARRELL^{7} (Wm.^{6}) & Olive BASS: (9)**<41>**

MICRO #8 of 18

Isaac PRINCE, b. 9 July 1654, Hull; d. 7 Nov. 1718, Boston <NEHGR 5:379,383>

CHILDREN OF Isaac PRINCE & Mary TURNER^{4} (Mary Brewster^{3}): (5 of 11)* <Hull VR:31,32>**<42>**

Alice PRINCE^{5}, b. 17 Dec. 1680

Joseph PRINCE^{5}, d. betw. 20 Jan. 1758 (will) - 27 Jan. 1758 (prob.) <Suffolk Co.Prob.#11708>**<43>**

Mary PRINCE^{5}, b. 2 Dec. 1685; d. 7 Feb. 1769/70

Ruth PRINCE^{5}, b. 10 June 1698

Onner PRINCE^{5}, b. 26 Oct. 1701; d. 18 Jan. 1777 <Weymouth VR 2:299>

John PRINCE, d. betw 25 May 1792 (will) - 14 Aug. 1792 (prob.) <Suffolk Co.Prob.91:541>**<44>**

Joseph GOULD, b. 6 Nov. 1695* (son of Robert & Judith); d. ?21 Dec. 1769* <Gould Gen.(1895):337>

CHILDREN OF Joseph GOULD & Mary PRINCE^{5}: (7) <Hull, Gould Gen.(1895):338>

Joseph GOULD^{6}, b. 27 Jan. 1715

Samuel GOULD^{6}, b. 21 Nov. 1717; d. aft. 1769*

Elisha GOULD^{6}, b. 7 Sept. 1719; d. 12 Feb. 1777*

Mary GOULD^{6}, b. 21 May 1721; d. 25 Feb. 1744***<45>**

Jane GOULD[6], b. 20 Feb. 1722/3; d. 18 Oct. 1795* (wf of Sam. Loring)
Caleb GOULD[6], b. 20 Dec. 1724; aft. 1769*
Joshua GOULD[6], b. 26 Feb. 1728

CHILDREN OF Elisha GOULD[6] & Experience LORING: (9) <Gould Gen.(1895):339>

Elisha GOULD[7], b. 1 Sept. 1745
Jane GOULD[7], b. 13 Sept. 1747, d. 30 Jan. 1797 (wf of Stephen Greenleaf of Boston)
Mehitable GOULD[7], b. 13 Aug. 1750 (m. John Loring of Hull)
Experience GOULD[7], b. 12 Oct. 1752 (m. Abel Barker of Pembroke)
Elizabeth GOULD[7], b. 31 Mar. 1755 (m. John Fillebrown of Boston)
Olive GOULD[7], b. 31 Mar. 1757 (m. Samuel Lovell)
James GOULD[7], b. 28 July 1760, d. 26 Nov. 1774
Lydia GOULD[7], b. 6 Apr. 1763 (m. Jonathan Loring)
Sarah GOULD[7], b. 27 Sept. 1765 (m. Ebenezer Pool of Weymouth)

Francis LOUD, (*son of Francis & Sarah), b. 26 July 1700* <Ipswich VR 1:256>;d. 2 or 3 Jan. 1774* <Weymouth VR 2:298>

CHILDREN OF Francis LOUD & Onner PRINCE[5] (Mary Turner[4]): (13)* <Weymouth VR>

Jacob LOUD[6], b. 24 May 1723 <VR 1:173>; d. 15 Nov. 1779*, Weymouth <VR 2:298>
Deborah LOUD[6], b. 25 June 1725
Onner LOUD[6], b. 5 Feb. 1727
Sarah LOUD[6], b. 19 July 1728/9 (m. Amasa Wade)
Mary LOUD[6], b. 9 Jan. 1731 <Weymouth VR 1:174>; d. ?28 Jan. 1781 (?wf of Elisha Jones?)
Francis LOUD[6], b. 23 Dec. 1732
Mercy LOUD[6], b. 28 Mar. 1735
John LOUD[6], b. 23 Feb. 1737
William LOUD[6], b. 1 Feb. 1739; d. 6 Aug. 1810 <Weymouth VR>
Son, b. 1 Feb. 1741; d. 2 Feb. 1741; d. 8 Feb. 1741
Alice LOUD[6], b. 30 Mar. 1742; d. 5 July 1742
Elliot LOUD[6], b. 28 July 1743; d. 28 Mar. 1813
Caleb LOUD[6], b. 18 Apr. 1747 <VR 1:171>; d. 4 May 1782, Weymouth <VR 2:297>

Susanna BATES, (*dau of Abraham & Sarah), b. 9 Dec. 1752* <Weymouth VR 1:22>

CHILDREN OF Caleb LOUD[6] (Onner Prince[5]) & Susanna BATES: (1 of 5)***<46>**

Caleb LOUD[7], b. 5 Oct. 177(2)* <Weymouth VR 1:171>

Joanna DYER, (*dau of Jos. & Jane (Stevens?)), b. 2 July 1737, Weymouth

CHILDREN OF Francis LOUD[6] (Onner Prince[5]) & Joanna DYER: (3) <Weymouth>

Lucy LOUD[7], b. 21 May 1757
Alice LOUD[7], b. 29 Mar. 1762
Joanna LOUD[7], b. 26 Mar. 1765

Mary SMITH, (*dau of John & Hannah), b. 6 Jan. 1726*, Weymouth; d. 5 Jan. 1797*<Weymouth VR 2:298

CHILDREN OF Jacob LOUD[6] (Onner Prince[5]) & Mary SMITH*: (5) <Weymouth VR>

Jacob LOUD[7], b. 6 Mar. 1747 <VR 1:173>
Esau LOUD[7], b. 17 Sept. 1750 <VR 1:172>; d. 24 Mar. 1798 <Weymouth VR 2:298>
Peleg LOUD[7], b. 29 Nov. 1752, d. 28 Aug. 1776 <VR 1:175, 2:299>
Eliphalet LOUD[7], b. 30 Dec. 1755 <VR 1:172>
Reuben LOUD[7], b. 1 Oct. 1761 <VR 1:175>; d. ?8 or 10 Oct. 1795*, London, Eng.

Capt. Jacob LOUD, d. pre 2 Sept. 1837 (adm.) <Norfolk Co.Prob.#11914>

CHILDREN OF Capt. Jacob LOUD & Ruth BLANCHARD: (4) <Weymouth VR 1:173>

Jacob LOUD, b. 21 June 1803
John White LOUD, b. 27 June 1809
Oliver LOUD, b. 2 Mar. 1809
Samuel Blanchard LOUD, b. 26 Apr. 1812

Nehemiah JOY, d. pre 1 Jan. 1803 (div.) <Norfolk Co.Prob.#10825>

CHILD OF Nehemiah JOY & Miriam TURNER:**<47>**

Lydia JOY, bpt. 12 June 1748 <Thomas Joy & His Desc.(1900):76>

CHILD OF Jacob LOUD[7] (Jacob[6]) & Lydia JOY:

Jacob LOUD[8], b. 16 Dec. 1773 <Weymouth VR 1:173>

Huldah PALMER, (*? dau of Bezeleel), bpt. 5 Oct. 1755* <Scituate VR 1:286>; d. 25 July 1819*<Weymouth VR 2:298>

CHILDREN OF Esau LOUD[7] (Jacob[6]) & Huldah PALMER: (8) <Weymouth VR>**<48>**

Bezaleel LOUD[8], b. 21 Sept. 1782 <VR 1:171>; d. 7 Feb. 1839 <Abington VR 2:313>

Samuel LOUD[8], b. 16 Nov. 1783 <VR 1:176>

Achsah LOUD[8], b. 30 Dec. 1785 <VR 1:170>

Nathaniel LOUD[8], b. 12 Oct. 1787 <VR 1:175>

Horatio LOUD[8], b. 12 June 1790 <VR 1:173>; d. 19 or 20 Oct. 1825

Percis LOUD[8], b. 28 Oct. 1792 (son) <VR 1:175>

Reuben LOUD[8], b. 1794, d. 15 Mar. 1798 <Hist.Weymouth 3:376>

Esau LOUD[8], b. 10 Dec. 1797 <VR 1:172>

Abiah HARRIS, (dau of Abiel & Susannah (Snell)), b. 2 June 1789 <Abington VR 1:101>; d. 1 Apr. 1857, Abington <Mass.VR 112:265>

CHILDREN OF Bezaleel LOUD[8] & Abiah HARRIS: (7) <3-7, Abington VR 1:136>

Alden S. LOUD[9], b. 13 Sept. 1810 <Weymouth VR 1:170>

Samuel Dexter LOUD[9], b. 23 Jan. 1815 <Weymouth VR 1:176>

Charles Southworth LOUD[9], b. 25 Sept. 1820

Susannah Snell LOUD[9], b. 16 Apr. 1823

Harriet Jane LOUD[9], b. 29 July 1825

Thomas Remington LOUD[9], b. 20 Mar. 1829

Lydia Augusta LOUD[9], b. 19 July 1831

CHILDREN OF John LOUD[6] (Onner Prince) & Mercy VINING: (7) <Weymouth VR>

John Randel LOUD[7], b. 13 Nov. 1758 <VR 1:173>

Sylvanus LOUD[7], b. 1 Oct. 1759 <VR 1:176>, d.y.

Sylvanus LOUD[7], b. 1 June 1760 <VR 1:176>

James LOUD[7], b. 17 May 1762 <VR 1:173>

Asa LOUD[7], b. 16 Nov. 176(4) <VR 1:171>

Mary LOUD[7], b. 18 July 1766 <VR 1:174>

Betsey LOUD[7], b. 9 Sept. 1770 <VR 1:171>

CHILDREN OF Sylvanus LOUD[7] & Lydia LOVELL: (5) <Weymouth VR>

Lydia LOUD[8], b. 29 Sept. 1782 <VR 1:174>

John LOUD[8], b. 25 Oct. 1785 <VR 1:173>

Solomon LOUD[8], b. 2 Aug. 1787 <VR 1:176>

Silvanus LOUD[8], b. 27 Feb. 1791 <VR 1:176>

Ebenezer LOUD[8], b. 6 Oct. 1792 <VR 1:172>

Mary C. WHITTEMORE, d. 8 Mar. 1892, ae 70y3m, cancer of stomach, wf of John, lived & died at 43 Chester Sq., Boston, dau of Solomon Loud & Abigail Keith <Mass.VR 429:97>

CHILDREN OF William LOUD[6] (Onner Prince[5]) & Lucy VINING: (4) <Weymouth VR 1:171>**<49>**

David LOUD[7], b. 27 Sept. 1761

William LOUD[7], b. 13 Apr. 1764

Benjamin LOUD[7], b. 28 Jan. 1767

Daniel LOUD[7], b. 29 Apr. 1769

Mary/Polly LOUD[7], b. c1771, d. 28 Aug. 1857, Weymouth <Mass.VR 112:258>

Caleb LOUD, (son of Wm. & Lucy), d. 28 July 1787, ae 3 <Weymouth VR 2:297>

Jonathan WHITE, (son of Ben.), b. c1774, Weymouth, d. 3 Mar. 1857, ae 83 <Mass.VR 112:258>

CHILDREN OF Jonathan WHITE & Mary/Polly LOUD^{7}: (8) <Weymouth VR>

George Washington WHITE^{8}, b. 12 Dec. 1797 <VR 1:339>; d. 16 Apr. 1879, Weymouth, boot cutter <Mass.VR 311:256>

Mary Ann WHITE^{8}, b. 1 Dec. 1799 <VR 1:343> (m. Beriah Torrey)

Jonathan WHITE^{8}, b. 16 Jan. 1801 <VR 1:341>

Boylston Adams WHITE^{8}, b. 7 Nov. 1803 <VR 1:337>

Lucy Eldridge WHITE^{8}, b. 9 Apr. 1806 <VR 1:342> (m. David Vining)

William Loud WHITE^{8}, b. 27 Jan. 1811 <VR 1:347>

Charles Volentine WHITE^{8}, b. 21 June 1834(?) <VR 1:337>

Mary Vining WHITE^{8}, b. 10 Sept. 1836(?) <VR 1:343>

John SOPER, (*son of John & Mary), b. 28 Nov. 1694* <Hull VR:34>; d. ?12 Dec. 1742* <Hull VR:73>

CHILDREN OF John SOPER & Ruth PRINCE^{5} (Mary Turner^{4}): (5)* <Hull VR:34>

John SOPER^{6}, b. Sept. 1721

James SOPER^{6}, b. 20 June 1723

Elizabeth SOPER^{6}, b. 11 Dec. 1724; d. 3 Feb. 1724/5 <Hull VR:73>

Elizabeth SOPER^{6}, b. 21 Dec. 1733

( ) SOPER^{6}, b. 26 Feb. 1736 (name too faint)

CHILDREN OF Thomas PRINCE & Ruth TURNER^{4} (Mary Brewster^{3}): (5)* <2-5, Boston Rcd.Com.>

Thomas PRINCE^{5}, b. 10 July 1686 <Scituate VR 1:300>; d. 2 Nov. 1754, Duxbury g.s. <MD 9:161>

James PRINCE^{5}, b. 23 Nov. 1687 <9:175>, unm.

Ruth PRINCE^{5}, b. d.y. <9:190,193>

Benjamin PRINCE^{5}, b. 28 Feb. 1693/4 <9:208; Scituate VR 1:300>; d. 1 Dec. 1737* <Yarmouth ChR:14>

Job PRINCE^{5}, b. 14 Apr. 1695 <Scituate VR 1:300>; d. Apr. 1731*, Jamaica <Kingston VR:371>

Israel SILVESTER, (*son of Israel), b. 23 Sept. 1674*

CHILDREN OF Israel SILVESTER & Ruth (TURNER^{4}) Prince: (3) <Duxbury, MD 9:24>

Ruth SILVESTER^{5}, b. 26 June 1701 **<50>**

Israel SILVESTER^{5}, b. 5 May 1705 <MD 8:234>; d. betw 8 Feb. 1771 (will) - 3 Mar. 1788 (adm.), Duxbury (1785* in ChR)

Grace SILVESTER^{5}, b. Nov. 1706; d. 2 Apr. 1768, Duxbury g.s. <MD 9:161>

MICRO #9 of 18

Abiel NELSON, d. 15 Sept. 1744* <N. Yarmouth 1st ChR:15>

CHILDREN OF Benjamin PRINCE^{5} (Ruth Turner^{4}) & Abiel NELSON: (6 of 9) <Duxbury, 1-5, MD 11:78> **<51>**

Benjamin PRINCE^{6}, b. 14 Apr. 1718

Paul PRINCE^{6}, b. 14 May 1720; d. 25 Nov. 1809*

Silvanus PRINCE^{6}, b. 17 Sept. 1722; d. 18 Sept. 1790* <NEHGR 5:12>

Sarah PRINCE^{6}, b. 8 Apr. 1725

John PRINCE^{6}, b. 20 May 1727

Lydia PRINCE^{6}, b. 11 Apr. 1735*

Elizabeth JOHNSON, b. c1729, d. 7 Apr. 1800*, ae 71 <NEHGR 5:12> (wf of Silvanus Prince^{6})

Hannah CUSHING, b. 8 May 1722, Hingham <MD 1:34>; d. 6 Feb. 1814 <MD 1:35>

CHILDREN OF Paul PRINCE^{6} & Hannah CUSHING: (10) <Bible, MD 1:35>

Sarah PRINCE^{7}, b. 29 Feb. 1744

Cushing PRINCE^{7}, b. 29 Oct. 1745

Rachel PRINCE^{7}, b. 22 July 1747

Hannah PRINCE^{7}, b. 20 Jan. 1749

Ruth PRINCE^{7}, b. 12 Apr. 1751

David PRINCE^{7}, b. 17 May 1753

Else PRINCE^{7}, b. 13 Feb. 1756

Paul PRINCE^{7}, b. 13 Nov. 1758

Pyam PRINCE^{7}, b. 26 Oct. 1760

Ammi PRINCE^{7}, b. 1 Aug. 1763 (son)

Abigail KIMBALL, (*dau of Christopher & Sarah (Jolls)), b. 28 Jan. 1703* <Boston Rcd.Com.24:22>; d. 6 Sept. 1780, Kingston g.s. <MD 7:85>

CHILDREN OF Job PRINCE^{5} (Ruth Turner^{4}) & Abigail KIMBALL: (6)*

Thomas PRINCE^{6}, b. Oct. 1720, d. 5 Jan. 1768, Kingston g.s. <MD 7:169>

Job PRINCE^{6}, b. ( )

James PRINCE^{6}, b. ( ); d. 1759, N. Carver

Kimball PRINCE^{6}, b. 28 Apr. 1726, Kingston <Gen.Adv.2:39>; d. 10 Apr. 1814, Kingston <MD 7:169>

Christopher PRINCE^{6}, b. 8 Mar. 1729/30 <Gen.Adv.2:39>

Ruth PRINCE^{6}, b. ( )

CHILDREN OF Job PRINCE^{6} & Elizabeth ALLEN: (9) <Boston Rcd.Com.>

Hezekiah Blanchard PRINCE^{7}, b. 15 Aug. 1749* <24:271>

Job PRINCE^{7}, b. 28 Sept. 1751* <24:277>

Elizabeth PRINCE^{7}, b. 28 May 1753* <24:282>

Thomas PRINCE^{7}, b. 27 Sept. 1754* <24:285>; d. 1790*

Sarah PRINCE^{7}, b. 29 Mar. 1756* <24:289>

James PRINCE^{7}, b. 20 Feb. 1758* <24:295>

Samuel PRINCE^{7}, b. 2 Apr. 1761* <24:302>, d.y.

Samuel PRINCE^{7}, b. 9 Mar. 1766* <24:313>

Abigail PRINCE^{7}, b. 14 Mar. 1767* <24:315>

CHILDREN OF James PRINCE^{7} & Agnes GORDON: (2) <Boston Rcd.Com.24:391>

James PRINCE^{8}, b. 15 Jan. 1790*

Caroline PRINCE^{8}, b. 9 Mar. 1791*

Deborah FULLER^{5} (John^{4}, Sam.$^{3-2-1}$), b. 14 Dec. 1729 <Kingston VR:80>; d. 4 Mar. 1826, Kingston g.s. <MD 7:169>

CHILDREN OF Kimball PRINCE^{6} (Job^{5}) & Deborah FULLER: (9) <Kingston, Gen.Adv.4:14>

Christopher PRINCE^{7}, b. 11 July 1751*

Kimball PRINCE^{7}, b. 20 July 1753*

Sarah PRINCE^{7}, b. 15 Jan. 1756*

Ruth PRINCE^{7}, b. 7 May 1758*

Deborah PRINCE^{7}, b. 13 July 1760*

Noah PRINCE^{7}, b. 18 Jan. 1763*

Job PRINCE^{7}, b. 22 Mar. 1765*

John PRINCE^{7}, b. 23 Feb. 1768*; d. 30 June 1824*

Hezekiah PRINCE^{7}, b. 7 Feb. 1771*

Lydia DELANO^{6} (Joshua^{5}, Martha Simmons^{4}, Mercy Pabodie^{3}, Eliz. Alden^{2}), b. 12 July 1723, Duxbury <MD 10:185>; d. 22 Oct. 1809, Kingston g.s. <MD 7:169>

CHILDREN OF Thomas PRINCE^{6} (Job^{5}) & Lydia DELANO: (6) <2-6, Kingston VR>

Abigail PRINCE^{7}, b. 21 Oct. 1747, Duxbury <MD 12:165>

Thankful Delano PRINCE^{7}, b. 6 Mar. 1749/50*; d. 19 Sept. 1840, Kingston g.s. <MD 7:84>

Thomas PRINCE^{7}, b. 9 Sept. 1756*; d. 17 Oct. 1783, Kingston g.s. <MD 7:169>, unm.

James PRINCE^{7}, b. 10 Aug. 1758*

Lydia PRINCE^{7}, b. 6 Apr. 1762*

Sylvia PRINCE^{7}, b. 20 June 1765*

Theophilus *STETSON*^{6} (*Elisha^{5}, Abigail Brewster^{4}, Wrestling^{3}, Love^{2}), b. 10 July 1742*, Kingston (hus of Abigail Prince^{7})**<52>**

Job DREW, b. c1744, d. 16 Mar. 1833, Kingston g.s. <MD 7:84>

CHILDREN OF Job DREW & Thankful Delano PRINCE^{7} (Tho.^{6}): (14) <Kingston VR>

Prince DREW^{8}, b. 7 Feb. 1768*; d. 28 June 1776, Kingston g.s. <MD 7:84>

Job DREW^{8}, b. Sept. 1769, d. 17 Dec. 1769, ae 2m24d, Kingston g.s. <MD 7:84>

Fanny DREW^{8}, b. 20 Oct. 1770* (m. Philemon Sampson)

Job DREW^{8}, b. 14 Jan. 1773*; d. 17 Aug. 1838*, Boston<53>

Kezia DREW^{8}, b. 13 Dec. 1775*

Lebbeus DREW^{8}, b. 11 Jan. 1777*

Nehemiah DREW^{8}, b. 16 Nov. 1778*

Charles DREW^{8}, b. 11 Feb. 1781*

Sophia DREW^{8}, b. 15 Oct. 1782* (m. Ira Thomson)

Thomas Prince DREW^{8}, b. 15 Sept. 1784*; d. 14 July 1788, Kingston g.s. <MD 7:84>

Ira DREW^{8}, b. 21 Aug. 1786*

Ezra DREW^{8}, b. 15 Dec. 1788*

Sukey DREW^{8}, b. 6 Mar. 1791* (m. Elisha Ford)<54>

Harvey DREW^{8}, b. 15 Apr. 1793*; d. 18 Dec. 1795, Kingston g.s. <MD 7:84>

CHILDREN OF Job DREW^{8} & Sarah LAWRENCE: (2)* <Boston><54>

Ellen Prince DREW^{9}, b. 2 Jan. 1807; d. 4 Feb. 1885, Westford (wf of Seth Wilson)

Joseph Lawrence DREW^{9}, b. 25 Aug. 1808; d. 26 Apr. 1882, Boston<55>

CHILD OF Thomas PRINCE^{5} (Ruth Turner^{4}) & Judith FOX*:

Hannah PRINCE^{6}, b. 22 Oct. 1730 <MD 11:237>

Micah HOLMES, d. 16 July 1870, ae 70y1m22d, Plymouth, mariner, b. Kingston <Mass.VR 230:332><56>

Isaac PARTRIDGE, (son of John (& Mary*)), b. 2 Mar. 1704/5, Duxbury <MD 9:26>; d. 26 Jan. 1794* <Duxbury VR:397> (g.s. says he d. 2 Feb.)

CHILDREN OF Isaac PARTRIDGE & Grace SILVESTER^{5} (Ruth Turner^{4}): (4) <Duxbury, MD 12:30>

Ruth PARTRIDGE^{6}, b. 23 Mar. 1730/1; d. 15 Jan. 1756, Duxbury g.s., unm. <MD 9:161>

John PARTRIDGE^{6}, b. 28 May 1732; d. 14 Sept. 1755, Duxbury g.s. <MD 9:161>

Lucretia PARTRIDGE^{6}, b. 2 Mar. 1734/5

Calvin PARTRIDGE^{6}, b. 29 Mar. 1739

Abigail SNELL, (dau of Josiah), b. c1703, d. 22 July 1775*, ae 72

CHILDREN OF Israel SILVESTER^{5} (Ruth Turner^{4}) & Abigail SNELL: (6)

Joseph SILVESTER^{6}, b. 9 July 1735*; d. aft. 1770*

Israel SILVESTER^{6}, b. 1 Nov. 1737*; d. aft. 1770*

Seth SILVESTER^{6}, b. 30 Aug. 1740*; d. 11 Dec. 1756*

Josiah SILVESTER^{6}, b. 14 May 1742*; d. 13 Sept. 1768*, unm.

Zachariah SILVESTER^{6}, b. 24 Feb. 1744/5; d. aft. 1770*

Abigail SILVESTER^{6}, b. 17 Apr. 1747*; d. aft. 1770*

John PICKETT, d. 16 Aug. 1667 (at sea, returning from Barbadoes) <NEHGR 8:326,9:44>

CHILDREN OF John PICKETT & Ruth BREWSTER^{3}: (5) <3-5, New London VR>

Mary PICKETT^{4}, b. ( )

Ruth PICKETT^{4}, b. c1654, d. 14 Sept. 1690*, ae 36, Old Lyme g.s.

John PICKETT^{4}, b. 25 July 1656 <4:328>

Adam PICKETT^{4}, b. 15 Nov. 1658 <4:328>

Mercy PICKETT^{4}, b. 16 Jan. 1660 <4:327>

CHILDREN OF Charles HILL & Ruth (BREWSTER^{3}) Pickett: (5) <New London CT VR>

Jane HILL^{4}, b. 9 Dec. 1669 <4:323>

Charles HILL^{4}, b. 16 Oct. 1671 <4:321>; d. pre 12 Nov. 1711 (inv.) <New London CT Prob.#2614><57>

Ruth HILL^{4}, b. & bur. Oct. 1673 <4:319>

Jonathan HILL^{4}, b. Dec. 1674 <4:318>; d. pre 13 July 1725 <New London CT Prob.#2623><58>

Son, b. 27 Apr. 1677, lived half hour <4:315>

Hannah WETHERELL^{4} (Grace Brewster^{3}, Jonathan^{2}), b. 21 Mar. 1659/60, d. 16 Sept. 1689 <New London CT VR 4:327, 299>

CHILDREN OF Adam PICKETT^{4} (Ruth Brewster^{3}) & Hannah WETHERELL: (3) <New London CT VR>

Adam PICKETT^{5}, b. 7 Sept. 1681 <4:309>

John PICKETT^{5}, b. 28 July 1685 <4:303>

Hannah PICKETT^{5}, b. 6 June 1689 <4:299>

Benjamin SHAPLEY, (son of Nicholas), d. betw 5 July 1706 (will) - 18 Sept. 1706 (inv.) <New London CT Prob.#4758>

CHILDREN OF Benjamin SHAPLEY & Mary PICKETT^{4} (Ruth Brewster^{3}): (7) <1-6, New London CT VR>

Ruth SHAPLEY^{5}, b. 21 Dec. 1672 <4:320>

Benjamin SHAPLEY^{5}, b. 20 Mar. 1675 <4:317>; d. pre 5 July 1706* (father's will)

Mary SHAPLEY^{5}, b. 26 Mar. 1677 <4:315>

Joseph SHAPLEY^{5}, b. 15 Aug. 1681 <4:309>

Anne SHAPLEY^{5}, b. 31 Aug. 1685 <4:303>; d. pre 22 June 1751 (bond) <New London CT Prob.#3718>

Daniel SHAPLEY^{5}, b. 14 Feb. 1689 <4:299>; d. betw 6 Jan. 1753 (will) - 2 July 1753 (prob.) <New London CT Prob.#4761>**<59>**

Jane SHAPLEY^{5}, b. ( )

James MORGAN, d. betw 29 Mar. 1745 (will) - 11 May 1748 (prob.) <New London CT Prob.#3733> (3rd hus of Anne Shapley^{5})

CHILDREN OF Benjamin SHAPLEY^{5} & *Ruth DYMOND*: (2) <New London CT Prob.#4759>**<60>**

Benjamin SHAPLEY^{6}, b. c1703

Joseph SHAPLEY^{6}, b. c1705

John MORGAN, d. betw 30 May 1744 (will) - 16 Mar. 1746 (prob.) <New London CT Prob.#3736> (hus. of Ruth Shapley^{5})**<61>**

Samuel FOSDICK, d. 27 Aug. 1702*, New London CT <prob.#2041>

CHILDREN OF Samuel FOSDICK & Mercy PICKETT^{4} (Ruth Brewster^{3}): (8) <1-4, New London CT VR>

Samuel FOSDICK^{5}, b. 16 Aug. 1683, d. 18 Nov. 1683 <4:305>

Samuel FOSDICK^{5}, b. 18 Sept. 1684 <4:303>

Mercy FOSDICK^{5}, b. 30 Nov. 1686 <4:303>

Ruth FOSDICK^{5}, b. 27 June 1689 <4:299>

Anna FOSDICK^{5}, b. 8 Dec. 1691 (m. Tho. Latham)

John FOSDICK^{5}, b. 1 Feb. 1693/4

Thomas FOSDICK^{5}*, b. 20 Aug. 1696*; d. 17 July 1774***<62>**

Mary FOSDICK^{5}*, b. 7 July 1699*

CHILD OF John ARNOLD & Mercy (PICKETT^{4}) Fosdick:

Lucretia ARNOLD^{5}*, b. 26 Aug. 1703*

Susanna TURNER^{5} (Ezekiel^{4}, Mary Brewster^{3}, Jonathan^{2}), b. 2 Jan. 1685 <New London CT VR 4:303>

CHILDREN OF Samuel FOSDICK^{5} & Susanna TURNER: (8)* <New London CT VR>

Mercy FOSDICK^{6}, b. 28 Mar. 1708

Samuel FOSDICK^{6}, b. 11 Mar. 1710

William FOSDICK^{6}, b. 4 Feb. 1712

Ruth FOSDICK^{6}, b. 25 Jan. 1713/4

James FOSDICK^{6}, b. 20 Nov. 1716

Ezekiel FOSDICK^{6}, b. 17 Feb. 1719/20

Jesse FOSDICK^{6}, b. 7 Nov. 1722

Susanna FOSDICK^{6}, b. 11 Oct. 1724

Rev. Moses NOYES, d. betw 19 Aug. 1719 (will) - 21 Nov. 1729 (prob.) <New London CT Prob.#3845>

CHILDREN OF Rev. Moses NOYES & Ruth PICKETT^{4} (Ruth Brewster^{3}): (2 of 4)

Moses NOYES^{5}, d. betw 13 Jan. 1786 (will) - 6 Mar. 1786 (prob.) <New London CT Prob.#3847>**<63>**

John NOYES^{5}, d. betw 20 July 1733 (will) - 18 Sept. 1733 (prob.) <New London CT Prob.#3840>**<64>**

Ruth NOYES^{5}, b. ( ) (m. Wadsworth)

Sarah NOYES^{5}, b. ( )

James WADSWORTH^{7} (James^{6}, Ruth Noyes^{5}), d. betw 22 Apr. 1776 (will) - 13 Sept. 1727 (prob.) <Middleton Prob.#3629>**<65>**

LOVE BREWSTER^{2} (William^{1})

Dr. John BREWSTER, b. c1739, d. 18 Aug. 1823, ae 84 <"Hinman":330,331>
Mary DURKEE, (dau of Wm.), d. 4 June 1783
CHILDREN OF Dr. John BREWSTER & 1st Mary DURKEE: (5) <"Hinman":330,331>
Mary BREWSTER, b. 9 Sept. 1762
William BREWSTER, b. 17 June 1764
John BREWSTER, b. 30 May 1766 (deaf & dumb, portrait painter)
Augustus BREWSTER, b. 30 May 1768
Dr. Royal BREWSTER, b. 13 July 1770
CHILDREN OF Dr. John BREWSTER & 2nd Ruth AVERY: <"Hinman":330,331>
William Augustus BREWSTER, b. 10 Dec. 1791
Sophia BREWSTER, b. 9 Apr. 1795, d. 24 Apr. 1800
Betsey A. BREWSTER, b. 11 Sept 1798, d. 17 Oct. 1833
MICRO #10 of 18
CHILDREN OF Love BREWSTER^{2} & Sarah COLLIER: (4)**<66>**
Sarah BREWSTER^{3}, b. ( )**<67>**
Nathaniel BREWSTER^{3}, b. ( ), d. pre 1 Nov. 1676 <Plymouth Co.Court Orders, 5:146>
William BREWSTER^{3}, b. c1645, d. 3 Nov. 1723, near 78yr, Duxbury g.s. <VR:356, MD 9:160>
Wrestling BREWSTER^{3}, b. ( ), d. 1 Jan. 1696/7, Duxbury <MD 20:113>
Lydia PARTRIDGE, (dau of George & Sarah (Tracy)), d. 2 Feb. 1742/3, Duxbury <VR:355, MD 12:31>
CHILDREN OF William BREWSTER^{3} & Lydia PARTRIDGE: (8) <Duxbury>
Sarah BREWSTER^{4}, b. 25 Apr. 1674 <MD 9:173>
Nathaniel BREWSTER^{4}, b. 8 Nov. 1676 <MD 9:173>; d. betw 11 Feb. 1755* (will) - 7 Apr. 1755*(prob)
Lydia BREWSTER^{4}, b. 11 Feb. 1680 <MD 9:229>
William BREWSTER^{4}, b. 4 May 1683 <MD 9:229>; d. 26 Dec. 1768*, Lebanon CT <Brewster Gen.>
Mercy BREWSTER^{4}, b. 7 Dec. 1685 <MD 9:229>
Benjamin BREWSTER^{4}, b. 7 July 1688 <MD 9:229>
Joseph BREWSTER^{4}, b. 17 Mar. 1693/4; d. 20 Apr. 1767, S. Duxbury g.s. <MD 9:232,160>
Joshua BREWSTER^{4}, b. ( )
Elizabeth TURNER^{5} (Ben.^{4}, Mary Brewster^{3}, Jonathan^{2}), b. c1703, d. Apr. 1786, 83rd yr, S. Duxbury g.s. <MD 9:160>
CHILDREN OF Joseph BREWSTER^{4} & Elizabeth TURNER: (5) <Duxbury, MD 12:120>
Truelove BREWSTER^{5}, b. 16 May 1726, d. 21 Feb. 1726/7
Lemuel BREWSTER^{5}, b. 23 Oct. 1727, d. 13 Nov. 1727
Lemuel BREWSTER^{5}, b. 28 June 1729; d. pre 18 Apr. 1774 (bond) <Plymouth Co.Prob.#2764>**<68>**
Eunice BREWSTER^{5}, b. 12 Mar. 1731 (m. Timothy Walker)
Truelove BREWSTER^{5}, b. 27 Jan. 1735/6, unm.
Abigail BREWSTER^{5} (John^{4}, Wrestling^{3}, Love^{2}), b. 17 Dec. 1736*; d. betw 30 Feb. 1780 (will) - 3 July 1780 (prob.) <Plymouth Co.Prob.#2730> (wf of Lemuel Brewster^{5})**<68>**
Deborah JACKSON, (dau of Eleazer), b. 11 Mar. 1703/4, Plymouth <MD 3:124>
CHILDREN OF Joshua BREWSTER^{4} & Deborah JACKSON: (4) <Duxbury, MD 12:21>
Job BREWSTER^{5}, b. 11 Jan. 1723, d. Nov. 1727
Nathan BREWSTER^{5}, b. 21 Dec. 1724; d. 3 Nov. 1808* <Brewster Gen.>
Sarah BREWSTER^{5}, b. 11 Feb. 1727 (m. Joseph Wright)
Job BREWSTER^{5}, b. 17 Dec. 1729
CHILDREN OF Capt. John BURGESS & Susanna SAMSON: (5) <Plymouth VR 2:40>**<69>**
Susan BURGESS, b. 28 Nov. 1808
Anna BURGESS, b. 30 Sept. 1810
Catharine BURGESS, b. 11 Dec. 1815

Mary Ann BURGESS, b. 23 Aug. 1817

John BURGESS, b. 10 Dec. 1819

CHILDREN OF Capt. John BURGESS & 2nd Sophia SAMPSON: (2) <Plymouth VR 2:40>

Albert Thomas BURGESS, b. 3 Sept. 1825

Sophia BURGESS, b. 1 July 1828

Rachel PARTRIDGE, (*dau of John), b. 25 Oct. 1726*, Lebanon CT; d. (26 Apr.) 1757*, Duxbury

CHILDREN OF Nathan BREWSTER^5 (Joshua^4) & 1st Rachel PARTRIDGE*: (3) <Duxbury, MD 12:169>

John Partridge BREWSTER^6, b. 23 Feb. 1753, d. 10 Mar. 1753

Rachel Partridge BREWSTER^6, b. 27 Jan.1754

Anna BREWSTER^6, b. 16 Dec. 1755

CHILDREN OF Nathan BREWSTER^5 & 2nd Hannah ( ): (2 of 4) <1-2, Duxbury, MD 12:169,170>**<70>**

Joshua BREWSTER^6, b. 2 May 1761

William BREWSTER^6, b. 23 Aug. 1763

Mary DWELLY, b. 29 Mar. 1684* <Scituate VR 1:141>; d. 29 July 1764* <Duxbury VR:355>

CHILDREN OF Nathaniel BREWSTER^4 (Wm.^{3}) & Mary DWELLY: (5) <Duxbury, MD 12:30>

Samuel BREWSTER^5, b. 5 Apr. 1708

Mercy BREWSTER^5, b. 5 Apr. 1708 (twins)

Ruth BREWSTER^5, b. 9 Dec. 1711 (m. Joseph Morgan)

William BREWSTER^5, b. 14 Feb. 1714/5, d. c1775* <Brewster Gen.1:54,84>

Joseph BREWSTER^5, b. 3 July 1718; d. 3 or 5 Sept. 1791 <Duxbury VR:355>

Jedidah WHITE, b. 6 Nov. 1721, Marshfield; d. 26 Mar. 1794 <Duxbury VR:356>

CHILDREN OF Joseph BREWSTER^5 & Jedidah WHITE: (6) <Duxbury ChR 1:8, 29>

Zadock BREWSTER^6, b. 15 Mar. 1742; d. 21 May 1811

Mary BREWSTER^6, b. ( )

Joseph BREWSTER^6, d. 19 Sept. 1814

Ruth BREWSTER^6, d. pre 1822

Nathaniel BREWSTER^6, b. 4 July 1755; d. 2 Oct. 1827

Truelove/Freelove BREWSTER^6, bpt. 13 Jan. 1760

Priscilla SAMPSON^4 (John^3, Stephen^2), b. 21 May 1724, Duxbury <MD 11:237>

CHILDREN OF William BREWSTER^5 (Nath.^{4}) & Priscilla SAMPSON: (5) <1-3, Duxbury, MD 12:167>

Daniel BREWSTER^6, b. 12 Sept. 1747

Nathaniel BREWSTER^6, b. 23 Nov. 1748

Steven BREWSTER^6, b. 3 Oct. 1750

( ) BREWSTER^6*, b. 3 July 1757* (name too faint)

( ) BREWSTER^6*, b. 12 Sept. 1759* (name too faint)

Hopestill WADSWORTH, b. c1687, d. 23 (Mar.) 1773*, 86th yr, Lebanon CT <Brewster Gen.:55>

CHILDREN OF William BREWSTER^4 (Wm.^{3}) & Hopestill WADSWORTH: (6) <Duxbury, MD 9:232>

Oliver BREWSTER^5, b. 16 July 1708

Ichabod BREWSTER^5, b. 15 Jan. 1710/11; d. 27 July 1797, Lebanon CT

Elisha BREWSTER^5, b. 29 Oct. 1715

Seth BREWSTER^5, b. 20 Dec. 1720

Lot BREWSTER^5, b. 25 Mar. 1723/4

Huldah BREWSTER^5, b. 20 Feb. 1725/6

Lydia BARSTOW, (dau of Sam. & Lydia (Randall)), b. 1 Apr. 1717* <Scituate VR 1:33>; d. 6 Feb. 1813, Lebanon CT

CHILDREN OF Ichabod BREWSTER^5 & Lydia BARSTOW: (8) <1-3, Pembroke; 4-8, Lebanon CT>

Bathsheba BREWSTER^6, b. 3 Sept. 1737; d. ae 90*, Marlborough CT (wf of 3rd hus, Peter Huxford)

Lydia BREWSTER^6, b. 7 Aug. 1739; d. Granville MA* (m. Asahel Clark)

William BREWSTER^6, b. 13 Aug. 1741; d. 10 July 1821, near Rome NY

Huldah BREWSTER^6, b. 23 Apr. 1744; d. 11 Sept. 1830, Fort Ann NY (m. Ogias Coleman)

Betty BREWSTER^{6}, b. 10 Aug. 1746 (m. Amos Thomas Jr.)

Prince BREWSTER^{6}, b. 19 June 1749; d. 30 Oct. 1816, Windsor CT

Ichabod BREWSTER^{6}, b. 6 Mar. 1753; d. 27 July 1841, Lebanon CT

Hopestill BREWSTER^{6}, b. 27 May 1760; d. 7 Feb. 1843, Oxford NY (wf of 2nd hus, Jared Hinckley)

Mary ( ), b. Nov. 1661, d. 12 Nov. 1742, ae 80y11m27d, Kingston g.s. <MD 7:168>

CHILDREN OF Wrestling BREWSTER^{3} & Mary ( ): (8) <MD 20:111>

Mary BREWSTER^{4}, b. 1679, d. 17 Apr. 1761, ae 82y1m24d, Kingston g.s. <MD 7:89>

Sarah BREWSTER^{4}, b. ( )

Abigail BREWSTER^{4}, b. Mar. 1683, d. 6 May 1761, ae 78y1m16d, Kingston g.s. <MD 7:172>

Hannah BREWSTER^{4}, b. c1688; d. 8 Jan. 1763, Duxbury <MD 8:233>

Elizabeth BREWSTER^{4}, b. c1690, d. 5 Dec. 1741, 51st yr, Kingston g.s. <MD 7:23>

Jonathan BREWSTER^{4}, d. 24 Nov. 1753, Windham CT

Wrestling BREWSTER^{4}, b. Aug. 1694, d. 1 Jan. 1767, ae 72y4m28d, Kingston g.s. <MD 7:24>**<71>**

John BREWSTER^{4}, d. betw 24 June 1766 (will) - 1 Jan. 1770 (prob.) <Plymouth Co.Prob.#2752>

CHILDREN OF John PARTRIDGE & Mary ( )BREWSTER: (2) <MD 9:26>

Benjamin PARTRIDGE, b. 5 Mar. 1700/1

Isaac PARTRIDGE, b. 2 Mar. 1704/5

Elisha STETSON, b. c1685, d. 11 Feb. 1755, ae 69y11m13d, Kingston g.s. <MD 7:172>

CHILDREN OF Elisha STETSON & Abigail BREWSTER^{4} (Wrestling^{3}): (5) <1-4, Plymouth, MD 7:178>

Sarah STETSON^{5}, b. 26 Aug. 1708 (m. Robert Bradford^{5})

Eglah STETSON^{5}, b. 7 Oct. 1710 (m. Ephraim Washburn^{5})

Zeresh STETSON^{5}, b. 29 Nov. 1712 (m. Benjamin Bradford^{4})

Hopestill STETSON^{5}, b. 21 May 1715

Elisha STETSON^{5}, bpt. 19 Mar. 1721* <Kingston VR:136>; d. 28 Aug. 1803, 85th yr, Kingston g.s. <VR:382; MD 7:172>

Sarah ADAMS, (*dau of Francis), b. c1721, d. 26 Oct. 1804, 83rd yr, Kingston g.s. <VR:383, MD 7:172> (wf of Elisha Stetson^{5})

CHILDREN OF John SIMMONS^{5} (*John^{4}, Mercy Pabodie^{3}, Eliz. Alden^{2}) & Hopestill STETSON^{5}: (4) <Kingston VR 1:18>

Faith SIMMONS^{6}, b. 27 June 1738

Noah SIMMONS^{6}, b. 15 Jan. 1739/40; d. betw 30 May 1824 (will) - 5 Oct. 1824 (prob.) <Plymouth Co. Prob.#18381, 58:364, 365>

Eunice SIMMONS^{6}, b. 8 Mar. 1742/3

John SIMMONS^{6}, b. 29 Aug. 1746

CHILDREN OF Noah SIMMONS^{6} & 1st Lydia HOWLAND: (3) <Kingston VR 2:52>

Elisabeth SIMMONS^{7}, b. 15 Sept. 1764, d. 20 July 1804 (m. Benjamin Snow)

John SIMMONS^{7}, b. 26 July 1766

Silvester SIMMONS^{7}, b. 28 June 1768 (dau)

CHILD OF Noah SIMMONS^{6} & 2nd Diana ( ): <Kingston VR 2:52>

Hezekiah SIMMONS^{7}, b. 17 June 1772

CHILDREN OF Noah SIMMONS^{6} & 3rd Molly ( ): (11) <Kingston VR 2:52>

Diana SIMMONS^{7}, b. 1 July 1774

Noah SIMMONS^{7}, b. 22 Nov. 1775, d. 27 Nov. 1776

William SIMMONS^{7}, b. 7 May 1777

Noah SIMMONS^{7}, b. 25 Dec. 1778; d. pre 30 May 1824 (father's will)

James SIMMONS^{7}, b. 12 Mar. 1781; d. pre 30 May 1824 (father's will)

Oliver SIMMONS^{7}, b. 19 Dec. 1782, d. 10 Feb. 1786

Joseph SIMMONS^{7}, b. 29 Mar. 1785, d. 19 Jan. 1807

Stevens SIMMONS^{7}, b. 21 Feb. 1787

Peleg SIMMONS^{7}, b. 30 Dec. 1788

Lydia SIMMONS^{7}, b. 17 Sept. 1791, d. 9 Nov. 1791

Martin SIMMONS^{7}, b. 26 Jan. 1794, d. 29 Nov. 1794

Rebecca BRADFORD^{5} (John$^{4-3}$, Wm.^{2}), b. 14 Dec. 1710, Plymouth <MD 12:13>

CHILDREN OF John BREWSTER^{4} & Rebecca BRADFORD: (4)* <Kingston>

John BREWSTER^{5}, b. 7 Oct. 1730; d. 31 July 1798, unm.

Rebecca BREWSTER^{5}, b. 25 Mar. 1733; d. pre 24 June 1766 (father's will) (m. John Samson^{4})

Abigail BREWSTER^{5}, b. 17 Dec. 1736 (m. Lemuel Brewster^{5})

Sarah BREWSTER^{5}?, (mentioned in father's will)

Mary PARTRIDGE, (*dau of John), b. 2 May 1693*, Duxbury <MD 9:26>

CHILDREN OF Jonathan BREWSTER^{4} (Wrestling^{3}) & Mary PARTRIDGE: (9)

James BREWSTER^{5}, b. May 1715; d. 2 Oct. 1755

Jonah BREWSTER^{5}, b. ( )

Peleg BREWSTER^{5}, b. 7 Feb. 1717; d. 2 Apr. 180(1)

Hannah BREWSTER^{5}, b. ( ) (m. John Barker)

Mary BREWSTER^{5}, d. 9 Aug. 1768 (wf of 2nd hus, Jeremiah Bingham)

Jerusha BREWSTER^{5}, d. 22 Sept. 1795 (wf of Zebulon Rudd)

Sarah BREWSTER^{5}, b. ( ) (m. Jehosephat Holmes)

Elijah BREWSTER^{5}, b. 12 Mar. 1731, Windham; d. pre 14 July 1755, unm.

Jonathan BREWSTER^{5}, b. 1 May 1737, d.y.

Joseph HOLMES, b. 1665, d. 26 June 1733, 68y23d, Kingston g.s. <MD 7:89>

CHILDREN OF Joseph HOLMES & Mary BREWSTER^{4} (Wrestling^{3}): (10) <1, 3-8, 10, Plymouth, MD 13:170>

Joseph HOLMES^{5}, b. 4 Oct. 1697; d. 26 Apr. 1756, Kingston g.s. <MD 7:89>

Wrestling HOLMES^{5}, b. 8 Feb. 1698 (not on rcds)

Ephraim HOLMES^{5}, b. 14 Mar. 1699; d. 10 Nov. 1780, Kingston g.s. <MD 7:89>

Mary HOLMES^{5}, b. 7 June 1701; d. 13 Aug. 1797, Dingley Cem., N. Duxbury <MD 11:56>

Sarah HOLMES^{5}, b. 11 Apr. 1703

Abigail HOLMES^{5}, b. 18 July 1705

Jonathan HOLMES^{5}, b. 5 July 1709 <"See Giles Memorial">

Micah HOLMES^{5}, b. 7 Apr. 1714

Lydia HOLMES^{5}, b. 5 June 1717 (not on rcds)

Keziah HOLMES^{5}, b. 23 Mar. 1719; d. 22 June 1787*

Sarah TILDEN, b. c1702, d. 27 Mar. 1773, 71st yr, Kingston g.s. <MD 7:90>

CHILDREN OF Ephraim HOLMES^{5} & Sarah TILDEN: (3)*

Ephraim HOLMES^{6}, b. 31 Oct. 1734

Sarah HOLMES^{6}, b. 23 Mar. 1740/1

Levi HOLMES^{6}, b. 28 Nov. 1747

Rebecca WATERMAN^{5} (Mary Cushman^{4}, Isaac^{3}, Mary Allerton^{2}), b. 9 Oct. 1710, Plympton <Halifax VR:40>; d. 14 July 1801, Kingston g.s. <MD 7:169>

CHILDREN OF Joseph HOLMES^{5} (Mary Brewster^{4}) & Rebecca WATERMAN: (11)* **<72>**

CHILDREN OF Isaiah THOMAS & Keziah HOLMES^{5} (Mary Brewster^{4}): (6)* <Kingston>

Micah THOMAS^{6}, b. 1 May 1746; d. 1775, at sea <Plymouth Co.Prob.#20426>

Isaiah THOMAS^{6}, b. 12 Nov. 1747, d.y.

Keziah THOMAS^{6}, b. 23 June 1751

Isaiah THOMAS^{6}, b. 24 Jan. 1753

Holmes THOMAS^{6}, bpt. 27 July 1755

Spencer THOMAS^{6}, bpt. 7 May 1758; d. pre 16 May 1842 <Plymouth Co.Prob.#20476>

Nathaniel CHURCHILL, (son of Wm.), b. c1717, d. 17 Aug. 1803, ae 85y2m25d <Plympton VR 2:573>

Susanna McFARLAND, b. c1726, d. 22 June 1765, 49th yr <Plympton VR 2:573>

CHILD OF Nathaniel CHURCHILL & Susanna McFARLAND:

Susannah CHURCHILL, b. 19 Jan. 1757 <Plympton VR 2:573>

CHILDREN OF Holmes THOMAS^{6} (Keziah Holmes^{5}) & Susannah CHURCHILL: (2) <Plympton ChR:105>
Kezia THOMAS^{7}, bpt. 29 Sept. 1782
Lydia THOMAS^{7}, bpt. 29 Sept. 1782
Jacob DINGLEY, (son of John & Sarah), b. 31 Oct. 1703, Marshfield <MD 8:177>; d. 24 Dec. 1772, Dingley Cem., N. Duxbury <MD 11:56>
CHILDREN OF Jacob DINGLEY & Mary HOLMES^{5} (Mary Brewster^{4}): (6) <1-2, Marshfield; 4-6, Duxbury>
Jacob DINGLEY^{6}, b. 8 Jan. 1727 <MD 30:156>
Joseph DINGLEY^{6}, bpt. 28 Dec.1729 <MD 31:169>
Abner DINGLEY^{6}, b. 21 Jan. 1731/2, d. 21 June 1807 <MD 11:148,56>
Mary DINGLEY^{6}, b. 10 Nov. 1735 <MD 11:148>
Sarah DINGLEY^{6}, b. 11 Apr. 1742, d. 11 June 1747 <MD 11:148, 12:148>
Abigail DINGLEY^{6}, b. 5 May 1745, d. 31 July 1747 <MD 11:148, 12:148>
Desire PHILLIPS, (dau of Ben.), d. pre 9 Feb. 1750 <Plymouth Co.Deeds 12:228>
CHILD OF Jacob DINGLEY^{6} & 1st Desire PHILLIPS:
William DINGLEY^{7}, b. 1749; bpt. 28 July 1751 <Marshfield 1st ChR>
Susanna FULLER^{5} (John^{4}, Sam.$^{3-2-1}$), b. c1734, d. 17 Mar. 1782, ae 48 <Duxbury VR>**<73>**
CHILDREN OF Jacob DINGLEY^{6} & 2nd Susanna FULLER: (8) <2-4,6-7, Duxbury VR>
Elkanah DINGLEY^{7}, b. 9 Nov. 1754 <VR:59>
Levi DINGLEY^{7}, b. 18 Oct. 1756
Desire DINGLEY^{7}, b. 7 Feb. 1758
Susanna DINGLEY^{7}, b. 26 Apr. 1764
Jacob DINGLEY^{7}, d. 9 July 1766, ae 6wks, N. Duxbury Cem. <MD 11:56>
Jacob DINGLEY^{7}, b. 1 Nov. 1767
Ezra DINGLEY^{7}, b. 5 Aug. 1770
John DINGLEY^{7}, b. 6 June 1773
CHILDREN OF Jacob DINGLEY^{6} & 3rd Alathea FULLERTON: (2)**<74>**
Joseph DINGLEY^{7}, b. ( )
Abner DINGLEY^{7}, b. ( ), d.y.
CHILDREN OF William DINGLEY^{7} & Sarah JORDAN: (8)**<75>**
John BEARSE, d. pre 6 Apr. 1761 (adm.)
CHILDREN OF John BEARSE & Sarah HOLMES^{5} (Mary Brewster^{4}): (12) <2-11, Halifax VR:44>
Joseph BEARS^{6*}, b. 26 Mar. 1721* <Plympton VR:17>
Gideon BEARS^{6}, b. 6 Mar. 1722/3* <Plympton VR:16>; d. pre June 1761*
John BEARS^{6}, b. 28 Oct. 1724
Lydia BEARS^{6}, b. 23 Feb. 1728/9
Mary BEARS^{6}, b. 17 Dec. 1730
Sarah BEARS^{6}, b. 10 Mar. 1732
Deborah BEARS^{6}, b. 10 Nov. 1735
Jerusha BEARS^{6}, b. 13 May 1738
Asa BEARS^{6}, b. 13 May 1740; d. 15 July 1829 <Halifax VR:60>
Keziah BEARS^{6}, b. 13 Jan. 1743/4
Levy BEARS^{6}, b. 13 June 1750
Rainy BEARS^{6}, b. pre 1750
Mary RANDALL, b. c1740, d. 15 Apr. 1825, ae 84y9m, Hebron ME g.s.
CHILDREN OF Asa BEARS^{6} & Mary RANDALL: (4 of 8) <Halifax>**<76>**
Asa BEARSE^{7}, b. 20 Jan. 1765; d. 8 Sept. 1856, Hebron ME
Charles BEARSE^{7}, b. c1771, d. 16 Jan. 1855, ae 83y9m10d, g.s.
Seth BEARSE^{7}, d. 13 Aug. 1861
Isaac BEARSE^{7}, b. 22 Aug. 1776; d. Dec. 1821* or Jan. 1822*
Abigail RIPLEY^{6} (*Hannah Sturtevant^{5}, Fear Cushman^{4}, Isaac$^{3-2}$), b. 28 May 1732*; d. aft.June 1761

CHILDREN OF Gideon BEARSE^{6} (Sarah Holmes^{5}) & Abigail RIPLEY: (3) <Halifax VR:38>
Jerusha BARSE^{7}, b. 13 Apr. 1752
Jonathan BARSE^{7}, b. 25 Aug. 1754
Gideon BARSE^{7}, b. 9 Feb. 1758; d. 18 June 1844*
CHILD OF Asa BEARCE^{7} & Rhoda WESTON:
Asa BEARCE^{8}, b. 24 Apr. 1796*; d. pre 1 July 1879 (will)
CHILDREN OF Caleb STETSON & Sarah BREWSTER^{4} (Wrestling^{3}): (7) <Plymouth, MD 13:167>
Abisha STETSON^{5}, b. 22 Feb. 1706
Elizabeth STETSON^{5}, b. 14 Oct. 1709
Barzilla STETSON^{5}, b. 17 Dec. 1711; d. 11 Jan. 1766* <Plymouth ChR 1:395>
Joshua STETSON^{5}, b. 21 Apr. 1714
Jerusha STETSON^{5}, b. 30 June 1716
John STETSON^{5}, b. 18 Dec. 1718
Jedediah STETSON^{5}, b. 12 Sept. 1721
CHILDREN OF Caleb STETSON & Abigail ( ): (2) <MD 18:216>
Caleb STETSON, b. 12 Aug. 1755
Bradford STETSON, b. 20 May 1757
Ruth KEMPTON, d. 27 Feb. 1768* <Plymouth ChR 1:397>
CHILDREN OF Barzilla STETSON^{5} (Sarah Brewster^{4}) & Ruth KEMPTON: (4) <Plymouth, MD 15:160>
Barzilla STETSON^{6}, b. 21 Dec. 1742; d. 1 Dec. 1782, Boston, drowned <Plymouth ChR 1:412>
Jedediah STETSON^{6}, b. 17 July 1745
Sarah STETSON^{6}, b. 26 June 1749
Mehitable STETSON^{6}, b. 30 Sept. 1751
Child of Barzilla STETSON's, d. 4 Nov. 1769 <Plymouth ChR 1:398>
Child of Barzilla STETSON's, d. 16 Nov. 1781 <Plymouth ChR 1:411>
MICRO #11 of 18
Hannah THOMAS^{5} (Mary Tilden^{4}, Hannah Little^{3}, Anna Warren^{2}), b. 30 Aug. 1698, Duxbury <MD 9:25>; d. 20 Aug. 1788, Kingston g.s. <MD 7:24>
CHILDREN OF Wrestling BREWSTER^{4} (Wrestling^{3}) & Hannah THOMAS: (7) <Plymouth, MD 13:168>
Wrestling BREWSTER^{5}, b. 29 Aug. 1724; d. 8 Feb. 1810, Kingston g.s. <MD 7:24>
Isaac BREWSTER^{5}, b. 17 Mar. 1727**<77>**
Thomas BREWSTER^{5}, b. 23 Dec. 1729**<78>**
Elijah BREWSTER^{5}, b. 10 Sept. 1732; d. 23 Sept. 1732, Kingston g.s. <MD 7:24>
Elisha BREWSTER^{5}, b. 9 Feb. 1733/4; d. 1 Sept. 1801
Hannah BREWSTER^{5}, b. 20 Oct. 1737; d. 1748**<79>**
Mary BREWSTER^{5}, b. 27 Nov. 1740; d. 25 Aug. 1795, unm., Kingston g.s. <MD 7:24>
Leonice SOULE^{5} (Aaron$^{4-3}$, John^{2}), b. 4 Jan. 1753 <Pembroke VR> (wf of Isaac Brewster^{5})**<80>**
Deborah SEABURY^{5} (Deborah Wiswall^{4}, Priscilla Pabodie^{3}, Eliz. Alden^{2}), b. 13 Apr. 1727, Duxbury <MD 9:25>; d. 23 Oct. 1802, Kingston g.s. <MD 7:24>
CHILDREN OF Wrestling BREWSTER^{5} & Deborah SEABURY: (2)
Hosea BREWSTER^{6}, d. pre 14 Nov. 1794 (bond) <Plymouth Co.Prob.#2745, 34:17>
Huldah BREWSTER^{6}, b. ( )

PATIENCE BREWSTER^{2} (William^{1})

Thomas PRENCE, b. c1600, d. 29 Mar. 1783, Plymouth <MD 3:203>
CHILDREN OF Thomas PRENCE & Patience BREWSTER^{2}: (4)
Rebecca PRENCE^{3}, b. pre 22 May 1627 <MD 1:150>
Thomas PRENCE^{3}, b. pre 22 May 1627 <MD 1:150>
Mercy PRENCE^{3}, b. c1631, d. 28 Sept. 1711, ae 80, Eastham g.s. <MD 8:2>

Hannah PRENCE^{3}, b. pre 1635* <MD 17:200>; d. pre 23 Nov. 1698 <MD 14:87>

Nathaniel MAYO, (son of Rev. John), d. betw. 19 Dec. 1661 (will) - 4 Mar. 1662 (prob.)<MD 17:215>

CHILDREN OF Nathaniel MAYO & Hannah PRENCE^{3}: (6) <Eastham, MD 17:200>

Thomas MAYO^{4}, b. 7 Dec. 1650; d. 22 Apr. 1729, Orleans g.s.

Nathaniel MAYO^{4}, b. 16 Nov. 1652; d. 30 Nov. 1709, Eastham <MD 4:33>

Samuel MAYO^{4}, b. 12 Oct. 1655; d. 29 Oct. 1738 , Eastham g.s.

Hannah MAYO^{4}, b. 17 Oct. 1657; d. aft. 15 June 1676* <MD 9:121>

Theophilus MAYO^{4}, b. 17 Dec. 1659; d. betw. 28 Mar. 1673 - 15 June 1676* <MD 3:204, 9:121>

Bathsheba MAYO^{4}, b. betw. 19 Dec. 1661 (father's will) - Mar. 1661/2 (prob.); d. aft. 15 June 1676* <MD 9:121>

Jonathan SPARROW, (son of Richard), b. c1634, d. 21 Mar. 1706/7, ae 73, Eastham g.s. <MD 8:4>

CHILDREN OF Jonathan SPARROW & Hannah (PRENCE^{3}) Mayo: (2)<81>

Patience SPARROW^{4}, b. pre 25 Oct. 1675, d. 25 Oct. 1745, "above 80", Barnstable <MD 14:195>

Richard SPARROW^{4}, b. c1675; d. 13 Apr. 1728, ae 53, Orleans g.s. <MD 15:56>

CHILD OF Richard SPARROW^{4} & Mercy COB:<82>

Priscilla SPARROW^{5}, b. 8 July 1722, Eastham <MD 7:19>; d. aft. 1 Feb. 1775 (hus. will)

David SNOW, d. 23 Feb. 1776, Eastham <MD 27:104>

CHILDREN OF David SNOW & Priscilla SPARROW^{5}: (9) <Eastham, MD 27:104>

Mercy SNOW^{6}, b. 6 Mar. 1748

Jonathan SNOW^{6}, b. 13 Sept. 1749

Eunice SNOW^{6}, b. 8 Feb. 1751

Stephen SNOW^{6}, b. 9 Nov. 1752

Phebe SNOW^{6}, b. 28 Aug. 1754

Priscilla SNOW^{6}, b. 19 May 1756

Mary SNOW^{6}, b. 28 Aug. 1758

David SNOW^{6}, b. 28 July 1760

Moses SNOW^{6}, b. 17 Feb. 1763

Elizabeth WIXAM, (dau of Robert & Alice), d. Dec. 1699, Eastham <MD 4:33>

CHILDREN OF Nathaniel MAYO^{4} (Hannah Prence^{3}) & Elizabeth WIXAM: (7) <Eastham, MD 4:32,33>

Nathaniel MAYO^{5}, b. 7 July 1681; d. aft. 1709 (father's will)

Bathshua MAYO^{5}, b. 23 Sept. 1683; d. 9 Jan. 1706, Eastham <MD 4:33>

Alice MAYO^{5}, b. 29 Apr. 1686

Ebenezer MAYO^{5}, b. 13 July 1689; d. 9 Nov. 1709 <MD 4:33>

Hannah MAYO^{5}, b. 16 June 1692 <MD 4:33>; d. aft. 26 Apr. 1729*

Elisha MAYO^{5}, b. 28 Apr. 1695 <MD 4:33>; d. aft 1 July 1734*

Robert MAYO^{5}, b. 23 Mar. 1697/98, d. 26 July 1707 <MD 4:33>

Thomas FREEMAN^{5} (Tho.^{4}, Mercy Prence^{3}, Patience Brewster^{2}), b. 11 Oct. 1676 (hus of Bathshua Mayo^{5})

John HIGGINS, (son of Ichabod), b. 8 June 1692, Eastham <MD 6:14>; d. aft. 7 July 1787*

CHILDREN OF John HIGGINS & Hannah MAYO^{5}: (6) <Eastham, MD 15:54>

Hannah HIGGINS^{6}, b. 6 Mar. 1714/5

Bathsheba HIGGINS^{6}, b. 13 June 1718

Abigail HIGGINS^{6}, b. 25 Oct. 1720

John HIGGINS^{6}, b. 25 Nov. 1722

Robert HIGGINS^{6}, b. 24 Aug. 1724

Ichabod HIGGINS^{6}, b. 26 Apr. 1729

Bethiah KNOWLES^{7} (Enos^{6}, Sam.^{5}, Mercy Freeman^{4}, Mercy Prence^{3}, Patience Brewster^{2}), b. 12 Jan. 1734/5, Eastham <MD 17:37>

CHILD OF Ichabod HIGGINS^{6} & Bethiah KNOWLES:

John HIGGINS^{7}, d. ?1801*

CHILDREN OF John HIGGINS[7] & Sarah HIGGINS: (2) <Eastham, MD 33:14>
Bethiah HIGGINS[8], b. 15 June 1787
Hannah Mayo HIGGINS[8], b. 16 July 1789; d. 23 July 1848
Edmund FREEMAN, (*son of Abner & Sarah), b. 1 Feb. 1780*, d. 1823, New Orleans <Freeman Gen.:183>
CHILDREN OF Edmund FREEMAN & Bethiah HIGGINS[8]: (6)* <Freeman Gen.>
Adaline FREEMAN[9], b. 8 June 1809
Edmund FREEMAN[9], b. 7 July 1811
Leander FREEMAN[9], b. 23 Oct. 1814
John Higgins FREEMAN[9], b. 1 June 1817
Reuben Higgins FREEMAN[9], b. 8 May 1819
Otis W. FREEMAN[9], b. 11 May 1821; d. 3 May 1851
Ruth DOANE[3] (Dan.[2], John[1]), d. betw 17 Nov. 1719 - 15 Mar. 1722
CHILDREN OF Nathaniel MAYO[5] (Nathaniel[4]) & Ruth DOANE: (4) <Eastham VR>
Elizabeth MAYO[6], b. 29 Sept. 1712
Nathaniel MAYO[6], b. 4 Aug. 1714
Abigail MAYO[6], b. 24 Sept. 1716; d. 8 Mar. 1724
Ruth MAYO[6], b. 17 Nov. 1719
CHILDREN OF Samuel MAYO[4] (Hannah Prence[3]): (7)
Samuel MAYO[5], b. c1689*; d. 7 Oct. 1761*, Orleans g.s.
Jonathan MAYO[5], d. 17 May 1768, Eastham <MD 15:140>
Mercy MAYO[5], b. pre 1712*; d. aft. 1740*
Rebecca MAYO[5], b. pre 1710*; d. aft. 1740*
Mary MAYO[5], b. c1694*; d. 13 July 1744*, Middle Haddam g.s.**<83>**
Hannah MAYO[5], d. 5 July 1719, Harwich <MD 6:56> (wf of Judah Hopkins[4], Stephen[3], Gyles[2])
Sarah MAYO[5], d. pre 9 Apr. 1734
Thankful TWINING[5] (Ruth Cole[4], Ruth Snow[3], Constance Hopkins[2]), b. 11 Jan. 1696/7, Eastham <MD 4:142>; d. 28 Aug. 1779, Eastham <MD 15:140>
CHILDREN OF Jonathan MAYO[5] & Thankful TWINING: (11) <Eastham, MD 15:140>
Ruth MAYO[6], b. 16 Mar. 1720/21
Hannah MAYO[6], b. 6 Dec. 1721; d. 16 May 1767, Eastham <MD 15:140>
Elizabeth MAYO[6], b. 1 Sept. 1723
Rebecca MAYO[6], b. 31 May 1725
Theophilus MAYO[6], b. 2 Apr. 1727
Jonathan MAYO[6], b. 17 Mar. 1728/9
Thankful MAYO[6], b. 4 Feb. 1731/2
Mary MAYO[6], b. 13 Apr. 1733
Ebenezer MAYO[6], b. 9 Feb. 1734/5
Constant MAYO[6], b. 8 Apr. 1737
Jerusha MAYO[6], b. 25 Aug. 1739 **<83>**
Ralph SMITH, (son of Tho.), b. 23 Oct. 1682, Eastham <MD 4:141>; d. 8 Apr. 1763*, Middle Haddam
CHILDREN OF Ralph SMITH & Mary MAYO[5] (Sam.[4]): (7) <Eastham VR, MD 8:15>
Isaac SMITH[6], b. 17 Nov. 1716
Phebe SMITH[6], b. 16 May 1720
Thomas SMITH[6], b. 14 June 1723; d. 19 Sept. 1759, Middletown CT
Enoch SMITH[6], b. 10 Nov. 1725
Mary SMITH[6], b. 7 Nov. 1728 <MD 8:16>
Jonathan SMITH[6], b. 30 Dec. 1730 <MD 8:16>
Ezra SMITH[6], b. 10 Dec. 1732 <MD 8:16>
Ruth MAYO[6] (Israel[5], Tho.[4], Hannah Prence[3], Patience Brewster[2]), b. 27 Apr. 1725, Eastham <MD 16:73>; d. 8 Nov. 1788*, Middle Haddam CT g.s. <Higgins Gen.:119>

CHILDREN OF Thomas SMITH^{6} & Ruth MAYO: (7) <Middletown CT, Barbour Coll.2:214>

Thomas SMITH^{7}, b. 4 June 1744

Mary SMITH^{7}, b. 10 Sept. 1746

Mercy SMITH^{7}, b. 5 Apr. 1749

Zoeth SMITH^{7}, b. 28 Mar. 1751

Enoch SMITH^{7}, b. 10 Apr. 1753

Jonathan SMITH^{7}, b. 25 Sept. 1756

Alice SMITH^{7}, b. 12 Nov. 1758

Urania WRIGHT^{6} (John$^{5-4}$, Adam^{3}, Hester Cooke^{2}), b. 12 Aug. 1741* <Plympton VR>

CHILDREN OF Thomas SMITH^{7} & Urania WRIGHT: (2)*

Rev. Bela SMITH^{8}, b. June 1783; d. 3 July 1847

Zoeth SMITH^{8}, b. ( )

Rhoda MERWIN, (dau of Miles & Mary), b. 11 Nov. 1780; d. 23 Sept. 1862

CHILDREN OF Rev. Bela SMITH^{8} & Rhoda MERWIN: (8)

Bela SMITH^{9}, b. 26 Sept. 1812; d. 19 Sept. 1881, Cornwallville NY

Rhoda SMITH^{9}, b. 26 Sept. 1812 (twins)

Charles D. SMITH^{9}, b. 11 Feb. 1815; d. 2 Jan. 1853

Merwin SMITH^{9}, b. 7 Feb. 1817

Joseph Merwin SMITH^{9}, b. 23 Jan. 1819; d. 12 Aug. 1865

Mary Urania SMITH^{9}, b. 6 May 1821; d. 12 Aug. 1865, unm.

Rev. Thomas Barrett SMITH^{9}, b. 15 Mar. 1823, Durham NY; d. 2 Oct. 1895, Yonkers NY

James Wright SMITH^{9}, b. 31 Aug. 1825; d. 22 Sept. 1886

CHILD OF Zoeth SMITH^{8} (Tho.^{7}) & Olive MERWIN, (dau of Miles & Mary):

Addison SMITH^{9}, b. ( )

Martha Morgan BUCK, b. 29 June 1829, Wethersfield CT; d. 7 Apr. 1894, bur.White Plains, NY

CHILDREN OF Rev. Thomas Barrett SMITH^{9} (Bela^{8}) & Martha Morgan BUCK: (4)

Thomas Valentine SMITH^{10}, b. 23 Dec. 1849, Durham NY; d. 9 July 1871

James Alzamora SMITH^{10}, b. 20 Mar. 1852, Liberty NY

Charles SMITH^{10}, b. 23 Sept. 1855, Crawford NY

Fred Milton SMITH^{10}, b. 1 June 1857, Milton NY

Amanda JEROME, b. c1815, d. 21 Feb. 1806, ae 91, Cornwallville NY (wf of Bela Smith^{9})

Elizabeth BERRY, d. 28 Apr. 1714, Eastham <MD 6:55>

CHILDREN OF Stephen COLE & 1st Elizabeth BERRY: (2) <Harwich, MD 5:90>

Samuel COLE, b. 8 Jan. 1712/3

Stephen COLE, b. 14 Apr. 1714

CHILD OF Stephen COLE & 2nd Rebecca MAYO^{5} (Sam.^{4}): <Harwich, MD 5:90>

Elizabeth COLE^{6}, b. 9 May 1726

John COLE, d. betw 12 Oct. 1753 (will) - 6 Nov. 1753 (prob.) <Barnstable Co.Prob.9:79,81>

CHILDREN OF John COLE & Mercy MAYO^{5} (Sam.^{4}): (4) <Eastham VR>

John COLE^{6}, b. 1 Feb. 1728/9; d. aft 4 Dec. 1753*

Theophilus COLE^{6}, b. 30 Oct. 1730; d. pre 12 Oct. 1753*

Rebecca COLE^{6}, b. 7 Apr. 1733; d. aft 12 Oct. 1753*

Mercy COLE^{6}, b. 11 Aug. 1735; d. pre 12 Oct. 1753*

CHILDREN OF Samuel MAYO^{5} (Sam.^{4}) & Abigail SPARROW^{4} (Jonathan$^{3-2}$, Rich.^{1}):(8) <Harwich, MD 7:195>

Rebecca MAYO^{6}, b. 19 Apr. 1714

Samuel MAYO^{6}, b. 3 June 1716

Thomas MAYO^{6}, b. 28 Oct. 1718

Phebe MAYO^{6}, b. 28 Feb. 1720/1

Abigail MAYO^{6}, b. 20 Feb. 1722/3

Reliance MAYO^{6}, b. 7 Mar. 1724/5

Sarah MAYO^{6}, b. 24 May 1727

Lois MAYO^{6}, b. 13 May 1731

James HIGGINS, b. 22 July 1688, Eastham <MD 6:15>; d. 11 July 1777, Eastham g.s., Orleans Cem. (hus of Sarah Mayo^{5} (Sam.^{4})

Barbara KNOWLES, (dau of Richard), b. 28 Sept. 1656, Eastham <MD 5:23>; d. 23 Feb. 1714/5, Eastham <MD 8:94>

CHILDREN OF Thomas MAYO^{4} (Hannah Prence^{3}) & Barbara KNOWLES: (10) <Eastham, MD 8:94>

Thomas MAYO^{5}, b. 3 Apr. 1678

Theophilus MAYO^{5}, b. 31 Oct. 1680; d. 6 Oct. 1763, Eastham <MD 15:53>

Mary MAYO^{5}, b. 6 Aug. 1683; d. 1777, Eastham <MD 7:185>

Mercy MAYO^{5}, b. 19 Jan. 1685; d. pre 7 Mar. 1765*

Ruth MAYO^{5}, b. 20 Jan. 1688

Judah MAYO^{5}, b. 25 Sept. 1691

Lydia MAYO^{5}, b. 12 June 1694

Richard MAYO^{5}, b. 13 Jan. 1696/7

Son, b. 1 Aug. 1699, d. 18 Aug. 1699

Israel MAYO^{5}, b. 12 Aug. 1700; d. pre 30 Oct. 1771*

Elizabeth AREY^{7} (Oliver^{6}, Mary Mayo^{5}, Tho.^{4}), b. 16 Feb. 1747

CHILDREN OF Nathaniel MYRICK & Elizabeth AREY^{7}: (8) <Bangor Hist.Mag.6:246>

Abigail MYRICK^{8}*, b. 10 Oct. 1769*

Joseph MYRICK^{8}, bpt. 25 Oct. 1772, Orleans <MD 10:230>, d.y.

Joseph MYRICK^{8}, b. 16 Apr. 1774*; bpt. 29 May 1774, Orleans <MD 10:231>

Molly MYRICK^{8}, b. 10 June 1776*; bpt. 21 July 1776, Orleans <MD 10:232>

Nathaniel MYRICK^{8}*, b. 7 July 1778*

Elizabeth MYRICK^{8}*, b. 12 Feb. 1781*

Solomon MYRICK^{8}*, b. 7 Feb. 1783*

Reuben MYRICK^{8}*, b. 12 Aug. 1786*

Eli STARR, b. 27 July 1794, Danbury

CHILD OF Eli STARR & Sally HURLBURT: ("2nd child") <Hist.Starr Fam., by Burgis Starr, (1879):336>

Harmon STARR, b. 13 June 1820, d. 15 May 1844 (lived Oneonta NY)

CHILDREN OF Israel MAYO^{5} (Tho.^{4}) & Mercy RIDER: (7) <Eastham, MD 16:73>

Ruth MAYO^{6}, b. 25 Apr. 1725; d. 8 Nov. 1788*

Mercy MAYO^{6}, b. 12 Apr. 1728; d. 25 Mar. 1760, Eastham <MD 15:229>

Thomas MAYO^{6}, b. 20 May 1730

Priscilla MAYO^{6}, b. 6 Oct. 1732

Alice MAYO^{6}, b. 6 Mar. 1734/5

Phebe MAYO^{6}, b. 31 July 1738

Esther MAYO^{6}, b. 12 Nov. 1740

Jonathan LINNELL, b. c1723, d. 9 June 1797, Orleans g.s. <MD 7:230>

CHILDREN OF Jonathan LINNELL & 1st Mercy MAYO^{6}: (5) <Eastham, MD 15:229>

Experience LINNELL^{7}, b. 18 Nov. 1748; d. 5 June 1819, Eastham g.s. <MD 9:67>

Thomas LINNELL^{7}, b. 8 Aug. 1750

Ruth LINNELL^{7}, b. 16 May 1752

Zeruiah LINNELL^{7}, b. 26 Apr. 1754

Uriah LINNELL^{7}, b. 16 Feb. 1756

CHILDREN OF Jonathan LINNELL & 2nd Rachel ( ) SMITH: (3) <Harwich, Eastham VR -MD 15:229>

Samuel LINNELL, b. 18 Mar. 1764

Marcy LINNELL, b. 18 Apr. 1766

Lettice LINNELL, b. 20 May 1768

James HICKMAN^{7} (*Mary Smith^{6}, Jos.^{5}, Sam.^{4}, Mary Hopkins^{3}, Giles^{2}), b. c1749, d. 15 Dec. 1820,

Eastham g.s. <MD 9:67>

CHILDREN OF James HICKMAN & Experience LINNELL^{7} (Mercy Mayo^{6}): (5) <1-4, Eastham, MD 33:84>

Samuel HICKMAN^{8}, b. 4 July 1776

Mercy HICKMAN^{8}, b. 28 Dec. 1777

John HICKMAN^{8}, b. 24 Nov. 1779

Mary HICKMAN^{8}, b. 26 June 1786

James HICKMAN^{8*}, b. 3 July 1790*

Eusebia SAWYER, (dau of Phineas & Hannah), b. c1793, Harvard MA, d. 4 Sept. 1857, ae 64, Boston <Mass.VR 113:60>

CHILD OF James HICKMAN$^{8?}$ & Eusebia SAWYER:

James E. HICKMAN, b. 26 Feb. 1824, Eastham; d. 6 May 1871, Melrose MA, unm. <Mass.VR 239:195>

MICRO #12 of 18

Nathaniel PAINE^{6} (Theophilus^{5}, John^{4}, Mary Snow^{3}, Constance Hopkins^{2}), b. 7 Sept. 1736 (hus of Phebe Mayo^{6}, Israel^{5})

CHILD OF Judah MAYO^{5} (Tho.^{4}) & Mary HAMILTON^{5} (Mary Smith^{4}, Mary Hopkins^{3}, Gyles^{2}):

Lydia MAYO^{6}, b. 23 Jan. 1722/3, Eastham <MD 16:30>

poss. Mary MAYO^{6*}, b. ( )

Samuel AREY^{3} (*Richard$^{2-1}$), b. c1688, d. 1773, ae 85, Eastham <MD 7:184>

CHILDREN OF Samuel AREY & Mary MAYO^{5} (Tho.^{4}): (8) <Eastham, MD 15:53>

Joseph AREY^{6}, b. 24 May 1715

Oliver AREY^{6}, b. 15 Sept. 1717; d. 30 Mar. 1760, Eastham, Orleans g.s.

Thomas AREY^{6}, b. 7 May 1719

Ruth AREY^{6}, b. 30 June 1721

Mary AREY^{6}, b. 30 June 1721 (twins)

Joshua AREY^{6}, b. 8 Mar. 1722

Zelotas AREY^{6}, b. 31 May 1724

Paul AREY^{6}, b. 22 Apr. 1726

Elizabeth GOULD, (dau of Nathaniel), b. 6 Jan. 1719/20, Harwich <MD 6:85>

CHILDREN OF Oliver AREY^{6} & Elizabeth GOULD: (7) <1-5, Eastham, MD 16:197>

Oliver AREY^{7}, b. 6 Nov. 1742; d. 24 Mar. 1813, Orleans g.s.

Abigail AREY^{7}, b. 20 Mar. 1745

Elizabeth AREY^{7}, b. 16 Feb. 1747

Thomas AREY^{7}, b. 10 Oct. 1751

Eunice AREY^{7}, b. 20 Apr. 1758

Mary AREY^{7}, b. ( )

Jedidah AREY^{7}, b. ( )

Joseph AREY, b. 22 May 1785, Eastham[<84>]

Dorothy ( ), b. 13 Mar. 1786, Harwich[<84>]

CHILDREN OF Joseph AREY & Dorothy ( ): (10)[<84>]

Thomas AREY, b. 29 Aug. 1808, Orleans

Josiah Snow AREY, b. 16 Sept. 1810

Oliver AREY, b. 16 Mar. 1813

James Hopkins AREY, b. 10 May 1815

Joseph AREY, b. 9 Nov. 1817, d. 16 Mar. 1819

Joseph AREY, b. 18 Aug. 1819

Joshua Taylor AREY, b. 25 Oct. 1822

Benjamin Higgens AREY, b. 17 June 1827, d. 18 July ( )

Salley Eldredg AREY, b. 17 June 1829

CHILD OF Nathaniel MYRICK & Elizabeth AREY^{7} (Oliver^{6}):[<85>]

Mary MYRICK^{8}, bpt. 21 July 1776, Eastham <MD 10:232>; d. Boston (m. Jesse Libby)[<86>]

Mary COLE, b. c1739, d. 22 June 1811, 72nd yr, Orleans g.s. (wf of Oliver Arey^{7})

Jonathan GODFREY, (son of George), b. 24 June 1682, Eastham <MD 4:30>; d. Mar.or Apr. 1765

CHILDREN OF Jonathan GODFREY & Mercy MAYO^{5} (Tho.^{4}): (1 of 9)**<87>**

Ruth GODFREY^{6}, b. c1719, d. 22 July 1796, 77th yr, Chatham <MD 13:178> (wf of 2nd hus Tho.Mirick)

John GOULD^{5}, (Nathaniel^{4}, John$^{3-2}$, Zacheus^{1}), b. 21 June 1718, Harwich <MD 6:85>; d. betw 1746 - 1750 (wf remarried)

CHILDREN OF John GOULD & Ruth GODFREY^{6}: (4) <Harwich, MD 24:112>

John GOULD^{7}, b. 15 Sept. 1741

Thomas GOULD^{7}, b. 26 Mar. 1743; lost at sea, pre 1 Apr. 1785 <Barnstable Co.Prob.22:209>**<88>**

Richard GOULD^{7}, b. 9 Dec. 1744

Abigail GOULD^{7}, b. 22 Apr. 1746; d. 3 or 30 Apr. 1820, Chatham g.s. ("oldest cem.")

CHILDREN OF Joseph DOANE & Abigail GOULD^{7}: (11) <Chatham, MD 16:213>

Mercy DOANE^{8}, b. 25 Sept. 1767

Joseph DOANE^{8}, b. 11 July 1769, d.y.

Dorcas DOANE^{8}, b. 20 July 1771

John DOANE^{8}, b. 23 July 1773

Elisha DOANE^{8}, b. 11 Apr. 1776

Abigail DOANE^{8}, b. 28 Jan. 1778

Isaiah DOANE^{8}, b. 7 Apr. 1779

Joseph DOANE^{8}, b. 19 Aug. 1780

Thomas Gould DOANE^{8}, b. 24 Dec. 1784

Hezekiah DOANE^{8}, b. 26 Sept. 1786

Nehemiah DOANE^{8}, b. 17 Feb. 1789 <MD 16:214>

CHILDREN OF John GOULD^{7} (Ruth Godfrey^{6}) & Apphia COLE: (2) <Orleans, MD 13:82>

Joseph GOULD^{8}, bpt. 26 June 1791

Patty GOULD^{8}, bpt. 26 June 1791

CHILDREN OF Thomas GOULD^{7} (Ruth Godfrey^{6}) & Phebe COLE: (9) <1-4, Eastham, MD 31:175; 5-9, Orleans, MD 10:230-233>

Mary GOULD^{8}, b. 6 Nov. 1764

Thomas GOULD^{8}, b. 11 Sept. 1765

Ruth GOULD^{8}, b. 11 Aug. 1767

Paine GOULD^{8}, b. 6 June 1770

Nathaniel GOULD^{8}, bpt. 2 May 1773 <MD 10:230>

James GOULD^{8}, bpt. 13 Nov. 1774 <MD 10:231>

Phebe GOULD^{8}, bpt. 4 Aug. 1776 <MD 10:232>

Solomon GOULD^{8}, bpt. 12 Aug. 1778 <MD 10:233>, d.y.

David GOULD^{8}, bpt. 5 Mar. 1780 <MD 11:252>, d.y.

Mercy NICKERSON, d. 2 Jan. 1829* <Mt. Vernon ME VR>

CHILDREN OF Nathaniel GOULD^{8} & Mercy NICKERSON: (9) <1-6, b. Cape Cod; 1-9, Mt.Vernon ME VR 2:49>

Armina GOULD^{9}, b. 30 Mar. 1793

David GOULD^{9}, b. 1 Feb. 1795; d. Vienna ME*

Nathaniel J. GOULD^{9}, b. 6 Aug. 1797

Mercy GOULD^{9}, b. 14 Nov. 1800; d. 1875

Phebe GOULD^{9}, b. 11 Jan. 1803

Ruth GOULD^{9}, b. 4 Sept. 1805

Lurenda GOULD^{9}, b. 19 Dec. 1807

Thomas GOULD^{9}, b. 6 Dec. 1809; d. 1 Dec. 1889

James GOULD^{9}, b. 15 Oct. 1814

Ruth (HIGGINS)(Godfrey) Smith, (dau of Silvanus), b. 18 Feb. 1772* (?2nd wf of Nath. Gould^{8})**<89>**

Laura HOOKER, (*dau of Zibeon & Mary), b. ?7 Sept. 1809 <Sherborn VR:50> (wf of Tho.Gould^{9})

Benjamin HURD, (*son of Jos. & Mary), b. 6 Sept. 1770*, Eastham <MD 34:184>

CHILDREN OF Benjamin HURD & Phebe GOULD^{8} (Tho.^{7}): (11) <Eastham, MD 33:132>

Solomon HURD^{9}, b. 21 Dec. 1793

Joanna HURD^{9}, b. 28 June 1797

Gould HURD^{9}, b. 28 May 1799

Phebe HURD^{9}, b. 17 Oct. 1802, d.y.

Joseph HURD^{9}, b. 22 Jan. 1801, d.y.

Benjamin HURD^{9}, b. 22 Jan. 1801, (twin), d.y.

Phebe HURD^{9}, b. 14 Oct. 1804

Benjamin HURD^{9}, b. 27 Sept. 1806

Rutha Gould HURD^{9}, b. 20 Feb. 1809

Joseph HURD^{9}, b. 22 Dec. 1810

Eunice HURD^{9}, b. 6 Mar. 1804 (1814?)

Joshua GOULD^{6} (Nath.$^{5-4}$, John$^{3-2}$, Zacheus^{1}), b. 10 Feb. 1747; d. 19 June 1826, Orleans g.s.

Mary HURD, b. c1748, d. 1 Dec. 1843, ae 95, Orleans g.s. <Gould Gen.>

CHILDREN OF Joshua GOULD & Mary HURD: (8) <Eastham, MD 33:183>

Rebecca GOULD, b. 7 Aug. 1772

Josiah GOULD, b. 23 Sept. 1774

Joshua GOULD, b. 3 Sept. 1776, unm.

Jonathan GOULD, b. 18 May 1779, unm.

Nathaniel GOULD, b. 16 Feb. 1782; d. betw 16 Nov. 1843 (will) - 9 Jan. 1844 (witness)<Gould:106>

Thomas GOULD, b. 26 Nov. 1784

Molly GOULD, b. 23 Sept. 1787

Benjamin GOULD, b. 7 June 1790; d. 1807

Hannah KNOWLES, b. 1786, d. 1872 <Gould Gen.:106>

CHILDREN OF Nathaniel GOULD, (son of Joshua) & Hannah KNOWLES: (10) <Orleans, MD 34:61>

Jonathan GOULD, b. 6 Mar. 1807; d. 27 Dec. 1843

Mary GOULD, b. 28 Nov. 1809

Nathaniel GOULD, b. 23 Nov. 1811; d. 19 Dec. 1855, bur. at sea <Orleans VR: 11,12>**<90>**

Joseph Knowles GOULD, b. 2 Feb. 1813

Franklin GOULD, b. 11 July 1816

Joshua GOULD, b. 12 Aug. 1818; d. 28 Nov. 1838, Boston

Hannah Knowles GOULD, b. 3 Aug. 1820

Sally W. GOULD, b. 8 Sept. 1822; d. 1850

Benjamin GOULD, b. 22 Jan. 1824

Nancy GOULD, b. 18 Nov. 1828

CHILDREN OF Thomas GOULD (son of Joshua) & Thankful HURD*: (5) <Eastham, MD 34:60>

Clement GOULD, b. 13 Sept. 1811

Rebecca GOULD, b. 3 Dec. 1817

Thankful GOULD, b. 3 Apr. 1822

Eliza C. GOULD, b. 24 Feb. 1826

Thomas GOULD, b. 15 Feb. 1828

Nathaniel GOULD, (son of Nath.), b. c1772, Eastham; d. 5 or 7 Dec. 1855, ae 83, Orleans, pauper, heart disease <Mass.VR 93:10>

Ruth HIGGINS, (dau of Gideon & Ruth), bpt. 29 May 1774, Orleans <MD 10:231>**<91>**

CHILD OF David GODREY & Ruth HIGGINS:

Sally GODFREY, b. 8 Dec. 1793 <Eastham/Orleans VR 6:160>

CHILDREN OF Lewis SMITH & Ruth (HIGGINS) Godfrey: (5) <Eastham/Orleans VR 6:160>

Olive SMITH, b. 20 Feb. 1798

David Godfrey SMITH, b. 8 Dec. 1799

Gideon SMITH, b. 6 May 1802

Silvanus Higgins SMITH, b. 28 Sept. 1804

Lewis SMITH, b. 22 May 1810

Rebecca SMITH^{3} (Tho.^{2}, Ralph^{1}), b. 31 Mar. 1685,Eastham, d. 22 Dec. 1748, Eastham<MD 4:141,24:91>

CHILDREN OF Theophilus MAYO^{5} (Tho.^{4}) & Rebecca SMITH: (9) <Eastham, MD 7:13>

Asa MAYO^{6}, b. 29 July 1706 <MD 7:12>; d. early 1780, Eastham <MD 7:186>

Isaac MAYO^{6}, b. 16 June 1708

Rebecca MAYO^{6}, b. 2 Dec. 1710

Ebenezer MAYO^{6}, b. 1 Mar. 1712/3

Experience MAYO^{6}, b. 3 Apr. 1716 (dau)

Theophilus MAYO^{6}, b. 17 Sept. 1718

( )h MAYO^{6}, b. 30 July 1721 (dau)

( ) MAYO^{6}, b. 22 Sept. 1724, d. 13 Oct. 1724

Benjamin MAYO^{6}, b. 21 July 1726 <MD 15:53>

CHILDREN OF Asa MAYO^{6} & Experience YATES^{5} (Abigail Rogers^{4}, James^{3}, Jos.^{2}):(6)<Eastham, MD 17:36>

Abigail MAYO^{7}, b. 12 July 1732/3 (sic)

Lydia MAYO^{7}, b. 9 May 1734

Sarah MAYO^{7}, b. 13 Oct. 1736

Deborah MAYO^{7}, b. 17 Aug. 1738

Experience MAYO^{7}, b. 27 Apr. 1741

Asa MAYO^{7}, b. 28 Aug. 1743; d. betw 28 May 1775 - 16 July 1775, Eastham <MD 7:185,15:14>

CHILDREN OF Asa MAYO^{7} & Hannah COVEL: (5) <Eastham, MD 10:232>**<92>**

Isaac MAYO^{8}, b. 27 Oct. 1763 <MD 31:175>

Sarah MAYO^{8}, bpt. 9 July 1775

Shubael MAYO^{8}, bpt. 9 July 1775

Asa MAYO^{8}, bpt. 9 July 1775

Ruth MAYO^{8}, bpt. 9 July 1775

Elizabeth HIGGINS, d. 4 Nov. 1721, Eastham <MD 9:10>**<93>**

CHILDREN OF Thomas MAYO^{5} (Tho.^{4}) & 1st Elizabeth HIGGINS: (7) <Eastham, MD 9:9; 4-7, MD 9:10>

Elizabeth MAYO^{6}, b. 1 May 1702

Thankful MAYO^{6}, b. 10 Jan. 1703/4

Bathsheba MAYO^{6}, b. 27 Apr. 1705

Eliakim MAYO^{6}, b. 1 Apr. 1707

Sarah MAYO^{6}, b. 12 June 1710, d. 27 July 1711

Joshua MAYO^{6}, b. 28 May 1712

Mercy MAYO^{6}, b. 27 Feb. 1718/9

CHILD OF Thomas MAYO^{5} & 2nd Elizabeth ROGERS:**<94>**

Hannah MAYO^{6}, b. 8 Nov. 1724, Eastham <MD 9:10>

Joseph PAINE^{4} (Mary Snow^{3}, Constance Hopkins^{2}), d. 1 Oct. 1712, Eastham <MD 7:236>

CHILDREN OF Joseph PAINE & Patience SPARROW^{4} (Hannah Prence^{3}): (11) <Eastham, MD 4:209>

Ebenezer PAINE^{5}, b. 8 Apr. 1692

Hannah PAINE^{5}, b. 5 July 1694

Joseph PAINE^{5}, b. 29 Mar. 1697

Richard PAINE^{5}, b. 25 Mar. 1699

Dorcas PAINE^{5}, b. 27 May 1701

Phebe PAINE^{5}, b. 30 July 1703

Reliance PAINE^{5}, b. 27 Jan. 1705/6

Thomas PAINE^{5}, b. 1 Dec. 1708

Mary PAINE^{5}, b. 1 Dec. 1708 (twins)

Jonathan PAINE^{5}, b. 10 Dec. 1710

Experience PAINE[5], b. 27 May 1713 <MD 4:210>
John JENKINS, d. 8 July 1736, "above 70" <Barnstable East ChR:41>**<95>**
CHILD OF John JENKINS & Patience (SPARROW[4]) Paine:
Patience JENKINS[5], bpt. 6 Oct. 1717 <Barnstable ChR>
Mercy COB[3] (James[2], Henry[1]), b. 9 Apr. 1685, Barnstable <MD 3:73>
CHILDREN OF Richard SPARROW[4] (Hannah Prence[3]) & Mercy COB: (9) <Eastham, 1-8, MD 7:19>
Richard SPARROW[5], b. 10 Nov. 1702; d. 5 June 1774, Orleans g.s.
Rebecca SPARROW[5], b. 12 Oct. 1704
Mercy SPARROW[5], b. 6 Dec. 1706; d. 14 Feb. 1739/40 <Eastham VR:69>
Sarah SPARROW[5], b. 20 July 1708; d. 21 Aug. 1790, Eastham, Orleans g.s.
Hannah SPARROW[5], b. 12 Oct. 1711
Elizabeth SPARROW[5], b. 18 Apr. 1717
Mary SPARROW[5], b. 10 Mar. 1718/9
Priscilla SPARROW[5], b. 8 July 1722
Jonathan SPARROW[5], b. 17 Dec. 1724; d. pre 23 Feb. 1727/8
Josiah COOK[5] (Joshua[4], Deborah Hopkins[3], Gyles[2]), b. 30 Aug. 1707, Eastham**<96>**
CHILDREN OF Josiah COOK & Hannah SPARROW[5]: (5) <Eastham VR:95>
Elijah COOK[6], b. 26 Jan. 1731/2, d.y.
Elizabeth COOK[6], b. 24 Feb. 1733/4
Josiah COOK[6], b. 3 Dec. 1735
Elijah COOK[6], b. 8 June 1737
Joshua COOK[6], b. 12 Apr. 1740
Elisha DOANE, (son of Joseph), b. 3 Feb. 1705/6, Eastham <MD 3:179>
CHILDREN OF Elisha DOANE & Elizabeth SPARROW[5] (Richard[4]): (6) <Eastham, MD 17:140>
Rebecca DOANE[6], b. 21 Feb. 1735/6
Mercy DOANE[6], b. 31 Apr. 1738, d. Feb. 1739/40
Silvanus DOANE[6], b. 20 Jan. 1739/40
Mercy DOANE[6], b. 27 Jan. 1741/2
Elisha DOANE[6], b. 9 Sept. 1744 <MD 17:141>
Sarah DOANE[6], b. 15 Jan. 1747 <MD 17:141>
Edmund FREEMAN[5], (Edmund[4], Mercy Prence[3], Patience Brewster[2]), b. c1702, d. 22 July 1782, Eastham, Orleans g.s.
CHILD OF Edmund FREEMAN[5] & 1st Lois PAINE[5] (Nicholas[4], Mary Snow[3], Constance Hopkins[2]):
Lois FREEMAN[6], b. 3 Sept. 1726
CHILDREN OF Edmund FREEMAN[5] & 2nd Sarah SPARROW[5] (Richard[4]): (2) <Eastham VR:66>
Jonathan FREEMAN[6], b. 22 Feb. 1729/30
Edmund FREEMAN[6], b. 13 Feb. 1731
Mehitable NICKERSON, (dau of Ben. & Sarah), b. 15 Oct. 1744 <Harwich VR 2:86> (poss. wf of Elisha Doane[6] <Doane Gen.73,111>)
CHILDREN OF Zebulon YOUNG & Mercy SPARROW[5] (Richard[4]): (6) <Eastham VR:69>
Thankful YOUNG[6], b. 8 Jan. 1725/6
Nathaniel YOUNG[6], b. 14 Oct. 1728
Thankful YOUNG[6], b. 18 Sept. 1731
Zebulon YOUNG[6], b. 30 Sept. 1733
Isaac YOUNG[6], b. 23 Sept. 1735
Mercy YOUNG[6], b. 14 Sept. 1737
CHILDREN OF Isaac YOUNG[6?] & Priscilla HOPKINS: (3) <Eastham>
Thankful YOUNG, b. 16 Aug. 1764
Rebecca YOUNG, b. 15 Jan. 1766
Mercy YOUNG, b. 7 Aug. 1768

CHILDREN OF Richard MAYO & Rebecca SPARROW^{5} (Richard^{4}): (5) <Eastham, MD 16:203>

Richard MAYO^{6}, b. 22 Oct. 1729

Eunice MAYO^{6}, b. 22 Oct. 1731

Rebecca MAYO^{6}, b. 18 Feb. 1733/4

Sarah MAYO^{6}, b. 19 June 1736

Ruth MAYO^{6}, b. 8 July 1739

MICRO #13 of 18

Hannah SHAW, b. ?20 June 1698, Eastham <MD 3:229>; d. aft. 28 Jan. 1774 (hus. will)

CHILDREN OF Richard SPARROW^{5} (Richard^{4}) & Hannah SHAW: (5) <Eastham, MD 16:33>

Isaac SPARROW^{6}, b. 4 Apr. 1725; d. 19 June 1808, Orleans g.s. <MD 8:147>

Rebecca SPARROW^{6}, b. 27 Jan. 1726/7

Hannah SPARROW^{6}, b. 5 Mar. 1730/1, d. 26 Aug. 1736

Hannah SPARROW^{6}, b. 7 Aug. 1737

Mercy SPARROW^{6}, b. 27 June 1739

Rebecca KNOWLES^{6} (Sarah Paine^{5}, John^{4}, Mary Snow^{3}, Constance Hopkins^{2}), b. 23 May 1726, Eastham <MD 15:71>; d. 23 Nov. 1809, Orleans g.s.

CHILDREN OF Isaac SPARROW^{6} & Rebecca KNOWLES^{6}: (8) <Eastham, MD 24:190>

Richard SPARROW^{7}, b. 5 Dec. 1747; d. 19 Oct. 1811, Orleans g.s.

Sarah SPARROW^{7}, b. 13 Sept. 1749

Isaac SPARROW^{7}, b. 7 June 1752

Mercy SPARROW^{7}, b. 25 Apr. 1754; d. 6 May 1794, Orleans g.s.

Rebecca SPARROW^{7}, b. 2 Oct. 1756

Josiah SPARROW^{7}, b. 10 Feb. 1759; d. 14 July 1849, Orleans g.s.

Hannah SPARROW^{7}, b. 8 Dec. 1761

Elizabeth SPARROW^{7}, b. 12 Aug. 1764

Elizabeth ( ) SPARROW, d. 29 Oct. 1795, 43rd yr, Eastham g.s. <MD 7:229>

CHILDREN OF Richard SPARROW^{7} & Elizabeth ( ): (9) <Eastham>

Mary SPARROW^{8}, b. 21 Aug. 1772 <MD 33:81>

Elizabeth SPARROW^{8}, b. 3 Sept. 1774 <MD 33:81>

Isaac SPARROW^{8}, b. 27 Sept. 1776 <MD 33:81>

Rebecca SPARROW^{8}, b. 25 Apr. 1779 <MD 33:81>

Tabitha SPARROW^{8}, b. 18 May 1781 <MD 33:81>**[<97>]**

Lucy SPARROW^{8}, b. 27 June 1783 <MD 33:84>

Richard SPARROW^{8}, b. 31 Aug. 1785 <MD 33:84>

Joshua Knowles SPARROW^{8}, b. 21 Aug. 1787 <MD 33:84>

Jesse SPARROW^{8}, b. 13 Oct. 1790 <MD 33:84>

Sally GODFREY, (dau of David & Ruth), b. c1793, Orleans, d. 25 May 1855, ae 62, Orleans <Mass VR 93:10>

CHILDREN OF Jesse SPARROW^{8} & Sally GODFREY: (2) <Orleans>

Olive SPARROW^{9}, b. c1819, d. 17 Dec. 1890, Somerville, bur. Orleans, ae 71y10m9d, anemia & old age, widow of Solomon Higgins <Mass.VR 410:267>

Jesse SPARROW^{9}, b. c1821, d. 18 Aug. 1867, ae 46y2m7d, Orleans, widower, shoemaker <Mass.VR 202:10>

CHILDREN OF Heman LINNELL & Sarah SPARROW^{7} (Isaac^{6}): (5) <Eastham, MD 6:66>

Heman LINNELL^{8}, b. 11 Sept. 1775

James LINNELL^{8}, b. 6 Dec. 1776

Joshua LINNELL^{8}, b. 9 Oct. 1778

Isaac LINNELL^{8}, b. 22 Oct. 1780

Sally LINNELL^{8}, b. 10 Sept. 1782

John FREEMAN^{2} (Edmund^{1}), b. c1621, d. 28 Oct. 1719, 98th yr, Eastham g.s. <MD 5:143>

CHILDREN OF John FREEMAN & Mercy PRENCE^{3}: (11) <1-5, Eastham; MD 5:145>
John FREEMAN^{4}, b. 2 Feb. 1650, d.y. <MD 17:199>
John FREEMAN^{4}, b. Dec. 1651 <17:199>; d. 27 July 1721, Harwich g.s.
Thomas FREEMAN^{4}, b. Sept. 1653; d. 9 Feb. 1715/6, Harwich <MD 6:56>
Lieut. Edmund FREEMAN^{4}, b. June 1657; d. 10 Dec. 1717, Eastham <MD 8:66>
Mercy FREEMAN^{4}, b. July 1659; d. 1744, Eastham g.s.
Hannah FREEMAN^{4}, b. c1664; d. 15 Feb. 1743/44, Harwich, Brewster g.s.
Patience FREEMAN^{4}, b. ( )
William FREEMAN^{4}, b. ( ); d. pre 31 May 1687 <MD 3:177>
Prence FREEMAN^{4}, b. 3 Feb. 1665
Nathaniel FREEMAN^{4}, b. 20 Mar. 1669**<98>**
Bennet FREEMAN^{4}, b. Feb. 1670/1 <MD 9:138>; d. 30 May 1716, Eastham g.s. <MD 8:4>**<99>**

CHILDREN OF Jonathan FREEMAN & Eunice ( ): (4) <Orleans 6:97>
Catherine FREEMAN, b. 31 July 1805
Meris FREEMAN, b. 29 Apr. 1807 (son)
Eunice FREEMAN, b. 9 Mar. 1812
Polly King FREEMAN, b. 20 Oct. 1813

John PAINE^{4} (Mary Snow^{3}, Constance Hopkins^{2}), b. 14 Mar. 1660/61 <MD 9:50>, d. 26 Oct. 1731,Eastham g.s. <Eastham VR say 18 Oct.- MD 15:143>**<100>**

CHILDREN OF John PAINE & Bennet FREEMAN^{4} (Mercy Prence^{3}): (13) <1-5,7-13, Eastham, MD 8:14,15>
John PAINE^{5}, b. 18 Sept. 1690
Mary PAINE^{5}, b. 28 Jan. 1692/3
William PAINE^{5}, b. 6 June 1695
Benjamin PAINE^{5}, b. 22 Feb. 1696/7, d. 15 Dec. 1713
Sarah PAINE^{5}, b. 14 Apr. 1699; d. 12 July 1772 <MD 15:71>
Stillborn, b. 28 Jan. 1700/1 <MD 8:227>
Elizabeth PAINE^{5}, b. 2 June 1702
Theophilus PAINE^{5}, b. 7 Feb. 1703/4
Josiah PAINE^{5}, b. 8 Mar. 1705/6 <MD 8:15>; d. 7 May 1728
Rebecca PAINE^{5}, b. 30 Oct. 1709 <MD 8:15>
Mercy PAINE^{5}, b. 3 Apr. 1712 <MD 8:15>
Benjamin PAINE^{5}, b. 18 May 1714 <MD 8:15>; d. 14 Jan. 1716/7**<101>**

Sarah MAYO, (dau of Samuel), d. betw. 26 Mar. 1736/7 (will) - 5 Mar. 1745/6 (inv.), Harwich <MD 14:44,8:69,70>

CHILDREN OF Lieut. Edmund FREEMAN^{4} (Mercy Prence^{3}) & Sarah MAYO: (12) <MD 8:68>
Ruth FREEMAN^{5}, b. pre 1685*; d. 7 June 1728, Eastham <MD 8:245>
Sarah FREEMAN^{5}, b. c1681-85*; d. 21 Jan. 1743/44, Eastham <MD 20:155>
Isaac FREEMAN^{5}, b. pre 1687* (eldest son)
Ebenezer FREEMAN^{5}, b. c1687; d. 11 June 1760, Wellfleet g.s. <MD 10:207>
Mary FREEMAN^{5}, b. betw. 1681-91*
Experience FREEMAN^{5}, b. pre 1697*; d. betw.12 Feb. 1718 (father's estate) <MD 8:68> - 24 Apr. 1728 (hus.inv.) <Barnstable Co.Prob.4:408-9>**<102>**
Mercy FREEMAN^{5}, b. c1692; d. 2 Dec. 1759, 67th yr, Truro g.s. <MD 12:6>
Thankful FREEMAN^{5}, b. pre 1702*
Elizabeth FREEMAN^{5}, b. pre 1701*; d. betw. 12 Feb. 1718 (father's estate) - 26 Mar. 1736/7 (will of mother) <MD 8:68,69> (m. Isaac Pepper)
Hannah FREEMAN^{5}, b. c1697; d. 7 July 1751, Eastham g.s. <MD 8:4>
Lieut. Edmund FREEMAN^{5}, b. c1702; d. 22 July 1782, 80th yr, Orleans g.s.
Rachel FREEMAN^{5}, b. c1709-13*; d. aft. 20 Sept. 1765 (hus will) <Barnstable Co.Prob.13:204>

Jonathan SNOW^{5} (Nicholas^{4}, Mark^{3}, Constance Hopkins^{2}), b. 30 Jan. 1691/2, Eastham <MD 3:180>

CHILDREN OF Jonathan SNOW & Thankful FREEMAN^{5}: (3) <Eastham, MD 15:74>

Isaac SNOW^{6}, b. 4 Feb. 1719/20

Experience SNOW^{6}, b. 31 May 1721

Lydia SNOW^{6}, b. 22 Oct. 1722

Abigail YOUNG, (dau of David), b. 28 Dec. 1688, Eastham <MD 7:237>; d. 12 June 1781, Wellfleet g.s. <MD 10:207>

CHILDREN OF Ebenezer FREEMAN^{5} (Edmund^{4}) & Abigail YOUNG: (4) <Eastham, MD 6:13>

Jennet FREEMAN^{6}, b. 17 Dec. 1711; d. 3 Feb. 1771, Wellfleet g.s. <MD 10:207>

Thankful FREEMAN^{6}, b. 15 Feb. 1714/5

Anne FREEMAN^{6}, b. 6 June 1716

Ebenezer FREEMAN^{6}, b. 30 Nov. 1719; d. 18 Sept. 1774, Wellfleet g.s. <MD 10:207>

Isaac FREEMAN, b. c1733, d. 6 Aug. 1807, ae 74, Wellfleet g.s. <MD 10:207>**<103>**

Thankful HIGGINS, b. c1737, d. 29 Jan. 1824, ae 87, Wellfleet g.s.<" "> (wf of Isaac Freeman)

CHILD OF Lieut. Edmund FREEMAN^{5} (Edmund^{4}) & 1st Lois PAINE^{5} (Nicholas^{4}, Mary Snow^{3}, Constance Hopkins^{2}): <Eastham, MD 16:74>**<104>**

Lois FREEMAN^{6}, b. 3 Sept. 1726; d. 1790, Eastham <MD 7:228>

Sarah SPARROW^{5} (Richard^{4}, Hannah Prence^{3}, Patience Brewster^{2}), b. 20 July 1708, Eastham <MD 7:19> d. 21 Aug. 1790, Orleans g.s.

CHILDREN OF Lieut. Edmund FREEMAN^{5} & 2nd Sarah SPARROW: (2) <Eastham, MD 16:74>

Jonathan FREEMAN^{6}, b. 22 Feb. 1729/30; d. 2 July 1768, Eastham <MD 24:192>

Edmund FREEMAN^{6}, b. 13 Feb. 1731

Thankful LINNELL, b. c1731, d. 28 May 1810, Orleans g.s.

CHILDREN OF Jonathan FREEMAN^{6} & Thankful LINNELL: (8) <Eastham, MD 24:192>

Edmund FREEMAN^{7}, b. 15 Dec. 1752; d. 31 Dec. 1777, g.s.

Abner FREEMAN^{7}, b. 12 June 1755; d. 8 June 1833, Orleans g.s.

Rebecca FREEMAN^{7}, b. 26 Mar. 1757

Sarah FREEMAN^{7}, b. 6 June 1759

John FREEMAN^{7}, b. 10 Nov. 1761; d. 1817* <Freeman Gen.:184>

Hannah FREEMAN^{7}, b. 6 Mar. 1764

Thankful FREEMAN^{7}, b. 1 May 1766; d. 25 July 1769, g.s.

Lois FREEMAN^{7}, b. 7 July 1768

Sarah HIGGINS, b. c1757, d. 24 Dec. 1832, ae 75, Orleans g.s.

CHILDREN OF Abner FREEMAN^{7} & Sarah HIGGINS: (11) <Eastham/Orleans, MD 34:58>

Jonathan FREEMAN^{8}, b. 25 Aug. 1778; d. 22 Jan. 1839*

Edmund FREEMAN^{8}, b. 1 Feb. 1780

Sarah FREEMAN^{8}, b. 16 Mar. 1782

Mercy FREEMAN^{8}, b. 16 Apr. 1784

Bathsheba FREEMAN^{8}, b. 20 Aug. 1786

Tamsa FREEMAN^{8}, b. 5 Mar. 1789

Thankful FREEMAN^{8}, b. 2 May 1791

Rachel FREEMAN^{8}, b. 16 July 1793

Infant, d. 1795 <MD 7:229>

Hitta FREEMAN^{8}, b. 27 Apr. 1797

Samuel FREEMAN^{8}, b. 4 Feb. 1800

Abigail HOPKINS^{6} (Joshua^{5-4-3}, Gyles^{2}), b. 19 Dec. 1764*, Eastham; d. 1829* <Freeman Gen.:184>

CHILDREN OF John FREEMAN^{7} (Jonathan^{6}) & Abigail HOPKINS: (11) <Eastham, MD 34:58,59>

Joshua FREEMAN^{8}, b. 8 Oct. 1784 <MD 34:58>

Thomas FREEMAN^{8}, b. 6 Apr. 1787

Lydia FREEMAN^{8}, b. 10 Mar. 1789

Rebecca FREEMAN^{8}, b. 25 May 1791; d. 1818*

Benjamin FREEMAN^{8}, b. 30 June 1793

Nabby FREEMAN^{8}, b. 16 Apr. 1795

John FREEMAN^{8}, b. 23 Aug. 1797

Polly FREEMAN^{8}, b. 11 Dec. 1799; d. June 1819*, unm.

William FREEMAN^{8}, b. 21 Jan. 1802

James FREEMAN^{8}, b. 27 Jan. 1805

Marcy FREEMAN^{8}, b. 9 Mar. 1808

Jesse SNOW^{5} (Micajah^{4}, Stephen^{3}, Constance Hopkins^{2}), b. 27 Oct. 1709, Eastham <MD 9:11>

CHILDREN OF Jesse SNOW & Lois FREEMAN^{6} (Edmund^{5}): (9) <Eastham, MD 16:145>**<105>**

Sarah SNOW^{7}, b. 15 Sept. 1750

Edmund SNOW^{7}, b. 6 Jan. 1752

Ephraim SNOW^{7}, b. 3 May 1754

Lois SNOW^{7}, b. 12 Sept. 1757

Micajah SNOW^{7}, b. 14 Nov. 1759

Thankful SNOW^{7}, b. 24 Feb. 1761

Paine SNOW^{7}, b. 6 Apr. 1763

Tamsin SNOW^{7}, b. 9 Mar. 1765

Freeman SNOW^{7}, b. 30 May 1768

Isaac PEPPER, (son of Isaac), b. 29 July 1693, Eastham <MD 5:196> (m. Eliz. Freeman^{5} (Edmund^{4}))

Thomas GROSS, b. 4 Feb. 1677/8* <Hist.Hingham 1:280>; d. pre 14 Mar. 1727/8 (adm.)

CHILDREN OF Thomas GROSS & Experience FREEMAN^{5} (Edmund^{4}): (4)

Freeman GROSS^{6}, b. c1710/11*

Sarah GROSS^{6}, b. 27 Nov. 1713*

Elizabeth GROSS^{6}, b. 5 (June) 1716*

Thomas GROSS^{6}, b. 9 Oct. 1718

CHILDREN OF Christian REMICK & Hannah FREEMAN^{5} (Edmund^{4}): (9) <Eastham, 1701-81:19>

Mercy REMICK^{6}, b. 30 Nov. 1718

Hannah REMICK^{6}, b. 21 Mar. 1720/1

Elizabeth REMICK^{6}, b. 2 Jan. 1722/3

Christian REMICK^{6}, b. 18 Apr. 1726

Daniel REMICK^{6}, b. 11 July 1729

Isaac REMICK^{6}, b. 9 Feb. 1732/3

Joseph REMICK^{6}, b. 21 Mar. 1738/9, d.y.

Sarah REMICK^{6}, b. 9 Apr. 1742

Joseph REMICK^{6}, b. 8 June 1744

Samuel HINCKLEY^{4} (Sam.^{3}, Tho.^{2}, Sam.^{1}), b. 24 Sept. 1684, Barnstable <MD 6:98>

CHILDREN OF Samuel HINCKLEY & Mary FREEMAN^{5} (Edmund^{4}): (11) <1-6, Harwich, MD 4:208>

Seth HINCKLEY^{6}, b. 25 Dec. 1707

Shubael HINCKLEY^{6}, b. 15 Mar. 1708/9; d. 2 Feb. 1798 <Hallowell VR>

Samuel HINCKLEY^{6}, b. 12 Feb. 1710/11; d. pre 18 June 1767 (adm.)<Lincoln Co.Prob.:347>

Mary HINCKLEY^{6}, b. 12 Feb. 1710/11 (twins); d. Mar. 1710/11

Edmund HINCKLEY^{6}, b. 20 Nov. 1712

Reliance HINCKLEY^{6}, b. 21 Nov. 1714

Aaron HINCKLEY^{6}, b. 13 Sept. 1715 <Truro VR:33>; d. 8 Mar. 1792, Brunswick ME <VR 1:516>

Mehitable HINCKLEY^{6}, b. 25 Dec. 1718 <Truro VR:33>

Experience HINCKLEY^{6}, b. 16 Jan. 1720/1 <Truro VR:33>

Mary HINCKLEY^{6}, bpt. 12 Apr. 1724 <MD 9:76>

Isaac HINCKLEY^{6}, bpt. 27 Mar. 1726 <MD 9:76>

Mary LARRABEE, (dau of Ben. & Mary), b. 7 Apr. 1728 <Brunswick ME VR 1:349>

CHILDREN OF Aaron HINCKLEY^{6} & Mary LARRABEE: (12) <Brunswick ME VR 1:374>

Isabella HINCKLEY^{7}, b. 27 Apr. 1747

Benjamin HINCKLEY^{7}, b. 27 Dec. 1748

Reliance HINCKLEY^{7}, b. 26 Dec. 1750, d. 26 Oct. 1753

Lois HINCKLEY^{7}, b. 30 May 1753

Nathaniel HINCKLEY^{7}, b. 4 Aug. 1755

Theophilus HINCKLEY^{7}, b. 22 Dec. 1757

Stephen HINCKLEY^{7}, b. 9 Jan. 1760

Aaron HINCKLEY^{7}, b. 3 Nov. 1762, d. 3 Jan. 1763

John HINCKLEY^{7}, b. 1 Dec. 1763

Mary HINCKLEY^{7}, b. 12 June 1766

Jeremiah HINCKLEY^{7}, b. 7 Apr. 1769

Rachel HINCKLEY^{7}, b. 7 Apr. 1769 (twins)

CHILDREN OF Benjamin LARRABEE & Mary ( ): (8) <Brunswick ME VR 1:349>

Mary LARRABEE, b. 7 Apr. 1728

Nathaniel LARRABEE, b. 23 Dec. 1729

Isabella LARRABEE, b. 27 Nov. 1731

Abigail LARRABEE, b. 9 Jan. 1733/4

Hannah LARRABEE, b. 10 Dec. 1735

Elisabeth LARRABEE, b. 10 Jan. 1737/8

Benjamin LARRABEE, b. 5 Feb. 1739/40

Stephen LARRABEE, b. 12 July 1742

CHILDREN OF Aaron HINKLY & 1st Bethiah LOMBARD: (5) <Brunswick ME VR 1:473>

Jazaniah HINKLY, b. 12 June 1789

Rebecca HINKLY, b. 30 Jan. 1792

Elnathan HINKLY, b. 6 Mar. 1794

Mary HINKLY, b. 29 Aug. 1796

Nathaniel HINKLY, b. 1 Mar. 1799

CHILD OF Aaron HINKLY & 2nd Anne ( ) <Brunswick ME 1:473>

Joel HINKLY, b. 3 Apr. 1801

CHILDREN OF Samuel MELCHER & Isabella ( ): (10) <Brunswick ME VR 1:380>

Reliance MELCHER, b. 15 Nov. 1768

Mary MELCHER, b. 1 Aug. 1771

Aaron MELCHER, b. 23 Feb. 1773

Samuel MELCHER, b. 8 May 1775

Elisabeth MELCHER, b. 8 May 1775

Lois MELCHER, b. 2 July 1780

Rebecca MELCHER, b. 6 Mar. 1783

John MELCHER, b. 19 May 1785

Noah MELCHER, b. 30 May 1788, d. 27 Oct. 1788

Rachel MELCHER, b. 23 Feb. 1793

CHILDREN OF Edmund HINCKLEY^{6} (Mary Freeman^{5}) & Sarah SMITH: (10) <Brunswick ME VR 1:365>

Edmund HINCKLEY^{7}, b. 9 Sept. 1745; d. 5 Aug. 1762 <VR 1:503>

Sarah HINCKLEY^{7}, b. 22 Aug. 1747

Elnathan HINCKLEY^{7}, b. 19 Jan. 1749

Isaac HINCKLEY^{7}, b. 19 Dec. 1751

Thankful HINCKLEY^{7}, b. 23 Aug. 1755

Priscilla HINCKLEY^{7}, b. 10 Aug. 1757

Samuel HINCKLEY^{7}, b. 12 Aug. 1759

Lemuel HINCKLEY^{7}, b. 17 Dec. 1762

Edmund HINCKLEY[7], b. 17 Mar. 1764

Aaron HINCKLEY[7], b. 17 Mar. 1764 (twins)

CHILD OF Isaac HINCKLEY[6] (Mary Freeman[5]) & Agnes SMITH:**<106>**

Mehitable HINCKLEY[7], b. 28 Jan. 1751 <Brunswick ME VR 1:370>

CHILDREN OF Thomas COTTEN & Agnes (SMITH) Hinckley: (5) <Brunswick ME VR 1:370>

Mary COTTEN, b. 24 Apr. 1759

Martha COTTEN, b. 18 May 1761

Sarah COTTEN, b. 16 July 1764

Isaac Hinkly COTTEN, b. 7 Sept. 1767

Ruth COTTEN, b. 6 Mar. 1770

Joseph THOMPSON, (son of James & Eliz (Frye)), b. 23 Mar. 1713/4; d. pre 1759

CHILDREN OF Joseph THOMPSON & Mary HINCKLEY[6] (Mary Freeman[5]): (2 of 6)**<107>**

William THOMPSON[7], b. 19 May 1741 <Brunswick ME VR 1:357>

Judith THOMPSON[7], b. 8 Feb. 1743 (m. James Stackpole)

CHILDREN OF Cornelius THOMPSON & Phebe ( ): (4) <Brunswick ME VR 1:418>

Thomas Hinkley THOMPSON, b. 18 Aug. 1797

Shubael Trenik THOMPSON, b. 2 July 1799

Harlow THOMPSON, b. 10 May 1801

Adeline THOMPSON, b. 14 Aug. 1803

CHILDREN OF Thomas THOMPSON & Mehitable ( ): (3) <Brunswick ME VR 1:381>

Lois THOMPSON, b. 15 Dec. 1769

Cornelius THOMPSON, b. 26 Apr. 1772

Hannah Smith THOMPSON, b. 14 Feb. 1774

(The following 2 pages contain the family history of George Ernest Bowman as found in the files.)

Tobias LORD[8] (Mehitable Scammon[7], Mehitable Hinckley[6], Mary Freeman[5]),b. 17(2)8*, d. 3 Jan. 1799*

CHILD OF Tobias LORD[8] & Hannah Perkins:

Nathanial LORD[9], b. ( )

CHILDREN OF Nathaniel LORD[8] (Mehitable Scammon[7], Mehitable Hinckley[6], Mary Freeman[5]) & Phebe WALKER: (1 of 9)**<108>**

Charles Austin LORD[9], b. 11 May 1806, Kennebunkport ME; d. 1878, Portland ME

Ernestine LIBBY, b. 9 June 1809, Scarborough ME; d. 8 Mar. 1898, Hancock Point ME

CHILDREN OF Charles Austin LORD[9] & Ernestine LIBBY: (7)

Ernestine LORD[10], b. 1832, Kennebunkport ME, d.y.

Ernestine LORD[10], b. 4 May 1834, Kennebunkport ME; d. 13 Dec. 1919, Brookline MA

Frances Ellen LORD[10], b. 11 Nov. 1835, New York City; d. 1 Aug. 1920, unm., Wakefield*

Claire Austin LORD[10], b. 7 June 1838, Portland ME; d. 7 Jan. 1885, Danvers MA

Lydia Arabelle LORD[10], b. 2 Jan. 1845, St. Louis, MO; d. 5 Mar. 1904, Brooklyn NY

Nathalie LORD[10], b. 12 July 1847, Kennebunkport ME; d. 3 Feb. 1928, Wakefield MA, unm.

Agnes McCartney LORD[10], b. 30 Oct. 1848, Kennebunkport ME; d. 5 Jan. 1935, Wakefield MA, unm.

Rev. Charles Baker RICE, (son of Austin & Charlotte (Baker)), b. 29 June 1829, Conway MA; d. 1913 Danvers MA

CHILDREN OF Rev. Charles Baker RICE & Claire Austin LORD[10]: (5)

Lily Sherman RICE[11], b. 30 Mar. 1862, Conway; d. 2 Nov. 1936, Melrose MA (m. Frank Foxcroft)

Natalie Lord RICE[11], b. 20 Dec. 1867, Danvers Centre MA (m. Frank Clark)

Austin RICE[11], b. 25 Sept. 1871, Danvers

Caleb RICE[11]*, b. 25 Sept. 1871* (twin), d. next day

Charles RICE[11]*, b. c1873*, d. ae 10 days

Laura Agnes LYMAN, (dau of Darwin & Julia (Stevens)), b. 5 May 1874, Cunnington MA (1st wf of Austin Rice[11])

Rev. George Augustus BOWMAN, b. 3 Dec. 1820, Bath ME; d. 17 July 1906, Waltham

CHILDREN OF Rev. George Augustus BOWMAN & Ernestine LORD^{10} (Charles^{9}): (5)
Caroline North BOWMAN^{11}, b. 29 Feb. 1856, Portland ME
George Ernest BOWMAN^{11}, b. 5 Jan. 1860, Manchester NH; d. 5 Sept. 1941**<109>**
Austin Lord BOWMAN^{11}, b. 14 Nov. 1861, Manchester NH; d. 3 June 1915, New York NY <PN&Q 3:90>
Ernestine Libby BOWMAN^{11}, b. 30 Oct. 1863, d. 5 Aug. 1864
Bernard Davis BOWMAN^{11}, b. 5 July 1868, Windsor CT; d. 12 Dec. 1885
Ida Van Horne, d. 28 May 1905, New York NY (1st wf of Austin Lord Bowman)
CHILDREN OF Austin Lord BOWMAN^{11} & 2nd Eleanor HEAGAN: (2) <New York NY>
Austin Lord BOWMAN^{12}, b. 11 Jan. 1910; d. 26 Apr. 1910
Ernestine Jane BOWMAN^{12}, b. 23 Jan. 1912 <PN&Q 1:33>
William Dwight PARKINSON, b. 10 Aug. 1857, Falmouth
CHILDREN OF William Dwight PARKINSON & Caroline North BOWMAN^{11} (Rev. George^{10}): (4)
Royal PARKINSON^{12}, b. 10 Feb. 1884, Fergus Falls, Minn.
Dana PARKINSON^{12}, b. 27 June 1885, Fergus Falls, Minn.
Taintor PARKINSON^{12}, b. 27 Oct. 1886
Herman Owen PARKINSON^{12}, b. 3 Feb. 1891
CHILDREN OF Herman Owen PARKINSON^{12} & Constance DYER: (3)
Samuel PARKINSON^{13}, b. 7 Aug. 1922, Stockton CA
Nancy PARKINSON^{13}, b. 22 Aug. 1924, Stockton CA
Jean PARKINSON^{13}, b. 3 June 1927, Taunton MA

MICRO #14 of 18

Lucy Robinson BACON^{10} (Clarence^{9}, Lucy Robinson^{8}--), b. 11 Mar. 1889, Jamaica Plain
CHILDREN OF Dana PARKINSON^{12} (Caroline Bowman^{11}) & Lucy Robinson BACON: (4)
Dwight PARKINSON^{13}, b. 14 May 1916, Boise, Idaho <PN&Q 4:101>
Elizabeth Bacon PARKINSON^{13}, b. 3 Sept. 1917, Salmon, Idaho <PN&Q 5:93>
Caroline Bowman PARKINSON^{13}, b. 3 Oct. 1921, Salt Lake City, Utah
Ruth PARKINSON^{13}, b. 29 Mar. 1928
CHILD OF Royal PARKINSON^{12} (Caroline Bowman^{11}) & Loretta Catherine MUNRO:
Dorothy Lucy PARKINSON^{13}, b. 2 Feb. 1919, Worcester
Ida (STUBBLEFIELD) Still, b. 31 Aug. 1890, Oregon (2nd wf of Royal Parkinson)
Stephen Albert EMERY, (son of Stephen & Jennett (Loring)), b. 4 Oct. 1841, Paris Hill ME; d. 15 Apr. 1891, Boston
CHILDREN OF Stephen Albert EMERY & Lydia Arabelle LORD^{10} (Charles^{9}): (5) <1-4, Malden MA>
Stephen EMERY^{11}, b. 24 Dec. 1868
Charles Austin Lord EMERY^{11}, b. 9 Feb. 1870; d. 1 July 1888, Rockport MA
Sidney Sheppard EMERY^{11}, b. 5 May 1871, Malden MA; d. 1 Oct. 1932
Moritz Hauptmann EMERY^{11}, b. 19 Nov. 1875
Ernestine EMERY^{11}, b. 24 Sept. 1877, Newton MA
Nellie Babbitt THALHEIMER, (dau of William & Sarah Pritchard (Coolidge)), b. 11 May 1869, Cincinnati OH
CHILDREN OF Stephen EMERY^{11} & Nellie Babbitt THALHEIMER: (3)
William Thalheimer EMERY^{12}, b. 7 July 1900, Newton MA
Stephen Albert EMERY^{12}, b. 14 Aug. 1902, Chicago IL
Mary Elizabeth EMERY^{12}, b. 21 Mar. 1906, New York City
Anna Payne BUTLER, (dau of Nathaniel & Jennette Loring (Emery)), b. 24 Aug. 1862, Auburn ME
CHILD OF Sidney Sheppard EMERY^{11} & Anna Payne BUTLER:
Loring Lord EMERY^{12}, b. 25 July 1899, Winchester MA
Albert Funk MESCHTER, b. 24 Feb. 1880, Palm PA
CHILDREN OF Albert Funk MESCHTER & Ernestine EMERY^{11} (Lydia Lord^{10}): (2)
Emery MESCHTER^{12}, b. 26 Apr. 1910, Philadelphia PA

Helen MESCHTER[12], b. ( )

(The end of the family genealogy of George Ernest Bowman as found in the files.)

James THOMPSON, (son of James), b. 22 Feb. 1707, Kittery ME; d. 22 Sept. 1791, Topsham ME

CHILDREN OF James THOMPSON & 1st Reliance HINCKLEY[6] (Mary Freeman[5]): (10) <Brunswick ME VR 1:350>

Elizabeth THOMPSON[7], b. 13 Mar. 1733, Biddeford

Samuel THOMPSON[7], b. 22 Mar. 1735, Biddeford

James THOMPSON[7], b. 22 Feb. 1737, Biddeford; d. 14 June 1737

Reliance THOMPSON[7], b. 27 June 1738, Biddeford

Adrian THOMPSON[7], b. 29 Mar. 1740, Biddeford

Rachel THOMPSON[7], b. 3 June 1741, Biddeford; d. 27 Dec. 1762 <VR 1:503>

Ruth THOMPSON[7], b. 27 May 1743, Biddeford

Aaron THOMPSON[7], b. 29 May 1745

Isaiah THOMPSON[7], b. 17 Apr. 1747

James THOMPSON[7], b. 23 May 1751

Lydia (BROWN) Harris, d. 10 Feb. 1764

CHILDREN OF James THOMPSON & 2nd Lydia (BROWN) Harris: (6) <Brunswick ME VR 1:380>

Benjamin THOMPSON, b. 26 Oct. 1753

Jemima THOMPSON, b. 18 Oct. 1755

Ezekiel THOMPSON, b. 16 Sept. 1757

Sarah THOMPSON, b. 16 Sept. 1760

Ruth THOMPSON, b. 29 Dec. 1763

Rachel THOMPSON, b. 29 Dec. 1763 (twins); d.y.

CHILDREN OF Samuel THOMPSON[7] & Abiel ( ): (8) <Brunswick ME VR 1:375>

Reliance THOMPSON[8], b. 31 Nov. 1758

Rachel THOMPSON[8], b. 19 Feb. 1761, d.y.

Rachel THOMPSON[8], b. 9 July 1763

James THOMPSON[8], b. 15 June 1765

Humphrey THOMPSON[8], b. 11 Dec. 1767

Aaron THOMPSON[8], b. 18 Oct. 1769, d. 25 Oct. 1769

Aaron THOMPSON[8], b. 16 Nov. 1770

Thomas Cheney THOMPSON[8], b. 14 July 1774

CHILDREN OF Daniel WEED & Elizabeth THOMPSON[7] (Reliance Hinckley[6]): (3) <Brunswick ME VR 1:368>

James WEED[8], b. 17 July 1753

Reliance WEED[8], b. 7 Oct. 1754

Patience WEED[8], b. 3 Aug. 1756

CHILDREN OF James CURTIS & 1st Rachel THOMPSON[7] (Reliance Hinckley[6]): (2) <Brunswick ME VR 1:372>

Hannah CURTIS[8], b. 14 Sept. 1760

William CURTIS[8], b. 25 Feb. 1762

CHILDREN OF James CURTIS & 2nd Mary ( ): (10) <Brunswick ME VR 1:372>

Rachel CURTIS, b. 15 Mar. 1765

Molley CURTIS, b. 15 Mar. 1767; d. 12 Sept. 1774 <VR 1:503>

James CURTIS, b. 11 Nov. 1768

Sarah CURTIS, b. 11 Jan. 1771

John CURTIS, b. 14 Dec. 1772

Theodore CURTIS, b. 12 Jan. 1775; d. 12 Sept. 1775 <VR 1:503>

Molley CURTIS, b. 9 July 1777

Lucy CURTIS, b. 21 May 1779

Theodore CURTIS, b. 1 Oct. 1781

Daniel CURTIS, b. 26 Jan. 1784

Samuel WELCH, b. 3 Oct. 1760, Bath ME, d. 30 Oct. 1834 <Bath VR 1:39>

Lydia ( ) WELCH, b. 23 June 1758, d. 4 Aug. 1805 <Bath VR 1:39>

CHILDREN OF Samuel WELCH & 1st Lydia ( ): (13) <Bath ME VR 1:39>

William WELCH, b. July 1782, drowned 15 Apr. 1793

Edward WELCH, b. 26 Sept. 1783

Daniel WELCH, b. 1 Feb. 1785

Samuel Reed WELCH, b. 30 May 1786

Ruth WELCH, b. 16 July 1787

Jemima WELCH, b. 28 Sept. 1788

James WELCH, b. 1 Jan. 1790, d. 20 July 1812

Robert WELCH, b. 24 Nov. 1792

Ezekiel WELCH, b. 30 Apr. 1794

Sarah WELCH, b. 14 Aug. 1795

Martha WELCH, b. 4 Jan. 1797

Humphry WELCH, b. 9 May 1798

Lydia WELCH, b. 1 Apr. 1800, d. 4 Nov. 1815

Hannah ANDREWS, b. 20 May 1762, d. 10 Mar. 1834 (2nd wf of Samuel Welch)

Lettice DURGIN, b. c1788, Topsham ME, d. 26 Aug. 1873, old age, Boston <Mass.VR 258:182>

CHILD OF Samuel Reed WELCH & Lettice DURGIN:

Marilla WELCH, b. 11 Aug. 1809 <Brunswick ME VR:230>

CHILDREN OF Samuel HINCKLEY^{6} (Mary Freeman^{5}) & Sarah MILLER*: (11) <1-5, Brunswick ME VR 1:351, 6-11, Georgetown ME VR:13>

Capt. John HINCKLEY^{7}, b. 11 Sept. 1733, "killed at seige of Bagaduce"

Mehitable HINCKLEY^{7}, b. 26 Oct. 1735

Samuel HINCKLEY^{7}, b. 17 Mar. 1738

Mary HINCKLEY^{7}, b. 6 Nov. 1740

Josiah HINCKLEY^{7}, b. 18 Feb. 1742/3

Edmund HINCKLEY^{7}, b. 29 June 1745; d. 18 Aug. 1807, Georgetown

William HINCKLEY^{7*}, b. 4 June 1747*

Seth HINCKLEY^{7*}, b. 27 Mar. 1749* **<110>**

Matthew HINCKLEY^{7*}, b. 26 Aug. 1752*; d. 29 Aug. 1809*, at sea

Sarah HINCKLEY^{7*}, b. 8 Aug. ( )

Reliance HINCKLEY^{7*}, b. 8 May 175()

Mary PETTINGILL, b. 8 July 1746, Salisbury MA; d. 27 Apr. 1839, Georgetown ME

CHILDREN OF Edmund HINCKLEY^{7} & Mary PETTINGILL: (7) <Georgetown ME VR:13>

Elizabeth Clark HINCKLEY^{8}, b. 7 Jan. 1768

John HINCKLEY^{8}, b. 28 Feb. 1769

Edmund HINCKLEY^{8}, b. 6 Jan. 1778

Mary HINCKLEY^{8}, b. 10 June 1780

Matthew HINCKLEY^{8}, b. 29 June 1782; d. 11 Jan. 1845, Bath ME

Rebecca HINCKLEY^{8}, b. 29 July 1787

Sarah HINCKLEY^{8}, b. 18 May 1790

CHILDREN OF Shubael HINCKLEY^{6} (Mary Freeman^{5}) & 1st Mary SMITH (dau of James): (4) <Brunswick ME VR 1:351>

Ebenezer HINCKLEY^{7}, b. 10 Feb. 1733

Thomas HINCKLEY^{7}, b. 7 Dec. 1737; d. 10 Dec. 1821, Hallowell ME

Shubael HINCKLEY^{7}, b. 7 Dec. 1737 (twins)

James HINCKLEY^{7}, b. 4 Jan. 1739/40

CHILDREN OF Shubael HINCKLEY^{6} & 2nd Sarah YOUNG: (2)

Aaron HINCKLEY^{7}, b. 25 Mar. 1762 <Brunswick ME VR 1:351>

Lois HINCKLEY^{7}, b. 9 Dec. 1763 <Georgetown ME VR:13>

CHILDREN OF James HINCKLEY^{7} & Mary McKENNY (dau of Matthew): (10) <Hallowell ME, NEHGR 8:170>
James HINCKLEY^{8}, b. 14 Aug. 1769, Topsham ME, d. Mar. 1840
Thomas HINCKLEY^{8}, b. 3 Apr. 1772, living Jan. 1854
Mercy HINCKLEY^{8}, b. 17 Dec. 1775
Nicholas HINCKLEY^{8}, b. 1 Apr. 1778
Ebenezer HINCKLEY^{8}, b. 20 Oct. 1780
Clark HINCKLEY^{8}, b. 10 May 1783
Levi HINCKLEY^{8}, b. 29 May 1785
Oliver Osgood HINCKLEY^{8}, b. 24 Aug. 1787
Mehitable HINCKLEY^{8}, b. 18 May 1790, living Jan. 1854
Mary HINCKLEY^{8}, b. 18 Mar. 1793, living Jan. 1854
Joanna NORCROSS, (dau of Jonathan & Martha), b. 3 June 1773, poss. Bath ME, d. June 1842
CHILDREN OF James HINCKLEY^{8} & Joanna NORCROSS: (8) <Hallowell ME, Reg. of Fam.:90; NEHGR 8:170>
Owen HINCKLEY^{9}, b. 27 Mar. 1794
Mary McKenney HINCKLEY^{9}, b. 7 July 1796
Smith HINCKLEY^{9}, b. 1 Aug. 1798
Nicholas HINCKLEY^{9}, b. 25 Oct. 1799
Thomas HINCKLEY^{9}, b. 15 Dec. 1802, d. 5 Sept. 1803
Pamela HINCKLEY^{9}, b. 25 May 1805
Henry Kendall HINCKLEY^{9}, b. 20 May 1807
Martha Ann HINCKLEY^{9}, b. 11 Aug. 1814
Sarah PILSBURY, (dau of Isaac & Mary), b. 6 Dec. 1791, London NH
CHILDREN OF Oliver Osgood HINCKLEY^{8} (James^{7}) & Sarah PILSBURY: (3) <Hallowell ME Reg.of Fam.:91>
Sarah Elizabeth HINCKLEY^{9}, b. 26 Oct. 1815
Helen Loisa HINCKLEY^{9}, b. 9 Oct. 1817
Amos HINCKLEY^{9}, b. 21 July 1823
CHILDREN OF Ebenezer HINCKLEY & Susanna ( ): (4) <Brunswick ME VR 1:369>
Hipzibah HINCKLEY, b. 23 July 1755
Susanna HINCKLEY, b. 7 Feb. 1758
Ebenezer HINCKLEY, b. 10 Apr. 1760
Nehemiah HINCKLEY, b. 16 Oct. 1762
CHILDREN OF Samuel HINKLEY & Sarah ( ): (5) <Brunswick ME VR 1:351>
John HINKLEY, b. 11 Sept. 1733
Mehitable HINKLEY, b. 26 Oct. 1735
Samuel HINKLEY, b. 17 Mar. 1738
Mary HINKLEY, b. 6 Nov. 1740
Josiah HINKLEY, b. 18 Feb. 1742/3
CHILDREN OF Shubael HINCKLEY^{7} (Shubael^{6}) & 1st Mary CLEW (dau of Prince): (3 of 7) <Hallowell ME Register of Fam.:19>**<111>**
Jane HINCKLEY^{8}, b. 1 July 1760
Stephen HINCKLEY^{8}, b. 27 Aug. 1762
Mary HINCKLEY^{8}, b. May 1771
CHILDREN OF Shubael HINCKLEY^{7} & 2nd Abigail (NORCROSS) Robinson: (5) <Hallowell ME VR 1:294>
Shubael HINCKLEY^{8}, b. 8 Oct. 1786
Harriet HINCKLEY^{8}, b. 30 Aug. 1788
Charles Albert HINCKLEY^{8}, b. 18 Jan. 1792
Cornelius Thompson HINCKLEY^{8}, b. 26 Feb. 1796
Joseph White HINCKLEY^{8}, b. 24 Aug. 1802
CHILDREN OF Shubael HINCKLEY^{8} & Betsey SPADE: (3) <Hallowell ME Reg. of Fam.:142>
Elizabeth HINCKLEY^{9}, b. 27 Aug. 1813

Elijah Robinson HINCKLEY[9], b. 16 May 1815

Mariah HINCKLEY[9], b. 2 Oct. 1818

CHILDREN OF Thomas HINCKLEY[7] (Shubael[6]) & 1st Elizabeth MITCHEL (dau of Christopher & Deborah): (4) <Hallowell ME Register of Fam.:19>

David HINCKLEY[8], b. 8 Jan. 1766, Georgetown ME

James HINCKLEY[8], b. 2 Feb. 1768, Georgetown ME

William HINCKLEY[8], b. 2 Apr. 1770, Georgetown ME

Samuel HINCKLEY[8], b. 6 July 1772

Mary TAYLOR (dau of Elias & Mary), b. c1759, d. 24 Feb. 1856, nearly 97

CHILDREN OF Thomas HINCKLEY[7] & 2nd Mary TAYLOR: (6) <Hallowell ME VR 1:291>

Thomas HINCKLEY[8], b. 26 Oct. 1781

Aaron Taylor HINCKLEY[8], b. 1 Apr. 1784

Joseph HINCKLEY[8], b. 30 Apr. 1786

Elizabeth HINCKLEY[8], b. 6 Oct. 1788, d. 6 Sept. 1803

Royal Ariel HINCKLEY[8], b. 3 Feb. 1791

Benjamin HINCKLEY[8], b. 29 Apr. 1793

CHILDREN OF James HINKLEY & Mary MEIGGS: (5) <Family Bible>[<112>]

Holmes HINKLEY, b. 24 June 1793

Mary HINKLEY, b. 16 Aug. 1799

Hannah HINKLEY, b. 7 May 1801, d. 12 June 1801

Jesse HINKLEY, b. 20 Oct. 1802, d. 15 Aug. 180(2?)

James HINKLEY, b. 24 Mar. 1805, d. 4 Apr. 1807

Elijah COUCH, b. 16 July 1793, d. 17 Feb. 1868 <Family Bible>

CHILDREN OF Elijah COUCH & Mary HINKLEY: (6) <Hallowell ME, Family Bible>[<112>]

Mary Jane COUCH, b. 8 July 1821

Adeline Tompson COUCH, b. 6 Jan. 1825, d. 17 Jan. 1840

William James COUCH, b. 5 Apr. 1828, d. 5 Aug. 1844

Hannah Holmes COUCH, b. 17 Jan. 1832

Catherine Ellen COUCH, b. 22 June 1835

Olive Ann COUCH, b. 17 Feb. 1842, d. 8 Mar. 1848

Daniel NORCROSS, b. 28 Feb. 1761, d. 16 Aug. 1822 <Family Bible>[<113>]

Mary NORCROSS, b. 24 Sept. 1770[<113>]

Thomas COBB, b. c1692, d. 9 Feb. 1768, Truro g.s. <MD 12:6>

CHILDREN OF Thomas COBB & Mercy FREEMAN[5] (Edmund[4]): (9) <3-9, Truro VR:37>

Mercy COBB[6], b. ( )

Thomas COBB[6], b. 4 July 1720 <VR:36>

Richard COBB[6], b. 28 Feb. 1721/2

Tamsin COBB[6], b. 9 Jan. 1723/4; d. 18 Sept. 1793, N. Truro g.s. <MD 13:104>

Joseph COBB[6], b. 22 Aug. 1726; d. 21 July 1807*, S. Truro g.s.

Freeman COBB[6], b. 25 Oct. 1728

Elisha COBB[6], b. 27 Oct. 1730

Betty COBB[6], b. 22 Dec. 1732

Sarah COBB[6], b. 15 Aug. 1735

Rachel (TREAT[5]) Mulford (John[4], Sam.[3], Robert[2], Richard[1]), b. 5 Nov. 1725*, d. 23 Dec. 1809*

CHILDREN OF Joseph COBB[6] & Rachel (TREAT) Mulford: (6) <Truro VR:83>

Sarah COBB[7], b. 15 Feb. 1752

Joseph COBB[7], b. 28 Oct. 1754

Tamson/Thomasine COBB[7], b. 31 Jan. 1757; d. 22 Nov. 1794, Truro g.s., Old North Cem. <MD 13:197> (wf of Daniel Lombard)

Freeman COBB[7], b. 16 Jan. 1759

Mulford COBB[7], b. 25 Mar. 1761

Richard COBB[7], b. 11 Dec. 1763

CHILD OF Richard COBB[7] & "Excy" ( ):

Hope COBB[8], b. 11 July 1797 <Truro VR:168>; d. 17 Oct. 1850 <Rich Family Bible>

CHILD OF Nehemiah RICH & Hope COBB[8]:

Martha A. RICH[9], b. 15 Nov. 1826 <Truro VR:287>; d. 21 Jan. 1900 <Rich Family Bible>

Daniel LOMBARD, b. c1753, d. 13 Jan. 1797, 44th yr, Truro g.s., Old North Cem. <MD 13:195> (hus of Tamson/Thomasine Cobb[7])

Lot HARDING, b. c1721, d. 29 Oct. 1802, ae 81, N. Truro g.s. <MD 13:104>

CHILDREN OF Lot HARDING & Tamsin COBB[6] (Mercy Freeman[5]): (11) <Truro VR:28>

Ester HARDING[7], b. 25 Dec. 1748, d. ae 2 yrs.

Tamson HARDING[7], b. 22 Apr. 1750

Ester HARDING[7], b. 2 Apr. 1752

Hannah HARDING[7], b. 25 May 1754

Mercy HARDING[7], b. 15 Aug. 1756

Huldah HARDING[7], b. 16 Aug. 1758

Sarah HARDING[7], b. 27 July 1760

Martha HARDING[7], b. 27 July 1764; d. 31 Aug. 1843 <Truro VR:301>

Bettee HARDING[7], b. 31 July 1766

Nathaniel HARDING[7], b. 7 Mar. 1769

Lot HARDING[7], b. 31 Aug. 1771; d. 2 Apr. 1840 <Truro VR:284>

Thomas GRAY, d. betw. 20 Sept. 1765 (will) - 12 Mar. 1766 (prob.) <Barnstable Co.Prob.13:204>

CHILDREN OF Thomas GRAY & Rachel FREEMAN[5] (Edmund[4]): (8) <Harwich, MD 13:149>

Susanna GRAY[6], b. 18 Oct. 1732; d. pre 20 Sept. 1765, unm. (father's will)

Elizabeth GRAY[6], b. 6 Sept. 1734 (m. Ebenezer Bangs)

Joshua GRAY[6], b. 18 Sept. 1736; d. betw. 8 Oct. 1808 (will) - 10 Oct. 1809 (prob.) <Barnstable Co Prob.35:81>**<114>**

Hannah GRAY[6], b. c27 Apr. 1739

Sarah GRAY[6], b. 8 Oct. 1741; d. pre 20 Sept. 1765, unm. (father's will)

Rachel GRAY[6], b. Apr. 1744; d. pre 20 Sept. 1765, unm. (father's will)

Mehitable GRAY[6], b. Apr. 1747; d. pre 20 Sept. 1765, unm. (father's will)

Mary GRAY[6], b. 20 Apr. 1749; unm. in 1808 (brother Joshua's will)

Ebenezer BANGS[7] (Ann Sears[6], Mercy Freeman[5], Tho.[4], Mercy Prence[3], Patience Brewster[2]), b. 28 Oct. 1729, Harwich <MD 13:57> (m. Elizabeth Gray[6])

CHILDREN OF Israel DOANE & Ruth FREEMAN[5] (Edmund[4]): (6) <Eastham, MD 8:244>

Israel DOANE[6], b. 2 Nov. 1701

Prence DOANE[6], b. 20 Mar. 1703/4

Abigail DOANE[6], b. 29 Dec. 1706

Elnathan DOANE[6], b. 9 Apr. 1709

Daniel DOANE[6], b. 9 Aug. 1714 <MD 8:245>

Edmund DOANE[6], b. 20 Apr. 1718 <MD 8:245>; d. 20 Nov. 1806 <Barrington N.S. VR>

Elizabeth (OSBORN)(Merrick) Paine, b. Jan. 1716, Eastham, d. 24 May 1798 <Barrington N.S. VR>

CHILDREN OF Edmund DOANE[6] & Elizabeth (OSBORN)(Merrick) Paine: (7) <Barrington N.S. VR>**<115>**

Israel DOANE[7], b. 20 Dec. 1750

Samuel Osborn DOANE[7], b. 7 June 1752

Prince DOANE[7], b. 14 Sept. 1753, lost at sea Sept. 1779

Jedidah DOANE[7], b. 8 Dec. 1754

Ruth DOANE[7], b. 7 Apr. 1756

Abigail DOANE[7], b. 18 Apr. 1758

Edmund DOANE[7], b. 14 Sept. 1759

CHILDREN OF Samuel Osborn DOANE^{7} & Sarah HARDING: (6) <Barrington N.S., MD 8:141,9:142>
Samuel Osborn DOANE^{8}, b. 28 Jan. 1775
James DOANE^{8}, b. 20 Nov. 1776
Harvey DOANE^{8}, b. 15 Feb. 1779
Prince DOANE^{8}, b. 19 Oct. 1781
Josiah DOANE^{8}, b. 31 Aug. 1784
Sarah DOANE^{8}, b. 13 May 1787
CHILDREN OF Prence DOANE^{6} (Ruth Freeman^{5}) & Elizabeth GODFREY: (5) <Eastham, MD 16:75>
Prince DOANE^{7}, b. 12 Nov. 1726
Ruth DOANE^{7}, b. 20 Sept. 1728
Phebe DOANE^{7}, b. 10 Dec. 1730
Abigail DOANE^{7}, b. 17 June 1732
Mary DOANE^{7}, b. 3 May 1734
Benjamin HIGGINS^{3} (Ben.^{2}, Richard^{1}), b. 15 Sept. 1681; d. aft. 1 July 1760 (will) <MD 18:189>
CHILDREN OF Benjamin HIGGINS & Sarah FREEMAN^{5} (Edmund^{4}): (14) <Eastham, MD 7:15>
Priscilla HIGGINS^{6}, b. 17 Nov. 1702
Thomas HIGGINS^{6}, b. 24 June 1704
Sarah HIGGINS^{6}, b. 13 July 1706
Paul HIGGINS^{6}, b. 25 June 1708
Reliance HIGGINS^{6}, b. 13 May 1710
Elizabeth HIGGINS^{6}, b. 1 Apr. 1712
Experience HIGGINS^{6}, b. 31 Jan. 1713/4
Benjamin HIGGINS^{6}, b. 1 Mar. 1715/6; d. betw. 17 Sept. 1777 (will) - 15 Oct. 1777 (prob.) <Barnstable Co.Prob.20:9>
Thankful HIGGINS^{6}, b. 28 Oct. 17717
Zaccheus HIGGINS^{6}, b. 15 Aug. 1719 <MD 15:143>; d. aft. 1779, Bar Harbor ME?
Solomon HIGGINS^{6}, b. 8 Sept. 1721 <MD 15:143>
Lois HIGGINS^{6}, b. 6 Aug. 1723 <MD 15:143>
Isaac HIGGINS^{6}, b. 12 July 1725 <MD 15:143>
Freeman HIGGINS^{6}, b. 28 July 1727 <MD 15:143>; d. aft. 18 Jan. 1770 <Middletown CT Deeds 22:121>

MICRO #15 of 18

CHILDREN OF Benjamin HIGGINS^{6} & Hannah HIGGINS (dau of James & Sarah (Mayo)): (5) <1-3, Eastham, MD 16:143>
Edmund HIGGINS^{7}, b. 21 Dec. 1740
Benjamin HIGGINS^{7}, b. 29 Nov. 1743
Lot HIGGINS^{7}, b. 21 Feb. 1745/6
Elisha HIGGINS^{7}, b. c1750 <Higgins Gen.:126>
Sarah HIGGINS^{7}, b. ( ), unm. 1777 <Higgins Gen.:126>
CHILDREN OF Isaac HIGGINS^{6} (Sarah Freeman^{5}) & Rebecca MAYO (dau of Richard & Rebecca (Sparrow)): (3) <Eastham, Higgins Gen.:129>
Reliance HIGGINS^{7}, b. 3 May 1750
Rebecca HIGGINS^{7}, b. 30 Aug. 1753
Isaac HIGGINS^{7}, b. 6 Oct. 1755
CHILDREN OF Paul HIGGINS^{6} (Sarah Freeman^{5}) & Rebecca MAYO (dau of Sam. & Abigail (Sparrow)): (7) <Harwich, Higgins Gen.:125>
Abigail HIGGINS^{7}, b. 27 Nov. 1738
Samuel HIGGINS^{7}, b. 28 Feb. 1739/40
Thankful HIGGINS^{7}, b. 17 Sept. 1743
Rebecca HIGGINS^{7}, b. 18 Aug. 1745, d.y.
Eunice HIGGINS^{7}, b. 20 May 1747

Paul HIGGINS^{7}, b. 1 Sept. 1751, prob. d.y.

Rebecca HIGGINS^{7}, b. 16 Apr. 1754, unm. 1779

Abigail PAINE^{5} (*Nicholas^{4}, Mary Snow^{3}, Constance Hopkins^{2}), b. 3 Aug. 1707*

CHILDREN OF Thomas HIGGINS^{6} (Sarah Freeman^{5}) & Abigail PAINE: (8) <Eastham, MD 16:197>

Philip HIGGINS^{7}, b. 28 Jan. 1727/8

Thomas HIGGINS^{7}, b. 1 Jan. 1729/30

Benjamin HIGGINS^{7}, b. 8 Feb. 1731/2

Jonathan HIGGINS^{7}, b. 10 Apr. 1734

Jesse HIGGINS^{7}, b. 21 Feb. 1736

Thankful HIGGINS^{7}, b. 9 Apr. 1738 <MD 16:196>

Sarah HIGGINS^{7}, b. 17 July 1740 <MD 16:196>

Solomon HIGGINS^{7}, b. 15 July 1743 <MD 16:196>

CHILDREN OF Solomon HIGGINS^{7} & 2nd Abigail PIERCE: (6) <Higgins Gen.>

Solomon HIGGINS^{8}, b. 21 July 1774

Nathaniel HIGGINS^{8}, b. 21 Aug. 1776

Sarah HIGGINS^{8}, b. 23 Sept. 1778

Thankful HIGGINS^{8}, b. 22 Feb. 1781; d. 30 Apr. 1801 <MD 11:143>

Mary HIGGINS^{8}, b. 23 Jan. 1785

Isaac HIGGINS^{8}, b. 1 Apr. 1789

CHILDREN OF Solomon HIGGINS^{8} & Elizabeth DYER: (5) <Higgins Gen.:191,293>

Barzillai HIGGINS^{9}, b. 28 Nov. 1794 <Truro VR:166>

Louisa S. HIGGINS^{9}, d. 10 Sept. 1847

Nathaniel HIGGINS^{9}, b. 30 Jan. 1797, d. 28 Apr. 1800

Solomon HIGGINS^{9}, b. 12 Oct. 1799

Nathaniel HIGGINS^{9}, b. 12 Aug. 1803, d. 29 Nov. 1804

Bethiah CHASE, d. betw. 28 Nov. 1772 - 1774

CHILDREN OF Zaccheus HIGGINS^{6} (Sarah Freeman^{5}) & 1st Bethiah CHASE: (7) <Eastham>

Solomon HIGGINS^{7}, b. 4 July 1758

Obadiah HIGGINS^{7}, b. 21 Mar. 1761, d. 1784

Henry HIGGINS^{7}, b. 15 Dec. 1762, d. 4 Jan. 1768

Mary HIGGINS^{7}, b. 10 Dec. 1765

Bethiah HIGGINS^{7}, b. 15 Apr. 1769

Rebecca HIGGINS^{7}, b. 26 Jan. 1771

Zaccheus HIGGINS^{7}, b. 28 Nov. 1772

CHILDREN OF Zaccheus HIGGINS^{6} & 2nd Esther DEAN, (*dau of James?): (3) <Eastham>

James Dean HIGGINS^{7}, b. 11 Sept. 1774

Reliance HIGGINS^{7}, b. 12 Sept. 1777

Abijah HIGGINS^{7}, b. 12 May 1779

CHILDREN OF ?Zaccheus HIGGINS? & Rebecca YOUNG, (dau of Nathan & Rebecca (Shaw)): (3) <Higgins Gen.:126,128>**<116>**

Israel HIGGINS, b. c1742

Nathan HIGGINS, b. 6 June 1755

Mary HIGGINS, b. ( )

CHILDREN OF Henry YOUNG & Elizabeth HIGGINS^{6} (Sarah Freeman^{5}): (9) <Eastham, 1701-81:100>

Seth YOUNG^{7}, b. 6 Apr. 1734

Solomon YOUNG^{7}, b. 14 Oct. 1735, d.y.

Solomon YOUNG^{7}, b. 18 May 1737

Josiah YOUNG^{7}, b. 14 May 1739

Anne YOUNG^{7}, b. 4 Dec. 1740

Eunice YOUNG^{7}, b. 15 Jan. 1742/3

Sarah YOUNG^{7}, b. 6 Feb. 1744/5
Elizabeth YOUNG^{7}, b. ( ) <Grandfather's will>
Henry YOUNG^{7}, b. ( ) <Grandfather's will>
CHILDREN OF Freeman HIGGINS^{6} (Sarah Freeman^{5}) & 1st Martha COLE: (2) <Eastham, MD 16:30>
Timothy HIGGINS^{7}, b. 28 Mar. 1749; d. 27 Jan. 1829, Standish ME g.s.
Apphia HIGGINS^{7}, b. 1 Oct. 1752
Thankful (HOPKINS^{5}) Paine (Caleb$^{4-3}$, Gyles^{2}), b. 30 May 1724 <Truro VR:47>; d. aft. 18 Jan. 1770
CHILDREN OF Freeman HIGGINS^{6} & 2nd Thankful (HOPKINS) Paine: (6) <Eastham, MD 16:76>
Martha HIGGINS^{7}, b. 9 Apr. 1758
Thankful HIGGINS^{7}, b. 9 Apr. 1758 (twins)
Zedekiah HIGGINS^{7}, b. 11 Apr. 1760
Priscilla HIGGINS^{7}, b. 1 Mar. 1762
Marcy HIGGINS^{7}, b. 9 Aug. 1764
Elisha HIGGINS^{7}, b. 9 Nov. 1766
CHILDREN OF Ithiel BLAKE* & Apphia HIGGINS^{7}: (10*) <Gorham ME VR>
Apphia BLAKE^{8}, b. 23 July 1770
Elizabeth BLAKE^{8}, b. 15 Dec. 1772
Martha BLAKE^{8}, b. 19 Feb. 1775
Mary BLAKE^{8}, b. 24 Feb. 1778
Nathaniel BLAKE^{8}, b. 1 Oct. 1780
Freeman BLAKE^{8}, b. 25 July 1786
Timothy BLAKE^{8}, b. 22 May 1789; d. 7 Jan. 1883*, Gorham ME
Lydia BLAKE^{8}, b. ( ) <Hist.Gorham:402>
Fanny BLAKE^{8}, b. 1793 <Hist.Gorham:402>
Israel BLAKE^{8}, b. ( ) <Hist.Gorham:402>
Susanna HIGGINS, (*dau of Ebenezer), b. c1789, d. 12 Apr. 1862, ae 73
CHILDREN OF Timothy BLAKE^{8} & Susanna HIGGINS: (6*) <Hist.Gorham:404>
Miriam F. BLAKE^{9}, b. 4 Jan. 1812
Ebenezer Higgins BLAKE^{9}, b. 27 Dec. 1813
Ithiel BLAKE^{9}, b. 30 Jan. 1816
Apphia Higgins BLAKE^{9}, b. 21 May 1818
Adeline BLAKE^{9}, b. 21 Feb. 1822
Fanny H. BLAKE^{9}, b. 24 Jan. 1824
CHILDREN OF David SEAR*? & Mercy HIGGINS^{7} (Freeman^{6}): (6*) <Boston Rcd.Com.>
Sarah SPEAR^{8}, b. 20 Mar. 1788 <24:337>
Mercy SPEAR^{8}, b. 23 Aug. 1792 <24:340>
Thomas Stoddard SPEAR^{8}, b. 4 Jan. 1794 <24:342>
Julia Maria SEAR^{8}, b. 14 Nov. 1797 <24:346>
Susan SPEAR^{8}, b. 5 July 1800 <24:349>
John Ingersol SPEAR^{8}, b. 12 Oct. 1802 <24:350>
CHILDREN OF Thomas Stoddard BOARDMAN & Thankful HIGGINS^{7} (Freeman^{6}): (2*) <Boston Rcd.Com.>
William BOARDMAN^{8}, b. 17 Apr. 1783 <24:332>
Caleb BOARDMAN^{8}, b. 6 June 1784 <24:333>
Reliance YATES, (*dau of John & Thankful (King)), b. c1751, d. 14 Dec. 1825,Standish ME g.s.**<117>**
CHILDREN OF Timothy HIGGINS^{7} (Freeman^{6}) & Reliance YATES: (6) <Eastham>
Prince HIGGINS^{8}, b. 25 Sept. 1772
Ephraim HIGGINS^{8}, b. 11 Oct. 1775
Experience HIGGINS^{8}, b. 20 Sept. 1777, d. 8 Sept. 1865
Thankful HIGGINS^{8}, b. 29 Sept. 1779, d. 22 July 1823, ae 43
Freeman HIGGINS^{8}, b. 21 June 1787, d. 17 Nov. 1809, ae 22y4m27d

Timothy HIGGINS[8], b. 10 June 1791, Standish ME; d. 21 May 1863, Standish ME g.s.

Rosanna F. HIGGINS, wf of Timothy[8], d. 14 Dec. 1858, ae 60, Standish ME g.s.

Rebecca HIGGINS, wf of Ephraim, d. 1834 <Standish ME VR, Book 2>

CHILDREN OF Ephraim HIGGINS & Rebecca HIGGINS: (8) <Standish ME VR 1:322>

Daniel HIGGINS, b. 9 June 1799

Timothy HIGGINS, b. 8 Mar. 1802

Stephen HIGGINS, b. 20 Aug. 1803

Louisa HIGGINS, b. 3 Mar. 1806; d. 15 May 1842 <VR 2:12>

Martha HIGGINS, b. 3 Mar. 1808

Reliance HIGGINS, b. 9 Feb. 1811

Catherine HIGGINS, b. 13 Sept. 1813

Rebecca HIGGINS, b. 17 Sept. 1816

Higgins Inscriptions, Standish ME Cemetery: (13)

Seth HIGGINS, d. 4 Dec. 1898, ae 93y4m3d

Rebecca HIGGINS, wf of Seth, d. 30 Apr. 1886, ae 83y11m

Timothy HIGGINS, d. 27 Jan. 1829, ae 80

Reliance HIGGINS, wf of Timothy, d. 14 Dec. 1825, ae 74

Experience LOWELL, wf of Daniel, late of Bridgton, d. 8 Sept. 1865, ae 88y6m

Timothy HIGGINS Jr., d. 21 May 1863, ae 71y11m20d

Rosanna HIGGINS, wf of Timothy Jr., d. 14 Dec. 1858, ae 60

George F. HIGGINS, son of Seth & Rebecca, d. May 1833, ae 3

Infant son of Seth & Rebecca Higgins, d. 12 July 1832, ae 1 week

George F. HIGGINS, son of Seth & Rebecca, d. Oct. 1828, ae 10 mths.

Freeman HIGGINS, son of Timothy & Reliance, d. 17 Nov. 1809, ae 22y4m27d

Thankful HIGGINS, d. 22 July 1823, ae 43

John Deane HIGGINS, 1826-1897

Sarah WHITNEY, wf of Robert Higgins, d. 1834 <Standish ME VR 2>

CHILDREN OF Robert HIGGINS & Sarah WHITNEY: (9) <Standish ME VR 1:319>

Hannah HIGGINS, b. 4 Feb. 1791

Thankful HIGGINS, b. 11 Oct. 1793, "deceased"

William HIGGINS, b. 9 June 1796, "deceased"

Simeon HIGGINS, b. 25 Ar. 1798

Jerusha Morton HIGGINS, b. 24 July 1800

Sarah HIGGINS, b. 9 Jan. 1803

Marcy HIGGINS, b. 9 Oct. 1805, "deceased"

Adaline HIGGINS, b. 11 Mar. 1808

Mary HIGGINS, b. 1 Dec. 1810, "deceased"

CHILDREN OF William HIGGINS & Phebe PAINE: (11) <Standish ME VR 1:320>

Eliza HIGGINS, b. 15 Oct. 1795, "deceased"

Phebe HIGGINS, b. 13 Apr. 1797

Huldah HIGGINS, b. 20 May 1799

Abigail HIGGINS, b. 8 June 1801

Lucy HIGGINS, b. 23 May 1803

Joseph HIGGINS, b. 2 July 1805

Nancy HIGGINS, b. 20 July 1807

William HIGGINS, b. 12 Apr. 1809

Robert HIGGINS, b. 1 Oct. 1811

Almira HIGGINS, b. 23 Apr. 1813

Ansel HIGGINS, b. 6 Nov. 1815

Enoch F. HIGGINS, d. 25 Jan. 1834, ae 44 <Standish ME VR 2:14>

CHILDREN OF Enoch F. HIGGINS & Miriam ( ): (4) <Standish ME VR 2:14>
Harriet Maria HIGGINS, b. 19 Aug. 1814
Mary HIGGINS, b. 26 May 1818
Caroline HIGGINS, b. 7 Apr. 1820
John Dean HIGGINS, b. 23 Jan. 1826
CHILDREN OF Elkanah HIGGINS & Jemima ( ): (11) <Standish ME VR 1:324>
Samuel HIGGINS, b. 2 Feb. 1791
Elizabeth HIGGINS, b. 25 Jan. 1793
Ebenezer HIGGINS, b. 20 July 1795
Abner HIGGINS, b. 25 Nov. 1797
Yates HIGGINS, b. 11 June 1799
Jonathan HIGGINS, b. 20 Apr. 1801
Elkanah HIGGINS, b. 13 Nov. 1802
Heman HIGGINS, b. 29 Apr. 1804
Reliance HIGGINS, b. 25 Jan. 1806
Experience HIGGINS, b. 11 Feb. 1808
Curtis HIGGINS, b. 19 Aug. 1810
CHILDREN OF Ebenezer HIGGINS & Rebecca ( ): (6) <Standish ME VR 1:307>
Ebenezer HIGGINS, b. 24 July 1775, Truro
Rebekah HIGGINS, b. 11 Apr. 1780, Provincetown
Hannah Atkins HIGGINS, b. 20 Aug. 1782, Pearsontown
Martha HIGGINS, b. 21 June 1784, Pearsontown
David HIGGINS, b. 3 Nov. 1787 <1:308>
Susanna HIGGINS, b. 14 Apr. 1789 <1:308>
CHILDREN OF Seth HIGGINS & Rebecca ( ): (2) <Standish ME VR 1:328> (See Cemetery Rcds.p.239)
George Francis HIGGINS, b. 1 Dec. 1827, d. 10 Oct. 1828
George Francis HIGGINS, b. 13 May 1830, d. 1833
Selina HIGGINS, b. 12 June 1773, Eastham <Standish ME VR 1:314>
CHILDREN OF Prince HIGGINS[8] (Timothy[7]) & Selina HIGGINS: (7) <Standish ME VR 2:12>
Mary HIGGINS[9], b. 12 Aug. 1800
Lewis HIGGINS[9], b. 18 Jan. 1803; d. 11 Mar. 1888
Martha HIGGINS[9], b. 31 Jan. 1805, d.y.
Esther HIGGINS[9], b. 18 Sept. 1806
Lucinda HIGGINS[9], b. 15 Sept. 1808, d.y.
Freeman HIGGINS[9], b. 14 June 1812, d. 1 Mar. 1824
Chesley HIGGINS[9], b. 4 July 1816
CHILDREN OF Lewis HIGGINS[9] & Susan WHITNEY, (dau of Edmond & Martha (Merserve)): (11) <Standish ME VR 2:14>
Ivory Fessenden HIGGINS[10], b. 15 Aug. 1828, d. 2 Oct. 1847
Freeman HIGGINS[10], b. 11 Jan. 1830
Orlando Melvin HIGGINS[10], b. 22 Aug. 1831
Elijah Lewis HIGGINS[10], b. 23 June 1833, d. 17 Nov. 1862
Martha Ellen HIGGINS[10], b. 7 June 1835
Merrill Whitney HIGGINS[10], b. 11 July 1837
Arravesta HIGGINS[10], b. 10 Apr. 1840
Arramantha HIGGINS[10], b. 10 Apr. 1840 (twins)
Milton Foss HIGGINS[10], b. 7 Dec. 1842
Edwin F. HIGGINS[10], b. 13 Mar. 1847
Hadley F. HIGGINS[10], b. 28 July 1849
CHILDREN OF Jesse SMITH, (son of Tho. & Mary) & Sarah HIGGINS[6] (Sarah Freeman[5]): (7) <Eastham,

MD 16:71>**<118>**

Ruth SMITH^{7}, b. 18 July 1725

David SMITH^{7}, b. 28 Jan. 1726/7

Priscilla SMITH^{7}, b. 20 July 1729

Sarah SMITH^{7}, b. 19 July 1731

Eunice SMITH^{7}, b. 23 Feb. 1732/3

Jerusha SMITH^{7}, b. 1 Mar. 1734/5

Jesse SMITH^{7}, b. 1 Feb. 1736/7

John MAYO^{3}, (Sam.^{2}, Rev. John^{1})b. c1656, d. 1 Feb. 1725/6, Harwich, Brewster g.s.

CHILDREN OF John MAYO & Hannah FREEMAN^{4} (Mercy Prence^{3}): (8) <Hist.Hingham 3:66>

Hannah MAYO^{5}, b. 8 Jan. 1681/2*

Samuel MAYO^{5}, b. 16 July 1684*

Mercy MAYO^{5}, b. 23 Ar. 1688*

John MAYO^{5}, b. 10 May 1691*

Rebecca MAYO^{5}, b. 18 Sept. 1692*

Mary MAYO^{5}, b. 26 Oct. 1694*

Joseph MAYO^{5}, b. 22 Dec. 1696*; d. aft. 14 Apr. 1744*

Elizabeth MAYO^{5}, b. 16 July 1706, Harwich <MD 4:177>; d. 27 Feb. 1789, Provincetown g.s. <MD 10:29>

Ebenezer NICKERSON^{5} (Mary Snow^{4}, Mark^{3}, Constance Hopkins^{2}), b. 13 June 1697, Harwich <MD 4:209>; d. 15 Feb. 1768, Provincetown g.s. <MD 10:29> (hus of Eliz. Mayo^{5})

CHILDREN OF John MAYO^{5} & Susanna FREEMAN^{5} (John^{4}, Mercy Prence^{3}, Patience Brewster^{2}): (9)<Harwich VR, MD 5:203>

Rebecca MAYO^{6}, b. 10 Oct. 1713

Susanna MAYO^{6}, b. 13 Mar. 1714/5

Samuel MAYO^{6}, b. 17 Mar. 1717

John MAYO^{6}, b. 11 Apr. 1719

Mercy MAYO^{6}, b. 2 Mar. 1721/2

Prence MAYO^{6}, b. 26 Oct. 1723

Benjamin MAYO^{6}, b. 23 Sept. 1725

Hannah MAYO^{6}, b. 11 Aug. 1727

Mary MAYO^{6}, b. 23 Jan. 1729/30

Joshua SEARS^{4} (Paul$^{3-2}$, Richard^{1}), b. 20 Nov. 1708 (hus of Rebecca Mayo^{6})**<119>**

CHILDREN OF Joseph MAYO^{5} (Hannah Freeman^{4}) & Abigail MYRICK^{5} (Ben.^{4}, Abigail Hopkins^{3}, Gyles^{2}): (10) <Harwich, MD 8:106>

Joseph MAYO^{6}, b. 11 Nov. 1718

Moses MAYO^{6}, b. 1 Feb. 1720/1

Lydia MAYO^{6}, b. 23 Mar. 1721/2

Thomas MAYO^{6}, b. 1 Apr. 1725; d. 1778, Newport RI**<120>**

Abigail MAYO^{6}, b. 1 Dec. 1728

Elizabeth MAYO^{6}, b. 28 Mar. 1731, d.y.

Isaac MAYO^{6}, b. 28 Mar. 1733

Elizabeth MAYO^{6}, b. 28 Mar. 1733 (twins)

Nathan MAYO^{6}, bpt. 15 June 1735 <MD 7:94>, d.y.

Nathan MAYO^{6}, b. 5 Apr. 1736

Eunice MAYO^{6}, b. 7 Apr. 1738

Phebe FREEMAN^{8} (*Watson^{7}, Edmund^{6}, Tho.^{5}, John^{4}, Mercy Prence^{3}, Patience Brewster^{2}), b. 1 June 1725* <Harwich VR>; d. 6 Jan. 1791*, Brewster g.s.

CHILDREN OF Moses MAYO^{6} & Phebe FREEMAN^{8}*: (11)**<121>**

CHILDREN OF Nathan MAYO & Anna (   ): (8) <Brewster Ch.>

Elizabeth WING, (*dau of Elnathan & Hannah (Allen)), b. 28 Feb. 1729*; d. 11 Feb. 1816*

CHILDREN OF Thomas MAYO^{6} (Jos.^{5}) & Elizabeth WING: (11) <1-9, Harwich>

Thomas MAYO^{7}, b. 8 Oct. 1753 <MD 24:152>

Asa MAYO^{7}, b. 7 Feb. 1755 <MD 24:152>; 4 or 24 Dec. 1823 <Brewster VR:53,54>

Ebenezer MAYO^{7}, b. 22 Mar. 1757 <MD 24:152>

Isaac MAYO^{7}, b. 21 Nov. 1758 <MD 24:152>; d. 12 Oct. 1844

Maria MAYO^{7}, b. 4 Feb. 1761; unm. <MD 24:152>

Elnathan MAYO^{7}, bpt. 4 July 1763 <MD 12:157>

Desire MAYO^{7}, bpt. 7 Aug. 1768 <MD 13:98>, d.y.

Elizabeth MAYO^{7}, bpt. 24 Nov. 1771 <MD 13:100>

John MAYO^{7}, bpt. 21 Aug. 1774 <MD 13:102>

Child*, b. ( )

Desire MAYO^{7}*, b. 3 July 1772*

CHILDREN OF Isaac MAYO^{7} & Hannah CAHOON: (9) <Mayo Gen. mss., by Charles Mayo>

Randall MAYO^{8}, b. 1783, d. 1800

Mary MAYO^{8}, b. 1783 (sic)

Allen MAYO^{8}, b. 1785, d. 1860

Isaac MAYO^{8}, b. 1787, d. 1815

Hannah MAYO^{8}, b. 1790

Reuben MAYO^{8}, b. 7 Apr. 1794, Provincetown, d. 10 May 1882, Princeton Minn.

Jacob MAYO^{8}, b. 2 Nov. 1796, d. 1852

Lydia MAYO^{8}, b. 1799

Maria MAYO^{8}, b. 3 June 1803

CHILDREN OF Reuben MAYO^{8} & Dorcas MORRILL: (13) <Mayo Gen., mss., by Charles Mayo>**<122>**

Moses Hall MAYO^{9}, b. 22 Feb. 1824, d. 12 Mar. 1824

Sarah Thurston MAYO^{9}, b. 26 Mar. 1825

Emily Ann MAYO^{9}, b. 19 Feb. 1827

Hannah Maria MAYO^{9}, b. 18 Mar. 1829

Reuben Morrill MAYO^{9}, b. 9 May 1831

Charles Hall MAYO^{9}, b. 14 May 1833, d. 20 Dec. 1890

George Fred MAYO^{9}, b. 24 May 1835

Jacob Allen MAYO^{9}, b. 15 Apr. 1837, d. Aug. 1851, unm.

Ellen Mercy MAYO^{9}, b. 2 June 1839

Peter Morrill MAYO^{9}, b. 20 June 1841, d. Oct. 1850

Frances Snow MAYO^{9}, b. 31 Mar. 1843

Viola Adeli() MAYO^{9}, b. 2 May 1845

Arthur Melvin MAYO^{9}, b. 26 Aug. 1849, d. Oct. 1850

MICRO #16 of 18

Stephen HALL, d. betw. 25 Dec. 1854 (will) - 20 Mar. 1855 (prob.) <Paris ME Probate> (1st hus. Sarah Thurston Mayo^{9})

Sally SEABURY^{6} (Ichabod^{5}, Jos.^{4}, Martha Pabodie^{3}, Eliz. Alden^{2}), b. 2 Aug. 1760, d. 14 July 1835 <Brewster VR 24,54>

CHILDREN OF Asa MAYO^{7} (Tho.^{6}) & Sally SEABURY: (13) <Brewster VR:24,54>

John MAYO^{8}, b. 28 May 1779

Gideon MAYO^{8}, b. 21 Jan. 1781; d. 6 July 1800, at sea

Rhoda MAYO^{8}, b. 21 Feb. 1784

Jeremiah MAYO^{8}, b. 29 Jan. 1786

Sally MAYO^{8}, b. 10 Dec. 1787; d. 10 June 1866, Syracuse NY, "suddenly at church"

Asa MAYO^{8}, b. 1 Dec. 1789; d. 15 Feb. 1817

Benjamin MAYO^{8}, b. 29 Apr. 1791; d. 16 Mar. 1838, St. Pieres <Brewster VR:93>

Seabury MAYO^{8}, b. 18 Dec. 1792; d. 9 Aug. 1821

Josiah MAYO^{8}, b. 13 Sept. 1795

Elisha MAYO^{8}, b. 20 June 1797; d. 25 Dec. 1816

David MAYO^{8}, b. 15 June 1800

Temperance MAYO^{8}, b. 27 Feb. 1802

Catharine MAYO^{8}, b. 21 Feb. 1808; d. 10 Sept. 1809

Hannah GRAY, (dau of Lot & Rhoda), b. 18 May 1792 <Brewster VR:48,93>

CHILD OF Benjamin MAYO^{8} & Hannah GRAY:

Asa MAYO^{9}, b. 2/3 Jan. 1818 <Brewster VR:93>

Samuel HIGGINS, b. 20 July 1786*, Harwich (hus of Sally Mayo^{8})

Lydia LAHA, (*dau of James & Lydia), b. 28 May 1780, Harwich <Brewster VR:25,56>

CHILDREN OF John MAYO^{8} (Asa^{7}) & Lydia LAHA: (4) <Brewster VR:69>

James Laha MAYO^{9}, b. 27 May 1803

John MAYO^{9}, b. 21 Nov. 1804

Charles MAYO^{9}, b. 10 Feb. 1809

Catharine MAYO^{9}, b. 10 Jan. 1812

CHILD OF James Laha MAYO^{8} & Laura SNOW:

James H. MAYO^{9}, b. 3 Dec. 1834, Harwich, d. 22 Jan. 1915, ae 80y1m19d, Springfield MA, valvular heart disease, widowed, mining engineer <Mass.VR 74:390>

Jason WOOD, b. 8 Sept. 1774, Stoughton, d. 15 Sept. 1848

CHILDREN OF Jason WOOD & Desire MAYO^{7} (Tho.^{6}): (10)

Elisha WOOD^{8}, b. 18 Aug. 1798

Hannah WOOD^{8}, b. 18 Oct. 1799

Eben WOOD^{8}, b. 30 Oct. 1801

Jason WOOD^{8}, b. 13 Nov. 1803

Theodate WOOD^{8}, b. 12 Sept. 1805

Phineas WOOD^{8}, b. 20 Oct. 1807

Samuel WOOD^{8}, b. 9 Dec. 1809

John M. WOOD^{8}, b. 6 Jan. 1812

Clarissa WOOD^{8}, b. 22 Jan. 1814

Catherine WOOD^{8}, b. 9 Nov. 1817

Sarah MERRICK, (dau of Wm.), b. 1 Aug. 1654, Eastham <MD 5:23>; d. 21 Apr. 1696, Eastham, consumption <MD 8:182>

CHILDREN OF John FREEMAN^{4} (Mercy Prence^{3}) & 1st Sarah MERRICK: (10) <1-7, Eastham, MD 3:180>

John FREEMAN^{5}, b. 3 Sept. 1674, d.y.

Sarah FREEMAN^{5}, b. Sept. 1676; d. 23 Apr. 1739 <Freeman Gen.:50>

John FREEMAN^{5}, b. July 1678; d. aft. 27 Aug. 1747 (deed)

Rebecca FREEMAN^{5}, b. 28 Jan. 1680; d. pre 22 Apr. 1721 (father's will)

Nathaniel FREEMAN^{5}, b. 17 Mar. 1682/3; d. 2 Aug. 1735, Harwich <MD 13:70>

Benjamin FREEMAN^{5}, b. July 1685; d. 14 Mar. 1758*, Brewster g.s.

Mercy FREEMAN^{5}, b. 3 Aug. 1687; d. 7 July 1720, Harwich <MD 6:56>

Patience FREEMAN^{5}, b. ( ), d. 28 Jan. 1731/2, Harwich <MD 13:70>

Susanna FREEMAN^{5}, b. ( )

Mary FREEMAN^{5}, b. c1693, d. 18 Aug. 1719, ae about 26, Harwich <MD 6:56>

Mercy (HEDGE) Watson, b. c1658, d. 27 Sept. 1721, 63rd yr, Harwich g.s.

CHILD OF John FREEMAN^{4} & 2nd Mercy (HEDGE) Watson:

Elizabeth FREEMAN^{5}, b. July 1698 <MD 31:151>; d. aft. 8 May 1770* (dau Mercy's will)

CHILDREN OF John MAYO^{5} (Hannah Freeman^{4}, Mercy Prence^{3}, Patience Brewster^{2}) & Susanna FREEMAN^{5}: (9) <Harwich, MD 5:203>

Rebecca MAYO^{6}, b. 10 Oct. 1713

Susanna MAYO^{6}, b. 13 Mar. 1714/5

Samuel MAYO^{6}, b. 17 Mar. 1717

John MAYO^{6}, b. 11 Apr. 1719

Mercy MAYO^{6}, b. 2 Mar. 1721/2

Prence MAYO^{6}, b. 26 Oct. 1723

Benjamin MAYO^{6}, b. 23 Sept. 1725

Hannah MAYO^{6}, b. 11 Aug. 1727 <MD 5:204>

Mary MAYO^{6}, b. 23 Jan. 1729/30 <MD 5:204>

Edward SNOW^{4} (Jabez^{3}, Constance Hopkins^{2}), b. 26 Mar. 1672, Eastham <MD 4:32>; d. betw. 8 Apr. 1754 (will) - 20 Sept. 1758 (prob.)

CHILDREN OF Edward SNOW & Sarah FREEMAN^{5} (John^{4}): (7) <Harwich ChR.>

Thomas SNOW^{6}, bpt. 19 Oct. 1707 <MD 4:247>; d. pre 8 Apr. 1754*

Jabez SNOW^{6}, bpt. 19 Oct. 1707 <MD 4:247>

Rebecca SNOW^{6}, bpt. 19 Oct. 1707 <MD 4:247>; d. 2 Apr. 1723 <MD 8:34>

Martha SNOW^{6}, bpt. 19 Oct. 1707 <MD 4:247>

Nathaniel SNOW^{6}, bpt. 8 Jan. 1709/10 <MD 4:248>

Nathan SNOW^{6}, bpt. 27 May 1716 <MD 5:17>

Joseph SNOW^{6}, bpt. 14 Sept. 1718 <MD 5:18>

Temperance DIMOCK^{5} (Desire Sturgis^{4}, Temperance Gorham^{3}, Desire Howland^{2}), b. June 1689, Barnstable <MD 4:221>; d. 29 ( ) 1773*, Brewster g.s.

CHILDREN OF Benjamin FREEMAN^{5} (John^{4}) & Temperance DIMOCK: (10) <Harwich, 1-6,9,10, MD 5:87>

Desire FREEMAN^{6}, b. 20 Apr. 1711

Rebecca FREEMAN^{6}, b. 27 Mar. 1713

Temperance FREEMAN^{6}, b. Oct. 1715

Benjamin FREEMAN^{6}, b. 10 Jan. 1717/18; d. 10 Dec. 1786*

Sarah FREEMAN^{6}, b. 11 Mar. 1719/20

Fear FREEMAN^{6}, b. 23 Mar. 1721/22

Isaac FREEMAN^{6}, bpt. 4 Apr. 1725, d.y. <MD 6:152>

Isaac FREEMAN^{6}, bpt. 26 Mar. 1727 <MD 6:154>

John FREEMAN^{6}, b. 29 July 1729

Mehitable FREEMAN^{6}, b. 4 Nov. 1731

Sarah DILLINGHAM, (*dau of John), b. 10 Feb. 1719/20*; d. ae about 60

CHILDREN OF Benjamin FREEMAN^{6} & Sarah DILLINGHAM: (7) <Harwich, MD 24:151>**<123>**

Mary FREEMAN^{7}, b. 23 Mar. 1737**<124>**

Thankful FREEMAN^{7}, b. 30 Sept. 1741

Temperance FREEMAN^{7}, b. 17 July 1744

Edward FREEMAN^{7}, b. 19 Oct. 1746

Lydia FREEMAN^{7}, b. 28 Apr. 1752

Rebecca FREEMAN^{7}, b. 6 July 1754

Benjamin FREEMAN^{7}, b. 2 Aug. 1757

John BACON^{5} (Mary Hawes^{4}, Desire Gorham^{3}, Desire Howland^{2}), b. 24 Mar. 1696/7, Barnstable <MD 2:215>; d. 24 May 1745, Barnstable g.s.

CHILDREN OF John BACON & Elizabeth FREEMAN^{5} (John^{4}): (10) <Barnstable, MD 31:151>

Mary BACON^{6}, b. 24 Mar. 1727, d. 17 July 1727

John BACON^{6}, b. 22 Apr. 1728

Barnabas BACON^{6}, b. 18 Apr. 1729, d. 15 July 1729

Daughter, b. 3 Jan. 1729/30, d. ae 1/2 hr.

Elizabeth BACON^{6}, b. 8 May 1731; d. 17 Oct. 1811*

Isaac BACON^{6}, b. 25 Dec. 1732; d. 24 June 1819

Mercy BACON^{6}, b. 27 Jan. 1734; d. 21 Mar. 17(68)*, unm.

Simeon BACON[6], b. 26 July 1736, d. 21 Mar. 1739/40

Desire BACON[6], b. 20 May 1738; d. 2 Mar. 1811*

Mary BACON[6], b. 23 Aug. 1740

Mercy WATSON[4] (Elkanah[3], Geo.[2], Robert[1]), b. Oct. 1683, Plymouth <MD 5:55>; d. aft. 27 Aug. 1747

CHILDREN OF John FREEMAN[5] (John[4]) & Mercy WATSON: (11) <1-9, Harwich <MD 4:175>

Elkanah FREEMAN[6], b. 28 Oct. 1702; d. 21 Jan. 1713/4 <MD 6:55>

Sarah FREEMAN[6], b. 26 Jan. 1704

Mercy FREEMAN[6], b. 24 Apr. 170()

John FREEMAN[6], b. 13 Aug. 1709; d. 24 Jan. 1804*, Hardwick Ch.

Phebe FREEMAN[6], b. 28 Nov. 171()

Thankful FREEMAN[6], b. 6 Oct. 1714

Elkanah FREEMAN[6], b. 8 Feb. 1716/17

Mary FREEMAN[6], b. 13 Oct. 1719

Eli FREEMAN[6], b. 27 Apr. 1722 <MD 7:195>

Elishua FREEMAN[6], b. 21 May 1724 <MD 7:195>

Hannah FREEMAN[6], bpt. ( ) July 1728*, Harwich <MD 6:156>

Constant MYRICK[5] (Nath.[4], Abigail Hopkins[3], Gyles[2]), d. 17 Mar. 1792*, ae 91, Hardwick

Joanna RICKARD, b. c1710, d. 29 Mar. 1797*, Hardwick ChR

CHILDREN OF John FREEMAN[6] & Joanna RICKARD: (8) <Rochester, 1-4, VR 2:6>

Mercy FREEMAN[7], b. 15 July 1732

Watson FREEMAN[7], b. 25 Oct. 1734

John FREEMAN[7], b. 17 Sept. 1736

Sarah FREEMAN[7], b. 15 Oct. 1737

Thankful FREEMAN[7]*, bpt. 24 Jan. 1741*

Susanna FREEMAN[7]*, bpt. 9 Sept. 1744*

Mary FREEMAN[7]*, bpt. 8 June 1746*

Eli FREEMAN[7]*, b. 3 July 1749*; d. 10 May 1816*

Thomas ASHLEY, (son of Jos.), d. pre 15 Oct. 1762 <Plymouth Co.Prob.#544, 16:466>

CHILDREN OF Thomas ASHLEY & Phebe FREEMAN[6] (John[5]): (6*) <Rochester VR>

Thankful ASHLEY[7], b. 28 Jan. 1729

Miriam ASHLEY[7], b. 14 July 1732

Thomas ASHLEY[7], b. 5 June 1738

John ASHLEY[7], b. 30 Aug. 1740

Elkanah ASHLEY[7], b. 13 June 1744

Isaac ASHLEY[7], b. 13 Apr. 1747

Judah BERRY, d. betw. 21 Nov. 1769 (will) - 11 May 1773 (prob.) <Barnstable Co.Prob.17:96>

CHILDREN OF Judah BERRY & 1st Mary FREEMAN[5] (John[4]): (3) <Harwich, MD 5:204>

Lemuel BERRY[6], b. 21 Feb. 1713/4; d. 27 Aug. 1767*, Brewster g.s.

Theophilus BERRY[6], b. 12 Oct. 1715; d. aft. 21 Nov. 1769 (father's will)

Mary BERRY[6], b. 15 Dec. 1717; d. aft. 21 Nov. 1769 (father's will)

CHILDREN OF Judah BERRY & 2nd Rebecca HAMLEN: (3 of 7) <Harwich, MD 5:204>**<125>**

Ruth BERRY, b. 19 Mar. 1720/21; d. pre 21 Nov. 1769 (father's will)

Hannah BERRY, bpt. 19 May 1723 "with 4 others"

Mercy BERRY, b. 29 Apr. 1725

CHILDREN OF Lemuel BERRY[6] & Lydia CLARK*: (10)

Mary BERRY[7], bpt. 31 Aug. 1746

Judah BERRY[7], bpt. 31 Aug. 1746

Scotoway BERRY[7], bpt. 31 Aug. 1746; d. 12 July 1832*, ae 87, Brewster g.s.

Rebecca BERRY[7], bpt. 6 Mar. 1747/8 <MD 8:247>

Mehitable BERRY[7], bpt. 18 Mar. 1749/50 <MD 9:210>

Lemuel BERRY^{7}, bpt. 12 Apr. 1752 <MD 10:130>

Lydia BERRY^{7}, bpt. 28 July 1754 <MD 10:132>

Sarah BERRY^{7}, bpt. 3 Oct. 1756 <MD 10:251>

Reliance BERRY^{7}, bpt. 13 Aug. 1758 <MD 10:252>

Dau., bpt. 27 July 1760 <MD 12:52>

Hannah MAYO^{7} (*Moses^{6}, Phebe Freeman^{5}-), b. c1751, d. 12 Dec. 1806*, 56th yr, Brewster g.s.

CHILDREN OF Scotoway BERRY^{7} & Hannah MAYO*: (3 of 9) <Harwich>**<126>**

Issacher BERRY^{8}, bpt. 19 Apr. 1787 <MD 13:140>

Olive BERRY^{8}, bpt. 19 Apr. 1789 <MD 13:140>

Eunice BERRY^{8}, bpt. 21 Aug. 1791 <MD 13:141>

CHILDREN OF Theophilus BERRY^{6} (Mary Freeman^{5}) & Hannah LINCOLN: (4) <Harwich, MD 33:63>

Benjamin BERRY^{7}, b. 10 Jan. 1737

Priscilla BERRY^{7}, b. 15 Nov. 1738

Jonathan BERRY^{7}, b. 27 Dec. 1743

Hannah BERRY^{7}, b. 24 Dec. 1745

Chillingsworth FOSTER, (son of John), b. 11 July 1680, Marshfield <MD 2:249>; d. 22 Dec. 1764, Brewster g.s.

CHILDREN OF Chillingsworth FOSTER & 1st Mercy FREEMAN^{5} (John^{4}): (7) <Harwich, MD 3:175,176>

James FOSTER^{6}, b. 21 Jan. 1705/6

Chillingsworth FOSTER^{6}, b. 25 Dec. 1707

Mary FOSTER^{6}, b. 5 Jan. 1709/10

Thomas FOSTER^{6}, b. 15 Mar. 1711/12

Nathan FOSTER^{6}, b. 10 June 1715 <MD 3:176>

Isaac FOSTER^{6}, b. 17 June 1718 <MD 3:176>; d. 10 Sept. 1777*, Brewster g.s.

Mercy FOSTER^{6}, b. 20 May 1720 <MD 3:176>; d. 28 Aug. 1720 <MD 6:56>

Susanna (GRAY) Sears, d. 7 Dec. 1730, Harwich <MD 8:35>

CHILDREN OF Chillingsworth FOSTER & 2nd Susanna (GRAY) Sears: (4) <MD 8:160>

Mercy FOSTER, b. 29 July 1722

Nathaniel FOSTER, b. 17 Apr. 1725

Jerusha FOSTER, b. 9 Dec. 1727

Son, b. Mar. 1729/30, stillborn

Joseph O. BAKER, (son of Jos. & Catherine), b. c1817, Harwich, d. 23 June 1885, ae 68, Harwich, pneumonia, married, trader <Mass.VR 364:11>

Joseph GOULD, (son of Jos.), b. 1746, d. 14 Sept. 1803 <Gould Fam.:107>**<127>**

CHILDREN OF Joseph GOULD & Susanna FOSTER^{7} (Nathan^{6}, Chillingsworth^{5}): (10) <Gould Fam.:107>**<127>**

Hannah GOULD^{8}, b. 3 Nov. 1769, d. 15 Sept. 1770

Hannah GOULD^{8}, b. 10 July 1771, d. 10 June 1794

Sarah GOULD^{8}, b. 10 June 1773, d. 20 Aug. 1790

Solomon GOULD^{8}, b. 3 Nov. 1775, d. 10 Nov. 1777

Lucy GOULD^{8}, b. 15 June 1777, d. 28 Nov. 1777

Solomon GOULD^{8}, b. 3 Nov. 1779, d. at sea

Joseph GOULD^{8}, b. 3 Sept. 1781, d. 16 Sept. 1835, unm.

Susanna GOULD^{8}, b. 13 Nov. 1783, d. 1869

Benjamin GOULD^{8}, b. 3 Sept. 1784

Lucy GOULD^{8}, b. 23 July 1787, d. 19 Aug. 1847

Thomas ALLEN, b. c1803, Harwich, d. 27 Apr. 1871, ae 68, Harwich, hemorrhage of kidneys, married, farmer <Mass.VR 238:12>

CHILDREN OF Thomas ALLEN & Lucy GOULD^{8}: (4) <Gould Fam.:174>**<127>**

Freeman Doane ALLEN^{9}, b. 21 June 1814, d. 13 Apr. 1829

John ALLEN^{9}, b. 23 Nov. 1816, d. Nov. 1860, lost at sea

Lucy G. ALLEN^{9}, b. 30 July 1821

Hannah Gould ALLEN^{9}, b. 27 Jan. 1825, living 1874

CHILDREN OF Chillingsworth FOSTER^{6} (Mercy Freeman^{5}) & Mercy WINSLOW: (3) <Harwich, MD 19:56>

Thankful FOSTER^{7}, b. 14 June 1733

Mercy FOSTER^{7}, b. 2 May 1735, Barnstable

Chillingsworth FOSTER^{7}, b. 17 July 1737, Barnstable

CHILDREN OF Chillingsworth FOSTER^{6} & Mary ( ): (2) <Harwich, MD 19:56>[<128>]

Mehitabel FOSTER^{7}, b. 18 Apr. 1746

Sarah FOSTER^{7}, b. 26 Nov. 1747

Hannah SEARS^{5} (Ruth Merrick^{4}, Abigail Hopkins^{3}, Gyles^{2}), b. 3 June 1720, Harwich <MD 5:86>; d. 31 Oct. 1760*, Brewster g.s.

CHILDREN OF Isaac FOSTER^{6} (Mercy Freeman^{5}) & Hannah SEARS: (7) <Harwich, MD 13:60>

Isaac FOSTER^{7}, b. 29 May 1739; d. 29 Feb. 1824*, Brewster g.s.

Samuel FOSTER^{7}, b. 31 May 1741

David FOSTER^{7}, b. 24 Mar. 1742/3

Lemuel FOSTER^{7}, b. 24 Feb. 1744

Seth FOSTER^{7}, b. Mar. 1747

Hannah FOSTER^{7}, b. 4 May 1749

Nathaniel FOSTER^{7}, b. 8 Apr. 1751

CHILDREN OF Seth FOSTER^{7} & Sarah COBB: (8) <Brewster VR:61>

Sally FOSTER^{8}, b. 27 Aug. 1774

Abigail FOSTER^{8}, b. 22 June 1776

Seth FOSTER^{8}, b. 18 Feb. 1778

Sears FOSTER^{8}, b. 20 Mar. 1784; d. 1834, lost at sea <Brewster VR:100>

Jerusha FOSTER^{8}, b. 11 June 1786

Rebecca FOSTER^{8}, b. 28 Nov. 1788

Barnabas Cobb FOSTER^{8}, b. 10 Mar. 1792; d. 1828

Betsey FOSTER^{8}, b. 5 Dec. 1796

CHILDREN OF Sears FOSTER^{8} & Betsey ( ): (12) <Brewster VR:100>

Elijah FOSTER^{9}, b. 6 Mar. 1804, d. 17 Feb. 1810

Tempy M. FOSTER^{9}, b. 7 Sept. 1805, d. 18 Mar. 1807

Betsy FOSTER^{9}, b. 29 July 1807

Hannah FOSTER^{9}, b. 19 Feb. 1809

Tempy M. FOSTER^{9}, b. 19 June 1811

Sarah C. FOSTER^{9}, b. 19 Jan. 1812, d. 27 June 1837, unm.

Elijah FOSTER^{9}, b. 24 Jan. 1815, d. 17 Mar. 1815

Sears FOSTER^{9}, b. 12 Aug. 1816, d. 20 Sept. 1836

Elijah FOSTER^{9}, b. 24 June 1818

Isaac C. FOSTER^{9}, b. 16 Aug. 1820 or 1822

Barna FOSTER^{9}, b. 17 July 1823 or 1824

Thaddeus FOSTER^{9}, b. 7 Nov. 1825, d. 27 Nov. 1827

William Whittemore GOSS, b. 11 June 1802, Weston VT <Brewster VR:102>

CHILDREN OF William Whittemore GOSS & Hannah FOSTER^{9}: (12) <Brewster VR:102>

William Freeman Myrick GOSS^{10}, b. 4 July 1827

Hannah Jane GOSS^{10}, b. 27 Jan. 1829

Betsy Foster GOSS^{10}, b. 25 Feb. 1830

Franklin GOSS^{10}, b. 17 July 1831

Loisa F. GOSS^{10}, b. 18 Aug. 1834, d. 14 Sept. 1834

Walter Scott GOSS^{10}, b. 31 Dec. 1832

Warren GOSS^{10}, b. 19 Aug. 1835

Mary GOSS^{10}, b. 28 July 1837
Ellen GOSS^{10}, b. 27 Apr. 1839
Ellery GOSS^{10}, b. 27 Aug. 1840, d. 25 Mar. 1841
Maria Antoinette GOSS^{10}, b. 26 Feb. 1842
Abba E. GOSS^{10}, b. 1 Feb. 1849 <VR:200>
Sarah THATCHER^{5} (*Ben.^{4}, Lydia Gorham^{3}, Desire Howland^{2}), b. 1 Dec. 1741*, Harwich; d. 2 Oct. 1777*, Brewster g.s. (wf of Isaac Foster$^{7-6}$)
CHILDREN OF James FOSTER^{6} (Mercy Freeman^{5}) & Lydia WINSLOW: (11) <Rochester VR 1:129,130>
Mercy FOSTER^{7}, b. 4 July 1730
Mary FOSTER^{7}, b. 11 Apr. 1732
Chillingsworth FOSTER^{7}, b. 8 Dec. 1733
James FOSTER^{7}, b. 17 Apr. 1735, d. 29 May 1735
Lydia FOSTER^{7}, b. 13 Apr. 1736
James FOSTER^{7}, b. 12 Apr. 1737
Edward FOSTER^{7}, b. 3 July 1738
Nathan FOSTER^{7}, b. 4 Apr. 1740, d. 28 Oct. 1742
John FOSTER^{7}, b. 5 Aug. 1742, d. 9 Sept. 1742
Nathan FOSTER^{7}, b. 26 Jan. 1743/4
John FOSTER^{7}, b. 30 July 1745
CHILDREN OF Nathaniel HASKELL & Lydia FOSTER^{7}: (4) <Hardwick VR>
Prince HASKELL^{8}, b. 26 Apr. 1758 <VR:53>
George HASKELL^{8}, b. 23 Apr. 1761 <VR:54>
Nathaniel HASKELL^{8}, b. 15 July 1762 <VR:53>
Mary HASKELL^{8}, b. 1 July 1765 <VR:54>
David PADDOCK (*Zachariah & Bethiah), b. 12 Aug. 170(), Yarmouth <MD 4:189> (1703-08)
CHILDREN OF David PADDOCK* & Mary FOSTER^{6} (Mercy Freeman^{5}): (8) <MD 13:56>
Mercy PADDOCK^{7}, b. 11 Aug. 1728
Bethiah PADDOCK^{7}, b. 27 Aug. 1729
Mary PADDOCK^{7}, b. 25 Sept. 1730
Sarah PADDOCK^{7}, b. 20 Nov. 1731
Mercy PADDOCK^{7}, b. 7 Feb. 1732/3
David PADDOCK^{7}, b. 12 Dec. 1734
Anthony PADDOCK^{7}, b. 4 Oct. 1736
Betey PADDOCK^{7}, b. ( )
Mary WATSON^{4} (Elkanah^{3}, George^{2}, Robert^{1}), b. Oct. 1688, Plymouth <MD 5:55>
CHILDREN OF Nathaniel FREEMAN^{5} (John^{4}) & Mary WATSON: (5) <Harwich, MD 5:202>
Daughter, b. 7 July 1711, d. 25 Aug. 1711
Prence FREEMAN^{6}, b. 22 July 1712; d. 16 Dec. 1790*, Harwich
Mary FREEMAN^{6}, b. 24 Nov. 1714
Lemuel FREEMAN^{6}, b. 18 Apr. 1717
Daughter, b. 14 Oct. 1719, d.c 5 Jan. 1719/20
Abigail DILLINGHAM, b. 9 June 1713*; d. 30 July 1803*, Harwich (m. Prence Freeman^{6})
Eleazer CROSBY, (son of Tho.), b. 31 Mar. 1680, Eastham <MD 4:31>; d. 8 Oct. 1759*? <MD 24:111>
CHILDREN OF Eleazer CROSBY & Patience FREEMAN^{5} (John^{4}): (13) <1-10, Harwich, MD 4:208>
Keziah CROSBY^{6}, b. 15 May 1708; d. 7 May 1824*, Brewster
Rebecca CROSBY^{6}, b. 12 May 1709
Eleazer CROSBY^{6}, b. 5 Jan. 1710/11; d. betw. 24 Mar. 1784 (will) - 6 Oct. 1784 (prob.)
Silvanus CROSBY^{6}, b. 15 Nov. 1712, d.y.
Phebe CROSBY^{6}, b. 18 Dec. 1714; d. aft. 21 May 1787
Sarah CROSBY^{6}, b. 8 Dec. 1716, d. 29 or 31 July 1724 <MD 8:34,35>

Isaac CROSBY^{6}, b. 18 Oct. 1719 <MD 4:209>

Mary CROSBY^{6}, b. 28 Nov. 1722 <MD 4:209>

Sarah CROSBY^{6}, b. 18 Mar. 1725/6 <MD 4:209>

Patience CROSBY^{6}, b. 29 Oct. 1728 <MD 4:209>

Eunice CROSBY^{6}, d. 29 Jan. 1731/2 (day after mother died)

Zerviah CROSBY^{6}, b. ( ) (mentioned in father's will)

Prince CROSBY^{6}, b. ( ) (mentioned in father's will)

CHILDREN OF Eleazer CROSBY^{6} & Lydia GODFREE: (8) <Harwich, MD 23:56>

Eleazer CROSBY^{7}, b. 14 Oct. 1736; d. pre 24 Mar. 1784 (father's will)

Keziah CROSBY^{7}, b. 6 Jan. 1739/40; d. 7 May 1824* <Brewster VR:41>

Watson CROSBY^{7}, b. 23 Mar. 1741; d. pre 24 Mar. 1784 (father's will)

Rebecca CROSBY^{7}, b. 15 May 1744; unm. in 1784

Isaac CROSBY^{7}, b. 15 May 1744 (twins); d. aft. 24 Mar. 1784 (father's will)

Reuben CROSBY^{7}, b. 12 May 1747; d. pre 24 Mar. 1784 (father's will)

Lydia CROSBY^{7}, b. 2 Jan. 1749; d. aft. 5 Apr. 1806* <Brewster VR:23>

Richard CROSBY^{7}, b. 16 May 1752; d. pre 24 Mar. 1784 (father's will)

Eleazer COBB^{6} (*Sarah Hopkins^{5}, Stephen$^{4-3}$, Gyles^{2}), b. 28 Dec. 1734*, Harwich; d. 23 Aug. 1813* <Brewster VR:41>

CHILD OF Eleazer COBB & Keziah CROSBY^{7}:

Mercy COB^{8}, b. 29 Sept. 1762, Harwich <MD 24:151>

CHILDREN OF James LAHA & Lydia CROSBY^{7}: (5) <Brewster VR:25>

Richard LAHA^{8}, b. 20 July 1776

Tamsey LAHA^{8}, b. 23 Feb. 1778

Lydia LAHA^{8}, b. 28 May 1780

James LAHA^{8}, b. 11 May 1783

John LAHA^{8}, b. 13 Nov. 1786

CHILDREN OF John MAYO & Lydia LAHA^{8}: (4) <Brewster VR:69>

James Laha MAYO^{9}, b. 27 May 1803

John MAYO^{9}, b. 21 Nov. 1804

Charles MAYO^{9}, b. 10 Feb. 1809

Catharine MAYO^{9}, b. 10 Jan. 1812

Joseph CLARK, d. betw. 21 May 1787 (will) - 9 Oct. 1787 (prob.)

CHILDREN OF Joseph CLARK & Phebe CROSBY^{6} (Patience Freeman^{5}): (8) <Brewster>

Mary CLARK^{7}, bpt. 13 Sept. 1747 <MD 8:247>

Nathaniel CLARK^{7}, bpt. 13 Sept. 1747 <MD 8:247>

Silvanus CLARK^{7}, bpt. 13 Sept. 1747 <MD 8:247>

Phebe CLARK^{7}, bpt. 13 Sept. 1747 <MD 8:247>; d. aft. 21 May 1787 (father's will)

Joseph CLARK^{7}, bpt. 13 Sept. 1747 <MD 8:247>

Prince CLARK^{7}, bpt. 30 July 1749 <MD 9:209>; d. pre 21 May 1787 (father's will)

Sarah CLARK^{7}, bpt. 9 June 1751 <MD 10:124>

Patience CLARK^{7}, bpt. Dec. 1753 <MD 10:135>; d. pre 21 May 1787 (father's will)**<129>**

Capt. Solomon CROSBY, (son of Edmund & Thankful (Myrick)), b. c1775, d. 5 Mar. 1811, Boston, Brewster g.s. <VR:47>

Phebe ( ) CROSBY, b. c1778, d. 17 Feb. 1819, ae 41, Brewster g.s.

CHILDREN OF Capt. Solomon CROSBY & Phebe ( ): (3) <Brewster VR:47>

Emily CROSBY, b. 25 Mar. 1803

Joseph Clark CROSBY, b. 15 Dec. 1804, shoemaker

Solomon CROSBY, b. 21 Mar. 1808, lost at sea Jan. ( )

Samuel KNOWLES, (son of Richard), b. 17 Sept. 1651, Plymouth <MD 16:237>; d. 19 June 1737, Eastham g.s. <MD 17:147>

CHILDREN OF Samuel KNOWLES & Mercy FREEMAN^{4} (Mercy Prence^{3}): (10) <Eastham, MD 6:205>
James KNOWLES^{5}, b. 13 Aug. 1680
Mercy KNOWLES^{5}, b. 13 Sept. 1681
Samuel KNOWLES^{5}, b. 15 Jan. 1682; d. 30 Jan. 1750*, Boston, Granary g.s.
Nathaniel KNOWLES^{5}, b. 15 May 1686
Richard KNOWLES^{5}, b. latter end July 1688
Rebecca KNOWLES^{5}, b. middle Mar. 1690
John KNOWLES^{5}, b. middle Apr. 1692
Ruth KNOWLES^{5}, b. Nov. 1694
Cornelius KNOWLES^{5}, b. Oct. 1695
Amos KNOWLES^{5}, b. 1702, d. 9 Dec. 1788, Orleans g.s. <MD 7:227 says 1786>
Rebecca DILLINGHAM, d. 3 Nov. 1772, Eastham <MD 7:184>
CHILDREN OF Amos KNOWLES^{5} & Rebecca DILLINGHAM: (7) <Eastham, MD 17:149>
Amos KNOWLES^{6}, b. 18 Dec. 1730; d. 30 Nov. 1796, Orleans g.s.
Lydia KNOWLES^{6}, b. 1 Aug. 1733
Rebecca KNOWLES^{6}, b. 20 Apr. 1736
Ruth KNOWLES^{6}, b. 10 Dec. 1738
Isaac KNOWLES^{6}, b. 3 June 1741
Rachel KNOWLES^{6}, b. 15 Jan. 1743/4
Richard KNOWLES^{6}, b. 22 Sept. 1746
John KNOWLES^{6}, b. 1 June 1749

MICRO #17 of 18

Eastham Church, S. Parrish, Bill of Mortality: (5)
Wife of Amos KNOWLES, d. 1772 <MD 7:184>
Wife of Amos KNOWLES, d. 1785 <MD 7:187>
Amos KNOWLES, d. 1786 <MD 7:227>
Infant of Amos KNOWLES, d. 1790 <MD 7:228>
Amos KNOWLES, d. 1796 <MD 7:230>
Abigail PEPPER^{6} (Phebe Paine^{5}, Jos.^{4}, Mary Snow^{3}, Constance Hopkins^{2}), b. 27 Oct. 1738, Eastham <MD 16:72>; d. pre 10 Apr. 1786 (will of Solomon Pepper)
CHILDREN OF Amos KNOWLES^{6} & 1st Abigail PEPPER: (8) <Eastham, MD 32:64>
James KNOWLES^{7}, b. 17 Nov. 1765
Richard KNOWLES^{7}, b. 13 Sept. 1767; d. 19 Dec. 1771*
Lydia KNOWLES^{7}, b. 4 Aug. 1768
Amos KNOWLES^{7}, b. 19 Sept. 1769
Solomon KNOWLES^{7}, b. 24 Oct. 1770
Lydia KNOWLES^{7}, b. 22 Aug. 1772
Phebe KNOWLES^{7}, b. 24 July 1774; d. 1825, Orleans <MD 9:37>
Edward KNOWLES^{7}, b. 22 Aug. 1778
Peter KNOWLES^{7}, b. ( )
CHILD OF Amos KNOWLES^{6} & 2nd Mary BROWN: <Eastham, MD 32:64>
George Brown KNOWLES^{7}, b. 20 Jan. 1788
Elisha SMITH, bpt. 18 Oct. 1772, Orleans 1st Ch. <MD 10:230>; d. 1821, Orleans <MD 9:37>
CHILDREN OF Elisha SMITH & Phebe KNOWLES^{7}: (7) <Orleans, MD 34:187>
Amos Knowles SMITH^{8}, b. 12 Oct. 1799
Perlina/Paulina SMITH^{8}, b. 1 July 1801; d. 11 Dec. 1852, Orleans
James SMITH^{8}, b. 19 July 1803
Mary Knowles SMITH^{8}, b. 2 Feb. 1806
Lucinda SMITH^{8}, b. 27 June 1808
Elisha SMITH^{8}, b. 23 Sept. 1810

Phebe Knowles SMITH[8], b. 24 May 1814

Gould LINNELL, b. 1 Jan. 1797*, Orleans <bpt.- MD 13:64>; d. 24 July 1865, Orleans

CHILDREN OF Gould LINNELL & Paulina SMITH[8]: (8) <Eastham VR 2:131>

Gould LINNELL[9], b. 20 Jan. 1823*

Sally LINNELL[9], b. 7 Oct. 1825*

Joseph LINNELL[9], b. 27 Feb. 1828*, d.y.

Paulina LINNELL[9], b. 23 Nov. 1830*

Mary LINNELL[9], b. 26 Oct. 1833*

Joseph LINNELL[9], b. 25 Jan. 1836*

Phebe A. LINNELL[9], b. 14 Sept. 1839*

Rebecca LINNELL[9], b. 10 Sept. 1842*

CHILDREN OF Thomas RICH & Mercy KNOWLES[5] (Mercy Freeman[4]): (12) <1-9, Eastham, MD 7:236>

Thomas RICH[6], b. 22 Dec. 1702

Mercy RICH[6], b. 8 Aug. 1704

James RICH[6], b. 10 Jan. 1705/6

Joseph RICH[6], b. 1 Jan. 1707/8

David RICH[6], b. 17 Mar. 1710

Sarah RICH[6], b. 1 Sept. 1712

John RICH[6], b. 14 Sept. 1714

Thankful RICH[6], b. 14 Oct. 1716

Samuel RICH[6], b. 14 May 171()

Cornelius RICH[6], b. ( )

Rebecca RICH[6], b. ( )

Ruth RICH[6], b. ( )

CHILDREN OF George SHAW & Mercy RICH[6]: (4) <Eastham VR:82>

Elkanah SHAW[7], b. 21 Nov. 1724

John SHAW[7], b. 16 Sept. 1727

James SHAW[7], b. 12 Oct. 1728

Mary SHAW[7], b. 7 June 1731

Martha COBB[3] (James[2], Henry[1]), b. 6 Feb. 1682, Barnstable <MD 3:73>; d. 31 Oct. 1763, Chatham g.s <MD 8:238>

CHILDREN OF Richard KNOWLES[5] (Mercy Freeman[4]): (6) <Chatham, MD 4:182>

Martha KNOWLES[6], b. 28 Jan. 1713/4

Richard KNOWLES[6], b. 26 Mar. 1715; d. 20 Aug. 1736, Chatham g.s. <MD 8:238>

Mercy KNOWLES[6], b. 9 Aug. 1717; d. 14 May 1758, Chatham g.s. <MD 8:237>

James KNOWLES[6], b. 11 Nov. 1719

Cornelius KNOWLES[6], b. 10 Apr. 1722 <MD 4:183>

Rebecca KNOWLES[6], b. 2 Mar. 1723/4

Sarah ( ) KNOWLES, d. 26 Dec. 1748, 29th yr, Chatham g.s. <MD 8:238> (*1st wf of James Knowles[6])

Ruth ( ) KNOWLES, d. 17 Sept. 1766, 46th yr, Chatham g.s. <MD 8:238> (*2nd wf of James Knowles[6])

George GODFREE[5] (Deborah Cook[4], Deborah Hopkins[3], Gyles[2]), b. c1706, d. 4 Dec. 1768, Chatham g.s. <MD 8:237> (hus. of Mercy Knowles[6] - children listed under Hopkins)

Jane ( ) GODFREE, d. 16 Aug. 1768, Chatham g.s. <MD 8:237> (2nd wf of George Godfree[5])

CHILDREN OF Samuel KNOWLES[5] (Mercy Freeman[4]) & Bethiah BROWN: (6) <Eastham, MD 7:239>

Enos KNOWLES[6], b. 30 Apr. 1712; d. 1784, Eastham <MD 7:187>

Azubah KNOWLES[6], b. 6 Feb. 1713/4

Samuel KNOWLES[6], b. 6 Oct. 1715

Nathaniel KNOWLES[6], b. 6 Oct. 1717

Jerusha KNOWLES[6], b. 9 Mar. 1719/20

Seth KNOWLES[6], b. 20 Jan. 1721/2; d. 18 Mar. 1787*, Orleans g.s.

Sarah SPARROW^{5} (Rebecca Merrick^{4}, Abigail Hopkins^{3}, Gyles^{2}), d. 1784, Eastham <MD 7:187>

CHILDREN OF Enos KNOWLES^{6} & Sarah SPARROW: (3)

Bethiah KNOWLES^{7}, b. 12 Jan. 1734/5, Eastham <MD 17:37>

Jerusha KNOWLES^{7*}, b. ( ) <NEHGR 80:119>

Nathaniel KNOWLES^{7*}, b. ( ) <NEHGR 30:119>

Ichabod HIGGINS^{6} (Hannah Mayo^{5}, Nathaniel^{4}, Hannah Prence^{3}, Patience Brewster^{2}), b. 26 Apr. 1729, Eastham <MD 15:54>

CHILD OF Ichabod HIGGINS & Bethiah KNOWLES^{7}:

John HIGGINS^{8*}, b. ( )

CHILDREN OF Samuel KNOWLES^{6} (Sam.^{5}) & Hannah FREEMAN: (4) <Eastham, MD 20:95>

Prince KNOWLES^{7}, b. 30 Oct. 1736 <MD 15:141>

Samuel KNOWLES^{7}, b. 14 Sept. 1738

Azubah KNOWLES^{7}, b. 11 Nov. 1740

Hatsel KNOWLES^{7}, b. 5 Nov. 1742

Ruth FREEMAN^{6} (Nath.$^{5-4}$, Mercy Prence^{3}, Patience Brewster^{2}), b. 30 Sept. 1727, Eastham <MD 15:230>; d. 12 May 1812, Orleans g.s.

CHILDREN OF Seth KNOWLES^{6} (Sam.^{5}) & Ruth FREEMAN: (13) <Eastham, 1-9, MD 33:14>

Freeman KNOWLES^{7}, b. 24 Nov. 1745

Nathaniel KNOWLES^{7}, b. 14 Mar. 1750

Seth KNOWLES^{7}, b. 20 Apr. 1752

Ruth KNOWLES^{7}, b. 3 Aug. 1754

Samuel KNOWLES^{7}, b. 6 Nov. 1756

Amasa KNOWLES^{7}, b. 15 Apr. 1758

Abiathar KNOWLES^{7}, b. 5 Feb. 1760

Mary KNOWLES^{7}, b. 14 Dec. 1762

Hannah KNOWLES^{7}, b. 4 Oct. 1764

Chloe KNOWLES^{7}, b. 28 Dec. 1766 <MD 33:15>

Jerusha KNOWLES^{7}, b. 15 Oct. 1768 <MD 33:15>

Abner KNOWLES^{7}, b. 1 Feb. 1770 <MD 33:15>

Exxa KNOWLES^{7}, b. 2 Nov. 1773 (dau.)

Mary ( ) FREEMAN, d. 29 Jan. 1742/3, 77th yr, Orleans g.s. <MD 8:91>

CHILDREN OF Nathaniel FREEMAN^{4} (Mercy Prence^{3}) & Mary ( ): (6) <Eastham, MD 8:91>

Abigail FREEMAN^{5}, b. 22 Feb. 1692/3

Nathaniel FREEMAN^{5}, b. 11 Feb. 1693/4; d. 27 Sept. 1767, Orleans g.s.

John FREEMAN^{5}, b. 15 June 1696; d. 9 June 1772*

Mary FREEMAN^{5}, b. 3 Oct. 1698

Eliezer FREEMAN^{5}, b. 23 Apr. 1701; d. betw. 11 Dec. 1782* (will) - 9 May 1784* (prob.)

Lydia FREEMAN^{5}, b. 14 Oct. 1703; d. 30 Dec. 1755* <Rochester VR 2:381>

Thomison SEARS, (dau of Sam.), b. c1692, d. 17 July 1761* <Freeman Gen.:68,69>

CHILDREN OF John FREEMAN^{5} & Thomison SEARS: (11*) <Freeman Gen.:68,69>

John FREEMAN^{6}, b. 30 Jan. 1719/20, d. 1 Apr. 1753

Mary FREEMAN^{6}, b. 27 Mar. 1721

Mercy FREEMAN^{6}, b. 8 May 1722

Abigail FREEMAN^{6}, b. 6 June 1723

Joseph FREEMAN^{6}, b. 26 Jan. 1724/5; d. 1778*

Gideon FREEMAN^{6}, b. 3 May 1726

Hannah FREEMAN^{6}, b. 12 July 1728

Joshua FREEMAN^{6}, b. 1 May 1730, d.y.

Eunice FREEMAN^{6}, b. 1 May 1730 (twins)

Joshua FREEMAN^{6}, b. 29 Nov. 1731

Tamzin FREEMAN^{6}, b. 2 July 1734

CHILDREN OF Nathaniel FREEMAN^{5} (Nath.^{4}) & Hannah MERRICK: (7) <Eastham, MD 15:230>

Nathaniel FREEMAN^{6}, b. 9 Mar. 1722/3

Elizabeth FREEMAN^{6}, b. 12 Apr. 1725

Ruth FREEMAN^{6}, b. 30 Sept. 1727

Martha FREEMAN^{6}, b. 28 Feb. 1737 (m. Prince Freeman^{6}, Eliezer^{5}, below)

Susanna FREEMAN^{6}, b. 4 Nov. 1739

Mary FREEMAN^{6}, b. 4 Jan. 1742/3

Hannah FREEMAN^{6}, b. 17 Dec. 1746

Phebe PAINE^{6} (Rich.^{5}, Jos.^{4}, Mary Snow^{3}, Constance Hopkins^{2}), b. 1727*, d. 1812*, ae 85

CHILDREN OF Joseph FREEMAN^{6} (John^{5}) & Phebe PAINE: (7) <Eastham/Harwich, MD 33:13,34:108>

Nathaniel FREEMAN^{7}*, b. 18 Nov. 1749*, Harwich, d.y. <Freeman Gen.:114>

Joseph FREEMAN^{7}, b. 16 May 1751

John FREEMAN^{7}, b. 3 Mar. 1758

Josiah FREEMAN^{7}, b. 24 Feb. 1761

Nathaniel FREEMAN^{7}, b. 7 Apr. 1764

Thomas FREEMAN^{7}, b. 7 Dec. 1767

Mary FREEMAN^{7}, b. 7 Mar. 1770

CHILDREN OF Eliezer FREEMAN^{5} (Nath.^{4}) & Rebecca YOUNG: (8) <1-6, Eastham, MD 16:144>

Rebecca FREEMAN^{6}, b. 27 Dec. 1726, d. 4 Nov. 1730

Eliezer FREEMAN^{6}, b. 16 June 1728

Phebe FREEMAN^{6}, b. 24 Mar. 1729/30; d. pre 1785*

Rebecca FREEMAN^{6}, b. 21 Mar. 1733, d. Apr. 1733

Seth FREEMAN^{6}, b. 19 Jan. 1733/4, d. Aug. 1734

Mary FREEMAN^{6}, b. 27 July 1735; d. pre 1785*

Prince FREEMAN^{6}, b. ( ) (m. Martha Freeman^{6}, Nath.^{5}, above)

Elizabeth FREEMAN^{6}, b. ( )

Elizabeth SNOW^{6} (Jabez^{5-4-3}, Constance Hopkins^{2}), b. 12 Jan. 1730/1, Eastham <MD 15:230> (1st wf of Eliezer Freeman^{6})

Ruth KNOWLES^{7} (Seth^{6}, Sam.^{5}, Mercy Freeman^{4}, Mercy Prence^{3}, Patience Brewster^{2}), b. 3 Aug. 1754, Eastham <MD 16:145> (2nd wf of Eliezer Freeman^{6})

Family Sampler, (Elisha & Phebe Freeman's Family):<130>

Elisha FREEMAN, b. 5 Nov. 1792

Phebe NICKERSON, b. 5 Oct. 1793

CHILDREN OF Elisha FREEMAN & Phebe NICKERSON: (10)

Priscilla P. FREEMAN, b. 12 Nov. 1815, d. 11 Oct. 1829

Phebe FREEMAN, b. 19 Feb. 1817

Betsy FREEMAN, b. 24 Sept. 1891

Eliza N. FREEMAN, b. 10 July 1820, d.y.

Eliza FREEMAN, b. 23 Mar. 1822

Phinehas FREEMAN, b. 14 Dec. 1824, d.y.

Charles R. FREEMAN, b. ( ), d.y.

Charles R. FREEMAN, b. 3 Mar. 18( )

Calvin N. FREEMAN, b. 3 Sept. 1829

Simeon N. FREEMAN, b. 26 July 1831, d. 17 Feb. 1832

Elisha FREEMAN^{4} (Sam.$^{3-2-1}$), b. 9 Dec. 1701, Eastham <MD 6:202> (removed to Liverpool N.S.)

CHILDREN OF Elisha FREEMAN & Lydia FREEMAN^{5} (Nath.^{4}): (12) <1-11, Rochester VR>

Eunice FREEMAN^{6}, b. 5 June 1727*

Mary FREEMAN^{6}, b. 4 Apr. 1729*

Lydia FREEMAN^{6}, b. 6 Feb. 1730/1*

Simeon FREEMAN^{6}, b. 28 Feb. 1732/3*
Elisha FREEMAN^{6}, b. 12 Feb. 1734/5*
Barnabas FREEMAN^{6}, b. 21 Jan. 1737/8*
Nathaniel FREEMAN^{6}, b. 5 Mar. 1739/40*
Phebe FREEMAN^{6}, b. 21 June 1742*
Lothrop FREEMAN^{6}, b. 28 Mar. 1744*, d. 3 Apr. 1745*
Lothrop FREEMAN^{6}, b. 16 Oct. 1746*
Zoheth FREEMAN^{6}, b. 18 Sept. 1749*
Joan FREEMAN^{6}, bpt. 24 Sept. 1749*

Rebecca SPARROW^{3} (Jonathan^{2}, Richard^{1}), b. 30 Oct. 1655, Eastham <MD 14:194>; d. Feb. 1740, Brewster g.s.

CHILDREN OF Thomas FREEMAN^{4} (Mercy Prence^{3}) & Rebecca SPARROW: (10) <Eastham, MD 8:93>
Mercy FREEMAN^{5}, b. last wk Oct. 1674; d. 30 Aug. 1747, Harwich
Thomas FREEMAN^{5}, b. 11 Oct. 1676; d. 22 Mar. 1716/17, Harwich <MD 6:56>
Jonathan FREEMAN^{5}, b. 11 Nov. 1678; d. 27 Apr. 1714, Harwich <MD 3:174,6:55>
Edmund FREEMAN^{5}, b. 11 Oct. 1680; d. 10 Mar. 1745/6, Brewster g.s.
Joseph FREEMAN^{5}, b. 11 Feb. 1682; d. betw. 10 Mar. 1756 (will) - 18 Mar. 1756 (prob.) Harwich
Joshua FREEMAN^{5}, b. 7 Mar. 1684/5
Hannah FREEMAN^{5}, b. 28 Sept. 1687, d. 25 Aug. 1707
Prence FREEMAN^{5}, b. 3 Jan. 1689; d. 14 Apr. 1769*, E. Hampton CT
Hatsuld FREEMAN^{5}, b. 27 Mar. 1691; d. betw. 13 May 1773 (will) - 13 July 1773 (prob.), Harwich
Rebecca FREEMAN^{5}, b. 26 Apr. 1694 <MD 3:175>

Phebe WATSON, (dau of Elkanah), b. June 1681, Plymouth <MD 5:55>; d. pre 4 July 1749 (adm.)

CHILDREN OF Edmund FREEMAN^{5} & Phebe WATSON: (4) <Harwich, MD 3:175>
Watson FREEMAN^{6}, b. 24 Sept. 1704
Joshua FREEMAN^{6}, b. latter end May 1706; d. 23 Sept. 1770*
Hannah FREEMAN^{6}, b. 28 Feb. 1708/9; d. 11 Dec. 1730*
Edmund FREEMAN^{6}, b. 28 Nov. 1710

Mary CLARK, (*dau of Scotto & Mary (Haskell)), b. 17 Apr. 1712*, Harwich <MD 5:203>; d. betw. 20 Feb. 1797 (will) - 29 Mar. 1797 (prob.)

CHILDREN OF Edmund FREEMAN^{6} & Mary CLARK: (7)
Hannah FREEMAN^{7}, b. 25 Oct. 1732*
Edmund FREEMAN^{7}, b. 10 Oct. 1734*
Scotto FREEMAN^{7}, b. 20 Feb. 1736*
Mary FREEMAN^{7}, b. 12 June 1739*
Phebe FREEMAN^{7}, bpt. 25 Oct. 1761 <MD 12:53>
Seth FREEMAN^{7}, bpt. 25 Oct. 1761 <MD 12:53>
Haskell FREEMAN^{7}, bpt. 25 Oct. 1761 <MD 12:53>

CHILDREN OF Seth FREEMAN^{7} & Abigail ROGERS*: (9*) <Freeman Gen.:177>
Hannah FREEMAN^{8}, b. 25 Aug. 1774
Edmund FREEMAN^{8}, b. 31 Jan. 1777, d. 1798
Scotto FREEMAN^{8}, b. 23 Aug. 1779
Betsy FREEMAN^{8}, b. 2 Sept. 1781
Abigail FREEMAN^{8}, b. 11 Mar. 1784
Seth FREEMAN^{8}, b. 7 July 1786
( ) FREEMAN^{8}, b. 20 Oct. 1788 (too faint to read)
Haskell FREEMAN^{8}, b. 7 May 1792
Clark FREEMAN^{8}, b. 11 Feb. 1795

CHILDREN OF Joshua FREEMAN^{6} (Edmund^{5}) & Patience ROGERS*: (2*)
Joshua FREEMAN^{7}, b. 1730, d. 11 Nov. 1796

George FREEMAN^{7}, b. 1739

CHILDREN OF Watson FREEMAN^{6} (Edmund^{5}) & Sarah GRAY, (dau of John & Susanna): (6) <Harwich>

Phebe FREEMAN^{7}, b. 1 June 1725 <MD 13:58>

Elkanah FREEMAN^{7}, b. 31 Mar. 1727 <MD 13:58>

Sarah FREEMAN^{7}, b. 29 Mar. 1729 <MD 13:58>

Isaac FREEMAN^{7}, b. 26 Oct. 1733 <MD 13:58>

Hannah FREEMAN^{7}, b. 8 Apr. 1736 <MD 13:58>

Watson FREEMAN^{7}, bpt. 25 Feb. 1738/39 <MD 7:98>; d. pre 1777*

Olive BERRY, (dau of Scoto & Hannah), b. c1790, Brewster, d. 8 Feb. 1869, at 397 Fourth St., Boston, pneumonia, ae 79y10m, buried Brewster <222:22> (Mass.VR?)**<131>**

CHILDREN OF Elkanah FREEMAN^{7} & Abigail MAYO*: (5) <Brewster>

Christian FREEMAN^{8}, bpt. 20 Apr. 1760 <MD 12:52>

William FREEMAN^{8}, bpt. 20 Apr. 1760 <MD 12:52>

Elkanah FREEMAN^{8}, bpt. 20 Apr. 1760 <MD 12:52>

Barnabas FREEMAN^{8}, bpt. 22 Nov. 1761 <MD 12:53>

Abigail FREEMAN^{8}, bpt. 31 July 1768 <MD 13:98>

Elizabeth COB^{6} (Sarah Hopkins^{5}, Stephen$^{4-3}$, Gyles^{2}), b. 30 Apr. 1738, Harwich <MD 8:220> (wf of Isaac Freeman^{7}, Watson^{6})

Thankful FREEMAN^{7} (*Ben.$^{6-5}$, John^{4}, Mercy Prence^{3}, Patience Brewster^{2}), b. 1741*, d. 1809*

CHILDREN OF Watson FREEMAN^{7} (Watson^{6}) & Thankful FREEMAN: (3) <Harwich>

Watson FREEMAN^{8}, bpt. 28 May 1764 <MD 12:252>

Joshua FREEMAN^{8}, bpt. 13 July 1766 <MD 13:37>

Edward FREEMAN^{8}, bpt. 7 Aug. 1768 <MD 13:98>

CHILDREN OF Hatsuld FREEMAN^{5} (Tho.^{4}) & Abigail ( ): (7 of 9) <1-6, Harwich, MD 8:160>**<132>**

David FREEMAN^{6}, b. 18 July 1720

Abigail FREEMAN^{6}, b. 26 May 1723

Jonathan FREEMAN^{6}, b. 11 May 1725

Sarah FREEMAN^{6}, b. 10 Dec. 1727; d. pre 13 May 1773 (father's will)

Bette FREEMAN^{6}, b. 11 Mar. 1729/30

Mercy FREEMAN^{6}, b. 27 Mar. 1735

Jerusha FREEMAN^{6}, b. ( ) (mentioned in father's will)

CHILDREN OF Seth PERRY & Mercy ( ): (3) <Rochester VR 1:235>**<133>**

Abigail PERRY, bpt. 27 May 1764

Freeman PERRY, bpt. 27 May 1764

Sarah PERRY, bpt. 27 May 1764

Mercy BRADFORD^{4} (John^{3}, Wm.^{2}), b. 20 Dec. 1681, Plymouth <MD 1:147>; d. 27 June 1738, Plympton g.s. <MD 10:112>

CHILDREN OF Jonathan FREEMAN^{5} (Tho.^{4}) & Mercy BRADFORD: (4) <Harwich, MD 5:86>

Jonathan FREEMAN^{6}, b. 26 Mar. 1709/10

Mercy FREEMAN^{6}, b. 24 Apr. 1711

Bradford FREEMAN^{6}, b. 15 Aug. 1713

Ichabod FREEMAN^{6}, b. 2 Aug. 1714

Lydia THACHER^{4} (Lydia Gorham^{3}, Desire Howland^{2}), b. 11 Feb. 1684/5 <MD 13:221>; d. 3 Sept. 1724, Brewster g.s. <MD 8:34>

CHILDREN OF Joseph FREEMAN^{5} (Tho.^{4}) & Lydia THACHER: (6) <Harwich, MD 5:87>

Thacher FREEMAN^{6}, b. 3 Dec. 1710

Elizabeth FREEMAN^{6}, b. 14 Dec. 1712

Joseph FREEMAN^{6}, b. 25 Mar. 1714/5

Lydia FREEMAN^{6}, b. 22 Oct. 1717

Rebecca FREEMAN^{6}, b. 23 Apr. 1720

Thomas FREEMAN^{6}, b. 23 Mar. 1721/2

Paul SEARS, b. 15 June 1669, Yarmouth; d. 14 Feb. 1739/40, Harwich

CHILDREN OF Paul SEARS & Mercy FREEMAN^{5} (Tho.^{4}): (12) <Yarmouth, 1-6, MD 7:149; 7-12, MD 7:250>

Ebenezer SEARS^{6}, b. 15 Aug. 1694

Paul SEARS^{6}, b. 21 Dec. 1695; d. aft. 28 Dec. 1770*, Rochester (deed)

Elizabeth SEARS^{6}, b. 27 Aug. 1697

Thomas SEARS^{6}, b. 6 June 1699

Rebecca SEARS^{6}, b. 2 Apr. 1701

Mercy SEARS^{6}, b. 7 Feb. 1702

Deborah SEARS^{6}, b. 11 Mar. 1705

Ann SEARS^{6}, b. 27 Dec. 1706

Joshua SEARS^{6}, b. c20 Nov. 1708

Daniel SEARS^{6}, b. 16 July 1710

Edmund SEARS^{6}, b. 6 Aug. 1712; d. 12 Aug. 1796, W. Brewster g.s.

Hannah SEARS^{6}, b. 6 Mar. 1714/5; d. 7 Nov. 1739, Yarmouth

Olive (BANGS) Sears, (dau of Elkanah & Sally), b. c1803, Brewster, d. 4 Apr. 1889, ae 86y6m25d, heart disease, Brewster, housewife <Mass.VR 400:7>

Thomas HOWES, (son of Prince & Dorcas (Joyce)), b. 27 June 1706

CHILDREN OF Thomas HOWES & Hannah SEARS^{6}: (2)

Sarah HOWES^{7}, b. 8 June 1735

Thomas HOWES^{7}, b. 17 July 1737

Ebenezer BANGS^{4} (Edw.^{3}, Jonathan^{2}, Edw.^{1}), bpt. 8 Feb. 1702, Harwich <MD 4:245>

CHILDREN OF Ebenezer BANGS & Ann SEARS^{6} (Mercy Freeman^{5}): (9) <Harwich>

Barnabas BANGS^{7}, b. 11 Mar. 1727/8 <MD 13:57>

Ebenezer BANGS^{7}, b. 28 Oct. 1729 <MD 13:57>

Ruth BANGS^{7}, b. 28 Sept. 1731 <MD 13:57>

Silvanus BANGS^{7}, b. 10 Feb. 1734/5 <MD 13:57>

Edmund BANGS^{7}, bpt. 18 May 1746 <MD 8:121>

Edward BANGS^{7}, bpt. 18 May 1746 <MD 8:121>

Ann BANGS^{7}, bpt. 18 May 1746 <MD 8:121>

Jonathan BANGS^{7}, bpt. 29 June 1746 <MD 8:121>

Willard BANGS^{7}, bpt. 23 Oct. 1748 <MD 9:208>

Gideon HIGGINS, (son of Moses & Eliz. (Arey)), b. 22 July 1738, Eastham <MD 17:143>; d. 1816, Orleans ChR <MD 8:149>

CHILDREN OF Gideon HIGGINS & Ruth (   ): (6) <Orleans>**<134>**

Lucia HIGGINS, bpt. 25 Oct. 1772 <MD 10:230>

Ruth HIGGINS, bpt. 29 May 1774 <MD 10:231>

Joseph HIGGINS, bpt. 23 Aug. 1778 <MD 10:233>

Godfrey HIGGINS, bpt. 16 July 1780 <MD 11:253>; d. 1781? <MD 7:187>

Miriam HIGGINS, bpt. 27 Oct. 1782 <MD 12:151>

Sally HIGGINS, bpt. 8 Apr. 1787 <MD 13:90>

CHILDREN OF Jonathan BANGS^{7} (Ann Sears^{6}) & Deborah HURD: (7)

Jonathan BANGS^{8}, b. 1767/68

Willard BANGS^{8}, bpt. 3 Dec. 1769; d. 5 Jan. 1827, Buxton ME

Ezekiel BANGS^{8}, bpt. 8 July 1773

Thankful BANGS^{8}, bpt. 16 June 1775

Deborah BANGS^{8}, bpt. 17 Sept. 1777

Ann BANGS^{8}, b. 1778/79

Sylvanus BANGS^{8}, b. 17 June 1781; d. Jan. 1836

Dorcas THOMPSON, d. 2 Nov. 1838, Buxton ME

CHILDREN OF Willard BANGS[8] & Dorcas THOMPSON: (6) <poss. Buxton ME>
Sally BANGS[9], b. 22 Apr. 1795; d. 15 Aug. 1828
Ezekiel BANGS[9], b. 20 Apr. 1797
Deborah BANGS[9], b. 16 Jan. 1798; d. 28 Aug. 1798
Samuel BANGS[9], b. 22 Nov. 1799; d. 18 Feb. 1855
Ebenezer BANGS[9], b. 24 Nov. 1802; d. 28 Apr. 1821
Frederick BANGS[9], b. 21 Oct. 1806
Rebecca HARMON, b. 15 Jan. 1802, Buxton ME
CHILDREN OF Samuel BANGS[9] & Rebecca HARMON: (9) <poss. Buxton ME>
Sarah BANGS[10], b. 10 May 1821
Harriet Frances BANGS[10], b. 21 Dec. 1822; d. 23 Apr. 1860, Sweden ME
Ebenezer F. BANGS[10], b. 12 Mar. 1825
James W. BANGS[10], b. 27 July 1827; d. 14 Feb. 1832
Mary E. BANGS[10], b. 10 Dec. 1829; d. 28 Feb. 1832
Ellen M. BANGS[10], b. 2 Oct. 1832; d. 18 Feb. 1851
Emily J. BANGS[10], b. 17 June 1835
Esther M. BANGS[10], b. 23 May 1838
James H. BANGS[10], b. 17 Nov. 1839
William Henry GREENE, b. 10 Mar. 1815, Greene's Hill, Sweden ME; d. 4 July 1857, Sweden ME
CHILDREN OF William Henry GREENE & Harriet Frances BANGS[10]: (4) <poss. Sweden ME>
Frances E. GREENE[11], b. 28 Mar. 1848; d. 1890
Henry Eugene GREENE[11], b. 14 Aug. 1851; d. 21 Aug. 1905, Bridgton ME
Samuel B. GREENE[11], b. 19 June 1854; d. 15 Mar. 1892
Lucy M. GREENE[11], b. 29 June 1856
Florence Adelaide KNIGHT, b. 27 Feb. 1857, Naples ME; d. 28 Feb. 1939, Bridgton ME
CHILD OF Henry Eugene GREENE[11] & Florence Adelaide KNIGHT:
Harriet Frances GREENE[12], b. 21 Dec. 1880, unm. in 1944
Elizabeth GRAY[6] (Rachel Freeman[5], Edmund[4], Mercy Prence[3], Patience Brewster[2]), b. 6 Sept. 1734, Harwich <MD 13:149>
CHILDREN OF Ebenezer BANGS[7] (Ann Sears[6]) & Elizabeth GRAY: (9) <Harwich>
Thomas BANGS[8], bpt. 18 July 1756 <MD 10:133>
Sylvanus BANGS[8], bpt. 4 June 1760 <MD 12:52>
Susanna BANGS[8], bpt. 27 Mar. 1763 <MD 12:156>
Ebenezer BANGS[8], bpt. 31 Mar. 1765 <MD 12:252>
Sarah BANGS[8], bpt. 22 Oct. 1769 <MD 13:99>
Barnabas BANGS[8], bpt. 11 Aug. 1771 <MD 13:100>
Joshua BANGS[8], bpt. 21 Nov. 1773 <MD 13:101>
Elizabeth BANGS[8], bpt. 8 Sept. 1776 <MD 13:136>
Betsey BANGS[8], bpt. 21 Feb. 1779 <MD 13:137>
Mercy SNOW[5] (Micajah[4], Stephen[3], Constance Hopkins[2]), b. 26 Sept. 1713, Eastham <MD 9:11> (wf of Daniel Sears[6], Mercy Freeman[5]) (no issue shown)
Charity WHITTREDGE, b. 10 Oct. 170()* <Rochester VR 1:305>; d. aft. 26 Mar. 1741*<Sears Gen.:55>
CHILDREN OF Paul SEARS[6] (Mercy Freeman[5]) & Charity WHITTREDGE: (7) <2-6, Rochester VR>
Paul SEARS[7], b. 1722 or 1728 <Sears Gen.:81>
Marcy SEARS[7], b. 28 Apr. 1724 <VR 1:260>
William SEARS[7], b. 14 Jan. 1725 <VR 1:261>
Mary SEARS[7], b. 20 Apr. 1730 <VR 1:260>
Nathaniel SEARS[7], b. 1 Sept. 1738 <VR 1:260>
Elizabeth SEARS[7], b. 26 Mar. 1741 <VR 1:259>
Hannah SEARS[7], b. 6 Aug. 1731 <Sears Gen.:81>

CHILDREN OF Nathaniel SEARS & Elizabeth WINSLOW: (10) <Rochester VR>
Elizabeth SEARS, bpt. 28 July 1771 <VR 1:259>
Jesse SEARS, bpt. 28 July 1771 <VR 1:260>
Nathaniel SEARS, bpt. 28 July 1771 <VR 1:260>
Prince SEARS, bpt. 28 July 1771 <VR 1:261>
Silas SEARS, bpt. 28 July 1771 <VR 1:261>
Paul SEARS, bpt. 4 Apr. 1773 <VR 1:261>
Susanna SEARS, bpt. 4 June 1775 <VR 1:261>
Mary SEARS, bpt. 19 Aug. 1781 <VR 1:260>
John SEARS, bpt. 11 Sept. 1785 <VR 1:260>
Hannah CROWELL, b. 9 Sept. 1725; d. 22 June 1802, W. Brewster g.s.
CHILDREN OF Edmund SEARS^6 (Mercy Freeman^5) & Hannah CROWELL: (10) <Dennis, MD 6:93>
Edmund SEARS^7, b. 3 Jan. 1743/4; d. 16 Mar. 1832
Elizabeth SEARS^7, b. 16 Oct. 1745; d. 1819
Jane SEARS^7, b. 17 Nov. 1748; d. July 1799
Joshua SEARS^7, b. 21 July 1751; d. 1751
Joshua SEARS^7, b. 1 July 1753; d. 31 Mar. 1825
Christopher SEARS^7, b. 16 Aug. 1756; d. Feb. 1809
Elkanah SEARS^7, b. 21 Oct. 1758; d. 1 June 1836
Mercy SEARS^7, b. 7 Mar. 1761; d. 27 Jan. 1849
Temperance SEARS^7, b. 9 Aug. 1764
Hannah SEARS^7, b. 8 Dec. 1766

MICRO # 18 of 18

Mary DOANE, (dau of Jos.), b. 15 Nov. 1691, Eastham <MD 31:178>
CHILDREN OF Prence FREEMAN^5 (Tho.^{4}) & Mary DOANE: (10) <Harwich, MD 5:204>
Nathaniel FREEMAN^6, b. 9 Mar. 1712/3; d. 6 Sept. 1791, E. Hampton CT, Hog Hill g.s.**<135>**
Priscilla FREEMAN^6, b. 6 May 1714/5
Hatsel FREEMAN^6, b. 7 Mar. 1716/7, d. July 1739
Hannah FREEMAN^6, b. 31 May 1719
Mary FREEMAN^6, b. May 1721
Susanna FREEMAN^6, b. May 1723
Barnabas FREEMAN^6, b. 20 Feb. 1724/5
Keziah FREEMAN^6, b. middle of Oct. 1726
Moses FREEMAN^6, b. 11 Nov. 1730
Elizabeth FREEMAN^6, b. 15 Oct. 1733
CHILDREN OF Isaac SMITH & Mary FREEMAN^6: (5) <Chatham>**<136>**
Priscilla SMITH^7, b. 26 Nov. 1746 <MD 11:40>
Freeman SMITH^7, b. 1 Feb. 1748 <MD 11:40>
Azuba SMITH^7, b. 10 Aug. 1752 <MD 11:40>
Molly SMITH^7, b. 3 Dec. 1755 <MD 12:171>
Thankful SMITH^7, b. 29 Jan. 1759 <MD 12:171>
Martha BROWN, (dau of Sam. & Lydia (Fish)), b. 8 July 1720, Eastham <MD 16:70>; d. 31 Mar. 1801, Middle Haddam <Freeman Gen.:59; Doane Gen.:51>**<137>**
CHILDREN OF Nathaniel FREEMAN^6 (Prence^5) & Martha BROWN: (6) <Middletown CT VR 2:326>**<138>**
Silvanus FREEMAN^7, b. 16 Apr. 1740 <MD 7:99>
Martha FREEMAN^7, b. 22 July 1742; d. 9 Jan. 1819, Haddam Neck CT g.s. (photo)
Priscilla FREEMAN^7, b. 24 Sept. 1745
Lydia FREEMAN^7, b. 17 Oct. 1746
Hatsuld FREEMAN^7, b. 18 Dec. 1749; d. 1 Nov. 1774*
Dr. Nathaniel FREEMAN^7, b. 8 Nov. 1751; d. 31 Oct. 1799***<137>**

Leah BRAINERD, b. 12 Dec. 1740, Haddam Neck CT <Brainerd Gen.(1908) 1:2:45>

CHILDREN OF Silvanus FREEMAN[7] & Leah BRAINERD: (10) <Chatham CT, Brainerd Gen.(1908) 1:2:59>

Charity FREEMAN[8], bpt. 23 Sept. 1759

Lydia FREEMAN[8], bpt. 31 Aug. 1760

Leah FREEMAN[8], bpt. 4 Dec. 1763, d. 6 July 1766

Sylvanus FREEMAN[8], b. 29 May 1765

Thankful FREEMAN[8], b. 25 Apr. 1767

Martha FREEMAN[8], b. 25 Apr. 1767 (twins)

Leah FREEMAN[8], b. 26 Feb. 1769

Philena/Paulina FREEMAN[8], b. 24 Jan. 1771

Festus FREEMAN[8], b. 1778, drowned with brother Hatsell, 21 Sept. 1798, off Saybrook, boat upset

Hatsell FREEMAN[8], b. 1781, d. 21 Sept. 1798, drowned

CHILD OF Dr. Nathaniel FREEMAN[7] (Nath.[6]) & Olivia CORNWALL:

Annie FREEMAN[8], b. c1807, d. 4 July 1843, ae 50y2m24d (m. Stephen Brainerd)<Brainerd Gen.:2:1:78>

Jabez ARNOLD, b. c1738, d. 4 July 1822, Haddam Neck CT g.s. (photo)

CHILDREN OF Jabez ARNOLD & Martha FREEMAN[7] (Nath.[6]): (1 of 9)**<139>**

Gideon ARNOLD[8], b. c1769, d. 24 Aug. 1843, Haddam Neck CT g.s. (photo)

Lucy ( ) ARNOLD, d. 12 Aug. 1856, ae 79, Haddam Neck CT g.s. (photo)

CHILD OF Gideon ARNOLD[8] & Lucy ( ):

Mary Bowers ARNOLD[9], b. c1808, d. 28 Sept. 1883*, ae 75, Haddam Neck CT g.s. See <135>

Warren Sylvester WILLIAMS, b. c1819, d. 25 Sept. 1890*, ae 71, Haddam Neck CT g.s. See <135>

CHILDREN OF Warren Sylvester WILLIAMS & Mary Bowers ARNOLD[9]: (2) <Haddam CT Epitahs> See <135>

Titus WILLIAMS[10], b. c1843, d. 14 Sept. 1861, ae 18

Mary Gertrude WILLIAMS[10], b. c1846, d. 7 Feb. 1924, ae 78

John WING, b. c1688, d. 12 June 1758*, 78th yr, Brewster g.s.

Bethiah WINSLOW, (*dau of Kenelm), b. c1691, d. 19 June 1720*, ae 29

CHILDREN OF John WING & 1st Bethiah WINSLOW: (4) <Harwich, MD 6:55>

Mercy WING, b. 25 Dec. 1713

Bethiah WING, b. 22 Jan. 1715/6

Rebecca WING, b. 26 Mar. 1718

John WING, b. 8 June 1720

CHILDREN OF John WING & 2nd Rebecca (FREEMAN[5]*) Vicory (*Tho.[4]): (6) <1-5, Harwich, MD 6:55>

Hannah WING[6], b. 7 May 1724

Thankful WING[6], b. 20 Aug. 1725

Phebe WING[6], b. 20 Jan. 1726/7

Joseph WING[6], b. 21 Aug. 1728

David WING[6], b. 10 Aug. 1732

Thomas WING[6]*, b. ( ) <Wing Gen.:79>

David FOSTER[7] (*Phebe Wing[6]), b. c1758, d. 3 Jan. 1821, 63rd yr, Williamstown MA g.s. <Bible>

Susanna ( ) FOSTER, b. c1758, d. 20 Apr. 1829*, ae 71 <Bible>

CHILDREN OF David FOSTER[7] & Susanna ( ): (9) <2-9, Williamstown VR:38>**<140>**

David FOSTER[8], b. 18 June 1784; d. 30 Oct. 1860, dropsy, Williamstown MA <Mass.VR 138:63**<141>**>

Nathaniel FOSTER[8], b. 2 June 1786

John FOSTER[8], b. 2 June 1786 (twins), d. 24 Aug. 1786

John FOSTER[8], b. 19 Mar. 1788

Eli FOSTER[8], b. 6 Feb. 1790

Charlotte FOSTER[8], b. 9 May 1792

Dorcas FOSTER[8], b. 22 Oct. 1795

Susanna FOSTER[8], b. 7 Nov. 1797

Lydia FOSTER[8], b. 6 Mar. 1800

Polly TREADWELL, b. 22 May 1786; d. 15 July 1841
CHILDREN OF David FOSTER^{8} & Polly TREADWELL: (11)
Phebe FOSTER^{9}, b. 25 Feb. 1805
Clarissa FOSTER^{9}, b. 9 Sept. 1807
Luna FOSTER^{9}, b. 14 Dec. 1810
Charlotte FOSTER^{9}, b. 9 May 1812, d. 26 Nov. 1817
David FOSTER^{9}, b. 26 June 1815
John A. FOSTER^{9}, b. 10 July 1817
Joshua FOSTER^{9}, b. 17 July 1819, d. 1 Apr. 1820
John FOSTER^{9}, b. 17 July 1819 (twins), d. 5 Apr. 1820
Angeline Burlingame FOSTER^{9}, b. 28 Aug. 1821
Samuel D. FOSTER^{9}, b. 9 Jan. 1825
Caroline R. FOSTER^{9}, b. 27 Sept. 1831
Bathsheba MAYO^{5} (Nath.^{4}, Hannah Prence^{3}, Patience Brewster^{2}), b. 23 Sept. 1683, Eastham<MD 4:32>; d. 9 Jan. 1706, Eastham <MD 4:33> (1st wf of Tho. Freeman$^{5-4}$) (d. 5 mths after marriage)
Mary SMITH, b. 24 May 1685 <Smith Fam.Rcd.>
CHILDREN OF Thomas FREEMAN^{5} (Tho.^{4}) & 2nd Mary SMITH: (4) <Harwich>
Thomas FREEMAN^{6}, b. 13 Sept. 1708 <MD 5:86>; d. 19 July 1766, Harwich <MD 24:111>
James FREEMAN^{6}, b. 9 Oct. 1710 <MD 5:86>
Bathsheba FREEMAN^{6}, b. 22 Mar. 1713 <MD 5:87>
Samuel FREEMAN^{6}, b. 8 Aug. 1715 <MD 5:87>
CHILDREN OF Thomas FREEMAN^{6} & Dorothy COLE: (7) <2-7, Harwich, MD 19:57>
Thomas FREEMAN^{7}, b. 26 Apr. 1731, Cape Cod <MD 19:57>
James FREEMAN^{7}, b. 23 June 1734
Isaac FREEMAN^{7}, b. 12 Feb. 1736/7
Sarah FREEMAN^{7}, b. 23 Nov. 1739; d. 23 Feb. 1753 <MD 24:111>
Marah FREEMAN^{7}, b. 9 Apr. 1742
Obed FREEMAN^{7}, b. 27 Nov. 1744; d. 19 Jan. 1754 <MD 24:111>
Timothy FREEMAN^{7}, b. 4 May 1747
Lydia SPARROW^{3} (Jonahan^{2}, Richard^{1}), d. aft. 16 Mar. 1708/9 <MD 14:4>
CHILDREN OF William FREEMAN^{4} (Mercy Prence^{3}) & Lydia SPARROW: (2) <MD 5:144,145>
William FREEMAN^{5}, b. c1685, d. 13 Mar. 1772, 87th yr, Orleans g.s. <MD 12:60>
Lydia FREEMAN^{5}, b. pre 1687, <MD 12:60>
Richard GODFREE, (son of George), b. 11 June 1677, Eastham <MD 4:30>
CHILDREN OF Richard GODFREE & Lydia FREEMAN^{5}: (6) <Harwich, MD 3:175>
Hannah GODFREE^{6}, b. 26 Jan. ( )
Elizabeth GODFREE^{6}, b. 20 Dec. 1704
Mary GODFREE^{6}, b. 23 Aug. 170()
Lydia GODFREE^{6}, b. 27 July 170()
Phebe GODFREE^{6}, b. 24 June 17( )
Rebecca GODFREE^{6}, b. 7 July 1709
Mercy PEPPER, (dau of Isaac), b. 7 Aug. 1690, Eastham <MD 5:196>; d. 9 Oct. 1769, Orleans g.s.
CHILDREN OF William FREEMAN^{5} (Wm.^{4}) & Mercy PEPPER: (10) <1-9, Harwich, MD 5:88>
Mercy FREEMAN^{6}, b. 6 Mar. 1712/3, d. 11 May 1713
William FREEMAN^{6}, b. 12 May 1715
Daniel FREEMAN^{6}, b. 30 Dec. 1717
Mercy FREEMAN^{6}, b. 19 Feb. 1719/20
Apphia FREEMAN^{6}, b. 21 Mar. 1721/2
Isaac FREEMAN^{6}, b. 22 Dec. 1724
Lydia FREEMAN^{6}, b. 7 Feb. 1730/1; d. 11 Oct. 1757

Solomon FREEMAN[6], b. 30 Jan. 1732/3

Simeon FREEMAN[6], b. 28 Sept. 1735; d. 1798*?

Jonathan FREEMAN[6]*?, b. 3 Aug. 1738* <Freeman Gen.:67>

Edmund FREEMAN, (son of Edmund), d. pre 5 Jan. 1703/4 (adm.)

CHILDREN OF Edmund FREEMAN & 1st Rebecca PRENCE[3]: (2)

Patience FREEMAN[4], b. c1647; d. 16 Apr. 1738

Rebecca FREEMAN[4], b. c1650; d. aft. 9 June 1705*

CHILDREN OF Edmund FREEMAN & 2nd Margaret PERRY: (6) <Sandwich>

Margaret FREEMAN, b. 2 Oct. 1652 <MD 14:69>

Edmund FREEMAN, b. 5 Oct. 1655 <MD 14:109>

Alice FREEMAN, b. 29 Mar. 1658 <MD 14:109>

Rachel FREEMAN, b. 4 Sept. 1659 <MD 14:110>

Sarah FREEMAN, b. 6 Feb. 1662 <MD 14:110>

Deborah FREEMAN, b. 9 Aug. 1665 <MD 14:110>

Joseph BURGE, d. Aug. 1695

CHILDREN OF Joseph BURGE & Patience FREEMAN[4] (Rebecca Prence[3]): (5) <1-4, Sandwich, MD 14:171>

Rebecca BURGE[5], b. 17 Jan. 1667

Dorothy BURGE[5], b. 12 Nov. 1670

Joseph BURGE[5], b. 18 Nov. 1673; d. pre 5 Aug. 1695*

Benjamin BURGE[5], b. 5 May 1681

Ichabod BURGE[5], b.( )

Ezra PERRY, (son of Ezra), b. 11 Feb. 1652, Sandwich <MD 14:171>

CHILDREN OF Ezra PERRY & Rebecca FREEMAN[4] (Rebecca Prence[3]): (9) <Sandwich, MD 30:64>

Ebenezer PERRY[5], b. 18 Nov. 1673 <MD 14:110>

Mary PERRY[5], b. 21 Dec. 1675 <MD 14:110>

Ezra PERRY[5], b. 2 Feb. 1679

Hannah PERRY[5], b. 10 Sept. 1681

Edmund PERRY[5], b. 20 Oct. 1683

Freelove PERRY[5], b. 28 Nov. 1685 (dau)

Samuel PERRY[5], b. 20 Mar. 1688

Rebecca PERRY[5], b. 2 Oct. 1689

Patience PERRY[5], b. 2 Feb. 1691/2

* * * * *

FOOTNOTES

<1> p.175, NEHGR 124:150 states that William Brewster was very possibly the son of William & Mary (Smythe). His date of birth has not been found, but it is believed to be c1566<NEHGR 18:18>.
<2> p.175, A great deal has been written about the identity of Mary and although many possibilities have shown up in print none have been verified. See Plymouth Colony, 1620-1691 by Eugene Stratton (1986), p.250 for discussion.
<3> p.177, Jonathan's will, dated 14 Mar. 1748 mentions eight children, viz: Peleg, Jonah, Hannah Barker, Mary (wf of Jeremiah Bingham), Jerusha (wf of Zebulon Rudd), Sarah Holmes, Elijah (b. 12 Mar. 1731) and Jonathan (b. 5 May 1737).
<4> p.178, Ann (Addis) Darte, bpt. 17 Mar. 1628, Frampton on Severne, Gloucestershire, Eng. <TAG 57:183>.
<5> p.178, The children of Benjamin Payne and Mary Brewster are shown in his will dated 11 Jan. 1755, viz: Benjamin (eldest son), 3 sons under age - Stephen, Daniel and Seth, and daughters - Mary, Lydia, Hannah and Sarah. <Windham Prob.#2879>
<6> p.181, Here we have an interesting story for its time. Christopher's wife Mary died 13 July 1676, ae 55. At the County Court of New London CT, 16 Sept. 1673, Elizabeth "Brawly" widow, was found guilty of committing fornication with Christopher Christophers, "which sin of hers is highly aggravated as being the second of y[t] nature with the same party who is a married man. This Court having seriously considered the haniousness of the offence and alsoe considering her present condition being neare the time of delivery, whereby shee is incaple of undergoing such punishment as the haniousness of the transgression may deserve, doe adjudg her to pay five pound fine and to weare a papour on her hatt on some publique day where on shall be written in capitall letters, Let the punishment of my whore dome be a warning to others; or else to pay fifteene pound fyne..." Elizabeth chose to pay the fifteen pounds. <New London CT Court Records 3:63> Despite this fact, the Brewsters recorded the birth of John Christophers as the son of Christopher

Christopher and his wife Elizabeth. <Brewster Book, MD 1:77>
<7> p.182, No dates accompany the names of the seven Christophers children, viz: Joseph (b. 14 July 1692), Mary, Jonathan (dy), Grace, Lydia, Ruth and Joanna.
<8> p.182, This list is derived from a ten page list containing births from the New London CT VR. Although I have arranged them under families, I have not attempted to show line of descent as most of these families will turn up later.
<9> p.183, Charles Hill had remarried, 12 June 1678 to Rachel Mason, dau of John.
<10> p.185, The entire page is written faintly in pencil, with these two names too faint to make out. The first, a daughter, could read Mary, with the second possibly being Deborah.
<11> p.186, A later note states Hawkins Turner married Lucy Starr, b. 18 July 1708 & d. 16 Mar. 1809, ae 100 yrs. Nine children are listed without dates, viz: Lucretia, Dorothy, Hawkins, Starr, Lucy, Grace, Betty, Catharine and Molly. <Source - A History of the Starr Family of New England, From the Ancestor, Dr. Comfort Starr, of Ashford, County of Kent, England, Who Emigrated to Boston Mass. in 1635. Hartford CT. 1879. p.43>
<12> p.187, No dates accompany the names of the four Turner children (poss. b. Hull), viz: Elisha, Lucy A., Eliza and Adeline W.
<13> p.187, No children are listed here for Grace Dwelly who divorced her 1st husband Jesse Turner^{5} (Jonathan^{4}, Mary Brewster^{3}, Jonathan^{2}). She married 2nd husband Joseph Church^{5} (Nathaniel$^{4-3}$, Eliz. Warren^{2}) in 1742. See the Warren family for her children.
<14> p.187, You have to give John Turner credit for refusing to act his age! He married his 2nd wife when he was 76 yrs old and fathered four children, the last when he was 83. Tongues must have wagged when his 1st child was born only three months after his marriage!
<15> p.188, Both John's will and The Dillingham Family of New England (typewritten mss. compiled by Winthrop Alexander, 1923) name his nine children, viz: Lydia (wf of Jos. Reccord), Elisha (of Smithfield RI), Elizabeth (wf of Joshua Simmons), Jael (wf of Jonathan Peterson), John (dec'd of NY), Mary Stertevant, Henry, and Princess (wf of Nehemiah Peterson of Duxbury). The Dillingham Family lists a son Jeremiah who is not mentioned in John's will

The above family history also gives a lineage for John Dillingham^{4}: John^{4}, b. c1695, Sandwich; John^{3}, b. 1656 or 58, (married ? Lydia Hatch); Henry^{2}, bpt. 1624, d. 1705, Sandwich (married Hannah Perry, 1652); Edward^{1} of Sandwich.
<15a>p.189, The Records of the Second Church of Scituate (Norwell) are printed in Mayflower Source Records, by Gary Boyd Roberts, pp.312-430.
<16> p.189, Elizabeth Prouty had an illegitimate child, Eleanor Prouty in 1730. She is called deceased at Eleanor's baptism, 20 June 1731, Norwell Ch <NEHGR 59:78>. Eleanor d. 20 Apr. 1766, the wf of Samuel Curtis.
<17> p.190, Four Clapp children are listed without dates, viz: Michael T., James S., Eunice and Sarah. <Clapp Memorial:167>
<18> p.190, This birth is crossed out.
<19> p.190, His unnamed widow died 8 Nov. 1831, ae 81. <Norwell ChR:9>
<20> p.190, There appears to be some question as to the parentage of this Thomas Silvester. The marriage records call him "Jr." and his son is called Thomas Silvester "3d".
<21> p.191, The eight Smith children are listed without additional data, (b. Lyme), viz: Asa, Clement, Amos, Russell, Elizabeth, Grace, Lucy and Olive.
<22> p.192, Ezekiel Turner's 1st marriage to Theoda Williams in 1723 produced no known children.
<23> p.193, The Coit Genealogy:49 calls her Elizabeth Ely, dau of David.
<24> p.193, This same David Coit is also given an entirely different list of children, taken from the Coit Gen.:98. On a following page reads "He is supposed to have married Betsy Calkins, 28 Apr. 1797" - this statement is crossed out and there are faint scribbles thru the following six children, viz: Charlotte, b. 22 May 1798; John Calkins, b. 27 July 1799; David Gardiner, b. 28 Dec. 1800; Betsey, b. 28 Oct. 1802; Julia, b. 4 Mar. 1805, d. 8 Dec. 1805; and Julia, b. 22 Apr. 1808, d. 5 Oct. 1808.
<25> p.194, Bowman questions whether or not she was Lydia, the dau of John & Abigail Turner who was b. 5 July 1699.
<26> p.194, The names are so faint the following are an educated guess from the visible letters viz: (?), b. 6 Jan. 1712/3; Samuel, bpt. 9 July 1716; John, bpt. 2 Dec. 1718 and Abigail, bpt. 21 Jan. (July?) 1723. <Scituate VR 1:59>
<27> p.194, Descendants of Walter Woodworth of Scituate Mass., by William A. Woodworth, White Plains NY 1898.
<28> p.194, (Ibed.,:12) Because of the way the names are numbered, it is not clear whether the list names all of Samuel's childen, or if some of those listed are his childrens' children. Refer to the above Woodworth Descendants.
<29> p.194, Six of the Turner children were baptized 20 Dec. 1751, prob. Scituate, at "the house of their father who was sick...Jemima upon her desire", viz: Jemima, Consider, John, Joseph, Ruth and Vine. Deborah was baptized 21 June 1752.
<30> p.195, She is shown as the 2nd wife of Polycarpus Jacobs. He is called Charles Jacobs in Nantucket VR 3:306, 4:86, with no marriage date given.
<31> p.196, See <13>
<32> p.196, The names and dates are written very faintly in pencil and are difficult to read; therefore the data has been verified from the Norwell ChR, printed in Mayflower Source Records. The page numbers, in order of baptisms, are: 356,360,363,364,368,370,373,376 and 382. Data from these pages is also included in the text in brackets.
<33> p.196, Jemima, dau of Thomas & Jemima Farrow, bpt. Norwell Ch., Scituate <Mayflower Source Records:389>
<34> p.196, Bathsheba, dau of Rev. Peter & Rebecca Hobart <MD 19:187-190>.
<35> p.199, Stetson is spelled "Sturtson" in the records <Mayflower Source Records:324>.

<36> p.199, She is called Sally Jones Turner in the birth records, but Sally James Turner in the marriage records.
<37> p.199, She is called Mercy James Turner in the marriage records.
<38> p.200, The baptisms can be found in the Norwell ChR, printed in Mayflower Source Records, pp.(in order): 368,373,379,381,383 and 390. Data from these pages is also included in the text in brackets.
<39> p.201, d. 30 May 1734 <Scituate VR>
<40> p.201, The baptisms can be found in the Norwell ChR, printed in Mayflower Source Records, pp.(in order): 366,366,370,373,375,379 and 384.
<41> p.202, Nine children are listed between the years 1771-1790 but the writing is too faint to hazard a guess as to the names and dates. On the preceeding pages the names of eight Barrell children are shown, viz: Susanna, Jennet, William, Samuel, Elijah, Azor, Charles & Paschal.
<42> p.202, The eleven children and dates of birth are too faint to determine. The five names included here are taken from proceeding pages.
<43> p.202, The children of Joseph Prince are named in his will, viz: Sarah "Province", Joseph, Isaac, Caleb, James, Mary (wf of Joseph Ballard), Elizabeth and Abigail.

He is said to have married Mary Townsend in the files. His will mentions his wife Mary and "former wife Mary", so it is not clear if Mary Townsend was the mother.
<44> p.202, He is possibly the husband of Sarah Prince[6], mentioned in her father's will as Sarah Province (see <43>). The will of John Province of Boston mentions wife Sarah and children Sarah (wf of John Larain of Annapolis Royal, NS), and Elizabeth (wf of Samuel Dexter of Albany NY).
<45> p.202, If the dates are correct, Mary died six weeks after her marriage to Nathaniel Dill (29 Dec. 1743). He died 10 Aug. 1749 <Gould Gen.:338>.
<46> p.203, No dates accompany the pencilled names of the remaining four Loud children, viz: Charles, John, Olive and Susan. <Loud Family>
<47> p.204, Seven additional children are named in the will of Nehemiah Joy, viz: Benjamin, Turner, Caleb, Jesse, Nehemiah, Sarah and Olive.
<48> p.204, He is called Esau <u>Cloud</u> in the Hanover ChR.
<49> p.204, The will of William Loud also mentions his married daughters, Polly White, Lucy Penniman & Naomi Hobart <Norfolk Co.Prob.#11934, 18:295>.
<50> p.205, Although her parents were married in Oct. 1701, a check of MD 9:24 shows her birth was indeed recorded as June 1701.
<51> p.205, No dates accompany the remaining three pencilled Prince children, viz: Ruth, Lydia (d.y.) and John.
<52> p.206, The accompanying note reads "See Stetson Fam:68 for 11 children".
<53> p.207, Death Certificate, City of Boston #2854. It also states he died of "scirrhus of prostrate gland" and was buried at "141 South Ground".
<54> p.207, An excerpt from a manuscript family record is included, which appears to be recollections by the wife of Joseph Lawrence Drew[8] on her husband's family. She states Sarah Lawrence was the daughter of Samuel Lawrence & Mary Dawes, b. 26 Jan. 1777, Boston, d. 3 Dec. 1833, Covington, near New Orleans.

The following excerpt gives a little personal data on Sukey (Drew) Ford: "Sukey got her mother's gold beads because she staid home the longest. She was about thirty when she married a Mr. Ford. He was a widower and quite well off. He had a child, a boy I think, when he married Sukey."
<55> p.207, Mass. Death Certificate 339:105, #2789. It also states he died of "paralysis-apoplexy" and he resided at 159 K. Street, Boston.
<56> p.207, He is shown to be an 8th generation descendant of Brewster. His entry here seems misplaced and out of order.
<57> p.207, The children of Charles Hill and Abigail Fox are listed in the division of his estate, 5 Apr. 1720, viz: Charles (only son), Hannah (eldest dau.) and Abigail (youngest dau.).
<58> p.207, The children of Jonathan Hill & Mary Sharswood are listed in the division of his estate, 9 Jan. 1727/8, viz: Charles (eldest son), Jane (eldest dau.), Mary, George, John and Ruth.
<59> p.208, The will of Daniel Shapley lists 8 children, viz: John, Daniel, Joseph, Benjamin, Adam, Mary, Abigail and Ruth.
<60> p.208, The inventory of Benjamin Shapley's[5] estate was taken 11 Feb. 1713/4. His two sons, aged 11 and 9 are the only children named.
<61> p.208, The will of John Morgan mentions "two children of my daughter Ruth Brewster, dec'd" and the following seven children, viz: John, Mary, Sarah, Hannah, Rachel, Martha and Elizabeth.
<62> p.208, The will of Thomas Fosdick mentions wife Grace and six children, viz: Thomas, Katharine, Sarah, Clement, Samuel and Grace. In 1779, wife Grace was the wife of Ezekiel Fox, and by 1791 son Samuel had died and daughter Grace is called Grace Beebe.
<63> p.208, The will of Moses Noyes mentions wife Hannah and children, viz: Calvin, Moses, Eliakim, Esther (widow of Elias Miner & her 3 sons, Joseph , Benjamin & Selden), Hannah (wf of Seth Stoddard), "Mendwell"(?), Elizabeth (wf of Abraham Avery) and Eunice.
<64> p.208, The will of John Noyes mentions wife Mary and "my child if Providence of God shall continue its life".
<65> p.208, The will of James Wadsworth mentions eldest son James, daughter Ruth "Atwater" and youngest son John Noyes (& his sons, John Noyes, William and James).
<66> p.209, Sarah Collier's name is not mentioned in the files but has been added here. She was baptized 30 Apr. 1616, Southwark, Surrey, Eng. and died 26 Apr. 1691, Plymouth, wife of 2nd husband Richard Parke. <Plymouth 1st ChR 3:22, MD 3:192>
<67> p.209, Sarah Brewster, b. c1635, d. betw. 5 Mar. 1668 - 21 Jan. 1678/9, probably Duxbury.

<PCR 4:80>. She married Benjamin Bartlett^{3} (Mary Warren^{2}). See Warren family.
<68> p.209, The will of Abigail Brewster mentions five children, viz: Elizabeth, Rebecca, Royal/Ariel, Joseph and John.
<69> p.209, Capt. John Burgess Jr., b. 26 Mar. 1785, d. 4 May 1850, Plymouth g.s. Mrs. "Susanner" Burgess, wife of Capt. John, d. 20 Dec. 1819, ae 33y5m, 10 days after the birth of her 5th child. The inscription on her tombstone is quite touching, it reads:

"Thou lovely chief of all my joys,
Thou sov'reign of my heart.
How could I bear to hear thy voice
Pronounce the sound depart!"

<Burial Hill, by Benjamin Drew:279>
<70> p.210, A second wife (d. 1776) and third wife are written too faintly in pencil to read. The third child could read Benjamin but the 4th child is too faint.
<71> p.211, The grave stone inscription gives his year of death as 1761, ae 72y4m28d, not 1767. <Mayflower Source Records:236>
<72> p.212, Eleven children are listed but the majority of the names (no dates) are too faint to read. Giles Mem.:188 is written across this page.
<73> p.213, b. 18 Nov. 1731 <Kingston VR>. Her Duxbury g.s. gives her age at death as 50th yr.
<74> p.213, She is called Althea Joice, widow in the Marshfield VR 2:66 where their marriage is recorded, 14 Oct. 1782.
<75> p.213, Eight Dingley children are listed, only two with dates, viz: William (b. 1776), Jeremiah (b. 14 Jan. 1779, Cape Elizabeth), Abigail, Polly, Lucy, Esther, Sarah and Susanna <Maine Hist.Gen.Recorder 2:123>.
<76> p.213, The four remaining Bearse children are listed without dates, all born Halifax except Lydia, viz: Ursala, Job, Polly & Lydia (b. Shepardsville Planation, Hebron ME).
<77> p.214, d. 20 Dec. 1810 <Kingston VR>
<78> p.214, Is he the Thomas Brewster who died 10 Aug. 1815, ae 85, Kingston g.s.? <MD 7:24>
<79> p.214, A Hannah Brewster, dau of Wrestling and Hannah, d. 2 Sept. 1743, ae 10y10m2d, Kingston g.s. <MD 7:24>
<80> p.214, d. 11 Feb. 1825 <Kingston VR>
<81> p.215, Jonathan Sparrow, b. 9 July 1665, d. 9 Mar. 1739/40, Eastham "sixth child of Capt. Jonathan Sparrow by his second wife Hannah..." <Mayflower Source Records:436>
<82> p.215, The remaining 7 children of Richard Sparrow & Mercy Cob can be found in the Eastham VR, MD 7:19, viz: Richard, b. 10 Nov. 1702; Rebecca, b. 12 Oct. 1704; Mercy, b. 6 Dec. 1706; Sarah, b. 20 July 1708; Hannah, b. 12 Oct. 1711; Elizabeth, b. 18 Apr. 1717; Mary, b. 10 Mar. 1718/19.
<83> p.216, History of Middlesex Co., Conn. 1884. NY (p.213).
<84> p.219, Family Records. The passport of Joseph Arey, 1811, describes his appearance - 6 ft dark complexion, brown hair, blue eyes with a scar on left thigh.
<85> p.219, A complete list of children is given within on the previous page.
<86> p.219, She is possibly the Mary Libby who d. 18 Feb. 1850, ae 73y9m, b. Hampden ME, dau of Nathaniel Myrick <Mass.VR 50:12>.
<87> p.220, The remaining eight Godfrey children are listed without dates, viz: Hannah, Mercy, Thomas, Lydia, Jephtha L., Mehitable, Anna and Barbara.
<88> p.220, "...my late Husband Thomas Gould late of Eastham went a voyage to sea two years ago and the vessels nor any of the ships company being two hundred in number have not been hear of since...", 26 Aug. 1791. <Barnstable Co.Prob.27:192>
<89> p.220, Her line of descent is later shown thus: Ruth Higgins^{6} (Sylvanus^{5}, Sam.^{4}, Jonathan$^{3-2}$, Richard^{1}). The only source listed for a possible 3rd marriage to Nathaniel Gould is the Gould Genealogy (Lynn, 1895) which states Ruth was 58 yrs. old when she marr. Nathaniel in 1830 and bore him three children. See <91> for questions regarding her identification.
<90> p.221, Five children are listed for Nathaniel Gould and Hannah K. Crosby with no dates,viz: Joshua, Nathaniel, Sarah, Nancy and Theresa.
<91> p.221, There appear to be two Ruth Higgins with the files assuming they are both the same person as they are both attributed to marrying the same three men. First we have Ruth, b. 18 Feb. 1772, Orleans, dau of Sylvanus & Abigail <MD 33:83>. Then there is Ruth, bpt. 29 May 1774, Orleans, dau of Gideon & Ruth <MD 10:231>. The records clearly show two seperate families, each having a daughter Ruth. I had thought a clue to the parentage of this particular Ruth might be found in the names of her children, hoping she had named a son after her father. No such luck! Two of her sons are named Sylvanus Higgins Smith and Gideon Smith!
<92> p.222, A handwritten page with no source listed contains the following information. Hannah Covel, dau of Joseph Covel & Hannah Bassett (dau of Nathaniel & Hannah Bassett), m. Asa Mayo^{7} Jr., who d. 15 June 1775. They were the parents of Sarah Mayo (b. 3 Apr. 1765, d. 27 Aug. 1843). Joseph Covel, husband of Hannah Bassett, died soon after their marriage. Several years later (1756) Hannah (Bassett) Covel married Asa Mayo^{6} as his 2nd wife. Asa Mayo^{6} d. 1 Jan. 1780.
<93> p.222, Elizabeth Higgins^{4} (Hannah Rogers^{3}, Jos.^{2}) b. 11 Feb. 1680/1, Eastham. Her husband *Thomas Mayo d. July 1769, Eastham* <MF5G 2:187>.
<94> p.222, Elizabeth Rogers d. 10 May 1772, Eastham <MF5G 2:187>.
<95> p.223, John Jenkins, son of John & Mary, b. 13 Nov. 1659, Barnstable <MD 6:236>.
<96> p.223, MD 6:15
<97> p.224, Tabitha's year of birth in MD 33:81 is given as 1787, however this clearly seems to be an error and is also questioned by Bowman. Her entry follows that of Rebecca b. in 1779.
<98> p.225, d. 4 Jan. 1760, Orleans g.s. <Mayflower Source Rcds.:438>
<99> p.225, The journal of her husband, John Paine, says she died 13 May 1716 <MD 9:138>.
<100> p.225, Descendants of this family will find interesting reading in "Deacon John Paine's

Journal", printed in Vols.8 & 9 of the Mayflower Descendant (MD). (See the reference list at the end of the Brewster Family).

The following excerpt from the journal was written by John after the death of his wife: "On the 13th day of May 1716 My dearly beloved wife Bennet departed this life being five and fourty years two months five and twenty dayes old, being great with child and within two weeks of the time of her travel...She was indeed the desire of my Eyes and the Joy of my heart, a most profitable and pleasant companion, a most loving and obedient wife, a tender and compationate mother, a kind mistress, a curtious neighbour and steady and fast friend but above all and that which Crowned all she was a good christian..."

<101> p.225, John Paine writes of his son's death in his journal, "...a most lovly & pleasant child of about 2 yrs & 8 mth old...I hope in heaven my precious Babe is blest and that with Jesus he is now at rest." <MD 9:139>

<102> p.225, The probate records of Thomas Gross name wife Jane/Joan, so Experience was deceased by this date. Thomas & Experience's four minor children were put in the care of Sarah Freeman.

<103> p.226, He is shown as the son of Ebenezer Freeman[5] & Abigail Young but is not included in the list of their children. His year of birth casts doubt as to his belonging to this family.

<104> p.226, Lois Paine, b. 29 Sept. 1705, Eastham, dau of Nicholas Paine & Hannah Higgins <MD 4:33>. She died pre Sept. 1729 when Edmund remarried (probably after birth of dau. Lois, 1726).

<105> p.227, Lois Freeman had an illegitimate son, Philip Young, b. 5 Mar. 1744, Eastham, no father named. <MD 24:138>

<106> p.229, A pencilled footnote from the Brunswick ME VR 1:370 states Isaac Hinkley was killed by Indians. This would have taken place between 1750 and Nov. 1757.

<107> p.229, The remaining four Thompson children are listed without dates, viz: Joseph, John, Cornelius and Margaret.

<108> p.229, The remaining eight Lord children are listed without dates, viz: Mehitable Scammon, Daniel Walker, Louise Walker, Phebe, Nathaniel, Betsey Watts, Susan & Lucy Jane (d.y.).

<109> p.230 , George Ernest Bowman, the compiler of The Bowman Files.

<110> p.232, Maine Hist. & Gen. Recorder 9:135 states Deacon Samuel Hinckley's "oldest son" (?) Seth was killed by Indians, no date.

<111> p.233, The remaining eight Hinckley children are listed without dates, viz: Thomas, Mercy, Nicholas, Ebenezer, Clark, Levi, Mehitable and Mary.

<112> p.234, Family Bible (printed 1816) belonging to Miss Katharine Ellen Couch of Hallowell ME, 1907.

<113> p.234, (Ibed.,) Is this Mary (Hinckley) Norcross who married Daniel Norcross in 1814?

<114> p.235, Joshua Gray and wife Mary do not appear to have had children. His will mentions several nephews and sister Mary.

<115> p.235, The Barrington, Nova Scotia records state the Doane family moved from New England to Nova Scotia in 1761. The records also state all the children but Prince were living in Mar. 1832. "Signed by Samuel O. Doane, Town Clerk". (One of the children.)

<116> p.237, The identification of Rebecca Young's husband appears to be incorrect. The Zaccheus Higgins shown here is shown to be the son of Benjamin Higgins & Sarah Freeman[5], while their son Zaccheus has already been accounted for with two marriages (same page as Young marriage.) Careful examination of the files shows Rebecca Young's husband is possibly Solomon Higgins[6], brother of Zaccheus.

<117> p.238, Later in the files are four copies of a typed sheet listing the children of Timothy Higgins and two of his sons. Two of these sheets list Reliance as "Reliance (Hopkins) Yates, while the other two copies have the name Reliance striken out with the name "Alliance" inserted.

<118> p.241, A note from Higgins Gen.:87 states this family moved to Dutchess Co. NY

<119> p.241, An accompanying note states Joshua Sears and Rebecca Mayo had twelve children and moved to Middletown CT, 1746. <Sears Gen.:83,84>

<120> p.241, An accompanying note from A Mayo Genealogy, mss., by Charles E. Mayo states Thomas Mayo "was imprisoned for a time on board the noted prison ship 'Jersey' at New York. Was discharged sick and died on his way home at Newport RI".

<121> p.241, The eleven Mayo children are listed without dates, viz: Phebe, Moses, Mary, Hannah, Issacher, Elkanah, Edmund, Phebe, Watson, Katherine and Benjamin.

<122> p.242, The Files contain a copy of a record from the Probate Court, Elk River, Sherburne co., Minn. It is dated 23 Dec. 1911 and shows that Reuben Mayo's remaining eight children were still alive on this date. The names of the eight are given here to note the married names of the daughters and slight variations in first names, viz: Emily A. McClellan, Hannah M. Tibbetts, Sarah T. Thomas, Reuben M. Mayo, Mercy Ellen Heath, Fannie Heath, Viola Wedgewood and Frederick G. Mayo.

<123> p.244, Benjamin and Sarah were married 15 Mar. 1738/9, one year after the birth of their 1st child Mary, 23 Mar. 1737. They made a publick confession, 8 Apr. 1739 <MD 7:98>

<124> p.244, Mary Freeman's date of death is given as 20 Feb. 1789*, Harwich g.s. with her will dated 29 Sept. 1787. She is called a single woman and mentions only nieces and nephews in her will (viz: Mary & Barnabas Atwood, Watson Freeman). Bowman attributes a marriage to James Crosby, 27 Oct. 1787, with no issue.

<125> p.245, Judah Berry's will mentions three additional children, viz: Experience Bangs (deceased), Sarah Hinckley and Aznba Crosby. This accounts for nine of his ten children.

<126> p.246, The remaining six Berry children were baptized the same day, 29 July 1786, viz: Barns, Rebecca, Mehitable, Willis Scotto, Hannah Watson and Joshua. <MD 13:140> (See p.255 for additional data on Olive Berry[8]).

<127> p.246, The Family of Zaccheus Gould of Topsfield, by Genjamin Apthorp Gould. 1895.Lynn.

<128> p.247, It is not clear if these two children are by his wife Mercy Winslow or a second wife, Mary. These two are called the children of Chillingworth & "Mary", however, the names Mary

and Mercy were sometimes interchanged. The nine year span between these two sets of children does suggest a second marriage.
<129> p.249, Her father's will (1787) mentions her son Benjamin Myrick.
<130> p.253, From a Family Sampler (stitched by the Betsy Freeman in sampler), owned in 1910 by Miss Phebe Elizabeth Freeman, daughter of Calvin N. (in sampler), of Provincetown MA.
<131> p.255, She is called the widow of Elijah Bailey with an added note stating she was the widow of Thomas Snow. See p.246 for her Mayflower descent.
<132> p.255, Two Freeman children are listed too faintly in pencil to read (before Jerusha), Their baptism dates are 4 June 1732 and 3 July 1737.
<133> p.255, She is possibly Mercy Freeman^{6} who is called Mary Perry in her father's will.
<134> p.256, This chart states Gideon Higgins possibly married Ruth Bangs^{7}, the source appears to be the Higgins Gen.:172,173. Also cited are MD 27:108 giving the marriage of Gideon Higgins & "Ruth Burges", 28 Jan. 1760 and the Bangs Gen.:35 with the marriage of Gideon Higgins & Mehitable Bangs (dau of James & Bethiah (Wing)), 18 Apr. 1760.

Four additional children are added uncertainly in pencil (from Higgins Gen.?),viz: Josiah, Jerusha, and Azubah. The fourth name is very faint but could read "Aquila", b. 24 Oct. 1767.
<135> p.258, East Hamton CT Epitahs, by Lucius B. Barber, 1931 (mss., no paging).
<136> p.258, Mary Freeman^{6} had an illegitimate child, James Freeman^{7}, bpt. 8 June 1740, Brewster <MD 7:99>, the father being James Freeman^{6} (Tho$^{5-4}$, Mercy Prence^{3}, Patience Brewster^{2}).
<137> p.258, See <135>.
<138> p.258, A letter from the Historian-General of the General Society of Mayflower Descendants, 1935, states new evidence had come to light proving Nathaniel Freeman's wife was Martha Brown not Martha Dunham as had been previously accepted. The files show that the Descendants of Deacon John Doane, and The Brainerd Family of America (1908) both incorrectly state her maiden name was Dunham.
<139> p.259, The remaining eight Arnold children are listed without dates, viz: Samuel B.P., Solomon, Nathaniel, Elijah, Martha, Lydia, Sophia and Polly.
<140> p.259, A note from the Foster Gen.:562 states David Foster married Lydia White and had David, b. 18 June 1784 and Nathaniel, b. May 1786.
<141> p.259, Mass.VR 138:63 states David Foster was born in Rhode Island.

* * * * *

REFERENCE LIST

GENEALOGICAL ARTICLES PERTAINING TO BREWSTER FAMILY RESEARCH

Mayflower Descendant (MD) (1899-1937)

1:1-8 - The Brewster Book
(cont-d, 1:71-77, 168-74, 193-97; 2:21-24, 112-13 and cont-d below)
1:224-27 - Hannah (Brewster^{3}) Starr
2:203-06 - Will & Inventory of Love Brewster^{2}
3:15-30 - Inventory & Settlement of Estate of Elder William Brewster
3:203-16 - Will & Inventory of Gov. Thomas Prence (incl. death rcds.)
4:17-19 - A Calkins Family Record
4:65-67 - John Doty^{2}'s Deed to Wrestling Brewster^{3}
4:100-09 - William Brewster (his life)
5:24-27 - The Brewster Book
5:41-46 - Will & Inventory of John Turner Sr.
5:143-51 - Will & Inventory of Maj. John Freeman
6:44-49 - Will & Inventory of Benjamin Bartlett
6:57-58 - Jonathan Brewster's 1st Wife & Child
(Note: This claim has been disproved.)
8:65-72 - Estate of Lt. Edmund Freeman & Will of Wife Sarah, 1718,1737
8:80-84 - Rev. Jonathan Scott's Family Bible (1744-1850)
8:164-65 - Letter from Jonathan Brewster^{2} to Sarah, Widow of Love, 1656
8:227-31 - Deacon John Paine's Journal
8:234-36 - Will of Abigail Illsley, 1828
9:49-51 - Deacon John Paine's Journal
9:52-53 - Family Bible Record of James Scammon Emery
9:97-99 - Deacon John Paine's Journal
9:119-22 - Estate of Rev. John Mayo
9:136-40 - Deacon John Paine's Journal (end)
9:246-51 - Aaron Soule^{3}'s Wife Mary Wadsworth And The Marriage of Five of Her Sisters
11:1-5 - Richard & Mercy Sparrow's Children & Marriages
13:19-23 - Freeman Notes: Thomas & William Freeman^{4}
14:40-43 - Freeman Notes: Deeds (sons of Lt. Edmund Freeman)
14:193-03 - Capt. Jonathan Sparrow's Wives And Their Children (Hannah Prence^{3})
18:177-83 - The Will of Benjamin Bartlett of Duxbury And The Division of His Real Estate
18:189-91 - The Will of Benjamin Higgins (m. Sarah Freeman^{5})
19:91-92 - Paine Notes: Samuel Paine^{4} (m. Patience Freeman^{4})
19:97-100 - The Estate of John James of Scituate (m. Lydia Turner^{4})
19:145-49 - The Estate of William Barrell of Scituate And The Will of Widow Lydia (Turner^{4})
19:187-90 - Hobart/Bradford/Rogers/Turner Notes: (Bathsheba Hobart m. Joseph Turner^{4})

20:84-88 - Will of Jonathan Turner[4] of Scituate MA
20:112-16 - Estate of Wrestling Brewster[3] And His Son Wrestling's Will
20:153-55 - Will of Capt. John James[4] of Scituate MA
20:168-69 - Will of Joseph Holmes Sr. of Kingston MA (m. Mary Brewster[4])
21:159-61 - Autograph of Maj. John Freeman (m. Mercy Prence[3])
22:1-2 - Another Brewster Imprint Identified With A Brewster Autograph On Its Title Page (Elder William Brewster)
23:172-73 - Family Record of Joseph Holmes Sr. (m. Mary Brewster[4])
24:97-101 - William Brewster's Autograph signature On A Lease Of Scrooby Manor House
24:130-31 - Miscellaneous Death Records: Fourth wife of Gov. Thomas Prence
25:124-26 - Estate of Ensign Joseph Paine (m. Patience Sparrow[4])
29:138-41 - Freeman Notes: Deeds (James, Samuel & Thomas)
30:97-98 - Deaths of Patience (Brewster[2]) Prence & Fear (Brewster[2]) Allerton
31:1-2 - Mary (Brewster[3]) Turner
32:28-32 - John Turner Sr. and Mary Brewster[3], Their Marriage And Their Children
32:49-50 - Autographs of Major John Freeman, Assistant, And His Wife Mercy Prence[3]
32:71-80 - Elisha Turner[4] And Elizabeth Jacob And Their Six Children
33:97-100 - A Receipt of Heirs of Gov. Thomas Prence
33:100-14 - John Freeman[4] of Eastham and Harwich, His Wives, His Children, His Will and His Widow's Estate
34:14-15 - False & Faked Mayflower Claims (Elisha and Zebulon Sylvester[6])
PN&Q 2:158 - Mary (Brewster[3]) Turner

Mayflower Descendant (MD) (1985-1990)

36:119-24 - Nathan Brewster[6] of Killingly, CT
37:59-60 - Nathan Brewster[6] of Killingly, CT
39:37-40 - Records of the James Jones & Daniel Denison Families
40:71-79 - Thomas Caswell of Taunton & His Descendants

Mayflower Quarterly (MQ) (1975-1990)

44:39-44 - Pilgrim Ancestry of Revolutionary Soldiers: The Taylor Family of Virginia
44:122-24 - The Brewster Family: Where Did These Brewster Descendants Go?
45:201-02 - The Identity of Mercy Mayo, Wife of John Cole (Correction to MF5G 2:247, #166 - Mercy Mayo, dau of Samuel Mayo[4] & wife Ruth Hopkins <Barnstable Co.Prob.5:450-56>.)
45:219-20 - The Brewster Family: Where Did These Brewster Descendants Go?
47:19-22 - The Grays of Dorset, VT (Capt. John[8])
49:74-81 - The Shelleys of Raynham MA (Benjamin Shelley m. Mary Turner[6])
51:131-34 - Sarah (Brewster[3]) Bartlett
51:161-67 - Jonathan Brewster In Leiden Documents, Part 1
52:6-16 - Jonathan Brewster In Leiden Documents, Part 2
52:57-63 - Jonathan Brewster In Leiden Documents, Part 3 (Not Jonathan Brewster's Wife & Child)
52:72-83 - Jonathan Brewster & His Family (Correction to MD 6:57, no 1st wife & child)
52:132-36 - Three Generations of Paines From Cape Cod To Maine And Back Again
53:175 - Queries (Was Ruhamah Turner who m. John Jennings the dau of John Turner & Mary Brewster[3]?)
53:238-40 - Jeptha Nickerson's Dilemma (Sally Doan[8])
54:10-14 - The Haskell Bible (Benjamin Franklin Haskell)
54:117 - The Identity of Hannah Freeman[6], wf of Elijah Caswell
54:276-79 - Some Brewster Descendants in Canada (Alexander Hyde[8])
55:208 - Comstock Correction (Bible record of Oliver Comstock)
56:104-06 - Thomas Howes[5], Husband of Bathsheba Sears[5] of Yarmouth & Ashfield, MA: A Case of Mistaken Identity
56:216-17 - Bible Records: Harvey Barrelle[8]

Miscellaneous

NEHGR 18:18 - The True Date of the Birth & Death of Elder Brewster
NEHGR 53:109 - Early Generations of the Brewster Family
NEHGR 111:242 - The baptism of Lucretia (Oldham) Brewster
TAG 41:1 - New Light On The Brewsters of Scrooby & New England
Detroit Society for Genealogical Research Magazine, Spring 1985 - (maiden name of Mrs. Mary Brewster)

* * * * * * *

PETER BROWN

MICRO #1 of 5

CHILDREN OF Peter BROWN[1] & 1st Martha ( ) FORD: (2) <Plymouth><1>

Mary BROWN[2], b. c1626; d. aft. 17 Jan. 1683 (hus. will) <MD 4:122><2>

Priscilla BROWN[2], b. c1629; d. aft. 17 Feb. 1697/8 (hus. will) <MD 33:36>

CHILDREN OF Peter BROWN[1] & 2nd Mary ( ): (2) <Plymouth><1>

Rebecca BROWN[2], b. betw. 1627-33; d. aft. 9 Mar. 1698/9 (hus. will) <MD 8:101>

Child, b. pre 1633, d. pre 1647

MARY BROWN[2] (Peter[1])

Ephraim TINKHAM, d. betw. 17 Jan. 1683 (will) - 20 May 1685 (inv.) <MD 4:122>

CHILDREN OF Ephraim TINKHAM & Mary BROWN[2]: (8) <Plymouth>

Ephraim TINKHAM[3], b. 5 Aug. 1649 <MD 16:120>; d. 13 Oct. 1714,Middleboro,Nemasket g.s.<MD 15:101>

Ebenezer TINKHAM[3], b. 30 Sept. 1651 <MD 16:237>; d. 8 Apr. 1718, Middleboro <MD 4:73,15:100>

Peter TINKHAM[3], b. 25 Dec. 1653 <MD 17:70>; d. 30 Dec. 1709, Middleboro, Nemasket g.s.<MD 15:102>

Helkiah TINKHAM[3], b. 8 Feb. 1655 <MD 17:71>; d. betw. 20 May 1718 (codicil) - 25 Sept. 1731 (witness sworn) <MD 12:145>

John TINKHAM[3], b. 7 June 1658 <MD 17:72>, d.y.

Mary TINKHAM[3], b. 5 Aug. 1661 <MD 17:186>; d. 1731, Middleboro Green g.s.

John TINKHAM[3], b. 15 Nov. 1663 <MD 17:186>

Isaac TINKHAM[3], b. 11 Apr. 1666 <MD 18:56>; d. betw. 25 Feb. 1708/9 (will) - 12 Apr. 1732(prob.)

John TOMSON[3] (Mary Cooke[2]), b. 24 Nov. 1649, Plymouth; d. 25 Nov. 1725, Middleboro Green g.s.

CHILDREN OF John TOMSON & Mary TINKHAM[3]: (12) <Middleboro; 4-11, MD 2:104>

Mary TOMSON[4], b. 2 May 1681 <MD 1:221>, unm.

John TOMSON[4], b. 9 Aug. 1682 <MD 1:221>

Ephraim TOMSON[4], b. 16 Oct. 1683 <MD 1:221>; d. 13 Nov. 1744 <Halifax VR:1>

Shubael TOMSON[4], b. 11 Apr. 1686; d. 7 July 1733 <MD 13:5>

Thomas TOMSON[4], b. 29 July 1688

Martha TOMSON[4], b. 4 Jan. 1689/90, unm.

Sarah TOMSON[4], b. 3 Mar. 1691/2, unm.

Peter TOMSON[4], b. 11 May 1694, unm.

Isaac TOMSON[4], b. 10 Mar. 1696/7

Ebenezer TOMSON[4], b. 19 June 1699, unm.

Francis TOMSON[4], b. 27 Jan. 1700/01

Jacob TOMSON[4], b. 24 June 1703 <MD 2:104>

Elizabeth BURROUGHS, (dau of Jeremiah), b. 5 Mar. 1654, Marshfield <MD 2:6>; d. 8 Apr. 1718, Middleboro, Nemasket g.s. <MD 4:74,15:101>

CHILDREN OF Ebenezer TINKHAM[3] & Elizabeth BURROUGHS: (7) <Middleboro VR>

Ebenezer TINKHAM[4], b. 23 Mar. 1679 <MD 1:221>; d. pre 7 Nov. 1726 (adm.)<3>

Jeremiah TINKHAM[4], b. 7 Aug. 1681 <MD 1:221>; d. 5 Apr. 1715, Middleboro <MD 4:74>

Peter TINKHAM[4], b. 20 Apr. 1683 <MD 1:221>

Joanna TINKHAM[4], bpt. 1685; d. 29 Apr. 1766, ae 81st yr, Marshfield g.s. <MD 17:165>

Elizabeth TINKHAM[4], bpt. 1688; d. 27 Mar. 1715 <MD 4:74>

Priscilla TINKHAM[4], bpt. 1690; d. 16 Apr. 1715 <MD 4:74>

Shubael TINKHAM[4], bpt. 1692; d. 29 Mar. 1739, 47th yr, Middleboro g.s. <MD 15:103>

Patience PRATT, b. c1681, d. 29 Mar. 1718, 37th yr, Middleboro g.s. <MD 15:102>

CHILDREN OF Ebenezer TINKHAM[4] & Patience PRATT: (6) <1-4, Middleboro, MD 2:202>

Elizabeth TINKHAM[5], b. 13 Oct. 1704

Mary TINKHAM^{5}, b. 30 Jan. 1705/6

Peter TINKHAM^{5}, b. 5 Sept. 1709; d. 10 Oct. 1745, Nemasket g.s., Middleboro <MD 15:102>

Jabez TINKHAM^{5}, b. 29 Dec. 1711; d. pre 9 June 1727

Priscilla TINKHAM^{5}, b. aft. 22 July 1712/3*<4> <5>

Patience TINKHAM^{5}, b. aft. 22 July 1712/3* (c1717); d.? 9 Apr. 1791*, Middleboro g.s. <MD 15:109>

Hannah (HATCH^{3}) Turner, (Mary Doty^{2}), b. 15 or 16 Feb. 1681/2 <MD 21:98>; d. 13 Apr. 1771 (2nd wf Ebenezer Tinkham^{4})

Rebecca TINKHAM, (dau of Eben. & Hannah), b. 20 Dec. 1739 <Middleborough VR 1:188>

David THOMAS, (son of Israel & Phebe), b. 4 Nov. 1743, d. 9 Feb. 1825 <Middleborough VR 2:120>

CHILD OF David THOMAS & Rebecca TINKHAM:

Asel THOMAS, b. 17 Feb. 1768 <Middleborough VR 2:114>

Edmund WOOD, (*son of David & Joanna), b. 28 Nov. 1721*, Middleboro <MD 3:235>; d. 29 Dec. 1805*, Nemasket g.s., Middleboro <MD 15:107>

CHILDREN OF Edmund WOOD & Patience TINKHAM^{5} (Eben.^{4}): (3) <MD 18:153><6>

Priscilla WOOD^{6}, b. 4 Jan. 1752

Joshua WOOD^{6}, b. 27 Dec. 1753

Francis WOOD^{6}, b. 6 Sept. 1756

Eunice THOMAS, (dau of Wm.), b. 15 Feb. 1708/9, Middleboro <MD 2:202>; d. 8 Apr. 1778, Nemasket g.s., Middleboro <MD 15:101>

CHILD OF Peter TINKHAM^{5} (Eben.^{4}) & Eunice THOMAS:

Eunice TINKHAM^{6}, b. 6 July 1730*

CHILDREN OF Jeremiah TINKHAM^{4} (Eben.^{3}) & Joanna PARLOUR: (3) <Middleboro><7>

Joanna TINKHAM^{5}, b. 8 Dec. 1711 <MD 3:84>

Jeremiah TINKHAM^{5}, b. 20 Feb. 1712/13 <MD 3:84>; d. 4 June 1790, Middleboro g.s.<MD 15:101>

Ebenezer TINKHAM^{5}, b. 16 Dec. 1714 <MD 3:86>; d. 17 Nov. 1801, Middleboro g.s. <MD 15:100>

CHILDREN OF Robert MACKFUN & Joanna (PARLOUR) Tinkham: (4) <Middleboro>

Agnes MACKFUN, b. 23 June 1721 <MD 6:180>

Elizabeth MACKFUN, b. 1 Mar. 1722/3 <MD 6:180>

Patience MACKFUN, b. 1 Jan. 1724/5 <MD 6:227>

Robert MACKFUN, b. 24 Jan. 1726/7 <MD 6:229>

Naomi WARREN^{5} (John^{4}, Rich.^{3}, Nath.^{2}), b. c1716, d. 21 June 1795, Middleboro g.s. <MD 15:102>

CHILDREN OF Jeremiah TINKHAM^{5} & Naomi WARREN: (10) <Middleboro; 4-9, MD 20:36>

Jeremiah TINKHAM^{6}, b. 27 Oct. 1740 <MD 15:221>

Elisha TINKHAM^{6}, b. 18 Aug. 1742, d. 6 Dec. 1835, Middleboro g.s. <MD 15:221,101>

Joanna TINKHAM^{6}, b. 6 Dec. 1743, d. 2 June 1761, Middleboro g.s. <MD 15:221,101>

James TINKHAM^{6}, b. 8 May 1745; d. 22 July 1836, Middleboro g.s. <MD 15:101>

Abigail TINKHAM^{6}, b. 25 Dec. 1746; d. 2 July 1822, unm.

Anna TINKHAM^{6}, b. 9 Oct. 1748

Jesse TINKHAM^{6}, b. 25 July 1750

Benjamin TINKHAM^{6}, b. 6 Jan. 1755; d. 23 Aug. 1775, Middleboro g.s. <MD 15:100>

Huldia TINKHAM^{6}, b. 18 Dec. 1756; d. 25 May 1835, unm., Middleboro g.s. <MD 15:101>

Ebenezer TINKHAM^{6}, b. 26 Aug. 1758, d. 1 Mar. 1820, Middleboro g.s. <MD 20:38, 15:101>

Hannah SHAW, (dau of Benoni), b. c1715, d. 15 Sept. 1794, 79th yr, Middleboro g.s. <MD 15:101>

CHILDREN OF Ebenezer TINKHAM^{5} (Jeremiah^{4}) & Hannah SHAW: (9) <Middleboro>

Rebecca TINKHAM^{6}, b. 20 Dec. 1739 <MD 14:246>

Isaac TINKHAM^{6}, b. 26 Nov. 1741 <MD 15:223>

Zebedee TINKHAM^{6}, b. 24 Jan. 1744, d. 2 Oct. 1820, Middleboro g.s. <MD 16:108,15:103>

Hannah TINKHAM^{6}, b. 26 July 1747 <MD 20:36>

Lydia TINKHAM^{6}, b. 4 Dec. 1749 <MD 20:37>

Lucia TINKHAM^{6}, b. 22 Apr. 1752 <MD 20:37>

Ruth TINKHAM^{6}, b. 17 Apr. 1755 <MD 20:37>; d. 9 Oct. 1805, unm.

Betty TINKHAM^{6}, b. 4 Apr. 1757 <MD 20:38>

Priscilla TINKHAM^{6}, b. 5 June 1760; d. 3 July 1770 <MD 15:102>

Sarah (GREEN*?) TINKHAM, b. c1748, d. 10 Aug. 1776, ae 28y5m28d, Middleboro g.s. <MD 15:103>**<8>**

CHILD OF Elisha TINKHAM^{6} (Jeremiah^{5}) & Sarah (GREEN*?):**<8>**

Naomi TINKHAM^{7}*, b. 2 Jan. 1775*, d. 1850* <Richmond Gen.:96>

Reliance (RICHMOND*^{7}) (*John$^{6-5}$, Jos.^{4}, Abigail Rogers^{3}, John^{2}), b. June 1749*, Middleboro; d. 12 Oct. 1791, 43rd yr, Middleboro, Nemasket g.s. <MD 15:103>

CHILDREN OF Elisha TINKHAM^{6} & 2nd Reliance (RICHMOND*): (8*) <Richmond Gen.:96>

Jeremiah TINKHAM^{7}, b. 1() Aug. 1778, d. 21 Oct. 185(8)

Thomas TINKHAM^{7}, b. 20 Jan. 1780

John TINKHAM^{7}, b. 21 June 1781

Hannah TINKHAM^{7}, b. 26 Apr. 1784

Sally TINKHAM^{7}, b. ( )

( ) TINKHAM^{7}, b. 18 Sept. 1787 (name too faint)

Lucy TINKHAM^{7}, b. 1 Mar. 1789

Elisha TINKHAM^{7}, b. 21 Aug. 1791

Sarah (RICHMOND*^{7}), (sister of Reliance above), b. c1749, d. 3 June 1796, 47th yr, Middleboro Nemasket g.s. <MD 15:103>

CHILD OF Elisha TINKHAM^{6} & 3rd Sarah (RICHMOND*^{7}):

Isaac TINKHAM^{7}*, b. 19 Mar. 1795* <Richmond Gen.:96>

Sarah REDDING, b. c1752, d. 2 Apr. 1774, 22nd yr, Middleboro, The Green g.s. <MD 14:221>

CHILDREN OF James TINKHAM^{6} (Jeremiah^{5}) & 1st Sarah REDDING: (2) <Middleboro VR 4:1:62, MD 33:75>

Louisa TINKHAM^{7}, b. 30 Nov. 1771

James TINKHAM^{7}, b. 28 Mar. 1774

Chloe RICKARD, (dau of Sam & Zuruiah), b. 16 Sept. 1754, Middleboro, d. 29 Dec. 1822, Middleboro, Nemasket g.s. <MD 20:37, 15:100>

CHILDREN OF James TINKHAM^{6} & 2nd Chloe RICKARD: (11) <Middleboro VR 4:1:62, MD 33:75>

Sarah TINKHAM^{7}, b. 26 Feb. 1779

Chloe TINKHAM^{7}, b. 3 May 1780

Jacob TINKHAM^{7}, b. 13 Aug. 1781

Asenath TINKHAM^{7}, b. 12 May 1782

Lazarus TINKHAM^{7}, b. 5 Jan. 1784

Anna TINKHAM^{7}, b. 14 Sept. 1785; d. 1 Apr. 1871, Randolph, general dropsy & paralysis of heart <Mass.VR 239:298>

Jenney TINKHAM^{7}, b. 25 Aug. 1787; d. 11 Apr. 1813, unm. <"Jane", Middleboro VR 7:210>

Jeremiah TINKHAM^{7}, b. 19 Sept. 1790

Andrew TINKHAM^{7}, b. 5 Sept. 1792

Enoch TINKHAM^{7}, b. 4 Sept. 1795

Lewis TINKHAM^{7}, b. 6 Oct. 1797 <MD 33:76>

Nathaniel HOWARD, b. c1787, d. 28 Jan. 1857, ae 70y6m17d, Easton MA

CHILD OF Nathaniel HOWARD & Anna TINKHAM^{7}:

Jane Tinkham HOWARD^{8}, b. ( )

CHILDREN OF Rev. James Porter & Jane Tinkham HOWARD^{8}: (4) <Family Bible>

Jane Frances PORTER^{9}, b. 4 Nov. 1835

James Frederic PORTER^{9}, b. 26 Aug. 1837

Emma R. PORTER^{9}, b. 29 Aug. ( )*

George Henry PORTER^{9}, b. 30 Sept. 1847

Thomas MACOMBER, (son of Tho.), b. 2 July 1684, Marshfield <MD 2:251>; d. 5 Oct. 1771, Marshfield g.s. <Marshfield VR 2:109, MD 13:48>

CHILDREN OF Thomas MACOMBER & Joanna TINKHAM^{4} (Eben.^{3}): (6) <Marshfield VR>

Thomas MACOMBER^{5}, b. 28 Apr. 1710, d. 8 Jan. 1749, Marshfield g.s.<MD 7:134,13:48>

Ursula MACOMBER^{5}, b. 10 Dec. 1711, d. 10 Nov. 1748, unm., Marshfield g.s.<MD 8:179,13:48>

Sarah MACOMBER^{5}, b. 27 Oct. 1713 <MD 8:179> (See <9>)

Elizabeth MACOMBER^{5}, b. 22 Feb. 1715, d. 16 Mar. 1800, Marshfield g.s. <MD 7:134,13:134>

Onesimus MACOMBER^{5}, b. 18 June 1720, d. 26 Aug. 1749, Marshfield g.s. <MD 7:120,13:48>

Joanna MACOMBER^{5}, b. 20 Apr. 1727, d. 2 Mar. 1791, unm., Marshfield g.s. <MD 7:121,13:48>

Molly MACUMBER, b. c1777, d. 6 Jan. 1796, 19th yr <Hanover ChR:200>

Mrs. Bettey MACOMBER, b. c1764, d. 22 July 1807, ae 43 <Hanover ChR:262>

Job WINSLOW^{5} (Mercy Snow^{4}, Josiah^{3}, Abigail Warren^{2}), b. c1715, d. 19 May 1787, 72nd yr, Marshfield g.s. <MD 13:134>

CHILDREN OF Job WINSLOW & Elizabeth MACOMBER^{5}: (3)

Mercy WINSLOW^{6*}, b. ( )

Benjamin WINSLOW^{6}, b. c1744, d. 4 Dec. 1761, 17th yr, Marshfield g.s. <MD 13:134>

Joanna WINSLOW^{6*}, b. ( )

CHILDREN OF Onesimus MACOMBER^{5} (Joanna Tinkham^{4}) & Lucy BARKER: (2) <Marshfield VR 2:111>

Thomas MACOMBER^{6}, b. 31 May 1746; d. 15 July 1833* <Hanson VR:8>

Onesimus MACOMBER^{6}, b. 20 July 1748; d. 24 Apr. 1791, Marshfield g.s. <MD 13:48>

Leah TILDEN, b. c1746, d. 3 Apr. 1831*, ae 85 <Hanson VR>

CHILDREN OF Thomas MACOMBER^{6} & Leah TILDEN: (3) <Marshfield VR 2:79>

Thomas MACOMBER^{7}, b. 20 July 1768

John MACOMBER^{7}, b. 28 Jan. 1770

Onesimus MACOMBER^{7}, b. ( )

CHILDREN OF Josiah BARKER & Sarah MACOMBER^{5} (Joanna Tinkham^{4}): (7)**<9>**

Ebenezer BARKER^{6}, b. 3 Aug. 1739*

Deborah BARKER^{6}, b. 5 Oct. 1741*

Thomas BARKER^{6}, b. 29 Oct. 1743*

Joanna BARKER^{6}, b. 2 Sept. 1747*

Ursula BARKER^{6}, b. 5 Mar. 1749*

Sarah BARKER^{6}, b. 6 Aug. 1751*

Lydia BARKER^{6}, b. 6 Feb. 1754*

Mercy TILDEN^{5} (Desire Oldham^{4}, Mercy Sprout^{3}, Eliz. Samson^{2}), bpt. 9 Sept. 1722*, Scituate

CHILDREN OF Thomas MACOMBER^{5} (Joanna Tinkham^{4}) & Mercy TILDEN: (2) <Marshfield VR, MD 31:70>

William MACOMBER^{6}, b. 1 May 1746

Thomas MACOMBER^{6},b. 2 Aug. 1748**<10>**

Prudence STETSON^{6} (*Mary Eames^{5}, Mary Oakman^{4}, Eliz. Doty^{3}, Edw.^{2}), b. 19 Mar. 1750* <Scituate VR 1:349>**<10>**

CHILDREN OF Thomas MACOMBER^{6} & Prudence STETSON: (3) <Marshfield VR 2:78, MD 29:110>

Joanna MACOMBER^{7}, b. 20 Aug. 1769

Mercy MACOMBER^{7}, b. 23 July 1771

Thomas MACOMBER^{7}, b. 17 Aug. 1773

Priscilla CHILDS, (dau of Jos.), b. 5 Nov. 1693, Marshfield <MD 6:19>; d. 11 July 1739, Nemasket g.s., Middleboro <MD 15:102>

CHILDREN OF Shubael TINKHAM^{4} (Eben.^{3}) & Priscilla CHILDS: (6) <Middleboro VR>

Elizabeth TINKHAM^{5}, b. 1 Oct. 1719 <MD 5:40>

Joseph TINKHAM^{5}, b. 16 Dec. 1721, d. 28 Apr. 1767, Middleboro, Nemasket g.s. <MD 5:40,15:102>

Sarah TINKHAM^{5}, b. 23 Feb. 1723/4 <MD 6:180>

Priscilla TINKHAM^{5}, b. 10 June 1726, d. 15 Apr. 1769, Middleboro, The Green g.s.<MD 6:229,12:199>

Ebenezer TINKHAM^{5}, b. 2 Jan. 1728/9 <MD 7:242>

Perez TINKHAM^{5}, b. 4 Aug. 1736, d. 25 Nov. 1760, Middleboro g.s. <MD 8:248,15:102>

John COBB^{5} (John^{4}, Rachel Soule^{3}, John^{2}), b. 31 May 1722, Middleboro <MD 6:226>; d. 22 June 1750, Middleboro, The Green g.s. <MD 12:144>

CHILDREN OF John COBB & Priscilla TINKHAM^{5}: (2) <Middleboro VR, MD 16:134>

John COBB^{6}, b. 9 Nov. 1745; d. 23 Jan. 1822, Middleboro, The Green g.s. <MD 12:144>

Martha COBB^{6}, b. 9 June 1748

CHILDREN OF William CUSHMAN^{5} (Ichabod^{4}, Isaac^{3}, Mary Allerton^{2}) & Priscilla (TINKHAM) Cobb: (7) <Middleboro VR>

Priscilla CUSHMAN^{6}, b. 23 Oct. 1751 <MD 18:154>

Isaac CUSHMAN^{6}, b. 27 Feb. 1754 <MD 18:155>

Susanna CUSHMAN^{6}, b. 13 Jan. 1756 <MD 18:155>

Andrew CUSHMAN^{6}, b. 26 Mar. 1757 <MD 20:35>

Perez CUSHMAN^{6}, b. 26 Jan. 1759 <MD 23:44>

Patience CUSHMAN^{6}, b. 16 Sept. 1764 <MD 23:44>

Welthea CUSHMAN^{6}, b. 13 Sept. 1767; d. 3 June 1768 <MD 12:200>

CHILDREN OF Joseph TINKHAM^{5} (Shubael^{4}) & Agnes MACKFUN: (4) <Middleboro VR>

Priscilla TINKHAM^{6}, b. 9 Aug. 1741 <MD 15:223>

Shubael TINKHAM^{6}, b. 26 Mar. 1743 <MD 15:223>

Elisabeth TINKHAM^{6}, b. 26 July 1746, d. 28 June 1748 <MD 17:19,15:101>

Ebenezer TINKHAM^{6}, b. 28 July 1748, d. 19 Sept. 1749 <MD 15:100>

Esther WRIGHT^{3} (Hester Cooke^{2}), b. 1649, Plymouth <MD 16:121>; d. 28 May 1717, Middleboro, Nemasket g.s. <MD 15:101>

CHILDREN OF Ephraim TINKHAM^{3} & Esther WRIGHT: (6) <Middleboro>

Martha TINKHAM^{4}, b. c1678, d. 16 Feb. 1758, 80th yr, Middleboro, The Green g.s.

John TINKHAM^{4}, b. 22 Aug. 1680, d. 14 Apr. 1766, Middleboro, Nemasket g.s. <MD 1:221,15:102>

Ephraim TINKHAM^{4}, b. 7 Oct. 1682 <MD 1:221>; d. pre 27 July 1713 (inv.) <MD 17:163>

Isaac TINKHAM^{4}, b. last June 1685; d. 7 Apr. 1750, Halifax, Thompson St. g.s. <MD 1:222,14:10>

Samuel TINKHAM^{4}, b. 19 Mar. 1687 <MD 1:223>; d. 16 Mar. 1775, Middleboro, Green g.s.<MD 14:221>

Mary TINKHAM^{4}, b. ( )

<u>Middleboro VR: (misc.)</u> (10)

Mary WOOD, (dau of Ephraim & Mary), b. 8 Aug. 1756

CHILDREN OF John TINKHAM & Mary WOOD: (7) <VR 4:14>

Joseph TINKHAM, b. 10 Jan. 1779

Susannah TINKHAM, b. 25 May 1780

Amasa TINKHAM, b. 21 Aug. 1782

Joanna TINKHAM, b. 24 Jan. 1785

Ariel TINKHAM, (son), b. 6 Nov. 1787

Oren TINKHAM, b. 26 Dec. 1790

John TINKHAM, b. 28 Jan. 1794

Mary Wood THOMPSON, (dau of Nathaniel & Mary), b. 16 Mar. 1812 <VR 7:177>

David THOMAS, (son of Capt. Asel & Phebe), b. 9 Apr. 1807 <VR 7:53>

Hannah COBB, b. 27 Feb. 1699 <Family Gen., mss.:136> (m. Jacob Tinkham)

William CURTIS, (son of William & Martha), b. 28 Aug. 1742 <Pembroke TR>

Capt. William CURTIS, d. 1 Oct. 1821 <Pembroke TR>

<u>MICRO #2 of 5</u>

Dr. Sebra CROOKER, d. 11 Apr. 1839, China ME <Family Record>

CHILD OF Dr. Sebra CROOKER & Lydia CURTIS:

Sebra CROOKER, b. 12 Aug. 1800, Wiscasset ME, d. 17 Mar. 1891, S. Brookfiled N.S. <Family Record>

Pamelia DURLAND, b. 12 Sept. 1810, Willmont, N.S., d. 8 Mar. 1886, Augusta ME <Family Record> (wf of Sebra Crooker)

Martha COBB^{4} (Rachel Soule^{3}, John^{2}), b. 23 Mar. 1691/2 <Middleboro VR>

CHILDREN OF Ephraim TINKHAM^{4} (Ephraim^{3}) & Martha COBB: (2) <Middleboro VR, MD 2:202>

Moses TINKHAM^{5}, b. 16 Aug. 1709; d. 27 Apr. 1730, Middleboro, The Green g.s. <MD 14:221>

Ephraim TINKHAM^{5}, b. 13 Feb. 1711/2; d. 13 May 1730, Plympton g.s. <MD 11:165>

John SOULE^{3} (John^{2}), b. c1674, d. 19 May 1743, 69th yr, Middleboro, The Green g.s. (hus of Martha Tinkham^{4} (Ephraim^{3}))

Abijah WOOD, (dau of Abiel), b. 20 Feb. 1688/9, Middleboro, d. 25 Dec. 1777, Halifax, Thompson St. g.s. <MD 2:106,14:10>

CHILDREN OF Isaac TINKHAM^{4} (Ephraim^{3}) & Abijah WOOD: (5) <1-4, Middleboro VR>

Ephraim TINKHAM^{5}, b. 8 Nov. 1718, d. 10 Jan. 1734/5, Middleboro, The Green g.s. <MD 3:233,14:221>

Isaac TINKHAM^{5}, b. 21 Apr. 1720, d. 28 Oct. 1779, Middleboro, The Green g.s. <MD 3:235,14:221>

Noah TINKHAM^{5}, b. 25 July 1722, d. 12 June 1765, Halifax, Thompson St. g.s. <MD 4:68,14:10>

Nathan TINKHAM^{5}, b. 18 Apr. 1725 <MD 6:228>

Moses TINKHAM^{5}, b. c1730, d. 15 Apr. 1750, 20th yr, Halifax, Thompson St. g.s. <MD 14:10>

Sarah SOULE^{5} (Zachariah^{4}, Ben.^{3}, John^{2}), b. 15 June 1727, Plympton <MD 2:121>

CHILDREN OF Nathan TINKHAM^{5} & Sarah SOULE: (6) <Halifax VR:54>

Ephraim TINKHAM^{6}, b. 21 Apr. 1748 <VR:53>

Ruth TINKHAM^{6}, b. 14 Aug. 1750

Sarah TINKHAM^{6}, b. 2 June 1753

Nathan TINKHAM^{6}, b. 26 Jan. 1756

Isaiah TINKHAM^{6}, b. 19 Sept. 1757

Zenas TINKHAM^{6}, b. 10 July 1763

Sarah PORTER, b. c1722, d. 27 July 1795, 73rd yr, Halifax g.s. <MD 3:159>

CHILDREN OF Noah TINKHAM^{5} (Isaac^{4}) & Sarah PORTER: (5) <Halifax VR:53>

Moses TINKHAM^{6}, b. 16 Nov. 1752; d. 13 May 1754, Halifax g.s. <MD 3:157>

Sarah TINKHAM^{6}, b. 20 Apr. 1756; d.? 12 June 1832, unm., Halifax g.s.

Mary TINKHAM^{6}, b. 15 June 1758

Noah TINKHAM^{6}, b. 15 Sept. 1761; d. 29 Nov. 1786, Halifax g.s. <MD 3:159>

Joseph TINKHAM^{6}, b. 24 Nov. 1764; d. 18 Dec. 1841, Halifax g.s.

Lucy LUCAS, b. c1760, d. 6 Oct. 1792, 32nd yr, Halifax g.s. <MD 3:159> (wf of Jos. Tinkham^{6})

Hannah HOWLAND^{3} (Isaac^{2}), b. 6 Oct. 1694, Middleboro, d. 25 Mar. 1792, Middleboro, Nemasket g.s. <MD 1:224,15:101>

CHILDREN OF John TINKHAM^{4} (Ephraim^{3}) & Hannah HOWLAND: (10) <Middleboro VR>

Cornelius TINKHAM^{5}, b. 31 Aug. 1717, d. 16 Apr. 1739, Middleboro, Nemasket g.s. <MD 3:86,15:100>

John TINKHAM^{5}, b. 8 May 1719, d. 22 ( ) 1793, Middleboro, Nemasket g.s. <MD 3:233,15:101>

Esther TINKHAM^{5}, b. 26 Apr. 1721 <MD 3:234>

Hannah TINKHAM^{5}, b. 10 Apr. 1723 <MD 4:69>

Susanna TINKHAM^{5}, b. 19 Mar. 1724/5 <MD 6:228>

Abishai TINKHAM^{5}, b. 23 May 1727 <MD 6:229>

Amos TINKHAM^{5}, b. 10 July 1729, d. 25 Apr. 1776, Middleboro, Nemasket g.s. <MD 7:242,15:100>

Mary TINKHAM^{5}, b. 17 Jan. 1731/2 <MD 9:48>; d. 6 Aug. 1808

Seth TINKHAM^{5}, b. 27 Aug. 1734 <MD 12:232>; d. pre 13 Feb. 1766 (father's will)<Plymouth Co.Prob. #20870, 19:370>

Zilpah TINKHAM^{5}, b. 25 July 1737, d. 26 Nov. 1818, Middleboro, The Green g.s. <MD 8:249,13:120>

Sarah TINKHAM, (*?dau of Peter & Eunice), b. c1735, d. 13 Feb. 1820, ae 85, Middleboro, Nemasket g.s. <MD 15:103>

CHILDREN OF Amos TINKHAM^{5} & Sarah TINKHAM: (6) <Middleboro VR>

Eunice TINKHAM^{6}, b. 20 May 1753, d. 22 May 1756 <MD 20:36,16:247>

Sarah TINKHAM^{6}, b. 4 Apr. 1757 <MD 20:38>

Zilpha TINKHAM^{6}, b. 2 Aug. 1759 <MD 22:148>

Seth TINKHAM^{6}, b. 28 Sept. 1761 <MD 23:44>

Amos TINKHAM^{6}, b. 21 May 1765 <MD 25:105>

Squire TINKHAM^{6}, b. 17 Oct. 1772 <MD 32:89>

John MILLER^{6} (John^{5}, Lydia Coombs^{4}, Francis^{3}, Sarah Priest^{2}), b. 27 Nov. 1737, Middleboro, d. 1 Dec. 1807, Middleboro, The Green g.s. <MD 14:244,13:119> (hus of Zilpah Tinkham^{5} (John^{4}))

Jerusha VAUGHAN, b. c1721, d. 25 Nov. 1787, Middleboro, Nemasket g.s. <MD 15:101>

CHILDREN OF John TINKHAM^{5} (John^{4}) & Jerusha VAUGHAN: (9) <1-6, Middleboro VR>

Jael TINKHAM^{6}, b. 24 Jan. 1743/4 <MD 16:15>

Cornelius TINKHAM^{6}, b. 20 Oct. 1745 (O.S.) <MD 18:152>

Daniel TINKHAM^{6}, b. 26 Jan. 1746 (O.S.) <MD 18:152>

Susanna TINKHAM^{6}, b. 27 Nov. 1748 <MD 18:152>; d. 6 June 1753* <*MD 15:102>

Joseph TINKHAM^{6}, b. 18 Aug. 1750 <MD 18:152>

John TINKHAM^{6}, b. 16 Apr. 1754 <MD 18:152>

Huldah TINKHAM^{6}, b. c1760, d. 6 Aug. 1787, ae 27y7d, unm., Middleboro, Nemasket g.s. <MD 15:101>

Amasa TINKHAM^{6}, b. c1762, d. 27 Sept. 1778, ae 16y1m12d, Middleboro <MD 15:100>

Levi TINKHAM^{6}, b. c1754, d. 17 Sept. 1857, ae 91y10m, Middleboro, Nemasket g.s., mechanic, old age <MD 15:102, Mass.VR 112:305>

Mary FOSTER^{6} (Tho.^{5}, Faith Oakman^{4}, Eliz. Doty^{3}, Edw.^{2}), b. 21 Dec. 1765, Marshfield; d. 19 Mar. 1826, Middleboro, Nemasket g.s. <MD 15:102>

CHILD OF Levi TINKHAM^{6} & Mary Foster:

Mary TINKHAM^{7}, b. c1810, d. 7 Nov. 1887, ae 77y10m22d, Middleboro, (widow Wood) <Mass.VR 383:366>

CHILDREN OF Henry WOOD & Mary TINKHAM^{4} (Ephraim^{3}): (6) <Middleboro VR>

Samuel WOOD^{5}, b. 27 Sept. 1718 <MD 3:233>

Esther WOOD^{5}, b. 31 Jan. 1720/1, d. 9 May 1721 <MD 6:179,4:74>

Joanna WOOD^{5}, b. 30 Mar. 1722 <MD 6:179>

Susanna WOOD^{5}, b. 24 Apr. 1724 <MD 8:29>

Henry WOOD^{5}, b. 27 Feb. 1726/7 <MD 8:29>

Moses WOOD^{5}, b. 3 Feb. 1730/1 <MD 8:29>; d. 26 July 1779

Lydia WATERMAN^{6} (Jos.^{5}, Lydia Cushman^{4}, Eleazer^{3}, Mary Allerton^{2}),b. 29 Aug. 1740;d. 30 Oct. 1790

CHILDREN OF Moses WOOD^{5} & Lydia WATERMAN: (5)

Son, b. Sept. 1763, d.y.

Moses WOOD^{6}, b. 3 Mar. 1765, d. 9 Jan. 1811

Deliverance WOOD^{6}, b. 28 Aug. 1769, d. 5 Oct. 1786

Isaiah WOOD^{6}, b. 3 July 1773, d. 1 Apr. 1834

Bathsheba WOOD^{6}, b. 9 Sept. 1776, d. 20 Mar. 1778

Patience COBB^{4} (Rachel Soule^{3}, John^{2}), b. 23 Sept. 1693, d. 4 Nov. 1727, Middleboro, The Green g.s. <MD 2:42,5:38> (1st wf of Sam. Tinkham^{4} (Ephraim^{3}))

Melatiah EDDY, b. c1704, d. 8 Oct. 1798, 94th yr, Middleboro, The Green g.s. <MD 14:221>

CHILDREN OF Samuel TINKHAM^{4} (Ehpraim^{3}) & 2nd Melatiah EDDY: (8) <Middleboro VR>

Ephraim TINKHAM^{5}, b. 30 Apr. 1733 <MD 12:31>; d. 5 Nov. 1769, Middleboro, Green g.s.<MD 14:221>

Patience TINKHAM^{5}, b. 9 Jan. 1734/5 <MD 12:233>

Samuel TINKHAM^{5}, b. 16 Apr. 1737 <MD 8:249>

Silas TINKHAM^{5}, b. 25 Apr. 1739 <MD 14:245>

Fear TINKHAM^{5}, b. 14 Mar. 1740/1 <MD 15:120>

Martha TINKHAM^{5}, b. 27 Mar. 1743 <MD 15:220>

Lois TINKHAM^{5}, b. 2 Oct. 1745 <MD 16:107>

Sarah TINKHAM^{5}, b. 18 June 1748 <MD 18:151>

Sarah STANDISH^{5} (Moses^{4}, Eben.^{3}, Alex.^{3}), b. 26 Apr. 1736 <Halifax VR:42>

CHILDREN OF Ephraim TINKHAM^{5} & Sarah STANDISH: (7) <Middleboro VR; 1-6, MD 26:24>

Abigail TINKHAM^{6}, b. 20 July 1758

Samuel TINKHAM^{6}, b. 16 Mar. 1760, d. 2 Aug. 1761

Joshua TINKHAM^{6}, b. 24 Apr. 1762, d. 24 Oct. 1762

Sarah TINKHAM^{6}, b. 11 Sept. 1763

Ephraim TINKHAM^{6}, b. 2 Aug. 1765

Susanna TINKHAM^{6}, b. 27 Aug. 1767; d. 3 Nov. 1769 <MD 26:25>

Samuel TINKHAM^{6}, b. 17 July 1769 <MD 29:189>

CHILDREN OF Caleb LEACH & Abigail TINKHAM^{6}: (2*) <Davis' Landmarks>

Ebenezer LEACH^{7}, b. 1783

Abigail LEACH^{7}, b. 1785

CHILDREN OF Helkiah TINKHAM^{3} & Ruth (   ): (9) <Plymouth VR, MD 4:111>

Helkiah TINKHAM^{4}, b. 15 Aug. 1685; d. pre 17 Dec. 1746 (adm.) <Plymouth Co.Prob.#20856>

Mary TINKHAM^{4}, b. 13 Aug. 1687; d. 17 Mar. 1717, Plymouth g.s. <Drew:210>

John TINKHAM^{4}, b. 27 Mar. 1689; d. 12 May 1730

Jacob TINKHAM^{4}, b. 15 June 1691; d. aft. 1731* (father's will)

Caleb TINKHAM^{4}, b. 12 Oct. 1693

Sarah TINKHAM^{4}, b. 30 Jan. 1696; d. 22 Feb. 1714/5

Ebenezer TINKHAM^{4}, b. 3 May 1698

Ruth TINKHAM^{4}, b. 13 Feb. 1701

Peter TINKHAM^{4}, b. 1 Apr. 1706

CHILDREN OF Caleb TINKHAM^{4} & Mercy HOLMES, (*dau of Nathaniel): (7) <Plymouth, 1-6, MD 15:114>

Mercy TINKHAM^{5}, b. 8 May 1726 <MD 15:113>

Patience TINKHAM^{5}, b. 16 July 1729

Fear TINKHAM^{5}, b. 5 Nov. 1731

Sarah TINKHAM^{5}, b. 28 Dec. 1733

Nathaniel TINKHAM^{5}, b. 12 Aug. 1736

Caleb TINKHAM^{5}, b. 20 Mar. 1738

Eleanor TINKHAM^{5}, b. ( )

CHILDREN OF Samuel BRYANT & Eleanor TINKHAM^{5}: (3) <Plymouth, MD 20:71>

Sarah BRYANT^{6}, b. 23 Dec. 1758

Samuel BRYANT^{6}, b. 14 Apr. (   ) (no yr given in rcds.)

Lydia BRYANT^{6}, b. ( ) (no date given in rcds.)

Mary BONNEY^{3} (Wm.^{2}, Tho.^{1}), b. 9 May 1704, Plympton <MD 3:166>

CHILDREN OF Ebenezer TINKHAM^{4} (Helkiah^{3}) & 1st Mary BONNEY: (2) <Plymouth, MD 15:113>

Sarah TINKHAM^{5}, b. 22 Nov. 1733

Ebenezer TINKHAM^{5}, b. 20 Feb. 1735/6

CHILDREN OF Ebenezer TINKHAM^{4} & 2nd Jane PRATT: (7) <Plymouth, MD 15:113>

Mary TINKHAM^{5}, b. 7 Oct. 1737, d. 18 Apr. 1739

Mary TINKHAM^{5}, b. 9 Apr. 1739

Ebenezer TINKHAM^{5}, b. 14 Apr. 1741

James TINKHAM^{5}, b. 19 Jan. 1743/4

Phebe TINKHAM^{5}, b. 12 July 1746

Susanna TINKHAM^{5}, b. 15 Sept. 1748

Priscilla TINKHAM^{5}, b. 26 July 1755

Elizabeth (*HEITER), d. aft. 1 Sept. 1750 <Plymouth Co.Prob.2:441>[<11>]

CHILDREN OF Helkiah TINKHAM^{4} (Helkiah^{3}) & Elizabeth HEITER: (12) <Plymouth; 1-8, MD 5:99>

Hannah TINKHAM^{5}, b. 31 Oct. 1710

Elizabeth TINKHAM^{5}, b. 5 July 1713

Isaac TINKHAM^{5}, b. 27 Dec. 1715

Sarah TINKHAM^{5}, b. 5 Aug. 1718

Zedekiah TINKHAM^{5}, b. 11 July 1721

John TINKHAM^{5}, b. 29 Sept. 1723, d. 13 Oct. 1723

Mary TINKHAM^5, b. 14 Sept. 1724
Martha TINKHAM^5, b. 29 Dec. 1726
Ruth TINKHAM^5, b. 9 July 1729 <MD 5:100>
Lydia TINKHAM^5, b. 9 July 1729 (twins), d. 22 Oct. 1732 <MD 5:100>
Ebenezer TINKHAM^5, b. 26 June 1732 <MD 5:100>; d. pre 1 Sept. 1760*
Lydia TINKHAM^5, b. 10 Mar. 1734/5 <MD 5:100>

CHILDREN OF Jonathan SANDERS, (*son of Henry & Ann) & Elizabeth TINKHAM^5: (3) <MD 15:162>
Mary SANDERS^6, b. 22 Mar. 1741/2
Elizabeth SANDERS^6, b. 12 Aug. 1744
Jonathan SANDERS^6, b. 5 Feb. 1746/7, d. 1 Oct. 1747

CHILDREN OF Thomas SILVESTER & Martha TINKHAM^5 (Helkiah^4): (3) <MD 18:212>
Thomas SILVESTER^6, b. 11 Feb. 1750/1
Sarah SILVESTER^6, b. 5 June 1753
Hannah SILVESTER^6, b. 4 Mar. 1756

Hannah COBB, (dau of Eben.), b. 27 Feb. 1699, Plymouth <MD 2:19>; d. pre 2 Nov. 1725 (hus.2nd marr. int.) <MD 18:124>

CHILDREN OF Jacob TINKHAM^4 (Helkiah^3) & Hannah COBB: (2) <Plymouth, MD 13:115>
Mercy TINHAM^5, b. 27 Sept. 1722, d. 20 Apr. 1724
Jacob TINKHAM^5, b. 28 Feb. 1723/4

Lydia DUNHAM, (dau. of Josiah), b. 8 Feb. 1724/5, Plymouth <MD 13:34>

CHILDREN OF Jacob TINKHAM^5 (Jacob^4) & Lydia DUNHAM: (4) <Plymouth, MD 4:10>
Hannah TINKHAM^6, b. 31 Oct. 1747; d. 2 Aug. 1815, Marshfield, Plainville g.s. <MD 14:49>
Lydia TINKHAM^6, b. 15 Nov. 1749
Mary TINKHAM^6, b. 28 Nov. 1751
Jacob TINKHAM^6, b. 10 Sept. 1754

William CURTIS, b. 28 Aug. 1742, d. 1 Oct. 1821 <Pembroke VR:399>

CHILDREN OF William CURTIS & Hannah TINKHAM^6 (Jacob^5): (7) <1-3, MD 22:182>
William CURTIS^7, b. 19 Aug. 1769; d. ae 43, (c1811), Plainville g.s., Marshfield <MD 14:49>
(Hannah) CURTIS^7, b. 3 Sept. 1771 (Lydia?)<12>
Lydia CURTIS^7, bpt. 15 Aug. 1773<12> (m. Dr. Sebra Crooker, see p.272)
James CURTIS^7, b. 25 Nov. 1773
Stoddard CURTIS^7, b. 15 Aug. 1775 <Pembroke VR:71>; d. pre 19 Aug. 1818 (father's will) <Plymouth Co.Prob.54:230>
Hannah CURTIS^7, b. 24 May 1781 <Pembroke VR:71>
Jacob CURTIS^7, b. 30 May 1784 <Pembroke VR:71>
Polly CURTIS^7, b. 5 Mar. 1787 <Pembroke VR:71>

Olive ( ) CURTIS, d. 8 Nov. 1837, 70th yr, Plainville g.s., Marshfield <MD 14:49> (wf of Wm^7)

Ann GRAY^5 (John^4, Mary Winslow^3, Mary Chilton^2), b. 5 Aug. 1691, Plymouth <MD 1:145>; d. 6 Sept. 1730, Kingston g.s. <MD 7:221>

CHILDREN OF John TINKHAM^4 (Helkiah^3) & Ann GRAY: (6)
Mary TINKHAM^5, b. 25 June 1718, Plymouth <MD 13:33>; d. 25 July 1730, Kingston g.s. <MD 7:221>
Edward TINKHAM^5, b. 2 Feb. 1719/20, Plymouth <MD 13:33>
John TINKHAM^5, b. c1722, d. 15 Sept. 1748, ae 26y9m29d, Kingston g.s. <MD 7:221>
Ephraim TINKHAM^5, b. 25 Mar. 1724 <Kingston VR, Gen.Adv.2:39>
Ann TINKHAM^5, b. 6 Aug. 1726 <Kingston VR, Gen.Adv.2:39>
Joseph TINKHAM^5, b. 14 May 1728 <Kingston VR, Gen.Adv.2:39>

CHILDREN OF Joseph TINKHAM$^{5?}$ & Deborah FULLER: (4) <Kingston VR, Gen.Adv.3:80>
John TINKHAM, b. 9 Nov. 1754
Joseph TINKHAM, b. 26 May 1757
Levi TINKHAM, b. 17 Feb. 1762

Seth TINKHAM, b. 22 Mar. 1764

CHILD OF John TINKHAM^{5} (John^{4}) & Sarah EVERSON:

Anne TINKHAM^{6}, b. 3 Jan. 1748/9, d. 6 Jan. 1754 <Kingston VR 1:43>

CHILDREN OF Edward TINKHAM^{5} (John^{4}) & Lydia RIDER, (*dau of Ben.): (2) <Gen.Adv.2:121>

Salvenis TINKHAM^{6}, b. 1 Aug. (1743) (parents married in Sept.)

Rebecca TINKHAM^{6}, b. 11 June 1745

CHILDREN OF Ebenezer CURTIS & Mary TINKHAM^{4} (Helkiah^{3}): (4) <Plymouth, MD 7:208>

Jacob CURTIS^{5}, b. 11 Oct. 1710

Caleb CURTIS^{5}, b. 15 Aug. 1712, d. 19 Nov. 1729

Mary CURTIS^{5}, b. 21 Dec. 1714

Sarah CURTIS^{5}, b. 19 Aug. 1717

Mary BENNET, (dau of Jos.), b. 5 Nov. 1708, Middleboro <MD 2:203>

CHILDREN OF Peter TINKHAM^{4} (Helkiah^{3}) & Mary BENNET: (2) <Plymouth, MD 12:223>

Jacob TINKHAM^{5}, b. 29 May 1738

Arthur TINKHAM^{5}, b. 7 June 1742

Sarah ( ) TINKHAM, d. aft. 10 Apr. 1759 (deed) <Bristol Co.Prob.53:383>

CHILDREN OF John TINKHAM^{3} & Sarah ( ): (5) <Dartmouth VR:185>

John TINKHAM^{4}, b. ( )

Mary TINKHAM^{4}, b. ( )

Martha TINKHAM^{4}, b. 19 May 1722; d. aft. 26 Feb. 1790 <Bristol Co.Deeds 69:136>

Peter TINKHAM^{4}, b. 8 Feb. 1723/4; d. aft. 1778*

Elkiah TINKHAM^{4}, b. 10 Nov. 1725

MICRO #3 of 5

CHILDREN OF Peter TINKHAM^{4} & Eunice CLARK: (4) <Dartmouth VR:185>**<13>**

Charles TINKHAM^{5}, b. 16 June 1747; d. 18 Nov. 1822*, Rochester

Clark TINKHAM^{5}, b. 7 Feb. 1748/9

Ephraim TINKHAM^{5}, b. 27 Jan. 1750/1

Sarah TINKHAM^{5}, b. 14 Dec. 1753

CHILDREN OF John TINKHAM^{4} (John^{3}) & Mary ( ): (7) <Dartmouth VR:273>**<14>**

Elizabeth TINKHAM^{5}, b. 17 July 1741

John TINKHAM^{5}, b. 10 May 1743

Almy TINKHAM^{5}, b. 15 Sept. 1745

Mary TINKHAM^{5}, b. 4 Sept. 1747

Barbary TINKHAM^{5}, b. 14 July 1749

Deborah TINKHAM^{5}, b. 22 May 1751

Hannah TINKHAM^{5}, b. 3 Dec. 1754

Joseph ELLIS, d. aft. 26 Feb. 1790 <Bristol Co.Deeds 69:136>

CHILDREN OF Joseph ELLIS & Martha TINKHAM^{4} (John^{3}): (1 of 4)**<15>**

Luke ELLIS^{5}, b. ( )

CHILDREN OF Luke ELLIS^{5} & 1st Naomi BRIGGS^{8}: (7)**<16>**

CHILD OF Luke ELLIS^{5} & 2nd Elizabeth MACOMBER: <New Bedford>

Naomi ELLIS^{6}, b. c1785, d. 29 Mar. 1864, ae 79, paralysis, New Bedford, unm. <Mass.VR 174:116>

CHILD OF Charles TINKHAM^{5} (Peter^{4}) & Jane ELLIS:

Andrew TINKHAM^{6}, b. 4 Apr. 1777, <Rochester VR 1:293>, d. Feb. 1853, Sydney ME

Jemima WILBOR, b. July 1785*, Sydney ME, d. 19 July 1833*, Sydney ME

CHILD OF Andrew TINKHAM^{6} & Jemima WILBOR:

David Wilbor TINKHAM^{7}, b. 10 Apr. 1814, d. 4 May 1889

Mercy MENDALL, (dau of John), b. 3 Aug. 1666, Marshfield <MD 3:42>

CHILDREN OF Peter TINKHAM^{3} & Mercy MENDALL: (4)

Mercy TINKHAM^{4}, b. c1692, d.? 17 Apr. 1723*, ae 31, Middleboro, The Green g.s. <MD 14:84>

Joanna TINKHAM^{4}, b. c1696, d. 28 June 1738, 42nd yr, Middleboro, The Green g.s. <MD 12:68>

Samuel TINKHAM^{4}, b. betw. 1696-1703; d. betw. 1741 - 1747**<17>**

Seth TINKHAM^{4}, b. 15 May 1704, Middleboro <MD 7:242>; d. 9 Feb. 1751, Middleboro, Nemasket g.s. <MD 15:103,18:81>

Joseph BATES, b. c1692, d. 31 Aug. 1778, 86th yr, Middleboro, The Green g.s. <MD 12:69>

CHILDREN OF Joseph BATES & Joanna TINKHAM^{4}: (6) <Middleboro VR>

Joanna BATES^{5}, b. 28 May 1718 <MD 4:68>

Mercy BATES^{5}, b. 8 Aug. 1719 <MD 4:68>

Joseph BATES^{5}, b. 18 Mar. 1721/2 <MD 4:68>

Elizabeth BATES^{5}, b. 12 Jan. 1722/3 <MD 6:227>

Thomas BATES^{5}, b. 9 Nov. 1724 <MD 6:227>

Priscilla BATES^{5}, b. 6 Jan. 1726/7 <MD 7:241>

Eunice TINKHAM^{6} (Peter^{5}, Ebenezer$^{4-3}$, Mary Brown^{2}), b. c1729, d. 14 Oct. 1785, 56th yr,Middleboro The Green g.s. <MD 12:68>

CHILDREN OF Joseph BATES^{5} & Eunice TINKHAM: (6) <Middleboro VR>

Peter BATES^{6}, b. 22 Dec. 1750

Joanna BATES^{6}, b. 2 Aug. 1752

Elizabeth BATES^{6}, b. 20 July 1754

Sarah BATES^{6}, b. 26 Feb. 1756

Joseph BATES^{6}, b. Mar. 1758, d. 14 May 1758 <MD 12:69>

Samuel BATES^{6}, b. June 1759, d. 17 May 1760 <MD 12:69>

CHILDREN OF Samuel TINKHAM^{4} (Peter^{3}) & Mary STAPLES: (9) <Middleboro VR>

Martha TINKHAM^{5}, b. 23 Aug. 1720, d. 20 Mar. 1743/4, Middleboro <MD 4:69,16:18>

Peter TINKHAM^{5}, b. 16 May 1722 <MD 4:69>; d. pre 9 May 1757* <Plymouth Co.Deeds 47:51>

Samuel TINKHAM^{5}, b. 13 Mar. 1723/4, d. 28 Mar. 1796, Middleboro, Nemasket g.s. <MD 6:229,15:103>

Mercy TINKHAM^{5}, b. 24 Apr. 1726 <MD 6:229>

Deborah TINKHAM^{5}, b. 7 Sept. 1728 <MD 9:49>

Gideon TINKHAM^{5}, b. 24 Apr. 1731 <MD 9:49>

Joanna TINKHAM^{5}, b. 15 May 1734 <MD 12:233>

Keziah TINKHAM^{5}, b. 15 Aug. 1738 <MD 14:244>

Lydia TINKHAM^{5}, b. 10 May 1741, d. 24 Dec. 1747 <MD 15:217,18:80>

Hope COBB^{5*} (*Gershom^{4}, Hope Chipman^{3}, Hope Howland^{2}), b. 10 Nov. 1727*, Middleboro; d. 3 June 1760, 33rd yr, Middleboro, The Green g.s. <MD 14:221>

CHILD OF Samuel TINKHAM & Hope COBB: <Middleboro>

Lazarus TINKHAM, b. 28 Feb. 1745/6, d. Nov. 1762 <MD 16:20,14:221>

CHILD OF Samuel SNOW & Deborah TINKHAM^{5*}: ("apparently not married")

Samuel SNOW^{6*}, b. 10 May 1753 <MD 18:154>

CHILD OF Nathaniel WOOD & Martha TINKHAM^{5} (Sam.^{4}):

Joshua WOOD^{6}, b. 17 Mar. 1744, d. 20 Oct. 1744, Middleboro <MD 16:20,16:18>

Mary ( ) TINKHAM, b. c1700, d. 6 ( ) 1745, 45th yr, Middleboro g.s. <MD 15:102>**<18>**

CHILDREN OF Seth TINKHAM^{4} (Peter^{3}) & Mary ( ): (9) <Middleboro VR>

Bathsheba TINKHAM^{5}, b. 10 July 1726 <MD 6:228>

Ebenezer TINKHAM^{5}, b. 21 Mar. 1727/8, d. 16 May 1729 <MD 7:241,15:100>

Son, b. 26 Jan. 1729/30, stillborn <MD 13:5>

Dau, b. 12 Feb. 1730/1, stillborn <MD 13:5>

Mercy TINKHAM^{5}, b. 25 July 1732 <MD 9:49>

Seth TINKHAM^{5}, b. 13 Nov. 1734, d. 13 Feb. 1808, Middleboro, Nemasket g.s. <MD 12:233,15:103>

Elizabeth TINKHAM^{5}, b. 11 May 1737 <MD 8:249>

Dau, b. 10 June 1739, stillborn <MD 15:24>

Joanna TINKHAM^{5}, b. 1 Jan. 1740/1 <MD 15:120>

Eunice SOULE^{5} (Zachariah^{4}, Ben.^{3}, John^{2}), b. 1 Feb. 1735/6* <Plympton VR>; d. 11 May 1808,Middleboro, Nemasket g.s. <MD 15:101>

CHILD OF Seth TINKHAM^{5} & Eunice SOULE:

Hazael TINKHAM^{6}, b. 20 Apr. 1763 (son) <Middleboro VR 2:76>; d. 9 May 1839, Middleboro, Nemasket g.s. <MD 15:103>

Susanna PRATT, (*dau of Eben & Deborah (Morse)), b. c1759, d. 5 Dec. 1840, ae 81y2m4d, Middleboro Nemasket g.s. <MD 15:103>

CHILDREN OF Hazael TINKHAM^{6} & Susanna PRATT: (4) <Middleboro>

Sophia TINKHAM^{7}, b. 12 Mar. 1785, d. 28 Nov. 1785 <MD 32:89,15:103>

Hazael TINKHAM^{7}, b. 18 Mar. 1787, d. 16 Oct. 1865 <MD 32:140,15:101>

George Washington TINKHAM^{7}, b. 14 Aug. 1791, d. 15 Oct. 1838 <MD 33:76,15:101>

Hervey TINKHAM^{7}, b. 5 Oct. 1795

PRISCILLA BROWN^{2} (Peter^{1})

William ALLEN, d. 1 Oct. 1705, Sandwich <Barnstable Co.Prob.2:211, MD 31:26> (m. Priscilla Brown, no issue)

REBECCA BROWN^{2} (Peter^{1})

William SNOW, d. 31 Jan. 1708, Bridgewater <MD 8:103>

CHILDREN OF William SNOW & Rebecca BROWN^{2}: (8) <MD 8:101-2>

William SNOW^{3}, b. ( ); d. pre 7 Nov. 1726 (adm.) <MD 22:47>

Joseph SNOW^{3}, d. 18 Dec. 1753, Bridgewater <MD 14:209>

Benjamin SNOW^{3}, d. 28 May 1743* <Bridgewater VR 2:558>

Mary SNOW^{3}, b. ( )

Lydia SNOW^{3}, b. ( )

Hannah SNOW^{3}, b. ( ) (no issue)[<19>]

Rebecca SNOW^{3}, b. c1671, d. 4 Apr. 1740, Plympton g.s. <MD 11:116>

James SNOW^{3}, d. 1690 <MD 31:17>

MICRO #4 of 5

Snow Inscriptions, Middleboro, Green Cem.:

Sarah SNOW, wf of Jonathan, d. 12 Apr. 1743, ae 39y8m4d

Aaron SNOW, son of Jonathan & Sarah, d. 4 Jan. 1741/2, ae near 12y

Jonathan SNOW, d. 17 Jan. 1783, 81st yr

Samuel SNOW, d. 22 June 1781, 51st yr

Aaron SNOW, d. 1 May 1879, 82nd yr

Snow Inscriptions, Middleboro, Warrentown Cem.:

Judith SNOW, dau of Venus & Olive, d. 26 Aug. 1847, ae 2mths

Snow Inscriptions, Middleboro, Central Cem.:

George R. SNOW, son of Russell & Amelia A., d. 7 Sept. 1848, ae 1y3m

Snow Inscriptions, Acushnet, Central Cem.:

John H. SNOW, d. 27 Mar. 1848, ae 47

Lucy SNOW, wf of John H., & dau of N. & H. Sears, d. 1 Nov. 1838, ae 36

Snow Inscriptions, Marion, Central Cem.:

Lemuel SNOW, d. 29 Apr. 1847, ae 65y19d

Delia SNOW, wf of Lemuel, d. 8 Sept. 1843, ae 68y4m27d

Snow Inscriptions, Raynham, Town Cem.:

Solomon SNOW, d. 30 May 1821, ae 79

Betsey SNOW, widow of Solomon, d. 12 Jan. 1834, ae 80

Snow Inscriptions, Kingston, Central Cem.:

Elizabeth SNOW, wf of Benjamin, d. 20 July 1804, 39th yr

Snow Inscriptions, Mattapoisett, Old Cem. in field:

Joseph SNOW, d. 31 Aug. 1808, 75th yr

Rachel SNOW, wf of Joseph, d. 18 May 1807

Joseph SNOW, d. 31 May 1800, ae 27

Priscilla SNOW, wf of Thomas, d. 16 Feb. 1806, 30th yr

Nancy SNOW, wf of Thomas, d. 4 Dec. 1812, 29th yr

Snow Inscriptions, Mattapoisett, Marion Rd. Cem.:

Rebecca SNOW, wf of Joseph Jr., d. 17 Sept. 1898, ae 74y1m23d

Snow Inscriptions, Mattapoisett, Central Cem.:

Joseph SNOW, d. 1 Mar. 1835, ae 33y9m, on stone with:

Ann Eliza SNOW, dau of Joseph & Eunice H., d. 17 Sept. 1835, ae 14mths

Priscilla SNOW, 1st wf of Deacon Thomas, & dau of Capt. John Hammond, d. 16 Feb. 1806, 30th yr

Nancy SNOW, 2nd wf of Deacon Thomas, & dau of Capt. James Hatch, d. 4 Dec. 1812, 29th yr

Mary W. SNOW, wf of Capt. Martin, b. 8 Jan. 1814, d. 28 Feb. 1843, ae 29y1m22d

Rachel SNOW, wf of Wyatt, d. 27 Sept. 1836, ae 31y4m10d

Thomas SNOW, d. 12 Nov. 1849, ae 56y2m23d

Dennis SNOW, son of James & Anna, d. 15 Apr. 1841, ae 39y8m10d

Ephraim SNOW, son of James & Anna, d. 29 Jan. 1818, ae 21y1m9d

James W. SNOW, son of James & Anna, lost at sea 1836, 24th yr

Snow Inscriptions, East Bridgewater:

Mrs. Martha SNOW, dau of Isaac, & wf of Capt. Simeon Whitman, d. 30 Aug. 1781, ae 53

Snow Inscriptions, Rochester, Central Cem.:

Mark SNOW, d. 2 Sept. 1799, 69th yr

Isaac SNOW, d. 19 Apr. 1789, ae 71

Thankful SNOW, widow of Isaac, d. 6 Oct. 1817, 99th yr

Freeman SNOW, son of Freeman & Sarah, d. 25 May 1793, 20th yr

Dr. Isaac Newton SNOW, lost at sea 19 Aug. 1812, 23rd yr

Capt. Jonathan SNOW, d. 27 Mar. 1810, 55th yr

Hannah SNOW, widow of Capt. Jonathan, d. 13 Sept. 1813, 50th yr

Jonathan SNOW, son of Capt. Jonathan & Hannah, d. 1 Nov. 1813, 19th yr

George W. SNOW, son of Capt. Jonathan & Hannah, d. 20 Sept. 1808, ae 9y10m

Walter SNOW, son of Capt. Jonathan & Hannah, d. 1 June 1806, ae 19y7d, Lisbon

Sarah SNOW, wf of Deacon Thomas, d. 26 Nov. 1843, ae 67

Elizabeth Pitson SNOW, 3rd wf of Deacon Thomas, d. 27 May 1817, 39th yr

Snow Inscriptions, Rochester, Union Church Cem.:

Nathaniel SNOW, d. 12 Mar. 1841, ae 54y6m

Snow Inscriptions, "Old Parish Cem. in woods near N. Rochester":

Samuel SNOW, (rest of stone missing)

Hannah SNOW, wf of Samuel, d. 14 Nov. 1795, 41st yr

* * * * *

Elizabeth ALDEN^3 (Jos.^{2}), d. 8 May 1705, Bridgewater <MD 14:203>

CHILDREN OF Benjamin SNOW^3 & 1st Elizabeth ALDEN: (5) <Bridgewater, MD 14:203>

Rebecca SNOW^4, b. 7 Nov. 1694

Benjamin SNOW^4, b. 23 June 1696

Solomon SNOW^4, b. 6 Apr. 1698

Ebenezer SNOW^4, b. 29 Mar. 1701

Elizabeth SNOW^4, b. 5 May 1705; d. 6 July 1755 <Bridgewater VR 2:444>

CHILD OF Benjamin SNOW^3 & 2nd Sarah ( ):

Sarah SNOW^4, b. 20 Aug. 1706, Bridgewater <MD 14:203>**<20>**

Joseph CARVER, d. 24 Sept. 1778 <Bridgewater VR 2:444>

CHILDREN OF Joseph CARVER & Elizabeth SNOW^4: (8) <Bridgewater VR>

Joseph CARVER^5, b. 23 Mar. 1727 <VR 1:65>

Benjamin CARVER^5, b. 28 Feb. 1728/9 <VR 1:65>

Elizabeth CARVER^5, b. 10 Sept. 1731 <VR 1:65>

Abiezer CARVER^5, b. 14 Sept. 1734, d. 31 Aug. 1755 <VR 1:65,2:444>

Sarah CARVER^5, b. 14 Feb. 1736/7 <VR 1:66>

Experience CARVER^5, b. 2 May 1739 <VR 1:65>

Robert CARVER^5, b. 2 June 1742 <VR 1:66>

Rebecca CARVER^5, b. 28 Sept. 1744 <VR 1:66>

CHILDREN OF Joseph CARVER$^{5?}$ & Sarah HARTWELL: (4) <Bridgewater VR>

Hannah CARVER^6, b. 19 May 1747 <VR 1:65>

Rhoda CARVER^6, b. 9 Oct. 1749 <VR 1:66>

Oliver CARVER^6, b. 12 May 1751 <VR 1:66>

Bernice CARVER^6, b. 8 Dec. 1753 <VR 1:65>

Brig. Gen. William BARTON, (son of Ben.), b. 26 May 1748, Warren; d. 22 Oct. 1831, Providence

CHILDREN OF Brig. Gen. William BARTON & Rhoda CARVER$^{6?}$: (9) <Family Record>

William BARTON^7, b. 16 Dec. 1771; d. 16 Jan. 1818, Enfield CT <Arnold VR 18:259>

Benjamin BARTON^7, b. 20 Dec. 1773; d. Oct. 1797, Port au Riffe, W.I. <Arnold VR 13:163>

George Washington BARTON^7, b. 6 Feb. 1776

Daniel BARTON^7, b. 20 July 1778, d. 9 Apr. 1780

Henry BARTON^7, b. 18 Nov. 1780; d. 11 Nov. 1814, Savannah GA <Arnold VR 18:259>

Lieut. Robert Carver BARTON^7, b. 19 Dec. 1782; d. Sept. 1824, near Marietta OH <Arnold VR 13:163>

John BARTON^7, b. 3 Apr. 1785

Anna Maria BARTON^7, b. 5 Mar. 1788

Sarah BARTON^7, b. 30 Aug. 1790

CHILD OF Nathaniel PRATT & Sarah SNOW^4 (Ben.^{3}):**<21>** **<22>**

Seth PRATT^5, b. ( ), d. betw. 29 Nov. 1794 (will) - 6 Jan. 1796 (prob.)<Plymouth Co.Prob.35:448>

CHILDREN OF Joseph SNOW^3 & Hopestill ALDEN^3 (Jos.^{2}): (7) <Bridgewater, MD 14:208>

Joseph SNOW^4, b. 7 Sept. 1690; d. betw. 12 Jan. 1765 (will)- 31 July 1773 (inv.)**<23>**

Mary SNOW^4, b. 1 Nov. 1691

James SNOW^4, b. 16 Aug. 1693**<24>**

Rebecca SNOW^4, b. 25 June 1696

Isaac SNOW^4, b. 22 July 1700; d. 10 July 1737 <Bridgewater VR 2:559>

Jonathan SNOW^4, b. 27 Sept. 1703; d. 17 Jan. 1783, Middleboro, Nemasket g.s. <MD 15:7>

David SNOW^4, b. 27 Sept. 1703 (twins)

Hannah SHAW, (dau of Jos.), b. 31 July 1704, d. 30 Mar. 1762 <Bridgewater VR 1:288,2:578>

CHILDREN OF Isaac SNOW^4 & Hannah SHAW: (6) <E. Bridgewater>

Hannah SNOW^5, bpt. 8 Aug. 1725

Isaac SNOW^5, bpt. 17 Apr. 1726

Martha SNOW^5, bpt. 29 Dec. 1728

Peter SNOW^5, bpt. 29 Aug. 1731

Joseph SNOW^5, bpt. 30 June 1734

Judah SNOW^5, bpt. 13 Feb. 1736/7

Elizabeth BOWDITCH^5 (*?Mary Bass^4, Sam.^{3}, Ruth Alden^2), d. 4 Nov. 1783*, Haverhill

CHILDREN OF Isaac SNOW^5 & Elizabeth BOWDITCH: (11*) <Haverhill VR>

Mary SNOW^6, bpt. 16 July 1749, E. Bridgewater

Elizabeth SNOW^6, b. 9 Apr. 1751

Hannah SNOW^6, b. 31 Mar. 1753

Isaac SNOW^{6}, b. 17 Nov. 1754; d. 31 Mar. 1756

James SNOW^{6}, b. 21 Sept. 1756

Isaac SNOW^{6}, b. 14 Apr. 1758; d. 25 Apr. 1759

Sarah SNOW^{6}, b. 14 Dec. 1759; d. 28 Nov. 1793

Joseph SNOW^{6}, b. 1 Sept. 1761; d. 18 June 1791

Judith SNOW^{6}, b. 23 Ar. 1763

Isaac SNOW^{6}, b. 21 Mar. 1765

Susanna SNOW^{6}, b. 16 Feb. 1767

CHILDREN OF James SNOW^{4} (Jos.^{3}) & 1st Ruth SHAW: (1 of 11)**<25>**

Ruth SNOW^{5}, b. 12 May 1720 <Bridgewater VR> <MD 15:87>

CHILD OF James SNOW^{4} & 2nd Hannah HOVEY:

James SNOW^{5}, b. ( )

Perez BONNEY^{3} (John^{2}, Tho.^{1}), b. 10 Mar. 1709

CHILDREN OF Perez BONNEY & Ruth SNOW^{5} (James^{4}): (7) <Pembroke VR>

Joel BONNEY^{6}, b. 14 Aug. 1740 <VR:42>

Perez BONNEY^{6}, b. 13 July 1742 <VR:45>

Titus BONNEY^{6}, b. 1 June 1744 <VR:38>

Celia BONNEY^{6}, b. 16 Apr. 1746 <VR:39>

Jairus BONNEY^{6}, b. 14 Feb. 1747 <VR:42>

Asa BONNEY^{6}, b. 16 Sept. 1751 <VR:39>

James BONNEY^{6}, b. ( )

Sarah SOULE^{4} (John$^{3-2}$), b. 8 Oct. 1703, Middleboro <MD 2:105>; d. 12 Apr. 1743, Middleboro, Green g.s. <MD 14:133>

CHILDREN OF Jonathan SNOW^{4} (Jos.^{3}) & Sarah SOULE: (7) <Bridgewater, MD 15:196>

Samuel SNOW^{5}, b. 20 Sept. 1729; d. 22 June 1781, Middleboro, Nemasket g.s. <MD 15:7>

Jesse SNOW^{5}, b. 8 Feb. 1730/1

Sarah SNOW^{5}, b. 3 Dec. 1732

Rebecca SNOW^{5}, b. 16 Oct. 1734

Jonathan SNOW^{5}, b. 10 Mar. 1735/6

Moses SNOW^{5}, b. 27 Sept. 1737 <MD 15:197>

Aaron SNOW^{5}, b. 1740 <MD 15:197>; d. 4 Jan. 1741/2 <MD 14:133>

Deborah TINKHAM^{5} (Sam.^{4}, Peter^{3}, Mary Brown^{2}), b. 7 Sept. 1728 <Middleboro VR>

CHILD OF Samuel SNOW^{5} & Deborah TINKHAM: ("apparently not married")

Samuel SNOW^{6}, b. 10 May 1753, Middleboro <MD 18:154>

Elizabeth FIELD, (dau of John & Eliz.), b. 4 Aug. 1698, Bridgewater <MD 7:55>

CHILDREN OF Joseph SNOW^{4} (Jos.^{3}) & Elizabeth FIELD: (6) <Bridgewater; 1-5, MD 15:84>

Rev. Joseph SNOW^{5}, b. 26 Mar. 1715; d. 10 Apr. 1803, Providence <Arnold VR 2:1:274>

John SNOW^{5}, b. 19 Apr. 1717

Elizabeth SNOW^{5}, b. 4 May 1719

Susanna SNOW^{5}, b. 12 Dec. 1722

Sarah SNOW^{5}, b. 3 Feb. 1725

Daniel SNOW^{5}, b. 1727

James SNOW^{5}, b. c1730*; d. 8 Oct. 1812*, Providence RI (mentioned in father's will)

Hannah (SEARLE*), b. 14 Nov. 1823*, Providence RI

CHILDREN OF James SNOW^{5} & Hannah (SEARLE*): (2 of 5)**<26>**

Joseph SNOW^{6}, b. 31 May 1765*; d.? 2 Jan. 1812, 47th yr <Arnold VR 14:291>

Daniel SNOW^{6}, d. pre 1 Dec. 1784 (inv.) <Provindence RI Prob.#A1197, W:6:450>**<27>**

Rebecca ( ) SNOW, b. 14 Feb. 1765

CHILDREN OF Joseph SNOW^{6} & Rebecca ( ):

William Downing SNOW^{7}, b. 16 Apr. 1786; d. 24 Feb. 1854

Stephen Wardwell SNOW^{7}, b. 28 Dec. 1788; d. 17 Apr. 1818

Henry SNOW^{7}, b. 4 Aug. 1791

Joseph SNOW^{7}, b. 3 Nov. 1794

Hannah SNOW^{7}, b. 9 Feb. 1797

Nancy Downing SNOW^{7}, b. 7 Sept. 1799

Joseph Valentine SNOW^{7}, b. 14 Feb. 1802; d. 28 Oct. 1856

Abigail SNOW^{7}, b. 13 Dec. 1804

Edward SNOW^{7}, b. 26 Mar. 1806; d. 26 Sept. 1859

CHILDREN OF William Downing SNOW^{7} & Lydia HORSWELL: (2)

Amanda SNOW^{8}, b. c1819, d. 23 May 1880, ae 61, Fall River

William Downing SNOW^{8}, b. 20 June 1820, d. 10 Mar. 1893 <Bible Rcd.>

CHILD OF William READ & Amanda SNOW^{8}:

Julia A. READ^{9}, b. ( ), d. c1932, Fall River

Ann WARHURST, b. 19 Sept. 1820, d. 4 Nov. 1889 <Bible Rcd.>

CHILDREN OF William Downing SNOW^{8} (Wm.^{7}) & Ann WARHURST: (9)

Rebecca A. SNOW^{9}, b. 27 Apr. 1837

Amanda M. SNOW^{9}, b. 24 May 1839, d. 21 Sept. 1880

Amelia Josephine SNOW^{9}, b. 30 Oct. 1841, d. 17 July 1931

George W. SNOW^{9}, b. 15 Oct. 1843, d. 11 Feb. 1923

Mary E. SNOW^{9}, b. 7 Dec. 1848, d. 17 Feb. 1908

Josephine SNOW^{9}, b. 11 Mar. 1852, d. 4 Sept. 1852

Henry C. SNOW^{9}, b. 10 Jan. 1854

Ida SNOW^{9}, b. 29 Apr. 1858, d. 3 Aug. 1858

Edward C. SNOW^{9}, b. 17 Oct. 1859, d. 31 Aug. 1860

Sarah FIELD, b. 9 Aug. 1710, d. 19 July 1753 <Arnold VR 3:1:246,274>

CHILDREN OF Rev. Joseph SNOW^{5} (Jos.^{4}) & 1st Sarah FIELD:(9) <Arnold VR 2:1:246>

Sarah SNOW^{6}, b. 27 Oct. 1738; d. 23 Apr. 1752

John SNOW^{6}, b. 3 Feb. 1740

Joseph SNOW^{6}, b. 22 Sept. 1741; d. 10 Oct. 1741

Lydia SNOW^{6}, b. 8 Jan. 1744; d. 22 Mar. 1763

Susanna SNOW^{6}, b. 14 Oct. 1745; d. 21 Mar. 1766

Elizabeth SNOW^{6}, b. 10 Oct. 1747

Abigail SNOW^{6}, b. 26 Mar. 1749; d. 10 Aug. 1752

Josiah SNOW^{6}, b. 24 Feb. 1750

Rebecca GRANT, d. 30 Sept. 1774 <Arnold VR 10:229>

CHILDREN OF Rev. Joseph SNOW^{5} & 2nd Rebecca GRANT: (4) <Arnold VR 2:1:246>

Rebecca SNOW^{6}, b. 13 Feb. 1756

Samuel SNOW^{6}, b. 1 Aug. 1758

Edward SNOW^{6}, b. 9 May 1760

Benjamin SNOW^{6}, b. 6 Dec. 1761

Margaret PROCTOR, b. c1734, d. 21 Apr. 1817, 83rd yr, Attleboro <Arnold VR 14:291> (3rd wf of Rev. Joseph Snow^{5})

Samuel RICKARD^{3} (Giles$^{2-1}$), b. 14 Jan. 1662, Plymouth; d. 7 Sept. 1727, Plympton g.s. <MD 11:116>

CHILDREN OF Samuel RICKARD & Rebecca SNOW^{3}: (9) <1,2,4-7, Plymouth>

Rebecca RICKARD^{4}, b. 9 Feb. 1690/1 <MD 1:211>

Hannah RICKARD^{4}, b. 25 Sept. 1693 <MD 1:211>; d. 1771 (widow), Bridgewater

Samuel RICKARD^{4}, b. May 1696, d. 18 Aug. 1768, ae 72y2m27d <MD 11:116>

Bethiah RICKARD^{4}, b. 15 Oct. 1698 <MD 3:15> **<27a>**

Henry RICKARD^{4}, b. 4 Feb. 1700 <MD 3:15> **<27a>**

Mary RICKARD^{4}, b. 8 Apr. 1702 <MD 3:15>

Elkanah RICKARD^4, b. 7 June 1704 <MD 3:15>**<27a>**

Mehitable RICKARD^4, b. 1 Apr. 1707, Plympton <MD 3:94>

Eleazer RICKARD^4, b. 8 Mar. 1709/10, Plympton <MD 3:94>

CHILDREN OF Josiah BYRAM & Hannah RICKARD^4: (5) <Bridgewater, MD 15:87>

Susanna BYRAM^5, b. 27 Apr. 1721 <MD 15:86>

Josiah BYRAM^5, b. 5 Mar. 1722/3

Theophilus BYRAM^5, b. 8 Aug. 1725

Mehitable BYRAM^5, b. 25 May 1730

Rebecca BYRAM^5, b. 26 Aug. 1732

Rachel ( ) RICKARD, b. c1700, d. 30 Jan. 1792, 92nd yr, Plympton g.s. <MD 11:116>**<28>**

CHILDREN OF Samuel RICKARD^4 & Rachel ( ): (7) <1-3, Plympton, MD 2:52>**<29>**

Lemuel RICKARD^5, b. 6 Nov. 1722; d. 21 Sept. 1756, Plympton g.s. <MD 11:116>

Theophilus RICKARD^5, b. 26 Jan. 1725

Samuel RICKARD^5, b. 12 Oct. 1727; d. 9 Nov. 1815, Plympton g.s. <MD 11:116>

Lazarus RICKARD^5, b. 1730

Elizabeth RICKARD^5, b. 1732

Rachel RICKARD^5, b. 1736

Rebecca RICKARD^5, b. 1740; d. 23 Feb. 1757, Plympton g.s. <MD 11:116>

CHILDREN OF William SNOW^3 & Naomi WHITMAN, (dau of Tho.): (6) <Bridgewater VR, MD 15:47>

Bethiah SNOW^4, b. 28 Sept. 1688

James SNOW^4, b. 14 Oct. 1691

Susanna SNOW^4, b. 27 Sept. 1694; d. pre 1731*

William SNOW^4, b. 14 Aug. 1697

Eleazer SNOW^4, b. 14 July 1701; 18 Feb. 1796 <Brewster VR 3:217>

John SNOW^4, b. 14 Aug. 1704

CHILDREN OF Elisha HAYWARD & 1st Experience ( ): (5)

Experience HAYWARD, b. 3 May 1710

Elisha HAYWARD, b. 3 May 1710 (twins)

Hannah HAYWARD, b. 2 July 1711

Tabitha HAYWARD, b. 26 July 1714

(Onner) HAYWARD, b. 26 July 1714 (twins)

CHILDREN OF Elisha HAYWARD & 2nd Bethiah SNOW^4 (Wm.^{3}): (3) <Bridgewater, MD 14:208>

Bethiah HAYWARD^5, b. 7 Apr. 1722

Naomi HAYWARD^5, b. 25 Mar. 1726

Ezra HAYWARD^5, b. 16 Nov. 1729

Mercy KING, b. 16 Feb. 1707; d. 29 Mar. 1789 <Bridgewater VR 3:217>

MICRO #5 of 5

CHILDREN OF Eleazer SNOW^4 (Wm.^{3}) & Mercy KING:(5) <Bridgewater VR>

Bettie SNOW^5, b. 9 Mar. 1729

Reuben SNOW^5, b. 16 Apr. 1731

Eleazer SNOW^5, b. 30 Oct. 1734; d. 1 Feb. 1797*, Brockton g.s.

Mercy SNOW^5, b. 22 Mar. 1737; d. 16 July 1829*, Sharon CT g.s.

Daniel SNOW^5, b. 30 Apr. 1742

CHILD OF Reuben SNOW^5 & Hannah WILLIS*, (*dau of Stoughton):

Rhoda SNOW^{6}*, b. 1769

Hannah DUNBAR, (*dau of Sam. & Melatiah), b. 17 Oct. 1743*, d. 1812*

CHILDREN OF Daniel SNOW^5 (Eleazer^4) & Hannah DUNBAR*: (9)**<30>**

Mary WOOD, (*dau of John), d. 18 Feb. 182(?) (4 or 9?), ae 90, Brockton g.s.

CHILDREN OF Eleazer SNOW^5 (Eleazer^4) & Mary WOOD*: (10)**<31>**

Jacob JOHNSON, b. c1734, d. Apr. 1777, ae 43, Sharon CT g.s.

CHILDREN OF Jacob JOHNSON & Mercy SNOW^5 (Eleazer^4): (4*) <Sharon CT>

Oliver JOHNSON^6, bpt. 20 July 1761

Jacob JOHNSON^6, bpt. 25 Dec. 1763 <Stoughton & Canton VR:93>

David JOHNSON^6, b. 21 July 1766

Mercy JOHNSON^6, bpt. 2 Aug. 1773

CHILDREN OF Israel ALGER^3 (*Israel^2, Tho.^{1}) & Susanna SNOW^4 (Wm.^{3}): (3*)

Israel ALGER^5, bpt. 1727

Daniel ALGER^5, bpt. 1727

James ALGER^5, bpt. 1729

Mary WASHBURN^5 (James^4, Eliz. Mitchell^3, Jane Cook^2), b. 28 Oct. 1694, Bridgewater <MD 14:205>; d. 31 Mar. 1774, Bridgewater, Scotland g.s. (wf of Wm. Snow$^{4-3}$)

* * * * *

FOOTNOTES

<1> p.268, A listing of Peter Brown's children is not given in the files so has been added here for easier reference to the ensuing generations.
<2> p.268, MFIP, Brown:1 states she d. aft. Nov. 1689 when she gave consent to a land sale between sons John and Helkiah.
<3> p.268, Ebenezer d. 31 Aug. 1726 <Middleboro Deaths (1947):201>.
<4> p.269, bpt. 22 Apr. 1716 <Middleboro 1st ChR:2>.
<5> p.269, bpt. 11 Apr. 1714 <Middleboro 1st ChR:2>.
<6> p.269, Edmund and Patience were married in 1744, so the additional three children mentioned in Edmund's will (1791) were probably born between their marriage and Priscilla's birth in 1752. The three are Edmond Jr., Peter and Patience. <Plymouth Co.Prob.#23342, 40:38>
<7> p.269, MFIP, Brown:17 calls her Joanna Parlow, dau. of Thomas Parlow & Elizabeth Gibbs. She married 2nd Robert Mackfun.
<8> p.270, An accompanying pencilled note reads: "Richmond Gen.:96 says 1st wf was Naomi Green! & had one child Naomi b. 2 Jan. 1775, d. 1850, m. Andrew Thomas, no issue."
<9> p.271, A note from the Barker Family (1900) by Barker Newhall states Josiah Barker d. 15 June 1774, Marshield (p.18) and his wife Sarah Macomber d. 6 Jan. 1786, Marshfield (p.26).
<10> p.271, Pencilled notes show a Thomas & Prudence Macomber who were alive in 1801 when they sold land. On 16 Jan. they were called "of Bridgewater" and on 26 May they were called "of Jay ME". Source given is "92:2 and 92:257" - possibly Bridgewater Co.Deeds.
<11> p.275, Is she the Elizabeth Tinkham, widow who d. 27 May 1762? <Plymouth ChR 1:392>
<12> p.276, According to the Plymouth ChR 1:460, William & Lydia were bpt. 15 Aug. 1773. As there is no mention of Lydia's birth in the Pembroke VR it is quite possible the Hannah b. in 1771 is an error and should read Lydia.
<13> p.277, MFIP, Brown:32 states this family moved to Rochester MA and had additional children.
<14> p.277, Bowman suggests John maried Mary Peckham, dau of John. He cites a deed dated 24 Jan. 1745 in which John Tinkham of Dartmouth sold to Stephen Taber land "that doth belong to me in Right of heirship by Lineal Decent from my hon^d father John Peckham Late of s^d Dartmouth." The witnesses were Peter Tinkham & Hezekiah Tinkham. <Bristol Co.Deeds 49:234>
MFIP, Brown:30 however, states John married Mary Allen (dau of Wm.) on 13 May 1741, Dartmouth (no source). (This marriage date is two months before the birth of the 1st child.) Mary Allen was b. 9 July 1718, Dartmouth. <Mayflower Source Rcds.:149>
<15> p.277, The remaining three Ellis children are listed without dates, viz: Seth, Elijah and John.
<16> p.277, There are no dates for the remaining seven Ellis children, viz: Joseph Phinney, Sarah E., Benjamin R., Mary, Lavina, Eliza and Deborah M.
<17> p.278, Samuel Tinkham d. betw. May 1741 (birth of his last child) <MD 15:217> and the child's death 24 Dec. 1747 when he was called deceased. <MD 18:80>
<18> p.278, Middleboro Deaths:201 gives her date of death as 16 June 1745.
<19> p.279, d. 29 Mar. 1723, prob. Yarmouth <NEHGR 100:32>.
<20> p.281, MFIP, Brown:43 shows Sarah d. 28 Apr. 1732, Bridgewater.
<21> p.281, MFIP, Brown:43 identifies Nathaniel Pratt as the son of Joseph & Sarah (Benson), b. 23 Mar. 1700/01, Weymouth and d. 24 Dec. 1749, Bridgewater. Also given are three additional children, viz: Anna, and unnamed twins. who probably died soon after birth, in May 1732 (mother d. 28 Apr. 1732.).
<22> p.281, No children are listed for Seth Pratt and his wife Hannah Washburn^7 (Jos.^{6}, Josiah^5, John^4, Eliz. Mitchell^3, Jane Cook^2), however, his will mentions six sons and two daughters, viz: Nathaniel, Simeon, Sylvanus, Asa, Joseph, Seth, Chloe (wf of Jeremiah Conant) and Joanna Bessee, widow.
<23> p.281, d. 24 July 1773, Providence RI <MFIP, Brown:36>.
<24> p.281, A pencilled death date for James Snow of 28 Aug. 1749, 58th yr, Bridgewater g.s. <VR:217> belongs to another - James Snow^4 (Wm.^{3}, Rebecca Brown^2). The James Snow in question here d. betw. 19 Mar. 1760 (will) - 12 May 1760 (presented) <Plymouth Co.Prob.#18684>.
<25> p.282, The remaining ten Snow children are listed without dates, viz: Ruth, Abijah, Mary, Nathan, Abigail, Susanna, Jedediah, Sarah, James and John. See MFIP, Brown:38 for dates.

<26> p.282, The remaining three Snow children are listed without dates, viz: John, Daniel & an unnamed child.
<27> p.282, Six children are listed without dates for Daniel Snow & wf Sarah ( ), viz: Daniel, Elizabeth, Susanna, Lydia, Rebecca and Sarah.
<27a>p.283, Recent research (1991) on the Peter Brown family has proven that Bethiah & Henry Rickard and probably Elkanah are not descendants of Peter Brown. MQ 57:69 states the following: "It should be noted that these three children did not participate in the 17 May 1739 deed and no later deed, selling their rights to Samuel Rickard's estate, has been found."
<28> p.284, MFIP, Brown:44 states he married Rachel Whiton, 19 Oct. 1721, Hingham. She was the dau. of Thomas & Joanna (May)(Gardner) Whiton, b. 12 July 1700, Hingham.
<29> p.284, MFIP, Brown:44 provides the missing birthdates for the last four children, viz: Lazarus, b. 29 May 1730; Elizabeth, b. 2 Mar. 1732/3; Rachel, b. 17 May 1736 & Rebecca, b. 17 Apr. 1740.
<30> p.284, The nine Snow children are listed too faintly in pencil to read. Years of birth only are given, which range from 1765-1782.
<31> p.284, The ten Snow children are listed too faintly in pencil to read (no dates).

* * * * *

REFERENCE LIST

GENEALOGICAL ARTICLES PERTAINING TO BROWN FAMILY RESEARCH

Mayflower Descendant (MD) (1899-1937)

1:79-82 - Inventory of Peter Brown
4:122-25 - Will & Inventory of Ephraim Tinkham, 1684
4:128 - Mary ( ) Brown, widow of Peter
5:29-37 - Settlement of Peter Brown's Estate
8:101-03 - Will & Inventory of William Snow, 1698/9
12:145-48 - Tinkham Notes: Helkiah Tinkham[3]
17:162-66 - Tinkham Notes: Ebenezer[3], Isaac[3] & Ephraim[3]
17:186-87 - Burrowes/Tinkham Notes: (Elizabeth Burrowes m. Ebenezer Tinkham[3])
19:16-21 - Thomas Macomber's Will And The Estates of His Sons Thomas & Onesimus (hus. of Joanna Tinkham[4])
19:136-41 - The Wills of John Soule[3], His Widow Martha (Tinkham[4]) And His Daughters Rebecca and Esther
21:97-101 - Hannah Hatch's Three Husbands, Japhet Turner, Ebenezer Tinkham[4] and Capt. Ichabod Tupper
22:47-48 - Estate of William Snow[3]
22:99-100 - Will of Benjamin Snow[3]
32:26-27 - Will of William Allen (m. Priscilla Brown[2])
PN&Q 2:55 - Will of John Mendall (dau Mercy m. Peter Tinkham[3])

Mayflower Quarterly (MQ) (1975-1990)

44:80-84 - Pilgrim Ancestry of Revolutionary Soldiers: Mercy Raymond Bedford of N.C., Patriot
53:10-13 - Some New Information About Pilgrim Peter Brown
53:84-86 - The Five Harvey Farringtons

Miscellaneous

Mayflower Familes In Progress: Peter Brown of the Mayflower and His Descendants for Four Generations (MFIP), pub. by General Society of Mayflower Descendants, 2nd Ed., 1988.

TAG 42:35 - Goodwife Martha Ford Alias Widow Ford, Her Second Husband Peter Browne & Her Children
NGSQ 67:253 - Peter Brown of Windsor, Conn., Not A Mayflower Descendant

* * * * * * * * *

JAMES CHILTON

(There are 16 pages of data on the James Chilton family found on microfiche #5 of the Peter Brown family. The following are transcribed from these pages after which I will continue with the Chilton microfiche.)

James CHILTON, d. 8 Dec. 1620 (O.S.), Cape Cod Harbor, Provincetown <MD 30:3>
Mrs. James CHLTON, d. 1621, Plymouth<1>
CHILDREN OF James CHILTON[1] & ( ): (2)<2>
Isabella CHILTON[2], bpt. 15 Jan. 1586/7, Canterbury, Eng.
Mary CHILTON[2], d. betw. 23 Oct. 1678 <Suffolk Deeds 9:42> - May 1679, Boston <MD 1:65><3>
St. Paul's Church, Canterbury, Kent co., England:
Anne CHILTON, dau of Lionel, bpt. 8 Aug. 1566
Margaret CHILTON, dau of Lionel, bpt. 26 Sept. 1569
Lionel CHILTON, son of John, bpt. 28 May 1581
Richard CHILTON, bpt. 27 Jan. 1582
Joel CHILTON, bpt. 16 Aug. 1584
Sisley CHILTON, bpt. 28 Feb. 1584
Isabel CHILTON, dau of James, bpt. 15 Jan. 1586
John CHILTON, son of John, bpt. 3 Sept. 1587
Jane CHILTON, dau of James, bpt. 8 June 1589
Ingle CHILTON, dau of James, bpt. 29 Apr. 1599
Anne CHILTON, dau of John, bpt. 23 Sept. 1599
Lionel CHILTON, bur. 27 Feb. 1581
Lionel CHILTON, bur. 25 Jan. 1582
Edith CHILTON, bur. 25 Nov. 1579
Dorothie CHILTON, bur. 26 May 1593
Anne CHILTON, wf of John, bur. 19 Oct. 1601

ISABELLA CHILTON[2] (James[1])

Roger CHANDLER, d. pre 11 Oct. 1665 <PCR 4:110>
CHILDREN OF Roger CHANDLER & Isabella CHILTON: (3)
Samuel CHANDLER[3], b. ( )
Sarah CHANDLER[3], b. ( )
Martha CHANDLER[3], d. 1 May 1674, Taunton <PCR 8:36>
John BUNDY, b. c1617, d. aft. 29 Oct. 1681 (will, ae 64) <PCR 4:1:99>
CHILDREN OF John BUNDY & 1st Martha CHANDLER[3]: <3-6, Taunton, NEHGR 16:324>
Martha BUNDY[4], b. 2 Nov. 1649 <Boston Rcd.Com.9:29>
Mary BUNDY[4], b. 5 Oct. 1653 <Boston Rcd.Com.9:41>
James BUNDY[4], b. 29 Sept. 1664 (PCR 8:36 says 29 Dec.)
Patience BUNDY[4], b. ( ), d. 27 Mar. 1665
Sarah BUNDY[4], b. 4 Mar. 1668
Samuel BUNDY[4], b. 4 Oct. 1670
CHILDREN OF John BUNDY & 2nd Ruth GURNEY: (3) <Taunton, NEHGR 16:324>
John BUNDY, b. 6 Oct. 1677
Joseph BUNDY, b. 1 Jan. 1679
Edward BUNDY, b. 13 Aug. 1681

(The end of the Chilton data on the Peter Brown microfiche.)

MICRO #1 of 7

MARY CHILTON^{2} (James^{1})

John WINSLOW^{2} (Edw.^{1}), d. betw. 12 Mar. 1673 (will) - 21 May 1674 (prob.), Boston <MD 3:131>**<4>**

CHILDREN OF John WINSLOW & Mary CHILTON^{2}: (10)

Susanna WINSLOW^{3}, b. pre 1634* <MD 1:66>; d. betw. 31 July 1676* - 6 Mar. 1685***<4a>**

Mary WINSLOW^{3}, b. pre 1635* <MD 3:131>; d. betw. 28 Oct. 1663 - Nov. 1665

Edward WINSLOW^{3}, b. c1634; d. 19 Nov. 1682*, 48th yr, Boston <MD 12:129>

Sarah WINSLOW^{3}, b. c1638*; d. 9 Apr. 1726*, ae 88 <NEHGR 15:308>

Isaac WINSLOW^{3}, b. pre 1644*, d. betw. 26 Aug. 1670 (will) - 29 Aug. 1670 (prob.), Port Royal, Jamaica <Middlesex Co.Prob.>

John WINSLOW^{3}, b. pre 1644*; d. betw. 3 Oct. 1683 (will) - 12 Oct. 1683 (prob.), Boston<MD 10:54>

Joseph WINSLOW^{3}, b. ( ); d. pre 3 Oct. 1679 (adm.)

Samuel WINSLOW^{3}, b. ( ); d. 14 Oct. 1680, Copp's Hill g.s., Boston

Child, b. pre 1651* <Bradford>; d. pre 12 Mar. 1673*

Benjamin WINSLOW^{3}, b. 12 Aug. 1653*, Plymouth <PCR:17>; d. betw. 12 Mar. 1673* - 31 July 1676*, unm. <MD 17:70,1:65>

CHILD OF John WINSLOW & Mary ( ):

John WINSLOW, b. 13 Dec. 1768 <Boston Rcd.Com.24:317>

CHILD OF John WINSLOW & Margaret ( ):

Joseph WINSLOW, b. 6 Oct. 1766 <Boston Rcd.Com.24:313>

Margaret WINSLOW, d. 17 Nov. 1820, ae 87, Dorchester <Boston Rcd.Com.21:367>

CHILDREN OF Joseph WINSLOW & Mary ( ): (2) <Boston Rcd.Com.>

Abigail WINSLOW, b. 20 Jan. 1750 <24:275>

Sarah WINSLOW, b. 7 Dec. 1752 <24:280>

CHILD OF Josiah WINSLOW & Sarah ( ):

John Hayward WINSLOW, b. 21 Mar. 1737 <Boston Rcd.Com.24:231>

CHILD OF Samuel WINSLOW & Ayme ( ):

Samuel WINSLOW, b. 28 June 1692 <Boston Rcd.Com.9:202>

CHILDREN OF John WINSLOW: (2) <Malden VR:105 (printed)>

Mary WINSLOW, b. 27 (11mth) 1659

Jonathan WINSLOW, b. 27 (8mth) 1666

CHILDREN OF Jacob WINSLOW & Elizabeth WHITTEMORE: (3) <Malden VR:105 (printed)>

Mary WINSLOW, b. 7 Jan. 1693/4

John WINSLOW, b. 25 Mar. 1699

Jacob WINSLOW, b. 3 Apr. 1702

CHILDREN OF John WINSLOW & Elizabeth ( ): (6) <Malden VR:105 (printed)>

Mary WINSLOW, b. 8 Apr. 1721

John WINSLOW, b. 8 Mar. 1723

Huldah WINSLOW, b. 17 July 1725

Thomas "WINSLED", b. 9 Jan. 1727/8

Elizabeth WINSLOW, b. 28 May 1732

Naomi WINSLOW, b. 12 Mar. 1734/5

CHILDREN OF Capt. George WINSLOW & Elizabeth REID: (5) <Malden VR:105 (printed)>

George Reed WINSLOW, b. 30 Oct. 1821

Catherine Elizabeth WINSLOW, b. 2 May 1832

Caroline Barrett WINSLOW, b. 24 Feb. 1836

Margaret Goodwin WINSLOW, b. 21 Sept. 1837

Thomas Forbes WINSLOW, b. 29 Jan. 1839; d. 5 June 1839 <VR:393>

Caroline BARRETT, (dau of Wm.), b. c1809, d. 28 Oct. 1836, ae 27 <Malden VR:393>

CHILD OF Capt. Caleb S. WINSLOW & Caroline BARRETT:

Mary Elizabeth WINSLOW, b. 17 May 1834, d. 23 May 1834 <Malden VR:105,393 (printed)>

John WINSLED, b. c1655, d. 10 Jan. 1683, ae 28, g.s. <Malden VR:393>

John WINSLOW, d. 21 Jan. 1780 <Malden VR:393>

CHILD OF John WINSLOW & Sarah ( ):

John WINSLOW, b. 5 Mar. 1724 <Boston Rcd.Com.24:168>

Sarah HILTON, d. 4 Apr. 1667, Boston, Copp's Hill g.s.**<5>**

CHILDREN OF Edward WINSLOW^3 & 1st Sarah HILTON: (3) <Boston Rcd.Com.9:80>

John WINSLOW^4, b. 18 June 1661

Sarah WINSLOW^4, b. 10 Apr. 1663

Mary WINSLOW^4, b. 30 Apr. 1665

Elizabeth HUTCHINSON, b. 4 Nov. 1639, Boston, d. 16 Sept. 1728, Boston <MD 12:129>

CHILDREN OF Edward WINSLOW^3 & 2nd Elizabeth HUTCHINSON: (5) <Boston, MD 12:129>

Edward WINSLOW^4, b. 1 Nov. 1669; d. 1 Dec. 1753, Boston, goldsmith <MD 24:165>

Katherine WINSLOW^4, b. 2 June 1672

Elizabeth WINSLOW^4, b. 22 Mar. 1673/4

Susanna WINSLOW^4, b. 31 July 1675

Ann WINSLOW^4, b. 7 Aug. 1678; d. 24 May 1773, Milton MA <Milton Hist.:254>

Hannah MOODY, (dau of Rev. Joshua), b. 17 Sept. 1672, Boston; d. betw. 1709-1712**<6>**

CHILDREN OF Edward WINSLOW^4 & 1st Hannah MOODY: (10) <Boston Rcd.Com.>

Edward WINSLOW^5, b. 15 Apr. 1693, d.y. <9:208>

Joshua WINSLOW^5, b. 12 Feb. 1694 <9:216>; d. 9 Oct. 1769, Boston

Hannah WINSLOW^5, b. 8 Mar. 1697 <9:234>

John WINSLOW^5, b. 24 Dec. 1698, d. 22 Apr. 1699 <9:242,252>

John WINSLOW^5, b. 14 Apr. 1700 <24:4>

William WINSLOW^5, b. 24 Mar. 1701, d.y. <24:12>

Edward WINSLOW^5, b. 8 Feb. 1703 <24:24>

Samuel WINSLOW^5, b. 29 May 1705 <24:38>; d. pre 6 Dec.1745 (adm.) <MD 10:106, Suffolk Prob.>

William WINSLOW^5, b. 13 Feb. 1707 <24:52>; d. 1746 <Suffolk Prob.>

Isaac WINSLOW^5, b. 2 May 1709 <24:64>; d. pre 28 Oct. 1785, Halifax N.S. <Suffolk Co.Prob.84:643>

CHILD OF Edward WINSLOW^4 & 2nd Elizabeth (DIXIE) Pemberton:**<7>**

Elizabeth WINSLOW^5, b. 16 Feb. 1712/3 <Boston Rcd.Com.24:87>**<8>**

CHILD OF David FARNUM & Dorothy ( ):

Susanna FARNUM, b. 7 Apr. 1687 <Boston Rcd.Com.9:173>**<9>**

CHILD OF John FARNUM & Dorothy ( ):

Susanna FARNUM, b. 1 Aug. 1688 <Boston Rcd.Com.9:179>**<9>**

CHILD OF Jonathan FARNUM & Ann ( ):

Susanna FARNUM, b. 16 June 1711 <Boston Rcd.Com.24:75>

Richard CLARKE, d. 27 Feb. 1795, London, Eng. <NEHGR 5:50>**<10>**

CHILDREN OF Richard CLARKE & Elizabeth WINSLOW^5 (Edw.^{4}): (12) <Boston Rcd.Com.>

Hannah CLARKE^6, b. 27 Feb. 1733/4 <24:219>

William CLARKE^6, b. 21 Feb. 1734/5 <24:224>

Elizabeth CLARKE^6, b. 8 Mar. 1735/6 <24:227>

Edward CLARKE^6, b. 30 Nov. 1737 <24:231>

Joseph Lee CLARKE^6, b. 28 Apr. 1740 <24:241>

Mary CLARKE^6, b. 17 Aug. 1741 <24:244>

Jonathan CLARKE^6, b. 20 May 1749 <24:255>

Susanna Farnum CLARKE^6, b. 20 May 1745 <24:255

Isaac Winslow CLARKE^6, b. 27 Oct. 1746 <24:259>

Sarah CLARKE^6, b. 9 Apr. 1750 <24:273>

lLucy CLARKE^6, b. 19 May 1752 <24:279>

Richard CLARKE^6, b. 19 May 1756 <24:288>

CHILDREN OF Isaac WINSLOW^5 (Edw.^{4}) & 1st Lucy WALDO: (7) <Roxbury, Boston Rcd.Com.>

Lucy WINSLOW^6, b. ( )

Hannah WINSLOW^6, b. 28 Feb. 1755 <24:288>

Samuel WINSLOW^6, b. 9 June 1757 <24:293>

Elizabeth WINSLOW^6, b. 11 June 1759 <24:298>

Grizel WINSLOW^6, b. 9 Sept. 1760 <24:300>

Isaac WINSLOW^6, b. 27 Apr. 1763 <24:307>

Sarah Tyng WINSLOW^6, bpt. 31 Mar. 1765 <6:159>

CHILD OF Isaac WINSLOW^5 & 2nd Jemima DEBUKE:

Thomas WINSLOW^6, bpt. 16 Feb. 1772, Roxbury <Boston Rcd.Com.6:166>

Elizabeth SAVAGE, (dau of Tho & Margaret), b. 29 Set. 1704 <Boston Rcd.Com.24:32>**<11>**

CHILDREN OF Joshua WINSLOW^5 (Edw.^{4}) & Elizabeth SAVAGE: (12) <Boston Rcd.Com.>

Rev. Edward WINSLOW^6, b. 8 Nov. 1722 <24:158>

Margaret WINSLOW^6, b. 28 Apr. 1724 <24:168>

Hannah WINSLOW^6, b. 8 Mar. 1725 <24:173>

Elizabeth WINSLOW^6, b. 29 Apr. 1729 <24:195>

Susanna WINSLOW^6, b. 25 Feb. 1730 <24:200>

Mary WINSLOW^6, b. 23 June 1732 <24:210>

Katharine WINSLOW^6, b. 8 Sept. 1733 <24:214>; d. aft. 4 Sept. 1816 (of Newport RI) <Suffolk Co. Deeds 254:273> (Katharine Malbone)

Martha WINSLOW^6, b. 20 Jan. 1734 <24:219>; d. aft. 1786, unm. <Suffolk Co.Prob.#18763>

Ann WINSLOW^6, b. 20 Jan. 1734 (twins) <24:219>; d. pre 29 Sept. 1769

Joshua WINSLOW^6, b. 1 Jan. 1736 <24:227>

John WINSLOW^6, b. ( )

Isaac WINSLOW^6, b. 24 Sept. 1743*

CHILDREN OF Joshua WINSLOW & Anna ( ): (2) <Boston Rcd.Com.24:295>

George Scot WINSLOW, b. 14 Nov. 1758

Anna Green WINSLOW, b. 29 Nov. 1759

Jane Isabella ALLEYNE, b. 21 Oct. 1721, Barbados <Bible>

CHILDREN OF Rev. Edward WINSLOW^6 (Joshua^5) & Jane Isabella ALLEYNE: (6) <Rev.'s Bible>

Elizabeth WINSLOW^7, b. 13 Jan. 1746/7, Barbados, d. 19 Dec. 1748

Joshua WINSLOW^7, b. 20 Sept. 1749, Boston, d. 14 Oct. 17(worn)

Mary WINSLOW^7, b. 1 Jan. 1750/1

Edward WINSLOW^7, b. 14 Mar. 1752

Margaret Alford WINSLOW^7, b. 7 Aug. 1753

Isabel Alleyne WINSLOW^7, b. 20 Oct. 1754

MICRO #2 of 7

Isaac WINSLOW^7 (Isaac^6, Josh.^{5}), b. c1754, d. 26 July 1856, Roxbury

CHILDREN OF Samuel WINSLOW^5 & Rebecca CLARKE: (1 of 4)**<12>**

Rebecca WINSLOW^6, b. c1742, Westminster, d. 11 Aug. 1788, 46th yr, Eustis St. g.s.

John WILLIAMS, (son of John), b. 25 Dec. 1719, Dorchester; d. 8 Feb. 1794, Roxbury

CHILDREN OF John WILLIAMS & Rebecca WINSLOW^6: (4)

Lucy WILLIAMS^7, b. Feb. 1772

Sarah WILLIAMS^7, b. ( )

Rebecca WILLIAMS^7, b. 1781, d. 4 Jan. 1865, ae 83y9m6d, 6 Vernon St., Roxbury, widow <Mass.VR 184:232> (wf of Stephen Childs)

Samuel WILLIAMS^7, b. ( )

CHILD OF Joseph SCOTT* & Elizabeth WINSLOW^4 (Edw.^{3}):

Joseph SCOTT^{5}, b. 23 Nov. 1694 <Boston Rcd.Com.9:216>

CHILDREN OF Samuel HINCKS & Elizabeth (WINSLOW^{4}) Scott: (2) <NEHGR 29:315><13>

Katharine Ann HINCKS^{5}, b. c1716*

Samuel HINCKS^{5}, b. c1718*

CHILDREN OF Samuel HINCKS^{5} & Susanna DYER: (10) <Truro, 4-10, VR:139>

Elizabeth HINCKS^{6}, b. 21 July 1757 <VR:76>

Susanna HINCKS^{6}, b. 14 Aug. 1759 <VR:76>

John HINCKS^{6}, b. 17 Oct. 1760 <VR:76>

Phebe HINKS^{6}, b. 15 Jan. 1764

Anna HINKS^{6}, b. 10 Jan. 1765

Winslow HINKS^{6}, b. 22 Apr. 1766; d. 21 Mar. 1847*, N. Bucksport ME g.s.<Bangor Hist.Mag. 7:27>

Samuel HINKS^{6}, b. 24 Apr. 1769

Ruth HINKS^{6}, b. 14 Aug. 1771

Elisha HINKS^{6}, b. 14 July 1774; d. 15 Mar. 1851*, Bucksport ME g.s. <Bangor Hist.Mag.7:27>

Jesse Young HINKS^{6}, b. 1 Jan. 1776; d. 29 Dec. 1853, Bucksport ME g.s. <Bangor Hist.Mag.7:27>

Mary ( ) HINCKS, d. 14 May 1844*, ae 67y11m, Bucksport ME g.s. (wf of Elisha Hincks^{6})

Ruth P. RICH, b. 5 July 1780; d. 19 Apr. 1856*, Bucksport ME g.s. <Bangor Hist.Mag.7:27>

CHILDREN OF Jesse Young HINKS^{6} & Ruth P. RICH: (12) <Family Bible><14>

Mary HINKS^{7}, b. 16 Dec. 1797

Ruth HINKS^{7}, b. 17 Apr. 1801, d. Apr. 1832

Jesse HINKS^{7}, b. 28 Feb. 1802, d. 28 Feb. 1802

Elizabeth P. HINKS^{7}, b. 15 Dec. 1803

Jesse HINKS^{7}, b. 13 Jan. 1806; d. 1 Feb. 1883<15>

Rebecah R. HINKS^{7}, b. 15 July 1808

Betsey HINKS^{7}, b. 19 Feb. 1811

Reuben G. HINKS^{7}, b. 23 Feb. 1813

John W. HINKS^{7}, b. 23 Aug. 1817

Joseph F. HINKS^{7}, b. 8 Mar. 1820, d. 25 July 1820

Hannah HINKS^{7}, b. 4 Aug. 1821

Joshua Y. HINKS^{7}, b. 29 Mar. 1824, d. 28 May 1826

Eliza ELDRIDGE, b. 31 Aug. 1807, d. 17 Nov. 1881<15>

CHILDREN OF Jesse HINKS^{7} & Eliza ELDRIDGE: (10) <Family Bible><15>

Julia S. HINKS^{8}, b. 6 Jan. 1829, d. 18 Feb. 1861

Mary N. HINKS^{8}, b. 10 Mar. 1830

Elizabeth G. HINKS^{8}, b. 30 Nov. 1832

Jesse Y. HINKS^{8}, b. 20 Apr. 1834

Jane L. HINKS^{8}, b. 15 Sept. 1836, d. 19 June 1840

Josephine HINKS^{8}, b. 15 Feb. 1839

Louisa HINKS^{8}, b. 19 May 1841, d. 17 June 1893

Phebe L. HINKS^{8}, b. 25 Dec. 1843, d. 1 July 1900

Emma D. HINKS^{8}, b. 13 Mar. 1846

John L.R. HINKS^{8}, b. 26 Apr. 1849, d. 5 May 1886

Thomasin COLLINGS, b. c1765, d. 11 July 1857*, ae 92y7m9d, N. Bucksport ME g.s.<Bangor Hist.Mag.>

CHILDREN OF Winslow HINCKS^{6} (Sam.^{5}) & Thomasin COLLINGS: (2) <Truro VR:160>

Hannah HINCKS^{7}, b. 11 Oct. 1791

Thomasin HINCKS^{7}, b. 9 Oct. 1793

CHILDREN OF Samuel WINSLOW^{3} & Hannah BRIGGS, (dau of Walter): (2)

Richard WINSLOW^{4}, b. on or before 31 Mar. 1676, d. c1707 <MD 10:52-56>

Mary WINSLOW^{4}, b. 8 June 1678 <Boston Rcd.Com.9:147>; d. 2 June 1681, Copp's Hill g.s., Boston

John TAYLOR, (son of John & Rebecca (Taintor)), b. 21 Nov. 1674, Boston <MD 1:90>; d. betw. 9 Apr

1703 (will) - 29 Jan. 1719/20 (letter), Jamaica W.I. <MD 21:121>

CHILDREN OF John TAYLOR & Ann WINSLOW[4]: (5) <2-5, Jamaica, MD 7:121>

Rev. John TAYLOR[5], b. 30 Aug. 1704, <Boston Rcd.Com.24:31>; d. 26 Jan. 1750*<Hist.Milton:257>

Elizabeth TAYLOR[5], b. 8 Nov. 1712; d. 5 June 1793 <Bible, MD 32:145>

William TAYLOR[5], b. 18 May 1714

Rebecca TAYLOR[5], b. 25 Feb. 1715

Ann TAYLOR[5], b. 14 May 1718

CHILDREN OF Moses EMERSON & Rebecca TAYLOR: (3)**<16>**

Nathaniel GREENE, (son of Nath. & Ann), b. 14 May 1709, Boston, d. 4 Jan. 1738, Surinam, South America, mariner <MD 32:145-47>

CHILDREN OF Nathaniel GREENE & Elizabeth TAYLOR[5]: (5) <MD 32:146>

Nathaniel GREENE[6], b. 15 Apr. 1730, d. 7 May 1730

Ann GREENE[6], b. 8 Aug. 1731, d. 1 Nov. 1733 <Boston Rcd.Com.24:202>

Nathaniel GREENE[6], b. 16 Aug. 1733 <Boston Rcd.Com.24:212>, d. 30 Mar. 1773, Boston

Elizabeth GREENE[6], b. 25 Dec. 1734 <Boston Rcd.Com.24:217>, d. 1735

John GREENE[6], b. 29 Nov. 1736; d. 1 Jan. 1813*, Stafford CT

Rev. Peter COFFIN, b. 9 Dec. 1713, Exeter NH <NEHGR 24:310>, d. 13 Dec. 1777, ae 64, Exeter NH (2nd hus of Eliz.Taylor[5])

CHILDREN OF John HENDERSON & Rachel CRANMER: (2) <Boston Rcd.Com.>

Rachel HENDERSON, b. 11 Oct. 1719 <24:137>

Mary HENDERSON, b. 4 Sept. 1726 <24:176>

Azubah WARD, (*dau of Daniel), b. 30 Oct. 1737*, Worcester, d. 27 Sept. 1814*, Stafford CT <Ward Fam.(1851):42,76>

CHILDREN OF John GREENE[6] & Azubah WARD: (10*) <1-6, Woodstock CT, 7-10, Stafford CT; Ward Fam.>

Elizabeth GREENE[7], b. 2 Sept. 1759

Rufus GREENE[7], b. 4 June 1761

Martha GREENE[7], b. 10 Mar. 1763

Daniel GREENE[7], b. 28 Mar. 1765

Mary GREENE[7], b. 17 May 1767

Lucretia GREENE[7], b. 20 Feb. 1770

Azubah GREENE[7], b. 27 July 1772

Sarah GREENE[7], b. 13 Dec. 1774

John Taylor GREENE[7], b. 25 May 1777

Dolly GREENE[7], b. 25 Feb. 1783

Elizabeth ROGERS, (dau of Rev. Nath.), b. c1708, d. 17 Apr. 1735, ae 27, Milton MA

CHILDREN OF Rev. John TAYLOR[5] (Ann Winslow[4]) & 1st Elizabeth ROGERS: (4) <Milton>

John TAYLOR[6], b. 15 June 1731*

Ann TAYLOR[6], b. 16 July 1732*

Nathaniel TAYLOR[6], b. 4 Mar. 1733*

William TAYLOR[6], b. 8 Apr. 1735*

CHILDREN OF Rev. John TAYLOR[5] & 2nd Dorothy (SHERBURNE)(Pymes) Rogers: (4)**<17>**

Mary NORWELL, (dau of Increase & Parnell), b. 26 May 1643; d. betw. 14 Apr. 1720 (will) - 23 Jan. 1729 (prob.)

CHILDREN OF Isaac WINSLOW[3] & Mary NORWELL: (2)

Parnell WINSLOW[4], b. 14 Nov. 1667; d. 1751

Isaac WINSLOW[4], b. 22 July 1670; d. Aug. 1670 <Boston Cem.Dep't>

Richard FOSTER, (son of Wm. & Ann), b. 10 Aug. 1663, Charlestown, d. 1745

CHILDREN OF Richard FOSTER & Parnell WINSLOW[4]: (10) <Charlestown, NEHGR 25:69>

Parnell FOSTER[5], b. 23 Feb. 1687, d. 11 Nov. 1687

Richard FOSTER[5], b. 28 Nov. 1689, d. 11 Feb. 1694

Mary FOSTER^5, b. 16 Feb. 1692, d. 23 Dec. 1718

Richard FOSTER^5, b. 23 Mar. 1694, d. 29 Aug. 1774

Parnell FOSTER^5, b. 25 Aug. 1696, d. 15 Sept. 1752

Anne FOSTER^5, b. 8 Nov. 1699<18>

Sarah FOSTER^5, b. 16 Nov. 1701, d. c1736

Isaac FOSTER^5, b. 30 Jan. 1704, d. 27 Dec. 1781, Charlestown

Elizabeth FOSTER^5, b. 21 Aug. 1706

Katharine FOSTER^5, b. 6 Apr. 1713, d. 11 Feb. 1716

Rev. Daniel PERKINS, d. 29 Sept. 1782, Bridgewater <MD 15:88>

CHILDREN OF Rev. Daniel PERKINS & Anne FOSTER^5: (6) <Bridgewater, MD 15:88>

Daniel PERKINS^6, b. 17 Nov. 1722, d. 29 Mar. 1726

Anne PERKINS^6, b. 1 May 1724

Sarah PERKINS^6, b. 13 Feb. 1725/6, d. 22 Dec. 1745

Daniel PERKINS^6, b. 1 Dec. 1727, d. 27 Dec. 1745

Richard PERKINS^6, b. 2 Mar. 1729/30

William PERKINS^6, b. 14 Feb. 1731/2, d. 7 Jan. 1745/6

Eleanor WYER, (dau of Wm. & Eleanor), b. c1714, d. 5 Mar. 1798, ae 84, Charlestown

CHILDREN OF Isaac FOSTER^5 (Parnell Winslow^4) & Eleanor WYER: (7) <Charlestown>

William FOSTER^6, b. 27 May 1733, d. 3 Dec. 1759

Isaac FOSTER^6, bpt. 28 May 1738, d.y.

Isaac FOSTER^6, b. 28 Aug. 1740; d. 27 Feb. 1782, Boston?

Thomas FOSTER^6, bpt. 27 Dec. 1741

Edward FOSTER^6, bpt. 6 May 1744

Eleanor FOSTER^6, b. 4 Aug. 1746

Richard FOSTER^6, bpt. 4 Dec. 1748

Martha MASON, (dau of Thaddeus), b. c1743, d. 21 Sept. 1770, ae 27

CHILDREN OF Isaac FOSTER^6 & 1st Martha MASON: (4)

Martha FOSTER^7, b. 11 May 1766, d. 4 May 1768

Eleanor FOSTER^7, b. 4 Nov. 1767

Martha FOSTER^7, b. 19 Sept. 1769

Nancy FOSTER^7, b. ( )<19>

Mary RUSSELL, (dau of Richard), b. c1749, d. 14 Jan. 1786, ae 37

CHILD OF Isaac FOSTER^6 & 2nd Mary RUSSELL:

Mary Beal FOSTER^7, bpt. 23 Aug. 1774

Sarah EMERSON, (dau of John & Sarah), b. c1695, d. 16 Nov. 1724, ae 29<20>

CHILDREN OF Richard FOSTER^5 (Parnell Winslow^4) & 1st Sarah EMERSON: (4)

Sarah FOSTER^6, bpt. 4 May 1718

Richard FOSTER^6, b. 8 Oct. 1720, d. 22 Jan. 1722

Mary FOSTER^6, bpt. 4 Nov. 1722

Katharine FOSTER^6, b. 16 Aug. 1724, d. ae 5mths

Mary FOYE, (dau of John & Sarah), d. 26 Oct. 1774, ae 72<21>

CHILDREN OF Richard FOSTER^5 & 2nd Mary FOYE: (8)

Elizabeth FOSTER^6, b. 17 Sept. 1726, d. pre 1760

Richard FOSTER^6, b. 17 Feb. 1728

Parnell FOSTER^6, b. 24 Aug. 1729

Hannah FOSTER^6, bpt. 28 Feb. 1731

William FOSTER^6, bpt. 27 Dec. 1732

Margaret FOSTER^6, b. 19 May 1734, d. 15 Dec. 1789

Ann FOSTER^6, b. 24 July 1736

Katherine FOSTER^6, bpt. 19 Mar. 1738

CHILD OF John WINSLOW^3 & 1st Elizabeth ( ):<22>

John WINSLOW^4, b. 22 May 1669 <Boston Rcd.Com.9:112>; d. betw. 21 Apr. 1690 (will) - 4 Nov. 1695 (prob.)<23>

Judith ( ) WINSLOW, b. c1625, bur. 18 Dec. 1714, ae near 90, Boston <Sewall's Diary, Mass.Hist. Col.5:7:30> (2nd wf of John Winslow^3)

CHILDREN OF John WINSLOW^4 & Abigail ATKINSON: (2) <Boston Rcd.Com.>

Elizabeth WINSLOW^5, b. 2 Apr. 1693 (1692?) <9:208>

John WINSLOW^5, b. 31 Dec. 1693 <9:209>

John WINSLOW, d. betw. 27 Sept. 1773 (will) - 17 Dec. 1773 (prob.), hatter, Boston <Suffolk Co. Prob.73:316-17><24>

MICRO #3 of 7

CHILDREN OF Alexander TODD & Elizabeth WINSLOW^5: (2) <Boston Rcd.Com.>

Abigail TODD^6, b. 14 Nov. 1721 <24:153>

Elizabeth TODD^6, b. 23 Sept. 1723 <24:162>

CHILDREN OF Joseph WINSLOW^3 & Sarah LAWRENCE: (2) <MD 1:67>

Mary WINSLOW^4, b. 25 Sept. 1674

Joseph WINSLOW^4, b. 16 June 1677 <25>

Edward GRAY, b. c1629, d. "ye last of" June 1681, ae abt 52, Plymouth g.s.<Burial Hill, Drew:95>

CHILDREN OF Edward GRAY & 1st Mary WINSLOW^3: (6) <Plymouth>

Desire GRAY^4, b. 6 Nov. 1651 <MD 16:237>; d. 4 Dec. 1690, Plymouth <MD 16:62>

Mary GRAY^4, b. 18 Sept. 1653 <MD 17:70>; d. pre 24 Aug. 1681 (father's estate)

Elizabeth GRAY^4, b. 11 Feb. 165() <MD 17:183>; d. aft. 22 Dec. 1721

Sarah GRAY^4, b. 12 Aug. 1659 <MD 17:183>; d. 14 Feb. 1736/7 <Bristol RI VR 2:75>

John GRAY^4, b. 1 Oct. 1661 <MD 17:183>; d. 29 May 1732, Kingston g.s. <MD 7:88>

Anna GRAY^4, b. c1663/4 <MD 1:66,67>; bur. 30 July 1728 <NEHGR 31:50>

Dorothy LETTICE, (dau of Tho.), d. aft. 5 Mar. 1684/5 <Plymouth Court Orders 6:2:21>

CHILDREN OF Edward GRAY & 2nd Dorothy LETTICE: (2 of 6)<26>

Edward GRAY, b. 31 Jan. 1666, Plymouth <MD 18:56>

Susanna GRAY, b. 15 Oct. 1668, Plymouth

Samuel LITTLE^3 (Anna Warren^2), b. c1657, d. 16 Jan. 1707 <Bristol RI VR 2:70>

CHILDREN OF Samuel LITTLE & Sarah GRAY^4 (Mary Winslow^3): (4) <1-3, Marshfield, MD 5:234>

Thomas LITTLE^5, b. 28 June 1683 <Duxbury VR>

Sarah LITTLE^5, b. 23 July 1685

Samuel LITTLE^5, b. 7 Nov. 1691

Edward LITTLE^5, b. ( )

CHILDREN OF William GRAY & Elizabeth HALL: (2)

Edward GRAY, b. 16 July 1764, d. 27 Dec. 1810 <Gray Gen.:195><27>

Rev. Thomas GRAY, b. ( )

Susanna TURELL, (dau of "Madame Turrell"), d. 10 Sept. 1816 <Gray Gen.:195><27>

CHILDREN OF Edward GRAY, (son of Wm.) & Susanna TURELL: (1 of 6) <Gray Gen.:195><27,28>

Mary Ann GRAY, b. 27 Nov. 1793; d. 22 Feb. 1850, Boston <Mass.VR 50:12>

CHILD OF Rev. Thomas GRAY (son of Wm.) & Deborah STILLMAN: <Gray Gen.:195><27>

Dr. Thomas GRAY, b. 1801, Jamaica Plains; d. 7 Mar. 1849, ae 46, Boston <Mass.VR 41:138>

CHILDREN OF William A. FALES & Mary Ann GRAY, (dau of Edw.): (4) <Gray Gen.:195><27>

Edward Gray FALES, b. ( )

Jane FALES, b. ( ), m. George Lamb of New Orleans

Mary Turell FALES, b. ( ), m. Dr. Thomas Gray (above son of Rev. Thomas)

Caroline Danforth FALES, b. ( )

CHILDREN OF Dr. Thomas GRAY & Mary Turell FALES: (4) <Gray Gen.:197><27>

Mary Ann GRAY, m. Guy Byram Schott of Philadelphia

Alice GRAY, m. Sidney K. Richardson of Boston

Caroline Fales GRAY, m. J.B.F. Davidge of Washington D.C.

T. Fales GRAY, b. 4 July 1849

James LEBLOND, d. betw. 17 Oct. 1700 (will) - 23 Oct. 1713 (account) <Suffolk Co.Prob.18:185>**<29>**

CHILDREN OF James LEBLOND & Anna GRAY^4 (Mary Winslow^3): (9) <2nd Church, Boston>

James LEBLOND^5, bpt. 21 Apr. 1690, d.y.

James LEBLOND^5, bpt. 7 June 1691

Ann LEBLOND^5, bpt. 9 Apr. 1693, d.y.

Peter LEBLOND^5, bpt. 6 Jan. 1694

Gabriel LEBLOND^5, bpt. 6 Mar. 1698

Ann LEBLOND^5, bpt. 15 Dec. 1700

Philippa LEBLOND^5, bpt. 23 Apr. 1704

Mary Ann LEBLOND^5, bpt. 10 Mar. 1706

Alexander LEBLOND^5, bpt. 4 Sept. 1709

Lieut. Nathaniel SOUTHWORTH^3 (Constant^2, Edw.^{1}), b. c1648, d. 14 Jan. 1710, 62nd yr, Nemasket g.s., Middleboro <MD 15:7>

CHILDREN OF Lieut. Nathaniel SOUTHWORTH & Desire GRAY^4 (Mary Winslow^3): (6) <1-4, Plymouth>

Constant SOUTHWORTH^5, b. 12 Aug. 1674 <MD 1:142>; d. betw. 14 Jan. 1702 (will) - 5 Feb. 1705 (prob.), unm. <Bristol Co.Prob.2:147>

Mary SOUTHWORTH^5, b. 3 Apr. 1676 <MD 1:142>; d. 2 Feb. 1757, Plymouth <MD 1:142, 31:114>

Ichabod SOUTHWORTH^5, b. middle of Mar. 1678 <MD 1:142>; d. 20 Sept. 1757, Middleboro g.s<MD 15:7>

Capt. Nathaniel SOUTHWORTH^5, b. 18 May 1684 <MD 1:142>; d. 8 Apr. 1757, Middleboro g.s.<MD 15:8>

Elizabeth SOUTHWORTH^5, bpt. 1687, Plymouth**<30>**

Edward SOUTHWORTH^5, bpt. 1690, Plymouth; d. 26 Apr. 1749, 61st yr, Middleboro g.s. <MD 15:7>

Bridget BOSWORTH, (dau of Nath. & Mary), b. 2 June 1691 <Hull VR:12>

CHILDREN OF Edward SOUTHWORTH^5 & Bridget BOSWORTH: (9) <Middleboro VR>

Constant SOUTHWORTH^6, b. 25 July 1712 <MD 3:86>

Bridget SOUTHWORTH^6, b. 3 Apr. 1714 <MD 3:86>

Ebenezer SOUTHWORTH^6, b. 13 Aug. 1716 <MD 3:86>

Edward SOUTHWORTH^6, b. Dec. 1718 <MD 3:233>

Theophilus SOUTHWORTH^6, b. 10 Feb. 1720/1 <MD 3:234>

Sarah SOUTHWORTH^6, b. 16 Jan. 1723/4 <MD 6:179>

Benjamin SOUTHWORTH^6, b. 27 Apr. 1728 <MD 7:240>

Lemuel SOUTHWORTH^6, b. 27 Apr. 1728 (twins) <MD 7:240>

Mary SOUTHWORTH^6, b. 2 Jan. 1731/2 <MD 9:48>

Thomas COLLIER, (*son of Gershom & Eliz. (Pool)), b. 27 Jan. 1705/6* <Hull VR:15>

CHILDREN OF Thomas COLLIER & Bridget SOUTHWORTH^6: (7*) <Scituate VR>

Thomas COLLIER^7, b. 17 Apr. 1736 <1:91>

Gershom COLLIER^7, b. 31 Apr. 1738 <1:90>

Bridget COLLIER^7, b. 9 May 1740 <1:90>

William COLLIER^7, b. 11 May 1742 <1:91>; d. 22 Dec. 1790 <Hull VR:64>

Jane COLLIER^7, b. 9 Apr. 1744 <1:90>

Mary COLLIER^7, b. 22 Apr. 1746 <1:90>

Ephraim Bosworth COLLIER^7, b. 13 June 1748 <1:90>

Daniel WHEELOCK, (son of Paul & Lois) b. c1800, Sutton, d. 25 Aug. 1865, ae 65y9m18d, Grafton, accidentally, stone cutter <Mass.VR 185:210>

Jerome WHEELOCK, (son of Dan. & Susan P.), b. c1834, Grafton, engineer <Mass.VR 118:174>

Lydia Ann ROBINSON, (dau of Henry & Myra (Haynes), wf of Jerome Wheelock), b. c1832, Concord, d. 19 June 1899, ae 67y4m29d, Worcester <Mass.VR 494:522>

CHILDREN OF Constant SOUTHWORTH^6 (Edw.^{5}) & Martha KEITH^3 (*Jos.^{2}, James^1): (10) <Bridgewater,

MD 16:42>

Bettie SOUTHWORTH^7, b. 19 Jan. 1734/5

Nathaniel SOUTHWORTH^7, b. 16 Feb. 1737

Ezekiel SOUTHWORTH^7, b. 10 Mar. 1738/9

Martha SOUTHWORTH^7, b. 18 Apr. 1741, d. 1 July 1741

Mary SOUTHWORTH^7, b. 18 Apr. 1741 (twins), d. 24 May 1741

Desire SOUTHWORTH^7, b. 7 Sept. 1742, d. 28 Feb. 1746/7

Jedediah SOUTHWORTH^7, b. 6 Jan. 1744/5

Constant SOUTHWORTH^7, b. 29 Jan. 1746/7

Sarah SOUTHWORTH^7, b. 9 Dec. 1749

Ichabod SOUTHWORTH^7, b. 9 June 1751, d. 27 Jan. 1756

CHILDREN OF Ebenezer SOUTHWORTH^6 (Edw.^{5}) & Elizabeth ( ): (4) <Middleboro VR>

Peleg SOUTHWORTH^7, b. 20 June 1741 <MD 15:221>

Ebenezer SOUTHWORTH^7, b. 17 Sept. 1744 <MD 16:106>

Sarah SOUTHWORTH^7, b. 2 Oct. 1747 <MD 17:19>

Lurayna SOUTHWORTH^7, b. 8 Jan. 1749 <MD 18:85>

Esther HODGES, (dau of Henry), b. 17 Feb. 1677, Taunton<31>; d. betw. 26 Dec. 1759 (will) - 1 July 1760 (prob.) (poss. Feb. 1760) <MD 21:73>

CHILDREN OF Ichabod SOUTHWORTH^5 (Desire Gray^4) & Esther HODGES: (6) <Middleboro VR>

Desire SOUTHWORTH^6, b. 23 Nov. 1707 <MD 3:84>

Priscilla SOUTHWORTH^6, b. 11 Feb. 1709/10 <MD 3:84>; d. 30 Oct. 1793*, Lakeville g.s.

Nathaniel SOUTHWORTH^6, b. 23 Jan. 1711/12 <MD 3:84>; d. 23 Aug. 1731, Middleboro g.s. <MD 15:7>

Mary SOUTHWORTH^6, b. 30 Nov. 1713 <MD 8:28>

Abigail SOUTHWORTH^6, b. 6 July 1716 <MD 8:28>

William SOUTHWORTH^6, b. 30 Nov. 1719 <MD 8:28>; d. 2 Apr. 1750, Middleboro g.s. <MD 15:8>

CHILDREN OF Samuel SHAW & Desire SOUTHWORTH^6: (10*)

Samuel SHAW^7, b. 29 Dec. 1731

Ichabod SHAW^7, b. 10 June 1734; d. 25 Aug. 1821<32>

Elijah SHAW^7, b. 28 June 1736, Plympton; d. 24 July 1806, Greene ME

William SHAW^7, b. 9 July 1738; d. 7 Mar. 1807 <MD 14:131>

Joshua SHAW^7, b. 12 Apr. 1741

Ebenezer SHAW^7, b. ( ), d.y.

James SHAW^7, b. 22 May 1746

Benoni SHAW^7, b. ( )

Desire SHAW^7, b. 1 Feb. 1751; d. VT

Zebediah SHAW^7, b. ( )

Nathaniel THOMAS, d. 22 Mar. 1838*, ae 81 <Plymouth VR 3:101><33>

Jane THOMAS, d. betw. 24 May 1843 (will) - 17 Feb. 1851 (prob.) (2nd wf of Nath. Thomas)<34>

CHILDREN OF Ichabod SHAW^7 & Priscilla ATWOOD: (13) <Plymouth, 1-9, MD 18:215><35>

Priscilla SHAW^8, b. 11 Jan. 1758

Mary SHAW^8, b. 2 Aug. 1760

Experience SHAW^8, b. 1 July 1762

Desire SHAW^8, b. 7 June 1765

Lydia SHAW^8, b. 15 Aug. 1767

Ichabod SHAW^8, b. 21 Nov. 1769<36>

Southworth SHAW^8, b. 3 Feb. 1772, d.y.<37>

Lucy SHAW^8, b. 2 June 1773

Southworth SHAW^8, b. 28 July 1775<38>

Sarah SHAW^8, b. 4 May 1778 <MD 18:216>

Nancy SHAW^8, b. 4 Jan. 1781 <MD 18:216>

John Atwood SHAW^{8}, b. 18 Apr. 1783 <MD 18:216>

Samuel SHAW^{8}, b. 22 Sept. 1785 <MD 18:216>

Nathaniel MACUMBER, b. c1708, d. 10 Nov. 1787*, 79th yr, Lakeville g.s. <Macomber Gen.:16>

CHILDREN OF Nathaniel MACUMBER & Priscilla SOUTHWORTH^{6} (Ichabod^{5}): (6*)**<39>**

Joseph RIDER, b. c1671, d. 29 Dec. 1766, 95th yr, Plymouth g.s. <MD 31:114>

CHILDREN OF Joseph RIDER & Mary SOUTHWORTH^{5} (Desire Gray^{4}): (4)**<40>**

Joseph RIDER^{6}, b. c1714, d. 13 May 1779, 65th yr, Plymouth g.s.**<41>**

Jemima RIDER^{6}, b. ( ), d. aft. 21 Apr. 1764***<42>**

Philippa RIDER^{6}, d. aft. 19 Apr. 1780* <Plymouth Co.Deeds 64:226, Phillippe Loring, "spinster">

Hannah RIDER^{6}, b. Nov. 1710, d. 14 Mar. 1763*, ae 52y4m18d, Plymouth g.s. <Kingman:37>**<43>**

MICRO #4 of 7

CHILDREN OF Joseph RIDER^{6} & Elizabeth CROSSMAN: (10) <Plymouth VR, MD 22:105>

Hannah RIDER^{7}, b. 14 Feb. 1739/40

Mary RIDER^{7}, b. 8 Nov. 1741

Nathaniel RIDER^{7}, b. 13 June 1744

Job RIDER^{7}, b. 9 June 1746

Elizabeth RIDER^{7}, b. 16 Sept. 1748

Bathsheba RIDER^{7}, b. 7 Nov. 1750

Sarah RIDER^{7}, b. 15 Apr. 1753

Desire RIDER^{7}, b. 10 Mar. 1755

Phebe RIDER^{7}, b. 7 Mar. 1757

Huldah RIDER^{7}, b. 1 May 1760, d. Sept. 1760

Paul LEONARD, (son of Tho. & Sarah), b. 17 Nov. 1735, d. 5 Jan. 1799 <Raynham VR 1:40,93>

CHILD OF Paul LEONARD & Mary RIDER^{7}:

Mary/Polly LEONARD^{8}, b. c1763, d. 27 Oct. 1797, 34th yr, Westmoreland NH g.s.

Isaac HALL, b. c1761, d. 30 June 1836, ae 75, Westmoreland NH g.s.

CHILDREN OF Isaac HALL & Mary/Polly LEONARD^{8}: (5)

Alfreda HALL^{9}, b. 27 Sept. 1788

Philip HALL^{9}, b. 18 Jan. 1791

Betsy HALL^{9}, b. 21 Dec. 1792, d. 18 Mar. 1878, Chesterfield

Ellehu HALL^{9}, b. 30 June 1795

Polly HALL^{9}, b. 2 Oct. 1797

John COOPER, (son of Richard & Hannah (Wood*)), b. 12 Dec. 1697, Plymouth <MD 2:18>; d. 7 Dec. 1760*, Plymouth g.s. <Burial Hill by Drew:208>

CHILDREN OF John COOPER & Hannah RIDER^{6} (Mary Southworth^{5}): (1 of 5)**<44>**

Richard COOPER^{7}, b. 29 June 1740 <Family Rcd.>; d. 10 Sept. 1819, Plymouth g.s. <Kingman:134>

Hannah SAMSON^{5} (Eben.^{4}, David^{3}, Caleb^{2}), b. 2 Oct. 1744, Plymouth <MD 15:160>; d. 23 Sept. 1826, Plymouth g.s. <Kingman:155>

CHILDREN OF Richard COOPER^{7} & Hannah SAMSON: (13) <1-3, Plymouth VR, MD 21:22>**<45>**

Hannah COOPER^{8}, b. 1 July 1761

Richard COOPER^{8}, b. 30 Jan. 1763; d. 30 Jan. 1844*, Old Cem. g.s., Plympton <MD 9:217>

Elizabeth COOPER^{8}, b. 25 July 1764

Priscilla COOPER^{8}, b. 10 July 1767

Capt. Joseph COOPER^{8}, b. 1 July 1769; d. 25 Nov. 1851***<46>**

Polly COOPER^{8}, b. 13 Oct. 1770

George COOPER^{8}, b. 11 July 1773, d. ae 1y9m

Calvin COOPER^{8}, b. 14 May 1775, d. ae 1y5m

Esther COOPER^{8}, b. 29 Oct. 1777

John COOPER^{8}, b. 30 Mar. 1780

Lusha COOPER^{8}, b. 1 July 1782, d. ae 1y

Nancy COOPER[8], b. 10 Jan. 1785, d. ae 2y
Calvin COOPER[8], b. 20 Sept. 1788

Gravestones at "Forest Hills": (7)

Hayward Pierce HALL, 1836-1892, Boston
Sarah B. HALL, 1835-1916
Thomas HALL, b. 6 Nov. 1869, d. 19 Aug. 1911, son of :
Dr. Thomas HALL, b. 5 Nov. 1841, d. 14 May 1909, his wife:
Mary P. HALL, b. 30 Apr. 1843, d. 29 Oct. 1913
Thomas HALL, b. 2 Sept. 1812, d. 9 Oct. 1879, his wife:
Sara W. HALL, b. 5 Feb. 1813, d. 2 Sept. 1872 (parents of Dr. Thomas)
Hannah SAMSON[6] (Zabdiel[5], Hannah Soule[4], Ben.[3], John[2]), b. c1762, d. 7 Mar. 1813, ae 51y4d, Old Cem. g.s., Plympton <MD 9:217>

CHILDREN OF Richard COOPER[8] (Rich.[7]) & Hannah SAMSON: (8)

Richard COOPER[9], b. 1 Dec. 1784*; d. 29 Dec. 1851, 67y28d, Plympton g.s. <MD 9:217>
Hannah COOPER[9]*, b. 13 Dec. 1786*
Eleanor COOPER[9]*, b. 3 Apr. 1788*
Polly COOPER[9]*, b. 5 Oct. 1791*
Betsy COOPER[9], b. 6 Aug. 1793*; d. 25 Aug. 1799, ae 6y7d, Plympton g.s. <MD 9:217>
Priscilla Virgil COOPER[9]*, b. 11 Apr. 1797*
Eliza COOPER[9], b. 23 Sept. 1799*; d. 28 Jan. 1816, ae 16y4m5d
John Dexter COOPER[9]*, b. 1 Dec. 1802*
Philip VINCENT, d. pre 25 Feb. 1756 <Yarmouth VR 3:287>

CHILDREN OF Philip VINCENT & Philippa RIDER[6] (Mary Southworth[5]): (3) <Yarmouth VR 3:161>

Sarah VINCENT[7], b. 18 Oct. 1745, d. 23 Feb. 1756 <VR 3:287>
Joshua VINCENT[7], b. 3 Feb. 1747/8, d. 21 Nov. 1750
Philip VINCENT[7], b. 24 Mar. 1750
Mercy VINCENT, widow, d. 15 Mar. 1756 <Yarmouth VR 3:287>
Abigail VINCENT, wf of David, d. 29 June 1756 <Yarmouth VR 3:287>

CHILD OF Jonathan DEXTER & 1st Hannah VINCENT:**<47>**

Isaac DEXTER, b. 15 Oct. 1751, Dartmouth

CHILD OF Jonathan DEXTER & 2nd Philippa (RIDER[6])(Vincent) Loring:**<47>**

John DEXTER[7]*, b. 4 June 1759* <Barnstable Fam.1:326>

CHILDREN OF Benjamin DEXTER & Hannah BARROW: (6)

Peleg DEXTER, b. 16 Apr. 1722
John DEXTER, b. 30 Apr. 1724, Rochester**<47>**
Enoch DEXTER, b. 6 Mar. 1726
Ebenezer DEXTER, b. 6 Aug. 1728
Joseph DEXTER, b. 27 Feb. 1731
Isaac DEXTER, b. 19 July 1734
Jael HOWLAND[3] (Isaac[2]), b. 13 Oct. 1688, Middleboro <MD 1:223>; d. 9 Nov. 1745, Nemasket g.s., Middleboro <MD 15:7>

CHILDREN OF Nathaniel SOUTHWORTH[5] (Desire Gray[4]) & Jael HOWLAND: (6) <Middleboro VR>

Fear SOUTHWORTH[6], b. 3 Feb. 1709/10 <MD 2:107>; d. aft. 25 Dec. 1755 (father's will)**<48>**
Ichabod SOUTHWORTH[6], b. 12 Apr. 1711, d. 22 or 23 Nov. 1727, g.s. <MD 3:84,15:7>
Hannah SOUTHWORTH[6], b. 24 Oct. 1714 <MD 3:84>; d. aft. 25 Dec. 1755 (father's will)**<48>**
Gideon SOUTHWORTH[6], b. 5 Sept. 1718, d. 25 Oct. 1788, Nemasket g.s., Middleboro <MD 3:234,15:7>
Samuel SOUTHWORTH[6], b. 18 Jan. 1721/2 <MD 6:180>; d. pre 25 Dec. 1755 (father's will)**<48>**
Nathaniel SOUTHWORTH[6], b. 26 Jan. 1728/9 <MD 7:242>; d. 31 July 1762, Middleboro g.s. <MD 15:8>

CHILDREN OF Joseph LEONARD & Fear SOUTHWORTH[6]: (5) <Middleboro VR>

Joseph LEONARD[7], b. 29 July 1732 <MD 12:232>

Timothy LEONARD^{7}, b. 19 Mar. 1733/4 <MD 12:232>

Hannah LEONARD^{7}, b. 3 July 1736 <MD 15:222>

Abiah LEONARD^{7}, b. 8 May 1738 <MD 15:222>

Gideon LEONARD^{7}, b. 15 Oct. 1739 <MD 15:223>

Rebecca ELLIS, b. c1720, d. 19 June 1781, ae 61, Nemasket g.s., Middleboro <MD 15:8>

CHILDREN OF Gideon SOUTHWORTH^{6} (Nath.^{5}) & Rebecca ELLIS: (4) <Middleboro VR>

Jael SOUTHWORTH^{7}, b. 23 Sept. 1742 <MD 15:220>

Elizabeth SOUTHWORTH^{7}, b. 28 Feb. 1744/5 <MD 16:107>

Rebecca SOUTHWORTH^{7}, b. 26 Dec. 1746 <MD 17:19>

Gideon SOUTHWORTH^{7}, b. 16 May 1750 <MD 18:85>

CHILDREN OF Robert SPROUT^{4} (James^{3}, Eliz. Samson^{2}) & Hannah SOUTHWORTH^{6} (Nath.^{5}): (3)<Middleboro>

Zebedee SPROUT^{7}, b. 14 Mar. 1741/2 <MD 16:19>

Samuel SPROUT^{7}, b. 8 Jan. 1743/4 <MD 16:19>

Robert SPROUT^{7}, b. 14 Apr. 1748 <MD 17:19>; d. Apr. 1782

Susanna SMITH, (dau of Jonathan), b. 30 Ar. 1726*

CHILDREN OF Nathaniel SOUTHWORTH^{6} (Nath.^{5}) & Susanna SMITH: (7) <Middleboro>

Mary SOUTHWORTH^{7}, b. July 1749, d. 6 Oct. 1752, ae 3y4m <MD 15:7>

Rebecca SOUTHWORTH^{7}, b. 1751, d. 4 May 1753, ae 1y5m27d <MD 15:8>

John SOUTHWORTH^{7}, b. 1754, d. 27 Sept. 1754, ae 7m <MD 15:7>

Susanna SOUTHWORTH^{7}, b. Aug. 1755, d. 26 June 1758, ae 2y10m <MD 15:8>

Bathsheba SOUTHWORTH^{7}, b. 1757, d. 29 June 1764, 7th yr <MD 15:7>

Nathaniel SOUTHWORTH^{7}, b. 1760, d. 3 Aug. 1761, ae 11m20d <MD 15:8>

Hannah SOUTHWORTH^{7}, b. Oct. 1762*; d. 16 July 1821*

CHILDREN OF Samuel SOUTHWORTH^{6} (Nath.^{5}) & Elizabeth CASWELL: (3) <Middleboro VR>

Hannah SOUTHWORTH^{7}, b. 19 Oct. 1746 <MD 17:19>

Lucia SOUTHWORTH^{7}, b. 19 July 1748 <MD 17:19>

Samuel SOUTHWORTH^{7}, b. 9 July 1750 <MD 18:85>

Seth ARNOLD, (son of Rev. Sam.), d. betw. 30 Sept. 1720 - 31 Oct. 1721 (will sworn)<MD 25:35>**<49>**

CHILDREN OF Seth ARNOLD & Elizabeth GRAY^{4} (Mary Winslow^{3}):(6)

Edward ARNOLD^{5}, b. 20 Mar. 1679/80, Marshfield <MD 2:249>

Penelope ARNOLD^{5}, b. 21 Apr. 1682, Marshfield <MD 2:251>; d. pre 11 Dec. 1715 (father's will)

Desire ARNOLD^{5}, b. ( ); d. pre 11 Dec. 1715 (father's will)

Benjamin ARNOLD^{5}, b. ( )

Deacon James ARNOLD^{5}, bpt. 20 Oct. 1700, Marshfield <MD 11:122>; d. 25 Sept. 1755, 56th yr, Duxbury g.s. <MD 9:159>

Elizabeth ARNOLD^{5}, b. ( )

CHILDREN OF Ichabod BARTLETT^{4} (Ben.^{3}, Mary Warren^{2}) & Desire ARNOLD^{5}: (2)

Sarah BARTLETT^{6}, b. 24 Dec. 1710, Marshfield <MD 6:19>

Seth BARTLETT^{6}, b. ( )

Anthony WATERMAN^{4} (Sarah Snow^{3}, Abigail Warren^{2}), b. 4 June 1684, Marshfield, d. 3 Apr. 1715, Marshfield g.s. <MD 2:183,10:50>

CHILDREN OF Anthony WATERMAN & Elizabeth ARNOLD^{5} (Eliz. Gray^{4}): (2) <Marshfield, MD 7:119>

Thomas WATERMAN^{6}, b. 29 Apr. 1710

Joseph WATERMAN^{6}, b. 3 Jan. 1711

CHILDREN OF Jonathan ALDEN^{3} (Jonath.^{2}) & Elizabeth (ARNOLD^{5}) Waterman: (4) <Marshfield, MD 30:15>

Jonathan ALDEN^{6}, b. 14 Jan. 1718

Anthony ALDEN^{6}, b. 3 Aug. 1720

Seth ALDEN^{6}, b. 3 Jan. 1721

Josiah ALDEN^{6}, b. 3 June 1724

CHILD OF Benjamin ARNOLD^{5} (Eliz. Gray^{4}) & Hannah BARTLETT^{5} (*Sam.^{4}, Ben.^{3}, Mary Warren^{2}):

Samuel ARNOLD^{6}, b. 1 Feb. 1715/16, Duxbury <MD 8:233>

Mercy BREWSTER^{4} (Wm.^{3}, Love^{2}), b. 7 Dec. 1685, Duxbury <MD 8:229>

CHILDREN OF Edward ARNOLD^{5} (Eliz. Gray^{4}) & Mercy BREWSTER: (2) <Duxbury, MD 9:26>

Ezra ARNOLD^{6}, b. 30 July 1707; d. 18 Feb. 1780, S. Duxbury g.s. <MD 9:159>

William ARNOLD^{6}, b. 6 May 1718; d. 26 May 1718 <MD 9:26>

Rebecca SPRAGUE, b. c1711, d. 25 Oct. 1805*, ae 95 <Duxbury VR>**<50>**

CHILDREN OF Ezra ARNOLD^{6} & Rebecca SPRAGUE*: (6)

Seth ARNOLD^{7}, b. 12 June 1733*; d. 17 Mar. 1819*

Gamaliel ARNOLD^{7}, b. 8 Aug. 1735*

Lucy ARNOLD^{7}, b. ( )

Rebecca ARNOLD^{7}, bpt. 31 July 1743*; d. 23 Dec. 1763, ae 20y5m

Edward ARNOLD^{7}, bpt. 7 May 1749*

William ARNOLD^{7}, bpt. 12 Aug. 1750*; d. 13 Aug. 1836*

Joanna SPRAGUE, b. c1715, d. 19 Mar. 1766, 51st yr, Duxbury g.s. <MD 9:159>**<50>**

CHILDREN OF James ARNOLD^{5} (Eliz. Gray^{4}) & Joanna SPRAGUE: (5) <1-4, Duxbury VR>

Bildad ARNOLD^{6}, b. 20 Nov. 1735 <MD 11:150>

Luther ARNOLD^{6}, b. Sept. 1737 <MD 11:150>

James ARNOLD^{6}, b. 23 Sept. 1740, d. 9 Sept. 1742 <MD 11:238,9:159>

James ARNOLD^{6}, b. 1745 <MD 11:150>

Benjamin ARNOLD^{6}*, bpt. 12 Apr. 1752; d. 18 Jan. 1776*, Roxbury

Joanna MORTON^{3} (Ephraim^{2}, George^{1}), d. aft. 23 Aug. 1738*

CHILDREN OF John GRAY^{4} (Mary Winslow^{3}) & Joanna MORTON: (7) <Plymouth VR, MD 1:145>

Edward GRAY^{5}, b. 21 Sept. 1687, d. 20 Feb. 1687/8

Mary GRAY^{5}, b. 7 Dec. 1688; d. 17 Mar. 1703

Ann GRAY^{5}, b. 5 Aug. 1691

Desire GRAY^{5}, b. 1 Dec. 169(), d. 6 Dec. 1695

Joanna GRAY^{5}, b. 29 Jan. 1695/6

Samuel GRAY^{5}, b. 23 Dec. 1701/02; d. Oct. 1738, Kingston g.s. <MD 7:88>

Mercy GRAY^{5}, b. 4 Feb. 1703/4; d. 5 ( ) 1782, Kingston g.s. <MD 7:87>

Patience WADSWORTH, (dau of Elisha), b. 20 Aug. 1706, Duxbury; d. 23 Apr. 1782, Kingston<MD 7:88>

CHILDREN OF Samuel GRAY^{5} & Patience WADSWORTH: (6) <Kingston VR 1:27>

Mary GRAY^{6}, b. 10 Sept. 1728, d. 15 Oct. 1728

John GRAY^{6}, b. 3 Dec. 1729; d. 26 Apr. 1810, Kingston g.s. <MD 7:88>

Mary GRAY^{6}, b. 11 Nov. 1731; d. 15 July 1812, Kingston g.s. (wf of Ben. Cooke^{5}) <MD 7:26>

Elizabeth GRAY^{6}, b. 28 Apr. 1734; d. 4 Nov. 1740 <MD 7:88>

Samuel GRAY^{6}, b. 28 Oct. 1736; d. 1818*, Duxbury

Capt. Wait GRAY^{6}, b. 17 Mar. 1739; d. pre 22 July 1771*

Desire CUSHMAN^{6} (*Tho.^{5}, Rob.^{4}, Tho.^{3}, Mary Allerton^{2}), b. 24 July 1748 <Kingston VR>; d. 25 Oct. 1822, Kingston g.s. <MD 7:88>

CHILDREN OF John GRAY^{6} & Desire CUSHMAN: (4) <1-3, Kingston VR>

John GRAY^{7}, b. 5 May 1777 <VR:85>

Betsey GRAY^{7}, b. 20 July 1785 <VR:85>

Lewis GRAY^{7}, b. 3 May 1790 <VR:86>

Amaziah GRAY^{7}, b. ( )

Sabra RIPLEY, b. c1742, d. 31 Dec. 1786*, ae 44 (wf of Zenas Drew) <Kingston ChR.>

CHILD OF Capt. Wait GRAY^{6} (Sam.^{5}) & Sabra RIPLEY:

Wait GRAY^{7}, bpt. 15 May 1763 (dau., named after dec. father)

CHILDREN OF Samuel GRAY^{6} (Sam.^{5}) & Eunice DELANO, (*dau of Elkanah): (10*) <Kingston VR, ChR.>

Mary GRAY^{7}, b. 26 July 1763; d. 24 Oct. 1768

Abigail GRAY^{7}, b. 25 July 1765; d. 23 Oct. 1768

Sarah GRAY^{7}, b. 5 Sept. 1767

Elizabeth GRAY^{7}, b. 17 Sept. 1769

Lucy GRAY^{7}, b. 24 Oct. 1771

Bethiah GRAY^{7}, bpt. 27 Mar. 1774

Sophiah GRAY^{7}, bpt. 3 Mar. 1776

Hannah GRAY^{7}, bpt. 23 Aug. 1778

Samuel GRAY^{7}, bpt. 26 Nov. 1780

Eunice GRAY^{7}, bpt. 25 Apr. 1784

Myles STANDISH^{2}, d. 1660/61, at sea (1st hus. of Sarah Winslow^{3})

Tobias PAYNE, d. 12 Sept. 1669, Boston

CHILD OF Tobias PAYNE & Sarah (WINSLOW^{3}) Standish:

William PAYNE^{4}, b. 21 Jan. 1668/9, Boston <MD 3:130>; d. betw. 25 Jan. 1733* (will) - 1 July 1735 (prob.) <Suffolk Co.Prob.B.32:176>

Richard MIDDLECOTT, d. 13 June 1704

CHILDREN OF Richard MIDDLECOTT & Sarah (WINSLOW^{3})(Standish) Payne: (4)

Mary MIDDLECOTT^{4}, b. 1 July 1674 <Boston Rcd.Com.9:133>; d. pre 26 May 1729<51>

Sarah MIDDLECOTT^{4}, b. 20 May 1678 <Boston Rcd.Com.9:146>; d. aft. 26 May 1729*<52> (See p.315)

Jane MIDDLECOTT^{4}, b. 16 Sept. 1682; d. Sept. 1743

Edward MIDDLECOTT^{4}, b. ( )

CHILDREN OF William PAYNE^{4} (Sarah Winslow^{3}) & 1st Mary TAYLOR, (dau of James): (4) <NEHGR 42:256>

William PAYNE^{5}, b. 25 Nov. 1695, d. Feb. 1705*

Tobias PAYNE^{5}, b. 25 June 1697; d. 1733*, near Virgin Islands

Sarah PAYNE^{5}, b. Jan. 1699, d.y.

Mary PAYNE^{5}, b. 6 Jan. 1700; d. aft. 1744*

CHILDREN OF William PAYNE^{4} & 2nd Margaret STEWART, (dau of Wm.): (12) <Boston, NEHGR 32:256>

Sarah PAYNE^{5}, b. 15 June 1704; d. aft. 1744*

William PAYNE^{5}, b. 19 Sept. 1706, d.y.

William PAYNE^{5}, b. 26 Jan. 1707

Edward PAYNE^{5}, b. 17 Mar. 1708, d.y.

Ann PAYNE^{5}, b. 8 June 1711

John PAYNE^{5}, b. 9 Feb. 1712

Edward PAYNE^{5}, b. 7 Oct. 1714, d.y.

Margaret PAYNE^{5}, b. 22 May 1716

Richard PAYNE^{5}, b. 4 Apr. 1718

Thomas PAYNE^{5}, b. 23 Apr. 1720, d.y.

Edward PAYNE^{5}, b. 4 Feb. 1721; d. 5 Mar. 1788*, Boston

Jane PAYNE^{5}, b. 17 Feb. 1723

Rebecca AMORY, (dau of Tho.), b. c1724, d. 14 Feb. 1799*, ae 73

CHILDREN OF Edward PAYNE^{5} & Rebecca AMORY: (5)

Mary PAYNE^{6}, b. 1 Dec. 1757; d. 6 Nov. 1834*, unm.

Sarah PAYNE^{6}, b. 1 Dec. 1757 (twins); d. 22 Jan. 1833*, unm.

Rebecca PAYNE^{6}, b. 28 Aug. 1759; d. 22 Jan. 1833* (m. Christopher Gore, Gov. of Mass., no issue)

William PAYNE^{6}, b. 18 July 1762; d. 21 July 1827*

Edward PAYNE^{6}, b. 11 Oct. 1765, d. 31 Dec. 1765

Lucy (GRAY) Dobell, d. 13 Mar. 1809*

CHILDREN OF William PAYNE^{6} & 1st Lucy (GRAY) Dobell: (4)

Edward William PAYNE^{7}, b. 8 Apr. 1804*; d. 7 Mar. 1832*, unm.

William Edward PAYNE^{7}, b. 8 Apr. 1804* (twins); d. 5 July 1838*, Paris, France

Christopher Gore PAYNE^{7}, b. 8 May 1807*, d. 5 Oct. 1807*

Ellis Gray PAYNE^{7}, b. 8 May 1807* (twins), d. 25 Sept. 1807*

Jonathan SEWALL, (son of Stephen), d. Nov. 1731*

CHILDREN OF Jonathan SEWALL & Mary PAYNE^{5} (Wm.^{4}): (3)

Margaret SEWALL^{6}, b. 6 Oct. 1725*

Jonathan SEWALL^{6}, b. Aug. 1728*

Jane SEWALL^{6}, b. Nov. 1731*

CHILDREN OF John COLMAN & Sarah PAYNE^{5} (Wm.^{4}): (5)

Sarah COLMAN^{6}, b. July 1736*

John COLMAN^{6}, b. 18 Jan. 1737*

William COLMAN^{6}, b. Aug. 1739*, d.y.

William COLMAN^{6}, b. Aug. 1744*

Benjamin COLMAN^{6}, b. July 1748*

Sarah WINSLOW^{5} (Abigail Waterman^{4}, Sarah Snow^{3}, Abigail Warren^{2}), b. 3 Dec. 1704, Marshfield <MD 6:20>; d. 8 Feb. 1770, Wellfleet g.s.

CHILD OF Tobias PAYNE^{5} (Wm.^{4}) & Sarah WINSLOW:

Mary PAYNE^{6}, b. ( )

Elisha COOKE, (son of Elisha & Eliz.), b. 20 Dec. 1678 <Boston Rcd.Com.9:145>; d. 24 Aug. 1737

CHILDREN OF Elisha COOKE & Jane MIDDLECOTT^{4} (Sarah Winslow^{3}): (5 of 10)**<53>**(See p.315)

Elisha COOKE^{5}, b. 3 Nov. 1703* <Boston Rcd.Com.24:30>, d.y.

Middlecott COOKE^{5}, b. 3 Aug. 1705* <Boston Rcd.Com.24:33>

Elizabeth COOKE^{5}, b. Feb. 1708*

Sarah COOKE^{5}, b. Apr. 1711*; d. 11 July 1740*

Mary COOKE^{5}, b. 1723*

CHILDREN OF John PHILLIPS & Sarah COOKE^{5}: (5*)

Elisha PHILLIPS^{6}, b. Sept. 1733

John PHILLIPS^{6}, b. Apr. 1735

William PHILLIPS^{6}, b. Aug. 1736

Thomas PHILLIPS^{6}, b. Oct. 1737, d. Feb. 1741

Mary PHILLIPS^{6}, b. May 1739, d. Feb. 1741

CHILDREN OF Henry GIBBS & Mary MIDDLECOTT^{4} (Sarah Winslow^{3}): (3)**<54>**

Sarah GIBBS^{5}, b. 13 Sept. 1696 <Boston Rcd.Com.9:227>

John GIBBS^{5}, b. 10 Dec. 1697 <Boston Rcd.Com.9:232>, unm.

Henry GIBBS^{5}, b. c1699 (father's will)

CHILDREN OF Othniel HAGGET & Mary (MIDDLECOTT^{4}) Gibbs: (4)**<55>**

MICRO #5 of 7

Louis BOUCHER, d. pre 12 May 1726**<56>**

CHILDREN OF Louis BOUCHER & Sarah MIDDLECOTT^{4} (Sarah Winslow^{3}): (6)

Ann BOUCHER^{5}, b. Apr. 1703; d. 31 Mar. 1736

Sarah BOUCHER^{5}, b. Sept. 1705; d. aft. 10 July 1770***<57>**

Mary BOUCHER^{5}, b. 1708, d.y.

Mary BOUCHER^{5}, b. 1710, d.y.

Lewis BOUCHER^{5}, b. 1713, d.y.

Jane BOUCHER^{5}, b. May 1716

Nathaniel CUNNINGHAM, d. 7 Sept. 1748, London Eng.

CHILDREN OF Nathaniel CUNNINGHAM & Ann BOUCHER^{5}: (5)

Nathaniel CUNNINGHAM^{6}, b. 10 Apr. 1725

Ann CUNNINGHAM^{6}, b. ( )

Ruth CUNNINGHAM^{6}, b. 15 Jan. 1728; d. 15 Nov. 1789* (m. James Otis^{5} -see Doty family)

Sarah CUNNINGHAM^{6}, b. 6 Sept. 1731

Timothy CUNNINGHAM^{6}, b. 1732-36*

John FOYE, d. betw. 10 July 1770 (will) - 16 Dec. 1771 (prob.)

CHILDREN OF John FOYE & Sarah BOUCHER^{5} (Sarah Middlecott^{4}): (6)

Sarah FOYE^{6}, b. 2 Jan. 1731

Ann FOYE^{6}, b. 2 Sept. 1733, d.y.

John FOYE^{6}, b. 15 Sept. 1734

Elizabeth FOYE^{6}, b. 8 Dec. 1735

Ann FOYE^{6}, b. 3 Apr. 1737

Lewis FOYE^{6}, b. 6 Jan. 1738; d. aft. 1784 (will)

Francis DISER, (*son of Francis), d. pre 1789*

CHILDREN OF Francis DISER & Ann FOYE^{6}: (4*)

Francis DISER^{7}, bpt. 25 Nov. 1759

Sarah DISER^{7}, bpt. 2 May 1762; d. 6 Oct. 1840, unm., alms house

John Foye DISER^{7}, bpt. 5 May 1765; d. aft. 1802

James DISER^{7}, bpt. 2 July 1769

Anna SWAN^{7} (Josh.^{6}, Eben.$^{5-4}$, Mary Pratt^{3}, Mary Priest^{2}), b. 1 Apr. 1769*, d. aft. 1802* (wf of John Foye Diser^{7})

CHILDREN OF David MUNROE, (*son of David) & Elizabeth FOYE^{6} (Sarah Boucher^{5}): (5*)

Louis MUNROE^{7}, b. 15 July 1766, d. at sea aft. 1794

Eliza MUNROE^{7}, b. 24 Sept. 1767

Jane Boucher MUNROE^{7}, b. 26 Feb. 1770; d. 1840

Abigail MUNROE^{7}, b. 10 July 1771; d. 1843

David MUNROE^{7}, bpt. 7 Mar. 1772; d. 1 Mar. 1835

Robert LATHAM, d. betw. 14 Nov. 1685 (deed) - 28 Feb. 1688/9 <PN&Q 1:10>

CHILDREN OF Robert LATHAM & Susanna WINSLOW^{3}:(8)**<58>**

Mercy LATHAM^{4}, b. 2 June 1650, Plymouth <MD 1:67>; d. betw. 31 July 1676 - June 1698 <MD 1:67>

James LATHAM^{4}, b. c1658*; d. 1738*, ae 80 <Bridgewater Epitaphs:210> (adm.-MD 22:118>

Hannah LATHAM^{4}, b. aft. 1656* (see Cooke Family)

Joseph LATHAM^{4}, b. pre 1667*

Chilton LATHAM^{4}, b. c1671; d. 6 Aug. 1751*, 80th yr, Bridgewater

Susanna LATHAM^{4}, b. pre 1673*; d. aft. 31 July 1676* <MD 3:131>

Elizabeth LATHAM^{4}, b. c1664; d. 16 Nov. 1730, 66th yr, Kingston g.s. <MD 7:26> (see Cooke Fam.)

Sarah LATHAM^{4}, b. pre 1672

Susanna KINGMAN, (dau of John), b. c1679, d. 23 June 1776, ae 97, Bridgewater

CHILDREN OF Chilton LATHAM^{4} & Susanna KINGMAN: (8) <Bridgewater, MD 14:46>

Charles LATHAM^{5}, b. 18 Mar. 1701; d. 5 July 1788 <Bridgewater VR 3:348>

Jane LATHAM^{5}, b. 13 June 1703

Arthur LATHAM^{5}, b. 16 Sept. 1705; d. 1736*

James LATHAM^{5}, b. 16 Aug. 1708**<59>**

Robert LATHAM^{5}, b. 16 Aug. 1711; d. 10 Dec. 1788

Joseph LATHAM^{5}, b. 24 July 1714; d. 1777*

Susanna LATHAM^{5}, b. 20 May 1717

Mary LATHAM^{5}, b. 6 July 1720

CHILDREN OF James LATHAM^{5} & Abigail HARVEY: (3) <Bridgewater VR 3:266> (See pg.305)

Abigail LATHAM^{6}, b. 27 June 1740

Arthur LATHAM^{6}, b. 8 Aug. 1742

Mary LATHAM^{6}, b. 20 June 1744

Mary JOHNSON, (dau of David), b. c1729, . 20 Apr. 1752, 23rd yr <Bridgewater VR 3:286>

CHILD OF Robert LATHAM^{5} (Chilton^{4}) & Mary JOHNSON: <Bridgewater VR 3:283>

Robert Johnson LATHAM^{6}, b. 10 Apr. 1752, d. 15 May 1756

CHILDREN OF Thomas LATHAM & Abigail (   ): (4) <Bridgewater VR 3:363>

Nabbe LATHAM, b. 6 Sept. 1753

William LATHAM, b. 3 Jan. 1756

Bettie LATHAM, b. 12 Mar. 1758

Thomas LATHAM, b. 20 Sept. 1759

CHILDREN OF Joseph LATHAM Jr. & Mary ( ): (5) <Bridgewater VR 3:374>

James LATHAM, b. 7 Sept. 1748

Hannah LATHAM, b. 27 Dec. 1750

Molley LATHAM, b. 2 Mar. 1756, d. 11 May 1759

Isaac LATHAM, b. 22 May 1760

Joseph LATHAM, b. 26 Dec. 1761

CHILDREN OF Chilton LATHAM & Mary ( ): (2) <Bridgewater VR 3:419>

Chilton LATHAM, b. 3 July 1771

Mary LATHAM, b. 14 Dec. 1772

Alice ALLEN, (dau of Nehemiah), b. 8 Oct. 1707, Bridgewater <MD 14:208>

CHILDREN OF Arthur LATHAM[5] (Chilton[4]) & Alice ALLEN: (2) <Bridgewater VR 3:283>

Nehemiah LATHAM[6], b. 1 Nov. 1733; d. 21 Nov. 1807

Jane LATHAM[6], b. 3 July 1736

CHILDREN OF Jonathan CONANT & Jane LATHAM[6]: (6)**<60>**

Lucy HARRIS[7] (Arthur[6], Isaac[5], Mercy Latham[4], Susanna Winslow[3], Mary Chilton[2]), d. 1797*

CHILDREN OF Nehemiah LATHAM[6] (Arthur[5]) & Lucy HARRIS: (10)<1-3, Bridgewater VR 3:241; 4-10, Ch.R>

Arthur LATHAM[7], b. 16 Feb. 1758

Alice LATHAM[7], b. 5 Apr. 1760

Mehitable LATHAM[7], b. 7 Jan. 1761/2; d. 9 May 1788 <1st Ch. E.Bridgewater>

Lucia LATHAM[7], bpt. 11 Mar. 1764

Nehemiah LATHAM[7], bpt. 19 Apr. 1767

Bethiah LATHAM[7], bpt. 8 Oct. 1769

Allen LATHAM[7], bpt. 1 Sept. 1771, d. 23 Sept. 1798

Robert LATHAM[7], bpt. 12 Sept. 1773, d. 1 Sept. 1782

Bela LATHAM[7], bpt. 10 Mar. 1776, d. 8 Sept. 1793

Consider LATHAM[7], bpt. 18 June 1780, d. 8 Sept. 1782

Susanna WOODWARD, (dau of Nath.), b. 30 May 1709, d. 18 Feb. 1761 <Bridgewater VR:3:348>

CHILDREN OF Charles LATHAM[5] (Chilton[4]) & Susanna WOODWARD: (6) <Bridgewater 3:348>

Bettie LATHAM[6], b. 14 Dec. 1725

Susanna LATHAM[6], b. 11 Oct. 1727

Woodward LATHAM[6], b. 24 Dec. 1729; d. 13 Dec. 1802*

Mary LATHAM[6], b. 24 Oct. 1735

Chilton LATHAM[6], b. 5 Sept. 1739; d. 1792*

Jane LATHAM[6], b. 5 Sept. 1739 (twins)

CHILDREN OF Chilton LATHAM[6] & Mary HAWARD/HOWARD, (*dau of James): (2) <Bridgewater VR 3:419>

Chilton LATHAM[7], b. 3 July 1771; d. 1811*

Mary LATHAM[7], b. 14 Dec. 1772

Rebecca DEAN, (*dau of Seth), b. c1740, d. 8 July 1820 <Bridgewater VR 3:341>

CHILDREN OF Woodward LATHAM[6] (Charles[5]) & Rebecca DEAN: (6) <Bridgewater VR 3:341>

Eliab LATHAM[7], b. 11 June 1764

Susanna LATHAM[7], b. 29 Jan. 1766

George LATHAM[7], b. 9 Nov. 1768

Dean LATHAM[7], b. 3 Apr. 1771; d. 10 Feb. 1835*

Gallen LATHAM[7], b. 13 Feb. 1775; d. 25 May 1844 <Bridgewater Epitaphs:210>

Barzillai LATHAM[7], b. 3 Apr. 1778

Mary WASHBURN[7] (Ben.[6-5], Jonathan[4], Eliz. Mitchell[3], Jane Cooke[2]), b. 29 June 1780 (wf of Barzillai Latham[7])

Susanna KEITH, (*dau of Eleazer), b. 14 Aug. 1780, d. 16 Oct. 1869 <Bridgewater Epitaphs:210> (wf of Gallen Latham^{7})

CHILDREN OF James LATHAM^{5} (Chilton^{4}) & Abigail HARVEY: (5) <1-3, Bridgewater VR 3:266>

Abigail LATHAM^{6}, b. 27 June 1740

Arthur LATHAM^{6}, b. 8 Aug. 1742 (removed to Winchester NH)

Mary LATHAM^{6}, b. 20 June 1744

James LATHAM^{6}, b. ( )

Susanna LATHAM^{6}, b. ( )

Deliverance ALGER, (dau of Tho. & Eliz. (Packard)), d. pre 1 Jan. 1749 (adm.) <MD 22:120>

CHILDREN OF James LATHAM^{4} (Susanna Winslow^{3}) & Deliverance ALGER: (5)**<61>**

Thomas LATHAM^{5}, b. pre 1692*; d. betw. 1759 - 1769*

Anne LATHAM^{5}, b. c1693; d. 1770*, ae 77

Joseph LATHAM^{5}, b. ( ); d. betw. 2 June 1758 (will) - 19 Jan. 1759 (inv.)

Susanna LATHAM^{5}, b. ( )

Betty LATHAM^{5}, b. ( ); d. 14 Oct. 1782, Bridgewater <MD 15:89>

Nicholas WADE, d. betw. 20 Jan. 1767 (will) - 22 May 1767 (prob.) <Plymouth Co.Prob.19:476>

CHILDREN OF Nicholas WADE & Anne LATHAM^{5}: (1 of 6)**<62>**

Amasa WADE^{6}, b. c1743, d. 15 May 1804*, ae 61 <Weymouth VR 2:->

Sarah LOUD^{6} (Onner Prince^{5}, Mary Turner^{4}, Mary Brewster^{3}, Jonathan^{2}), b. 19 July 1728/9*; d. 1790 <Weymouth VR 2:361>

CHILDREN OF Amasa WADE^{6} & Sarah LOUD: (1 of 6)**<63>**

Amasa WADE^{7}, b. 17 July 1768 <Weymouth VR 1:329>

CHILDREN OF Daniel JOHNSON & Betty LATHAM^{5} (James^{4}): (6) <Bridgewater, MD 15:89>

Daniel JOHNSON^{6}, b. 21 Oct. 1726

James JOHNSON^{6}, b. 7 Nov. 1728

Joseph JOHNSON^{6}, b. 17 Nov. 1730, d. 26 Dec. 1745

Isaiah JOHNSON^{6}, b. 18 Oct. 1734

Levet JOHNSON^{6}, b. 27 Oct. 1736

Bettie JOHNSON^{6}, b. 1 Feb. 1738/9

Sarah HAYWARD, (dau of Nath.), b. 28 June 1696 <Bridgewater VR 2:44>; d. 25 Apr. 1781<Bridgewater Epitaphs:210>

CHILDREN OF Joseph LATHAM^{5} (James^{4}) & Sarah HAYWARD: (7)

James LATHAM^{6}, bpt. 1732; d. pre 1758*

Betty LATHAM^{6}, b. c1722, d. 1808*, ae 86

Joseph LATHAM^{6}, bpt. 1732

Thomas LATHAM^{6}, b. c1729, d. 1778*, ae 49

Nathaniel LATHAM^{6}, bpt. 1732; d. ?1776, army, NY

Sarah LATHAM^{6}, bpt. 1733; d. 1785*

Seth LATHAM^{6}, bpt. 1738; d. 1825*, ae 87

CHILDREN OF Joseph LATHAM^{6} & Mary PRYER: (7) <1-5, Bridgewater VR 3:374>

James LATHAM^{7}, b. 7 Sept. 1748

Hannah LATHAM^{7}, b. 27 Dec. 1750

Molley LATHAM^{7}, b. 2 Mar. 1756, d. 11 May 1759

Isaac LATHAM^{7}, b. 22 May 1760

Joseph LATHAM^{7}, b. 26 Dec. 1761

Nanny LATHAM^{7*}, b. 1763*

Winslow LATHAM^{7*}, b. ( )

CHILDREN OF James LATHAM^{7} & Esther BAKER: (4*) <Pelham MA>**<64>**

Esther Cutter LATHAM^{8}, b. 30 Oct. 1781

Eunice LATHAM^{8}, b. 2 Apr. 1787

Hannah LATHAM^{8}, b. 18 Apr. 1789

Robert LATHAM^{8}, b. 22 Feb. 1791

CHILDREN OF Nathaniel LATHAM^{6} (Jos.^{5}) & Mercy LEACH, (dau of Nehemiah): (2)

Nathaniel LATHAM^{7}, b. ( )

Levi LATHAM^{7}, b. ( )

CHILDREN OF Levi LATHAM^{7} & Hannah ALDEN, (dau of Eleazer): (7)**<65>**

Rachel HOUSE, b. c1744, d. 1797*, ae 53 (1st wf of Seth Latham^{6}, Jos.^{5})

Elizabeth ( ) HANKS, b. c1750, d. 1825*, ae 75 (2nd wf of Seth Latham^{6})

CHILDREN OF Nathaniel HARDEN & Susanna LATHAM^{5} (James^{4}): (3*) <Mitchell:170>**<66>**

CHILDREN OF Thomas LATHAM^{5} (James^{4}) & Deborah HARDIN: (7)**<67>**

CHILDREN OF Isaac HARRIS, (son of Arthur) & Mercy LATHAM^{4} (Susanna Winslow^{3}): (5 of 8)**<68>**

Desire HARRIS^{5}, b. ( ), d. betw. 11 Feb. - 1 Dec. 1698, Bridgewater <MD 2:146>

Jane HARRIS^{5}, b. 19 July 1671, Bridgewater (2nd dau.) <MD 2:243>

Isaac HARRIS^{5}, b. ( ), d. aft. 3 Oct. 1738 (deed)

Samuel HARRIS^{5}, b. ( ); d. pre 27 June 1731 (bpt. of last child) <E. Bridgewater VR:62>

Mary HARRIS^{5}, b. ( ); d. 22 Apr. 1727, Bridgewater <MD 15:46>

John KINGMAN, b. c1660, d. 8 Jan. 1755, 95th yr, Bridgewater <MD 5:249>

CHILDREN OF John KINGMAN & 1st Desire HARRIS^{5}: (5) <Bridgewater, MD 5:249>

Desire KINGMAN^{6}, b. 17 June 1690; d. 22 Dec. 1739*

Mary KINGMAN^{6}, b. 7 Apr. 1692; d. aft. 30 Aug. 1748*

John KINGMAN^{6}, b. 7 Feb. 1694, d.y.

Seth KINGMAN^{6}, b. 10 Jan. 1696

Deliverance KINGMAN^{6}, b. 11 Feb. 1698

CHILDREN OF John KINGMAN & 2nd Bethiah NEWCOMB: (7) <Bridgewater, MD 5:249>

Isaac KINGMAN, b. 14 Sept. 1699

John KINGMAN, b. 16 Mar. 1702

Abigail KINGMAN, b. 28 May 1705

David KINGMAN, b. 21 May 1708

Ebenezer KINGMAN, b. 21 Jan. 1711

Josiah KINGMAN, b. 9 Oct. 1713

Bethiah KINGMAN, b. 23 Apr. 1716

MICRO #6 of 7

CHILDREN OF Ebenezer ORCUTT & Deliverance KINGMAN^{6} (Desire Harris^{5}): (9*)

Ebenezer ORCUTT^{7}, b. 10 Aug. 1727

Samuel ORCUTT^{7}, b. 21 Dec. 1729

Micah ORCUTT^{7}, b. 25 Oct. 1731; d. 1760

Mary ORCUTT^{7}, b. 20 Aug. 1733

Jonathan ORCUTT^{7}, b. 23 Oct. 1735

Jacob ORCUTT^{7}, b. 19 June 1737

Hosea ORCUTT^{7}, b. 17 Set. 1739

Hannah ORCUTT^{7}, b. 24 Nov. 1741

Keziah ORCUTT^{7}, b. 11 Nov. 1744

Ann PHILLIPS, d. aft. 23 Nov. 1779*

CHILDREN OF Micah ORCUTT^{7} & Ann PHILLIPS: (4)

Anna ORCUTT^{8}, b. ?20 July 1755*; d. 14 Jan. 1807, ae 52 <MD 8:104>

Micah ORCUTT^{8}, b. 14 Sept. 1756*

Hannah ORCUTT^{8}, b. 20 Oct. 1757*

Mary ORCUTT^{8}, bpt. 8 June 1760*

CHILD OF John HEWES & Anna ORCUTT^{8}:

Nathaniel Phillips HEWES^{9}, b. 2 Dec. 1773 <MD 8:104>; d. pre 26 Oct. 1812* (adm.)

Charles WILLIS, (son of Charles & Abigail (Belknap*)), b. 27 June 1753* <Boston VR>; d. 14 Jan. 1831, ae 77 <MD 8:105>

CHILDREN OF Charles WILLIS & Anna (ORCUTT^{8}) Hewes: (11) <Boston, MD 8:104>**<69>**

Nancy WILLIS^{9}, b. 13 Mar. 1780, d. 27 May 1783

Charles WILLIS^{9}, b. 19 July 1781; d. 13 July 1789 <MD 8:105>

John Phillips WILLIS^{9}, b. 23 Oct. 1782; d. 27 Aug. 1783 <MD 8:105>

Nancy WILLIS^{9}, b. 13 Jan. 1784; d. 5 Sept. 1864, Newton MA

Sally Belknap WILLIS^{9}, b. 27 Aug. 1785; d. 10 May 1855, Cambridge, heart disease <Mass.VR 94:38>

Nabby Belknap WILLIS^{9}, b. 31 Mar. 1787; d. 1798 <MD 8:105>

Charles WILLIS^{9}, b. 22 May 1789, d. 18 Jan. 1845, Chelsea, bur. Old Granary, Boston<MD 8:105>**<70>**

Polly Jones WILLIS^{9}, b. 3 June 1791

William Bothan WILLIS^{9}, b. 2 Mar. 1794

Henry Phillips WILLIS^{9}, b. 21 Jan. 1797

John Phillips WILLIS^{9}, b. 12 May 1799

CHILD OF Nathaniel Phillips HEWES^{9} (Anna Orcutt^{8}) & Sally EATON:

Sally HEWES^{10}, b. c1798, d. 14 Jan. 1814, ae 16 <Boston VR>

Eliza EATON, b. 22 Jan. 1789*

CHILDREN OF Charles WILLIS^{9} (Anna Orcutt^{8}) & Eliza EATON: (14*)

Child, b. June 1811, d. June 1811 <Morse Gen.Reg.2:213>

Nathaniel Phillips Hewes WILLIS^{10}, b. 14 Feb. 1813

Charles WILLIS^{10}, b. 14 Feb. 1813 (twins)

Andrew Jackson WILLIS^{10}, b. 16 Feb. 1815, d. 23 Feb. 1815

Eliza Ann WILLIS^{10}, b. 27 May 1816

Frances Maria Adeline WILLIS^{10}, b. 16 July 1817

Charlotte Eaton WILLIS^{10}, b. 11 Mar. 1819

George Henry WILLIS^{10}, b. 26 Aug. 1820

Frederick Augustus WILLIS^{10}, b. 27 Jan. 1822

Elmira Sarah Eaton WILLIS^{10}, b. 1 Nov. 1823

Caroline Clarissa Churchill WILLIS^{10}, b. 9 June 1825

Mary Jackson WILLIS^{10}, d. ae 9 mths

James Davis Knowles WILLIS^{10}, b. 24 Sept. 1829

Cyrus Pitts G. WILLIS^{10}, b. 24 Sept. 1829 (twins)

Larkin SNOW^{7} (*Elisha^{6}, Isaac^{5}, John$^{4-3}$, Constance Hopkins^{2}), b. 24 Jan. 1778*, Harpswell*; d. 30 Mar. 1846*, Boston*

CHILDREN OF Larkin SNOW & Nancy WILLIS^{9} (Anna Orcutt^{8}): (5)

Ephraim Larkin SNOW^{10}, b. 20 May 1805*

Margaret Ann SNOW^{10}, b. 25 Dec. 1806*

George Murdock SNOW^{10}, b. 7 May 1812*

Henry Augustus SNOW^{10}, b. 26 Aug. 1817*

Mary Brown SNOW^{10}, b. 28 June 1819*

John Phillips ORCUTT, b. c1782, d. 18 Oct. 1825*, ae 43 <Morse Gen.Reg.2:211>

CHILDREN OF John Phillips ORCUTT & Sally Belknap WILLIS^{9} (Anna Orcutt^{8}):(8*)<Morse Gen.Reg.2:211>

John Paton ORCUTT^{10}, b. 1 Apr. 1809

William Henry ORCUTT^{10}, b. 5 July 1810

Alfred Holmes ORCUTT^{10}, b. 10 Aug. 1811

Ira Brown ORCUTT^{10}, b. 23 Oct. 1812

Caroline Sally Ann ORCUTT^{10}, b. 4 Aug. 1815

Edwin Augustus ORCUTT^{10}, b. 17 May 1818, d. 23 Sept. 1843

Alansa Foster ORCUTT^{10}, b. 7 Oct. 1820

Alexander Black ORCUTT^{10}, b. 2 Mar. 1822, d. 20 Nov. 1822

CHILDREN OF John ORCUTT & Desire KINGMAN^{6} (Desire Harris^{5}): (6*)

Son, b. 14 Apr. 1722, d. same day

Experience ORCUTT^{7}, b. 24 Mar. 1722/3

Dau., b. 23 Dec. 1724, stillborn

John ORCUTT^{7}, b. 7 Sept. 1726

Hannah ORCUTT^{7}, b. 24 Sept. 1729, d. 17 Dec. 1735

Susanna ORCUTT^{7}, b. 15 Jan. 1732/3

Samuel COPELAND, (*son of John & Ruth Newcomb)), b. 20 Sept. 1686* <Braintree VR:663>; d. pre 6 Jan. 1746 (adm.), Braintree <Suffolk Co.Prob.#8648,39:307>

CHILDREN OF Samuel COPELAND & Mary KINGMAN^{6} (Desire Harris^{5}): (12) <Braintree VR>

Samuel COPELAND^{7}, b. 28 Oct. 1711* <VR:691>; d. 1799*, Washington NH

Mary COPELAND^{7}, b. 7 July 1713* <VR:697>

Desire COPELAND^{7}, b. 22 Oct. 1715* <VR:699>

John COPELAND^{7}, b. 27 May 1718* <VR:703>

Abigail COPELAND^{7}, b. 6 Aug. 1720* <VR:707>

Ruth COPELAND^{7}, b. 21 Mar. 1722* <VR:710>; d. pre 1748* <Suffolk Co.Prob.#8648,41:449>

Susanna COPELAND^{7}, b. 22 Feb. 1724* <VR:753>

Isaac COPELAND^{7}, b. 27 Mar. 1726* <VR:757>; d. 19 June 1795

Hannah COPELAND^{7}, b. 29 Feb. 1727/8* <VR:760>

Bethiah COPELAND^{7}, b. 27 July 1729* <VR:763>

Seth COPELAND^{7}, b. 21 Apr. 1731*

Daniel COPELAND^{7}, b. 30 July 1733* <VR:769>; d. pre 1748* <Suffolk Co.Prob.#8648,41:449>

CHILDREN OF Samuel COPELAND^{7} & Mary OWEN, (*dau of Nath. & Deborah (Parmenter)): (11)<Braintree>

Abraham COPELAND^{8}, b. 25 June 1736 <VR:776>

Mary COPELAND^{8}, b. 23 May 1738 <VR:777>

Hannah COPELAND^{8}, b. 12 July 1740 <VR:783>

Ruth COPELAND^{8}, b. 26 Apr. 1742 <VR:785>

Sarah COPELAND^{8}, b. 26 Apr. 1742 (twins) <VR:785>

Isaac COPELAND^{8}, b. 11 Apr. 1744 <VR:788>

Jacob COPELAND^{8}, b. 10 July 1746 <VR:791>

Sarah COPELAND^{8}, b. 20 Sept. 1748 <VR:795>

Nathaniel COPELAND^{8}*, b. 9 Sept. 1750* <Copeland Ms.1:54>

Silence COPELAND^{8}*, b. 4 May 1755* <Copeland Ms.1:54>

Samuel COPELAND^{8}*, b. 24 July 1757* <Copeland Ms.1:54>

Lydia THAYER, (dau of John & Lydia (Copeland*)), b. 12 Aug. 1730*; d. Mar. 1799

CHILDREN OF Isaac COPELAND^{7} (Mary Kingman^{6}) & Lydia THAYER: (2 of 11)**<71>**

Isaac COPELAND^{8}, b. 17 Oct. 1753

Samuel COPELAND^{8}, b. 15 June 1758*?

Ruth WHITMARSH, b. 20 June 175()*, Concord; d. 10 Oct. 1849*, ae 90y3m20d

CHILDREN OF Samuel COPELAND^{8} & Ruth WHITMARSH: (8*) <Copeland Ms.1:57,133>

Ruthy COPELAND^{9}, b. 29 Jan. 1785; d. aft. 5 June 1847, unm. (will) <Suffolk Co.Prob.#35174>

Betsy/Eliza COPELAND^{9}, b. 27 Nov. 1787

Thomas COPELAND^{9}, b. 11 Oct. 1789

Samuel COPELAND^{9}, b. 4 Mar. 1792

Nancy COPELAND^{9}, b. 2 Mar. 1794

Mary/Polly COPELAND^{9}, b. 15 Sept. 1796

Sally COPELAND^{9}, b. 14 May 1798

Abigail COPELAND^{9}, b. 15 June 1800

CHILDREN OF Hezekiah ADAMS & Nancy COPELAND^{9} (Sam.^{8}): (4)**<72>**

Jane COOKE4 (Caleb3, Jacob2), b. 16 Mar. 1688/9, Plymouth <MD 4:111>; d. 8 Feb. 1716/7, Bridgewater <MD 14:204>

CHILDREN OF Isaac HARRIS^{5} (Mercy Latham^{4}) & 1st Jane COOKE: (5) <Bridgewater, MD 14:204>

Arthur HARRIS^{6}, b. 25 June 1708

Abner HARRIS^{6}, b. 29 July 1710

Anne HARRIS^{6}, b. 25 Sept. 1712

Elizabeth HARRIS^{6}, b. 1 Dec. 1714

Jane HARRIS^{6}, b. 10 Jan. 1716/17

CHILD OF Isaac HARRIS^{5} & 2nd Elizabeth (SHAW) Washburn:

Isaac HARRIS^{6}, b. 22 July 1720, Bridgewater <MD 14:204>

James DUNBAR, (son of Robert), d. 12 Dec. 1690, Bridgewater <MD 2:243>

CHILD OF James DUNBAR & Jane HARRIS^{5} (Mercy Latham^{4}):

Robert DUNBAR^{6}, b. 30 Nov. 1689; d. 16 May 1736

Pelatiah SMITH, d. 10 or 18 Sept. 1727*, <Bellingham VR>

CHILDREN OF Pelatiah SMITH & Jane (HARRIS^{5}) Dunbar: (11) <Bridgewater>

Jane SMITH^{6}, b. 22 May 1692 <MD 2:243>

Pelatiah SMITH^{6}, b. 25 Apr. 1695 <MD 2:243>

James SMITH^{6}, b. 18 Jan. 1696/7 <MD 2:243>

Samuel SMITH^{6}, b. 5 May 1699 <MD 2:243>

Desire SMITH^{6}, b. 22 Oct. 1701 <MD 2:244>

Sarah SMITH^{6}, b. ( )

Joanna SMITH^{6}, b. 16 Dec. 1703 <MD 14:181>

Ruhamah SMITH^{6}, b. 13 Dec. 1705 <MD 14:182>; m. John Thayer

Robert SMITH^{6}, b. 8 Aug. 1708 <MD 14:182>; d. aft. 21 Feb. 1784* (will) <Suffolk Co.Prob.#18864>

Joseph SMITH^{6}, b. 5 Apr. 1710 <MD 14:182>

Eleanor SMITH^{6}, b. ( )

Smith THAYER^{6} (Palatia^{5}, John^{4}, Tho.^{3}, Ferdinando^{2}, Tho.^{1}), b. 15 Dec. 1770, d. 31 Mar. 1818<73>

Abigail DRAKE, b. 1770, Uxbridge MA, d. 13 Mar. 1839, New Ipswich NH<73>

CHILD OF Smith THAYER & Abigail DRAKE:

Stephen THAYER, b. 24 July 1803, Upton MA, d. 11 Jan. 1890 (m. Joanna Pond below)<73>

Joab POND, (son of Daniel), b. 17 Mar. 1756, Wrentham<74>

Joanna PERRY, b. 22 July 1755, Wrentham, d. 19 Oct. 1805 (1st wf of Joab Pond, no issue)<74>

Mary BALCH, b. 10 Feb. 1770, d. 14 Oct. 1838, New Ipswich NH<74>

CHILDREN OF Joab POND & 2nd Mary BALCH: (2 of 10)

Joanna POND, b. 13 Feb. 1808, Keene NH; d. 15 Apr. 1878<74>

Permelia Hammond POND, b. 23 Feb. 1830

Rhoda BATES, b. 1 May 1800, d. 24 Nov. 1836

CHILDREN OF Rev. Silas KENNEY & Rhoda BATES: (2) <Bellingham>

Silas Emmons KENNEY, b. 20 Oct. 1825

Charles KENNEY, b. 14 Aug. 1827

MICRO #7 of 7

Sarah ( ) SMITH, b. c1757, d. 29 May 1832, ae 75, g.s. <Arlington VR:151>

CHILDREN OF Samuel SMITH^{6} (Jane Harris^{5}) & Sarah ( ): (12) <Hist.Cambridge:656>

Sarah SMITH^{7}, b. 13 Apr. 1717

Susanna SMITH^{7}, b. 24 Aug. 1720, d. 26 Apr. 1721

Anna SMITH^{7}, b. 6 Nov. 1726

Pelatiah SMITH^{7}, b. 8 Jan. 1727/8

Samuel SMITH^{7}, b. 8 Dec. 1729

Michael SMITH^{7}, b. 12 June 1732

Joseph SMITH^{7}, b. 7 July 1734

Benjamin SMITH^{7}, b. 13 Jan. 1735/6

Robert SMITH^{7}, bpt. 31 Dec. 1738; d. 19 May 1740

Thomas SMITH^{7}, b. 25 Mar. 1740

Robert SMITH^{7}, b. 10 Dec. 1741

Daniel SMITH^{7}, bpt. 8 June 1746, d. 23 July 1746

Levina COOK, b. c1758, d. 16 Aug. 1841, ae 83 (widow of 2nd hus Ezekiel Bates)

CHILDREN OF Pelatiah SMITH^{7} & Eunice THAYER: (2) <Bellingham MA>

Robert SMITH^{8}, b. 5 Nov. 1752; d. 3 Jan. 1794 <Norfolk Co.Prob.#17020,1:86>

Margaret SMITH^{8}, b. 10 Nov. 1754

CHILDREN OF Robert SMITH^{8} & Levina COOK: (8*) <Bellingham MA>

Pelatiah SMITH^{9}, b. 25 June 1776; d. 25 Aug. 1864, old age, Bellingham <Mass.VR 175:214>

Margaret SMITH^{9}, b. 20 Mar. 1778

Abner SMITH^{9}, b. 1 May 1780

Robert SMITH^{9}, b. 30 Mar. 1782; d. ae 70

Levina SMITH^{9}, b. 13 Apr. 1784

Simon SMITH^{9}, b. 1 July 1787, d. 3 Aug. 1790

Samuel SMITH^{9}, b. 28 Mar. 1789

Ruel SMITH^{9}, b. 23 Apr. 1790

Ezekiel BATES, b. c1738, d. 5 Sept. 1816, ae 78 or 79 (2nd hus of Levina Cook)

CHILDREN OF Robert SMITH^{9} & Sally FAIRBANKS: (3*)

Eliza Brooks SMITH^{10}, b. 17 Nov. 1810, d. c1890, Wareham (m. Horace Rockwood)

Julia SMITH^{10}, b. ( )

Amanda SMITH^{10}, b. c1826, d. 1922, ae about 96 or 97

Joanna THAYER, (?dau of Ben. & Sarah (Bosworth)), b.? 8 Mar. 1777, Mendon <Thayer Gen.:577>; d. 18 Jan. 1850, ae 72y10m10d, bronchitis, Bellingham MA <Mass.VR 49:110>

CHILDREN OF Pelatiah SMITH^{9} (Robert^{8}) & Joanna THAYER: (9) <Bellingham MA>

Margaret SMITH^{10}, b. 1 Nov. 1797; d. Sept. 1847, dropsy, Bellingham <Mass.VR 33:105>

Sarah SMITH^{10}, b. 22 Mar. 1800

Joanna SMITH^{10}, b. 29 Aug. 1803

Pelatiah SMITH^{10}, b. 25 Mar. 1806; d. 21 Jan. 1892, pneumonia, Bellingham <Mass.VR 428:443>

Levina Bates SMITH^{10}, b. 22 Aug. 1808

Zilpha Thayer SMITH^{10}, b. 22 Mar. 1811

Ruth Alden SMITH^{10}, b. 4 Oct. 1813

Olive Abigail SMITH^{10}, b. 22 May 1817

Milatiah Wales SMITH^{10}, b. 17 Jan. 1820

Samuel DARLING, (son of Sam. & Mary (Burr)), b. 15 Aug. 1793, Bellingham, d. 22 Nov. 1874, farmer <Mass.VR 266:227>

CHILDREN OF Thomas BURCH & Sarah SMITH^{6} (Jane Harris^{5}): (5*) <Bellingham MA VR>

Jeremiah BURCH^{7}, b. 10 Feb. 1718/19

Mary BURCH^{7}, b. 21 Feb. 1720

Sarah BURCH^{7}, b. 24 Oct. 1721

Hannah BURCH^{7}, b. 21 Sept. 1723

Abigail BURCH^{7}, b. 5 Dec. 1728

CHILDREN OF Daniel PACKARD & Mary HARRIS^{5} (Mercy Latham^{4}): (7) <Bridgewater, MD 15:46>

Sarah PACKARD^{6}, b. 28 Aug. 1714; d. 1792*

Mary PACKARD^{6}, b. 23 July 1716

Susanna PACKARD^{6}, b. 3 Apr. 1718

Martha PACKARD^{6}, b. 13 Jan. 1720

Daniel PACKARD^{6}, b. 11 Sept. 1722

Isaac PACKARD^{6}, b. 3 Apr. 1724

Nehemiah PACKARD^{6}, b. 22 Mar. 1727

Zachariah SHAW, b. c1711, d. 1790*, ae 79

CHILDREN OF Zachariah SHAW & Sarah PACKARD^{6}: (8*)<75>

Sarah SHAW^{7}, b. 25 June 1734

Ruth SHAW^{7}, b. 29 Jan. 1738

Martha SHAW^{7}, b. 29 Aug. 1740, d. 1825, unm.

Daniel SHAW^{7}, b. 29 Sept. 1742

Elizabeth SHAW^{7}, b. 30 Sept. 1744

Judith SHAW^{7}, b. 24 May 1749, Bridgewater

Zachariah SHAW^{7}, b. 12 Dec. 1751

Nehemiah SHAW^{7}, b. 31 Mar. 1753

CHILDREN OF John EDSON^{5} (*Joseph^{4-3-2}, Sam.^{1}) & Judith SHAW^{7}: (12*) <Bridgewater>

Isaac EDSON^{8}, b. 5 Dec. 1770

Martha EDSON^{8}, b. 24 May 1772

Mary EDSON^{8}, b. 24 May 1772 (twins)

Sarah EDSON^{8}, b. 3 Mar. 1776

Ruth EDSON^{8}, b. 31 Jan. 1778

Isaiah EDSON^{8}, b. 10 Feb. 1781

Sylvia EDSON^{8}, b. 4 Dec. 1782

Hannah EDSON^{8}, b. 8 Sept. 1784, d. 27 Sept. 1785

Jacob EDSON^{8}, b. 2 Nov. 1786

Nehemiah Shaw EDSON^{8}, b. 9 Jan. 1789

Joseph EDSON^{8}, b. 23 Dec. 1792

James EDSON^{8}, b. 25 Mar. 1795

John BISBEE, b. c1747, d. 1 Nov. 1817*, ae 70 <Bridgewater VR 2:438> (m. Mary Edson^{8})

CHILD OF Paul HAMMOND & Sarah EDSON^{8}:

Paul HAMMOND^{9}, b. 14 May 1795 <Rochester VR 1:153>

Jonathan RIDER, b. c1750, d. 7 May 1799, ae 49 <Rochester VR 2:424>

CHILDREN OF Jonathan RIDER & Sarah (EDSON^{8}) Hammond: (2) <Rochester VR>

Samuel RIDER^{9}, b. 27 May 1797 <VR 1:251>

Jonathan RIDER^{9}, b. 17 Apr. 1799 <VR 1:250>; d. 21 Dec. 1875, Marion, farmer <Mass.VR 275:318>

CHILDREN OF Joseph Bates SMITH & Sarah (EDSON^{8})(Hammond) Rider: (7) <1-3, Rochester VR 1:271><76>

Isaac SMITH^{9}, b. 6 Sept. 1801; d. 28 Feb. 1849, suicide, shoemaker <Rochester VR 2:432>

Royal SMITH^{9}, b. 2 or 7 Nov. 1803

Joseph Edson SMITH^{9}, b. 24 Apr. 1807; d. 15 Jan. 1891, Mattapoisett <Mass.VR 419:539>

Sarah SMITH^{9}, b. 18 Sept. 1809

Permelia SMITH^{9}, b. 21 Apr. 1813; d.?24 June 1820

Sylva Cipher SMITH^{9}, b. 21 Aug. 1814

Julia Ann SMITH^{9}, b. 19 Apr. 1817

Almira Wheaton RICHMOND^{7} (Josiah^{6-5-4}, Jos.^{3}, John$^{2-1}$), b. 9 Jan. 1810, Marion<Richmond Gen.:103>

CHILDREN OF Jonathan RIDER$^{9?}$ (?Sarah Edson^{8}) & Almira Wheaton RICHMOND: (4) <Richmond Gen.:219>

Josiah T. RIDER, b. 1826, Rochester now Marion

Sarah RIDER, b. 1830, NY

Royal S. RIDER, b. 1834, NY

Mary E. RIDER, b. 1840

Sarah Crandall SKIFFE, (dau of James & Betsey (Ames)), b. 1799, New Bedford, d. 14 Jan. 1894, ae 94y5m11d, Mattapoisett <Mass.VR 446:614>

CHILDREN OF Joseph Edson SMITH^{9} (Sarah Edson^{8}) & Sarah Crandall SKIFFE: (3) <Rochester VR>

James Edward SMITH^{10}, b. 1 Dec. 1831 <VR 1:271>

Nathan SMITH^{10}, b. 14 Oct. 1835 <VR 1:272>

Sylvia Cyher SMITH^{10}, b. 22 July 1837 <VR 1:272>

CHILDREN OF Samuel HARRIS^{5} (Mercy Latham^{4}) & Abigail HARDING: (6)

Susanna HARRIS^{6}, bpt. 5 Sept. 1725

Abigail HARRIS^{6}, bpt. 5 Sept. 1725

Mary HARRIS^{6}, bpt. 5 Sept. 1725

Seth HARRIS^{6}, bpt. 27 Mar. 1726

Samuel HARRIS^{6}, bpt. 24 Mar. 1727/8

Isaac HARRIS^{6}, bpt. 27 June 1731

CHILDREN OF John HOWARD, (*son of John) & Sarah LATHAM^{4} (Susanna Winslow^{3}): (1 of 6)<77>

Edward HAWARD^{5}, b. 7 Feb. 1686/7, d. 14 July 1776, Bridgewater <MD 15:50>

Mary BYRAM, d. 11 Jan. 1767, Bridgewater <MD 15:50>

CHILDREN OF Edward HAWARD^{5} & Mary BYRAM: (6) <Bridgewater, MD 15:50>

Sarah HAWARD^{6}, b. 2 Nov. 1714

Mary HAWARD^{6}, b. 23 Mar. 1717

Bethiah HAWARD^{6}, b. 20 Apr. 1719

Jane HAWARD^{6}, b. 10 Aug. 1719

Edward HAWARD^{6}, b. 11 Mar. 1723/4

James HAWARD^{6}, b. 1 May 1726

Henry HAWARD, (son of Jonathan & Sarah), b. 6 Sept. 1710, Bridgewater <MD 5:248>

CHILD OF Henry HAWARD & Mary HAWARD^{6}:

Mary HAWARD^{7}, b. 27 Jan. 1733/4 <MD 15:200>

* * * * * *

FOOTNOTES

<1> p.287, The identity of James Chilton's wife has long been sought, in fact, Bowman himself said he had spent a quarter of a century searching. He mentions no foundation for the claim that her name was "Susanna", except for an early statement in Mitchell's History of Bridgewater, published in 1840, page 222. Bowman's notes state that Dr. Nathaniel B. Shurtleff of Boston wrote to Judge Mitchell asking his source for the name and received the following reply: "I cannot now say how I learnt the name of James Chilton's wife, but I am very certain I had good authority for calling it Susanna - perhaps I may stumble upon it again".

MF5G 2:3-5, suggests the possibility that James m. Susanna Furner, daughter of his step-mother, Isabell by her first husband Francis Furner.

<2> p.287, James Chilton had ten known children but only Mary & Isabella have known children.

<3> p.287, Mary Chilton was bpt. 31 May 1607, St. Peter's Parish, Sandwich, Kent co., England. Both she and her husband, John Winslow, are buried in King's Chapel Burying Ground, Boston <MF5G>

<4> p.288, John Winslow, son of Edward Winslow & Magdalen Ollyver, b. 16 Apr. 1597, Droitwich, Worcestershire, England <MF5G 2:6>.

<4a> p.288, In his will, dated 3 Oct. 1683, John Winslow^{3} called his sister Susanna deceased. However, on 6 Mar. 1685, Robert & Susanna Latham acknowledged a deed. <Plymouth Co.Deeds 5:28>

<5> p.289, Sarah Hilton, dau. of William Hilton & Sarah Greenleaf, b. June 1641, Newbury <MF5G>

<6> p.289, d. 25 Apr. 1711, Boston <MF5G 2:40>

<7> p.289, Elizabeth Dixie, dau. of John Dixey & Elizabeth Allen, b. 3 Oct. 1669, d. 18 Sept. 1740 <MF5G 2:40>.

<8> p.289, d. 22 Aug. or 3 Sept. 1765, ae 53, Boston <MF5G 2:98>.

<9> p.289, Edward Winslow^{4} married as his 3rd wife Susanna (Farnum) Lyman (widow of Caleb whom she m. 1709, Boston). In attempting to identify her, Bowman has found two possibilities in the Boston records. MF5G 2:40 states Susanna was b. 1687 or 1688.

<10> p.289, Son of William Clarke & Hannah Appleton, b. 1 May 1711, Boston <MF5G 2:98>.

<11> p.290, d. 7 Aug. 1778, Boston <MF5G 2:95>.

<12> p.290, The three additional Winslow children are listed without dates, viz: Sarah, Edward, and Joshua. <MD 10:108>

<13> p.291, MF5G 2:43 gives three Hinkes children with baptism dates, viz: Elizabeth, bpt. 26 July 1713; Katharine Ann, bpt. 2 Jan. 1714/5 and Samuel, bpt. 19 Apr. 1717, d. 1804, Bucksport ME

<14> p.291, Bible of "Jesse J. & Ruthy Hinks", printed at Brattleboro VT, 1822. In 1905 the bible was in the possession of Jesse Young Hinks of Oldtown ME.

<15> p.291, Family Bible, "New Testament, 1832". In 1905 in the possession of Elizabeth G. (Hinks) Stickney of Bangor ME (dau of Jesse & Eliza and wf of Thomas Stickney).

<16> p.292, The three Emerson children are listed in pencil without dates, viz: Moses, Ann and Edward Winslow. Bowman questions whether Rebecca married Edward or Moses Emerson and includes a pencilled marriage date of 2 Oct. 1744. MF5G 2:104 confirms she married Rev. Moses Emerson (pre 1643), the son of Jonathan Emerson & Hannah Day, b. 22 Dec. 1717, Haverhill, d. 14 May 1779, Philadelphia.

<17> p.292, MF5G 2:102 states Dorothy's name is Dorothy (Sherbourne)(Rymes) Rogers. Her name is

written in pencil in the files, and while it appears to read as Pymes, it could be Rymes.
The three Taylor children are listed without dates, viz: Dorothy, Ann Sherburne and Edward Sherburne.
<18> p.293, d. 7 July 1750 <W. Bridgewater VR>.
<19> p.293, The files do not show if Nancy was a child by Isaac's first or second wife.
<20> p.293, b. 7 Aug. 1695, Charlestown <MF5G 2:113>.
<21> p.293, b. 9 Apr.1704, Charlestown (& d. there) <MF5G 2:113>.
<22> p.294, Very little has been uncovered concerning John Winslow and his two wives. MF5G 2:13 gives John and 1st wife Elizabeth four children born in Boston, viz: Richard, b. 18 Apr. 1664, d.y.; Elizabeth, b. 14 Mar. 1665; John; and Ann, b. 7 Aug. 1670, prob. d.y.
<23> p.294, d. 1 Jan. 1694/5, Boston <MF5G 2:29>.
<24> p.294, This John Winslow is not identified in the files. His will mentions wife Elizabeth and children John, Sarah and Elizabeth.
<25> p.294, The gravestone of Edward Gray is the oldest original stone still standing on Burial Hill.
<26> p.294, The remaining four Gray children are listed without dates, viz: Rebecca, Lydia, Thomas and Samuel.
<27> p.294, Gray Genealogy, by M.D. Raymond. 1887. Tarrytown NY.
<28> p.294, The remaining five Gray children are listed without dates, viz: Edward, Eliza, Susanna, John and Frederick Turell.
<29> p.295, On 28 Aug. 1721, in the account of the executor, Anne Leblond mentions the bringing up of her children from "23 Oct. 1713 to 1 May last past which is seven years." <Suffolk Co.Prob.#3515, 22:220>
<30> p.295, The children of James Sprout[3] (Eliz. Samson[2]) and Elizabeth Southworth will be found under the Samson family.
<31> p.296, Dau. of Henry Hodges & Easter Gollup. <Mayflower Source Rcds.:640>
<32> p.296, Plymouth g.s. <Burial Hill by Drew:107>.
<33> p.296, Nathaniel Thomas is not identified. On the same page is written two marriages, one to Priscilla Shaw, 9 Dec. 1781, Plymouth <VR 2:264> and another to Jane (Downs) Jackson, 1 July 1796, Plymouth <VR 2:291>. Nathaniel's will, dated 8 May 1830 and probated Aug. 1838, mentions wife Jane and children not named here. <Plymouth Co.Prob.#20436,80:261>
A later pencilled, rough chart shows Nathaniel's 1st wife Priscilla to be the dau of Ichabod Shaw[7] and Priscilla Atwood. Seven children are listed on this chart but it is not clear by which wife, viz: William, Nathaniel, Mary Ann, Harriet, Deborah, Nancy and John. See the will of Nathaniel's widow Jane below <34>.
<34> p.296, Jane's will mentions daughters Harriet Jones (wf of Samuel), Jane Reed, Mary Ann Callaway and Deborah Macomber (wf of Elijah Jr.). Deborah's portion was to be held in trust "for her sole use, separate and independant of her husband". See above <33>.
<35> p.296, Priscilla Atwood, b. c1740, d. 24 July 1824, ae 84, Plymouth g.s. <Burial Hill by Drew:107>.
<36> p.296, d. 26 July 1837, Plymouth g.s. The same source lists the following: Betsey Shaw, wf of Ichabod, d. 6 Dec. 1795, ae 20 with dau. Betsy Holmes, ae 7m15d; Esther Shaw, widow of Ichabod, d. 1 Nov. 1840, 78th yr. <Burial Hill by Drew:164>
<37> p.296, d. 9 Sept. 1772, ae 7m6d, Plymouth g.s. <Burial Hill by Drew:107>.
<38> p.296, d. 18 Jan. 1847, Plymouth g.s.; wife Maria Shaw, b. 20 Mar. 1778, d. 5 Oct. 1850, Plymouth g.s. <Burial Hill by Drew:163>.
<39> p.297, The six Macumber childen are listed in pencil without dates, viz: Job, George, Nathaniel, Ichabod, Ezra and John.
<40> p.297, MF5G 2:86 lists an additional child, Desire.
<41> p.297, Burial Hill by Drew:119.
<42> p.297, b. 3 Apr. 1712 <Hull VR>.
<43> p.297, Burial Hill by Drew:208 shows her g.s. date as 14 Mar. 1765 ae 59y4m18d.
<44> p.297, The remaining four Cooper children are listed without dates, viz: Joseph, Nathaniel, John and Thomas.
<45> p.297, All thirteen children with birth & death dates are found in a family bible, printed in 1791, said to have belonged to Capt. Richard Cooper.
<46> p.297, Plymouth g.s.; also Mrs. Lucy Cooper, wf of Capt. Joseph, d. 13 Oct. 1842, ae 70 yr <Burial Hill by Drew:172>.
<47> p.298, John Dexter, b. 30 Apr. 1724 is shown to be the Jonathan Dexter who m. 1st Hannah Vincent, 2nd Philippa Rider.
<48> p.298, Plymouth Co.Prob.#18938, 14:318.
<49> p.299, On 30 Sept. 1720 Seth took inventory of the estate of Samuel Thomas of Marshfield <Plymouth Wills 4:254>.
<50> p.300, Daughters of John Sprague and Bethiah Snow[4] (Josiah[3], Abigail Warren[2]) <Plymouth Co.Prob. 8:147>.
<51> p.301, MF5G 2:45 states Mary d. June 1718 at sea from Barbados to Boston after living in Barbados from 1701-18.
<54> p.302, MF5G 2:45 identifies Henry Gibbs as the son of Robert & Elizabeth, of Barbados, b. 8 Oct. 1668, Boston. His will (dated 2 Dec. 1698, probated 24 Oct. 1705) mentions children John and Sarah and the child "my wife is now carrying".
<55> p.302, The four Hagget children are listed without dates, viz: Othaniel, Nathaniel, Mary and William. Nathaniel Hagget was living in Barbados in 1733 and later Boston. See NEHGR 15:308.
<56> p.302, d. at sea on way to England, 1715 <MF5G 2:48>.
<57> p.302, d. pre 2 Dec. 1771, Charlestown <MF5G 2:109>.

<58> p.303, MF5G 2:14 discounts the claim of a daughter Sarah and adds a daughter Mary based on the will of Mary (Chilton) Winslow who named a grandaughter, Mary Pollard.
<59> p.303, d. 8 July 1792, Chesterfield NH <MF5G 2:84>.
<60> p.304, The six Conant children are listed in pencil without dates, viz: Jane, Sally, Jerusha, Josiah, Lydia and Alice.
<61> p.305, A 6th child, Lucretia, is written in pencil with a question mark, the source being Mitchell:222.
<62> p.305, The remaining five Wade children are listed without dates, viz: Samuel, Thomas, John, James and Nicholas.
<63> p.305, The remaining five Wade children are listed without dates, viz: Nabby, Polly, Lot, Hannah and Thomas.
<64> p.305, James and Esther's marriage intentions are dated 1769, a 12 year gap before the 1st child. The children on their chart are entered in such a way as to leave room for earlier ones.
<65> p.306, The seven Latham children are listed without dates, viz: Nathaniel, Cyrus, Susanna Alden, Robert, Marcus, Lewis and Hannah. "Moved to Windsor" is written on this page.
<66> p.306, Nathaniel Harden, son of John & Hannah, b. 7 Jan. 1691/2 <Braintree VR:666>.
The three Harden children are listed without dates, viz: Nathaniel (b.1727*), Abraham and Seth (b. 1731*).
<67> p.306, Deborah Hardin, dau. of John & Anna Hardin, b. 29 July 1694 <Braintree VR:671>.
The seven Latham children are listed without dates, viz: Joseph, Rotheus, Beriah, Anne, Deliverance, Jennet and Rhoda. MF5G 2:72 (addendum) finds no evidence for son Joseph.
<68> p.306, MF5G identifies Isaac Harris as the son of Arthur & Martha, b. c1644, Duxbury, d. 22 Jan. 1706/07, Bridgewater.
The remaining five Harris children are listed without dates, viz: Samuel, Desire, Susanna, Mary, Mercy and Arthur. Two unnamed chldren are included in pencil.
<69> p.307, Charles Willis possibly remarried after his wife's death in 1807. Two children are pencilled in on his page, viz: Eliza Badger Willis, b. 1 Jan. 1810 and Mary Ann Willis, b. 13 Dec. 1812.
<70> p.307, Charles Willis Jr. was named William Parsons Willis at his birth in May 1789, however, possibly as a result of the death of his 8 yr. old brother Charles in July 1789, his name was changed.
<71> p.308, The remaining nine Copeland children are listed without dates, viz: John (d.y.), Abigail (d.y.), John, Abigail, Seth, Lydia, Elkanah, Lawrence and Mary. <Thayer Mem.1:88>
<72> p.308, The four Adams children are listed in pencil without dates, viz: Ruth, Sally, Mary and George. <Copeland Mss.1:133,305-07>
<73> p.309, History of New Ipswich NH, by Chandler & Lee, p.664.
<74> p.309, Daniel Pond and His Descendants, by E.D. Harris (1873), pp.68-69.
<75> p.311, The files give the years of birth only, full dates have been added from the Bridgewater VR <MD 16:39>. The records also list a 9th child, Joseph, b. 8 Nov. 1736, d. 18 Dec. 1760.
<76> p.311, The last four children are listed on the same page but separate from the first three, with the heading "Of Joseph Smith Only". This refers to the VR in which the 1st three are called "Of Joseph & Sarah". While these last four appear to belong to this family, the files do not specifically state this fact.
<77> p.312, The remaining five Howard children are listed in pencil without dates, viz: Susanna, Robert, Martha, Sarah and Bethiah.

* * * * *

REFERENCE LIST

GENEALOGICAL ARTICLES PERTAINING TO CHILTON FAMILY RESEARCH

Mayflower Descendant (MD) (1899-1937)

1:65-71 - Will & Inventory of Mary Chilton
1:89-90 - The John Taylor Bible
3:129-34 - John Winslow's Will
8:103-05 - Family Bible of Charles Willis Jr.
10:52-56 - Chilton/Winslow Notes
10:106-11 - Chilton/Winslow Notes
11:129 - Marriage of Roger Chandler & Isabel Chilton
17:82-87 - Little Notes: (Samuel Little[3] & Sarah Gray[4])
21:1-10 - Sarah Winslow[3]'s Three Husbands
21:24-28 - Wills of Lieut. Nathaniel Southworth & His Son Constant - (m. Desire Gray[4])
21:40-42 - Latham/Washburn Notes: (Hannah Latham[4] & Joseph Washburn)
21:62-64 - Will of John Gray[4] of Kingston MA
21:73-76 - Estate of Capt. Ichabod Southworth[5] & The Will of His Widow Esther
21:121-24 - Wills of John Taylor of Boston and Rev. John Taylor of Milton - (m. Ann Winslow[4])
22:118-21 - Estates of James Latham[4] & His Widow Deliverance
24:165 - Miscellaneous Death Records: The Boston Post-boy (Edward Winslow[4])
25:35-37 - Will of Seth Arnold (m. Elizabeth Gray[4])
32:145-47 - A Green/Taylor Record - (John Taylor & Ann Winslow[4], Nathaniel Greene & Elizabeth Taylor[5])

PN&Q 4:21-22 - Memorial to Mary Chilton

Mayflower Quarterly (MQ) (1975-1990)

43:56 - The Baptism of Mary Chilton
43:81-82 - James Chilton (from upcoming MF5G book)
46:182 - The Historian General's Column
- (MF5G 2:21 - Mary Leonard[5])
47:66-68 - The Historian General's Column
- (MF5G 2:71 - Mary Packard[6], MF5G 2:22 - Sarah Leonard[5])
47:205 - Dan Leonard's Family Bible (MF5G 2:55-56)
52:114 - Gravestone of Mary Chilton

OTHERS

Mayflower Families Through Five Generations (MF5G): James Chilton of the Mayflower. Vol.2. pub. by General Society of Mayflower Descendants. 3rd Ed., 1986.

TAG 38:244 - Origins of the Chiltons of the Mayflower

* * * * * * * *

The following footnotes were inadvertently omitted from the Chilton family:

<52> p.301, d. 27 Dec. 1764. <Cambridge VR>
<53> p.302, The remaining five COOKE children died young, viz: two sons named Elisha and three daughters named Jane.

* * * * * * * *

FRANCIS COOKE

MICRO #1 of 30

Francis COOKE, d. 7 Apr. 1663, Plymouth <MD 3:95>**<1>**

Hester MAHIEU, d. betw. 8 June 1666 - 18 Dec. 1675 <MD 3:103,242>**<2>**

CHILDREN OF Francis COOKE & Hester MAHIEU: (5)

John COOKE^2, b. ( ); d. 23 Nov. 1695, Dartmouth <MD 2:116,3:33>

Jane COOKE^2, b. pre 1613**<2a>**

Jacob COOKE^2, b. c1618 (deposition) <MD 2:45>; d. betw. 11-18 Dec. 1675, Plymouth <MD 3:236>

Hester COOKE^2, b. pre 22 May 1627 (cattle division); d. betw. 8 June 1666 - 7 Dec. 1675 (will of son John) <MD 3:105>

Mary COOKE^2, b. betw. 1624 - 22 May 1627 <MD 1:149,3:98>; d. 21 Mar. 1714, Halifax g.s.

HESTER COOKE^2 (Francis^1)

Richard WRIGHT, d. 9 June 1691, Plymouth <MD 16:62>

CHILDREN OF Richard WRIGHT & Hester COOKE^2: (6) <Plymouth>

Adam WRIGHT^3, b. c1645, d. 20 Sept. 1724, 79th or 80th yr, Plympton g.s. <MD 1:178>

John WRIGHT^3, b. pre 1656; d. betw. 7 Dec. 1675 (will) - 7 June 1676 (prob.) <MD 3:105>**<3>**

Esther WRIGHT^3, b. 1649, d. 28 May 1717, 68th yr <MD 16:121>

Isaac WRIGHT^3, b. 26 Aug. 1652 <MD 16:238>; d. betw. 7 Dec. 1675 - 7 June 1676, unm.**<3>**

Samuel WRIGHT^3, b. ( ); d. betw. 7 Dec. 1675 - 7 June 1676, unm.**<3>**

Mary WRIGHT^3, b. ( )

CHILDREN OF Eleazer DUNHAM & Bathsheba ( ): (9) <MD 1:141>

Eleazer DUNHAM, b. 15 Jan. 1682

Nathaniel DUNHAM, b. 20 Mar. 1685

Mercy DUNHAM, b. 10 Dec. 1686

Israel DUNHAM, b. Oct. 1689

Elisha DUNHAM, b. Aug. 1692

Josiah DUNHAM, b. June 1694

Bathshua DUNHAM, b. 26 Apr. 1696

Susanna DUNHAM, b. June 1698

Joshua DUNHAM, b. 1 Apr. 1701

Sarah SOULE^3 (John^2), d. betw. 16 Mar. 1690/1 - 1699 <MD 4:160,11:242>

CHILDREN OF Adam WRIGHT^3 & 1st Sarah SOULE: (6) <MD 4:240>

John WRIGHT^4, b. c1680, d. 31 May 1774, 94th yr, Plympton g.s. <MD 11:197>

Isaac WRIGHT^4, b. Jan. 1685/6, d. 11 Jan. 1766, ae 80 wanting 8 days, Plympton g.s. <MD 11:196>

Rachel WRIGHT^4, b. c1688, d. 7 Dec. 1779, 91st yr <Rochester VR 2:341>

Mary WRIGHT^4, b. ( ); d. aft. 14 Nov. 1738* <"E.H.W. notes">

Sarah WRIGHT^4, b. ( ); d. betw. 9 Apr. 1725 - 1738**<4>**

Esther WRIGHT^4, b. ( ); d. betw. 1 Oct. 1703 - Oct. 1706 (b. last child & hus. 2nd marr.)

Mehitable BARROW, (dau of Robert), d. aft. 2 Nov. 1744 <MD 4:241>

CHILDREN OF Adam WRIGHT^3 & 2nd Mehitable BARROW: (4) <MD 4:240>

Samuel WRIGHT^4, b. c1699, d. 5 Jan. 1773, 74th yr, Plympton g.s. <MD 11:197>

Moses WRIGHT^4, b. pre 9 Apr. 1702*

James WRIGHT^4, b. aft. Apr. 1702*

Nathan WRIGHT^4, b. 12 May 1711 <MD 5:183>; d. pre 7 Apr. 1762 (adm.) <Plymouth Co.PR #23535>

CHILDREN OF Isaac WRIGHT: <ChR. - unidentified>

Rachel WRIGHT, b. 6 May 1733

Isaac WRIGHT, b. 12 Sept. 1736

Mary COLE, (dau of John & Susanna), b. c1696, d. 20 July 1759, 63rd yr, Plympton g.s. <MD 11:197>

CHILDREN OF Isaac WRIGHT^{4} (Adam^{3}) & Mary COLE: (5) <Plympton VR, MD 5:209>

Susanna WRIGHT^{5}, b. 9 Dec. 1719; d. 14 Mar. 1736/7, Plympton g.s.

Joseph WRIGHT^{5}, b. 16 June 1721; d. betw. 27 Feb. 1788 (will) - 4 Sept. 1804 (prob.)

Mary WRIGHT^{5}, b. 30 Jan. 1726

Rachel WRIGHT^{5}, b. 23 Mar. 1732

Isaac WRIGHT^{5}, b. 3 Sept. 1736; d. 29 Oct. 1796, Plympton g.s.**<5>**

Ebenezer BARLOW, b. c1691, d. 4 May 1754, 63rd yr <Rochester VR 2:341>**<6>**

CHILDREN OF Ebenezer BARLOW & Rachel WRIGHT^{4} (Adam^{3}): (5) <Rochester VR>

Moses BARLOW^{5}, b. 6 Sept. 1720, d. 10 Aug. 1721 <VR 1:21>

Moses BARLOW^{5}, b. 29 May 1722, d. c1st Oct. 1723 <VR 1:21>

Seth BARLOW^{5}, b. 29 Mar. 1725, d. about mid June 1726 <VR 1:22>

Sarah BARLOW^{5}, b. 7 July 1727 <VR 1:22>

Mary BARLOW^{5}, b. 20 Dec. 1730 <VR 1:21>

CHILD OF Seth FULLER & Sarah WRIGHT^{4} (Adam^{3}):**<7>**

Archippus FULLER^{5}, b. 17 May 1721, Plympton <MD 3:92>; d. aft. 1742*

CHILD OF Seth FULLER & Deborah ( ):

Sarah FULLER, b. 27 Jan. 1727/8 <MD 5:209>

Daniel PRATT, b. c1680, d. 7 May 1739, 59th yr, Plympton g.s. <MD 10:221>

CHILDREN OF Daniel PRATT & 1st Esther WRIGHT^{4} (Adam^{3}): (2) <Plympton VR, MD 5:183>

Joshua PRATT^{5}, b. 27 Dec. 1701

Sarah PRATT^{5}, b. 1 Oct. 1703

CHILDREN OF Daniel PRATT & 2nd Mary WASHBURN^{3} (Philip^{2}, John^{1}): (2) <Plympton VR, MD 5:183>

Benjamin PRATT, b. 28 ( ) 1707

Esther PRATT, b. 30 Mar. 1709

Annis ( ) PRATT, b. c1683, d. 21 Feb. 1760, 77th yr, Plympton g.s. <MD 10:220>

CHILDREN OF Daniel PRATT & Annis ( ): (4)**<8>**

Joshua DUNHAM, (*?son of Eleazer & Bathshua), b. ?1 Apr. 1701*

CHILDREN OF Joshua DUNHAM & Sarah PRATT^{5} (Esther Wright^{4}): (10) <Plymouth VR 1:106, MD 13:166>

James DUNHAM^{6}, b. 16 Dec. 1723

Sarah DUNHAM^{6}, b. 26 Jan. 1725/6

Joshua DUNHAM^{6}, b. 27 Nov. 1727

Marcy DUNHAM^{6}, b. 8 Nov. 1729

Bathshua DUNHAM^{6}, b. 7 Jan. 1731/2

Elizabeth DUNHAM^{6}, b. 10 June 1733

Joshua DUNHAM^{6}, b. 15 Feb. 1735/6

Luce DUNHAM^{6}, b. 18 Feb. 1737/8

Levi DUNHAM^{6}, b. 1 June 1743

Elisha DUNHAM^{6}, b. 25 Nov. 1744

Faith CHANDLER, (dau of Zebedee), b. c1740, d. 12 May 1821, ae 80y9m3d, Plympton g.s.**<9>**

CHILDREN OF Isaac WRIGHT^{5} (Isaac^{4}) & Faith CHANDLER: (9)**<10>**

MICRO #2 of 30

Sarah BREWSTER^{5} (Joshua^{4}, Wm.^{3}, Love^{2}), b. 11 Feb. 1727 <Duxbury VR>

CHILDREN OF Joseph WRIGHT^{5} (Isaac^{4}) & Sarah BREWSTER: (5)**<11>**

CHILD OF Joseph SAMPSON^{7} (Mary Wright^{6}, Jos.^{5}): <Plymouth>

Rufus SAMPSON^{8}, b. c1801, d. 12 Dec. 1858, ae 57, Plymouth, "of gravel", mariner<Mass.VR 121:261>

Nancy WHITING, b. c1798, Plymouth, d. 2 Dec. 1866, ae 68y5m, congestion of lungs, Plymouth,<Mass. VR 193:328>**<12>**

CHILD OF Rufus SAMPSON^{8} & Nancy WHITING: <Plymouth>

Rufus SAMPSON^{9}, b. c1828, d. 8 Sept. 1903, ae 75y3m25d, Plymouth, grocer <"Deaths 45:72">

Esther JORDAN, (dau of John & Ellen (Royal)), b. c1836, England, d. 23 May 1930, ae 94y4m10d, Plymouth <Plymouth Dths.8:207>

CHILDREN OF Rufus SAMPSON^{9} & Esther JORDAN: (2)

George SAMPSON^{10}, b. ( )

Nancy W. SAMPSON^{10}, b. c1860, d. 28 Sept. 1862, ae 2y9m2d, Plymouth <Mass.VR 157:370>

Mary LUCAS, (dau of Benoni), b. c1683, d. 24 Sept. 1759, 76th yr, Plympton g.s. <MD 11:197>

CHILDREN OF John WRIGHT^{4} (Adam^{3}) & Mary LUCAS: (6) <Plympton VR, MD 3:164>**<13>**

Esther WRIGHT^{5}, b. 4 Mar. 1709; d. 18 June 1743 <Duxbury VR:387>

John WRIGHT^{5}, b. 11 Oct. 1711; d. pre 3 Apr. 1780, of Chatham CT (adm.)<Middletown CT PR #3969>

Repentance WRIGHT^{5}, b. 8 Oct. 1713; d. 7 May 1800, unm., Plympton g.s. <MD 11:197>

Benjamin WRIGHT^{5}, b. 20 Mar. 1715/6; d. 10 Mar. 1792, unm., Plympton g.s., Old Cem. <MD 11:196>

Sarah WRIGHT^{5}, b. 17 Nov. 1719; d. 10 May 1809, unm., Plympton g.s. <MD 11:197>

Adam WRIGHT^{5}, b. 27 Sept. 1724; d. pre 4 Mar. 1776 (adm.) <Plymouth Co.PR, 23:83>**<14>**

CHILDREN OF John HUNT, (son of Tho. & Honor (Stetson)) & 1st Esther WRIGHT^{5}: (3) <Duxbury VR>

John HUNT^{6}, b. 6 Oct. 1734*

Judah HUNT^{6}, b. 18 Nov. 1737*; d. 18 Apr. 1826*

Mary HUNT^{6}, b. 28 Nov. 1741*; d. 7 Mar. 1810*, Plympton, unm.

Deborah SOULE^{4} (Moses^{3}, John^{2}), d. 14 Oct. 1805, Duxbury

CHILDREN OF John HUNT & 2nd Deborah SOULE: (4) <Duxbury>

Samuel HUNT, b. 24 Jan. 1746/7

Deborah HUNT, bpt. 9 May 1756

Lot HUNT, bpt. 9 May 1756

Asa HUNT, bpt. 31 Oct. 1756; d. 1776, ae 19 <ChR>

Mary COOMER, *(dau of Wm. & Joanna), d. pre 8 Apr. 1780*

CHILDREN OF John WRIGHT^{5} (John^{4}) & Mary COOMER: (3) <1-2, Plympton VR:241>

William WRIGHT^{6}, b. 19 Feb. 1738/9*

Urania WRIGHT^{6}, b. 12 Aug. 1741*

Ezekiel WRIGHT^{6}, b. ( )

Thomas SMITH^{7} (Ruth Mayo^{6}, Israel^{5}, Tho.^{4}, Hannah Prence^{3}, Patience Brewster^{2}), b. 4 June 1744 <Middletown CT VR> (m. Urania Wright^{6}, see Brewster family)

CHILDREN OF Adam WRIGHT^{5} (John^{4}) & 1st Ruth SAMSON (dau of Tho.): (4) <Plympton>

Esther/Hester WRIGHT^{6}, b. 26 Sept. 1754; d. 3 Apr. 1806, Plympton g.s. <MD 10:146>

Levi WRIGHT^{6}, b. 10 Aug. 1756 <VR:236>

Lydia WRIGHT^{6}, b. 28 Oct. 1758 (m. Daniel Thrasher)

John WRIGHT^{6}, b. 16 Oct. 1766

CHILD OF Adam WRIGHT^{5} & 2nd Sarah (STANDISH^{5}) Tinkham, (Moses^{4}, Eben.^{3}, Alex.^{2}):

Benjamin WRIGHT^{6}, b. 11 July 1774 <Plympton VR:231>; d. 2 Sept. 1842 <Barnstable VR 4:280>

Sarah CROCKER, b. c1779, d. 3 Dec. 1840, ae 61, Barnstable

CHILDREN OF Benjamin WRIGHT^{6} & Sarah CROCKER: (14) <Barnstable VR 4:280>

Temperance WRIGHT^{7}, b. 24 Sept. 1799

William WRIGHT^{7}, b. 22 Mar. 1801

Asa WRIGHT^{7}, b. 4 Aug. 1802; d. 1 Feb. 1868, Holliston MA, mariner <Mass.VR 212:132>

Benjamin WRIGHT^{7}, b. 9 Sept. 1804

Sophia WRIGHT^{7}, b. 27 Dec. 1805

Lois WRIGHT^{7}, b. 4 Feb. 1807, d. 25 June 1810

Nelson WRIGHT^{7}, b. 29 Oct. 1808, d. 1 June 1810

Betsy Crocker WRIGHT^{7}, b. 23 May 1810

Chloe Hall WRIGHT^{7}, b. 10 Nov. 1811, d.y.

Martha Crocker WRIGHT^{7}, b. May 1812

Nelson WRIGHT^{7}, b. 15 Aug. 1815, d. 23 Nov. 1839

Lot Crocker WRIGHT[7], b. 25 Apr. 1817, d. 25 Oct. 1823

Nancy Crocker WRIGHT[7], b. 5 Dec. 1818

Chloe Hall WRIGHT[7], b. 5 May 1823, d. 16 Apr. 1833

CHILDREN OF Benjamin WRIGHT[7] & Eunice ( ): (3) <Barnstable VR 6:274>

Benjamin C. WRIGHT[8], b. 19 Jan. 1834, d. 14 June 1854

William W. WRIGHT[8], b. 11 May 1837, d. 3 Aug. 1854

Persis C. WRIGHT[8], b. 14 Feb. 1839

Mary CROCKER, b. c1807, d. 28 Nov. 1835*, ae 29y4m, Barnstable g.s.

CHILDREN OF Asa WRIGHT[7] (Ben.[6]) & 1st Mary CROCKER: (2) <Barnstable>**<15>**

William WRIGHT[8], b. c1832, d. 1 Jan. 1836, ae 4y5m15d

Mary H. WRIGHT[8], b. c1833, d. 5 July 1834, ae 13m6d

Hodiah J. CROCKER, (dau of Sam & Thankful (Percival)), b. c1815, Barnstable, d. 20 Feb. 1908, ae 92y5m29d, at 34 Elm St., Andover, bur. Holliston, widow of Asa Wright[7] <Mass.VR Dths 2:140>

Asa HOOPER, d. 25 Oct. 1807* <Plympton VR:487>

CHILDREN OF Asa HOOPER & Esther WRIGHT[6] (Adam[5]): (4) <Plympton VR:120>

Ruth HOOPER[7], b. 4 May 1774*

Asa HOOPER[7], b. 30 Sept. 1782*

Esther HOOPER[7], b. 4 June 1788*

Polly HOOPER[7], b. 18 Mar. 1793*

Betty WEST[7] (Sam.[6], Bethiah Keen[5], Josiah[4], Abigail Little[3], Anna Warren[2]), b. c1759, d. 20 Mar. 1820*, 66th yr <Plympton VR:535>

CHILDREN OF Levi WRIGHT[6] (Adam[5]) & Betty WEST: (6) <Plympton VR>

Josiah WRIGHT[7], b. 3 Apr. 1780* <VR:235>

Levi WRIGHT[7], b. 9 May 1781* <VR:236>

Adam WRIGHT[7], b. 6 Mar. 1784* <VR:230>

Betsey WRIGHT[7], b. 15 Apr. 1786* <VR:231>

Ruth Sampson WRIGHT[7], b. 24 Oct. 1791* <VR:239>

John WRIGHT[7], b. 18 May 1795* <VR:235>

Jeremiah GIFFORD[3] (Robert[2], Wm.[1]), d. betw. 3 Mar. 1768 <Bristol Co.LR 53:115> - 21 Jan. 1771* (inv.) <Bristol Co.PR, 22:21>

CHILDREN OF Jeremiah GIFFORD & Mary WRIGHT[4] (Adam[3]): (13) <Dartmouth VR 1:316>

Jonathan GIFFORD[5], b. 25 Mar. 1704; d. betw. 30 Dec. 1756 (will) - 3 May 1757 (prob.) <Bristol Co PR, 15:330>**<16>**

Gideon GIFFORD[5], b. 19 Mar. 1705/6; d. betw. 10 Dec. 1759 (will) - 14 Apr. 1760 (prob.) <Bristol Co.PR, 17:6>**<17>**

John GIFFORD[5], b. 7 Mar. 1707/8; d. 18 Dec. 1802 <VR RI 10:80>

Sarah GIFFORD[5], b. 3 Oct. 1710

Elizabeth GIFFORD[5], b. 13 Oct. 1712

Joseph GIFFORD[5], b. 13 Oct. 1712 (twins); d. pre 24 May 1777*

William GIFFORD[5], b. 19 Jan. 1714

Benjamin GIFFORD[5], b. 14 May 1716/17?; d. pre 16 Dec. 1807* (adm.)**<18>**

Isaac GIFFORD[5], b. 16 May 1717; d. 3 Mar. 1812 <Westport VR>

Peleg GIFFORD[5], b. 1 Dec. 1719

Margaret GIFFORD[5], b. 15 Apr. 1722

Adam GIFFORD[5], b. 3 Jan. 1725; d. betw. 26 Sept. 1778 (will) - 4 May 1779 (prob.)<Bristol Co.PR, 26:6>

David GIFFORD[5], b. 5 Apr. 1728

Mary CORNELL, d. 13 July 1792 <Westport VR> (wf of Isaac Gifford[5])

Alice CORNELL, (dau of Wm. & Mehitable), b. 14 Mar. 1726 <Dartmouth VR 1:63>; d. 1811 (wf of Peleg Gifford[5])

Mehitable FISH, (dau of Tho.), b. 22 July 1784 (Cornell Gen.(1902):41>

William CORNELL, d. 1775

CHILDREN OF William CORNELL & Mehitable FISH: (10) <Dartmouth VR>

Benjamin CORNELL, b. 13 Nov. 1711 <VR 1:63>

George CORNELL, b. 25 Dec. 1713 <VR 1:64>

Caleb CORNELL, b. 24 Mar. 1716 <VR 1:63>

Rebecca CORNELL, b. 9 Mar. 1718 <VR 1:66>

Joseph CORNELL, b. 8 Dec. 1720 <VR 1:63>

Daniel CORNELL, b. 17 Sept. 1723 <VR 1:63>

Alse CORNELL, b. 14 Mar. 1726 <VR 1:63>

Mary CORNELL, b. 8 June 1728 <VR 1:66>

Rachel CORNELL, b. 22 ( ) 1733 <VR 1:66>

Elizabeth CORNELL, b. 25 Jan. 1736 <VR 1:64>

CHILDREN OF Benjamim GIFFORD[5] (Mary Wright[4]) & Elizabeth PETTIS: (3)**<19>**

CHILDREN OF Ichabod GIFFORD[6] (Ben.[5]) & Sarah PETTEY: (6) <Dartmouth VR 4:105>

James GIFFORD[7], b. 12 Aug. 1767

Jeremiah GIFFORD[7], b. 8 Nov. 1773

Elisha GIFFORD[7], b. 27 Mar. 1774, d. 12 Apr. 1774

Sarah GIFFORD[7], b. 17 June 1775, d. 17 Nov. 1777

Sarah GIFFORD[7], b. 9 Apr. 1779

Ichabod GIFFORD[7], b. 7 Oct. 1789

CHILDREN OF Jeremiah GIFFORD[7] & Judith REED: (3) <1-2, Dartmouth VR 4:105>

Elizabeth GIFFORD[8], b. 14 Sept. 1794

Ebenezer GIFFORD[8], b. 11 July 1796

George Washington GIFFORD[8], b. Oct. 1802, Westport, d. 31 May 1881, ae 78y7m29d, apoplexy, Fall River, carpenter, married <Mass.VR 328:102>

Betsey GIFFORD, b. c1806, Westport, d. 7 June 1882, ae 76y6m, Bright's Disease, widow, Fall River dau. of Abner & Sophia (?) (her maiden name not given) <Mass.VR 337:98>

CHILDREN OF James GIFFORD 2nd & Anner READ: (2) <Dartmouth VR 4:105>

Phillip GIFFORD, b. 14 Apr. 1790

Leviana GIFFORD, b. 4 June 1794

CHILDREN OF James GIFFORD & Elizabeth ( ): (2) <Dartmouth VR>

Zervia GIFFORD, b. 11 Dec. 1785

George GIFFORD, b. 10 Nov. 1788

CHILDREN OF John GIFFORD & Bathsheba ( ): (9) <Friends'Rcds., Dartmouth:33>**<20>**

Lydia GIFFORD, b. 14 3mth 1743, d. 8 4mth 1754

Phebe GIFFORD, b. 20 6mth 1745

Meribah GIFFORD, b. 6 5mth 1748

Rowland GIFFORD, b. 6 5mth 1748 (twins)

Jesse GIFFORD, b. 22 7mth 1750, d. 14 4mth 1754

Benjamin GIFFORD, b. 29 9mth 1755

John GIFFORD, b. 29 9mth 1755 (twins), d. 3 10mth 1755

John GIFFORD, b. 20 Mar. 1758; d. 9 Nov. 1834, Westport g.s.

Bathsheba GIFFORD, b. 20 3mth 1758 (twins)

Isabel MILK, b. c1753, d. 6 Aug. 1846, ae 93, Westport g.s.

CHILDREN OF John GIFFORD (son of John & Bathsheba) & Isabel MILK: (4 of 12) <Westport>**<21>**

Alden GIFFORD, b. 2 May 1792* <Westport VR 1:46>

Rebecca M. GIFFORD, b. c1795, d. 16 June 1863, ae 68, 53 Hillman St., New Bedford, heart disease <Mass.VR 165:112>

Squire GIFFORD, b. 14 Oct. 1795, d. 6 Mar. 1878

John GIFFORD, b. 9 Mar. 1800, Westport, d. 10 Sept. 1880 (living Watertown NY in 1822)
John F. UNDERWOOD, (son of Nicholas & Phebe (Brownell)), b. 29 Aug. 1791, Westport; d. 28 Dec. 1874, consumption, 500 Hillman St., New Bedford <Mass.VR 265:138>
CHILD OF John F. UNDERWOOD & Rebecca M. (GIFFORD) Cornell: <New Bedford>
Mary A. UNDERWOOD, b. c1831, d. 20 May 1902, ae 71y3m, Danvers <Mass.VR 528:454>
Gravestones from the "Gifford & Richmond Lot", Westport MA: (12)
Patience TRIPP, wf of Rufus, d. 2 Nov. 1875, ae 90y5m (dau of John)
Rufus TRIPP, d. 19 June 1856, ae 73y5m
Ellen GIFFORD, dau of Elkanah & Mary, d. 5 July 1843, ae 6m7d
Isabel GIFFORD, d. 6 Aug. 1856, ae 93
Martha M. GIFFORD, dau of Leonard & Esther, d. 8 Jan. 1847, ae 4y8m7d
Sarah Amanda GIFFORD, dau of Lemuel & Phebe Ann, d. 17 Feb. 1849, ae 3y3m14d
Frederick C. MOULTON, son of Othinal & Lauretta, d. 5 Feb. 1846, ae 3y4m20d
Dr. Thomas RICHMOND, b. 25 Jan. 1779, d. 3 Apr. 1839
Mary (SHEARMAN) Richmond, b. 15 Apr. 1786, d. 18 May 1850
Charles W. RICHMOND, son of Dr. Thomas & Mary, d. 12 May 1821, ae 3y4m
Sophia S. RICHMOND, dau of Thomas & Mary, b. 27 Feb. 1823, d. 10 Apr. 1840
Three infant children of Dr. Thomas & Mary RICHMOND, no dates
CHILDREN OF Moses WRIGHT^4 (Adam^3) & Thankful BOALS: (3) <Plympton VR:234>
Hannah WRIGHT^5, b. 22 Sept. 1735
Ebenezer WRIGHT^5, b. 14 Feb. 1736/7; d. 20 Mar. 1816, Plympton g.s., Old Cem. <MD 11:196>
Moses WRIGHT^5, b. 15 June 1739
Anna TRIPP, d. May 1772
CHILDREN OF Ebenezer WRIGHT^5 & 1st Anna TRIPP: (6) <Plympton VR>
Elizabeth WRIGHT^6, b. 17 Dec. 1758 <VR:233>
Thankful WRIGHT^6, b. Sept. 1760 <VR:240>
Ebenezer WRIGHT^6, b. 15 June 1763 <VR:232>
Moses WRIGHT^6, b. 14 June 1765 <VR:237>
Lemuel WRIGHT^6, b. 1765-70 <VR:236>
Hannah WRIGHT^6, b. 12 Mar. 1770 <VR:234>
CHILDREN OF Ebenezer WRIGHT^5 & 2nd Deliverance CHURCHILL, (dau of Perez): (4) <Plympton VR>
Lemuel WRIGHT^6, b. 23 Mar. 1777
Anna WRIGHT^6, b. 31 Aug. 1779
Isaiah WRIGHT^6, b. 13 June 1781
Zebedee WRIGHT^6, b. 24 Aug. 1786
Hannah COOKE^5 (Wm.^{4}, Jacob$^{3-2}$), b. 8 Nov. 1707, Plymouth <MD 5:54>; d. 25 Feb. 1784, Kingston
CHILDREN OF Nathan WRIGHT^4 (Adam^3) & Hannah COOKE: (6)
Nathan WRIGHT^5, b. 10 Sept. 1737; d. 8 Oct. 1748
Zadock WRIGHT^5, b. 3 Apr. 1739; d. 7 Oct. 1748
Tabitha WRIGHT^5, b. 16 Mar. 1740/1
Hannah WRIGHT^5, b. 27 June 1743
Priscilla WRIGHT^5, b. 3 July 1746; d. 11 July 1746
Lydia WRIGHT^5, b. 26 Jan. 1749/50
Ann TILSON, b. c1703, d. 16 Nov. 1792, 89th yr, Plympton g.s. <MD 11:196>
CHILDREN OF Samuel WRIGHT^4 (Adam^3) & Ann TILSON: (4) <Plympton, 1-3, MD 2:52>
Sarah WRIGHT^5, b. 3 June 1726; d. 12 May 1777, Plympton g.s. (wf of James Hall) <MD 10:144>
Samuel WRIGHT^5, b. 6 Oct. 1728; d. 22 Dec. 1814, Plympton g.s. <MD 11:197>
Edmund WRIGHT^5, b. 28 Oct. 1730
Jacob WRIGHT^5, b. ( )
Abigail STANDISH^5 (Zachariah^4, Eben.^{3}, Alex.^{2}), b. 16 Dec. 1731, Plympton <MD 2:53>; d. 1 Dec.

1774, Plympton g.s. <MD 11:196>

CHILDREN OF Samuel WRIGHT[5] & Abigail STANDISH: (6) <Plympton VR>**<22>**

Sarah WRIGHT[6], b. pre 1756

Samuel WRIGHT[6], b. 9 July 1756

Abigail WRIGHT[6], b. 9 July 1756 (twins)

Nathan WRIGHT[6], b. ( )

Peleg WRIGHT[6], b. 25 Jan. 1764, d. 10 Oct. 1770

Peleg WRIGHT[6], b. 6 Feb. 1771

JACOB COOKE[2] (Francis[1])

Damaris HOPKINS[2], d. betw. 1665-1669

CHILDREN OF Jacob COOKE[2] & 1st Damaris HOPKINS: (7) <Plymouth>

Elizabeth COOKE[3], b. 18 Jan. 1648 <MD 15:27>; 21 Nov. 1692, Plymouth <MD 16:63>

Caleb COOKE[3], b. 29 Mar. 1651 <MD 16:237>; d. d. 13 Feb. 1721/2, Plymouth<Burial Hill by Drew:23>

Jacob COOKE[3], b. 26 Mar. 1653 <MD 17:70>; d. 24 Apr. 1747, Kingston g.s.

Mary COOKE[3], b. 12 Jan. 1657 <MD 17:72>; d. 28 Aug. 1712, Plymouth g.s.**<22a>**

Martha COOKE[3], b. 16 Mar. 1659 <MD 17:182>

Francis COOKE[3], b. 5 Jan. 1662; d. betw. May 1736 (cod.)-18 Sept. 1746 (prob.)<MD 17:183,18:147>

Ruth COOKE[3], b. 17 Jan. 1665 <MD 18:57>

Elizabeth LETTICE, (dau of Tho.), d. 31 Oct. 1693, Swansea (wf of 3rd hus Hugh Cole)

CHILDREN OF Jacob COOKE[2] & 2nd Elizabeth (LETTICE) Shurtleff: (2) <Plymouth>

Sarah COOKE[3], b. c1671, d. 8 Feb. 1744/5, 74th yr

Rebecca COOKE[3], b. ( )

MICRO #4 of 30

John DOTY[2], b. c1640, d. 8 May 1701, Plymouth <MD 16:63>

CHILDREN OF John DOTY[2] & Elizabeth COOKE[3]: (9) <MD 1:144> <See Doty Family>

CHILDREN OF Elkanah CUSHMAN[3] (Mary Allerton) & Martha COOKE[3]: (5) <MD 1:142><See Allerton Family>

Robert BARTLETT[4] (Jos.[3], Mary Warren[2]), b. c1663, Plymouth, d. 3 Jan. 1718, 55th yr

CHILDREN OF Robert BARTLETT[4] & Sarah COOKE[3]: (12) <MD 1:212> <See Warren Family>

Jane ( ) COOKE, d. Apr. 1736, Kingston <MD 15:139>

CHILDREN OF Caleb COOKE[3] & Jane ( ): (9) <Plymouth, MD 4:111>

John COOKE[4], b. 5 Feb. 1682/3; d. betw. 6 May 1741 (will) - 6 July 1741 (prob.) <MD 17:56>

Mercy COOKE[4], b. 21 Feb. 1683/4, d. 11 Feb. 1713/14, unm., Plymouth

Ann COOKE[4], b. 21 Aug. 1686

Jane COOKE[4], b. 16 Mar. 1688/9; d. 8 Feb. 1716/7, Bridgewater <MD 14:204>

Elizabeth COOKE[4], b. 30 Nov. 1691; d.? 14 Jan. 1754*, N. Yarmouth <Old Times:1108>

Mary COOKE[4], b. 20 Aug. 1694

Caleb COOKE[4], b. 17 Apr. 1697; d. 15 Mar. 1724, Kingston g.s. <MD 7:26>

James COOKE[4], b. 19 Aug. 1700

Joseph COOKE[4], b. 28 Nov. 1703

CHILDREN OF Isaac HARRIS[5] (Mercy Latham[4], Susanna Winslow[3], Mary Chilton[2]) & Jane COOKE[4]: (5) <See Chilton Family, p.309>

Robert JOHNSON, d. aft. 25 Apr. 1758*

CHILDREN OF Robert JOHNSON & Elizabeth COOKE[4]: (4) <Plymouth>

Jane JOHNSON[5], b. 15 Aug. 1716 <MD 13:168>

Joseph JOHNSON[5], b. 1 Jan. 1717/18 <MD 13:168>; d. betw. 22 Jan. 1763* - 20 Aug. 1774*

Sarah JOHNSON[5], b. 9 Feb. 1719/20 <MD 13:169>; d. 26 Sept. 1761, Plymouth <MD 31:114>

Caleb JOHNSON[5], b. 2 Apr. 1722 <MD 13:169>

"Old Times", N. Yarmouth ME: (5)

Elizabeth JOHNSON, dau of widow Esther, bpt. 4 Oct. 1778 <:858>

Esther JOHNSON, dau of widow Esther, bpt. 4 Oct. 1778 <:858>

Mary JOHNSON, dau of David, bpt. 7 Aug. 1791 <:941>

Joseph GRAY, bpt. 4 Nov. 1770 <:1117>

Andrew GRAY, b. 12 Jan. 1736, d. 8 Dec. 1810 <:1118>

Cornelius MORTON[5] (Ephraim[4], Geo.[3], Ephraim[2], Geo.[1]), b. 18 Aug. 1713, Plymouth <MD 3:13>

CHILDREN OF Cornelius MORTON & Jane JOHNSON[5]: (6) <Gen.Adv.2:122-23; Kingston VR>

Robert MORTON[6], b. ( ),d. 10 Apr. 1742 <VR:368>

Maria MORTON[6], b. ( ), d. 24 Apr. 1742 <VR:368>

Cornelius MORTON[6], b. 1 Sept. 1740 <VR:111>

Joshua MORTON[6], b. 10 Set. 1743 <VR:112>

Sarah MORTON[6], b. 31 Jan. 1745/6 <VR:112>

Deborah MORTON[6], b. 27 Feb. 1752 <VR:111>

Mary RING[5] (Andrew[4], Eleazer[3], Deborah Hopkins[2]), b. 23 Feb. 1724/5 <Kingston VR:121>; d. Dec. 1808*, N. Yarmouth ME <Old Times:1157>

CHILDREN OF Joseph JOHNSON[5] (Eliz. Cooke[4]) & Mary RING: (11) <N. Yarmouth ME, Old Times:1157>

Content JOHNSON[6], bpt. 23 May 1742*

Nathan JOHNSON[6], bpt. 22 May 1743*

Andrew Ring JOHNSON[6], bpt. 3 Nov. 1745*

Annah JOHNSON[6], bpt. 29 May 1748*

Joseph JOHNSON[6], bpt. 11 June 1749*; d. aft. 17 Oct. 1774* <Cumberland Co.Deeds:8:451>

Joshua JOHNSON[6], bpt. 8 Dec. 1751*

Mercy JOHNSON[6], bpt. 23 Feb. 1755* (poss. the child who d. 30 Jan. 1761, :1109>

Elizabeth JOHNSON[6], bpt. 28 May 1758*; d. 1 Apr. 1759* <:1109>

Mercy JOHNSON[6], bpt. 1 June 1760*

Lucretia JOHNSON[6], bpt. 29 Aug. 1762*

Sarah Newland JOHNSON[6], bpt. 15 May 1768* <:1158>

CHILD OF Joseph JOHNSON[6] & Abigail BUCKNAM, (dau of Wm.):

Joshua JOHNSON[7], b. ( ); d. pre 25 Mar. 1837, of Portland ME <Cumberland Co.Deeds 151:211>

Sally/Sarah RANDALL, (dau of Stephen & Lydia), b. 13 May 1793*, Cape Elizabeth ME <VR>; d. 20 Oct. 1879*, Cape Elizabeth ME

CHILDREN OF Joshua JOHNSON[7] & Sally/Sarah RANDALL: (7)[<23>]

Thomas DAVEE, (son of Rob. & Deborah), b. 19 Nov. 1718, Plymouth <MD 13:35>; d.? 2 Feb. 1779* <Plymouth ChR 1:409>

CHILDREN OF Thomas DAVEE & 1st Sarah JOHNSON[5] (Eliz. Cooke[4]): (8) <Plymouth, MD 15:212>

Robert DAVEE[6], b. 13 Sept. 1741

Thomas DAVEE[6], b. 20 Oct. 1743; d. 5 Mar. 1771, at sea <Burial Hill by Kingman:42>

William DAVEE[6], b. 20 Apr. 1746; d. pre 18 Feb. 1804*

Deborah DAVEE[6], b. 28 May 1749, d. 4 May 1759

Betty DAVEE[6], b. 29 Jan. 1751/2

Joseph DAVEE[6], b. 29 Aug. 1756

Solomon DAVEE[6], b. 12 July 1759

John DAVEE[6], b. 12 Sept. 1761

Hannah ROGERS[6] (*Tho.[5], Eleazer[4], Tho.[3], Jos.[2]), b. 10 Aug. 1734*

CHILDREN OF Thomas DAVEE & 2nd Hannah ROGERS: (2) <Plymouth, MD 15:212>

Johnson DAVEE[6], b. 16 July 1762

George DAVEE[6], b. 10 Mar. 1764

Jane HOLMES[7], (Eleazer[6], Hannah Sylvester[5], Hannah Bartlett[4], Jos.[3], Mary Warren[2]), b. c1748, d. 25 Jan. 1824, ae 76 <Plymouth ChR 2:671>

CHILDREN OF Thomas DAVEE^{6} & Jane HOLMES: (2)

Deborah DAVEE^{7}, b. ( )

Thomas DAVEE^{7}, b. c1771, d. 6 Apr. 1797, ae 26, Plymouth g.s. <Drew:266>

Betsey BARNES^{7} (Corban^{6}, John^{5}, Mary Bartlett^{4}, Jos.^{3}, Mary Warren^{2}), b. 26 Jan. 1771, Plymouth <MD 23:12>; d. 16 June 1864, New Bedford MA g.s. (m. 1st Tho.Davee^{7}, 2nd Jeremiah Mayhew)

Lydia HARLOW^{7} (John$^{6-5}$, Sam.^{4}, Rebecca Bartlett^{3}, Mary Warren^{2}), b. 9 June 1748, Plymouth <MD 15:39>; d. 11 Oct. 1825 <Plymouth ChR 2:673>

CHILDREN OF William DAVIE^{6} (Sarah Johnson^{5}) & Lydia HARLOW: (2 of 5)**<24>**

William DAVIE^{7}, b. c1772, Plymouth, d. 8 Feb. 1856, ae 84, Boston, bur. Plymouth <Plymouth VR>

Ebenezer DAVIE^{7}, b. c1775, d. 10 Feb. 1832*, 56y11m, Plymouth g.s. <Drew:296>

CHILDREN OF Isaac DAVIE & Rhoda PERRY, (dau of John): (2)

Isaac Lewis DAVIE, b. ( )

Mary B.C. DAVIE, b. ( )

CHILDREN OF Joseph DAVIE^{7} (Wm.^{6}) & Hannah FAUNCE, (dau of Peleg): (7)**<25>**

Lydia CURTIS^{4} (Zaccheus$^{3-2}$, Francis^{1}), b. c1777, d. 29 June 1840, ae 63, Plymouth g.s. <Drew:296>

CHILDREN OF Ebenezer DAVIE^{7} (Wm.^{6}) & Lydia CURTIS: (11) <Plymouth>

Ebenezer DAVIE^{8}, b. 25 Dec. 1798; d. 30 Dec. 1885, Plymouth, mariner <Mass.VR 365:351>

Lydia DAVIE^{8}, b. 14 Nov. 1801*, Plymouth; d. 18 Feb. 1870*, Plymouth

Jane DAVIE^{8}, b. c1803, d. 11 Oct. 1841, ae 38y1m11d (m. Frederick Robbins)

Capt. William DAVIE^{8}, b. 23 Apr. 1806*; d. 1887*, Hammonton NJ

John DAVIE^{8}, b. c1808, d. 27 June 1841, ae 32y11m15d, Plymouth g.s. <Drew:295>

Deborah Curtis DAVIE^{8}, b. c1813, d. 13 July 1838, ae 25y5m27d, unm.**<26>**

George DAVIE^{8}, b. c1813, d. 11 Aug. 1831, ae 18, drowned at sea**<27>**

Susan DAVIE^{8}, b. ( ), (m. Oliver Edes)

Patience C. DAVIE^{8}, b. ( ), (m. Geo. Hathaway)

Curtis DAVIE^{8}, b. ( )

Nathaniel Curtis DAVIE^{8}, b. c1819, d. 6 Oct. 1839, ae 19y10m6d**<28>**

Priscilla H. SNOW, (dau of Leonard), b. c1819, d. 10 Dec. 1838*, ae 19y10m, Plymouth g.s.<:295>

CHILD OF John DAVIE^{8} & Priscilla H. SNOW:

John L. DAVIE^{9}, b. c1838, d. 20 Jan. 1839, ae 5m20d, Plymouth g.s. <Drew:295>

Thomas TORREY, b. 28 Feb. 1799*, Plymouth; d. 8 Aug. 18(47)*, Boston (m. Lydia Davie^{8})

Mercy Bartlett BRADFORD, (dau of Wm. & Nancy (Boylston)), b. c1804, Plymouth, d. 27 Oct. 1882, ae 78y5m9d, Plymouth <Mass.VR 338:327>

CHILDREN OF Ebenezer DAVIE^{8} (Eben.^{7}) & Mercy Bartlett BRADFORD: (4) <Plymouth, MD 23:10>**<29>**

Curtis DAVIE^{9}, b. 12 Sept. 1827

Mercy Ann DAVIE^{9}, b. 6 Sept. 1829; unm

Sarah W. DAVIE^{9}, b. 29 Sept. 1833 (m. Albert Barnes)

Emeline DAVIE^{9}, b. 6 Sept. 1835; unm.

Marcia WESTON, (dau of Lewis), b. 19 Dec. 1809*; d. 12 May 1843 <Plymouth ChR 2:685>

CHILDREN OF Capt. William DAVIE^{8} (Eben.^{7}) & 1st Marcia WESTON: (2) <Plymouth, MD 22:34>

George DAVIE^{9}, b. 1 Aug. 1832; d. 25 Feb. 1849*

Marcia Torrey DAVIE^{9}, b. 26 Aug. 1834

Lydia Ann BAKER, d. June 1879*, Hammonton NJ

CHILDREN OF Capt. William DAVIE^{8} & 2nd Lydia Ann BAKER: (3)

George Henry DAVIE^{9}, b. 4 Dec. 1853, Plymouth; d. Dec. 1931, "Kinderhook"

William DAVIE^{9}, b. 4 June 1856*, Plymouth

Emma Woodward DAVIE^{9}, b. 4 Feb. 1861*, Hammonton NJ

Experience STETSON^{7} (Barzillai$^{6-5}$, Sarah Brewster^{4}, Wrestling^{3}, Love^{2}), b. c1775, d. 22 Oct. 1819 ae 44, consumption, bur. South Ground, Boston

CHILDREN OF William DAVIE^{7} (Wm.^{6}) & Experience STETSON: (5)

Child, d. 1 Aug. 1795 <Plymouth ChR 1:423>

Deborah DAVIE^{8}, b. ( )

Ellen DAVIE^{8}, b. ( )

Eliza Bowes DAVIE^{8}, b. 22 Dec. 1817*, Boston; d. 12 Nov. 1866, St. Louis MO(wf of Henry Whitmore)

Child, b. ( )

CHILDREN OF James COOKE^{4} (Caleb^{3}) & Abigail ( ): (4) <Kingston VR 1:20>**<30>**

Hannah COOKE^{5}, b. 22 July 1733

Lucy COOKE^{5}, b. 29 Aug. 1736

Lewrany/Lusanna COOKE^{5}, b. 24 Jan. 1738/9

Elijah COOKE^{5}, b. 24 July 1741**<31>**

Elizabeth SEARS^{3} (Silas^{2}, Richard^{1}), d. pre Apr. 1727*

CHILDREN OF John COOKE^{4} (Caleb^{3}) & Elizabeth SEARS: (4) <Plymouth, MD 13:169>

Silas COOKE^{5}, b. 1 Dec. 1708; d. betw. 12 June 1750 (will) - 1 Aug. 1750 (inv.), of Norton <Bristol Co.PR, 12:392,395>

Paul COOKE^{5}, b. 8 May 1711; d. betw. 5 Dec. 1785 (will) - 5 Dec. 1787 (citation), of Billerica <Middleboro Co.PR #5028>

Robert COOKE^{5}, b. June 1714

Mercy COOKE^{5}, b. Mar. 1718

Joanna HOLMES, (dau of Nath.), b. 7 Oct. 1715, Plymouth <MD 2:81>

CHILDREN OF Paul COOKE^{5} & Joanna HOLMES: (9) <1-6, Kingston VR>

Nathaniel COOKE^{6}, b. 28 Mar. 1736, d. 1 Oct. 1736

John COOKE^{6}, b. 3 Sept. 1737; d. 9 Feb. 1810, Claremont NH

Abigail COOKE^{6}, b. 1 Dec. 1739; d. aft. father's will (m. James Pearson)

Mercy COOKE^{6}, b. 5 Dec. 1741; d. aft. father's will

Paul COOKE^{6}, b. 22 Mar. 1743/4; d. pre father's will

Sears COOKE^{6}, b. 4 May 1746; d. 1 Sept. 1816*, g.s. <Billerica VR>

Nathaniel COOK^{6*}, b. 29 May 1752*, d. 22 Oct. 1778* <Norton VR>

Lothrop COOK^{6*}, b. 25 July 1754*, d. pre father's will

Sarah COOK^{6}, b. ( ); mentioned in father's will

Archelans JAY, (*son of Wm. & Susanna), b. 29 Oct. 1751*, d. 22 Oct. 1776* <Woburn VR>

CHILD OF Archelans JAY & Sarah COOK^{6}:

Sarah JAY^{7}, b. 9 Oct. 1775* <Woburn VR>

William LAWS, (*?son of James & Eunice (Hosley)), b. 10 Apr. 1746* <Billerica VR> (2nd hus of Sarah Cook^{6})

Jonathan KNAPP, (*son of Jonathan & Mehitable (Tucker)), b. 20 Dec. 1735* <Norton VR> (m. Mercy Cooke^{6})

MICRO #5 of 30

Mary GODFREY, b. 4 May 1738, Norton; d. 18 Dec. 1795, Claremont NH

CHILDREN OF John COOKE^{6} (Paul^{5}) & Mary GODFREY: (11) <Norton VR:41>

James COOK^{7}, b. 12 Jan. 1760; d. 22 July 1812

Matilda COOK^{7}, b. 12 May 1761; d. 3 Apr. 1826

Paul COOK^{7}, b. 1 Jan. 1763; d. 3 Jan. 1817

Mary COOK^{7}, b. 26 Apr. 1766; d. 4 July 1844

Rachel COOK^{7}, b. 8 Apr. 1769; d. 16 Dec. 1827

Rhoda COOK^{7}, b. 8 Apr. 1769 (twins); d. Feb. 1796

John COOK^{7}, b. 11 Sept. 1771; d. 10 Aug. 1785

George COOK^{7}, b. 29 June 1773; d. 29 June 184()**<32>**

Nancy COOK^{7}, b. 23 Aug. 1775; d. 23 Jan. 1777

Nathaniel COOK^{7}, b. 9 Jan. 1779; d. 22 Jan. 1852

Godfrey COOK^{7}, b. 22 July 1781; d. 5 Apr. 1849

Josiah STEVENS, b. 12 Aug. 1752, Guilford CT, d. 10 Apr. 1827 <Hist.Claremont NH:464>

CHILD OF Ebenezer BREWER & Matilda COOK^{7}:

Ebenezer BREWER, b. 13 Sept. 1785

CHILDREN OF Josiah STEVENS & Matilda (COOK^{7}) Brewer: (7)**<33>**

Abigail CROSBY, (*dau of Francis & Sarah (Richardson)), b. 14 Dec. 1743*, d. 31 Dec. 1836 <Billerica VR>

CHILDREN OF Sears COOK^{6} (Paul^{5}) & Abigail CROSBY*: (4*) <Billerica VR>

Abigail COOK^{7}, b. 11 Feb. 1773

Francis COOK^{7}, b. 25 Aug. 1775; d. 5 July 1831

(   ) COOK^{7}, b. 6 May 1778 (name too faint)

Susanna COOK^{7}, b. 6 May 1778 (twins)

CHILDREN OF Robert COOKE^{5} (John^{4}) & Patience (   ): (6) <Kingston VR 1:18>**<34>**

Hannah COOKE^{6}, b. 25 July 1736, d. 3 Sept. 1736

Caleb COOKE^{6}, b. 14 Oct. 1737, d. 3 Mar. 1737/8

Seth COOKE^{6}, b. 14 Feb. 1738/9

Silas COOKE^{6}, b. 20 Mar. 1739/40

Joseph COOKE^{6}, b. 9 Aug. 1744, d. 18 Aug. 1744

Ebenezer COOKE^{6}, b. 6 Apr. 1745

CHILDREN OF Ebenezer COOKE^{6}: (2) <Norton VR 1:41>

Patience COOKE^{7}, bpt. 14 June 1767

Susanna COOKE^{7}, bpt. 17 Sept. 1769

CHILDREN OF Silas COOKE^{5} (John^{4}) & Elizabeth STETSON: (6) <1-4, Kingston VR 1:22>

Sarah COOKE^{6}, b. 15 Nov. 1731

Elizabeth COOKE^{6}, b. 16 July 1735

Deborah COOKE^{6}, b. 12 Nov. 1737

Rubee COOKE^{6}, b. 25 May 1740; d. pre 1765

Joshua COOKE^{6}, bpt. 23 Oct. 1744* <VR:45>

Eunice COOKE^{6}*, bpt. 14 Nov. 1742* <VR:47>

Mary MOREY, (dau of George), b. 16 Jan. 1752*, Norton (m. Joshua Cooke^{6})

Zebediah SHEPARDSON, (*son of Amos & Margaret (Pidge)), b. 17 Nov. 1737* <Attleboro VR:234>; d. betw. 16 Apr. 1810 (will) - 4 Sept. 1810 (prob.) <Bristol Co.PR, 45:541>

CHILDREN OF Zebediah SHEPARDSON & Deborah COOKE^{6}: (2)**<35>**

CHILD OF Joseph COOKE^{4} (Caleb^{3}) & Experience HODGES^{4} (*Sam.^{3}, John^{2}, Wm.^{1}):**<36>**

Ann COOKE^{5}, b. 14 Aug. 1733 <Kingston VR>

Robert CARVER, (son of John & Mary), b. 30 Sept. 1694 <Plymouth VR>

CHILDREN OF Robert CARVER & Mary COOKE^{4} (Caleb^{3}): (3) <Plymouth, MD 13:169>

Elizabeth CARVER^{5}, b. 22 Feb. 1717/8

Mary CARVER^{5}, b. 14 Sept. 1721

Robert CARVER^{5}, b. 19 Aug. 1723

Richard ADAMS, (*son of Francis & Mary (Buck)), b. 14 June 1719* <Plymouth VR>

CHILDREN OF Richard ADAMS & Mary CARVER^{5}: (12*) <Kingston VR>

Robert ADAMS^{6}, b. 30 May 1745; d. at sea

Eliphalet ADAMS^{6}, b. 8 Aug. 1746; d. at sea

Celia ADAMS^{6}, b. 8 Dec. 1747

Ruby ADAMS^{6}, b. 19 Aug. 1749; d. Dec. 1833

Margaret ADAMS^{6}, b. 29 Mar. 1751

Mary ADAMS^{6}, b. 15 Jan. 1753, d.y.

Richard ADAMS^{6}, b. 6 Feb. 1755

James ADAMS^{6}, b. 1756; d. at sea

Thomas ADAMS^{6}, b. 1758; d. 12 Oct. 1795

George ADAMS^{6}, b. 1761; d. 8 Aug. 1846
Hope ADAMS^{6}, b. 1763; d. 15 Sept. 1853
Lucy ADAMS^{6}, b. 1769; d. June 1848
Elizabeth LATHAM^{4} (Susanna Winslow^{3}, Mary Chilton^{2}), b. c1664~~, d.~~ 16 Nov. 1730, 66th yr, Kingston g.s. <MD 7:26>
CHILDREN of ~~Francis~~ COOKE^{3} & Elizabeth LATHAM: (6) <MD 18::148>
Susanna COOKE^{4}, b. c1689*; d. Oct. 1769, 80th yr, Halifax g.s. <MD 10:11>
Robert COOKE^{4}, b. ( ); d. 20 Jan. 1731/2 <Kingston VR 1:9>
Caleb COOKE^{4}, b. c1694*, d. 19 Aug. 1762, 68th yr, Kingston g.s. <MD 7:26>
Francis COOKE^{4}, b. c1696*, d. 4 May 1724, 28th yr, Kingston g.s. <MD 7:26>**<37>**
Sarah COOKE^{4}, b. c1698*; d. 26 Oct. 1730, ae about 32, Plymouth g.s.
Elizabeth COOKE^{4}, b. c1707, d. 6 June 1750, 43rd yr <Bridgewater Epitaphs:94>
Hannah SHURTLEFF, (dau of Abiel & Lydia), b. 31 July 1705, Plymouth <MD 2:79>; d. 4 or 14 Nov. 1789, Kingston g.s. <MD 7:26>
CHILDREN OF Caleb COOKE^{4} & Hannah SHURTLEFF: (12) <1-11, Kingston VR 1:33>
Caleb COOKE^{5}, b. 4 July 1727; d. 26 Sept. 1756, Kingston <Gen.Adv.2:121>
Benjamin COOKE^{5}, b. 18 May 1729; d. 25 Dec. 1799, Kingston g.s. <MD 7:26>
Lydia COOKE^{5}, b. 8 Apr. 1731, d. 2 Nov. 1733
Isaac COOKE^{5}, b. 18 Mar. 1732/3; d. 1736, ae 3 <VR 1:35>
Ephraim COOKE^{5}, b. 1 June 1737; d. 1821
Hannah COOKE^{5}, b. 8 Apr. 1739
Rebecca COOKE^{5}, b. 5 Feb. 1741/2
Lydia COOKE^{5}, b. 21 Aug. 1744
Sarah COOKE^{5}, b. 21 May 1747, d. 18 Dec. 1754
Fear COOKE^{5}, b. 15 Feb. (no yr), d. same day <VR 1:35>
Amos COOKE^{5}, b. 3 Jan. 1749, d. 14 Dec. 1754
Elkanah COOKE^{5}, b. ( ), d. ae 13mths <VR 1:35>
Huldah COOKE, (dau of Wm. & Tabitha), d. 7 Feb. 1730/1 <Kingston VR 1:35>
William COOKE Jr., d. 18 Apr. 1731 <Kingston VR 1:35>
Phebe COOKE, (wf of Jacob), "and their child" d. 15 July 1728 <Kingston VR 1:35>
Mary GRAY^{6} (Sam.^{5}, John^{4}, Mary Winslow^{3}, Mary Chilton^{2}), b. 11 Nov. 1731 <Kingston VR>; d. 15 July 1812, Kingston g.s. <MD 7:26>
CHILDREN OF Benjamin COOKE^{5} (Caleb^{4}) & Mary GRAY: (10) <Kingston VR 1:58>
Elizabeth COOKE^{6}, b. 19 Aug. 1755
Sarah COOKE^{6}, b. 20 May 1757; d. 27 Jan. 1828, unm., Kingston g.s. <MD 7:27>
Elkanah COOKE^{6}, b. 17 May 1759; d. 11 Sept. 1839, Kingston g.s. <MD 7:26>
Faith COOKE^{6}, b. 24 Apr. 1761, d. 16 Sept. 1768
Caleb COOKE^{6}, b. 26 May 1763; d. 5 Oct. 1782, Kingston g.s. <MD 7:26>
Lettice COOKE^{6}, b. 12 Oct. 1765; d. 27 Aug. 1831, Kingston g.s. <MD 7:85>
Eunice COOKE^{6}, b. 22 Sept. 1767; d. 2 Jan. 1851, unm., Kingston g.s. <MD 7:26>
Priscilla COOKE^{6}, b. 25 Jan. 1770, d. 2 Jan. 1780
Patience COOKE^{6}, b. 9 Jan. 1773; d. 22 or 29 Dec. 1837, unm., Kingston g.s. <MD 7:27>
Molly COOKE^{6}, b. 19 Nov. 1774; d. pre 6 Oct. 1800* (father's div.)<Plymouth Co.PR #4855,37:316>
Christiana HOLMES, (*dau of Jonathan Jr. & Rebecca), b. 17 July 1760* <Kingston VR>; d. 27 Feb. 1796, 30th yr, Kingston g.s. <MD 7:26>
CHILDREN OF Elkanah COOK^{6} & 1st Christiana HOLMES*: (2)**<38>**
Polly WASHBURN, b. c1778, d. 13 Feb. 1821, ae 43, Kingston g.s. <MD 7:27>
CHILDREN OF Elkanah COOKE^{6} & 2nd Polly WASHBURN*: (1 of 7)**<38>**
Peleg COOK^{7}, b. 4 Jan. 1814*, Kingston; d. 2 Jan. 1901, Raynham <Mass.VR 516:345>
CHILDREN OF Caleb COOKE^{5} (Caleb^{4}) & Sarah ADAMS: (2) <Gen.Adv.4:16>

Bartlit COOKE^{6}, b. 9 Sept. 1754

Amos COOKE^{6}, b. 12 Mar. 1756

Eunice EATON^{5} (David^{4}, Ben.$^{3-2}$), b. 12 Apr. 1759 <Kingston VR>; d. 1799 <Kingston ChR> (m. Amos Cooke^{6})

David LEACH^{3} (David^{2}, Giles^{1}), d. pre 6 Dec. 1756 (adm.) <Plymouth Co.PR #12422,14:184>**<39>**

CHILDREN OF David LEACH & Elizabeth COOKE^{4} (Francis^{3}): (5) <1-4, Kingston VR>

James LEACH^{5}, b. 6 May 1734

Elizabeth LEACH^{5}, b. 2 Mar. 1734/5

Mercy LEACH^{5}, b. 16 Feb. 1737/8

Sarah LEACH^{5}, b. 17 Mar. 1739/40

Susannah LEACH^{5}, b. 1743, Bridgewater

Ruth SILVESTER^{5} (Ruth Turner^{4}, Mary Brewster^{3}, Jonathan^{2}), b. 26 June 1702 <Scituate VR 1:321>

CHILDREN OF Francis COOKE^{4} (Francis^{3}) & Ruth SILVESTER: (2) <Plympton VR, MD 2:52>

Ruth COOKE^{5}, b. 4 Feb. 1721/2; d. 23 May 1790, Kingston g.s. <MD 7:90>

Susanna COOKE^{5}, b. 28 July 1723; d. 6 Jan. 1766, Kingston g.s. <MD 7:25> (wf of Gershom Cobb)

Josiah HOLMES, (*son of John & Mercy), b. 15 Dec. 1716*, Plymouth; d. 12 Dec. 1782, Kingston g.s. <MD 7:89> (hus. of Ruth Cooke^{5})

Abigail HARLOW^{5} (Abigail Church^{4}, Nath.^{3}, Eliz. Warren^{2}), b. 27 Jan. 1692/3, Plymouth <MD 2:17>; d. 25 Oct. 1727, Kingston g.s. <MD 7:26>

CHILDREN OF Robert COOKE^{4} (Francis^{3}) & 1st Abigail HARLOW: (5) <1-4, Plymouth VR, MD 13:171>

Charles COOKE^{5}, b. 4 Oct. 1717

Nathaniel COOKE^{5}, b. 19 Dec. 1719; d. 4 Nov. 1758 <Kingston VR:332>

Robert COOKE^{5}, b. 12 Mar. 1721; d. 2 Sept. 1743 <Kingston VR>

Sarah COOKE^{5}, b. 18 June 1724; d. aft. 21 Dec. 1744*

Francis COOKE^{5}, b. c1727; d. pre 17 Oct. 1762* (wf called widow) <Bridgewater ChR>

Lydia TILDEN^{4} (*Samuel^{3}, Jos.^{2}, Nath.^{1}), b. 23 Apr. 1700, Marshfield <MD 8:177>; d. aft. 4 May 1741

CHILDREN OF Robert COOKE^{4} & 2nd Lydia TILDEN: (2) <Kingston VR 1:9>

Samuel COOKE^{5}, b. 1 July 1729, d. 30 July 1729

Simeon COOKE^{5}, b. 21 Sept. 1730; d. aft. 20 Dec. 1744

CHILDREN OF Francis COOKE^{5} (Robert^{4}) & Sarah BRYANT, (*dau of Ichabod): (5*) <Bridgewater VR>

Ruth COOKE^{6}, b. 30 July 1751

Rhoda COOKE^{6}, b. 4 Mar. 1753

Sarah COOKE^{6}, b. 28 Feb. 1755

Phebe COOKE^{6}, b. 9 May 1757

Gamaliel COOKE^{6}, b. 9 June 1759

Perez RANDALL, b. c1716, d. 11 Mar. 1786*, 70th yr, Kingston g.s.<MD 7:169>(?hus of Sarah Cooke^{5})

Hannah FAUNCE^{5} (Lydia Cooke^{4}, Jacob$^{3-2}$), b. 30 May 1718, Plymouth <MD 5:100>; d. 24 Dec. 1747, Kingston g.s. <MD 7:26>

CHILDREN OF Charles COOKE^{5} (Robert^{4}) & 1st Hannah FAUNCE: (3) <Kingston VR 1:27>

Abigail COOKE^{6}, b. 25 Sept. 1739

Lydia COOKE^{6}, b. 3 Dec. 1741

Josiah COOKE^{6}, b. 28 July 1745; d. 24 Apr. 1827, Kingston g.s. <MD 7:26>

CHILDREN OF Charles COOKE^{5} & 2nd Sarah ( ): (9) <Kingston VR 1:27>

Hannah COOKE^{6}, b. 31 Aug. 1750, d. 25 Dec. 1754

Asenath COOKE^{6}, b. 13 Oct. 1751

John COOKE^{6}, b. 13 Dec. 1752

Zadoc COOKE^{6}, b. 4 Apr. 1754

Hannah COOKE^{6}, b. 28 July 1755

Zenus COOKE^{6}, b. 12 Nov. 1756; d. pre 29 July 1794 (request) <Plymouth Co.PR #4926>

Francis COOKE^{6}, b. 26 July 1758

Anne COOKE^{6}, b. 12 Feb. 1761

Sarah COOKE^{6}, b. 8 Aug. 1762

MICRO #6 of 30

Joanna FAUNCE, (dau of John & Hannah), b. 27 Jan. 1757, d. 19 Mar. 1837 <Kingston VR, Gen.Adv. 2:124> (m. Zenas Cooke^{6})

Lydia FAUNCE, (dau of John & Hannah), b. 12 Apr. 1746, Kingston <Gen.Adv.2:124>; d. 10 Dec. 1836, Kingston g.s. <MD 7:26> (m. Josiah Cooke^{6})

Mary SAMSON^{5} (Peleg^{4}, Lydia Standish^{3}, Alex.^{2}), b. 6 Jan. 1724* <Pembroke VR:182>

CHILDREN OF Nathaniel COOKE^{5} (Robert^{4}) & Mary SAMSON: (7) <Kingston VR 1:28>

Mary COOKE^{6}, b. 10 Sept. 1742; d. 18 Aug. 1762, unm., Kingston <Gen.Adv.2:119>

Peleg COOKE^{6}, b. 9 July 1745; d. 1 Aug. 1767* <Kingston VR>

Nathaniel COOKE^{6}, b. 11 Apr. 1747

Susanna COOKE^{6}, b. 11 Feb. 1750

Isaac COOKE^{6}, b. 7 Jan. 1752; d. 9 Jan. 1782, "ae 32", consumption <Kingston ChR>

Deborah COOKE^{6}, b. 18 Feb. 1755

Levi COOKE^{6}, b. 8 Sept. 1757

CHILDREN OF Isaac COOKE^{6} & Rebecca BRADFORD: (2)

Molly COOKE^{7}, b. 15 Nov. 1779

Isaac COOKE^{7}, b. 23 Dec. 1781

Hannah FULLER, b. c1749, d. 23 Mar. 1819, ae 70 <Kingston ChR> (m.1st Peleg Cooke^{6}, 2nd Sam.Drew)

Hannah BISBE, (*dau of Elijah), b. c1722, d. 10 Feb. 1799, ae 77, Kingston g.s. <MD 7:85>

CHILD OF Robert COOKE^{5} (Robert^{4}) & Hannah BISBE: <Kingston VR 1:47>

Robert COOKE^{6}, b. 15 Sept. 1743; d. 10 Sept. 1828, Kingston g.s. <MD 7:27>

John FAUNCE, d. 30 Nov. 1768*, ae 52y7m6d, Kingston g.s. <MD 7:85> (2nd hus of Hannah Bisbe)

Lydia ADAMS^{6} (Thankful Washburn^{5}, Lydia Billington^{4}, Isaac^{3}, Francis^{2}), b. 25 Feb. 1755* <Kingston VR:14>; d. 17 Aug. 1812, Kingston g.s. <MD 7:26>

CHILDREN OF Robert COOKE^{6} & Lydia ADAMS: (1 of 5)**<40>**

Robert COOKE^{7}, b. 13 July 1775*; d. 2 Jan. 1844, Kingston g.s. <MD 7:27>

Judith ADAMS^{7} (John^{6}, Thankful Washburn^{5}, Lydia Billington^{4}, Isaac^{3}, Francis^{2}), b. c1783, d. 1 June 1824, Kingston g.s. <MD 7:26> (wf of Robert Cooke^{7})

CHILDREN OF Simeon COOKE & Mary DINGLEY: (6) <Kingston VR>

Lydia COOKE, b. 23 Jan. 1757 <VR:49>

Spencer COOKE, b. 21 June 1761 <VR:51>

Frederick COOKE, bpt. 19 May 1765 <VR:48, ChR>

Pelham COOKE, bpt. 13 Mar. 1768 <VR:50, ChR>

Melzar COOKE, b. 4 Apr. 1772 <VR:49>

CHILDREN OF Ephraim COLE & Sarah COOKE^{4} (Francis^{3}): (4) <1,3,4, Plymouth VR, MD 13:32>**<41>**

Ephraim COLE^{5}, b. 12 Oct. 1718

Sarah COLE^{5}, b. c1723, d. 1730, ae 7

Rebecca COLE^{5}, b. June 1727

Sarah COLE^{5}, b. June 1730

James STURTEVANT, b. c1687, d. 8 May 1756, ae 69, Halifax g.s. <MD 10:10>

CHILDREN OF James STURTEVANT & Susanna COOKE^{4} (Francis^{3}): (2 of 8)**<42>**

Caleb STURTEVANT^{5}, b. c1716, d. 7 Oct. 1793, 78th yr, Halifax g.s. <MD 10:9>

Elizabeth STURTEVANT^{5}, b. c1735, d. 28 July 1747, ae 13y3m10d, Halifax g.s. <MD 10:9>

Patience CUSHMAN^{5} (Isaac$^{4-3}$, Mary Allerton^{2}), b. 8 Apr. 1721, Plympton <MD 3:165>; d. 1 Jan. 1769 Halifax g.s. <MD 10:10>

CHILDREN OF Caleb STURTEVANT^{5} & 1st Patience CUSHMAN: (6) <Halifax VR:47>

Jabez STURTEVANT^{6}, b. 12 Feb. 1740

Rebecca STURTEVANT^{6}, b. 21 Jan. 1741/2
Jane STURTEVANT^{6}, b. 18 Nov. 1743
Susanna STURTEVANT^{6}, b. 3 Mar. 1745/6
Betty STURTEVANT^{6}, b. 27 Oct. 1748
Patience STURTEVANT^{6}, b. 12 May 1758
CHILDREN OF Caleb STURTEVANT^{5} & 2nd Abigail ( ) BEARCE: (3) <Halifax VR:47>
Caleb STURTEVANT^{6}, b. 14 Feb. 1771; d. 2 Oct. 1793, Halifax g.s. <MD 10:9>
Abigail STURTEVANT^{6}, b. 14 Feb. 1771 (twins)
Winslow STURTEVANT^{6}, b. 26 June 1773
CHILD OF Jabez STURTEVANT^{6} & Azubah WOOD:
Samuel STURTEVANT^{7}, b. 25 May 1772 <Halifax VR:51>
Lydia MILLER, b. 18 May 1661 <NEHGR 55:33>; d. 1 Mar. 1727/8, Kingston g.s. <MD 7:26>
CHILDREN OF Jacob COOKE^{3} & Lydia MILLER: (8) <Plymouth VR, MD 2:81>
William COOKE^{4}, b. 5 Oct. 1683; d. aft. 30 Nov. 1740 (deed)
Lydia COOKE^{4}, b. 18 May 1685; d. 7 July 1738, Kingston g.s. <MD 7:85>
Rebecca COOKE^{4}, b. 19 Nov. 1688; d. 14 Apr. 1769, Kingston g.s. <MD 7:171>
Jacob COOKE^{4}, b. 16 June 1691; d. aft. 1742**<43>**
Margaret COOKE^{4}, b. 3 Nov. 1695
Josiah COOKE^{4}, b. 14 May 1699
John COOKE^{4}, b. 23 May 1703; d. 8 Dec. 1745, Kingston g.s. <MD 7:26>
Damaris COOKE^{4}, b. 23 May 1703 (twins)
Phebe HALL, b. c1688, d. 15 July 1728, 40th yr, Kingston g.s. <MD 7:27>**<44>**
CHILDREN OF Jacob COOKE^{4} & 1st Phebe HALL: (5) <Kingston VR 1:17>
Jesse COOKE^{5}, b. 14 Nov. 1717
Asa COOKE^{5}, b. 12 June 1720
Phebe COOKE^{5}, b. 5 Aug. 1722
Jacob COOKE^{5}, b. 19 Apr. 1725
Child, b. ( ), d. 15 July 1728 <MD 7:27>
CHILDREN OF Jacob COOKE^{4} & 2nd Mary HERCY: (2) <Kingston VR 1:17>**<45>**
Stephen COOKE^{5}, b. 7 Mar. 1729/30
Mary COOKE^{5}, b. 20 Aug. 1733
Phebe CROSMAN, b. c1712, d. 25 Mar. 1805, ae 93, Kingston g.s. <MD 7:90>
CHILDREN OF John COOKE^{4} (Jacob^{3}) & Phebe CROSMAN: (6) <Kingston VR 1:22>
Lydia COOKE^{5}, b. 7 July 1732, d. 30 July 1732, ae 23d, Kingston g.s. <MD 7:26>
Sarah COOKE^{5}, b. 21 Oct. 1733
Lydia COOKE^{5}, b. 17 Feb. 1735/6
Silvanus COOKE^{5}, b. 1 May 1738; d. 12 Nov. 1814, Kingston g.s. <MD 7:27>
Margaret COOKE^{5}, b. 26 July 1741
Molly COOKE^{5}, b. 29 Oct. 1743
Samuel KENT, b. c1703, d. 11 June 1786, ae 83, Kingston g.s. <MD 7:90> (2nd hus. Phebe Crosman)
Samuel KENT, (son of Sam.), d. betw. 11 Jan. 1755* (deed) - 4 Sept. 1756* (adm.)
CHILD OF Samuel KENT & Sarah COOKE^{5}:
Sarah KENT^{6}, b. 30 June 1756; d. 9 Jan. 1835, Kingston g.s. <MD 7:90>
Abner HOLMES, b. c1754, d. 30 Jan. 1814, ae 60, Kingston g.s. <MD 7:88> (hus. of Sarah Kent^{6})
John FAUNCE, (son of Jos.), b. 3 Dec. 1683, Plymouth <MD 1:142>; d. 18 Nov. 1751, Kingston g.s. <MD 7:85>
CHILDREN OF John FAUNCE & Lydia COOKE^{4} (Jacob^{3}): (7) <Plymouth VR, MD 5:100>
Judith FAUNCE^{5}, b. 1 Jan. 1710/11
Lydia FAUNCE^{5}, b. 10 June 1714
John FAUNCE^{5}, b. 13 Apr. 1716

Hannah FAUNCE^{5}, b. 30 May 1718

Mary FAUNCE^{5}, b. 25 Apr. 1720

Mehitable FAUNCE^{5}, b. 11 Apr. 1722

Rebecca FAUNCE^{5}, b. 15 Sept. 1724

Simon LAZELL^{3} (Joshua^{2}, John^{1}), b. 12 Sept. 1688 <Hist.Hingham 2:424>

CHILDREN OF Simon LAZELL & Margaret COOKE^{4} (Jacob^{3}): (7) <1-3, Plymouth; 4-7, Middleboro>

Joshua LAZELL^{5}, b. 5 May 1717, d. 9 July 1718 <MD 12:225>

Joshua LAZELL^{5}, b. 30 Sept. 1719 <MD 12:225>

Lydia LAZELL^{5}, b. 5 Jan. 1722/3 <MD 12:225>

Jacob LAZELL^{5}, b. 25 Mar. 1729 <MD 13:6>

William LAZELL^{5}, b. 30 Apr. 1732 <MD 13:6>

Sarah LAZELL^{5}, b. 30 Apr. 1732 <MD 13:6>

Abner LAZELL^{5}, b. 22 Aug. 1734 <MD 13:6>

Tabitha HALL, (dau of Elisha & Lydia), d. aft. 1739/40**<46>**

CHILDREN OF William COOKE^{4} (Jacob^{3}) & Tabitha HALL: (7) <Plymouth VR, MD 5:54>

Hannah COOKE^{5}, b. 8 Nov. 1707; d. 25 Feb. 1784*

Lydia COOKE^{5}, b. 4 Feb. 1710; d. 30 Apr. 1793* <Kingston ChR>

Huldah COOKE^{5}, b. 12 Aug. 1712; d. 7 Feb. 1730/1, Kingston g.s. <MD 7:26>

William COOKE^{5}, b. 15 Jan. 1714/5; d. 18 Apr. 1731, Kingston g.s. <MD 7:27>

Elisha COOKE^{5}, b. 10 Mar. 1716/7; d. betw. 25 Jan. 1799 (will) - 2 Nov. 1799 (prob.)

Tabitha COOKE^{5}, b. 8 July 1719

Priscilla COOKE^{5}, b. 13 Mar. 1721/2

Benjamin ORCUTT^{3} (*Ben.^{2}, Wm.^{1}), b. 12 Feb. 1707/8*, Weymouth

CHILDREN OF Benjamin ORCUTT & Tabitha COOKE^{5}: (4*)

Elizabeth ORCUTT^{6}, b. 30 Nov. 1740, Weymouth

Tabitha ORCUTT^{6}, b. 1744

Consider ORCUTT^{6}, b. 1746

Priscilla ORCUT^{6}, b. 1750

Nathan WRIGHT^{4} (Adam^{3}, Hester Cooke^{2}), b. 12 May 1711, Plympton <MD 5:183>; d. pre 7 Apr. 1762 (adm.) (hus. of Hannah Cooke^{5})

Rebecca EGERTON, (dau of Denis & Experience), b. 11 May 1723 <Halifax VR:47>

CHILDREN OF Elisha COOKE^{5} (Wm.^{4}) & Rebecca EGERTON: (18!) <poss. Halifax>

William COOKE^{6}, b. 7 Oct. 1742 <Kingston VR 1:29>

Huldah COOKE^{6}, b. 25 Nov. 1743 <Kingston VR 1:29>

Consider COOKE^{6}, b. 4 Feb. 1745

Rebecca COOKE^{6}, b. 18 Nov. 1746; d. pre 1753

Levi COOKE^{6}, b. 29 Apr. 1748

Tabitha COOKE^{6}, b. 21 May 1750

Experience COOKE^{6}, b. 8 Aug. 1751; d. pre 25 Jan. 1799* (father's will)

Rebecca COOKE^{6}, b. 1 Apr. 1753

Abner COOKE^{6}, b. 4 Mar. 1755; d. pre 25 Jan. 1799* (father's will)

Hannah COOKE^{6}, b. 22 Oct. 1756

Phebe COOKE^{6}, b. 3 Mar. 1758

Meirem COOKE^{6}, b. May 1759

Lydia COOKE^{6}, b. 27 Nov. 1760

Simeon COOKE^{6}, b. 4 Jan. 1762; d. pre 25 Jan. 1799* (father's will)

Elisha COOKE^{6}, b. 8 Dec. 1764

Daniel COOKE^{6}, b. 5 Dec. 1766

James COOKE^{6}, b. 7 Dec. 1772

Mary COOKE^{6}, b. 26 June 1774

MICRO #7 of 30

Kingston ChR, Baptisms:

Eunice COOKE, dau of Silas & Elisabeth, bpt. 14 Nov. 1742 <:117>

Molly COOK, dau of John & Phebe, bpt. 6 Nov. 1743 <:117>

Solomon COOK, son of Asa & Lusanna, bpt. 13 Nov. 1743 <:117>

Maria COOK, dau of James & Abigail, bpt. 22 Jan. 1743/4 <:118>

Lydia COOKE, dau of Caleb, bpt. 23 Oct. 1744 <:118>

Joshua COOKE, dau of Silas & Elizabeth, bpt. 23 Oct. 1744 <:118>

Ebenezer COOKE, son of Robert, bpt. 7 Apr. 1745 <:118>

Dau. of Moses & Lydia BASSET, bpt. 14 July 1745 <:118>

Bethiah COOKE, dau of James, bpt. 24 Aug. 1746 <:120>

Sarah COOK, dau of Caleb, bpt. 5 July 1747 <:120>

Zelak BASSET, son of Moses, bpt. 1 Nov. 1747 <:120>

James COOKE, son of James, bpt. 15 Sept. 1748, in private <:121>

Amos COOKE, son of Caleb, bpt. 12 Mar. 1748/9 <:121>

Crocker SAMPSON, son of Cornelius, bpt. 2 July 1749 <:121>

James BASSET, son of Moses, bpt. 5 Nov. 1749 <:121>

James COOKE, son of James, bpt. 24 Dec. 1749 <:122>

Hannah COOKE, dau of Charles, bpt. 2 Sept. 1750 <:122>

Priscilla BASSET, dau of Moses, bpt. 26 July 1752 <:123>

Dau. of Cornelius SAMSON, bpt. 13 Oct. 1752 <:123>

John COOKE, son of Charles, bpt. 18 Mar. 1753 <:123>

Zadock COOKE, son of Charles, bpt. 16 June 1754 <:124>

Kingston ChR, Deaths:

Isaac COOKE, d. 9 Jan. 1782, ae 32, consumption <:252>

Widow of Benjamin SAMSON, d. 17 June 1782, ae 45 <:252>

Deborah COOK, d. 16 July 1782, ae 30, consumption <:252>

Caleb COOK, d. 13 Aug. 1782, ae 19, consumption <:252>

Lydia COOK, wf of Amos, d. Feb. 1785, ae 25, consumption <:253>

Zadock COOK, son of John, d. 12 Feb. 1786, ae 3, putrid fever <:254>

Daniel COOK, son of Josiah, d. 3 May 1786, ae 3, putrid fever <:254>

Hannah COOK, widow, d. 14 Nov. 1789, ae 84, old age <:255>

Wife of Moses BASSETT, d. 30 Apr. 1793, ae 83, old age <:256>

Asa COOK, son of John, d. 4 Sept. 1793, ae 5, stoppage worms <:257>

Cornelius SAMPSON Jr., d. 23 June 1794, ae 23, shot himself <:257>

John COOK, d. 26 Apr. 1795, ae 42, spinal decay <:257>

Son of widow Joanna COOK, d. 20 Jan. 1796, ae 2, canker rash <:258>

Christianna COOK, wf of Capt. Elkanah, d. 27 Feb. 1796, ae 29, consumption <:258>

Cornelius SAMPSON, d. 1 Mar. 1796, ae 72, urinary <:258>

Lydia SAMSON, wf of Samuel, d. 3 May 1796, ae 44, scrofulous humour <:258>

Lois COOK, wf of John, d. 18 Feb. 1798, ae 24, childbed & pleurisy <:258>

Molly COOK, widow, d. 17 Sept. 1798, ae 43 <:259>

John COOK Jr., d. 24 Mar. 1799, ae 14, slow putrid fever <:259>

Eunice COOK, wf of Amos, d. Apr. 1799, ae 40, influenza <:259>

Benjamin COOK, d. 25 Dec. 1799, ae 70, stranguary <:259>

Moses BASSETT, b. 15 Nov. 1712*; d. 1806*, ae 92 <Kingston ChR>

CHILDREN OF Moses BASSETT & Lydia COOKE^5 (Wm.^{4}): (6*) <Kingston VR:21>

Huldah BASSETT^6, b. <u>31</u> June 1739

Welthea BASSETT^6, b. 4 July 1742

Sarah BASSETT^6, b. 12 May 1745; d. 23 May 1761

Zelak BASSETT^{6}, b. 26 Sept. 1747; d. 1824
James BASSETT^{6}, b. 9 Sept. 1749; d. 6 Mar. 1825
Priscilla BASSETT^{6}, b. 29 May 1752
John RICKARD^{3} (John^{2}, Giles^{1}), b. 24 Nov. 1657, Plymouth; d. 25 Apr. 1712, Plymouth**<47>**
CHILDREN OF John RICKARD & Mary COOKE^{3}: (7) <Plymouth, 1-3,5,6,, MD 1:144>
John RICKARD^{4}, b. last of Feb. 1679; d. pre 1685
Mercy RICKARD^{4}, b. 3 Feb. 1682
John RICKARD^{4}, b. 3 Feb. 1684
Mary RICKARD^{4}, bpt. 1688
Esther RICKARD^{4}, b. first of Apr. 1691
James RICKARD^{4}, b. 25 or 26 Sept. 1696
Elizabeth RICKARD^{4}, b. ( )
Ignatius CUSHING, (son of Jeremiah), b. 1689, Scituate
CHILDREN OF Ignatius CUSHING & Mercy RICKARD^{4}: (3) <Plymouth, MD 12:12>
Hannah CUSHING^{5}, b. 1 Jan. 1710, d. c8 Jan. 1710, "about 7 dayes after"
Ignatius CUSHING^{5}, b. 7 Feb. 1711, d. 23 Jan. 1717/8
Hannah CUSHING^{5}, b. 25 Aug. 1714

JANE COOKE^{2} (Francis^{1})**<48>**

Mitchell's Epitaphs in Bridgewater:<49>
Nathan MITCHELL, d. 2 Mar. 1789, ae 59 <:182>
Experience MITCHELL, d. 1689, of Elmwood <:186>
Anna MITCHELL, wf of John, d. 17 Feb. 1794, ae 37 <:69>
Mary MITCHELL, dau of Nathan & Ann, b. 23 Aug. 1760, d. 10 Oct. 1768
Thomas MITCHELL, d. 1 Sept. 1727, ae 69 <:66>
Maj. Thomas MITCHELL, d. 1 Apr. 1776, ae 50 <:84>
Elisha MITCHELL, d. 6 Jan. 1790, ae 44 <:214>
Elizabeth MITCHELL, wf of Col. Edward, d. 9 May 1799, ae 85 <:214>
Hannah MITCHELL, wf of Capt. Elisha, d. 16 July 1787, ae 36 <:214>
Jannett MITCHELL, wf of Cushing, d. 25 Feb. 1774, ae 26 <:214>
Persis MITCHELL, wf of Bradford, d. 20 Mar. 1799, ae 43 <:214>
CHILDREN OF Samuel WASHBURN & Hannah HAVEN: (9) <"Natick" VR>
Miriam WASHBURN, b. 22 June 1780
Elijah WASHBURN, b. 11 or 19 Mar. 1782
Hannah WASHBURN, b. 8 Feb. 1784
Polly WASHBURN, b. 6 Aug. 1786
Samuel WASHBURN, b. 28 July 1788
Jediah WASHBURN, b. 12 July 1790
Joseph WASHBURN, b. 30 June 1792
Joshua WASHBURN, b. 11 Apr. 1795
Sally WASHBURN, b. 23 July 1797

MICRO #8 of 30

Experience MITCHELL, d. betw. 5 Dec. 1684 (will) - 14 May 1689 (inv.) <MD 4:150>
CHILDREN OF Experience MITCHELL & 1st Jane COOKE^{2}: (2)**<48>**
Elizabeth MITCHELL^{3}, b. ( )
Thomas MITCHELL^{3}, b. pre 1650 ; d. betw. Aug. 1672* - Dec. 1688* <MD 3:104>
CHILDREN OF Experience MITCHELL^{1} & 2nd Mary ( ): (6)**<50>**
Mary MITCHELL, b. pre 1636
Sarah MITCHELL, b. c1641*; d. aft. Dec. 1731***<50a>**

Jacob MITCHELL, b. pre 1650*; d. 1675, Dartmouth <MD 21:185>

Edward MITCHELL, b. pre 1650*; d. 15 Mar. 1716/7 <MD 20:141>

John MITCHELL, b. pre 1656*

Hannah MITCHELL, b. c1656

CHILDREN OF Edward MITCHELL^{2} (Experience^{1}) & Alice BRADFORD^{4}: (3) <Bridgewater, MD 14:184>

Mary MITCHELL, b. 19 July 1709

Alice MITCHELL, b. 23 Dec. 1714; d. 20 Dec. 1779* <Hingham 2:302>

Edward MITCHELL, b. 7 Feb. 1715/6; d. 23 Dec. 1801*, E. Bridgewater g.s. <VR:372>

John WASHBURN, (son of John), d. 12 Nov. 1686, Bridgewater <MD 15:251>**<51>**

CHILDREN OF John WASHBURN & Elizabeth MITCHELL^{3}: (11) <Bridgewater, MD 15:249>

Samuel WASHBURN^{4}, b. c1651, d. 24 Mar. 1719/20, 69th yr, Bridgewater <MD 16:49>

Joseph WASHBURN^{4}, b. c1653, d. 20 Apr. 1733, ae about 80 <Bridgewater ChR 2:572>

Thomas WASHBURN^{4}, b. pre 1662*; d. betw. Mar. 1729/30 (will) - 4 Dec. 1732 (prob.) <MD 16:51>

John WASHBURN^{4}, b. pre 1663*; d. c1719-1724*

Benjamin WASHBURN^{4}, b. c1661*; d. betw. 28 July 1690 (will) - 17 Mar. 1690/91 (prob.) <MD 16:47>

Jonathan WASHBURN^{4} b. ( ); d. pre 10 Jan. 1725/26 (adm.) <MD 16:50>

James WASHBURN^{4}, b. 15 May 1672 <MD 2:291>; d. 11 June 1749, Bridgewater g.s. <Epitaphs:74>

Mary WASHBURN^{4}, b. ( ); d. aft. 9 Oct. 1722 <MD 30:23>**<51a>**

Elizabeth WASHBURN^{4}, b. ( ); d. 27 Feb. 1741/2 <Norton:393>

Jane WASHBURN^{4}, b. pre 1678*; d. pre 1698*

Sarah WASHBURN^{4}, b. pre 1682*, d. 1746*, ae 71, <Bridgewater Epitaphs:26>

Joseph MITCHELL, b. c1737, d. 30 Dec. 1791, ae 54, Plymouth g.s.**<52>**

Mary TINKHAM^{5} (*Eben.^{4}, Helkiah^{3}, Mary Brown^{2}), b. c1739, d. 22 May 1790, ae 51, Plymouth**<52>**

CHILDREN OF Joseph MITCHELL & Mary TINKHAM: (4) <Plymouth, MD 21:164>

Joseph MITCHELL, b. 14 Nov. 1760

James MITCHELL, b. 23 Mar. 1763

Ebenezer MITCHELL, b. 23 Aug. 1765

Mary MITCHELL, b. 3 Feb. 1768

Hannah WASHBURN, b. pre 1709*; d. 1756 <Bridgewater VR 2:434>

Nathan BASSETT^{4} (Wm.^{3}, Jos.^{2}, Wm.^{1}), b. 5 Sept. 1702 <Bridgewater VR 1:42>

CHILDREN OF Nathan BASSETT & Hannah WASHBURN: (7) <Bridgewater VR 1:43>

John BASSETT, b. 29 Aug. 1734

Nathan BASSETT, b. 4 Sept. 1737 <VR 1:44>; d. 1756 <VR 2:435>

Ruth BASSETT, b. 11 May 1740 <VR 1:44>

David BASSETT, b. 27 Feb. 1742/3; d. 1756 <VR 2:434>

Hannah BASSETT, b. 5 May 1745

Joseph BASSETT, b. 27 Oct. 1747/26 Oct. 1748; d. 13 or 14 Mar. 1817 <VR 2:435>

Jonathan BASSETT, b. 25 May 1750

CHILDREN OF Benjamin MITCHELL: (4) <Old Times, ME>

Mehitable MITCHELL, bpt. 28 July 1746 <:615>

Betty MITCHELL, bpt. 4 Oct. 1747 <:616>

Hannah MITCHELL, bpt. 13 Mar. 1750 <:617>

Joanna MITCHELL, bpt. 15 Dec. 1754 <:664>

Noah HERSEY, b. 24 Feb. 1709/10*, d. 29 June 1755* <Hingham 2:302>

CHILDREN OF Noah HERSEY & Alice MITCHELL^{3} (Edward^{2}, Experience^{1}): (6*)

Peleg HERSEY, b. 22 Nov. 1737

Sarah HERSEY, b. 28 Aug. 1741

Jacob HERSEY, b. 23 Apr. 1744, d. Jan. 1747/8

Noah HERSEY, b. 6 Oct. 1746

Jacob HERSEY, b. 6 Aug. 1748; d. 7 Aug. 1773

Levi HERSEY, b. 23 July 1751

Elizabeth CUSHING, b. 21 May 1714*, Kingston; d. 9 May 1799*, E. Bridgewater g.s. <VR:372>

CHILDREN OF Edward MITCHELL^{3} (Edw.^{2}, Experience^{1}) & Elizabeth CUSHING: (10)<Bridgewater VR 3:243>

Cushing MITCHELL, b. 8 Dec. 1740; d. 4 June 1820 <Bridgewater VR>

Alice MITCHELL, b. 5 Apr. 1744

Elisha MITCHELL, b. 28 Mar. 1746

John MITCHELL, b. 8 Mar. 1747/8

William MITCHELL, b. 13 Mar. 1749/50

Bradford MITCHELL, b. 17 May 1752; d. 20 May 1842

Molly MITCHELL, b. 4 Apr. 1754

Sele MITCHELL, b. 20 Aug. 1757

Sarah MITCHELL, b. 26 Apr. 1759

Bela MITCHELL, b. 30 Oct. 1761

Jennet ORR, (dau of Hugh), b. 14 Apr. 1748* <Bridgewater VR 1:236>; d. 25 Feb. 1774 <Bridge. VR>

CHILDREN OF Cushing MITCHELL^{4} (Edw.$^{3-2}$, Experience^{1}) & 1st Jennet ORR: (3)<Bridgewater VR 3:236>

Alice MITCHELL, b. 18 Apr. 1767

Nahum MITCHELL, b. 12 Feb. 1769

Jennet MITCHELL, b. 17 May 1771

CHILDREN OF Cushing MITCHELL^{4} & 2nd Hannah ( ): (5) <Bridgewater VR 3:236>

Hannah MITCHELL, b. 2 Feb. 1781

Celia MITCHELL, b. 25 May 1783

Cushing MITCHELL, b. 31 Dec. 1784

Charles MITCHELL, b. 2 Mar. 1788

Newton MITCHELL, b. 20 Aug. 1789

Bathsheba CHURCHILL, b. c1762, d. 13 July 1788*, ae 26, Plymouth g.s. (wf of Ben.Washburn)

Washburn Deaths, Middleboro VR:

Lydia WASHBURN, dau of Capt. Amos, d. 4 July 1799, ae 34 <4:160>

George WASHBURN, son of Col. Abiel & Betsey, d. 29 Nov. 1803, ae 2 <7:4>

Benjamin WASHBURN, d. 5 Apr. 1822, ae 70 <7:26>

Alice WASHBURN, widow of Benjamin, d. 28 July 1823, ae 69 <7:27>

Deacon Jonathan WASHBURN, d. 21 Oct. 1824, ae 71 <7:27>

Polly WASHBURN, 3d wf of Capt. Linus, d. 25 Jan. 1825, ae 43 <7:27>

George WASHBURN, youngest son of Gen. Abial, d. 19 Jan. 1826, ae 22 <7:28>

Thomas J. WASHBURN, son of Thomas 2d, d. 22 Nov. 1822 <7:29>

Marriet WASHBURN, dau of Lewis, d. 8 Oct. 1825, ae 3 <7:29>

Gilman WASHBURN, son of Nathan, d. 11 Jan. 1807, ae 2 <7:29>

Cordelia WASHBURN, dau of Nathan, d. 2 June 1815, ae 3 <7:29>

Sarah WASHBURN, dau of Nathan, d. 12 Aug. 1820 <7:29>

Mary A.S. WASHBURN, dau of Nathan, d. 5 Aug. 1821 <7:29>

Hiram WASHBURN, son of Nathan, d. 1 Aug. 1825, ae 19 <7:29>

Solomon WASHBURN, d. 29 Aug. 1825 <7:34>

Anna WASHBURN, widow of Solomon, d. 12 Dec. 1832 <7:34>

Harrison WASHBURN, son of Tho. & Charity, d. 29 Sept. 1838, Charlestown SC <14:2>

CHILDREN OF Jonathan WASHBURN & Rebecca ( ): (2) <Bridgewater VR, MD 15:48>

Silas WASHBURN, b. 11 Feb. 1712/3

Lemuel WASHBURN, b. 18 Aug. 1714

MICRO #9 of 30

James HAWARD, d. 1690, "expedition to Canada" <MD 30:187>

CHILDREN OF James HAWARD & Elizabeth WASHBURN^{4} (Eliz. Mitchell^{3}): (3) <Bridgewater VR, MD 5:247>

Elizabeth HAWARD^{5}, b. 16 Jan. 1685/6; d. 8 Jan. 1760, Bridgewater <MD 15:170>

Mercy HAWARD^{5}, b. 27 Feb. 1687/8, d. 26 Jan. 1704/5

James HAWARD^{5}, b. 26 Jan. 1689/90

CHILDREN OF Edward SEALY & Elizabeth (WASHBURN^{4}) Haward: (2) <Bridgewater VR, MD 5:247>

Benjamin SEALY^{5}, b. 5 Mar. 1693

John SEALY^{5}, b. 10 Apr. 1697

Thomas BUCK, d. 4 Apr. 1755, Bridgewater <MD 15:170>

CHILDREN OF Thomas BUCK & Elizabeth HAWARD^{5} (Eliz. Washburn^{4}): (6) <Bridgewater VR, MD 15:170>

Mary BUCK^{6}, b. 6 Nov. 1713

Thomas BUCK^{6}, b. 11 Oct. 1715

Elizabeth BUCK^{6}, b. 17 Oct. 1717

John BUCK^{6}, b. 29 Apr. 1721

Matthew BUCK^{6}, b. 4 June 1724

Tabitha BUCK^{6}, b. 1 Oct. 1728

Sarah LANE, (dau of John), b. 22 June 1701, Norton <Lane Fam.(1897),2:15>

CHILDREN OF Benjamin SEALY^{5} (Eliz. Washburn^{4}) & Sarah LANE: (2) <Lane Fam.2:15>

Sarah SEALY^{6}, b. 19 Apr. 1720

Hannah SEALY^{6}, b. 24 Dec. 1725

Mary BOWDEN, b. c1669, d. 18 Dec. 1747, 78th yr, Bridgewater g.s. <Epitaphs:74>

CHILDREN OF James WASHBURN^{4} (Eliz. Mitchell^{3}) & Mary BOWDEN: (9) <Bridgewater VR, MD 14:205>

Mary WASHBURN^{5}, b. 28 Oct. 1694; d. 31 Mar. 1774*, Scotland g.s., Bridgewater

Anna WASHBURN^{5}, b. 1 Feb. 1695/6

James WASHBURN^{5}, b. 6 Oct. 1698; d.? 4 Aug. 1741*, 44th yr <Taunton VR 3:210>

Edward WASHBURN^{5}, b. 8 Dec. 1700

Moses WASHBURN^{5}, b. 9 Sept. 1702

Gideon WASHBURN^{5}, b. 16 Aug. 1704; d. 1794*

Sarah WASHBURN^{5}, b. 2 Oct. 1706

Martha WASHBURN^{5}, b. 10 Jan. 1708/9

Elizabeth WASHBURN^{5}, b. 5 Apr. 1710

Edward WASHBURN Jr., d. pre 25 Mar. 1767 (adm.) <Plymouth Co.PR #21952, 17:180>**<53>**

Elizabeth RICHMOND^{5} (Eben.^{4}, Abigail Rogers^{3}, John^{2}), b. 1 Sept. 1708, Middleboro <MD 2:106>

CHILDREN OF Edward WASHBURN^{5} & Elizabeth RICHMOND: (5) <1-3,5, Middleboro VR>

Abigail WASHBURN^{6}, b. 25 Mar. 1730 <MD 15:121>

James WASHBURN^{6}, b. 13 Jan. 1731/2 <MD 15:121>

Edward WASHBURN^{6}, b. 17 June 1734 <MD 15:121>**<54>**

Abiel WASHBURN^{6}*, b. ( ), d. "in French War" <Richmond Gen.:30>

Capt. Amos WASHBURN^{6}, b. 8 Apr. 1742 <MD 23:45>; d. pre 24 Oct. 1794 (adm.)**<55>**

CHILD OF Edward WASHBURN^{6} & Hannah JONES:**<56>**

Gen. Abiel WASHBURN^{7}, b. 13 Dec. 1762, d. 17 June 1843, Nemasket g.s., Middleboro <MD 15:105>

Elizabeth PIERCE^{4} (Job^{3}, Eben.^{2}, Isaac^{1}--), b. 6 Jan. 1766, d. 23 Mar. 1850, Nemasket g.s., Middleboro <MD 15:105>

CHILDREN OF Gen. Abiel WASHBURN^{7} & Elizabeth PIERCE: (11) <1-5, Middleboro VR, MD 33:78>**<57>**

Abiel WASHBURN^{8}, b. 29 Dec. 1788; d. 1 June 1866 <NEHGR 20:379>

Betsy P. WASHBURN^{8}, b. 2 June 1791

Polly WASHBURN^{8}, b. 13 Oct. 1792

William R. Pierce WASHBURN^{8}, b. 29 Mar. 1794

Abigail WASHBURN^{8}, b. 13 June 1796; d. 16 Mar. 1863, unm.

Philander WASHBURN^{8}, b. 22 Mar. 1798*

Orville WASHBURN^{8}, b. 24 Jan. 1799*; d. 9 Oct. 1819, Middleboro g.s. <MD 15:105>

George WASHBURN^{8}, b. 13 Nov. 1801, d. 29 Nov. 1803, Middleboro g.s. <MD 15:105>

Lucy Ann WASHBURN^{8}, b. Aug. 1805*; d. 5 Dec. 1854*

Caroline WASHBURN^{8}, b. 19 June 1807*

Louisa Jane WASHBURN^{8}, b. ( )

Elizabeth LEONARD, (dau of Josiah), b. c1701, d. 14 Oct. 1783*, 81st yr (wf of Joseph Crossman)

CHILDREN OF James WASHBURN^{5} (James^{4}) & Elizabeth LEONARD: (1 of 5)**<58>**

Jonah WASHBURN^{6}, b. 16 Feb. 1733, Middleboro; d. 12 Mar. 1810*, Randolph VT

Huldah SEARS, (dau of David & Phebe), b. 10 Aug. 1737 <Middleboro ChR:97>; d. 22 Mar. 1816*, VT

CHILDREN OF Jonah WASHBURN^{6} & Huldah SEARS: (8) <1-6, Middleboro VR>

Abner WASHBURN^{7}, b. 12 Oct. 1757 <MD 18:153>

Jonah WASHBURN^{7}, b. 3 Jan. 1760 <MD 23:45>

Josiah WASHBURN^{7}, b. 23 Jan. 176() <MD 23:45>

Azel WASHBURN^{7}, b. 26 Apr. 1764 <MD 24:41>

Huldia WASHBURN^{7}, b. 27 June 1766 <MD 25:108>

Lucy WASHBURN^{7}, b. 16 Mar. 1769 <MD 29:189> (1st name worn in rcds.)

Elizabeth WASHBURN^{7*}, b. 3 May 1772*

Daniel WASHBURN^{7*}, b. 27 Mar. 1776*; d. Stowe VT

Hannah CUSHMAN^{5} (Robert^{4}, Tho.^{3}, Mary Allerton^{2}), b. 25 Dec. 1705, Plymouth <MD 4:111>

CHILDREN OF Moses WASHBURN^{5} (James^{4}) & Hannah CUSHMAN: (6) <1-4, Bridgewater VR, MD 15:199>

Peter WASHBURN^{6}, b. 16 June 1728

Moses WASHBURN^{6}, b. 9 Dec. 1730; d. pre 8 Oct. 1813*

Robert WASHBURN^{6}, b. 24 Jan. 1733

Ira WASHBURN^{6}, b. 10 Jan. 1734/5

Bezaleel WASHBURN^{6*}, b. ( )

Thomas WASHBURN^{6*}, b. ( )

Abigail POPE, (dau of Tho.), b. 15 Jan. 1724/5, d. 8 Jan. 1784 <Dartmouth VR 1:182,3:77> (wf of Peter Washburn^{6})

CHILDREN OF Moses WASHBURN^{6} & Sarah POPE: (1 of 7*)**<59>**

Lettice WASHBURN^{7}, b. c1757, d. 3 Apr. 1844*, ae 87, Fairhaven <Mass.VR 8:45> <see next pg.>**<60>**

CHILD OF Lettice WASHBURN^{7} & 1st Mercy SPOONER:

Amaziah WASHBURN^{8}, b. ( ) See <61>

Sarah SPOONER, b. c1764, Dartmouth, d. 11 Aug. 1845, ae 81, Fairhaven <Mass.VR 20:45><see nxt pg>

CHILDREN OF Lettice WASHBURN^{7} & 2nd Sarah SPOONER: (12)**<61>**

James WASHBURN^{8}, b. 21 Apr. 1784, d. 10 Oct. 1784

John WASHBURN^{8}, b. 21 Apr. 1784 (twins), d. 12 Mar. 1842

William WASHBURN^{8}, b. 14 May 1786, d. 20 Nov. 1869

Mercy WASHBURN^{8}, b. 18 May 1789, d. 17 Aug. 1852

Susan WASHBURN^{8}, b. 21 Oct. 1791, d. Nov. 1853

Lettice WASHBURN^{8}, b. 6 Dec. 1793; d. 23 Aug. 1867, ae 77y7m11d, Acushnet <Mass.VR 202:62>

Elizabeth WASHBURN^{8}, b. 29 Nov. 1795

Israel WASHBURN^{8}, b. 24 Nov. 1796, d. 23 Apr. 1864

Nancy WASHBURN^{8}, b. 14 Jan. 1799, d. 1823

Sarah WASHBURN^{8}, b. 23 June 1801, d. 1802

Sarah WASHBURN^{8}, b. 24 June 1805

Joseph WASHBURN^{8}, b. 30 Sept. 1808, d. 1818

Joseph SPOONER, b. c1718, d. betw. 3 Oct. 1770 (will) - 17 Feb. 1771 (prob.) <Spooner Gen.:66,83>

CHILDREN OF Joseph SPOONER & Deborah SPOONER (dau of Simson & Sarah (Jenney) Spooner): (8)**<62>**

"Acushnet Cemetery" (NY 1831, p.20): (9)

Abigail WASHBURN, consort of Peter, d. 8 Jan. 1782, ae 57

Abbie H. WASHBURN, dau of Reuben, d. 11 Dec. 1851, ae 7mths

John S. WASHBURN, d. 12 Mar. 1842, ae 58

Desire WASHBURN, wf of John, d. 29 Nov. 1849, ae 64

Bazabiel WASHBURN, d. 2 Oct. 1843, ae 43

Lettice WASHBURN, "soldier of the Revolution", d. 3 Apr. 1844, ae 86

Sarah WASHBURN, his wife, "soldier of Jesus", d. 11 Aug. 1845, ae 83

Gilbert T. WASHBURN, son of Bazaliel Jr., d. 9 Aug. 1844, ae 5

Lettice WASHBURN, son of Wm., infant, d. 18 Jan. 1845

CHILD OF Lettice WASHBURN^{8} (Lettice^{7}) & Annie CHASE:

William WASHBURN^{9}, b. c1818, d. 26 Feb. 1903, ae 84y4m16d, Acushnet <Mass.VR 540:103>

Hannah ALLEN, (dau of Noel & Hannah), b. c1822, Westport, d. 18 Mar. 1889, ae 67y1m18d <Mass.VR 400:140> (wf of Wm. Washburn^{9})

CHILDREN OF John WASHBURN^{4} (Eliz. Mitchell^{3}) & Rebecca LAPHAM: (6) <Bridgewater, MD 2:93>**<63>**

Josiah WASHBURN^{5}, b. 11 Feb. 1679 <MD 2:92>; d. pre 24 May 1734 (adm.) <Plymouth Co.PR #22029>

Lieut. John WASHBURN^{5}, b. 5 Apr. 1682; d. 6 July 1746*, Bridgewater g.s.

Joseph WASHBURN^{5}, b. 7 July 1683

William WASHBURN^{5}, b. 16 Feb. 1686; d. 16 Mar. 1756, Bridgewater <MD 15:49>

Abigail WASHBURN^{5}, b. 2 June 1688

Rebecca WASHBURN^{5*}, b. ( )

MICRO #10 of 30

Margaret PACKARD, (*dau of Nath.), b. c1682, d. 10 Dec. 1743*, ae 61, Bridgewater g.s.

CHILDREN OF Lieut. John WASHBURN^{5} & Margaret PACKARD: (8) <Bridgewater VR, MD 14:208>

Lieut. John WASHBURN^{6}, b. 9 July 1711; d. 3 June 1797*

Nathaniel WASHBURN^{6}, b. 3 Sept. 1713; d. 17 Mar. 1750*, Bridgewater g.s.

Robert WASHBURN^{6}, b. 23 May 1715

Abraham WASHBURN^{6}, b. 19 Apr. 1717; d. pre 11 July 1746 (father's will)

Margaret WASHBURN^{6}, b. 22 Aug. 1718; d. pre 11 July 1746 (father's will)

Abishai WASHBURN^{6}, b. 16 June 1720

Jane WASHBURN^{6}, b. 28 Mar. 1722

Content WASHBURN^{6}, b. 22 Apr. 1724

Mary PRATT^{5} (Sam.$^{4-3}$, Mary Priest^{2}), b. 11 July 1716, Middleboro <MD 6:180>

CHILDREN OF Nathaniel WASHBURN^{6} & Mary PRATT: (4)**<64>**

CHILDREN OF Josiah WASHBURN^{5} (John^{4}) & Mercy TILSON: (7) <Bridgewater VR, MD 14:182>

Joanna WASHBURN^{6}, b. 14 Nov. 1703

Joseph WASHBURN^{6}, b. 22 July 1705; d. 12 Dec. 1766, Bridgewater g.s. <Bridgewater VR 2:154>

Lydia WASHBURN^{6}, b. 16 Aug. 1707

Jemima WASHBURN^{6}, b. 27 June 1710

Rebecca WASHBURN^{6}, b. 15 Feb. 1711/12

Josiah WASHBURN^{6}, b. 3 June 1716; d. pre 4 Dec. 1789 (adm.) <Plymouth Co.PR #22031>

Mercy WASHBURN^{6}, b. 29 May 1718

CHILDREN OF David JOHNSON & Rebecca WASHBURN^{5} (John^{4}): (5) <Bridgewater VR, MD 15:168>

Isaac JOHNSON^{6}, b. 9 Aug. 1721; d. 2 May 1807

David JOHNSON^{6}, b. 8 Aug. 1724

Mary JOHNSON^{6}, b. 29 Aug. 1729

Sarah JOHNSON^{6}, b. 19 July 1732

Rebecca JOHNSON^{6}, b. 22 June 1734

Mary WILLIS, (dau of Tho.), b. c1725, d. 27 Oct. 1799, W. Bridgewater g.s.

CHILDREN OF Isaac JOHNSON^{6} & Mary WILLIS: (6) <Bridgewater VR>

Huldah JOHNSON^{7}, b. 23 May 1745

Thomas JOHNSON^{7}, b. 6 July 1747

Elizabeth JOHNSON^{7}, b. 27 Mar. 1749

Mary JOHNSON^{7}, b. 4 Nov. 1751

Isaac JOHNSON^{7}, b. 27 Feb. 1755; d. pre Oct. 1828*

Rebecca JOHNSON^{7}, b. 26 Dec. 1758

Mary WRIGHT, b. 25 Oct. 1763; d. 5 Oct. 1828, widow <Bridgewater ChR>

CHILDREN OF Isaac JOHNSON^{7} & Mary WRIGHT: (3)<65>

Deliverance ORCUTT* (*dau of Wm.), b. c1707, d. 5 Dec. 1790*, ae 83, Bridgewater g.s.(widow of 2nd hus. Abiel Packard)

CHILDREN OF Joseph WASHBURN^{6} (Josiah^{5}) & Deliverance ORCUTT*: (8) <1-5,8, Bridgewater VR 2:154>

Joseph WASHBURN^{7}, b. 28 Sept. 1729

Jeremiah WASHBURN^{7}, b. 7 Sept. 1731

Hannah WASHBURN^{7}, b. 6 Sept. 1733

Joanna WASHBURN^{7}, b. 30 Jan. 1735/6

Silvanus WASHBURN^{7}, b. 24 Feb. 1737/8

Eliab WASHBURN^{7}, b. ( )

Eliphalet WASHBURN^{7}, b. ( )

Martha WASHBURN^{7}, b. 11 June 1744

Solomon BARTLETT, b. 12 Feb. 1757; d. 26 Apr. 1838*, Plainfield VT

CHILDREN OF Solomon BARTLETT & 1st Huldah WASHBURN: (4)

Darius BARTLETT, b. 3 Mar. 1783, d. 14 May 1809

Thomas BARTLETT, b. 22 Feb. 1785, d. 27 Dec. 1805

Chauncy BARTLETT, b. 1 Oct. 1787

Joel BARTLETT, b. 16 Mar. 1790, d. 7 Nov. 1820

Mercy OLDS, b. 2 Jan. 1763, d. 21 Nov. 1812

CHILDREN OF Solomon BARTLETT & 2nd Mercy OLDS: (6)

Child, bur. 14 May 1794

Huldah BARTLETT, b. 21 June 1795

Caroline BARTLETT, b. 22 July 1796

Fanny BARTLETT, b. 28 Aug. 1798, d. 8 Aug. 1800

Levi BARTLETT, b. 5 Nov. 1800

Fanny BARTLETT, b. 12 June 1803, d. 19 Aug. 1821

CHILDREN OF Samuel WEST & Lydia WASHBURN^{6} (Josiah^{5}): (3*) <Bridgewater VR>

Ezra WEST^{7}, b. 30 June 1739

Mehitable WEST^{7}, b. 21 Sept. 1741

John WEST^{7}, b. 4 Mar. 1743

CHILDREN OF William WASHBURN^{5} (John^{4}) & Experience MAN: (9) <Bridgewater VR, MD 15:49>

Abigail WASHBURN^{6}, b. 11 Dec. 1715

Alice WASHBURN^{6}, b. 6 Jan. 1716/17, d. 17 May 1736

William WASHBURN^{6}, b. 14 Apr. 1718

Experience WASHBURN^{6}, b. 14 Oct. 1719, d. 3 July 1724

Zipporah WASHBURN^{6}, b. 17 Aug. 1721

Thankful WASHBURN^{6}, b. 13 Aug. 1723

Philip WASHBURN^{6}, b. 26 May 1726, d. 8 May 1736

Ezekiel WASHBURN^{6}, b. 22 May 1728; d. pre 1785*, Bridgewater

Job WASHBURN^{6}, b. 3 June 1733, d.y.

Experience CURTIS, d. aft. 10 Dec. 1785*

CHILDREN OF Ezekiel WASHBURN^{6} & Experience CURTIS: (6) <Bridgewater VR>

Zipporah WASHBURN^{7}, b. 16 Aug. 1750 <VR 1:337>; d. 18 Apr. 1751

Ezekiel WASHBURN^{7}, b. 11 Mar. 1752 <VR 1:329>; d. pre 5 Apr. 1785 (adm.)

Alice WASHBURN^{7}, b. 15 Apr. 1754 <VR 1:326>

Betty/Betsey WASHBURN^{7}, b. 11 Jan. 1756 <VR 1:326>; d. 4 July 1828

Experience WASHBURN^{7}, b. 30 Aug. 1758 <VR 1:328>

Deliverance WASHBURN^{7}, b. 30 Aug. 1758 (twins) <VR 1:327>

Naomi THAYER, d. aft. 10 Dec. 1785

CHILDREN OF Ezekiel WASHBURN[7] & Naomi THAYER: (2) <Brockton VR>

Arba WASHBURN[8], bpt. 19 Sept. 1791 <VR 1:50>

Sophia WASHBURN[8], bpt. 19 Sept. 1791 <VR 1:51>

Lt. Nathaniel PRATT, (son of Seth & Hannah (Washburn)), b. c1754, d. 11 May 1828, ae 74 <Bridgewater VR 2:545>

CHILDREN OF Lt. Nathaniel PRATT & Betsey WASHBURN[7] (Ezekiel[6]): (8)**<66>**

William SHAW, (son of Wm. & Hannah), b. 24 Jan. 1757 <Bridgewater VR 1:290> (hus. of Deliverance Washburn[7])

CHILDREN OF John KINSLEY & Thankful WASHBURN[6] (Wm.[5]): (7) <Norwich CT VR 1:294>

John KINSLEY[7], b. 27 Aug. 1749, d. 28 Dec. 1753

Rhoda KINSLEY[7], b. 12 Apr. 1751

William KINSLEY[7], b. 16 Apr. 1753, d. 29 Dec. 1753

Thankful KINSLEY[7], b. 26 Sept. 1754

Mary KINSLEY[7], b. 30 Oct. 1756

Bethiah KINSLEY[7], b. 10 Oct. 1758, d. 4 Mar. 1759

Roger KINSLEY[7], b. 7 Feb. 1760

CHILDREN OF Jonathan WASHBURN[4] (Eliz. Mitchell[3]) & Mary VAUGHAN, (dau of George): (10) <Bridgewater VR, MD 15:48>

Elizabeth WASHBURN[5], b. 12 Oct. 1684

Josiah WASHBURN[5], b. 12 May 1686

Benjamin WASHBURN[5], b. 17 Jan. 1687/8; d. 25 Aug. 1740, Bridgewater <MD 14:204>

Ebenezer WASHBURN[5], b. 23 Feb. 1690; d. 10 Oct. 1727*, prob. unm.<Plymouth Co.PR #21948>

Martha WASHBURN[5], b. 27 Feb. 1692

Joanna WASHBURN[5], b. 12 Oct. 1693

Daughter, b. 29 Nov. 1696, d. 16 Dec. 1696

Nathan WASHBURN[5], b. 29 Jan. 1699; d. pre 1728* (div. of brother Ebenezer's estate)

Jonathan WASHBURN[5], b. 29 Aug. 1700; d. pre 1728*(div. of brother Ebenezer's estate)

Cornelius WASHBURN[5], b. 6 May 1702; d. 12 Feb. 1779*, Bridgewater g.s.

Phebe HAYWARD, (dau of Tho.), b. 26 Apr. 1725 <Bridgewater VR 1:153>

CHILD OF Josiah WASHBURN[6] (Josiah[5]) & Phebe HAYWARD:

Solomon WASHBURN[7], b. 24 Oct. 1754*

CHILD OF Solomon WASHBURN[7] & Anne MITCHELL:

Zenas WASHBURN[8], b. c1775, d. 18 Feb. 1824*, ae 49, lung fever <E.Bridgewater VR:397>

CHILDREN OF Zenas WASHBURN[8] & Lydia WHITMAN, (*dau of Noah): (7*)

Lysander WASHBURN[9], b. 1802, d. 19 or 26 Feb. 1809

Freelove Whitman WASHBURN[9], bpt. Oct. 1808

Sarah Whitman WASHBURN[9], bpt. Oct. 1808

Selden WASHBURN[9], bpt. Oct. 1808

Lysander WASHBURN[9], bpt. 13 May 1810

Angelina WASHBURN[9], bpt. 18 Apr. 1813

Lydia WASHBURN[9], bpt. 11 May 1817

Martha KINGMAN, (dau of Henry), b. 10 July 1699, Bridgewater <MD 15:47>;d. Feb. 1793, Bridgewater <MD 14:204>

CHILDREN OF Benjamin WASHBURN[5] (Jonathan[4]) & Martha KINGMAN: (3) <Bridgewater VR, MD 14:204>

Mary WASHBURN[6], b. 24 Mar. 1729/30

Martha WASHBURN[6], b. 23 Oct. 1731

Benjamin WASHBURN[6], b. 6 July 1735; d. 5 Jan. 1796* <Bridgewater Epitaphs:90>

Desire SEARS, (dau of Edw.), b. 15 Mar. 1742/3 <Halifax VR:42>; d. 15 Nov. 1800* <Bridge.Ep.:90>

CHILDREN OF Benjamin WASHBURN[6] & Desire SEARS: (10*)

Oliver WASHBURN[7], b. 30 Aug. 1763; d. 1 Aug. 1818
Azel WASHBURN[7], b. Apr. 1765; d. 15 Nov. 1805
Sally/Sarah WASHBURN[7], b. 14 July 1767
Lydia WASHBURN[7], b. 1 June 1769
Deborah WASHBURN[7], b. 15 Jan. 1771; d. 15 Jan. 1775
Desire WASHBURN[7], b. 20 June 1773; d. Jan. 1775
Sears WASHBURN[7], b. 19 May 1777; d. aft. 1800 (father's estate) <Plymouth Co.PR #21926,36:547>
Mary/Polly WASHBURN[7], b. 29 June 1780; d. aft. 1800 " " "
Huldah WASHBURN[7], b. 24 Apr. 1784; d. aft. 1800 " " "
Benjamin WASHBURN[7], b. 15 Apr. 1786; d. 21 May 1786
Experience ( ) WASHBURN, b. c1706, d. 1 Apr. 1786*, 80th yr, Bridgewater g.s.
CHILDREN OF Cornelius WASHBURN[5] (Jonathan[4]) & Experience ( ): (9) <Bridgewater VR, MD 15:173>
Nathan WASHBURN[6], b. 25 Dec. 1728, d. 25 Sept. 1747 <MD 15:172,173>
Daniel WASHBURN[6], b. 21 July 1730 <MD 15:172>; d. 14 Feb. 1801*, Bridgewater g.s.
Robert WASHBURN[6], b. 25 Jan. 1736, d. "12th day"
Robert WASHBURN[6], b. 6 Feb. 1735, d. 11 June 1737
Experience WASHBURN[6], b. 1 Feb. 1743, d. 10 Feb. 1743
Experience WASHBURN[6], b. 8 Mar. 1744
Joanna WASHBURN[6], b. 28 May 1747
Ebenezer WASHBURN[6], b. c1735, d. 12 Oct. 1747
Cornelius WASHBURN[6], b. 29 Dec. 1739, d. 27 Sept. 1747
Experience HARLOW, b. c1733, d. 27 May 1816*, ae 83
CHILD OF Daniel WASHBURN[6] & Experience HARLOW*:
Cornelius WASHBURN[7], b. c1753*
Hannah LATHAM[4] (Susanna Winslow[3], Mary Chilton[2]), b. c1650-62*; d. aft. 24 Aug. 1723* <Plymouth Co.Deeds 18:109>
CHILDREN OF Joseph WASHBURN[4] (Eliz. Mitchell[3]) & Hannah LATHAM: (8)
Jonathan WASHBURN[5], b. pre 1687*
Joseph WASHBURN[5], b. pre 1696, d. 1759 <Leicester VR:280>
Ebenezer WASHBURN[5], b. ( ), d. pre 1755* (adm.)
Miles WASHBURN[5], b. pre 1678*; d. aft. 6 Sept. 1738*
Ephraim WASHBURN[5], b. ( ); d. pre 16 July 1755* (adm.) <Plymouth Co.PR, 14:487>
Edward WASHBURN[5], b. ( ), d. aft. 6 Sept. 1738*
Benjamin WASHBURN[5], b. ( ); d. aft. 7 Nov. 1753*
Hephzibah WASHBURN[5], b. pre 1687*; d. 4 Apr. 1750* <Bridgewater VR 2:515>

MICRO #11 of 30

Zerviah PACKARD, (dau of Israel & Hannah), b. 22 May 1713, Bridgewater <MD 15:46>; d. aft. 1753*
CHILDREN OF Benjamin WASHBURN[5] & Zerviah PACKARD: (3) <Bridgewater VR>
Hannah WASHBURN[6], b. 19 Jan. 1743/4*
Sarah WASHBURN[6], b. 19 Apr. 1748*
Ebenezer WASHBURN[6], b. 18 Dec. 1750*
Mary POLEN, d. pre 9 Sept. 1784* (div. of dower)
CHILDREN OF Ephraim WASHBURN[5] (Jos.[4]) & Mary POLEN: (10) <Plympton VR:217>[<67>]
William WASHBURN[6], b. 26 Oct. 1726*; d. 21 Dec. 1810, 85th yr, Union Cem., S. Carver
Lydia WASHBURN[6], b. 4 May 1728*
Elizabeth WASHBURN[6], b. 9 Mar. 1732*
Mercy WASHBURN[6], b. 5 Mar. 1734*; unm. in 1784
Stephen WASHBURN[6], b. 24 Sept. 1736*
Isaac WASHBURN[6], b. 12 Nov. 1738*
Phebe WASHBURN[6], b. 27 Jan. 1740*

Japhet WASHBURN^{6}, b. 11 Sept. 1746 <Bible Rcd.>

John WASHBURN^{6}, b. c1748*

Jemima WASHBURN^{6}, b. ( ); d. pre Sept. 1784*

Consider BENSON, (*son of Sam. & Keziah), b. 16 Apr. 1730*, Middleboro <MD 15:120> (See below)

CHILDREN OF Consider BENSON & Elizabeth WASHBURN^{6}: (7) <Middleboro VR>

Son, b. 7 Mar. 1754 <MD 22:149>

William BENSON^{7}, b. 4 June 1756 <MD 22:149>

Patience BENSON^{7}, b. 2 Mar. 1758 <MD 22:149>

Molly BENSON^{7}, b. 17 Apr. 1760 <MD 22:149>

Samuel BENSON^{7}, b. 17 July 1762 <MD 23:46>

Consider BENSON^{7}, b. 4 Sept. 1764 <MD 23:71>

Peleg BENSON^{7}, b. 18 Dec. 1766 <MD 26:26>

CHILDREN OF Samuel BENSON & Keziah ( ): (5) <Middleboro VR, MD 15:120>

Consider BENSON, b. 16 Apr. 1730

Patience BENSON, b. 27 June 1732

John BENSON, b. 23 Aug. 1734

Lydia BENSON, b. 27 Aug. 1736

Jemima BENSON, b. 7 May 1739

Priscilla COOMBS, b. 1 Nov. 1745 <Bible Rcd.> (wf of Japhet Washburn^{6})

Samuel NORRIS, d. aft. Apr. 1794*

CHILD OF Samuel NORRIS & Lydia WASHBURN^{6} (Ephraim^{5}):

Jemima NORRIS^{7}, b. 30 Oct. 1770, d. 11 Apr. 1863 <Giddings Lane Family Bible; dth. Leeds ME VR>

Giddings LANE, b. 4 May 1770, d. 29 Jan. 1836 <Lane Family Bible; dth. Leeds ME VR>

CHILDREN OF Giddings LANE & Jemima NORRIS^{7}: (13) <Leeds ME VR>

Molly/Polly LANE^{8}, b. 6 Feb. 1790, d. 6 Sept. 1870

Alpheus LANE^{8}, b. 5 Dec. 1791

Lydia LANE^{8}, b. 13 Apr. 1794

Jemima LANE^{8}, b. 1 Mar. 1796

Dorcas LANE^{8}, b. 19 July 1798

Fanny LANE^{8}, b. 12 Sept. 1800

Giddings LANE^{8}, b. 16 Aug. 1802

Samuel LANE^{8}, b. 7 May 1806

Susannah LANE^{8}, b. 15 July 1808

Ruth LANE^{8}, b. 11 July 1810

Esther LANE^{8}, b. 31 May 1812

Calvin LANE^{8}, b. 6 Sept. 1814

Nancy LANE^{8}, b. 5 Jan. 1817

Uriah FOSS, b. 6 Mar. 1760, d. 16 June 1825 <Uriah Foss Family Bible>

Sarah GOODRIDGE, b. 24 Aug. 1759, d. 28 June 1830 <Foss Family Bible>

CHILD OF Uriah FOSS & Sarah GOODRIDGE:

Cyrus FOSS, b. 21 June 1785, d. 16 Oct. 1836 <Foss Family Bible>

Sarah ( ) WASHBURN, b. c1737, d. 26 Mar. 1805, 68th yr, Union Cem., S. Carver

CHILDREN OF William WASHBURN^{6} (Ephraim^{5}) & Sarah ( ): (8) <Carver VR>

William WASHBURN^{7}, b. 18 Sept. 1760; d. 20 Dec. 1783, Union Cem., S. Carver

Thomas WASHBURN^{7}, b. 5 Apr. 1762

Rowland WASHBURN^{7}, b. 2 July 1764; d. pre 5 Aug. 1794 <Plymouth Co.PR #22078, 34:9>**<68>**

Lydia WASHBURN^{7}, b. 14 July 1766

Perez WASHBURN^{7}, b. 25 Dec. 1768

Jemima WASHBURN^{7}, b. 6 May 1771

Asaph WASHBURN^{7}, b. 18 Feb. 1776

Benjamin LEACH, (son of Giles), d.? 13 July 1764* <Bridgewater VR 2:513>

CHILDREN OF Benjamin LEACH & Hephzibah WASHBURN^{5} (Jos.^{4}): (11) <Bridgewater VR, MD 14:182>

Anne LEACH^{6}, b. 19 July 1703

Joseph LEACH^{6}, b. 9 Oct. 1705; d. 12 Nov. 1760*

Mary LEACH^{6}, b. 1 May 1708

Sarah LEACH^{6}, b. 29 Apr. 1711

Benjamin LEACH^{6}, b. 14 Sept. 1713; d. 29 Feb. 1755/56, Bridgewater**<69>**

Ichabod LEACH^{6}, b. 8 May 1716, d. 11 Dec. 1722

Jerahmeel LEACH^{6}, b. 4 May 1718

Benanuel LEACH^{6}, b. 4 May 1718 (twins)

Nokes LEACH^{6}, b. 30 Mar. 1720

Susanna LEACH^{6}, b. 25 Oct. 1722

Hannah LEACH^{6}, b. 4 Mar. 1725

CHILDREN OF Samuel PACKARD & Anne LEACH^{6}: (9) <MD 15:171; (no dates rec. for 4>

Anne PACKARD^{7}, b. 1 Aug. 1723

Mary PACKARD^{7}, b. 16 Apr. 1725

Bettie PACKARD^{7}, b. 15 Oct. 1727

Samuel PACKARD^{7}, b. ( )

Hephzibah PACKARD^{7}, b. ( )

Caleb PACKARD^{7}, b. 10 Aug. 1735

Joshua PACKARD^{7}, b. 10 Aug. 1735 (twins)

Chloe PACKARD^{7}, b. ( )

Desire PACKARD^{7}, b. ( )

CHILDREN OF Joseph LEACH^{6} (Hephzibah Washburn^{5}) & Anna HARRIS^{6} (*?Isaac^{5}, Mercy Latham^{4}, Susanna Winslow^{3}, Mary Chilton^{2}): (4 of 9)**<70>**

Benjamin LEACH^{7}, b. c1743, d. 24 Jan. 1830*, ae 87 <Bridgewater ChR>

Jephtha LEACH^{7}, b. pre 1758; d. pre 7 Dec. 1779, lost at sea (adm. bond)**<71>**

Isaiah LEACH^{7}, b. pre 1758; d. 22 Mar. 1778* <adm. 7 Dec. 1778, Plymouth Co.PR #12441,23:182>

Orpha LEACH^{7}, b. ( )

Edward FOBES, (son of Wm. & Thankful), b. 14 Mar. 1737/8 <Bridgewater VR 1:113>

CHILDREN OF Edward FOBES & Orpha LEACH^{7}: (8) <5-8, Chesterfield VR 1:2>

John FOBES^{8}, b. 4 Nov. 1761* <Bridgewater VR 1:115>; d. pre 20 Nov. 1838 (adm.), N.Y.

Sylvester FOBES^{8}, b. 23 Apr. 1764* <Bridgewater VR 1:119>

Olive FOBES^{8}, b. 16 Feb. 1766*

Martha FOBES^{8}, b. 2 Feb. 1768*; d. 16 Dec. 1861*

Barzillai FOBES^{8}, b. 16 Nov. 1770, Bridgewater

Lucy FOBES^{8}, b. 19 May 1775, Bridgewater

Eber FOBES^{8}, b. 8 Dec. 1777, Chesterfield

Eunice FOBES^{8}, b. 14 Jan. 1780, Chesterfield

Edward FOBES, son of John & Abigail, b. 22 May 1707 <Bridgewater VR 1:113>

Edward FOBES, son of John & Martha, b. 12 Aug. 1739 <Bridgewater VR 1:113>

Edward FOBES, son of Abner & Phebe, b. 25 Oct. 1755 <Bridgewater VR 1:113>

Mary KEITH, b. c1744, d. 30 Nov. 1791*, 47th yr, Vernon St. cem., Bridgewater

CHILDREN OF Benjamin LEACH^{7} (Jos.^{6}) & 1st Mary KEITH: (10*)**<72>**

CHILDREN OF Benjamin LEACH^{7} (Jos.^{6}) & 2nd Anna SHORT*: (3*)

Anna LEACH^{8}, b. 13 Apr. 1793

Eunice LEACH^{8}, b. 18 May 1796

Chloe LEACH^{8}, b. 16 Mar. 1799

Timothy LEACH^{3} (John^{2}, Giles^{1}), b. 15 Oct. 1707, Bridgewater <MD 14:207>

CHILDREN OF Timothy LEACH & Sarah LEACH^{6} (Hephzibah Washburn^{5}): (9) <4-9, Bridgewater VR 3:255>

Rebecca LEACH[7], b. 24 July 1733, Bridgewater <MD 14:181>

Ichabod LEACH[7], b. 25 July 1735, Bridgewater <MD 14:181>

Timothy LEACH[7], b. 28 Aug. 1737, Bridgewater <MD 14:181>; d.y.

Sarah LEACH[7], b. 18 Feb. 1739

Jonathan LEACH[7], b. 20 Nov. 1741

Levi LEACH[7], b. 7 Apr. 1744

Nathan LEACH[7], b. 22 Dec. 1746

Ann LEACH[7], b. 21 Nov. 1749

Timothy LEACH[7], b. 23 Oct. 1751

MICRO #12 of 30

CHILDREN OF Ezra WASHBURN & Susanna LEACH[6] (Hephzibah Washburn[5]): (2)

Ezra WASHBURN[7], b. ( ), d. 16 Apr. 1793 <Stafford CT VR A:179>

Susanna WASHBURN[7], b. ( ), d. aft. 18 Sept. 1805

CHILDREN OF Ezra WASHBURN[7] & Lucy FULLER: (10) <Stafford CT VR A:53>

Keziah WASHBURN[8], b. 8 July 1768

Lucy WASHBURN[8], b. 22 Dec. 1769

Silas WASHBURN[8], b. 4 Oct. 1772

Son, b. 27 Oct. 1774, d. "about four weeks after"

Ezra WASHBURN[8], b. 19 Mar. 1776

Libeas WASHBURN[8], b. 5 July 1778

Simon WASHBURN[8], b. 21 May 1780

Peter WASHBURN[8], b. 24 Oct. 1782

Andrew WASHBURN[8], b. 31 May 1784

Vodisa WASHBURN[8], b. 7 Aug. 1786

Andrew WASHBURN, b. 31 May 1784; d. 22 May 1846, Chaplin CT

CHILD OF Andrew WASHBURN:

Mary WASHBURN, b. 14 Mar. 1815, Hampton CT

Zadock LEACH, (*son of Jesse & Alice), b. 12 July 1741*, d. 17 Mar. 1788* <Bridgewater VR>

CHILDREN OF Zadock LEACH & Susanna WASHBURN[7] (Susanna Leach[6]): (8)[<73>]

CHILDREN OF Abraham LEACH[8] (Susanna Washburn[7]) & Mary KEITH, (dau of Amos): (5)[<74>]

CHILDREN OF Zadock LEACH[8] (Susanna Washburn[7]) & Polly FROST: (4)[<75>]

CHILDREN OF Beza LEACH[8] (Susanna Washburn[7]) & Betsy SHAW: (3)[<76>]

Rebecca PERRY[5] (Rebecca Freeman[4], Rebecca Prence[3], Patience Brewster[2]), b. 2 Oct. 1689, Sandwich <MD 30:64>

CHILDREN OF Jonathan WASHBURN[5] (Jos.[4]) & Rebecca PERRY: (2*) <Bridgewater VR>

Silas WASHBURN[6], b. 11 Feb. 1712/3

Lemuel WASHBURN[6], b. 18 Aug. 1714

Hannah JOHNSON, b. 17 Jan. 1694/5, Hingham; d. 1780 <Leicester VR:280>

CHILDREN OF Joseph WASHBURN[5] (Jos.[4]) & Hannah JOHNSON: (6) <Hist. Leicester (1860)>

Seth WASHBURN[6], b. 19 May 1723, Bridgewater, d. 12 Feb. 1794 <MD 2:67>

Elijah WASHBURN[6], b. ( )

Ebenezer WASHBURN[6], b. 1734, Bridgewater; d. 24 Jan. 1795 <Hardwick VR:332>

Abiel WASHBURN[6], b. c1726, d. 30 June 1812, ae 86 <Hardwick VR:335>

Sarah WASHBURN[6], b. ( ), d. 1817

Mary WASHBURN[6], b. ( )

Dorothy NEWHALL, b. 8 Apr. 1740 <Leicester VR:66>; d. 29 Oct. 1807 <Hardwick VR:331>

CHILDREN OF Ebenezer WASHBURN[6] & Dorothy NEWHALL: (7) <3-7, Hardwick VR:118>

Susanna WASHBURN[7], b. 9 Apr. 1759 <Spencer VR:108>

Artemus WASHBURN[7]*, b. 16 Oct. 1767*, d. 23 Sept. 1792*

Dolley WASHBURN[7], b. 31 Jan. 1770

Ebenezer WASHBURN^7, b. 25 Oct. 1772

Cyrus WASHBURN^7, b. 5 Nov. 1774; d. 2 Mar. 1860, Vernon VT <VT Gazetteer 5:282>

Clarissa WASHBURN^7, b. 26 May 1777

Hannah WASHBURN^7, b. 30 Oct. 1779

Electa STRATTON, d. 26 Jan. 1806

CHILDREN OF Cyrus WASHBURN^7 & 1st Electa STRATTON: (4 or 5)

Cyrus WASHBURN^8, b. 12 Nov. 1800, Northfield; d. 28 Mar. 1802

Electa WASHBURN^8, bpt. 5 Mar. 1803, Northfield; d. 9 Mar. 1803

Albert Alden WASHBURN^8, b. ( ) VT

Roxanna Stratton WASHBURN^8, b. ( ) VT

Clarissa WASHBURN^8, b. (?) VT (poss. by 2nd wf below); d. 1878, Vernon VT

Rhoda FIELD, b. 6 Feb. 1785, Northfield <Field Gen.(1901) 1:304>; d. 1826, Vernon VT

CHILD OF Cyrus WASHBURN^7 & 2nd Rhoda FIELD:

Artemus Henry WASHBURN^8, b. 9 Sept. 1810; d. 6 Jan. 1896

Jacob WICKER, (son of Wm. below), b. 5 Jan. 1723, d. 9 Mar. 1789* <Leicester VR:107, 282>

CHILDREN OF Jacob WICKER & Abiel WASHBURN^6 (Jos.^{5}): (3)

William WICKER^7, b. ( )

James WICKER^7, b. ( )

Joseph WICKER^7, b. 14 Sept. 1769; d. 10 Dec. 1795 <Hardwick VR:335>

CHILDREN OF William WICKER & Rebecca ( ): (5) <Leicester VR:107>

Rebecca WICKER, b. 25 Nov. 1720

Jacob WICKER, b. 5 Jan. 1723 (see above)

John WICKER, b. 2 May 1726

James WICKER, b. 12 May 1729

Mercy WICKER, b. 1 Feb. 1740

CHILDREN OF James WICKER^7 (Abiel Washburn^6) & Martha ( ): (5) <Hardwick VR:125>

Lucinda WICKER^8, b. 22 Oct. 1773

Patty WICKER^8, b. 3 Apr. 1775

Joel WICKER^8, b. 1 Oct. 1779

Betsey WICKER^8, b. 8 Apr. 1781

Sophia WICKER^8, b. 6 Apr. 1783

CHILDREN OF William WICKER^7 (Abiel Washburn^6) & Susanna PARKER: (10) <Hardwick VR:125>[<77>]

Jacob WICKER^8, b. 20 Feb. 1773

Susanna WICKER^8, b. 7 Sept. 1774

John WICKER^8, b. 18 Aug. 1776

Levina WICKER^8, b. 7 Feb. 1779

Pliny WICKER^8, b. 23 Apr. 1781

Lemuel WICKER^8, b. 9 July 1783; d. 20 July 1825, Orwell VT <Hist.Addison Co.:743>

Ira WICKER^8, b. 26 July 1785

William WICKER^8, b. 22 Apr. 1788

Lucy WICKER^8, b. 9 Oct. 1790

Melinda WICKER^8, b. 2 Aug. 1796

CHILD OF Ira WICKER^8 & Mary HASKELL:

Lydia Emaline WICKER^9, b. c1817, d. 31 Jan. 1818, ae 1y <Hardwick VR:335>

Mary Parmer HUNT, (dau of Moses), b. c1790, d. 14 Oct. 1812, ae 22 <Hardwick VR:335>

CHILD OF Lemuel WICKER^8 (Wm.^{7}) & 1st Mary Parmer HUNT:

Mary WICKER^9, bpt. 12 Oct. 1812, d. 28 Oct. 1812 ae 11wks <Hardwick VR:125,335>

Sarah HASKELL, (dau of Geo.), b. 23 Dec. 1791 <Hardwick VR:54>; d. 22 July 1831, Orwell VT <Hist. Addison Co.:743> (wf of 2nd hus Geo. Rowley)

CHILDREN OF Lemuel WICKER^8 & 2nd Sarah HASKELL: (2 of 5) <Hardwick VR:125>[<78>]

Cyrus Washburn WICKER^{9}, bpt. 9 Oct. 1814 (b. 12 Aug. 1814, Hist.Addison Co.:743)

Charles WICKER^{9}, b. 7 May 1816

CHILD OF David WICKER & Ann DAVIS:

Esther WICKER, b. 12 Jan. 1762 <Leicester VR:107>

MICRO #13 of 30

CHILDREN OF John WICKER^{8} (Wm.^{7}) & Priscilla COLLINS: (2) <Hardwick VR:125>

Charles Augustus WICKER^{9}, b. 3 Sept. 1804

Daniel Wright WICKER^{9}, b. 28 Feb. 1806

Dorothy KNAPP, (dau of Abram), b. 26 Jan. 1772, Norfolk CT; d. 27 Nov. 1836, Isle La Motte VT (m. 1st Joseph Wicker^{7} (Abiel Washburn^{6}), 2nd Samuel Jordan)

Mary HARWOOD, b. 19 Dec. 1728, Lunenburg MA, d. 16 Sept. 1787, Leicester <MD 2:67>

CHILDREN OF Seth WASHBURN^{6} (Jos.^{5}) & Mary HARWOOD: (10) <MD 2:67>

Seth WASHBURN^{7}, b. 1 Feb. 1751, d. 17 Aug. 1776

Stillborn, b. 30 Dec. 1753

Joseph WASHBURN^{7}, b. 18 May 1753, d. 27 Mar. 1807

Asa WASHBURN^{7}, b. 25 July 1757 <Leicester VR:99>, d. 6 Oct. 1834, Putney VT

Maray WASHBURN^{7}, b. 16 June 1759, d. 1849

Hannah WASHBURN^{7}, b. 5 June 1762, d. 1850

Sarah WASHBURN^{7}, b. 22 Oct. 1764, d. 14 Dec. 1850

Amity WASHBURN^{7}, b. 17 Apr. 1766, d. 22 June 1794

Lucy WASHBURN^{7}, b. 11 Nov. 1769, d. 26 Nov. 1796

Elizabeth WASHBURN^{7}, b. 12 Oct. 1774, d. 30 June 1777

Sally UPHAM, (dau of Jacob & Zerviah), b. 13 Dec. 1758 <Spencer VR:107>, d. 11 Sept. 1804, Putney VT <MD 2:68>

CHILDREN OF Asa WASHBURN^{7} & Sally UPHAM: (11) <MD 2:68>

Reuben WASHBURN^{8}, b. 30 Dec. 1781

Levi WASHBURN^{8}, b. 20 Oct. 1783, d. 12 Dec. 1792

Elizabeth WASHBURN^{8}, b. 18 Dec. 1785, d. 3 June 1815

Seth WASHBURN^{8}, b. 27 Jan. 1788, d. 6 Feb. 1841

Lucy WASHBURN^{8}, b. 11 Jan. 1790

Asa WASHBURN^{8}, b. 31 Dec. 1791

Sallie WASHBURN^{8}, b. 21 Mar. 1794

Jacob WASHBURN^{8}, b. 13 Mar. 1796, d. 26 Oct. 1855

Amity WASHBURN^{8}, b. 29 Jan. 1798

Lucretia WASHBURN^{8}, b. 2 Aug. 1801

Child, b. 19 July 1803, d.y.

Persis BOUTELL, b. 29 Mar. 1760, d. June 1837 <MD 2:68> (2nd wf of Asa Washburn^{7})

Samuel KINSLEY, d. 17 Dec. 1713 <MD 30:17>

CHILDREN OF Samuel KINSLEY & Mary WASHBURN^{4} (Eliz. Mitchell^{3}): (8) <MD 30:16>

Samuel KINSLEY^{5}, b. pre July 1693

Hannah KINSLEY^{5}, b. ( )

Sarah KINSLEY^{5}, b. c1691; d. 14 May 1735*, 47th yr <Bridgewater Epitaphs:82>

Mary KINSLEY^{5}, b. ( ); d.? Dec. 1784*

Susanna KINSLEY^{5}, b. ( )

Benjamin KINSLEY^{5}, b. 16 May 1701; d. 13 Mar. 1759

Abigail KINSLEY^{5}, b. aft. 1707 (under 14 in 1722)

Bethiah KINSLEY^{5}, b. aft. 1707 (under 14 in 1722)

CHILDREN OF William HAYWARD^{4} (*Jos.$^{3-2}$, Tho.^{1}) & Abigail KINSLEY^{5}: (5*)

Abigail HAYWARD^{6}, b. 1730

Lois HAYWARD^{6}, b. 1732

Sarah HAYWARD^{6}, b. 1735

Keziah HAYWARD^{6}, b. 1740

Ann HAYWARD^{6}, b. 1743

CHILDREN OF William BRETT & Bethiah KINSLEY^{5} (Mary Washburn^{4}): (4*)

Ephraim BRETT^{6}, b. 1733

Mary BRETT^{6}, b. 1734

Silence BRETT^{6}, b. 1738

Daniel BRETT^{6}, b. 1740

Thomas WILLIS, (*son of Ben. & Susanna), b. c1694, d.? 13 Jan. 1784*, ae 92

CHILDREN OF Thomas WILLIS & Mary KINSLEY^{5} (Mary Washburn^{4}): (8*)

Susanna WILLIS^{6}, b. 1718

Thomas WILLIS^{6}, b. 1721

Jonah WILLIS^{6}, b. 1723

Mary WILLIS^{6}, b. 1725

Rhoda WILLIS^{6}, b. 1727

Betty WILLIS^{6}, b. 1731

Zephaniah WILLIS^{6}, b. 1733

Nathan WILLIS^{6}, b. 1738

Sarah (MAGOUN) Forbes, b. c1843, NH, d. 25 Jan. 1923, ae 80y7m28d, 43 Appleton St., Cambridge, myocarditis, dau of Aaron B. Magoun & Harriet (Adams), widow of Henry D. Forbes <Mass.VR>

Sally COLE, dau of Charles & Esther, b. 10 July 1787 <Scituate VR 1:86>

Sally COLE, dau of David & Charlotte, b. 12 July 1779 <Scituate VR 1:86>; d. 25 Dec. 1811<Bridgewater VR 2:497> (wf of Edward Howard)

Edward HOWARD, d. 15 Nov. 1820 <Bridgewater VR 2:496> (hus. of Sally Cole)

Josiah HAYWARD, (son of Nath.), b. 1 Mar. 1688, Bridgewater <MD 15:48>; d. 4 Feb. 1764* <Bridgewater Epitaphs:82>

CHILDREN OF Josiah HAYWARD & 1st Sarah KINSLEY^{5} (Mary Washburn^{4}): (6) <Bridgewater VR, MD 14:46>

Child, b. 26 Oct. 1715, d. 12 Nov. 1715

Josiah HAYWARD^{6}, b. 13 Apr. 1717; d. 21 Dec. 1797* <Bridgewater VR>

Nathan HAYWARD^{6}, b. 28 Apr. 1720; d. 29 June 1794*, Bridgewater g.s.

Abraham HAYWARD^{6}, b. 22 Dec. 1722, d. 30 Mar. 1723

Sarah HAYWARD^{6}, b. 3 Nov. 1724

Martha HAYWARD^{6}, b. 22 Sept. 1727, d. 18 Feb. 1727/8

Sarah PRIOR, (dau of John), d.?2 June 1761* <Bridgewater VR 2:489>

CHILD OF Josiah HAYWARD & 2nd Sarah (PRIOR) Moore:

Hannah HAYWARD, b. 26 Nov. 1739* <Bridgewater VR>

Mary PERKINS, (*dau of Tho. & Mary (Washburn)), b. 10 Jan. 1717/8, Bridgewater <MD 15:84>; d. 17 May 1756* <Bridgewater VR 2:488>

CHILDREN OF Josiah HAYWARD^{6} & 1st Mary PERKINS: (7)

Mary HAYWARD^{7}, b. 13 Nov. 1742*, d. 29 Aug. 1747*

Josiah HAYWARD^{7}, b. 20 July 1744*, d. 1 Oct. 1745*

Lemuel HAYWARD^{7}, b. 17 May 1746*, d. 3 Sept. 1747*

Hephzibah HAYWARD^{7}, b. 24 Apr. 1748*, d. 27 Nov. 1748*

Josiah HAYWARD^{7}, b. aft. 1751* (minor in 1765) and pre Nov. 1756*; d. 15 Oct. 1773*, unm.

Lois HAYWARD^{7}, b. aft. 1751* (minor in 1765) and pre 1758*; (m. Moses Simmons*)

Sarah HAYWARD^{7}, b. aft. 1751* (minor in 1765) and pre 1758*; (m.Plato Turner*)

Mary DUNHAM, b. pre 1740, d. pre Aug. 1768 (hus. remarried)

CHILDREN OF Josiah HAYWARD^{6} & 2nd Mary DUNHAM: (2)

Hepzibah HAYWARD^{7}, b. ( )

Molly HAYWARD^{7}, b. ( )

Dinah MUXHAM, (dau of Edmund), b. 15 Jan. 1746/7; d. 3 or 4 Dec. 1822 <Bridgewater VR 2:484>

CHILDREN OF Josiah HAYWARD[6] & 3rd Dinah MUXHAM: (3 of 7)**<79>**

Phineas HAYWARD[7], b. c1770, d. 15 June 1848, 78th yr, Otto g.s., Cattaraugus Co., NY

Cyrus HAYWARD[7], b. pre Dec. 1779; d. aft. 5 Dec. 1804* <Plymouth Co.Deeds 100:97>

Kinsley HAYWARD[7], b. ( )

CHILD OF Kinsley HAYWARD[7] & Hannah POOL:

Hannah Kinsley HAYWARD[8], b. 12 Mar. 1807 <Halifax VR:88>

Cyrus HAYWARD, son of Ezra & Lydia, b. 19 Sept. 1772 <Bridgewater VR 1:145>

Cyrus HAYWARD/HOWARD, b. 25 Oct. 1776 <Bridgewater VR 1:167> (m. Deborah Ripley)

CHILD OF Cyrus HAYWARD/HOWARD & Deborah RIPLEY:

Cyrus HOWARD, b. 20 Mar. 1807 <Bridgewater VR 1:167>

John HAYWARD, b. c1771, d. 24 Nov. 1836, ae 65 <Middleboro VR 14:9>

Robert EDSON[3] (Ezra[2], Sam.[1]), b. 24 July 1757 <Bridgewater VR 1:106> (m. Molly Hayward[7], Josiah[6])

Mehitabel GREEN, b. c1778, d. 9 May 1817, 39th yr, Old Cem., Sodus NY

CHILDREN OF Phineas HAYWARD[7] (Josiah[6]) & Mehitabel (GREEN*): (5) <1-4, Windsor VR:36>

Josiah HAYWARD[8*], bpt. 4 Jan. 1801*

Otis HAYWARD[8*], bpt. 4 Jan. 1801*

Joseph HAYWARD[8*], bpt. 13 Sept. 1801*

Mehitable HAYWARD[8], bpt. 2 Oct. 1803*

Child, d. 1817

Susanna LATHAM[6] (*Charles[5], Chilton[4], Susanna Winslow[3], Mary Chilton[2]), b. 11 Oct. 1720* <Bridgewater VR 3:348>; d. 23 Nov. 1811*, Bridgewater g.s.

CHILDREN OF Nathan HAYWARD[6] (Sarah Kinsley[5]) & Susanna LATHAM*: (8*)

Adam HAYWARD[7], b. 11 Oct. 1749, d. 7 May 1750

Beza HAYWARD[7], b. 20 Jan. 1751/2

Cephas HAYWARD[7], b. 20 Aug. 1754, d. 1 Mar. 1756

Susanna HAYWARD[7], b. 20 Jan. 1757

Sarah HAYWARD[7], b. 24 Oct. 1759, d. 27 Aug. 1760

Eunice HAYWARD[7], b. 25 Oct. 1761, d. 23 Sept. 1762

Nathan HAYWARD[7], b. 17 Sept. 1762

Betsy HAYWARD[7], b. 6 Sept. 1767, d. 25 Sept. 1775

CHILDREN OF Silas WILLIS, (*son of Joshua) & Sarah HAYWARD[6] (Sarah Kinsley[5]):(8*)<Bridgewater VR>

Sarah WILLIS[7], b. 13 July 1746

Silas WILLIS[7], b. 28 July 1748

Adam WILLIS[7], b. 25 Dec. 1750

Edmund WILLIS[7], b. 24 June 1753

Olive WILLIS[7], b. 10 Feb. 1756

Hannah WILLIS[7], b. 8 Sept. 1758

Betty WILLIS[7], b. 1761

Abraham WILLIS[7], b. 1764

Samuel PACKARD, d.? 21 Sept. 1774*

CHILDREN OF Samuel PACKARD & Susanna KINSLEY[5] (Mary Washburn[4]): (7*)

Child, b. 16 July 1730, d. 14 Sept. 1730

Samuel PACKARD[6], b. 29 Sept. 1731, d. 8 Mar. 1732

Charity PACKARD[6], b. 25 Feb. 1732/3

Samuel PACKARD[6], b. 21 Dec. 1734

Susanna PACKARD[6], b. 2(4) Aug. 1736

Jedediah PACKARD[6], b. 1 Oct. 1738

Abijah PACKARD[6], b. 25 May 1740

MICRO #14 of 30

Deborah PACKARD, (dau of Sam.), d. aft. 13 Mar. 1720 (hus. will) <MD 16:49>

CHILDREN OF Samuel WASHBURN^4 (Eliz. Mitchell^3) & Deborah PACKARD: (6) <Bridgewater>

Samuel WASHBURN^5, b. 6 Apr. 1678 <MD 2:145>

Noah WASHBURN^5, b. 11 July 1682 <MD 2:145>; d. 17 Oct. 1716, Bridgewater <MD 15:48>

Israel WASHBURN^5, b. 24 Feb. 1683 <MD 2:145>; d. pre 13 Mar. 1720 (father's will) <MD 16:49>

Nehemiah WASHBURN^5, b. 20 May 1686 <MD 2:146>; d. 17 Dec. 1748* <W.Bridgewater VR:219>

Benjamin WASHBURN^5, b. pre Sept. 1697*; d. aft. 16 Jan. 1770 <Plymouth Co.Deeds 55:85>

Hannah WASHBURN^5, b. c1689, d. 4 Mar. 1766*, 77th yr, Old Cem. <Bridgewater Epitaphs:91>

Bethiah KINGMAN, (dau of Henry), b. 6 June 1693, Bridgewater <MD 15:47>; d. aft. 16 Jan. 1770

CHILDREN OF Benjamin WASHBURN^5 & Bethiah KINGMAN: (2*)

Benjamin WASHBURN^6, b. Dec. 1718, d. 3 Aug. 1812, Bridgewater g.s. <PN&Q 2:76>

Henry WASHBURN^6, b. ( )

Susanna BATTLES, (*dau of Edw. & Experience), b. 2 June 1723*, Hingham; d. 26 Jan. 1744, Bridgewater g.s. <VR 2:575> (1st wf of Ben. Washburn^6)

Mary CUSHMAN^5 (Moses^4, Eleazer^3, Mary Allerton^2), b. 4 Oct. 1725, Plympton <MD 5:209>; d. 28 Nov. 1808, Bridgewater g.s. <PN&Q 2:76>

CHILDREN OF Benjamin WASHBURN^6 & Mary CUSHMAN: (8) <PN&Q 2:76>

Susanna WASHBURN^7, b. 29 May 1749

Mary WASHBURN^7, b. 17 June 1751, d. 2 Oct. 1804

Eunice WASHBURN^7, b. 5 Sept. 1753

Asa WASHBURN^7, b. 9 Oct. 1756

Joshua WASHBURN^7, b. 24 Sept. 1759, d. 14 May 1832 <Bible Rcd.>

Benjamin WASHBURN^7, b. 14 Jan. 1763, d. 5 Apr. 1798 <2:77>

Olive WASHBURN^7, b. 26 May 1765 <2:77>

Keziah WASHBURN^7, b. 16 Oct. 1769 <2:77>

Lovice (RECORDS*), b. 16 Feb. 1763, d. 10 Dec. 1831 <Bible Rcd.>

CHILDREN OF Joshua WASHBURN^7 & Lovice (RECORDS*): (7) <PN&Q 2:77>

Susanna WASHBURN^8, b. 14 Dec. 1787, d. 5 Nov. 1874

Marsena WASHBURN^8, b. 8 Dec. 1789, d. 13 Apr. 1876

Joshua WASHBURN^8, b. 10 Dec. 1791, d. 26 Feb. 1865

Benjamin WASHBURN^8, b. 30 Apr. 1796, d. 12 Nov. 1867

Isaac WASHBURN^8, b. 13 July 1799, d. 24 Sept. 1838

Eunice WASHBURN^8, b. 4 Nov. 1801, d. 2 July 1856

Charles WASHBURN^8, b. 7 Mar. 1807

Lucy GIFFORD, (dau of Elihu), b. 28 Sept. 1803, d. 30 Sept. 1853

CHILDREN OF Marsena WASHBURN^8 & Lucy GIFFORD: (5)

Caroline E. WASHBURN^9, b. 7 Oct. 1824, d. 7 Oct. 1908

Mary Gifford WASHBURN^9, b. 24 Oct. 1826, d. 19 July 1906, unm.

Lucy Merritt WASHBURN^9, b. 12 Oct. 1830, d. 27 June 1903, unm.

Frederick Augustus WASHBURN^9, b. 5 Jan. 1834, d. 23 Jan. 1908

Annie M. WASHBURN^9, b. 23 Apr. 1838

John KEITH, b. c1688, d. 11 June 1761*, Old Cem. <Bridgewater Epitaphs:91>

CHILDREN OF John KEITH & Hannah WASHBURN^5 (Sam.^{4}): (8) <Bridgewater VR, MD 15:45>

John KEITH^6, b. 1 Aug. 1712

James KEITH^6, b. 16 June 1716

Israel KEITH^6, b. 9 Jan. 1719

Hannah KEITH^6, b. 7 Apr. 1721

Keziah KEITH^6, b. 25 Aug. 1723

Daniel KEITH^6, b. 2 May 1725

Susanna KEITH^{6}, b. 27 May 1727; d. 5 Apr. 1750* (wf of Eben. Hinds) <Bridgewater Epitaphs:86>

Zephaniah KEITH^{6}, b. 8 Mar. 1730

Polly PRATT^{8} (Polly Keith^{7}, Dan.^{6}), d. 28 Sept. 1874, ae 88, Middleboro, widow of William Pratt <Bridgewater VR:50>

Waitstill SUMNER, d. pre 6 Mar. 1729/30* <Plymouth Co.Prob.#21999, 5:758>(wf of 2nd hus Ebenezer Pratt)

CHILDREN OF Israel WASHBURN^{5} (Sam.^{4}) & Waitstill SUMNER: (5) <Bridgewater VR, MD 14:206>

Sarah WASHBURN^{6}, b. 14 Aug. 1709; d. aft. 5 June 1729 (father's estate)<Plymouth Co.PR #21999>

Son, b. 6 Jan. 1710/11, d. 22 Jan. 1710/11

Deborah WASHBURN^{6}, b. 1 June 1712; d. aft. 5 June 1729 (" ")

Seth WASHBURN^{6}, b. 11 July 1714; d. pre 5 June 1729 (" ")

Israel WASHBURN^{6}, b. aft. 1718 (minor under 14 in 1722), d. aft. 5 June 1729 <" " & #21200>

Jane HAWARD, (*dau of Ephraim), d. 26 Jan. 1715, Bridgewater <MD 5:249>

CHILDREN OF Nehemiah WASHBURN^{5} (Sam.^{4}) & Jane HAWARD: (2) <Bridgewater VR, MD 5:248>

Silence WASHBURN^{6}, b. 26 July 1713

Jane WASHBURN^{6}, b. 6 Jan. 1715

Zenas WASHBURN, (*son of Eleazer), b. 18 Dec. 1774*, Bridgewater <Plympton VR:218>; d. 18 Feb. 1824* <E. Bridgewater:397> (m. Sarah Shurtliff)

CHILDREN OF Noah WASHBURN^{5} (Sam.^{4}) & Elizabeth SHAW: (3) <Bridgewater VR, MD 15:48>

Hannah WASHBURN^{6}, b. 13 July 1711

Eliezer WASHBURN^{6}, b. 8 Feb. 1713; d. 24 Feb. 1762* <Bridgewater Epitaphs:218>

Noah WASHBURN^{6}, b. 18 July 1716

Zachariah WHITMARSH^{4} (*Ezra^{3}, John$^{2-1}$), b. 1 Apr. 1707* <Weymouth VR 1:352>; d. 6 Feb. 1797* <Weymouth VR 2:373>

CHILDREN OF Zachariah WHITMARSH & Hannah WASHBURN^{6}: (9) <Weymouth VR>

Lucy WHITMARSH^{7}, b. 8 Sept. 1731* <VR 1:351>

Silvanus WHITMARSH^{7}, b. 16 June 1734* <VR 1:352>

Huldah WHITMARSH^{7}, b. 19 May 1736* <VR 1:350>

Ezra WHITMARSH^{7}, b. 28 Aug. 1740* <VR 1:350>

Hannah WHITMARSH^{7}, b. 4 Jan. 1741/2* <VR 1:350>

Zachariah WHITMARSH^{7}, b. 11 Sept. 1744* <VR 1:352>

John WHITMARSH^{7}, b. 1 Jan. 1746/7*, d. 5 Oct. 1751* <VR 1:351, 2:372>

Child, b. 5 July 1749*

Anna WHITMARSH^{7}*, bpt. 6 Apr. 1755*

Anna ALDEN^{5} (Eben.^{4}, Isaac^{3}, Jos.^{2}), b. 19 Feb. 1717/18, Bridgewater <MD 15:85>; d. 13 Feb. 1788* <Bridgewater Epitaphs:218>

CHILDREN OF Eliezer WASHBURN^{6} (Noah^{5}) & Anna ALDEN: (8)**<80>**

Huldah WOOD, d. c1770* <Southworth Gen.:92>

CHILDREN OF Eleazer WASHBURN^{7} (Eliezer^{6}) & 1st Huldah WOOD*:

Eleazer WASHBURN^{8}, b. ( )

Sarah SOUTHWORTH^{7} (*Eben.^{6}, Edw.^{5}, Desire Gray^{4}, Mary Winslow^{3}, Susanna Chilton^{2}), b. 2 Oct. 1747 Middleboro <Southworth Gen.:92>

CHILDREN OF Eleazer WASHBURN^{7} (Eliezer^{6}) & 2nd Sarah SOUTHWORTH: (4 of 8*)**<81>**

Sally WASHBURN^{8}, b. 1780

Sampson WASHBURN^{8}, bpt. 30 Mar. 1783* <E. Bridgewater ChR>

Bethiah WASHBURN^{8}, b. 1788*

Josiah WASHBURN^{8}, b. 1788*; d. 1834*, unm.

Rebecca SOULE^{6} (John^{5}, James^{4}, John$^{3-2}$), b. 15 Feb. 1784; bur. E. Bridgewater, (7 Pleasant St.) (wf of Sampson Washburn^{8})

Abigail LEONARD, (dau of Jacob), b. 11 Nov. 1680*, Weymouth

CHILDREN OF Samuel WASHBURN^{5} (Sam.^{4}) & Abigail LEONARD: (7) <Bridgewater VR, MD 14:204>
David WASHBURN^{6}, b. 30 Apr. 1704
Deliverance WASHBURN^{6}, b. 7 Oct. 1706
Solomon WASHBURN^{6}, b. 1 Oct. 1708
Samuel WASHBURN^{6}, b. 2 June 1710
Abigail WASHBURN^{6}, b. 3 Mar. 1712
Susanna WASHBURN^{6}, b. 13 Mar. 1714
Tabitha WASHBURN^{6}, b. 28 Aug. 1716
CHILDREN OF Solomon WASHBURN^{6} & Martha ORCUT: (4) <Bridgewater VR, MD 15:91>
Lydia WASHBURN^{7}, b. 17 Dec. 1732
Solomon WASHBURN^{7}, b. 1 Sept. 1734
Tabitha WASHBURN^{7}, b. 1 June 1736
Martha WASHBURN^{7}, b. 27 May 1738
John AMES, (son of John), b. 14 Apr. 1672, Bridgewater <MD 2:241>; d. 1756, Bridgewater <MD 6:8>
CHILDREN OF John AMES & Sarah WASHBURN^{4} (Eliz. Mitchell^{3}): (9) <Bridgewater VR, MD 6:8>
Elizabeth AMES^{5}, b. 9 Dec. 1697
John AMES^{5}, b. 19 Mar. 1700
Sarah AMES^{5}, b. 23 Jan. 1702; d. 20 July 1770*, Ashland Cem. <Brockton VR:352>
Abigail AMES^{5}, b. 9 Feb. 1705
Jonathan AMES^{5}, b. 10 June 1707
Deborah AMES^{5}, b. 1 Apr. 1710
Daniel AMES^{5}, b. 7 Oct. 1712
Benjamin AMES^{5}, b. 24 Feb. 1714/5
Joshua AMES^{5}, b. 9 Apr. 1718
Abiel PACKARD, (son of Zaccheus & Sarah), b. 29 Apr. 1699, Bridgewater<MD 14:206>; d. 1 June 1774*, Ashland Cem. <Brockton VR:346>
CHILDREN OF Abiel PACKARD & Sarah AMES^{5}: (10) <Bridgewater VR, MD 14:48>
Josiah PACKARD^{6}, b. 2 Oct. 1723
Abiel PACKARD^{6}, b. 19 Mar. 1728, d. 18 Jan. 1759
Joshua PACKARD^{6}, b. 26 July 1730
Thomas PACKARD^{6}, b. 21 Sept. 1732
Timothy PACKARD^{6}, b. 12 Apr. 1735
Sarah PACKARD^{6}, b. 30 Sept. 1737
Bettie PACKARD^{6}, b. 6 Oct. 1739
Daniel PACKARD^{6}, b. 9 May 1742
Eliab PACKARD^{6}, b. 28 July 1745
Benjamin PACKARD^{6}, b. 11 Nov. 1749
Deliverance (ORCUTT) Washburn, (dau of Wm.), b. c1707, d. 5 Dec. 1790*, ae 83, Old Cem., Bridgewater (2nd wf of Abiel Packard)
CHILDREN OF Thomas PACKARD & Mary HOWARD: (8) <Bridgewater>
Parmenas PACKARD, b. 26 Nov. 1757
Silines PACKARD, b. 11 Feb. 1760
Mary PACKARD, b. 8 May 1762
Thomas PACKARD, b. 20 Aug. 1764
Zeba PACKARD, b. 6 Mar. 1766
Elijah PACKARD, b. 21 Nov. 1769
Cyrus PACKARD, b. 18 Jan. 1772
Daniel PACKARD, b. 22 Oct. 1776
CHILDREN OF Thomas WASHBURN^{4} (Eliz. Mitchell^{3}) & Deliverance PACKARD, (dau of Sam.): (7)<82>
CHILDREN OF Ephraim JENNINGS & Deliverance WASHBURN^{5} (Tho.^{4}): (3) <Bridgewater VR, MD 5:248>

Mary JENNINGS^{6}, b. 1 Jan. 1719/20
Ephraim JENNINGS^{6}, b. 27 Sept. 1722
Sarah JENNINGS^{6}, b. 28 Sept. 1728
CHILD OF Josiah CONANT & Elizabeth WASHBURN^{5} (Tho.^{4}):
Prudence CONANT^{6}, b. 3 Mar. 1707, Middleboro <MD 4:68>; d. 4 Jan. 1766* <Plymouth ChR 1:395>
Thomas WESTON, d. pre 19 May 1743 (adm.) <Plymouth Co.PR #22448, 9:74>
CHILDREN OF Thomas WESTON & Prudence CONANT^{6}: (3*)
Thomas WESTON^{7}, b. ( ); d. pre 16 Oct. 1765
Mary WESTON^{7}, b. c1736, d. 28 July 1805, 69th yr (wf of "Wm. Weston^{5}")
Sarah WESTON^{7}, b. ( )
CHILDREN OF Thomas WASHBURN^{5} (Tho.^{4}) & Elizabeth HOWLAND^{4}* (*?James^{3}, Jos.^{2}): (2) <MD 15:88>
Mary WASHBURN^{6}, b. 25 May 1722, Bridgewater
Bettie WASHBURN^{6}, b. 22 Mar. 1723/4, Bridgewater
CHILDREN OF Thomas WASHBURN & Elizabeth ( ): (2) <N. Yarmouth Old Times:491>
Thomas WASHBURN, bpt. 29 Aug. 1731
Timothy WASHBURN, bpt. 29 Aug. 1731
CHILDREN OF Timothy WASHBURN^{5} (Tho.^{4}) & Hannah ( ): (3) <Bridgewater VR, MD 15:90>
Timothy WASHBURN^{6}, b. 26 Oct. 1721
Hannah WASHBURN^{6}, b. 28 Feb. 1723/4
Mary WASHBURN^{6}, b. 15 Oct. 1725
Joseph HAYWARD, d. 20 June 1718, Bridgewater <Plymouth Co.PR 4:136>
CHILD OF Joseph HAYWARD & 1st Alice (BRETT*), (*dau of Wm.):
Joseph HAYWARD, b. 15 Dec. 1673 <MD 5:248>

(**NOTE:** Line of descent for the following Hannah Mitchell^{2} line has been changed to show descent from Experience Mitchell^{1}, not Jane Cooke^{2}. This is not a Cooke Mayflower line. See <48>)

CHILDREN OF Joseph HAYWARD & 2nd Hannah MITCHELL^{2} (Experience^{1}): (8) <Bridgewater VR, MD 5:248>
Alice HAYWARD, b. 20 Mar. 1682/3; d. 30 Jan. 1715/6, Bridgewater <MD 15:47>
Mary HAYWARD, b. 18 Mar. 1684/5
Thomas HAYWARD, b. 6 Mar. 1686/7; d. pre 4 Nov. 1754 (adm.) <Plymouth Co.PR #9866, 13:360>
Edward HAYWARD, b. 24 July 1689
Hannah HAYWARD, b. 25 Sept. 1691
Susanna HAYWARD, b. 17 May 1695
Peter HAYWARD, b. 10 Nov. 1699
Abigail HAYWARD, b. 3 Aug. 1702; d. 30 Apr. 1796*, Brockton g.s. (m. Zachariah Snell)
MICRO #15 of 30
Zachariah SNELL, b. c1704, d. 6 May 1768*, Brockton g.s. (hus of Abigail Hayward^{3})
Israel ALGER, d. 13 Nov. 1762, Bridgewater <MD 15:47>
CHILDREN OF Israel ALGER & Alice HAYWARD^{3} (Hannah Mitchell^{2}): (2) <Bridgewater VR, MD 15:47>
Patience/Alice ALGER, b. 20 Sept. 1713 (name changed to Alice)
Son, b. 26 Jan. 1715/6, d. 16 Feb. 1715/6
CHILDREN OF Thomas AMES & Mary HAYWARD^{3} (Hannah Mitchell^{2}): (9) <Bridgewater VR, MD 3:143>
Thomas AMES, b. 6 Feb. 1706/7
Solomon AMES, b. 16 Jan. 1708/9
Joseph AMES, b. 6 May 1711; d. 14 May 1790 <Bridgewater VR 2:431>
Ebenezer AMES, b. 15 Apr. 1715
Mary AMES, b. 20 June 1717
Susanna AMES, b. 4 May 1720
Nathan AMES, b. 4 July 1722

Sarah AMES, b. 31 Dec. 1724

Bettie AMES, b. 15 Dec. 1727

Susanna LITTLEFIELD, d. 1 June 1753 <Bridgewater VR 2:432>

CHILDREN OF Joseph AMES[4] (Mary Hayward[3]) & 1st Susanna LITTLEFIELD: (8) <Bridgewater VR>

Phebe AMES, b. 8 Mar. 1736/7 <VR 1:34>

Ebenezer AMES, b. 15 Mar. 1738/9 <VR 1:32>

Nathaniel AMES, b. 10 Feb. 1740/1 <VR 1:34>

Elijah AMES, b. 7 Jan. 1742/3 <VR 1:32>

Susanna AMES, b. 8 Dec. 1744 <VR 1:36>

Joseph AMES, b. 24 May 1747 <VR 1:33>

Bethia AMES, b. 1 July 1749 <VR 1:31>

William AMES, b. 1 June 1751 <VR 1:36>

Ruth PACKARD, d. 30 Apr. 1768 <Bridgewater VR 2:431>

CHILD OF Joseph AMES[4] & 2nd Ruth PACKARD: <Bridgewater VR 1:36>

Zephania AMES, b. ( )

Abihail LATHROP, (dau of Sam.), d. 1 Sept. 1803 <Bridgewater VR 2:430>**<83>**

CHILDREN OF Joseph AMES[4] & 3rd Abihail LATHROP: (3) <Bridgewater VR>

Olive AMES, b. 22 July 1769 <VR 1:34>

James AMES, b. 5 Apr. 1771 <VR 1:33>

Fisk AMES, b. 15 Mar. 1773 <VR 1:32>

CHILDREN OF David GLAZIER & Cylinda MARCY: (2) <Willington CT VR>**<84>**

Carlos GLAZIER, b. 25 Oct. 1811

Caroline GLAZIER, b. 25 Oct. 1811 (twins), d. 19 Mar. 1868, Willington CT, consumption,<VR>

CHILD OF Charles AMES & Caroline GLAZIER, (dau of David):

Caroline AMES, b. c1846, d. 8 June 1921, ae about 75, Stonington CT (wf of David Miller)

Son, b. 13 July 1849 <Mansfield TR>

CHILD OF Thomas AMES[4] (Mary Hayward[3]) & Keziah HOWARD*:

John AMES, b. 1738, d. 17 July 1805, N. Easton MA g.s.

Susannah ( ) AMES, b. 1735, Bridgewater, d. 11 Jan. 1821, widow of John, N. Easton MA g.s.

CHILDREN OF Thomas HAYWARD[3] (Hannah Mitchell[2]) & Bethiah WALDO: (6) <Bridgewater VR 2:125>

Edmund HAYWARD, b. 12 May 1720; d. c1781* <MD 15:89>

Jane HAYWARD, b. 12 May 1720 (twins) <MD 15:89>

Elijah HAYWARD, b. 10 Feb. 1721/2; d. 1800* <MD 15:89>

Hannah HAYWARD, b. 5 Dec. 1723 <MD 15:90>

Bethiah HAYWARD, b. 14 Sept. 1724 <MD 15:90>

Rebecca HAYWARD, b. 24 Aug. 1727 <MD 15:90>

Anna SNELL, (*dau of Josiah), b. 19 Mar. 1732*, d. 14 May 1776* <Bridgewater VR 1:294,2:483>

CHILDREN OF Edmund HAYWARD[4] (Tho.[3]) & Anna SNELL*: (7*)

Mary HAYWARD, b. 1753

Isaiah HAYWARD, b. 1755

Waldo HAYWARD, b. 27 Mar. 1758

Edmund HAYWARD, b. 1762

Elijah HAYWARD, b. 1763

Anna HAYWARD, b. 1766

Hannah HAYWARD, b. 1770

CHILDREN OF Waldo HAYWARD[5] (Edmund[4]) & Lucy BARTLETT: (7) <Bridgewater VR>

Ira HAYWARD, b. 18 Sept. 1782 <VR 1:148>

Abbie HAYWARD, b. 16 Feb. 1786 <VR 1:142>

Bela HAYWARD, b. 16 Nov. 1787 <VR 1:144>

Zina HAYWARD, b. 3 May 1789 <VR 1:155>

Waldo HAYWARD, b. 24 Aug. 1794 <VR 1:155>
Otho HAYWARD, b. 3 Apr. 1796 <VR 1:153>
Lucinda HAYWARD, b. 22 Nov. 1800 <VR 1:150>
CHILDREN OF Ira HAYWARD & Sarah EDSON: (5) <Bridgewater VR>
Otis HAYWARD, b. 9 Dec. 1806 <VR 1:153>
Ambrose HAYWARD, b. 6 Jan. 1810 <VR 1:143>
Sumner Augustus HAYWARD, b. 20 July 1812 <VR 1:154>
Julia HAYWARD, b. 4 Oct. 1814 <VR 1:149>
Sarah Reliance HAYWARD, b. 8 Mar. 1818 <VR 1:154>
CHILDREN OF Samuel BARTLETT & Susanna DUNBAR: (9) <Bridgewater VR 1:41>
Susanna BARTLETT, b. 1 June 1758
Sarah BARTLETT, b. 7 Mar. 1760
Lucy BARTLETT, b. 28 Mar. 1762
Job Packard BARTLETT, b. 22 Jan. 1764; d. 19 Dec. 1774 <VR 2:434>
Samuel BARTLETT, b. 27 Dec. 1766
Hannah BARTLETT, b. 6 May 1769
Rachel BARTLETT, b. 8 June 1772
Keziah BARTLETT, b. 4 Aug. 1775
David BARTLETT, b. 28 Jan. 1778

(**NOTE:** Line of descent for the following Jacob Mitchell^{2} line has been changed to show descent from Experience Mitchell^{1} not Jane Cooke^{2}. This is not a Cooke Mayflower line. See <48>.

CHILDREN OF Jacob MITCHELL^{2} & Susanna POPE, (dau of Tho.): (3)
Thomas MITCHELL, b. c1658, d. 1 Sept. 1727, ae 69, Bridgewater g.s. <MD 14:47>
Jacob MITCHELL, b. c1671, d. 21 Dec. 1744, 73rd yr, N. Yarmouth ME g.s. <MD 18:130>
Mary MITCHELL, b. ( ); d. aft. 1710 (birth last child)
Deliverance KINGMAN, (dau of John), b. 12 Mar. 1676* <Weymouth VR 1:161>; d. pre Nov. 1701
CHILD OF Jacob MITCHELL^{3} (Jacob^{2}) & 1st Deliverance KINGMAN:
Jacob MITCHELL, b. 28 Dec. 1696 <Bridgewater VR, MD 14:48>
Rebecca CUSHMAN^{4} (Isaac^{3}, Mary Allerton^{2}), b. 30 Nov. 1678, Plymouth <MD 1:210>; d. 8 July 1756, N. Yarmouth ME**<85>**
CHILDREN OF Jacob MITCHELL^{3} & 2nd Rebecca CUSHMAN: (9) <Bridgewater VR, MD 2:224>
Susanna MITCHELL, b. 15 Jan. 1702/3
Rebecca MITCHELL, b. 19 Oct. 1704
Seth MITCHELL, b. 16 Mar. 1705/6
Mary MITCHELL, b. 7 Mar. 1707/8
Lydia MITCHELL, b. 20 June 1710
Noah MITCHELL, b. 16 Sept. 1712
Isaac MITCHELL, b. 20 Jan. 1714/5
Sarah MITCHELL, b. 29 Apr. 1717
Elizabeth MITCHELL, b. 27 Apr. 1722
Mary (HOWLAND*), b. c1704, d. 29 Jan. 1725/6, 22nd yr, Pembroke g.s. <MD 10:158>
CHILDREN OF Jacob MITCHELL^{4} (Jacob^{3}) & 1st Mary (HOWLAND*): (2*)
Mary MITCHELL, b. 29 July 1723 <Pembroke VR:153>
Jonathan MITCHELL, b. ( ) <Small Gen.:413>
CHILDREN OF Jacob MITCHELL^{4} & 2nd Rachel (LEWIS*) Cushing*: (4) <Pembroke VR:153>
Rachel MITCHELL, b. 10 Dec. 1730, d.y.
Jacob MITCHELL, b. 30 Sept. 1732
Rachel MITCHELL, b. 10 Dec. 1732

Sarah MITCHELL, b. 18 Aug. 1736

Samuel KINGMAN, (*son of John & Eliz.), b. 28 May 1670* <Weymouth VR 1:163>; d. betw. 3 June 1740 (will) - 12 May 1742 (inv.) <MD 31:27>

CHILDREN OF Samuel KINGMAN & Mary MITCHELL[3] (Jacob[2]): (6) <Bridgewater VR, MD 14:46>

Susanna KINGMAN, b. 12 Apr. 1697; d. aft. 3 June 1740 (father's will)

John KINGMAN, b. 4 June 1699

Joanna KINGMAN, b. 7 May 1701; d. pre 3 June 1740 (father's will)

Jane KINGMAN, b. 3 July 1704

Mary KINGMAN, b. 16 Apr. 1706

Samuel KINGMAN, b. 13 May 1710

CHILDREN OF Isaac KINGMAN & Jane KINGMAN[4] (Mary Mitchell[3]): (5) <Bridgewater VR, MD 15:173>

Abigail KINGMAN, b. 9 May 1730

Lemuel KINGMAN, b. 30 Nov. 1732

Jane KINGMAN, b. 20 Oct. 1736

Bethia KINGMAN, b. 16 May 1743

Isaac KINGMAN, b. 11 Oct. 1747

CHILDREN OF Akerman PETTINGALE & Joanna KINGMAN[4] (Mary Mitchell[3]): (4)

Daniel PETTINGALE, b. 10 Oct. 1726*

Nathan PETTINGALE, b. 1732*

Jacob PETTINGALE, b. 1734*

Hannah PETTINGALE, b. ( )

CHILDREN OF Benjamin VICKERY & Mary KINGMAN[4] (Mary Mitchell[3]): (6*) <Bridgewater VR 1:321>

Mary VICKERY, b. 17 Oct. 1740

Elizabeth VICKERY, b. 25 July 1743

Eliab VICKERY, b. 20 Oct. 1745

Benjamin VICKERY, b. 31 Dec. 1749

Olive VICKERY, b. 9 Aug. 1753

Huldah VICKERY, b. 28 Sept. 1759

CHILD OF Benjamin VICKERY Jr. & Rhoda HOLBROOK:

Amasa VICKERY, b. 1 Sept. 1777 <Mendon VR:198>

Solomon PACKARD, (son of Zaccheus), b. 20 Mar. 1689, Bridgewater <MD 14:206>; d. aft. 3 June 1740

CHILDREN OF Solomon PACKARD & Susanna KINGMAN[4] (Mary Mitchell[3]): (11) <Bridgewater VR, MD 15:168>

Sarah PACKARD, b. 23 May 1719

Jacob PACKARD, b. 2 Sept. 1720

Nathan PACKARD, b. Mar. 1722/3, d.y.

Susanna PACKARD, b. 11 Mar. 1724

Joanna PACKARD, b. 24 Nov. 1725

Martha PACKARD, b. 27 Nov. 1727

Solomon PACKARD, b. 17 Oct. 1729

Nathan PACKARD, b. 19 Feb. 1732/3

Benjamin PACKARD, b. 20 Oct. 1734

Zebulon PACKARD, b. 5 Aug. 1736

Micah PACKARD, b. 13 Aug. 1738

CHILD OF Levi CHURCHILL & Cynthia PACKARD[6] (Solomon[5], Susanna Kingman[4]):

Asaba CHURCHILL, b. c1800, E. Bridgewater, d. 2 Apr. 1875, ae 74y7m24d, paralysis, E. Bridgewater <Mass.VR 275:304> (wf of Lewis Keith)

Elizabeth KINGMAN, (*dau of John), b. 9 July 1673*, Weymouth; d. 1733*

CHILDREN OF Thomas MITCHELL[3] (Jacob[2]) & Elizabeth KINGMAN: (8) <Bridgewater VR, MD 14:47>

Thomas MITCHELL, b. 22 Sept. 1696

Henry MITCHELL, b. 25 Aug. 1698; bur. 6 Apr. 1712

Timothy MITCHELL, b. 7 Dec. 1700, d. 30 Sept. 1733
Susanna MITCHELL, b. 10 Feb. 1703
Edward MITCHELL, b. July 1705
Elizabeth MITCHELL, b. 12 May 1710
Mary MITCHELL, b. 11 May 1713
Seth MITCHELL, b. 2 Oct. 1715; d. 1802*

CHILDREN OF Seth MITCHELL[4] (Tho.[3]) & 1st Ann LATHAM[6] (*Tho.[5], James[4], Susanna Winslow[3], Mary Chilton[2]): (11*)

Jacob MITCHELL, b. 1740
Reuben MITCHELL, b. 1741, d. pre 1757
Seth MITCHELL, b. 1744
Zenas MITCHELL, b. 1746
Phineas MITCHELL, b. 1747
Eliphaz MITCHELL, b. 1749; d. 1820, unm.
Timothy MITCHELL, b. 1751
Rotheus MITCHELL, b. 1753
Ann MITCHELL, b. 1755
Reuben MITCHELL, b. 1757
Betty MITCHELL, b. 1759; unm.
Mary WADE, (*dau of Nicholas), b. c1726, d. 1809*, ae 83

CHILDREN OF Seth MITCHELL[4] & 2nd Mary WADE: (4*)

Molly MITCHELL, b. 1761; unm.
Nabby MITCHELL, b. 1762
Susanna MITCHELL, b. 1766

CHILDREN OF Rotheus MITCHELL[5] (Seth Mitchell[4]) & Hephzibah HAYWARD[7] (Josiah[6], Sarah Kinsley[5], Mary Washburn[4], Eliz. Mitchell[3], Jane Cooke[2]): (4) <Mitchell:244>

Cynthia MITCHELL, b. 1784
Eliphalet MITCHELL, b. 1785
Horatio MITCHELL, b. 1787
Betsy MITCHELL, b. 1791

CHILDREN OF Thomas MITCHELL[5] (Tim.[4], Tho.[3]) & Keziah SWIFT[6] (Wm.[5], Abigail Gibbs[4], Alice Warren[3], Nath.[2]): (7) <Bridgewater VR 3:219>

Timothy MITCHELL, b. 31 Aug. 1758
William MITCHELL, b. 16 Aug. 1760
Lusanna MITCHELL, b. 29 Aug. 1762
Thomas MITCHELL, b. 13 June 1765
Calvin MITCHELL, b. 3 Aug. 1767
Luther MITCHELL, b. 13 Sept. 1769, d. 9 Mar. 1771
Zilpha MITCHELL, b. 6 Aug. 1772

(**NOTE:** Line of descent for the following John Mitchell[2] line has been changed to show descent from Experience Mitchell[1] not Jane Cooke[2]. This is not a Cooke Mayflower line. See <48>.

CHILD OF John MITCHELL[2] & 1st Mary BONNEY:

Experience MITCHELL, b. 2 Jan. 1676 <MD 4:151>

CHILDREN OF John MITCHELL[2] & <u>3rd</u> Mary PRIOR: (8) <MD 9:229>

Mary MITCHELL, b. 28 Feb. 1682 <MD 9:174>
Hannah MITCHELL, b. 13 Feb. 1683
Joseph MITCHELL, b. 13 Mar. 1683/4; d. 24 Nov. 1754 <Kingston VR>
Elizabeth MITCHELL, b. 25 Mar. 1684/5, d.y.

Elizabeth MITCHELL, b. 29 Mar. 1686 <MD 9:175>

John MITCHELL, b. 13 Jan. 1688/9

Sarah MITCHELL, b. 9 May 1690

Esther MITCHELL, b. 22 Jan. 1691/2 <MD 9:230>

CHILDREN OF Joseph MITCHELL[3] (John[2]) & Bathshua LUMBERT: (13) <1-12, Plymouth VR, MD 7:178>

Sarah MITCHELL, b. 16 Aug. 1711; d. June 1712 <Gen.Adv.2:1>

Hannah MITCHELL, b. 14 Feb. 1712/3

Joseph MITCHELL, b. 28 Oct. 1714, d. 16 July 1715

John MITCHELL, b. 18 June 1716; d. 5 July 1732 <Gen.Adv.2:122>

Mary MITCHELL, b. 2 Feb. 1717/18; d. 3 Oct. 1743 <Gen.Adv.2:122>

Sarah MITCHELL, b. 14 Oct. 1719

Bathsheba MITCHELL, b. 10 Aug. 1721

Alice MITCHELL, b. 21 July 1723; d. 5 Sept. 1724 <Gen.Adv.2:2>

Joseph MITCHELL, b. 4 Jan. 1724/5

Benjamin MITCHELL, b. 5 Feb. 1727/8; d. 27 Nov. 1802, 76th yr, Kingston g.s <MD 7:168>

Martha MITCHELL, b. 14 June 1731

Ruth MITCHELL, b. ( )

Phebe MITCHELL*, b. ( )

CHILDREN OF Japhet RICKARD & Martha MITCHELL: (2) <Gen.Adv.4:16>

Lusanna RICKARD, b. 8 July 1752, Middleboro

Martha RICKARD, b. 18 Aug. 1755, Parting Ways

Mary PHILIPS, b. 9 Feb. 1731, d. Apr. 1811*, ae 80 <Kingston ChR:367>

CHILDREN OF Benjamin MITCHELL[4] (Jos.[3]) & Mary PHILIPS: (11) <Kingston VR:110-11, Gen.Adv.4:16>

Bathsheba MITCHELL, b. 8 Mar. 1752, d. 25 Mar. 1752 <Kingston ChR:367>

Benjamin MITCHELL, b. 6 Mar. 1753

Abigail MITCHELL, b. 5 May 1755

Molly MITCHELL, b. 24 Nov. 1757; d. 29 Jan. 1846, unm., Kingston g.s. <MD 7:168>

Rebecca MITCHELL, b. 26 Mar. 1760

John MITCHELL, b. 10 Apr. 1762; d. 19 Nov. 1822, Kingston g.s. <MD 7:168>

Ezra MITCHELL, b. 19 Dec. 1764; d. 16 Mar. 1812, Kingston g.s. <MD 7:168>

Sarah MITCHELL, b. 13 Mar. 1767; d. 19 Aug. 1854, Kingston g.s. <MD 7:168>

Hannah MITCHELL, b. 4 Apr. 1770

Joseph MITCHELL, b. 1 Jan. 1773; d.? 30 Apr. 1834* <Kingston ChR:367>

Thomas MITCHELL, b. 13 Sept. 1775; d. Jan. 1812, consumption

Joanna ( ) MITCHELL, b. c1761, d. 3 June 1843, ae 82, Kingston g.s.

CHILD OF John MITCHELL[5] (Ben.[4]) & Joanna ( ):

Benjamin MITCHELL, b. 1798, d. 25 Apr. 1811, ae 13y4m17d, Kingston g.s.

Lucy SAMPSON[7] (Gideon[6], Zabdiel[5], Hannah Soule[4], Ben.[3], John[2]), b. c1784, Plympton, d. 3 Feb. 1875, Halifax <Mass.VR 275:306> (wf of Joseph Mitchell[5] (Ben.[4]))

CHILD OF James SHAW & Mary MITCHELL[2] (Experience[1]):

James SHAW, b. 6 Dec. 1754, Plymouth <MD 17:71>

(**NOTE:** Line of descent for the following Sarah Mitchell[2] line has been changed to show descent from Experience Mitchell[1] not Jane Cooke[2]. This is not a Cooke Mayflower line. See <48>.

John HAYWARD, d. pre 21 Nov. 1710 (adm.) <Plymouth Co.PR #9806, 3:14>

CHILDREN OF John HAYWARD & Sarah MITCHELL[2] (Experience[1]): (12) <Bridgewater VR, MD 2:92>

Dau., b. June 1662, d. few days later

Sarah HAYWARD, b. 25 Oct. 1663; d. 11 July 1737, Bridgewater <MD 14:184>

Son, b. Jan. 1665, d. ae 5wks

John HAYWARD, b. 20 Apr. 1667; d. 14 Apr. 1705, Bridgewater <MD 5:250>

Joseph HAYWARD, b. 23 Nov. 1669; d. 23 Mar. 1758*, Bridgewater g.s. "Old Graveyard"

Mary HAYWARD, b. 20 Apr. 1672; d. 5 Nov. 1712, Bridgewater <MD 6:8>

Thomas HAYWARD, b. 10 Jan. 1674; d. 20 Mar. 1741, Bridgewater <MD 7:55>

Benjamin HAYWARD, b. 26 Nov. 1677; d. 4 Oct. 1684 or 85

Susanna HAYWARD, b. 10 Aug. 1680; d. 19 June 1746, Bridgewater <MD 14:183>

Elizabeth HAYWARD, b. 16 Apr. 1683

Benoni HAYWARD, b. 17 Mar. 1686

Mercy HAYWARD, b. 29 Oct. 1687

MICRO #16 of 30

Edmund RAWSON, b. 8 July 1689*, Mendon

CHILDREN OF Edmund RAWSON & Elizabeh HAYWARD^{3} (Sarah Mitchell^{2}): (3*)

Edmund RAWSON, b. 15 Aug. 1718

Abner RAWSON, b. 24 Apr. 1721

Nathan RAWSON, b. 4 Aug. 1724

Susanna EDSON, (son of Sam.), b. 15 Jan. 1678/9, Bridgewater <MD 3:143>

CHILDREN OF John HAYWARD^{3} (Sarah Mitchell^{2}) & Susanna EDSON: (2) <Bridgewater VR, MD 5:250>

Susanna HAYWARD, b. 13 Sept. 1699

Sarah HAYWARD, b. 7 Aug. 1703; d. 23 Apr. 1779*, Stoughton (wf of Edw. Wentworth)

Josiah WINSLOW^{4} (*Josiah^{3}, Kenelm$^{2-1}$), b. 9 June 1697*, Freetown; d. pre Dec. 1745*

CHILDREN OF Josiah WINSLOW & Sarah HAYWARD^{4} (John^{3}): (5*)

Susanna WINSLOW, b. 6 Oct. 1724

Josiah WINSLOW, b. ( ), d. Oct. 1805, N. Vineyard ME

Ezra WINSLOW, b. c1736, d. c1796

John Hayward WINSLOW, b. 22 Mar. 1738

Asa WINSLOW, b. ( )

Edward WENTWORTH, (*son of John & Martha), b. c1693, d. 12 Feb. 1767*, ae 74, Stoughton (2nd hus of Sarah Hayward^{4} (John^{3}))

CHILDREN OF Joseph HAYWARD^{3} (Sarah Mitchell^{2}) & Mehitable DUNHAM: (9) <Bridgewater VR, MD 5:250>

Mehitable HAYWARD, b. 17 May 1701

Thomas HAYWARD, b. 23 Sept. 1702

Joanna HAYWARD, b. 15 Aug. 1704

Malatiah HAYWARD, b. 31 Aug. 170()

Hannah HAYWARD, b. 9 Nov. 1708

Sarah HAYWARD, b. 14 Dec. 1710

Joseph HAYWARD, b. 19 Oct. 1713; d. 17 Oct. 1738

Daniel HAYWARD, b. 29 Nov. 1715; d. 25 June 1749

Benjamin HAYWARD, b. 22 Feb. 1717; d. 15 Dec. 1773* <Bridgewater VR 2:484> (g.s. says 1777 ae 55)

CHILDREN OF Samuel DUNBAR^{5} (Sarah Thaxter^{4}, Abigail Church^{3}, Eliz. Warren^{2}) & Malatiah HAYWARD^{4} (Jos.^{3}): (5)**<86>**

CHILDREN OF Benjamin HAYWARD^{4} (Jos.^{3}) & Sarah CAREY*, (*dau of Recompence): (9) <Bridgewater>

Mary HAYWARD, b. 8 Dec. 1742*, d. 15 June 1749*

Sarah HAYWARD, b. 25 June 1744*

Joseph HAYWARD, b. 27 June 1746*; d. 16 Jan. 1836*, N. Bridgewater

Benjamin HAYWARD, b. 11 Sept. 1748*, d. 15 Feb. 1750/1*

Mary HAYWARD, b. 3 Sept. 1750*

Daniel HAYWARD, b. 1 Feb. 1752*

Benjamin HAYWARD, b. 13 Jan. 1754*

Mehitable HAYWARD, b. 7 July 1757*, d. 16 Jan. 1771*

Cary HAYWARD, b. 15 June 1759*

Daniel MANLEY, (son of Tho. & Lydia), b. 8 Oct. 1721 <Easton VR:20> (see below)

Rebecca MANLEY, (dau of Nath. & Hannah), b. 29 May 1714 <Easton VR:30> (see below)

CHILD OF Daniel MANLEY & Rebecca MANLEY:

Olive MANLEY, b. 31 Oct. 1750* <Easton VR:20>; d. 24 Oct. 1813*, Bridgewater (see below)

CHILDREN OF Joseph HAYWARD[5] (Ben.[4]) & Olive MANLEY: (9) <Bridgewater VR>

Child, b. 25 Oct. 1769*, d.y.

Asaph HAYWARD, b. 3 Oct. 1770*

Hannah HAYWARD, b. 30 Aug. 1772*

Olive HAYWARD, b. 19 June 1774*

Sarah HAYWARD, b. 9 June 1776*

Rebecca HAYWARD, b. 17 June 1778

Sylva HAYWARD, b. 18 Mar. 1780*

Manley HAYWARD, b. 24 June 1782*; d. 25 Oct. 1825 (see below)

Mary HAYWARD, b. 31 Oct. 1787*

Coweeset Cem., Marshall's Corner, Brockton (N. Bridgewater): (8)

Rebecca MANLEY, wf of Daniel, d. 30 Apr. 1790, 76th yr

Daniel MANLEY, d. 18 Jan. 1804, 83rd yr "S.A.R. 1775"

Olive HAYWARD, wf of Joseph, d. 24 Oct. 1813, 63rd yr

Joseph HAYWARD, d. 16 Jan. 1836, 90th yr "S.A.R. 1775"

Manley HAYWARD, d. 25 Oct. 1825, ae 43 "1812 War"

Mary HAYWARD, wf of Manley, d. 29 Jan. 1834, ae 49

Lyman DRAKE, d. 5 Oct. 1844, 28th yr<87>

Mary Ann DRAKE, wf of Lyman, d. 5 Feb. 1906, 85th yr<87>

William AMES, (son of John), b. 6 Nov. 1673, Bridgewater, d. 20 Nov. 1712, Bridge. <MD 2:241,6:8>

CHILDREN OF William AMES & Mary HAYWARD[3] (Sarah Mitchell[2]): (6) <Bridgewater VR, MD 6:8>

Mary AMES, b. 18 Dec. 1699

William AMES, b. 18 Sept. 1701

Martha AMES, b. 7 Mar. 1704

Bethiah AMES, b. 25 Apr. 1706

Sarah AMES, b. 27 July 1708

Hannah AMES, b. 21 Sept. 1710

Nathaniel BRETT, d. 19 Nov. 1740, Bridgewater <MD 14:184>

CHILDREN OF Nathaniel BRETT & Sarah HAYWARD[3] (Sarah Mitchell[2]): (12) <Bridgewater VR, MD 3:8>

Stillborn son, b. 2 Jan. 1684/5

Alice BRETT, b. 29 Jan. 1685/6; d. 7 Mar. 1685/6

Son, b. 9 Dec. 1686, d. same day

Seth BRETT, b. 24 Feb. 1687/8; d. 11 Feb. 1721/2, smallpox <MD 14:84>

Son, b. 9 June 1690, d. 11 June 1690

Son, b. 15 June 1691, d. same day

Mehitable BRETT, b. 12 Aug. 1692; d. 1736*

Sarah BRETT, b. 28 Jan. 1694/5; d. 28 Dec. 1774, unm. <MD 14:184>

Son, b. 4 Feb. 1697/8, d. 15 Feb. 1697/8

Hannah BRETT, b. 18 Oct. 1699; d. 1777* <MD 3:9>

William BRETT, b. 26 Apr. 1702 <MD 3:9>

Nathaniel BRETT, b. 3 Nov. 1704 <MD 3:9>; d. 1779*

Son, b. 11 Jan. 1706/7, d. same day

CHILDREN OF Joseph GANNETT* & Hannah BRETT[4] (Sarah Hayward[3]): (2*)

Seth GANNETT, b. 1734

Thomas GANNETT, b. 1736

CHILDREN OF Samuel EDSON & Mehitable BRETT[4] (Sarah Hayward[3]): (2*)

Samuel EDSON, b. 1722, d. 1800, unm.

Nathaniel EDSON, b. 1725

CHILDREN OF Nathaniel BRETT[4] (Sarah Hayward[3]) & Rebecca* ( ): (3*)

Hannah BRETT, b. 1733

Deborah BRETT, b. 1736

Uriah BRETT, b. 1740

CHILDREN OF Seth BRETT[4] (Sarah Hayward[3]) & Sarah ALDEN[4]: (See p.37)

CHILDREN OF William BRETT[4] (Sarah Hayward[3]) & Bethiah KINSLEY, (*dau of Sam. & Mary): (5*)

Ephraim BRETT, b. 5 Feb. 1732/3 <Norwich CT VR 1:55>

Mary BRETT, b. 8 Sept. 1734 < " " >

Silence BRETT, b. 27 May 1738 < VR 1:56 >

Daniel BRETT, b. 26 Jan. 1739/40 < VR 1:55>

Sarah BRETT, b. 19 Sept. 1743 < " " >

Jacob HAZEN, b. 30 Nov. 1729 <NEHGR 33:233>

CHILDREN OF Jacob HAZEN Jr. & Mary BRETT[5] (Wm.[4]): <Norwich CT VR 2:178>

Jacob HAZEN, b. 20 June 1753

William HAZEN, b. 19 July 1755

Plylena HAZEN, b. 14 May 1758

Lydia HAZEN, b. 24 Apr. 1760

Frederick HAZEN, b. 25 Sept. 1763

Celinda HAZEN, b. 10 July 1765

Lavinia HAZEN, b. 29 Apr. 1768

Jabin HAZEN, b. 14 Dec. 1770

John HAZEN, b. 20 Dec. 1773 <VR 3:170>

Thomas HAYWARD, (*son of Nath.), d. 18 May 1746, Bridgewater <MD 14:183>

CHILDREN OF Thomas HAYWARD & Susanna HAYWARD[3] (Sarah Mitchell[2]): (9) <Bridgewater VR, MD 14:183>

Susanna HAYWARD, b. 24 Aug. 1703, d. 10 Feb. 1703/4

Jacob HAYWARD, b. 29 Jan. 1704/5, d. May 1705

Thomas HAYWARD, b. 28 Mar. 1705/6, d. 23 May 1706

Elizabeth HAYWARD, b. 13 Mar. 1706/7; d. 2 May 1772 <MD 14:182>

Thomas HAYWARD, b. 25 Dec. 1708

Susanna HAYWARD, b. 10 Jan. 1711

John HAYWARD, b. 18 Sept. 1713

Jacob HAYWARD, b. 21 Mar. 1716/17

Jemima HAYWARD, b. 11 Oct. 1721

David DUNBAR[5] (Sarah Thaxter[4], Abigail Church[3], Eliz. Warren[2]), b. 27 Jan. 1711,Bridge.<MD 5:250>

CHILD OF David DUNBAR & Susanna HAYWARD[4] (Susanna Hayward[3]):

Susanna DUNBAR, b. ( )

Bethiah BRETT, d. 14 Aug. 1745, Bridgewater <MD 7:55>

CHILDREN OF Thomas HAYWARD[3] (Sarah Mitchell[2]) & Bethiah BRETT: (7) <Bridgewater, MD 7:55>

Alice HAYWARD, b. 7 Apr. 1707; d. 13 Oct. 1803, Japan Cem., Bridgewater**[<88>]**

Son, b. 22 Sept. 1709, d. same day

Son, b. 22 May 1712, d. 23 June 1712

Bethiah HAYWARD, b. 22 Sept. 1715

Mary HAYWARD, b. 4 Jan. 1718/19

Seth HAYWARD, b. 3 Dec. 1721

Phebe HAYWARD, b. 26 Apr. 1725

(**NOTE:** End of the non-Mayflower line of the children of Experience Mitchell[1] by his 2nd wife.)

MICRO #17 of 30

JOHN COOKE^{2} (Francis^{1})

Sarah WARREN^{2}, d. aft. 15 July 1696

CHILDREN OF John COOKE^{2} & Sarah WARREN: (5)

Sarah COOKE^{3}, b. c1634/5; d. aft. 1710*

Elizabeth COOKE^{3}, b. c1640; d. 6 Dec. 1715, Tiverton RI <Arnold 4:7:115>

Esther COOKE^{3}, b. 16 Aug. 1650 <MD 16:235>; d. aft. 16 Apr. 1671 (birth of last child)

Mary COOKE^{3}, b. 25 July (worn) <PCR 8:16>; d. betw. 26 Apr. 1708-25 Jan. 1714/5 <MD 16:229>

Mercy COOKE^{3}, b. c1656, d. 22 Nov. 1733, 77th yr <MD 3:33; Dartmouth VR:205>

CHILDREN OF John HATHAWAY: (9) <Dartmouth, NEHGR 20:339>

Sarah HATHAWAY, b. 24 Feb. 1683/4

Joannah HATHAWAY, b. 28 Jan. 1685

John HATHAWAY, b. 18 Mar. 1687

Son, b. 3 Apr. 1690

Hannah HATHAWAY, b. 16 Feb. 1692

Mary HATHAWAY, b. 11 June 1694

Jonathan HATHAWAY, b. 23 June 1697

Richard HATHAWAY, b. 21 May 1699

Thomas HATHAWAY, b. 5 Feb. 1700

Dartmouth Deaths <NEHGR 21:266>: (12)

John CANNON, son of John, d. 11 Sept. 1726

John CANNON, d. 28 Mar. 1750

John COOKE, d. 23 Nov. 1695

Joanna HATHAWAY, wf of John, d. 9 Mar. 1728/9

Samuel TABER, son of Thomas, d. 9 Oct. 1718

Thomas TABER, d. 14 July 1748

Tucker TABER, son of Philip & Susannah, d. 25 June 1749

Jabez DELANO, d. 23 Dec. 1735 <21:267>

Elizabeth HATHAWAY, dau of Jonathan & Susanna, d. 29 Apr. 1703 <21:267>

Paul HATHAWAY, son of Jonathan & Susanna, d. 2 Jan. 1722/3 <21:267>

Jonathan HATHAWAY Sr., d. 17 Sept. 1727 <21:267>

Joanna HATHAWAY, wf of John, d. 25 Oct. 1695 <21:267>

CHILDREN OF John CANNON: (6) <Dartmouth, NEHGR 22:66>

Cornelius CANNON, b. 18 July 1711

John CANNON, b. 11 Aug. 1714

Elizabeth CANNON, b. 20 Mar. 1716/7

Mary CANNON, b. 3 Apr. 1719

Philip CANNON, b. 11 Sept. 1721 <22:67>

Joanna CANNON, b. 27 Mar. 1728 <22:67>

William SPOONER, son of Sam., b. 13 Feb. 1688, Dartmouth <NEHGR 21:268>

Barker LITTLE, son of Nath. & Lydia, b. 24 Oct. 1747, Darmouth <NEHGR 22:66>

CHILDREN OF Arthur HATHAWAY: (2) <Dartmouth, NEHGR 22:66>

Simon HATHAWAY, b. 26 Dec. 1711

Joanna HATHAWAY, b. 5 Nov. 1713

CHILDREN OF William SPOONER: (5) <Dartmouth, NEHGR 22:67>

Benjamin SPOONER, b. 31 Mar. 1690

Joseph SPOONER, b. 18 Feb. 1692

Joshua SPOONER, b. 16 Mar. 1694

Sarah SPOONER, b. 6 Oct. 1700

Abagail SPOONER, b. 6 Dec. 1702

John TRIP, son of Joseph, b. 6 July 1668, Dartmouth <NEHGR 22:67>

CHILDREN OF John TABER, (son of Philip) & Mary ( ): (2) <Dartmouth, NEHGR 22:69>

Meribah TABER, b. 27 Sept. 1753

John TABER, b. 12 Jan. 1756

Hannah POPE, dau of Seth, b. 14 Dec. 1693, Dartmouth <NEHGR 22:69>

CHILDREN OF Thomas TABER: (3) <Dartmouth, NEHGR 22:69>

Priscilla TABER, b. 28 Jan.1701/2

Jonathan TABER, b. 24 Feb. 1702/3

Amaziah TABER, b. 9 July 1704

CHILDREN OF John TRIPP: (7) <Dartmouth, NEHGR 30:56>

George TRIPP, b. 16 June 1716

Timothy TRIPP, b. 22 Feb. 1717

Ruth TRIPP, b. 4 Apr. 1720

Elizabeth TRIPP, b. 23 Aug. 1722

Rebecca TRIPP, b. 27 July 1724

CHILDREN OF John TRIPP & Hannah ( ) <Dartmouth, NEHGR 30:56>

Hannah TRIPP, b. 25 Aug. 1738

Mary TRIPP, b. 20 Mar. 1741

CHILDREN OF Jonathan TABER, (son of Philip) & Robey ( ): (6) <Dartmouth, NEHGR 30:57>

Jonathan TABER, b. 20 Mar. 1735

Margaret TABER, b. 10 July 1740

Gardner TABER, b. 20 May 1742

Benjamin TABER, b. 20 Feb. 1747

Peleg TABER, b. 27 Jan. 1751

Eseck TABER, b. 5 Nov. 1755

CHILDREN OF Thomas TABER: (7) <Dartmouth, NEHGR 30:57>

Priscilla TABER, b. 28 June 1701

Jonathan TABER, b. 24 Feb. 1702/3

Amaziah TABER, b. 9 July 1704

Esther TABER, b. 6 Mar. 1709/10

Mary TABER, b. 12 Nov. 1711

Samuel TABER, b. 4 Dec. 1714

Seth TABER, b. 5 July 1719

CHILDREN OF Thomas TABER, (son of Jos.) & Ruth ( ): (2) <Dartmouth, NEHGR 30:57>

Peace TABER, b. 5 Nov. 1745

Ruth TABER, b. 7 May 1748

CHILDREN OF William SPOONER: (12) <Dartmouth; 1-4, NEHGR 30:58; 5-12, NEHGR 32:20>

Jemima SPOONER, b. 7 Dec. 1700

Jane SPOONER, b. 12 May 1703

Elizabeth SPOONER, b. 22 May 1705

Micah SPOONER, b. 2 Apr. 1707

Nathaniel SPOONER, b. 21 Apr. 1709

Rebecca SPOONER, b. 17 Nov. 1710

Sarah SPOONER, b. 18 Jan. 1711/2

Mercy SPOONER, b. 8 Jan. 1713/4

Isaac SPOONER, b. 9 Jan. 1715/6

Alice(?) SPOONER, b. 27 Mar. 1718

William SPOONER, b. 29 Jan. 1719/20

Ebenezer SPOONER, b. 29 May 1724

CHILDREN OF Nathan DELANO & Sarah ( ): (2) <Dartmouth, NEHGR 32:20>
Thomas DELANO, b. 18 Oct. 1754
Rebecca DELANO, b. 18 Oct. 1754 (twins)
CHILDREN OF Philip TABER & Susannah ( ): (9) <Dartmouth; 1-3, NEHGR 32:20, 4-9, NEHGR 34:198>
Richard TABER, b. 25 Nov. 1711
Thomas TABER, b. 18 Nov. 1713
Zephaniah TABER, b. 1 Oct. 1715
Tucker TABER, b. 10 Oct. 1717
Jesse TABER, b. 21 Nov. 1719
Peace TABER, b. 22 Feb. 1722 (dau)
Huldah TABER, b. Mar. 1724
Noah TABER, b. 7 July 1727
Philip TABER, b. 31 Oct. 1730
Eleanor TABER, dau of Wm., b. 24 Jan. 1752, Dartmouth <NEHGR 34:406>
CHILDREN OF Thomas TABER: (12) <Dartmouth, NEHGR 35:32>
Thomas TABER, b. 22 Oct. 1668
Esther TABER, b. 17 Apr. 1671
Lydia TABER, b. 8 Apr. 1673
Sarah TABER, b. 28 Jan. 1674
Mary TABER, b. 18 Mar. 1677
Joseph TABER, b. 7 Mar. 1679
John TABER, b. 22 Feb. 1681
Jacob TABER, b. 26 July 1683
Jonathan TABER, b. 22 Sept. 1685
Bethiah TABER, b. 3 Sept. 1687
Philip TABER, b. 7 Feb. 1689
Abigail TABER, b. 2 May 1693
CHILDREN OF Philip TABER: (8) <Dartmouth, NEHGR 35:32> (See pg.369)
Mary TABER, b. 28 Jan. 1668
Sarah TABER, b. 26 Mar. 1671
Lydia TABER, b. 28 Sept. 1673
Philip TABER, b. 29 Feb. 1675
Abigail TABER, b. 27 Oct. 1678
Esther TABER, b. 23 Feb. 1680
John TABER, b. 18 July 1684
Bethiah TABER, b. 18 Apr. 1689
CHILDREN OF Jonathan DELANO Jr.: (2) <Dartmouth, NEHGR 35:33>
Sarah DELANO, b. 18 Mar. 17( )
Jane DELANO, b. 16 Dec. ( )
Daniel WILCOX, d. 2 July 1702, Tiverton RI <MD 16:243>
CHILDREN OF Daniel WILCOX^1 & 1st ( ): (2)**<89>**
Daniel WILCOX, b. ( )
Samuel WILCOX, b. ( ); d. pre 9 June 1702* (father's will)
CHILDREN OF Daniel WILCOX & 2nd Elizabeth COOKE^3: (2 of 8) <MD 16:239-41>**<90>**
Mary WILCOX^4, b. ( ), d. betw. 26 Apr. 1735 (will) - 28 May 1735 (prob.), Tiverton <MD 17:63>
Edward WILCOX^4, b. ( ), d. betw. 19 May 1718 (will) - 29 May 1718 (inv.), Tiverton <Bristol Co. PR 3:433-34>
CHILDREN OF Daniel WILCOX^2 (Dan.^{1}) & Hannah COOK, (dau of John): (5) <Austin:423>
Daniel WILCOX, b. ( )
Mary WILCOX, b. 25 Feb. 1682*

Hannah WILCOX, b. 11 Apr. 1684*

Joseph WILCOX, b. 28 Oct. 1687*

Eliphal WILCOX, b. ( )

Samuel SANFORD^{3} (John$^{2-1}$), b. 5 Oct. 1677, Portsmouth RI, d. 3 Sept. 1738,Tiverton RI<2:1389>**<91>**

CHILD OF Samuel SANFORD^{3} & Deborah MANCHESTER: (5) <Tiverton RI, 2:1389**<91>**

Restcome SANFORD, b. 27 July 1704

Peleg SANFORD, b. 8 Mar. 1708

Mary SANFORD, b. 7 May 1710

Samuel SANFORD, b. 21 Nov. 1716

Eliphal SANFORD, b. 12 May 1714

Elizabeth LAKE, d. 6 May 1749

CHILDREN OF Restcome SANFORD^{4} (Sam.^{3}) & Elizabeth LAKE: (1 of 9) <Tiverton RI, 2:1392>**<91>**

William SANFORD, b. 17 June 1725, Tiverton RI <2:1393>

Restcome SANFORD, b. 18 June 1727

Abigail SANFORD, b. 19 Feb. 1729, d. 6 Dec. 1736

David SANFORD, b. 28 Sept. 1730, d. 27 Nov. 1736

Peleg SANFORD, b. 24 Jan. 1733, d. 10 Dec. 1736

Mary SANFORD, b. 24 Sept. 1735

Samuel SANFORD, b. 11 Oct. 1737

Deborah SANFORD, b. 23 Dec. 1739

Sarah SANFORD, b. 7 Nov. 1741

CHILDREN OF William SANFORD^{5} (Restcome^{4}) & Mary WAIGHT: (6) <Tiverton RI, 2:1393>**<91>**

Joseph SANFORD, b. 15 June 1746

Abigail SANFORD, b. 28 Nov. 1748

Peleg SANFORD, b. 23 Oct. 1751

Eliphal SANFORD, b. 22 Apr. 1755

William SANFORD, b. 27 Sept. 1757, d. 26 Oct. 1837

Thomas SANFORD, b. 30 June 1761

CHILDREN OF Peleg SANFORD^{6} (Wm.^{5}) & Lillis WILCOX, (dau of Cuthbert): (4) <7:304>**<92>**

Mary SANFORD, b. 22 Mar. 1776

Samuel SANFORD, b. 26 May 1777

Restcome SANFORD, b. 26 Sept. 1779

Stephen SANFORD, b. 26 Oct. 1781

CHILDREN OF Daniel WILCOX (d.1721) & Sarah ( ): <Friends' Rcds. at New Bedford Library>

Sarah WILCOX, b. 15 Jan. 1704/5

Stephen WILCOX, b. 28 May 1707

Daniel WILCOX, b. 25 Aug. 1709

William WILCOX, b. 22 Nov. 1711

Mary WILCOX, b. 17 Dec. 1712

Hannah WILCOX, b. 1 Nov. 1715

Katherine WILCOX, b. 25 Feb. 1717/8

Lemuel WILCOX, b. 30 May 1720, d. 19 Jan. 1727

CHILDREN OF Edward WILCOX^{4} (Eliz. Cooke^{3}) & Sarah MANCHESTER: (4) <Tiverton RI, Arnold 4:7:115>

Josiah WILCOX^{5}, b. 22 Sept. 1701*

Ephraim WILCOX^{5}, b. 9 Aug. 1704*

William WILCOX^{5}, b. 26 Dec. 1706*

Freelove WILCOX^{5}, b. 18 Dec. 1709*

CHILDREN OF Ephraim WILCOX^{5} & Mary PRICE: (6*)

Edward WILCOX^{6}, b. 13 Apr. 1730

John WILCOX^{6}, b. 22 Oct. 1733

Ephraim WILCOX^6, b. 20 July 1737

Sarah WILCOX^6, b. 16 July 1740

Elizabeth WILCOX^6, b. 19 May 1745

Oliver WILCOX^6, b. 20 May 1747

John EARLE, b. betw. 12 Feb. 1718/9 (will) - 2 Feb. 1727/8 (inv.) <MD 17:61>

CHILDREN OF John EARLE & Mary WILCOX^4 (Eliz. Cooke^3): (6) <Tiverton RI>

John EARLE^5, b. 7 Aug. 1687

Daniel EARLE^5, b. 28 Oct. 1688

Benjamin EARLE^5, b. 21 May 1691; d. 15 June 1770 <Earle Fam.:36>

Mary EARLE^5, b. 6 June 1693

Rebecca EARLE^5, b. 17 Dec. 1695

Elizabeth EARLE^5, b. 6 Sept. 1699; d. pre 10 June 1764 <MD 18:253>

Rebecca WESTGATE, b. 8 Jan. 1697, d. 17 Nov. 1779 <Earle Fam.:36>

CHILDREN OF Benjamin EARLE^5 & Rebecca WESTGATE: (4) <Warwick RI VR:93>

William EARLE^6, b. 12 Feb. 1726/7

John EARLE^6, b. 27 Jan. 1728/9

Sarah EARLE^6, b. 8 Feb. 1730/1

Benjamin EARLE^6, b. 25 Nov. 1733

Mary BROWN, (dau of George), b. 21 Jan. 1733, d. 22 Aug. 1800 <Earle Fam.:50>

CHILD OF William EARLE^6 & Mary BROWN:

William EARLE^7, b. 17 Feb. 1758, Providence RI <Earle Fam.:50>

CHILDREN OF Daniel EARLE^5 (Mary Wilcox^4) & Grace HIX, (dau of Jos.): (5) <Tiverton RI VR>

Mary EARLE^6, b. 10 Sept. 1719

Sarah EARLE^6, b. 1 July 1723

Daniel EARLE^6, b. 27 Mar. 1726

John EARLE^6, b. 25 July 1732

Benjamin EARLE^6, b. 22 June 1736

CHILDREN OF George WESTGATE & Elizabeth EARLE^5 (Mary Wilcox^4): (5) <Warwick RI VR 1:67>

George WESTGATE^6, b. 16 Sept. 1728

John WESTGATE^6, b. 1 Feb. 1730/1

Priscilla WESTGATE^6, b. 8 Sept. 1732

Mary WESTGATE^6, b. 7 Jan. 1734/5

Earl WESTGATE^6, b. 26 Feb. 1735/6; d. pre 10 June 1764*

CHILDREN OF Earl WESTGATE^6 & Elizabeth GIFFORD: (2*) <Portsmouth RI VR>

Mary WESTGATE^7, b. 18 Feb. 1758

Joseph WESTGATE^7, b. 10 June 1761

CHILDREN OF George WESTGATE^6 (Eliz. Earle^5) & Elizabeth DURFEE*, (*dau of David): (4*)<Tiverton>

Rebecca WESTGATE^7, b. 11 Aug. 1761

Abigail WESTGATE^7, b. 13 June 1763

Eliphal WESTGATE^7, b. 19 Sept. 1764

Elizabeth WESTGATE^7, b. 2 Oct. 1766

CHILDREN OF John WESTGATE^6 (Eliz. Earle^5) & Grace CHURCH: (6*) <Tiverton RI VR>

Elizabeth WESTGATE^7, b. 16 Aug. 1757

John WESTGATE^7, b. 7 June 1759

Lydia WESTGATE^7, b. 1(6) Aug. 1761

Earl WESTGATE^7, b. 26 Nov. 1763

Priscilla WESTGATE^7, b. 28 June 1766

George WESTGATE^7, b. 1 Nov. 1768

CHILDREN OF John EARLE^5* (*Mary Wilcox^4) & Sarah POTTER: (4) <Kingston VR>

Benjamin EARLE, b. 18 Dec. 1712

Susanna EARLE, b. 25 June 1715

Abigail EARLE, b. 7 Aug. 1724

Lydia EARLE, b. 30 Dec. 1726

CHILD OF Daniel SHERMAN & Susanna EARLE, (dau of John):

Daniel SHERMAN, b. 28 Aug. 1735 <Kingstown RI VR>

Isaac SHELDON, (dau of Isaac & Susanna), b. 4 Mar. 1715/6 <S. Kingstown RI VR>

CHILDREN OF Isaac SHELDON & Abigail EARLE, (dau of John): (5) <S. Kingstown RI VR>

Samuel SHELDON, b. 30 June 1747

Lydia SHELDON, b. 23 Aug. 1749

Sarah SHELDON, b. 17 Aug. 1751

Isaac SHELDON, b. 22 July 1755

Benjamin SHELDON, b. 28 July 1758

CHILDREN OF Samuel WILCOX[2], (son of Dan.[1]) & Mary ( ): (3) <Dartmouth VR 1:19, NEHGR 22:67>

Jeremiah WILCOX, b. 24 Sept. 1683*; d. betw. 31 Dec. 1765* (will) - 10 May 1768* (prob.)

William WILCOX, b. 2 Feb. 1685*; d. pre 24 Sept. 1705*

Mary WILCOX, b. 14 Feb. 1688*

CHILDREN OF Jeremiah WILCOX[3] (Sam.[2]) & 1st Mary ( ): (2) <Darmouth VR 1:304>

Mary WILCOX, b. 10 Feb. 1709 (??); d. 14 Nov. 1757 <Dartmouth Rcds.> (wf of Humphry Smith)

Sarah WILCOX, b. 13 Nov. 1734 (??)

CHILDREN OF Jeremiah WILCOX[3] & 2nd Judith BRIGGS[5] (Eliz. Fobes[4], Martha Pabodie[3], Eliz.Alden[2]): (3) <Dartmouth VR 1:304>

Samuel WILCOX, b. 30 Sept. 1739*

William WILCOX, b. 23 May 1741*

Benjamin WILCOX, b. 24 Sept. 1747*; d. pre 5 Apr. 1816

Patience TUCKER, (dau of Henry), b. 18 Sept. 1746* (see below)

CHILDREN OF Benjamin WILCOX[4] (Jeremiah[3]) & Patience TUCKER: (5) <Dartmouth VR 4:8>

Jeremiah WILCOX, b. 6 Sept. 1770*

Phebe WILCOX, b. 27 Nov. 1771*

Willard WILCOX, b. 23 Feb. 1773*

Patience WILCOX, b. 21 June 1776*

Benjamin WILCOX, b. 26 Feb. 1785*

CHILDREN OF Henry TUCKER Jr. & Elizabeth ( ): (7) <Dartmouth VR:354>

William TUCKER, b. 12 Jan. 1734/5

Phebe TUCKER, b. 18 Nov. 1736

Eliphal TUCKER, b. 28 Feb. 1739 (dau)

Susanna TUCKER, b. 14 Jan. 1741

Meribah TUCKER, b. 24 May 1745

Patience TUCKER, b. 18 Sept. 1746 (see above)

Elisabeth TUCKER, b. 18 Aug. 1749

MICRO #18 of 30

Deliverence SMITH, d. 30 June 1729 <Friends' Rcds., Dartmouth 125:76>

CHILDREN OF Deliverence SMITH & Mary ( ):

John SMITH, b. 11 July 1693

Deborah SMITH, b. 13 July 1695

Ann SMITH, b. 16 Dec. 1696

Alice SMITH, b. 29 Oct. 1698, d. 22 Oct. 1783

Peleg SMITH, b. 27 May 1700, d. 8 Oct. 1778

George SMITH, b. 27 Aug. 1701, d. 17 Sept. 1769

Hope SMITH, b. 23 Jan. 1703

Humphry SMITH, b. 13 Apr. 1705, d. 4 Nov. 1777 (m. Mary Wilcox, p.366)

Mary SMITH, b. 14 Jan. 1706/7

Abigail SMITH, b. 10 Apr. 1709

CHILD OF Willard WILCOX^{5} (Ben.^{4}) & Ruth LAWRENCE:

Henry WILCOX, b. 22 Apr. 1795*; d. 10 Mar. 1870, Westport, heart disease <Mass.VR 229:147>

CHILDREN OF Isaac LAWRENCE & Elizabeth (   ): (2) <Dartmouth VR 4:25>

Ruth LAWRENCE, b. Feb. 1775

Abigail LAWRENCE, b. 13 May 1776

George SMITH, b. 21 June 1790 <Friends' Rcds., Dartmouth:759>

Sarah E. (   ) SMITH, b. 22 June 1791 < " " >

CHILDREN OF George SMITH & Sarah E. (   ): (8) < " " >

Joseph E. SMITH, b. 18 10mth 1817

Sarah SMITH, b. 10 9mth 1819

David W. SMITH, b. 25 8mth 1821

Leander SMITH, b. 4 4mth 1825

Hannah W. SMITH, b. 30 11mth 1827

Franklin SMITH, b. 9 3mth 1832, d. 2mth 1836

Emily SMITH, b. 5 9mth 1834, d. 9 2mth 1836

Charles SMITH, b. 14 4mth 1837

Thomas TABER, d. betw. 15 June 1723 (will) - 20 Mar. 1732/3 (prob.)

CHILDREN OF Thomas TABER & Esther COOKE^{3}: (2) <Dartmouth VR:5>

Thomas TABER^{4}, b. 22 Oct. 1668; d. betw. 2 Aug. 1722 (will) - 4 Sept. 1722 (prob.) <Bristol Co. PR 4:103>

Esther TABER^{4}, b. 17 Apr. 1671; d. aft. 15 June 1723* (father's will)

Samuel PERRY, (son of Ezra), b. middle Mar. 1667, Sandwich <MD 14:171>; d. betw. 2 Aug. 1750 (will) - 7 Sept. 1751 (prob.) <Barnstable Co.PR 8:490>

CHILDREN OF Samuel PERRY & Esther TABER^{4}: (9) <Sandwich VR, MD 30:61>

Elizabeth PERRY^{5}, b. 17 July 1690; d. May 1759*, South Amenia NY

Deborah PERRY^{5}, b. 16 June 1692

Thomas PERRY^{5}, b. 24 Feb. 1693/4; d. pre 2 Aug. 1750 (father's will)

Sarah PERRY^{5}, b. 8 June 1696; d. pre 2 Aug. 1750 (father's will)

Nathan PERRY^{5}, b. 12 Jan. 1700/01; d. betw. 5 May 1769 (will) - 29 Nov. 1769 (prob.)<Barnstable Co.PR 13:488, 12:413>

Mary PERRY^{5}, b. 10 Dec. 1702

Ebenezer PERRY^{5}, b. 5 Mar. 1705/6

Seth PERRY^{5}, b. 24 Feb. 1707/8; d. 18 Oct.1729*, Sandwich g.s.

Mercy PERRY^{5}, b. 8 Dec. 1710; d. pre 2 Aug. 1750

Peleg BARLOW, b. 25 Feb. 1692*, Sandwich; d. Oct. 1759*, South Armenia NY

CHILDREN OF Peleg BARLOW & Elizabeth PERRY^{5}: (6) <Sandwich VR 2:76>

Thomas BARLOW^{6}, b. 17 May 1718; d. 3 Apr.* 1768, Sandwich

Seth BARLOW^{6}, b. 24 Sept. 1720

Mary BARLOW^{6}, b. 10 Dec. 1724

Nathan BARLOW^{6}, b. 25 Aug. 1726

Moses BARLOW^{6}, b. 25 Nov. 1728

Sarah BARLOW^{6}, b. 1 Oct. 1731

CHILDREN OF Nathan BARLOW & Joan (   ): (3) <Sandwich VR 2:144>

Mercy BARLOW, b. 9 Oct. 1749

Joanna BARLOW, b. 22 Aug. 1751

Fear BARLOW, b. 16 Feb. 1755

CHILDREN OF Thomas BARLOW^{6} (Eliz. Perry^{5}) & Mehitable WING, (*dau of Eben.):(9)<Sandwich VR 2:137

Levi BARLOW^{7}, b. 12 Nov. 1747*

Jesse BARLOW^{7}, b. 12 Sept. 1749*; d. 10 Dec. 1815*, Newport RI <VR RI 13:157>

Obed BARLOW^{7}, b. 13 July 1751*; d. 17 July 1839*

Sarah BARLOW^{7}, b. 3 June 1753*; d. 1 Jan. 1829*

Mary BARLOW^{7}, b. 21 Feb. 1756*

Nathan BARLOW^{7}, b. 20 Apr. 1758*; d. 28 Sept. 1795*

Elizabeth BARLOW^{7}, b. 16 July 1760*; d. 10 Jan. 1858*

Moses BARLOW^{7}, b. 21 Nov. 1762*

Mehitable BARLOW^{7}, b. 27 May 1765*; d. 14 Mar. 1835*

CHILD OF James WITHERLY & Mary BARLOW^{7}:

Mehitable WITHERLY^{8*}, b. aft. 1777*

Nathan HAMMOND, (*son of Josiah & Rebecca), b. 26 Feb. 1766* <Rochester VR 1:152>; d. 8 Apr. 1803 Hammondstown Cem., Mattapoisett <Rochester VR 2:388>

CHILDREN OF Nathan HAMMOND & Mehitable BARLOW^{7} (Tho.^{6}): (2*)

Nathan HAMMOND^{8}, b. c1791, d. 5 Sept. 1798, 7th yr, Hammondstown Cem.<Rochester VR 2:388>

Sarah HAMMOND^{8}, b. c1797, d. 11 Sept. 1798, ae 12 mths, Hammondstown Cem.<Rochester VR 2:388>

Sarah NYE, (*dau of Solomon), b. 20 Oct. 1750*, Falmouth

CHILDREN OF Jesse BARLOW^{7} (Tho.^{6}) & Sarah NYE*: (10) <Barlow Gen., mss.:59>

Silvina BARLOW^{8}, b. 6 Sept. 1770, d. 7 May 1838

Charlotte BARLOW^{8}, b. 27 Oct. 1772

Calvin BARLOW^{8}, b. 15 Mar. 1775

Joseph Warren BARLOW^{8}, b. 6 Mar. 1777

Arnold BARLOW^{8}, b. 9 July 1779, d. 21 Nov. 1835, Philadelphia

Jesse BARLOW^{8}, b. 7 Aug. 1781 <Sandwich VR 2:223>, d. 9 June 1837

Sally BARLOW^{8}, b. 6 June 1784

Huldah BARLOW^{8}, b. 11 Jan. 1789, d. 4 Apr. 1862, Stonington CT

Thomas BARLOW^{8}, b. 6 June 1791

Nathan BARLOW^{8}, b. 1 Sept. 1793

Deaths, from Providence Gazette (VR RI 13:157): (4)

Capt. Moses BARLOW, of Newport, d. 29 Nov. 1810, Havana

Joel BARLOW, late U.S. minister to France, on his way from Wilma to Paris (paper of 13 Mar. 1813)

Calvin BARLOW, of Newport, d. 7 May 1823, drowned off Seconnet Pt., ae 44

Mrs. Joel BARLOW, (widow of Hon.Joel late mininster to France) d. near Washington ("13 June 1818)

Ann BRITTIN, b. 1791*, Falmouth, d. 1878*, Philadelphia

CHILDREN OF Arnold BARLOW^{8} (Jesse^{7}) & Ann BRITTIN*: (1 of 11*)**<93>**

Susan BARLOW^{9}, b. 22 July 1820*, d. 25 Aug. 1890*

MICRO #19 of 30

CHILD OF Levi BARLOW^{7} (Tho.^{6}) & Rachel NYE:

Anson BARLOW^{8}, b. 5 Mar. 1773*, Falmouth <VR RI 4:2:82>

Rebecca HARLOW^{5} (Samuel^{4}, Rebecca Bartlett^{3}, Mary Warren^{2}), b. 27 Feb. 1678, Plymouth <MD 2:17>

CHILDREN OF Thomas TABER^{4} (Esther Cooke^{3}) & Rebecca HARLOW: (7) <Dartmouth VR:30,36>

Priscilla TABER^{5}, b. 28 June 1701

Jonathan TABER^{5}, b. 24 Feb. 1702/3

Amaziah TABER^{5}, b. 9 July 1704

Esther TABER^{5}, b. 6 Mar. 1709/10

Mary TABER^{5}, b. 12 Nov. 1711

Samuel TABER^{5}, b. 4 Dec. 1714, d. 9 Nov. 1718

Seth TABER^{5}, b. 5 (July) 1719

Philip TABER, d. pre 27 Feb. 1692/3 <MD 10:45>

CHILDREN OF Philip TABER & Mary COOKE^{3}: (8) <Dartmouth VR:9>

Mary TABER^{4}, b. 28 Jan. 1668

Sarah TABER^{4}, b. 26 Mar. 1671

Lydia TABER^{4}, b. 28 Sept. 1673; d. aft. 23 Mar. 1754*

Philip TABER^{4}, b. 29 Feb. 1675; d. betw. 14 July 1749 (will) - 5 Nov. 1751 (prob.) <Bristol Co.PR 13:6, 9>

Abigail TABER^{4}, b. 27 Oct. 1678

Esther TABER^{4}, b. 23 Feb. 1680

John TABER^{4}, b. 18 July 1684; d. betw. 18 June 1718 (will) - 28 Aug. 1727 (inv.)

Bethiah TABER^{4}, b. 18 Apr. 1689; d. betw. 11 Sept. 1776 (will) - 3 Oct. 1780 (prob.)

John MACOMBER, (son of Wm.), d. betw. 7 Oct. 1723 (will) - 28 Oct. 1723 (prob.) <Bristol Co.PR 4:232>**<94>**

CHILDREN OF John MACOMBER & Bethiah TABER^{4}: (7)**<95>**

Philip MACOMBER^{5}, b. 11 Sept. 1712; d. betw. 17 Feb. 1798 (will) - 5 May 1801 (prob.) <Bristol Co.PR 38:152>

Mercy MACOMBER^{5}, b. 28 Mar. 1714

Mary MACOMBER^{5}, b. 4 May 1715

Abiel MACOMBER^{5}, b. 4 Oct. 1717; d. betw. 22 May 1740 (will) - 17 June 1740 (prob.), unm.<Bristol Co.PR 9:423>

John MACOMBER^{5}, b. 8 Jan. 1719/20

William MACOMBER^{5}, b. 15 Mar. 1721/2

Job MACOMBER^{5}, b. 13 Feb. 1723/4

CHILDREN OF John TABER^{4} (Mary Cooke^{3}) & Susanna MANCHESTER: (5)**<95a>**

Joseph MOSHER^{3} (Hugh$^{2-1}$), d. betw. 15 Nov. 1743 (will) - 7 May 1754 (widow's petition)

CHILDREN OF Joseph MOSHER & Lydia TABER^{4} (Mary Cooke^{3}): (9) <1-8, Dartmouth VR>

Rebecca MOSHER^{5}, b. 28 Dec. 1695 <1:170>; d. pre Nov. 1743 (father's will)

Philip MOSHER^{5}, b. 20 Dec. 1697 <1:170>; d. aft. 24 Mar. 1760

Jonathan MOSHER^{5}, b. 13 Mar. 1699 <1:167>; d. betw. 10 May 1760 (will) - 4 July 1760 (inv.)<Bristol Co.PR 17:105>

Joseph MOSHER^{5}, b. 23 June 1701 <1:167>

James MOSHER^{5}, b. 14 Dec. 1704 <1:167>

Ruth MOSHER^{5}, b. 17 Sept. 1707 <1:170>

Benjamin MOSHER^{5}, b. 22 Feb. 1708/9 <1:164>; d. pre 1743 (father's will)

William MOSHER^{5}, b. 29 July 1713 <1:171>; d. pre 1743 (father's will)

Lydia MOSHER^{5}, b. ( )

Abigail MAXFIELD, (*dau of Timothy), b. 17 Aug. 1710* <Dartmouth VR>

CHILDREN OF Benjamin MOSHER^{5} & Abigail MAXFIELD*: (4) <1-3, Dartmouth VR>

Priscilla MOSHER^{6}, b. 22 Sept. 1729 <1:170>

Ede MOSHER^{6}, b. 17 Dec. 1731 <1:165>

Job MOSHER^{6}, b. 30 Apr. 1734 <1:167>

Rebecca MOSHER^{6}, b. ( )

CHILDREN OF Benjamin MOSHER 2d & Phebe BROWNELL: (9) <Dartmouth VR>**<96>**

Philip MOSHER, b. 7 June 1755 <1:170>

Thomas MOSHER, b. 7 June 1755 (twins) <1:171>

Desire MOSHER, b. 12 Mar. 1757 <1:165>

Richard MOSHER, b. 4 May 1759 <1:170>

Phebe MOSHER, b. 19 May 1761 <1:169>

Stephen MOSHER, b. 22 July 1763 <1:171>

Lydia MOSHER, b. 9 Mar. 1765 <1:168>

James MOSHER, b. 3 Nov. 1766 <1:167>

Jonathan MOSHER, b. 18 Apr. 1768 <1:167>

CHILDREN OF Thomas BROWNELL (1679-1752) & Mary CRANDALL (1689-1732): (6) <Little Compton RI VR>

Richard BROWNELL, b. 1715

Mary BROWNELL, b. 1717

Thomas BROWNELL, b. 1720; d. Nov. 1808

Sarah BROWNELL, b. 1722

Gideon BROWNELL, b. 1724; d. 1741

Phebe BROWNELL, b. 16 Feb. 1726 <VR 4:6:86>

CHILDREN OF Charles BROWNELL & Mary WILBOR: (5) <Little Compton RI VR 4:6:87>

Lemuel BROWNELL, b. 1719; d. 1780

James BROWNELL, b. 1722; d. 1736

Mary BROWNELL, b. 1724

Ruth BROWNELL, b. 1727

Phebe BROWNELL, b. 22 Sept. 1730

CHILDREN OF Giles BROWNELL & Elizabeth SHAW: (10) <Little Compton RI VR 4:6:87>

Isaac BROWNELL, b. 1726

Charles BROWNELL, b. 1728

Giles BROWNELL, b. 1729

William BROWNELL, b. 1731

Alice BROWNELL, b. 1733

Phebe BROWNELL, b. 10 June 1735

George BROWNELL, b. 1737

Mary BROWNELL, b. 1741

James BROWNELL, b. 1743

Joseph BROWNELL, b. 1744; d. 1824

CHILDREN OF James MOSHER[5] (Lydia Taber[4]) & Sarah DIVEL*: (5*) <Dartmouth VR>

Eunice MOSHER[6], b. 1 Mar. 1731 <1:166>

Gideon MOSHER[6], b. 26 June 1732 or 52 <1:166>

Peter MOSHER[6], b. 1 Jan. 1740/1 <1:169>

Anna MOSHER[6], b. 25 Aug. 1745 <1:163>

Benjamin MOSHER[6], b. 24 May 1749 <1:163>

Isabel POTTER, (dau of Stokes), b. 19 Oct. 1703* <Dartmouth VR 1:188>; d. aft. 4 Nov. 1760*

CHILDREN OF Jonathan MOSHER[5] (Lydia Taber[4]) & Isabel POTTER: (9) <1-7, Dartmouth VR>

Elizabeth MOSHER[6], b. 20 Sept. 1721* <1:165>

Judah MOSHER[6], b. 1 June 1723* <1:168>

Lydia MOSHER[6]*, b. 21 Mar. 1725* <1:168>, d. 9 Mar. 1727*

Jonathan MOSHER[6], b. 25 Nov. 1726* <1:167>

Isabel MOSHER[6], b. 2 Mar. 1730* <1:167>

Joseph MOSHER[6], b. 12 5mth 1732* <Uxbridge VR:111>

Job MOSHER[6], b. 4 Dec. 1737* <1:167>

Wesson MOSHER[6], b. ( )

Rebecca MOSHER[6], b. ( )

Meribah ALLEN, (dau of Zebulon), b. 16 1stmth 1739, d. 3 July 1778 <Uxbridge VR:111,389>

CHILD OF Joseph MOSHER[6] & Meribah ALLEN:

Allen MOSHER[7], b. 25 Sept. 1755 <Dartmouth VR 1:163>

CHILDREN OF Jonathan MOSHER[6]* (Jonathan[5]) & Ann MOTT: (3) <Dartmouth VR>

Hope MOSHER[7], b. 17 Apr. 1751 <1:166>

Garner MOSHER[7], b. 30 Aug. 1752 <1:166>

Elizabeth MOSHER[7], b. Nov. 1754 <1:165>

CHILDREN OF Philip MOSHER[5] (Lydia Taber[4]) & Abigail (TRIPP*), (*dau of Jonathan): (9*)<Dartmouth>

Israel MOSHER[6], b. 20 May 1720* <1:167>**<97>**

Caleb MOSHER[6]*, b. 8 Sept. 1721* <1:164>; d. betw. 8 Feb. 1786 (will) - 31 Aug. 1793 (prob.), of

Charlotte NY <Dutchess Co.PR A:366>
Maxson MOSHER[6*], b. 13 Jan. 1722* <VR 1:169>
Philip MOSHER[6], b. 8 May 1724* <VR 1:170>
Martha MOSHER[6*], b. 16 Oct. 1727* <1:168>, d.y.
Abigail MOSHER[6*], b. 4 Sept. 1730* <1:163>
Benjamin MOSHER[6*], b. 21 Apr. 1735* <1:164>
Lydia MOSHER[6*], b. 27 July 1738* <1:168>
Martha MOSHER[6*], b. 28 Dec. 1745* <1:168>

MICRO #20 of 30

Elizabeth WILBOR, (Sam. & Eliz. (Carr)), b. 23 July 1723* <Little Compton RI VR>; d. aft. 26 Mar. 1764* <mother's will> (see below)

CHILDREN OF Caleb MOSHER[6] & Elizabeth WILBOR: (1 of 8)[<98>]
Tripp MOSHER[7], b. Sept. 1744, d. 5 Nov. 1822, ae 78y1m9d
Samuel WILBOR, b. 7 Nov. 1692, d. May 1752, of Little Compton RI <Wilbores in America (1907)>
Elizabeth CARR, b. 29 July 1691, d. Mar. 1764 <will - 26 Mar. 1764, Little Compton RI PR 2:16>

CHILDREN OF Samuel WILBOR & Elizabeth CARR: (13) <Little Compton, RI VR 4:6:184>
Robert WILBOR, b. 14 Jan. 1715
Thomas WILBOR, b. 14 Sept. 1716
Susanna WILBOR, b. 10 June 1718
Mary WILBOR, b. 14 Mar. 1720
Abishai WILBOR, b. 22 Nov. 1722
Elizabeth WILBOR, b. 23 July 1723 (see above)
Martha WILBOR, b. 11 Mar. 1725
Ruth WILBOR, b. 20 Nov. 1726
Esek WILBOR, b. 22 Dec. 1728
Samuel WILBOR, b. 10 Oct. 1730
Joanna WILBOR, b. 29 May 1732
Ebenezer WILBOR, b. 3 Sept. 1735
David WILBOR, b. 31 July 1740

CHILDREN OF Daniel TRIPP & Rebecca MOSHER[5] (Lydia Taber[4]): (7)
Constant TRIPP[6], b. 25 May 1721* <Dartmouth VR 1:279>
Hannah TRIPP[6], b. 20 Oct. 1722* <Dartmouth VR 1:280>
Rebecca TRIPP[6], b. ( )
Daniel TRIPP[6], b. 19 July 1724* <Dartmouth VR 1:280>
Joseph TRIPP[6], b. ( )
Thomas TRIPP[6], b. 19 May 1734* <Dartmouth VR 1:283>
Charles TRIPP[6], b. ( )
William TRIPP, d. betw. 25 Nov. 1770 (will) - 4 Jan. 1771 (inv.) <Bristol Co.PR 21:497,499>

CHILDREN OF William TRIPP & Ruth MOSHER[5] (Lydia Taber[4]): (9*) <Dartmouth VR>
Desire TRIPP[6], b. 12 July 1729 <1:280>
Ede TRIPP[6], b. 24 Dec. 1730 <1:280>
Martha TRIPP[6], b. 27 Oct. 1732 <1:282>
Ruth TRIPP[6], b. 20 Nov. 1734 <1:283>
William TRIPP[6], b. 27 Feb. 1736/7 <1:284>
Abigail TRIPP[6], b. 12 Aug. 1738 <1:279>
Jonathan TRIPP[6], b. 30 Jan.1740/1 <1:281; Westport VR:94>
Lydia TRIPP[6], b. 1 Aug. 1747 <1:282>
Elijah TRIPP[6], b. 3 July1749 <1:280>
Abigail MOSHER, b. 13 Oct. 1743* <Westport VR:91>

CHILDREN OF Jonathan TRIPP[6] & Abigail MOSHER: (2) <Westport VR:91>

Abraham TRIPP^7, b. 10 Aug. 1765

Edey TRIPP^7, b. 1 Sept. 1768

Margaret ( ) TABER, d. betw. 16 May 1755 (will) - 3 May 1757 (prob.) <Bristol Co.PR 15:337-38>

CHILDREN OF Philip TABER^4 (Mary Cooke^3) & Margaret ( ): (10)<98a>

Benjamin BOWERS, d. aft. 13 Sept. 1772 (will) <Taunton PR 23:511>

CHILDREN OF Benjamin BOWERS & Comfort TABER^5 (Philip^4): (9)<99>

Stephen WEST, b. c1654, d. 12 Aug. 1748, 94th yr <Dartmouth VR:205>

CHILDREN OF Stephen WEST & Mercy COOKE^3: (9) <Dartmouth VR:11>

Katharine WEST^4, b. 9 Sept. 1684

Sarah WEST^4, b. 1 Aug. 1686

Ann WEST^4, b. 9 July 1688

Bartholomew WEST^4, b. 31 July 1690; d. betw. 15 Apr. 1767 (codicil) - 5 Oct. 1779 (prob.) <Bristol Co.PR 26:144,151>

Amy WEST^4, b. 22 May 1693

Stephen WEST^4, b. 19 May 1695; d. 7 July 1769, Dartmouth

John WEST^4, b. 27 Apr. 1697

Eunice WEST^4, b. 21 June 1699

Lois WEST^4, b. 12 Apr. 1701

CHILDREN OF Bartholomew WEST^4 & Ann ELDRIDGE: (6) <1-4, Dartmouth VR 1:293>

Andria WEST^5, b. 2 Jan. 1748/9*

William WEST^5, b. 1 Feb. 1750/1*

Bartholomew WEST^5, b. 26 Nov. 1753*, d.y.

Bartholomew WEST^5, b. 30 May 1756*

Edward WEST^5, b. ( )

Thomas WEST^5, b. ( ), d.y.

CHILDREN OF John WEST & Rebecca ( ): (2*) <Dartmouth VR 1:248>

Katherine WEST, b. 22 May 1730

Marcy WEST, b. 19 Feb. 1732

Susanna JENNEY, (dau of Sam. & Hannah), b. 3 Apr. 1697 <Dartmouth VR 1:140>

CHILDREN OF Stephen WEST^4 (Mercy Cooke^3) & Susanna JENNEY: (8) <Dartmouth VR 1:205>

Hannah WEST^5, b. 21 Apr. 1720

Mercy WEST^5, b. 7 July 1722

Samuel WEST^5, b. 3 Apr. 1723

Anne WEST^5, b. 8 Oct. 1727

Almy WEST^5, b. 11 Jan. 1729/30

Stephen WEST^5, b. 14 Mar. 1732

Bartholomew WEST^5, b. 8 Nov. 1734

MICRO # 21 of 30

CHILDREN OF Stephen WEST^5 & Salome ELDRIDGE: (5*) <Dartmouth VR 1:190>

Matthew WEST^6, b. 18 Feb. 1750/1, d. 15 Feb. 1753

Elnathan WEST^6, b. 20 Dec. 1753

Stephen WEST^6, b. 3 Feb. 1756

Rhoda WEST^6, b. 2 Jan. 1758

Samuel WEST^6, b. 14 Feb. 1762

CHILDREN OF Jethro HATHAWAY & Hannah WEST: (3) <Dartmouth VR><100>

Hephzibah HATHAWAY, b. 3 Apr. 1742

Stephen HATHAWAY, b. 28 Feb. 1743

Clark HATHAWAY, b. 25 Oct. 1747

Arthur HATHAWAY, d. 11 Dec. 1711, Dartmouth <MD 16:111>

CHILDREN OF Arthur HATHAWAY & Sarah COOKE^3: (4 of 7) <Plymouth><101>

John HATHAWAY[4], b. 17 Sept. 1653 <MD 17:70>; d. 11 July 1732, Dartmouth

Sarah HATHAWAY[4], b. 28 Feb. 1655 <MD 17:71>

Hannah HATHAWAY[4], b. ( ); d. betw. 13 Feb. 1748/9 (will) - 14 Mar. 1748/9 (inv.) <MD 22:2>

Lydia HATHAWAY[4], b. 1662, d. 23 June 1714 <Austin's Dict.:181>

Stephen PECKHAM[1], d. 23 Apr. 1724 <Peckham Gen.:224>**<102>**

Stephen PECKHAM[2], (Stephen[1]), b. 23 Feb. 1683, d. June 1764, Dartmouth <Peckham Gen.:234>**<103>**

CHILDREN OF Stephen PECKHAM[2] & 1st Content (?SISSON): (5) <Peckham Gen.:234>**<104>**

James PECKHAM, b. 4 Oct. 1716

Stephen PECKHAM, b. 4 Sept. 1718, d. 18 Mar. 1797

Seth PECKHAM, b. 29 Nov. 1723, d.y.

Content PECKHAM, b. 16 Feb. 1729, d.y.

George PECKHAM, b. 25 Oct. 1732, d.y.

CHILDREN OF Stephen PECKHAM[2] & 2nd Keturah ARTHUR, (dau of John & Mary (Folger)): (3) <Peckham>

Elizabeth PECKHAM, b. 5 July 1741

Eunice PECKHAM, b. 6 Dec. 1742

Richard PECKHAM, b. 16 Dec. 1744

CHILDREN OF Stephen PECKHAM[3] (Stephen[2]) & Sarah BOSS/BASS: (2 of 11*) <Peckham Gen.:272>**<104a>**

Elizabeth PECKHAM, b. 22 Dec. 1740

Seth PECKHAM, b. 31 Oct. 1750, d. 1826

CHILDREN OF Seth PECKHAM[4] (Stephen[3]) & Mercy SMITH: (1 of 6*) <Peckham Gen.:327>**<105>**

Dr. Hazael PECKHAM, b. 16 Nov. 1777, d. 1837, Killingly CT

Susanna THORNTON, b. 8 Oct. 1776 <Peckham Gen.:415>

CHILDREN OF Dr. Hazael PECKHAM[5] (Seth[4]) & Susanna THORNTON: (9*) <Peckham Gen.:416>

Paris PECKHAM, b. 1798, unm.

Smith PECKHAM, b. 1800

Amy PECKHAM, b. 1802

James PECKHAM, b. ( )

Susan PECKHAM, b. 1810

Hazael PECKHAM, b. 1811

Horatio PECKHAM, b. ( )

Pamelia PECKHAM, b. 1815

Dr. Fenner Harris PECKHAM, b. 20 or 27 Jan. 1820, d. 17 Feb. 1887

Catharine Davis TORREY, b. 13 June 1819, d. 22 Feb. 1853 <Peckham Gen.:493>

CHILDREN OF Dr. Fenner Harris PECKHAM[6] (Hazael[5]) & Catharine Davis TORREY: (1 of 4*)**<106>**

Ella L. T. PECKHAM, b. 12 Sept. 1846 <Peckham Gen.:496>

George CADMAN, (son of Wm.), d. 17 Nov. 1718* <Dartmouth VR 3:22>

CHILD OF George CADMAN & Hannah HATHAWAY[4] (Sarah Cooke[3]):

Elizabeth CADMAN[5], b. ( ) <MD 22:2>; d. aft. 6 Jan. 1768 (husband's will)

William WHITE[4] (Silvanus[3], Peregrine[2]), b. pre July 1684; d. betw. 6 Jan. 1768 (will)<Bristol Co. PR 26:286> - 17 Feb. 1777* (son William's will) <MD 22:7>

CHILDREN OF William WHITE & Elizabeth CADMAN[5]: (4 of 11)**<107>**

George WHITE[6], b. ( ); d. betw. 28 Dec. 1762 (will) - 29 Mar. 1764 (prob.) <Bristol Co.PR 18:318>

Christopher WHITE[6], b. ( ); d. betw. 18 Dec. 1793 (will) - 5 Oct. 1795 (prob.), Tiverton **<108>**

Sarah WHITE[6], b. ( ); d. aft. 6 Jan. 1768* <MD 22:8>

William WHITE[6], b. ( ); d. betw. 17 Feb. 1777 (will) - 9 Sept. 1780 (prob.) <MD 22:7>

David D. WHITE, b. 11 Oct. 1799, d. 20 July 1849, Little Compton <RI VR 4:6:181>

Patience BROWN, b. 31 Sept. 1804, Portsmouth <RI VR 4:6:181>

CHILDREN OF David D. WHITE & Patience BROWN: (12) <RI VR 4:6:181>

Christopher T. WHITE, b. 22 Mar. 1826

Ruth D. WHITE, b. 15 May 1827, d. 5 July 1866

Harriet A. WHITE, b. 10 Mar. 1829
Mary C. WHITE, b. 8 Feb. 1831
Benjamin B. WHITE, b. 29 Jan. 1833, d. 14 May 1835
Elizabeth W. WHITE, b. 13 Jan. 1835
Thomas E. WHITE, b. 5 Nov. 1836
Benjamin B. WHITE, b. 22 Jan. 1838
Martha L. WHITE, b. 8 Jan. 1840, d. 5 Apr. 1852
Pardon B. WHITE, b. 9 Mar. 1842, d. 19 Oct. 1865
Susan F. WHITE, b. 5 Mar. 1843
Charles G. WHITE, b. 19 May 1846
Elizabeth THURSTON, (dau of Edward), b. 24 or 29 Sept. 1719, Little Compton RI[<109>]
CHILDREN OF Christopher WHITE[6] (Eliz. Cadman[5]) & Elizabeth THURSTON: (12) <RI VR 4:6:181>
Sarah WHITE[7], b. 28 Sept. 1740
Thurston WHITE[7], b. 28 Oct. 1741
William WHITE[7], b. 26 May 1742
Mary WHITE[7], b. 26 May 1744
Noah WHITE[7], b. 26 Mar. 1745
Peregrine WHITE[7], b. 19 Nov. 1748; d. Sept. 1832
Susanna WHITE[7], b. 11 Aug. 1751
Elizabeth WHITE[7], b. 27 Feb. 1753; d. 22 Jan. 1844
Lucy WHITE[7], b. 24 Jan. 1755
Pardon WHITE[7], b. ( ); d. July 1789
Thomas WHITE[7], b. ( ); d. 7 Dec. 1841
Ruth WHITE[7], b. ( )
CHILDREN OF Noah WHITE[7] & Rhoda SHAW: (7) <Newport, VR RI 4:2:123>
William WHITE[8], b. 15 July 1777 <Little Compton RI VR>
Elizabeth WHITE[8], b. 28 Mar. 1779 <Little Compton RI VR>
Susanna WHITE[8], b. 9 Feb. 1782
Simeon WHITE[8], b. 16 Mar. 1785
Nicholas WHITE[8], b. 7 Oct. 1786
Pardon WHITE[8], b. 17 Feb. 1788
Roby WHITE[8], b. 21 Jan. 1795
Deborah SHAW, d. betw. 15 Jan.1766 (will) - 24 Nov. 1766 (prob.) <Bristol Co.PR 19:438>
CHILDREN OF George WHITE[6] (Eliz. Cadman[5]) & Deborah SHAW: (11) <New Bedford VR:161>
Israel WHITE[7], b. 27 Nov. 1730
Peleg WHITE[7], b. 14 Sept. 1732
Silvanus WHITE[7], b. 26 June 1734, d.y.
Ruth WHITE[7], b. 19 May 1736
Sarah WHITE[7], b. 25 Apr. 1740
William WHITE[7], b. 28 Feb. 1741/2
Hannah WHITE[7], b. 28 Mar. 1744
Mary WHITE[7], b. 4 June 1746
Eunice WHITE[7], b. 11 Aug. 1748
Silvanus WHITE[7], b. 14 Dec. 1750
Obed WHITE[7], b. ( ) (in father's will)
CHILDREN OF Israel WHITE[7] & Sibyl (WOODWARD) Hicks: (4) <New Bedford VR:290>
Theophilus WHITE[8], b. 10 Apr. 1755
Jerathmeel WHITE[8], b. 28 July 1757
John WHITE[8], b. 12 Oct. 1759
Cornelius WHITE[8], b. 14 Sept. 1762

CHILDREN OF Peleg WHITE[7] (Geo.[6]) & Rachel CORNELL: (5) <Dartmouth VR; also New Bedford VR:293>

Sarah WHITE[8], b. 17 Nov. 1755 <1:297>

Hannah WHITE[8], b. 1 Aug. 1757 <1:296>

Roger WHITE[8], b. 10 Oct. 1760 <1:297>; d. 4 Feb. 1829*, Ledyard, Cayuga Co., NY

George WHITE[8], b. 17 Nov. 1762 <1:296>

Peleg WHITE[8], b. 16 Oct. 1770 <1:297>

CHILDREN OF Roger WHITE[8] & Lydia PECKHAM, (dau of Stephen): (3) <Dartmouth & Westport VR>

Sarah P. WHITE[9], b. 28 Sept. 1783

Mehitable WHITE[9], b. 26 Oct. 1785

Elizabeth WHITE[9], b. 1 Feb. 1790

Culbert WILCOX, (*son of Stephen & Mary), b. 13 Apr. 1732* <Dartmouth VR 1:301> (hus of Ruth White[7] (Geo.[6]))

John BROWN, (son of Tobias), b. 1705, Little Compton RI; d. aft. 13 Feb. 1748/9* <MD 22:6>

CHILDREN OF John BROWN & Sarah WHITE[6] (Eliz. Cadman[5]): (9) <Little Compton, RI VR 4:6:95>

William BROWN[7], b. 12 May 1727*

Elizabeth BROWN[7], b. 10 Nov. 1728*

Abigail BROWN[7], b. 23 Oct. 1730*

Mary BROWN[7], b. 5 Mar. 1733*

John BROWN[7], b. 9 Nov. 1734*

Ruth BROWN[7], b. 23 Aug. 1737*; d. 5 Oct. 1805, Waterford RI g.s.

George BROWN[7], b. 17 Aug. 1739*

Thomas BROWN[7], b. 1741*; d. Mar. 1802*

Sarah BROWN[7], b. 1743*

Wanton HOWLAND, b. 2 Jan. 1732/3*, Tiverton <RI VR 4:7:89>

CHILD OF Wanton HOWLAND & Ruth BROWN[7]:

Benjamin HOWLAND[8]*, b. 7 July 1755*, d. 9 May 1821*

Gilbert DEVOL, b. c1739, d. 5 June 1824, 85th yr, Waterford RI g.s.<2nd hus. Ruth Brown[7])

Abigail THURSTON, (dau of Jonathan & Sarah), b. 7 May 1700 <Thurston Gen.:264>

CHILDREN OF William WHITE[6] (Eliz. Cadman[5]) & Abigail THURSTON: (2 of 5) <New Bedford VR:162>**<110>**

Sarah WHITE[7], b. 31 ( ) 1730

Hannah WHITE[7], b. 1731

Joanna POPE, (dau of Tho.), d. 25 Dec. 1695 <Dartmouth VR 3:36>

CHILDREN OF John HATHAWAY[4] (Sarah Cooke[3]) & 1st Joanna POPE: (6) <Dartmouth VR>

Sarah HATHAWAY[5], b. 24 Feb. 1683/4 <1:114>

Joanna HATHAWAY[5], b. 28 Jan. 1685 <1:112>

John HATHAWAY[5], b. 18 Mar. 1687 <1:112>

Arthur HATHAWAY[5], b. 3 Apr. 1690 <1:110>

Hannah HATHAWAY[5], b. 16 Feb. 1692 <1:111>

Mary HATHAWAY[5], b. 4 June 1694 <1:113>

CHILDREN OF John HATHAWAY[4] & 2nd Patience ( ): (10) <Dartmouth VR>**<111>**

Jonathan HATHAWAY[5], b. 23 June 1697 <1:112>; d. 11 May 1759*

Richard HATHAWAY[5], b. 21 May 1699 <1:113>

Thomas HATHAWAY[5], b. 5 Feb. 1700 <1:114>

Hunewell HATHAWAY[5], b. 21 Apr. 1703 <1:112>; d. betw. 2 Mar. 1772 (will) - 10 June 1772 (inv.) <Bristol Co.PR 22:244,259>

Abiah HATHAWAY[5], b. 21 Oct. 1705 <1:110>

Elizabeth HATHAWAY[5], b. 6 May 1708 <1:111>

Patience HATHAWAY[5], b. 27 Apr. 1710 <1:113>

Benjamin HATHAWAY[5], b. 10 Jan. 1712 <1:110>

James HATHAWAY[5], b. 24 Jan. 1713/4 <1:112>

Ebenezer HATHAWAY^5, b. 12 May 1717 <1:111>; d. pre 17 May 1774 <Bristol Co.Deeds 56:420>

MICRO #22 of 30

CHILDREN OF Ebenezer HATHAWAY^5 & Ruth HATCH: (7) <Dartmouth VR>

Lucee HATHAWAY^6, b. 17 Apr. 1742 <1:112>

Samuel HATHAWAY^6, b. 9 Dec. 1744 <1:;114>

James HATHAWAY^6, b. 9 July 1747 <1:112>

Ebenezer HATHAWAY^6, b. 6 Sept. 1749 <1:111>

Abiah HATHAWAY^6, b. 7 July 1751 <1:110>

Ruth HATHAWAY^6, b. 13 Apr. 1754 <1:114>

Timothy HATHAWAY^6, b. 24 Mar. 1756 <1:114>

CHILDREN OF Hunewell HATHAWAY^5 (John^4) & Mary (WORTH*): (8) <Dartmouth VR>

William HATHAWAY^6, b. 19 Jan. 1733/4* <1:114>; d. 27 Aug. 1765*, Dartmouth

Anna HATHAWAY^6, b. 1 Mar. 1735/6* <1:110>; d. pre 2 Mar. 1772* (father's will)

Lydia HATHAWAY^6, b. 29 Mar. 1738* <1:112>; d. pre 2 Mar. 1772* (father's will)

Obed HATHAWAY^6, b. 31 Dec. 1740*, <1:113>

Hunewell HATHAWAY^6, b. 30 Oct. 1743* <1:112>

James HATHAWAY^6, b. 21 Sept. 1747* <1:112>

Richard HATHAWAY^6, b. 28 Sept. 1750* <1:114>; d. 2 Aug. 1827*, New Bedford <Friends' Rcds.>

Paul HATHAWAY^6, b. ( )

Ruth BARKER, (dau of Jos.), d. 26 Mar. 1769*, Dartmouth

CHILD OF William HATHAWAY^6 & Ruth BARKER:

William HATHAWAY^7, b. 10 Oct. 1765*; d. 17 July 1770*

CHILD OF James BATES & Anna HATHAWAY^6 (Hunewell^5):

Worth BATES^7, b. c1759-70

CHILDREN OF William RUSSEL & Lydia HATHAWAY^6 (Hunewell^5): (2)

William RUSSEL^7, b. c1764-72*

Jonathan RUSSEL^7, b. 1764-72*

CHILDREN OF Paul HATHAWAY^6 (Hunewell^5) & Sarah WINSLOW: (8) <Dartmouth VR>

Mary HATHAWAY^7, b. 16 Oct. 1779

Anna HATHAWAY^7, b. 14 June 1781 <1:110>

Rhoda HATHAWAY^7, b. 22 Sept. 1783 <1:113>

Obed HATHAWAY^7, b. 3 Feb. 1786 <1:113>

James HATHAWAY^7, b. 17 Sept. 1790 <1:112>

Sarah HATHAWAY^7, b. 9 Apr. 1793 <1:114>

Phebe HATHAWAY^7, b. 20 Jan. 1798 <1:113>

Hunewell HATHAWAY^7, b. 11 May 1800 <1:112>

Sarah (HATHAWAY*), d. 14 July 1837*, ae 87, New Bedford <Friends' Rcds.>

CHILDREN OF Richard HATHAWAY^6 (Hunewell^5) & Sarah HATHAWAY: (7) <New Bedford VR>

William HATHAWAY^7, b. 22 June 1775*

Ebenezer HATHAWAY^7, b. 3 Feb. 1778* <1:220>

John HATHAWAY^7, b. 7 July 1782* <1:222>; d. pre Mar. 1825* (father's will)

Ezra HATHAWAY^7, b. 9 Oct. 1785* <1:221>; d. 1 July 1865, bur. Hathaway Farm <New Bedford VR 3:56>

Wesson HATHAWAY^7, b. 30 Apr. 1787* <1:226>; d. 21 Aug. 1825* <Northbridge VR:187>

Sarah HATHAWAY^7, b. 22 Feb. 1789* <1:225>

Lydia HATHAWAY^7, b. 27 Mar. 1791* <1:223>

Abigail (WANTON) Thurston, (dau of John), d. pre 4 July 1848 (adm.) <Bristol Co.PR 92:269>

CHILDREN OF Ezra HATHAWAY^7 & Abigail (WANTON) Thurston: (4 of 7) <New Bedford>**<112>**

Elizabeth Thurston HATHAWAY^8, b. 15 Jan. 1809*; d. 30 Apr. 1846*, New Bedford

Hannah W. HATHAWAY^8, b. c1823, New Bedford, d. 14 Mar. 1880, ae 57, New Bedford, married (Hannah King) <Mass.VR 319:126>

Adelaide HATHAWAY^{8}, b. ( ), d. pre 1851* (*1st wf of James Beetle below, no issue)

Ann Amelia HATHAWAY^{8}, b. 27 Oct. 1825, d. 20 Aug. 1889, New Bedford g.s. <Mass.VR 400:100>

CHILDREN OF Joseph C. TEW & Sarah A. HATHAWAY^{8} (Ezra^{7}): (2*) <New Bedford>

Edward C. TEW^{9}, b. 2 Dec. 1843

Emily TEW^{9}, b. 30 Oct. 1846

James BEETLE, (son of Henry & Martha), b. 8 Feb. 1812; boat builder, bur. New Bedford

CHILDREN OF James BEETLE & Ann Amelia HATHAWAY^{8} (Ezra^{7}): (3*)**<113>**

CHILDREN OF Benjamin KING, (b. c1808*) & Lydia Ann HATHAWAY^{8} (Ezra^{7}): (2)**<114>**

Adeline H. KING^{9}, b. aft. 1834*

Georgiana KING^{9}, b. aft. 1834*

Ezra HATHAWAY, son of Isaac, b. c1782, d. 26 Oct. 1864, ae 82, New Bedford <Mass.VR 174:126>

MICRO #23 of 30

CHILDREN OF George Cornell TEW & Elizabeth Thurston HATHAWAY^{8} (Ezra^{7}): (1 of 6)**<115>**

Sarah Thurston TEW^{9}, b. 5 May 1839

Mercy Ann ( ) HATHAWAY, b. 16 Nov. 1791* <Uxbridge VR>

CHILDREN OF Wesson HATHAWAY^{7} (Richard^{6}) & Mercy Ann ( ): (5) <Uxbridge VR:86>

Elizabeth Bowen HATHAWAY^{8}, b. 29 Mar. 1814*

Sarah Ann HATHAWAY^{8}, b. 20 Mar. 1816*

Nancy Almy HATHAWAY^{8}, b. 29 June 1818*

William HATHAWAY^{8}, b. 11 July 1820*

Thomas Smith HATHAWAY^{8}, b. 25 Sept. 1822*

Hannah PECKHAM, b. 6 Sept. 1782, RI; d. 28 Dec. 1867, of Tiverton RI, wf of Jos. Church <Mass. VR 202:92>

Mr. PECKHAM, native of Block Island, drowned at Bannister's Wharf, Newport, ae 60, 6 May 1807 <Providence Phenix, RI VR 19:52>

John CANNON, d. 28 Mar. 1750* <NEHGR 21:266>

CHILDREN OF John CANNON & Sarah HATHAWAY^{5} (John^{4}): (6) <NEHGR 22:66>

Cornelius CANNON^{6}, b. 18 July 1711

John CANNON^{6}, b. 11 Aug. 1714

Elizabeth CANNON^{6}, b. 20 Mar. 1716/7

Mary CANNON^{6}, b. 3 Apr. 1719

Philip CANNON^{6}, b. 11 Sept. 1721 <22:67>

Joanna CANNON^{6}, b. 27 Mar. 1728 <22:67>

Susanna POPE^{3} (Seth^{2}, Tho.^{1}), b. 31 July 1681, Dartmouth, d. 5 Feb. 1760, Dartmouth <NEHGR 42:52>

CHILDREN OF Jonathan HATHAWAY^{4} (Sarah Cooke^{3}) & Susanna POPE: (10) <Dartmouth VR:97>

Elizabeth HATHAWAY^{5}, b. 11 Mar. 1703, d. 29 Apr. 1703

Abigail HATHAWAY^{5}, b. 14 Dec. 1704

Gamaliel HATHAWAY^{5}, b. 10 Oct. 1707; d. betw. 3 June 1793 (will) - 2 Mar. 1797 (prob.)

Hannah HATHAWAY^{5}, b. 8 Nov. 1709

Seth HATHAWAY^{5}, b. 17 Aug. 1711

Deborah HATHAWAY^{5}, b. 10 July 1713

Jonathan HATHAWAY^{5}, b. 17 Oct. 1715

Silas HATHAWAY^{5}, b. 10 Dec. 1717

Elnathan HATHAWAY^{5}, b. 16 Jan. 1719/20

Paul HATHAWAY^{5}, b. 6 Oct. 1722, d. 2 Jan. 1722/3

CHILDREN OF Gamaliel HATHAWAY^{5} & Hannah HILLMAN*: (4) <Dartmouth VR 1:113>**<116>**

Obed HATHAWAY^{6}, b. 25 Mar. 1737*; d. betw. 15 Aug. 1805 (will) - 6 May 1806 (prob.) <Bristol Co. PR 42:110,111>

Eleazer HATHAWAY^{6}, b. 1 Aug. 1739*

Anna HATHAWAY^{6}, b. 3 Aug. 1741***<117>**

Micah HATHAWAY[6], b. 1 Oct. 1743*; d. 6 Jan. 1816*, Acushnet Cem.

Benjamin DILLINGHAM, d. betw. 25 June 1821 (will) - 25 July 1826 (prob.) <Bristol Co.PR 63:451> (hus. of Anna Hathaway[6])<117>

Mary MYRICKS, b. c1748, d. 3 Jan. 1793*, 45th yr, Acushnet Cem.

CHILDREN OF Micah HATHAWAY[6] & Mary MYRICKS*: (4 of 12)<118>

Thomas HATHAWAY[7], b. aft. 1764*

Nathan HATHAWAY[7], d. pre 1 May 1827 (adm.) <Bristol Co. PR 65:105> (1782-1826 - Fairhaven g.s.)

Micah HATHAWAY[7], b. ( )

Obed HATHAWAY[7], b. ( )

Elizabeth KEMPTON, (dau of James & Phebe), b. c1784, d. 23 July 1867, ae 83, Fairhaven <Mass.VR 202:72> (1784-1867 - Fairhaven g.s.)

CHILDREN OF Nathan HATHAWAY[7] & Elizabeth KEMPTON: (2)<119>

Phebe Kempton HATHAWAY[8], b. c1810, d. 20 Nov. 1888, ae 78, New Bedford, bur. Fairhaven (widow of Benjamin Jenne Crapo, below) <Mass.VR 391:167> (1810-1888 - Fairhaven g.s.)<120>

Daniel K. HATHAWAY[8], b. aft. 1813<121>

James KEMPTON, b. c1848, d. 11 Jan. 1816, 68th yr, Acushnet Cem.

Phebe STODDARD, b. c1853, d. 31 Dec. 1821, ae 68, Acushnet Cem.

CHILDREN OF James KEMPTON & Phebe STODDARD: (3) <g.s.>

Daniel KEMPTON, b. c1780, d. 21 Nov. 1814, 34th yr, at Halifax N.S., Acushnet Cem.

Hannah KEMPTON, d. 13 Apr. 1802, (no age), Acushnet Cem.

James KEMPTON, b. c1782, d. 24 May 1801, ae 19 wanting 18 days, in NY, Acushnet Cem.

Benjamin Jenne CRAPO, b. c1801, d. 22 Apr. 1864, ae 63, Fairhaven (hus of Phebe K. Hathaway[8]) <Mass.VR 174:87> (1801-1864 - Fairhaven g.s.)

CHILDREN OF Obed HATHAWAY[6] (Gamaliel[5]) & Desire HAWES: (4)<122>

James SISSON, d. betw. 15 June 1734 (will) - 2 Dec. 1734 (inv.) <Bristol Co.PR 8:168,180>

CHILDREN OF James SISSON & Lydia HATHAWAY[4] (Sarah Cooke[3]): (2 of 10) <Dartmouth VR 1:235><123>

Richard SISSON[5], b. 19 Feb. 1682*

Mary SISSON[5], b. 26 Feb. 1684/5*

CHILDREN OF Stephen PECKHAM & Content ( ): (5) <Dartmouth VR> (see p.373)

James PECKHAM, b. 4 Oct. 1716

Stephen PECKHAM, b. 14 Sept. 1718

Seth PECKHAM, b. 29 Nov. 1723

Content PECKHAM, b. 16 Feb. 1728/9

George PECKHAM, b. 25 Oct. 1732

CHILDREN OF Stephen PECKCOM & Keturah ( ): (3) <Dartmouth VR> (see p.373)

Elizabeth PECKCOM, b. 5 July 1741

Eunice PECKCOM, b. 6 Dec. 1742

Richard PECKCOM, b. 16 Nov. 1744

William DAVOL, d. 1772 (pre 14 Feb.- prob.)

CHILDREN OF William DAVOL & Sarah SISSON[5] (Lydia Hathaway[4]): (1 of 7)<124>

Hannah DAVOL[6], b. 13 Jan. 1712*

Samuel HAMMOND, d. betw. 12 July 1728 (will) - 20 Sept. 1728 (prob.)<Plymouth Co.PR 5:477>

CHILDREN OF Samuel HAMMOND & Mary HATHAWAY[4] (Sarah Cooke[3]): (11) <Rochester VR>

Benjamin HAMMOND[5], b. 18 Dec. 1682 <1:145> (1681?)

Seth HAMMOND[5], b. 13 Feb. 1683 <1:154>

Rosamond HAMMOND[5], b. 8 May 1684 <1:154>

Samuel HAMMOND[5], b. 8 Mar. 1685 <1:154>

Thomas HAMMOND[5], b. 16 Sept. 1687 <1:156>

Jedidiah HAMMOND[5], b. 19 Sept. 1690 <1:149>

Josiah HAMMOND[5], b. 15 Sept. 1692 <1:150>

Barnabas HAMMOND^{5}, b. 20 Jan. 1694/5 <1:144>

Meriah HAMMOND^{5}, b. 27 Jan. 1697/8 <1:152>

John HAMMOND^{5}, b. 4 Oct. 1701 <1:150>

Jedidah HAMMOND^{5}, b. 30 Sept. 1703 <1:149>

MICRO #24 of 30

CHILDREN OF Seth HAMMOND^{5} & Mercy RANDEL: (3) <Rochester VR>

Jerusha HAMMOND^{6}, b. 2 May 1708 <VR 1:144>

Aculus HAMMOND^{6}, b. 15 Dec. 1709 <VR 1:149>

Jedediah HAMMOND^{6}, b. 16 Dec. 1711 <VR 1:149>

Elizabeth JENNEY, d. 14 Dec. 1747 <Dartmouth VR 3:34>

CHILDREN OF Jedediah HAMMOND^{6} & 1st Elizabeth JENNEY: (5) <Dartmouth VR>

Zilpha HAMMOND^{7}, b. 5 July 1738 <1:106>

Jeduthan HAMMOND^{7}, b. 14 Apr. 1740 <1:105>

Eliphel HAMMOND^{7}, b. 14 June 1742 <1:105>

Jenne HAMMOND^{7}, b. 30 ( ) 1744 <1:105>

Elisabeth HAMMOND^{7}, b. 12 June 1747 <1:105>

CHILDREN OF Jedediah HAMMOND^{6} & 2nd Mary BOWLS: (12)

Child, bpt. 1749 <Rochester VR 1:157>

Deborah HAMMOND^{7}, b. 30 May 1749 <Dartmouth VR 1:105>

Symson HAMMOND^{7}, bpt. 14 Oct. 1750 <Rochester VR 1:156>

Simson HAMMOND^{7}, b. 14 Sept. 1751 <Dartmouth VR 1:106>

Child, bpt. 5 July 1752 <Rochester VR 1:157>

Phinehas HAMMOND^{7}, b. 15 Mar. 1753 <Dartmouth VR 1:105>

Patience HAMMOND^{7}, b. 21 Jan. 1755 <Rochester VR 1:153>

Anna HAMMOND^{7}, b. 28 Mar. 1758 <Rochester VR 1:144>

Pernal HAMMOND^{7}, b. 21 Apr. 1760 <Rochester VR 1:153>

Ruth HAMMOND^{7}, bpt. 16 Oct. 1763 <Rochester VR 1:154>

Ruth HAMMOND^{7}, b. 4 Sept. 1764 <Rochester VR 1:154>

Jedidiah HAMMOND^{7}, b. 4 July 1767 <Rochester VR 1:149>

Mary JENNE, (dau of Lettis & Mary), b. 7 May 1749 <Dartmouth VR 1:139> (m. Jeduthan Hammond^{7})

Margaret HAMMOND, b. c1785, Springfield, d. 22 Apr. 1861, ae 76, E. Brookfield, widow <Mass.VR 149:213>

Hephzibah STARBUCK, b. 2 Apr. 1680, Nantucket; d. 2 July or Sept. 1740*, Nantucket**<125>**

CHILDREN OF Thomas HATHAWAY^{4} (Sarah Cooke^{3}) & Hephzibah STARBUCK: (10) <Dartmouth VR:207>

Antipas HATHAWAY^{5}, b. 5 Oct. 1698

Apphia HATHAWAY^{5}, b. 13 May 1701

Pernel HATHAWAY^{5}, b. 3 June 1703; d. 6 Nov. 1715

Elizabeth HATHAWAY^{5}, b. 18 Oct. 1706

Mary HATHAWAY^{5}, b. 3 Oct. 1709

Thomas HATHAWAY^{5}, b. 25 Dec. 1711; d. 7 Nov. 1785

Nathaniel HATHAWAY^{5}, b. 23 June 1715

Hephzibah HATHAWAY^{5}, b. 18 Mar. 1718

Jethro HATHAWAY^{5}, b. 31 July 1720; d. 15 June 1803 <New Bedford TR 2:303> (see below)

Stephen HATHAWAY^{5}, b. aft. 1720***<126>**

Lois TABER^{5} (Jacob^{4}, Mary Tomson^{3}, Mary Cooke^{2}), b. 23 Aug. 1719 (wf of Tho. Hathaway^{5}, no issue)

Patience (COOK) Church, b. c1698, d. 17 Jan. 1764*, Newport RI

CHILD OF Antipas HATHAWAY^{5} & Patience (COOK) Church*:

Nathaniel HATHAWAY^{6}, b. 10 Jan. 1738/9 <Dartmouth VR 1:113>; d. pre 28 Sept. 1784 (inv.) <Bristol Co.PR 33:130>

CHILDREN OF Nathaniel HATHAWAY^{6} & Elizabeth PEIRCE, (dau of Clothier): (4)

Martha HATHAWAY^{7}, b. 11 Oct. 1771, Newport RI; d. 4 Apr. 1863, ae 91y5m23d, Westport <Mass.VR 165:143>

Elizabeth HATHAWAY^{7}, b. 22 Dec. 1776*

Patience HATHAWAY^{7}, b. 17 Oct. 1778* <Howland Gen.:214>

Nathaniel HATHAWAY^{7}, b. 1 Jan. 1782* <Nantucket VR 2:129 (Folger)>

Noah GIFFORD, b. 8 Feb. 1758*; d. 2 Nov. 1835*

CHILD OF Noah GIFFORD & Martha HATHAWAY^{7}:

Nathaniel GIFFORD^{8}, b. 26 Apr. 1798*, Little Compton RI

Mercy Anthony MACOMBER, (dau of Nathaniel & Susanna), b. c1799, Westport, d. 24 Nov. 1889, ae 89y9m17d, New Bedford, bur. Westport <Mass.VR 400:88>

CHILD OF Nathaniel GIFFORD^{8} & Mercy Anthony MACOMBER:

Abbie L. GIFFORD^{9}, b. c1844, Little Compton RI, d. 29 Dec. 1927, ae 83y9m20d, Westport <Mass.VR 80:585>

CHILD OF John H. BAKER & Abbie HOPKINS:

Jehiel BAKER, b. 26 Dec. 1837, Brewster, d. 12 Mar. 1915, ae 77y2m14d, Westport <Mass.VR 87:403>

CHILD OF Jehiel BAKER & Abbie L. GIFFORD^{9}:

Mercie E. BAKER^{10} b. 17 Aug. 1876, Westport <Mass.VR 277:161>

Susanna MAYHEW, b. 28 Apr. 1797* <Nantucket VR 2:129 (Folger)> (*wf of Nath. Hathaway^{7} above)

Resolved HOWLAND, b. 11 Sept. 1769* (m. Patience Hathaway^{7} above)

CHILD OF Adam MOTT & Apphia HATHAWAY^{5} (Tho.^{4}):

Jacob MOTT^{6}*, b. 27 Aug. 1721*

Anne WEST^{5} (Stephen^{4}, Mercy Cooke^{3}, John^{2}), b. 8 Oct. 1727*; d. 26 Dec. 1810*

CHILDREN OF Jacob MOTT^{6} & Anne WEST: (5*)

Starbuck MOTT^{7}, b. 17 Feb. 1748

Joseph MOTT^{7}, b. 16 May 1751

Stephen MOTT^{7}, b. 7 June 1754

Susannah MOTT^{7}, b. 3 Apr. 1758

Benjamin MOTT^{7}, b. 2 Oct. 1762

CHILDREN OF Samuel WING & Hepzibah HATHAWAY^{5} (Tho.^{4}): (6*) <Wing Gen.:82,95>**<127>**

CHILDREN OF Jethro HATHAWAY^{5} (Tho.^{4}) & Hannah WEST^{5} (Stephen^{4}, Mercy Cooke^{3}, John^{2}): (3)**<128>**

Hephzibah HATHAWAY^{6}, b. 3 Apr. 1742 <New Bedford VR:230>; d. aft. 13 May 1809* (deed)

Stephen HATHAWAY^{6}, b. 28 Feb. 1743 <New Bedford VR:230>; d. 4 Nov. 1825, New Bedford <Friends' Rcds.1:73>

Clark HATHAWAY^{6}, b. 25 Oct. 1747 <New Bedford VR:230>

Timothy DAVIS, (*son of Nicholas & Ruth), b. 9 Apr. 1730* <Rochester VR 1:102>; d. 18 July 1798 <Friends' Rcds.>

CHILDREN OF Timothy DAVIS & Hephzibah HATHAWAY^{6}: (3 of 11)**<129>**

Nicholas DAVIS^{7}, b. c1769, d. 30 Nov. 1839, ae 70, bur. Long Plain

Almy/Emma DAVIS^{7}, b. c1775, Dartmouth, d. 17 June 1856, ae 81, New Bedford <VR> (widow of Robert Cook)

Ruth DAVIS^{7}, b. ( ), d. 27 Nov. 1864, New Bedford

Nathaniel TABER, b. c1777, Fairhaven, d. 1 Nov. 1844, ae 67, Fairhaven, consumption, farmer <Mass.VR 14:45>

CHILDREN OF Nathaniel TABER & Ruth DAVIS^{7}: (2)

Almy TABER^{8}, b. ( )

Sarah W. TABER^{8}, b. c1804, Rochester, d. 22 June 1885, ae 81y1m9d, Rochester, bur. Mattapoisett (Sarah W. Gammons) <Mass.VR 356:327>

Ebenezer GAMMONS, (son of Wm. & Abigail), b. c1802, Taunton, d. 5 Sept. 1885, ae 83y6m20d, Rochester, bur. Mattapoisett <Mass.VR 356:327>

CHILDREN OF Nicholas DAVIS & Mary ( ): (2) <New Bedford, Friends' Rcds.2:2>

Nathan DAVIS, b. 25 11mth 1715

Elizabeth DAVIS, b. 20 11mth 1718

CHILDREN OF Nicholas DAVIS & Ruth ( ): (8) <New Bedford, Friends' Rcds.>

Timothy DAVIS, b. 9 2mth 1730

Nicolas DAVIS, b. 10 3mth 1732

Abraham DAVIS, b. 30 12mth 1735

Mary DAVIS, b. 30 5mth 1742

James DAVIS, b. 11 3mth 1744

Sumers DAVIS, b. 19 4mth 1742, d. 3 2mth 1759

Elizabeth DAVIS, b. 17 4mth 1744

Nathan DAVIS, b. 14 4mth 1748

Anne ( ) DAVIS, d. 16 5mth 1767 <New Bedford, Friends' Rcds.>

CHILDREN OF Nathan DAVIS & Anne ( ): (7) <New Bedford, Friends' Rcds.>

Hannah DAVIS, b. 23 4mth 1754

Nicholas DAVIS, b. 24 3mth 1756

John DAVIS, b. 30 7mth 1758

Richard DAVIS, b. 22 12mth 1760

Ruth DAVIS, b. 22 1mth 1762

Anna DAVIS, b. 8 8mth 1763

Mary DAVIS, b. 31 12mth 1765

Ruth SPOONER^{5} (Alden^{4}, Walter^{3}, Sam.^{2}, Wm.^{1}), b. 23 Sept. 1770* <Howland Gen.:277>

CHILDREN OF Nicholas DAVIS^{7} (Hepzibah Hathaway^{6}) & Ruth SPOONER*: (1 of 5)[<130>]

Jane S. DAVIS^{8}, b. 5 Jan. 1805*; d. 4 Dec. 1882*

Abigail SMITH, (dau of Humphrey), b. 21 June 1743 <Darmouth VR>; d. 29 June 1831, New Bedford <Friends' Rcds.1:73>

CHILDREN OF Stephen HATHAWAY^{6} (Jethro^{5}) & Abigail SMITH: (15) <Sandwich, Friends' Rcds. 2:19>

Humphrey HATHAWAY^{7}, b. 13 Apr. 1765; d. pre 7 Aug. 1821 (adm.)

Jethro HATHAWAY^{7}, b. 13 Sept. 1766; d. aft. 18 Aug. 1824* (father's will)

Mary HATHAWAY^{7}, b. 20 Dec. 1767; d. 27 Aug. 1856*, Fairhaven <Mass.VR 102:65>

Hannah HATHAWAY^{7}, b. 21 June 1769; d. 3 June 1857*, New Bedford

Thomas HATHAWAY^{7}, b. 30 Jan. 1771; d. 26 July 1793

Rebecca HATHAWAY^{7}, b. 18 Aug. 1772; d. aft. 4 Apr. 1830* (mother's will)

Abigail HATHAWAY^{7}, b. 15 Mar. 1774; d. 12 July 1867*, New Bedford

Stephen HATHAWAY^{7}, b. 4 Sept. 1775; d. aft. 18 Aug. 1824* (father's will)

Hepzibah HATHAWAY^{7}, b. 13 Apr. 1777; d. aft. 4 Apr. 1830* (mother's will)

Alice HATHAWAY^{7}, b. 13 Mar. 1779; d. pre 18 Aug. 1824* (father's will)

Nathaniel HATHAWAY^{7}, b. 18 Feb. 1781; d. 26 Oct. 1802, New Bedford <Friends' Rcds.1:52>

Elizabeth HATHAWAY^{7}, b. 9 Dec. 1782; d. 1860*

Smith HATHAWAY^{7}, b. 25 Dec. 1787; d. pre 18 Aug. 1824* (father's will)

Sylvia HATHAWAY^{7}, b. 20 Sept. 1790; d. 17 Apr. 1883*, Acushnet

George S. HATHAWAY^{7}, b. ( ); d. aft. 4 Apr. 1830* (mother's will)

MICRO #25 of 30

Rcds. of Monthly Meeting of Friends of New Bedford: (3)

Stephen S. HATHAWAY, b. 13 Mar. 1805

William H. HATHAWAY, b. 11 Mar. 1807

Lydia Ann HATHAWAY, b. 24 Nov. 1808

Mary ( ) SMITH, d. pre 9 Aug. 1764 (dau. Abigail's marriage) <Friends' Rcds., Dartmouth>

CHILDREN OF Humphry SMITH & Mary ( ): <Dartmouth VR 1:270>

Henry SMITH, b. 22 Sept. 1738

Humphry SMITH, b. 4 Feb. 1740

Abigail SMITH, b. 21 June 1743 (m. Stephen Hathaway^{6} (Jethro^{5}), p.381)

Daniel SMITH, b. 26 Sept. 1745

Weston HOWLAND, d. 8 June 1841*, New Bedford <Howland Gen.:153>

CHILDREN OF Weston HOWLAND & Abigail HATHAWAY^{7} (Stephen^{6}): (11*)

Thomas HOWLAND^{8}, b. 10 Sept. 1794, d. 1849

Hannah HOWLAND^{8}, b. 1796, d. 1876

Abraham HOWLAND^{8}, b. 1798, d. 1800

Weston HOWLAND^{8}, b. 1800, d. 1801

Abraham H.HOWLAND^{8}, b. 1802, d. 1867

Stephen H. HOWLAND^{8}, b. 1804, d. 1839

Alice R. HOWLAND^{8}, b. 1806, d. 1834

Weston HOWLAND^{8}, b. 1808, d. 1808

Susanna HOWLAND^{8}, b. 1809, d. 1871

William HOWLAND^{8}, b. 1812, d. 1872

Weston HOWLAND^{8}, b. 1815

Jireh SWIFT, b. 26 Sept. 1773*; d. 15 Oct. 1857* <Swift Gen.:27,54>

CHILDREN OF Jireh SWIFT & Elizabeth HATHAWAY^{7} (Stephen^{6}): (12*)

Elizabeth SWIFT^{8}, b. 1806

Sylvia SWIFT^{8}, b. 1807

Jireh SWIFT^{8}, b. 1809

Ezra H. SWIFT^{8}, b. 1810, d. 1813

George H. SWIFT^{8}, b. 1813, d. 1837

Mary SWIFT^{8}, b. 1815

William R. SWIFT^{8}, b. 1817, d. 1840

Humphrey H. SWIFT^{8}, b. 1819

Nancy S. SWIFT^{8}, b. 1822

Rebecca D. SWIFT^{8}, b. 1824, 1893

Nathaniel H. SWIFT^{8}, b. 1826

Franklin SWIFT^{8}, b. 1827, d. 1828

Thomas NYE, d. 22 June 1842*, New Bedford

CHILDREN OF Thomas NYE & Hannah HATHAWAY^{7} (Stephen^{6}): (12*)

William C. NYE^{8}, b. 1792

Betsey H. NYE^{8}, b. 1796

Nancy NYE^{8}, b. 1797

Philip NYE^{8}, b. 1797, d. 1858

Hannah NYE^{8}, b. 1800

Nathaniel H. NYE^{8}, b. 1803, d. 1859

Thomas NYE^{8}, b. 1804, d. 1882

James S. NYE^{8}, b. 1806, d. 1881

Humphrey H. NYE^{8}, b. 1807, d. 1860

Asa Russell NYE^{8}, b. 1809, d. 1858

George NYE^{8}, b. 1811, d. 1811

George H. NYE^{8}, b. 1812, d. 1847

Pardon HOWLAND, b. 1 Jan. 1777* ("not Mayflower")

CHILDREN OF Pardon HOWLAND & Hepzibah HATHAWAY^{7} (Stephen^{6}): (8*)**<131>**

Abigail SMITH, (*dau of Deliverance & Hannah), d. aft. 1 Feb. 1834* (swore to div.)

CHILDREN OF Humphrey HATHAWAY^{7} (Stephen^{6}) & Abigail SMITH: (5)

Thomas Schuyler HATHAWAY^{8}, b. 2 Mar. 1796*

Nathaniel HATHAWAY^{8}, b. ( )

Francis S. HATHAWAY^{8}, b. 14 Nov. 1803*

Alice R. HATHAWAY^{8}, b. ( )

Andrew Ritchie HATHAWAY^{8}, b. ( ), d. pre 18 July 1833*

CHILDREN OF John TABER & Mary HATHAWAY^{7} (Stephen^{6}): (4*)

Thomas Nye TABER^{8}, b. 1801, d. 1802

Silas TABER^{8}, b. 1802, d. 1816

Sarah Russell TABER^{8}, b. ?1806

George Hathaway TABER^{8}, b. 1808

Gideon NYE, d. 12 Mar. 1875*, Acushnet

CHILDREN OF Gideon NYE & Sylvia HATHAWAY^{7} (Stephen^{6}): (10*)

Gideon NYE^{8}, b. 1812

Sylvia Hathaway NYE^{8}, b. 1814, d. 1902

Hannah M. NYE^{8}, b. 1816

Clement Drew NYE^{8}, b. 1818

Thomas S.H. NYE^{8}, b. 1820

Elizabeth S. NYE^{8}, b. 1822, d. 1863

Edwin Coffin Hussey NYE^{8}, b. 1825, d. 1885

Lydia S.H. NYE^{8}, b. 1826

Jane Swift NYE^{8}, b. 1829

Clara Gordon NYE^{8}, b. 1831

Thomas KEMPTON, d. 29 Dec. 1768*, Dartmouth

CHILDREN OF Thomas KEMPTON & Mary HATHAWAY^{5} (Tho.^{4}): (7) <Dartmouth VR:321,322>

Esther KEMPTON^{6}, b. 25 Oct. 1736*

Capt. Thomas KEMPTON^{6}, b. 20 Apr. 1740*; d. 27 Jan. 1806*

Hepzibah KEMPTON^{6}, b. 10 Mar. 1743*

Ephraim KEMPTON^{6}, b. 26 Jan. 1745/6*; d. 25 Jan. 1802* (below)

Mary KEMPTON^{6}, b. 21 Dec. 1750* <VR:322>

David KEMPTON^{6}, b. 6 Mar. 1753* <VR:322>

Jonathan KEMPTON^{6}, b. 10 Sept. 1754*

Acushnet Cemetery Memorial Record:11: (6)

Ephraim KEMPTON, d. 19 Dec. 1803, ae 70, and

Capt. Ephraim KEMPTON, his son, d. 30 Oct. 1798, ae 29, Norfolk VA

Ephraim KEMPTON, d. 25 Jan. 1802, ae 55, and

Elizabeth KEMPTON, his wife, d. 29 Nov. 1848, ae 95

Thomas KEMPTON, d. 29 Dec. 1768, ae 65, and

Ruth KEMPTON, his wife, d. 6 Dec. 1771, ae "25" (error?)

Ephraim KEMPTON, d. c1733, d. 19 Dec. 1803*, ae 70 (above)

Ann NYE^{4} (Tho.^{3}, Jonathan^{2}, Ben.^{1}), b. 14 Nov. 1734 <Nye Gen.:77>

CHILDREN OF Ephraim KEMPTON & Ann NYE: (2 of 8)**<132>**

Lydia KEMPTON, b. 16 Feb. 1753 <Dartmouth VR:185>

Capt. Ephraim KEMPTON, b. c1769, d. 30 Oct. 1798*, ae 29 (see above)

Elizabeth TUPPER^{3} (*Roland^{2}, Israel^{1}), b. 22 Sept. 1753* <Sandwich VR>; d. 24 Nov. 1848* (p.383)

CHILDREN OF Ephraim KEMPTON^{6} (Mary Hathaway^{5}) & Elizabeth TUPPER: (6) <New Bedford>**<133>**

Lydia KEMPTON^{7}, b. 1774, d. 24 Feb. 1864, ae 89y10m, New Bedford <Mass.VR 174:114> (widow of Peter Foster)

Mary KEMPTON^{7}, b. 1777*

David KEMPTON^{7}, b. 1779*; d. 30 Aug. 1830*

Thomas KEMPTON^{7}, b. 1783*

Ephraim KEMPTON^{7}, b. 1789, d. 19 Aug. 1863, ae 73, dropsy, 189 Kempton St., New Bedford <Mass. VR 165:116>

Elizabeth KEMPTON^{7}, b. 1794

CHILD OF David KEMPTON^{7} & Joanna MAXFIELD:

David Batchelder KEMPTON^{8}, b. 1818, d. 4 Mar. 1899, ae 80y10m7d, cirrhosis of liver, New Bedford <Mass.VR 492:308>

CHILD OF Abner KIRBY^{6} (Justus^{5}, Nath.^{4}, Rob.^{3}, Richard$^{2-1}$) & Thankful SOULE, (dau of Jos):

Phebe KIRBY, b. 18 Feb. 1798, d. 31 May 1880, New Bedford <Kirby Gen.:297>

<u>MARY COOKE^{2}</u> (Francis^{1})

John TOMSON, b. c1616, d. 16 June 1696, 80th yr, Middleboro g.s. <MD 19:95>

CHILDREN OF John TOMSON & Mary COOKE^{2}: (11) <5-10, Barnstable>

Adam TOMSON^{3}, b. pre 26 Sept. 1646, d. c1648, ae about 1y6m

John TOMSON^{3}, b. 1648, d. 11 Feb. 1648, Plymouth <MD 15:27,28>

John TOMSON^{3}, b. 24 Nov. 1649, Plymouth <MD 16:121>; d. 25 Nov. 1725, Middleboro <MD 14:219>

Mary TOMSON^{3}, b. ( ); d. 3 May 1734* <Austin's Gen.Dict. RI:195>

Esther TOMSON^{3}, b. 28 July 1652 <MD 14:86>; d. betw. 26 Oct. 1705 - 12 Sept. 1706 <MD 23:72,74>

Elizabeth TOMSON^{3}, b. 28 Jan. 1654 <MD 14:86>

Sarah TOMSON^{3}, b. 4 Apr. 1657 <MD 14:86>; d.? 2 Dec. 1730*, ae 73, unm.**<134>**

Lydia TOMSON^{3}, b. 5 Oct. 1659 <MD 14:86>; d. 14 Mar. 1741/2, The Green Cem.,Middleboro<MD 14:134>

Jacob TOMSON^{3}, b. 24 Apr. 1662 <MD 14:86>; d. 1 Sept. 1726, Middleboro, g.s. <MD 14:219>

Thomas TOMSON^{3}, b. 19 Oct. 1664 <MD 14:86>; d. 26 Oct. 1742, Halifax <MD 14:9>**<134a>**

Peter TOMSON^{3}, b. ( ), d. pre 29 Apr. 1731 (adm.) <MD 22:135>

Mercy TOMSON^{3}, b. c1671, d. 19 Apr. 1756. 85th yr, Thompson St. Cem., Halifax <MD 14:8>

<u>MICRO #26 of 30</u>

Elizabeth THOMSON, wife of Tho., d. 24 Feb. 1779, ae 75, Plymouth g.s. <Kingman:51>

George D. THOMSON, d. 2 Apr. 1798, ae 24, Plymouth g.s. <Kingman:79>

James SOULE^{3} (John^{2}), b. c1659, d. 27 Aug. 1744, 85th yr, The Green Cem., Middleboro <MD 14:134>

CHILDREN OF James SOULE & Lydia TOMSON^{3}: (See micro #5 of Soule Family)

(**NOTE:** Line of descent for the following William Swift line has been changed to show descent from William Swift^{3}, not Elizabeth Tomson^{3}. This is not a Cooke Mayflower line.)**<135>**

William SWIFT^{3} (Wm.$^{2-1}$), b. 28 Aug. 1654, Sandwich <MD 14:173>; d. betw. 17 June 1700 (will) - 1 May 1701 (inv.) <MD 30:112>

CHILDREN OF William SWIFT^{3} & Elizabeth ( ): (10) <Sandwich VR; 3-10, MD 30:64>

William SWIFT, b. 24 Jan. 1679 <MD 14:172>; d. pre 13 Oct. 1750 (adm.) <Barnstable Co.PR 7:190>

Benjamin SWIFT, b.? c1682*

Joseph SWIFT, b. Nov. 1687; d. betw. 13 Jan. 1755 (will) - 1 July 1760 (prob.) <Barnstable Co.PR 12:85,86>

Samuel SWIFT, b. Dec. 1690

Joanna SWIFT, b. 9 Mar. 169()

Thomas SWIFT, b. Dec. 169(); d. 24 Dec. 1770*, 79th yr, Old Parish Cem., Rochester

Elizabeth SWIFT, b. 11 Jan. 169()

Thankful SWIFT, b. 11 Jan. 1690/() (twins)

Josiah SWIFT, b. (no date); d. aft. 31 Mar. 1718* <Barnstable Co. Deed>

Ebenezer SWIFT, b. (no date)

CHILDREN OF Benjamin MOREY^{5} & Thankful SWIFT^{4} (Wm.^{3}): (See micro #26, Warren Family)

CHILDREN OF Benjamin SWIFT^{4} (Wm.^{3}) & Hannah WING: (4 of 7) <Sandwich VR, MD 30:104> **<136>**

Samuel SWIFT, b. 11 Sept. 1704

Mary SWIFT, b. 11 Oct. 1706

Content SWIFT, b. 12 Dec. 1708

Zebulon SWIFT, b. 15 Apr. 1712

CHILDREN OF Ebenezer SWIFT^4 (Wm.^{3}) & Abigail GIBBS: (3)

Abigail SWIFT, b. ( )

Jabez SWIFT, b. Feb. 1732

Ebenezer SWIFT, b. 1 July 1733

CHILDREN OF Joseph SWIFT^4 (Wm.^{3}) & 1st Mercy* ( ): (7)

William SWIFT, b. 26 Feb. 1711*

Jean SWIFT, b. 4 Dec. 1713*; d.? 11 Mar. 1779 <ChR 1:409 (not identified, prob. Plymouth)>

Joseph SWIFT, b. 4 Sept. 1716*; d. pre 6 Dec. 1782 (wife's dth.)

Joshua SWIFT, b. 14 Feb. 1717/8*; d. 15 Feb. 1777*, Plymouth <ChR 1:407>

Martha SWIFT*, b. 4 May 1719*

Mercy SWIFT*, b. 16 Mar. 1721/2*

Joanna SWIFT*, b. ( )

Rebecca (CLARKE)(Ellis*) Morton, b. 2 June 1694, Plymouth <MD 1:141>

CHILD OF Joseph SWIFT^4 (Wm.^{3}) & 2nd Rebecca (CLARKE)(Ellis*)Morton*:

Thomas SWIFT, b. c1730*, d. 10 Jan. 1806*, ae 76, Sandwich g.s.

Mordecai ELLIS, (son of Freeman), d. pre 29 Mar. 1718 (adm.) <MD 29:23>

CHILD OF Mordecai ELLIS & Rebecca CLARKE:

Freeman ELLIS, b. 1718

Nathaniel MORTON^4 (Eleazer^3, Ephraim^2, George^1), d. c1727, at sea

CHILDREN OF Nathaniel MORTON & Rebecca (CLARKE) Ellis: (4) <Plymouth, MD 13:167>

Elizabeth MORTON, b. 12 Nov. 1720

Nathaniel MORTON, b. 10 Jan. 1722/3

Eleazer MORTON, b. 26 Sept. 1724

Ichabod MORTON, b. 28 Dec. 1726

CHILDREN OF Joseph BARTLETT^5 & Jean SWIFT^5 (Jos^4): (8) <See micro #21 of the Warren Family>

Thomas GLOVER, b. 28 Jan. 1719*, Lebanon CT

CHILDREN OF Thomas GLOVER & Joanna SWIFT^5 (Jos.^{4}): (1 of 6*)**<137>**

Mary GLOVER, b. 18 Nov. 1744

Sarah (BARTLETT^5) Lebaron (Jos.$^{4-3}$, Mary Warren^2), b. 24 Mar. 1702/03, Plymouth**<138>**; d. 6 Dec. 1782, Plymouth <ChR 1:412>

CHILD OF Joseph SWIFT^5 (Jos.^{4}) & Sarah (BARTLETT) Lebaron:

Mary SWIFT, b. Aug. 1738, d. Dec. 1738 <MD 13:302>

Abigail PHILLIPS, b. c1733, d. 6 Jan. 1804, ae 71, Sandwich g.s.

CHILDREN OF Thomas SWIFT^5 (Jos.^{4}) & Abigail PHILLIPS: (9) <Sandwich VR; Swift Gen.>

William SWIFT, b. c1753, d. 23 Nov. 1776*, ae 23y9m19d

Clark SWIFT, b. 23 Sept. 1755

Rebecca SWIFT, b. 12 Feb. 1760

Joseph SWIFT, b. 30 June 1762

Nathaniel SWIFT, b. 31 Dec. 1764

Maria SWIFT, b. 28 Apr. 1767

Thomas SWIFT, b. 13 May 1772

William SWIFT, b. 1 May 1777

Levi SWIFT, b. 13 Mar. 1780

Jonathan BEALE, bpt. 10 July 1757*; d. 18 June 1834*, ae 77, Quincy

CHILDREN OF Jonathan BEALE & Maria SWIFT^6 (Tho.^{5}): (10)

William Swift BEALE, b. 27 Apr. 1789, Quincy <Bible Rcd.>; d. 24 Sept. 1848 <g.s.>

Jonathan BEALE, b. 1790, d. 21 Jan. 1793, ae 3, Hancock Cem. <Hist.Braintree & Quincy (1878):129>

Thomas BEALE, b. 1793, d. 24 Sept. 1794, ae 1y6m21d <Hist.Braintree & Quincy:129>

Jonathan BEALE, b. 1794; d. aft. 1835 ("went west")

Peter BEALE, b. 1797, d. 1798

Benjamin BEALE, b. 1799, Quincy, d. 9 May 1854, ae 55, Milton, suicide by hanging<Mass.VR 85:167>

Joseph Swift BEALE, b. 1800, d. aft. 1835

Maria A.P. BEALE, b. 1803, Quincy, d. 19 July 1856, ae 53, Quincy, cancer <Mass.VR 103:162>

Cynthia Ann BEALE, b. 1805, d. aft. 1835, unm.

Caroline BEALE, b. 1807, d. pre 1835

Elizabeth HOLBROOK, b. 8 June 1791, Braintree; d. 8 Feb. 1849, ae <u>56</u>, Milton <Mass.VR 41:33>

CHILDREN OF William Swift BEALE^{7} (Maria Swift^{6}) & Elizabeth HOLBROOK: (9) <3-9, Milton>

William Swift BEALE, b. 26 Dec. 1813, Braintree

Elizabeth Holbrook BEALE, b. 27 Oct. 1816, Quincy; d. 22 Mar. 1876, Randolph

Caroline BEALE, b. 29 May 1818

Esther B. BEALE, b. 20 Dec. 1819

Maria Swift BEALE, b. 15 Dec. 1821

Jonathan T. BEALE, b. 9 Oct. 1823

Cynthia A. Swift BEALE, b. 8 Aug. 1827

Mary Tucker Ware BEALE, b. 21 Jan. 1832

Ada Gordon Byron BEALE, b. 18 Aug. 1833

Otis SPEAR, d. pre 4 Aug. Aug. 1844 (prob.), of Randolph

CHILDREN OF Otis SPEAR & Elizabeth Holbrook BEALE^{8} (Wm.^{7}): (1 of 4) **<139>**

Nancy Emogene SPEAR, b. 9 Jan. 1838, Randolph; d. 20 Apr. 1918, Randolph

Jane FAUNCE, bpt. 11 Aug. 1717*, Plymouth <ChR 1:217>; d. aft. 7 Apr. 1777* (hus. prob.)

CHILDREN OF Joshua SWIFT^{5} (Jos.^{4}) & Jane FAUNCE: (9) <Plymouth; 1-5, MD 15:210; 6-10, ChR>

Abigail SWIFT, b. 8 Mar. 1739

Joseph SWIFT, b. 5 Feb. 1742

Jean/Jane SWIFT, b. 6 June 1744

John SWIFT, b. 15 Sept. 1746

Lusanna SWIFT, b. 9 Feb. 1748/9

Joanna SWIFT, bpt. 14 July 1751 <ChR 1:447>

Mercy SWIFT, bpt. 7 July 1754 <ChR 1:449>

Joshua SWIFT, bpt. 23 Jan. 1757 <ChR 1:451>

Rebecca SWIFT, bpt. 24 Feb. 1760 <ChR 1:452>

Samuel RIDER, (*son of Ezekiel), d. betw. 26 Dec. 1803 (will) - 7 Feb. 1804 (prob.) <Plymouth Co. PR 38:514>

CHILDREN OF Samuel RIDER & Jane SWIFT^{6} (Joshua^{5}): (8) <Plymouth ChR>

Samuel RIDER, bpt. 26 Mar. 1775 <1:461>

George RIDER, bpt. 26 Mar. 1775 <1:461>

Jenny RIDER, bpt. 26 Mar. 1775 <1:461>

Joshua RIDER, bpt. 14 Sept. 1777 <1:462>

Ezekiel RIDER, bpt. 25 Mar. 1781 <1:464>

Susanna RIDER, bpt. 25 Apr. 1784 <1:466>

Lucy RIDER, b. ( )

Sarah Bartlett RIDER, bpt. 7 July 1790 <2:478>

CHILDREN OF Samuel SWIFT^{4} (Wm.^{3}) & Abigail ( ): (4) <2-4, Plymouth, MD 13:168>

Mary SWIFT*, b. 28 Apr. 1715*

Elizabeth SWIFT, b. c22 Jan. 1717/8

James SWIFT, b. 1 Mar. 1720/1

Samuel SWIFT, b. 16 Jan. 1723/4

Thankful MOREY^{5} (Jonathan^{4}, Mary Bartlett^{3}, Mary Warren^{2}), b. Mar. 1695/6, Plymouth <MD 2:18>

CHILDREN OF Thomas SWIFT^{4} (Wm.^{3}) & Thankful MOREY: (9) <Plymouth VR, MD 13:34>

Lydia SWIFT, b. 20 Aug. 1718 <MD 13:33>

Deborah SWIFT, b. 1 or 2 Sept. 1720 <MD 13:33>; d. aft. 25 July 1755 (guardianship of children)

Elizabeth SWIFT, b. 28 May 1723; d. 30 Mar. 1748/9*, Sandwich

Thomas SWIFT, b. 11 Jan. 1724/5; d. 17 Apr. 1795 <Rochester ChR>

Jerusha SWIFT, b. 11 May 1727

Phineas SWIFT, b. 25 Feb. 1731/2

Rhoda SWIFT, b. 10 Mar. 1733/4

Thankful SWIFT, b. 26 Feb. 1737/8, d. c26 May 1754

Lemuel SWIFT, b. 26 Feb. 1737/8 (twins)

CHILDREN OF Thomas SWIFT^{5} (Tho.^{4}) & Rebecca CLARK, (dau of James): (8) <2-6, Rochester VR>

Jonathan SWIFT, b. 4 July 1747, Plymouth <MD 12:226>

Lucy SWIFT, b. 14 Feb. 174()

Meribah SWIFT, b. 18 Aug. 175()

Thomas SWIFT, b. 8 Aug. 1755

James SWIFT, b. 24 Dec. 1758

Mary SWIFT, b. 12 Apr. 1764

Joseph SWIFT, b. 12 Apr. 1764 (twins)

Rebecca SWIFT, b. ( )

MICRO #27 of 30

Jonathan TOBEY^{3} (Jonathan^{2}, Tho.^{1}), b. 6 Aug. 1718; d. pre 15 Jan. 1755 (adm.)

CHILDREN OF Jonathan TOBEY & Deborah SWIFT^{5} (Tho.^{4}): (2 of 8) <Tobey Gen.:46>**<140>**

Jonathan TOBEY, b. 24 Dec. 1740; d. pre 1781

Thomas TOBEY, b. 26 Mar. 1753

Thomas TOBEY^{3} (Sam.^{2}, Tho.^{1}), b. 14 Aug. 1720; d. pre 14 Oct. 1761*

CHILDREN OF Thomas TOBEY^{3} & Elizabeth SWIFT^{5} (Tho.^{4}): (3)

Sylvanus TOBEY, b. 19 June 1741

Thomas TOBEY, b. 5 Jan. 1745/6

Seth TOBEY, b. 29 Nov. 1748

Benjamin CORNISH^{3} (*Ben.^{2}, Sam.^{1}), b. 17 July 1727*, Plymouth <MD 13:202>; d. aft. 1780*

CHILDREN OF Benjamin CORNISH & Rhoda SWIFT^{5} (Tho.^{4}): (10) <Plymouth, MD 18:214>

Deborah CORNISH, b. 25 June 1753

Susanna CORNISH, b. 4 Mar. 1755

William CORNISH, b. 3 Mar. 1757

Rhoda CORNISH, b. 16 Jan. 1759

Stephen CORNISH, b. 25 Dec. 1760

Nancey CORNISH, b. 22 Dec. 1762

Benjamin CORNISH, b. 25 Jan. 1765

Sarah CORNISH, b. ( ); d. 7 Feb. 1806, Plymouth <ChR 2:631>

George CORNISH, b. 1 Nov. 1767

Lemuel CORNISH, b. ( )

Nehemiah SAVERY, b. c1768, d. 20 Jan. 1846, ae 78, bur. Plymouth <TR 4:326>

CHILDREN OF Nehemiah SAVERY & 1st Sarah CORNISH^{6} (Rhoda Swift^{5}): (7) <Plymouth VR 2:323>

Elizabeth SAVERY, b. 14 July 1794; d. 10 Nov. 1872, Randolph <Mass.VR 248:333>

Thomas SAVERY, b. 24 Dec. 1795

Nehemiah SAVERY, b. 11 May 1797; d. aft. 18 May 1877 (will) <Plymouth Co.PR #17724>**<141>**

Mary SAVERY, b. 5 Oct. 1799

Windsor SAVERY, b. 10 Sept. 1801

Sarah Cornish SAVERY, b. 11 Jan. 1804

Infant, d. 7 Feb. 1806 (with mother) <Plymouth ChR 2:631>

CHILDREN OF Nehemiah SAVERY & 2nd Deborah SMITH: (5) <Plymouth VR 3:323>

Deborah Smith SAVERY, b. 16 May 1807

Louisa SAVERY, b. 18 Feb. 1810

Zenus SAVERY, b. 14 Oct. 1811

Mercy SAVERY, b. 23 Oct. 1813

Cordelia SAVERY, b. 18 May 1817

Sylvanus PRATT, (son of Matthew & Mary), b. 1800, Weymouth, d. 7 Aug. 1870, ae 70y7m26d,Randolph, dropsy, manufacturer <Mass.VR 230:280>

Lydia WEEKS, d. aft. 26 Nov. 1750* <Barnstable Co.PR 8:426, hus. estate>

CHILDREN OF William SWIFT[4] (Wm.[3]) & Lydia WEEKS: (2) <Plymouth, MD 12:224>

Solomon SWIFT, b. 9 June 1715

William SWIFT, b. 11 Apr. 1719

(**NOTE:** This ends the lineage of William Swift[3] which is not a Mayflower Cooke line.)

William REED, (son of Wm.), b. 15 Dec. 1639 <Weymouth VR 1:252>; d. betw. 26 Oct. 1705 (will) - 12 Sept. 1706 (prob.) <MD 23:72>

CHILDREN OF William REED & Esther TOMSON[3]: (9) <Weymouth VR>

Bathshua REED[4], b. pre 1682

John REED[4], b. 21 Oct. 1680; d.y. <1:249>

William REED[4], b. 24 May 1682 <1:252>; d. 3 June 1753, ae 74y4m3d, bur. Mt.Zion Cem <Abington VR>

Mercy REED[4], b. pre 1690**<142>**

John REED[4], b. 10 July 1687 <1:249>; d. betw. 20 Mar. 1733 (will) - 16 May 1739 (adm.) <Plymouth Co.PR #16619>

Mary REED[4], b. c1681-90; d. betw. 1 Oct. 1751 (will) - 2 Apr. 1759 (prob.)<Plymouth Co.PR 15:267>

Hester REED[4], b. ( )

Jacob REED[4], b. 6 Nov. 1691 <1:249>; d. 1766

Sarah REED[4], b. 21 Mar. 1694 <1:251>

CHILDREN OF Josiah ALLEN & Mary READ/REED[4]: (8) <Bridgewater VR, MD 14:182>**<143>**

Micah ALLEN[5], b. 2 Dec. 1708; d. betw. 11 Dec. 1744 (will) - 1 Apr. 1745 (prob.) <Plymouth Co.PR #311, 9:437,439>

Josiah ALLEN[5], b. 10 Jan. 1711/2; d. 6 Jan. 1744/5

Mary ALLEN[5], b. 27 Apr. 1714

Esther ALLEN[5], b. 7 June 1717

Sarah ALLEN[5], b. 23 May 1719

Nathan ALLEN[5], b. 16 Sept. 1721

Bettie ALLEN[5], b. 9 Feb. 1724

William ALLEN[5], b. 13 Sept. 1726

CHILDREN OF Micah ALLEN[5] & Hannah EDSON: (4) <Bridgewater VR, MD 16:44>

Mary ALLEN[6], b. 9 Dec. 1737; d. 1820

Micah ALLEN[6], b. 9 Feb. 1739/40

Joseph ALLEN[6], b. 7 Sept. 1742; d. 3 June 1826

Daniel ALLEN[6], b. 3 Sept. 1744

CHILDREN OF Dr. Micah ALLEN & Hannah CUSHING: (9) <Halifax VR:39>

Hannah ALLEN, b. 24 Sept. 1764

Seth ALLEN, b. 15 Sept. 1766

Charity ALLEN, b. 15 Sept. 1766 (?twins)

Cushing ALLEN, b. 2 Dec. 1768

Salome ALLEN, b. 18 Dec. 1770

Deborah ALLEN, b. 17 July 1773

William ALLEN, b. 22 Mar. 1776

Horatio Gates ALLEN, b. July 1778

Mary ALLEN, b. 4 Sept. 1781

Micah ALLEN, d. betw. 26 Mar. 1822 (will) - 4 Nov. 1823 (prob.) <Bristol Co.PR 61:95>; wife: Catherine EVERETT, (dau of Jos.), b. 20 May 1743**<144>**

CHILDREN OF Micah ALLEN & Catherine EVERETT: (1 of 9)**<145>**

Otis ALLEN, b. c1784, Mansfield, d. 30 Aug. 1874, ae 90y5m, Mansfield, farmer <Mass.VR 265:113>

Susan DEANE, (dau of Wm. & Abigail), b. 27 June 1787; d. 13 Feb. 1848, Mansfield <Mass.VR 32:51>
(wf of Otis Allen who is not identified)

CHILD OF Nicholas WHITMARSH & Mercy REED[4] (Esther Tomson[3]):**<146>**

Nicholas WHITMARSH[5], b. 20 Mar. 1698/9 <Weymouth VR 1:351>

CHILDREN OF Nicholas PORTER & Bathsheba REED[4] (Esther Tomson[3]): (10) <2-10, Abington VR>

Nicholas PORTER[5], b. 27 Oct. 1699 <Weymouth VR 1:218>

Nicholas PORTER[5], b. 26 Oct. 1700

William PORTER[5], b. 19 Aug. 1702 <also on Weymouth VR 1:220>

Bathsheba PORTER[5], b. 17 Sept. 1707

Daniel PORTER[5], b. 15 June 1708

Susanna PORTER[5], b. 20 Mar. 1711

Job PORTER[5], b. 6 June 1713

Esther PORTER[5], b. 20 June 1716

Abner PORTER[5], b. 27 Nov. 1718

Sarah PORTER[5], b. 3 Apr. 1722

Sarah HERSEY, (dau of Wm.), b. 26 Sept. 1692, Hingham

CHILDREN OF Jacob REED[4] (Esther Tomson[3]) & 1st Sarah HERSEY: (6)

Sarah REED[5], b. 2 May 1718

Jacob REED[5], b. 7 July 1720

Hannah REED[5], b. 26 Feb. 1722/3

William REED[5], b. 20 Sept. 1725; d. 4 Dec. 1807*

Elijah REED[5], b. 14 Feb. 1727/8

Betty REED[5], b. 1 Mar. 1731, d.y.

CHILD OF Jacob REED[4] & 2nd Hannah (   ) NOYES:**<147>**

Betty REED[5], b. 1 Oct. 1734

CHILD OF Nathan DRAKE[1] & Jane TOLMAN: <Drake Fam.:82>**<148>**

Ebenezer DRAKE, b. 26 Feb. 1803, d. 18 Aug. 1885

Welthea SAMPSON, b. c1802, d. 25 Feb. 1829 <Drake Fam.:163>

CHILDREN OF Ebenezer DRAKE[2] & 1st Welthea SAMPSON:

Mary Jane DRAKE, b. 25 Sept. 1825, d. 28 Aug. 1842

Aaron Sampson DRAKE, b. 15 Feb. 1829

Lucy REED, (dau of Noah & Lucy (Hayward))b. 24 Jan. 1807, d. 30 Oct. 1876

CHILDREN OF Ebenezer DRAKE[2] & 2nd Lucy REED: (8) <Drake Fam.:163>

Ebenezer Hayward DRAKE, b. 12 Mar. 1831, d. 21 June 1887

Noah Reed DRAKE, b. 20 Oct. 1832, d. 14 June 1853

Stephen DRAKE, b. 25 Nov. 1834, d. 11 Feb. 1835

Elizabeth DRAKE, b. 14 Nov. 1835, d. 22 Mar. 1856

Harriet DRAKE, b. 19 July 1839

Jeremy DRAKE, b. 2 Feb. 1842, d. 2 Nov. 1858

Lucy Reed DRAKE, b. 27 Oct. 1844

Albert Henry DRAKE, b. 16 Aug. 1846, d. 29 Sept. 1876

Phebe S. LUNN, (dau of Robert & Sarah (Newcomb)), b. 18 Sept. 1833

CHILDREN OF Ebenezer Hayward DRAKE[3] & Phebe S. LUNN: (2) <Drake Fam.:250>

Sarah Elizabeth DRAKE, b. 12 Feb. 1856

Nellie Vernon DRAKE, b. 31 Oct. 1866

CHILDREN OF Ellery C. WRIGHT, (son of Isaiah & Harriet (Bowman)) & Sarah Elizabeth DRAKE^{4}: (4)

Hattie Drake WRIGHT, b. 2 Aug. 1878, Stoughton <Drake Fam.:250>

Mary Alice WRIGHT, b. 17 Mar. 1881, Stoughton "

Frank Ray WRIGHT, b. 19 Oct. 1882, Campello "

Louie Forest WRIGHT, b. 12 Jan. 1886 "

Charles Edward BEALS, (son of Charles & Susan (Fisher)), b. 15 July 1869

CHILD OF Charles Edward BEALS & Nellie Vernon DRAKE^{4}: <Drake Fam.:250>

Helen Drake BEALS, b. 5 Jan. 1895

Silence NASH, (*dau of James), b. 19 Apr. 1726*; d. 9 Mar. 1807*

CHILDREN OF William REED^{5} (Jacob^{4}) & Silence NASH: (1 of 8*)**<149>**

Lt. James REED^{6}, b. 6 Oct. 1764; d. 30 Oct. 1855, Mt. Zion Cem.

Ruth PORTER, (dau of Sam & Hannah (Jackson)), b. 1 Feb. 1766 <Bridgewater VR 1:266>; d. 13 Apr. 1848, Mt. Zion Cem. <Abington VR 2:343>

CHILDREN OF Lt. James REED^{6} & Ruth PORTER: (8) <Reed Gen.(1901):118>

Mehitable REED^{7}, b. 10 May 1784, d. 8 Sept. 1846

Hannah REED^{7}, b. 12 Mar. 1786

James REED^{7}, b. 13 Aug. 1788 <Abington VR>; d. 23 Dec. 1810, Colebrook Cem.<Abington VR 2:340>

Jane REED^{7}, b. 10 June 1791, d. 3 Feb. 1869

Samuel Porter REED^{7}, b. 14 May 1793, d. 9 Sept. 1815

Timothy REED^{7}, b. 22 Mar. 1796

Maj. Marcus REED^{7}, b. 23 Aug. 1798

Cyrus REED^{7}, b. ( )

CHILD OF John REED^{4} (Esther Tomson^{3}) & 1st Sarah ( ):

John REED^{5}, b. 10 Aug. 1713 <Abington VR 1:185>

Mary WHEELER, d. aft. 12 July

CHILDREN OF John REED^{4} & 2nd Mary WHEELER: (10) <Abington VR 1:185>

James REED^{5}, b. 12 Oct. 1716; d. pre 5 Nov. 1753 (adm.) <Plymouth Co.PR #16603, 13:141>

Joseph REED^{5}, b. 13 Feb. 1717/8

Mary REED^{5}, b. 21 Dec. 1719

Ezekiel REED^{5}, b. 14 Nov. 1722 (1721?); d. at sea 1763

Peter REED^{5}, b. 29 Mar. 1723

Squire REED^{5}, b. 25 May 1725

Silence REED^{5}, b. 10 Aug. 1728, d. 24 Aug. 1728

Benjamin REED^{5}, b. 8 Apr. 1730

Samuel REED^{5}, b. 13 July 1732

Ruth (FORD) Pool, (*dau of Hezekiah & Ruth (Whitmarsh)), b. 3 May 1716*, d. 9 Jan. 1791* <Abington VR 1:77, 2:332>

CHILDREN OF James REED^{5} (John^{4}) & Ruth (FORD) Pool: (6) <1-5, Abington VR>

Joseph REED^{6}, b. 4 Aug. 1742 <1:185>; d. betw. 1 Sept. 1776 (will) - 5 May 1777 (inv.), unm.<Plymouth Co.PR #16633, 24:306>

Hezekiah REED^{6}, b. 23 Feb. 1744/5 <1:184>; d. 1 Mar. 1789, Bridgewater <Plymouth Co.PR #16579, 30:530>

Jeremiah REED^{6}, b. 4 Oct. 1746 <1:185>; d. 11 Dec. 1747

Jeremiah REED^{6}, b. 11 Apr. 1747 <1:185>

Olive REED^{6}, b. 2 Feb. 1748/9 <1:190>; d. pre 4 Mar. 1769*

Naomi REED^{6}, b. aft. 1751* (mentioned in father's will)

Deborah M. TIRRELL, b. c1747, d. 21 Dec. 1820*, Bridgewater

CHILDREN OF Hezekiah REED^{6} & Deborah M. TIRRELL: (9) <Reed Gen.(1901):107>

Deborah REED^{7}, b. 1768

Olive REED^{7}, b. 1770

James REED^{7}, b. 1772, d. 13 Aug. 1791

Isaac REED^{7}, b. 1774, Bridgewater; d. 17 Oct. 1867, ae 92y9m25d, E. Bridgewater <Mass.VR 203:291>

Jeremiah REED^{7}, b. 1777

Calvin REED^{7}, b. 1780

Joseph REED^{7}, b. 18 Oct. 1782

Jared REED^{7}, b. 1785, d. 1855

Nancy REED^{7}, b. 1789

Sally STETSON^{4} (*Peleg$^{3-2}$, Isaac^{1}), b. 31 Oct. 1777* <Abington VR>; d. 15 Feb. 1840* <E. Bridgewater VR:384>

CHILDREN OF Isaac REED^{7} & Sally STETSON: (3)

Sally REED^{8}*, b. 22 Oct. 1803*; d. 29 Feb. 1869*

Isaac REED^{8}*, b. 26 Jan. 1805*

James Thaxter REED^{8}, b. c1815, d. 22 Feb. 1875, ae 59y4m14d, bootmaker, E. Bridgewater <Mass.VR 275:303>

Eliza Ann KEITH, b. c1822, E. Bridgewater, d. 16 Feb. 1851, ae 28, bur. New Central Cem., E. Bridgewater <Mass.VR 58:171>

CHILD OF James Thaxter REED^{8} & Eliza Ann KEITH:

Sarah Scott REED^{9}, b. c1846, E. Bridgewater, d. 23 May 1884, ae 38, Brockton, bur. E. Bridgewater <Mass.VR 356:294> (wf of Henry Cushman Harding)

Alice NASH, (dau of Jacob & Abigail), b. Mar. 1684*, d. 5 Dec 1751*, ae 67y8m13d, bur. Mt. Zion cem. <Abington VR>

CHILDREN OF William REED^{4} (Esther Tomson^{3}) & Alice NASH: (10) <2-10, Abington VR>

Alice REED^{5}, b. 19 Oct. 1703, d. 24 Oct. 1703 <Boston Rcd.Com.24:23>

William REED^{5}, b. 15 Dec. 1705; d. 21 Nov. 1724, unm.

Obadiah REED^{5}, b. 14 Mar. 1706/7

Ebenezer REED^{5}, b. 13 July 1709 <VR 1:182>; d. 16 Apr. 1790* <Abington VR 2:328>

Alice REED^{5}, b. 4 Apr. 1711; d. 29 Sept. 1724

Daniel REED^{5}, b. 6 Dec. 1713

James REED^{5}, b. 3 Mar. 1716; d. 24 July 1762, Mt. Zion cem., Abington

Solomon REED^{5}, b. 22 Oct. 1719

Moses REED^{5}, b. 15 Jan. 1722/3

Alice REED^{5}, b. 19 Apr. 1725

Hannah TOMSON^{4} (Jacob^{3}, Mary Cooke^{2}), b. 10 Mar. 1708/9, Middleboro <MD 2:201>; d. 27 Nov. 1787* <Abington VR 2:339>

CHILDREN OF Ebenezer REED^{5} & Hannah TOMSON: (10) <Abington VR; dth. dates from Reed Gen.:43,44>

Ebenezer REED^{6}, b. 11 Dec. 1733 <1:182>; d. 7 June 1740*

William REED^{6}, b. 23 Oct. 1735 <1:193>; d.? 29 Mar. 1778*

Ichabod REED^{6}, b. 26 Apr. 1738 <1:184>; d. in French war

David REED^{6}, b. 9 July 1740 <1:181>; d. 10 May 1808*, ?Cunnington

Jonathan REED^{6}, b. 9 July 1740 <1:186> (twins)

Paul REED^{6}, b. 3 Mar. 1743 <1:190>; d. 15 Mar. 1743*

Silas REED^{6}, b. 3 Mar. 1743 (twins) <1:192>; d. 11 Aug. 1744*

Abigail REED^{6}, b. 10 Apr. 1745 <1:179>

Barnabas REED^{6}, b. 30 Apr. 1748 <1:180>

Ebenezer REED^{6}, b. 13 Dec. 1751 <1:182>; d. 18 Dec. 1751*

Mercy FORD, (*dau of Andrew & Sarah), b.? 7 June 1744*; d. pre 9 Jan. 1788 (hus.2nd marr.)

CHILDREN OF David REED^{6} & Mercy FORD: (10) <1-6, Abington VR>

Ichabod REED^{7}, b. 25 Nov. 1763 <1:184>; d. 12 Jan. 1778

Abigail REED^{7}, b. 4 June 1765 <1:179>; d. 13 Apr. 1781

David REED^{7}, b. 3 May 1767 <1:181>
Ebenezer REED^{7}, b. 27 Mar. 1769 <1:182>
Andrew REED^{7}, b. 25 June 1771 <1:180>
Paul REED^{7}, b. 12 Oct. 1773 <1:190>
William REED^{7}, b. 7 May 1777
Barnabas REED^{7}, b. 16 Oct. 1779
Ichabod REED^{7}, b. 12 May 1782
Thaxter REED^{7}, b. ( )

MICRO #28 of 30

Abigail NASH, (dau of James & Experience), b. c1717, d. 15 or 17 Jan. 1808, ae 91, bur. Mt. Zion cem. <Abington VR 2:337>

CHILDREN OF James REED^{5} (Wm.^{4}) & Abigail NASH: (9) <Abington VR>
Tabitha REED^{6}, b. 3 Mar. 1740 <1:193>
Experience REED^{6}, b. 23 Oct. 1741 <1:183>
Solomon REED^{6}, b. 25 Oct. 1743 <1:192>
Adam REED^{6}, b. 19 Aug. 1745 <ChR>
Stephen REED^{6}, b. 5 July 1748 <1:192>
Huldah REED^{6}, b. 25 Apr. 1751 <1:184>; d. 20 Feb. 1791, unm. <ChR>
Abel REED^{6}, b. 15 Apr. 1754 <1:179>
Molly REED^{6}, b. 3 Mar. 1756 <1:189>
James REED^{6}, b. 24 June 1758 <1:185>; d. 16 Feb. 1827, "pauper" <ChR>

Abigail WADSWORTH, (dau of John), b. 25 Oct. 1670, Duxbury <MD 9:172>; d. 15 Jan. 1744, The Green cem., Middleboro <MD 14:217>

CHILDREN OF Jacob TOMSON^{3} & Abigail WADSWORTH: (10) <Middleboro VR>
Jacob TOMSON^{4}, b. 17 Apr. 1695, d. 10 Mar. 1789, Green Cem., Middleboro <MD 2:41, 14:219>
Abigail TOMSON^{4}, b. 14 Feb. 1696/7 <MD 2:41>
Mercy TOMSON^{4}, b. 13 Oct. 1699, d. 4 Sept. 1799, Green Cem., Middleboro <MD 2:41, 12:70>
John TOMSON^{4}, b. 19 Mar. 1700/1, d. 6 Dec. 1790, Thompson St. Cem., Halifax <MD 2:41, 14:7>
Lydia TOMSON^{4}, b. 22 Apr. 1703 <MD 2:42>
Barnabas TOMSON^{4}, b. 28 Jan.1704/5 <MD 2:42>; d. 20 Dec. 1798, Halifax g.s. <MD 14:6>
Esther TOMSON^{4}, b. 18 Feb. 1706/7 <MD 2:105>; d. 5 July 1776, Green Cem., Middleboro <MD 12:69>
Hannah TOMSON^{4}, b. 10 Mar. 1708/9 <MD 2:201>
Mary TOMSON^{4}, b. 19 May 1711, d. 19 July 1769 <MD 2:201, 14:9>
Caleb TOMSON^{4}, b. 4 Nov. 1712, d. 19 Jan. 1787, Green Cem., Middleboro <MD 3:84, 14:217>

CHILD OF Jonathan INGLEE & Abigail TOMSON^{4}: **<150>**
Moses INGLEE^{5}, b. c1721, d. 18 Jan. 1809, 88th yr, Thompson St. cem., Halifax <MD 13:150>

Jonathan PACKARD, (son of Zaccheus & Sarah), b. 7 Dec. 1684 <Bridgewater VR> **<151>**

CHILDREN OF Jonathan PACKARD & Abigail TOMSON^{4}: (5) <Bridgewater VR>
Jonathan PACKARD^{5}, b. 28 Aug. 1724; d. 19 Mar. 1726
Susanna PACKARD^{5}, b. 21 Feb. 1726; d. 29 Oct. 1808*
Jacob PACKARD^{5}, b. 12 Apr. 1728
Jonathan PACKARD^{5}, b. 12 Nov. 1730
Abigail PACKARD^{5}, b. 13 May 1735

Anna RANSOM, (*?dau of Robert & Sarah), b.? 7 Sept. 1736*, Middleboro <MD 20:37>; d. 13 Feb. 1810, Halifax g.s. <MD 13:150>

CHILDREN OF Moses INGLEE^{5} (Abigail Tomson^{4}) & Anna RANSOM: (11) <Halifax VR:37>
Solomon INGLEE^{6}, b. 18 Oct. 1758
Sarah INGLEE^{6}, b. 5 Apr. 1760, d. 4 Feb. 1766 <VR:5, MD 13:150>
Abigail INGLEE^{6}, b. 14 July 1762
Ebenezer INGLEE^{6}, b. 7 Mar. 1764

Moses INGLEE^{6}, b. 16 June 1766

Sarah INGLEE^{6}, b. 23 Mar. 1768

Annah INGLEE^{6}, b. 2 Feb. 1772, d. 13 May 1787 <VR:7, MD 13:150>

Lemuel INGLEE^{6}, b. 4 Mar. 1774

Olive INGLEE^{6}, b. 23 Feb. 1776

Jesse INGLEE^{6}, b. 14 Mar. 1778

Robert INGLEE^{6}, b. 30 Mar. 1784

Hannah PORTER, (dau of Sam. & Mary), b. 16 Dec. 1712 <Abington VR 1:172>; d. 2 May 1787, Halifax g.s. <VR:6, MD 14:7>

CHILDREN OF Barnabas TOMSON^{4} (Jacob^{3}) & Hannah PORTER: (14) <Halifax VR:47>

Abigail TOMSON^{5}, b. 12 Feb. 1740/1; d. 31 Mar. 1747 <VR:2, MD 14:5>

Barnabas TOMSON^{5}, b. 13 Feb. 1741/2; d. 7 Sept. 1742 <VR:1, MD 14:6>

Jacob TOMSON^{5}, b. 14 Mar. 1743, d. same day <MD 14:7>

Samuel TOMSON^{5}, b. 14 Mar. 1743 (twins); d. 29 Apr. 1747 <VR:2, MD 14:9>

Jabez TOMSON^{5}, b. 26 Mar. 1744; d. 8 Apr. 1747 <VR:2, MD 14:7>

Asa TOMSON^{5}, b. 3 Sept. 1745; d. 5 Apr. 1747 <VR:2, MD 14:6>

Noah TOMSON^{5}, b. 20 Mar. 1746/7

Hannah TOMSON^{5}, b. 30 May 1748

Isaac TOMSON^{5}, b. 29 May 1749; d. 6 Dec. 1782, Halifax g.s. <MD 14:7>

David TOMSON^{5}, b. 2 Sept. 1750; d. 13 Sept. 1750 <VR:3, MD 14:6>

Olive TOMSON^{5}, b. 10 Apr. 1752; d. 12 Feb. 1776, unm., Halifax g.s. <VR:5, MD 14:8>

Abel TOMSON^{5}, b. 10 Apr. 1752 (twins); d. 28 July 1754 <VR:4, MD 14:5>

Adam TOMSON^{5}, b. 24 Apr. 1754; d. 20 Aug. 1821, Halifax g.s. <MD 14:5>

Ichabod TOMSON^{5}, b. 23 Apr. 1756 <VR:48>; d. 31 Aug. 1821, Halifax g.s. <MD 14:7>

Molly TOMSON^{5} (Amasa^{4}, Tho.^{3}, Mary Cooke^{2}), b. 13 Dec. 1756 <Halifax VR:50>; d. 12 June 1835, Halifax g.s. <MD 14:8>

CHILDREN OF Adam TOMSON^{5} & Molly TOMSON: (4) <Halifax VR>

Samuel TOMSON^{6}, b. 24 Sept. 1778 <VR:27>

Adam TOMSON^{6}, b. 27 May 1784 <VR:27>

Ward TOMSON^{6}, b. 4 Sept. 1786 <VR:28>

Zadock TOMSON^{6}, b. 4 Jan. 1790 <VR:28>

Lydia HALL, b. c1747, d. 20 Apr. 1821, 74th yr, Halifax g.s. <MD 14:8>

CHILDREN OF Ichabod TOMSON^{5} (Barnabas^{4}) & Lydia HALL: (3) <Halifax VR:28>

James TOMSON^{6}, b. 13 Apr. 1780

Hannah TOMSON^{6}, b. 14 Oct. 1782

Sarah TOMSON^{6}, b. 1 Mar. 1785

Huldah STURTEVANT, (*dau of Lemuel & Deborah), b. 11 Jan. 1751/2* <Halifax VR:46>; d. 16 Mar. 1839* <Tomson Gen.:44>

CHILDREN OF Isaac TOMSON^{5} (Barnabas^{4}) & Huldah STURTEVANT: (5) <Halifax VR:48>

Jabez TOMSON^{6}, b. 3 Nov. 1772; d. 7 Feb. 1845*, Plympton

Isaac TOMSON^{6}, b. 17 Nov. 1774; d. 1858*

Olive TOMSON^{6}, b. 17 Mar. 1777

Abigail TOMSON^{6}, b. 26 Sept. 1779

Jacob TOMSON^{6}, b. 26 June 1782

Betsy WOOD, (dau of Israel & Priscilla), b. 3 Oct. 1775 <Middleboro VR 4:88> (m. Jabez Tomson^{6})

Phebe SOULE, b. c1777, d. 5 Dec. 1823*, 46th yr <Tomson Gen.:69>

CHILDREN OF Isaac TOMSON^{6} & Phebe SOULE: (10*) <Tomson Gen.:69>

Sabina TOMSON^{7}, b. 1801

Roxanna TOMSON^{7}, b. 1802

Deborah TOMSON^{7}, b. 1804

Christopher C. TOMSON^{7}, b. 1807
Abigail TOMSON^{7}, b. 1809
Phebe TOMSON^{7}, b. 1811
Mary TOMSON^{7}, b. 1813
Isaac TOMSON^{7}, b. 1815
Hiram TOMSON^{7}, b. 1818
Joseph S. TOMSON^{7}, b. 1823
CHILDREN OF Noah TOMSON^{5} (Barnabas^{4}) & Priscilla HOLMES: (10) <Halifax VR:51>
Barnabas TOMSON^{6}, b. 20 Nov. 1769
David TOMSON^{6}, b. 16 Mar. 1772
Noah TOMSON^{6}, b. 3 July 1774
Abel TOMSON^{6}, b. 3 Oct. 1776
John Holmes TOMSON^{6}, b. 26 Sept. 1779
Priscilla TOMSON^{6}, b. 19 Sept. 1781
Betty TOMSON^{6}, b. 16 Feb. 1784
Cromwell TOMSON^{6}, b. 27 Apr. 1786
Elihu TOMSON^{6}, b. 1 Aug. 1788
Charles TOMSON^{6}, b. 30 Apr. 1792
Abigail CROSMAN, b. c1714, d. 23 Nov. 1791, Green Cem., Middleboro <MD 14:217>
CHILDREN OF Caleb TOMSON^{4} (Jacob^{3}) & Abigail CROSMAN: (8) <Middleboro VR>
Hannah TOMSON^{5}, b. 24 July 1737, d. 21 Sept. 1737 <MD 8:249, 14:218>
Sarah TOMSON^{5}, b. 15 Nov. 1738 <MD 14:244>
Lucia TOMSON^{5}, b. 12 July 1741 <MD 15:121>
Hannah TOMSON^{5}, b. 8 Aug. 1743 <MD 15:221>
Molly TOMSON^{5}, b. 12 Aug. 1745 <MD 16:107>
William TOMSON^{5}, b. 15 Feb. 1747/8 <MD 17:20>; d. 14 Mar. 1816, Green Cem., Middleboro<MD 14:220>
Nathaniel TOMSON^{5}, b. 13 Sept. 1750; d. 31 Jan. 1833 <MD 2:154>
Caleb TOMSON^{5}, b. 18 Oct. 1752
Hannah THOMAS^{5} (Mary Alden^{4}, John^{3}, Jos.^{2}), b. 9 Jan. 1749, d. 7 Apr. 1821 <MD 2:154>
CHILDREN OF Nathaniel THOMPSON^{5} (Caleb^{4}) & Hannah THOMAS: (6) <MD 2:152>
Rev. Otis THOMPSON^{6}, b. 14 Sept. 1776; d. 26 June 1859 <MD 2:154>
Sally THOMPSON^{6}, b. 5 Mar. 1778; d. 28 Feb. 1841 <MD 2:154>
Sybil THOMPSON^{6}, b. 27 Apr. 1780
Polly THOMPSON^{6}, b. 5 Apr. 1782
Nancy THOMPSON^{6}, b. 9 Sept. 1784
Sabina THOMPSON^{6}, b. 7 May 1787; d. 7 Sept. 1790 <MD 2:154>
Rachel CHANDLER, b. c1780, d. 16 Sept. 1827, ae 47y6m24d <MD 2:154>
CHILDREN OF Rev. Otis THOMPSON^{6} & 1st Rachel CHANDLER: (9) <MD 2:154>
Sabina THOMPSON^{7}, b. 7 Nov. 1802
Lucena THOMPSON^{7}, b. Feb. 1804, d. 7 Aug. 1851, ae 47
Fidelia THOMPSON^{7}, b. 9 Dec. 1805, d. 31 Mar. 1840
Rachel Chandler THOMPSON^{7}, b. 17 May 1807
Charlotte Wright THOMPSON^{7}, b. 17 Mar. 1811
Otis Chandler THOMPSON^{7}, b. 9 Oct. 1813
Josiah THOMPSON^{7}, b. 19 June 1816
Lucius THOMPSON^{7}, b. 20 July 1819
Alden THOMPSON^{7}, b. 2 Apr. 1822, d. 30 Dec. 1823
Charlotte FALES, b. 5 Jan. 1786, d. 12 Dec. 1848 <MD 2:154> (2nd wf. Rev. Otis Thompson^{6})
Polly SHAW, b. c1791, d. 3 Feb. 1874, ae 82y10m20d <MD 2:154>
Deborah STURTEVANT, (dau of Lemuel), b. 30 Sept. 1748 <Halifax VR:45>; d. 25 Dec. 1842, Green

Cem., Middleboro <MD 14:218> (m. Wm. Tomson^{5})

Ebenezer BENNET, (son of John), b. 20 Feb. ( ), Middleboro <MD 1:220>; d. 26 Aug. 1751, 51st yr, Bay of Honduras, Green Cem., Middleboro <MD 12:69>

CHILDREN OF Ebenezer BENNET & Esther TOMSON^{4} (Jacob^{3}): (8) <Middleboro>

Patience BENNET^{5}, b. 16 Sept. 1738, d. 11 Nov. 1781 <MD 14:244, 12:70>

John BENNET^{5}, b. 2 May 1740 <MD 14:246>

Son, stillborn, b. 1 May 1741 <MD 15:122>

Esther BENNET^{5}, b. 26 Mar. 1742, d. 29 Aug. 1743 <MD 15:217, 15:24>

Lydia BENNET^{5}, b. 15 July 1743, d. 13 Aug. 1743 <MD 15:221>

Dau., stillborn, b.12 July 1744 <MD 16:133, 12:69>

Dau., stillborn, b. 21 Aug. 1746 <MD 16:133, 12:69>

Ebenezer BENNET^{5}, b. 31 Jan. 1747, d. 10 Nov. 1778 <MD 16:133, 12:69>

Elizabeth (TILSON) Holmes, (dau of Edmund & Eliz. (Waterman)), b. 6 May 1700, Plymouth <MD 2:19>; d. 8 Aug. 1773, Green Cem., Middleboro <MD 14:218>

CHILDREN OF Jacob TOMSON^{4} (Jacob^{3}) & Elizabeth (TILSON) Holmes: (3) <Middleboro VR>

Abigail TOMSON^{5}, b. 26 Nov. 1735 <MD 13:3>

Jacob TOMSON^{5}, b. 28 Mar. 1738, d. 30 Nov. 1805, Green Cem., Middleboro <MD 4:70, 14:219>

Elizabeth TOMSON^{5}, b. 29 June 1741, d. 4 Dec. 1747 <MD 15:121, 14:218>

Freelove PHINNEY^{6} (Pelatiah^{5}, Jos.^{4}, Mary Rogers^{3}, Jos.^{2}), b. 27 Jan. 1740*<Bridgewater VR 1:262> d. 7 Nov. 1826, Green Cem., Middleboro <MD 14:218> (wf of Jacob Tomson^{5})

Joanna ADAMS, (dau of Jos. & Alice), b. 6 Jan. 1705, Marshfield; d. 10 Jan. 1779, Thompson St. Cem. <Halifax VR:6; MD 14:7>

CHILDREN OF John TOMSON^{4} (Jacob^{3}) & Joanna ADAMS: (5) <Halifax>

Son, b. & d. 10 Sept. 1736 <MD 10:103>

Son, stillborn, b. 11 June 1738 <MD 10:103>

Son, stillborn, b. 7 Mar. 1740 <MD 10:103>

Zaccheus TOMSON^{5}, b. 22 July 1743 <Halifax VR:49>; d. 19 Apr. 1747 <MD 10:103>

Joanna TOMSON^{5}, b. 9 Aug. 1751 <Halifax VR:49>; d. 10 Sept. 1833, Thompson St. Cem., Middleboro <MD 14:11>

Freeman WATERMAN^{6} (Tho.^{5}, Mary Cushman^{4}, Isaac^{3}, Mary Allerton^{2}), b. c1748, d. 5 Apr. 1830, Thompson St. Cem., Halifax <MD 14:11>

CHILDREN OF Freeman WATERMAN & Joanna TOMSON^{5}: (See Allerton Family, p.80)

Nehemiah BENNET, (son of John), b. 10 Nov. ( ), Middleboro <MD 1:220>; d. 15 Aug. 1769, 74th yr, Green Cem., Middleboro <MD 12:70>

CHILDREN OF Nehemiah BENNET & Mercy TOMSON^{4} (Jacob^{3}): (6) <Middleboro VR>

Abigail BENNET^{5}, b. 5 Jan. 1723/4, d. 11 Oct. 1801 <MD 6:179, 14:222>

Jacob BENNET^{5}, b. 29 Apr. 1725, d. 26 Nov. 1799 <MD 6:227, 12:69>

William BENNET^{5}, b. 2 July 1727 <MD 6:229>

Patience BENNET^{5}, b. 29 June 1730, d. 15 Sept. 1735 <MD 8:28, 13:5>

Martha BENNET^{5}, b. 8 Dec. 1733 <MD 12:230>

Hannah BENNET^{5}, b. 13 Jan. 1735/6 <MD 13:4>

Mary TINKHAM^{3} (Mary Brown^{2}), b. 2 Aug. 1661, Plymouth <MD 17:186; d. 1731, Green Cem., Middleboro <MD 14:219>

CHILDREN OF John TOMSON^{3} & Mary TINKHAM: (12) <Middleboro VR; 4-11, MD 2:41>

Mary TOMSON^{4}, b. 2 May 1681 <MD 1:221>; d. pre 3 Dec. 1745 (adm.), unm. <Plym.Co.PR #20608>**<152>**

John TOMSON^{4}, b. 9 Aug. 1682 <MD 1:221>; d. betw. 11 May 1757 (will) - 2 July 1757 (inv.) <Plymouth Co.PR #20585, 14:312,370>

Ephraim TOMSON^{4}, b. 16 Oct. 1683 <MD 1:221>; d. 13 Nov. 1744, Thompson St. Cem.,Halifax <MD 14:6>

Shubael TOMSON^{4}, b. 11 Apr. 1686; d. 7 July 1733, Green Cem., Middleboro <MD 13:5>

Thomas TOMSON^{4}, b. 29 July 1688; d. betw. 7 July 1759 (will) - 7 Apr. 1760 (prob.) <Plymouth Co.

PR #20656, 15:479>

Martha TOMSON[4], b. 4 Jan. 1689/90; d. betw. 1 July 1760 (will) - 16 May 1770 (prob.), unm. <Plymouth Co.PR #20605, 20:360>

Sarah TOMSON[4], b. 3 Mar. 1691/2; d. betw. 1 July 1760 (will) - 7 Jan. 1771 (prob.), unm.<Plymouth Co.PR #20639, 20:456>

Peter TOMSON[4], b. 11 May 1694; d. pre 23 June 1726 (adm.), unm. <MD 25:56; Plymouth Co.PR #20624>

Isaac TOMSON[4], b. 10 Mar. 1696/7; d. pre 19 Oct. 1724 (father's will)

Ebenezer TOMSON[4], b. 19 June 1699; d. pre 22 Mar. 1726/7 (adm.), unm.<MD 25:56; Plym. PR #20536>

Francis TOMSON[4], b. 27 Jan. 1700/01; d. 24 July 1734, unm.

Jacob TOMSON[4], b. 24 June 1703, d. 17 Feb. 1750/1, Thompson St. Cem., Halifax <MD 2:104, 14:8>

Joanna THOMAS, (dau of Jonathan), b. 28 Feb. 1707/8, Middleboro <MD 2:202>**<153>**

CHILDREN OF Ephraim TOMSON[4] (John[3]) & Joanna THOMAS: (4) <Halifax VR:42>

Child, b. 3 Dec. 1735; d. 5 Dec. 1735 <MD 10:103>

Joanna TOMSON[5], b. 23 July 1738; d. 17 Dec. 1744 <MD 3:30>

Ephraim TOMSON[5], b. 8 Apr. 1742; d. Apr. 1742, ae 21 days <MD 10:103>

Ephraim TOMSON[5], b. 8 May 1744; d. 25 May 1744 <MD 3:30>

Mary HAYWARD, d. 18 Mar. 1769, 44th yr, Thompson St. Cem., Halifax <MD 14:8>**<154>**

CHILDREN OF Jacob TOMSON[4] (John[3]) & Mary HAYWARD: (7) <1-4, Halifax VR:43>

Jacob TOMSON[5], b. 9 July 1736; d. 12 Nov. 1815*

Ebenezer TOMSON[5], b. 14 Oct. 1737; d. 10 May 1832*

Nathaniel TOMSON[5], b. 23 July 1740; d. pre 6 Apr. 1761, unm. <Plymouth Co.PR #20620>

Mary TOMSON[5], b. 7 Sept. 1743; d. 21 Aug. 1747 <Halifax VR:2>

Martha TOMSON[5], b. 1 Jan. 1745/6, d. 7 Sept. 1747 <Halifax VR:51,2>

Ephraim TOMSON[5], b. 1 Aug. 1748 <Halifax VR:51>

Daniel TOMSON[5], b. 24 Oct. 1750 <Halifax VR:51>

Elizabeth THOMAS[4] (Lydia Howland[3], John[2]), b. 19 Nov. 1690, Middleboro <MD 2:107>

CHILDREN OF John TOMSON[4] (John[3]) & Elizabeth THOMAS: (3) <Plympton VR, MD 2:51>

John TOMSON[5], b. 18 Feb. 1724/5; d. 18 Jan. 1777*

Elizabeth TOMSON[5], b. 7 Aug. 1726; d. 1794*

Lydia TOMSON[5], b. 13 Aug. 1730; d. 29 Aug. 1771

Betty FULLER, (dau of Eben.), d. betw. 1 Mar. 1777* - 3 May 1779***<155>**

CHILDREN OF John TOMSON[5] & Betty FULLER: (6)

Susanna TOMSON[6], b. c1761*

Thaddeus TOMSON[6], b. 1 July 1765*

Nathan TOMSON[6], b. 1767*

Zaccheus TOMSON[6], b. 1769*

Elizabeth TOMSON[6], b. 177()*

Stephen TOMSON[6], b. 1774*

Susanna PARLOUR, b. c1687, d. 9 June 1734, 47th yr, Green Cem., Middleboro <MD 14:220>

CHILDREN OF Shubael TOMSON[4] (John[3]) & Susanna PARLOUR: (5) <Middleboro VR>

Isaac TOMSON[5], b. 24 Sept. 1714 <MD 3:86>; d. 30 Apr. 1740, unm.

Shubael TOMSON[5], b. 27 Mar. 1716 <MD 3:86>; d. 18 June 1734, Green Cem., Middleboro,unm.<MD 13:5>

John TOMSON[5], b. 11 June 1717 <MD 3:86>; d. 22 June 1766, Green Cem., Middleboro <MD 14:219>

Mary TOMSON[5], b. 24 Sept. 1719 <MD 6:227>; d. 23 June 1734, Green Cem., Middleboro <MD 13:5>

Thomas TOMSON[5], b. 28 July 1721; d. 8 Feb. 1756* <Bridgewater VR 2:566>

Lydia WOOD, (*dau of Elnathan & Mary), b. 1 July 1722*, Middleboro <MD 4:68>; d. 28 Jan. 1761, Green Cem., Middleboro <MD 14:219>

CHILDREN OF John TOMSON[5] & 1st Lydia WOOD: (10) <1-8, Middleboro VR>

Shubael TOMSON[6], b. 11 Mar. 1741/2 <MD 15:220>; d. betw. 20 Jan. 1770 (will) - 17 Mar. 1770 (inv) <Plymouth Co.PR #20641, 20:358,359>**<156>**

Susanna TOMSON^{6}, b. 1 Nov. 1743 <MD 15:221>; d. 4 Sept. 1822*

Hon. Isaac TOMSON^{6}, b. 1 Feb. 1745/6 <MD 20:35>; d. 21 Dec. 1819, Green Cem., Middleboro

John TOMSON^{6}, b. 6 May 1748 <MD 20:35>

Ezra TOMSON^{6}, b. 4 July 1750 <MD 20:35>; d. 1778*

Lydia TOMSON^{6}, b. 21 June 1752 <MD 20:36>

Sarah TOMSON^{6}, b. 6 Oct. 1754 <MD 20:36>; d. 10 Nov. 1777*

Uzza TOMSON^{6}, b. Dec. 1756, d. 11 June 1758, ae 18m1d <MD 14:220>

Fear TOMSON^{6}, b. 6 Nov. 1757*, d. 10 Nov. 1796*

Priscilla TOMSON^{6}, b. 11 Apr. 1760*

Sarah (BRYANT) Soule, (dau of George & Sarah), b. 31 Oct. 1731 <Plympton VR>; d. 20 Aug. 1805, Halifax g.s. <VR:94> (widow of 3rd hus. Reuben Tomson^{4} (Tho.^{3}, Mary Cooke^{2}))

CHILD OF John TOMSON^{5} & 2nd Sarah (BRYANT) Soule:

Mary TOMSON^{6}, b. c1763

Lucy (STURTEVANT*), b. c1753, d. 4 Nov. 1834, 81st yr, Green Cem., Middleboro

CHILDREN OF Hon. Isaac TOMSON^{6} (John^{5}) & Lucy (STURTEVANT*): (4) <Middleboro VR 4:114>

George TOMSON^{7}, b. 12 Aug. 1788

Polly TOMSON^{7}, b. 14 Apr. 1790

Ezra TOMSON^{7}, b. 8 Mar. 1792

Harriet TOMSON^{7}, b. 19 Dec. 1795

Jane WASHBURN^{6} (John$^{5-4}$, Eliz. Mitchell^{3}, Jane Cooke^{2}), b. 28 Mar. 1722, Bridgewater <MD 14:208>; 22 Mar. 1793*, Bridgewater g.s. <VR 2:566> (m. Thomas Tomson^{5} (Shubael^{4}))

MICRO #29 of 30

Martha SOULE^{4} (John$^{3-2}$), b. 11 Apr. 1702, Middleboro <MD 2:105>; d. 18 Mar. 1772, Green Cem., Middleboro <MD 12:66>

CHILDREN OF Thomas TOMSON^{4} (John^{3}) & Martha SOULE: (5) <2-5, Halifax VR:46>

Peter TOMSON^{5}, b. 8 Oct. 1733, Middleboro <MD 12:230>; d. 21 June 1800, Halifax g.s. <MD 14:8>

Francis TOMSON^{5}, b. 15 Mar. 1734/5; d. 17 Dec. 1798, Green Cem., Middleboro <MD 14:218>**<157>**

Nathan TOMSON^{5}, b. 10 Dec. 1736

James TOMSON^{5}, b. 11 Nov. 1739

Thomas TOMSON^{5}, b. 1 June 1743; d. 16 Sept. 1747 <Halifax VR:2>

Rebecca SNOW^{5} (Jonathan^{4}, Jos.^{3}, Rebecca Brown^{2}), b. 16 Oct. 1734, Bridgewater <MD 15:196>; d. 27 Aug. 1766, Green Cem., Middleboro <MD 14:220> (1st wf of Francis Thomson^{5})**<157>**

Mary ( ) THOMSON, b. c1744, d. 17 Dec. 1829, 85th yr, Green Cem., Middleboro <MD 14:219> (2nd wf of Francis Thomson^{5})**<157>**

Rebecca THOMAS, b. c1736, d. 16 Oct. 1792, 56th yr, Halifax g.s. <MD 14:9>

CHILDREN OF Peter TOMSON^{5} (Tho.^{4}) & Rebecca THOMAS: (4) <Halifax VR:37>

Levi TOMSON^{6}, b. 6 Jan. 1764

Ezekiel TOMSON^{6}, b. 4 May 1766

Eliab TOMSON^{6}, b. 8 Dec. 1768; d. 2 Oct. 1835 <MD 14:6>

Aseph TOMSON^{6}, b. 2 Sept. 1771

CHILDREN OF Ezekiel TOMSON^{6} & Mary BOSWORTH: (2) <Halifax VR:25>

Polly TOMSON^{7}, b. 20 Aug. 1791 <MD 7:110>

Peter TOMSON^{7}, b. 1 Aug. 1793 <MD 7:111> (moved to N.Y.)

Thomas TABER, d. betw. 15 June 1723 (will) - 20 Mar. 1732/3 (prob.) <MD 16:231>**<158>**

CHILDREN OF Thomas TABER & Mary TOMSON^{3}: (10) <Dartmouth VR>

Lydia TABER^{4}, b. 8 Aug. 1673

Sarah TABER^{4}, b. 28 Jan. 1674

Mary TABER^{4}, b. 18 Mar. 1677

Joseph TABER^{4}, b. 7 Mar. 1679; d. betw. 20 Dec. 1748 (will) -1753 (prob.) <Bristol Co.PR 13:289>

John TABER^{4}, b. 22 Feb. 1681

Jacob TABER[4], b. 26 July 1683; d. 4 Apr. 1773* <Dartmouth VR 3:72>
Jonathan TABER[4], b. 22 Sept. 1685
Bethiah TABER[4], b. 3 Sept. 1687; d. aft. 24 Apr. 1753*
Philip TABER[4], b. 7 Feb. 1689; living Middletown NJ, 1751
Abigail TABER[4], b. 2 May 1693; living Tiverton RI 28 Aug. 1752* <Bristol Co.Deeds 41:6>
Ebenezer TABER, d. aft. 28 Aug. 1752* <Bristol Co.Deeds 41:6>
CHILDREN OF Ebenezer TABER & Abigail TABER[4]: (9) <Tiverton RI VR 1:73>
Paul TABER[5], b. 30 Mar. 1716
Thomas TABER[5], b. 28 Oct. 1717
Mary TABER[5], b. 24 Aug. 1719
Joseph TABER[5], b. 21 Sept. 1721
Hannah TABER[5], b. 13 Sept. 1723
Water TABER[5], b. 4 Sept. 1725; d. 17 June 1730
Lydia TABER[5], b. 24 Oct. 1728
Water TABER[5], b. 1 Oct. 1731
Jacob TABER[5], b. 2 Oct. 1735
CHILDREN OF Paul TABER[5] & Sarah ( ): (10) <Tiverton RI VR 1:121>
Pardon TABER[6], b. 16 July 1739
Samuel TABER[6], b. 11 Mar. 1741
Rhoda TABER[6], b. 19 Apr. 1743
Ebenezer TABER[6], b. 16 Mar. 1745
Abigail TABER[6], b. 18 May 1747
Susannah TABER[6], b. 4 Mar. 1750
Lydia TABER[6], b. 11 June 1752
Sarah TABER[6], b. 28 Nov. 1754
Thopson TABER[6], b. 2 Oct. 1757 (Thompson?)
John TABER[6], b. 28 Jan. 1760
Sarah WEST[4] (Mercy Cooke[3], John[2]), b. 1 Aug. 1686, d. 5 Dec. 1775 <Dartmouth VR>
CHILDREN OF Jacob TABER[4] (Mary Tomson[3]) & Sarah WEST: (8) <Dartmouth VR 1:76>
Eunice TABER[5], b. 10 July 1711, d. 4 June 1762
Stephen TABER[5], b. 22 Feb. 1712/3; d. aft. 9 Feb. 1778*
Jerusha TABER[5], b. 27 Aug. 1715; d. aft. 4 Jan. 1763* (father's will)
Bartholomew TABER[5], b. 11 Sept. 1717; d. betw. 27 Jan. 1801* (will) - 1 Oct. 1804* (inv.)<Bristol Co.PR 40:400, 41:12>
Lois TABER[5], b. 23 Aug. 1719; d. aft. 4 Jan. 1763* (father's will)
Sarah TABER[5], b. 23 July 1721, d. 16 Apr. 1745
Jacob TABER[5], b. 21 May 1723; d. aft. 24 Apr. 1780*
John TABER[5], b. 28 Nov. 1726, d. 27 Aug. 1761
Mercy (BOWDITCH*), d. aft. 27 Jan. 1801* (hus. will)**<159>**
CHILDREN OF Bartholomew TABER[5] & Mercy (BOWDITCH*): (4) <Dartmouth VR 4:2>
Sarah TABER[6], b. 13 May 1771
John TABER[6], b. 23 May 1773; d. aft. 17 Mar. 1847* (will) <Bristol Co.PR 91:292>
Jacob TABER[6], b. 12 Oct. 1775
Bartholowmew TABER[6], b. 2 Aug. 1779
Mary HATHAWAY, (dau of Stephen & Abigail), b. c1768, Fairhaven, d. 27 Aug. 1856, ae 88y8m7d, Fairhaven, widow <Mass.VR 102:65>
CHILDREN OF John TABER[6] & Mary HATHAWAY: (2*)
Sarah H. TABER[7], b. ( )
George H. TABER[7], b. ( )
CHILDREN OF Benjamin AKIN, (son of John "from Scotland") & Eunice TABER[5] (Jacob[4]): (1 of 10)**<160>**

Jacob AKIN^6, b. 1 Oct. 1740, d. 1756, ae 16

CHILDREN OF Bartholomew AKIN^6 (Eunice Taber^5) & Mercy DELANO, (dau of Nathaniel): (8)**<161>**

CHILDREN OF Edward BENNETT & Elizabeth AKIN^6 (Eunice Taber^5): (10)**<162>**

CHILDREN OF John TABER^4 (Mary Tomson^3) & Phebe SPOONER: (9) <Dartmouth VR 1:94>

Thomas TABER^5, b. 18 July 1712

Deborah TABER^5, b. 29 Apr. 1714

Rebecca TABER^5, b. 24 Jan. 1715/6

Mary TABER^5, b. 25 Aug. 1717

Elnathan TABER^5, b. 15 Sept. 1720

Phebe TABER^5, b. 6 Mar. 1723

Amaziah TABER^5, b. 23 Nov. 1724; d. betw. 14 Oct. (will) - 18 Dec. 1809 (prob.) <Bristol Co.PR 45:245,251>

Jabez TABER^5, b. 22 June 1727

Deborah TABER^5, b. 25 May 1731

CHILD OF Amaziah TABER^5 & Sarah WING: <Dartmouth VR 1:116>**<163>**

Phebe TABER^6, b. 7 Oct. 1751

Elizabeth SPOONER, b. 19 June 1683, Dartmouth, d. 14 July 1734*, Dartmouth <Taber Gen.:8>

CHILDREN OF Joseph TABER^4 (Mary Tomson^3) & Elizabeth SPOONER: (13) <Dartmouth VR:42; MD 3:218>

Amos TABER^5, b. 29 Apr. 1703

Sarah TABER^5, b. 2 Mar. 1704/5

Benjamin TABER^5, b. 2 Dec. 1706; d. betw. 1 Sept. 1774 (will) - 7 May 1782 (prob.) <Bristol Co.PR 27:87>

Mary TABER^5, b. 6 June 1708

Joseph TABER^5, b. 15 Feb. 1709/10; d. aft. 25 Jan. 1772* (will)**<164>**

Rebecca TABER^5, b. 11 Oct. 1711

Elenor TABER^5, b. 28 Mar. 1713

John TABER^5, b. 8 Aug. 1715

Thomas TABER^5, b. 20 Sept. 1717; d. 14 July 1748 <Dartmouth VR>

Elizabeth TABER^5, b. 2 Nov. 1718

Peter TABER^5, b. 6 Apr. 1721

William TABER^5, b. 15 Mar. 1722/3

Abigail TABER^5, b. 6 Apr. 1725

CHILDREN OF Benjamin TABER^5 & Susanna LEWIS: (13) <Dartmouth VR>

Elizabeth TABER^6, b. 17 Sept. 1730; unm. in 1774

Joseph TABER^6, b. 28 Feb. 1731/2

Benjamin TABER^6, b. 10 Oct. 1733; d. 5 Feb. 1820, New Bedford <Friends' Rcds.>

John TABER^6, b. 9 Oct. 1735

Archelus TABER^6, b. 26 July 1737

Joshua TABER^6, b. 28 Jan. 1739/40, d. 23 Feb. 1753

Mary TABER^6, b. 14 June 1741

Jeduthan TABER^6, b. 15 Mar. 1742/3

Rebecca TABER^6, b. 28 Feb. 1744/5

Thomas TABER^6, b. 28 Mar. 1747; d. 15 Oct. 1820 <Bible>

Jeremiah TABER^6, b. 3 Apr. 1749

Lewis TABER^6, b. 7 Oct. 1751

Seth TABER^6, b. ( )

CHILDREN OF Benjamin TABER^6 & 1st Hannah ( ): (3) <Dartmouth VR>

Barnabas TABER^7, b. 17 June 1761, d. 1767

Daniel TABER^7, b. 23 June 1764

Benjamin TABER^7, b. 2 Feb. 1766; d. 1846, New Bedford <Friends' Rcds.>

Eunice (WORTH) Gardner, d. 31 Jan. 1814, ae 85 <New Bedford VR; Friends' Rcds.>

CHILDREN OF Benjamin TABER[6] & 2nd Eunice (WORTH) Gardner: (2) <Dartmouth VR>

Barnabas TABER[7], b. 24 Apr. 1768; d. 10 May 1853, New Bedford, boat builder <Mass.VR 75:81>

Susanna TABER[7], b. 7 Apr. 1770

Francis TABER[7], b. 16 Sept. 1772

Mary CONGDON, b. c1778, d. 26 July 1852, ae 74, New Bedford, consumption <Mass.VR 66:80>

CHILD OF Barnabas TABER[7] & Mary CONGDON: <New Bedford>

William Congdon TABER[8], b. 24 Feb. 1797; d. 23 Mar. 1886, at 66 Fourth St., New Bedford, merchant <Mass.VR 373:129>

Benjamin TABER, d. 20 June 1821, New Bedford <Friends' Rcds.>

Charles TABER, (son of William C. & Hannah T.), b. c1822, New Bedford, d. 17 Nov. 1887, ae 65, 465 County St., New Bedford, merchant <Mass.VR 382:148>

Mary BENNET, b. 14 May 1749, d. Sept. 1776 <Bible>

CHILDREN OF Thomas TABER[6] (Ben.[5]) & 1st Mary BENNET: (4) <Bible>

Admiral TABER[7], b. 12 Apr. 1767

Elihu TABER[7], b. 16 May 1769, d. 8 Mar. 1828

Lydia TABER[7], b. 14 Aug. 1772, d. 22 Mar. 1847

Job TABER[7], b. Aug. 1774, d. Nov. 1774

Hannah DAVIS, (dau of Nathan & Anne), b. 24 Apr. 1754, d. 4 Jan. 1832, Lincoln VT <Bible>

CHILDREN OF Thomas TABER[6] & 2nd Hannah DAVIS: (10) <Bible>

Mary TABER[7], b. 27 Sept. 1779, d. 7 Dec. 1857

Nathan TABER[7], b. 6 Jan. 1781, d. 11 Apr. 1836

Charles TABER[7], b. 27 Mar. 1783, d. 17 Dec. 1853

Joseph TABER[7], b. 30 June 1785, d. 9 Apr. 1855

Dr. Benjamin TABER[7], b. 30 June 1785 (twins), d. 3 June 1866**<165>**

Anna TABER[7], b. 9 Oct. 1787, d. 13 Dec. 1862

Isaac TABER[7], b. 19 Nov. 1789, d. 27 May 1884

James TABER[7], b. 17 Mar. 1792, d. 23 May 1817

Hannah TABER[7], b. 30 Sept. 1794, d. 27 Apr. 1881

Thomas TABER[7], b. 17 Oct. 1796

Phebe CARPENTER, b. 4 Jan. 1789, d. 21 Sept. 1851 <Bible>

CHILDREN OF Dr. Benjamin TABER[7] & Phebe CARPENTER: (9) <Bible>

Russel TABER[8], b. 8 Nov. 1809, d. 7 Mar. 1894

Louis TABER[8], b. 2 Sept. 1811, d. 7 Dec. 1887

Silas TABER[8], b. 24 Apr. 1813

Sarah TABER[8], b. 11 Mar. 1815

James TABER[8], b. 21 Dec. 1817, d. 23 Apr. 1832

Phebe L. TABER[8], b. 23 Nov. 1819, d. 15 Mar. 1892

David C. TABER[8], b. 15 Mar. 1822

Benjamin J. TABER[8], b. 8 Nov. 1825

Seman TABER[8], b. 14 Mar. 1827

Martha ( ) TABER, d. 22 May 1868 (2nd wf of Dr. Ben. Taber[7]) <Bible>

MICRO #30 Of 30

CHILD OF Benjamin J. TABER[8]:

Adelbert Eugene TABER[9], b. 24 Jan. 1857, d. 27 July 1924

Lottie Ellen VAN CAMP, b. 31 Aug. 1856, Marion, Minn.

CHILDREN OF Adelbert Eugene TABER[9] & Lottie Ellen VAN CAMP: (3)

George Henry TABER[10], b. 6 Oct. 1881

Phoebe Jane TABER[10], b. 2 Dec. 1883

Boyd Irwin TABER[10], b. 8 Nov. 1885, d. 8 Sept. 1887

CHILDREN OF Peter TABER[5] (Jos.[4]) & Sarah ( ): (8) <Dartmouth VR>

Abigail TABER^{6}, b. 2 Nov. 1740

Elener TABER^{6}, b. 16 May 1742

Amos TABER^{6}, b. 19 Apr. 1744

Jethro TABER^{6}, b. 26 Jan. 1745/6

David TABER^{6}, b. 14 Nov. 1747

Lydia TABER^{6}, b. 20 July 1749

Keturah TABER^{6}, b. 1 Nov. 1751

Daniel TABER^{6}, b. 31 Jan. 1754

CHILDREN OF Thomas TABER^{5} (Jos.^{4}) & Ruth ( ): (2) <Dartmouth VR:36>

Peace TABER^{6}, b. 5 Nov. 1745

Ruth TABER^{6}, b. 7 May 1748

CHILDREN OF John KENEY & Lydia TABER^{4} (Mary Tomson^{3}): (5) <Dartmouth VR:71>

Ruth KENEY^{5}, b. 3 Aug. 169(worn)

Thomas KENEY^{5}, b. 9 Sept. 1698

Jonathan KENEY^{5}, b. 12 Mar. 1703

Mary KENEY^{5}, b. 22 Nov. 1705

Hannah KENEY^{5}, b. 27 May 1709

Manasseh MORTON^{4} (Geo.^{3}, Ephraim^{2}, Geo.^{1}), b. 3 Feb. 1669, Plymouth <MD 5:53> (m. Mary Taber^{4} (Mary Tomson^{3}))

CHILDREN OF Philip TABER^{4} (Mary Tomson^{3}) & Susannah TUCKER: (8) <Dartmouth>**<166>**

Richard TABER^{5}, b. 25 Nov. 1711

Thomas TABER^{5}, b. 18 Nov. 1713

Zephaniah TABER^{5}, b. (10 Oct. 1717)**<166>**

Jesse TABER^{5}, b. 21 Nov. 1719

Peace TABER^{5}, b. 22 Feb. 1722

Huldah TABER^{5}, b. 3 Mar. 1724

Noah TABER^{5}, b. 7 July 1727

Philip TABER^{5}, b. 31 Oct. 1730

William HART, d. aft. 1 Feb. 1733/4* (will) <Bristol Co.PR 8:269>

CHILDREN OF William HART & Sarah TABER^{4} (Mary Tomson^{3}): (7) <Dartmouth VR>

Archippus HART^{5}, b. 24 Jan. 1703**<167>**

Richard HART^{5}, b. ( )

Thomas HART^{5}, b. 18 Aug. 1706; d. 8 Nov. 1729

Luke HART^{5}, b. 25 Sept. 1708

William HART^{5}, b. 1 Dec. 1710; d. pre 4 Feb. 1797 (wife's will)

Hannah HART^{5}, b. 9 June 1713

Mary HART^{5}, b. 7 Nov. 1715

Mary ( ) HART, d. betw. 4 Feb. 1797 (will) - 2 Oct. 1810 (prob.) <Bristol Co.PR 46:7>

CHILDREN OF William HART^{5} & Mary ( ): (2) <Dartmouth VR 1:297>**<168>**

Annie HART^{6}, b. 1 Apr. 1741**<169>**

William HART^{6}, b. 18 Nov. 1742

CHILDREN OF William HART^{6} & Esther ( ): (12) <Dartmouth VR 4:72>**<170>**

Joseph HART^{7}, b. 8 Dec. 1767

Mary HART^{7}, b. 3 July 1770, d. 6 Dec. 1775

Hannah HART^{7}, b. 11 July 1772

Phebe HART^{7}, b. 12 Sept. 1775

Elisabeth HART^{7}, b. 22 Apr. 1777

William HART^{7}, b. 29 June 1779

Esther HART^{7}, b. 13 Oct. 1780

Stephen HART^{7}, b. 23 Dec. 1782

Mary HART^7, b. 22 Nov. 1784

Ruth HART^7, b. 21 May 1786

Benjamin HART^7, b. 28 Feb. 1788

Esther HART^7, b. 17 Nov. 1789; d. 21 Nov. 1866, Westport, consumption (Esther Sherman) <Mass.VR 192:129>

Sarah ( ) TOMSON, b. c1669, d. 24 Oct. 1742, 73rd yr, Halifax g.s. <MD 14:9>**<171>**

CHILDREN OF Peter TOMSON^3 & Sarah ( ): (4) <Plymouth VR, MD 4:111>**<171>**

Sarah TOMSON^4, b. 30 Oct. 1699; d. 9 May 1776, Halifax g.s. <MD 12:241>

Peter TOMSON^4, b. 30 June 1701; d. 28 Nov. 1791, Halifax g.s. <MD 14:8>

James TOMSON^4, b. 2 Feb. 1702/3; d. 23 Nov. 1739 <Halifax VR:1>

Joseph TOMSON^4, b. 3 June 1706

Hannah BOLTON, b. c1722, d. 6 July 1755, 33rd yr, Halifax g.s. <MD 14:7>

CHILDREN OF Peter TOMSON^4 & Hannah BOLTON: (2) <Halifax VR:48>

Hannah TOMSON^5, b. 12 Dec. 1741; d. 28 July 1747, Halifax g.s. <MD 14:7>

Peter TOMSON^5, b. 27 Apr. 1747; d. 2 Mar. 1749/50, Halifax g.s. <MD 14:8>

Lydia COWING, b. c1725, d. 12 May 1800, 75th yr, Halifax g.s.<MD 14:8> (2nd wf. of Peter Tomson^4)

Nehemiah BOZWORTH^4 (David^3, Hannah Howland^2), b. c1702, d. 22 Dec. 1762, 60th yr <Halifax VR:4>

CHILDREN OF Nehemiah BOSWORTH & Sarah TOMSON^4 (Peter^3): <See Howland Family, Micro #7>

Elizabeth BOLTON, (dau of John & Ruth (Hooper)), b. 23 Sept. 1714 <Bridgewater VR>; d. 11 June 1792, Thompson St. Cem., Halifax <MD 14:6>

CHILDREN OF Joseph TOMSON^4 (Peter^3) & Elizabeth BOLTON: (5) <Halifax VR:41>

Betty TOMSON^5, b. 16 May 1734

Joseph TOMSON^5, b. 3 Mar. 1735/6

John TOMSON^5, b. 14 Oct. 1737

Sarah TOMSON^5, b. 17 Apr. 1744

Hannah TOMSON^5, b. 19 May 1748; d. 7 Mar. 1755, Halifax g.s. <MD 14:7>

CHILDREN OF Joseph TOMSON^5 & Jerusha WOOD: (4) <Halifax VR:40>

Joseph TOMSON^6, b. 28 Apr. 1763; d. 29 Dec. 1808, Halifax g.s. <MD 14:7>

Hannah TOMSON^6, b. 5 Nov. 1766; d. 31 Dec. 1771, Halifax g.s. <VR:5>

Timothy TOMSON^6, b. 29 Jan. 1769

Hannah TOMSON^6, b. 23 Mar. 1774; d. 27 Apr. 1847, Halifax g.s. <MD 14:7>

Mary MORTON^4 (Mary Ring^3, Deborah Hopkins^2), b. 15 Dec. 1689, Plymouth <MD 1:209>; d. 20 Mar. 1781, Thompson St. Cem., Halifax <MD 14:8>

CHILDREN OF Thomas TOMSON^3 & Mary MORTON: (7) <Middleboro VR>

Reuben TOMSON^4, b. 11 Oct. 1716 <MD 3:85>; d. 28 Sept. 1793, Halifax g.s. <MD 14:9>

Mary TOMSON^4, b. 8 May 1718 <MD 3:86>; d. 9 Apr. 1756 <MD 10:105>

Thomas TOMSON^4, b. 21 Apr. 1720 <MD 3:234>; d. 14 Sept. 1769, Halifax g.s. <MD 14:9>

Amasa TOMSON^4, b. 18 Apr. 1722 <MD 4:68>; d. 7 May 1807, Halifax g.s. <MD 14:5>

Andrew TOMSON^4, b. 20 Mar. 1724/5 <MD 6:228>; d. pre 1743*

Ebenezer TOMSON^4, b. 11 Mar. 1725/6 <MD 6:228>; d. 10 Sept. 1813, Halifax g.s. <MD 14:6>

Zebadiah TOMSON^4, b. 18 Aug. 1728 <MD 7:242>; d. 30 Sept. 1775, Halifax <MD 3:158>

Lydia COBB^5 (John^4, Rachel Soule^3, John^2), b. 7 July 1718, Middleboro <MD 6:226>; d. 22 Aug. 1809 Halifax g.s. <MD 14:8>

CHILDREN OF Amasa TOMSON^4 & Lydia COBB: (4) <Halifax VR:50>

Ruth TOMSON^5, b. 14 Jan. 1744/5; d. 8 May 1831

Zadock TOMSON^5, b. 11 May 1747; d. 4 Dec. 1786, Halifax g.s. <MD 14:9>

Lydia TOMSON^5, b. 9 May 1752

Molly TOMSON^5, b. 13 Dec. 1756; d. 12 June 1835

Mary WRIGHT^5 (Isaac^4, Adam^3, Hester Cooke^2), b. 30 Jan. 1726, Plympton <MD 5:209>; d. 29 Nov. 1804, Thompson St. Cem., Halifax <MD 14:8>

CHILDREN OF Ebenezer TOMSON^{4} (Tho.^{3}) & Mary WRIGHT: (5) <Halifax VR:54>
Susanna TOMSON^{5}, b. 4 June 1749
Josiah TOMSON^{5}, b. 9 June 1751
Ebenezer TOMSON^{5}, b. 18 Oct. 1753
Mary TOMSON^{5}, b. 28 Apr. 1757
Eunice TOMSON^{5}, b. 10 Sept. 1765
Stephen ELLIS, d. betw. 19 Sept. 1823 (will) - 6 Apr. 1824 (prob.)
Mary TOMSON^{4} (Jacob^{3}, Mary Cooke^{2}), b. 19 May 1711, Middleboro <MD 2:201>; d. 19 July 1769, Halifax g.s. <MD 14:9>
CHILDREN OF Reuben TOMSON^{4} (Tho.^{3}) & 1st Mary TOMSON: (5) <Halifax VR>
Deborah TOMSON^{5}, b. 27 July 1740 <VR:46>
Andrew TOMSON^{5}, b. 18 Jan. 1741 <VR:46>; d. 23 May 1773, Halifax g.s. <MD 14:9>
Mercy TOMSON^{5}, b. 21 Sept. 1745 <VR:47>; d. 1 Sept. 1747, Halifax g.s. <MD 14:8>
Abigail TOMSON^{5}, b. 25 Oct. 1748 <VR:47>; d. 2 Apr. 1757, Halifax g.s. <MD 14:5>
Lucy TOMSON^{5}, b. 4 Dec. 1755 <VR:47>; d. 5 Jan. 1818 <MD 12:243>
Sarah (BRYANT)(Soule) Tomson, (dau of Geo. & Sarah), b. 31 Oct. 1731, Plympton <MD 2:121>; d. 20 Aug. 1805, Halifax g.s. <MD 14:9>
CHILD OF Reuben TOMSON^{4} & 2nd Sarah (BRYANT)(Soule) Tomson:
Joanna TOMSON^{5}, b. 19 Jan. 1772 <Halifax VR:47>
CHILDREN OF Micah REED^{6} (*Dan.^{5}, Wm.^{4}, Esther Tomson^{3}, Mary Cooke^{2}) & Deborah TOMSON^{5}: (8)
Susanna REED^{6}, b. 6 Sept. 1770
Mehitable REED^{6}, b. 23 Dec. 1771
Mercy REED^{6}, b. 21 Apr. 1772
Enoch REED^{6}, b. 11 Feb. 1773
Seth REED^{6}, b. 9 Jan. 1776
Ruth REED^{6}, b. 3 July 1778
Noah REED^{6}, b. 22 Apr. 1781
Abigail REED^{6}, b. 13 Nov. 1784
Judith NOYES, b. c1741, d. 1 Apr. 1832, ae 91, Halifax g.s. <MD 14:8>
CHILDREN OF Andrew TOMSON^{5} (Reuben^{4}) & Judith NOYES: (5) <Halifax VR:52>
Dau., b. 16 Mar. 1765, d. 27 Mar. 1765
Abigail TOMSON^{6}, b. 26 Mar. 1766
Reuben TOMSON^{6}, b. 9 May 1768
Abel TOMSON^{6}, b. 15 July 1770
Andrew TOMSON^{6}, b. 28 Aug. 1772
CHILDREN OF Nathaniel MORTON & Joanna TOMSON^{5} (Reuben^{4}): (7) <Halifax VR:18, MD 6:50>
Nathaniel MORTON^{6}, b. 3 Nov. 1791
Lloyd MORTON^{6}, b. 24 Feb. 1794
Cyrus MORTON^{6}, b. 14 Jan. 1797
Joanna MORTON^{6}, b. 10 Oct. 1799
Albert MORTON^{6}, b. 26 Apr. 1802
Elbridge Gerry MORTON^{6}, b. 21 Dec. 1804
Charles MORTON^{6}, b. 27 Oct. 1810
Mary LORING, b. c1725, d. 17 May 1802, 77th yr, Thompson St. Cem., Halifax <MD 14:8>
CHILDREN OF Thomas TOMSON^{4} (Tho.^{3}) & Mary LORING: (12) <Halifax VR:52>
Joshua TOMSON^{5}, b. 22 July 1746
Asa TOMSON^{5}, b. 4 Mar. 1747/8; d. 4 Feb. 1830, Thompson St. Cem., Halifax <MD 14:6>
Ignatius TOMSON^{5}, b. 24 Aug. 1750; d. 22 Jan. 1770, unm. <Halifax VR:5>
Sarah TOMSON^{5}, b. 5 Apr. 1752; d. 27 Nov. 1769, unm. <Halifax VR:5>
Mary TOMSON^{5}, b. 16 Sept. 1754

Loring TOMSON[5], b. 25 Apr. 1756

Lois TOMSON[5], b. 12 Apr. 1758

Seth TOMSON[5], b. 18 June 1760

Thomas TOMSON[5], b. 27 May 1762

Bezer TOMSON[5], b. 27 Feb. 1765; d. 24 Mar. 1773 <Halifax VR:5>

Caleb TOMSON[5], b. 23 Mar. 1767

Sarah TOMSON[5], b. 12 Jan. 1770

CHILDREN OF Thomas TOMSON[5] & Ruhamah BARROWS: (4*)**<172>**

Rebecca CAMBELL, b. c1734, d. 23 Oct. 1803, 69th yr, Thompson St. Cem., Halifax <MD 14:9>

CHILDREN OF Asa TOMSON[5] (Tho.[4]) & Rebecca CAMBELL: (5) <Halifax VR:28>

Rev. Ignatius TOMSON[6], b. 11 Mar. 1774; d. 11 Sept. 1848, Halifax g.s., unm. <MD 14:7>

Nehemiah TOMSON[6], b. 9 May 1775

Asa TOMSON[6], b. 19 Aug. 1776

Eliab TOMSON[6], b. 8 Dec. 1778

Rebecca TOMSON[6], b. 15 Mar. 1782

Zerviah STANDISH[5] (Moses[4], Eben.[3], Alex.[2]), b. 26 Aug. 1728, d. 25 July 1769 <Halifax VR:42,5>

CHILDREN OF Zebadiah TOMSON[4] (Tho.[3]) & Zerviah STANDISH: (9) <Halifax VR:53>

Rebecca TOMSON[5], b. 5 Mar. 1746/7

Rachel TOMSON[5], b. 22 Jan. 1748/9; d. 7 May 1751 <Halifax VR:3>

Zerviah TOMSON[5], b. 17 Mar. 1750/1

Zebediah TOMSON[5], b. 17 Dec. 1752; d. 7 Nov. 1753 <Halifax VR:4>

Thomas TOMSON[5], b. 17 Nov. 1754

Mercy TOMSON[5], b. 28 Oct. 1756

Zebadiah TOMSON[5], b. 15 Dec. 1758

Moses TOMSON[5], b. 1 July 1762

Rachel TOMSON[5], b. 22 Oct. 1767

* * * * * * * * * * *

FOOTNOTES

<1> p.316, Francis Cooke was born aft. Aug. 1583, England. He died "above 80 yrs.". <MFIP:1>
<2> p.316, Hester Mahieu, dau. of Jennie le Mahieu of Canterbury, England. <Ibed.>
<2a> p.316, Bowman states she died pre 8 June 1666 but it is almost certain she d. pre 1650/1. See <48>.
<3> p.316, The will of John Wright[3], dated 7 Dec. 1675, mentions leaving all his lands to his brothers Samuel and Isaac. He also states he is "being now to goe forth to warr" which undoubtedly refers to King Phillips War. <Plymouth Co.Wills 3:1:177> John's heirs acknowledged receipt on 7 June 1676, but the lands left to Samuel and Isaac were settled upon brother Adam. Isaac's estate was settled the same day. <Plymouth Co.Court Orders 5:139> Although it is not stated, Samuel and Isaac probably went "forth to warr" also.
<4> p.316, d. 7 June 1726. <Plympton VR:480>
<5> p.317, MD 11:196.
<6> p.317, b. 10 May 1692, Rochester, son of Moses Barlow & Mary Dexter. <Gen.Adv.4:68>
<7> p.317, b. 30 Aug. 1692, Plymouth <MD 3:14>, son of Samuel Fuller & Mercy Eaton (both Mayflower descendants).
<8> p.317, Although Bowman attributes these four children to Daniel's 2nd wife, MFIP, Cooke:65 states they are probably by his 3rd wife, Annis, viz: Nathaniel, Jabez (b. pre 1718), James and Joshua (b. aft. 1717).
<9> p.317, MD 11:196.
<10> p.317, Although no children are listed for Isaac Wright & Faith Chandler, MD 11:196 lists a son Caleb who d. 22 Jan. 1769, 7th yr., Plympton g.s. Also, Isaac's will, dated 20 Sept. 1796 mentions the following children, viz: Billey, Isaac, Chandler, Nathaniel, Caleb, Winslow, Molley and Hannah. <Plymouth Co.PR 36:31>
<11> p.317, No children are listed, however Joseph Wright's will, dated 27 Feb. 1788 mentions the following, viz: Deborah Churchill (eldest dau., marr.), Susanna (wf of Abner Rickard), Mary (wf of Sylvanus Samson), Joshua, and Joseph who had "disappeared". <Plymouth Co.PR 40:94>
<12> p.317, An accompanying note states her g.s. at Chiltonville, at the 4th Cong. Church, gives her date of death as 29 Nov. 1866.
<13> p.318, John Wright had an illegitimate child by Elizabeth Barber before their court appearance Dec. 1703. <MF5G 3:44 (Addendum:5)>

<14> p.318, d. Feb. 1776 <Plympton VR>.
<15> p.319, "Hinckley Copy, Barnstable Memorial Inscriptions, Baptist Cem., Hyannis 4:106."
<16> p.319, The will of Jonathan Gifford mentions children, viz: Dele Cornell, Dinah Potter, Mary Case and Jeremiah. Also mentioned is Timothey Potter, son of his deceased wife.
<17> p.319, The will of Gideon Gifford mentions wife Elizabeth and many relatives, but no chil.
<18> p.319, The records are not clear as to the year of birth. MF5G 3:143 states Benjamin and brother were twins, b. 1717, but does not explain the 2 day difference.
<19> p.320, Three Gifford children are listed without dates, viz: Ichabod, James and William. The files later give the marriage of another son, Benjamin, to Rhoda Potter (dau of Joshua and Lydia), 3 July 1783. <Friend's Rcds., Dartmouth:550>
<20> p.320, The family of John Gifford[5] (Mary Wright[4]) given here clearly does not jibe with his account in MF5G 3:141-42. MF5G gives John's marriage intentions to Comfort Hart (dau of Richard & Amy), 24 May 1730, with five unrecorded children born between 1731-38. It would therefore seem plausible that the wife and children Bowman attributes to John were his 2nd family, since their births did not begin until 1743. Unfortunately, two facts seem to refute this idea. First, MF5G states Comfort Hart died c1790 (no source). Second, and more important, the will of John Gifford mentions the children of John & Comfort and does not mention any of the nine children of John & Bathsheba. Since it appears these two John Giffords were not the same person, I have not included the line of descent that Bowman gives to the John with wife Bathsheba.
<21> p.320, The eight Gifford children are listed without dates, viz: Amy, Patience, Peace, Sylvia, Nancy, Zaccheus, David and Nicholas. <Gifford Gen., 1626-1896. (1896):53-54>
<22> p.322, MFIP, Standish:83 gives three additional children, viz: Hannah; Mercy, b. 27 June 1765; and Daniel, b. c1767, d. 27 Dec. 1794, 27th yr, Martinico.
<22a> p.322, Burial Hill by Drew:150. The VR say she died on the 25th.
<23> p.323, The seven Johnson children are listed without dates, viz: Daniel, Elbridge, Leonard, Ann B., William R., Andrew J., and Isabella.
<24> p.324, The remaining three Davie children are listed without dates, viz: Isaac, Lydia and Joseph. Plymouth ChR 1:410 gives the death of a child 20 Aug. 1780.
<25> p.324, The seven Davie children are listed without dates, viz: Lydia W., Mary F., Amanda, Hannah, Matilda, Betsey F. and Joseph.
<26> p.324, Burial Hill by Drew:296 states she was 28y5m27d when she died. This would place her birth at c1820.
<27> p.324, Plymouth g.s. <Burial Hill by Drew:296>.
<28> p.324, d. at Amsterdam, Plymouth g.s. <Ibed.>.
<29> p.324, All four Davie children were still living when Ebenezer Davie made his will (c1885). <Plymouth Co.Prob.#2408>
<30> p.325, MFIP, Cooke:50 identifies her as Abigail Hodges, dau of William Hodges & Hannah Tisdale, b. 4 May 1713, Norton. Six additional Cooke children are also given, viz: Susanna, Maria, Bethia, James (d.y.), James and Zenas.
<31> p.325, Was Elijah Cooke the unnamed "Cook" who d. 10 Nov. 1820, ae 79, at a poor house in Bridgewater? <E. Bridgewater VR:347>
<32> p.325, The files contain two original pages with the inscription, "From the George Cooke Bible owned by Dr. John H. Lang (Long?), Brooklyn NY. Great great grandson of John Cooke[6] (Francis Cooke)". Unfortunately the entries on the pages are not legible.
<33 p.326, The seven Stevens children are listed without dates, viz: Alfred (d.y.), Godfrey, Alvah, Edwin, Paran, Matilda and Miranda (d. 26 May 1882).
<34> p.326, On the page immediately following is a Samuel Cook, son of Robert & Patience, b. 11 July 1753, d. 5 July 1756 <Norton VR:42>. He appears to belong to this family but I hesitate to include him because Bowman did not.
<35> p.326, No children are listed for Zebediah Shepardson and wife Deborah Cooke[6], however, Zebediah's will (cited within) mentions oldest daughter Nancy (wf of Simeon Cobb) and youngest daughter Elona (wf of Caleb Abell), as well as grandaughter Elona Hodges.
<36> p.326, MFIP, Cooke:50 gives four additional Cooke children, viz: Joseph, Caleb, Mary and Susanna.
<37> p.327, Francis Cooke "drownded on Plimouth shore" with Benjamin Briant and John Ransom. <MD 2:141>
<38> p.327, The children of Elkanah Cooke and his two wives are listed in pencil and are too faint to read.
<39> p.328, b. 20 May 1706, Bridgewater. <MD 1:207>
<40> p.329, The remaining four Cooke children are listed without dates, viz: Eli, Sarah, Ira and Levi.
<41> p.329, Ephraim Cole, son of Ephraim & Rebecca, b. 3 Feb. 1691, Plymouth <MD 2:20>.
Burial Hill by Drew:197 gives the death of wife Sarah, son Ephraim who d. 1730, ae 12 and daughter Sarah "aged 7 years decd 1739". The footstone reads "Sarah Cole & 5 children, 3 of them decd in infancy".
<42> p.329, The remaining six Sturtevant children are listed without dates. The Plympton VR provides dates for seven children, viz: Francis, b. 15 Jan. 1711/2; Caleb, b. 16 Mar. 1715/6; James, b. 15 Sept. 1718; Susanna, b. 4 Feb. 1720/1; Lydia, b. 2 Mar. 1723/4; Mary, b. 16 Feb. 1728 (Kingston) and Sarah, bpt. 2 Apr. 1732.
<43> p.330, d. 20 Nov. 1753, Mendham NJ <MFIP, Cooke:52>.
<44> p.330, b. 3 Mar. 1689, dau of Elisha & Lydia. <Yarmouth VR:10>
<45> p.330, MFIP, Cooke:52 identifies her as Mary (Tirrell) Hearsey, dau of William Tirrell & Abigail Pratt, b. 22 Aug. 1689, Yarmouth.
<46> p.331, b. 18 Dec. 1683. <Yarmouth VR:10>
<47> p.333, Birth - PCR 8:17; death - Burial Hill by Drew:150. Drew states John's grave stone

is "shattered & ruined". Based on Kingman's book he states the date at one time read 25 Mar. 1712, while Plymouth VR <MD 16:64> state he died in April.

<48> p.333, Bowman states, "...in years of study of the original records I have not seen an item which seemed to indicate that Experience Mitchell's second wife Mary was the mother of any of his children." Researchers today however feel differently.

MFIP, Cooke:3 states Elizabeth Mitchell was b. 1628 and Thomas Mitchell c1631. These two have been accepted by the General Society of Mayflower Descendants as Jane Cooke's children. Since Thomas was the only Mitchell child known to have received land from grandfather, Francis Cooke, doubt is cast on the remaining Mitchell children who were born later than Thomas. (See the Forward for further discussion.)

Line of descent for the remaining Mitchell children has been changed to show non-Mayflower descent from Experience Mitchell[1] instead of Jane Cooke[2].

<49> p.333, "Mitchell's Epitaphs" poss. refers to "History of the Early Settlement of Bridgewater Including an Extensive Family Register", Nahum Mitchell. Boston, 1840.

<50> p.333, The files do not show these children as being by Experience's second wife so this omission has been corrected here for easier reference. The birthdates given these Mitchell children were given by Bowman on the assumption Jane Cooke was their mother, so may not be totally accurate. See <48> above.

<50a> p.333, Court records dated Dec. 1731 show Sarah was about 90 years old and had been bed-ridden for about four years. At this time, daughter Sarah Brett and her husband Nathaniel petioned the court to have the other children ordered to help pay for their mother's maintenance, which they had "utterly refused".

<51> p.334, bpt. 26 Nov. 1620, Bengeworth, Worcestershire, Eng., son of John Washburn and Margaret Moore. <MFIP, Cooke:9>

<51a> p.334, MFIP, Cooke:42 states she d. 28 Feb. 1740, Easton.

<52> p.334, Burial Hill by Drew:302.

<53> p.336, Although not identified, Edward Washburn Jr. left minor children Abigail & Abiel who had guardians appointed 10 Dec. 1766. <Plymouth Co.PR #21915, 19:407> See <54,56>.

<54> p.336, He is called Edward Washburn Jr. and appears to be the same mentioned in <53,56>.

<55> p.336, Three children are listed without dates for Capt. Amos & Prudence Washburn, viz: James (oldest son), Amos & Luther. <Plymouth Co.PR #21921>

<56> p.336, Edward & Hannah were married in 1765, three years after this child's birth <MD 25:87>. Perhaps this is the reason Bowman later questions the parentage of Abiel saying, Edward "is not father of Gen. Abiel", although he gives him the line of descent thru Edward.

However, the files also show reason to believe that this Edward Washburn is the same Edward Jr. who had died pre 1766 leaving two minor children, Abiel & Abigail. See <53>. Also shown is an Edward Washburn Jr. and wife Phebe who had a child, Abigail, b. 21 Sept. 1760, Middleboro <MD 23:45>. From this data it would be logical to assume Edward Washburn[6] married 1st Phebe ( ) and had two children, Abigail in 1760 and Abiel in 1762. When Phebe died, Edward remarried in 1765 to Hannah Jones.

<57> p.336, The source for the remaining children appears to be the Pierce Family (1870), pp. 135, 228.

<58> p.337, The remaining four Washburn children are listed without dates, viz: Reuben, Simeon, Ebenezer & Mary. All five children are mentioned in their father's will, dated 14 Jan. 1747 <MD 16:52>.

<59> p.337, The remaining six Washburn children are listed in pencil without dates, viz: Bezaleel, Nehemiah, Moses, Israel, Reliance and Abigail.

<60> p.337, The files contain a transcript of an item from an Acushnet newspaper, c1887 (The Standard) which states Lettice Washburn was a private in a Minute company commanded by Capt. Thomas Kempton which marched from Dartmouth 21 Apr. 1775.

<61> p.337, Descriptive & Biographical Record of Bristol Co., Mass. (1899) states their son Lettice was b. 6 Dec. 1793.

<62> p.337, The eight Spooner children are listed with year of birth only, viz: Ruth, 1750; Lois, 1752; Simpson, 1754; Caleb, 1755; Lucy, 1757; Mercy, 1759; Elizabeth, 1761 and Zoeth.

<63> p.338, In giving the marriage of John Washburn, his wife's name is omitted <Bridgewater VR MD 2:92>. See NEHGR 115:83 which questions a marriage to Rebecca Lapham.

<64> p.338, The four Washburn children are listed without dates, viz: Lucy, Abraham, Hannah and Nathaniel (who d. unm. before father).

<65> p.339, The three Johnson children are listed without dates, viz: Nahum, Isaac & Polly Lothrop.

<66> p.340, The eight Pratt children are listed without dates, viz: Sally, Hannah, Betsy, Elijah, Albertina, Seth, Chloe and Nathaniel.

<67> p.341, All the children except Jemima were still living 9 Sept. 1784. <Plymouth Co.Deeds 69:144>

<68> p.342, The probate records mention "Abigail Stevens, widow and Paul Stevens" and minor daughter Sally Stevens Washburn, under 14. <#22080, 26:306>

<69> p.343, Record of Deaths, 1749-1850 in Middleborough, Raynham, Bridgewater, Taunton and Norwich, (p.23), mss. copy, kept by Rev. Isaac Backus, deposited with the NEHGS.

No children are listed for Benjamin Leach & wife Hannah Keith. The probate records state his widow was left with a family of small children. <Plymouth Co.PR #12415, 14:;436> On 4 Feb. 1760, Jedediah Leach, minor above fourteen, son of Benjamin, chose his guardian. <PR # 12445, 15:459>

<70> p.343, The remaining five Leach children are listed without dates, viz: Rhoda, Dinah, Lois, Eunice & Chloe.

<71> p.343, His date of death was not known by his family. The records state that Jephtha

Leach was "supposed to have been lost at sea" and "hath for several years absented himself". In an affadavit signed 1 Jan. 1780 at Raynham, Kemrick Wilber testified that "while at Yorke in the first campaign, a man told him that he saw Jephtha Leach in North Corliner not long before". Mentioned are widow Anna Leach & Jephtha's only brother Benjamin. <Plymouth Co.PR #12446>
<72> p.343, The ten Leach children are listed in pencil without dates, viz: Joseph, Luke, Silas, Jephthah, Isaiah, Mary, Orpha, Lois, Hebzibah and Dinah.
<73> p.344, The eight Leach children are listed without dates, viz: Susanna, Beza, Abraham (who died pre 1840, NY), Zebedee, Parnel, Rufus, Zadock and Ezekiel.
<74> p.344, The five Leach children are listed in pencil without dates, viz: Eliza, Libeus, Susanna, Jesse and Eveline.
<75> p.344, The four Leach children are listed in pencil without dates, viz: Jane, Vesta, Betsy, and Zadock Washburn.
<76> p.344, The three Leach children are listed in pencil without dates, viz: Ezra, Isaac and Anne.
<77> p.345, Line of descent for William Wicker[7]'s line has been added on the basis of data shown in the files. Also, the full listing of his children was found on micro #13 but included here to preceed files on his children for easier reference.
<78> p.345, The remaining three Wicker children are listed without dates, viz: Mary, Abigail and Eliza.
<79> p.348, The remaining four Hayward children are listed without dates, viz: Independance (son), Otis, Eliza and Lucy.
<80> p.350, No children are listed for Eliezer & Anna Washburn however, the division of his estate, 10 Nov. 1764, mentions eight children, viz: Eleazer, Susannah Byram, Asa, Anna, Levi, Oliver, Alden and Isaac. <Plymouth Co.PR #21955, 19:280>
<81> p.350, The remaining four Washburn children are listed in pencil without dates, viz: Southworth, Zenas, Eliphalet and Hiram.
<82> p.351, The seven Washburn children are listed without dates, viz: Nathaniel, Thomas, Timothy, Elizabeth, Hephzibah, Patience and Deliverance. <MD 16:51>
<83> p.353, She m. 1st Israel Alger Jr., 2nd Jonathan Bozworth. <Mitchell:102>
<84> p.353, The Glazier data comes from a letter from the Town Clerk of Willington, dated 1928 in which he states "the Glazier family was prominent in Willington. Our records of the family go back to 1730. The old Glazier Tavern is one of the landmarks of the town; located at Willington Hill - in splendid condition still".
<85> p.354, MFIP, Allerton:32 states she was b. 30 Nov. 1676.
<86> p.358, It is not clear whether the five Dunbar children (without dates) are by 1st wife Melatiah or 2nd wife Mary Hayward[4] (Tho.[3], Sarah Mitchell[2], Experience[1]), viz: Sarah, Mehitable, Samuel, Melatiah and Hannah.
<87> p.359, The Files contain an affidavit signed in 1933 by Marion Drake, grand-daughter of Lyman Drake and Mary Ann Hayward. She states Mary Ann was b. 20 Aug. 1820, N. Bridgewater and d. in Chicago IL at her (Marion's) home. In 1876, Mary Ann had her husband's remains removed from Sharon CT (with an infant, Emily) to be re-interred in Brockton.
<88> p.360, Alice had an illegitimate son by Thomas Cushman. See p.87.
<89> p.363, Although Bowman attributes sons Daniel and Samuel to Daniel Wilcox's 2nd wife, Elizabeth Cooke, MFIP, Cooke:7 states they are most probably by an earlier 1st wife. The line of descent of these two sons has been corrected to show non-Cooke Mayflower descent.
<90> p.363, The remaining six Wilcox children are listed without dates, viz: John, Stephen, Susanna, Edward, Thomas, Lydia and Sarah.
<91> p.364, Thomas Sanford, the Emigrant to New England, 1632-4, Sketches of four other pioneer Sanfords and some of their descendants, by Carlton E. Sanford. 2 Vols, Rutland VT, 1911.
<92> p.364, The Rhode Island Historical Magazine, 1886-1887. Newport RI. (7:304).
<93> p.368, The remaining ten Barlow children are listed in pencil without dates, viz: Sarah Ann, Thomas, Thomas Arnold, Amanda, Joseph, Calvin, Caroline, Sylvina, Elizabeth and Bennett.
<94> p.369, b. 11 July 1687 <Dartmouth VR; MFIP, Cooke:35>.
<95> p.369, Year of birth only is given in the files. Full birth dates for the Macomber children has been added from the Dartmouth VR.
<95a> p.369, No dates accompany the names of the five Taber children. MFIP, Cooke:35 gives eight children with dates for the first five from Dartmouth VR. The last three were b. after 1718 (father's will), viz: Mary, b. 21 Mar. 1707; Phillip, b. 14 Dec. 1708; William, b. 28 Apr. 1711; Sarah, b. 13 Sept. 1713; Thomas, b. 30 Apr. 1716; John, Joseph & Lydia.
<96> p.369, Bowman attempts to identify her in the three families immediately following.
<97> p.370, He is possibly the Israel Mosher of Westport who d. betw. 4 Jan. 1798 (will) - 21 Sept. 1798 (inv.); mentioned is wife Sarah and sons Joseph (who received only $1.00) and Maxson. <Bristol Co.PR 35:491,492>
<98> p.371, The remaining seven Mosher children are listed without dates, viz: Philip, Samuel, Esek, Israel, Martha, Abigail and Elizabeth.
<98a> p.372, MFIP, Cooke:33 identifies her as Margaret Wood, dau. of William Wood & Martha Earle. The birthdates for the Taber children are not given, Dartmouth VR provides the full listing, viz: Martha, b. 6 Oct. 1700; Philip, b. 4 Oct. 1702; William, b. 18 Feb. 1704/5; Comfort, b. 3 Aug. 1707, d. aft. 5 Dec. 1782 <will - Taunton PR 30:65>; Mary, b. 25 Feb. 1710; Jonathan, b. 5 Oct. 1712; Josiah, b. 4 June 1715; Rebecca, b. 18 Apr. 1719; John, b. 7 Feb. 1723 and Margaret, b. 8 Apr. 1727.
<99> p.372, The will of Benjamin Bowers (1772) names eight children, viz: Philip (dec'd), Benjamin, Jonathan, Anna, Roby and married daughters, Elizabeth Clark, Comfort Huntington and Martha King. The will of wife Comfort (1782) calls daughter Elizabeth deceased.
<100> p.372, This family is out of order here. See p.380

<101> p.372, The remaining three Hathaway children are listed without dates, viz: Thomas[4], Jonathan[4] and Mary. The files later show Thomas Hathaway[4] d. betw. 5 Apr. 1742 (will) - 1 Apr. 1748 (inv.). <MD 16:112> and Jonathan Hathaway[4] d. 17 Sept. 1727* <Dartmouth VR:97>.
<102> p.373, The Peckham Genealogy by Stephen Farnum Peckham & Byron J. Peckham, NY, no date, received at NEHGS, 8 Nov. 1922.
<103> p.373, Stephen's will was dated 19 Mar. 1757, inventory taken 26 June 1764. <Bristol Co.PR 18:345,423>
<104> p.373, The will of James Sisson of Dartmouth, 15 June 1734, names deceased daughter Content and her unnamed children. <Bristol Co.PR 8:168>
<104a> p.373, The remaining nine Peckham children are listed in pencil without dates, viz: Peleg, Mercy, Stephen, Jonathan, James, Sarah, Lydia, Amy and Joseph.
<105> p.373, The remaining five Peckham children are listed in pencil without dates, viz: Thomas, Sarah, Seth, Mercy and John.
<106> p.373, The remaining three Peckham children are listed in pencil without dates, viz: Catharine F., Rosa and Fenner Harris.
<107> p.373, The remaining seven White children are listed without dates, viz: Hannah, Roger, Thomas, Elizabeth, Oliver, Abner and Susanna.
<108> p.373, MF5G 1:206 states he d. Aug. 1795.
<109> p.374, Bowman states Elizabeth's mother was Susanna Pearce, however MF5G 1:184 states she was Sarah Carr; 1:206 states Elizabeth d. July 1785 and a son George d. Aug. 1785.
<110> p.375, The remaining three White children are listed without dates, viz: Elizabeth, Abigail and Jonathan.
<111> p.375, MFIP, Cooke:22 identifies his 2nd wife as Patience Hunnewell, dau. of Richard Hunnewell and Elizabeth Stover.
<112> p.376, The remaining four Hathaway children are listed without dates, viz: George W., Sarah A. and Lydia Ann (d. pre 1848, see <114>).
<113> p.377, The three Beetle children are listed in pencil without dates, viz: Charles, Clarence and John.
<114> p.377, Benjamin King was appointed guardian of his two children 3 Oct. 1848, indicating his wife Lydia Ann was deceased. <Bristol Co.PR 136:160,140:171>. Immediately following this page is a 1848 marriage entry for an unidentified Benjamin King, widower age 40, son of Ebenezer & Nancy, to Lucy Manchester.
<115> p.377, Guardianship papers dated 5 Sept. 1848 state two children were above 14 - George Henry and Mary E. (who was living in Spencer NY), with the remaining Tew children under 14, viz: John L., Henrietta M., Helen L. and Sarah T. (all living New Bedford).
<116> p.377, All four Hathaway children were alive when Gamaliel made his will 3 June 1793. <Bristol Co.PR 4:441>
<117> p.377,378, No children are listed for Benjamin Dillingham and wife Anna Hathaway, however, ten children are mentioned in Benjamin's will, viz: (married daughters) Nabby Hawes, Ester Crandon, Priscilla Kempton and Hannah Terry and (sons) Paul, Benjamin, Lemuel, Edward and Asa. He also names wife Freelove, so 1st wife Anna was deceased by this time.
<118> p.378, The will of Micah Hathaway, dated 12 Feb. 1812, mentions the four sons and six unnamed single daughters. <Bristol Co.PR 52:8>

Representative Men & Old Families of Southeastern, Mass., J.H. Beers & Co. Chicago. 1912. (3:1:502), lists thirteen Hathaway children as follows, viz: Gamaliel, Nathan, Thomas, Jonathan, Mary, Sarah, Susan (d.y.), Hannah (m. Reuben Taber), Susan (m. John Kendricke), Lydia & Elizabeth (1st & 2nd wives of Enoch Jenney), Elois and Obed.
<119> p.378, Guardianship papers, dated 2 Oct. 1827, state Phebe was over 14 and Daniel under 14 years of age. <Bristol Co.PR 133:426>
<120> p.378, The death record states Benjamin & Phebe lived at 48 N. Second St., New Bedford.
<121> p.378, d. Dec. 1879. <Old Families 3:1502; See <118> for source>
<122> p.378, Obed's will (cited within) mentions wife Desire and four Hathaway children, viz: Hannah, Anna, Sarah Shearman and Elizabeth Washburn.
<123> p.378, The remaining eight Sisson children are listed without dates, viz: James, Jonathan, Philip, Thomas, Content, Sarah, Hannah and Rebecca.
<124> p.378, The remaining six Davol children are listed without dates, viz: Lydia, Sarah, Phebe, Joshua, David and William.
<125> p.379, MFIP, Cooke:25 states she d. 7 Apr. 1740.
<126> p.379, Bowman placed Stephen in this family on the basis that he was "mentioned in will of brother Thomas". However, the files give two separate transcriptions from Thomas' will, both differing slightly. The first mentions the name Stephen Hathaway twice, viz: as one of the children of "my brother Jethro" and "to Thomas Hathaway, the third son of Stephen Hathaway". Although a Stephen Hathaway was executor of the will, he is not named in this transcription as a brother. The second transcription (on a separate page) states, "Thomas Hathaway, 3d son of brother Stephen". <Bristol Co.PR 29:76> (Note: MFIP, Cooke:25 does not include Stephen in this family.)
<127> p.380, The six Wing children are listed in pencil without dates, viz: Joseph, Abigail, Joseph, Ebenezer, Hepzibah and Lydia.
<128> p.380, On 2 Oct. 1798, Stephen Hathaway was appointed guardian of his father, 78 year old Jethro Hathaway, who was certified "by reason of old age & infirmity" to be "really insane". (Stephen had requested the assessment.) <Bristol Co.PR 35:412>

As a matter of interest, Jethro made his will 16 Aug. 1798 - two months before he was declared "insane". His bequests were very specific and showed no signs of incompetence.
<129> p.380, The remaining two Davis children are listed without dates, viz: Jethro and Thomas. On the following page is another listing of eleven children with no dates, viz: Timothy, Stephen,

Almy, Ruth, Jethro, Nicholas, Hepzibah, Thomas, Daniel, Mary and Hannah.
<130> p.381, The remaining four Davis children are listed without dates, viz: Thomas, Alden S., Nicholas and Richard.
<131> p.382, The eight Howland children are listed in pencil without dates, viz: Pardon, Hepsebeth (d.y.), Hepsebeth, Elizabeth, Benjamin Franklin, Henry S., Hannah and Mary.
<132> p.383, The remaining six Kempton children are listed without dates, viz: Lemuel, Obed, Elijah, Wealthy, Silvia and Nancy.
<133> p.383, A note from Ricketson's History of New Bedford (1858), p.210, also states Elizabeth Tupper's mother was Zerviah Willis, dau. of Col. Samuel Willis. The children of Ephraim and Elizabeth are called the "great-grandchildren of Ephraim, whose wife Patience died in this place in 1779, aged 105 years".
<134> p.384, "In old cemetery on Pleasant St. opposite Pleasant St. schoolhouse, S. Weymouth."
<134a> p.384, Thomas' epitaph is given from his gravestone at the Thompson St., cemetery in Halifax <MD 14:9>, viz:

His days were spent in doing good
In life & death Faith was his food
Like him be pious, just and kind
Then peace & joy at death you'll find.

<135> p.384, This is a case where Bowman's research has been superceded by work done by later genealogists. Bowman believed Elizabeth Tomson married William Swift, as is shown in MD 30:110. However, MFIP, Cooke:19 clearly states that Elizabeth married Thomas Swift, <u>not</u> "William Swift as stated in MD 30:110". MFIP also states Thomas & Elizabeth Swift had one son, Thomas, b. 15 Nov. 1687, Weymouth. In his will, John Tomson mentions daughter Elizabeth Swift and grandson Thomas Swift. <MD 4:24>

William Swift and his wife Elizabeth (   ) had ten children, with all (or most) of these children carried on in the Files with Mayflower descent from Elizabeth Tomson[3]. Since this is incorrect, descent for William Swift's line has been changed to show descent from himself, William Swift[3] instead of Elizabeth Tomson[3].

(**Note:** In **Mayflower Marriages**, companion volume to this book, p.146, line 4 should be corrected to read, "Elizabeth Tomson[3] and Thomas Swift, c1687". Accordingly, all the fourth generation Swift entries on pp.146,147 should be corrected to show descent from William Swift[3] instead of Elizabeth Tomson[3].)
<136> p.384, The remaining three Swift children are listed without dates, viz: Hannah, Elizabeth and Benjamin.
<137> p.385, The remaining five Glover children are listed in pencil without dates, viz: Joanna, Gamaliel, Marcia, Elizabeth and Alexander.
<138> p.385, MD 2:18.
<139> p.386, The remaining three Spear children are listed without dates, viz: Janette B., George C. and William B.
<140> p.387, The remaining six Tobey children are listed without dates, viz: Deborah, Lemuel, Bathsheba, Lydia, Elizabeth and Mercy.
<141> p.387, No children are listed for Nehemiah Savery, however his will names his son and three married daughters, viz: Nehemiah Lewis, Sarah S. Thompson, Esther S. Bartlett and Irene F. Peterson.
<142> p.388, d. 4 Feb. 1737/8 <Abington VR>.
<143> p.388, On the chart which lists the children of William Reed and Esther Tomson[3], Josiah Allen is written as the husband of their daughter, Mary. However, in the listing of the children of Josiah Allen & Mary Reed, Mary is not identified, nor are her children given a Cooke line of descent. Recent research (MD 40:197-199) has shown that Josiah's wife, Mary Reed, was indeed the daughter of William & Esther Reed. On this basis, Mayflower descent for the Allen children has been added.
<144> p.389, Descendants of Richard Everett of Dedham, Mass., by Edward Franklin Everett. Boston. 1902. (p.40).
<145> p.389, Micah Allen's will mentions wife Catherine and the following nine children, viz: Catharine (wf of John Cobb), Micah, Polly (wf of Capt. Daniel Cobb), Elijah, Nancy (wf of Peleg Francis), Fanny (wf of Amasa Copeland), Oliver, Otis and Cloe (wf of George Lane).
<146> p.389, Bowman states that Mercy married a "Whitmarsh", his first name (Nicholas) has been added. He was the son of Nicholas Whitmarsh & Hannah Reed, b. 21 Aug. 1673, Weymouth and d. pre 27 Nov. 1706 when wife Mercy remarried. <MFIP, Cooke:78>
<147> p.389, MFIP, Cooke:79 states she was Hannah Noyes, dau. of Nicholas Noyes & Sarah Lunt, b. 23 July 1709, Newbury, poss. d. 5 Jan. 1777, Abington.
<148> p.389, The Drake Family in England & America, 1360-1895 and The Descendants of Thomas Drake of Weymouth, Mass., 1635-1691, by Louis Stoughton Drake. Boston. 1896.
<149> p.390, The remaining seven Reed children are listed in pencil without dates, viz: Silence, William, Jane, Betsy, Susanna, Timothy and Mehitable.
<150> p.392, Jonathan & Abigail were not married. <Plymouth Co. Court Rcds.2:21>
<151> p.392, Although a pencilled death date of "aft. 1750" is given with the source Mitchell, Bridgewater Epitaphs by William Latham (repr.1976), p.15 states he d. 7 June 1746.
<152> p.395, MFIP, Cooke:17 states she d. 30 May 1742, Halifax.
<153> p.396, MFIP, Cooke:70 states she d. 9 Mar. 1795, Asford CT, wife of 2nd husband Joseph Works.
<154> p.396, MFIP, Cooke:72 states she was b. 24 July 1718, Bridgewater, dau. of Joseph Hayward and Sarah Crossman.
<155> p.396, On 1 Mar. 1777, Betty requested an administrator for her husband's estate. <Plymouth Co.PR #20586>; 3 May 1779 her father, Ebenezer Fuller, requested the same for her estate.

<Plymouth Co.PR #20522>
<156> p.396, No children are listed for Shubael Tomson and wife Ruth Hall, however Shubael's will mentions wife Ruth and two children, viz: Shubael (under 7 yrs.) and Susanna (under 9 yrs).
<157> p.397, No children are listed for Francis Thomson and his two wives. His will, dated 20 Nov. 1798, mentions the following six children but does not identify their mother, viz: Thomas, Elias, Ruel, Zelpah (wf of Noah Cushman), Cynthia (wf of John Cox) and Molley. <Plymouth Co.PR #20550, 36:473>
<158> p.397, MFIP, Cooke:18 identifies him as "apparently" the son of Philip Taber and Lydia Masters, b. Feb. 1646, Yarmouth or Martha's Vineyard and d. 11 Nov. 1730.
<159> p.398, The Files later show a Mercy Bowdish, dau. of William Jr. & Mary, b. 2 Apr. 1737 <Dartmouth VR 1:123>. It is possible she was Bartholomew Taber's wife but it is not stated.
<160> p.398, The remaining nine Akin children are listed in pencil without dates, viz: Benjamin, Stephen, Sarah, Lydia, Elizabeth, Jerusha, Eunice, Bartholomew and Lois.
<161> p.399, The eight Akin children are listed in pencil without dates, viz: Mary (d.y.), Ebenezer (b. c1764), Nancy, Lemuel, Bartholomew, Eunice, Nathaniel and Henry.
<162> p.399, The ten Bennett childen are listed without dates, viz: Caleb, Jacob, Benjamin, Ebenezer, Edward, Eunice, Sarah, Lois, Betsey and an unnamed child.
<163> p.399, Amaziah Taber's will (cited within) mentions one daughter, Thankful (wf of Gideon Wood) and her two sons, Thomas & Amaziah Wood.
<164> p.399, No children are given for Joseph Taber and wife Mary, however his will mentions the following five, viz: William, Elisabeth, Jemima and married daughters, Rubee Brightman and Hannah Eldredge. Wife Mary made her will 23 May 1785, Dartmouth and mentions all five children; by this time Elizabeth was called Elizabeth Hart and Jemima was still single.
<165> p.400, History of Addison Co. VT (1886), p.509, states Benjamin was b. in Montpelier VT and his wife Phebe was from Starksboro VT. He moved to Lincoln in 1817, the first physician to settle and practise there.
<166> p.401, Bowman questions whether Susanna's maiden name was Tucker or Wilcox, MFIP, Cooke: 76 has Susanna Tucker. The list of children, which appears to have come from The Taber Genealogy (1924), p.10, also differs slightly from that in MFIP. Bowman has Zephaniah b. 10 Oct. 1717, while MFIP states Tucker Taber was b. 10 Oct. 1717, with Zephaniah b. 1 Oct. 1715. Bowman's list omits Tucker as well as Daniel and Amy who are given in MFIP.
<167> p.401, MFIP, Cooke:73 states he was b. 24 <u>Aug</u>.
<168> p.401, Is she the Mary Shepard who m. William Hart, 19 June 1740, Dartmouth?
<169> p.401, The Hart Gen.:191, states she had an illegitimate child, Simpson Hart, although no date is given here. (She m. 18 Aug. 1778, Dartmouth, to Samuel Joy.)
<170> p.401, Is she the Esther Slade who m. William Hart 15 July 1766, Dartmouth?
<171> p.402, Sarah's maiden name is not given, however in pencil with question markes are the names "Wood" and "Morton" - two possiblities.
<172> p.404, The four Tomson children are listed in pencil without dates, viz: Deborah, Lois, Thomas and Moses.

* * * * *

REFERENCE LIST

GENEALOGICAL ARTICLES PERTAINING TO COOKE FAMILY RESEARCH

Mayflower Descendant (MD) (1899-1937)

2:24-27 - Will & Inventory of Francis Cooke
2:152-54 - The Family Records of Nathaniel Thompson And His Son Rev. Otis Thompson
3:33-36 - Will & Inventory of John Cooke[2]
3:95-105 - Francis Cooke & His Descendants
3:135-38 - Bible Records of Sewall C. Allen & William Jones Hastings
3:236-42 - Will & Inventory of Jacob Cooke[2]
4:22-29 - Will & Inventory of Lt. John Tomson
4:128 - Hester ( ) Cooke
4:165-67 - Will & Inventory of Richard Wright
4:239-41 - Will & Inventory of Adam Wright
8:48-50 - Mayflower Marriages at Leyden
9:246-51 - Aaron Soule[3]'s Wife Mary Wadsworth and the Marriages of Five of Her Sisters
10:44-46 - Cooke Notes: John Cooke[2]; Taber/Wilcox/Hathaway
11:242-47 - Adam Wright[3]'s Wives & Their Children
13:44-45 - Cooke deed: John Cooke, 1658
15:136-39 - Wills of Caleb[3] & Jane Cooke
15:247-53 - Will of John Washburn
- (m. Elizabeth Mitchell[3])
15:253-56 - Will of Samuel Packard
- (dau. Deborah m. Samuel Washburn[4], dau. Deliverance m. Thomas Washburn[4])
16:47-53 - Washburn Notes: Sons of Elizabeth (Mitchell[3]) Washburn
16:110-14 - Will of Arthur Hathaway
- (m. Sarah Cooke[3])
16:148-56 - Cooke Notes: Estates of Caleb[4], Francis[4], Robert[4]
16:226-34 - Taber Notes: Phillip & Thomas Taber
16:239-43 - Wilcox Notes: Daniel Wilcox

16:248-53 - Washburn Notes: John Washburn
17:55-60 - Wills of John Cooke[4] & Robert Cooke[5]
17:60-64 - Wills of John Earle and his wife Mary Wilcox[4]
17:76-78 - Will of Jethro Hathaway[5]
18:115-17 - Will of George Vaughan
- (dau. Mary m. Jonathan Washburn[4])
18:129-32 - Will & Inventory of Thomas Pope
- (dau. Joanna m. John Hathaway[4])
18:147-50 - Will & Inventory of Francis Cooke[3]
18:253-55 - Earle/Westgate Notes: Mary (Wilcox[4]) Earle & dau. Elizabeth
18:256 - Notes: Hannah Cooke[5] m. Nathan Wright[4]
19:95 - Will of Lieut. John Tomson
- (m. Mary Cooke[2])
19:135-36 - Estate of Mercy Tomson[3]
20:140-42 - Will of Edward Mitchell[3]
- (Error, this is a non-Mayflower line)
20:150-52 - Will of Edward Wilcox[4]
20:159-63 - Will of John Tomson[3] of Middleborough MA
21:42-44 - Will of Jacob Cooke[3]
21:53-54 - Will of Isaac Wright[4]
21:185-86 - Estate of Jacob Mitchell[3]
- (Error, this is a non-Mayflower line)
22:2-7 - Wills of George Cadman & His Widow Hannah (Hathaway[4])
22:12-14 - Mayflower Marriage Records at Leyden & Amsterdam
22:135-42 - Estates of Peter Tomson[3] And His Son James[4]
23:49-55 - Wills of James Soule[3] And His Daughter Rebecca [4]
(m. Lydia Tomson[3])
23:72-74 - Will of William Read
(m. Hester Tomson[3])
24:44 - Estate of Noah Washburn[5]
24:83-86 - Children of Richard And Hester (Cooke[2]) Wright
24:167-78 - Estate of Jacob Tomson[3], Esq. of Middleborough MA
25:20-25 - Will of Abigail (Wadsworth) Tomson
(m. Jacob Tomson[3])
25:56-59 - Estates of Peter[4] & Ebenezer[4] Tomson
25:175-86 - Estate of Thomas Tomson[3] of Halifax And The Will Of His Widow Mary
27:145-55 - New Light On Francis Cooke, His Wife Hester Mahieu And Their Son John
30:16-23 - Estate of Samuel Kinsley
(m. Mary Washburn[4])
30:23-27 - Will of Joseph Mosher
- (m. Lydia Taber[4])
30:49-53 - Children of Lieut. John Tomson & Mary Cooke[2]
30:110-15 - The Wills of William[2] And William[3] Swift of Sandwich MA
- (Error, this is a non-Mayflower line)
32:97-101 - Will of Samuel Kingman
(m. Mary Mitchell[4], non-Mayflower)
32:101-03 - Deed: Experience Mitchell, 1672
MD 33:1-5 - Family Records of Elisha Cooke[5]

PN&Q 3:63 - Family Records of Godfrey Cooke[7]
PN&Q 3:101-04 - Two Mitchell Letters
PN&Q 4:127 - Family Records of Caleb Thompson[5]
PN&Q 5:1-3 - Seven Benjamin Washburns

Mayflower Descendant (MD) (1985-1990)

38:148-50 - The Paternity of Elisha Bennet Jr.
38:187-89 - Thomas Mitchell of Malden, Not A Mayflower Descendant
39:187-94 - Thomas Caswell of Taunton & His Descendants
40:197 - Josiah Allen's Wife Was William Read's Daughter

Mayflower Quarterly (MQ) (1975-1990)

45:70-80 - Joseph Howland of North Yarmouth, ME & Burton N.B. (1717-96)
46:18-19 - Two Matthew Allens of Bridgewater MA
47:68-70 - The Problem of Confused Identities: (II) Daniel Wilcox Jr. & Tyle Wilcox
48:12-17 - Which Josiah Washburn Married Sarah Richmond[5]?
- (typo error, p.15, line of descent for Josiah Washburn[5] should be from Jane Cooke[2] not Sarah Cooke[2])
[illegible] William Wilson[6] [illegible]
49:122-29 - Which John Rickard Married Mary Cooke[3]?
49:130-34 - Some Descendants of Francis Cooke, Mayflower Passenger
- (discusses the Mitchell children)
50:21-30 - Judah Fuller, The Bloomer's Daughter
50:188-90 - Susannah (Briggs) Palmer of Plymouth Colony & Little Compton RI

- (not the daughter of John Cooke & Sarah Warren)

55:114 - Esek Mosher[7]'s Family Bible

MISCELLANEOUS

Mayflower Families In Progress: Francis Cooke of the Mayflower and His Descendants for Four Generations (MFIP), pub. by General Society of Mayflower Descendants, 2nd Ed. 1987.

NEHGR 107:61 - Hester LeMayhieu, Wife of Francis Cooke
NEHGR 127:94 - Comments on the Two Wives of Experience Mitchell of Plymouth MA.
TAG 12:193 - Gaining Experience - A Problem in the Mitchell Family
TAG 59:28 - Not All The Children of Experience Mitchell Are Mayflower Descendants
TAG 59:165 - Richard Wright of Plymouth MA

* * * * * * * * *

EDWARD DOTY/DOTEN<1>

MICRO #1 of 6

Edward DOTY^{1}, d. 23 Aug. 1655, Plymouth <MD 17:72>

Faith CLARK, bur. 21 Dec. 1675, Marshfield <MD 2:181> (wf. of 2nd hus. John Phillips)

CHILDREN OF Edward DOTY & Faith CLARK: (9)

Edward DOTY^{2}, b. ( ); d. 8 Feb. 1689/90 <MD 5:210>

Mary DOTY^{2}, b. ( ); d. pre 13 June 1728 (hus. will) <MD 7:29> (See <37>)

Elizabeth DOTY^{2}, b. ( )

Desire DOTY^{2}, b. c1646, d. 22 Jan. 1731, ae 80, Marshfield g.s. <MD 12:48, 13:129>

John DOTY^{2}, b. ( ); d. 8 May 1701, Plymouth <MD 16:63>

Isaac DOTY^{2}, b. 8 Feb. 1648, Plymouth <MD 15:27>; d. 1728/9, Oyster Bay NY

Joseph DOTY^{2}, b. last of Apr. 1651, Plymouth <MD 16:237>; d. pre 18 Sept. 1734**<2>**

Thomas DOTY^{2}, b. ( ) ; d. 4 or 5 Dec. 1678, Plymouth <MD 4:233>

Samuel DOTY^{2}, b. ( )

John ROUSE^{2} (John^{1}), b. 28 Sept. 1643; d. 3 Oct. 1717, Winslow Cem., Marshfield <MD 10:49>

CHILDREN OF John ROUSE & Elizabeth DOTY^{2}: (2)

George ROUSE^{3}, b. ( ); bur. 19 Dec. 1676, Marshfield <MD 2:182>

George ROUSE^{3}, b. 25 Dec. 1679 <MD 2:249>; bur. 26 Feb. 1682 <MD 2:250>

John ROUSE Jr., d. 26 or 27 May 1704, ae 26, Winslow Cem., Marshfield <MD 8:177, 10:49>

DESIRE DOTY^{2} (Edward^{1})

William SHERMAN Jr., bur. 17 Nov. 1680, Marshfield <MD 4:171>

CHILDREN OF William SHERMAN Jr. & Desire DOTY^{2}: (6) <Marshfield VR, MD 6:21>

Hannah SHERMAN^{3}, b. 21 Feb. 1668**<3>**

Elizabeth SHERMAN^{3}, b. 11 Mar. 1670/1; d. July 1695, unm. <MD 7:118>

William SHERMAN^{3}, b. 19 Apr. 1672; d. 26 Feb. 1739/40, Marshfield g.s. <MD 13:110>

Patience SHERMAN^{3}, b. 3 Aug. 1674; d. pre 30 July 1723 (mother's will, MD 12:48>

Experience SHERMAN^{3}, b. 22 or 24 Sept. 1678 <+MD 3:42>

Ebenezer SHERMAN^{3}, b. 21 Apr. 1680; d. 1 Feb. 1759, Marshfield Hills g.s. <MD 9:203>

Israel HOLMES, d. 24 Feb. 1684 (drowned Plymouth Harbor) <MD 3:88, 4:171>**<4>**

CHILDREN OF Israel HOLMES & Desire (DOTY^{2}) Sherman: (2) <Marshfield VR, MD 6:21>

Israel HOLMES^{3}, b. 17 Feb. 1682; d. 8 Sept. 1760, Marshfield g.s. <MD 13:46>

John HOLMES^{3}, b. 15 June 1684; d. 6 Apr. 1754, Old cem., Plympton <MD 10:146>

CHILDREN OF Alexander STANDISH^{2} & Desire (DOTY^{2})(Sherman) Holmes: (3) <See Standish micro #1>

CHILDREN OF William RING^{3} (Deborah Hopkins^{2}) & Hannah SHERMAN^{3}: (6) <See Hopkins micro #10>

CHILDREN OF Miles STANDISH^{3} (Alex.^{2}) & Experience SHERMAN^{3}: (5) <See Standish micro #4>

Margaret DECRO, b. c1680, d. 17 Mar. 1726, ae 46, Marshfield g.s. <MD 13:110>

CHILDREN OF Ebenezer SHERMAN^{3} & 1st Margaret DECRO: (10) <1-6, Marshfield VR, MD 9:183>**<5>**

Eleazer SHERMAN^{4}, b. 21 Mar. 1700/1; d. pre 13 Apr. 1723 (adm.), unm.

Rachel SHERMAN^{4}, b. 29 Apr. 1702; d. aft. 10 Jan. 1759*

William SHERMAN^{4}, b. 27 Feb. 1704

Elizabeth SHERMAN^{4}, b. 27 Jan. 1706

Joseph SHERMAN^{4}, b. 28 July 1709; d. 3 Nov. 1732, Marshfield g.s., unm. <MD 13:110>

Abigail SHERMAN^{4}, b. 26 Dec. 1710

Ebenezer SHERMAN^{4}, b. 1712, d. 14 Jan. 1786, 74th yr, Marshfield Hills cem. <MD 9:203>

Robert SHERMAN^{4}, b. ( )

John SHERMAN^{4}, b. c1718*; d. 6 Nov. 1780*, 62nd yr, Marshfield Hills cem. <MD 9:203>

Elisha SHERMAN[4], b. c1722, d. 24 Feb. 1797, 75th yr, Marshfield <MD 14:52>

CHILD OF Ebenezer SHERMAN[3] & 2nd Bathsheba FORD:

Bathsheba SHERMAN[4], b. 18 May 1733*; d. 20 ( ) 1811*, ae 78

Lusanna ( ) SHERMAN, b. c1728, d. 4 Nov. 1780*, 52nd yr, Marshfield Hills cem. <MD 9:203>(*wf of John Sherman[4])

CHILDREN OF John SHERMAN & Elizabeth ( ): (6) <MD 30:130>**<6>**

Nathaniel SHERMAN, b. 9 Feb. 1748/9

Ruth SHERMAN, b. 22 Jan. 1750/1

Rufus SHERMAN, b. 29 June 1754

Asa SHERMAN, b. 12 Oct. 1756

Elizabeth SHERMAN, b. 14 Nov. 1758

John SHERMAN, b. 9 June 1762 <MD 30:131>

CHILDREN OF John SHERMAN & Lusanna ( ): (2) <MD 29:155>**<6>**

Urana SHERMAN, b. Mar. 1765

Elisha SHERMAN, b. 28 Feb. 1768

Caleb CARVER, (son of John & Mary), b. 5 Apr. 1715, Marshfield <MD 8:43>

CHILDREN OF Caleb CARVER & Abigail SHERMAN[4] (Eben.[3]): (9) <MD 30:149>

Caleb CARVER[5], b. 26 Apr. 1734

Ruth CARVER[5], b. 11 Oct. 1736, d. 11 Dec. 1738

John CARVER[5], b. 19 Oct. 1738; d.? 5 July 1782* <MD 30:132>

Israel CARVER[5], b. 2 Nov. 1740

Stephen CARVER[5], b. 2 Apr. 1743

Joseph CARVER[5], b. 28 Apr. 1745

Charles CARVER[5], b. 24 June 1746

Amos CARVER[5], b. 12 Nov. 1748

Abigail CARVER[5], b. 26 Feb. 1751 <MD 30:131>

CHILDREN OF Caleb CARVER[5] & Abigail ( ): (4)

Abigail CARVER[6], b. 5 Jan. 1764 <MD 30:131>

Melzar CARVER[6], b. 15 Nov. 1756 <MD 30:132>

Ruth CARVER[6], b. 10 Oct. 1758

John CARVER[6], b. ( )

Isaiah WALKER, (*son of Isaac & Bethiah (Norcut)), b. 12 Aug. 1724*; d. 1793*

CHILDREN OF Isaiah WALKER & Bathsheba SHERMAN[4] (Eben.[3]): (9*) <Walkers of Old Colony:371-5>

Gideon WALKER[5], b. 20 Dec. 1750

Bathsheba WALKER[5], b. 7 Dec. 1752

Isaiah WALKER[5], b. 3 Mar. 1755, d. in Revolution

Bethiah WALKER[5], b. 15 Nov. 1757

Daniel WALKER[5], b. 15 July 1760

Asa WALKER[5], b. 21 May 1763, d. 8 Apr. 1820

Levi WALKER[5], b. 9 July 1766, d. 20 Dec. 1851

Sarah WALKER[5], b. 22 May 1769, d. 16 Mar. 1854

James WALKER[5], b. 7 Oct. 1771, d. 23 May 1844

Elizabeth WORMALL, b. c1720, d. 20 May 1790, 70th yr, Marshfield Hills cem. <MD 9:203>

CHILDREN OF Ebenezer SHERMAN[4] (Eben.[3]) & Elizabeth WORMALL: (5) <Marshfield VR, MD 29:154>**<7>**

Huldah SHERMAN[5], b. 5 Nov. 1750

Deborah SHERMAN[5], b. 11 Sept. 1752

Keziah SHERMAN[5], b. 9 Sept. 1755

Ichabod SHERMAN[5], b. 21 Mar. 1758

Ebenezer SHERMAN[5], b. 31 Dec. 1760; d. 28 Aug. 1786, Marshfield Hills cem. <MD 9:203>

Lydia WALKER, (*dau of Isaac), b. 13 Mar. 1721*, Marshfield; d. 24 Oct. 1797, 76th yr, Plainville

Cem., Marshfield <MD 14:52>

CHILDREN OF Elisha SHERMAN^{4} (Eben.^{3}) & Lydia WALKER: (3) <Marshfield VR 2:110, MD 31:26>

Margaret SHERMAN^{5}, b. 11 Nov. 1745

Abiel SHERMAN^{5}, b. 23 June 1747

Ebenezer SHERMAN^{5}, b. 10 Nov. 1748; d. 23 Dec. 1834, Plainville Cem., Marshfield <MD 14:52>

Mary SIMMONS, b. c1755, d. 8 Aug. 1802, 47th yr, Plainville Cem., Marshfield

CHILDREN OF Ebenezer SHERMAN^{5} (Elisha^{4}) & 1st Mary SIMMONS: (9) <Marshfield VR 2:93, MD 29:162>

Aaron SHERMAN^{6}, b. 5 Dec. 1773

Sarah SHERMAN^{6}, b. 21 Oct. 1775

Elisha SHERMAN^{6}, b. 30 Aug. 1777

Lydia SHERMAN^{6}, b. 7 Sept. 1779; d. 15 Sept. 1844, unm.

Mary SHERMAN^{6}, b. 4 June 1782

Ebenezer SHERMAN^{6}, b. 10 Jan. 1785; d. 1862, Marshfield Hills g.s. <MD 9:203>

Isaac Winslow SHERMAN^{6}, b. 12 June 1788

Betsy Winslow SHERMAN^{6}, b. 12 Mar. 1790

Beulah SHERMAN^{6}, b. 23 June 1794

CHILD OF Ebenezer SHERMAN^{5} & 2nd Mercy JOYCE:

Thomas Joyce SHERMAN^{6}, b. 14 Jan. 1802

CHILDREN OF Aaron SHERMAN^{6} & Lydia MITCHELL: (7) <Marshfield 3:13>

Aaron Simmons SHERMAN^{7}, b. 20 Oct. 1798

Lydia Hatch SHERMAN^{7}, b. 29 Jan. 1801

Christopher Mitchell SHERMAN^{7}, b. 16 Nov. 1803

Isaac Winslow SHERMAN^{7}, b. 16 Aug. 1805

Celia Mitchell SHERMAN^{7}, b. 5 Mar. 1809

Elisha James SHERMAN^{7}, b. 16 Apr. 1813

Beulah SHERMAN^{7}, b. 10 Feb. 1816

Grace ( ) SHERMAN, 1796-1882, Marshfield Hills cem. <MD 9:203>

CHILDREN OF Ebenezer SHERMAN^{6} (Eben.^{5}) & Grace ( ): (6) <Marshfield VR 3:->

Lorenzo SHERMAN^{7}, b. 28 May 1818

Leander SHERMAN^{7}, b. 30 May 1820; d. 1902, Marshfield Hills cem. <MD 9:203>

Alexander SHERMAN^{7}, b. 5 July 1822

Albion Parris SHERMAN^{7}, b. 4 Nov. 1824; d. 1870, Marshfield Hills cem. <MD 9:203>

Albina SHERMAN^{7}, b. 16 Oct. 1827

Laura C. SHERMAN^{7}, b. 25 Nov. <u>1841</u>

Celia H. ( ) SHERMAN, 1821-1856, Marshfield Hills cem. <MD 9:203>

CHILD OF Leander SHERMAN^{7} & Celia H. ( ):

Adan Theron SHERMAN^{8}, b. Aug. 1843, d. 20 Jan. 1848, ae 4y5m5d, Marshfield Hills cem. <MD 9:203>

CHILDREN OF Seth JOYCE & Rachel SHERMAN^{4} (Eben.^{3}): (4) <Marshfield VR>

David JOYCE^{5}, b. 26 Nov. 1727, d. 16 Dec. 1727 <VR 2:106>

Margaret JOYCE^{5}, b. 14 Nov. 1729 <VR 2:106>

Seth JOYCE^{5}, b. 19 Oct. 1731 <VR 2:107>

Jonathan JOYCE^{5}, b. 11 Oct. 1733 <VR 2:107>

CHILD OF William SHERMAN & Mary ( ): **<8>**

Anthony SHERMAN, b. 21 Dec. 1722 <Marshfield VR:104>

Josiah WORMALL, d. pre 3 Nov. 1738 <Plymouth Co.PR #23493, 7:449>

CHILDREN OF Josiah WORMALL & Patience SHERMAN^{3}: (6) **<9>**

Mercy WHITE[illegible] (Peregrine[illegible]), b. c1676, d. 12 June [illegible] <MD 13:110>

CHILDREN OF William SHERMAN^{3} & Mercy WHITE: (4) <Marshfield VR>

Thankful SHERMAN^{4}, b. 10 Apr. 1699, d. 28 Sept. 1739, Marshfield g.s. <MD 6:18,13:50>

Sarah SHERMAN^{4}, b. 8 May 1701, d. 7 Aug. 1768, Marshfield g.s. <MD 8:179,12:251>

Mary SHERMAN^{4}, b. 1 June 1711 <MD 7:119>; d. aft. 11 Jan. 1782, unm. <Plymouth Co.Deeds 64:268>

Abigail SHERMAN^{4}, b. 1 June 1711 <MD 7:119>; d. aft. 11 Jan. 1782, unm. <Plym. Co. Deeds 64:268>

CHILDREN OF Adam HALL & Sarah SHERMAN^{4}: (2 of 8*)**<10>**

Adam HALL^{5}, b. c1729, d. 11 Oct. 1806, Marshfield Centre cem. <MD 8:197>

Sarah HALL^{5}, b. 1732, d. 30 Apr. 1735, ae 3, Marshfield g.s. <MD 12:251>

CHILDREN OF Adam HALL^{5} & Keziah FORD^{3*} (Sam.^{2}, Wm.^{1}): (7*)

Adam HALL^{6}, b. 1757

Mercy HALL^{6}, b. 1759

Susanna HALL^{6}, b. 1761; d. 1834, unm.**<11>**

Keziah HALL^{6}, b. 1764

Luke HALL^{6}, b. 1767; d. 28 June 1815, ae 48, Staten Island NY, Marshfield g.s. <MD 8:197>

Samuel HALL^{6}, b. 1770

William HALL^{6}, b. 1774

Anna (TUELS*), (*dau of Barnard & Experience (Taylor)), b. c1760, d. 20 July 1848, ae 88,E.Boston bur. Marshfield <MD 8:197>

CHILDREN OF Luke HALL^{6} & Anna (TUELS*): (3*)

Luke HALL^{7}, b. ( )

William HALL^{7}, b. ( )

Samuel HALL^{7}, b. c1800

Alice CARVER, b. c1800***<12>**

CHILDREN OF Luke HALL^{7} & Alice CARVER: (2 of 8*)**<13>**

Ellen HALL^{7}, b. 28 Dec. 1835

Albert HALL^{7}, b. 1839

John POLDEN, (*son of John & Lydia (Tilson)), b. 20 Jan. 1702*, Plymouth <MD 3:122>

CHILDREN OF John POLDEN & Thankful SHERMAN^{4} (Wm.^{3}): (2)

Mary POLDEN^{5}, b. ( )

John POLDEN^{5}, b. ( )

Elizabeth (TURNER^{*3}), (*Dan.^{2}, Humphrey^{1}), b. c1682, d. 10 Jan. 1754, 72nd yr, Marshfield g.s. <MD 13:46>

CHILD OF Israel HOLMES^{3} & Elizabeth (TURNER*):

Israel HOLMES^{4}, b. ( )

Joanna SPRAGUE, (dau of Sam.), d. pre 1720* (1st wf. of John Holmes^{3}, no issue)

Sarah THOMAS, (*dau of Sam.), b. c1686, d. 15 Sept. 1761*, 75th yr, Thompson St. cem., Halifax <MD 13:14>

CHILDREN OF John HOLMES^{3} & Sarah THOMAS: (6) <Marshfield VR, MD 30:147>

Thomas HOLMES^{4}, b. 15 Oct. 1720

Sarah HOLMES^{4}, b. 17 Sept. 1722

Samuel HOLMES^{4}, b. 20 Nov. 1724

Lydia HOLMES^{4}, b. 24 Apr. 1727

Ruth HOLMES^{4}, b. 30 Jan. 1735

John HOLMES^{4}, b. 14 Mar. 1738

EDWARD DOTY^{2} (Edward^{1})

Sarah FAUNCE, (dau of John), d. 27 June 1695, Plymouth (wf of 2nd hus. John Buck) <MD 16:63>

CHILDREN OF Edward DOTY^{2} & Sarah FAUNCE: (11) <Plymouth VR, MD 1:143>

Edward DOTY^{3}, b. 20 May 1664; d. betw. 3 Mar. 1689/90 - 3 Dec. 1696

Sarah DOTY^{3}, b. 9 June 1666

John DOTY^{3}, b. 4 Aug. 1668; d. 8 Feb. 1689/90*

Mary DOTY^{3}, b. 9 July 1671

Martha DOTY^3, b. 9 July 1671 (twins); d. betw. 12 Sept. 1748 - 26 Aug. 1741

Elizabeth DOTY^3, b. 22 Dec. 1673; d. 16 or 17 Dec. 1745, Marshfield Hills cem. <MD 9:168,31:24>

Patience DOTY^3, b. 7 July 1676

Mercy DOTY^3, b. 6 Feb. 1678; d. 30 Nov. 1682

Samuel DOTY^3, b. 17 May 1681

Mercy DOTY^3, b. 23 Sept. 1684

Benjamin DOTY^3, b. 30 May 1689

MICRO #2 of 6

Tobias OAKMAN, b. c1664, d. 16 June 1750, 86th yr, Marshfield Hills cem. <MD 9:169>**<14>**

CHILDREN OF Tobias OAKMAN & Elizabeth DOTY^3: (8) <1-6, Marshfield VR>

Faith OAKMAN^4, b. 15 May 1697 <MD 8:179>; d. 26 Dec. 1758, Marshfield g.s. <MD 12:150>

Samuel OAKMAN^4, b. 15 Mar. 1698/9 <MD 8:179>; d. 21 or 22 Nov. 1739, Marshfield Hills cem. <MD 9:169,31:24>

Elizabeth OAKMAN^4, b. 10 May 1701 <MD 8:177>; d. 5 Nov. 1768, Marshfield g.s. <MD 12:149>

Sarah OAKMAN^4, b. ( ) <MD 8:177>

Susanna OAKMAN^4, b. Jan. 1705/6 <MD 6:20>

Mary OAKMAN^4, b. 3 May 17( ) <MD 6:20> (pre 9 Mar. 1712/3 when 6 chil bpt., MD 31:119)

Mercy OAKMAN^4, b. ( )

Edward OAKMAN^4, bpt. 28 Oct. 1716 <MD 31:122>; d. 28 May 1791, 75th yr, Marshfield Hills cem. <MD 9:168>

Bethiah OAKMAN, wf of Christopher, d. 21 Jan. 1830 <Marshfield VR 3:deaths>

Harriet OAKMAN, wf of Christopher, d. 17 July 1831 <Marshfield VR 3:deaths>

Hatch OAKMAN, d. 31 May 1843, ae 46 <Marshfield VR 3:deaths>

Christopher F. OAKMAN, (son of Wm. C.), d. 21 Oct. 1837, ae 4 <Marshfield VR 3:deaths>

Sarah (DOGGETT^{*5}) (*Bethiah Waterman^4, Sarah Snow^3, Abigail Warren^2), b. c1716, d. 22 Jan. 1794, 78th yr, Marshfield Hills cem. <MD 9:169>

CHILDREN OF Edward OAKMAN^4 (Eliz. Doty^3) & Sarah (DOGGETT*): (10) <Marshfield VR, PN&Q 4:111>

Elizabeth OAKMAN^5, b. 20 Sept. 1737

Bethiah OAKMAN^5, b. 10 Dec. 1739

Sarah OAKMAN^5, b. 12 Oct. 1741

John OAKMAN^5, b. 29 June 1743

Samuel OAKMAN^5, b. 15 Sept. 1745

Joseph OAKMAN^5, b. 28 Apr. 1749

Tobias OAKMAN^5, b. 13 Mar. 1751

Alice OAKMAN^5, b. 10 June 1753

Abiah OAKMAN^5, b. 26 Apr. 1756

Amos OAKMAN^5, b. 26 Jan. 1759

Elisha FORD, (son of Michael & Bethiah (Hatch)), b. 16 Jan. 1696, Marshfield <MD 5:235>; d. 14 Nov. 1758, Marshfield g.s. <MD 12:149>

CHILDREN OF Elisha FORD & Elizabeth OAKMAN^4 (Eliz. Doty^3): (7)

Lemuel FORD^5, b. 20 Jan. 1720 <MD 7:121>; d. 22 Oct. 1812, Marshfield g.s. <MD 12:149>

Patience FORD^5, b. 1 Jan. 1722 <MD 30:152>

Jerusha FORD^5, b. 7 Dec. 1727 <MD 31:22>

Priscilla FORD^5, b. 20 July 1730 <MD 31:22>; d. 3 Aug. 1801, unm.

Elisha FORD^5, b. 16 Nov. 1734 <MD 31:22>; d. ()1 Oct. 1803, Marshfield Centre cem. <MD 13:243>

Isaac FORD^5, b. 19 July 1738 <MD 31:22>

Tabitha FORD^5, b. 13 Aug. [illegible]; d. 11 May 178[illegible]

CHILDREN OF Josiah FORD & Sarah ( ): <Marshfield VR>

William FORD, b. 8 July 1692 <MD 6:68>; d. Aug. 1696 <MD 7:118>

William FORD, b. 14 Feb. 1702 <MD 6:68>

CHILD OF John FORD & Hannah ( ): <Marshfield VR>

William FORD, b. 12 Apr. 1684 <MD 7:121>

CHILD OF William FORD Jr. & Elinor ( ): <Marshfield VR>

William FORD, b. Sept. 1696 <MD 5:237>

CHILDREN OF William FORD & Elizabeth ( ): <Marshfield VR>

Samuel FORD, b. 11 May 1701 <MD 8:179>

Elizabeth FORD, b. 27 Feb. 1703 <MD 7:119>

Deacon William FORD, d. 7 Feb. 1721, Marshfield <MD 7:133> (he is not indentified)

William FORD, d. 22 Dec. 1761, Marshfield <MD 31:25> (he is not identified)

CHILDREN OF William FORD Jr. & Hannah ( ): <Marshfield VR>

Silence FORD, b. 22 Nov. 1722 <MD 30:155>

Abner FORD, b. 8 Nov. 1724 <MD 30:155>

Nathan FORD, b. 15 Jan. 1727 <MD 30:156>

Elijah FORD, b. 2 May 1731 <MD 31:20>

Abigail FORD, b. 24 Sept. 1( ) <MD 30:156>

Levi FORD, b. ( ), bpt. 20 July 1735 <MD 9:185,31:170>

Elizabeth (TILDEN*), b. c1733, d. 17 May 1813, ae 80y2m6d, Marshfield Centre cem. <MD 13:243> (wf. of Elisha Ford[5] (Eliz. Oakman[4])

Priscilla TURNER, b. c1725, d. 29 May 1803*, ae 78, Marshsfield g.s. <MD 12:150>

CHILD OF Lemuel FORD[5] (Eliz. Oakman[4]) & Priscilla TURNER:

Molborough FORD[5], b. c1753, d. 21 Nov. 1842, ae 89y6m

Anna ( ) FORD, b. c1758, d. 15 July 1820, ae 62 (wf of Molborough Ford[5])

CHILDREN OF Benjamin WHITE[4] & Faith OAKMAN[4] (Eliz. Doty[3]): <See White Family micro #1>

Thomas FOSTER, (son of Deacon John), b. c1686, d. 6 Feb. 1758, Marshfield g.s. <MD 12:150>

CHILDREN OF Thomas FOSTER & Faith (OAKMAN[4]) White (Eliz. Doty[3]): (2) <Marshfield VR>

Thomas FOSTER[5], b. 4 May 1735 <MD 9:187>

Deborah FOSTER[5], b. 10 Mar. 1736, <MD 9:184>

CHILDREN OF Thomas FOSTER[5] & Mary (THACHER*) (*dau of Rev. Peter): (8) <Marshfield>

Thomas FOSTER[6], b. 16 Apr. 1758 <PN&Q 4:36>; d. 29 May 1759 <MD 12:150>

John FOSTER[6], b. 3 Feb. 1760 <PN&Q 4:36>; d. 5 Oct. 1760 <MD 12:150>

Peter FOSTER[6], b. 16 July 1761 <PN&Q 4:36>

Nathaniel FOSTER[6], b. 15 June 1763 <PN&Q 4:36>; d. 2 June 1772

Mary FOSTER[6], b. 21 Dec. 1765 <PN&Q 4:36>; d. 19 Mar. 1826, Nemasket cem., Middleboro <MD 15:102> (wf of Levi Tinkham[6] (John[5-4], Ephraim[3], Mary Brown[2])

Mercy Thatcher FOSTER[6], b. 13 Aug. 1768 <PN&Q 4:37>; d. 24 Mar. 1773

Susanna FOSTER[6], b. 8 June 1771 <PN&Q 4:37>

Rebecca FOSTER[6], b. 24 Sept. 1773 <PN&Q 4:37>

Jedediah EAMES, (son of Jonathan & Hannah), b. 19 Apr. 1701, Marshfield <MD 8:178>; d. pre 15 May 1738 (adm.) <Plymouth Co.PR 7:409>

CHILDREN OF Jedediah EAMES & Mary OAKMAN[4] (Eliz. Doty[3]): (4) <Marshfield VR, MD 31:22>

Jane EAMES[5], b. 20 Oct. 1734; d. 22 July 1778, Marshfield Hills cem. <MD 9:95>

Mary EAMES[5], b. 17 Nov. 1726

Jedediah EAMES[5], b. 23 Apr. 1729; d. 7 Oct. 1793, Marshfield Hills cem. <MD 9:92>

Penelope EAMES[5], b. 17 Apr. 1731

Robert SHERMAN[4] (Eben.[3], Desire Doty[2]), d. aft. 9 Feb. 1761 <MD 30:166>

CHILDREN OF Robert SHERMAN & Mary (OAKMAN[4]) Eames: (3) <Marshfield VR>

Sarah SHERMAN[5], b. 3 Apr. 1741 <MD 30:136>

Valentine SHERMAN[5], b. 4 Oct. 1742 <MD 31:23>

Betty Doty SHERMAN[5], b. 11 Apr. 1746 <MD 30:133>

Erastus RICHARDS, (*son of Wm. & Hannah), b. 28 July 1744* <Pembroke VR:177> (hus. of Betty Doty

Sherman^{5})

Seth EWELL, b. c1719, d. 25 Feb. 1804, ae 84y7m, Marshfield Hills cem. <MD 9:95> (hus of Jane Eames^{5} (Mary Oakman^{4}))

CHILDREN OF Joseph STETSON & Mary EAMES^{5} (Mary Oakman^{4}): (4*) <Scituate VR>

Joseph STETSON^{6}, bpt. 19 Jan. 1744/5 <1:333>

Lusanna STETSON^{6}, b. 28 Feb. 1745 <1:348>

Molly STETSON^{6}, b. 15 Aug. 1748 <1:349>

Prudence STETSON^{6}, b. 19 Mar. 1750 <1:349>

CHILDREN OF Lemuel LITTLE^{5} & Penelope EAMES^{5} (Mary Oakman^{4}): <See Warren Family micro #5>

Bethiah TILDEN, b. c1726, d. 9 Sept. 1811, ae 85, Marshfield Hills cem. <MD 9:92>

CHILDREN OF Jedediah EAMES^{5} (Mary Oakman^{4}) & Bethiah TILDEN: (6) <Marshfield VR 2:115>

Susanna EAMES^{6}, b. 5 Sept. 1753; d. 22 Sept. 1814, Marshfield Hills cem., unm. <MD 9:92>

Mary EAMES^{6}, b. 14 Aug. 1756

Jemima EAMES^{6}, b. 18 Jan. 1759

Jedediah EAMES^{6}, b. 12 June 1761; d. 5 June 1834, Marshfield Hills cem. <MD 9:92>

John Tilden EAMES^{6}, b. 15 June 1764; d. 19 Feb. 1847, Marshfield Hills cem. <MD 9:92>

Bethiah EAMES^{6}, b. 6 June 1767; d. 9 Dec. 1792, Marshfield Hills cem. <MD 9:92>**<15>**

Sarah ROGERS, b. 29 July 1771; d. 1 Jan. 1846, Marshfield Hills cem. <MD 9:92>

CHILDREN OF John Tilden EAMES^{6} & Sarah ROGERS: (4) <Marshfield VR 2:115>

Sally EAMES^{7}, b. 15 May 1794

Tilden EAMES^{7}, b. 11 Dec. 1795

Polly EAMES^{7}, b. 4 Apr. 1798

Betsy EAMES^{7}, b. 18 July 1800

CHILD OF John HAMBELTON & Mercy OAKMAN^{4} (Eliz. Doty^{3}):**<16>**

John HAMELTON^{5}, b. 20 Dec. 1745 <Marshfield VR 2:110>

Elizabeth HATCH, (*dau of Israel), b. c1703, d. 28 Dec. 1788, Marshfield Hills cem. <MD 9:168> (wf of 3rd hus Peter Ripley)

CHILDREN OF Samuel OAKMAN^{4} (Eliz. Doty^{3}) & Elizabeth HATCH: (4) <1-2, Marshfield VR 2:105,110>

Samuel OAKMAN^{5}, b. 4 Aug. 1727 <MD 31:25>; d. 17 July 1791, Main St. cem., Norwell

Tobias OAKMAN^{5}, b. 12 May 1729 <MD 31:25>

Israel OAKMAN^{5}*, bpt. 24 June 1732*, Norwell Ch., Scituate; d.y.

Elizabeth OAKMAN^{5}*, bpt. 4 Aug. 1734*, Norwell Ch., Scituate; d.y.

Deborah TURNER^{6} (John^{5}, Ben.^{4}, Mary Brewster^{3}, Jonathan^{2}), b. c1723, d. 29 Oct. 1795, Main St. cem., Norwell

CHILDREN OF Samuel OAKMAN^{5} & Deborah TURNER: (7) <Marshfield VR, MD 31:74>

Betty OAKMAN^{6}, b. 9 Feb. 1748; d. pre Sept. 1796

Melzar Turner OAKMAN^{6}, b. 29 June 1750**<17>**

Deborah OAKMAN^{6}, b. 1 Jan. 1752

Samuel OAKMAN^{6}, b. 17 Mar. 1753; d. 3 May 1756 <MD 31:76>

Mercy OAKMAN^{6}, b. 13 Feb. 1756

Seth OAKMAN^{6}, b. 11 Dec. 1757; d.29 June 1759

Samuel OAKMAN^{6}, b. 20 Oct. 1768; d. 7 Oct. 1776

Eunice OAKMAN^{6}, b. ( )

Ruth LITTLE^{5} (Constant Fobes^{4}, Martha Pabodie^{3}, Eliz. Alden^{2}), b. c1723, d. 2 July 1804, ae 81y4m Two Mile cem., Marshfield <MD 10:247>

CHILDREN OF Tobias OAKMAN^{5} (Sam.^{4}) & Ruth LITTLE: (7) <Marshfield VR 2:114>

[illegible]

Israel OAKMAN^{6}, b. 20 May 1751; d. 8 Mar. 1753

Alathea OAKMAN^{6}, b. 5 Nov. 1753

Hope OAKMAN^{6}, b. 12 Jan. 1756; d. 5 Feb. 1827, unm. <Marshfield VR 3:deaths>

Constant Fobes OAKMAN^{6}, b. 5 Apr. 1759

Ruth OAKMAN^{6}, b. 27 Dec. 1761

Elizabeth Hatch OAKMAN^{6}, b. 28 June 1765

CHILDREN OF Constant Fobes OAKMAN^{6} & Rachel HATCH: (9) <Marshfield VR 2:114>

Christopher OAKMAN^{7}, b. 23 Jan. 1785

Hatch OAKMAN^{7}, b. 23 Aug. 1787

Samuel OAKMAN^{7}, b. 18 Sept. 1790

Rachel OAKMAN^{7}, b. 7 Jan. 1793

Silima OAKMAN^{7}, b. 20 Oct. 1795; d.y.

Alithua OAKMAN^{7}, b. 24 Oct. 1798; d.y.

Hiram OAKMAN^{7}, b.3 May 1801

Constant OAKMAN^{7}, b. 6 Dec. 1803

Fobes OAKMAN^{7}, b. 14 June 1807

CHILDREN OF Christopher OAKMAN^{7} & Bethiah CLIFT: (9) <Marshfield VR 3:14>

William Clift OAKMAN^{8}, b. 20 Jan. 1809

Alathea OAKMAN^{8}, b. 28 May 1812

Thomas MORTON, d. betw. 26 Aug. 1741 (will) - 12 Sept. 1748 (prob.) <Plym.Co.PR 11:69, MD 27:135>

CHILDREN OF Thomas MORTON & Martha DOTY^{3}: (6) <Plymouth VR, MD 3:12>**<18>**

Thomas MORTON^{4}, b. 12 Feb. 1700; d. 10 July 1731*, Plymouth g.s. <Kingman:17>

Lydia MORTON^{4}, b. 15 Nov. 1702; d. 21 Oct. 1739 <MD 15:213>

Lemuel MORTON^{4}, b. 21 Oct. 1704

Sarah MORTON^{4}, b. 6 July 1706

Nathaniel MORTON^{4}, b. 2 Oct. 1710

Mary MORTON^{4}, b. 30 Aug. 1712

MICRO #3 of 6

CHILDREN OF John NELSON^{5} & Mary MORTON^{4}: <See Warren Family micro #25>

CHILDREN OF Joseph BARTLETT^{5} & Sarah MORTON^{4}: <See Warren Family micro #23>

CHILDREN OF Nathaniel MORTON^{4} (Martha Doty^{3}) & Mary ELLIS*:**<19>**

CHILDREN OF Nathaniel MORTON & Mary ( ): (3) <MD 19:151>**<20>**

Nathaniel MORTON, b. 13 Apr. 1747, d. 8 Aug. 1758

Nathaniel MORTON, b. 3 July 1749, d. 17 July 1753 (two Nathaniel's living?)

Lemuel MORTON, b. 9 July 1757, d. 1827

CHILDREN OF Lemuel MORTON & Azubah CUSHMAN: (5) <MD 24:14>**<21>**

Nathaniel MORTON, b. 27 May 1789

Lemuel MORTON, b. 9 Apr. 1792

Elizabeth Cushman MORTON, b. 8 Nov. 1796

Mary Ellis MORTON, b. 5 Sept. 1799

Nancy MORTON, b. 5 Feb. 1801

Hannah NELSON^{5} (Sam.^{4}, Lydia Bartlett^{3}, Mary Warren^{2}), b. 15 Dec. 1707, Plymouth <MD 12:222>

CHILDREN OF Thomas MORTON^{4} (Martha Doty^{3}) & Hannah NELSON: (2) <Plymouth VR, MD 13:203>

Bathsheba MORTON^{5}, b. 18 Sept. 1727

Martha MORTON^{5}, b. 24 Feb. 1729/30; d. 12 Dec. 1782*, Plymouth g.s. <Kingman:55>

Silas MORTON, (son of Timothy & Mary), b. 17 Apr. 1727, Plymouth <MD 12:13>; d. 30 Oct. 1782*, Plymouth g.s. <Kingman:55>

CHILDREN OF Silas MORTON & Martha MORTON^{5}: (10) <Plymouth VR, MD 3:13>

Hannah MORTON^{6}, b. 17 Aug. 1749; d.y.

Silas MORTON^{6}, b. 10 July 1752

Timothy MORTON^{6}, b. 30 Aug. 1754

Martha MORTON^{6}, b. 21 Sept. 1757

Job MORTON^{6}, b. 29 June 1760

Oliver MORTON^{6}, b. 5 Sept. 1763
Thomas MORTON^{6}, b. 21 Oct. 1765
Ezra MORTON^{6}, b. 21 Jan. 1768
Hannah MORTON^{6}, b. 13 Aug. 1770
Lemuel MORTON^{6}, b. 23 Feb. 1775
Joseph ALLEN/ALLYN, b. 7 Apr. 1671, Barnstable <MD 2:213>; d. pre 6 Apr. 1742*(adm.,Wethersfield)
CHILDREN OF Joseph ALLYN & Mary DOTY^{3}: (7) <3-7*, Doty Gen.:33,34>
Elizabeth ALLYN^{4}, b. 29 Sept. 1700, Plymouth <MD 3:12>
Mary ALLYN^{4}, b. 10 Nov. 1702, Plymouth <MD 3:12>
Hannah ALLYN^{4}, b. 17 May 1705
Samuel ALLYN^{4}, b. 24 Feb. 1706/7
Sarah ALLYN^{4}, b. 17 Aug. 1708 (See p.422)
Martha ALLYN^{4}, b. 22 Oct. 1710
Abigail ALLYN^{4}, bpt. 11 Sept. 1715
CHILDREN OF Zepheniah HATCH: (12) <Wethersfield CT>**<22>**
Lucy HATCH, b. 6 May 1752
Jerusha HATCH, b. 11 June 1755
James HATCH, b. 26 Oct. 1757
Moses HATCH, b. 15 Mar. 1760
Mary HATCH, b. 13 Apr. 1762
John HATCH, b. 22 Aug. 1764
Simeon HATCH, b. 26 Nov. 1766
Samuel HATCH, b. 19 Feb. 1768
Levi HATCH, b. 13 Oct. 1770
Esther HATCH, b. 10 Sept. 1772
Elias HATCH, b. 19 Mar. 1775
Daniel HATCH, b. 26 Aug. 1778
CHILDREN OF Simeon HATCH, (son of Zepheniah) & Rebecca KILBORN: (3)<Stiles' Ancient Wethersfield>
George HATCH, bpt. 21 Aug. 1791
Lucy HATCH, bpt. 31 Jan. 1796
Mary HATCH, bpt. 12 Nov. 1797
James OTIS^{4} (John^{3-2-1}), b. 4 or 14 June 1702, Barnstable <MD 11:130,132>; d. 9 Nov. 1778*
CHILDREN OF James OTIS & Mary ALLYN^{4} (Mary Doty^{3}): (13) <4-12, NEHGR 2:292; pencilled dates>
James OTIS^{5}, b. 5 Feb. 1724/5 <2:289>; d. 23 May 1783*, Andover MA
Joseph OTIS^{5}, b. 6 Mar. 1725/6 <2:291>
Mercy OTIS^{5}, b. 14 Sept. 1728 <2:291>
Mary OTIS^{5}, b. 9 Sept. 1730
Hannah OTIS^{5}, b. 31 July 1732
Nathaniel OTIS^{5}, b. 9 July 1734, d. 13 Jan. 1735
Martha OTIS^{5}, b. 9 Oct. 1736, d. 25 Nov. 1736
Abigail OTIS^{5}, b. 30 June 1738, d. 30 July 1738
Elizabeth OTIS^{5}, b. 1 Sept. 1739
Samuel Allyne OTIS^{5}, b. 24 Nov. 1740, d. 22 Apr. 1814
Sarah OTIS^{5}, b. 11 Apr. 1742, d. 5 May 1743
Nathaniel OTIS^{5}, 9 Apr. 1743, d. 30 Apr. 1763
Dau., b. ( ), d.y.
Ruth CUNNINGHAM^{6} (Ann Boucher^{5}, Sarah Middlecott^{4}, Sarah Winslow^{3}, Mary Chilton^{2}), b. 15 Jan. 1728*; d. 15 Nov. 1789*
CHILDREN OF James OTIS^{5} & Ruth CUNNINGHAM: (3)
James OTIS^{6}, b. 1755*; d. 1777* "on the Jersey"

Elizabeth OTIS^{6}, b. ( ); d. aft. 1821*
Mary OTIS^{6}, b. ( )
Benjamin LINCOLN, b. 1 Nov. 1756*
CHILDREN OF Benjamin LINCOLN & Mary OTIS^{6}: (2)
Benjamin LINCOLN^{7}, b. ( )
James Otis LINCOLN^{7}, b. ( )
CHILDREN OF George STILLMAN & Rebecca ( ): (3) <Ancient Wethersfield 2:669>
Rebecca STILLMAN, b. 14 Jan. 1688
Mary STILLMAN, b. 12 July 1689
Capt. Nathaniel STILLMAN, b. 1 July 1691; d. 1 Jan. 1770 <2:671>
Anna SOUTHWAYD, (dau of Wm.), b. c1684, d. 6 Jan. 1729/30, ae 35 (1st wf. Capt. Nath. Stillman) +
Sarah ALLYN, (dau. of Jos. & Mary (Doty)), b. c1708, d. 4 Mar. 1794, ae 85 (2nd wf Capt. Nath. Stillman) <Ancient Wethersfield 2:671>

ISAAC DOTY^{2} (Edward^{1})

CHILDREN OF Isaac DOTY^{2} & Elizabeth ENGLAND: (6) <Oyster Bay NY>
Isaac DOTY^{3}, b. c1673*
Joseph DOTY^{3}, b. c1680*; d. 1716 (will, 7 July 1716, Oyster Bay)
Jacob DOTY^{3}, b. c1682*
Solomon DOTY^{3}, b. c1691*; d. 1761/2
James DOTY^{3}, b. 21 Dec. 1693; d. 4 Feb. 1773
Samuel DOTY^{3}, b. c1695*; d. 1740/1*
CHILDREN OF Joseph DOTY^{3} & Sarah ( ): (4) <Oyster Bay NY>
Sarah DOTY^{4}, b. c1703-6*
Joseph DOTY^{4}, b. c1708*; d. Lansingburgh NY*
Isaac DOTY^{4}, b. c1711*; prob. d.y.*
Elizabeth DOTY^{4}, b. c1716*
CHILD OF Samuel DOTY^{3} & Charity MUDGE:
Elias DOTY^{4}, b. c1732*, Littleworth, Oyster Bay, NY; d. 16 Mar. 1806
John JACKSON, b. 9 Mar. 1701
CHILDREN OF John JACKSON & Sarah DOTY^{4} (Jos.^{3}): (1 of 9)**<23>**
Hannah JACKSON^{5}, b. 2 Mar. 1744; d. Ross co., OH
Taylor WEBSTER, b. 18 Nov. 1748, Plainfield NJ; d. Ross co., OH
CHILD OF Taylor WEBSTER & Hannah JACKSON^{5}:
William WEBSTER^{6}, b. 31 Jan. 1773, Plainfield NJ; d. 29 Dec. 1846, Butler co., OH
Mary MARSH, b. 5 Feb. 1779, Rahway NJ; d. 8 May 1864, Butler co., OH
CHILD OF William WEBSTER^{6} & Mary MARSH:
Joseph Samuel Marsh WEBSTER^{7}, b. 24 Oct. 1819; d. 14 Apr. 1889
Amy DEAN, d. 25 May 1782, Clinton NY
CHILD OF Elias DOTY^{4} (Sam.^{3}) & Amy DEAN:
Amy DOTY^{5}, b. 13 Feb. 1766; d. 18 Sept. 1829, Wolcott NY (bur. Rose NY)
Thomas HALL, b. 26 Apr. 1764; d. 2 Dec. 1843, bur. Hubbard cem., Rose NY
CHILDREN OF Thomas HALL & Amy DOTY^{5}: (1 of 6)**<24>**
Mercy HALL^{6}, b. 20 May 1796; d. 14 Sept. 1853, Rose NY g.s.
Winthrop ALLEN, b. 18 Sept. 1781, Montgomery MA; d. 22 Sept. 1854, Rose NY g.s.
CHILDREN OF Winthrop ALLEN & Mercy HALL^{6}: (1 of 4)**<25>**
William Henry ALLEN^{7}, b. 24 Oct. 1825; d. 26 July 1903, Coldwater, Michigan
Charlotte AUSTIN, d. 8 Feb. 1859, Rose NY g.s. (1st wf Wm. Henry Allen^{7})
Mary BARNES, b. 17 Feb. 1826, Rose NY; d. 12 Aug. 1888, Coldwater, Michigan

CHILDREN OF William Henry ALLEN^{7} & Mary BARNES: (2)
Elmer J. ALLEN^{8}, b. 19 Feb. 1865; d. 29 Sept. 1917
Robert Webster ALLEN^{8}, b. ( ); unm. June 1943

JOHN DOTY^{2} (Edward^{1})

Elizabeth COOKE^{3} (Jacob^{2}), b. 18 Jan. 1648, Plymouth, d. 21 Nov. 1692, Plymouth <MD 15:27,16:63>
CHILDREN OF John DOTY^{2} & 1st Elizabeth COOKE: (9) <Plymouth VR, MD 1:144>
John DOTY^{3}, b. 24 Aug. 1668; d. betw. 29 Apr. 1746 (will) - 14 July 1747 (prob.) <MD 20:27>
Edward DOTY^{3}, b. 28 June 1671; d. pre 15 Apr. 1701 (father's will)
Jacob DOTY^{3}, b. 24 or 27 May 1673; d. pre 15 Apr. 1701 (father's will)
Elizabeth DOTY^{3}, b. 10 Feb. 1675/6
Isaac DOTY^{3}, b. 25 Oct. 1678; d. 15 Apr. 1725, Plymouth g.s. <MD 25:164>
Samuel DOTY^{3}, b. last of Jan. 1682; d. pre 20 May 1740 (adm.) <Plymouth Co.PR #6629, 8:189,270>
Elisha DOTY^{3}, b. 13 July 1686; d. betw. 24 Dec. 1753 (will) - 17 July 1754 (prob.) <MD 19:176>
Josiah DOTY^{3}, b. Oct. 1689; d. pre 22 Feb. 1771 (adm.) <Plymouth Co.PR #6597, 20:483>
Martha DOTY^{3}, b. Oct. 1692
CHILDREN OF John DOTY^{2} & 2nd Sarah JONES^{4} (Patience Little^{3}, Anna Warren^{2}): (3) <Plymouth VR>
Sarah DOTY^{3}, b. 19 Feb. 1695/6 <MD 1:206>
Patience DOTY^{3}, b. 3 July 1697 <MD 1:206>; d. 18 Feb. 1784, Marshfield g.s. <MD 12:55>
Desire DOTY^{3}, b. 19 Apr. 1699 <MD 1:206>
George BARROWS, d. aft. 29 Sept. 1757 <MD 21:74>
CHILDREN OF George BARROWS & Desire DOTY^{3}: (2*) <Plympton>
Patience BARROWS^{4}, b. 26 Apr. 1724
George BARROWS^{4}, b. 5 Dec. 1727
Kenelm BAKER^{4} (Sarah Bradford^{3}, Wm.^{2}), b. 3 Nov. 1695, Marshfield <MD 5:235>; d. 22 May 1771, Marshfield g.s. <MD 12:55>
CHILDREN OF Kenelm BAKER & Patience DOTY^{3}: (8) <Marshfield VR>
John BAKER^{4}, b. 18 Oct. 1719 <MD 30:154>
Allis BAKER^{4}, b. 26 Jan. 1722 <MD 30:154>
Kenelm BAKER^{4}, bpt. 4 Oct. 1724 <MD 31:164>
Sarah BAKER^{4}, b. 21 Apr. 1726 <MD 9:186>
Kenelm BAKER^{4}, b. 1 July 1728 <MD 9:186>
Elizabeth BAKER^{4}, b. 29 June 1730 <MD 9:186>
William BAKER^{4}, b. 16 Oct. 1734 <MD 30:147>
Lucy BAKER^{4}, b. 15 May 1737 <MD 30:147>
CHILDREN OF Elisha DOTY^{3} & Hannah HORTON: (9) <Plymouth VR, MD 5:100>**<26>**
Elisha DOTY^{4}, b. 20 Oct. 1709
Samuel DOTY^{4}, b. 16 June 1712; d. pre 24 Dec. 1753* (father's will)
Hannah DOTY^{4}, b. 10 Oct. 1714, d.y.
Edward DOTY^{4}, b. 7 Oct. 1716; d. aft. 1757*
Hannah DOTY^{4}, b. 5 Sept. 1718; d. pre 24 Dec. 1753 (father's will)
Paul DOTY^{4}, b. 28 Nov. 1721; d. Jan. 1777, Plymouth <MD 3:13>
Lois DOTY^{4}, b. 26 Aug. 1724
Stephen DOTY^{4}, b. 24 June 1726; d. 27 May 1802*, Chiltonville cem., Plymouth
James DOTY^{4}, b. 27 Aug. 1728; d. 25 July 1786*, Plymouth g.s. <Drew:271>
Ruth FINNEY^{5} (John^{4}, Eliz Warren^{3}, Jos.^{2}), b. 1 Oct. 1729, Plymouth <MD 13:114>; d. 29 Mar. 1752* Plymouth g.s. <Drew:12> (1st wf James Doty^{4})
CHILDREN OF Edward DOTY^{4} & Phebe FINNEY: (6) <Plymouth VR, MD 15:163>**<27>**
Elisha DOTEN^{5}, b. 21 Nov. 1743

Edward DOTEN^{5}, b. 13 Oct. 1745
Thomas DOTEN^{5}, b. 6 Mar. 1747/8
John DOTEN^{5}, b. 9 Aug. 1750
Lemuel DOTEN^{5}, b. 7 Aug. 1753
James DOTEN^{5}, b. 18 Nov. 1757
Ruth (FAUNCE*) Rider*, d. Mar. 1785, Plymouth <MD 3:13>
CHILDREN OF Paul DOTEN^{4} (Elisha^{3}) & Ruth (FAUNCE*) Rider*: (5) <Plymouth, MD 3:113>
Paul DOTEN^{5}, b. 13 July 1750; d. Dec. 1774
Ruth DOTEN^{5}, b. 18 May 1752; d. 24 June 1791
Bathsheba DOTEN^{5}, b. 10 July 1756
Lydia DOTEN^{5}, b. 12 July 1758
Susanna DOTEN^{5}, b. 1 Oct. 1764, "Liverpool N.S."
Hannah BARTLETT^{6} (John^{5}, Robert^{4}, Jos.^{3}, Mary Warren^{2}), b. 13 Dec. 1727, Plymouth <MD 13:166>; d. 1 Apr. 1778, Chiltonville cem., Plymouth
CHILDREN OF Stephen DOTEN^{4} (Elisha^{3}) & Hannah BARTLETT: (8) <1-5, Plymouth, MD 7:208>
Mary DOTEN^{5}, b. 16 July 1746
Stephen DOTEN^{5}, b. 4 Dec. 1748
Sarah DOTEN^{5}, b. 26 Jan. 1750/1
Mercy DOTEN^{5}, b. 9 Mar. 1753
Hannah DOTEN^{5}, b. 8 July 1755
James DOTEN^{5}, b. c1762* <MD 19:180>; d. 6 June 1794*, Plymouth g.s. <Kingman::71>
John DOTEN^{5}, b. 1766, Plymouth; d. Aug. 1825, Sheffield MA
Joseph DOTEN^{5}, b. ( )
Sarah ANDREWS, b. c1762, d. 7 Dec. 1806*, 44th yr, Plymouth g.s. <Kingman:108>
CHILD OF James DOTEN^{5} & Sarah ANDREWS:
Susanna Andrews DOTEN^{6}*, b. 14 June 1793*, Plymouth; d. 1 Mar. 1880*, Chelsea <MD 17:182>
CHILDREN OF John DOTEN^{5} (Stephen^{4}) & Mary WRIGHT, (dau of Isaac & Faith (Chandler)): (6)
James DOTEN^{6}, b. 13 Nov. 1797, Plympton <Doty/Doten Fam.:173>
Mary DOTEN^{6}, b. 28 Aug. 1799, Plymouth < " " >
Faith Chandler DOTEN^{6}, b. 26 Mar. 1802 < " " >
John DOTEN^{6}, b. 1 Oct. 1804 < " " >
Bartlett DOTEN^{6}, b. 16 Feb. 1807, d. 16 Aug. 1867 <" " >
Caleb DOTEN^{6}, b. 2 May 1809, d. 25 Nov. 1818 <" " >
CHILDREN OF Joseph DOTEN^{5} (Stephen^{4}) & Elizabeth ALLEN* (b. 1772*): (4*)
Bathsheba Jones DOTEN^{6}, b. 1795
Elizabeth DOTEN^{6}, b. 1797
Joseph DOTEN^{6}, b. 1799, d. 1802
Joseph DOTEN^{6}, b. 1802
CHILDREN OF Stephen DOTEN^{5} (Stephen^{4}) & 1st Betsey HOLMES*: (9*)
Stephen DOTEN^{6}, b. 1774
Paul DOTEN^{6}, b. 1776
Betsey DOTEN^{6}, b. 1779, d.y.
Bartlett DOTEN^{6}, b. 1782, d.y.
Mercy DOTEN^{6}, b. 1785
Hannah DOTEN^{6}, b. 1788; unm.
Deborah DOTEN^{6}, b. 1791
Mary DOTEN^{6}, b. 1793; unm.
Esther DOTEN^{6}, b. 1796; unm.
CHILDREN OF Stephen DOTEN^{5} (Stephen^{4}) & 2nd Abigail CLARK*: (3*)
Betsey DOTEN^{6}, b. 1800; unm.

Joseph DOTEN[6], b. 1803

Eliza DOTEN[6], b. 1804; unm.

CHILDREN OF Joshua MORS & Elizabeth DOTY[3]: (7) <Plymouth VR, MD 2:163>

Joshua MORS[4], b. 12 Sept. 1699

Elizabeth MORS[4], b. 8 Oct. 1701

Edward MORS[4], b. 25 July 1704

Joseph MORS[4], b. 29 Dec. 1706

Newberrey MORS[4], b. 28 July 1709

Abigail MORS[4], b. 22 Sept. 1711

Theodorus MORS[4], b. 20 Aug. 1714

CHILDREN OF Edward MORS[4] & Margerett ( ): (9) <Rochester General Rcds. 2:6>

Joshua MORS[5], b. 29 Mar. 1728

Edward MORS[5], b. 19 May 1730

Mercy MORS[5], b. 9 July 1732; d. Feb. 1733 <VR 2:100>

Mercy MORS[5], b. 2 Mar. 1735/6

Malletiah MORS[5], b. 19 Dec. 1733; d. 11 Jan. 1757

John MORS[5], b. 22 Apr. 1738

Benjamin MORS[5], b. 9 Apr. 1740; d. 18 Aug. 1740

Benjamin MORS[5], b. 22 Apr. 1742

Ebenezer MORS[5], b. 31 Jan. 1747

CHILD OF Joshua MORSS & Elizabeth ( ):**<28>**

Susanna MORSS, b. 8 July 1724 <Rochester General Rcds. 2:6>

CHILDREN OF Joshua MORSS[5] (Edw.[4]) & Mary GOODNUF: (3) <Rochester General Rcds.2:3>

Malletiah MORSS[6], b. 5 Sept. 1765

Abigail MORSS[6], b. 21 Nov. 1779

Lucy MORSS[6], b. 21 Nov. 1779 (twins)

CHILDREN OF Malletiah MORSS/MORSE[6] (Joshua[5]) & Joanna SWIFT: (2) <Rochester VR>

Mary MORSE[7], b. Mar. 1789, d. 5 Dec. 1790, ae 1y9m, Rochester Center cem. <VR 2:414>

Joshua MORSE[7], b. 10 Sept. 1793 <VR 1:220>

Martha FAUNCE, (dau of Elder Thomas), b. 16 Dec. 1680, Plymouth <MD 1:147>; d. 9 Sept. 1745, Plymouth g.s. <MD 25:164>

CHILDREN OF Isaac DOTY[3] & Martha FAUNCE: (9) <Plymouth VR, MD 22:224>

Elizabeth DOTY[4], b. 24 Apr. 1704

Jeane DOTY[4], b. 10 Nov. 1706

Isaac DOTY[4], b. 30 Mar. 1709; d. betw. 6 May (will) - 16 May 1770 <Plymouth Co.PR #6585, 20:367>

Rebecca DOTY[4], b. 10 Mar. 1711; d. 21 Jan. 1766, Plymouth g.s. <Kingman:38> (wf of 2nd hus. David Turner)

Neriah DOTY[4], b. 8 Mar. 1712/3 (son); d. betw. 22 June 1738 (will) - 4 Dec. 1738 <MD 25:173>

Jabez DOTY[4], b. 1 Jan. 1716

Hope DOTY[4], b. 11 Nov. 1718; d. 5 Apr. 1720

Ichabod DOTY[4], b. 13 Jan. 1720/1, "4:00 a.m." <MD 2:225>; d pre 14 or 19 Aug. 1749*, unm.

Mary DOTY[4], b. 13 Jan. 1720/1, "2:00 p.m." (twins) <MD 2:225>

CHILDREN OF Lemuel BARTLETT[5] & Mary DOTY[4]: (8) <See Warren Family micro #23>

David TURNER, b. c1693, d. 18 Jan. 1769, 76th yr, Plymouth g.s. <Kingman:41>

Mary LANMAN, (*dau of James & Joanna), b. 12 Mar. 1718*<Boston Rcd.com.24:124>; d. 10 Mar. 1809*, ae 90, Plymouth g.s. <Drew:142>

CHILDREN OF Isaac DOTEN[4] (Isaac[3]) & Mary LANMAN: (14) <Plymouth VR, 3-11, MD 15:111>

Isaac DOTEN[5], b. 11 July 1735 <MD 15:110>; d. 6 Mar. 1809***<29>**

James DOTEN[5], b. 22 Jan. 1736/7 <MD 15:110>; d. betw. 10 June 1817 (will) - 30 Aug. 1817 (inv.) <Plymouth Co.PR #6591, 49:25,226>

Hope DOTEN^5, b. 19 Feb. 1738/9 <MD15:111>

Mary DOTEN^5, b. 12 Feb. 1740/1, d. 24 Apr. 1741

Jean DOTEN^5, b. 12 Feb. 1740/1 (twins), d. 5 May 1741

Ichabod DOTEN^5, b. 15 Sept. 1742, d. 28 Sept. 1747

Thomas DOTEN^5, b. 24 Dec. 1744

Mary DOTEN^5, b. 4 Feb. 1746/7

Jean DOTEN^5, b. 16 Apr. 1749, d. 10 Aug. 1750

William DOTEN^5, b. 21 July 1751

Rebecca DOTEN^5, b. 20 Apr. 1754, d. 5 Sept. 1754

Jabez DOTEN^5, b. 27 Dec. 1755 <MD 15:112>

John Palmer DOTEN^5, b. 19 June 1758, d. 21 Sept. 1760 <MD 15:112>

Rebecca DOTEN^5, b. 2 Apr. 1762 <MD 15:112>

CHILDREN OF James DOTEN^5 (Isaac^4) & Elizabeth KEMPTON: (1 of 11)**<30>**

Hope DOTEN^6, b. 15 June 1765 <MD 21:162>

CHILDREN OF Samuel SMITH* & Hope DOTEN^6: (4*) <Smithfield RI VR*>

Lucy SMITH^7, b. 27 Mar. 1792

Doten SMITH^7, b. 13 June 1793

Harriet SMITH^7, b. 21 Feb. 1795

Chandler Robbins SMITH^7, b. 17 Nov. 1797

Mehitable NELSON, (dau of John), b. 5 Apr. 1670, Plymouth or Middleboro <MD 1:141,220>

CHILDREN OF John DOTY^3 & Mehitable NELSON: (6) <Plymouth VR, MD 2:163>

Mehitable DOTY^4, b. 4 Nov. 1694

Edward DOTY^4, b. 1 Nov. 1697

John DOTY^4, b. 5 Feb. 1700; d. betw. 19 Jan. 1748 (will) - 3 Apr. 1749 (prob.) <Plymouth Co.PR # 6594, 12:102, 103>

Sarah DOTY^4, b. 14 Oct. 1707

Susanna DOTY^4, b. 20 Apr. 1710; d. aft. 16 Nov. 1750*

Lydia DOTY^4, b. 10 Feb. 1712/3

CHILD OF John DOTY^3:**<31>**

Jacob DOTY^4, b. ( ); d. betw. 29 Apr. 1746 - 26 June 1747 (inv.)<Plymouth Co.PR #6587,10:449>

MICRO #4 of 6

CHILD OF Jacob DOTY^4 & Deborah ( ):**<32>**

Jacob DOTY^5, b. ( ); d. pre 30 Aug. 1785 (inv.) <Plymouth Co.PR #6588, 29:289>

CHILDREN OF John DOTY^4 (John^3) & Lydia DUNHAM: (4)

Edward DOTEN^5, b. 4 May 1725; d. pre 27 Apr. 1765 (adm.) <Plymouth Co.PR #6573>

Ebenezer DOTEN^5, b. c1727*; d. pre 2 Dec. 1786 (bond) <Plymouth Co.PR #6572, 27:219>

Elizabeth DOTEN^5, b. c1729*

Nathaniel DOTEN^5, b. c1730*

CHILDREN OF Ebenezer DOTEN^5 & 1st Mercy WHITTEN: (4)

Caleb DOTEN^6, b. 11 Apr. 1751 <Plymouth VR:93>; d. 19 Apr. 1804

Elizabeth DOTEN^6, b. c1752* <Plymouth VR:308>

Amaziah DOTEN^6, b. 17 May 1756; d. 24 Jan. 1833

Ebenezer DOTEN^6, b. 15 Aug. 1762*; d. 22 Feb. 1856

CHILDREN OF Ebenezer DOTEN^5 & 2nd Mary RICKARD*^{6} (*Theophilus^5, Samuel^4, Rebecca Snow^3, Rebecca Brown^2): (5)

Sarah DOTEN^6, b. c1765*

Phebe DOTEN^6, b. ( ); removed to Irasburgh VT

Lydia DOTEN^6, b. c1767*

Edward DOTEN^6, b. ( )

Mercy DOTEN^6, b. ( ); not mentioned in div. of father's estate, 1787

CHILDREN OF John FINNEY^4 & Susanna DOTY^4 (John^3): (6) <See Warren Family micro #17>

CHILDREN OF Josiah DOTY^3 & Abigail ( ): (5) <Plymouth VR, MD 13:171>

Josiah DOTY^4, b. 18 Apr. 1715

Abigail DOTY^4, b. 3 Dec. 1716

Experience DOTY^4, b. 4 Jan. 1718/9

Patience DOTY^4, b. 10 Feb. 1720/1

Sarah DOTY^4, b. 2 June 1723

CHILDREN OF Ebenezer CURTIS, (*son of Francis & Hannah) & Martha DOTY^3: (4)<Plymouth VR,MD 7:208>

Eunice CURTIS^4, b. 23 June 1723

Martha CURTIS^4, b. 3 July 1725

Seth CURTIS^4, b. 22 Oct. 1727

Ebenezer CURTIS^4, b. 14 Oct. 1731

CHILDREN OF Samuel DOTY^3 & Mercy COBB: (5) <Plymouth VR, MD 14:240>

Samuel DOTY^4, b. 15 Aug. 1729

Child, b. 9 Feb. 1731/2, d. beginning Mar. 1731/2

Mercy DOTY^4, b. 14 Jan. 1732/3

Hannah DOTY^4, b. 8 Mar. 1734/5

Sarah DOTY^4, b. 5 Aug. 1736

JOSEPH DOTY^2 (Edward^1)

Deborah ( ) DOTY, d. 21 June 1711 <Rochester General Rcds.1:7>**<33>**

CHILDREN OF Joseph DOTY^2 & Deborah ( ): (9) <1-2, Sandwich VR, MD 14:108; 4-9, Rochester VR 1:5>**<33>**

Theophilus DOTY^3, b. 22 Feb. 1674

Ellis DOTY^3, b. 16 Apr. 1677

Elizabeth DOTY^{3*}, b. ( )

Joseph DOTY^3, b. 31 Mar. 1683

Deborah DOTY^3, b. 31 Mar. 1685

John DOTY^3, b. 1 Mar. 1688

Mercy DOTY^3, b. 12 Jan. 1691

Faith DOTY^3, b. 18 Jan. 1696

Mary DOTY^3, b. 28 July 1699

CHILDREN OF John ELLIS & Elizabeth FREEMAN: (5) <Sandwich>

Bennet ELLIS, b. 27 Feb. 1648/9

Mordecai ELLIS, b. 24 Mar. 1650

Joel ELLIS, b. 20 Mar. 1654

Matthias ELLIS, b. 2 June 1657

Freeman ELLIS, b. ( )

CHILDREN Ellis DOTY^3 & Elliner ( ): (6) <Rochester VR 1:46>

Edward DOTY^4, b. 7 May 1705

Barnabas DOTY^4, b. 17 May 1707**<34>**

John DOTY^4, b. 16 July 1709

Joseph DOTY^4, b. 4 Sept. 1712

Elliner DOTY^4, b. 25 Sept. 1715

Elijah DOTY^4, b. 1 Jan. 1717/8

CHILDREN OF Edward DOTY^{4*} & Mary ANDREWS: (8) <Rochester VR 2:16>

Thomas DOTY^{5*}, b. 25 Oct. 1727

Edward DOTY^{5*}, b. 25 Aug. 1729

Zurishaddai DOTY^{5*}, b. 19 Nov. 1731

John DOTY[5*], b. 7 Aug. 1734
Theodorus DOTY[5*], b. 25 Dec. 1736
Betty DOTY[5*], b. 14 Aug. 1739
Abigail DOTY[5*], b. 30 June 1741
Elener DOTY[5*], b. 22 Mar. 1743/4

CHILD OF John DOTY[3] & Elizabeth ( )*:
Samuel DOTY[4], b. ( )

CHILDREN OF Samuel DOTY[4] & Zeruiah LOVELL: (10) <Sharon CT VR:36>**<35>**
Mary DOTY[5], b. 31 Dec. 1739
David DOTY[5], b. 12 May 1741
Bette DOTY[5], b. 10 Mar. 1743
Reuben DOTY[5], b. 8 Feb. 1745
Asa DOTY[5], b. 6 Nov. 1746
Sarah DOTY[5], b. 5 Oct. 1748
Abigail DOTY[5], b. 17 Mar. 1750
Lucy DOTY[5], b. 27 Dec. 1751
Dilly DOTY[5], b. 5 Sept. 1753
Huldah DOTY[5], b. 25 Apr. 1755

CHILDREN OF Samuel DOTY & Elizabeth ( ): (2) <Sharon CT VR:36>**<35>**
Zerviah DOTY, b. 8 Feb. 1763, Amenia
John DOTY, b. 28 Dec. 1769, d. 21 Apr. 1775, Amenia

CHILDREN OF Joseph DOTY[3] & Hannah EDWARDS: (11) <Rochester General Rcds.1:57>
Sarah DOTY[4], b. 16 Aug.1709
Isaac DOTY[4], b. 2 May 1711; d. pre 8 May 1740* (adm.) <Plymouth Co.PR #6622, 8:188>
Ellis DOTY[4], b. 30 Jan. 1712/3
Deborah DOTY[4], b. 10 Apr. 1715, d. middle Sept. 1726
Elizabeth DOTY[4], b. 6 Apr. 1717
Hannah DOTY[4], b. 17 Apr. 1719
Silas DOTY[4], b. 3 Mar. 1721/2
Joseph DOTY[4], b. 12 May 1723
Faith DOTY[4], b. 31 May 1725
Deborah DOTY[4], b. c25 Dec. 1727
Timothy DOTY[4], b. 3 July 1730

CHILDREN OF Theophilus DOTY[3] & Ruth MENDALL, (dau of John): (7) <Rochester VR 1:51>**<36>**
Ebenezer DOTY[4], b. 7 Oct. 1697
Ruth DOTY[4], b. 1 Mar. 1698/9
Deborah DOTY[4], b. 29 July 1702
Lydia DOTY[4], b. 19 Aug. 1704
Elizabeth DOTY[4], b. 3 Sept. 1706
Caleb DOTY[4], b. 30 Mar. 1709
Phebe DOTY[4], b. 11 June 1711

MARY DOTY[2] (Edward[1])

Samuel HATCH[3] (*Walter[2], Wm.[1]), b. 22 Dec. 1653* <Scituate VR>; d. betw. 13 June 1728 (will) - 7 July 1735 (prob.) <MD 7:29>

CHILDREN OF Samuel HATCH & Mary DOTY[2]: (9) <Scituate VR 4:3:53>
Samuel HATCH[3], b. 10 Nov. 1678; d. betw. 23 Oct. 1766 (will)- 2 Feb. 1767 (prob.), of Scituate <Plymouth Co.PR 19:425>
Josiah HATCH[3], b. 30 May 1680; d. 12 Jan. 1714/5* <Rochester VR>

Hannah HATCH^{3}, b. 15 or 16 Feb. 1681/2; d. 13 Apr. 1771, Nemasket cem., Middleboro <MD 15:103> (wf of 3rd hus. Ichabod Tupper)

Ebenezer HATCH^{3}, b. 6 Apr. 1684; d. betw. 7 Jan. 1724 (will) - 21 Apr. 1724 (inv.), of Pembroke <Plymouth Co.PR #9490, 4:419,420>

Isaac HATCH^{3}, b. 20 Dec. 1687; d. betw. 11 Dec. 1756 (will) - 3 Dec. 1759 (prob.), of Pembroke <Plymouth Co.PR #9506, 15:446> (poss. d. 1 Nov. 1759)[<37>]

Elizabeth HATCH^{3}, b. 16 June 1690

Elisha HATCH^{3}, b. 7 Nov. 1692

Ezekiel HATCH^{3}, b. 14 May 1695; d. betw. 19 June 1765 (will) - 1 July 1768 (inv.) <MD 22:155>

Desire HATCH^{3}, b. 25 Sept. 1698

Abigail JONES^{5} (Joseph^{4}, Patience Little^{3}, Anna Warren^{2}), b. 13 Apr. 1694, Hingham

CHILDREN OF Ebenezer HATCH^{3} & Abigail JONES*: (2)

Ebenezer HATCH^{4}, b. aft. 1704 (under 21, father's will)

Sarah HATCH^{4}, b. aft. 1706 (under 18, father's will)

John BONNEY, (son of John), b. 27 June 1690* <Pembroke VR>; d. betw. 26 July 1763 (will)- 31 Jan. 1765

CHILDREN OF John BONNEY & Elizabeth HATCH^{3}: (5)

Elizabeth BONNEY^{4}, b. 16 Mar. 1719*; d. 16 Sept. 1723*

Zerviah BONNEY^{4}, b. 11 Mar. 1723*; d. aft. 1762*

John BONNEY^{4}, b. 30 Oct. 1725*; d. aft. 1762*

Rachel BONNEY^{4}, b. 21 Mar. 1727/8*

Thomas BONNEY^{4}*, b. 3 Nov. 1732*

Ruth CHURCH^{5} (Richard^{4}, Nath.^{3}, Eliz. Warren^{2}), b. 8 Dec. 1701 <Scituate VR 4:3:72>; d. aft. 19 June 1765 (hus. will)

CHILDREN OF Ezekiel HATCH^{3} & Ruth CHURCH: (6) <Rochester VR>

Ruth HATCH^{4}, b. 23 June 1719*; d. 31 May 1789*, Hardwick

Mary HATCH^{4}, b. 29 Nov. 1721*

Hannah HATCH^{4}, b. 29 Mar. 1724*

Isaiah HATCH^{4}, b. 11 Sept. 1729*

Luse HATCH^{4}, b. 10 Sept. 1732*

Sarah HATCH^{4}, b. 6 June 1736*

Japhet TURNER^{4} (Japhet^{3}, John^{2}*, Humphrey^{1}*), b. 4 Jan. 1682, Duxbury <MD 9:229>; d. pre 29 Jan. 1710 (adm.) <MD 21:98>

CHILDREN OF Japhet TURNER & Hannah HATCH^{3}: (4)

Hannah TURNER^{4}, b. 8 Sept. 1702 <Pembroke VR:211>; d. pre 26 Aug. 1766*(mother's will)<MD 21:101>

Japhet TURNER^{4}, bpt. 17 Sept. 1704* <Scitute VR 1:3:375>; d. pre 14 Sept. 1748 (adm.)

Israel TURNER^{4}, b. 6 July 1706 <Pembroke VR:212>; d. 24 Sept. 1760,Pembroke Centre cem.<MD 11:30>

Elizabeth TURNER^{4}, b. 28 Nov. 1709 <Pembroke VR:211>; d. aft. 26 Aug. 1766* (mother's will)

CHILDREN OF John PRATT^{5} & Elizabeth TURNER^{4}: (5) <See Priest Family micro #2>

CHILDREN OF William THOMAS, (*son of Wm. & Sarah (Pratt)) & Hannah TURNER^{4}: (9) <Middleboro VR, 1-6, MD 13:4; 7-9, MD 16:20>

Isaiah THOMAS^{5}, b. 13 Sept. 1722

Susanna THOMAS^{5}, b. 1 Sept. 1724

Thankful THOMAS^{5}, b. 26 Jan. 1726/7

Mary THOMAS^{5}, b. 22 Feb. 1728/9

Hannah THOMAS^{5}, b. 20 Apr. 1731

Ruth THOMAS^{5}, b. 25 Dec. 1733; d. 9 Feb. 1801*, Woodstock VT g.s.

Sarah THOMAS^{5}, b. 15 Sept. 1736 <MD 16:20>

William THOMAS^{5}, b. 16 Jan. 1738/9 <MD 16:20>

Huldah THOMAS^{5}, b. 18 June 1742 <MD 16:20>

Thomas WOOD, (*? Hannah Alden[4],John[3], Jos.[2]), b.? 24 Feb. 1731/2*, Middleboro <MD 8:29>
CHILDREN OF Thomas WOOD & Sarah THOMAS[5]: (3) <Middleboro VR, MD 23:45>
Hannah WOOD[6], b. 5 Sept. 1754
Sarah WOOD[6], b. 11 June 1757
Amasa WOOD[6], b. 5 Aug. 1760
CHILDREN OF Thomas PADDOCK & Hannah THOMAS[5] (Hannah Turner[4]): (4) <Middleboro VR, MD 16:246>
William PADDOCK[5], b. 6 Nov. 1748
Ichabod PADDOCK[5], b. 28 Mar. 1751
Hannah PADDOCK[5], b. 11 June 1752
Joanna PADDOCK[5], b. 27 Feb. 1755
Thomas ELLIS, (*son of Joel & Eliz.), b. 1 Jan. 1728/9*, Middleboro <MD 9:47>; d. 4 Apr. 1799*, Woodstock VT g.s.
CHILDREN OF Thomas ELLIS & Ruth THOMAS[5] (Hannah Turner[4]): (6) <1-2, Middleboro VR, MD 18:156>
Thomas ELLIS[6], b. 22 Sept. 1757
William ELLIS[6], b. 10 Mar. 1760
Susanna ELLIS[6], b. 22 Apr. 1762
Samuel ELLIS[6], b. 21 Aug. 1764
Southworth ELLIS[6], b. 18 Feb. 1769
Joshua ELLIS[6], b. 28 July 1777
Abigail HOLMES[5] (Mary Brewster[4], Wrestling[3], Love[2]), b. 18 July 1705 <MD 23:173>; d. 24 Oct. 1787 Pembroke Centre cem. <MD 11:30>
CHILDREN OF Israel TURNER[4] (Hannah Hatch[3]) & Abigail HOLMES: (9) <Pembroke VR>
Deborah TURNER[5], b. 20 June 1731 <:211>
Jonathan TURNER[5], b. 24 Mar. 1732 <:212>; d.? 18 Sept. 1796, 65th yr <Pembroke VR:458>
Abigail TURNER[5], b. 7 May 1735 <:209>; d. 24 Apr. 1748, Pembroke Centre cem. <MD 11:30>
Priscilla TURNER[5], b. 31 Dec. 1736 <:213>
Elizabeth TURNER[5], b. 27 May 1739 <:210>
Christiana TURNER[5], b. 20 June 1741 <:210>
Israel TURNER[5], b. 6 Apr. 1743 <:212>
Daniel TURNER[5], b. 7 Feb. 1744 <:210>; d. 30 July 1779, Pembroke Centre cem. <MD 11:30>
Capt. Elisha TURNER[5], b. ( ); d. aft. 9 Apr.1790*

MICRO #5 of 6

CHILDREN OF Poole SPEAR & Christiana TURNER[5]: (6) <NEHGR 18:161>**<38>**
Abigail SPEAR[6], b. c1777, Boston, d. 29 June 1852, ae 75y2m5d, Leominster MA <Mass.VR 68:121>
Samuel ABBOTT, b. c1765, Boston, d. 15 Oct. 1856, ae 91, Leominster MA <Mass.VR 104:157>
CHILD OF Samuel ABBOTT & Abigail SPEAR[6]: <Abbot/Sibley Family Bibles>
James P. ABBOT[7], b. 23 Nov. 1813, Boston
Sarah Smith SIBLEY, (dau of John & Sarah (Brooks)), b. 6 Apr. 1813, Bridgeton NJ <Bible>
CHILD OF James P. ABBOT[7] & Sarah Smith SIBLEY: <Abbot/Sibley Family Bibles>
Charles Sibley ABBOT[8], b. 26 June 1846, Louisville KY
Marietta McMULLEN, (dau of Dan. & Sophia (Butler)), b. 3 Dec. 1848, Louisville KY <Bible>
CHILD OF Charles Sibley ABBOT[8] & Marietta McNULLEN: <Abbot/Sibley Family Bibles>
Marietta ABBOT[9], b. 28 June 1878, Louisville KY (m. Jos. Henry Burnett)
Joseph Henry BURNETT, (son of Jos. Herndon & Laura (Duff)), b. 6 May 1872, Auburn KY <Bible>
Sarah KEEN[4] (Josiah[3], John[2], Josiah[1]), b. 5 Oct. 1758* <Pembroke VR:131>
CHILDREN OF Capt. Elisha TURNER[5] (Israel[4]) & Sarah KEEN: (9) <Pembroke VR>
Josiah TURNER[6], b. 16 Oct. 1782 <:213>
Mary TURNER[6], b. 13 Jan. 1784 <:213>
Elisha TURNER[6], b. 4 Nov. 1787 <:211>
Robert TURNER[6], b. 3 Oct. 1789 <:214>

David Tilden TURNER^{6}, b. 7 Feb. 1791 <:211>

Sarah TURNER^{6}, b. 5 May 1793, d. 25 May 1793 <:214,459>

Sarah TURNER^{6}, b. 20 Nov. 1794 <:214>

Joseph Tilden TURNER^{6}, bpt. 26 Sept. 1802 <:212>

Rebecca Tilden TURNER^{6}, bpt. 7 Apr. 1808 <:214>

Elizabeth MORSE^{4*} (*? Eliz. Doty^{3}, John^{2}), b.? 8 Oct. 1701*, Plymouth <MD 2:163>

CHILDREN OF Japhet TURNER^{4} (Hannah Hatch^{3}) & Elizabeth MORSE: (9) <Middleboro VR>

Betty TURNER^{5}, b. 12 May 1726 <MD 6:228>

Hannah TURNER^{5}, b. 30 June 1729 <MD 7:241>

Abigail TURNER^{5}, b. 11 Aug. 1731 <MD 9:47>

Japheth TURNER^{5}, b. 24 Sept. 1733 <MD 12:131>

Joshua TURNER^{5}, b. 3 Mar. 1735/6 <MD 13:4>

Joseph TURNER^{5}, b. 23 July 1738 <MD 13:6>

Samuel TURNER^{5}, b. 17 Apr. 1742 <MD 15:217>

Dau., still born, 6 Apr. 1744 <MD 15:222>

Mary TURNER^{5}, b. 31 May 1745 <MD 16:106>

CHILDREN OF Job BRYANT, (son of Ichabod & Ruth (Staples)) & Mary TURNER^{5}: (11) <1-5, Bridgewater VR; 6-11, Brockton VR:25>

Anna BRYANT^{6}, b. 12 Nov. 1764 <1:58>

Nathan BRYANT^{6}, b. 15 Sept. 1766 <1:60>

Calvin BRYANT^{6}, b. 16 Dec. 1768 <1:58>

Job Staples BRYANT^{6}, b. 19 July 1772 <1:59>

Thirza BRYANT^{6}, b. 4 Oct. 1774 <1:60>

Oliver BRYANT^{6}, bpt. 3 Sept. 1780

Samuel BRYANT^{6}, bpt. 3 Sept. 1780

David BRYANT^{6}, bpt. 30 Sept. 1781

Asa BRYANT^{6}, bpt. 30 Aug. 1783

Clement BRYANT^{6}, bpt. 16 Apr. 1786

Harriet BRYANT^{6}, bpt. 16 Apr. 1786

Thomas REYNOLDS, (son of Nath.), b. 1718, d. 1795, ae 77, Bridgewater

CHILDREN OF Thomas REYNOLDS & *Betty TURNER^{5*} (Japhet^{4}): (8) <Bridgewater VR>[<39>]

Amy REYNOLDS, b. 29 Oct. 1749, d. 9 May 1752 <1:276,2:548>

Joseph REYNOLDS, b. 21 June 1751 <1:276>; d. 15 Mar. 1831*, Auburn ME

Amy REYNOLDS, b. 21 Feb. 1753 <1:276>

Elizabeth REYNOLDS, b. 22 June 1755 <1:276>

Susanna REYNOLDS, b. 24 Apr. 1757 <1:277>

Martha REYNOLDS, b. 23 Mar. 1759 <1:276>

Thomas REYNOLDS, b. 27 Jan. 1762 <1:277>

Josiah REYNOLDS, b. 1 July 1766 <1:276>

CHILDREN OF Thomas LINDSAY & Elizabeth TURNER: (5) <marr. at Bridgewater>[<40>]

William LINDSAY, b. 1747

Mary LINDSAY, b. 1749

Hannah LINDSAY, b. 1752

James LINDSAY, b. 1755

Thomas LINDSAY, b. 1758

CHILD OF Joseph TURNER^{5*} (Japhet^{4}) & Mercy FRENCH:

Joshua TURNER^{6*}, b. 13 Dec. 1757 <MD 20:38>

James LeBARON, (son of James), b. 10 Dec. 1726, Middleboro <MD 8:28>; d. 3 Oct. 1780*, Middleboro

CHILDREN OF James LeBARON & Hannah TURNER^{5} (Japhet^{4}): (11) <2-7, Middleboro VR, MD 23:46>

James LeBARON^{6*}, b. 4 Jan. 1748* <LeBaron Gen.:25>

Japhet LeBARON^{6}, b. 20 July 1750
Elizabeth LeBARON^{6}, b. 24 Mar. 1752
Martha LeBARON^{6}, b. 30 Nov. 1755
William LeBARON^{6}, b. 20 Apr. 1757
James LeBARON^{6}, b. 30 Nov. 1759
Francis LeBARON^{6}, b. 31 Apr. 1762
Isaac LeBARON^{6*}, b. 20 Apr. 1764* <LeBaron Gen.:26>
Hannah LeBARON^{6*}, b. 11 Sept. 1766* <LeBaron Gen.:26>
Abigail LeBARON^{6*}, b. 17 May 1768* <LeBaron Gen.:26>
Lazarus LeBARON^{6*}, b. 7 Feb. 1771* <LeBaron Gen.:26>
Lydia CLIFT, (dau of Wm. & Lydia), b. 13 July 1697* <Scituate VR>; d. betw. 30 Sept. 1722* -1725*
CHILDREN OF Isaac HATCH^{3} & 1st Lydia CLIFT: (2) <MD 7:30>
Isaac HATCH^{4}, bpt. 30 Sept. 1722; d. 9 Dec. 1799, 83rd yr, Pembroke Centre cem. <MD 9:238>
Josiah HATCH^{4}, bpt. 30 Sept. 1722
Penelope EWELL, (dau of Gershom), d. pre 1 Jan. 1776 (adm.) <Plymouth Co.PR #9585, 23:78>**<41>**
CHILDREN OF Isaac HATCH^{3} & 2nd Penelope EWELL: (7) <Norwell Ch., Scitute>**<42>**
Penelope HATCH^{4}, bpt. 20 Feb. 1725*
Seth HATCH^{4}, bpt. 24 Dec. 1727* (See <43>)
Lydia HATCH^{4}, bpt. 4 Jan. 1729/30*
Mary HATCH^{4}, bpt. 23 Apr. 1732*, Marshfield
Sarah HATCH^{4}, bpt. 15 Sept. 1734*; d. 18 Aug. 1791*, unm.
Samuel HATCH^{4}, bpt. 1 Aug. 1736*; d. c1777*
Josiah HATCH^{4*}?, bpt. 3 June 1739*
Ann FISHER, (*? dau of John & Sarah), b.? 24 Oct. 1718* <Boston Rcd.com.24:129>
CHILDREN OF Isaac HATCH^{4} & 1st Ann FISHER: (12) <Pembroke VR>
Ann HATCH^{5}, b. 29 June 1739*
Lydia HATCH^{5}, b. 11 Jan. 1740*
Isaac HATCH^{5}, b. 4 Oct. 1742*; d. 1763*
Judith HATCH^{5}, b. 16 Feb. 1744*; d. pre 1799*
Sarah HATCH^{5}, b. 9 June 1747*
Clift HATCH^{5}, b. 23 June 1749*
Fisher HATCH^{5}, b. 28 June 1751*
Walter HATCH^{5}, b. 28 June 1751* (twins)
William HATCH^{5}, b. 3 Dec. 1754*
John HATCH^{5}, b. 17 June 1756*
Jabez HATCH^{5}, b. 20 Dec. 1759*
Harris HATCH^{5}, b. 30 Sept. 1760*
Sarah (HUMPHREYS) Cushing, b. c1722, Hingham; d. 30 May 1804, 82nd yr,Pembroke Ctr.cem.<MD 9:238>
CHILD OF Isaac HATCH^{4} & 2nd Sarah (HUMPHREYS) Cushing:
Isaac HATCH^{5}, b. 10 Nov. 1764* <Pembroke VR>
Sarah HATCH^{5} (Seth^{4}, Isaac^{3}), b. 3 Feb. 1764* (See p.433)
CHILDREN OF Isaac HATCH^{5} & Sarah HATCH: (6) <Pembroke VR>
Sarah HATCH^{6}, b. 23 Mar. 1792
Abigail HATCH^{6}, b. 30 June 1794
Isaac HATCH^{6}, b. 17 July 1796
Martin HATCH^{6}, b. 13 Dec. 1798
Josiah HATCH^{6}, b. 26 Sept. 1801
Caroline HATCH^{6}, b. 19 Jan. 1807
Josiah HATCH, b. c1711, d. 16 Sept. 1758, 47th yr, Pembroke Centre cem. <MD 9:238>
Mercy REDDING, (dau of Eben. & Mercy (Miller)), b. 30 Mar. 1708, Middleboro <MD 3:84>; d. 19 Sept

1779, Pembroke Centre cem. <MD 9:238>

CHILDREN OF Josiah HATCH & Mercy REDDING: (2) <Pembroke VR>

Zephaniah HATCH, b. 11 Dec. 1732 <:103>

Mercy HATCH, b. 23 May 1746 <:102>

Josiah HATCH, b. c1755, d. 2 Dec. 1834, ae 79y2m9d, Dingley cem, N. Duxbury <MD 11:57>, his wife:

Sarah ( ) HATCH, b. c1792, d. 30 Aug. 1848, ae 56y5m14d, Dingley cem., N. Duxbury <MD 11:57>

Job CLAPP[4] (*Jos.[3], Sam.[2], Tho.[1]), b. 6 Nov. 1712* <Clapp Gen.:113>

CHILD OF Job CLAPP & Penelope HATCH[4] (Isaac[3]):

Sarah CLAPP[5]*, b. 4 June 1759* <Scituate VR 1:74>

CHILDREN OF Seth HATCH[4] (Isaac[3]) & Mary TURNER*: (7) <Pembroke VR>**<43>**

Seth HATCH[5], b. 25 Aug. 1755 <:103>; d. 1836 (See <37> for poss. gravestone)

Penelope HATCH[5], b. 24 Nov. 1759 <:103>

Mercy HATCH[5], b. 14 Dec. 1761 <:102>

Sarah HATCH[5]*, b. 3 Feb. 1764* <:103> (m. Isaac Hatch[5], p.432)

Abigail HATCH[5], b. 16 Jan. 1766 <:100>; d. 16 Dec. 1831, unm.

Mary HATCH[5], b. 26 Aug. 1768 <:102>

Josiah HATCH[5], b. 5 Aug. 1773 <:102>

Desire HAWES[4] (Desire Gorham[3], Desire Howland[2]), b. last of Feb. 1681, Yarmouth <MD 2:207>; d. 8 Feb. 1723/4, Provincetown g.s. <MD 8:23> (wf of 2nd hus John Cowing)

CHILDREN OF Josiah HATCH[3] & Desire HAWES: (7) <1-5, Rochester VR>

Desire HATCH[4], b. 3 Feb. 1703*

Edmund HATCH[4], b. 10 July 1705*

Zerviah HATCH[4], b. 10 Sept. 1707*

Jabez HATCH[4], b. 21 May 1709*

Ebenezer HATCH[4], b. 8 Mar. 1710/1*; d. pre 13 June 1728

Josiah HATCH[4], b. ( )

Mary HATCH[4], b. ( )

Elizabeth OLDHAM, (dau of Tho. & (Mary Witherell)), b. 5 May 1677*

CHILDREN OF Samuel HATCH[3] & Elizabeth OLDHAM: (3) <Scituate VR>

Lydia HATCH[4], b. 24 May 1706

Ruth HATCH[4], b. 12 Oct. 1709

Samuel HATCH[4], b. 24 May 1723; d. pre 1766

CHILDREN OF John JONES[5] & Ruth HATCH[4]: (4) <See Warren Family micro #9>

John MITCHELL (*son of Wm.), d. pre 16 Oct. 1779* (adm.) <Plymouth Co.PR #14083, 27:45>

CHILDREN OF John MITCHELL & Lydia HATCH[4]: (4) <1-3, Scituate VR

John MITCHELL[5], b. 24 Mar. 1739

William MITCHELL[5], b. 3 Aug. 1741

Job MITCHELL[5], b. 19 July 1743

Elizabeth MITCHELL[5], b. ( )

MICRO #6 of 6

THOMAS DOTY[2] (Edward[1])

Mary CHURCHILL, (dau of John), b. 1 Aug. 1654, Plymouth <MD 17:71>; d. aft. 11 Oct. 1725 <Plymouth Co.Deeds 19:152> (widow of 2nd hus Henry Churchill)

CHILDREN OF Thomas DOTY[2] & Mary CHURCHILL: (3)

Martha DOTY[3], b. 1672

Hannah DOTY[3], b. Dec. 1675 <MD 1:143>

Thomas DOTY[3], b. 22 July 1679 <MD 21:59>; d. betw. 9 May 1721 (will) - 16 Feb. 1721/2 <Barnstable Co.PR 4:45-49>

Elizabeth HARLOW^{5} (Wm.^{4}, Rebecca Bartlett^{3}, Mary Warren^{2}), b. 3rd wk Feb. 1683, Plymouth <MD 1:207>; d. c1704/5

CHILD OF Thomas DOTY^{3} & Elizabeth HARLOW:

Thomas DOTY^{4}, b. 26 Jan. 1704, Plymouth <MD 4:112>

Elizabeth COOK^{5} (Richard^{4}, Deborah Hopkins^{3}, Gyles^{2}), b.? 30 Nov. 1704*, Eastham <MD 9:13>

CHILD OF Thomas DOTY^{4} & Elizabeth COOK:

Elizabeth DOTY^{5}, b. c1724, d. 8 Nov. 1756, 32nd yr

CHILD OF Perez TILSON & Elizabeth DOTY^{5}:

Elizabeth TILSON^{6}, b. c1746, d. 26 Oct. 1753, 7th yr

* * * * * * *

FOOTNOTES

<1> p.413, There are several variations of the Doty surname (Dotte, Dolton, Dotten, etc.), the most common being Doten. A child might be born a Doty but may use Doten when marrying (or vice versa), which in most cases means his children would carry the surname used at marriage. Keep this in mind when you come across both a Doty and Doten surname for the same person.

<2> p.413, Joseph Doty^{2} (late of Rochester) was deceased by 18 Sept. 1734 when his 2nd wife Sarah petitioned the courts. Records such as this are sometimes all we have to give us insight into our ancestors so are worth mentioning. The petition reads in part:

> "...That wheras my sd Decased Husband In his lifetime by Reason of old age & adverse Providences was Reduced to such Circumstances as to be obliged to live with & be supported In a measure by his son Joseph Doty & Dyed there, & so all the moveables we had was In our sd sons House and since My sd Husband's Death I Cannot Comfortably Dwell with him but might live with more Comfort with my own son Joseph Edwards, could I obtain such Beding & other necessary household stuff as My Husband & I had at his Decease which he my sd son In Law Joseph Doty withholds (as I apprehend) very Unjustly from me, Knowing I am through my own Poverty unable to take administration..."

<Plymouth Co.PR #6624> See <33> for an additional note concerning Joseph's death date.

<3> p.413, d. 8 July 1745, Plymouth. <MD 15:213>

<4> p.413, The records state Israel Holmes & Joseph Truant "were cast away saleing into Plimouth harbor & were drowned...& buried at Plimouth".

<5> p.413, Ebenezer & Margaret were married 18 Sept. 1702, a year and a half after the birth of their first child. The Church Records state: "Ebenezer Sherman & Margaret Decro being guilty of ye sin of...together made their peace with this church Sept. 28, 1701. <MD 11:240>

The Files contain a transcript of the court record and it is interesting to note the stand the courts took to illegitimacy. Whenever possible they made sure the town would not be liable should the mother not be able to support her child. Ebenezer was ordered to provide Margaret with financial support until the child reached eight years of age. (It was generally accepted that by this age a child could be put out to work and earn his keep.) The record from the Plymouth Quarter Sessions, 1687-1721, dated the third Tues. June 1701, reads:

> (p.176) "Margaret Decrow abovesd convict by her own confession of having a Bastard child by fornication Is Sentenced to pay a fine of three pound and ten shillings fees & charges or be Publickly whipped ten stripes who chose the former & payd sd fine & was dismist.
>
> Ordered by the Court that Ebenezer Sherman of Marshfield putative father of the Bastard child lately Borne of ye Body of Margaret Decrow Pay unto her the sum of two shillings pr weeke from ye day of the Birth of sd child untill it comes to ye age of two years & thenceforth the sum of eighteene pence per weeke till sd child shall attaine to ye age of Eight years Provided sd child shall so long live (p.177) & the same to be paid in money or other pay to ye acceptance of ye sd Margaret The sd weekly sums to be paid quarterly vizt at four payments in ye year in equall proportions unless the sd Ebenezer shall otherways with the concent of one of ye next Justices of the peace and overseers of ye poore in said Town of Marshfield Dispose of & provide for sd child. And sd Ebenezer to become bound in the sum of forty pound with sureties for ye performance of the abovesaid order....who became bound accordingly."

<6> p.414, The suggestion is made that these were a first and second wife of John Sherman^{4} (Ebenezer^{3}).

<7> p.414, Along with these birth entries in the Marshfield VR 2:84 is an entry immediately preceeding Huldah's birth in 1750: "Sarah Bruster alias Wormwood the Daughter of Elisabeth Wormwood was Born March ye 3rd 1743". (Illegitimate child?)

<8> p.415, This entry follows the blank chart for William Sherman^{4} (Eben.^{3}) but does not identify him.

<9> p.415, The six Wormall children are listed without dates, viz: Desire, Josiah, Mehitable, Mercy, Samuel & Ichabod.

<10> p.416, The six remaining Hall children are listed in pencil with birth year only, viz:

William, 1726; Thomas(?), 1728; Joseph, 1733; Sarah, 1735; Mercy 1739 and Levi, 1744.
<11> p.416, d. 4 Dec. 1834, 74th yr, Marshfield g.s. <MD 8:197>.
<12> p.416, Probably the Alice Hall who d. 4 Jan. 1840, ae 39y5m, Marshfield g.s. <MD 8:197>
<13> p.416, The remaining six Hall children are listed in pencil without dates, viz: Alice, Nancy, Emeline, Luke, Malinda and Matilda (who d. 10 Nov. 1835, ae 1y6m, Marshfield g.s. <MD 8:197>)
<14> p.417, A letter from the Town Clerk of Marshfield dated 1897 states Tobias was born in Scarboro ME. His source was "Col. H.D. Oakman who visited him that afternoon".
<15> p.419, On the following page her death date is given as 25 Oct. 1842, ae 74, unm. <Marshfield VR 2:deaths>
<16> p.419, Mercy m. 1st Matthew Simonton but no children are listed.
<17> p.419, He m. 1st Persis Rogers^{5} (Amos^{4}, Tim.$^{3-2}$, John^{1}), "not Mayflower". His second wife was his 1st cousin Louisa Oakman^{6} (Tobias^{5}, San.^{4}, Eliz Doty^{3}, Edw.^{2}), who was b. 30 Nov. 1749 <Marshfield VR>. No chldren are listed.
<18> p.420, The Files give a short transcription of the Plymouth Quarter Sessions 1687-1721, p.55, dated 3rd Tues. Sept. 1690 as follows:

> "Martha Doten of Plimouth Daughter of Tho. Doten presented for comitting fornication and thereof Convict p^{r} her own confession fined five pound and pay court fees: or be publickly whipt."

<19> p.420, Three children are listed without dates on Nathaniel Morton's chart, viz: Lemuel, Mary and Mercy. They would have been born after 1740 when he married Mary. (See <20>)
<20> p.420, On the page immediately following the chart of Nathaniel Morton^{4} is a listing of three children to "Nathaniel Morton & Mary ( )". Although not identified they are probably the same.
<21> p.420, Lemuel is not identified, but is probably the son of Nathaniel Morton^{4} & Mary Ellis (daughter named "Mary Ellis Morton").
<22> p.421, Annals of Winchester CT by John Boyed. 1873. p.190,191. Alsto stated is Zepheniah came from England and settled in Wethersfield. Sons Moses & Simeon moved from Wethersfield to Winchester c1791, Simeon moved from there to Vernon NY c1800.
<23> p.422, The remaining eight Jackson children are listed without dates, viz: Elizabeth, Joseph, John, Sarah, Phebe, Jemima, Rebecca and James.
<24> p.422, The remaining five Hall children are listed in pencil without dates, viz: Joshua, Benjamin, Elias, Stephen and Peter.
<25> p.422, The remaining three Allen children are listed without dates, viz: Ovid, Oscar and Amanda.
<26> p.423, A check of MD 5:100 shows the VR include the name "Harlow" added above Hannah's name. Since Bowman states Elisha m. Hannah Horton not Harlow, an explanation for the discrepancy was found in MD 19:177. Bowman discovered that William T. Davis (author of Ancient Landmarks of Plymouth) made a copy of the vital records for the town and when doing so, added the word "Harlow" above Hannah's name. Bowman goes on to say that Davis repeated this error in the second edition of his book.
<27> p.423, Is she Phebe Finney^{5} (Jon^{4}, Eliz. Waren^{3}, Jos.^{2}), b. 8 Feb. 1724/5, Plymouth? <MD 13:114>
<28> p.425, He is not identified but is possibly Joshua Mors^{4} (Eliz. Doty^{3}).
<29> p.425, Plymouth g.s. <Burial Hill by Drew:143>
<30> p.426, Eleven Doten children are mentioned in James' will (cited within), viz: Hope, James, Isaac, John, Elizabeth, Daniel, Mary, Thomas, Lucy, Lois and Elenor.
<31> p.426, Next to Jacob's name in pencil are the words "child of Lydia Jackson?" On the following page is an entry from the Plymouth Quarter Sesions, c1718-1723, p.12 as follows:

> "1st Tues. Mar. 1719, John Doty Senr of Plimton Moving to ye Court Concerning ye Child of Lydia Jackson of Plymouth of which he was Convict to be ye reputed Father at ye Sessions of this Court on ye 1st Tuesday of March 1718."

<32> p.426, No children are listed for Jacob Doty, however the division of his estate, Feb. 1753, mentions widow Deborah and the following six children, viz: Solomon (eldest son), Hannah (wf of Seth Fuller Jr.), Jemima, Zephaniah, Sarah and Jacob. <Plymouth Co.PR #6587, 13:98>
<33> p.427, Joseph m. Deborah Ellis, c1674. <Mayflower Increasings:57> On the same page with Deborah's death date is written "Joseph Doty, d. 21 July 1825, ae 74 yrs". Is this an error for 1725, referring to Deborah's husband Joseph Doty^{2}?? (His age fits.)<Rochester General Rcds.5:553> (See <2>).
<34> p.427, The files suggest he may be the Barnabas Doty whose estate was adm. 21 May 1759 by his "former wife Sarah, now the wife of Barzillai Hammond". No children are mentioned. <Plymouth Co.PR #6618, 15:190,191>
<35> p.428, A second marriage is indicated on Samuel Doty^{4}'s chart with no name given. The entries for the children of Samuel and Elizabeth appear to be the second marriage but it is not stated as so in the files.
<36> p.428, Ruth Mendall, b. 20 Sept. 1675, Marshfield <MD 3:42>, d. aft. 8 Feb. 1720 (father's will) <PN&Q 2:55>.
<37> p.429, The files contain an interesting letter dated 27 Oct. 1908 from Mr. Israel Hatch of Marshfield, concerning the burial site and gravestones of Isaac Hatch, his wife Penelope and some of their children. The letter in part reads:

> "Some years ago they stood upon the top of a small hill used for a burial place...on the farm first occupied by Samuel Hatch, father of Isaac. This farm was bought of (Cornet?) Robert Stetson by Walter Hatch and given to his son Samuel. It is in the extreme North end of Pembroke, partly in Marshfield, the town line running through the farm...It is about 2 1/2 miles from Hanover Station...the sixth house lot on the Westerly side of Water St...BUT the place has had quite a number of different owners in the last 100

> years. The burial lot was not enclosed and has been used as a cow pasure for many years and nearly all the stones are gone. I copied some of them some years ago and was astonished when visiting it two or three years ago to find so little left. I am not sure that the stones can be found today but think likely fragments may remain...several graves apparently of the ancestors, marked by common field stones at the head and foot. I can imagine Samuel the first and Mary Dotey are there and possibly Walter Hatch and Elizabeth as there was no other burial place, as far as we have knowledge, within several miles. But I suppose this may not interest you."

(One can only imagine Bowman's response to this last line, I'm sure he would have been extremely interested in finding the gravestone of Mary Doty[2]!!)

The gravestones he copied were the following: Isaac Hatch, d. 1 Nov. 1759, 73rd yr; Penelope, wife of Isaac, d. 1775, ae 79; Samuel Hatch, 1776; Sarah Hatch, 1791; Capt. Seth Hatch, 1836, ae 82 and his wife, 1835, ae 77.

The farm mentioned by Israel Hatch in his letter above, is also mentioned in the will of Isaac Hatch (1756): "The Farm on which I now Dwell Both upland & meadow...which I purchased of my Father Sam[ll] Hatch Deces[d]" was left to his son Samuel. (The list of expenses in the probate records includes "a pare of Grave Stones". (See <43> for further data.)

<38> p.430, The remaining five Spear children are listed in pencil without dates, viz: Joseph, Daniel, Oliver, Paul and Christiana.

<39> p.431, Thomas Reynolds married Elizabeth Turner, but the files are not certain if Elizabeth was Betty Turner[5], daughter of Japhet. Line of descent for these children is not given in the files due to this uncertainty.

<40> p.431, An accompanying pencilled note reads "Mitchell says Elizabeth dau. of Wm. (d.1747) and Eleanor".

<41> p.432, See <37>.

<42> p.432, Mayflower Source Records by Roberts, source for birthdates as follows: Penelope (p.364), Seth (p.429), Lydia (p.368), Mary (p.371), Sarah (p.374) and Samuel (p.376). See <37> for possible gravesites of Seth, Sarah and Samuel.

<43> p.433, The files later give some additonal data concerning the gravestone mentioned in <37> above. This data also appears to be from Mr. Israel Hatch. First is a picture (poorly reproduced) with the caption "Old Hatch Cemetery, Two Mile, Pembroke Mass." Next is a page with the following gravestone inscriptions which give a little more detail than that given in <37>:

"Erected in memory of Mr. Isaac Hatch
He died November 1st 1759 in ye 73rd year of his age
Erected in memory of Mrs. Penelope
latter wife of Mr. Isaac Hatch
She died Jan. 13 1775 in the 77th year of her age
In Memory of Capt. Seth Hatch
he died Aug. 12th 1799 aged 71yrs9mos12days
In memory of Mrs. Mary Hatch
Wife of Capt. Seth Hatch
She died Oct. 19th 1802 71st yr of her age"

* * * * * * *

REFERENCE LIST

GENEALOGICAL ARTICLES PERTAINING TO DOTY/DOTEN FAMILY RESEARCH

Mayflower Descendant (MD) (1899-1937)

3:87-91 - Will & Inventory of Edward Doty & wife
4:65-67 - Deed: John Doty[2]
4:171-74 - Estates of William Sherman & Israel Holmes
4:233-34 - Will & Inventory of Thomas Doty[2]
5:111-13 - Samuel Hatch's Wife Mary Doty[2]
5:210-14 - Estate of Edward Doty[2]
6:77-82 - Will & Inventory of John Doty[2]
7:29-33 - Will & Inventory of Samuel Hatch, 1728
12:48-52 - Will & Inventory of Desire (Doty[2])(Sherman)(Holmes) Standish
14:127 - Wives of Thomas Doty[4-3]
15:129 - Family Record of Eleazer Morton
- (m. Lucy Doty[5] (Sam.[4]))
19:190-92 - Will of John Nelson
- (dau. Mehitable m. John Doty[3])
20:27-31 - The Wills of John Doten[3] And His Widow
21:97-101 - Hannah Hatch[3]'s Three Husbands Japhet Turner, Ebenezer Tinkham & Capt.Ichabod Turner
22:36-37 - Will of Tobias Oakman
- (m. Elizabeth Doty[3])
22:155-56 - Will of Ezekiel Hatch[3]
25:133-35 - Will of William Sherman[3]
25:164-75 - Estates of Isaac Doty[3] of Plymouth And His Sons Neriah[4] And Ichabod[4]
27:96 - Deed: Faith (Clark) Doty
27:97-101 - Estate of Josiah Hatch[3] of Rochester MA
30:165-71 - Will of Ebenezer Sherman[3] of Marshfield MA

32:5-9 - Estate of Israel Holmes of Marshfield The Second Husband of Desire Doty[2]
33:114-15 - Guardians of John Doty[2]'s Children
PN&Q 2:55 - Will of John Mendall
- (dau. Ruth m. Theophilus Doty[3])
PN&Q 4:36-7 - Family Records From the Barrows Papers

Mayflower Descendant (MD) (1985-1990)

39:187-94 - Thomas Caswell of Taunton & His Descendants

Mayflower Quarterly (MQ) (1975-1990)

47:23-29 - The Elusive Luces - A Doty Line
- (William Luce[6])
49:135-37 - Ebenezer[4] & Lydia (Delano)(Wormall) Delano, A New Sampson Line
51:15-27 - Josiah & Desire (Hawes[4]) Hatch, A Howland-Doty Line
57:10-15 - The Winegar Family, A Doty And Howland Line

Miscellaneous

NEHGR 51:35 - Jabez Hatch, Ancestry & Descendants
NEHGR 119:161 - Lt. John & Elizabeth (Freeman) Ellis of Sandwich MA
TAG 36:1-11 - Notes on the Doty & Churchill Families

* * * * * * * * * *

Now available: Mayflower Families In Progress: Edward Doty Of The Mayflower and His Descendants for Four Generations (MFIP), pub. by General Society of Mayflower Descendants. 1991.

- (*Note: As this publication was not available at the time the Doty family was transcribed, it should be referred to by the reader.*)

FRANCIS EATON

MICRO #1 Of 4

Francis EATON[1], d. pre 8 Nov. 1633, Plymouth (inv.) <PCR 1:19, MD 1:197>

Sarah ( ) EATON, d. 1621, Plymouth <MD 1:15>

CHILD OF Francis EATON[1] & 1st Sarah ( ):<1>

Samuel EATON[2], b. 1620, England

CHILDREN OF Francis EATON[1] & 3rd Christian ( ): (3) <Plymouth><1>

Rachel EATON[2], b. c1625; d. pre Oct. 1661*

Benjamin EATON[2], b.. aft. 1 June 1627 <Cattle Division, MD 1:153>; d. 16 Jan. 1711/2, Plympton, "aged" <MD 2:140,10:113><2>

Child, b. ( ), d. aft. 1650, unm.

BENJAMIN EATON[2] (Francis[1])

Sarah HOSKINS, d. aft. July 1690 (will of son Wm.)<3>

CHILDREN OF Benjamin EATON[2] & Sarah HOSKINS: (4)<4>

Benjamin EATON[3], b.? pre 29 Oct. 1664; d. betw. 3 or 23 Apr. 1745 (will) - 20 Dec. 1745 (prob.) of Kingston <Plymouth Co.PR #7036, 10:70,73><5>

William EATON[3], b. pre July 1669; d. betw. July 1690 (will) - 18 Mar. 1690/1 (inv.) <Plymouth Co. PR, MD 12:227><6>

Ebenezer EATON[3], b. pre 1685*

Rebecca EATON[3], b. c1675, d. 13 Nov. 1770, 95th yr, Plympton g.s. <MD 11:116>

Mary COOMBS, b. c1665, d. 2 July 1728, 63rd yr, Plympton g.s. <MD 10:113><7>

CHILDREN OF Benjamin EATON[3] & Mary COOMBS: (11) <1-5, Plymouth VR, MD 2:78>

William EATON[4], b. 1 June 1691 ("non compos mentis" in father's will)

Hannah EATON[4], b. 10 Feb. 1692; d. 4 Mar. 1723/4, Plympton <MD 2:141>

Jabez EATON[4], b. 8 Feb. 1693; d. 19 May 1722, Plympton g.s. <MD 2:141,10:113>

Sarah EATON[4], b. 20 Oct. 1695; d. 13 Sept. 1737, Plympton g.s. <MD 10:112>

John EATON[4], b. 6 Oct. 1697; d. 30 Mar. 1766, Halifax g.s. <MD 12:243>

Benjamin EATON[4], b. c1698, d. 3 May 1751, ae 53, Kingston g.s. <MD 7:85>

Mary EATON[4], b. c1699, d. 14 May 1773, 74th yr, Nemasket cem., Middleboro <MD 15:7>

Francis EATON[4], b. ( ); d. betw. 3 Apr. 1745 - 15 June 1748 (div. father's estate)

Rev. Elisha EATON[4], b. c1702, d. 22 Apr. 1764, 62nd yr, Harpswell ME g.s.

Elizabeth EATON[4], b. ( )

David EATON[4], b. c1708, d. 8 July 1759, 51st yr, Kingston g.s. <MD 7:85>

Susanna (LEWIS) Beal, b. c1669, d. 13 Apr. 1739, ae 70, Kingston g.s. <MD 7:85> (2nd wf Ben. Eaton[3])

CHILDREN OF Jesse SNOW & Mary EATON: (3)<8>

Sarah SNOW, b. 20 Mar. 1758 <MD 19:176>

Bethania SNOW, b. 6 Sept. 1760 <MD 22:152>

Lavinia SNOW, b. 9 Apr. 1762

CHILDREN OF Andrew BEARCE & Margaret DAWES, (dau of Jonathan & Lois): (8) <Halifax VR:44>

Lois BEARS, b. 30 Oct. 1737; d. 30 Oct. 1747 <VR:2>

Margaret BEARS, b. 31 Jan. 1739/40

Ruth BEARS, b. 30 Oct. 1742

Lydia BEARS, b. 15 Nov. 1744

Experience BEARS, b. 1 Feb. 1746/7

Deborah BEARS, b. 26 Sept. 1749

Abthiah BEARS, b. 22 Aug. 1752

Andrew BEARS, b. 19 Feb. 1756

John TILSON^{3} (Ephraim^{2}, Edmund^{1}) b. c1672, d. pre 2 May 1718 (prob.)

CHILDREN OF John TILSON & Lydia RICKARD: (6) <Tilson Gen.:388>

Timothy TILSON, b. 24 Feb. 1707

Mary TILSON, b. 13 Dec. 1708 (m. Ben. Eaton$^{4-3}$)

Lydia TILSON, b. 9 May 1711

John TILSON, b. 23 Mar. 1713; d. 18 July 1785

Jonathan TILSON, b. 29 Sept. 1715

Patience TILSON, b. 18 Jan. 1718

Nehemiah STURTEVANT^{3} (Sam.$^{2-1}$), b. c1681 (bpt.1689), Plymouth, d. 22 Aug. 1744, 63rd yr, Plympton g.s. <MD 11:164>

Ruth SAMSON^{3} (George^{2}, Abraham^{1}), b. 22 Dec. 1684, Plympton <MD 5:183>; d. May 1766, Plympton g.s. <MD 11:164>

CHILDREN OF Nehemiah STURTEVANT & Ruth SAMSON: (10) <Plympton VR <MD 3:164>

Cornelius STURTEVANT, b. 10 Nov. 1704 <also on Plymouth VR>; d. 17 Dec. 1769*, Plympton g.s. (m. Eliz Eaton^{4}, see p.440)

Mercy STURTEVANT, b. 24 May 1706; d. 2 Aug. 1741 <MD 7:85>; d. 2 Aug. 1741, Kingston g.s. <MD 7:85> (m. Ben.Eaton$^{4-3}$ below)

Paul STURTEVANT, b. 24 Oct. 1708

Nehemiah STURTEVANT, b. 18 Nov. 1710

Noah STURTEVANT, b. 17 Feb. 1712/3; d. 10 Aug. 1715 <MD 11:164>

Ruth STURTEVANT, b. 28 Apr. 1715

Noah STURTEVANT, b. 7 Oct. 1717; d. 1 Jan. 1792 <MD 11:164>

Abia STURTEVANT, b. 30 July 1720

George STURTEVANT, b. 14 Oct. 1725

Lusanna STURTEVANT, b. 18 Apr. 1728

Capt. Joseph VAUGHAN, b. c1653, d. 2 Mar. 1733/4, Nemasket cem., Middleboro <MD 15:104>

Joanna THOMAS, b. c1657, d. 11 Apr. 1718, ae 61, Middleboro <MD 5:37>

CHILDREN OF Capt. Joseph VAUGHAN & Joanna THOMAS: (11) <Middleboro VR; 1-7, MD 1:221>

Elisha VAUGHAN, b. 7 Feb. 1680; d. 23 May 1724 <MD 4:75>

Jabez VAUGHAN, b. 30 Apr. 1682

George VAUGHAN, b. 3 Oct. 1683

Ebenezer VAUGHAN, b. 22 Feb. 1684

Elizabeth VAUGHAN, b. 7 Mar. 1686

Hannah VAUGHAN, b. 18 Nov. 1688; d. 6 Apr. 1715, Middleboro, unm. <MD 5:37>

Joseph VAUGHAN, b. 2 Oct. 1690; d. 5 Apr. 1718, Middleboro <MD 4:75>

John VAUGHAN, b. 8 Sept. 1692 <MD 2:104>

Mary VAUGHAN, b. 6 Oct. 1694 <MD 2:104>

Josiah VAUGHAN, b. 2 Feb. 1698/9 <MD 2:104>; d. 13 Feb. 1723/4, Middleboro <MD 5:38>

Joanna VAUGHAN, b. 26 Jan. 1701/2 <MD 2:104>

CHILDREN OF Zachariah SOULE^{4} & Mary EATON^{4} (Ben.^{3}): (9) <See Soule Family Micro #4>

CHILDREN OF Benjamin EATON^{4} (Ben.^{3}) & 1st Mercy STURTEVANT (above): (5) <Kingston VR 1:9>

Ruth EATON^{5}, b. 21 Mar. 1726/7; d. 21 May 1727 <MD 10:113>

Jabez EATON^{5}, b. 7 Aug. 1728, d. 26 Sept. 1728

Noah EATON^{5}, b. 29 May 1734; d. 30 Nov. 1798 <MD 10:113>

Mary EATON^{5}, b. 6 Mar. 1734/5; d. 5 May 1735 <MD 7:85>

Seth EATON^{5}, b. 1 Jan. 1738/9; d. 20 Feb. 1823*, Purchade cem., Middleboro

CHILDREN OF Benjamin EATON^{4} & 2nd Mary TILSON (above): (3)

James EATON^{5}, bpt. 15 Apr. 1744*

Benjamin EATON^{5}, b. pre 6 Mar. 1749*; d. Mar. 1770*

Thaddeus EATON^{5}, b. ( ); d. pre 26 Apr. 1757 (div. father's estate)<Plymouth Co.PR #7037, 14:260>

Bethiah ( ) EATON, b. c1729, d. 16 Dec. 1803*, 74th yr, Purchade cem., Middleboro (wf of Seth^{5})

Deborah ( ) EATON, b. c1728, d. 25 July 1809, Kingston g.s. <MD 7:87>**<9>**

CHILDREN OF David EATON^{4} (Ben.^{3}) & Deborah ( ): (6) <Kingston VR>

Lot EATON^{5}, b. 18 May 1744; d. 1822* <Kingston ChR>

Jabez EATON^{5}, b. 2 Aug. 1746; d. aft. 7 May 1810*

Job EATON^{5}, b. 26 Oct. 1749; d. May 1811*, delirium & fever <Kingston ChR>

Consider EATON^{5}, b. 1 Mar. 1752; d. 25 Dec. 1776, Kingston g.s. <MD 7:85>

Joshua EATON^{5}, b. 12 July 1755; d. 23 Dec. 1777, Canada, bur. Kingston <MD 7:85>

Eunice EATON^{5}, b. 12 Apr. 1759; d. 1799* <Kingston ChR> (wf of Amos Cooke^{6})

MICRO #2 OF 4

Elizabeth EVERSON, b. 13 Mar. 1732* <Kingston VR>; d. 26 Dec. 1803, Kingston g.s. <MD 7:85> (wf of Lot Eaton^{5})

William CLOUGH, (*son of Eben. & Thankful), b. 21 Feb. 1706* <Boston Rcd.com.24:45>; d. pre 1734

Katherine BELCHER, (dau of Gregory & Eliz.), b. 24 Dec. 1706 <Braintree VR:686>; d. 12 Apr. 1767

CHILD OF William CLOUGH & Katherine BELCHER:

William CLOUGH, b. 26 Oct. 1733 <Braintree VR:769>

CHILDREN OF Elisha EATON^{4} (Ben.^{3}) & Katherine (BELCHER) Clough: (7) <Braintree VR>**<10>**

Elisha EATON^{5}, b. 12 Sept. 1735 <:772>

Samuel EATON^{5}, b. 22 Mar. 1736/7 <:776>; d. 5 Nov. 1822*, unm.

Mary EATON^{5}, b. 1 Dec. 1738 <:779>; d. 9 Oct. 1793*, unm.

Elizabeth EATON^{5}, b. 9 May 1740 <:782>; d. 13 Jan. 1806*, unm.

Hannah EATON^{5}, b. 31 May 1742 <:785>

Thaddeus EATON^{5}, b. 1 Apr. 1744 <:788>, d.y.

Thaddeus EATON^{5}, b. 26 Feb. 1747/8 <:794>

CHILD OF Cornelius STURTEVANT & Elizabeth EATON^{4} (Ben.^{3}):

Silas STURTEVANT^{5}, b. 27 June 1730, Plympton <MD 1:177>

Thankful ALDEN^{4} (John^{3}, Jos.^{2}), b. 30 May 1706, Middleboro <MD 2:201>; d. 29 Oct. 1732, Middleboro <MD 13:5>

CHILDREN OF Francis EATON^{4} (Ben.^{3}) & 1st Thankful ALDEN: (2)

Joseph EATON^{5}, b. 26 Nov. 1728* <Kingston VR:68>; d. aft. 20 Mar. 1784* <Plymouth Co.Deeds 67:80>

Jabez EATON^{5}, b. 29 Jan. 1730/1, Middleboro <MD 12:131>

CHILDREN OF Francis EATON^{4} & 2nd Lydia FULLER: (7) <Middleboro VR; 3-7, MD 16:15>**<11>**

Silvanus EATON^{5}, b. 8 May 1734 <MD 16:14>

Thankful EATON^{5}, b. 21 Dec. 1735 <MD 16:14>

John EATON^{5}, b. 12 Aug. 1737

Mary EATON^{5}, b. 16 Feb. 1738/9

Elijah EATON^{5}, b. 7 Nov. 1740; d. 20 Jan. 1831*, N. Middleboro g.s.**<12>**

Benjamin EATON^{5}, b. 26 Mar. 1742

Susanna EATON^{5}, b. 13 Sept. 1743

Sarah SHAW, b. c1742, d. 4 July 1819*, 77th yr, N. Middleboro g.s. (wf of Elijah Eaton^{5})

CHILDREN OF Joseph EATON^{5} & Hannah CROSSMAN, (dau of Barnabas & Hannah): (4) <Middleboro VR>

Joel EATON^{6}, b. 3 Aug. 1751 <MD 26:30>; d. 19 Oct. 1851*, N. Middleboro g.s.

Abigail EATON^{6}, b. 14 June 1754 < " ">

Francis EATON^{6}, b. 29 Oct. 1756 < " ">

Mary EATON^{6}, b. 23 Sept. 1760 < " ">; d. 5 Mar. 1857, Norton MA <Mass.VR 111:129>

Lucy LEONARD, b. c1748, d. 12 Mar. 1842*, ae 94, N. Middleboro g.s.

CHILDREN OF Joel EATON^{6} & Lucy LEONARD*: (5*)

Apollos EATON^{7}, b. 1775

Polycarpus EATON^{7}, b. 1777

Alfred EATON^{7}, b. 1779, d. 15 Aug. 1840, ae 61

Cynthia EATON^{7}, b. 1782

Caroline EATON^{7}, b. 1787

CHILDREN OF Apollos EATON^{7} & Parna LEACH: (9)**<13>**

John SHAW, d. 9 Apr. 1834*, Foxboro (m. Mary Eaton^{6} (Jos.^{5}))

Benjamin BRYANT, d. 4 May 1724 <Plympton VR, MD 2:141>**<14>**

CHILDREN OF Benjamin BRYANT & Hannah EATON^{4} (Ben.^{3}): (6) <Plympton VR, MD 3:93>**<15>**

Phebe BRYANT^{5}, b. 18 Sept. 1713; d. 9 Oct. 1779, Green cem., Middleboro <MD 14:131>

Mercy BRYANT^{5}, b. 3 Jan. 1714

Hannah BRYANT^{5}, b. 24 Mar. 1716/7

Micah BRYANT^{5}, b. 2 Apr. 1719

Jerusha BRYANT^{5}, b. 7 Feb. 1721/2; d. 20 or 25 Apr. 1743*, Bridgewater

Jesse BRYANT^{5}, b. 1723, bpt. 21 July 1723*, Kingston

CHILDREN OF David CURTIS & Hannah BRYANT^{5}: (5) <Halifax VR:43>

Japhet CURTIS^{6}, b. 4 Dec. 1735

Jesse CURTIS^{6}, b. 29 Nov. 1737

Ezekiel CURTIS^{6}, b. 19 Oct. 1739

David CURTIS^{6}, b. 13 Nov. 1741

Jonathan CURTIS^{6}, b. 30 Apr. 1744

CHILDREN OF Solomon LEACH & 1st Jerusha BRYANT^{5} (Hannah Eaton^{4}): (2*) <Bridgewater VR>

Abisha LEACH^{6}, b. 7 Mar. 1739, d. 10 Jan. 1743 <Bridgewater VR>

Tabitha LEACH^{6}, b. 28 May 1742, d. 6 Jan. 1742/3

CHILDREN OF Solomon LEACH & 2nd Hannah LEACH: (7) <Bridgewater VR>

Hannah LEACH, b. 8 May 1744, d.y.

Jerusha LEACH, b. 23 Feb. 1746

Solomon LEACH, b. 5 Mar. 1750

Israel LEACH, b. 19 Oct. 1752

Hannah LEACH, b. 6 June 1755

Susanna LEACH, b. 18 Aug. 1758

Joseph LEACH, b. 8 Nov. 1760

David SEARS^{4} (*Josiah^{3}, Silas^{2}, Richard^{1}), b. 2 Oct. 1710*, Yarmouth; d. 20 Aug. 1788*, Middleboro <Sears Gen.:108>

CHILDREN OF David SEARS & Phebe BRYANT^{5} (Hannah Eaton^{4}): (4) <Middleboro VR, MD 13:6>

Zebedee SEARS^{6}, b. 26 June 1734

Huldah SEARS^{6}, b. 10 Aug. 1737

Abner SEARS^{6},b . 19 Feb. 1738/9

David SEARS^{6}, b. 25 June 1741

Hannah WESTON, b. 21 Apr. 1723*, d. 14 Apr. 1802* (*2nd wf of David Sears)

CHILDREN OF Ebenezer EATON^{3} & Hannah RICKARD^{3} (Giles$^{2-1}$): (6) <Plymouth, MD 2:165>

Ebenezer EATON^{4}, b. 17 Sept. 1702

Benjamin EATON^{4}, b. 23 Nov. 1704

Mercy EATON^{4}, b. 15 Mar. 1705/6

Elisha EATON^{4}, b. 11 Oct. 1708; d. betw. 3 Nov. 1737 (will) - 3 July 1738 (letter) <Plymouth Co. PR #7043>

Gideon EATON^{4}, b. 5 Feb. 1711/2

Joanna EATON^{4}, b. 29 Apr. 1716

Josiah RICKARD^{3} (Giles$^{2-1}$), b. c1672, d. 22 Jan. 1765, 93rd yr, Plympton g.s. <MD 11:115>

CHILDREN OF Josiah RICKARD & Rebecca EATON^{3}: (6) <1-3, Plymouth VR; 4-6, Plympton VR>

Giles RICKARD^{4}, b. 14 Oct. 1700 <MD 3:13>

Benjamin RICKARD^{4}, b. 20 Feb. 1702 <MD 3:14>; d. 28 Mar. 1788, Plympton g.s. <MD 11:115>
Josiah RICKARD^{4}, b. 21 Oct. 1703 <MD 3:14>
Desire RICKARD^{4}, b. 18 Feb. 1706 <MD 3:163>
Rebecca RICKARD^{4}, b. 24 Aug. 1708 <MD 3:163>; d. 29 Mar. 1791 <Bridgewater Epitaphs:210>
David RICKARD^{4}, b. 24 Dec. 1711 <MD 3:163>
Thankful PINCHEON, b. c1702, d. 10 Feb. 1794, 92nd yr, Plympton g.s. <MD 11:116>
CHILDREN OF Benjamin RICKARD^{4} & Thankful PINCHEON: (2)
Elijah RICKARD^{5}, b. c1751, d. 11 July 1747, Plympton g.s. <MD 11:115>
Benjamin RICKARD^{5}, b. c1754, d. 10 July 1747, Plympton g.s. <MD 11:115>
Seth ALLEN, b. 1710, Bridgewater, d. 1760
CHILDREN OF Seth ALLEN & Rebecca RICKARD^{4}: (3)[<16>]
Betty ALLEN^{5}, b. 1739
Mary ALLEN^{5}, b. 1743
Rebecca ALLEN^{5}, b. 1743
Thomas WHITMAN, b. c1702, d. 15 Dec. 1788, 87th yr <Bridgewater Epitaphs:201> (2nd hus of Rebecca Rickard^{4})

SAMUEL EATON^{2} (Francis^{1})

CHILDREN OF Samuel EATON^{2} & 1st Elizabeth ( ): (2)
Dau., b. ( )
Dau., b. ( )
CHILDREN OF Samuel EATON^{2} & 2nd Martha BILLINGTON^{3} (Francis^{2}): (3)
Sarah EATON^{3}, b. pre 1663
Samuel EATON^{3}, b. c1663, d. 8 Mar. 1723/4, 61st yr, Middleboro <MD 4:74>
Mercy EATON^{3}, b. ( )
CHILDREN OF Samuel EATON^{3} & Elizabeth FULLER^{3} (Sam.$^{2-1}$): (4) <Middleboro VR, MD 2:42>
Mercy EATON^{4}, b. 16 Dec. 1695; d. pre 3 June 1724 (deed) <MD 12:227>
Keziah EATON^{4}, b. 16 May 1700; d. 7 Feb. 1709/10 <MD 2:159>
Elizabeth EATON^{4}, b. 26 July 1701; d. 5 May 1780, Middleboro
Barnabas EATON^{4}, b. 12 Apr. 1703; d. pre 7 Dec. 1796*
Mehitable ALDEN^{4} (Jos.$^{3-2}$), b. 18 Oct. 1707, Bridgewater <MD 3:143>; d. 11 Apr. 1739, Middleboro <MD 15:24>
CHILDREN OF Barnabas EATON^{4} & 1st Mehitable ALDEN: (5) <Middleboro VR>
Hannah EATON^{5}, b. 29 Oct. 1730 <MD 12:131>
Samuel EATON^{5}, b. 16 May 1732 <MD 12:131>; d. 18 Jan. 1820*, "Old cem. in woods on Centre St."
Mary EATON^{5}, b. 14 May 1735 <MD 14:244>
Sarah EATON^{5}, b. 16 June 1737 <MD 14:244>
Seth EATON^{5}, b. 6 Apr. 1739 <MD 14:245>
Elizabeth CLEMANS, b. c1716, d. 7 Dec. 1796, 80th yr <Middleboro VR 4:130>
CHILDREN OF Barnabas EATON^{4} & 2nd Elizabeth CLEMANS: (8) <Middleboro VR>
Lot EATON^{5}, b. 9 Nov. 1744 <MD 16:135>
Mehitable EATON^{5}, b. 30 Apr. 1747 <MD 16:135>
Elizabeth EATON^{5}, b. 22 Feb. 1748/9 <MD 16:135>
Ziba EATON^{5}, b. 14 Sept. 1750 <MD 18:156>
Nathan EATON^{5}, b. 11 Aug. 1753 <MD 18:156>
Wealthy EATON^{5}, b. 19 June 1755 <MD 18:156>
Keziah EATON^{5}, b. 8 Oct. 1757 <MD 18:156>
Meribah EATON^{5}, b. 10 Feb. 1760 <MD 18:156>
CHILDREN OF Nathan EATON^{5} & Margaret CHERRY: (9) <Middleboro VR; 3-9, 4:1:124>

Hannah EATON^{6}, b. 3 Jan. 1775 <4:1:6>

Martha EATON^{6}, b. 8 June 1777 <4:1:6>; d. 5 May 1853, consumption, Middleboro <Mass.VR 76:211>

Barnabas EATON^{6}, b. 22 Jan. 1782

Ziba EATON^{6}, b. 18 Mar. 1784

Sarah EATON^{6}, b. 6 Nov. 1786

Mehitabel EATON^{6}, b. 23 Feb. 1789

Nancy EATON^{6}, b. 3 June 1791

Luther EATON^{6}, b. 6 Oct. 1793

Elisabeth EATON^{6}, b. 7 Dec. 1796

CHILDREN OF Abner LEONARD (son of Ben. below) & Martha EATON^{6}: (4) <Middleboro VR 7:127>

Abner LEONARD^{7}, b. 23 Aug. 1807

Nancy Eaton LEONARD^{7}, b. 30 Mar. 1810

Sarah Pratt LEONARD^{7}, b. 22 Aug. 1812

Olive LEONARD^{7}, b. 23 Oct. 1816

CHILDREN OF Benjamin LEONARD & Hannah ( ): (8) <Middleboro VR 4:1:82>

Daniel LEONARD, b. 21 July 1771

Andrew LEONARD, b. 3 Mar. 1774

Abner LEONARD, b. 10 July 1776; d. 25 June 1890, Plymouth, heart failure <Mass.VR 410:445>

Olive LEONARD, b. 13 Feb. 1779

George LEONARD, b. 17 Aug. 1781

Benjamin LEONARD, b. 4 May 1784

Hannah LEONARD, b. 16 Feb. 1787

Zebulon LEONARD, b. 6 July 1790

CHILD OF Abner LEONARD & Zilpha MORTON:

Sumner LEONARD, b. c1739, Plymouth, d. 1 Sept. 1892, Plymouth, ulcer of stomach <Mass.VR 428:592>

Patience TINKHAM^{5*} (*Sam.^{4}, Ephraim^{3}, Mary Brown^{2}), b. 9 Jan. 1734/5*; d. 9 Jan. 1812*, ae 80, "Old cem. in woods on Centre St."

CHILDREN OF Samuel EATON^{5} (Barnabas^{4}) & Patience TINHAM: (8) <Middleboro VR 4:5>

Samuel EATON^{6}, b. 27 Oct. 1754

Barnabas EATON^{6}, b. 17 Mar. 1757

Israel EATON^{6}, b. 9 June 1760; d. 19 Mar. 1833*, Taunton St. cem., Middleboro

Mehitable EATON^{6}, b. 23 Dec. 1763

Daniel EATON^{6}, b. 14 Oct. 1767

Darius EATON^{6}, b. 9 Mar. 1770; d. 23 Mar. 1828*, Brookfield g.s.

Eunice EATON^{6}, b. 9 Mar. 1770 (twins); d. 26 Sept. 1843* <Brookfield VR>

Enos EATON^{6}, b. 15 Sept. 1773

CHILD OF Darius EATON^{6} & Phebe RICHMOND, (*dau of Rufus^{7}--):

Rufus EATON^{7}, b. ( )

CHILD OF Rufus EATON^{7} & Clarissa HORR:

Louisa EATON^{8}, b. ( )

CHILDREN OF Benjamin BOND & Louisa EATON^{8}: (2)

Rufus Eaton BOND^{9}, b. 12 June 1848

Henry BOND^{9*}, b. 7 July 1856*

Seth EDDY, (*son of John), b. 2 July 1765* <Brookfield VR>; d. 13 Nov. 1823*, W. Brookfield g.s.

CHILDREN OF Seth EDDY & Eunice EATON^{6} (Sam.^{5}): (6*) <Brookfield VR>

Saloma EDDY^{7}, b. 15 Jan. 1793

Titus EDDY^{7}, b. 12 July 1795

Patience EDDY^{7}, b. 9 July 1798

Eunice EDDY^{7}, b. 11 Feb. 1801

Mary EDDY^{7}, b. 22 Feb. 1806

Abiel EDDY[7], b. 31 July 1810

CHILDREN OF David BARLOW* & Patience EDDY[7]: (6*) <Brookfield VR>

Atwell BARLOW[8], b. 26 June 1817

Edwin BARLOW[8], b. 20 Apr. 1819

Salome E. BARLOW[8], b. 30 Aug. 1821

Laura L. BARLOW[8], b. 22 Oct. 1826

Larinda BARLOW[8], b. 20 Oct. 1830

Silas BARLOW[8], b. ( )

CHILD OF Gilbert F. LINCOLN* & Salome E. BARLOW[8]:

David Franklin LINCOLN[9]*, b. 20 July 1845* <Brookfield VR>

CHILDREN OF Titus EDDY[7] (Eunice Eaton[6]) & Elizabeth KENT*: (6*) <Brookfield VR>

Elijah EDDY[8], b. 23 Apr. 1818

Erastus EDDY[8], b. 24 July 1819

Sophronia EDDY[8], b. 27 Mar. 1822

John EDDY[8], b. 25 June 1826

George EDDY[8], b. 7 Jan. 1828

Almira EDDY[8], b. 29 Aug. 1830

CHILDREN OF Israel EATON[6] (Sam.[5]) & 1st Eunice RICKARD*: (6*)

Zenas EATON[7], b. 1782

Linda EATON[7], b. 1785

Eunice EATON[7], b. 1787, d. 28 Mar. 1832*, ae 45, unm.

Israel EATON[7], b. 1790

Andrew EATON[7], b. 1795

Oliver EATON[7], b. 1799

Keziah ( ) EATON, b. c1762, d. 27 Aug. 1837*, ae 75, Middleboro g.s.

CHILD OF Israel EATON[6] & 2nd Keziah ( ):

Daniel EATON[7], b. ( )

CHILDREN OF Ziba EATON[5] (Barnabas[4]) & Ruth LEONARD: (5) <Middleboro VR 4:6>

Dau., d. 2 June 17( ), ae 6 days <MD 12:201>

Solomon EATON[6], b. 9 Aug. 1774

Betty EATON[6], b. 20 Sept. 1777

Clemmons EATON[6], b. 3 Oct. 1780

Ruth EATON[6], b. 12 May 1783

Peggy (RANDALL*), b. 10 Nov. 1778, Topsham ME

CHILD OF Solomon EATON[6] & Peggy RANDALL*:

Martha EATON[7]*, b. 4 Mar. 1803*, Bowdin ME

William KANNADY, (son of Alexander & Eliz.), b. 8 Mar. 1689, Plymouth <MD 1:209>; d. 23 June 1774 <NEHGR 21:347>

CHILDREN OF William KANNADY & Elizabeth EATON[4] (Sam.[3]): (6)<17>

Thankful CANEDY[5], b. ( )

Hannah CANEDY[5], b. c1737; d. 10 June 1783, ae 46, S. Middleboro g.s.

William CANEDY[5], b. ( ); d. betw. 17 Mar. 1804 (will) - 11 Apr. 1804 (prob.), Middleboro

Barnabas CANEDY[5], b. ( )

Mercy CANEDY[5], b. ( )

Fear CANEDY[5], b. ( ); d. pre 6 Jan. 1825 <Bristol Co.LR 117:23>

Elizabeth BARNABY[6]* (*Ambrose[5], James[4], Lydia Bartlett[3], Mary Warren[2]*), b. 9 Feb. 1738*;d. 1784* "suicide in tub of water" (*wf of 2nd hus Elijah Burt of Berkley) (*m. 1st Barnabas Canedy[5])

David PERKINS[7] (*Alice Leach[6]--), b.? 3 Mar. 1739*; d. aft. 2 Oct. 1801 <Bristol Co LR 80:336>

CHILDREN OF David PERKINS & Fear CANEDY[5]: (4)

David PERKINS[6], b. pre 1776*; d. aft. 2 Oct. 1801, of Rochester <Bristol Co.LR 80:336>

William PERKINS^{6}, b. c1776*; d. 11 Feb. 1844*, Savoy MA

Barnabas PERKINS^{6}, b. aft. 1776*; d. aft. 2 Oct. 1801, of New Bedford <Bristol Co.LR 80:336>

Hannah PERKINS^{6}, b. ( ); d. aft. 2 Oct. 1801 <Bristol Co.LR 80:336>

David PERKINS^{6}* (*Martha Howard^{5}, Sarah Latham^{4}, Susanna Winslow^{3}, Mary Chilton^{2}), d. c1783*, Oakham

Alice LEACH, (*dau of David), d. 1781-83*, Oakham

CHILDREN OF David PERKINS^{6} (Martha Howard^{5}) & Alice LEACH: (5) <Bridgewater VR>

David PERKINS, b. 3 Mar. 1739 <1:252>

Zephaniah PERKINS, b. 7 Aug. 1742 <1:259>; d. 1777

John PERKINS, b. 10 May 1746 <1:254>

Robert PERKINS, b. 17 Feb. 1750 <1:257>

Asa PERKINS, b. 6 Oct. 1754 <1:251>

CHILDREN OF Abial PEIRCE & Hannah CANEDY^{5} (Eliz. Eaton^{4}): <"see NEHGR 21:349>

Charity LEONARD, (dau of Elkanah), b. 27 Feb. 1731/2, Middleboro <MD 12:130>; d. aft. hus. will

CHILDREN OF William CANEDY^{5} (Eliz. Eaton^{4}) & Charity LEONARD: (4) <Middleboro VR 4:1:151>

Charity CANEDY^{6}, b. 5 June 1754; d. 8 June 1844***<18>**

Bathsheba CANEDY^{6}, b. 20 Nov. 1755

William CANEDY^{6}, b. 8 Dec. 1757; d. betw. 28 Sept. 1836 (will) - Nov. 1837 (prob.) <Plymouth Co. PR #3539, 79:483>

Noble CANEDY^{6}, b. 1 Sept. 1759

Rufus HOWLAND^{5}* (*John^{4}, Joshua^{3}, Sam.^{2}, Henry^{1}*), b. 6 May 1751*; d. VT

CHILDREN OF Rufus HOWLAND & Bathsheba CANEDY^{6}: (7)**<19>**

Mary G. BROWN, d. 21 Mar. 1836 <Middleboro VR 7:206>

CHILDREN OF William CANEDY^{6} (Wm.^{5}) & Mary G. BROWN: (9) <Middleboro VR 4:1:65>

William CANEDY^{7}, b. 20 Dec. 1784

Elizabeth CANEDY^{7}, b. 6 Sept. 1786

Jannet/Jane CANEDY^{7}, b. 31 Jan. 1788

Alexander CANEDY^{7}, b. 26 Mar. 1790

Zebulon Leonard CANEDY^{7}, b. 11 Aug. 1792; d. 14 Jan. 1840 <Middleboro VR 14:20>

Mary CANEDY^{7}, b. 28 Sept. 1794

Hannah CANEDY^{7}, b. 2 Feb. 1798

CHILD OF William ASHLEY & Jane CANEDY^{7}: <Middleboro>

William H. ASHLEY^{8}, b. c1817, d. 24 Apr. 1895,ae 78y1m20d, Fall River <Mass.VR 454:191>

CHILDREN OF Zebulon Leonard CANEDY^{7} (Wm.^{6}) & Olive BISBEE: (4) <Middleboro VR 7:217>**<20>**

Mary Brown CANEDY^{8}, b. 21 Dec. 1817; d. 11 Apr. 1832 <VR 7:206>

William CANEDY^{8}, b. c1824, d. 13 Aug. 1889, ae 65y7m, heart disease, Lakeville <Mass.VR 401:375>

Betsey Woodbridge CANEDY^{8}, b. 29 Feb. 1828

Elkanah Leonard CANEDY^{8}, b. 5 Aug. 1829

Mary Brown CANEDY^{8}, b. 15 Sept. 1833

CHILDREN OF Hopestill BISBEE & Betsey ( ): (7) <Middleboro VR 7:33>

Betsey BISBEE, b. 16 Jan. 1797, Rochester

Olive BISBEE, b. 12 Nov. 1798, Rochester

Hopestill BISBEE, b. 22 Aug. 1800

Alden Clark BISBEE, b. 9 Aug. 1802

Abigail BISBEE, b. 8 Sept. 1804

Deborah BISBEE, b. 15 Dec. 1807

Hannah BISBEE, b. 1 May 1810

CHILDREN OF Philip BUMPUS & Sarah EATON^{3}: (5) <Bristol, VR of RI:66>**<21>**

Samuel BUMPUS^{4}, b. 20 Feb. 1687/88

Philip BUMPUS^{4}, b. 13 Feb. 1689/90

Lydia BUMPUS[4], b. 2 Apr. 1692
Mathew BUMPUS[4], b. 8 June 1695
Josiah BUMPUS[4], b. 9 Apr. 1698

RACHEL EATON[2] (Francis[1])

Joseph RAMSDEN, d. 25 May 1674 <MD 8:19>
CHILD OF Joseph RAMSDEN & Rachel EATON[2]:**<22>**
Daniel RAMSDEN[3], b. 14 Sept. 1649, Plymouth <MD 16:121>; d. aft. 1684
CHILDREN OF Abner RAMSDAL & Jerusha (   ): (3) <Truro VR:167>
Jerusha RAMSDAL, b. 17 Apr. 1794
Abner/Ebner RAMSDAL, b. 17 Nov. 1795
John RAMSDAL, b. 5 Jan. 1797
CHILDREN OF Abner RANDEL & Jerusa COLLINS: (3) <Truro VR:146>
Richard Collings RANDEL, b. 31 Oct. 1787
Rebecca RANDEL, b. 10 July 1789
Dau., d. 19 June 1792 <Damon Diary>
Hannah CASWELL, (dau of Tho.), b. 14 July 1661 <Taunton VR 1:83>
CHILDREN OF Daniel RAMSDEN/RAMSDELL[3] & Hannah CASWELL: (5) <1-4, Plymouth VR, MD 3:14>
Thomas RAMSDELL[4], b. c1680, d. 16 Sept. 1727, Hanover
Samuel RAMSDELL[4], b. 5 June 1690
Joseph RAMSDELL[4], b. 15 Aug. 1693
Benjamin RAMSDELL[4], b. 1 June 1699
Hannah RAMSDELL[4], b. 28 Sept. 1700
Sarah ALVERSON, (dau of Nicholas), b. c1682, d. 4 Aug. 1773, ae 91, Hanover
CHILDREN OF Thomas RAMSDELL[4] & Sarah ALVERSON: (4 of 8)**<23>**
Mary RAMSDELL[5], b. 9 May 1706, Pembroke
Joseph RAMSDELL[5], b. 29 May 1708, Pembroke
Jemimah RAMSDELL[5], b. 28 July 1710, Pembroke
Gideon RAMSDELL[5], b. 13 Sept. 1712, Scituate; d. 28 Feb. 1795, Mt. Zion cem. <Abington VR 2:335>
CHILDREN OF Gideon RAMSDELL[5] & Sarah FARRINGTON: (6) <Abington>
John RAMSDELL[6], b. 20 Sept. 1738; d. 29 Oct. 1816, Smead cem., Wardsboro VT
Content RAMSDELL[6], b. 12 Dec. 1741
Gideon RAMSDELL[6], b. 5 May 1744
David RAMSDELL[6], b. 11 May 1746
Job RAMSDELL[6], b. 11 Dec. 1748
Micah RAMSDELL[6], b. 7 June 1751
Eunice COBB, (dau of John & Ruth (Chard)), b. 5 July 1740; d. 14 Sept. 1816, Wardsboro VT
CHILDREN OF John RAMSDELL[6] & Eunice COBB: (10) <Warwick MA>
John RAMSDELL[7], b. 17 June 1762; d. 27 Apr. 1813, Shoreham VT
David RAMSDELL[7], b. 17 June 1762 (twins); d. 1815, ?Shoreham VT*
Robert RAMSDELL[7], b. 22 July 1765; d. 21 May 1825, Washington VT
Sarah RAMSDELL[7], b. 12 Apr. 1767; d. 18 Apr. 1837, "probably Wardsboro VT"
Farrington RAMSDELL[7], b. 13 May 1769; d. Washington VT
Ruth RAMSDELL[7], b. 17 Feb. 1772
Eunice RAMSDELL[7], b. 29 Aug. 1774; d. 17 June 1847, Wardsboro VT (wf of Ebenezer Eaton)
Joanna RAMSDELL[7], b. 16 Mar. 1777 (m. Peter Cleveland, moved to Cleveland OH)
Job RAMSDELL[7], b. 8 July 1779; d. 10 Nov. 1870, Wardsboro VT
Gideon RAMSDELL[7], b. ( ); moved to Ohio aft. 1826
CHILDREN OF Farrington RAMSDELL[7] & Lois (   ): (8)

Bethiah RAMSDELL^{8}, b. 6 Oct. 1797
Charlotte RAMSDELL^{8}, b. 14 Apr. 1799
John RAMSDELL^{8}, b. 3 May 1801
Prudence H. RAMSDELL^{8}, b. 25 May 1803
Farrington RAMSDELL^{8}, b. 10 June 1805
Robert RAMSDELL^{8}, b. 11 Feb. 1807
Lois RAMSDELL^{8}, b. 4 July 1809
Nathaniel F. RAMSDELL^{8}, b. 13 May 1811

CHILDREN OF Gideon RAMSDELL^{7} (John^{6}) & Sarah UNDERWOOD: (9) <Wardsboro VT>
Mary RAMSDELL^{8}, b. 30 May 1805
Alvin RAMSDELL^{8}, b. 26 Dec. 1808
Eunice RAMSDELL^{8}, b. 10 Mar. 1811
Asa RAMSDELL^{8}, b. 6 Nov. 1813
Leland RAMSDELL^{8}, b. 12 Jan. 1816
Gideon RAMSDELL^{8}, b. 8 Aug. 1818
Louisa RAMSDELL^{8}, b. 13 Sept. 1821
Franklin RAMSDELL^{8}, b. 30 Apr. 1824
Sarah RAMSDELL^{8}, b. 11 May 1826

Abigail WHITE, b. 1780, d. 16 Aug. 1844, Wardsboro VT

CHILDREN OF Job RAMSDELL^{7} (John^{6}) & Abigail WHITE: (11) <Wardsboro VT>
Joseph White RAMSDELL^{8}, b. 4 Dec. 1804; living 1884*
John Cobb RAMSDELL^{8}, b. 17 Sept. 1806
Alanson RAMSDELL^{8}, b. 14 Feb. 1808
Marie RAMSDELL^{8}, b. 3 Aug. 1809
Sylvia RAMSDELL^{8}, b. 3 Nov. 1811; d. 6 May 1885
Chester RAMSDELL^{8}, b. ( ); living 1884 Minnesota
Harriet RAMSDELL^{8}, b. ( ); living 1884 Wardsboro VT
3 Children, b. ( )
Roena RAMSDELL^{8}, b. 21 June 1825; d. 6 Oct. 1897

Chloe PRICE, b. c1763, d. 22 Jan. 1815, ae 52, Shoreham VT

CHILDREN OF John RAMSDELL^{7} (John^{6}) & Chloe PRICE: (2) <Wardsboro VT>
Lois RAMSDELL^{8}, b. 16 Aug. 1786
Daniel Hovey RAMSDELL^{8}, b. 5 Nov. 1788; d. 1863, Wisconsin

Mary JEFFERSON, d. 27 Mar. or 21 Nov. 1830, Washington VT

CHILDREN OF Robert RAMSDELL^{7} (John^{6}) & Mary JEFFERSON: (6) <Washington VT>
Mehitable RAMSDELL^{8}, b. 9 May 1785
Phebe RAMSDELL^{8}, b. 18 Sept. 1787
David RAMSDELL^{8}, b. 27 Mar. or Dec. 1791; d. 29 Nov. 1824
John RAMSDELL^{8}, b. 13 Mar. 1795
Mary RAMSDELL^{8}, b. 19 Dec. 1799
Eunice RAMSDELL^{8}, b. 20 Jan. 1802

MICRO #4 of 4

Rosina Aurelia RAMSDELL^{8}, b. 11 Jan. 1823, Washington VT; d. 11 Feb. 1884, Calliope, Iowa[<24>]
Daniel Marshall BURNHAM, b. 10 Aug. 1823, Williamstown VT

CHILD OF Daniel Marshall BURNHAM & Rosina Aurelia RAMSDELL^{8}:
Ellen Francelia BURNHAM^{9}, b. 19 Sept. 1844; d. 12 June 1916

CHILDREN OF Nathaniel FITTS & Sarah RAMSDELL^{7} (John^{6}): (7)[<25>]

* * * * * * *

FOOTNOTES

<1> p.438, The name of Francis' 2nd wife is not known. It is believed that she might be the unnamed maid servant who came with the Carver family on the Mayflower. Gov. Bradford said she had "married and died a year or two after". The files do not identify his 3rd wife, she was Christian Penn who married 2nd Francis Billington[2].
<2> p.438, MF5G 1:193 (addendum) states Benjamin was "apparently" born Mar. 1627/8.
<3> p.438, b. 16 Sept. 1637, dau. of William Hoskins & Sarah Cushman. <MF5G 1:7> The Genealogist (TG) 1:238 states Sarah was still alive in Plympton as late as 31 May 1711.
<4> p.438, MF5G 1:193 (addendum) adds a possible 5th child, dau. Experience Eaton.
<5> p.438, Benjamin signed a deed with his parents 29 Oct. 1685, therefore he would have been 21 yrs. old by this date. <Plymouth Co.Deeds 5:368>
<6> p.438, In his will William states he is "being cald forth to go against the ffrench".
<7> p.438, b. 28 Nov. 1666, Boston, dau. of John & Elizabeth Coombs. <MF5G 1:11>
<8> p.438, MF5G 1:194 identifies Mary as possibly the dau. of Barnabas Eaton[4] (Sam.[3-2]).
MF5G 3:182 identifies Jesse Snow as the son of Jonathan Snow & Sarah Soule[4](John[3-2]) Eight children can be found in both MF5G books.
<9> p.440, Deborah Fuller, b. 23 Nov. 1727, Plympton, dau. of Jabez Fuller & Priscilla Sampson. <MF5G 1:39>
<10> p.440, MF5G 1:38 gives an 8th child, Ruth Eaton, b. 21 Feb. 1746.
<11> p.440, MF5G 1:35 identifies her as Lydia Fuller[4] (John[3], Sam.[2-1]) and Mercy Nelson, b. c1709, bpt. 9 Nov. 1718, Middleboro and d. 24 Oct. 180, probably Middleboro.
<12> p.440, No children are listed for Elijah and his wife Sarah. However, on the following page are the probate records for an Elijah Eaton - will datd 31 Oct. 1825, inventory taken 2 Mar. 1831 with the following chldren mentioned in the will, viz: Barzillai, Lucretia (wf of Azel Perkins), Mersena (wf of Daniel Eaton), Bethana (Leonard), Zebina (son) and Salona (Fobes). <Plymouth Co.PR #7042, 70:116,229>
<13> p.441, The nine Eaton children are listed without dates, viz: Charles, Calvin, Henry, Adam, Diana, Lucy, Caroline, Alice and Parna.
<14> p.441, Benjamin "drowned on Plymouth shore" with Francis Cook Jr. & John Ransom.
<15> p.441, Benjamin died two months after wife Hannah, leaving six orphaned children between the ages of infancy to 10 years. Hannah's father Benjamin Eaton became guardian of the children. <Plymouth Co.PR #3177, 8:31>
<16> p.442, MF5G 1:44 gives full dates of birth (Bridgewater) for the three Allen children, viz: Betty, b. 23 Oct. 1739, and Mary & Rebecca, b. 25 Apr. 1743 (twins).
<17> p.444, All the children were living 26 Jan. 1774 when William made his will. <Bristol Co.PR 23:268> MF5G 1:10 gives baptism dates for all the children as well as a 7th child, Nathaniel Canedy, bpt. 1731.
<18> p.445, An entry is given from the Middleboro VR 7:52 for Hannah Canedy, dau. of Charity Canedy, b. 3 Dec. 1772. This is followed in the VR by the children of Ebenezer Hinds and Charity Canedy[6].
<19> p.445, The seven Howland children are listed in pencil without dates, viz: Betsey, Mercy, Noble, Bathsheba (d.y.), Bathsheba, Pardon and Lucy.
<20> p.445, In the division of Zebulon's estate (1863), the four surviving children are mentioned with Salmon S. Canedy of Lexington, Mich. - all five received one fifth part. The division also states Betsy was the wife of Thomas P.W. Perkins of Rochester and Mary was the wife of William T. Jenney of Lexington, Mich. <Plymouth Co.PR #3542>
<21> p.445, MF5G 1:8 provides three additional Bumpas children, viz: Jemima, b. 7 Jan. 1787, Bristol; Bethia, b. c1700, Quinebaug CT and Sarah, b. c1702.
<22> p.446, There are two interesting items pertaining to Joseph & Rachel in the Plymouth Colony Records. On 4 May 1652 Joseph was ordered to move his wife and family out of the woods, and live closer to a town. <PCR 3:6> Evidently he ignored the order for it was repeated four years later, 3 June 1656. On this occasion the records state, "Wheras Joseph Ramsdan hath lived long in the woods in an uncivil way...with his wife alone...the Court have ordered, that hee repaier downe to sum naighborhood betwixt this and October next, or that then his house bee pulled down." <PCR 3: 102>

Four yrs. before the Ramsdens were ordered to leave the woods, Rachel found herself in the courts testifyng in a murder trial, 22 July 1648. Alice Bishop had been accused of murdering her four year old daughter, Martha, by slashing her throat with a knife. Rachel (aged about 23 yrs.) testified that when she arrived at Richard Bishop's house on an errand, "the wife of the said Richard Bishope requested her to goe fetch her some buttermilke at Goodwife Winslows, and gave her a Ketle for that purpose, and shee went and did it; and before shee went, shee saw the child lyinge abed asleepe...but when shee came shee found (Alice Bishop) sad and dumpish; shee asked her what blood was that shee saw at the ladder's foot; shee pointed unto the chamber, and bid her looke, but shee perseived shee had killed her child, and being afraid, shee refused, and ran and tould her father and mother...shee saith the reason that moved her to thinke shee had killed her child was that when shee saw the blood shee looked on the bedd, and the child was not there." <PCR 2:132> Alice Bishop confessed and on 4 Oct. 1648 was sentenced to be hanged.
<23> p.446, The remaining four Ramsdell children are listed without dates. Mayflower Source Rcds. by Roberts:348 gives the birth of Sarah, 14 Aug. 1715, Scituate, while MF5G 1:27 provides the remaining three, viz: Mercy, b. 5 Nov. 1717, Scituate; Lydia, b. 5 Sept. 1719, Scituate and David, b. 24 Oct. 1721, Abington.
<24> p.447, Rosina is given a line of descent to Robert[7] (John[6]), but she is not listed among the children of Robert & Mary. Note her year of birth is 21 years after that of the last child of Robert & Mary. Her birth would fit in the family of Job Ramsdell[7] (John[6]) (as one of the un-

named children) but there is not indication suggesting this in the files.
<25> p.447, The seven Fitts children are listed without dates, viz: Levi, Nathaniel B., Amasa, Ebenezer, Sarah, Joanna and Laura.

* * * * * * * * *

REFERENCE LIST

GENEALOGICAL ARTICLES PERTAINING TO EATON FAMILY RESEARCH

Mayflower Descendant (MD) (1899 -1937)

2:172-73 - Will & Inventory of Samuel Eaton[2] & Settlement of His Estate
8:18-20 - Estate of Joseph Ramsden (1674)
12:226 - Eaton Notes: William & Samuel Eaton[3]
18:125-26 - Eaton Notes: Will of Samuel Eaton[5]

Mayflower Descendant (MD) (1985-1990)

35:111-20 - Thomas Caswell of Taunton & His Descendants
36:187 - The Ramsden Family of Plymouth MA
38:69-80 - Thomas Caswell of Taunton & His Descendants
38:189 - Another Grandchild of Francis Eaton[1]?
- (Experience Eaton[3] (Ben.[2]))
39:1-3 - Mary (Ramsden) Caswell: A New Francis Eaton Line?
39:17-20 - Silvanus Eaton[5] (1734-c1791/2)
(re: MF5G 1:35-36)

Mayflower Quarterly (MQ) (1975-1990)

41:64-65 - Francis, Sarah & Christian Eaton
45:203-04 - Who Was Jemima Hill[7] of Pembroke MA?
- (correction to MF5G 1:26-27)
50:21-30 - Judah Fuller[5], The Bloomer's Daughter
50:71-76 - The Additional Children of Joseph & Mercy (Canedy) Williams & Their Migrations to Western Mass. & Groton NY
55:296-7 - Sylvia Sturtevant And Her Seven Mayflower Lines
56:308-10 - Nathan Crooker/Crocker, Sixth Generation From Mayflower Passenger Francis Eaton
57:16-21 - Emma Eaton And Her Seven Mayflower Lines

* * * * * * * * * *

EDWARD FULLER

MICRO #1 of 1

Consider FULLER, d. betw 20 Apr. 1829 (will) - 16 Sept. 1829 (adm.) <Plymouth Co.Prob.#8204><1>

CHILDREN OF Isaac WADSWORTH & Susanna NICHOLS: (2)

Abigail WADSWORTH, b. 24 May 1732

Susanna WADSWORTH, b. 21 Sept. 1738

Susanna (NICHOLS)(Wadsworth) Fuller, (widow of Isaac Fuller), d. betw 14 June 1783 (will) - 9 Aug. 1783 (inv.) <Plymouth Co.Prob.#8293, 29:27, 28>

John FULLER, d. 15 Apr. 1809, ae 57, Middleboro Green g.s. <MD 13:25>

Betty ( ) FULLER, (wf of John), d. 3 Sept. 1832, ae 75, Middleboro Green g.s. <MD 13:25>

Betsey FULLER, d. 26 Feb. 1814, ae 28, unm., Middleboro Green g.s. <MD 13:24>

CHILDREN OF Edward FULLER^{1}: (2)

Matthew FULLER^{2}, d. betw. 25 July 1678 (will) - 22 Aug. 1678 (inv.) <MD 13:7,9> (See <13>)

Samuel FULLER^{2}, d. 31 Oct. 1683, Barnstable <MD 2:237>

SAMUEL FULLER^{2} (Edward^{1})

Jane LOTHROP, bpt. 29 Sept. 1614, Edgerton, Kent co., Eng.; d. betw 1659 - 31 Oct. 1683<2>

CHILDREN OF Samuel FULLER^{2} & Jane LOTHROP: (9)

Hannah FULLER^{3}, d. aft. Oct. 1683 (father's will) <MD 2:239>

Samuel FULLER^{3}, bpt. 11 Feb. 1637/8, Scituate <NEHGR 9:281>; d. pre 28 Dec. 1691(inv.)<MD 12:189>

Elizabeth FULLER^{3}, b. ( ), (marr. a Taylor), d. aft. Oct. 1683 (father's will) <MD 2:239>

Sarah FULLER^{3}, b. Scituate, bpt. 1 Aug. 1641 <NEHGR 9:282>; d.y.

Mary FULLER^{3}, bpt. 16 June 1644 <NEHGR 9:283><3>

Thomas FULLER^{3}, b. 18 May 1650 <MD 4:226>; probably d. pre Oct. 1683 (father's will)

Sarah FULLER^{3}, b. 14 Dec. 1654 <MD 4:226>

John FULLER^{3}, b. ( ) <MD 2:239>

Child, b. 8 Feb. 1658/9, bur. 15 days later <MD 4:226>

Nicholas BONHAM, d. betw 6 Feb. 1683/4 (will) - 2 July 1684 (inv.) <NJ Archives 1:21:72><4>

CHILDREN OF Nicholas BONHAM & Hannah FULLER^{3}: (4) <1-3, Barnstable VR><5>

Hannah BONHAM^{4}, b. 8 Oct. 1659 <MD 2:214, 18:198>

Mary BONHAM^{4}, b. 4 Oct. 1661 <MD 2:214, 18:198>

Sarah BONHAM^{4}, b. 16 Feb. 1664 <MD 2:214>

Edmund DUNHAM, (son of Benajah), b. 25 July 1661, Eastham <MD 7:237> (hus. of Mary Bonham^{4})

Mehitable ROWLEY, (dau of Moses & Elizabeth (Fuller)), b. 11 Jan. 1660, Barnstable <MD 18:203>

CHILDREN OF John FULLER^{3} & Mehitable ROWLEY: (11)<6>

Joseph WILLIAMS, (son of John & Jane), b. 18 Apr. 1647 <Haverhill VR 1:321>

CHILDREN OF Joseph WILLIAMS & Mary FULLER^{3}: (4) <Haverhill VR 1:321>

Sarah WILLIAMS^{4}, b. 17 Nov. 1675

Mary WILLIAMS^{4}, b. 29 Nov. 1677

Capt. John WILLIAMS^{4}, b. 17 Feb. 1679; d. 12 Jan. 1741/2, Pockatannock CT

Hannah WILLIAMS^{4}, b. 30 Sept. 1683

CHILDREN OF Capt. John WILLIAMS^{4} & ?Hannah KNOWLTON*:<7>

Anne FULLER^{3} (Matthew^{2}), d. pre 30 Dec. 1691 <MD 12:189>

CHILDREN OF Samuel FULLER^{3} & Anne FULLER: (6)<8>

CHILDREN OF Barnabas FULLER^{4} (Samuel^{3}) & Elizabeth YOUNG: (5) <Barnstable, MD 4:226><9>

Samuel FULLER^{5}, b. Nov. 1681

Isaac FULLER^{5}, b. Aug. 1684

Hannah FULLER^{5}, b. Sept. 1688

Ebenezer FULLER[5], b. "latter end" Aug. 1699

Josiah FULLER[5], b. Feb. 1709**<10>**

Ruth CROCKER[4] (Ruth Chipman[3], Hope Howland[2]), b. 3 Aug. 1693, Barnstable <MD 4:120>; d. 1723-26*

CHILDREN OF Samuel FULLER[5] & 1st Ruth CROCKER: (3) <Barnstable, MD 33:24>

Sarah FULLER[6], b. 16 Apr. 1719

Barnabas FULLER[6], b. 1 Apr. 1721

Eliezer FULLER[6], b. 9 Feb. 1722/3

CHILDREN OF Samuel FULLER[5] & 2nd Lydia LOVEL: (4) <Barnstable, MD 33:24>**<11>**

Joshua FULLER[6], b. 3 Oct. 1727

Elizabeth FULLER[6], b. 24 Jan. 1728/9

Rebecca FULLER[6], b. 3 Apr. 1731

Lot FULLER[6], b. 18 Sept. 1733

CHILDREN OF Benjamin FULLER[4] (Samuel[3]): (4) <Barnstable, MD 4:227>

Temperance FULLER[5], b. 7 Mar. 1702

Hannah FULLER[5], b. 20 May 1704

John FULLER[5], b. 25 Dec. 1706

James FULLER[5], b. 1 May 1711

Temperance PHINNEY[5] (Ben.[4], Mary Rogers[3], Jos.[2]), b. 28 Mar. 1710, Barnstable <MD 11:132>

CHILDREN OF James FULLER[5] & Temperance PHINNEY: (6) <Barnstable, MD 32:53>

Martha FULLER[6], b. 21 June 1734

John FULLER[6], b. 6 Feb. 1735

Mary FULLER[6], b. 5 Nov. 1741

James FULLER[6], b. 21 Feb. 1743

Joseph FULLER[6], b. 3 Mar. 1745

Benjamin FULLER[6], b. 21 Sept. 1748

Patience YOUNG, (dau of George), b. 3 Mar. 1673 <Scituate VR>

CHILDREN OF Matthew FULLER[4] (Samuel[3]) & Patience YOUNG: (7) <1-7, Barnstable MD 4:226>**<12>**

Anne FULLER[5], b. Nov. 1693

Jonathan FULLER[5], b. Oct. 1696

Content FULLER[5], b. 19 Feb. 1698/9

Jean FULLER[5], b. 1704, d. 1708

David FULLER[5], b. Feb. 1706/7

Young FULLER[5], b. 1708

Cornelius FULLER[5], b. 1710

MATTHEW FULLER[2] (Edward[1])<13>

CHILDREN OF Matthew FULLER[2] & Francis ( ): (5) <MD 13:8>

Lieut. Samuel FULLER[3], b. ( ), d. 25 Mar. 1676*, Rehoboth**<14>**

Dr. John FULLER[3], b. ( ), d. pre 16 July 1691 (inv.) <MD 12:187,188>

Mary FULLER[3], b. ( )

Anne FULLER[3], b. ( ), d. pre 30 Dec. 1691 <MD 12:189>

Elizabeth FULLER[3], b. ( ); d. after 1714*

Moses ROWLEY, d. betw. 16 Aug. 1704 (will) - 8 Mar. 1705/6 (prob.)**<15>**

CHILDREN OF Moses ROWLEY & Elizabeth FULLER[3]: (10) <1-5, Barnstable MD 18:203>**<16>**

Mary ROWLEY[4], b. 20 Mar. 1653

Moses ROWLEY[4], b. 10 Nov. 1654

Child, d. 15 Aug. 1656

Shubael ROWLEY[4], b. 11 Jan. 1660

Mehitable ROWLEY[4], b. 11 Jan. 1660 (twin); d. aft. 1704*

Sarah ROWLEY^{4}, b. 16 Sept. 1662
Aaron ROWLEY^{4}, b. 1 May 1666
John ROWLEY^{4}, b. 22 Oct. 1667
Matthew ROWLEY^{4*}, b. ( )
Nathan ROWLEY^{4*}, b. ( )
Mary ( ) FULLER, b. aft. 1630; d. aft. 25 July 1678 <MD 13:9>**<17>**
CHILDREN OF Lieut. Samuel FULLER^{3} & Mary ( ): (7) <MD 13:8>
Thomas FULLER^{4}, b. pre 1663*
Jabez FULLER^{4}, d. pre 15 Sept. 1711 (inv.)
Timothy FULLER^{4}, b. ( )
Matthias FULLER^{4}, b. pre Aug. 1675; d. 1696 or 1697**<18>**
Abigail FULLER^{4}, b. pre Aug. 1675*
Anne FULLER^{4}, b. pre Aug. 1675*
Samuel FULLER^{4}, b. 1676**<19>**
CHILDREN OF Dr. John FULLER^{3} & 2nd Hannah MORTON: (3) <Barnstable, MD 4:225>**<20>**
Bethiah FULLER^{4}, b. Dec. 1687
John FULLER^{4}, b. Oct. 1689
Reliance FULLER^{4}, b. 8 Sept. 1691
Mary HALLETT^{4} (Eliz. Gorham^{3}, Desire Howland^{2}), d. aft. 11 May 1721
CHILDREN OF Jabez FULLER^{4} (Sam.^{3}) & Mary HALLETT: (6) <Barnstable, MD 4:226>
Samuel FULLER^{5}, b. 23 Feb. 1687
Jonathan FULLER^{5}, b. 10 Mar. 1692
Mercy FULLER^{5}, b. 1 Apr. 1696
Mary FULLER^{5}, b. 1698*
Lois FULLER^{5}, b. 23 Sept. 1704
Ebenezer FULLER^{5}, b. 20 Feb. 1708
CHILDREN OF Jonathan FULLER^{5} & Hannah HARLOW: (2) <Middleboro>**<21>**
Elinor FULLER^{6}, b. 25 Feb. 1730/1 <MD 9:47>
Ebenezer FULLER^{6}, b. 22 July 1732 <MD 12:130>
Jabez FULLER^{6} (Jonathan^{5}), b. 22 July 1717, Middleboro; d. 1770, Medfield (see **<21>**)
CHILD OF Jabez FULLER^{6} & Hannah PRATT^{6} (John^{5}, Sam.$^{4-3}$, Mary Priest^{2}):
Sarah FULLER^{7}, b. ( ) <Fuller Gen.3:34>

* * * * * * * * * * *

FOOTNOTES

<1> p.450, The identity of Consider Fuller is not shown. He is possibly the same who marr. Hannah Eaton, 13 July 1806 <Halifax VR:81>. His will mentions wife Hannah and the following 11 children, viz: Ezra (eldest son), Betsey (wf of Linus Drake, & eldest dau.), Joanna (wf of Ichabod Bassett), Sally (wf of Elijah Bird), John, Nathan, Daniel W., Samuel, Hannah, Smith and Waldo Ames (youngest son).
<2> p.450, Jane Lothrop, dau of Rev. John Lothrop & Hannah Howes <MF5G 4:7>.
<3> p.450, d. 11 Nov. 1720 <Norwich CT VR 1:62>.
<4> p.450, d. 20 July 1684, Piscataway NJ <MF5G 4:13>.
<5> p.450, MF5G 4:14 gives the names of four additional Bonham children, (plus Hezekiah's birthdate), b. Piscataway NJ, viz: Elizabeth, b. c1666; Hezekiah, b. 6 May 1677; Samuel, b. 7 Sept. 1672, d. 1 Oct. 1682; Jane, b. 29 Jan. 1675/6, d. 25 Feb. 1675/6 and Priscilla, b. 11 Nov. 1677.
<6> p.450, Twelve Fuller children are listed without dates, the source being the Fuller Gen. 1:34-7. Included in this list are Deborah & Anne which MF5G 4:17 discounts on the basis of insufficient evidence. Aparently there were also two Benjamins, Bowman lists one. The first six were b. Barnstable, the rest at E. Haddam CT, viz: Thomas, Samuel & Shubael, bpt. Oct. 1688; Thankful, bpt. 19 May 1689; Edward, b. c1691; Elizabeth, b. c1693; John, b. 10 Nov. 1697; Joseph, b. 1 Mar. 1699/1700; Benjamin, b. 20 Oct. 1701; Benjamin, bpt. 19 May 1706 and Mehitable, b. 16 Apr. 1706.
<7> p.450, Hannah Knowlton is listed (with uncertainty) as John Williams' 1st wife, with Mary ( ) as his second <Hist.Norwich CT:253>. MF5G 4:43 states his wife was Mary Knowlton (dau of Thomas Knowlton & Hannah Green) with the possibility that because of the seven year gap between

marriage date (1707) and birth of first child (1714), Mary Knowlton died and John remarried, the children being those of his 2nd wife (also a Mary). John's widow, Mary, d. 9 Mar. 1749, ae 69. (Mary Knowlton was born 29 Mar. 1681 so would have been almost 68 if this was her death date.)

Bowman lists three children (no dates) - Joseph and two daughters. The births of five Williams children can be found in Norwich CT VR 1:62, viz: Mary, b. 17 Feb. 1713/4; Benjamin, b. 4 July 1715, d. 15 July 1732; Joseph, b. 22 Jan. 1717/18, d. 27 May 1719; Zipporah, b. 28 July 1720 and Joseph, b. 23 Apr. 1723.

<8> p.450, The six Fuller children are listed without dates, viz: Matthew, Barnabas, Joseph, Benjamin, Desire and Sarah (both daughters b. after 30 Dec. 1670) <MD 12:189>.

<9> p.450, The eleven year span between the 3rd and 4th child is unusual. Since his wife Elizabeth was mentioned in his will is it possible Barnabas Fuller had a second wife Elizabeth which could explain this gap?

<10> p.451, MF5G 4:40 questions whether the year of birth should read 1700/01.

<11> p.451, Lydia (Conant) Lovell, (dau of Nathaniel & Hannah Mansfield), b. 8 Nov. 1692 <Bridgewater VR 1:80>; d. 28 Dec. 1764, Bolton CT <MF5G 4:115>.

<12> p.451, Matthew Fuller[4] is given the death date of 12 Dec. 1754, Sharon CT (no source). However, MF5G 4:41 shows he died between 1734 (joined church) - 3 Feb. 1743/4 (widow's will).

An eighth child, Hannah Fuller, was b. 10 July 1713, Colchester CT <MF5G 4:41>.

<13> p.451, The files of the descendants of Matthew Fuller are mixed with those of his brother, Samuel and have had to be sorted out. There is also inconsistency in giving him a generation number; he is shown as both Matthew[1] and Matthew[2] (Edward[1]). A reason for this may be due to the controversy surrounding his parentage. He is presently accepted as the son of Edward[1] not on the basis of an original record which states this relationship but rather on the basis of a great deal of strong circumstantial evidence in original records which points to this conclusion. A very thorough discussion of this matter (citing evidence both pro and con) can be found in TAG 61:194-99.

<14> p.451, MF5G 4:8 gives his date of death as 26 Mar. not 25 as stated here. Lieut. Samuel Fuller was killed during King Phillip's War. For an account, see Soldiers in King Phillip's War by George Bodge, repr. 1976, Baltimore.

<15> p.451, Moses Rowley, (son of Henry & ( ) (Palmer)), d. 14 June 1705, E. Haddam CT <MF5G 4:10>. For more data on the Rowley family see NYGBR 37:58-61 and TAG 32:38:45.

<16> p.451, The births of the 1st eight children can be found in MD 12:153.

<17> p.452, The wife of Samuel Fuller[3], Mary was mentioned in the will of Samuel's father, Matthew in 1678. However, she is also mentioned in the will of her son Matthias so was still living 7 Aug. 1696 <MD 31:187>.

<18> p.452, d. betw. 7 Aug. 1696 (will) - 28 May 1697 (prob.) <MD 31:187>.

<19> p.452, b. 15 Aug. 1676, Barnstable <MF5G 4:9>.

<20> p.452, Apparently John Fuller had a daughter by his 1st wife, Bethiah ( ). In his will, dated 1691, he mentions eldest daughter Lydia, wf of Joseph Dimmick. <Barnstable Co.Prob.2:107>.

<21> p.452, Jonathan Fuller m. 1st Eleanor Bennett, 14 Feb. 1711/12, Middleboro <MD 2:158>. She was the daughter of John, b. 18 Dec. 1689, Middleboro <MD 1:224>, d. 28 Sept. 1727 <Middleboro Deaths:70 - "1721 in her 38th yr" an error for 1727?>. MD 5:38 indicates the original records say 1720.

Jonathan & Eleanor had six children, b. Middleboro, <MD 4:68>, viz: Margaret, b. 17 Nov. 1712; Abigail, b. 11 Mar. 1714/5; Jabez, b. 22 July 1717; Jonathan, b. 13 July 1719; Timothy b. 29 June 1721; and Molly, b. 11 Sept. 1725 <MD 6:228>.

* * * * * * *

REFERENCE LIST

GENEALOGICAL ARTICLES PERTAINING TO E. FULLER FAMILY RESEARCH

Mayflower Descendant (MD) (1899-1937)

2:237-41 - Will & Inventory of Samuel Fuller[2]
13:7-11 - Will & Inventory of Capt. Matthew Fuller
16:192 - Autograph of Samuel Fuller[2]

Mayflower Descendant (MD) (1985-1990)

36:169-72 - The Mary Butler (Bass) Smith Bible
38:113-18 - Descendants of Thomas Fuller[6] (1718-1808)

Mayflower Quarterly (MQ) (1975-1990)

44:105-08 - Two New Lines To Pilgrims John Howland & Edward Fuller - (Lydia Smith, wife of William Bassett of Rochester MA)
45:144-45 - The Identity of Deborah Pratt
49:137-38 - John & Sarah (Bonham[4]) Fitz Randolph of Belvidere NJ
54:204-05 - Abigail, The Wife of Israel Stowell
55:112-13 - Mending a Fuller Break - (John Fuller[6])
55:292-95 - Which Hannah Pratt Did Jabez Fuller (1717-1770) Marry?
56:208-11 - Francis Fuller[6] And His Wife Hannah Cobb Share Seven Lines To Edward Fuller and John Howland

Miscellaneous

Mayflower Families Through Five Generations: Edward Fuller, pub. by General Society of Mayflower Descendants. Vol. 4. 1990.

NYGBR 33:171 - John Fuller of Redenhall, Eng. And His Descendants in New England
TAG 15:39-40 - Fuller Families of Colchester, Wethersfield & Farmington CT
TAG 61:194 - Was Matthew Fuller of Plymouth Colony A Son of Pilgrim Edward Fuller?

* * * * * * * * * * * *

SAMUEL FULLER

MICRO # 1 of 3

Samuel FULLER[1], d. betw. 30 July 1633 (will) - 28 Oct. 1633 (prob.) <MD 1:24, 2:8><1>

CHILDREN OF Samuel FULLER[1] & 3rd Bridget LEE: (2) <MD 1:25><2>

Rev. Samuel FULLER[2], b. c1628/9; d. 17 Aug. 1695 <MD 8:256><3>

Mercy FULLER[2], b. aft. 22 May 1627 (Cattle Division) <MD 1:151>; d. aft. 1650

Fuller Inscriptions, Thompson St. Cemetery, Halifax:

John FULLER, d. 24 Apr. 1766, 74th yr

Hannah FULLER, wf of John, d. 10 Sept. 1760, 75th yr (notation - 20 Sept.)

John FULLER, son of John & Hannah, d. 2 Aug. 1747, 24th yr

Hannah FULLER, d. 18 Nov. 1769, 50th yr (notation - Mrs., 8 Nov.)

Ebenezer FULLER, d. 27 Nov. 1786, 98th yr

Ebenezer FULLER, d. 22 Dec. 1769, 49th yr (notation - Jr.)

Lydia FULLER, wf of Ebenezer, d. 22 Aug. 1766, 39th yr

Chipman FULLER, d. 23 Sept. 1796, 41st yr

Thankful FULLER, widow of Chipman, d. 6 Nov. 1815, 55th yr

Miss Lydia FULLER, d. 16 Feb. 1812, 57th yr

Miss Nancy FULLER, d. 25 Mar. 1826, 31st yr

Capt. Ebenezer FULLER, d. 20 Feb. 1844, ae 61

Rebecca FULLER, wf of Lieut. Ebenezer, d. 16 May 1816, 38th yr

Ephraim FULLER, d. 12 Mar. 1813, ae 68y4m

Zerviah FULLER, wf of Ephraim, d. 25 Mar. 1781, ae 30 wanting 2 days

Miss Hannah FULLER, d. 3 Nov. 1814, ae 42 yrs (notation - 42nd yr)

Betsey FULLER, d. 7 Jan. 1836, 24th yr (notation - ae 24)

Ephraim FULLER, d. 11 Dec. 1843, ae 31

Benjamin FULLER, d. 4 Jan. 1836, ae 39

Polly FULLER, wf of Benjamin, d. 11 Nov. 1821, 22nd yr

Samuel FULLER, d. 10 Nov. 1842, 80th yr

Sally FULLER, wf of Samuel, d. 28 Apr. 1840, ae 73

William Nelson FULLER, son of Ebenezer & Abigail, d. 8 May 1832, ae 2y8m19d

Nathan FULLER, d. 26 Jan. 1761, ae 36

Ephraim Henry FULLER, son of Ephraim & Rebecca, d. 7 Mar. 1841, ae 2y10m

Mary Ann Perkins FULLER, dau of Benjamin & Anna T., d. 27 Dec. 1835, ae 6y10m

Nelson FULLER, son of Capt. Ebenezer & Abigail, d. 16 Feb. 1824, ae 1y6m

Fuller Inscriptions, Monponset Pond Cemetery, Halifax:

Noah FULLER, son of Ebenezer & Elizabeth, d. 22 Apr. 1749, 17th yr

Thomas FULLER, d. 1 Nov. 1810, ae 64 (notation - 4 Nov.)

Hannah FULLER, widow of Thomas, d. 25 Aug. 1814, ae 68

Miss Abigail FULLER, d. 7 Dec. 1806, 60th yr (notation - Mrs.)

Thomas FULLER, d. 13 Oct. 1845, ae 67 (notation - 15 Oct.)

Sally FULLER, widow of Thomas, d. 23 Dec. 1845, ae 52

Cyrus FULLER, d. 23 Feb. 1816, ae 35

Miranda FULLER, d. 24 May 1847, ae 24

George FULLER, d. 16 Sept. 1838, 24th yr

Joshua T. FULLER, d. 25 Oct. 1842, ae 21y11m

Hannah FULLER, d. 25 Sept. 1843, ae 24y9m

Sarah Scott FULLER, wf of Sylvanus R., d. 5 May 1845, ae 21y6m

Fuller Inscriptions, Old Green Cemetery, Plympton:

Seth FULLER, d. 22 Nov. 1760, 46th yr

John FULLER, son of Abial & Annie, d. 18 May 1715, 12th yr

Benjamin FULLER, son of Abial & Annie, d. 25 May 1724, 19th yr

Abigail FULLER, d. 23 Oct. 1756, 47th yr

Anness FULLER, d. 24 Feb. 1737, 19th yr

Zerviah FULLER, dau of Ephraim & Zerviah & wf of Isaiah Ripley Jr., d. 27 Mar. 1810, 33y10m25d

Samuel FULLER, d. 6 Sept. 1728, 70th yr

Judith FULLER, wf of James, d. 23 Feb. 1725, 21st yr (notation - 1725/6)

Samuel FULLER, son of Nathaniel & Martha, d. 7 Mar. 1743, ae 13y3m26d

Priscilla FULLER, wf of Amos, d. 28 Feb. 1834, ae 26y1m10d

Philemon FULLER, d. 6 Dec. 1838, ae 75y1m16d

Mercy FULLER, wf of Philemon, d. 23 Oct. 1847, ae 81y4m1d

Ephraim FULLER, d. 7 Aug. 1847, 68th yr

Clara FULLER, dau of Ephraim & Zerviah, d. 3 Jan. 1840, ae 29y24d (notation - 13 Jan.)

Fuller Inscriptions, Green Cemetery, Middleboro:

Jabez FULLER, d. 14 Oct. 1728, 31st yr

Dr. Jonathan FULLER, d. 13 Mar. 1802, 54th yr

Lucy FULLER, wf of Dr. Jonathan, d. 17 Sept. 1839, 82nd yr

John FULLER, son of Dr. Jonathan & Lucy, d. 23 Feb. 1797, ae 11m

Thomas FULLER, son of Dr. Jonathan & Lucy, d. 16 July 1782, 20th month

Jonathan Hyller FULLER, son of Dr. Jonathan & Lucy, d. 23 May 1793, ae 14y4m4d

John FULLER, d. 15 Apr. 1809, 57th yr

Betsey FULLER, wf of John, d. 3 Sept. 1832, 75th yr

Miss Betsey FULLER, d. 26 Feb. 1814, 28th yr

Fuller Inscriptions, Nemasket Hill Cemetery:

Rev. Samuel FULLER, d. 17 Aug. 1695, ae 70 (notation - 71st yr)<3>

Thomas FULLER, d. 8 Dec. 1774, 17th yr

Fuller Inscriptions, South Middleboro Cemetery:

Capt. Gamaliel FULLER, d. 23 Aug. 1848, ae 83

Orpal FULLER, widow of Capt. Gamaliel, d. 27 Dec. 1843, ae 77

Capt. John B. FULLER, d. 11 June 1835, ae 33

Lurana FULLER, dau of John B. & Lurana, d. Oct. 1822, ae 5m

Mercy P. FULLER, wf of Abiel, d. 12 Oct. 1831, ae 25

Almira FULLER, wf of Abiel, d. 23 Feb. 1840, ae 40

Sarah C. FULLER, dau of Abiel & Mercy P., d. 17 Oct. 1831, ae 5m

Fuller Inscriptions, Old Pond Cemetery, Lakeville:

Ziba FULLER, d. 4 Apr. 1811, 48th yr

Samuel FULLER, son of Ziba, d. 16 Feb. 1843, ae 45y2m

Hannah FULLER, wf of John, d. 13 Sept. 1803, ae 30y7m1d

Fuller Inscriptions, Central Cemetery, Kingston:

Ebenezer FULLER, d. 2 May 1759, 65th yr

Capt. Josiah FULLER, d. 3 Sept. 1805, 84th yr

Lydia FULLER, wf of Josiah, d. 3 Apr. 1784, 58th yr

Deacon John FULLER, d. 25 Sept. 1778, 80th yr

Deborah FULLER, wf of Mr. John, d. 8 Nov. 1776, ae 63y3m15d

Mary FULLER, widow of Deacon John & formerly wf of Robert Cushman, d. 3 May 1796, ae 94y3d

Mercy FULLER, widow of John, d. 5 ( ) 1782, 79th yr

Capt. Gilbert FULLER, d. 3 Dec. 1844, ae 43 (on same stone with:)

Mary FULLER, his wife, d. 31 Aug. 1846, ae 38

Zephaniah FULLER Jr., d. 31 Oct. 1806, 23rd yr, in West Indies

Dr. Jabez FULLER, d. 12 Apr. 1813, ae 59

Lucy FULLER, d. 25 Oct. 1847, ae 89
Dr. Seth FULLER, son of Dr. Jabez & Lucy, d. 4 Sept. 1807, ae 25y13d
Sarah FULLER, wf of Consider, d. 19 Sept. 1805, ae 33
Sarah FULLER, wf of Capt. Eleazer R., d. 4 Jan. 1825, ae 38
Eleazer FULLER, son of Eleazer R. & Sarah, d. 20 July 1834, ae 22y6m, at sea
John FULLER, d. 20 Oct. 1828, ae 86
Rebecca FULLER, wf of John, d. 16 June 1845
Hannah FULLER, wf of Benjamin, d. 14 Jan. 1826, ae 52
Deborah FULLER, widow of Ebenezer & formerly wf of David Eaton, d. 25 July 1809, ae 81

Fuller Inscriptions, North Carver Cemetery, Carver:

Hannah FULLER, wf of Seth Jr., d. 23 May 1764, ae 32
Jane H. FULLER, wf of Ebenezer Jr., d. 26 Jan. 1843, 21st yr
Issachar FULLER, d. 31 Oct. 1822, ae 93y3m12d
Elizabeth FULLER, wf of Issachar, d. 2 July 1781, ae about 51
Lucy FULLER, wf of Issacher, d. 30 Apr. 1847, ae 95
Thomas FULLER, son of Dr. Thomas & Polly, d. 11 Jan. 1790, ae 1m4d
Betsey FULLER, dau of Dr. Thomas & Polly, d. 15 Sept. 1788, ae 2y8m3d
Ezra M.B. FULLER, son of Ezra & Elizabeth A., d. 22 Aug. 1847, ae 5m23d

Fuller Inscription, Pierce & Morton Cemetery, Freetown:

Mary Fuller, wf of Asa, d. 23 Sept. 1838, ae 34

Fuller Inscriptions, Bensontown Cemetery, Bridgewater:

William FULLER, d. 11 July 1847, ae 72y2m18d (on same stone with:)
Tabitha FULLER, his wife, d. 10 Sept. 1856, ae 75y6m28d

SAMUEL FULLER^{2} (Samuel^{1})

CHILD OF Rev. Samuel FULLER^{2} & 1st ( ):
Samuel FULLER^{3}, b. c1658 <MD 5:69>; d. 6 Sept. 1728, Plympton g.s. <MD 10:116>
Elizabeth ( ) BOWEN, d. 11 Nov. 1713, Plympton <MD 2:140>**<4>**
CHILDREN OF Rev. Samuel FULLER^{2} & 2nd Elizabeth ( ) BOWEN: (6) <MD 5:69>
John FULLER^{3}, b. pre Sept. 1674* <2nd son, MD 5:69>; d. pre 10 Mar. 1709/10 (prob.)
Mercy FULLER^{3}, b. c1672; d. 25 Sept. 1735*, 63rd yr, Eastham g.s. <MD 8:3> (wf of Daniel Cole)
Experience FULLER^{3}, b. pre 1678*; d. betw. 20 July 1718* - 21 Dec. 1728*
Elizabeth FULLER^{3}, b. pre 1679*
Hannah FULLER^{3}, b. ( ), d. betw. 11 June 1707 - 1709* <Middleboro ChR:82>
Dr. Isaac FULLER^{3}, b. aft. 25 Sept. 1681*; d. pre 16 Nov. 1727 (adm.)<Plymouth Co.PR 5:393>
Samuel EATON^{3} (Samuel^{2}), b. c1663, d. 8 Mar. 1723/4, 61st yr, Middleboro <MD 4:74>
CHILDREN OF Samuel EATON & Elizabeth FULLER^{3}: (4) <MD 2:42>
Mercy EATON^{4}, b. 16 Dec. 1695; d. pre 1728*
Keziah EATON^{4}, b. 16 May 1700; d. 7 Feb. 1709/10 <MD 2:159>
Elizabeth EATON^{4}, b. 26 July 1701
Barnabas EATON^{4}, b. 12 Apr. 1703
James WOOD, d. pre 21 Dec. 1728 <MD 18:227>
CHILDREN OF James WOOD & Experience FULLER^{3}: (7)**<5>**
Priscilla RICKARD^{5} (*Jos.^{4}, John^{3}, Giles$^{2-1}$), b. 21 Jan. 1709/10, Plympton <MD 5:183>
CHILDREN OF Benjamin WOOD^{4} (Exper. Fuller^{3}) & Priscilla RICKARD: (4) <Middleboro, MD 14:245>**<6>**
Samuel WOOD^{5}, b. 6 Jan. 1733/4
Barnabas WOOD^{5}, b. 26 July 1735
Benjamin WOOD^{5}, b. 6 July 1737
Priscilla WOOD^{5}, b. 1 July 1739

CHILDREN OF Jonathan WOOD^{4} (Exper. Fuller^{3}) & Persis ROBBINS: (4) <Middleboro>**<7>**

Jonathan WOOD^{5}, b. 13 Feb. 1726/7 <MD 7:242>

Jedediah WOOD^{5}, b. 25 May 1728 <MD 7:242>

Elizabeth WOOD^{5}, b. 9 Apr. 1730 <MD 9:48>

James WOOD^{5}, b. 12 Mar. 1731/2 <MD 9:48>

George HOLMES, d. betw. 11 Feb. 1746 (will) - 4 Mar. 1746 (prob.)**<8>**

CHILDREN OF George HOLMES & Lydia WOOD^{4} (Experience Fuller^{3}): (2) <Plymouth, MD 13:111>

George HOLMES^{5}, b. 20 Jan. 1720/1

Richard HOLMES^{5}, b. 22 Feb. 1723/4; d. pre 11 Feb. 1746*

Lydia WEST^{6} (Bethiah Keen^{5}, Josiah^{4}, Abigail Little^{3}, Anna Warren^{2}), b. 15 June 1725, Plymouth <MD 13:113>

CHILDREN OF George HOLMES^{5} & Lydia WEST: (12) <1-4, Plymouth, MD 15:161>

Lydia HOLMES^{6}, d.y.

George HOLMES^{6}, b. 8 Aug. 1742; d. 10 July 1819*, ae 77 <Plymouth ChR 2:667>

Lydia HOLMES^{6}, d. aft. 17 Jan. 1820 <brother Joshua's estate below, 50:489> (wf of Ben. Clark)

Richard HOLMES^{6}, b. 1 June 1745; d. 22 Oct. 1820, Plymouth g.s. <Burial Hill, Kingman:136>

Bethiah HOLMES^{6}, b. c1745, d. 6 Dec. 1806, 61st yr, Plymouth g.s. <Kingman:108>

Experience HOLMES^{6}, b. c1752; d. 22 Dec. 1813, ae 61, Kingston g.s. <MD 7:27>

Sarah HOLMES^{6}, b. c1753*, d. 18 Sept. 1827, Plymouth <Kingman:158> (widow of Samuel Lanman)

Joshua HOLMES^{6}, d. pre 7 May 1813 (adm.) <Plymouth Co.PR #10481, 39:408>

Barnabas HOLMES^{6}, b. 1756*, d. 20 Mar. 1837*, ae 81, Plymouth g.s. <Burial Hill, Kingman:190>**<9>**

Mary HOLMES^{6}, b. c1765, d. 5 Jan. 1838, ae 73, Plymouth g.s. <Kingman:191>

Elizabeth HOLMES^{6}, d. aft. 1820*

Rebecca HOLMES^{6}, d. aft. 17 Jan. 1820 <Joshua's estate above, 50:489> (wf of Richard Austin)**<10>**

CHILDREN OF Caleb BARTLETT & Elizabeth HOLMES^{6}: (9)**<11>**

Thomas COOPER, b. c1749, d. 11 Oct. 1808, ae 59, Kingston g.s. <MD 7:27> (hus of Exper. Holmes^{6})

Ansel CHURCHILL^{5} (Ephraim^{4}, Stephen^{3}, Eliezer^{2}, John^{1}), b. 29 Mar. 1745* <Churchill Gen.:60>

CHILDREN OF Ansel CHURCHILL & Bethiah HOLMES^{6} (George^{5}): (1 of 5) **<12>**

John CHURCHILL^{7}, b. 1775, Plymouth **<13>**

Nancy JACKSON, (dau of Isaac), b. 28 July 1784 <Plymouth VR 2:50>**<14>**

CHILDREN OF John CHURCHILL^{7} & Nancy JACKSON: (7) <Churchill Gen.:136>

Hannah CHURCHILL^{8}, b. 1802

George CHURCHILL^{8}, b. 1803

John CHURCHILL^{8}, b. June 1805, d. 15 May 1706**<15>**

Bethia CHURCHILL^{8}, b. 12 Apr. 1807

Nancy CHURCHILL^{8}, b. 1808, d. 1822**<16>**

Sally Ann CHURCHILL^{8}, b. 26 Aug. 1811

Lillis Barton CHURCHILL^{8}, b. 22 Nov. 1813

Anna RICH, (dau of Walter), b. c1745, d. Mar. 1829, ae 84 <Plymouth VR 2:431>(wf of Geo. Holmes^{6})

CHILDREN OF William SAVERY & Lydia HOLMES^{6} (George^{5}): (5)**<17>**

Peter LANMAN, b. c1759, Plymouth, d. 14 Sept. 1825, 66th yr, Plymouth g.s. <Kingman:149>

CHILDREN OF Peter LANMAN & Mary HOLMES^{6} (George^{5}): (9)*

Polly LANMAN^{7}, b. 1784

Peter LANMAN^{7}, b. 1786, d.y.

Sally LANMAN^{7}, b. 1788

Peter LANMAN^{7}, b. 1790

Nancy LANMAN^{7}, b. 1792

Isaac LANMAN^{7}, b. 1794

Samuel LANMAN^{7}, b. 1796

Thomas LANMAN^{7}, b. 1798

Eliza E. LANMAN^{7}, b. 1801

Abigail DAMMON, b. c1754, d. 8 Apr. 1807, 53rd yr, Plymouth g.s. <Burial Hill by Drew:120>

CHILDREN OF Richard HOLMES^{6} & Abigail DAMMON: (1 of 9)<18>

Abigail HOLMES^{7}, b. c1773, d. 4 Jan. 1821, 48th yr, Plymouth g.s. <Burial Hill by Kingman:137> (3rd wf of William Leonard below)

Ephraim BARTLETT^{7} (Ephraim^{6}, Robert$^{5-4}$, Jos.^{3}, Mary Warren^{2}), b. c1766, d. 9 Sept. 1800, 34th yr, drowned on the Grand Bank <Burial Hill by Drew:149>

CHILD OF Ephraim BARTLETT & Abigail HOLMES^{7}:<19>

William LEONARD, b. 1767

Rebecca BARTLETT^{7} (Ephraim^{6}- see above), b. 1769, d. 2 Oct. 1801, 32nd yr, Plymouth <Drew:149> (1st wf of William Leonard)

Susanna BARTLETT^{7} (Ephraim^{6}- see above), b. 1763, d. 14 Dec. 1808, 45th yr, Plymouth <Drew:149> (2nd wf of William Leonard)

CHILDREN OF William LEONARD: (2)<20>

Nathaniel COBB, b. 1747*, Plympton

CHILD OF Nathaniel COBB & Sarah HOLMES^{6} (George^{5}):

Sarah COBB^{7}, b. ( )<21>

CHILDREN OF Samuel LANMAN & Sarah (HOLMES^{6}) Cobb: (6)<22>

Eleazer LEWIS, d. pre 3 Feb. 1727 (adm.) <Plymouth Co.PR 5:352><23>

CHILDREN OF Eleazer LEWIS & 1st Hannah FULLER^{3}: (5)

Edward LEWIS^{4}, b. pre Feb. 1707*

Susanna LEWIS^{4},

Hannah LEWIS^{4}, b. 1703, d. 10 Feb. 1793, 89y7m <E. Bridgewater ChR> (wf of Thomas Snell)

Elizabeth LEWIS^{4}, b. ( )

Shubael LEWIS^{4}, b. ( )

CHILDREN OF Eleazer LEWIS & 2nd Mary ( ): (3)<24>

Thomas SNELL, b. 1696, d. 28 July 1772 <E. Bridgewater ChR>

CHILDREN OF Thomas SNELL & Hannah LEWIS^{4}:<25>

CHILD OF Shubael LEWIS^{4} (Hannah Fuller^{3}) & Hasadiah EDDY (dau of Jabez):<26>

Samuel LEWIS^{5}, b. 1739

CHILDREN OF Samuel LEWIS & Mary NICHOLLS: (2) <Brinfield VR:86><27>

Azubah LEWIS, b. 14 Jan. 1778

Elizabeth LEWIS, b. 1 Apr. 1780

Mary PRATT, d. aft. 11 Nov. 1729 <Plymouth Co.Deeds 24:193>

CHILDREN OF Dr. Isaac FULLER^{3} & Mary PRATT: (7) <Middleboro, 1-4, MD 7:239; 5-7, MD 7:240>

Reliance FULLER^{4}, b. 28 Dec. 1710 <also rec. Plympton, MD 3:163>

Isaac FULLER^{4}, b. 24 Sept. 1712 <also rec. Plympton, MD 3:163>

Elizabeth FULLER^{4}, b. 23 July 1715

Samuel FULLER^{4}, b. 29 Jan. 1717/18

Micah FULLER^{4}, b. 31 Jan. 1719/20

Dr. Jabez FULLER^{4}, b. 7 May 1723; d. 5 Oct. 1781 <Medfield VR>

Mary FULLER^{4}, b. 23 Aug. 1726

Sarah PACKARD^{5} (Susanna Kingman^{4}, Mary Mitchell^{3}, Jacob^{2}, Experience^{1}), b. 23 May 1719, Bridgewater <MD 15:168>

CHILDREN OF Isaac FULLER^{4} & Sarah PACKARD: (9) <Bridgewater VR 1:122>

Isaac FULLER^{5}, b. 15 Dec. 1738

Olive FULLER^{5}, b. 14 Oct. 1740

Lemuel FULLER^{5}, b. 29 Sept. 1742

Isaiah FULLER^{5}, b. 7 July 1744

Sarah FULLER^{5}, b. 23 Mar.1746

Susanna FULLER^{5}, b. 27 Nov. 1748

Lois FULLER^{5}, b. 13 Oct. 1751

Benjamin FULLER^{5}, b. 22 Sept. 1754

Reliance FULLER^{5}, b. 22 Dec. 1756

Huldah FULLER, d. 18 May 1849, ae 74y7m16d, dropsy, wf of Isaac, dau of Nehemiah Leonard, b. Scituate <Hanson VR:95> (also rec. Pembroke VR:408>

Isaac FULLER, d. 4 Nov. 1851, ae 81y10m20d, Hanson, apoplexy, widower, farmer, b. Easton, son of Isaac & Mary <Mass.VR 58:174>

Elizabeth HILLIARD, d. 22 Oct. 1801 <Medfield VR>**<28>**

CHILDREN OF Jabez FULLER^{4} (Isaac^{3}) & Elizabeth HILLIARD: (9) <Medfield VR>

Dr. Jonathan FULLER^{5}, b. 3 Oct. 1748; d. 13 Mar. 1802, The Green g.s., Middleboro <MD 13:25>

John FULLER^{5}, b. 28 July 1750; d. 22 Sept. 1830 <Medfield VR>

Elisabeth FULLER^{5}, b. 12 Apr. 1752

Dr. Jabez FULLER^{5}, b. 26 May 1753; d. 12 Apr. 1813, Kingston g.s. <MD 7:87>

Thomas FULLER^{5}, b. 27 June 1755

Mary FULLER^{5}, b. 9 June 1758; d. 11 June 1822 <Medfield VR>

Catherine FULLER^{5}, b. 2 Apr. 1760; d. 2 Dec. 1831 <Medfield VR>

Sara FULLER^{5}, b. 25 Feb. 1763

Experience FULLER^{5}, b. 1 June 1766

Lucy EDDY, b. c1757, d. 17 Sept. 1839, 82nd yr, The Green g.s., Middleboro <MD 13:25>**<29>**

CHILDREN OF Dr. Jonathan FULLER^{5} & Lucy EDDY: (3)**<30>**

Jonathan Hyller FULLER^{6}, b. 1779, d. 23 May 1793, ae 14y4m14d, drowned <MD 13:25>

Thomas FULLER^{6}, b. 1780, d. 16 July 1782, ae 20m

John FULLER^{6}, b. 1796, d. 23 Feb. 1797, ae 11m3d <MD 13:25>

MICRO #2 of 3

Lucy LORING^{5} (Anna Alden^{4}, John^{3}, Jonathan^{2}), bpt. 19 Nov. 1758*, Duxbury; d. 25 Oct. 1847, ae 89 Kingston g.s. <MD 7:87> (wf of Jabez Fuller$^{5-4}$)

Martha FULLER^{6} (*Barnabas^{5}, Nathaniel^{4}, Samuel^{3-2-1}), b. 11 Jan. 1754, Kingston; d. 20 Mar. 1804, Medfield (1st wf of John Fuller^{5} (Jabez^{4}))

CHILDREN OF John FULLER^{3} & Mercy NELSON, (dau of Wm): (5 of 9)**<31>**

Ebenezer FULLER^{4}, b. c1688, d. 27 Nov. 1786, 98th yr, Thompson St. Cem., Halifax <MD 13:11>

John FULLER^{4}, b. 20 Mar. 1692, Middleboro; d. 24 Apr. 1766**<32>**

Samuel FULLER^{4}, b. aft. 19 Sept. 1691

Jabez FULLER^{4}, b. 1697*, d. 14 Oct. 1728, 31st yr, Middleboro Green g.s. <MD 13:25>**<33>**

Joanna FULLER^{4}, d. aft. 19 Sept. 1712 (m. Tho. Doggett)

Deborah SOULE^{4} (Ben.^{3}, John^{2}), b. 23 Apr. 1702, Plymouth <MD 4:113>; d. 24 Jan. 1724/5, Plympton g.s. <MD 2:234, 10:115> (1st wf of Jabez Fuller^{4}, John^{3})**<33>**

Priscilla SAMSON^{4} (Lydia Standish^{3}, Alexander^{2}), b. 12 Nov. 1700, Plymouth <MD 3:123> (2nd wf of Jabez Fuller^{4}, John^{3})**<33>**

Hannah THOMAS, d. 20 Sept. 1760**<34>**

CHILDREN OF John FULLER^{4} (John^{3}) & 1st Hannah THOMAS: (4)

Hannah FULLER^{5}, b. 7 Feb. 1720; d. 8 Nov. 1769, unm**<35>**

Abigail FULLER^{5}, b. 1 July 1721; d. 17 Oct. 1723

John FULLER^{5}, b. 5 Sept. 1723**<36>**

Bathsheba FULLER^{5}, b. 19 Jan. 1726

Lydia (ALDEN) Eddy, d. 1 Mar. 1803 (2nd wf of John Fuller^{4})**<37>**

Daniel COLE^{2} (Dan.^{1}), b. c1666, d. 15 June 1736, 70th yr, Eastham g.s. <MD 8:3> (hus of Mercy Fuller^{3})

Mercy EATON^{3} (Samuel^{2}), d. aft. 27 Feb. 1704 (last child)

CHILDREN OF Samuel FULLER^{3} & Mercy EATON: (11) <Plymouth, MD 3:14>

Nathaniel FULLER^{4}, b. 14 Nov. 1687; d. betw. 16 Mar. 1749 (will) - 7 May 1750 (prob.)

Samuel FULLER^{4}, b. 30 Aug. 1689; d. pre 20 Dec. 1728 (adm.) <Plymouth Co.PR #8283>

William FULLER^{4}, b. 14 Feb. 1691; d. 26 Aug. 1692

Seth FULLER^{4}, b. 30 Aug. 1692

Ebenezer FULLER^{4}, b. 24 Mar. 1695; d. 2 May 1759, Kingston g.s. <MD 7:87>

Benjamin FULLER^{4}, b. 7 Mar. 1696

Elizabeth FULLER^{4}, b. 30 Mar. 1697

John FULLER^{4}, b. 19 Dec. 1698; d. 25 Sept. 1778, Kingston g.s. <MD 7:87>

Jabez FULLER^{4}, b. "beginning" June 1701

Marcey FULLER^{4}, b. 3 Oct. 1702

James FULLER^{4}, b. 27 Feb.1704

Jabez FULLER, b. 22 July 1717, Middleboro; d. 1770, Medfield

CHILDREN OF Jabez FULLER & Hannah PRATT: (11) <Middleboro, 1-4, MD 24:38, 5-11, MD 24:39>

Sarah FULLER, b. 22 July 1746

Lucy FULLER, b. 17 Jan. 1747; d.y.

Peter FULLER, b. 13 May 1748

Lucy FULLER, b. 13 May 1748 (twins)

Zenas FULLER, b. 8 July 1751

Betty FULLER, b. 13 Sept. 1753

John FULLER, b. 18 June 1754

Amasa FULLER, b. 6 Mar. 1755

Silas FULLER, b. 27 Apr. 1756

Andrew FULLER, b. 18 May 1758

Hannah FULLER, b. 6 Mar. 1764

Judith RICKARD, (dau of Henry & Mary), b. 2 Sept. 1705, Plympton <MD 10:115>; d. 23 Feb. 1725/6, Plympton <MD 2:235>

CHILD OF James FULLER^{4} (Sam.^{3}) & Judith RICKARD:

Elkanah FULLER^{5}, b. 9 Feb. 1725/6 <MD 1:245>

Samuel FULLER^{5} (Ben.^{4}, Sam.^{3}), d. pre 9 May 1758 (adm.), Plympton**<38>**

CHILDREN OF Samuel FULLER^{5} & Anna TINKHAM: (5) <Plympton VR>**<39>**

Mary FULLER^{6}, b. 23 Nov. 1748 <VR:106>

Rube FULLER^{6}, b. 20 Jan. 1750/1 <VR:107>

Benjamin FULLER^{6}, b. 10 Dec. 1752 <VR:103>

Silvanus FULLER^{6}, b. 16 Mar. 1755 <VR:107>

Anna FULLER^{6}, b. 4 May 1757 <VR:103>

Joanna GRAY^{5} (John^{4}, Mary Winslow^{3}, Mary Chilton^{2}), b. 29 Jan. 1695/6, Plymouth <MD 1:145>

CHILDREN OF Ebenezer FULLER^{4} (Sam.^{3}) & Joanna GRAY: (8) <1-3, Plymouth, MD 13:170; 3-8, Kingston, Gen.Adv.2:43>

Josiah FULLER^{5}, b. 15 May 1722; d. 3 Sept. 1805, Kingston g.s. <MD 7:87>

Samuel FULLER^{5}, b. 14 Oct. 1723; d. 22 Apr. 1724

Rebecca FULLER^{5}, b. 23 Apr. 1725

Hannah FULLER^{5}, b. 8 June 1727; d. 20 Aug. 1736

Mercy FULLER^{5}, b. 29 Aug. 1730; d. 8 Jan. 1733/4

Lois FULLER^{5}, b. 16 Nov. 1733

Eunice FULLER^{5}, b. 5 May 1736; d. 4 June 1781*, Plymouth (wf of Ebenezer Robbins**<40>**

Ebenezer FULLER^{5}, b. 16 Feb. 1737/8

Hannah COBB, b. c1771, d. 29 Apr. 1853, ae 82, widow, b. Plymouth <Plymouth TR 4:398>

CHILDREN OF Ansel ROBBINS & Hannah COBB: (12) <Plymouth TR 2:352>**<41>**

Amasa ROBBINS, b. 27 Aug. 1791

James ROBBINS, b. 10 Aug. 1793

Stephen ROBBINS, b. 18 Aug. 1795

Harvey ROBBINS, b. 12 Dec. 1797

Lemuel Cobb ROBBINS, b. 22 Sept. 1799; d. 2 Oct. 1800**<42>**

Betsey Cobb ROBBINS, b. 25 July 1801

Thaddeus ROBBINS, b. 4 Oct. 1803

Levi ROBBINS, b. 23 Sept. 1806; d. 2 Mar. 1869 <Plymouth TR 4:108>

Hannah Cobb ROBBINS, b. 2 Aug. 1808

John Flavill Cobb ROBBINS, b. 7 June 1810

Milton ROBBINS, b. ( )

Fear Cobb ROBBINS, b. ( )

Lydia CUSHMAN^{6} (Robert$^{5-4}$, Tho.^{3}, Mary Allerton^{2}), b. c1726, d. 3 Apr. 1784, 58th yr, Kingston g.s. <MD 7:87>**<43>**

CHILDREN OF Josiah FULLER^{5} (Eben.^{4}) & Lydia CUSHMAN^{6}: (5 of 12)**<44>**

Josiah FULLER^{6}, b. 15 Nov. 1747, d. 27 Nov.1747 <Gen.Adv.3:80>

Hannah FULLER^{6}, b. 15 Nov. 1747 <Kingston VR:81>

Josiah FULLER^{6}, b. 31 Oct. 1748 <Gen.Adv.3:80>

Angeline FULLER^{6}, bpt. 5 Mar. 1769 <Kingston VR:79>

Malachi FULLER^{6}, bpt. 5 Mar. 1769 <Kingston VR:83>

Elizabeth ( ) FULLER, b. 23 May 1750 (wf of Josiah Jr.)

CHILDREN OF Josiah FULLER Jr. & Elizabeth ( ): (5) <Kingston VR:80,81,81>**<45,46>**

John Holmes FULLER, b. 28 Oct. 1774

Content FULLER, b. 27 Nov. 1777**<47>**

Lemuel FULLER, b. 25 June 1781

Josiah FULLER, b. 11 Dec.1783

Ephraim Holmes FULLER, b. 6 Aug. 1786

CHILDREN OF Josiah FULLER Jr. & Lucy ( ): (3) <Kingston VR:80,82>**<46>**

Josiah FULLER, b. 16 Sept. 1808

Charles Warren FULLER, b. 29 Apr. 1810

Elizabeth Holmes FULLER, b. 12 Jan. 1812

Mercy GRAY^{5} (John^{4}, Mary Winslow^{3}, Mary Chilton^{2}), b. 4 Feb. 1703/4, Plymouth <MD 1:145>; d. 5 ( ) 1782, Kingston g.s. <MD 7:87>**<48>**

CHILDREN OF Jabez FULLER^{4} (Samuel^{3}) & Mercy GRAY: (6*) <*Gen.Adv.3:6>**<49>**

Thomas FULLER^{5}, b. 31 Aug. 1734, d. 2 Apr. 173()**<50>**

Joanna FULLER^{5}, b. 31 Mar. 173()**<51>**

James FULLER^{5}, b. 4 Dec. 1737; d. 1760

Jabez FULLER^{5}, b. 24 Feb.1739

John FULLER^{5}, b. 29 Sept. 1741

Mercy FULLER^{5}, b. 6 July 1747, Kingston

Elizabeth SHORT, (dau of Luke Jr. & Susanna), b. 1 Nov. 1693<Weymouth VR 1:275>;d. pre July 1785*

CHILDREN OF Ebenezer FULLER^{4} (John^{3}) & Elizabeth SHORT: (7) <1-6, Middleboro MD 13:4>

Susanna FULLER^{5}, b. 7 Dec. 1716 <MD 13:3>

Ruth FULLER^{5}, b. 18 Apr. 1719; d. 26 Jan. 1743, Halifax g.s. <MD 9:152>

Ebenezer FULLER^{5}, b. 18 Oct. 1721; d. 22 Dec. 1769, Thompson St. Cem., Halifax <MD 13:11>

Nathan FULLER^{5}, b. 22 Apr. 1725; d. 26 Jan. 1761, Thompson St. Cem., Halifax <MD 13:12>

Betty FULLER^{5}, b. 15 Aug. 1729

Noah FULLER^{5}, b. 7 Sept. 1732; d. 22 Apr. 1749, Monponsett Cem., Halifax <MD 9:153>

Lois FULLER^{5}, b. 22 July 1740 <Halifax VR:48>

Lydia CHIPMAN^{5} (Jacob^{4}, Sam.^{3}, Hope Howland^{2}), b. 19 Dec. 1728 <Halifax VR:41>; d. 22 Aug. 1766, Thompson St. Cem., Halifax <MD 13:12>

CHILDREN OF Ebenezer FULLER^{5} & 1st Lydia CHIPMAN: (5 of 6)**<52>**

Ruth FULLER^{6}, b. ( )

Lydia FULLER^{6}, d. 16 Feb. 1812, 57th yr, unm., Thompson St. Cem., Halifax <MD 13:12>

Chipman FULLER^{6}, b. c1755, d. 23 Sept. 1796, 41st yr, Thompson St. Cem., Halifax <MD 13:11>

Priscilla FULLER^{6}, b. c1758, d. 3 Jan. 1835, ae 76y5m17d, Plympton

Eunice FULLER^{6}, b. 7 Dec. 1760, Halifax; d. 27 July 1842

Deborah (FULLER) EATON, (dau of Jabez), b. 14 Dec. 1729, Kingston <Gen.Adv.2:2>; d. 21 July 1809, Kingston g.s. <MD 7:87> (2nd wf of Eben. Fuller^{5})

CHILDREN OF Ezekiel RIPLEY & Priscilla FULLER^{6}: (7)

Lydia RIPLEY^{7}, b. 27 Aug. 1789

Seba RIPLEY^{7}, b. 7 Aug. 1791

Coomer RIPLEY^{7}, b. 20 June 1793

Priscilla RIPLEY^{7}, b. 28 Aug. 1795

Ezekiel RIPLEY^{7}, b. 3 June 1797

Chipman RIPLEY^{7}, b. 1 June 1800

Ruth RIPLEY^{7}, b. 10 June 1802

Joel PERKINS, b. 6 Aug. 1761, E. Windsor CT; d. 26 Mar. 1841

CHILDREN OF Joel PERKINS & Eunice FULLER^{6} (Eben.^{5}): (7)

Ebenezer PERKINS^{7}, b. 7 Aug. 1790

Joel F. PERKINS^{7}, b. 22 Apr. 1792

Eunice PERKINS^{7}, b. 27 Nov. 1793

John PERKINS^{7}, b. 3 Mar. 1796

Ansel PERKINS^{7}, b. 29 May 1798

Nelson PERKINS^{7}, b. 4 July 1800

Alvah Chipman PERKINS^{7}, b. 4 Oct. 1803

Thankful WRIGHT^{6*} (*Eben.^{5}, Moses^{4}, Adam^{3}, Hester Cooke^{2}), b. c1760, Plympton; d. 6 Nov. 1815, 55th yr, Thompson St. Cem., Halifax <MD 13:12>

CHILDREN OF Chipman FULLER^{6} (Eben.^{5}) & Thankful WRIGHT: (5) <Halifax VR:19>

Ruth FULLER^{7}, b. 23 Oct. 1780; d. aft. 1804*

Ebenezer FULLER^{7}, b. 26 Nov. 1782; d. 20 Feb. 1844*, Thompson St. Cem., Halifax <MD 13:12>

Nathan FULLER^{7}, b. 23 Feb. 1785; d. 7 Jan. 1875, Halifax, farmer <Mass.VR 275:306>

Priscilla FULLER^{7}, b. 29 Nov. 1787

Nancy FULLER^{7}, b. 25 June 1795; d. 25 Mar. 1826, unm., Thompson St. Cem., Halifax <MD 13:12>

Faith SOULE^{6} (Jacob$^{5-4}$, James^{3}, John^{2}), b. c1784, Middleboro, d. 11 Nov. 1864, ae 79y11m, Halifax <Mass.VR 175:310>

CHILDREN OF Nathan FULLER^{7} & Faith SOULE: (3) <Halifax VR:90>

Chipman FULLER^{8}, b. 22 Mar. 1810

Nathan FULLER^{8}, b. 21 Dec. 1813

Alfred FULLER^{8}, b. 21 Apr. 1817; d. 30 June 1893, Bridgewater, widower <Mass.VR 437:583>

Mary P. FULLER, d. 30 May 1886, ae 73y11m18d, b. Kingston, dau of Joseph & Lucy Mitchell <Mass.VR 374:327> (wf of Alfred Fuller^{8})

MICRO #3 of 3

Ebenezer FULLER, b. c1782, d. 20 Feb. 1844, ae 61y2m24d, Thompson St. Cem., Halifax <MD 13:12>

Rebecca FULLER, b. c1778, d. 16 May 1816, 38th yr, Thompson St. Cem., Halifax <MD 13:12>

CHILD OF Ebenezer FULLER & 1st Rebecca FULLER:

Zerviah Nelson FULLER, b. 3 July 1811 <Halifax VR:92> (m. Calvin Gammon)

Abigail SAMSON^{7} (*Gideon^{6}, Zabdiel^{5}, Hannah Soule^{4}, Ben.^{3}),b. 6 Apr. 1794*,Plympton; d. pre 1864*

CHILDREN OF Ebenezer FULLER & 2nd Abigail SAMSON: (3)<1st 2, fath. will - Plymouth Co.Prob.#8212>

Rebecca FULLER, b. ( ) (m. Ephraim Fuller)

Ebenezer FULLER, b. aft. 1819

Nelson FULLER, b. 1822, d. 16 Feb. 1824, ae 1y6m

CHILDREN OF Elijah LEACH & Ruth FULLER^{6} (Eben.^{5}): (3) <Halifax VR:51>

Ebenezer LEACH^{7}, b. 11 Dec. 1772

Lucy LEACH^{7}, b. 31 Jan. 1775

Lois LEACH^{7}, b. 10 May 1777

Mary PARLOW, d. aft. 6 Apr. 1761* (wf of Nathan Fuller^{5})

CHILDREN OF Nathan FULLER^{5} (Eben.^{4}) & Mary PARLOW: (6)<53>

Joseph BOSWORTH, d. 1 Aug. 1769, 50th yr, Thompson St. Cem., Halifax <MD 12:240>

CHILD OF Joseph BOZWORTH & 1st Ruth FULLER^{5} (Eben^{4}):

James BOZWORTH^{6}, b. 16 Jan. 1743

Sarah COBB, b. c1721, d. 17 June 1804, ae 83, Thompson St. Cem., Halifax <MD 12:240>

CHILDREN OF Joseph BOZWORTH & 2nd Sarah COBB: (7)

Eli BOZWORTH, b. 10 Aug. 1745 <Halifax VR:49>

John BOZWORTH 2d, b. 28 Dec. 1746

Ruth BOZWORTH, b. 10 Sept. 1748

Richard BOZWORTH, b. 16 July 1750

Deborah BOZWORTH, b. 16 Jan. 1753

Joseph BOZWORTH, b. 15 Nov. 1756

Mary BOZWORTH, b. 5 Dec. 1758

Edmund WILLIS, (son of Silas), b. 24 June 1753 <Bridgewater VR 1:351><54>

Deborah RING^{4} (Eleazer^{3}, Deborah Hopkins^{2}), b. 10 July 1698, Plymouth <MD 1:208>; d. 8 Nov. 1763, Kingston g.s. <MD 7:87>

CHILDREN OF John FULLER^{4} (Sam.^{3}) & 1st Deborah RING: (10)<55>

Eleazer FULLER^{5}, b. 3 Nov. 1723; d. 20 Aug. 1736, Kingston g.s. <MD 7:87>

Issachar FULLER^{5}, b. 8 July 1725; d. 31 Oct. 1822, N. Carver g.s.

John FULLER^{5}, b. 16 Sept. 1727; d.y.

Deborah FULLER^{5}, b. 14 Dec. 1729

Susanna FULLER^{5}, b. 18 Nov. 1731

Noah FULLER^{5}, b. 21 May 1734

Ezra FULLER^{5}, b. 23 Apr. 1736; d. 24 May 1771, Kingston g.s. <MD 7:87>

Consider FULLER^{5}, b. 7 July 1738

Eleazer FULLER^{5}, b. 27 Apr. 1740

Hannah FULLER^{5}, b. 30 Apr. 1743

Jacob DINGLEY^{6} (Mary Holmes^{5}, Mary Brewster^{4}, Wrestling^{3}, Love^{2}), b. 8 Jan. 1727, Marshfield <MD 30:156> (hus. of Susanna Fuller^{5})

CHILDREN OF Consider FULLER^{5} & Lydia BRYANT: (2) <Halifax VR>

Luna FULLER^{6}, b. 17 Feb. 1760

Eliphalet FULLER^{6}, b. 23 Oct. 1761

Elizabeth DOTEN^{5} (John^{4-3-2}), b. c1730, d. 2 July 1781, ae about 51, N. Carver g.s.

CHILDREN OF Issachar FULLER^{5} (John^{4}) & 1st Elizabeth DOTEN: (11) <1-8, Kingston VR:80>

Lydia FULLER^{6}, b. 1 May 1749

Isaac FULLER^{6}, b. 8 Feb. 1751

John FULLER^{6}, b. 18 Mar. 1753

Deborah FULLER^{6}, b. 18 Feb. 1756

Noah FULLER^{6}, b. 26 Mar. 1758

Silvia FULLER^{6}, b. 13 Apr. 1760

Issachar FULLER^{6}, b. 22 Mar. 1762

Elizabeth FULLER^{6}, b. 10 Feb. 1764

Edward FULLER^{6}, b. 25 Aug.1768 <Carver VR:33>

Rebecca FULLER^{6}, b. 27 June 1772 <Carver VR:33>

Abigail FULLER^{6}, b. 18 July 1774 <Carver VR:33>

Lucy TINKHAM^{6} (Eben.^{5}, Jeremiah^{4}, Eben.^{3}, Mary Brown^{2}), b. 22 Apr. 1752, Middleboro <MD 20:37>; d. 30 Apr. 1847, N. Carver g.s.

CHILDREN OF Issachar FULLER^{5} & 2nd Lucy TINKHAM: (5) <Carver VR:34>

Lucy FULLER^{6}, b. 4 Nov. 1786; d. 3 Sept. 1864, Carver, dysentery <Mass.VR 175:305> (wf of E.Cobb)

Deborah FULLER^{6}, b. 3 Mar. 1788

Ebenezer FULLER^{6}, b. 26 Oct. 1789

Hannah FULLER^{6}, b. 4 Nov. 1786

Priscilla FULLER^{6}, b. 16 Feb. 1794

Ebenezer COBB, d. 30 Mar. 1864, N. Carver, ae 82y5m5d, palsy, farmer, son of Benjamin Cobb & Sarah Ransom <Mass.VR 175:304> (hus of Lucy Fuller^{6})

Martha SAMPSON^{3} (George^{2}, Abraham^{1}), b. 25 Oct. 1689

CHILDREN OF Nathaniel FULLER^{4} (Sam.^{3}) & Martha SAMPSON: (9) <Plympton, MD 3:164>

Sarah FULLER^{5}, b. 28 Sept. 1712 <MD 3:163>; d. 21 July 1763, Halifax g.s. <MD 9:152>

Ruth FULLER^{5}, b. 4 Mar. 1713/4

Elizabeth FULLER^{5}, b. 2 July 1716, d. 1716, Plympton g.s. <MD 10:115> (on stone with twin:)

William FULLER^{5}, b. 2 July 1716, d. 1716, Plympton g.s. <MD 10:116>

Amos FULLER^{5}, b. 12 Feb. 1718/9

Nathaniel FULLER^{5}, b. 26 May 1721; d. pre 9 Apr. 1748 (bond) <Plymouth Co.PR #8263>

Barnabas FULLER^{5}, b. 25 Sept. 1723

Jesse FULLER^{5}, b. 18 Feb. 1725/6

Samuel FULLER^{5}, b. 11 Nov. 1729; d. 7 Mar. 1743, Plympton g.s. <MD 10:116>

Abigail HARLOW^{6} (James^{5}, Abigail Church^{4}, Nath.^{3}, Eliz. Warren^{2}), b. c1722, d. 15 Apr. 1755, 33rd yr <Plympton VR>

CHILDREN OF Amos FULLER^{5} & 1st Abigail HARLOW: (6)*

Mary FULLER^{6}, b. 24 May 1745; d. 31 Oct. 1747

Martha FULLER^{6}, b. 15 Dec. 1746; d. Jan. 1746/7

Nathaniel FULLER^{6}, b. 12 Dec. 1747

Hannah FULLER^{6}, b. 1 Oct. 1749; d. 23 Mar. 1819

Sarah FULLER^{6}, b. 6 Apr. 1751

Abigail FULLER^{6}, b. 12 June 1753; d. 6 Feb. 1754

Rachel (STANDISH^{5}) Samson, b. 24 Apr. 1726; d. 13 Oct. 1809 <56>

CHILDREN OF Amos FULLER^{5} & 2nd Rachel (STANDISH) Samson: (2) <MD 2:45>

Amos FULLER^{6}, b. 27 Oct. 1760

Philemon FULLER^{6}, b. 20 Oct. 1763; d. pre 21 Jan. 1839 (adm.) <Plymouth Co.PR #8277, 10:235>

Isaac STURTEVANT^{5} (Fear Cushman^{4}, Isaac^{3}, Mary Allerton^{2}), b. 10 Aug. 1708, Plympton <MD 5:180>; d. 6 Feb. 1750, Halifax g.s. <MD 10:10>

CHILDREN OF Isaac STURTEVANT & Sarah FULLER^{5} (Nathaniel^{4}): (7) <Halifax VR:52>

Martha STURTEVANT^{6}, b. 18 Nov. 1735

Sarah STURTEVANT^{6}, b. 14 Mar. 1737/8; d. 25 Sept. 1747, Halifax <MD 3:32>

Isaac STURTEVANT^{6}, b. 11 Mar. 1739/40

Simeon STURTEVANT^{6}, b. 11 May 1742; d. 2 Mar. 1822, Halifax g.s. <MD 10:11>

Samuel STURTEVANT^{6}, b. 19 Jan. 1744/5; d. 8 Jan. 1839, Halifax g.s. <MD 10:10>

Jesse Fuller STURTEVANT^{6}, b. 27 Mar. 1748

Nathaniel STURTEVANT^{6}, b. 2 Aug. 1750

* * * * * * *

FOOTNOTES

<1> p.455, Samuel Fuller was bpt. 20 Jan. 1580, Redenhall, Norfolk co., Eng., son of Robert Fuller. <NEHGR 55:411> His 1st two marriages produced no known surviving children.
<2> p.455, Bradford tells us that Bridget Fuller brought a child with her when she came over in 1623. The Cattle Division of 1627 lists no children so the child apparently died young. Despite this fact, Bowman questions whether this child was the Bridget Fuller who m. Henry Sirkman in 1641, however this claim has never been proven.
<3> p.455,456 Was Samuel born in 1625 or 1629? The inscription on his gravestone says he died at the age of 70; Plymouth Church Records <MD 15:21> state he was "about 66 yrs" and Middleboro VR <MD 1:222> do not give his age. MF5G 1:51 amended his birth date from c1624 to aft. 22 May 1627 but repeat that he died in his 71st yr in 1695 which is contradictory. Since he was not mentioned in the Cattle Division of 1627 then it is safe to assume he was born c1629 and, as the Church Records state, was about 66 years old when he died in 1695.
<4> p.457, Elizabeth (Nichols^{3}) Bowen, (John^{2}, Francis^{1}).
<5> p.457, The seven Wood children are listed without data with the exception of #2-5 who were baptized 4 Nov. 1716, viz: Jonathan (eldest son), Benjamin, Barnabas, Abel, Ichabod, Lydia & James.
<6> p.457, MF5G 1:52-53 provides five additional Wood children born at Ashford CT, viz: Joseph, b. 15 Aug. 1743; Experience, b. 30 Apr. 1745; Deborah, b. 19 Dec. 1746; Noah, b. 3 Dec. 1749 and Sarah, b. 2 May 1752.
<7> p.458, Persis Robbins, dau of Jeduthan Robbins & Hannah Pratt, b. 27 Nov. 1699, Plymouth <MD 2:164>
<8> p.458, Son of John Holmes & Patience Bonum.
<9> p.458, Two wives are given for Barnabas Holmes - Anna Damon, 1787 and Margaret (Drew) Rickard, 1812. As no dates accompany the names of the three children (viz: Lydia West, Nancy & Judith) it is not clear who the mother was.
<10> p.458, The will of Experience (Holmes^{6}) Cooper calls Rebecca her half-sister.
<11> p.458, Mayflower descent is given to Caleb Bartlett in pencil with a line scribbled over it, viz: Caleb^{6} (Robert$^{5-4}$, Jos.^{3}, Mary Warren^{2})

The nine Bartlett children are listed in pencil without dates, viz: Caleb, Betsey, Isaac, Rebeca, Robert, Susan, George, Charles and Holmes.

<12> p.458, The remaining four Churchill children are listed without dates, viz: Ansell, Priscilla, Patience and Bethiah.
<13> p.458, John Churchill is given a date of death of 14 Oct. 1841, Plymouth, however this is clearly an error. Burial Hill by Drew:221, #1539 shows he d. 14 Oct. 1814, ae 39. His wife Nancy and two children are included with him.
<14> p.458, d. 11 June 1838, 54th yr <Burial Hill by Drew:221, #1540>.
<15> p.458, Ibed., p.221, #1540.
<16> p.458, d. 22 Aug. 1822, ae 14 <Ibed., p.221, #1542>
<17> p.458, The five Savery children are in pencil without dates, viz: William, Thomas, George Holmes, Sally and Joey. Lydia Holmes' second marriage to William Atwood produced one son, Wm.
<18> p.459, The names of the nine Holmes children were taken from their father's will <Plymouth Co.PR #10555, 53:168>. With the exception of Abigail, no dates accompany the names, viz: Richard, Thomas Cooper, Experience, Nancy, Elizabeth, Jane, Sarah and Polly.
<19> p.459, Ephraim Bartlett, b. 19 Feb. 1809, d. 3 Dec. 1832 <Drew:149> is the child credited to Ephraim & Abigail Bartlett. Unless one of these dates is an error, this could not be correct. Ephraim Sr. died, as is shown, in 1800. His alledged son could not have been born nine years later! Gravestone inscriptions are not infallible, could his year of birth, 1809, be an error for 1800 or is Bowman wrong in assigning this Ephraim to this family?
<20> p.459, Two children are listed for William Leonard, Rebecca & Eleanor, but without dates and no clue as to which of his wives was their mother. A third child can be found in Burial Hill by Drew:149 - Ephraim Bartlett Leonard, d. 31 Jan. 1809, ae 7m14d. He is listed here as the son of William & Susanna Leonard. The inscription is on the stone of his mother who died the previous month.
<21> p.459, Bowman shows Sarah Cobb^{7} as the wife of America Brewster. Burial Hill by Drew:120 lists "Sarah, widow of Capt. America Brewster, d. Dec. 22 1850, ae 75 yrs". (Her husband, America, is on the same page - d. 17 Nov. 1847, ae 74 yrs.)
<22> p.459, Burial Hill by Drew:145 gives a Samuel Lanman, d. 10 Jan. 1794, 73rd yr - no identification is given.

The six Lanman children are listed in pencil without dates, viz: Polly, Nathaniel Cobb, Elizabeth, Rebecca, Samuel and Lucy.

<23> p.459, Eleazer Lewis, b. 26 June 1664, Barnstable, son of Edward Lewis & Hannah Cobb <MD 10:250>
<24> p.459, The three Lewis children are listed without dates, viz: Keziah (bpt. 1713), Samuel and Mary.
<25> p.459, No children are listed. See MF5G 1:81 for a detailed account of the ten Snell children, viz: Deliverance, Thomas, Eleazer, Joseph, Hannah, Polycarpus, William, Barnabas, Lewis and Smith.
<26> p.459, No children are lsited. See MF5G 1:84-85 for a detailed account of the ten Lewis children, viz: Eleazer, Gideon, Jabez, Samuel, Hannah, Amasa, Abner, Elizabeth, Seth and Mary. Hasadiah Eddy is the dau. of Jabez Eddy & Mary Rickard.
<27> p.459, No identification is made as to whether this Samuel Lewis was the son of Shubael Lewis and Hannah Fuller.
<28> p.460, Elizabeth was b. 6 Oct. 1724, Boston, dau of John & Elizabeth Helyer <MF5G 1:90>.

<29> p.460, Lucy Eddy, b. 25 Mar. 1758, Middleboro, dau of Zachariah Eddy & Mercy Morton <Ibed.>
<30> p.460, MF5G 1:90 gives eight additional Fuller children, viz: Lucy Eddy, Sally, Thomas, Zachariah, Betsey, Jabez, Seth and Mercy Freeman.
<31> p.460, The additional four Fuller children are without additional data, viz: Elizabeth, Mary, Mercy and Lydia.
<32> p.460, bur. Thompson St. Cemetery, Halifax <MD 13:12>.
<33> p.460, Deborah Soule is mistakenly credited as the wife of Jabez Fuller[4] (Sam.[3]). She died the same day she gave birth to stillborn twins. No children are listed for Jabez Fuller & 2nd wife Priscilla Samson, however they did have one child, Deborah, b. 23 Nov. 1727, Plympton; d. 25 July or 1 Aug. 1809, Kingston, (wf of 2nd husband Ebenezer Fuller). <MF5G 1:72>.
<NOTE: This error of crediting wife Deborah Soule to Jabez Fuller[4] (Sam.[3]) is repeated in **Mayflower Marriages**, companion volume to this book. The corrected two lines on p.171 should read:
Jabez Fuller[4] (John[3]) & 1st Deborah Soule
Jabez Fuller[4] (Sam.[3]) & Mercy Gray[5]
Also, p.170, the entry should read: Jabez Fuller[4] (John[3]) & 2nd Priscilla Samson[4].>
<34> p.460, Hannah Thomas, dau of David Thomas & Abigail Wood, b. 22 Feb. 1684/5, Middleboro <MD 12:231>; bur. Thompson St. Cemetery, Halifax <MD 13:12>.
<35> p.460, Although Bowman states she d. 18 Nov. the records clearly say 8 Nov. She is buried at the Thompson St. Cemetery, Halifax <MD 13:12>.
<36> p.460, d. 2 Aug. 1747, bur. Thompson St. Cemetery, Halifax <MD 13:12>.
<37> p.460, b. 18 Dec. 1710, Middleboro, dau of John Alden & Hannah White <MD 2:201>.
<38> p.461, b. 14 May 1724 <Plympton VR>
<39> p.461, b. 6 Aug. 1726, dau of John Tinkham & Ann Gray <Kingston VR> (Chilton descendant).
<40> p.461, In Burial Hill by Drew:138, the gravestone inscription for Eunice Robbins states she died in her 40th yr. Also inscribed on her stone are son Ebenezer who "d. in captivity, 21st yr" (c1783) and four infant children, viz: Consider, Levi, Joanna & Levi.

Ebenezer Robbins & Eunice Fuller had seven children, Plymouth, viz: Levi, b. 21 Jan. 1761; Ebenezer, b. 4 Aug. 1762; Thaddeus, b. 25 Aug. 1764; Consider, b. 25 May 1766, d. 20 June 1766; James, b. 29 Oct. 1767; Ansell, b. 29 Sept. 1769; Levi, b. 29 Aug. 1771, d. 11 May 1772 <MD 23:8>.
<41> p.461, Ansell Robbins is not identified, however, he is quite possibly the son of Ebenezer & Eunice Robbins. (See <40> above)
<42> p.462, Burial Hill by Drew:139 states he died 2 Oct. 1801, ae 1yr10d. Bowman's date appears to be correct.
<43> p.462, b. 29 Sept. 1726, dau of Robert Cushman & Mercy Washburn. <MF5G 1:60>
<44> p.462, Seven Fuller children are listed as being baptized on 7 Mar. 1769, viz: James, Joanna, Josiah, Lemuel, Lydia, Thankful and Zephaniah <Kingston VR:81-84>.
<45> p.462, Josiah Fuller d. betw. 15 Sept. 1814 (will) - 3 July 1820 (prob.) <Plymouth Co.PR 53:10> His parentage is not given, could he be the Josiah Fuller[6] immediately preceeding his entry?
<46> p.462, The files do not show if these are a 1st and 2nd marriage for Josiah or unrelated.
<47> p.462, d. 19 May 1783, Kingston g.s. <MD 7:87>
<48> p.462, MF5G 1:66 gives her date of death as 13 Aug. 1782.
<49> p.462, Jabez Fuller[4] (Sam.[3]) is mistakenly credited with 1st wife Deborah Soule. See <33>.
<50> p.462, d. 1738 <MF5G 1:66>
<51> p.462, d. 1736 <Ibed.>
<52> p.462, MF5G 1:70 lists the sixth child as Ichabod Fuller while Bowman has Lois in pencil with the source being "grandfather's will". MF5G also gives the baptism years for the children, at Halifax, viz: Ruth, 1748; Lydia, 1749/50; Chipman, 1755; Priscilla, 1758; Eunice 1760 and Ichabod, 1766, d.y. (Lydia's baptism date does not agree with her date on g.s. - 57 in 1812, therefore b. c1755.)
<53> p.464, The six Fuller children are listed without dates, viz: Noah, Hannah, Lucy, Asenath, Thomas (b. c1757, d. 8 Dec. 1774, ae 17) and Susanna.
<54> p.464, Edmund Willis is listed in pencil as the husband of Mercy Fuller[5] (Jabez[4]). MF5G 1: 67 gives them a daughter Sally, b. 1783, Hardwick, before moving to Vermont.
<55> p.464, Kingston VR
<56> p.465, Rachel Standish[5] (Moses[4], Eben.[3], Alex.[2]), b. & d. Plympton <VR>.

* * * * * * * *

REFERENCE LIST

GENEALOGICAL ARTICLES PERTAINING TO S. FULLER FAMILY RESEARCH

Mayflower Descendant (MD) (1899-1937)

1:23-28 - Will of Dr. Samuel Fuller
2:8-10 - Inventory of Dr. Samuel Fuller
5:65-72 - Estate of Rev. Samuel Fuller[2]
8:129 - Mayflower Marriages in Leyden
10:1-2 - Marriage of Samuel Fuller to Agnes Carpenter
16:129-31 - An Autograph of Samuel Fuller The Mayflower Passenger
18:227-33 - The Settlement of James Wood's Estate and The Will of George Holmes
22:65-66 - Marriage Record of Samuel Fuller, Leyden

25:55 - Bridget & Samuel Fuller's Deed To The Church At Plymouth

Mayflower Descendant (MD) (1985-1990)

36:187-89 - The Ramsden Family of Plymouth, Mass.
38:69-80 - Thomas Caswell of Taunton & His Descendants
39:85-87 - Samuel Fuller[2] of Plymouth & Middleborough

Mayflower Quarterly (MQ) (1975-1990)

41:99-100 - Samuel & Bridget Fuller
- (from forthcoming MF5G)
46:183-85 - William Sturtevant, Descendant of Samuel Fuller
- (MF5G 1:57)
50:21-30 - Judah Fuller[5], The Bloomer's Daughter
54:102-06 - The Pilgrim Physician Doctor Samuel Fuller (1580-1633) of the Mayflower

Miscellaneous

Mayflower Families For Five Generations: Samuel Fuller of the Mayflower, (MF5G) pub. by General Society of Mayflower Descendants. Vol. 1. 1975, 1988.

NEHGR 55:192,410 - Early New England Families
- Fullers of Redenhall
TAG 15:39-40 - Fuller Families of Colchester, Wethersfield & Farmington CT
TAG 60:194-99 - Was Matthew Fuller Of Plymouth Colony A Son Of Pilgrim Edward Fuller?

* * * * * * * * *
* * * * * * *
* * * * *
* * *
*

INDEX

CPSIA information can be obtained
at www.ICGtesting.com
Printed in the USA
BVHW090215030719
552537BV00015B/128/P